THE BELFAST

AND

PROVINCE OF ULSTER

DIRECTORY FOR 1852,

CONTAINS

I. CALENDAR FOR THE YEAR.
II. HISTORICAL SKETCH OF THE TOWN AND TRADE.
III. BELFAST STREET DIRECTORY.
IV. BALLYMACARRETT DIRECTORY.
V. ALPHABETICAL DIRECTORY.
VI. PROFESSIONS AND TRADES DIRECTORY.
VII. COUNTRY RESIDENTS.
VIII. LOCAL INSTITUTIONS, &c.
IX. PROVINCE OF ULSTER DIRECTORY.

Vol. I.

BELFAST:
JAMES ALEXANDER HENDERSON, PUBLISHER,
NEWS-LETTER OFFICE.

1852.

This facsimile reprint published by
Books Ulster
2015

ISBN: 978-1-910375-27-3

TO THE READER.

In presenting to the public "THE BELFAST AND PROVINCE OF ULSTER DIRECTORY," the Publisher has to return his sincere thanks for the ready support afforded him, and for the kind assistance of those to whom he looked for information. Every exertion has been used to secure completeness and accuracy, and it is hoped the Work will be found to be a perfect Directory for Belfast and the principal towns in the Province of Ulster. Still, the Publisher has to crave indulgence for such errors and imperfections as are commonly incident to a first issue. He offers the present volume rather as an instalment of what he aspires to undertake, than as an average specimen of the series which it commences.

In the compilation of the Work every attention has been paid to the convenience of those for whose use the Directory is intended. In order to facilitate the progress of strangers and others through the Town, a MAP OF BELFAST, which will be found to embrace all the recent improvements of the town, has, at considerable expense, been *specially* prepared for the Directory.

It is the intention of the Publisher, relying on the patronage and support of the Inhabitants of Belfast, to issue the Directory periodically, with such alterations and improvements as may be necessary, until the Work shall become a standard book of reference for Belfast and the North of Ireland.

NEWS-LETTER OFFICE,
BELFAST, *27th May*, 1852.

☞ The Publisher requests that any Alterations or Corrections wished for by Subscribers or Purchasers, in future publications of the Directory, may be forwarded to the Office, 10 Bridge Street, Belfast.

GENERAL INDEX.

ALPHABETICAL DIRECTORY	204
Ballymacarrett	199
BELFAST (historical sketch)	25

BOROUGH OF BELFAST—

Anacreontic society	455
Antrim militia staff	453
Brown street schools	446
Bank of Ireland	429
Belfast academy	444
Belfast banking company	427
Belfast savings' bank	430
Belfast and Ballymena rail.	431
Belfast and co. Down do	432
Chamber of commerce	426
Committees, Town Council	424
Corporation	423
Custom house	433
Coaches, cars, &c.	460
Coast guard office	433
Chemico-agricul. society	439
Christ church schools	446
Charitable society	448
Constabulary officers	449
Consistorial court	450
County court house	451
Commerical club	454
Commercial buildings	454
Classical harmonist society	455
Deaf and Dumb institution	447
Donegall st. National school	445
Destitute sick society	448
District military staff	451
Essayists' club	452
Freemasons' club	453
Fine arts association	452
General Assembly's college	443
General hospital	436
Government school of design	444
Harbour commissioners	425
Harbour officers	426
Houses of public worship	458
Inland revenue office	433
Jews' society auxiliary	448
Ladies' clothing society	448
Library and society for promoting knowledge	440
Ladies' industrial school	445
Lying-in-hospital	447
Literary society	452
Local marine board	456
Lagan navigation company	457
Luggage porters	460
Lunatic asylum	437
Magdalen asylum	447
Medical society	435
Medical benevolent fund society	435
Magistrates	449
Manor court	450
Masonic lodges of Belfast	453
Master mariners' association	456
Markets and fairs	457
New jail	451
Natural history society	440
Northern banking company	428
Northern Sun. school asso.	446
Officers of health	437
Odd-fellows' societies	439
Public weigh-houses	425
Provincial bank	430
Poor-law union	434
Public baths & washhouses	441
Parochial schools	446
Petty sessions	449
Police office	449
Post office	450
Provincial masonic g. lodge	453
Provident building societies	455
Quarter sessions	449
Queen's College	442
Queen's College literary and scientific institute	452
Royal academical institution	444
Royal botanic society	441
Royal Flax society	438
Rifle club	454
Seaman's friend society	456
Society for prevention of cruelty to animals	448
St. George's Church schools	446
St. Malachy's seminary	445
St. Patrick's orphan society	447
Social inquiry society	452
Singing classes	455
Ship-owners' association	456
Steamers	460
Total abstinence association	455
Trustees sick, &c., seamen	456
Town mission	458
Union Club	454
Ulster female penitentiary	447
Ulster banking company	428
Ulster railway	432
Union dispensaries	435
Water commissioners	426
Working classes' association	441
CALENDAR	13

CONVEYANCES—

Railway time	421
Mail and stage coaches	422

GENERAL INDEX.

Country Residents...............	413
Professions and Trades—	
Academies & public schools	364
Accountants	365
Aerated water makers ...	365
Agents	365
Agricultural impt. makers	365
Alabaster manufacturers...	365
Apothecaries and surgeons	365
Architects	366
Artists............................	366
Asphalte & felt manufactrs.	366
Assurance offices	366
Attorneys	366
Auctioneers	366
Auctioneers and brokers ...	366
Baby linen warehouses......	366
Bakers	366
Banks............................	367
Barristers-at-Law.............	367
Basket makers	367
Baths	367
Bell hangers	367
Bleachers	367
Block, pump, & mast makers	368
Bobbin manufacturers	368
Bookbinders	368
Booksellers and stationers	368
Book agents	368
Boot and shoe shops.........	368
Brassfounders & gasfitters	369
Brewers	369
Brick and tile makers	369
Bricklayers (masters)	369
Brush makers	370
Builders and carpenters ...	370
Butchers........................	370
Butter merchants	371
Button blue manufacturers	372
Cabinet makers................	372
Canvass manufacturers ...	372
Carpenters	372
Carpet&damask warerooms	372
Carriers' quarters.............	372
Carvers, gilders, &c..........	372
Cheesemongers	372
Chemists, manufacturing...	372
Chimney sweepers	372
China & glass warehouses	372
Civil engineers................	372
Clock and watchmakers..	373
Clothes dealers	373
Clothes renovators	373
Clothiers	374
Coach factories.............	374
Coach offices	374
Coal merchants................	374
Commission merchants, &c.	374
Confectioners...................	375
Consuls and vice-consuls...	375
Copper and tinplate workers	375
Coopers	376
Cork cutters	376
Cotton spinners...............	376
Cotton yarn merchants......	376
Cutlers, &c.	376
Damask manufacturers	376
Dentists...........................	376
Designers........................	376
Distillers	376
Dress makers	376
Druggists and chemists.....	377
Drysalters,......................	377
Dyers..............................	377
Earthenware&glass dealers	377
Electrical manufacturer ...	377
Emigration agents............	377
Engravers & lithographers	377
Farriers	377
Feather merchants............	377
File cutters.....................	377
Fish (dried) merchants......	377
Fishmongers	377
Flax and tow merchants...	378
Flax spinners...................	378
Flour merchants..........	378
Fruiterers	379
Furniture brokers.........	379
Furriers	379
Gingham manufacturers....	379
Glass manufacturers......	379
Glue manufacturers.........	379
Grain merchants...........	379
Grocers (retail)...............	380
Grocers (wholesale)......	383
Gun & pistol manufacturers	384
Haberdashers............	384
Hackle and gill makers.....	385
Hairdressers...................	385
Harbour master..........	385
Hardware dealers.	385
Hardware merchants	385
Hatters, &c.....................	385
Hide merchants..........	385
Horse dealers.................	386
Horse shoers and farriers...	386
Hosiers and glovers.........	386
Hotels, &c......................	386
House, rent, & land agents	387
Insurance agents	387
Insurance companies' offices	388
Iron and brassfounders ...	389
Iron and tinplate merchants	389
Iron works......................	389
Ironmongers	390
Jewellers and opticians ...	390

GENERAL INDEX.

Last and boot tree makers 390
Leather and hide merchants 390
Lime burners............ 390
Linen and cotton printers 390
Linen & damask warehouses 390
Linen manufacturers, &c. 390
Linen ornament makers... 391
Linen thread manufacturers 391
Linen yarn merchants 391
Livery stable keepers 391
Lloyd's agent and surveyor 391
Looking-glass maker 391
Machine makers 391
Maltsters 391
Marble and stone cutters... 392
Masters in chancery, .. 392
Mattress makers.......... 392
Matting manufactory...... 393
Merchants 393
Mill banding manufactory 393
Millers................... 393
Milliners and dressmakers.. 393
Music sellers.............. 395
Muslin gas singers............ 395
Muslin manufacturers...... 395
Nail manufacturers........ 395
News agents.............. 396
Newspapers.............. 396
Nautical instrument makers 396
Notaries public............ 396
Nursery & seedsmen,.... 396
Nurse tenders 396
Oil merchants 396
Painters and glaziers 397
Paper makers & merchants 397
Patent saw mills 397
Pawnbrokers.......... .. 397
Pipe makers 397
Picture frame makers 397
Physicians and surgeons .. 398
Piano-forte makers, ... 398
Plasterers (masters)........ 398
Plumbers, &c. 398
Posting establishments ... 398
Post offices..................... 399
Potteries..................... 399
Poulterers 399
Printers 399
Provision dealers 399
Provision merchants........ 400
Publishers 400
Railway companies 400
Reading rooms and libraries 400
Rectifying distillers 400
Reed makers 400
Restaurants 400
Room paper warehouses ... 400
Rope and twine makers..... 400

Saddlers & harness makers 401
Saloons 401
Salt merchants 401
Saw makers and sharpers 401
Servants' registry offices.. 401
Ship brokers 401
Ship builders................. 401
Ship chandlers 401
Ship owners 401
Shirt makers............. 402
Shuttle makers 403
Silk manufacturers 403
Silk mercers 403
Sizing factories............ 403
Soap and candle makers... 403
Soda ash manufacturers ... 403
Solicitors and attorneys.... 403
Spirit dealers................ 404
Starch manufacturers 407
Stationers 407
Stay and corset makers ... 408
Steam packet agents 408
Stock and share brokers ... 408
Straw bonnet makers 408
Tailors 408
Tanners and curriers........ 409
Taverns and coffee houses 409
Teachers 409
Tea merchants, wholesale 410
Timber merchants 410
Tobacco and snuff dealers 410
Toy shops,..................... 410
Trimming warehouses.... 410
Umbrella makers 411
Undertakers 411
Universal parcels office ... 411
Upholsterers 411
Venetian blind makers...... 411
Veterinary surgeons 411
Watch glass manufacturers 411
Whip and thong makers ... 411
Whitesmiths 411
Woollen warehouses......... 411
Printed calico warehouses 411
Wholesale wine merchants 412
Wire cloth manufacture... 412
Woollendrapers 412

STREET DIRECTORY 49
VILLAGE DIRECTORY—
Ardoyne, Ballysillan, &c. 417
Dundonald 417
Dunmurry 417
Greencastle 418
Holywood 418
Newtownbreda 419
The Knock..................... 420
Whitehouse 420
Whiteabbey 420

ALPHABETICAL LIST OF STREETS,

WITH INDEX.

Street	Page
Abbey street, Peter's hill,	49
Abbotsford place, York street,	49
Academy street, Donegall st.,	49
Academy court, 33 Academy st.,	50
Adelaide place	50
Agnes' place, Shankhill road,	167
Albert place, Donegall pass,	50
Albert square, Donegall quay,	50
Albert st., Durham street,	51
Albert st. place, Albert street,	51
Albion lane, Donegall pass,	51
Albion place, Botanic road,	51
Alexander st., Frederick st.,	51
Alexander st. South, Peter's hill	52
Alfred st., Upper Arthur st.,	52
Allen's court, Peter's hill,	57
Anderson's court, Shankhill,	57
Anderson's court, Millfield,	57
Alton st., Old Lodge road,	149
Ann street	52-3
Annette street, Verner st.,	53
Antrim place, Antrim road,	54
Antrim road,	54
Apsley place, Donegall pass,	54
Ardmoulin place, Falls road,	54
Arnon st., Trinity st.,	56
Arthur lane, Upper Arthur st.,	54
Arthur place, Arthur st.,	55
Arthur square, Corn market,	55
Arthur st., Arthur square,	55-6
Arthur st. Upper, Arthur st.,	56
Artillery st., North Queen st.,	56
Ashmore st., Conway st.,	79
Ashley place, Ballymacarrett,	199
Aughton terrace, Donegall pass,	57
Back lane, Prince's street,	57
Bairn's court, Curtis street,	57
Ballynafeigh, Ormeau road,	151
Balmer's court, Verner street,	57
Bank lane, Castle place,	57
Barnes' court, Peter's hill,	62
Barker's court, Pilot street,	58
Barrack st., Mill street,	58
Bath place, Falls road,	58
Beattie's entry, Mill street,	59
Bedford st., Donegall sq. South,	90
Bell's lane, Smithfield,	59
Belvidere place, Gt. Victoria st.,	59
Berryhill ct., Little Donegall st.,	59
Berry st., Hercules st.,	59
Birch st., Little Donegall st.,	63
Black's place, Hercules street,	59
Blakely's lane, Tomb street,	60
Bogan's row, Falls road,	60
Bond street, Cromac street,	60
Bond st. New, Eliza street,	60
Botanic garden, Malone road,	61
Botanic road, Gt. Victoria st.,	60
Botanic view, Botanic road,	61
Bolton street, Verner street,	61
Boundary court, Boundary st.,	61
Boundary street, Falls road,	61
Boyd's court,	62
Boyd's court, Nile street,	62
Boyd street, Peter's hill,	62
Bradbury place, Botanic road,	62
Bradford's entry, Millfield,	63
Bradford square, Tomb street,	63
Bradford street, Dock street,	63
Breadalbane place, Gt. Victoria st.,	63
Bridge end,	63
Bridge end, Ballymacarrett,	199
Bridge street, High street,	63
Bridge st. place, Bridge street,	63
Brougham street, York street,	63
Brown's entry, Barrack street,	64
Brown's row, Academy street,	64
Brown's square, Peter's hill,	64
Brown street, Millfield,	64
Brunswick lane, Henry square,	65
Brunswick street, Howard st.,	65
Burn's Court, Mill street,	65
Byrne's lane, Lower Lagan st.,	65
Caddell's entry, High street,	65
Cahoon's court, Brown square,	65
Calendar street, Castle lane,	65
California st., Old lodge road,	65
Cambridge st., York road,	66
Camden terrace, Botanic road,	66
Campbell's buildings, Peter's hill,	66
Campbell's buildings, Conway st.,	79
Campbell's buildings	169
Campbell's court, Carrick hill,	66
Campbell's place, Old lodge road,	66
Campbell st., ditto.,	66
Canning street, York road,	66

LIST OF STREETS.

Street	Page
Cargill street, Townsend st.,	60
Caroline st., Gt. George's st.,	66
Carrick hill, North street,	67
Carr's row, Old Malone road,	75
The Castle, Castle buildings,	68
Castle buildings, Castle place,	68
Ditto., Donegall place,	68
Castle chambers, Castle place,	69
Castle court, ditto.,	69
Castle lane, Donegall place,	69
Castle market, Calendar st.,	69
Castle place, High street,	70
Castle street, Castle place,	70
Catherine st., Henrietta st.,	71
Catherine st. North, Lt. May st.,	71
Catherine court, Catherine st.,	71
Caxton street, Robert street,	71
Chapel lane, Mill street,	72
Chapel lane, Ballymacarrett,	200
Charlemont st., Berry st.,	72
Charles street, Union street,	72
Charlotte st., Donegall pass,	73
Charters' buildings, Falls road,	99
Chichester lane, Albert square,	73
Chichester st., Donegall sq. East,	73
Chichester street, Lower,	74
Church lane, High street,	74
Church lane, Upper,	74
Church street, Donegall st.,	74
Clarence place, Alfred street,	75
Clarendon place, ditto.,	75
Clarendon dock,	81
Clark's lane, Gt. Patrick st.,	75
Cliftonville, New lodge road,	75
Coates' street, Townsend st.,	75
Cole's alley, Church lane,	76
College court, College sq. North,	76
College place North, ditto.,	76
College square East,	76
College square North, King st.,	76
College street, College sq. East,	76-7
College st. South, Howard st.,	77
Collingwood street, Earl st.,	77
Commercial buildings	77
Commercial ct., Donegall st.,	78
Conley's court, Millfield,	78
Conlon street, Old lodge road,	78
Conway street, Falls road,	78
Cooney's court, Ann street,	79
Corn market, Castle place,	79
Coronation place, Little York st.,	80
Corporation sq., Gt. George's st.,	80
Corporation st., Victoria st.,	80-1
Corporation street.	82
Cotton court, Waring street,	82
Court street, New court-house,	82
Covent garden, Little Patrick st.,	82
Cranstone place, Antrim road,	82
Crawford street, Welsh street,	82
Crescent, Lower, Malone road,	82
Crescent, Upper, Malone road,	82
Cromac road, Cromac bridge.	82
Cromac st., Gt. Edward st.,	83
Crown entry, High street,	84
Crumlin place, Crumlin road,	84
Crumlin terrace, ditto,	84
Crumlin road, Antrim road,	85
Cuddy's row, New Lodge road,	85
Culbert's court, Little York st.,	85
Cullingtree st., Durham st.,	85
Cullingtree place, Cullingtree st.,	85
Cumberland place, Donegall pass,	85
Cunningham's court, Mill st.,	85
Curell's place, Townsend st. ,	85
Curell's row, Townsend st.,	85
Curtis st., York st.,	86
Damside, Millfield,	86
Davidson's court, Durham st.,	86
Dayton place, Townsend st.,	86
Devis street, Barrack street,	86
Dock lane, Dock street,	86
Dock street, York street,	86
Dominick street, Bolton street,	87
Donaldson's court, Barrack st.,	87
Donegall lane, Donegall st.,	87
Donegall pass, Cromac road,	87
Donegall place, Castle place,	87-8
Donegall place buildings,	88
Donegall quay,	88
Donegall square East,	89
Donegall square North,	89
Donegall square South,	89
Donegall square West,	90
Donegall street.	90-1-2
Donegall st. Little, John street,	92-3
Donegall st. place, Donegall st.,	93
Downshire place, Gt. Vic. st.,	93
Drake's lane, Union place,	93
Drummond's court, Carrick hill,	93
Dublin bridge, Old Malone road,	93
Duffin's court, Winetavern st.,	94
Duffy's place, Boundary st.,	94
Durham court, Durham st.,	94
Durham place, off Durham st.,	94
Durham street, Barrack street,	94-5
Durham st. New, Townsend st.,	95
Dyet's entry, Barrack street,	95
Eagleston place, Antrim road,	54
Earl lane, Earl street,	95
Earl street, York street,	95
East street, Verner street,	96
Economy place, Henry street,	96

LIST OF STREETS.

Edward street, Robert street,...	96	Grace street, Hamilton street,	108
Edward st. Gt., Victoria street,	97	Graham's entry, High street,...	108
Edward st. Little, Edward st.,...	97	Grattan court, Grattan street,...	108
Eglinton st., Crumlin road,......	97	Grattan place, Grattan st.,.......	108
Eliza court, Eliza street,.........	97	Grattan street, Gordon street,	108-9
Eliza place, Eliza street,.........	97	Greenland st., Shankhill road,	109
Eliza street, Cromac street,......	97	Green st.; Corporation street,...	109
Ellen's court, Nile street,......	98	Green's court, Green street,...	110
Elliott's court, Donegall street,	98	Gregg's lane, West street,......	110
Erskine's court, Durham street,	98	Grove st., North Queen st.,.......	110
Fairy place, Old Lodge road,...	98	Hagan's court, Grattan st.,.......	111
Falloon's court, Fleet street,...	98	Hamill court, Hamill street,...	111
Falls court, Falls road,............	98	Hamill street, Barrack street,...	111
Falls court, Durham street,......	98	Hamilton court, High street,....	111
Falls road, Townsend street,...	99	Hamilton place, Stephen st.,...	111
Ferguson's court, Smithfield,...	100	Hamilton's place, Boundary st.,	111
First street, Falls road,.........	100	Hamilton street, Cromac street,	111
Fisherwick place	100	Hammond's court, Corn market,	112
Fitzwilliam st., Malone road,...	100	Hanna's court, Shankhill road,	112
Fleet street, York street,.........	100	Hanna's lane, Peter's hill, ...	112
Fleming's place, Old Lodge road,	150	Hardinge st., North Queen st.,	145
Forcade's entry, Berry street,...	100	Harmony place, Dublin road,...	112
Fountain lane, Donegall place,	100	Harper's court, Curtis street,...	112
Fountain place, Old Dublin road,	101	Henrietta street, Cromac street,	112
Fountain st., Castle street,......	101	Henry place, Antrim road, ...	54
Fountainville, Old Malone road,	101	Henry square, Green street, ...	113
Fowl market, St. Geo.'s market,	101	Henry street, Corporation St.,...	113
Fox's row, Durham street,......	101	Hercules place, Castle place,...	113
Francis street, Smithfield,......	101	Hercules street, Hercules place,	114
Franklin place, Linenhall st.,...	102	Herdman's buildings	115
Frederick lane, Frederick st.,...	102	High street, Castle place, ...	115
Frederick place, Frederick st.,...	102	Hill street, Waring street, ...	117
Frederick st., York street,......	102	Holmes' court, Verner street,...	118
Friendly street, Welsh street,...	103	Hope's court, Millfield, ...	118
Fulton's entry, Hercules st.,...	103	Hope st., Breadalbane place,...	118
Gable street, Boundary street,	103	Hopeton place, Shankhill road,	118
Galway court, Galway street,...	103	Houston's lane, Seymour st.,...	118
Galway street, Durham street,	103	Howard st., Donegall sq. south,	118
Gamble st., Tomb street,......	103-4	Howard st., North, Falls road,	119
Garden place, Cromac road,...	104	Howard st., South, Cromac road,	119
Gardner street, Peter's hill,......	104	Hudson's court, Hudson's entry,	119
Garmoyle st., Corporation st.,...	104	Hudson's entry, North street,...	119
Gavin's buildings, Shankhill road,	168	Hudson's row, Shankhill road,	167
George's court, Frederick street,	104	Hunter's row, New lodge road,	119
George's lane, Montgomery st.,	104	Hutchinson street, Stanley st.,	119
George's street, Great,...........	105	Improvement place, Lancaster st.,	119
George's street, Little,............	105	Ingram place, Donegall pass,...	87
Gibb's court, Alexander st.,......	106	Institution place, Lettuce hill,	119
Glasshouse st., Boyd st.,.........	106	Jacobson's court, Mill street,...	119
Glenfield place, Ormeau road,...	106	James' court, Carrick hill, ...	119
Glengall place, Gt. Vic. st.,...	106	James' place, Nelson street, ...	119
Glengall st., Gt. Victoria st.,...	106	James' st. south, Howard street,	119
Glentilt place, Old Lodge road,	106	Johnny's entry, Talbot street,...	119
Gloucester st., Gt. Edward st.,	107	Johnston's buildings,...............	119
Gooseberry corner, B.macarrett,	200	Johnston's court, Gt. Edward st.,	120
Gordon street, Hill street,......	107	Johnston's court, Millfield,......	120

LIST OF STREETS.

Street	Page
John street, Donegall street,	120
Joy's court, Joy's entry,	121
Joy's entry, High street,	121
Joy's place, Dublin bridge,	121
Joy street, Montgomery street,	121
Keenan's court, Millfield,	122
Kennedy's court, North street,	122
Kennedy's entry, Devis street,	122
Kennedy's place, Shankhill road,	122
Kennedy's row, Smithfield,	122
Kent st. Lower, John street,	123
Kent street Upper, Union st.,	123
Killen street, College street,	123
King's court, Lancaster street,	123
King street, Mill street,	123
King st. court, King street,	124
King st. North, Brown street,	124
Lagan st., Cromac street,	124
Lagan st. Upper, Lagan street,	124
Lagan village, B.macarrett,	200
Lancaster street, York street,	124
Law's lane, North street,	125
Leadbetter place,	125
Leeds street, Cullingtree st.,	125
Legg's lane, High street,	125
Lemon's court, Smithfield,	125
Lemon's lane, Gt. Edward st.,	125
Letitia st., Wilson st.,	125
Lettuce hill, Barrack street,	126
Lewis's court, Brown square,	126
Liddy's court, Little Donegall st.,	126
Lilliput, Old Carrickfergus road,	126
Lindsay's place, Cromac road,	126
Linen Hall,	126
Linen Hall street,	126
Linfield and Linfield road,	127
Lisburn road, Malone,	127
Long lane, Church street,	127
Lynas's lane, Gt. Patrick st.,	127
Magee's lane, Gt. George's st.,	127
Malone place, Malone road,	127
Malone road Lower, Blackstaff,	127
Malone road Old,	129
Market st., May's market,	129
Marlborough st., Princes's st.,	130
Marquis st., Mill st.,	130
Marshall's lane, Lynas's lane,	130
Mary's place, North Queen st.,	145
Mary's market, Townsend st.,	130
Mary st., Park street,	131
Massey's court, Durham st.,	131
Mawhinney's court,	131
Maxwell's row, Sandy row,	133
May st., Clarence place,	131
May st. Little, Cromac st.,	132
Meadow lane, Meadow st.,	132
Meadow st., York street,	132
Meek's court, Barrack street,	132
Meeting-house lane, Wm. st.,	132
Melbourne court, Melbourne st.,	133
Melbourne st., Brown st.,	133
Michael st., Little Geo.'s st.,	133
Millar's lane, Berry street,	133
Millfield, Mill street,	133
Mill street, Castle street,	135
Millview place, Townsend st.,	136
Mitchel's entry, High street,	136
Mitchell street, Gardiner st.,	136
Moffet st., Henry street,	137
Molyneaux st., Little Geo.'s st.,	137
Montgomery st., Chichester st.,	137
Moore's place, Lower Malone,	137
Morrison's place, Pound street,	137
Morrow's entry, Hill street,	137
Mountcharles, Old Malone road,	138
Mount pottinger, Ballymacarrett,	200
Mountview terrace,	138
Mullan's lane, Trafalgar st.,	138
Murphy's lane, Verner street,	138
Murphy street, Verner street,	138
Murray's terrace, College sq.,	138
Mustard street, John street,	138
M'Adam's court, Carrick hill,	139
M'Allen's place, Shankhill,	139
M'Auley's place, M'Auley st.,	139
M'Auley street, Cromac street,	139
M'Clean's entry, Marquis st.,	139
M'Clelland's lane, Peter's hill,	139
M'Clennaghan's court, Mill st.,	139
M'Crory's row, Ballymacarrett,	201
M'Cully's gate, Peter's hill,	156
M'Dowell's court, Durham st.,	140
M'Kibbin's court, North street,	140
M'Larnon's buildings,	202
M'Master's row, Durham street,	140
M'Millan's place, Falls road,	140
M'Tier's court, North street,	140
M'Tier's street, Shankhill,	140
Napier's place,	141
Neeson's court, Mill street,	141
Nelson's buildings,	168
Nelson court, Nelson street,	141
Nelson street, Gt. Patrick st.,	141
New court, Tomb street,	142
New lodge place, Lodge road,	142
New lodge road, North Queen st.,	143
New road, Ballymacarrett,	202
New row, Berry street,	144
Nile street, Nelson street,	144
North Ann st., Corporation st.,	144
North Boundary st.,	144
North Howard Street,	167

LIST OF STREETS.

Northburn place, Old lodge road,	144
Northburn st., Old lodge road,	145
North Queen st., Carrick hill,	145
North Queen street place,	146
North Street, Bridge street,	146
O'Haggarty st., Boundary st.,	149
Old lodge place, Old lodge road,	149
Old lodge road, Peter's hill,	149
Ormeau place, Ormeau road,	150
Ormeau road, Cromac road,	150
Ormeau st., Newtownbreda road,	151
Ormond market, Patrick street,	153
Orr's entry, High street,	151
Oxford street, May street,	152
Pakenham place,	152
Park street, Stanhope street,	152
Patrick lane, Patrick street,	152
Patrick street, York street,	152
Patrick street Little, York st.,	153
Patterson's place,	154
Patterson's place, Donegall sq.,	155
Peel's place, Shankhill road,	155
Peter's hill, North street,	155
Pilot street, Corporation street,	156
Plunkett's court, Carrick hill,	156
Plunkett's place, Antrim road,	54
Police place, William st. South,	157
Police square, Victoria street,	157
Poplar court, Gratton street,	157
Portland place, Portland street,	157
Portland st., St. George's st.,	157
Portview, Ballymacarrett,	202
Posnett's place, Donegall pass,	87
Pound street, Barrack street,	158
Pottinger's entry, High street,	157
Pottinger's place, Ballymacarrett,	202
Prince's court, Prince's street,	158
Prince's dock	158
Prince's street, Queen's square,	159
Prospect terrace,	159
Queen's College, Malone road,	160
Queen's Island,	160
Queen's quay, Ballymacarrett,	202
Queen's square, High street,	160
Queen street, Castle street,	160
Queen st. Upper, Wellington pl.,	161
Quigley's court, Cromac street,	159
Quinn's entry, High street,	161
Raphael court, Raphael street,	161
Raphael street, Cromac street,	161
Renwick place, Malone road,	161
Riley's place, Cromac street,	161
Ritchie's place, North street,	162
River street, Welsh street,	162
Robert court, Mustard street,	162
Robert street, Hill street,	162
Rochfort place, College court,	162
Roundhill, Ballymacarrett,	203
Roseann place, Old Carrick road,	163
Rosemary street, Bridge street,	163
Ross street, Falls road,	164
Round entry, North street,	164
Royal terrace, Lisburn road,	164
Roy's court, Roy street,	165
Roy street, Stanfield street,	165
Russell street, Cromac street,	165
Sackville place, Sackville street,	165
Sackville street, Townsend st.,	166
Salter's court, Barrack street,	166
Saltpan row, Ballymacarrett,	203
Samuel street, Winetavern st.,	161
Sarah street, Frederick street,	166
Seaview place, B.macarrett,	203
Second st., North Howard st.,	167
Seymour lane, Seymour street,	167
Seymour st., Chichester street,	167
Shankhill road, Townsend st.,	167
Sheals' entry, Carrick hill,	169
Shipboy street, Nelson street,	169
Ship street, York street,	169
Ship st. Back, Ship street,	170
Ship street Little, Dock street,	170
Short street, Pilot street,	170
Short strand, Ballymacarrett,	203
Skipper street, High street,	170
Sir Henry's buildings,	203
Smithfield, Berry street,	170
Smith street, Lagan street,	173
Southwell st., Henry street,	173
Spamount, Old Carrick road,	173
Spencer street,	173
Stanfield court, Stanfield st.,	173
Stanfield street, Verner street,	173
Stanhope st., Old Lodge road,	174
Stanley lane, Little York st.,	175
Stanley place, Little York st.,	175
Stanley st., Albert street,	175
St. Ann's buildings, Donegall st.,	175
Staunton street, Verner street,	175
Steam Mill lane, Gamble st.,	176
Stephen st., Little Donegall st.,	176
Store lane, Queen's square,	176
Stormont court, Durham street,	176
Suffern's entry, North street,	177
Sugar House entry, High st.,	177
Sussex place, Alfred street,	177
Sussex st., York street,	177
Talbot court, Gratton street,	177
Talbot street, Donegall street,	177
Tanner's court, Millfield,	178
Taylor's row, Carrick hill,	178
Tea lane, Lower Malone,	178
Telfair's entry, Ann street,	178
Third street, Fall's road,	178

LIST OF STREETS.

Thomas court, George's lane,...	178	Waring st. place, Waring st.,...	190
Thomas street, Lancaster street,	178	Warehouse lane, Waring st.,...	190
Thomas street North, York st.,	179	Washington st., Frederick st.,...	190
Thompson's entry, Millfield,...	179	Waugh's court, North street,...	190
Tomb street, Waring street,...	179	Wellington court, Wellington st.,	190
Torrens's row, Hercules street,	180	Wellington place, Donegall sq.,	190
Torrens's market, Hercules st.,	180	Wellington square, Falls road,	191
Townsend place, Townsend st.,	180	Wellington st., Fisherwick place,	191
Townsend st., Shankbill road,	180	Wellwood place, Gt. Vic. street,	191
Trafalgar st., Corporation st.,...	181	Welsh street, Lagan street,.....	191
Trinity street, Antrim road,...	182	Wesley lane, Wesley street,.....	191
Union place, Lancaster street,	182	Wesley place, Botanic road,....	192
Union street, Donegall street,	183	West street, Smithfield,........	192
Unity street, Trinity street,......	183	Wheeler's place, B.macarrett,..	203
University square,...........	184	William's lane, Green street,...	192
Upton street, Wall street.....	184	Williams' place, Wellwood place,	193
Valentine street, Henry street,	184	Williams' row, Little Geo.'s st.,	193
Vere street, York street,......	184	William street, Church street,	193
Verner's lane, Verner street,...	185	William st. South, Arthur sq.,	194
Verner street, Cromac street,...	185	Wills' place, May's fields,....	194
Victoria court, off Durham st.,	186	Wilson street, Millfield,.......	194
Victoria place, Victoria street,	186	Windsor place, Gt. Victoria st.,	194
Victoria st., Corporation st.,...	186	Winecellar entry, High street,	193
Victoria st. Gt., Glengall place,	187	Winetavern st., North street,...	193
Victoria street Little,..........	187	Woodstock place, B.macarrett,	203
Victoria terrace, Old Malone road	193	York lane, York street,........	194
Walker's lane, Frederick st.,...	187	York road, York street,......	194
Wall street, Carrick hill,......	187	York st., Donegall street, ...	195
Waring street................	188	York st. Little, Gt. Patrick st.,..	197

INDEX TO PROVINCIAL DIRECTORY.

Antrim, County...............	463	Donegal, County	533
Antrim, Town	466	Down, County	536
Ardglass................	468	Downpatrick	540
Armagh, County	469	Dromore...............	545
Armagh, City...............	471	Dungannon	547
Aughnacloy	479	Enniskillen	554
Ballibay...............	481	Fermanagh, County...............	560
Ballycastle...............	483	Hillsborough...............	562
Ballymena...............	486	Larne...............	564
Ballymoney	491	Lisburn	567
Ballynahinch...............	494	Londonderry, County	572
Banbridge	496	Londonderry, City...............	575
Ballyclare	490	Lurgan	588
Bangor	500	Maghera...............	592
Blackwatertown...............	503	Monaghan, County	594
Carrickfergus...............	504	Monaghan, Town	596
Castleblayney	508	Moneymore	600
Castledawson...............	510	Moy and Charlemont	602
Cavan, County	512	Newry...............	605
Cavan, Town	514	Newtownards...............	615
Clones	517	Portadown	620
Coleraine	520	Randalstown	625
Comber	525	Saintfield	626
Cookstown...............	527	Tyrone, County...............	628
Donaghadee	531	Ulster, Province	461

THE CALENDAR.

1852.]		JANUARY.				[31 Days.	

Full Moon.................. 7th day, at 45m. past 5 Morning.
Last Quarter.............14th day, at 54m. past 12 Morning.
New Moon..................21st day, at 3m. past 7 Morning.
First Quarter............29th day, at 10m. past 10 Morning.

DAY OF MONTH	DAY OF WEEK	REMARKABLE EVENTS.	MOON.		HIGH WATER*	
			Rises.	Sets.	Morn.	Even.
			H. M.	H. M.	H. M.	H. M.
1	Th	Ireland and England united 1801.	0 E 49	1 M 32	5 47	6 1
2	Fri	Edmund Burke born 1730.	1 7	2 42	6 34	7 5
3	Sat	General G. Monk died 1670.	1 30	3 52	7 41	8 0
4	Su	2nd Sunday after Christmas.	1 58	5 5	8 31	8 53
5	Mo	Frederick Duke of York died 1827.	2 34	6 16	9 15	9 37
6	Tu	Epiphany—Twelfth Day.	3 23	7 22	9 50	10 16
7	We	General Penny Post estab. 1840.	4 25	8 21	10 30	10 59
8	Th	Battle of New Orleans 1815.	5 35	9 10	11 20	11 42
9	Fri	Trinity College, Dublin, opened 1593.	6 50	9 48	—	0 2
10	Sat	Archbishop Laud beheaded 1645.	8 19	10 18	0 25	0 49
11	Su	1st Sunday after Epiphany.	9 44	10 42	1 13	1 36
12	Mo	Duke of Newcastle died 1851.	11 E 8	11 2	2 7	2 35
13	Tu	Pres. Church, Cornwall, Jamaica, foun.	—	11 23	3 2	3 34
14	We	Lord Eldon d. 1838. [stone laid 1837	0 M 31	11 M 40	4 8	4 37
15	Th	John Aikin born 1747.	1 55	0 E 1	5 10	5 47
16	Fri	Battle of Corunna 1809.	3 16	0 23	6 9	6 45
17	Sat	Franklin born 1706, died 1790.	4 37	0 51	7 21	7 52
18	Su	2nd Sunday after Epiphany.	5 52	1 27	8 24	8 51
19	Mo	John Howard died 1790.	6 59	2 15	9 18	9 41
20	Tu	Miles Coverdale died 1568.	7 53	3 10	10 4	10 25
21	We	American Independence decl. 1783.	8 37	4 10	10 47	11 7
22	Th	Lord Bacon born 1561, died 1626.	9 9	5 26	11 27	11 46
23	Fri	Duke of Kent died 1820.	9 33	6 38	—	0 4
24	Sat	Frederick the Great born 1712.	9 53	7 50	0 21	0 40
25	Su	3rd Sunday after Epiphany.	10 9	8 58	0 58	1 17
26	Mo	Sunday Schools established 1784.	10 25	10 9	1 36	1 56
27	Tu	Mozart born 1756.	10 39	11 E 16	2 13	2 34
28	We	Sir Francis Drake died 1596.	10 55	—	2 55	3 19
29	Th	King George III. died 1820.	11 11	0 M 24	3 42	4 7
30	Fri	Charles I. Martyred 1649.	11 31	1 34	4 37	5 5
31	Sat	Ben Johnson born 1574.	11 M 55	2 M 45	5 37	6 6

REMEMBRANCER OF BUSINESS, ETC.

1st. Returns of Partners in all Banks in Ireland to be made to the Stamp Office in Dublin; penalty for omission, £50—8 & 9 Vic., c. 37.—Dividends on Bank of Ireland Stock due; payable 8th.

8th. Fire Insurance Premium due at Christmas, must be paid by this day, or the Policy becomes void.

10th. Borough Coroners to transmit to Lord Lieutenant a Return of Inquests held in year preceding—3 & 4 Vic., c. 108.—Partridge, Pheasant, Quail, Landrail, or Wild Turkey, not to be taken, killed, exposed for sale, or purchased, between this date and 20th Sept. following; Penalty £5 a head—27 Geo. III., c. 35, and 37 Geo. III., c. 21.

12th. Hilary Term begins; ends Jan. 31.

19th. Last day for making out and issuing half-yearly Receipts for Interest to Savings' Banks and Friendly Societies—7 & 8 Vic., c. 83.

* The Tide Tables are taken from "Smith's Belfast Almanac," published by Alexander Mayne.

THE CALENDAR.

[1852.] **FEBRUARY.** [29 Days.

Full Moon,................ 5th day, at 29m. past 6 Evening.
Last Quarter,............12th day, at 39m. past 9 Morning.
New Moon,................20th day, at 30m. past 12 Morning.
First Quarter............28th day, at 7m. past 5 Morning.

DAY OF MONTH	DAY OF WEEK	REMARKABLE EVENTS.	MOON. Rises.	Sets.	HIGH WATER. Morn.	Even.
			H. M.	H. M.	H. M.	H. M.
1	Su	4th Sunday after Epiphany.	0E27	3M55	6 40	7 18
2	Mo	Dr. Gregory died 1841.	1 9	5 3	7 49	8 22
3	Tu	Gt. Temp. Meet. Exeter-hall 1851.	2 3	6 5	8 49	9 14
4	We	Sir Joseph Banks born 1743.	3 12	6 58	9 37	9 58
5	Th	Sir Robert Peel born 1788.	4 29	7 42	10 21	10 44
6	Fri	Charles II. died 1685.	5 56	8 16	11 8	11 30
7	Sat	Queen Mary born 1515.	7 23	8 43	11 51	—
8	Su	Septuagesima Sunday.	8 51	9 7	0 11	0 34
9	Mo	Butler (poet) born 1612.	10 16	9 29	0 58	1 21
10	Tu	Queen Victoria married 1840.	11E41	9 46	1 45	2 11
11	We	Washington born 1732.	—	10 6	2 41	3 10
12	Th	Lady Jane Grey beheaded 1554.	1M 6	10 29	3 39	4 11
13	Fri	Revolution completed 1688.	2 26	10 54	4 38	5 8
14	Sat	Valentine's Day.	3 43	11M27	5 42	6 17
15	Su	Sexagesima Sunday.	4 52	0E10	6 57	7 35
16	Mo	Melancthon born 1497.	5 49	1 2	8 11	8 40
17	Tu	First Soiree of Whitting. Club 1847.	6 36	2 4	9 7	9 30
18	We	Luther died 1546.	7 11	3 12	9 52	10 12
19	Th	Voltaire born 1694.	7 37	4 24	10 32	10 52
20	Fri	21] Thurot landed at C.fergus 1760.	7 58	5 35	11 12	11 27
21	Sat	Resignation of Russell Ministry 1851.	8 16	6 46	11 45	—
22	Su	Shrove Sunday.	8 30	7 54	0 1	0 13
23	Mo	Sir J. Reynolds died 1792.	8 44	9 3	0 30	0 46
24	Tu	Shrove Tuesday.—Louis Philippe ab-	9 0	10 11	1 1	1 16
25	We	Ash Wednesday. [dicated 1848.	9 15	11E19	1 34	1 52
26	Th	Napoleon escaped from Elba 1815.	9 32	—	2 16	2 34
27	Fri	Hare hunting ends.	9 52	0M28	2 56	3 17
28	Sat	Brunswick Theatre fell 1828.	10 22	1 36	3 39	4 8
29	Su	Quadragesima—1st Sunday in Lent.	10M59	2M46	4 39	5 10

REMEMBRANCER OF BUSINESS, ETC.

Guardians of the Poor.—In this month, notice for the Election of Guardians of the poor, will be issued by the Returning Officer for each Union. Landlords who have not claimed to vote in respect of rent payable to them, and Clergymen or Impropriators who have not claimed to vote in respect of Tithe Rent-charge—also Occupiers liable to rents under the nett annual value of their tenements, who have not claimed to vote in respect of the beneficial interests so possessed—should send in statements of their claims to the Board of Guardians of the Union, on or before the 18th of this month.

1st. Accounts of Borough Income and Expenditure for preceding year, to be transmitted to Lord Lieutenant, by Town Councils, Commissioners, or Boards of Guardians of the Poor, in whichever the property shall have been vested—3 & 4 Vic., c. 108.

THE CALENDAR.

1852.] **MARCH.** [31 Days.

Full Moon.................. 6th day, at 6m. past 5 Morning.
Last Quarter.............12th day, at 5m. past 8 Evening.
New Moon..................20th day, at 10m. past 6 Evening.
First Quarter............28th day, at 26m. past 8 Evening.

DAY OF MONTH	DAY OF WEEK.	REMARKABLE EVENTS.	MOON. Rises.	Sets.	HIGH WATER. Morn.	Even.
			H. M.	H. M.	H. M.	H. M.
1	Mo	Quest. of Parl. Ref. introduced 1831.	11м46	3 50	5 48	6 30
2	Tu	Rev. John Wesley died 1791.	0е47	4 46	7 10	7 51
3	We	Resumption of Russell Admin. 1851.	1 59	5 34	8 23	8 51
4	Th	First Mission to Tahiti 1796.	3 20	6 11	9 18	9 40
5	Fri	John Arundel died 1848.	4 48	6 41	10 3	10 26
6	Sat	Michael Angelo born 1474.	6 19	7 6	10 49	11 11
7	Su	2nd Sunday in Lent.	7 40	7 27	11 32	11 53
8	Mo	William III. died 1702.	9 18	7 49	—	0 13
9	Tu	Peace bet. Britain and Lahore 1846.	10е46	8 8	0 35	0 57
10	We	Benjamin West died 1820.	—	8 29	1 18	1 46
11	Th	Bishops expelled Parliament 1640.	0м12	8 55	2 16	2 39
12	Fri	Chelsea Hospital founded 1682.	1 33	9 26	3 7	3 36
13	Sat	James II. landed in Ireland 1688.	2 46	10 7	4 6	4 42
14	Su	3rd Sunday in Lent.	3 48	10 56	5 14	5 56
15	Mo	Ralph Erskine born 1685.	4 37	11м50	6 35	7 16
16	Tu	Voluntary Discus. bet. Drs. Cooke and	5 15	1е 3	7 53	8 27
17	We	St. Patrick's Day. [Ritchie 1836.	5 43	2 13	8 53	9 14
18	Th	Dr. Chalmers born in Fife 1780.	6 4	3 23	9 34	9 54
19	Fri	Sir J. Denham, poet, died 1688.	6 23	4 35	10 13	10 33
20	Sat	Sir Isaac Newton died 1727.	6 38	5 44	10 47	11 3
21	Su	4th Sunday in Lent.	6 52	6 52	11 19	11 33
22	Mo	Plague in London 1605.	7 6	8 1	11 48	—
23	Tu	Shakspeare born 1564.	7 21	9 10	0 1	0 13
24	We	Queen Elizabeth died 1603.	7 38	10 19	0 20	0 43
25	Th	Ec. Titles Bill read 2nd time 1851.	7 57	11е28	1 1	1 18
26	Fri	Reform Bill read first time 1830.	8 22	—	1 38	1 57
27	Sat	Archbishop French died 1839.	8 54	0м36	2 17	2 42
28	Su	5th Sunday in Lent.	9 35	1 40	3 6	3 32
29	Mo	Charles Wesley died 1788.	10 28	2 38	4 2	4 40
30	Tu	Annexation of the Punjaub 1849.	11 34	3 27	5 19	6 1
31	We	Allied Sovereigns entrd. Paris 1814.	11м49	4м 8	6 44	7 27

REMEMBRANCER OF BUSINESS, ETC.

1st. Copious Returns of Partners in Banks in Ireland to be published in the Dublin Gazette, by Commissioners of Stamps—8 & 9 Vic. c. 37.

18th. Last day for serving Publican's notices to obtain spirit license at Belfast Easter Sessions.

25th. Free Mason Societies and Friendly Brothers, to register name of Society, place and time of meeting, and names and description of Members, with the Clerk of the Peace for the county, annually, on or before this day—2 & 3 Vic., c. 74.—Guardians of the Poor to be elected for each Union, and those previously in office, not re-elected, to retire—1 & 2 Vic., c. 56.—Officers of Health (not less than two, or more than five), to be appointed, by Vestry, within one month after this date, in every Town containing 1,000 inhabitants, or where the Lord Lieutenant shall direct—59 G. III., c. 41.

| 1852.] | | **APRIL.** | | | [30 Days. |

FULL MOON................. 4th day, at 2 Evening.
LAST QUARTER............11th day, at 35m. past 8 Morning.
NEW MOON...................19th day, at 21m. past 11 Morning.
FIRST QUARTER............27th day, at 39m. past 7 Morning.

DAY OF MONTH	DAY OF WEEK	REMARKABLE EVENTS.	MOON. Rises.	Sets.	HIGH WATER. Morn.	Even.
			H. M.	H. M.	H. M.	H. M.
1	Th	Expedition to North Pole 1818.	2E13	4M40	8 3	8 31
2	Fri	Battle of Copenhagen 1801.	3 41	5 6	8 54	9 20
3	Sat	Bishop Heber died 1826.	5 12	5 28	9 42	10 3
4	Su	PALM SUNDAY. [1811, aged 76.	6 43	5 48	10 25	10 49
5	Mo	R. Raikes, founder of S. Schools, died	8 14	6 4	11 10	11 29
6	Tu	Richard Cœur de Lion died 1199.	9 44	6 29	11 51	—
7	We	Electricity first known 1467.	11E11	6 52	0 10	0 32
8	Th	Bonaparte abdicated 1814.	—	7 22	0 56	1 20
9	Fri	GOOD FRIDAY.	0M32	7 59	1 46	2 13
10	Sat	Foundation st. laid of 1st Presby. Ch.	1 42	8 47	2 42	3 7
11	Su	EASTER SUNDAY. [in Antigua 1840.	2 37	9 45	3 40	4 11
12	Mo	Marquis of Downshire d. 1845, aged 57	3 18	10M51	4 51	5 29
13	Tu	Catholic Relief Bill passed 1829.	3 50	0E 3	6 12	6 50
14	We	Otway died 1685	4 12	1 13	7 28	8 1
15	Th	12] America discovered 1492.	4 30	2 24	8 27	8 50
16	Fri	Buffon, naturalist, died 1788.	4 51	3 34	9 7	9 27
17	Sat	Benjamin Franklin died 1790.	5 0	4 43	9 44	9 59
18	Su	1ST SUNDAY AFTER EASTER.	5 14	5 52	10 16	10 33
19	Mo	Siege of Derry commenced 1680.	5 29	7 1	10 48	11 3
20	Tu	Sir C. S. Hunter died 1851.	5 44	8 10	11 17	11 32
21	We	Duke of Sussex died 1843.	6 3	9 21	11 45	11 58
22	Th	Peter Abelard died 1142.	6 24	10 29	—	0 14
23	Fri	Wordsworth died 1850.	6 54	11E35	0 32	0 50
24	Sat	Castle of Belfast burned 1708.	7 30	—	1 10	1 30
25	Su	2ND SUNDAY AFTER EASTER.	8 19	0M34	1 51	2 14
26	Mo	David Hume born 1711.	9 18	1 27	2 43	3 9
27	Tu	Edward Gibbon 1737.	10 28	2 9	3 39	4 16
28	We	Wreck of the Exmouth 1847.	11M47	2 43	4 58	5 40
29	Th	Washington inaugurated 1784.	1E11	3 9	6 23	7 2
30	Fri	1st Stone London Univer. laid 1827.	2 38	3M32	7 39	8 5

REMEMBRANCER OF BUSINESS, ETC.

In this month, a copy of the Entries in every Marriage Register, kept in pursuance of Act, to be delivered to the Registrar of the District—7 & 8 Vic., c. 81.

5th. Dividends fall due on the following Government Securities:—3 per cent. Reduced, and New 3¼ per cent. Stock; payable 8th.

8th. Fire Insurance Premium due 25th March, must be paid on or before this day, or the Policy becomes void.

THE CALENDAR.

1852.]		MAY.				[31 Days.	

Full Moon.................. 3rd day, 59m. past 9 Evening.
Last Quarter................10th day, 59m. past 10 Evening.
New Moon....................19th day, 51m. past 2 Morning.
First Quarter...............26th day, 14m. past 3 Afternoon.

DAY OF MONTH	DAY OF WEEK	REMARKABLE EVENTS.	MOON. Rises.	Sets.	HIGH WATER. Morn.	Even.
			H. M.	H. M.	H. M.	H. M.
1	Sat	Great Industrial Exhibition op. 1851.	4e 6	3m51	8 33	8 53
2	Su	3rd Sunday after Easter.	5 38	4 10	9 17	9 39
3	Mo	Jamaica discovered 1495.	7 9	4 29	10 0	10 24
4	Tu	Clocks introduced 1368.	8 39	4 50	10 45	11 6
5	We	Napoleon died 1821.	10 7	5 16	11 27	11 50
6	Th	1] Duke of Wellington born 1769.	11e25	5 50	—	0 11
7	Fri	Monster Meeting at Kildare 1843.	—	6 33	0 34	0 59
8	Sat	Bonaparte landed at Elba 1814.	0m29	7 29	1 24	1 51
9	Su	4th Sunday after Easter.	1 18	8 35	2 17	2 43
10	Mo	Battle of Lodi 1796.	1 54	9 46	3 14	3 42
11	Tu	Earl Chatham died 1778.	2 19	10 59	4 18	4 57
12	We	New Orleans inundated 1849.	2 39	11m12	5 37	6 15
13	Th	Vaccination introduced 1796.	2 55	1e23	6 49	7 22
14	Fri	Grattan died 1820. [1644.	3 9	2 32	7 48	8 12
15	Sat	Belfast surrendered to Gen. Munro	3 23	3 41	8 32	8 47
16	Su	Rogation Sunday—O'Connell d. 1847.	3 43	4 50	9 6	9 22
17	Mo	Trial by Jury instituted 970.	3 51	5 58	9 39	9 59
18	Tu	Disruption of Scottish G. Assembly	4 8	7 9	10 16	10 34
19	We	Montrose executed 1650. [1843.	4 29	8 20	10 48	11 4
20	Th	Ascension Day—Holy Thursday.	4 56	9 28	11 24	11 36
21	Fri	Miss Edgworth died 1849.	5 30	10 31	11 51	—
22	Sat	Pope, poet, born 1688.	6 15	11e23	0 11	0 30
23	Su	Sunday after Ascension Day.	7 11	—	0 51	1 13
24	Mo	Queen Victoria born 1819.	8 17	0m11	1 33	1 58
25	Tu	Princess Helena Augusta born 1846.	9 32	0 47	2 27	2 57
26	We	Dr. Dodd executed 1777.	10m54	1 15	3 26	3 59
27	Th	Calvin died at Geneva 1574, aged 54.	0e16	1 39	4 41	5 18
28	Fri	William Pitt born 1759.	1 41	1 57	5 57	6 35
29	Sat	Restoration of Charles II. 1660.	3 8	2 15	7 7	7 35
30	Su	Pentecost—Whit Sunday.	4 37	2 34	8 0	8 24
31	Mo	Dr. Chalmers d. at Edinburgh 1847.	6 e 7	2m52	8 46	9 15

REMEMBRANCER OF BUSINESS, ETC.

1st. Dredging for Oysters prohibited, generally, between this date and 1st September following—5 & 6 Vic., c. 106.

22nd. Trinity Term begins this day, and ends on Saturday, 12th June.

24th. The Queen's birth-day. A holiday in the Banks and public offices. Bills due on this day payable on the 22nd.

29th. Anniversary of the restoration of Monarchy in Great Britain.

THE CALENDAR.

[1852.]   **JUNE.**   [30 Days.

Full Moon.................. 2nd day, at 2m. past 6 Morning.
Last Quarter............. 9th day, at 51m. past 2 Afternoon.
New Moon.................. 17th day, at 23m. past 4 Afternoon.
First Quarter............ 24th day, at 23m. past 8 Evening.

Day of Month	Day of Week	REMARKABLE EVENTS.	Moon Rises H. M.	Moon Sets H. M.	High Water Morn. H. M.	High Water Even. H. M.
1	Tu	First Census of Belfast in 1757: Pro-	7E36	3M15	9 38	10 3
2	We	[testant, 7993 ; Roman Catholic, 556	8 59	3 44	10 27	10 50
3	Th	The Siege of Rome began 1849.	10 12	4 22	11 11	11 33
4	Fri	Netherlands divided 1831.	11 9	5 11	11 55	—
5	Sat	King of Hanover born 1771.	11E51	6 13	0 17	0 41
6	Su	Trinity Sunday.	—	7 24	1 7	1 30
7	Mo	Reform Bill recd. Royal Assent 1832	0M23	8 40	1 55	2 19
8	Tu	Ebenezer Erskine died 1754.	0 45	9 54	2 46	3 13
9	We	Dr. Carey died 1834, aged 72.	1 3	11M 7	3 41	4 14
10	Th	Oxford shot at Queen Victoria 1840.	1 17	0E16	4 44	5 17
11	Fri	George I. died 1727.	1 30	1 26	5 49	6 19
12	Sat	Collins, poet, died 1756.	1 44	2 36	6 47	7 17
13	Su	1st Sunday after Trinity.	1 59	3 45	7 42	8 5
14	Mo	William III. landed at C.fergus 1690.	2 15	4 55	8 27	8 47
15	Tu	Luther excommunicated 1520.	2 33	6 6	9 7	9 28
16	We	Duke of Marlborough died 1722.	2 58	7 15	9 48	10 6
17	Th	John Wesley born 1703.	3 39	8 22	10 24	10 43
18	Fri	Battle of Waterloo 1815.	4 12	9 21	11 2	11 19
19	Sat	20] Ascen. of Queen Victoria 1837.	5 4	10 11	11 35	11 57
20	Su	2nd Sunday after Trinity.	6 8	10 50	—	0 16
21	Mo	Ibrahim Pacha visited Belfast 1846.	7 21	11 21	0 39	1 1
22	Tu	World's Peace Convention 1843.	8 41	11E45	1 24	1 49
23	We	Akenside died 1770.	10 3	—	2 17	2 44
24	Th	Midsummer day.	11M26	0M 5	3 12	3 43
25	Fri	Battle of Bannockburn 1314.	0E50	0 23	4 21	4 57
26	Sat	George IV. died 1830.	2 16	0 40	5 31	5 57
27	Su	3rd Sunday after Trinity.	3 42	0 58	6 29	7 1
28	Mo	Victoria crowned 1838.	5 9	1 18	7 35	8 3
29	Tu	Rousseau born 1712.	6 35	1 43	8 33	8 59
30	We	William Roscoe died 1831.	7E52	2M15	9 26	9 49

REMEMBRANCER OF BUSINESS, ETC.

In this month, half-yearly Return of Transfers, &c., to be made to the Registrar of Joint Stock Companies, by every Company completely registered under Act, and not afterwards incorporated—7 & 8 Vic., c. 110.

1st. Clerk of Peace in Counties to make out and print copy of Parliamentary Voters' Register for each barony separately; to deliver precept to Clerks of Unions requiring revision of Register and Supplemental List of rate-payers. Clerk of Peace in Boroughs to make out List of Parliamentary Voters for each Ward ; to deliver his precept to Town Clerk, for publication of Notices, &c., under Parliamentary Voters Act.

12th. Last day for serving Publicans' notices to obtain Spirit License at Belfast Summer Sessions.

25th. Auctioneers to take out Excise License—8 & 9 Vic., c. 15.

28th. The Queen's Coronation day. Holiday in Government Offices. Poor-Rate Collectors to attend in a place to be named and notified, for three days, for receipt of Rates in baronies and boroughs.

THE CALENDAR.

[1852.] **JULY.** [31 Days.

FULL MOON.................. 1st day, at 4m. past 3 Evening.
LAST QUARTER.............. 9th day, at 42m. past 7 Morning.
NEW MOON.................17th day, at 51m. past 3 Morning.
FIRST QUARTER............24th day, at 37m. past 12 Morning.
FULL MOON.................31st day, at 47m. past 1 Morning.

Day of Month	Day of Week	REMARKABLE EVENTS.	MOON. Rises.	MOON. Sets.	HIGH WATER. Morn.	HIGH WATER. Even.
			H. M.	H. M.	H. M.	H. M.
1	Th	Battle of the Boyne 1690.	8E56	2M58	10 13	10 38
2	Fri	Sir Robert Peel died 1850, aged 62	9 46	3 55	11 1	11 23
3	Sat	Cranmer born 1489.	10 22	5 2	11 57	—
4	Su	4TH SUNDAY AFTER TRINITY.	10 48	6 16	0 3	0 26
5	Mo	French army entered Rome 1849.	11 8	7 33	0 47	1 10
6	Tu	Strange, engraver, died 1792.	11 24	9 48	1 33	1 52
7	We	John Huss burnt 1415.	11 38	10 0	2 16	2 39
8	Th	Duke of Cambridge died 1850.	11E52	11M12	3 1	3 24
9	Fri	Gen. Taylor P.U.S. d. at Washington	—	0E20	3 51	4 23
10	Sat	John Calvin born 1509. [1850.	0M 6	1 29	4 51	5 22
11	Su	5TH SUNDAY AFTER TRINITY.	0 21	2 40	5 40	6 13
12	Mo	Erasmus died 1536.	0 39	3 50	6 43	7 18
13	Tu	William Penn died 1718.	0 59	4 59	7 48	8 16
14	We	Bastile (Paris) destroyed 1789.	1 28	6 7	8 39	9 0
15	Th	Reform Bill passed 1832.	2 5	7 10	9 21	9 42
16	Fri	Cromwell mar. against Scotland 1650.	2 54	8 5	10 2	10 23
17	Sat	Dr. Isaac Watts born 1674.	3 55	8 48	10 44	11 5
18	Su	6TH SUNDAY AFTER TRINITY.	5 6	9 23	11 26	11 44
19	Mo	Lord W. Russell beheaded 1683.	6 26	9 50	—	0 5
20	Tu	Union of England & Scotland 1706.	7 49	10 12	0 26	0 49
21	We	Robert Burns died 1796.	9M14	10 30	1 15	1 37
22	Th	Battle of Aughrim 1691.	10 38	10 48	2 3	2 29
23	Fri	Gibraltar taken 1704.	0E 2	11 5	2 57	3 26
24	Sat	Habeas Corpus sus. in Ireland 1848.	1 27	11 23	3 56	4 29
25	Su	7TH SUNDAY AFTER TRINITY.	2 53	11E46	5 2	5 34
26	Mo	Second French Revolution 1830.	4 17	—	6 3	6 40
27	Tu	Battle of Talavera 1809.	5 36	0M15	7 18	7 52
28	We	Siege of Derry ended 1689	6 44	0 52	8 24	8 52
29	Th	Ecclesiastical Titles Bill passed 1851.	7 40	1 43	9 15	9 41
30	Fri	Dr. Paley born 1743.	8 20	2 46	10 3	10 27
31	Sat	Greenwich Hospital founded 1696.	8E50	3M56	10 50	11 11

REMEMBRANCER OF BUSINESS, ETC.

1st. Last day for payment of poor rates due up to 1st January, to qualify for voting in Parliamentary elections,—13 & 14 Vic., c. 69.

8th. Clerks of Unions to furnish Town Clerks with Lists of £8 Ratepayers in Boroughs, &c.; on or before this day to enter objections on Register of Voters received from Clerk of Peace. Last day for returning same to Clerk of Peace; to make out Supplemental List of £12 rate-payers for Clerk of Peace.

20th. Town Clerk to make out Lists of Parliamentary voters, annually; to be published on 22nd July; last day for Clerk of Peace to enter objections to Parliamentary Voters on Register of barony; to be published on or before 22nd July.

AUGUST.

1852.] [31 Days.

LAST QUARTER............. 8th day, at 2m. past 1 Morning.
NEW MOON.................15th day, at 34m. past 1 Afternoon.
FIRST QUARTER............22nd day, at 38m. past 5 Morning.
FULL MOON................29th day, at 42m. past 2 Afternoon.

DAY OF MONTH	DAY OF WEEK	REMARKABLE EVENTS.	MOON. Rises.	MOON. Sets.	HIGH WATER Morn.	HIGH WATER Even.
			H. M.	H. M.	H. M.	H. M.
1	Su	8TH SUNDAY AFTER TRINITY.	9E12	5M13	11 30	11 49
2	Mo	Belfast Poor-house founded 1771.	9 29	6 28	—	0 8
3	Tu	Queen Victoria landed at Cork 1849.	9 44	7 43	0 26	0 45
4	We	Admiral Duncan died 1804.	9 59	8 55	1 4	1 20
5	Th	Lord Howe died 1799.	10 11	10 4	1 40	2 0
6	Fri	Queen Victoria entered Dublin 1849.	10 26	11M14	2 22	2 45
7	Sat	Queen Caroline died 1821.	10 41	0E24	3 4	3 25
8	Su	9TH SUNDAY AFTER TRINITY.	11 1	1 32	3 48	4 16
9	Mo	Defeat of the Hungarians 1849.	11 25	2 43	4 45	5 13
10	Tu	Disturbances in Ireland 1848.	11E59	3 51	5 47	6 21
11	We	Queen Victoria visited Belfast 1849.	—	4 50	6 56	7 35
12	Th	George IV. born 1762.	0M42	5 54	8 7	8 33
13	Fri	Queen Adelaide born 1792.	1 38	6 42	8 59	9 21
14	Sat	Printing first introduced 1437.	2 44	7 20	9 44	10 5
15	Su	10TH SUNDAY AFTER TRINITY.	4 3	7 51	10 26	10 52
16	Mo	Sir Walter Scott born 1771.	5 28	8 15	11 9	11 30
17	Tu	Duchess of Kent born 1786.	6 55	8 35	11 49	—
18	We	M. Delambre died 1822.	8 21	8 53	0 11	0 34
19	Th	Sir M. A. Shee, Pres. R.A., d. 1850.	9 47	9 10	0 55	1 18
20	Fri	Ashburton Treaty signed 1842.	11M13	9 29	1 40	2 4
21	Sat	The Royal George sunk 1782.	0E41	9 50	2 37	3 3
22	Su	11TH SUNDAY AFTER TRINITY.	2 6	10 16	3 32	4 3
23	Mo	Battle of Bosworth 1485.	3 27	10 52	4 30	5 3
24	Tu	Wallace beheaded 1305.	4 37	11E37	5 42	6 25
25	We	26] Louis Philippe died 1850.	5 35	—	7 3	7 41
26	Th	Prince Albert born 1819.	6 19	0M34	8 14	8 44
27	Fri	Battle of Dresden 1813.	6 52	1 42	9 8	9 34
28	Sat	29] Belfast first lighted with gas 1823.	7 16	2 56	9 53	10 14
29	Su	12TH SUNDAY AFTER TRINITY.	7 34	4 12	10 35	10 53
30	Mo	John Locke born 1632.	7 52	5 27	11 11	11 29
31	Tu	John Bunyan died 1688.	8 E 3	6M40	11 44	11 58

REMEMBRANCER OF BUSINESS, ETC.

Borough Taxes and Poor Rates due on or before 31st May preceding, must be paid in this month, to qualify Burgesses to vote at the next Municipal Election—3 & 4 Vic., c. 108.

1st. Town Commissioners for Paving, &c., to elect Chairman, who is to go out of office 31st July following—9 Geo. IV., c. 82.

4th. Notices of claim to vote as Parliamentary electors must be served on or before this day—13 & 14 Vic., c. 69.

9th. Clerks of Peace to prepare lists of claimants to vote as Parliamentary electors, and to publish same on or before 11th instant—13 & 14 Vic., c. 69

20th. Notices of objections to persons registered, or claiming to be registered, as Parliamentary voters, must be served on or before this date.

22nd. Clerks of Peace in counties, and Clerks in boroughs, to make out lists of persons objected to, as Parliamentary electors, and publish same.

THE CALENDAR. 21

| 1852.] | | **SEPTEMBER.** | | | [30 Days. |

Last Quarter................. 6th day, 10m. past 6 Evening.
New Moon.....................13th day, 14m. past 10 Evening.
First Quarter................20th day, 53m. past 12 Noon.
Full Moon ....28th day, 1m. past 6 Morning.

DAY OF MONTH	DAY OF WEEK	REMARKABLE EVENTS.	MOON. Rises.	Sets.	HIGH WATER. Morn.	Even.
			H. M.	H. M.	H. M.	H. M.
1	We	*Belfast News-Letter* com. 1737.	8E17	7M50	—	0 16
2	Th	Oliver Cromwell born 1599.	8 30	8 59	0 31	0 47
3	Fri	Oliver Cromwell died 1658.	8 46	10 9	1 1	1 18
4	Sat	Hudson River discovered 1609.	9 4	11M18	1 36	1 59
5	Su	13th Sunday after Trinity.	9 25	0E29	2 18	2 39
6	Mo	Lafayette born 1757.	9 53	1 36	3 0	3 23
7	Tu	Lieut. Gale, æronaut, killed 1850.	10 31	2 42	3 50	4 21
8	We	Queen Elizabeth born 1533.	11E19	3 42	4 58	5 37
9	Th	Mungo Park died 1771.	—	4 33	6 14	6 53
10	Fri	Pr. of Wales creat. Earl of Dub. 1849	0M22	5 17	7 32	8 8
11	Sat	William the Conqueror died 1087.	1 35	5 49	8 35	9 0
12	Su	14th Sunday after Trinity.	2 57	6 15	9 23	9 45
13	Mo	Wolfe killed 1759. Fox died 1806.	4 23	6 37	10 7	10 27
14	Tu	R. Raikes, founder of S. Sch. b. 1735.	5 54	6 56	10 49	11 9
15	We	Gold received from California 1849.	7 23	7 14	11 28	11 50
16	Th	James II. died 1701.	8 53	7 32	—	0 9
17	Fri	London and Bir. Rail. opened 1838.	10 23	7 52	0 31	0 52
18	Sat	Samuel Johnson born 1709.	11M52	8 18	1 16	1 42
19	Su	15th Sunday after Trinity.	1E17	8 49	2 3	2 36
20	Mo	Battle of Newbury 1643.	2 33	9 32	3 6	3 38
21	Tu	Sir W. Scott died 1832.	3 34	10 26	4 10	4 47
22	We	Great Britain st. stranded Dundrum	4 23	11E33	5 27	6 7
23	Th	Wallace executed 1305. [Bay 1846.	4 57	—	6 51	7 30
24	Fri	Ulster Inst. for Deaf, Dumb, & Blind,	5 22	0M44	8 6	8 32
25	Sat	Mrs Hemans born 1794. [op. 1845.	5 41	1 59	8 57	9 17
26	Su	16th Sunday after Trinity.	5 57	3 14	9 36	9 54
27	Mo	Philadelphia taken 1777.	6 11	4 27	10 12	10 30
28	Tu	George Buchanan died 1582.	6 24	5 39	10 47	11 2
29	We	Lord Nelson born 1758.	6 37	6 48	11 16	11 32
30	Th	G. Whitfield died 1770.	6E53	7M58	11 43	11 56

REMEMBRANCER OF BUSINESS, ETC.

8th. Revision Courts under Parliamentary Voters Act, to be held between this day and the 25th day of October, inclusive—13 & 14 Vic., c. 69.—Town Clerk of each Municipal Borough to prepare an alphabetical list of Burgesses; Collectors of local taxes attending to insert sums paid—6 & 7 Vic., c. 93.

18th. Publicans, Distillers, and Brewers, to give notice of application for renewal of license, on or before this day—6 Geo. IV., c. 81.

20th. Town Clerk to prepare Burgess lists for each ward, and allow access for perusal by all persons, without fee, until 30th, delivering a signed copy to Mayor on 20th—6 & 7 Vic., c. 93.

22nd. Town Clerk to have a copy of lists posted conspicuously from this day to 30th—6 & 7 Vic., c. 93.

29th. Ex-Officio Guardians of the Poor, to be selected for each Union, from qualified Justices, not being Clergymen, Assistant-Barristers, or Stipendiaries—1 & 2 Vic., c. 56.

OCTOBER.

1852.] [31 Days.

Last Quarter............. 6th day, at 12m. past 10 Morning.
New Moon................13th day, at 50m. past 6 Morning.
First Quarter............19th day, at 32m. past 11 Evening.
Full Moon................27th day, at 30m. past 11 Evening.

DAY OF MONTH	DAY OF WEEK	REMARKABLE EVENTS.	MOON. Rises.	Sets.	HIGH WATER Morn.	Even.
			H. M.	H. M.	H. M.	H. M.
1	Fri	London University opened 1828.	7 E 7	9 M 9	—	0 11
2	Sat	Dr. Channing died 1842.	7 27	10 17	0 27	0 44
3	Su	17th Sunday after Trinity.	7 51	11m26	1 3	1 21
4	Mo	John Rennie died 1821.	8 26	0E32	1 40	2 0
5	Tu	Marquis of Donegall died 1844.	9 8	1 34	2 22	2 40
6	We	Louis Philippe born in Paris 1773.	10 2	2 28	3 15	3 55
7	Th	Zimmerman died 1795.	11e10	3 11	4 21	4 59
8	Fri	Cortez entered Mexico 1519.	—	3 48	5 44	6 25
9	Sat	Eddystone Lighthouse compl. 1759.	0m26	4 19	7 7	7 41
10	Su	18th Sunday after Trinity.	1 50	4 38	8 19	8 36
11	Mo	Dr. Abercrombie born 1781.	3 18	4 58	8 59	9 20
12	Tu	National Guards visited London 1848	4 47	5 16	9 41	10 2
13	We	Canova died 1832.	6 19	5 34	10 25	10 46
14	Th	William Penn born 1644.	7 52	5 53	11 5	11 24
15	Fri	John Foster died 1843.	9 25	6 15	11 45	—
16	Sat	Houses of Parliament burnt 1834.	10m56	6 45	0 6	0 29
17	Su	19th Sunday after Trinity.	0E19	7 24	0 54	1 19
18	Mo	Dean Swift died 1745.	1 30	8 16	1 48	2 15
19	Tu	Meagher and others convicted 1848.	2 23	9 20	2 45	3 14
20	We	Sir Christopher Wren born 1632.	3 2	10 32	3 52	4 30
21	Th	Battle of Trafalgar 1805.	3 30	11e47	5 9	5 51
22	Fri	Lord Holland died 1840.	3 50	—	6 32	7 12
23	Sat	Irish Rebellion and Massacre 1641.	4 6	1 m 2	7 45	8 9
24	Su	20th Sunday after Trinity.	4 20	2 10	8 33	8 51
25	Mo	Battle of Agincourt 1415.	4 33	3 27	9 9	9 25
26	Tu	Sir G. Kneller died 1726.	4 45	4 38	9 41	9 58
27	We	25] 1st British Parliament 1707.	4 59	5 47	10 16	10 30
28	Th	Dr. Doddridge died 1751.	5 14	6 57	10 46	11 0
29	Fri	Sir Walter Raleigh beheaded 1618.	5 32	8 8	11 16	11 29
30	Sat	Tower of London burnt 1841.	5 54	9 18	11 44	11 59
31	Su	21st Sunday after Trinity.	6E26	10m25	—	0 17

REMEMBRANCER OF BUSINESS, ETC.

In this month, the Justices assembled at Quarter Sessions fix a day in each division of the county, for a special sessions to be held for the revision of the Jurors lists.

1st. Notices of Objections to Burgesses inserted in lists, and of claims to be inserted, must, on this day, be given to the Town Clerk, and the former left at premises of persons objected to—6 & 7 Vic., c. 93.

12th. Municipal Borough Lists of Objections and Claims, to be posted conspicuously in Borough, for 8 days next preceding 20th October.— Town Clerk to keep copies of lists, for perusal during same time, without fee—6 & 7 Vic., c. 93.

13th. Fire Insurance Premium due at Michaelmas, must be paid on or before this day, or the policy becomes void.

25th. County Revision Courts, under Parliamentary Voters Act, to be held between 8th September and this day—13 & 14 Vic., c. 69.

THE CALENDAR. 23

| 1852.] | | **NOVEMBER.** | | | [30 Days. | | |

LAST QUARTER............ 5th day, at 17m. past 12 Morning.
NEW MOON................11th day, at 17m. past 4 Evening.
FIST QUARTER............18th day, at 3m. past 2 Evening.
FULL MOON...............26th day, at 17m. past 6 Evening.

DAY OF MONTH	DAY OF WEEK	REMARKABLE EVENTS.	MOON. Rises.	Sets.	HIGH WATER Morn.	Even.
			H. M.	H. M.	H. M.	H. M.
1	Mo	Great monetary difficulty 1847.	7 E 4	11M29	0 34	0 51
2	Tu	Kauffman died 1807	7 52	0E26	1 11	1 31
3	We	Prince of Orange born 1650.	8 54	1 13	1 57	2 21
4	Th	Wm. III. landed in England 1690.	10 4	1 51	2 48	3 17
5	Fri	Gunpowder Plot.	11E23	2 20	3 55	4 31
6	Sat	Princess Charlotte died 1817.	—	2 43	5 13	5 56
7	Su	22ND SUNDAY AFTER TRINITY.	0M46	3 2	6 36	7 11
8	Mo	Milton died 1674.	2 13	3 20	7 41	8 8
9	Tu	Prince of Wales born 1841.	3 42	3 37	8 29	8 53
10	We	Martin Luther born 1483.	5 12	3 54	9 22	9 32
11	Th	French Republic established 1848.	6 46	4 14	9 54	10 19
12	Fri	Bishop Gardner died 1555.	8 21	4 40	10 41	11 2
13	Sat	Execution of the Mannings 1849.	9 52	5 14	11 24	11 46
14	Su	23RD SUNDAY AFTER TRINITY.	11M12	6 1	—	0 11
15	Mo	Old Parr died 1635, aged 152.	0E 16	7 1	0 32	1 2
16	Tu	Battle of Lutzen, Gustavus k., 1632.	1 2	8 14	1 29	1 50
17	We	Queen Mary died 1558.	1 35	19 31	2 24	2 57
18	Th	Ernest, King of Hanover, died 1851.	1 58	0E48	3 26	4 2
19	Fri	Charles I. born 1600.	2 16	—	4 36	5 16
20	Sat	Cape of Good Hope doubled 1497.	2 30	0M 4	5 54	6 29
21	Su	24TH SUNDAY AFTER TRINITY.	2 42	1 17	7 2	7 31
22	Mo	Lord Clive died 1774.	2 54	2 28	7 52	8 14
23	Tu	24] Flight of the Pope f. Rome 1848	3 7	3 36	8 31	8 48
24	We	John Knox died 1572, aged 67.	3 24	4 46	9 6	9 25
25	Th	Dr. Isaac Watts died 1748.	3 38	5 56	9 43	10 2
26	Fri	Great Storm in London 1703.	3 58	7 7	10 20	10 35
27	Sat	Princess Mary of Cambridge b. 1833.	4 25	8 16	10 51	11 6
28	Su	1ST SUNDAY IN ADVENT.	5 2	9 21	11 21	11 37
29	Mo	Oliver Goldsmith born 1731.	5 47	11 22	11 54	—
30	Tu	29] Siege of Drogheda com. 1641.	6E45	11M14	0 14	0 34

REMEMBRANCER OF BUSINESS, ETC.

15th. Clerks of the Peace, on or before this day, to post notice, of the times appointed for holding Quarter Sessions, for the year 1853.

20th. Town Clerks to have Burgess Roll completed this day, from revised Lists—5 & 6 Vic. c. 93.

25th. Borough Councillors to be elected—5 & 6 Vic., c. 93.

30th. Plans, Sections, and Books of Reference, relating to any projected line of Railway must be deposited on or before this day, with the Clerk of the Peace and at the Railway Board, London, prior to application to Parliament for Act of Incorporation.—Clerk of the Peace to deliver over to Returning Officer for Borough, and Sheriff for Levy, the Book containing the revised list of Parliamentary Voters, on or before this day.

[1852.] **DECEMBER.** [31 Days.

Last Quarter................. 4th day, 58m. past 11 Morning.
New Moon..................... 11th day, 8m. past 3 Morning.
First Quarter............... 18th day, 15m. past 8 Morning.
Full Moon.................... 26th day, 46m. past 12 Evening.

Day of Month	Day of Week	REMARKABLE EVENTS.	MOON. Rises.	Sets.	HIGH WATER. Morn.	Even.
			H. M.	H. M.	H. M.	H. M.
1	We	Ebenezer Elliott died 1849.	7E53	11M53	0 54	1 15
2	Th	Kildare-place Society establish. 1811.	9 7	0E25	1 38	2 7
3	Fri	James II. abdicated 1688.	10 28	0 49	2 31	2 59
4	Sat	Cardinal Richelieu died 1642.	11E49	1 9	3 29	4 7
5	Su	2nd Sunday in Advent.	—	1 26	4 41	5 18
6	Mo	General Monk born 1608.	1M14	1 42	5 57	6 32
7	Tu	Flaxman died 1826.	2 40	1 57	7 2	7 27
8	We	Richard Baxter died 1691.	4 10	2 15	7 53	8 18
9	Th	Milton born 1608.	5 43	2 37	8 43	9 12
10	Fri	Grouse shooting ends.	5 15	3 6	9 36	10 0
11	Sat	Charles XII. killed 1718.	8 40	3 45	10 24	10 49
12	Su	3rd Sunday in Advent.	9 57	4 39	11 10	11 33
13	Mo	Dr. Johnson died 1784.	10 56	5 48	11 55	—
14	Tu	General Washington died 1799.	11M35	7 6	0 21	0 48
15	We	Bonaparte born 1784.	0E 1	8 26	1 10	1 36
16	Th	Bonaparte's decree 1807.	0 22	9 45	2 2	2 31
17	Fri	Gray born 1724.	0 37	11E 0	2 58	3 24
18	Sat	Sir H. Davy born 1778.	0 51	—	3 54	4 24
19	Su	4th Sunday in Advent.	1 3	0M13	4 55	5 30
20	Mo	Louis Napoleon proclaimed 1848.	1 16	1 24	5 54	6 25
21	Tu	Shortest day.	1 29	2 33	6 51	7 20
22	We	T. Holcroft born, 1744.	1 45	3 44	7 48	8 14
23	Th	Duke of Guise assassinated 1588.	2 3	4 54	8 34	8 53
24	Fri	Peace with America 1804.	2 28	6 4	9 15	9 36
25	Sat	Christmas Day.	3 0	7 11	9 53	10 12
26	Su	1st Sunday after Christmas.	3 43	8 14	10 30	10 49
27	Mo	Charles Lamb died 1834.	4 37	9 9	11 8	11 26
28	Tu	Dr. C. Burney died 1817.	5 44	9 53	11 43	—
29	We	Thomas A'Beckett murdered 1174.	6 57	10 29	0 1	0 22
30	Th	Malthus died 1834.	8 15	10 56	0 45	1 7
31	Fri	Wycliffe died 1384.	9E37	11M16	1 30	1 54

REMEMBRANCER OF BUSINESS, ETC.

1st. Borough Council to elect a Mayor out of the Aldermen or Councillors—to enter office on the 1st of January—6 & 7 Vic. c. 93.

3rd. Borough Auditors and Assessors (two of each) to be elected by the whole body of qualified Burgesses; and two Assessors for each Ward to be elected by its Burgesses—5 & 6 Vic. c. 93.

25th. County Treasurers to transmit to Chief Secretary for Ireland, before this day, copies of all Presentments made and fiated; to be laid before Parliament. Forfeiture of office for neglect—6 & 7 Wm. IV. c. 116.

31st. Within twenty-one days after this date, the Owner or Master of every Ship trading to Foreign places or the Colonies, and of every British registered Ship of 80 tons or upwards, employed in the Fisheries, or trading between Ports within the United Kingdom—to furnish to a Collector of Customs, the original or copy of every agreement for Wages made in the preceding half-year with the seamen employed.

BELFAST.

HISTORICAL RETROSPECT.

The first historical notice of Belfast occurs in the records of the twelfth century. About the middle of that period, we find that a fort existed in this locality, which was destroyed in the year 1178, by the celebrated John de Courcy, to whom a grant of the entire province of Ulster had been made by Henry the Second. From that period, little is known of the place, or the changes it underwent, until the invasion of the celebrated Edward Bruce, in 1315, at which time we learn that Belfast was a " good town and stronghold," the ancient fort having given place to a substantial castle. It appears that the English and the native Ulster Chieftains held alternate possession of the town and castle, during a lengthened series of sanguinary conflicts, until the year 1575, when a large tract of territory, including the Castle of Belfast, which had been several times, during the civil wars, destroyed and re-built, was granted by Queen Elizabeth to Sir Thomas Smith on certain conditions. These conditions not having been fulfilled, the entire estate of the English was granted, in 1612, to the Lord Deputy Chichester. In the year following, a charter was granted to the sovereign, twelve burgesses, and commonalty of Belfast. This charter constituted Lord Chichester, then newly created a Baron, his heirs, &c., lords of the castle and manor, and authorised the borough to send two members to Parliament. The first Sovereign was Thomas Vesey, Esq., and the first Parliamentary representatives were Sir John Blennerhasset, Baron of the Exchequer, and George Trevallion, Esquire.

The population of Belfast and its vicinity, which was a distinct territory at this period, mainly consisted of English and Scotch settlers, according to the policy of James I., who resolved, wisely, to plant his Irish possessions with colonists from Great Britain. The town itself was still an exceedingly insignificant place, consisting only of the castle, a Church, and a collection of houses, known by the name of "the village." But under the new government it rapidly began to enlarge itself; and, from this era, symptoms of its future prosperity and importance began to manifest themselves.

In the year 1637, Belfast obtained, by purchase, from the Corporation of Carrickfergus, the right of importing commodities, at one-third of the duties payable at other places, and it thus became a port of considerable trade. Even in the midst of the alarms and misfortunes to which the inhabitants were subjected during the war between Charles I. and the Parliament, and the rage of sectarian strife, which reached even this remote quarter of English rule, the commerce of Belfast continued slowly but steadily to increase, so much so that, in the period from 1683 to 1686, we find that 67 vessels, with an aggregate tonnage of 3,307 tons, belonged to the port. Previously, the military defences of the town had been much strengthened by Charles I., who granted £1,000 to the then governor, Colonel Chichester, newly created Earl of Donegall, for that purpose. Belfast, during the civil war, was thrice in the hands of the Parliamentarians, and it was under the protectorate of Cromwell that it made its first and most rapid strides towards social and commercial importance.

The charter was renewed in 1688 by James II., the number of burgesses being raised to thirty-five. The policy of James was, however, so distasteful to the inhabitants generally, that they declared for the Prince of Orange immediately on his arrival. It was not, however, until after the reduction of James's adherents, by the Duke of Schomberg, that Belfast could be properly described as under the sway of the new monarch. On the 14th of June, 1690, King William the Third visited Belfast, where he remained for five nights, lodging in the house of Sir William Franklin, which stood on the present site of the Donegall Arms Hotel. It was during this visit that his Majesty authorised the grant of £1,200 a-year, to the Presbyterian ministers of Ulster, who had suffered greatly in his cause, and this was the origin of the *Regium Donum*. It was in 1642 that the first Presbytery had been held in Carrickfergus, and in 1645, that the first Presbyterian congregation was established in Belfast.

Though the trade of the town and port had greatly increased for some time previous to the Revolution settlement, the town itself was extremely insignificant. The houses were thatched; goods were exposed for sale chiefly in the open streets, and there were no public buildings save the Castle, the Church, the Market house, and the "Long Bridge," which had been just finished. Nevertheless, the population was becoming numerous, and soon began to prove how much they appreciated the blessings of peace and good government.

The progress of the town from this period until the time when Belfast became one of the most flourishing and prosperous communities in the island, will be chiefly noted by the history of each of its present institutions under their distinctive heads. During the reign of Queen Anne and the two first monarchs of the House of Hanover, the inhabitants were distinguished not more for their love of the arts of peaceful industry, than for their loyal attachment to the throne. The last remnant of the semi-barbarous period, through the mists of which we have to look for fragmentary notices of the early origin and progress of the

HISTORICAL RETROSPECT.

town—the celebrated castle of Belfast—was destroyed by fire in 1708, the three daughters of the then Earl of Donegall having perished in the conflagration. Volunteer corps were formed for the first time in the period rendered memorable by the menaced invasion of the Pretender, and these corps were effectually organised in 1760, when the French Admiral, Thurot, landed at Carrickfergus, and reduced the garrison there, as a preparatory step to the intended capture of Belfast. The Volunteers were again enrolled in 1779, on the rumour of another French invasion; and in the course of a few years, the movement being general throughout the country, they presented a well disciplined force of 5,000 men, exercising a political influence, which was at last considered so hostile to the English Government, that it was thought necessary to extinguish the corps in 1793. Notwithstanding the proclamations of the Government, the military organisation survived, and was directed to the vain effort of securing independence of English rule. Arrests and penalties were alike unavailing, and, in 1795, seventy-two associations of "United Irishmen" were represented at a meeting in Belfast, held with the view of completing arrangements for action. The news of another French invasion revived the spirit of loyalty in 1798, and, when the rebellion of that year broke out, the yeomanry of Belfast and the adjoining counties were found on the side of the Government troops at Antrim and Ballynahinch. After the passing of the Act of Union, the Municipal Government of Belfast was materially altered by the appointment of Police Commissioners and "Life Commissioners," in conjunction with the former Corporation; these new local bodies being invested, the former with the levying of taxes for public expenses, and the latter with powers for regulating the paving, lighting, and cleansing of the town. The first Sovereign, under the new order of things, was John Brown, Esq., and, under this local Government, the borough continued until the passing of the Municipal Act of 1841, in conformity with which, the Corporation now consists of a Mayor, ten Aldermen, and thirty Town Councillors. The first Mayor of Belfast was George Dunbar, Esq. Various other public bodies were incorporated at different times—such as the Harbour Commissioners, the Water Commissioners, &c., under whose management, in conjunction with the Town Council, the borough and port progressed to such a degree of prosperity, that Belfast has, at length, earned the acknowledged title of the commercial metropolis of Ireland.

SITE, EXTENT, POPULATION, ETC.

Belfast, properly so called, is situate in the Barony of Upper Belfast, in the County of Antrim; but the large suburb of Ballymacarrett, which is only separated from the town by the river Lagan, forms a portion of the County Down. The whole comprises an area of 1,872 acres, of which

576 acres are occupied by Ballymacarrett. Of this area, 1,542 acres are within the Municipal boundary, and 330 without.

The parish of Belfast, otherwise called Shankhill, in which the borough is included, lies chiefly in the Barony of Upper Belfast and partly in the Barony of Lower Belfast. It is nine miles and a quarter long, by five in breadth, and contains, according to the Ordnance survey, 19,559 statute acres—exclusive of the borough, 18,263 acres. The town is 80 Irish miles distant from Dublin, in lat. 54 deg. 36 min. 8·5 sec. North, and long. 5 deg. 55 min. 53·7 sec. West. It stands at the mouth of the Lagan, where that river expands into the Belfast Lough.

For the purposes of commerce, it is most commodiously situated, all the natural impediments to the navigation of the harbour and lough having been recently removed by the energy and industry of the inhabitants. The site of the town is low, a great portion of it consisting of land reclaimed from the sea, and few parts being more than six feet above high water mark; owing to which cause, the streets in the neighbourhood of the river are occasionally inundated, the fall not being sufficient to carry off the floods which descend, in rainy weather, from the hills in the vicinity. Except, however, during the prevalence of epidemics, the town is considered healthy, and, when the sanitary regulations, now contemplated and partly in operation, are completed, few manufacturing centres in the United Kingdom will, probably, be found more generally free from the noxious influences which induce disease. The scenery of the suburbs and adjacent districts is not surpassed in picturesqueness by the environs of any other Irish town. From every elevated point a series of splendid prospects may be obtained. The harbour commands a noble view down the Lough, which is twelve miles in length by five in width, bounded on the Northern shore by a range of basaltic mountains, one of which, Cave Hill, is broken on its South-Eastern face into abrupt precipices, and, overlooking the town at a distance of only three miles, forms a grand and peculiar feature in the landscape. The opposite, or County Down shore, rises gently from the level of the Lough in swelling uplands, whose wavy outline well contrasts with the sterner aspect of the Antrim hills. On both sides the eye rests with pleasure upon a succession of handsome villas, richly wooded slopes, well cultivated farms, and smiling towns. Westward and Southward, the view is equally striking. The valley of the Lagan, a broad and fertile tract, expands as far as the eye can reach along the base of a verdant and graceful range of mountains, of considerable elevation, with undulating outline. In every direction, the aspect of the suburban districts combines the charms of rural beauty and elegant retirement, with the enlivening evidences of manufacturing industry.

The river Lagan, which separates the counties of Antrim and Down, is crossed by three bridges, and several boat ferries. The Queen's

RELIGIOUS INSTITUTIONS.

Bridge, built on the site of the old Long Bridge, is a massive granite structure, with five arches. It was opened for public traffic in 1844.

The population of Belfast in 1834 amounted to 60,813, of which 16,388 were members of the Established Church; 23,576 Presbyterians; 19,712 of the Roman Catholic persuasion; and 1137 of other persuasions. In 1841, the population, within the municipal boundary, was 70,447: without, 4,861: total, 75,308, of which 68,611 were in Antrim, and 6,697 in Down; the total of inhabited houses being 10,906, averaging 6·9 persons to a house. Since the year 1834, there is no record of the proportions belonging to the different religious denominations. According to the census of 1851, the population is 99,660, including Ballymacarrett; the increase between 1841 and 1851 being no less than 24,352, a larger increase than that exhibited by any other town in Ireland within the same period, numerically, though the *rate* of increase in the town of Galway has been higher. This population of 99,660, consists of 46,443 males and 53,217 females. The total number of families is 20,553. The number of houses on the 31st of March, 1851, the date at which the census was taken, was 15,100, of which 13,965 were inhabited, 1,050 uninhabited, and 85 in process of building. The increase of inhabited houses since 1841, is 3,059, being at the rate of 28 per cent. The decrease of uninhabited houses, during the same period, has been 856, being at the rate of 44 per cent. The increase of houses in progress of building since 1841 has been 22, being at the rate of 34 per cent. Both in the census of 1841 and in that of 1851, Belfast is exhibited as a separate district.

RELIGIOUS INSTITUTIONS.

The total number of places of worship in Belfast is forty-eight: the prevailing denominations are those of the Established, Presbyterian, Wesleyan, and Roman Catholic Churches. The Established Church possesses ten religious edifices, viz.:—St. Anne's (the Parish Church), St. George's, Christ Church, Magdalen Church, Shankhill Church, Trinity Church, Malone Chapel of Ease, St. Paul's Church, Ballymacarrett, and the Military Chapel, Infantry Barracks. A new Episcopal Church (St. John's), is about to be erected near Oxford street. There are twenty-one Presbyterian Churches, of which there are, in connection with the General Assembly of the Presbyterian Church in Ireland, the following, viz.:—Rosemary Street, Fisherwick Place, May Street, Donegall Street, Linenhall Street, York Street, Alfred Street, Alfred Place, Townsend Street, Great George's Street, College Square, Ballymacarrett, Malone, Berry Street, Bethel Chapel, and Crumlin Road. In connection with the Unitarian body, the following:—First Unitarian, Second Unitarian (both in Rosemary Street), and Third Unitarian in York Street; in connection with the Covenanters, the following:—Dublin Road (Eastern Reformed), and College Square South (Reformed Presbyterian). There are seven houses of worship in connection with the Methodist Societies, viz.:—

Donegall (Wesleyan), York Street (New Connexion), Frederick Street (Wesleyan), Ballymacarrett (Wesleyan), Wesley Place (Wesleyan), Donegall Place (Primitive), and Melbourne Street. The Roman Catholic Chapels are four, viz.:—St. Mary's, St. Patrick's, St. Malachy's, and the Ballymacarrett Chapel. The Society of Friends have one Chapel, in Frederick Street; the Independents one, in Donegall Street; the Baptists one, in Academy Street; and the Latter-Day Saints, or Mormonites, one, in King Street. There are, besides, two Wesleyan Chapels about to be built—one in Shankhill, and the other to accommodate the dense manufacturing population on the Falls Road. The former is to be in connexion with the Frederick Street Congregation, and the latter with Donegall Square East Church. Almost every one of the leading congregations in the town, of whatever persuasion, has a Sabbath School, and many of them a daily school, in connexion with its place of public worship.

The greater number of the religious edifices are handsome structures, some of them built in a style of considerable architectural taste. St. Anne's Church, in Donegall Street, erected in 1778, has a fine Doric portico, Ionic tower, and Corinthian steeple. Trinity Church, near the Antrim Road, built in 1843, at private expense, is a handsome Gothic structure, with an exceedingly graceful octagonal spire. St. George's Church, in High Street, erected in 1812, possesses one of the finest Corinthian tetrastyle porticoes in Ireland—the gift of Dr. Alexander, then bishop of the diocese, and formerly the chief ornament of the palace of Ballyscullion, built by the celebrated Earl of Bristol, when Bishop of Derry. The Church of the First Presbyterian Congregation in connexion with the General Assembly, in Rosemary Street, is a noble edifice, with a grand Doric portico, reached by twenty steps, and finished in the interior in a style of costly magnificence. The Fisherwick Place Presbyterian Church, opened in 1827, boasts of an elegant portico of four Ionic columns, with capitals imitated from the temple of Ilyssus. It was erected by Mr. Millar, a native architect, at a cost of £10,000. The May Street Presbyterian Church, opened in 1829, has a recessed Ionic portico, with two massive fluted columns and four pilasters; it is of large dimensions, and its interior is very elegantly designed and decorated. Christ Church possesses a massive cut stone front, with an Ionic portico of two pillars surmounted by an entablature. The Wesleyan Church, Donegall Square East, is an exceedingly handsome edifice, the facade consisting almost entirely of a hexastyle Corinthian portico. The interior is light, cheerful, and finished with great attention to elegance and convenience. St. Malachy's Chapel, in M'Clean's fields, is a large brick building, in the Tudor style, cruciform in shape, with several turrets surmounting the gables, and decorated in the interior with an exquisite and elaborate traceried ceiling. The newly erected

Church of St. Paul's, in York Street, is a Gothic structure, in the early style, with lancet windows, cut stone belfry, and crocket finials.

EDUCATIONAL INSTITUTIONS.

Perhaps no town in the empire can boast of a greater number of educational establishments, in proportion to its size, than Belfast. They may be enumerated, according to their dates, as follow:—The Belfast Academy, the Royal Academical Institution, the Brown Street Schools, the Lancasterian or Ragged Schools, the National Schools, the Ulster Institution for the Deaf and Dumb and the Blind, the Educational and Industrial School, the Queen's College, and the Government School of Design.

The Belfast Academy—the first important seminary established in the town, was founded in 1786. It early obtained a high reputation, from the ability with which it was conducted under its successive principals, and is still regarded as one of the best seminaries for classical and mercantile education in the kingdom. The success of this academy first suggested the plan of the Royal Academical Institution.

The Royal Academical Institution was founded by voluntary subscription in 1810, when the proprietors became incorporated by Act of Parliament, and received a public grant of £1,500 per annum, increased, in 1834, to £3,500. A medical school was added in 1836. It originally included two schools, one for the education of pupils intended for the learned professions, and the other for instructions in the ordinary branches of education. Lectureships were included in the foundation to the number of seven, each professor receiving a salary of £150, besides two professorships of divinity with a salary of £100 a-year each. The government of the Institution consisted of a president, four vice-presidents, twenty managers, and eight visitors. For a long period of years the Royal Academical Institution continued to afford instruction to the students of the Orthodox Presbyterian bodies of Ulster, until the General Assembly ceased to be connected with it; and, in 1849, the collegiate department was dissolved and transferred to the Queen's College. The schools, however, still occupy the main portion of the building, and continue in a state of great efficiency, under six masters. The building is a large plain edifice of brick, pointed with stone-work, fronting the noble area of College Square on the South side.

The Brown Street Sunday, Daily, and Infant School was founded in 1812. It forms a commodious edifice, in which about 500 children of both sexes are instructed in the ordinary branches of a mercantile education, for the small sum of one penny per week for each pupil. The female schools are superintended by a committee of ladies. To this establishment, Belfast is indebted for the rescue of a large portion of its poorer population from vice and ignorance, and their introduction to the means of acquiring respectability and competence.

The Lancasterian school, in Frederick Street, was founded in 1811, for the instruction of the labouring classes. A few years since, a Female Industrial School, for the instruction of poor girls in needle-work and embroidery, was established in the building, supported partly by voluntary contributions, and partly by the proceeds of the work executed. The institution now feeds, clothes, and educates ninety poor girls, fitting them for domestic servants and other useful avocations. Here, also, is a "ragged" school, the first of the kind established in Ireland.

The Ulster Institution for the Education of the Deaf and Dumb and the Blind was opened in 1845, at the cost of £11,000, by voluntary subscription, having originated in a previous establishment situated in College Street, carried on upon a much smaller scale. It is capable of affording the blessings of religious and secular instruction to one hundred pupils. The Institution is under the management of a committee of the subscribers, a principal, and male and female assistants. The building is a superb structure in the Elizabethan style, situated in Malone, and occupying a considerable area.

The Queen's College was opened in October, 1849. It is a fundamental principle of the establishment that the religious opinions of the students shall not be in any way interfered with by the professors. The number of matriculated students at the opening was 108. The building is one of the finest in Ulster. It occupies a noble site on the Botanic Road, in the centre of elegantly laid-out grounds, neighbouring the Botanic Garden. The cost of the structure was nearly £30,000. It is an edifice in the Tudor style of architecture, with a facade in front of 600 feet in length. The material is a bright red brick, profusely ornamented with cut-stone. It consists of a lofty entrance tower, in the basement storey of which is the Hall, two slightly recessed ranges of building on either side, and two wings, extending backwards to a considerable depth, and forming the Northern and Southern faces of the edifice. In the rere, the extremities of the wings are connected together by the cloisters or ambulatories, the whole forming a square massive pile. The examination hall is an exceedingly large and lofty room, being eighty feet in length, by forty in width, and forty in height. The North wing contains the lecture-rooms, laboratory, &c., and the Southern, the apartments of the President and Professors. Its government consists of a President, Vice-President, thirteen Professors in the faculty of arts, which includes engineering and agriculture; five in the faculty of medicine; and two in the faculty of law. There are four Deans of Residences, a Registrar, a Librarian, and a Bursar. The College is endowed with thirty scholarships of £24; eleven, of £20; four, of £15; and ten senior scholarships of £40 each. The Queen's College, Belfast, as those of Cork and Galway, is constituted a College of the Queen's University in Ireland, and its Professors are considered Professors of that University.

LITERARY AND OTHER INSTITUTIONS.

The Government School of Design occupies the Northern wing of the Academical Institution. It is supported partly by a Government endowment, and partly by local aid. It gives instruction to pupils of both sexes in the arts of design and decoration, with a special view to the improvement of the staple manufactures of the country. The school was opened in 1850. It is under the management of a general committee, and is in connexion with the Parent School of Design in Somerset House, London.

There are twenty-eight National Schools in the town and vicinity of Belfast, besides a considerable number of schools under the patronage of the Church Education Society. A male and female school is attached to the institution of the Belfast Charitable Society, to the Union Workhouse, and to the Infantry Barracks.

LITERARY AND OTHER INSTITUTIONS.

Amongst the literary and scientific institutions now existing in Belfast, the first place must be given to the Natural History and Philosophical Society, which holds its meetings in the Museum, a neat building situate in College Square North. This Society was the first of its kind established in Ireland. A paper is read twice a month by each member in rotation, and, during the winter, a monthly lecture is given, which is open to the friends of the members. The Museum contains a fine collection, scarcely inferior to that of the Royal Dublin Society, or of the Trinity College Museum. It has latterly been much enriched by the contributions of Sir James E. Tennent, M.P., one of the most distinguished members of the Society. It is open to the public, at a moderate charge, every day except Sunday.

The Belfast Society for the Promotion of Knowledge, holds its meetings in the White Linen Hall, and possesses a library containing upwards of 10,000 volumes. There are also several minor literary societies connected with the greater educational establishments, and a Society called the Essayist Club, which meets once a month, for the reading and discussion of original papers by the members. The Belfast Working Classes' Association meets in temporary apartments in the Castle Chambers, where there is a news-room and the nucleus of a library. This Society has it in contemplation to found an Athenæum for Belfast.

The Belfast Medical Society meets once a month in the General Hospital, in the library of which building there is a valuable collection of books for the use of the members.

The Anacreontic Society, instituted for the cultivation of vocal and instrumental music, holds its meetings in the Music Hall, a spacious building in May Street. The members meet once a week, and, in the winter, give a series of concerts to the public.

At a short distance from the town, in the vicinity of Queen's

College, are the Gardens of the Royal Botanical and Horticultural Society, the grounds of which are of considerable extent, tastefully laid out, and containing a noble range of conservatories, and a large collection of native and exotic plants. Several times in the course of each year, there are exhibitions of plants and flowers in the Garden, at which prizes for successful competition are awarded.

In December 1851, was founded a Social Inquiry Society, on the plan of the Statistical Society of Dublin, the members of which hold their meetings in the rooms of the Chamber of Commerce.

The Royal Society for the Promotion and Improvement of the growth of Flax in Ireland, was established by a number of gentlemen connected with the flax trade in Belfast, in the year 1841, with the view of introducing a better system of handling flax in its growth and preparation, and to increase the quantity grown to the amount required for the British and Irish linen trade. The Society has latterly directed its attention chiefly to the provinces of Leinster, Munster, and Connaught. It keeps up a staff of agriculturists, who are trained in Belgium, in the most approved system of management, and who are sent to give instructions to all parts of Ireland, where there are farming societies or landed proprietors subscribing to its funds. The Lord Lieutenant has, during the last four years, annually placed a sum of £1,000 at the disposal of the Society, in aid of its operations in the South and West. The Queen and Prince Albert are patrons of the Society. The Lord Lieutenant vice-patron, and the Marquis of Downshire its president.

The Chemico-Agricultural Society of Ulster, instituted for the dissemination of practical knowledge on the connection of chemistry with agriculture, and for the analysis of soils and manures, &c., meets every Friday. The President is the Marquis of Downshire, and the chemist, who is its principal practical officer, and to whose labours its success from the commencement is mainly attributable, is Professor Hodges, M.D. To forward the views of this Society, a laboratory has been opened, where analyses and experiments are made, advice given, and pupils instructed. Arrangements are in progress for an appropriate museum and library. The newspapers published in Belfast are the following:— The *News-Letter*, published continuously since A.D. 1737 (three times a week); the *Commercial Chronicle* (three times a week); the *Northern Whig* (three times a week); the *Banner of Ulster* (twice a week); the *Mercury* (three times a week); the *Vindicator, Mercantile Register*, and *Ulster General Advertiser* (once a week). In the winter of 1850, an Association for the Promotion of the Fine Arts was founded, and its first exhibition of paintings and sculpture was opened with so much success, that there is reason to believe it will be a permanent Institution.

There are several news-rooms—viz., the Commercial News-room, in the Commercial Buildings; the Linen Hall News-room, in the White

LITERARY AND OTHER INSTITUTIONS. 35

Linen Hall; the People's News-room, 17 Castle Place; and others of a minor character. A public news-room, on a large scale and liberal terms, is about to be established in the magnificent hall of the newly-erected Corn Exchange, Victoria Street.

The monetary institutions of Belfast are the following:—The Belfast Banking Company, whose establishment, a beautiful structure in the Italian Palatial style, occupies the site of the Old Exchange, at the foot of Donegall Street; the Northern Banking Company, who have recently erected a magnificent Bank of cut Portland stone in the Ionic style, in Victoria Street, the most costly structure in the town, proportionally to its size; the Bank of Ireland, Donegall Place ; the Ulster Banking Company, Waring Street; the Provincial Banking Company, Donegall Street; and the Belfast Savings' Bank, King street.

The principal poor-relief institutions are those of the Belfast Charitable Society, and the Union Workhouse. The Charitable Society was incorporated by Act of Parliament, in 1774. Its Poorhouse and Infirmary constitute a handsome structure, ornamented with a turret and spire, on the Antrim Road, at the head of Donegall Street. It provides in-door relief to decayed persons of both sexes, besides many children who are instructed in useful avocations, and afterwards apprenticed out to the trading community. It originally derived its main support from annual subscriptions, but having, by its Act, obtained special privileges, grants of ground, &c., the proceeds therefrom, with the interest of bequests, render it nearly independent of the contributions of the public. The Union Workhouse was opened in 1841, but has since been nearly doubled in extent by the addition of new buildings for in-door relief, schools, and a large infirmary with 600 beds. It supports the great mass of the pauperism of the district. The Union comprises twelve electoral districts, for which there are twenty-two elected, and twelve ex-officio guardians. Besides these establishments, there is a Destitute Sick Society, a Clothing Society, a Ladies' Connaught Relief Society, a Girls' Industrial School, the Ulster Female Penitentiary (established 1831), and the Magdalen Asylum, founded in 1842, in connexion with which is an Episcopal Chapel, supporting a chaplaincy, in Donegall Pass.

The following are the principal benevolent associations:—The Association for Discountenancing Vice, the Auxiliary Bible Society, the Auxiliary to the Hibernian School Society, the Auxiliary to the Society for promoting Christianity among the Jews, and the Seamen's Friend Society.

HARBOUR AND QUAYS.

The Harbour of Belfast was originally a creek of the river Lagan, in the entrance to the stream now arched over in High Street, and was under no regular government. In 1637, the Earl of Stafford, having purchased from the Corporation of Carrickfergus the privilege of receiving to their use one-third of all the custom duties imported into that town, with other trading monopolies, the trade of Belfast for the first time became important, and in 1729, by Act of Parliament, a separate Corporation was appointed for the conservancy of the Harbour, whose powers were increased by the 25th George III. chap. 64. The artificial fords were soon after removed, and the river deepened. In 1791 a platform for graving was made, and one graving dock was opened in 1800, and another in 1826. Up to 1829, however, very little beyond this had been done for the improvement of the Harbour, notwithstanding the increasing trade of the port, partly because the proprietors of the town and all the property in its vicinity—the Donegall family—themselves wished to form the Harbour, and were, therefore, reluctant to lease any ground for the purpose to the Ballast Corporation ; and partly because the question was taken up and held in suspense by the Government for several years. The Government, however, having abandoned the undertaking, and the Corporation being left to their own resources, the latter obtained copies of all reports and estimates in possession of the Government, and, in addition called in the services of several eminent engineers. Amongst these were Messrs. Walker and Burges, whose plan having met with the approbation of all parties interested, was adopted by the Harbour Corporation, and an amended Act, obtained in August 1831, at length gave the necessary powers to carry into effect the improvement of the port. The old winding channel, always tedious of navigation, was superseded in 1840, by the first portion of a new channel, which was then completed to the extent of one mile, extending from Prince's Dock to below the Mile-end water. In 1841, another bill was obtained, for the purpose of completing this improvement, and under its provisions the New Cut was continued (with a short interval yet unfinished) to Garmoyle, by an embanked channel, which was opened on the 10th of July, 1849. The new channel has nine feet of water at low tides, thus enabling steamers and large sailing vessels to come up to the quays at neap tides, and vessels drawing eighteen feet of water, at spring tides. Within the last few years the most extensive improvements have been made in the quayage of the port, which now consists of two splendid quays, extending on either side of the river from Queen's Bridge to the Mile-water, and two capacious docks, called respectively the Prince's (formerly Dunbar's) and the Clarendon Docks. The former is reserved for foreign shipping. The latter was opened in September, 1850, by his Excellency the Earl of Clarendon, during a visit to the town. On the North, or Antrim side of the river, the quays are exclusively reserved for steamers and vessels in the foreign trade. These are flanked by extensive stores, offices, &c., and a range of handsome sheds. On the opposite side there are a coal exchange, and offices and yards,

HARBOUR AND QUAYS.

for the accommodation of the coal merchants; and the quay itself is reserved for colliers and coasting vessels. Opposite the Eastern extremity of the Southern, or Queen's Quay, is Queen's Island, upon which has been erected a Patent Slip, which gives accommodation to vessels of 1,000 tons register, whilst undergoing repairs. Adjoining the ship-building ground of Messrs. A. M'Laine and Sons, there is a second Patent Slip, for vessels under 400 tons register. The island is neatly planted and laid out with promenades, for the recreation of the public. There is a Battery at the Eastern extremity; and nearly in the centre was erected, in the summer of 1851, an elegant structure of glass and wood, for the purpose of annual bazaars, or fetes, in aid of the General Hospital. The cost of the recent improvements of the port amounted to £405,519, raised in loans, on the security of the harbour dues. Several ship-building yards occupy a large space in the vicinity of the docks. A screw-pile light-house, connected with which is a pilot establishment, stands near the embouchure of the river; it rises thirty feet above high water, and exhibits a fixed red light. There is a second light-house, besides beacons. There are thirty-nine pilots belonging to the harbour. The present Custom House is an old unsightly building, quite inadequate to the wants of the port; but it is to be replaced by a handsome and commodious structure. It may be mentioned here that, during the progress of the Harbour Improvements of Belfast, in deepening the river, the steam dredges then in use for that purpose turned up, in the course of those operations, some of the stones from which it is stated Belfast originally derived its name, *Beala-fearsad*, "The Town of the Ford." Mr. M'Williams, who has at present the charge of the Harbour Commissioners' machinery on Queen's Island, discovered that those stones were worn upon the upper surface, and that the causeway, or ford, had been about 40 feet in width. It was protected from the action of the influx and efflux of the tide by piles at either side, the removal of which, in the course of the Harbour Improvements, was a matter of very considerable difficulty, and one which, before the cause was discovered, very considerably injured the machinery of the river-deepening apparatus. We are not aware that the whole of these remarkable relics have been preserved, but we believe that the antiquarian can have access to some of them, on making inquiry in the proper quarter.

In 1786, the total number of ships that entered the port of Belfast amounted to 772 vessels, with a tonnage of 34,287 tons, and a tonnage revenue of £1,553; in 1850, the number of vessels entering the port was 4,490, with a tonnage of 624,113 tons, and a revenue of £29,012. At the close of the year 1851, the number of vessels registered as belonging to the port was 448, with an aggregate tonnage of 74,540 tons, of which, in the foreign trade, were 137 vessels, with a tonnage of 57,996 tons, and, in the coasting trade, 311 vessels, with a tonnage of 16,544 tons. During the year 1851, 17 vessels, with a registered tonnage of 10,506 tons, were added to the foreign-trade shipping; and, during the same period, 22 vessels, registered at 1,544 tons, were added to those engaged in the coasting trade. The aggregate tonnage of the steamers trading between Belfast, and England and Scotland, amounts to 7,298 tons. The total number of vessels which entered the harbour in 1851 was 5,016. The aggregate tonnage was 650,938: viz., steamers, 309,783; foreign vessels, 84,716; cross-Channel and coasters, 244,830; Irish Channel, 13,609. The harbour rates, on goods, in 1851, amounted to £8,330 9s. 10d., being an increase of £868 12s. 8d. over 1850. The tonnage dues in 1851 amounted to £10,735, being an increase of £422 over 1850. The quayage dues in 1851 amounted to £2,670 14s., being an increase of £326 12s. over 1850. The ballast dues in 1851 amounted to £2,670 14s., being an increase of £500 18s. over 1850. The quantity of coals delivered at the quays in 1851 was 295,513 tons, being an increase of nearly 42,000 tons over 1850—a fair test by which to form an opinion as to the increased manufacturing industry and general comfort of the community.

The customs duties paid at the port of Belfast, for each of the last three years, ending 5th Jan., amounted, for, 1849, to £346,426 16s. 2d.; for 1850, to £362,990 12s. 2d.; for 1851, to £369,415 12s. 1d. The increase of the year ending 5th January, 1852, over that ending 5th January, 1851, is, therefore, £6,424 19s. 11d.; and over the year preceding, £22,988 16s. 11d.

The commerce of Belfast is greater than that of any other port in Ireland. It ranks next to that of Leith. The principal exports consist of corn, meal, and flour, cured provisions, linen yarn, feathers, flax and tow, cotton manufactures, linen cloth, green and tanned hides, horses, eggs, &c. The chief articles of export, however, are the various linen fabrics, value £3,320,000; muslins and other cotton manufactures, £1,400,000; cured provisions, £400,000; flax and tow (unmanufactured), £40,000; and the total value of the general exports amounts to about £5,600,000. By much the largest proportion of the exports of Belfast are transferred, for re-shipment, to Liverpool, London, Greenock, &c., forming in value, perhaps, almost one-half of the entire value of exports from the first of those ports, thus establishing the character of Belfast as the chief commercial port of Ireland. The chief imports are timber, grain, flax, flaxseed, sugar, barilla, fruit, &c.

With the West Indian colonies of Great Britain the direct trade of the port is considerable, but principally with Demerara, Barbadoes, and Antigua. In the trade to these ports a large amount of the tonnage registered at Belfast is regularly engaged, in addition to chartered vessels. By far the largest proportion of the Colonial produce imported into Belfast is first landed at Liverpool, Greenock, or other ports, and conveyed across Channel by steamers.

An import trade from the East to this port, after having been in abeyance for a very considerable period, was re-opened about the year 1844, through the agency of an enterprising merchant of the town, to whom was consigned the first cargo of tea, directly imported, that has ever landed in Ireland. The bottom in which this cargo was brought to our shores had been chartered in China for the purpose. The commerce of Belfast with the Eastern possessions of Britain, as also with China, is steadily increasing, and, as late as last year, vessels owned by Belfast merchants are recorded in Lloyd's Register as engaged in the regular trade between ports in the East—as Bombay, Calcutta, Hong-Kong, Shanghae, Singapore, &c.—and British ports. Indeed, a very large amount of the tonnage registered as belonging to the port of Belfast is not engaged in its own trade. A number of the largest ships belonging to the port have never entered the harbour, but are engaged either in the cotton-carrying, the East India, or the African trades.

The general interests of Trade and Commerce are attended to by the Chamber of Commerce, a voluntary association formed in 1783. Its business is now transacted in suitable rooms in Waring Street. This association has, of late years, proved of essential advantage to the mercantile interests of the town, and it numbers in its body the great proportion of the respectable merchants and traders.

The amount of Postage collected in the town of Belfast was, in 1842, £4,588; in 1851, it was £7,246.

The Stamp Duties received in the Belfast collection were, in 1846, £22,021; in 1850, they amounted to £26,991.

The Inland Revenue collected in the Belfast district amounted, in 1850, to £206,278.

STEAM NAVIGATION.

Shortly after the introduction of Steam Navigation upon the Clyde, some enterprising gentlemen in Glasgow conceived that a cross-channel trade might, probably, prove remunerative, and speculation pointed out as the first point, the nearest commercial port of Ireland, to wit, Belfast. The only trade between those two ports, now so important in the annals of British commerce, was at that time conducted by casual vessels, the freight ships being, in general, those which, having discharged cargoes of coals, afterwards accepted an occasional freight. The passenger trade to Scotland or England was, generally, conducted by means of vessels trading between Donaghadee and Portpatrick, or Parkgate, in Cheshire. About the year 1819, after Steam Navigation had been tested upon the Clyde, and when the capability of steamers for cross channel, or deep sea navigation, had been proved, the merchants of Glasgow, always foremost in matters of judicious enterprise, started a small steamer, with the object of plying between two ports whose interests were so closely connected. The vessel chosen by them for this purpose was one which, in the present age of improvement, would be considered very small indeed, and quite insufficient for the object intended. She was named the *Clydesdale*, a small boat of about 100 tons, forty horse-power, flush-decked, and with far less shelter from a shower, or from the sea spray, than at present is to be had in a canvass tent—no bridge, no suitable convenience, in short, of any kind. The *Clydesdale* ran for two or three years, when she was replaced by another steamer, not larger or more elegant, named the *Rob Roy*. The *Clydesdale* was afterwards burned, during a voyage between the Clyde and Belfast, and her helmsman, by name Cochrane, had a pension awarded him by public subscription in Scotland, in recognition of his gallantry in holding by the wheel whilst the vessel was on fire under his feet. The *Rob Roy* was supplanted by the *George Canning* and the *Britannia*, worse boats than even the two former ones. The next vessel on the line was the *Eclipse*; and, shortly after, competition having commenced, the *Swift*, a Leith and London smack, converted into a steamer, was put into this trade by a rival company. The history of this competition is curious. It was carried on with very considerable spirit for some months; at last one of the vessels advertised that its rate of passage to Glasgow would be only 3d. Immediately upon this, the opposition steamer announced that it would carry passengers to Glasgow for nothing. It was then considered that the opposition was at an end. However, the morning previous to the departure of the next steamer on the other side, it was announced that the vessel would not only take deck passengers for nothing, but that, in order to enable them to proceed on their voyage comfortably, they would each be furnished with a pint of strong beer! The first steamer, however, which took cargo from Belfast to Glasgow, was the *Aimwell*, a small vessel not more than 100 tons burthen, and 40 horse-power. The *Aimwell* performed her voyages very unsatisfactorily to the Belfast merchants, inasmuch as, instead of being accomplished within the 12 hours, they were generally protracted to what would now be considered an extraordinary time, namely, 24 hours, if not, as sometimes happened, 36 hours. The present daily communication is eight hours from Greenock.

In 1826, the Messrs. Langtrys & Herdman (then Langtry & Co.) opened a line of steam communication from this port to Liverpool. Their first steamer, the *Chieftain*, was built at Port-Glasgow. She was a double-decked vessel of imposing appearance, with very tall masts, and rigged like an East Indiaman. On her arrival here, in 1826, thousands flocked to the quay to inspect her. The same firm have since then kept on the line a regular supply of first-class steamers, these being the *Corsair*—a favourite vessel—in 1827; *Falcon*, 1835; *Reindeer*, 1838; *Sea-King*, 1845; and *Blenheim*, 1848, which steamer at present runs regularly on the line. About 1830, the importance of Belfast, as a commercial port, became acknowledged by the Dublin Steam Packet Company, in consequence of which, they placed one of their vessels to ply once a week between Belfast and Liverpool. Previously to this, the only direct communication between Belfast and Liverpool was that afforded by the steamer of Messrs. Langtry & Co., until the year 1835. It is now proposed to establish a new company, for the purpose of having daily steam communication with Liverpool, under the immediate and sole control of the Belfast merchants, and steps have been already taken for carrying out the necessary arrangements.

In the year 1829, a trade was established between Belfast and London, with the provision that the vessels were to call at Plymouth, Devonport, and Dublin. The merchants of Belfast contracted with Messrs. Fawcett and Co., of Liverpool, for a steamer of 200 horse-power and 500 tons burthen, to be suited for the navigation between this port and London. This vessel, the *Erin*, was launched, and plied for two years. She did not turn out very well, proving a watery vessel. The *Erin* left London in the middle of June, 1844, on her last voyage, and was seen off Ilfracombe, drifting into the bay, and next morning struck on Lundy Island, where she was totally lost, with all hands. No other steamer replaced the *Erin* on this line. The next experiment in the opening of a trade between the two ports, was in that of screw-propelled steamers; previously, however, there had been a line of sailing vessels which made regular passages, calling occasionally at Whitehaven. Two screw steamers commenced plying in 1849. The first of these was built in the Thames, and having turned out very well, the system of screw-propulsion having been tested to advantage, and the trade between Belfast and London offering a reasonable investment for capital, the keel of a ship of considerable tonnage was laid down at Dumbarton, on a slip belonging to Messrs. Denny, Brothers, the builders of several steamers which have acquired a high reputation.

There are now thirty-two steamers regularly plying between this port and London, Liverpool, Fleetwood, Glasgow, Ardrossan, Morecambe, Whitehaven, Dublin, and Londonderry.

THE CORPORATION, &c.

The Borough of Belfast is governed by a Corporation, elected by the five Wards—St. Anne's, Dock, Smithfield, St. George's, and Cromac—each Ward returning two Aldermen and six Councillors; from the former a Mayor is annually chosen. The Corporation have recently effected the most salutary and extensive improvements in the town, under various acts of Parliament, which have enabled them to build new and handsome streets, purchase the sites and lots of the markets, and otherwise promote the convenience and prosperity of the inhabitants.

There are twelve principal markets, viz., May's Market, for the daily sale of grain and meal; George's Market, for butchers' meat, poultry, eggs, butter, cheese, &c., on Tuesdays and Fridays; the Flax and Fruit Market, daily ; the Bogwood, Turf, and Grass Market, daily ; the Cattle Market, Mondays, Wednesdays, and Fridays; the Pork Market, daily ; the Butter Market, daily; the Smithfield Market, miscellaneous produce, daily; the Potato Market, daily; Castle Market, fruit, vegetable, butchers' meat, &c., daily; Ormond Market, for similar sales, daily; the retail Fish Market, daily; and the Monthly Cattle and Horse Fair, on the first Wednesday of each month. The income arising from the tolls of these markets is increasing yearly, and is expected soon to form a considerable fund for Corporation purposes. The present Town-hall is a mean and inconvenient structure; but it is in contemplation to erect a new Town-hall, in a commanding site, and on a scale of great magnificence, which, if constructed according to the model of the Corporation architect, already completed, will be by far the noblest public building in the town.

The paving, lighting, and cleansing of the town are vested in a Police Committee, chosen by the Town Council under a special act; the average annual expenditure being £9,000.

WATER COMMISSIONERS.

The supply of pipe water, which is obtained from three capacious reservoirs, situate about one mile North of the town, is under a Board of Water Commissioners, incorporated in 1840, and elected by the ratepayers. The grounds belonging to the Commissioners are situated near the Antrim road, and are most beautifully laid out for the recreation of the respectable inhabitants. The view from the walk surrounding the principal sheet of water is unrivalled, comprehending the hills of the County Down, and an extensive view of the Lough down the channel.

The Commercial Buildings, erected by subscription, at a cost of £20,000, in 1820, are situate in front of the Southern extremity of Donegall Street, at the angle of Bridge Street and Waring Street. The building is of granite, and presents a fine, imposing appearance. It is adorned in front with eight Ionic pillars, supported on a broad cornice above the windows of the lower storey, the principal portion of which is occupied by a subscription News Room, which is furnished with a valuable collection of maps, charts, &c. In this room, the merchants meet on 'Change at two o'clock, on Mondays, Wednesdays, and Fridays. Above the News Room, on the upper floor, is the Assembly Room, a beautiful apartment, usually devoted to public meetings, exhibitions, &c. The roof and sides of this chamber are enriched with the most sumptuous decorations, coloured in imitation of the rarer marbles.

The Corn merchants of Belfast have recently formed themselves into an association, for the greater facility of business, and by private subscriptions have erected a Corn Exchange, situate in Victoria Street. This building is a chaste and elegant edifice, of cut stone, with an open balustrade in front, and a range of handsome shops in the basement storey. The Exchange occupies a large and elaborately decorated hall on the first floor, lighted by the side windows and a range of roof lights. It is contemplated to establish a public News Room in connexion with the Corn-Exchange.

Amongst the public buildings about to be erected in Belfast is an extensive and suitable range of offices, to contain the Customs, Inland Revenue, and Post Office departments, the premises now devoted to these purposes being altogether unsuited to the respectability, and inadequate to the wants, of the town.

BENEVOLENT INSTITUTIONS.

The Belfast General Hospital, the most extensive and important institution of its kind in Ulster, originated in a General Dispensary, which was founded in the year 1792, by voluntary subscriptions. In the year 1798, a project for establishing an hospital for fever cases, in connexion with the dispensary, was undertaken and accomplished; but it was not until 1815 that the first stone of the present Hospital was laid by the then Marquis of Donegall, the charity having become fully acknowledged as one of the necessary institutions of the town. The Hospital was completed and opened in 1817, and immediately gave accommodation to 212 intern patients. A medical school and chemical lectures were established in connection with it. In 1846, consequent upon the erection of the new Fever Hospital in Malone, the General Dispensary, hitherto connected with the Hospital, was placed under separate management, and the institution formally received the title of "The Belfast General Hospital," to be under the management of a president, vice-presidents, life governors, and a committee. The building, which is the principal ornament of that portion of the town in which it stands (Frederick Street), is 160 feet in length in front. It is surrounded by a considerable area, both in front and rere; it is flanked on the one side by the Dispensary rooms, and on the other by the Committee room and porter lodge. At the eastern wall runs a long shed, originally used for fever cases, and kept now as a reserve ward. The Hospital has, during recent years, received considerable aid from the public, through the proceeds of annual fetes.

The District Lunatic Asylum, for the Counties of Antrim and Down, and the County of the Town of Carrickfergus, is situate near the Falls Road, within a mile of the town. It is a handsome and commodious edifice with extensive grounds attached. It was opened in 1829. The number of patients is generally about 150.

The Lying-in-Hospital, a square building on the Antrim Road, was opened for the accommodation of poor women in 1830, at the cost of £1,200. It is supported by voluntary contributions, and is under the direction of a committee of benevolent ladies. It affords relief to an annual average of 191 patients.

COUNTY GAOL AND COURT-HOUSE.

The new County Gaol stands on an elevated and healthy situation on the Crumlin Road, on an area of ten acres. It was designed after the model of the Pentonville prison, near London. The central portion consists of board, reception, and waiting rooms, the governor's department, and the chapel and inspection. From the centre hall four wings diverge, two for males, with three storeys or ranges, and a like number for females. The Church is divided into compartments, which admit of 348 prisoners. The management of the gaol is under a board of superintendence; and the officers connected therewith, are those of an inspector, three chaplains, a surgeon, an apothecary, and a resident governor.

Opposite to the new Gaol, and connected with it by means of a subterranean passage, is the new County Court-house, built in consequence of the late transfer of the Assize business from Carrickfergus to Belfast, and the proclamation of Belfast as the county town. It is a truly splendid structure, and acknowledged to be the finest County Court-house in Ireland. It is in the Corinthian order of architecture, with an imposing portico of eight columns of 30 feet in height, in the centre of the front facade, and wings enriched with pilasters. A bold cornice is carried round three sides of the building, and on the apex of the pediment stands a fine figure of Justice. The public hall, in the interior, and the Crown and Record Courts, are models of chaste design. The whole building, as well as the Gaol, reflecting the greatest credit on the able architect, C. Lanyon, Esq., C.E. The Court-house was opened in the Summer of 1850.

Besides the Assize Courts, there are held in Belfast a Court of Quarter Sessions, a Manor Court, and daily Petty Sessions.

The town is the head quarters of the Northern military district of Ireland; and there are extensive Barracks for Cavalry and Infantry, situate in North Queen Street. The garrison usually consists of a troop of horse and a regiment of infantry. Belfast is also the residence of the County resident Magistrate, and is the head quarters of the Constabulary for the district, comprising the stations of Belfast, Lisburn, and Whitewell Brae.

RAILWAYS.

There are three Railways, the head offices and principal termini of which are situated in Belfast, viz.: the Ulster Railway (from Belfast to Armagh) ; the Belfast and Ballymena Railway, with branches to Carrickfergus and Randalstown ; and the Belfast and County Down Railway, with a branch to Holywood. The Belfast terminus of the Ulster Railway, in Great Victoria Street, is an imposing structure, with a central portico of four massive columns and two wings, and an exceedingly spacious and handsome Station-house in the rear. The terminus of the Belfast and County Down Railway, on the Queen's Quay, is an elegant cut stone edifice. That of the Belfast and Ballymena line is, as yet, only partially completed, but when finished will be most commodious.

The principal manufactures carried on in Belfast and its vicinity—at least those, to which it is chiefly indebted for its present state of prosperity—are, the linen yarn, linen, cotton, and sewed muslin manufactures.

THE LINEN TRADE.

The climate and soil of Ulster are admirably adapted for the cultivation of flax; but it is only, within recent years, that its culture has received any large share of attention. In 1841, the establishment of the Royal Flax Society greatly assisted in the development of this grand national resource, and the growth of flax has become concentrated in Ulster since the employment of machinery in spinning yarn. The flax planted in Ulster alone, in 1851, reached the very great breadth of 138,619 acres. So large a quantity, grown as it were at the very doors of the manufacturers, with an extensive local demand for their yarns, has given them considerable advantages over their rivals in other parts of the United Kingdom, who are obliged principally to depend upon the supply of the raw material from abroad. Improved modes of steeping the flax, and of scutching the fibre, of recent introduction, have also given a great stimulus to the trade; and its extent may be judged of from the fact, that the number of spindles in operation in Ireland for the spinning of flax, on the 1st of January, 1851, was 500,000, of which by far the greater proportion is employed in Belfast, and the districts adjacent; and that the number of persons engaged in connexion with the trade is estimated at 200,000; and the amount invested in buildings, machinery, and the requisite floating capital, at £3,000,000.

The exports of Irish linen manufactures have steadily increased almost from the earliest establishment of the trade, notwithstanding the apparent decline previous to the introduction of machinery. This increase became most apparent after the abolition of the bounties, which, under the Linen Board, were paid on the export of some description of linen fabrics. These bounties ceased in 1830. The apparent amount of exports of linen from Ireland is now small, arising from the fact that nearly all is sent by the cross Channel steamers to the English and Scotch ports, whence it is trans-shipped to foreign countries. The entire export from Ireland to Great Britain, and all foreign countries, reaches about 106,000,000 yards; value, £4,400,000.

The restrictive policy adopted by most of the European states, and which there seems little disposition to relax, is a bar to the more rapid progress of the linen trade, which now mainly depends upon the export to North and South America, and the West Indies, in addition to the home consumption, which has not kept pace with the increase of the export trade.

The establishment of Schools of Design is likely to benefit the damask and printed linen manufacture, and afford employment to an important class of individuals in a manufacturing community. The value attached to the ornaments used in preparing packets of linen for the foreign markets, and the taste with which it is thought necessary to get them up, render them no unimportant article of trade; and by the help of the School of Design, there is every prospect that the "linen bands" will become a home manufacture, and secure to the town of Belfast an annual expenditure of £60,000, now paid to strangers and foreigners.

Belfast is the great centre of the Irish flax spinning and linen trades. Of the sixty-six factories in connection with these manufacturies in Ulster, no fewer than thirty-five were located in Belfast and its suburbs, in 1851, and their number is constantly increasing. One of the Belfast factories employs 25,000 spindles, and several from 10,000 to 20,000. It is considered that the advantages which Belfast offers for the location of a flax factory, as being the centre of the trade, where the chief purchases of yarns are made by the manufacturers, and the greater convenience of obtaining skilled workers, are sufficient to counterbalance the greater cheapness of water power in other localities. Hence the chief increase of spinning machinery is found to be in and around Belfast.

It is estimated that the coal consumed in driving the steam engines of the flax mills in Belfast (upwards of thirty in number), and bleach greens, is above 160,000 tons annually, employing fifty vessels, and 300 seamen. 400,000 spindles are now at work, giving employment to about 20,000 operatives, and about £40,000 are annually paid in wages. The ratio of increase in the persons employed in factory labour here is fifty-two per cent, whilst in England it is $30\frac{1}{2}$; and in Scotland only $13\frac{1}{2}$ per cent.

In 1725, machinery was first applied to the operations of washing, rubbing and beetling linen, in the parish of Belfast. The only acid in the process of bleaching, up to 1761, was buttermilk. In 1764, Dr. Ferguson, of Belfast, received from the Linen Board a premium of £300, for the successful application of lime in the bleaching process. In 1770, he introduced the use of sulphuric acid ; in 1780, potash was first used ; and in 1795, chloride of lime was introduced. Recent improvements have enabled some bleachers to perfect the process in ten days, and very lately it was stated in the *Belfast News-Letter*, that in one establishment linen is perfectly bleached and finished, without injury to the fabric, in the short space of three days. The proprietors of the bleach greens either bleach linen for hire, are themselves manufacturers, bleaching and exporting their own fabrics, or are purchasers of brown linen, and export it when bleached.

LOCAL MANUFACTURES.

The articles manufactured by the trade are very numerous. Among these may be named, ordinary shirtings, light and heavy, of all degrees of texture; sheetings, drills, plain and striped; checks; bed-ticks; damasks and diapers ; grey damasks for stair and carpet coverings; mosquito netting; lawns; cambric and cambric handkerchiefs; printed lawns and cambrics; sacking; canvass; ropes and cordage; yarn for carpeting; sewing threads, &c.

The neighbourhoods of Belfast and Lisburn chiefly excel in the production of damask, as that of Lurgan excels in the manufacture of lawns and cambrics; Armagh of light linens; Ballymena of heavy linens, and so on. The damask manufacture was introduced into Ireland about 1764. Mr. Coulson, of Lisburn, received several sums of money from the Linen Board, to assist him in improving the manufacture. In 1828, the Ardoyne damask manufactory was established by Mr. Andrews. At the present time, the fabric has reached a high point of excellence, and the finest quality is not excelled, if it is even equalled, by the choicest products of Saxony. These productions consist of double and single damasks and diapers. The first named are considered articles of luxury, not so much from the intrinsic cost of manufacture, as from the great expense of getting up special designs for customers, to whom cost is no object. The second division comprises the great bulk of coarse goods for home sale and export.

There has of late been considerable improvement in the printing of linens and lawns for ladies' dresses, and of the borders of cambric handkerchiefs—a branch of the trade which is likely to become of extreme importance and value, when our native designs equal or excel those of fereign pattern drawers, as it is expected will be the case, when the pupils of the School of Design have had sufficient instruction and experience.

Mr. J. MacAdam, jun., to whose excellent papers in the fourth volume of the *Journal of Design* we are chiefly indebted for the information above given, says, " There are many reasons for believing that the future progress of the Irish linen trade will at least keep pace with its past development. One cause of linen fabrics being dearer than cotton is, that the great mass of the latter are woven by power, while all the former, except some of the coarsest kinds, are woven by hand. Although many attempts have been made to adapt the power loom to linens, they have hitherto not been successful, chiefly owing to the fact, that flax-fibre is not so elastic a substance as cotton-wool. Nevertheless, late experiments have given more satisfactory results, although not yet sufficiently matured to warrant the belief that the power-loom can be soon made generally available. A Belfast damask manufacturer has been able to produce some light damasks, of fair quality, by power, and is at present erecting a steam engine and factory to carry on the manufacture on a more extended scale. It is scarcely possible that the difficulties which have heretofore prevented power-loom weaving from being adopted in the linen manufacture, should prove insuperable. Mechanical science has achieved many triumphs, where much greater obstacles lay in the way. We may, therefore, conclude that, sooner or later, the system will be fully carried out, and its results will have a powerful effect on the advancement of the manufacture."

The greater number of the factories connected with this trade in Belfast are gigantic structures, erected at great expense, and some of them are of elegant architectural design. The forest of chimney stalks along the Falls Road, where the greater number of them are situated, is a very peculiar feature in the view of the town, from whatever direction it be taken. There are, however, few parts of the suburban districts where these immense foci of industry do not attract the attention of the passer by. The largest flax-mill in Belfast, which is also one of the largest in the United Kingdom, is that of the York Street Spinning Company. It employs 25,000 spindles, and 1,000 hands; and the value of the flax under process amounts to upwards of £100,000.

The Linen Hall, which was erected in 1785, at a cost of £10,000, for the accommodation of the Belfast linen merchants, is a spacious building, forming a quadrangle, two storeys in height, and occupying the area of Donegall Square. Its front, which faces Donegall Place, is ornamented with a pediment, clock—turret, and cupola. The extreme neatness of the edifice, both within and without, and the good taste displayed in the ordering of the ornamental grounds attached to it, enhance the interest which its attractions, as the seat of an immense traffic, distributing the blessings of industry to upwards of half-a-million of individuals, cannot fail to create.

In the Brown Linen Hall, situate in Donegall Street, considerable quantities of yard-wide brown linens are sold on each Tuesday and Friday.

PLAIN AND SEWED MUSLIN TRADE.

Next in importance to the linen trade, among the local manufactures of Belfast, are the plain and sewed muslin trades. The greatest part of the cotton yarn used in the manufacture is imported, chiefly from the neighbourhood of Manchester, and afterwards goes through its subsequent processes in the establishments here, passing through from fourteen to twenty hands in its different stages, viz., winding, warping, weaving, &c. The fabric is then printed with a lithographed impression of the pattern to be worked and given out to the embroiderers, among whom it passes through four or five stages.

This important trade, in all its branches, employs very nearly, 500,000 individuals, the embroiderers being exclusively females, great numbers of them living at remote distances from the seat of the manufacture. In the sewed muslin branch alone, wages to the amount of from £900,000 to one million sterling are annually paid by upwards of forty firms now established in Belfast; and in the plain muslin trade throughout the country, the annual expenditure in wages, altogether for manual labour, is from £300,000 to £400,000. The wages of learners average from 6d. to 1s. per week. Regular workers of the middling qualities of sewing earn from 2s. to 5s. per week ; and the better classes of workers from 6s. to 9s. weekly. The best descriptions of sewed muslins are produced by the Belfast establishments, or the Scotch houses which have branch establishments here. The importance to Ireland of this manufacture, in a social point of view, cannot be over-rated, since it gives employment to so many thousands of persons, and carries comfort and independence into many a cottage which would otherwise be the scene of misery and degradation.

The cotton mills in and about Belfast are five in number, viz.:—Messrs. Leppers', containing about 30,000 spindles ; Mr. M'Cracken's, 20,500 ditto; Mr. Gamble's (Ballynure), 17,000 ditto; Mr. Cochrane's (Bangor), 13,000 ditto; and Mr. Wallace's (Bangor), 9,000 ditto. These mills produce only the coarser kinds of yarn.

We have thus presented our readers with a mere general sketch of Belfast as it now is. In our next volume, it is our intention to enter into much more enlarged and minute particulars of the town and trade of Belfast.

BELFAST
STREET DIRECTORY,

CONTAINING

THE NAMES OF ALL INHABITANTS WHOSE HOUSES ARE VALUED ABOVE SIX POUNDS.

NOTE.—It is necessary to explain, that the principal streets of Belfast are numbered by taking the houses on both sides alternately, and not consecutively, on each side. Thus, in these streets, No. 1 is the first house on the right side, No. 2 the first house on the left side, and so on to the opposite extremity of the street.

Abbey Street, Peter's Hill
1 George Jamieson, night constable
2 Valentine M'Gibbon, publican
Several small houses

Abbotsford Place,
LOWER END OF YORK STREET.
1 Robt. S. Lepper, proprietor of cotton spinning mills, New Lodge Road
2 Mrs M'Donnell
3 Abraham Bell, ship agent
4 Robert Mackenzie, merchant
5 Samuel Woolsey, flax merchant
6 Edmund Getty, Secretary Harbour Commissioners

Academy Street
FROM 61 DONEGALL STREET TO 83 GREAT PATRICK STREET.
J. Walker, confectioner, hall door
1 Mrs Orr, servants' registry office
3 Sampson Kennedy, clerk post office
5 Thomas Bruce, gas fitter
7 Dr Robert Bryce, surgery
9 William Ross's seminary
11 Fraser, Tanner & Co., sewed muslin manufacturers
13 Mrs Lorimer, grocer
15 S. M'Cabe, carver and gilder
17 E. M'Cune, milliner
19 Mrs Holmes
21 John Richardson, clerk post office
23 Bridget Morris, clothes dealer
25 Charles Tumbelty, tailor
27 St Anne's Parochial School; Mr Robinson, master; Mrs Morrow, mistress
29 Andrew Macartney, gilder
31 Benjamin Alcorn, loom and general carpenter
33 Edward Walsh, plasterer
[*Academy Court.*
35 Samuel Adams, sailor
37 Dr Warren
" House and shop vacant
[*Robert Street.*
39, 41 John M'Kenna, grocer and spirit merchant
43 John Armstrong, painter
45 John Fulton, provision merchant
47, 49 M'Clinton & Thomson, chandlers
51, 53 Vacant
55 Letham, Blyth, and Letham, muslin manufacturers
57 John Briggs, plain and ornamental painter and decorator
57½ Miss Kane, milliner
59 John Cuddy, spirit store
Joseph M'Bride, sewed muslin manufacturer
[*Green Street.*
61 H. Clements, dress maker
63 David Nesbit, designer and lithographer
65 J. Millar, dressmaker
67 John Stewart, shoemaker
69 James Smylie, tailor
71, 73 Pat. Coleman, spirit merchant
[*Little Edward Street.*
75 Miss Sharkey, dress maker

E

" Mathew Scott, bricklayer
77 Gawn Robb, sea captain
79 Alex Rutherford, cabinet maker
81 Bernard Mariner, lodging house
83 Wm Hamilton's hall door
[*Great Patrick street.*]
50 Mrs Bruce, provision dealer
Brown's Row.]
46, 48 Thomas Shields, pawnbroker
44 BAPTIST CHAPEL
42 Rev. Mr Eccles, Baptist minister
40 Alexander Johnston, painter
38 Francis Kean, carver
" A. Kean, milliner
36 Vacant
34 Stephen Ryan, sailor
32 James M'Donnell, sawyer
30 Vacant
Curtis Street.]
28 J. Caldwell, muslin manufacturer
26 J. and W. Gamble, mill owners
22, 24 Samuel M'Connell, provision merchant
18, 20 Vacant
16 James Hutcheson & Co., muslin manufacturers
14 Samuel M'Millen, tow merchant
12 H. Morrison, tailor
10 Dr Gooden
8 Jas. Dowling, provision merchant
6 Vacant
2 Belfast Academy, Rev. Dr. Bryce, Principal

Academy Court
OFF 33 ACADEMY STREET.

5 John Graham, chimney sweep
Five small houses

Adelaide Place
FROM DONEGALL SQUARE SOUTH TO FRANKLIN PLACE.

1 F. D. Finlay, proprietor of *Northern Whig*
2 Charles Fiers, gentleman
3 Colonel Brough, assistant adjutant General
4 Mrs Montgomery
" Rev. R. Knox, Presbyterian minister
" William M'Neill, of Ireland and M'Neill's, Corn market
5 John Aickin, surgeon
6 Mrs Campbell
7 Mrs Craufurd's school

Albert Place
DONEGALL PASS.

1 James Aiken, merchant, 6 York street
2 James Blain, damask manufacturer, Corry's Crescent
3 Mrs Jamison
4 Charles Finlay, tea merchant, 5 Waring street
5 Vacant
6 Henry Dickson, wine, spirit, flax, and corn merchant, Victoria street

Albert square
(FORMERLY DONEGALL QUAY)
FOOT OF WARING STREET.
NORTH SIDE.

1 John Harrison, merchant; residence, Mertoun, Holywood
3 Robert Grogan, bonded warehouse; residence, 19, Dock street
9 Jasper Macauley and Co., merchants, brokers, and commission agents; residence, 15, College street south
11 John Gaussen & Co., merchants; residence, 6, Victoria place
13 Wm. C. Heron and Co., merchants; residence, Maryfield, County Down
15 T. G. Folingsby and Co., commission merchants, ship and insurance agents; T. G. Folingsby's residence, 1, Clarence place; A. Forrester's, 51, Corporation street
17 Henry Neill and Co., grain merchants; residence, 2, Albion place

SOUTH SIDE.

1 Francis Campbell, spirit dealer
3 John M'Kenna, butcher
5 Vacant
7 James Scott, provision merchant
9 William Larmour, flour and grain stores
Edward Porter and Son's iron stores
13 James Hamilton, bark and oil stores
15 James Lemon's patent rope and canvas stores
17 Richard M'Cune, spirit dealer
19 Bernard Fitzpatrick, spirit dealer
21 James Nichol, tavern keeper

STREET DIRECTORY.

WEST SIDE.
16 Peter Mackerall, lodging house
18 William M'Ferran, publican and lodging house keeper
20 James Shields, grocer
22 Patrick Moynes, publican
24 William Hanvey, publican

Albert Street
OFF DURHAM STREET.

Durham Street Flax Spinning Mill, John Hind & Sons, proprietors; residences: John Hind, The Lodge; John Hind, jun., Chichester street; James Hind, The Lodge
1 James M'Cullough, tinsmith
7 Sarah Boyd
9 John Hanlon, house carpenter
15 Bernard Lenaghan, pensioner
Machine works—Jas. Scrimgeour, proprietor
NORTH QUEEN PLACE.
Twelve small houses

Albert Street Place
3 John Burgess, shoemaker
Eleven small houses

Albion Lane
WEST CORNER OF DONEGALL PASS.
1 Mrs Waring, dealer
2 Henry Hamill, green grocer
3 Mrs. Robinson
4 John Dickson, labourer
5 Alexander Adams, blacksmith
  Edward Brown, revenue officer
  Henry Adams, car owner

Albion Place, Botanic Road
1 Arthur Collins Weir, merchant, 94¼ Bridge street
2 Robert Neill, jeweller, High street
3 Mrs. W. J. Moore
4 Wm. Neill Blow, paper merchant office, Rosemary street
5 Mrs Halliday
6 Rev. Robert Wilson, D.D.
7 Wm. Simms, agent; office, Linen hall
8 Thos. C. M'Indoe, sewed muslin manufacturer, Waring st. place
9 Jas. Torbitt, wine merchant, North street
10 John M'Entire, merchant; office, 15½ Fountain street
11 Forster Green, tea & coffee dealer, 3 High street
12 John Blackwood, Northern Bank
13 Miss Ross
14 Miss Caughey
15 William Kerr, merchant

Alexander Street
FROM NO. 7 FREDERICK STREET TO 68 GREAT GEORGE'S STREET.

1 John Bradley, whitesmith
3, 5 John Christy starch manufacturer
7 Mrs. Barnes
9 James Walker, labourer
11 Widow Kane
13 Henry M'Kean, labourer
15 Neal M'Grannell, shoemaker
  [*Walker's lane.*
17 William M'Donnell, shoemaker
19 Singleton Wilson, dealer
21 Luke Monaghan, labourer
23 Margaret Pollock, lodgings
25 Joseph Blair, tailor
27 Alexander Kerr, carpenter
29 Thomas Grimmea, grocer
[*Here Lancaster street intersects.*]
31 John Kennedy, spirit dealer and grocer
33 Mary Ann Willis, shirtmaker
35 John M'Cann, labourer
37 Michael Trollan, carter
  [*Mary's lane.*
39 Samuel Preston, dealer
41 John Hatton, labourer
43 Hugh Holmes, blacksmith
45 John M'Crisk, labourer
47 John Maxwell, dealer
49 Patrick M'Dermott, carter
51 Robert Magee, labourer
53 James Hughes, pensioner
55 Anne Crawford, eating house
57 Michael O'Neill, labourer
  [*Great George's street.*]
68 Michael Carraher, cow keeper
66 James Walls, labourer
64 Rebecca Boyd, lodging house
62 Thomas Magarry, sawyer
60 Toal Boyle, dealer
58 James Wright, dealer
52, 54 Hugh Burns, grocer
50 Ellen Boyd, confectioner
Drake's lane.]
44 William Trelford, baker
42 Matthew Boyle, pensioner

40 John Johnston, grocer
38 James Brennan, dealer
36 William Davis, coach painter
34 Hugh Cooper, cow keeper
32 Peter Mohan, labourer
Magee's lane.]
30 Hugh Britton, rag merchant
28 Patrick Sheridan, pensioner
26 Joseph M'Auley, bandbox maker
24 John M'Alister, pensioner
22 Daniel Hunter, labourer
20 Thomas M'Clean, pensioner
18 Mary M'Donnell, shoe shop
16 Patrick Feran, spirit dealer
12, 14 Samuel Walker, grocer
10 Samuel Kelly, shoemaker
8 Margaret Wild, lodgings
6 Thomas Loney, bricklayer
4 James Ritchie, shoemaker
2 Robert Boyle, labourer

Alexander Street South
PETER'S HILL.

1 Susannah Patton, winder
3 Thomas Stevenson, warper
5 Allen M'Alpin, travelling clerk
7 James Shanks, millwright
9 Andrew Young, watchman, Mr. Howie's bleach green
11 John Lappan, writing clerk
12 James Kerr, damask weaver
10 James Stirling, mechanic
8 Jane Milliken, sewer
6 John Stevenson, caretaker at Mr. Tilley's, Matier street
4 Francis Philips, mechanic
2 Thomas Morton, moulder
" Thomas Morton, sen., overlooker

Alfred Street
CONTINUATION OF ARTHUR STREET.
ALFRED PLACE PRESBYTERIAN CHURCH, Rev. Jas. Martin, Minister

1 Rev. George Shaw
ALFRED STREET PRESBYTERIAN CHURCH, Rev. George Shaw, Minister
2 Vacant
4 Wm. Lowry, linen merchant
6 Samuel Thompson, merchant; office, Corporation street
8 Henry Charley, merchant; office, Donegall quay
10 Mrs. Hanlon

12 John G. Megaw, merchant; office, Messrs. W. M'Clure and Sons, Corporation street
14 Miss Burden
16 Dr. Wm. Burden

Ann Street
CORN MARKET TO QUEEN'S BRIDGE.

1 H. W. Donaldson, spirit dealer
3 Vacant
5 James Bremner, upholsterer
7 James T. Campbell, cabinet maker
9 John Kelly, cabinet maker
11 Robert Henderson, white smith
13 Samuel Moore, grocer
[*Cooney's court.*
15, 17 William Haddock, spirit dealer and grocer
19 Robert Gilmore, grocer and spirit dealer
21 Charlotte Kerr, Star saloon
23 James Shaw, soap and candle manufacturer [*Telfair's entry.*
25 John Kennedy and Co., umbrella and parasol manufacturers
27 Samuel Cowan, merchant; residence, Cromac Lodge
27½ David Connor, flax and yarn commission agent; residence, Dundonald
29 John Martin and Co., merchants
" John Martin, Killileagh Mills
" Sam. Martin; residence, 7 Franklin place
31 John Finlay, soap & candle manufacturer; residence, Holywood
33 William H. Milligan, grocer, and tobacco and snuff manufacturer
35 Hugh Hamilton and Co., grocers
" Joseph Richardson, wine and spirit merchant, 4 Upper Church lane
37 Lough and Gregg, iron merchants
41 John Wightman, grocer
43 Vacant
45 W. and T. Hunter, leather merchant
47 Andrew Clarke, grocer
49 John Fetherston, publican; Portaferry and Downpatrick coach office [*Upper Church lane.*
51 Vacant
53 John H. Brown, wholesale grocer
55 Vacant
New houses building
....[*Victoria street intersects.*]....

STREET DIRECTORY.

Entrance to Pork Market.
Yards, stores, offices, &c., Town Council
[*Queen's Bridge.*]
136 Philip Jordan, publican
134 Catherine Birkmyre, bakery
132½ W. T. and R. S. Waterson, solicitors; Dublin address, 26 Lower Ormond quay; W. T. Waterson's residence, Seville Lodge, Strandtown
132 Burned
130½ Ann Street Brewery, Ledlie Clarke, proprietor; residence, Pakenham place
130 Jane Fee, publican
" David Fee, lighter owner
128 James Dixon, publican
126 Daniel M'Cullough, shoemaker
124 Bernard Reilly, grocer and provision merchant
122 Anne Webster, grocer
Princess Street.]
120 Ann Hill, publican
116 Allan R. Long, publican
114 William Bell, iron merchant
Space of vacant ground; W. Mullan, owner
.... [*Victoria Street intersects.*] ....
82 Vacant
80 Edwd. Stockdale, Victoria Hotel, and commercial boarding house
78 Wm. Carroll, grocer
76 John Moffett, chandler and soap boiler
74 Mrs M'Fadden, leather seller
72 James Sergison, copper and tinsmith
" Eliza Sergison, furrier
70 Amelia Bain, grocer
68 Hugh Millen, publican; Downpatrick, Portaferry, Bangor, &c. coach office
Church Lane.]
66 Mrs Pollock, haberdasher
62 John Graham, hair cutter
60 James Reid, grocer and publican
58 Isaac Bailie, boot and shoemaker, and leather seller
56 Jane Hepburn, haberdasher
54 John Lynn, painter and glazier
52 H. M'Keown, painter and glazier
50 Anne Ingle, bonnet and straw warehouse
48 R. M'Clure, boot and shoemaker

46 Sarah Crawford, milliner
Cole's Alley.]
44½ Robert Greenhill, currier and leather merchant
44 R. Ridgeway, boot and shoe maker
42 A. W. Budge, publican
Pottinger's Entry.]
40 Thomas Rainey, publican
38 T. H. Aikin, apothecary
36½ James Barry, dealer
36 Hugh Cuddy, spirit dealer
32 John Magee, plumber
30½ John Toman, grocer
30 William Hogg, grocer
Joy's Entry.]
26 James Black, boot and shoemaker
24 Bernard Peak, publican and lodging house keeper
Wilson's Court.]
22 Mrs Hazleton, haberdasher
20 Wm. Smylie, boot and shoemaker
18 Robert Feris, boot and shoemaker
16 Samuel Boyle, wine, spirit, ale, and porter merchant
14 Robert Hamilton, hair cutter
8 & 10 Vacant
12 Robert Heron, hair dresser
Crown Entry.]
6 Matilda M'Dowell, haberdasher
4 Joseph Sands, grocer
2 Geo. M'Afee, boot and shoemaker

Annette Street, off Verner street
3 James Hall, porter
5 James M'Ilneel, day constable
7 James Jamison, labourer
9 Bernard Doran, cowkeeper
44 Mrs Hamilton, shirtmaker
42 Henry Campbell, sawyer
38 Charles Jamison, porter
36 Samuel Campbell, porter
34 John Morrow, porter
32 Samuel M'Nally, labourer
30 Robert M'Cullough, porter
28 William Hogg, shoemaker
26 John Hatrick, sawyer
24 Patrick M'Cann, carter
22 William Wylie, boot & shoemaker
20 John M'Kittrick, carter
18 James Brown porter
16 John Campbell, sergt. day police
14 John Duffy, tailor
12 Henry Carroll, fancy biscuit manufacturer
" Joseph Lemon, iron founder

10 John Hutton, carter
8 Hugh Carson, bricklayer
6 Richard Hutton, labourer
4 Hugh Murdock, house agent
2 Patrick Greenan, sawyer

Antrim Road
FROM HEAD OF DONEGALL STREET.
1 James Carlisle, timber yard, 85 Donegall street
3 John Kennedy, publican
Thos. M'Cullough, carman's yard
Thomas Wilson, cart maker
Abel Gamble, stone yard, 19 Shipboy street
Trinity Street.]
5 John Kennedy, cartmaker
6 William Crawford, builder
7 James M'Gee, horse shoer and general jobber
Lying in Hospital, and Court house post-office receiving office
Cassino—Vacant
NEW BURYING GROUND
Several small houses [Henry's pl.
Mr Henry's residence
[*Henry's place.*
Patrick Mullen, confectionary
VICINAGE.
Roman Catholic Seminary
Domingo place.]
Lime Kiln
Rev. Wm. Bruce's, Farmhill
[*Antrim place.*
J. Beath, commission merchant, Antrim place cottage
P. Dale, Antrim cottage
Margaret Thompson, grocer
Mrs. Bruce, Thorndale
Mr. Pearce, iron founder, Pebble Lodge
[*Halliday's Row.*
Constabulary barracks
EAGLESTON PLACE.
1 Misses Houston
2 Mrs. Copeland
3 Misses M'Cammon
PLUNKET'S PLACE.
1 Wm. Gillespie, pensioner
2 Mary Blair
3 Mrs Smith
Gilbert Weir, Lodge view; muslin manufacturer, corner of Great Patrick street
James Hunter (Denis Wilson's), publcian

J. M'Laughlin, curds and cream house
Cliftonville.]
BELFAST WATER WORKS—John M'Quoid, caretaker

Antrim Place
ANTRIM ROAD.
1 Sam. Burns, commercial traveller
2 Thomas Mulligan, merchant; 6 Donegall street.
3 Miss Berwick
4 Elias Thomson, linen and yarn merchant
5 William Hamilton, manager at Messrs Sinclair's, Tomb street
6 Mrs Hodgens
7 Mrs David Ferguson, commission agent
8 Lamont Carson, glass manufacturer, High street
9 Mrs Fleming

Apsley Place
DONEGALL PASS.
1 Thomas Gaffikin, butcher, 13 Corn market
2 Mrs Atkinson
3 John Anderson, merchant; office, 19 Donegall street
4 Alfred Brownless, sea captain
5 William Tidd, master of Union Workhouse
6 Hugh Larmour, gentleman
" William Larmour, grain merchant, Victoria street
7 William Rodgers, general commission merchant, 31 Waring street
8 Alexander Knox, gentleman

Ardmoulin Place
FALLS ROAD.
1 James Combe, Falls Foundry
2 Robert Hamilton, engraver; office, Castle place
3 William M'Ilwrath, manufacturer; office, 4 Donegall street place; factory, Sackville street
4 Tobias Porter, manager Belfast flour mills

Arthur Lane
OFF 26 UPPER ARTHUR STREET.
1 Vacant
2 Anne Megarry
3 Vacant

4 Edward Hearty
5 Patrick Mars, coachman
6 Samuel Thomas, bell hanger
8 Samuel Kennedy, car owner
10 William Logue, coach washer

Arthur Place
OFF 14 AND 16 ARTHUR STREET.

1 Thos. K. Lowry, barrister-at-law; and Ballytrim, Killyleagh
" Thos. M'Quiston, painter
3 William Beattie, rent agent
5 Frederick Joy, solicitor
7 Hugh O'Connor, teacher
Plough Hotel Stables
9 Mrs M'Cullough, piano forte manufacturer
8 Jas. Keegan, rectifying distillery
6 William R. Black, teacher
2 John Clendinning, merchant; office, Donegall street place
" Orr R. Gamble, solicitor; Dublin address, 22 Middle Gardner street, and Train view, Whiteabbey

Arthur Square
CORN MARKET TO ARTHUR STREET.

1 David Dunlop, confectioner
3 James Young, solicitor; Dublin address, 51 Camden street; residence, 5 Dock street
5 Samuel Edgar, woollendraper and haberdasher
7 Robt. Gaffikin, carver and gilder; residence, 32 Arthur street Up.
9 William Reid, haberdasher
11 Modesto Silo, carver and gilder
Charles Blackwood, butcher; shop, Corn market
10 A. Welsh, printing office
8 Miss Donaldson, milliner
" William Donaldson, horse repository, Chichester street
6 John Hart, professor of music
4 Sam. Hanna, military boot maker
2 Eliza Gossan, provision dealer

Arthur Street
FROM ARTHUR SQUARE TO CHICHESTER STREET.

1 Theatre Royal, Thomas Cunningham, lessee
3 Tully M'Kenny, solicitor; Dublin address, 107 Capel street
" James M'Clean, solicitor; Dublin address, Leinster chambers, and 43 Dame street
3½ John Dyer, Northern servants' registry office
5 Mrs Horswill, baby linen and children's dress establishment
" John Cinnamoud, boot and shoemaker; shop, 9 Castle place
7 Chemico Agricultural Society Rooms, Dr. Hodges, chemist
" Mrs. J. Haslett, millinery and dress warehouse
9 Miss Culloden, baby linen warehouse
" Joseph Culloden, gentleman
11 Thomas K. Wheeler, physician and apothecary
13 John Kennedy, house and general agent, conveyancer, master extraordinary in chancery, and commissioner for taking affidavits
" John Keenan, solicitor; Dublin address, 18 Fleet street
" Francis H. O'Flaherty, proctor
15 Mrs Ann Murray
17 Samuel Kennedy, solicitor; Dublin address, 26 Lower Ormond quay
" Samuel Stevenson, tailor and clothier
19 Alex. Moore, house and ornamental painter
" James Tittle, solicitor; Dublin address, 19 Upper Ormond quay
21 Hugh H. Boyd, agent; residence, 1 Fitzwilliam street
" William M. Collins, solicitor; Dublin address, 103 Capel street residence, Fitzwilliam place
23 William Davis, solicitor; Dublin address, 185 Great Brunswick street; residence, Greenville
25 Samuel Moore, solicitor; Dublin address, 19 Upper Ormond quay
27 Thomas B. Johnston, solicitor; Dublin address, 103 Capel street
29 John Coates, solicitor; Dublin, address, 25 Upper Meckleburg street, and Newtownards

STREET DIRECTORY.

31 William Dillon, proctor and solicitor; Dublin address, 22, Middle Gardiner street; residence, Roseville, Whiteabbey
" Paul M'Henry, Civil Engineer
33 William and Alex. J. Cranston, solicitors; Dublin address, 29, Upper Ormond quay
[*Chichester Street.*]
28 Alexander Kilpatrick, agent for Blackie & Sons, publishers, Glasgow
26 George Browne, ladies' silk dyer, artificial florist, &c.; Arthur street district post office receiving house
24 Crawford and Russell, solicitors; Dublin address, 46 Lower Gardner street; W. Crawford's, Dalchoolin, Holywood
22 Charles Davis, dentist
*20 John Nocher, linen and damask warehouse
18 John Dinnen, solicitor; Dublin address, 22 Middle Gardner st.
" Surgeon Smith
†16 Thomas and John M'Quiston, glaziers and house painters
Arthur Place.]
14 Mrs Clendinning, (late Miss Lorimer) millinery warerooms
12 Saml. M'Dowell Elliott, solicitor, and Seneschal of Belfast; Dublin address, 15 Lower Ormond Quay; residence, the Old Lodge
10 Robert Campbell, baker
8 Robert Galbraith, hairdresser, wig maker, perfumer,&c.
CHRONICLE PLACE.
6½ *Commercial Chronicle* office, J. C. Anderson, proprietor; residence, 51 Upper Arthur st.
6 Alexander Robb, tailor
4 Joseph Gibson, solicitor; Dublin address, 103 Capel street
2½ William Young, shoe warehouse
" Patrick Savage, solicitor; Dublin address, 82 Jervis street
2 Samuel Edgar; shop, 5 Arthur square

---

* This house is lettered 16 both on shop and hall door, but stands No. 20 in the street, and is so rated.
† Numbered 14 but stands 16.

Arnon Street
OFF TRINITY STREET.
New street—no houses yet built

Arthur Street Upper
CONTINUATION OF ARTHUR STREET.
Patterson's Place.]
35, 37, 39, Vacant
41 Miss Grattan, milliner
43 Vacant
45 James M'Donald, agent for A. Fullarton & Co., publishers, Edinburgh
" Mons. Jules Festu, French master
47 James M'Kisack, linen and yarn agent; office, 10 Corporation st.
49 Mrs Henry, milliner
51 John C. Anderson, proprietor of *Belfast Commercial Chronicle*
53 Mrs Keith, milliner and dressmaker
55 Dr Henry Ferguson, surgeon
57 Mrs Allen
59 James T. May, professor of music
59½ Jas. Brown, land agent ⎫ Court
60 John Workman & ⎬ round
Sons, manufacturers ⎭ corner 59
Side of Music Hall.]
42 Dr. R. S. Dill, Surgeon
40 William M. Macartney, barrister-at-law
38 Miss Lamont and Miss Rook's boarding and day school
36 William Gilbert, watchmaker and jeweller; shop, 15 High street
34 Mrs M'Dowell
" J. B. M'Gregor, surgeon
32 Robert Gaffikin, carver and gilder; shop, 7 Arthur square
30 Miss Knowles' seminary.
28 Miss A. J. Williamson
26 Mary Sparling, dressmaker
Arthur Lane.]
24 Edward M'Hugh, haberdasher; shop, 12 Rosemary street

Artillery Street
ARTILLERY BARRACKS, NORTH QUEEN STREET.
2 Charles Raverty, labourer
4 Michael Malone, labourer
6½ John M'Ilvoy, porkcutter
8 Randal M'Donnell, bricklayer
10 Patrick Roddy, labourer
12 James Woods, night constable
14 James Irvine, labourer

16 Fanny Tumbelty
18 James Maxwell, millworker
20 James M'Coubrey, labourer
22 Mary Doran
   John M'Veigh, flax dresser
   Rose Loughran
   James Hamilton, millworker
   James Milliken, carter
   John Logan, labourer
   William Hall, labourer
   John Connor, labourer
   John Edgar, millworker
   Thomas Tierney, labourer
   Martin Higgins, labourer
   Thomas Curley, carter
   John Murphy, dealer
   Thomas Middleton, labourer
   Joseph Farley, labourer
   Francis Maxwell, labourer
   Mary M'Cann, dealer
   Thomas Walsh, moulder
   Alexander Ellis, caretaker grain store
   James Hughes, labourer
   John Doyle, labourer
   Samuel Smith, muslin printer
   Joseph Dodds, ship carpenter

Aughton Terrace
DONEGALL PASS.

1 George Holmes, Lieutenant Royal Engineers
2 Captain Allworthy, formerly in constabulary
3 Robert Greer, merchant, 13 Donegall street
4 William Agnew, solicitor
5 James M'Donald, agent to Fullartons, publishers and printers, Edinburgh
6 Mrs Fitzgerald
7 Mrs Isabella Aughton
8 James Moncrief, vitriol works, Ballymacarrett

Allen's Court
OFF PETER'S HILL.
About fifteen small houses

Anderson's Court
SHANKHILL ROAD.
A few small houses

Anderson's Court
OFF MILLFIELD.
About fifteen small houses

Back Lane
WEST SIDE PRINCE'S STREET
Mr Bell's grain store and stable
Mr Ireland's grain store and stable
21 Vacant

Bairn's Court
OFF CURTIS STREET.
Eight small houses

Balmer's Court
VERNER STREET.

1 Charles M'Mullan, seaman
3 Mrs Storey
5 Samuel Best, dealer
8 Robert Townsend, dealer
6 Robert M'Kee, fowl dealer
4 Anne M'Ginnity
2 John Mitchell, tanner

Bank Lane
FROM 29 CASTLE PLACE TO CHAPEL LANE.

1 M. Taggart, commercial traveller
3 Surgeon John Quin
5, 7 Cochrane, Brothers, and Co., sewed muslin manufacturers
9 James Stirrat, sewed muslin agent
11 Mrs Torney
13 Mathew Doland, whitesmith
15 James Sloan, car driver
17 Daniel M'Cann, labourer
19 Edward Gilmour, shoemaker
21 Arthur Maherg, cooper
23 Robert M'Quillen, servant
25 Geo. and James Magill, brewers
27 Store vacant
29 Mrs Hamill
31 John Donnelly, dyer
33 Bernard Brady, maltsman
35 James Fitzpatrick, coachman
37 Henry Slane, coachmaker
39 Rose Black
   [*Chapel lane.*]
   Side of Cunningham's brewry
42 Mrs Glasgow
40 Store vacant
38 John Brooks, servant
36 Hugh Kelly, wine and spirit store; residence, 13, North Queen st.
30, 32, 34 Vacant
28 Susan Lee
26 Wm. Butler, bootcloser
24 Edward M'Anally, labourer
22 Henry Dillon, basketmaker
16 Robert Saunders, carpenter

14 John Maguire, dyer
12 Robert Ross, dealer
10 Hugh Mullan, saddler
8 J. Rutherford, painter and glazier's
4, 2, Vacant [stores

Barnet's Court
NORTH SIDE PETER'S HILL.
Ten small houses

Barker's Court
SOUTH SIDE PILOT STREET
Six small houses

Barrack Street
FROM MILL STREET TO DURHAM ST.,
FALLS ROAD.
1 Isabella Erwin, grocer
3 Timothy O'Meely, haberdasher
5 Robert Meek, baker
7 James O'Kane, shoemaker
[Meek's Court.
9 Mary M'Cormac, dealer
11 John Hayes, butcher
13 John Higgins, shoemaker
15 William Kelly, butcher
17 P. Murphy, grocer and spirit dealer
19 James B. Owen, pawnbroker
Galway's entry.]
23, 25 Chas. Hilland, grocer and spirit dealer
27 Dr M'Gregor, accoucheur
29, 31 James M'Cracken, builder and grocer
33 Andrew Barnett, spirit dealer
[Brown's Entry.
35 Henry Davis, cooper
37, 39 J. Mackenzie, Shaw, & Co., Belfast Distillery
A. M. Shaw's residence
39 John Russell, grocer
39½ Philip Hamilton, labourer
41 Robert Milligan, pawnbroker
[Kennedy's Entry.
45 Ann Hagan, grocer
47 Patrick Cochrane, carman
49 James Devlin, tailor
51 Patrick O'Neill, carpenter
53 Francis Campbell, grocer
55 Henry Rippet, cattle dealer
57 William Hughes, do.
59 Henry Cochrane, labourer
61 Ann M'Grady
63 Bernard M'Anally, butcher
65 James M'Guigan
67 John O'Neill, grocer

69 David Campbell, pig dealer
71 Alexander Spence, dealer
73 Archibald M'Master, carpenter
75 John Mulholland, merchant
77 Richard Graham, merchant
79 Bernard Campbell, mason
81 Patrick M'Kenna, labourer
83 Patrick Grant, grocer
85, 87 Robert Williams, grocer
[Durham street.]
76 John Close, grocer
74 Felix Connelly, carman
72 Wm. J. M'Cormack, carman
70 Robert Williams, hay dealer
68 Patrick Grant, grocer
66 Samuel Coleman, grocer
64 Charles M'Geough, butcher
62 Mathew M'Geough, baker
60 Wm. Connolly, millworker
58 Betty Clarke, lodging house
Murphy's Row.]
56 Francis Harvey, carman
Old Barracks
52 Thomas M'Kee, cooper
50 James O'Neill, butcher
48 G. Rafferty, grocer and publican
46 Hugh Harper, pawnbroker
42, 44 Vacant
40 Bernard Lenard, engineer
38 John M'Adorey, grocer
36 H. Trelford, publican and grocer
34 Thomas M'Evoy, grocer
32 Sarah M'Cullough, dealer
30 William Mallen, weaver
28 Tobias M'Quade, baker
Dyas Court.]
26 Patrick Meekan, dealer
24 James O'Neill, dealer
22 William Gardner, green grocer
20 Thomas Mills, labourer
Donaldson's Court.]
18 James Carnes, watchman
14, 16 Alexander Withers, grocer
12 Patrick Woods, grocer
10 Hugh Mason, grocer
Lettuce Hill.]
8 Hugh M'Quillan, grocer
6 Robert Wright, publican
4 Peter Battersby, rag store
2 Elizabeth Savage, grocer

Bath Place, Falls Road
1 Patrick Savage, Bath House Tavern
2 Wm. M'Connell, calico printer
3 Wm. Spence, writing clerk

4 George Sibbin, pawnbroker
Public Baths and Wash Houses,
W. J. Livingston, superintend.

Beattie's Entry
SOUTH SIDE MILL STREET.
Twenty-two houses

Bell's Lane
EAST SIDE OF SMITHFIELD.
1 Patrick Noon, shoemaker
3 Wm. Ellis, schoolmaster
5 Patrick Kerr, shoemaker
7 Robert M'Cudden, huckster
9 Mary Frim, green grocer
11 George M'Cullough, carpenter
13 Vacant
15 Francis Frys, bailiff
17 Patrick Fox, dealer
19 Margaret Magee
21 Francis M'Cormack, shoemaker
23 Rodger M'Quillan, labourer
[*Torren's Row and Market at end.*
24 Mary M'Kavanagh, huckster
22 Ellen Hogshaw, fishmonger
20 Mick M'Conaghy, huckster
18 John Burns, dealer
16 Edward M'Garry, shoemaker
14 Samuel Robinson, shoemaker
12 Wm. Halliday, porter
10 Bernard Connor, tanner
8 James Brady, jun., shoemaker
6 James Brady, sen., shoemaker
4, 6 Henry Chapman, shoemaker

Belvidere Place
OPPOSITE VICTORIA PLACE.
1 Mrs Pentland
2 Richard Atkinson, book keeper
3 Hugh Morrow, Inspector, Belfast Bank
4 Mrs Arthur
5 Mrs Martin
6 Robt. Hamilton, in Messrs Richardson, Brothers' office, Corporation street

Berryhill Court
OFF 76 LITTLE DONEGALL STREET.
Thirty-four small houses

Berry Street
FROM HERCULES ST. TO SMITHFIELD.
1 Peter Magouran, spirit dealer
3 Peter Harkin, clothes dealer
5 James Griffith, do.
7 George Gordon, clothes dealer
9 Michael Grimes, do.
11 John Reilly, do.
13 John Stewart, do.
15 John Sheals, do.
17 Thomas Marshall, shoemaker
19, 21 Geo. M'Ginley, clothes dealer
23 George Fulton, clothes dealer
25 John Crawford, jun., grocer and publican [*New Row.*
27 Stephen M'Kenna, clothes dealer
29 Sarah M'Clean, clothes dealer
31 Richard Ledgett, clothes dealer
33 Vacant
35 John Drummond, clothes dealer
[*Charlemont street.*
37 Sarah Stewart, clothes dealer
39 James Griffith, clothes dealer
41 Elizabeth Griffith, do.
43 James Bogan, publican
45 Robert M'Dowell, clothes dealer
49 Ellen Hughes, do.
51 James Lyons, do.
53 James Stewart, do.
55 Hugh Ward, stocking dealer
Chapel Lane.] [*Millar's Lane.*
BERRY ST. PRESBYTERIAN CHURCH
TEETOTAL HALL
38 John Byrne, auctioneer
36 Wm. M'Laughlin, clothes dealer
34 George M'Ginley, clothes dealer
30 Vacant
28 William Porter and Son, clothiers and general outfitters
26 Henry Mallaghan, clothes dealer and auctioneer
24 Vacant
22 Richard Lennon, clothes dealer
20 Anne Jane Fulton, clothes dealer
18 Patrick Keenan, confectioner
16 Edward Stritch, haberdasher
14 Thomas Monaghan, clothes dealer
12½ Thomas Mallaghan
12 Samuel Campbell, grocer
10 John Gordon, clothes dealer
8½ Alexander Hamill, do.
8 Miles Dolan, do.
6 Richard Jones, do.
4 Thomas O'Reilly, do.
2 Peter Harkin, do.

Black's Place
OFF HERCULES STREET.
1 James Strickland, labourer
3 Hugh M'Grath, labourer

5 Robert Welsh, fishmonger
7 Francis M'Kee, chandler
9 Jane Menim
11 Michael Adrain, labourer
13 Mary Bradley, fishmonger
15 William Collins, fishmonger
17 Felix Cowan, labourer
19 Patrick Butler, coal factor
21 John Fee, labourer
23 Alice Finnigan
25 Jane Orem, clothes dealer
27 Patrick Lucas, comb maker
29 Patrick Mulholland, labourer
31 James Stewart, labourer
30 Mary M'Connell
28 Bryan Rock, labourer
26 John Woodward, cabinet maker
24 Robert Woods, labourer
18 James Murphy, chandler
18 Mrs Orem
16 Isabella Stitt
14 James Maginnis, bricklayer
12 Margaret M'Glenn, lodgings
10 William Butler
8 William Dogherty
6 William Stit
4 John Hungerford, carpenter
2 Michael Pentleton, labourer

Blakely's Lane
WEST SIDE TOMB STREET.
Eight houses and store

Bogan's Row, Falls Road
Fourteen small houses

Bond Street
OFF CROMAC STREET.
1 John Rogers, labourer
3 John Martin, labourer
5 John M'Court, dealer in old books
7 John Devenny, labourer
9 Daniel Moore, tile burner
11 Robert M'Auley, carpenter
13 John Doherty, labourer
15 Mrs M'Aree, mill worker
17 J. Caruthers, boot and shoemaker
19 John M'Cafferty, labourer
21 Widow Crean
23 Christopher Noddings, flax dresser
25 Daniel Barniff, carpenter
27 William Steed, tailor
29 Hugh Henan, baker
31 John Kearns, fowl dealer
33 John Thompson, porter
35 Felix Quin, servant

36 Lewis Cross, mechanic
34 William Gordon, labourer
32 Adam Hampton, cooper
30 John Sharkey, labourer
28 Richard Keys, labourer
26 Aaron Smith, labourer
24 Robert Donaghy, lamplighter
22 Henry Jordan, caretaker
20 Henry Doonegan, plate layer
18 Mary M'Kigan, cow keeper
16 Samuel M'Ilwaine, car owner
14 John Stevenson, porter
12 Mrs Osborne
10 Alex. Millen, house carpenter
8 Henry M'Convill, labourer
6 Thomas Jones, writing clerk
4 Robert Crooks, grocer
2 James Clarke, dealer

Bond Street, New
CONTINUATION OF BOND STREET TO ELIZA STREET.
1 Thomas Frith, flax spinner
3 Thomas Rice, meal dealer, Castle Market
5 James M. Fordyce, brewer, Cromac brewery
7 Thomas Gibson, travelling clerk, Belfast Chemical Works Company
9 Wm. Greig, delf merchant, High street
11 Thomas Carnes, travelling clerk, Messrs Dobbin's, druggists, 18 & 20 North street
15 John Gregg, buyer to Jas. Young and Co., woollen drapers, 19 Donegall street
17 Thomas Gilmore, pawnbroker, Cromas street

Botanic Road
RIGHT SIDE FROM VICTORIA PLACE
1 Vacant
2 John Percival Hudson, gentleman
3 Vacant
4 John Hoy, wine and spirit merchant; shop, Victoria street
5, 6 Vacant
7 John Hartley, notary public; office, Castle buildings
8 James Ewart, muslin manufacturer
9 Miss Hume
10 Dr Robert John Black, surgeon
11 Mrs Henderson

STREET DIRECTORY.

Botanic Cottage
Rev. George Hill

Botanic Garden.
D. Ferguson, curator
William M'Kechnie, gatekeeper

Botanic View
BOTANIC ROAD.
1 David Reimbach, second master in School of Design
2 Mrs Murray
3 Mrs Hall
4 Doctor Dickie, professor of natural history, in Queen's College
5 Mrs Stewart
6 Miss Greaves
7 Doctor James Thompson
8 James Connor, Ulster Bank
9 Mrs Cooper

Bolton Street
EAST SIDE VERNER STREET.
Four small houses

Boundary Court
OFF BOUNDARY STREET.
Eight small houses

Boundary Street
FROM FALLS ROAD TO PETER'S HILL.
1 Samuel Todd, smith
3 Johnston Fleming, grocer
5 John Burnside, ropemaker
7 Samuel Johnston, ropemaker
9 Andrew M'Mullan, ropemaker
11 Richard King, ropemaker
13 Andrew M'Mullan, ropemaker
15 Martha Henry, confectionary
17 William Rice, shoemaker
19 Robert Robinson, bootmaker
21 P. Devlin, labourer [*Reid's Place.*
23 Robert Windsor, labourer
25 James Magill, weaver
27 Nathaniel M'Adam, labourer
29 William Bickerstaff, labourer
31, 33, 35 William Spence, provision dealer and publican
37 William Arlow, carman
39 William Dickey, carpenter
41 Henry Louden, carpenter
43 William M'Clelland, shoemaker
45 Moses Livingstone, weaver
47 William Craw, ropemaker
49 James M'Culloch, engineer
[*Upper Cargill street.*

51 Alexander Green, dyer and grocer
53 William M'Namee, labourer
55 Peter Clarke, labourer
57 James Harvey, dyer
59 Denis Gartins, baker
61 John O'Neill, labourer
63 Mary Ann Ferguson
" Charlotte Campbell, millworker
" Patrick M'Laughlin, bricklayer
65 Patrick M'Evoy, labourer
67 Owen Doyle
[*Henrietta court.*
69 Mary Ann Jackson
71 Patrick Henry, labourer
73 James Morrison, milkman
75 Michael Leonard, mechanic
77 Daniel Dougherty, mechanic
79 Edward Donnelly, engineer
81 John Newell, porter
83 John Mullan, porter
[*Duffy's place.*
85 Patrick M'Cabe, grocer
87 James Lemon, ropemaker
89 Hugh Agnew, mechanic
91 William M'Laughlin, mechanic
93 Eliza M'Clusky, millworker
95 George Wilkinson, engineer
Wall of Campbell and Boomer's mill
[*Waste ground.*
60 James M'Corry, publican
58 Henry Donnelly, stonemason
56 James Porter, labourer
54 James Johnston, moulder
52 Mary Cronin
50 James Boyd, grocer
Cargill street.]
48 John M'Trustery, carpenter
46 William Hall, cabinet maker
44 Archibald Leinster, porter
42 Francis Green, watchman
Boundary court.]
40 Eliza Bunting, green grocer
38 Hugh Montgomery, labourer
36 Abraham Grattan, shoemaker
O'Haggarty street.]
34 Wm. M'Ilwrath, grocer
32 Abraham Neill, night constable
" John M'Knight, night constable
30 Wm. Humphreys, pork cutter
28 Alex. Blair, designer
26 Edward Linn, bootmaker
24 Wm. Rodgers
" Patrick Woods
22 William Johnston, carman

F

20 James M'Ilveen, mechanic
18 Spiers Muir, bookbinder
16 Hugh Sales, night constable
Gable street.]
14 Mary Ball, green grocer
12 Michael Halpan, tailor
10 Matthew Quail, starch maker
8 John Whisker, butcher
6 John M'Cartney, scavenger
4 Jeremiah Smith, shoemaker
2 John Savage, grocer
John Magee, moulder

Boyd's Court
AT BOYD'S BLACKSTAFF MILL.
Eleven houses

Boyd's Court
OFF NILE STREET.
Ten houses

Boyd Street
FROM PETER'S HILL TO MITCHELL ST.
1 John Hanna (grocer and spirit merchant) hall door
3 W. Sloane, smith
5 James Hall, constable
7 Daniel M'Keith, bootmaker
9 Robert Lithgow, shoemaker
11 Vacant
[*Boyd's court*—13 small houses.
13 William Boal, cabinet maker
15 Jane Gilliland, bonnet maker
17 James Mulholland, starch worker
19 William M'Auley, bricklayer
21 John Wilson, baker
23 Mary Ann M'Bride, grocer
[*Glasshouse street*—24 small houses.
25 John M'Anally, shoemaker
27 James Crow, plasterer
29 Robert M'Neice, cabinet maker
31 Thomas Moffett, shoemaker
33 John Smith, blacksmith
35, 37 Starch Works, James Boyd, proprietor; residence, Beech lodge
39 James Boyd's office
41 John Peacock, currier
43 Samuel Murray, painter
45 Daniel M'Conagill, boiler maker
47 John Harley, starch worker
49 Mary Blackburn, sempstress
51 Miss Cooper's school
[*Mitchell street.*]
60 John Lemon, porter
58 John Bell, printer
56 William Cooper, carpenter

54 Robert Newell, labourer
52 John Lockhart, smith
50 James M'Clarnen, carpenter
48 Robert Wiggins, blacksmith
46 John Harlin, carpenter
44 James Macklin, baker
42 Richard Jennings, carpenter
40 James Treaner, carpenter
38 Thomas Heaney, baker
36 John Martin, bootmaker
34 Robert Long, mill wright
32 Patrick Davison, porter
30 Samuel Anderson, hackler
28 Daniel Pettigrew, mill wright
26 John M'Clarnen, carpenter
24 Charles M'Crory, porter
22 David Ferguson, harness maker
20 Hugh Murray, mill wright
18 Alexander Vint, stone cutter
16 Archibald Adair, carpenter
14 Edward Echlin, cabinet maker
12 James Doyle, baker
10 George White, carpenter
8 Andrew Corrigan, painter
6 William Hincks, pensioner
4 Hugh Lappen, porter
2 E. Connor, grocer, hall door

Bradbury Place
FROM BOTANIC ROAD TO LISBURN ROAD
1 William Fawkner, grocery and spirit dealer
3 James Martin, grocer
7 Thomas Johnston, carpenter
9 Alex. Murphy, boot and shoemaker
11 Wm Goodwin, boot and shoemaker
13 John Rodgers, gardener
15 Alexander Stewart, gardener
17 Robert Carson
19 George M'Ilveen, labourer
21 William M'Kelvey, carpenter
23 Hugh Larmour, grocer
25 James Kennedy, linen inspector
27 John Patrick, porter Queen's Col.
29 Arthur Mackay, tailor
31 James M'Vey, labourer
33 Jane Homes, lodging house
35 Constabulary
37 Robert Kennedy, spirit store
39 George Mateer, Malone toll gate keeper

Barnes Court
BROWN'S ROW, SOUTH SIDE MILLFIELD.
Nine small houses

STREET DIRECTORY.

Bradford's Entry
WEST SIDE MILLFIELD.
Seven houses
7 Alex. Crawford's Starch Works

Bradford Square
EAST SIDE TOMB STREET.
1 Bernard Mooney, block and pump maker
3 Ann Lamb, lodging house
5 Margaret Black, lodging house
   [*Steam lane across east end.*
6 Sarah Massy, lodging house
4 Mary Dickson, lodging house
2 Jane Haddock, lodging house

Bradford Street
OFF DOCK STREET
Some new houses

Breadalbane Place
OPPOSITE VICTORIA PLACE
1 Mrs J. A. Wilson
2 Mrs Patterson
3 Jas. Siebert, linen, yarn merchant; office, Linen Hall

Bridge End
Ulster Canal Company's stores and landing

Bridge Street
FROM HIGH ST. TO BELFAST BANK.
1 Cooke Johnston & Co., hat warehouse
3 M. M'Cracken, boot and shoemaker; residence, 54 Great George's st.
5 John Jennings, woollendraper
7, 9, 11 John Arnott & Co., wholesale and retail woollendrapers, silk mercers, and general warehousemen; D. Taylor's residence, 2 Lower Cresent
13 Riddel & M'Callum (late Brown's), haberdashers and lacemen, and hosiery and Berlin wool establishment
15 John Craig, wholesale and retail ironmonger; residence, Great George's street
17, 17½ John Arnott & Co. (see above)
19 David Walker, confectioner and restaurant
21 Geo. W. Kyle, hosier, glove, shirt, and stock maker, outfitter, &c.
23 John B. M'Grotty & Co., woollendrapers, hatters, outfitters, and clothiers; residence, 26 College street
25 Thomas Ward, sub-stamp distributor; residence, Cherry hill, Malone
27 George Phillips, bookseller, stationer, and librarian; residence, 3 Linen hall street
   [*Commercial Buildings.*
28½ Hugh Graham & Co., hat and cap manufacturers
28 A. M'Cracken, boot and shoemaker
26 Edward M'Hugh, hat and cap warehouse
24½ A. C. Weir & Co., Manchester woollen warehouse; residence, 1 Albion place
24 John Kelly, brush, comb, and trunk manufacturer
22 Waring Curran, oil, colour, and dye stuff warehouse; residence, Donegall street
20 John M'Kenna (sign of the Golden Lamb), draper and haberdasher
18 A. & J. Marshall, hosiers and glovers
16, 14, 12 Thomas M'Kenna & Co., linen and woollendrapers
10 *News-Letter Office* (estd. 1737), James Alex. Henderson, publisher; residence, Mount Collyer Park
8 Alexander Wilson, basket manufacturer and toy merchant; residence, 76 Joy street
6 Robt. Pelan & Co., Prince of Wales Bazaar, and basket manufactory; residence, 15 York street
4 Robert Donnelly, confectioner and cigar dealer; residence, 9 Joy st.

Bridge Street Place
OFF NO. 22 BRIDGE STREET.
Falls Mills Co., flax spinners

Birch Street
OFF LITTLE DONEGALL STREET.
1 James M'Mannus, spirit store
45 Thomas Graham, chimney sweep
And 57 other small houses

Brougham Street
LEFT SIDE OF YORK STREET.
1 Alexander Douglass, salesman
3 Mrs Eliza Everett

5 Mrs Elizabeth Carr
7 David Parkhill, gentleman
9 James Porteous, sewed muslin manufacturer
11 James Sullivan, shipowner
13 John Smith, butter merchant
 Waste ground
21 Rev. Samuel Downing, Methodist minister
 Four new houses building

Brown's Entry
NORTH SIDE OF BARRACK STREET.
Nineteen houses

Brown's Row
Eleven houses

Brown's Square
FROM PETER'S HILL TO BROWN STREET.
1 John M'Laughlin, spirit dealer
3 William Bunting, market constable
5 Andrew Walker, carman
M'Kee's court.]
11 Walter Cahoon, pensioner
13 James Bell, weaver
17 John Hare, carpenter
21 Thomas Macnamee, day constable
25 Francis Williamson, day constable
29 James Hamilton's rag store
31, 33 Robert Carnduff, bakery establishment
53 James Macauley, whitesmith
55 Thomas Carmichael, carman
65 John M'Kever, gate keeper Messrs. Herdman's stores
 S. Bamford, spirit store (hall door) [*Peter's hill.*]
40 James Magee, grocer
26 to 20 S. & W. Thompson, foundry
 [*Lewis Court*—18 small houses. *M'Conkey's court.*]
10 Daniel Hall, brush manufacturer
Rowentree court.]
2 Robert Humphrey, house and rent agent [*Humphrey's court.*
 The remainder of the houses in this street are principally occupied by weavers.

Brown Street
FROM MILLFIELD TO MELBOURNE ST.
1 Geo. Hopes, grocer and spirit dealer
5 Ralph Russell, labourer
7 Samuel Walker, labourer
9 Thomas Hayes, house painter

11 Andrew M'Gimpsey, spirit dealer
13 William Bruce, wood turner
15 John M'Cracken, general dealer
17 Vacant
19 Neill M'Neill, bricklayer
21 Michael Conway, weaver
23 Robert Wilson, weigher at Smithfield weigh bridge
25 John M'Ilveen, engineman
27 Archibald Dixon, carman
29 Francis M'Cann, labourer
29½ Andrew Crozier, servant
31 Robert Canning, tailor
33 Thomas Hill, weaver
35 William Hall, house painter
37 Henry Murray, house painter
39 James Girven, weaver
41 John Downey, writing clerk
43 John M'Glaughlen's stores
45 John M'Glaughlen, grocer and spirit dealer
78 John O'Neill, carter
76 Samuel M'Burney
74 Sarah Irvin
72 Andrew Shaw, grocer
70 Robert Niblock, mechanic
68 Nathaniel Fleeton, day constable
66 Joseph M'Cracken, spirit dealer
64 Eliza Ewing
62 Robert Boyd, bleacher
60 Anne Coates
58 John Withers, carman
56 John Loughran, mechanic
54 Thomas Patterson, cabinetmaker
52 John Steen, house painter
50 James Black, labourer
48 Robert Morrison, porter
46 Agnes M'Ilwaine
44 Mary M'Ivor
42 William M'Gloughlen, whitesmith
40 Thomas Burnside, bricklayer
38 Wm Channon, garrison librarian
36 Charles Hagan
34 Wm John Davis, nailer
32 Wm Crook, carpenter
30 Laughlin M'Clean, nailer
28 Isaac Hayburn, ropemaker
26 Thomas Morgan, salesman
24 Charles Crawford, smith's helper
22 Sarah Connor
20 Charles Donoghey, shoemaker
18 John Leitch, sawyer
16 Charles Shiels, boot and shoemaker
14 John Short, labourer
12 Jane Daley

STREET DIRECTORY.

10 Henry Stewart, tanner
8 John Shaw, car driver
6 John M'Williams, night watchman
4 Eliza Reid, dealer
2 Eliza Scott, dressmaker

Brunswick Lane
WEST SIDE HENRY SQUARE.
Nine Houses

Brunswick Street
BETWEEN HOWARD STREET AND HOUSE OF CORRECTION.
1 James Mathewson, grocer; shop, Donegall place
2 Wm. White, linen commissioner
Ulster Female Penitentiary

Burn's Court, off Mill Street.
Ten small houses

Byrnes Lane
OFF LOWER LAGAN STREET.
Five houses

Caddell's Entry
FROM HIGH ST. TO ROSEMARY ST.
1 Peter Hughes, porter
3 Rose Campbell, huckster
5, 7 James Barnes, spirit dealer
9 Peter Fox, labourer
11 Vacant
13 Arthur Ward, boarding house
15 John M'Cready, tailor
17 John Murray, weaver
19 William Agar, butcher
21 Betsy Hammond, washerwoman
23 James Martin, labourer
25 David Hood, boarding house
27 Samuel Haddock, labourer
29 Vacant
30 James Hughes, cork cutter
28 Alexander Robinson, carman
26 Alexander Kerr, pensioner
24 James Hughes, eating house
22 Jane Rafferty, huckster
20 Mary M'Court, huckster
18 William Stewart, shoemaker
16 Robert Magee, spirit dealer
14 Catherine Hanna, boarding house
12 Mary Kearns, boarding house
10 Margaret Forster, boarding house
8 Feenan, boarding house
6 Jane Anderson, boarding house
4 Mary Gibson, eating house
2 John Henderson's printing office

Cahoon's Court
OFF BROWN'S SQUARE.
Four small houses

Calendar Street
FROM CASTLE LANE TO DONEGALL SQ.
1 James Crawford, wine and spirit merchant; residence, 26 Donegall place
3 James Coey's wholesale and retail boot and shoe warehouse
5 Richardson, Sons, and Owden's stores
7 Day and Bottomley, wholesale woollen merchants; Wm. Bottomley's residence, Fortbreda, county Down
9 William Stevenson, jun., and Co., general merchants; residence, Dunmurry
" J. Cameron, linen and ribbon manufacture; residence, 15 Victoria
11 Stables, vacant [place
13 A. & S. Henry & Co.'s back entrance to Donegall square north
[*Donegall square.*
16 John Ladley, solicitor; and 74 Dame street, Dublin; residence, 99 Joy street
14 Connolly Sherrard, house and land agent; residence, 2 Chichester st.
12 John Preston and Co., linen yarn and flax merchants; residence, 5 Pakenham place
10 John Dunville and Co., wholesale wine, tea, and spirit merchants; William Dunville's residence, Richmond lodge, county Down
8 Anne Murray's tobacco manufactory; residence, 15 Arthur st
6 *Northern Whig Office,* F. D. Finlay, proprietor; residences, 1 Adelaide place, and Ballynafeigh cottage, county Down
4 Peter Keegan, rectifying distiller, and wine and spirit merchant; residence, 12 Victoria place
2 Arthur Carmichael, Fox tavern
Samuel Clay, poulterer; residence, 6 Wellington street

California Street
19 WALL ST. TO OLD LODGE ROAD.
1 Mathew Maine, engineer
3 William Knox, plumber
5 Alexander Dixon, millwright

7 Robert Lawson, writing clerk
9 Richard Robinson, schoolmaster
11 Samuel Gordon, linen lapper
Five new houses
Park street.]
Six new houses
William Davis, message porter
Hugh Campbell, linen lapper
William Lavery, linen lapper
Oswald Reid, blacksmith
Four new houses
[*Park street.*
20 Moses Hutchinson, labourer
18 Andrew Thompson, linen lapper
16 Hugh Glass, linen lapper
14 Robert Fleming, tailor
12 Robert Carswell, bookbinder
10 William Sweeney, mechanic
8 John Black, shipping clerk
6 William Campbell, bookbinder
4 John Ritchie, foreman in muslin manufactory
2 James Scott, grocer and salesman

Cambridge Street
OFF CANNING STREET, YORK ROAD.
1 John M'Mullan, tailor
2 Hugh Renton, foreman hackler

Camden Terrace, Botanic Road
1 Rev. Charles Reichel
2 William G. Bell
3 Edward Masson, professor of Greek, Assembly's College
4 Mrs Savage
5 George Sibbald, Belfast Bank

Campbell's Buildings
PETER'S HILL AND TOWNSEND ST.
1 Alex. Edgar, foreman carpenter
3 David Imray, foreman in muslin warehouse
5 Wm. Guy, poor rate collector
7 Robert Clements, builder
9 Henry Johnston, engraver
11 George Wilson, mechanic
13 Robert Reynolds, warper
15 Robert Campbell, carpenter
17 James Withers, editor Belfast *Commercial Chronicle*
19 John Hodgson, grocer
21 James M'Keever, tobacco spinner
23 James Coates, water tax collector
12 James Sinclair, street inspector
10 Archibald Price, ironfounder

8 John Dornan, manager in foundry
6 E. Whitla, dressmaker
4 Noah Longworth, engineer
2 M. M'Coulery, dressmaker

Campbell's Court
OFF CARRICK HILL.
Several small houses

Campbell's Place
OFF THE OLD LODGE ROAD.
1 Conway M'Niece, cow keeper
3 Mrs Saunders
5 Mathew Fulton, cow keeper
4 William Falloon, blacksmith
2 John Saunders, horse dealer

Campbell Street
OFF OLD LODGE ROAD.
Twenty-two small houses.

Canning Street
OFF YORK ROAD.
1 John Williamson, carter
Seven new houses building

Cargill Street
OFF TOWNSEND AND BOUNDARY ST.
1 Addison Briggs, clerk
3 George Cameron, goldsmith
5 William Warnock, tobacco spinner
7 Robert M'Mechan, labourer
9 James Russell, grocer and publican
11 Mary M'Clusky, widow
13 William Bell, mechanic
30 David Law, brass founder
28 Robert Mawhinney, pork cutter
26 Stephen Houston, mill wright
24 John Donaldson, smith
22 John Montgomery, pork cutter
" M. Montgomery, dress maker
20 James M'Comb, dealer in butter
18 Susan Taylor, widow
16 Robert Taylor, iron moulder
14 Joseph White, mechanic
12 William Morrison, weaver
10 Alexander Riddell, shoemaker
8 George Ireland, tinsmith
6 Arthur Douglas, labourer
4 David Gamble, tinsmith
2 John M'Adam, cabinet maker

Caroline Street
FROM GREAT GEORGE'S STREET TO LITTLE PATRICK STREET.
1 Elizabeth Hunter, grocer

3 Edward Hughes, labourer
5 John Hawthorn, sailor
7 Hamilton Rowan, ship carpenter
9 Joseph M'Farland, cooper
11 William Lemon, ship carpenter
13 Alexander M'Kay, cooper
15 William Lattimore, sail maker
17 Charles Wardlow, sawyer
19 Matthew Shanks, carpenter
21 James Humphreys, porter
23 Edward Murray, cooper
25 Hugh Bole, stokerer
27 Mrs Moreland, waistcoat maker
26 John Kelly, sawyer
24 John Kelly, master of vessel
22 Samuel Reynolds, porter
20 Jane Hunter
18 Charlotte Brown, mill worker
16 James M'Cormick, cooper
14 James Tosh, cooper
12 Daniel M'Kee, master of vessel
10 Robert Gill, master of vessel
8 Robert Carmichael, sailor
6 James M'Clure, sawyer
4 Charles Webb, rigger
2 Robert Hunter, rag store

Carrick Hill
FROM NORTH ST. TO DONEGALL ST.
1 James Graham, hair dresser
3 Isaac Griffith, dealer in hay
5 Francis Mullan, lodging house
7 Hugh Casey, dealer in hay
9 Vacant
11 Hugh Kearney, lodging house
13 Alice Hegarty, lodging house
15 Elizabeth Kernaghan
17 John Lennon, grocer and baker
19 John M'Bride, labourer
21, 22 Wm M'Carter, grocer and baker
25 James Brennan, dealer
Upper Kent street.]
27 Francis Sherry, dealer
29 Thomas M'Ilveen, nailer
31 John Dougherty, labourer
33, 35 James M'Keown, musician
37 Patrick Rogan, spirit dealer
39 James Bruce, carter
41 Hugh M'Anally, lodging house
Pepperhill steps.]
43 Samuel M'Oracken, publican
45 James Hutton, marble polisher
47 Bridget Kellen, spirit dealer
49 Simon Dickson, bleacher
51 John Dogherty, labourer
53 Hugh M'Mullan, spirit dealer

55 Hannah M'Claverty, dealer
57 Maria Montgomery, grocer
59 Mary M'Gookin, lodging house
61 John M'Ilwee, letterpress printer
63 Thomas Taylor, iron moulder
65 James M'Goff, pensioner
67 Hugh M'Keown, lodging house
69 Thomas Garrity, lodging house
71 John Stewart, lodging house
73 James Armstrong, shoemaker
75 P. M'Shane, lodging house
77 Denis Toal, shoemaker
79 John M'Kee, labourer
81 E. Cushnahan, grocer
83 Peter Murphy, labourer
85 Laurence Flanagan, pensioner
87 John Hanley, shoemaker
89 John Carmichael, baker
91 Anthony Kennedy, musician
93 Samuel M'Cullough, shoemaker
95 Robt Kennedy, boot and shoemaker
97 Mary Ann M'Nair, mill worker
99 Mrs M'Keown, dealer
101 Jane Patrick, dealer
103 Mary Sheals, dressmaker
105 Patrick Graham, grocer
107 Patrick Graham, cotton spinner
109 James Dunlop, grocer
Little Donegall street.]
111 W. Vance, Indian corn steam mill; residence, 15 Gt. George's street
 [*Donegall street.*]
140 Thomas M'Cullough, publican
138 Henry Rogan, carter
136 John Kirker, tailor
134 Sarah Canning, widow
132 James Kelly, labourer
130 James M'Collam, pensioner
128 Jas. M'Cloy, house & rent agent
 [*Campbell's court.*
126 Timothy Mallon, pensioner
124 Margaret Pollock, huckster
122 Charlotte Corrigan, widow
120 George Nolan, publican
 [*Plunket's court.*
118 R. Sheilds, boot and shoemaker
116 George Smith, grocer
 [*James's court.*
114 William Scott, publican
112 John Potts, grocer
110 John Whilford and Neill Johnston, curriers
108½ John M'Blain, tanyard;   40
108 Vacant   [*Donegall street*
106 Catherine Martin, widow

104 John M'Crudden, labourer
102 Mary Cassidy, widow
100 John Brady, sailmaker
98 Denis M'Kendry, grocer
96 John Williamson, dealer
94 James M'Wade, grocer
92 Patrick Mulgrew, hackler
90 Sarah Gordon, widow
88 Alex. Bain, boot and shoemaker
86 Vacant
84 Patrick M'Cann, labourer
              [Drummond's court.
82 Felix Mallon, carpenter
80 John Johnston, clerk
78 Patrick Marlow, mechanic
76 Patrick O'Donnell, servant
74 Vacant   *[Wall street.*
72 Hugh Taylor, publican and grocer
70 Ann Taylor, widow
68 Margaret M'Keown, lodging house
66 Ann Johnston, grocer
64 Daniel M'Neill, dealer
62 Nelson Russell, publican and grocer
60 James Connor, pipemaker
58 George Munro, dealer
56 John M'Glaughlin, labourer
              [M'Adam's court.
54 Jane Rowan, widow
52 Peter Overend, plasterer
50 Mary Miller, dealer
48 Sarah Tucker, widow
46 John Wilson, labourer
44 James Malone, labourer
42 John Jamison, labourer
40 John Smith, labourer
38 H. Thompson, publican and grocer
36 John Robinson, confectioner
34 Alexender M'Creight, labourer
32 John Jones, stone cutter
30 John Phillips, whitesmith
28 John Whiteside, sailmaker
26 Eliza Wilson, widow
              [Carrickhill place.
24 James Pinkerton, boarding house
22 Ann M'Kechnie, widow
20 John Burke, labourer
18 William Crothers, labourer
16 Walter Wheeler, lime burner
14 Samuel Wilkinson, lime burner
12 Ann Hackett, widow
10 Edward M'Quillan, butcher
8 Robert Boyd, labourer
6 Archibald Martin, press and machine man, *News-Letter* office
4 Ann M'Curry, grocer

2 William M'Cloy, publican

The Castle, Castle Buildings
CASTLE PLACE.

John Cunningham; warehouse, Linen hall; residence, Macedon, Carrickfergus road

Young Men's Christian Association Back entrance to Union Club

1 John Hartley, notary public; residence, 7 Botanic road

" Wm. Hartley, agent and accountant; residence, 25 Chichester street

2 Robert Gunning, (private office) of Gunning & Campbell's mills, Falls road

3 Geo. K. & F. Smith, solicitors; residence, 3 Glengall place

" Orr & Montgomery, solicitors; A. Montgomery's residence, Mount Pottinger

Gunning & Campbell, of Mills, Falls road

Upper landings vacant

The Marquis of Donegal's rent and Cave-hill Railway offices, T. Verner, receiver; residence, Ormeau

THE CASTLE YARD.

John Grogan, Veterinary Institution and Horse Repository

Castle Buildings
CASTLE PLACE.

1 Robert Magill, woollendraper and hatter; residence, 1 Posnett's place, Donegall pass

2 James Magill, printseller and stationer, artist and colourman; residence, 33 King street

3 Daniel John Allen, French and English hat warehouse; residence, 2 Wellwood place

4 James Boucher, tea and coffee importer and family grocer; and 6 Castle buildings, Donegall place

5 M. Riddel, Berlin wool and fancy warehouse

DONEGALL PLACE.

6 James Boucher, grocer
7 Taken by Mr Magill, stationer
8 John Mullan, bookseller
9 Union Club, James Russell, resident attendant
10 Ross O'Connor & Co., glass manufacturers and china warehouse

STREET DIRECTORY.

Castle Chambers
FROM CASTLE PLACE TO ROSEMARY STREET.

1 Gordon and Crawford, agents to the Royal Exchange Assurance Office of London; R. F. Gordon's residence, Craigdarragh, county Down
" Bernard Ranaghan, hair cutter, wig maker, and ornamental hair worker
3 James Neild, commission agent
3 William Boyce, general commission merchant; residence, Laganville, county Down
  Robert Irwin, caretaker to the Castle Chambers
5 Vacant   [*Rosemary street.*
6 John M. Johnston, land agent, High-Sheriff's office
" Geo. Stephenson, solicitor, Lisburn
7 Sir William G. Johnson's office
17 Alexander Gordon and Son, wine merchants
16 Vacant
13 John Forsythe, land agent
4 People's Reading, Newspaper, and Library Rooms
  William Page's back hall door
  Joseph Braddell's back hall door

Castle Court
NORTH SIDE CASTLE PLACE.
1 James Moore, printer
  Four houses

Castle Lane
FROM DONEGALL PLACE TO ARTHUR SQUARE.

1 Imperial Hotel Restaurant, Dr Hurst, proprietor
  Bonded warehouses [*Calendar st.*
11 John Gordon, spirit dealer
13 James Carland, rent agent; residence, Ballynafeigh
15 James M'Cann, hair cutter
17 James Stewart, Theatre Tavern; residence, Bryansburn Cottage, near Bangor
21 Edward Prior Grey, Shakspeare Hotel
  Manager's residence, Theatre
      [*Arthur Square.*]
  William and Gilmore Agnew, letterpress, copperplate, and lithographic printers; booksellers, bookbinders, and stationers
18 Henry and Wm. Seeds, solicitors; Railway street, Lisburn, and 54 Upper Dorset street, Dublin
16 Henry James Ramsey and Thos. Garrett, solicitors; and 8 Inn's quay, Dublin
14 Alex. Charles Dobbin, solicitor; and 8 Inn's quay, Dublin
12 Adam Black, hotel keeper
*10 John B. Kennedy, solicitor; and 5 Summerhill, Dublin; residence, Holywood
8 James Kennedy Jackson, solicitor, coroner for the district of Belfast; and deputy clerk of the crown for Antrim; Dublin address, 37 Blessington street
6 John & Francis Teeling, solicitors
" Signor Pitchoni, artist
4 Mary Trevor, spirit dealer
Castle Market.]
3¾ Market Office, Francis Rea, clerk
3½ Jane Meenan, poulterer
  Castle Yard Veterinary establishment, John Grogan, proprietor
3 George Wm. Braddell, notary public, insurance office; residence, Howard street
2 John Devlin, auction mart

Castle Market
FROM CALENDAR STREET TO HAMMOND'S COURT.

1 David Ferguson, butcher
3 James Dinnen, butcher
4 Hiram Morgan, butcher
5 David Dinnen, butcher
6 A. Kennedy, meal and flour dealer
7 Thomas Rice, meal and flour dealer
8 Vacant
9 Bernard Meenan, fishmonger
10, 11 Vacant
12, 13 Catherine Curran, fruit dealer
14 Mrs Glasgow, green grocer
15 Patrick Flinn, flour dealer
16 Ann Loughran, butcher
17 John M'Donnell, green grocer
18 Alexander Dickson, nurseryman and fruit dealer
19, 20, 21 Vacant
22 Hannah Torrens, green grocer
23 Sarah O'Connor, green grocer
24 Mary Henry, green grocer
25, 26 David Ferguson, green grocer

Castle Place

FROM HIGH ST. TO CASTLE BUILDINGS.

1 James Cochran, grocer, tea, wine, and spirit merchant; residence, 6 Queen street
3 James Rolleston, watchmaker
5 Joseph Orr, seedsman; residence, 1 Little Victoria street
7 George Crawford Hyndman, broker, auction and commission mart; residence, 5 Howard street
9 John Cinnamond, boot and shoe warehouse; residence, 5 Arthur street
9½ Donegall Arms Posting Establishment
11 Donegall Arms Hotel, John Moore, proprietor
13 John Henderson, printer and stationer
15 Dublin Coach Office, Edward Greer, proprietor; residence, Newry
15¼ John Davidson & Co., grocers
Castle Chambers.]
17 Joseph Braddell, gun and pistol manufacturer
19 Wm. Page, haircutter, wigmaker, perfumer, and chiropodist
21 Wm. Millen, haberdashery; residence, 14 Fountain street
23, 25 George Macoun, furrier, silk mercer, and millinery
Castle Court:]
27, 29 Archer and Sons, wholesale stationers, paper makers, book binders, printers, and lithographers; proprietors of Ballyclare, Carnanee, and Kilgreel paper mills; residence, Milltown, Ballyclare
31 Eliza Gardner, confectioner
33 Archibald Sloan, cabinet maker
35 David Brown, hardware merchant and ironmonger
37 James M'Conagil, jeweller and watchmaker
Hercules Place.]
Front of the Northern Bank
Castle Buildings.]
26 Charles Morgan, trimming shop; residence, 71 Joy street
24 Charles Noah Davis, furrier, and boot and shoe warehouse; residence, 3 Posnett's place, Donegall pass
22 John Currie, hair dresser, wig maker, and perfumer
20 Mary and Sarah Oldrin, children's linen warehouse
18 John Gray, watch and clock maker and jeweller
16 Geo. Quin, surgeon and apothecary
14 Joseph Hart, pianoforte and music warehouse
12 Daniel Kerr, saddle and harness maker
10 Vacant
8½ Mary Banks, milliner
8 Henry Fegan, boot and shoemaker; residence, 57 Hill street
6 James M'Cleave and Son, saddle and harness makers
4 James O'Neill, printer and stationer, fancy toy warehouse
2 Patrick Read, tobacconist and cigar dealer; residence, Crown entry

Castle Street

FROM CASTLE PLACE TO MILL STREET.

1 Northern Bank
3 William B. Caughey, Northern Bank
" Surgeon Lamont
5 James Rutherford, painter, glazier, and paper hanger
7 Ann Smith, staymaker
9 George L. Hill, engraver
11 Alexander M'Mullan, painter
11½ William M'Ivor, brazier and gasfitter
13 Thomas Forbes, upholsterer and Venetian blind maker
" Mrs Forbes, staymaker
15 John Maguire, dyer; residence, 17 Cromac street
17 John M'Cloy, painter
19 Robert Gibson, haberdashery establishment
21 Belfast Gas Company's Office; Alex. Turnbull, collector
23 William Alldritt, brassfounder and gasfitter
25 J. and T. Smith, engravers
27 Joseph M'Carter, clerk
29 Thos. Stewart, provision merchant
" John White, carver
30½ William Adamson, hairdresser
31 Thomas Ferguson, house and rent agent
33 Robert Hamilton, engraver

35 Jacob Halliday and Co., hardware warehouse; residence, No. 20
37, 39 Francis Coates, house, sign, and ornamental painter, and stained glass warehouse
41 John Hood, surgeon
43 Barclay and Wallace, milliners, &c.
45 John O'Hanlon, tailor
47 Thomas Galloway, painter
49 Patrick Kennedy, tanner
[*Mill Street.*]
28 William M'Cleery, rent agent
26 Misses Byrne's school.
24 Wm Gavin, rent and house agent
22 William Miller, engraver, and manufacturer of linen ornaments
20 Jacob Halliday, hardware merchant
18½ David Carty, coach maker
18 Robert Thompson, manager in linen office
16 Robert Hughes, ribbon merchant
14 John Trueman, English baker and fancy biscuit manufacturer
12½ William M'Cune, builder
" Joseph Nimack, cabinet maker
12 William Coates, tinsmith, coppersmith, and gasfitter
10 William Thomson, engraver
8 Vacant
6 Samuel M'Cann, spirit dealer, Railway and Steam Packet Tavern
Fountain Street.]
4 Robert Thomson, engraver, dyesinker, and copperplate printer
2 Hugh B. Carr, Venetian and wire blind manufacturer, and general upholstery and bedding establishment

Catherine Street
FROM HENRIETTA ST. TO CROMAC ST.
[*Catherine court.*
1 Isabella Read, dressmaker
3 Mary O'Brien, dressmaker
5 John Graham, coachmaker
7 Vacant
9 Sarah Stafford
11 James Lowry, linen measurer
28 Patrick M'Ateer, carpenter
26 Arthur Gaffikin
24 William Brown, clerk
22 Henry M'Bride, compositor
20 Margaret Wilson
18 Hamilton Allan, mechanic
16 John M'Kenzie, brass founder
14 Vacant

12 John Brock, compositor
10 Thomas O'Brie, gilder
8 Vacant
6 Mr. Williamson
4 Edward Graham, clerk
2 Henry Downey, coach driver

Catherine Street North
FROM LITTLE MAY STREET TO HENRIETTA STREET.
1 Joseph Garner, servant
3 Alexander Jackson, musician
5 Wm. M'Crea, servant
7 Joseph Tottem
9 Mrs Scott
...[*Hamilton street intersects.*]...
11 Mrs Fletcher
13 Paul Macloskie, classical teacher
" C. H. Macloskie, travelling clerk *News-Letter* office
15 Samuel M'Cann, baker
17 James Colvin, lapper
19 Wm. Saunders, shopman
21 Mr. Vance, cabinet wareroom
.....[*Russell street intersects.*].....
23 Daniel M'Cann, printer
25 James Mullan, sawyer
27 David Johnston, plasterer
29 John Patterson, stone cutter
31 Edward M'Peak
...[*Henrietta Street intersects.*]....
26 Eliza Malone, washerwoman
24 Mrs Dunlop
22 G. Russell, tailor
20 Wm. M'Bratney
18 Edward Lloyd, cabinet maker
16 John Brown, boot and shoemaker
14 John Flood, carpenter
12 Mrs Mathews
10 Wm. Murray, clerk
8 Margaret M'Call
6 Henry Bradford, book keeper
4 John Murphy, grain merchant
2 Adam Smyrl, clerk

Catherine Court
OFF CATHERINE STREET.
2 James Campbell, joiner
4 Rose Ann M'Givern
6 Edward Killen, sawyer
Mr. Moss, mill worker

Caxton Street
FROM ROBERT STREET TO GREEN ST.
1 Robert Stewart, labourer
3 Edward M'Dermott

5 Daniel Crenard, guard on Ballymena Railway
7 Stables
9 Catherine Miller
11 Ann Smith
15 Ellen Crawford
21 Margaret Kearney
23 Patrick Smith, labourer
27 Wm. Fitzgerald, smith
29 Harvey Stanley sawyer
.....[*Green street intersects.*].....
C. & P. M'Glade's spirit store
33 Mary Crummie, sewer
35 John Hutchinson, carpenter
John M'Quade, porter
Daniel M'Cormack, labourer
28 Thomas Lynas, lumper
26 James M'Donnell, cooper
[*Ireland's court.*
Vacant
24 Charles M'Glaughlin, ferryman
22 Wm. John Kirkpatrick, blacksmith
20 Edward Gore, labourer
P. M'Donald's spirit store.
14 Bernard Collins, mason
12 James Adries, shoemaker
10 Wm. Spence, nailer
8 James Dargan, shoemaker
6 Wm. Reilly, labourer
2 Ann Smith

Chapel Lane
FROM MILL STREET TO BERRY STREET.
1 Mrs M'Kenna, dealer in wool
William Fegan, tailor
Thomas Clements, drayman
John M'Aree, car keeper
J. & T. Cunningham's grain stores
[*Bank lane.*
5 Rose Black, publican
7 John M'Keown, tailor
9 William Mathews, shoemaker
[*Back entrance to Bank lane brewery.*
11 Samuel Keatley, clothes dealer
13 John M'Vickar, constable
28 Samuel M'Cann, spirit dealer
26 James Lyons, clothes dealer
24 Henry Maguire, pawnbroker
20 Henry Maguire's pawnbroking establishment
20½ Ann Maguire, grocer and publican
18 Owen Kerr, Catholic bookseller
16 Hugh Hinds, sawyer
14 John M'Cormick, boot & shoemaker
12 John Edmonston, woodturner

10 ST. MARY'S ROMAN CATHOLIC CHAPEL—John Marley, sexton
8 Henry Dugan, car owner
6 William M'Kee, bookbinder
4 William Miller, stained paper manufactory
2 Chas M'Manamy, porter in brewery

Charlemont Street
FROM 35 BERRY ST. TO TORRENS' ROW.
1 Sarah Stewart, clothes dealer, 37 Berry street
3 Mary M'Mullan, bonnet maker
5 John M'Cleave, dealer in old iron, Smithfield
7 James Hughes, cork cutter
9 Hiram M'Conkey, tin smith
11 Hugh Hall, porter
13 David Wilard, painter
15 James Clements, slater
17 Mathew Mills, stone cutter
19 Widow Cochrane, tin worker
21 Patrick Reilly, labourer
23 Patrick M'Creight, card maker
25 Margaret Garrett, washerwoman
27 Peter Cunningham, breweryman
29 Jas. Ramsey, grocer and provision dealer
30 Elizabeth M'Peake, grocer
28 James Feris, carpenter
26 Mrs Erwin, fruit dealer
24 John Fea, pensioner
22 John Donnelly, gasfitter
20 Bernard Donaghy, labourer
18 Samuel Kilpatrick, labourer
16 John Burns, car owner
14 Jane M'Carty, cow keeper
12 Hugh Mills, tinsmith
10 James Black, painter
8 Samuel Thompson, dealer
6 Mrs O'Neill
4 Mary Godfrey, confectioner
2 Jas. Williamson, clothes dealer

Charles Street
FROM 21 UNION STREET TO STEPHEN STREET.
1 Robert M'Minn, shoemaker
3 William Stevenson, butcher
5 — Higgins
7 Robert M'Caughtry, shoemaker
9 James Black, chandler
11 James Morgan, general dealer
13 Mary Perry
15 Henry Killen, porter

17 John Hamill, stoker
19 Eliza M'Manus
21 Francis Brady, carpenter
23 Arthur Woods, baker
25 John Duffey, labourer
27 Amelia O'Hara, mill worker
30 Alex. Henderson, grocer and spirit dealer
28 James Ash, stoker
26 Thomas Donaghey, chandler
24 John Jones, carpenter
22 William Jones, clothlapper
20 James M'Fadden, cooper
18 Mary Carlisle
16 Ellen Parker
14 William Crow, carpenter
12 David Gibson, chainmaker
10 Thomas Hill, marketman
8 John M'Glade, labourer
6 John Johnston, labourer
4 Samuel Craig, labourer
2 William Craig, labourer

Charlotte Street
DONEGALL PASS.
Twenty-two houses
[*Little Charlotte street.*

Chichester Lane
WEST SIDE OF ALBERT SQUARE.
1 Ann Shaw, boarding house
3 William Andrews, shoemaker
5 Vacant
7 Bernard Vallely, shoemaker and boarding house
9 Sarah Fallon, boarding house
11 Mary Mooney
12 Hugh Donnelly, labourer
10 David Lindsay, labourer
8 Ann Kane, boarding house
6 John Clark, boarding house
4 Elizabeth M'Aleece, boarding house
2 John Robinson, boatman

Chichester Street
FROM DONEGALL SQUARE EAST.
1 Alexander S. Mayne, book and tract depository
" William Reid, piano forte tuner
3 James M'Clean, solicitor
5 Miss Barklie, milliner and dressmaker
7 Doctor James Moore, surgeon
9 Andrew Cowan, J.P., co. Down
11 J. Hind, jun., flax spinner and linen manufacturer, Durham st. mill
[*Upper Arthur street.*

13 Doctor Robert M'Kibbin; residence, Avoneil
" James Turner, dentist
15 Mrs Grogan
17 Richard Hooke, artist
19 William H. Haslett, solicitor; office, 14 Chichester street
21 Miss Maxwell
23 Doctor John Brennan, M.D.
25 Wm. Hartley; office, The Castle, Castle Buildings
27 Miss Cassidy, professor of dancing
" Mrs Irwin, professor of dancing
29 Miss Simms' boarding school
[*Montgomery street.*
31 Vacant
31½ M'Curtin and Riley, grain and flour merchants
33 Wm. Donaldson, horse repository
33½ John Grattan and Co., ærated water manufactory
5 Luke Eagle, Northern racket court and billiard room
37 Samuel Vance, secretary of Chamber of Commerce, 36 Waring st.
39 John Mark, Chichester street Academy
41 L. and T. Brown, timber and slate merchants; and Queen's bridge
[*Seymour Lane.*
Samuel M'Roberts, spirit dealer
[*Great Edward street.*]
34 T. S. Corry, surgeon, Victoria st. medical hall
34 James Agnew, timber and scantling yard; residence, 12 Hamilton street
32 Charles Devlin, stabling yard
30 Vacant
28 William Bathurst, coach factory
26 Graham and Magee, coach makers; Mr Graham's residence, 5 Catherine street; Mr Magee's residence, Pottinger's entry
24 James Low, spirit and alabaster stores
George's lane.]
22 Residence of Messrs. Smith & Waugh
20 Smith and Waugh, coach builders
18 William Moore, architect
16 John B. Shannon, gentleman
14 Wm. Henry Haslett, solicitor, office
12 Samuel Black, solicitor; and 54 Upper Dorset street, Dublin
Arthur street.]

G

10 Dr. Henry Murney, surgeon
8 Mrs Hill
6 Miss Lambert, boarding school
4 Miss Auchinleck
2 Connolly Sherrard, house and rent agent

Chichester Street, Lower
1 Francis M'Kay, grocer and spirit dealer
3 Mary Stewart, boarding house
May's market
Potato and vegetable market
LEFT SIDE.
Pork, Bogwood, and Turf market ;
John Brown, gate keeper
St. George's market
Victoria street.]

Church Lane
HIGH STREET TO UP. CHURCH LANE.
1 Archibald Ferguson, watch and clock maker
3 William Palmer, boot and shoemaker
5 James Mortimer, boot and shoemaker
7 Arthur Atkinson, boot and shoemaker
9 Robt. Brown, boot and shoemaker
11 J. M'Quoid, boot and shoemaker
13 Macveagh, Brothers, feather merchants
15 William Howard, wire worker
17 J. Riddell and Son, iron merchants
19 William Cowan, grocer and spirit retailer
21 Henry Love, wholesale grocer and commission agent
" John A. Clarke's flour stores
23 W. Kennedy, baker
25 Francis Raymond's boarding house
27, 29 James Wilson, wine and spirit dealer
[*Cole's alley.*
31 Joseph M'Clure, boot and shoemaker
33 Robert M'Hinch, wholesale grocer
35 Vacant
37 W. R. M'Clelland, grocer
39 M. Pollock, haberdashery
[*Ann street.*]
46 Hugh Millen, spirit dealer
44 Martin Harper, wholesale grocer
42 John Cuddy's plate and crown glass, paint, oil, and colour warehouse; residences, Summerhill, county Down, and 1 Clarendon place
40 William Fisher, wholesale and retail grocer
38 Samuel Shaw, hatter
36 John Brice, spirit dealer
34 J. Archer, comb manufacturer
32 John Allen, haberdasher
30 Eliza Patterson, dress maker
" Wm. Maguire, boot and shoemaker
28 G. Maguire, boot and shoemaker
26 Henry M'Namara, roper
24 Isabella Hyndman, confectioner
22 J. M'Gee, boot and shoemaker
20 William Hay, confectioner
18 R. Kirner, watch and clock maker
16 John M'Cord, leather dealer
14 A. Anderson, tailor
12 William Fox, haberdasher
10 Vacant
8 William Mortimer, boot and shoemaker
6 Thomas Palmer, boot and shoemaker
4 John Mortimer, boot and shoemaker
2 H. Palmer, boot and shoemaker

Church Lane, Upper
1 J. Fetherson, spirit dealer
3 James Grant, spirit dealer
5 Wm. M'Donnell, boarding house
7 R. Stewart, baker
Hugh Gelston, wholesale wine and spirit, and 35 Ann street
9 J. Cuddy's alabaster and Roman cement mills
11 E. Rodgers, spirit dealer & stabling
Left side.]
Two new houses, not finished
J. Richardson's wine and spirit stores

Church Street
FROM DONEGALL ST. TO NORTH ST.
1 Coleman and Dobbin, wine and spirit merchants ; Mr. Coleman's residence, 2 Crumlin terrace
3 Crawford and Co., ærated water manufacturers
5 Vacant
7 Robert Clements, publican
[*William Street.*
9 Town Council's store yard

11 Thomas Waugh, sewed muslin manufacturer; residence, 10 Lancaster street
13 William Hicks, sewed muslin manufacturer
15 James Porteus and Co., sewed muslin manufacturers; residence, 9 Brougham street
17 Richard Thompson, wine and spirit merchant; residence, The Mount, near Carrickfergus
17½ Vacant
19 Vacant
21 Eliza Robinson, milliner
20 Samuel Titley, publican
18 Nathaniel Dickey, grocer
16 William J. Elliott, manager of Belfast Public Bakery Company
14 Belfast Public Bakery
12¼ W. Rodgers, auctioneer and valuator
12 Wm John Moore, wine and spirit merchant
10 Vacant
Long Lane.]
8 James Sheils, publican
6 William Brown, grocer
4 Samuel Lattimore, cabinet maker
2 Daniel M'Henry, publican

Carr's Row, or Dublin Bridge.
OLD MALONE ROAD.

1 James M'Kane, labourer
2 John Duff, porter
3 Robert Huston, linen lapper
Six small houses

Clarence Place
FROM ALFRED STREET TO DONEGALL SQUARE SOUTH.

1 T. G. Folingsby, merchant; office, Albert square
3 William M'Comb, bookseller 1 High street
5 Samuel Browne, surgeon, R.N.
7 Henry Clarke
9 Dr. Samuel Hunter, surgeon and physician
2 James Stirling, gentleman

Clarendon Place
FROM ALFRED STREET TO JOY STREET.

MAY STREET PRESBYTERIAN CHURCH, Rev. Dr. Cooke, minister; residence, Ormeau road

1 John Cuddy, merchant; office, Church lane
3 Andrew J. Barnett, merchant
5 Thomas Corbitt, merchant
7 James Reid, gentleman
9 Miss Haloran
Hugh Morrison's undertaking and posting establishment
MUSIC HALL

Clark's Lane
FROM GREAT PATRICK STREET TO CURTIS STREET.

1 Back entrance to Henry Loughran's spirit store
Twenty small houses.

Cliftonville, New Lodge Road
OFF ANTRIM ROAD—LEFT SIDE.

Thos. Armstrong, writing master, Belfast Academy
Thomas Jackson, architect; office, 16 Donegall place
James Reid, of Messrs William Browne & Co., Waring street
George Ash, merchant; office, 40 Waring street
George Smith, engineer to Harbour Corporation
Rev. William Gibson, professor of Christian Ethics, Assembly's College
Miss Macnaughtan
William Herdman, of Messrs. Langtry & Herdman's, Waring street
Robert Lindsay, of Messrs. Lindsay, Brothers, Donegall place, and Robert Lindsay and Co., Victoria street
C. Hoffmeister, collector, Custom House

Coates Street
OFF TOWNSEND STREET.

1 John Hunter, waiter
3 William Freebairn, shoemaker
5 Hugh M'Murray, tailor
7 James Donnelly, sawyer
9 James Rowan, servant
11 Theophilus Bole, cabinet maker
13 Joseph Heasley, weaver
15 Thomas Murdoch, cloth lapper
17 William Baird, bricklayer
8 John Fitzpatrick, hackler
Mrs Gibson, widow

Mathew M'Cullough, currier
6 Robert M'Cullough, flax dresser
4 William Ritchie, mechanic
2 Lewis Ritchie, grocer

Cole's Alley
WEST SIDE CHURCH LANE.
James Wilson, spirit stores
James Reid, wholesale and retail wine and spirit stores
Twelve small houses

College Court
BEHIND COLLEGE SQUARE NORTH.
1 Robert Hamilton, weaving factory, Hamilton street
2 Henry Garrett, contractor and builder
3 John Hughes, labourer

College Place North
OFF COLLEGE SQUARE NORTH.
1 James D. O'Connor, Savings' bank
2 George Little, clerk
3 Robert Gamble, merchant
4 James Harrison, clerk
5 William O'Hara, coachman
6 George Terrier, mechanic
7 Alex. Thompson, coachman
8 James Major, flax bundler
9 Samuel M'Cord, surveyor
10 Mrs O'Neill

College Square East
OPPOSITE ACADEMICAL INSTITUTION.
1 Ann Boyd
2 Alexander Gordon, surgeon
3 Dr James Seaton Reid
4 James Keegan, wine merchant; High street
5 Mrs Mackay
6 Nathaniel Henry
7 Susanna Allen
8 James Mawhinny, surgeon; 113 Millfield
9 Vacant
10 Mrs. Ann M'Cully, boarding house
Wellington place.]
11 Thomas Grattan, Dentist
12 John Clarke, J.P.
13 Mrs. Rosetta Harrison
14 Wm. Booker, merchant
15 Richard Connery, agent
16 Rev. J. Scott Porter
17 Dr. Charles D. Purdon, surgeon

18 James M'Adam, Soho Foundry, Townsend street
19 Jas. M'Intyre, publisher, of Simms & M'Intyre, Donegall street

College Square North
KING STREET TO DURHAM STREET.
1 Thomas Chermside, flax merchant. Pottinger's entry
2 James T. M'Caw; merchant
3 Robert Patterson, hardware merchant, High street
4 Alex. O'Rorke, solicitor, 14 Donegall street
5 James Campbell, flax spinner, Falls mills
6 John Taylor, Ulster bank
7 MUSEUM—William Darragh, caretaker
8 Dr James Drummond
9 Samuel Græme Fenton, J.P., Mayor of Belfast
10 Mrs Mary Ann Sloan
11 Mrs Sloan
12 Sir William G. Johnson
13 Russell Kennedy, merchant
14 Mrs Stewart
15 Adam Dickey, poor rate collector
16 James Magill, brewer, Bank lane
17 Miss Anne Torbett
18 William Stevens, clerk
19 George Macoun, haberdasher, 23 and 25 High street
20 James Campbell, clerk
[*Killen street.*
21, 22, 23 New houses, not finished
24 William Cooper, linen merchant
25 William Ross, architect and builder
COLLEGE SQUARE PRESBYTERIAN CHURCH—Rev. Joshua Collins, minister
[*Durham street.*
LEFT SIDE.
CHRIST'S CHURCH—Rev. Dr Drew, Incumbent; residence, Victoria place
ENTRANCE TO THE GOVERNMENT SCHOOL OF DESIGN

College street
FROM COLLEGE SQUARE EAST TO FOUNTAIN STREET.
1 David M'Cahey, starch manufacturer; Boyd street
3 Mrs Ellen Pelan

5 Mary Ball
..... [*Queen street intersects.*].....
7 Vacant
9 Miss Brown, teacher of music
11 Eliza Carmichael, dressmaker
　　　　　　[*Fountain mews.*
13 Bernard Hughes' stables, Fountain mews
15 Miss Stewart
17 John Armstrong, surgeon
" Miss Kennedy, teacher of music
19 Miss Johnston, dressmaker
21 Miss Bridge
23 Lawson Brown, timber yard, Chichester street
25 Mrs Lyons
27 Mr Johnston's writing school
　　[*Fountain street at end.*]
38 James Bristow, Bank of Ireland
36 Mrs Oulton
34 Wm. H. Sproull, solicitor; and 19 Upper Ormond quay, Dublin
32 Mrs Eleanor Sproull
30 Wm. Low, Commission Office
28 Miss Disney
26 Mrs Bennett
24 J. B. M'Grotty, woollendraper; Bridge street
22 Martin Harper, grocer; 44 Church lane
20 Miss Stavely's seminary
18 Miss Sueter's Paris and London stay house
16 Misses Roe's boarding day school
14 Vacant
12 Vacant
10 Mrs M'Clelland
8 Daniel Hanna, civil engineer
6 Thomas Harroworth, brewer
4 Mrs. Margt. Dunlop, boarding house
2 Mrs Elizabeth Wilson

College Street South
FROM HOWARD ST. TO DURHAM ST.
1 Jeremiah O'Rorke, book keeper
3 Mrs Ellen Lowry
5 Lieutenant Calder
7 Miss Mason's, and the Misses Mulligan's school
9 Mrs Alice Knox
11 Henry N. Smith, attorney, 9 Donegall street
13 Foster Connor, linen manufacturer
15 Jasper Macauley, grain merchant, 9 Albert quay
17 Not finished
19 Not finished
21 Robert Cotter, grocer
14 John M'Dornan, pawnbroker, Durham street
12 Mrs Ridgeway
10 Robert Magee, clerk
8 Catherine Fox
　Rev. Wm. M'Carroll
　COVENANTER'S MEETING HOUSE
6 Mrs Margaret Linn
" Henry Linn, engineer
4 John Willis, professor of music
2 James M'Conkey

Collingwood Street
FROM EARL STREET TO SHIP STREET.
1 John Pelan, hackler
3 Philip Burns, iron moulder
5 Michael Murray, carpenter
7 Vacant
11 Jane Gillespie, lodging house
13 Alexander Dunlop, foreman, *Banner* jobbing office
15 Isabella Chignell, lodging house
17 Hugh Atkins, painter
19 James Cooke
21 Robert Kennedy, pilot
23 George Perry, tide waiter
25 Crawford Grattan, guard on the Ballymena railway
　Seven new houses
　Robert M'Clenaghan, master of the *Belfast*, steam tug
　Frederick Spiller, clerk
　James Adamson, clerk
26 Eliza Camac, grocer
24 Emily Gibson
22 James Bracegirdle, clerk
20 Mrs Wilson, lodgings
Fleet street.]
16 Mrs Bell
14 Charles Frazer, spirit store
12 Edward Hall, ship smith
10 Vacant
8 John M'Cartney, sailor
6 Alexander Duff, bookbinder
4 John Cooper, sawyer

Commercial Buildings
ROSEMARY STREET TO WARING ST.
1 Jackson S. Stevenson, bill and share broker, and commission agent; residence, 6 Mount View terrace
2 Vacant

3 J. M. Mercer, linen merchant; residence, 8 Upper Queen street
4 Ulster Deaf and Dumb Society's office; Rev. John Kinghan, assistant secretary
5, 6 Valentine Holmes, United States Consul
7 Royal Flax Society's office; James MacAdam, jun., secretary, and Vice Consul of Portugal; residence, Beaver Hall, Ballymacarret
8 Water Commissioners' office; Plato Oulton, secretary and clerk; residence, 36 College street
Commercial News Room; Henry Boyd, secretary
Commercial Hotel; P. Echlin, proprietor

Commercial Court
OFF DONEGALL STREET.

4 Robert M'Bride & Co., muslin manufacturs; R. M'Bride's residence, 19 Fountain place
6 James Hart, muslin manufacturer; residence, 26 Queen street
7 Clark and Drummond, cotton yarn merchants; residence, Glasgow—Samuel Hart, general manager, 5 Franklin place
13 J. & T. Kennedy, muslin manufacturers and bleachers; Jas. Kennedy's residence, Rosetta; Thos. Kennedy's residence, Wellington place
14 John A. M'Entire, silk manufacturer; residence, Carrickfergus road
20 Robert Hannay, porter
The remainder stores unoccupied

Conley's Court
OFF MILLFIELD.

Seven small houses, one occupied.

Conlon Street
OFF OLD LODGE ROAD.

Conway Minniece, labourer
John Saunders, horse dealer
Mrs Saunders, widow
William Falloon, blacksmith
Mathew Fulton, cow keeper
James M'Cann, boot and shoemaker

Henry O'Hara, carman
Hugh Quin, carman
Edward Shillington, law messenger

Conway Street
FALLS ROAD TO SHANKHILL ROAD.

1 Patrick Campbell, watchman
Entry
3 Thomas Rodgers, bundler
4 Mrs Hamilton
5 Widow M'Sherry
6 John Fishbourne, store keeper
7 Robert M'Coy, linen bundler
8 Denis Connery, machine master
9 John Walsh, labourer
10 John Thompson, labourer
11 Matthew M'Quillan, labourer
12 Michael Kelly, pensioner
13 Margaret Magee, widow
14 John M'Ardle
Kennedy's mill buildings
26 James Connor, grocer
27 James Stevenson, spinning master
28 Fanny Hanna, widow
29 Mrs. Corry
30 Patrick M'Cance, weaver
31 James M'Gowan, flax dresser
32 Jane Campbell
33 Alexander Dunwiddy, carman
34 Thomas Molloy, flax dresser
35 Mary Gutter
36 Eleanor M'Mullan
37 William C. Meharg, clerk
38 William Duncan
39 Mary Courtney
40 Francis Beatham, carman
41 Bernard M'Gow, weaver
42 Bernard Collins
43 Alexander Beverley, flax dresser
44 Francis Neill
45 Patrick M'Cance, engine driver
46 Daniel Curran, sawyer
47 Eliza Hawthorn
48 Hugh Finlay, hackler
49 Mrs M'Cance
50 John Harrison, labourer
52 Francis M'Kay
53 Patrick Dowd, overseer
54 Robert Lappan, labourer
55 Peter Hay, block printer
56 John Maguire, cooper
57 William Duncan, labourer
58 Owen Butler, hackler
59 John Boyd, flax dresser

61 William Fagan, gardener
Campbell's Buildings.
1 J.Mawhinney, preparing master
2 Thomas Aikin
3 Michael M'Clusky, foreman flax dresser
4 George M'Cann, flax dresser
5 Michael M'Phillips
6 Jas. M'Kibbin, reeling master
7 Wm. M'Camilly, time keeper
8 Robert Orr
9 Catherine Mawhinney
10 Patrick Lamb, engineer
11 Thomas Quillan, flax dresser
12 Samuel Moore, overseer
  Eliza Black, seamstress
  William Coates, publican
  Ashmore Street
  Alexander Wyley, cooper
  George Duncan, carman
  James Hughes, labourer
  Samuel Alexander, bakery, grocery, and provision store
  Michael M'Keown, hackler
  William Thompson, bleacher
  James Geddis, watchman
  William Hinch, bleacher
  James Trimble, teacher
  Samuel Rainey, bleacher
  Conway street National School
  John M'Larnon, mechanic
  Nevin Drennan, carpenter
  Alexander Elliott, shoemaker
  Patrick Devlin, shoemaker
  Henry Haslett
  Charles M'Crory, bleacher
  John Roberts, labourer
  Ann Lake
  Anna Little
  Gregory M'Loughlin, block printer
  John Davison, block cutter
  Benjamin Crowther, mechanic
  Nathaniel Kirk, mason
36 R. Carson, grocer and publican
37 James Donaldson, cow keeper
38 John Mallin, fireman
39 Robert Gordon, tow bundler
40 Vacant
41 John Bell, flax bundler
42 Vacant
43 James M'Govern, bleacher
44 James Todd, farmer
45 Robert Bell, overseer
46 Jane Adams, widow
  Maxwell's Houses.

Ann Jane Adams, widow
John M'Connell, calico printer
John Lafferty, calico printer
Jonathan Blake, mechanic
Joseph Greenwood, flax dresser
Robert Humphries, machine maker
Margaret Shiels
Alexander Reid, musician
Archibald Maxwell, carpenter
Ellen Black, shopkeeper
Thomas Cameron, cooper
John Bryson, clerk
John Adams, labourer
Benjamin Moore, weaver
William Gorman, colporteur
14 Thomas M'Ilroy, yarn bundler
13 William Lowden, weaver
12 Rosanna Wallace, seamstress
11 Mary Jane Chapman
10 David Horner, mechanic
9 William Kirkwood, mechanic
8 John Tolan, labourer
7 Thomas Keogh, brickmaker
6 Nancy Lilburn, widow
5 Thomas M'Mullan, flax dresser
4 Eliza Corry, seamstress
3 James M'Alish, carman
2 James Ferran, watchman
1 Michael Riley, hackler
  Gasometer, Peter Ronan
  [*Shankhill road.*]

Cooney's Court,
SOUTH SIDE ANN STREET.
43 Robert Henderson, whitesmith
7 George Todd, shoemaker
  James Agnew, carpenter
  Several small houses

Corn Market
FROM CASTLE PLACE TO ANN STREET.
1 John Colgan, butcher and poulterer
3 William Downing, Grape Tavern
5 to 9 Davis' Plough Hotel, George Davis, proprietor
11 Arthur Dowling, poulterer, and feather warehouse; residence, 6 Franklin place
13 Thomas Gaffikin, butcher; stores, Thomas court; residence, 1 Apsley place, Donegall pass
15 Thomas Bell, cutler and surgical instrument maker
17, 19 Ireland and M'Neill, house

furnishing ironmongers; James Ireland's residence, Clifden, Holywood; William M'Neill's, 4 Adelaide place
19 John Fehrenbach, clock maker, &c.
21 James D. Gaffikin, poulterer
83 Cuming, Brothers, tea dealers, grocers, &c.
23½ Vacant
25 John Gaffikin, butcher & poulterer
27 Thomas Mackin, publican and tobacconist
29 Surgeon Smyth, apothecary, medical hall
[*Arthur square.*]
32 William Bell, London Tavern
30 Joseph Whitaker, boot and shoemaker
28 Martha Yeates, baker
26 Pelan and M'Mullan, soap and candle manufacturers; window glass merchants; George Pelan's residence, Lisburn
24 Hugh Clarke & Co., letterpress printers
20 Charles Blackwood, victualler and poulterer, by special appointment, to her Majesty; residence, 11 Arthur square
18 S. R. M'Cleave, seal engraver
" John M'Afee, boot and shoemaker
16 William Linden, confectioner to the Queen
14 William Carson, wholesale grocer and general merchant; residence, 1 Howard street
12 Medical Hall, Grattan & Co., apothecaries and chemists
10 John Grattan's residence
8, 6 Marcus Ward & Co., wholesale & retail stationers, lithographers, binders, and account book manufacturers; John Ward's residence, 21 King street
2 Forster Green and Co., tea and coffee merchants

Coronation Place
OFF LITTLE YORK STREET.
Five small houses

Corporation Square
FOOT OF GEORGE STREET—EAST SIDE
CORPORATION STREET
1 James P. Corry and Co., timber and slate yard; residence, 4 Franklin place
Store and office vacant
7 Michael Hanlon, scantling yard
" Jasper Macauley's grain stores; office, 9 Albert square; residence, 15 College street south
61 The Longford Arms hotel and tavern, Mrs. Graham
63 Robert Austin, steam flour mills
[*Steam Mill Lane.*]
65 Charnock, Brothers, wine and spirit merchants
67 Arthur Dickson, spirit dealer
69 Mrs Potter, Marine Hotel and Tavern
[*Tomb street.*]
71 Thomas Wilson, spirit dealer
73 William Muirhead, ironmonger
75 Mrs Nugent, boardinghouse
77 Allen Waters, baker
79 Neill Blaney, boot and shoemaker
81 Captain Henry Harston, R.N., marine shipping office

Corporation Street
FROM VICTORIA STREET TO GARMOYLE STREET.
1, 3 Samuel Thomson, merchant; residence, 6 Alfred street
5 Robert Watters, engineer
7 Jas. M'Connell, commission agent
9 Joseph Abbott, ship chandler, patent rope maker, and canvass manufacturer; residence, Holywood
11 J. Montgomery & Son, merchant residence, Elmgrove
" Ferrie & Campbell, bonded stores; residence, Holywood
13, 15 James Crawford, ship chandler
17 Daniel Murphy, grocer and publican
19 John M'Tear, grocer, publican, and provision merchant
[*Gamble street.*]
19½ Jas. M'Kee, muslin manufacturer; residence, 13 Dock street
21 Joseph Scott, commercial traveller
23 William Weir, butter merchant
25 John W. M'Cracken, notary public; residence, 141 York street.
27 Thos. Waters, copper and tin smith
29 Dr. Warwick, surgeon
" Wm. J. M'Niece, medical hall
31 Peter Clarke, ship chandler

33 William Johnston, surgeon
35 William Connell, land agent
37 William Carlisle, emigration agent
39 James M'Ferran, ship broker
41 O'Neill Bayley, provision mercht.
43 David Kirwan, ship builder, of Thompsons and Kirwan, Queen's Island
45 Mrs Russell
47 Mrs Mullin
49 J. A. Alexander, surgeon
51 Alex. Forrester, of T. G. Folingsby and Co., Albert quay
53 T. Fraser
55 Dr Moreland, surgeon
57 Samuel M'Crea, emigration agent
59,61,63 Wm Douglass, provision merchant & general emigration office
65 James Trotter, seaman's clothier
67 Marine Board office, Commander Harston, R.N., examiner and shipping master

[*Corporation square.*
69 Capt. John Gowan, harbour master

GRAVING DOCKS.

Thomas Maguire, harbour police, gatekeeper
Alex. O'Neill, overseer of workers
Edward Connor, boat rigger

Alex. Connell & Co. (late Charles Connell & Sons), ship builders, &c.; residence, Rifle Lodge, Whiteabbey
Alexander M'Laine & Sons, ship builders, &c.; Alex. M'Laine's residence, Corporation street

---

CLARENDON DOCK.

---

71 Alex. M'Laine, ship builder
73 Miss Richey
 [*Garmoyle street.*]
38 Jane Gibson, clothier
36 Alexander Britten, plasterer
34 James Rutherford, publican
32 Wm. Redpath, boarding house
30 George Patton, house agent and accountant
28 Mary Mariner, grocer and publican
North Ann street.]
26 Timothy Bell, provision dealer
24 John M'Keldin, clothier
22 James Junk
20 Thomas Webb, machinist
18 Richard Clarke, spirit dealer

16 Patrick Rice, spirit dealer
Trafalgar street.]
 Enclosed ground
14 Dr. Samuel Snowdon
12 Thomas Brown, sea captain
10 Miss Clarke, boarding house
 Enclosed ground
Henry street.]
 Nicholas Fitzsimons, Lloyds' agent, and general merchant; residence, Dunsona, Whiteabbey
 Paul L. Munster, Danish, Swedish, and Norwegian consulates; residence, Holywood
 Richardson, Brothers, & Co., linen, flax, linen yarn, grain, and general commission merchants; residences: Joseph Richardson, Liverpool; J. G. Richardson, Bessbrook, Newry; Wm. Valentine, Whiteabbey; Joshua Pim, Sans Souci
Little Corporation street.]
8 Francis M'Manus, grocer & publican
6 I. & J. Wallace's sewed muslin warerooms; residence, 44 Nelson st.
4 J. Scott, ship chandler; residence, 4 Meadow street
2 Wm. Newett and Co., ship chandlers; residence, 9 York street
 Side of Mrs Arnold's clothing establishment
Great George's street.]
98 John Gillies, grocer and publican
96 Rt. Creen, rope, iron, & rag stores
94 J. & H. Wardlow & Co.'s timber yard
92,90,88 Vacant
86 Wm. J. and A. Duffield, provision store; Wm. J. Duffield's residence, 53 York street
84 Fergus O'Farrell, spirit dealer
Little Patrick street.]
 Side of Ormond's market
Great Patrick street.]
 Side of Butter market
 Wm. M'Clure and Son, merchants; residences: Thos. M'Clure, Belmont; John G. Megaw, 12 Alfred street
 Geo. A. Carruthers, wine and spirit merchant; 17 College sq. North
 Rt. Workman & Co.'s sewed muslin warerooms; residence, 52 York st.
 Young & Stevenson, coal and iron commission merchants; Andrew Young's residence, 4 U. Crescent

Corporation Street Little
CORPORATION STREET TO NELSON ST.
1 Henry Cameron, sea steward
2 Michael Lennon, shipwright
3 John Kane, bricklayer
4 Thomas Ryan, pilot
5 John Young, ship carpenter
6 John Sanderson, pattern maker
7 William Gordon, ship carpenter
8 Alexander Christie, mariner
9 Henry M'Lean, pilot
10 Thomas Owen, sawyer
11 Michael Rafferty, lath cutter
12 John Kennedy, sawyer
13 Robert Sloan, mariner
14 Matthew Orr, ship carpenter
12 Henry M'Lean, mariner
14 Martha Rails
16 James Loughrey, sawyer
18 John Fagan, sawyer
20 Robert M'Ferran, ship carpenter
22 Patrick M'Wade, soap boiler
24 William Auld, mariner
26 Edward Robinson, warper
OPPOSITE SIDE.
Richardson, Brothers, & Co's stores

Cotton Court.
OFF WARING STREET.
1 Thomas Starret, smith
2 Francis Hart, labourer
4 Robert Hart, labourer
6 Hugh M'Manus, labourer
8, 10 N. A. Prenter, drysalter, paint, oil, and colour stores
OTHER SIDE.
J. Hoy, Waring street
9 Thomas Collins, sailor
7 Robert Lindsay, labourer
5 Michael Aree, labourer
3 Mary Kane

Court Street
AT SIDE OF NEW COURT HOUSE.
Alexander Hunter, warehouseman

Covent Garden
SOUTH SIDE LITTLE PATRICK ST.
John Porter, whitesmith
Five small houses

Cranstone Place
(FORMERLY DOMINGO PLACE),
ANTRIM ROAD.
William Leck, of D. & J. Macdonald & Co.'s, York street
New house belonging to W. Leck, unoccupied
Thos. Dowling, customhouse officer
William Makepeace, excise officer
Five new houses building in the rear, by Daniel Murray, of Ballymacarrett

Robert Hope, bookbinder

Crawford Street
OFF WELSH ST., VERNER STREET.
Fourteen small houses.

Crescent, Lower
MALONE ROAD.
Four new houses
Mrs. Andrews
Claude Nursey, head master School of Design
Thomas A. Barnes
David Taylor, of Arnott & Co.'s, Bridge street
Wm. Bryson, manufacturer

Crescent, Upper
MALONE ROAD.
1 John Workman, muslin manufacturer
2 Professor Wm. P. Wilson, Queen's College
3 Thomas Grueber, merchant
4 Andw. Young, commission mercht.
5 James Green, custom-house
6 Robert Boag, of Albion cloth company; office, 22 High Street
7 William Browne, merchant; office, Waring Street
8 Henry Smith, of Smith & Weir, Donegall place
9 Robert Cassidy, solicitor; office, Donegall place
10 Robert Corry, merchant

Cromac Road
CROMAC BRIDGE TO DONEGALL PASS.
OLD PAPER MILL
1 Robert Anderson, sawyer
3 Lewis Marrs, clerk
5 Robert Hennan, linnen lapper
7 Thomas Brown, jeweller
9 John Mathews, clerk
11 Miss Fletcher, dress maker
13 John Coyle, grocer and spirit dealer
[*Little Howard street.*
13 John Taylor, grocer & spirit dealer

STREET DIRECTORY. 83

15 Mary Owens, washerwoman
17 James M'Conrid, butcher
19 Patrick Garrigan, slater
21 John Clarke, gasfitter
23 Henry Hull, civil bill officer
25 Mrs M'Mannus
27 James Ferris, carpenter
29 Henry Magee, proctor
1 David Malcolm, yarn merchant
LEFT SIDE.
Four small houses
22 Rachael Ewart, grocer and spirit dealer
20 William Stott, jobbing smith
18 Alexander Bingham, labourer
16 Samuel Baxter, labourer
BELFAST GAS COMPANY'S WORKS, William Barlow, manager
12 John Johnston, labourer
10 Samuel Lindsay, coal merchant
8 Patrick Lindsay, grocer
6 Cunningham King, cutler
King's place—five small houses.]
4 James Gray and Co., Coal Island firebrick and tile works, Bernard M'Callin, agent
2 Edward Martin, labourer

Cromac Street
FROM GREAT EDWARD STREET TO CROMAC ROAD.

1 G. Duncan, grocer and spirit dealer
3 Mary Strain, washerwomam
" Elizabeth Hanna
5 James Stewart, butcher
7 Henry M'Cann, coach driver
9 John Quart, green grocer & mason
11 James O'Neill, spirit dealer
[*Little May street.*
11¼ John Cavanagh, professor of music and provision dealer
11½ William Williams, builder; residence, 19 Cromac street
11¼ James Parker, butcher
11½ George Witherhead, grocer and spirit dealer
11½ John Dunlop, butcher
11½ John M'Camisky, marine store; residence, 34 Market lane
David M'Vea, green grocer
13 Mrs Agnes M'Roberts, shirtmaker
13½ John Adams, painter and glazier
15 Wm. Reid, grocer
17½ Fullerton, Brothers, grocers and spirit dealers
[*Hamilton street.*

17 Thomas Maguire, pawnbroker
19 William Williams, builder
21 William Haffern, linen measurer, Linen Hall
" Margaret Haffern, milliner and and dressmaker
23 William Finlay, linen yarn dealer
25 Mrs Mary Ann Spiller
27 Ann Thompson, thread manufacturer
29 Hugh M'Clements
31 Sarah Manning
33 James Rice, auctioneer
35 Margaret Shaw
[*Russell street.*
37 Archibald Kirker, baker and flour merchant
39 Anna Eid, milliner and dressmaker
41 Wm. Lenaghan, sawyer and provision dealer
43 Samuel Kelly, grocer and commission coal merchant
45 Abraham Mathews, grain merchant
47 John Jones, grocer and spirit dealer
[*Henrietta street.*
49 James Smith, pawnbroker
51 Mary Burke, fruiterer and confectioner
51¼ William Gowdy, spirit dealer
51½ Abraham Mathews, grain merchant; residence, 45 Cromac street
53¾ Thomas Rogan, blacksmith
53 John Wallace, printer and publisher of the *General Advertiser*; office, 6 Waring street
58 Archibald Kirker's flour store
55 Chancellor's Ladies' Day School
57 Bernard Quin, reporter, *Mercury*
59 Patrick M'Ateer, builder and spirit dealer
[*Catherine street.*
57 Gateway, vacant
59 Bernard Smith, labourer
61 Margaret M'Auley, grocer and spirit dealer
63 Cromac Street Constabulary Station
65 James John Hannan, attorney's clerk
67 Richard Aicken, architect
69 Michael Boomer, spirit dealer
71 Mary Verner
73 Catherine Smith
New houses building
112 Joseph Campbell, grocer

110 George Anderson, sewed muslin manufacturer
108 Thomas Sessions, excise officer
106 Robert Graham, linen manufacturer
104 John Ranson, writing clerk
102 Ellen Dunlop, boardinghouse
100 Mrs Ann Crymble
98 Vacant
Raphael street.]
96 Joseph Anderson, foreman of works to the Town Council
94 William Adams, car owner
92 Martin Simpson, car owner
88 William Carlile, car driver
86 Vacant
84 Fordyce and Mullen, brewers and wholesale spirit merchants; residences; Mr Mullen, 27 Eliza place; Mr Fordyce, 5 New Bond street
82 Bernard Muckian, cooper and grocer
80 Patrick Mooney, labourer
Eliza street.]
80 Edward Gordon, dealer
78½ Neal Clarke, spirit dealer
78 Young Clarke, grocer
76 Robert M'Crea, grocer
74 Thomas Gilmore, pawnbroker
72 John Mateer, evening & day school
70 John Clarke, confectioner
68 John Copeland, carpenter
66 Wm. Fletcher, silver plater
64 Hugh Young, chandler
62 Thomas Monteague, waiter
60 Mary Ann Crothers, grocer
58 Bernard Ferguson, provision dealer
56 Eliza Hunter, grocer
54 Robert Beggs, pawnbroker
52 Jas. Morrison, grocer and publican
50 Tully Magee, huckster
48 Patrick Roche, grocery and provision store
46 Henry Savage, grocer and spirit dealer
44 James Milliken, shoemaker
" Hugh M'Donnell, porter
42 John Jordan, leather cutter
40 William Russell, grocer and spirit dealer
38 Thomas Cochrane, saddler
36 Thomas Kilmartin, writing clerk and spirit dealer
Lagan street.]

34 Alexander Johnston, grocer and spirit dealer
32 John M'Kechnie, servant
30, 28 Nathaniel Duncan, grocer, provision, wine, and spirit merchant
26 Wm. Hull, grocer and spirit dealer
25 George M'Roberts, provision dealer
22 John M'Areavy,
20 Jane Steed, grocer and spirit dealer
Pump entry]
18 Samuel Quigley, grain merchant
16 William Quigley, grain merchant
14 William Corbett
" Jane and Eliza Corbett, dressmakers and milliners
12 John Campbell, accountant
10 James M'Connell, linen lapper
8 William Rorke
6 James Mullen, linen merchant
4 Charlotte Montgomery, dressmaker
2 Richard Atkinson, spirit dealer

Crown Entry
17 HIGH STREET TO ANNE ST.
3 Ann Jane M'Cracken, milliner
5 Thomas M'Cracken and Co., engravers
 Charles Hunter, Crown Tavern
11 William Gracey, oyster house
 R. and D. Read, printers and publishers
16 John Nimack, cabinet maker, of Arthur street

Crumlin Place
CRUMLIN ROAD, LEFT SIDE.
1 George Druitt, clerk
2 Robert Stitt Benson, manager of bleach green
3 Jas. Robie, jun., reporter *Banner*
4 Joseph Eaton, warehouseman
5 Alexander Fortune, plumber

Crumlin Terrace
CRUMLIN ROAD, RIGHT SIDE.
John Pim, merchant; office, Waring street
James Coleman, merchant, of Coleman and Dobbin's, Church street
Mrs. Pike
Thomas Scott, gentleman—Judges lodgings

Crumlin Road
RIGHT SIDE.
[*Mountview Terrace.*
Gordon Thomson, gentleman, Bedeque house
NEW COUNTY PRISON—J. Forbes, governor
[*Crumlin Terrace.*
[*Old Lodge Road.*
LEFT SIDE.
James Cameron, Glentilt Lodge
John Ritchey, printer
Thos. Haddock, turnkey in Gaol
Robert M'Culloch, Court House Tavern
NEW COUNTY COURT HOUSE—A. Rule, court keeper
Mrs Blair
Mrs Law, Fairview Cottage
Eglinton street—building.]
Presbyterian Church — building; Rev. James Martin, minister

Cuddy's Row
OFF NEW LODGE ROAD.
Eight small houses

Culbert's Court
MIDDLE OF LITTLE YORK STREET.
Fifteen small houses

Cullingtree Street
FROM DURHAM ST. TO STANLEY ST.
1 William Sheppard, mechanic
3 Robert Middleton, labourer
5 Adam Greer, weighmaster
7 James Moore, labourer
9 Thomas Patton, bleacher
11 Robert Hammond, weaver
13 John Stewart, night watchman
15 Charles Woods, reeling master
17 Daniel Nicholl, mechanic
19 William Lightbody, scutcher
21 James Falkner, porter
23 Alexander Livingston, labourer
26 John Craig, engineer
24 Robert M'Andrew, carpenter
22 Robert Kerr, warper
20 Timothy Bell, accountant
18 Ferrard Boyles, coachman
16 John Jamison, grocer
14 George Gibson, linen lapper
12 Richard Johnson, linen lapper
10 Samuel Elder, compositor
8 John M'Quiston, house painter
6 John Usher, butler
4 Margaret Malcomson, boarding house
2 Mary Brown, grocer

Cullingtree Place
OFF CULLINGTREE STREET.
1 Robert Morrison, brushmaker
3 Hugh Smyth, butler
5 John Boyd, carpenter
7 William Armstrong, carpenter
9 Mary M'Kee
11 Michael Boomer, carpenter
13 James M'Lean, coppersmith
15 Thomas Wilson, engineer
17 Arthur M'Ilveen, cloth lapper
19 Samuel Haynan, brass founder
21 Robert M'Cahan, grocer
16 Mrs. Creegan
14 William Hyde, mechanic
12 Elizabeth Gibson
10 James Reynolds, engineer
8 Thomas Kimpson, lapper
6 Joseph Bruce, brass founder
4 Vacant
2 Samuel Todd, bookbinder

Cumberland Place
DONEGALL PASS.
1 George Smyth, cashier in Lindsay, Brothers
2 Thomas Lloyd, haberdasher, of Murray, Greene, and Lloyd's, Donegall place
3 Mrs Mulligan
4 Robert M'Quiston, gentleman

Cunningham's Court
OFF MILL STREET.
Thirty-five small houses

Cunningham's Court
OFF MUSTARD STREET.
Four small houses

Currel's Place
TOWNSEND STREET.
47 William Ferris, spirit store
49 James M'Mullan, flax dresser
51 Ann Kane, widow
53 Patrick Hall, flax dresser
55 Edward Lanyon, coach painter
Several small houses

Currel's Row
OFF TOWNSEND STREET.
Six small houses

Curtis Street,
FROM 23 YORK STREET TO 28 ACADEMY STREET.
1 Hugh M'Call, pawnbroker
3 Vacant
5 John M'Laughlin, spirit store and grocery [*Harper's Court.*
7 Thomas Leeburn, clerk & huckster
9 William M'Connell, labourer
11 James Dooley, stone cutter and huckster [*Bairn's Court.*
13 Hugh M'Cormack, dealer
15 William M'Garry, pensioner
17 James Caldwell, sewed muslin manufacturer; residence, 28 Academy street
20 Eliza Donaldson, lodging house
18 Arthur Douglas, house painter
16 James Nugent, baker
14 Daniel M'Gallarty, lodging house
12 James Brown, plasterer
10 Robert Gracey, millwright
8 James Harrison, mechanic
Corr's Lane.]
6 John Chancellor & Co., sewed muslin manufacturers
4 Daniel Kennedy, gingham manufacturer
Clark's Lane.]
2 Vacant

Dam Side
OFF MILLFIELD.
15, 17 Robert Campbell, Dam Side Foundry

Davidson's Court
OFF DURHAM STREET.
Thirty small houses

Dayton Place
FROM TOWNSEND STREET TO GREENLAND STREET.
1 Thomas M'Ilvenny, carman
3 James Mack, dealer
5 William Reid, pensioner

Devis Street
BARRACK STREET TO FALLS ROAD.
1, 3 Side of John Russell's grocery and spirit store
5 John O'Neill, plasterer
7 John O'Neill, butcher
9 Margaret Cook, green grocer
[*Kennedy's entry.*
11 Patrick M'Larnon, shoemaker
13 Isaac Reid, labourer

15 Francis M'Cartney, linen lapper
17 Rodger Kane, labourer
19 Ann Dillon, lodgings
[*Houston's entry.*
21 John Houston, spirit dealer
23 Mark Benn, boarding house
25, 27 John Young, flax, tow, and yarn dealer
29 James John Belshaw, pawnbroker
31 Henry M'Clarnon, spirit dealer
Wm. Smith, carpenter
Mary Doyle
Emily Birch, teacher
22 Thomas Kirker, grocer and spirit dealer, receiving house of Post office
20 John Beatty, blacksmith
18 Mary M'Cleave
16 John Girvan, foreman in distillery
14 Hugh Beggs, miller
" Rice Beggs, dress maker
12 Michael Curran, miller
10 Joseph Marley, boot and shoemaker
8 James Quinn, green grocer
6 Hugh Kerr, car driver
2 James O'Neill, labourer

Dock Lane
SOUTH SIDE DOCK STREET.
1 Rose Ann Morris, boarding house
3 John M'Clements, carpenter
5 James Dunn, sailmaker
10 James Ferguson, master porter
8 Alexander Shaw, sawyer
6 James Hood, cooper
4 Andrew Mitchell, blockmaker
2 James Dougherty, tidewaiter

Dock Street
YORK STREET TO CORPORATION ST.
1 Robert Stevenson, grocer and publican
.. [*Little York street intersects.*]..
3 Vacant
5 James Young, solicitor
7 John Young, iron merchant
9 James M'Callum, merchant draper
11 Miss Bell
13 James M'Kee, muslin manufacture
15 Mrs Neill
17 William Cairncross, gentleman
19 Robert Grogan, ship broker
25 Thomas Robinson, grocer and publican
[*Nelson street.*

27 Robert Crawford, clerk
29 Henry Tousseant, foreman tailor
31 Robert Henry, blacksmith
33 David Moore, clerk
35 Arthur Gaffikin, provision mercht.
37 James Smyth, gentleman
39 Samuel Houston, ship owner
  New houses building
41 Nancy Murphy, green grocer
43 Oswald Roberts, boatbuilder
45 Ellen Charters, publican
22 Wm. Keegan, gardener
20 James M'Donald, ship broker
18 Hy. Hazard, custom house officer
16 Miss Falloon
14 Thomas Green, street inspector
12 Thomas Casement, ship carpenter
10 Rev. David Hamilton
8 Robert Hanna, salesman
6 James Behan, clerk
4 Wm. Vint, provision merchant
2 James Ferguson, linen draper

Dominick Street
(Formerly Cricket place.)
BOLTON STREET TO ANNETTE STREET.
Seven small houses

Donaldson's Court
OFF BARRACK ST.
Seven small houses

Donegall Lane
DONEGALL STREET TO YORK LANE.
Stables
Two offices vacant
Side of Roman Catholic Seminary

Donegall Pass
CROMAC ROAD TO OLD MALONE ROAD.
[*Aughton terrace.*
1 James Johnston
2 Hugh Carruthers, linen ornament
3 Mrs Briggs   [printer
4 Isabella Clark
5 Robert Smith, in distillery
6 George Biggar, gentleman
            [*Charlotte street.*
1 Jn. Dowling, law commissioner
2 Miss Larkin
3 Mrs Rook
4 Mrs Rippingham
  INGRAM PLACE.
1 Samuel Bullick, academy, 82
2 Mrs Heron   [High st.

3 Isaac M'Cune, in spirit store
4 Mrs M'Conkey
5 Wm. Boyce, clerk of the Union
6 James A. Crozier, gentleman
7 Francis Plunkett, commission
  agent, Donegall street
            [*Cumberland place.*
            [*Apsley place.*
MAGDALENE EPISCOPAL CHAPEL;
  Rev. E. J. Hartrick, parsonage
            [*Albert place*
Andrew Gilmore, gentleman
  SOUTH SIDE.
1 Wm. Finlay, Donegall Pass Tavern
Eight small houses
Rose Lodge.—Hutchinson Posnett,
  agent for Viscount Dungannon
  POSNETT'S PLACE.
1 Robert Magill, woollendraper,
  Castle buildings
2 Wm. Adamson, manager and
  agent for J. and W. Bradley's
  muslin warerooms, Waring st.
3 Chas. N. Davis, furrier, Castle pl.
Cromac Lodge—Samuel Cowan, gent.
  J. Nixon, inland revenue officer
  James Dixon, travelling clerk

Donegall Place
CASTLE PL. TO DONEGLAL SQ. NORTH.
1 Lindsay, Brothers, retail silk mercers, haberdashers, woollen drapers, &c.
3 Lindsay, Brothers, wholesale warerooms and offices
" James Lindsay's residence
3 John M'Vicker, merchant clothier
5 Bernard Hughes, Railway bakery
  residence, 35 Queen street
            [*Fountain lane.*
5 Jas. Moore, stationer and account
  book manufacturer; agent for
  John Cassell's coffee
7 Rev. Wm. Batt
9 Moses Staunton, wholesale and retail roompaper, carpet, damask,
  and house furnishing warehouse
" Wm. Benn, commission merchant;
  residence, Fitzwilliam street
" Robert and Alfred Cassidy, solicitors; residence, 9 Upper Crescent
11 Smith, Weir, & Co., linen manufacturers, bleachers, and merchants;
  Hy. Smith's residence, Crescent
" Thos. Henry Weir's residence

13 Murray, Greene, and Lloyd, silk mercers, haberdashers, &c.; residences: Mr Murray, Limerick; Mr. Greene, Ballymena; Mr. Lloyd, 2 Cumberland place
15 MASONIC HALL—Thomas Harper, steward
17 P. Lynch, M.D., and surgeon
19 George O'Brien
21 Gilmore, Brothers, cabinet makers and upholsterers
23 Davison and Torrens, solicitors; residences: Richard Davison, The Abbey, Whiteabbey; James Torrens, Woodbank, Whiteabbey
25 Wm. Coffey, piano forte and music warehouse
27 Royal Hotel—C. Kerns, proprietor [*Donegall square North.*]
28 John F. Ferguson, D.L., J.P., linen merchant; office, Linen Hall
26 James Crawford, wine merchant; stores, Calendar street
24 Robert Arthur, solicitor
22 Bank of Ireland—Edward Geoghegan, agent; J. Bristow, sub-agent
20 Vacant
18 Johnsons & Co., wholesale London and Manchester warehousemen
16 Thomas Jackson, architect; residence, Cliftonville Cottage
" John Taylor, agent for Standard Life Assurance Company, & for British Guarantee Association; residence, 6 College sq. North
" J. H. Burgess, drawing instructor
14 J. N. Richardson, Sons, & Owden, Lisburn & Newry, flax spinners, linen manufacturers and bleachers; residences: Jonathan Richardson, Glenmore, near Lisburn; John Grubb Richardson, Lisnegarvey, near Lisburn, and Bessbrook, near Newry; William Richardson, 4 Prospect Terrace, Belfast; Jn. Owden, Brooklands
12 J. Coey, Northern boot & shoehouse
10 Imperial Hotel, Dr. C. Hurst, proprietor; and Locust Lodge, Bal-
Castle lane.] [lynafeigh
8 Vacant
8½ John Devlin, auctioneer, &c.
6 J. N. Macartney, watchmaker, jeweller, and optician; residence, 1 Pakenham place

METHODIST CHAPEL AND SCHOOL
4 Jane Billsland, glass & china warehouse; residence, 23 Fountain st.
2 C. Thompson, cook & confectioner

Donegall Place Buildings
DONEGALL PLACE AND CASTLE ST.
1 Francis O'Hayer, saddler; residence, 2 Fountain street
2 John Maclurcan, silk mercer; residence, 13 Victoria place
3 Mathison, Brothers, wholesale and retail grocers; James Mathison's residence, Brunswick st
5, 6 James Armstrong & Co., tea importers and dealers
7 Entrance to offices
8 Miss Hill, milliner; residence, 8 Fountain street
9 Daniel M'Cann, soap and candle manufacturer; residence, 97 York street
10 Timothy Ivers, cabinet maker; residence, 21 Eliza street
OFFICES:
1, 2 STAMP OFFICE—Thos. R. Stannus, distributor of stamps; residence, Lisburn
3, 4, 5 INLAND REVENUE OFFICES —Evan Cameron, collector
6, 7 Vacant
8 Thomas Turner, architect; residence, 21 Queen street
9, 10 Vacant
11 Messrs Lynch, professor of dancing
12, 13 Arthur K. Forde, Stamp Office

Donegall Quay
CORPORATION SQ. TO QUEEN'S BRIDGE
61 The Longford Arms—Mrs Graham
59 Langtrys and Herdman's yard
57 Belfast Arms, W. Young, proprietor
49, 51, 53, 55 Charley and Malcolm, general steam packet & forwarding agents; John Charley's residence, Donegall sq. South; W. H. Malcolm's residence, 49 York st.
45 Sinclair and Boyd, West India and general merchants; R. Boyd's residence, Bloomfield
43 George C. Pim, broker and commission merchant; residence, University square
[*Gamble street.*

41 Crown and Anchor Hotel—John Blakley, proprietor
39 Charles Duffin & Co., flax and yarn stores; office, 28 Waring street
33, 35, 37 George M'Tear, merchant and steam-packet agent; residence, Hazlebank
29, 31 John and Thomas Sinclair's stores
23, 25, 27 Robert Henderson, general steam packet, forwarding and commission agent; residence, 74 York street, and Willow Bank, Malone [*Albert square.*
13 James Hamilton and Co.'s stores; office, 11 Queen's square
15 Royal Victoria Yacht Tavern—John Colville, proprietor
Side of Harbour office—entrance in 23 Queen's square, Edmund Getty, secretary; residence, 6 Abbotsford place
[*Queen's square.*
Side and stores of Custom House
[*Marlborough street.*
17 James Lemon, merchant; warehouse and stores, 15 Queen's square
23 John and James Martin and Co., shipowners; John Martin's residence, Glenview
25 Patrick M'Cormick, spirit dealer
27 Catherine Birkmyre's bakery, back entrance
29 James Tedford, ship chandler and provision dealer; residence, 34 Chichester street
31 Margaret Hughes, spirit dealer
33 Cherry Byrne, wine and spirit dealer
35 Queen's Bridge Tavern — Philip Jordan, proprietor

Donegall Square East

CHICHESTER STREET TO CLARENCE PLACE.

1 Alexander S. Mayne, depository of Ulster tract and book society, &c.
1 A. and J. Elliot and Co., general commission merchants and sewed muslin manufacturers, and Elliot, Brothers, and Co., Glasgow.
2 Wm. Watson, wholesale merchant; stores, 11 Hercules street
3 Vacant
4 Dr. James Patterson
5 WESLEYAN METHODIST CHAPEL and SCHOOLS
6 John M'Cance, gentleman
7 John Finlay, flax merchant; stores, Police square
8 Mrs Ashmore
9 John Workman, of Messrs. J. and R. Workman, manufacturers
10 Wm. M'Gee, M.D., surgeon, R.N.

Donegall Square North

CALENDAR ST. TO FOUNTAIN ST.

1, 2 A. and S. Henry & Co. (of Manchester), linen merchants
3 Charles Duffin, merchant; office, 28 Waring street
4 J. Dickinson&Co.(of Nottingham), wholesale stationers; manager, John Hutchinson
[*Donegall place.*
Public billiard room
5 Vacant
6 Edward Bruce, gentleman
7 Mrs Agnew
8 David Herd, linen manufacturer
9 Mrs Campbell
10 Robert Calwell, hardware mercht.; 14 Waring street

Donegall Square South

ADELAIDE PLACE TO LINENHALL ST.

1 Wm. Musgrave, barrister-at-law, and 67 Lower Mountjoy street, Dublin
" John R. and Jas. Musgrave, ironmongers; shop, High street
2 Francis M'Laughlin, tobacconist; shop, 65 High street
3 John Ferguson, linen merchant; office, 10 Waring street
4 A. and A. T. M'Clean, gentlemen
5 Major General Bainbrigge
6 Edward Tucker, starch and glue manufacturer; warehouse, 27 Waring street
7 John Praeger, linen merchant, Vice Consul for Austria and Bremen; office, Fountain lane
" A. and A. T. M'Clean's office
8 John Charley, merchant and steam-packet agent; office, Donegall quay
9 J. W. Anderson and Co., sewed muslin manufacturers

" Anderson and Gray, muslin manufacturers, and Linenhall street [*Linenhall street.*

BEDFORD STREET.

Thornton Huggins and Co., linen merchants; P. Ewing's residence, Bankmore

R. & J. Workman, manufacturers; Robert Workman's residence, 10 Pakenham place; J. Workman's, The Crescent

J. and T. Kennedy, muslin manufacturers and bleachers, and 13 Commercial court

John Leadbetter and Co., linen manufacturers, and York street

---

Donegall Square West

WELLINGTON PLACE TO HOWARD ST.

1 Mrs Thompson
" Robert Thompson, merchant; residence, Holywood
2 Robert Alexander, linen merchant; Vice-Consul for Venezuela
1¼ Robert Alexander's office
3 Chas. W. Shaw, merchant; office, 52 Waring street
Wellington street.]
4 T. Greer, merchant; warehouse, 18 Rosemary street
5 Dr T. Read, surgeon
6 James Girdwood, merchant; warehouse, High street
7 Robert Magee, gentleman
8 James Campbell, gentleman
9 Thomas Major, gentleman

Donegall street

COMMERCIAL BUILDINGS TO ANTRIM ROAD.

BELFAST BANK

---

1 Hill Smyth, stationer, bookbinder, and lithographer
" Clerical Rooms
" Robert Waring, woollendraper, &c.
3 James Grant, confectioner, pastry and biscuit baker; residence Cregagh Cottage, Castlereagh
5 James Marshall, clothier and draper; residence, Holywood
7 H. Blain, linen and damask house
9 Moses Cherry, saddler and American trunk manufactory

11 Dr. Washington Murphy, surgeon
11½ James Watt & Co., seedsmen
13 Hugh H. Hannay, wholesale woollen and Manchester warehouse; residence, 14 York street
13½ T. S. Major & Co., sewed muslin manufacturers; residence, Dunmurry
13¾ Greer and Oakman, Manchester and Scotch woollen warehouse; Robert Greer's residence, 3 Aughton terrace
15 Robert Gray and Co., woollendrapers, mercers, &c.
17 Thomas M. Sharp, general broker
19 James Young and Co., wholesale woollen and Manchester warehouse; William Young's residence, 18 Wellington place; John Anderson's, 3 Apsley place
21 Robert King, merchant tailor and hatter
[*Elliott's court.*
23 Alexander Hunter, confectioner
25 William M'Connell and Co., wholesale woollen merchts., &c.; Wm. M'Connell's residence, Charleville, near Castlereagh.
[*Commercial court.*
27 James Nichol, baker
29 Thomas Jackson, linen manufacturer
" James Ewart, architect
" Henry Milford, solicitor; 26 Lower Ormond quay, Dublin
" J. and J. Beath, commission merchants; J. Beath's residence, Antrim place cottage
31 MacAdam and Co., oil and guano merchants; Mr MacAdam's residence, Beaver hall
33 James Quirey and Co., wine and spirit merchants, leather dealers, &c.
" G. W. Kyle, hosier; shop, Bridge street
35 *Banner of Ulster* office
37 F. Todd, umbrella maker
[*Donegall street place.*
39 Dr Fryer, surgeon and apothecary
41 James Maxwell, cabinet maker
43 H. Bourns and Sisters, ladies' repository
45 John Reynolds, toy and fancy warehouse

STREET DIRECTORY.

47 James Cameron, plumber, lead merchant, &c.; residence, Glentilt place, Crumlin road
49 John Barclay and Co., boot and shoemaker
51 M. and A. M'Kibbin, and Co., silk mercers, milliners, and dress makers
" A. M'Kibbin, of Northern Bank.
53 J. and N. Carson, grocers and wine merchants
55 J. Cuming, grocer, wine, and spirit merchant
" George D. MacKeown, solicitor; 26 Lower Ormond quay, Dublin
[*Talbot street.*
57 The Vicarage—Rev. T. F. Miller, Vicar
ST. ANNE'S PARISH CHURCH
59 Dr. Halliday, surgeon
61 John Walker, confectioner
[*Academy street.*
63 Belfast Academy—The Rev. R. J. Bryce, LL.D., principal
" Robert Bryce, M.D., surgeon
65 John Robinson's, marble and stone establishment
67 Jenning's and Co., iron merchants
69 Moses Crothers, grocer
71 B. Hughes, bakery establishment
73 John M'Kenna, foreign fruit, tea, and Italian warehouse
[*York street.*
75 The Queen's Hotel—Thomas Cunningham, proprietor
" P. Macaulay, flax spinner, foreign agent; residence, Mills, Randalstown
77 Surgeon Henry M. Johnston
INDEPENDENT MEETING HOUSE
79 James B. Ferguson, starch manufacturer
81 Mrs Brown's commercial boarding house
83 Dr. Thos. Thompson, R.N., surgeon
85 James Carlisle, builder and millowner
87 J. Robinson, marble and stone yard
89 J. C. Graham and Co., sewed musmuslin manufacturers
89½ J. Arnott and Co.'s assistant boarding house
91 F. M'Cracken, jun., millowner
93 Wm. M'Cracken, of Northern Bank

95 John M'Connell, muslin warehouse, Kent street
[*Donegall lane.*
Donegall Street Male and Female National Schools, erected by the Right Rev. Dr. Crolly, 1833
ST. PATRICK'S ROMAN CATHOLIC CHAPEL
97 Right Rev. Dr. Denvir, Roman Catholic Bishop
" Rev. Henry O'Loughran
" Rev. Francis M'Kenna
" Rev. John Gallogly
" Rev. William Curoe
" Rev. John Maghaham, Dean of Seminary
" Edward Kelly, Professor of Classics and Mathematics
99 W. Curran, druggist; shop, Bridge st.
101 Mrs Cruikshank's school
103 Robert Gilmore, pawnbroker; shop, North street and Carrick hill
105 Elizabeth Lynn
107 Samuel Douglass
109 John Knox, manufacturer
111 John Black, gentleman
[*North Queen street.*
112 William Vance, starch manufacturer and miller
110 Belfast Foundry—Samuel Boyd, proprietor; residence, Little Donegall street
108 Horse Bazaar and Veterinary establishment—James King, veterinary surgeon, proprietor
" M. Folie, farrier
106 George Emerson, gentleman
" William Emerson, merchant
104 Mr Crang, surgeon
[*Union street.*
102 William Dobbin, druggist, &c.; shop, North street
100 Thomas Elliott, accountant
98 Francis Rea, clerk of markets
96 Dr. Black, surgeon
94 Miss Bell, upholsterer
" Mrs Eccles
92 Mr Thompson, electropist
90 Dr. John Clarke, surgeon
88 Joseph Bigger, provision merchant
86 William Suffern, gentleman
84 Hugh Porter, clerk
82 S. R. and T. Brown, of Glasgow
" David M'Kean, agent for ditto

80 Protestant Hall—James Dixon, caretaker
" Wm. Greer, muslin manufacturer
78 John Suffern's residence
76 John Suffern, solicitor; Dublin, office, 12 Upper Temple street
74 P. H. Mahir, confectioner
John street.]
72 Bernard Fitzpatrick, grocer, wine and spirit merchant
70 Hitchcock and Black, solicitors
68 Edward Dorrian, surgeon and apothecary
66 Dr. Pirrie, surgeon
64 Margaret Milliken, dress maker
62 Mrs Robinson, milliner and dressmaker
60 James Andrews, solicitor; Dublin, office, 103 Capel street
DONEGALL STREET PRESBYTERIAN CHURCH—Rev. Isaac Nelson, Minister
58 Mary Wilson, linen and damask warehouse
Wm. Eakin & Co.'s stores
56 James Gaskin, painter and glazier
54 Unoccupied
52 Wm. Eakin and Co., drug, oil, and colour merchants; residence, Great Patrick street
Church street.]
50 Daniel M'Henry, spirit dealer
48 Surgeon Charles Clarke Macmullan's medical hall
46 George Harrison, ladies' boot and shoemaker
" Andrews and Smith, solicitors; Dublin, office, 103 Capel street
44 J. M'Cullough & Co., solicitors
42 John Smyth, solicitor; Dublin, office, 43 Dame street, and branch office, Carrickfergus
40 John M'Blain's leather warehouse; tan-yard, 108½ Carrick hill
38 J. S. Johnston, baker
36 Provincial Bank of Ireland office; manager, Robert Trotter
34 William Quaile, cabinet maker
32 John Holden and Co., sewed musslin manufacturers; J. Holden's residence, Royal terrace
32 William and Robert Druitt, linen manufacturers and bleachers; Wm. Druitt's residence, Mount Pottinger

Thompson's court—Davis' buildings.]
30 Johnston and Pelling, sewed muslin manufacturers; C. Pelling's residence, 16 Great Patrick st.
28, 26 Simms and M'Intyre, publishers; John Simms' residence, Holywood; James M'Intyre's, 19 College square
24 Ewart and Son, manufacturers; residence, Mountview terrace
" M. A. Quirey and Co., haberdashers, &c.
St. Anne's buildings.]
22 Mearns and Co., paper stainers and room paper manufacturers
Removed to 10 Castle place
20 BROWN LINEN HALL
18 Robert Roddy, linen and damask manufacturer and bleacher, wholesale and retail family linen warehouse
16 Robert Bowman, solicitor; Dublin office, 8 Inn's quay; residence, Carrickfergus
14 Alexander and Daniel O'Rorke, solicitors; Dublin office, 39 Blessington street; Alexander O'Rorke's residence, 4 College Square North, and High street, Ballymena; Daniel O'Rorke's residence, Howard street
12 E. Hunter, confectioner
" John Rea, solicitor; Dublin, office, 22 Middle Gardiner street
8, 10 Dublin Bakery, James Canning, proprietor
6 J. and T. Mulligan, Manchester warehouse, cap manufacturers, &c.; T. Mulligan's residence, 2 Antrim place
4 John M'Laughlin, wholesale tobacconist
" William Dale, broker, auctioneer, &c.; residence, 109 Donegall st.
2 William Penton, seedsman, &c.; residence, 6 North street and Holywood.

Donegall Street, Little
JOHN STREET TO CARRICK HILL.
1 Duncan Campbell, jobbing smith
3 Alexander Guy, publican
5 Joseph Bigger, provision merchant
7 S. R. & T. Brown's sewed muslin warerooms, D. M'Kane, agent;

residence, 82 Donegall street
9 Margaret Mortimer, lodging house
11 William Milliken, ostler
13 Isabella M'Kay, lodging house
15 Terence Devlin, labourer
17 Mrs. O'Neill, lodging house
19 H. Thomson, file cutter
21 Wm. Kelly, labourer
23 R. & J. Bells's flax store
25 C. Martin, sizer
   A. Rutherford's sizing works
27 Saml. Martin, starch manufacturer
29 James Irvin, spirit dealer
.....[Union street intersects.]....
31 John Hunter, lodging house
37 John M'Dowell, chandler
39 James Steen, labourer
41 James Reid, cooper
43 Agnes Campbell, lodging house
45 David Watt, publican
47 Samuel Boyd, machine maker
49 Patrick M'Cann, maker of cordials, &c.
51 Wm. Scott, in Dublin mail coach office
   Side of Wm. Vance's corn mill
   [Carrick hill.]
74 John M'Clure, labourer
72 Mary Conway
64 Cornelius M'Fall, shoe maker
62 Allen Campbell, lodging house
60 John Crawford, lodging house
58 James M'Lorinan, labourer
Stephen street.]
56 Robert Gilmer, pawnbroker
54 Jonathan Vint, wine and spirit store
52 Anthony Campbell, carpenter
50 Anthony Houston, carpenter
Russell's court.]
48 Paul Semple, shoemaker
46 Thomas Gourly, baker
44 Gilbert Robinson, labourer
42 John Hamilton, paper works
40 David Blaney, labourer
38 Patrick Murney, musician
36 James Montgomery, shoemaker
34 Thomas M'Master, pork cutter
32 Robert Watson, grocer
30 Mr. Russell, huckster
28 John Gibson, nailer
26 Jane O'Neill, lodging house
24 Roddy Gillan, paver
22 Vacant
20 Starch works, Mr. Martin owner

18 Joseph Stevenson, labourer
16 William Duncan, night constable
14 John Conolly, flax and waste dealer
   Seven small houses

Donegall Street Place
BETWEEN 37 AND 39 DONEGALL ST.
Back entrance to *Banner* office
5 Gamble and Co., linen manufacturers and bleachers; residence, 2 Prospect terrace
7 John O. Macnish & Co., cotton yarn agent; residence, 7 Prospect terrace
9, 10 John Cuppage and Co., flax and yarn stores, flax spinners; residence, Lurgan
4 William M'Ilwrath and Co., linen manufacturers; residence, 2 Ardmoulin place
2 White and Clendinning, commission agents; Mr White's residence, 6 Brunswick street; John Clendinning's residence, 1 Arthur place
Dr. Fryer, surgeon, hall door

Downshire Place
OPPOSITE VICTORIA PLACE.
1 Robert Orr, excise officer
2 Elizabeth Campbell
3 George Smith, dentist in Mr Barnett's, Wellington place
4 Miss Mary Reid
5 Feaquhea Macrae, butler
6 Wm Magill, brewer in Bank lane
7 Margaret Dunlop, nursetender
" Misses Rodgers, dressmakers and milliners

Drake's Lane
OFF UNION PLACE, GREAT GEORGE'S STREET.
Thirteen small houses

Drummond's Court
OFF CARRICK HILL.
Twenty-eight small houses

Dublin Bridge, or Carr's Row
OLD MALONE ROAD.
1 James M'Kane, labourer
2 John Duff, porter
3 Robert Houston, linen lapper
   Six small houses

Duffin's Court
OFF WINETAVERN STREET.
Six small houses.

Duffy's Place
OFF BOUNDARY STREET.
1 Joseph Armstrong, night constable
2 James Magee, labourer
3 John M'Namee, flax dresser
4 James M'Gowan, mechanic
5 Charles Byrne, joiner
6 Hugh Shields, carpenter
7 Richard Downing, millworker
8 Mary Kirkwood, widow
9 Margaret Cooper, widow
10 Maria Olden, widow
11 William Armstrong, flax dresser
12 Patrick Heburn, widower
13 James Fitzpatrick, carpenter
14 James Fitzpatrick, carpenter
15 Thomas Gallagher, labourer
16 Wm Macloskie, flaxdresser

Durham Court
OFF DURHAM STREET.
Fourteen small houses

Durham Place
LEPPER'S MILL ROW, OFF DURHAM ST.
Thirteen small houses.

Durham Street
FROM SOUTH END OF BARRACK ST.
TO SANDY ROW.
1 Daniel M'Ilherron, spirit dealer
3 Bernard Macartney, dealer
5 John Kennedy, pork cutter
7 Patrick M'Alinden, cow keeper
9 Margaret Kean
[*Durham place.*
11, 13 Felix Kinney, grocer and spirit dealer
15 John Hanlon, whitesmith
17 William Quee, butcher
19 Owen M'Kenna, dealer
[*Durham court.*
21 J. Brown, ostler, Donegall Arms
23 Francis Donnelly, carpenter
25 Robert M'Comb, carpenter
27 Thomas Reilly, coachman
29 Andrew Coulter, grocer and spirit dealer
31 William Grubb, mechanic
33 Patrick Flanagan, labourer
35 William Cooper, labourer
37 James Larmour, labourer
39 William Gilmore, cattle dealer
41 S. Collier, grocer
43 John Hull, weaver
45 Margaret Hill, dealer
47 Catherine Hayes, housekeeper
49 Sturgeon Marshall, dealer
51 Wm King, spirit dealer
53 Ellen Fitzsimons, shop keeper
[*Falls court.*
55 George Macaulay, shoemaker
57 Margaret Stavely, grocer
59 Clark Gray, nailer
61 Elizabeth M'Call, white worker
63 Miss Ferguson
65 Thomas Oyston, manager of mill
67 Samuel Thompson
69 Constabulary Station—Head Constable Henderson
[*Albert street.*
71 Alex. Glenn, grocer [*Fox's row.*
73 Wm Steenson, weaver
75 Joseph Dugan, weaver
77 Thomas Kirker, spirit dealer
[*M'Master's row.*
79 Joseph M'Cullough, grocer and spirit dealer
Two new houses building
81 Joseph M'Cracken, day constable
83 Robert Clugston, weaver
85 James Patterson, labourer
87 John M'Millen, labourer
89 James M'Caul, spirit dealer
[*Cullingtree street.*
Six houses building
91 Ann Miller
93 Thomas Goodfellow, labourer
[*New road leading to Falls road.*
109 Elizabeth Vincent
111 John Frew, publican
113 John Moffett, grocer
115 Wm Alderdice, civil bill officer
117 David Alderdice, Victoria tavern
[*Victoria court.*
119 Wm M'Cleevy, warper
121 John Stewart, dealer
123 Robert Shaw, dealer
125 John Montgomery, book keeper
" Miss Montgomery, dressmaker
127, 129 Mrs Lattimer
131 John Smyth, teacher
133 John M'Dowell, carpenter
[*M'Dowell entry.*
135 John Campbell, spirit dealer
137 John Davison, builder
[*Davison's court.*

STREET DIRECTORY.

139 Thomas Pursely
141 John Hall, lodging house
143 Matthew Tewton, carpenter
145 David Law, publican
              [*Stormont court.*
147 Isaac Duffy, soap boiler
149 Thomas Rollands, carter
151 Henry Gregory, labourer
153 John M'Caw, labourer
155 James Millar, night constable
157 Mrs Massey   [*Massey's court.*
159 Robert Erskine, grocer
              [*Erskine's court.*
Ulster Railway goods stores
.... [*Ulster Railway intersects.*]....
161 John Boyd and Son, flax and tow spinners; residence, 4 Glengall place
Pelan's row—10 small houses.]
46 James Watson, grocer and publican
44 Thomas Shanks, tailor
42 Joseph Shane, car keeper
40 James Nelson, tailor
38 Mrs Surplus, shirtmaker
36 James Pelan, grocer and publican
Glengall street.]
    James Montgomery, gentleman
34 James Henry, weighmaster
32 Mrs South, dressmaker
30 William Dougherty, teacher
28 John M'Dornan, pawnbroker
College street south.]
    Robert Cotter, grocer
    Robert Thompson, mechanic
    Thomas Clarke, butler
    Jas. Plunkett, plasterer and builder
    Christ Church School Rooms
College square.]
Galway street.]
28 Robert Wood, tailor
26 Arthur Galway, gentleman
24 Samuel Douglass, butler
22 William Strain, publican
20 John Wiley, boot and shoemaker
18 Moses Graham, boot and shoemaker
16 John Todd, labourer
14 Hugh M'Mullan, labourer
12 Bernard Monaghan, labourer
10 James Horner, publican
 8 Edward Murney, fireman
 6 John M'Gimpsey
 4 Hugh Robinson, cow keeper
Robinson's court.]
 2 Vacant

Durham Street, New
TOWNSEND STREET TO POUND STREET
1 John Corr, flax dresser
3 David Walker, fireman
5 James Cahoon, turner
7 Eliza Boyle, shopkeeper
9 Ann Donaghy
M'Millan's place.]
11 Henry Taggart, carpenter
13 Thomas Macklin, turner
15 William M'Ateer, carpenter
17 James Chapman, tailor
19 John Fitzsimons, labourer
21 Philip Burns, hackler
23 John Midgley, reed maker
25 Hugh Allen, hair dresser
27 Thomas Martin, pensioner
29 Thomas Scott, grocer and publican
LEFT SIDE.
Fourteen small houses
Samuel Kelly, spirit dealer
James Mawhinney, surgeon

Dyet's Entry
OFF BARRACK STREET.
Four small houses

Earl Lane
OFF EARL STREET.
Robert Wilson, labourer
Robert Fulton, carpenter
John Devlin, blacksmith
George Reynolds, sea captain
James Paton, carpenter
Rose O'Hara, washerwoman
       [*North Thomas street.*
Ten small houses

Earl Street
CORPORATION STREET TO YORK ST.
1 Daniel Jacobson, clothier
3 John M'Donnell, butler
5 Patrick M'Bride, harbour master
7 Hugh Burnett, labourer
9 Elizabeth Ann Victor
11 Robert M'Cullough, labourer
13 Daniel Symington, teacher
15 Benjamin Duff, store keeper
17 Elizabeth O'Neill
19 Robert Wilson, shipowner
21 Rebecca Burnett, boarding house
23 James Daly, shipowner
25 James Moorehead, cooper
          [*Little York street.*
27 James Loughead, clerk
29 Charles Grant, carpenter

31 Thomas Leggit, sea captain
33 George Gainford, Custom-house officer
35 Martha Craig
50 Wm Alexander, *Mercury* office
48 John Smyth, sea captain
46 William Smyth, commercial traveller
44 William M'Mullan, sea captain
42 Edward Ring, doctor
40 Captain M'Cullough
38 Captain Wilson
Earl lane.]
36 Miss Murphy
34 Wm. Keir, gentleman
32 Thomas Berkley, ship smith
30 Joseph Henderson, in the Water Commissioners' office
28 Simon Chapman
26 James Roger, sea captain
24 Charles Bell, cabinet maker
22 George Montgomery, deputy harbour master
20 D. Smith, ticket writer
18 Miss Kirk
16 Hugh Brown, cooper
14 Hugh Liddy, accountant
12 Samuel Jamison, clerk
10 John Close, joiner
Nelson street.]
8 William Harper, cooper
6 Thomas Williamson, sea captain
4 Robert Bakewell, capenter
2 Jas. Barrett, Custom-house officer

East Street
EAST SIDE VERNER STREET.
1 John Connor, grocer
3 Bernard Smith, clerk
5 Wm. Finlay, plasterer
7 Mary A. M'Mahon
9 Jane Stewart, whiteworker
11 Samuel Kerr, carpenter
13 Grace Jamieson, quilter
15 Richard Anderson, sawyer
15 Francis Wilson, forgeman
17 Vacant
19 Alex. M'Bratney, weighmaster
21 Wm. Fenton, car driver
Seven small houses
New house building
John M'Areavy's store
[*Byrnes lane.*
10 Wm. Dougherty, lapper
8 Neill Byrne, labourer

6 Margaret Connelly
4 Susan Brannan
2 Bernard Kelly, labourer
Side of Fordyce and Co.'s new stores

Economy Place
OFF HENRY STREET.
1 John Magennis
3 Samuel Lyle, porter
5 Wm. Kidd, carpenter
7 Wm. Thompson, stone cutter
9 Bernard Curran, ship carpenter
11 Wm. Croan, brushmaker
12 Henry Hamill, cooper
10 Margaret Reid
8 Wm. M'Graw, servant
6 James Shannon, spinning master
4 Joseph Roberts, spinning master
2 John Smith, blacksmith

Edward Street
FROM ROBERT STREET TO GT. PATRICK STREET.
1 Hugh Dornan, musician
3 John M'Millan, saddler
5 Thomas Hughes, carver
7 James Thomson, cooper
9 Thomas Montgomery tailor
11 David Smylie, grocer
13 Hugh M'Graw, flax dealer
15 Patrick Reddington, servant
17 Robert White, confectioner
19 Francis Lyons, tailor
21 Joseph Hanna, shoemaker
23 John Conville, car driver
25 James Donaldson, sail maker
27 Francis Pinkerton, clerk
29 James Black, provision shop
31 John M'Kenna, butcher
[*Green street.*
33 Samuel M'Connell, grocer
35 John Perry, carpenter
37 Miss Anna Rea, milliner
39 William Vance, carpenter
41 Elizabeth Ferguson
43 Robert Adams, butcher
45 Patrick M'Cullough, carpenter
47 Peter M'Kenney, butter merchant
51 Wm. Rosbotham, grocer and spirit dealer
[*Little Edward street.*
53 Thomas Downey, ironmonger
55 Henry M'Glade, publican
57 Charles Goudy, cabinet maker
54 Samuel Todd, grocer

52 Samuel Johnston, tailor
50 James M'Murtry, provision dealer
48 John Morrow, shoemaker
Little Edward street.]
46 Clement Bell, butter merchant; residence, 22 Great Patrick st.
44 Vacant
42 Vacant
40 John M'Gonigal, cooper
38 James Devlin, porter
36 C. and P. M'Glade's residence
34 Charles & Patrick M'Glade, grocers and spirit dealers
Green street.]
32 Michael Peak, publican
30 Richard Rawe, shoemaker
28 John Hamill, labourer
26 Margaret Alexander, milliner
24 James Thompson, letter carrier
22 James Hill, carpenter
20 Mrs. Bingham, lodgings
18 Vacant
16 Jane Scott, lodging house
14 William Rogers, porter
12 George Bruce, coal factor
10 William Higgins, car driver
8 Edward Hector, boot closer
6 William Roy, carpenter
4 Thomas Mullan, shoemaker
2 John Campbell, publican

Edward Street, Great
VICTORIA STREET TO MAY STREET.
11 Samuel M'Roberts, publican and stabling yard
11½ Alexander Rea, hair cutter
13 John Graham, boarding house
15 James Frazer, stabling yard
17 James Frazer, spirit store
[*Johnston's court.*
19 Thomas Largy, butcher
19½ Patrick Carrol, butcher
21 John Scott, butcher
23 Edward D. Gribben, surgeon
25 Jane Anderson, Ballynahinch and Castlewellan coach office
[*Gloucester street.*
27 Alice Thompson, haberdasher
29 Robert Riley, boarding house
31, 31½ Denis Smyth, horse repository and publican, also Ballynahinch coach office
33 Benjamin Gordon, saddler
35 James O'Neill, confectioner
37 George Thompson, haberdasher

39 Daniel Browne, grocer
42 George Houston, boarding house
40 Margaret Martin, dressmaker
" Rose Reilly, stay maker
38 Sarah J. Thompson, haberdasher
36 James Warnock, tallow chandler
34½, 34 William Bell, baker & grocer
32 Thomas Harvey, grocer
30 John Griffith, pawnbroker
28 John O'Neill, haberdasher
26 Hugh Murnaghan, grocer, spirit dealer and engineer
Lennon's Lane.]
22 Margaret Gillespie, spirit dealer
20 Andrew Stewart, butcher
18 J. M'Cann, hair cutter
16 James Brady, butcher
14 William Cochran, tinsmith
12 Hugh & Joseph Millen, wholesale and retail spirit stores
10 Thomas Quigley, fruiterer
8 Agnes Martin, boarding house
6 Jane Chambers, boarding house
4 William Shaw, boarding house
2½ Mary Wilson, boarding house
2 Francis M'Keys, publican

Edward Street, Little
EAST SIDE EDWARD STREET.
Two small houses
20 Samuel Nicholl, porkcutter
18 Jane Cowan, boarding house
16 Hugh Houston, canvass weaver
14 James M'Cracken, bricklayer
12 Wm. Dolway, tobacco spinner

Eglinton Street
CRUMLIN ROAD.
New houses building, Robert Henderson, owner
PRESBYTERIAN CHURCH (building)
—Rev. James Martin, Minister

Eliza Court
ELIZA STREET.
Eleven small houses

Eliza Place
ELIZA STREET.
15 Simon O'Regan, engineer
15 Samuel Moore, gentleman

Eliza Street
EAST SIDE CROMAC STREET.
1 Hugh Strain, dealer
3 Wm M'Connell, labourer

5 James M'Connell, car driver
[*Eliza court.*
7 Hugh Orr, sawyer
9 Robert Tweedly, painter
11 John Workman, bootmaker
13 Richard Robinson, agricultural implement and bobbin manufacturer
[*Eliza place.*
19 Mrs Ferguson
21 Timothy Ivers, cabinet maker, Castle street
23 Rev. David Maginnis
25 John M'Donald, tobacconist, 4 North street
27 Matthew Mullan, brewer, Cromac brewery
29 Richard Robinson, machine maker, 13 Eliza street
Thomas Firth, Eliza street flax mill; residence, 1 Bond street
THE BELFAST IRON WORKS—Robert Pace, jun., and Thomas N. Gladstone, managers; Robert Pace's residence, 43 High street
LEFT SIDE.
Gilbert Robb, clerk
Robert Stevenson, grain merchant, 5 Gloucester street
James Munce, builder
Miss Cahoun
Robert M'Caig, salesman in J. & D. Lindsay's, Donegall place
James Maddox, tailor
New house building
Four small houses
24 Stewart Oliver, grocer and spirit dealer
22 Daniel Dyer, labourer
20 James M'Clarnon, carpenter
Lindsay, Brothers, & Co., silk manufactory establishment
18 James Entwisle, architect
Five new houses building
Murphy street.]
16 John Johnston, gardener
14 Elizabeth Girvan
12 Agnes Watson, dressmaker
10 Charles Bell, broker
8 George Johnston, sawyer
6 Joseph Harrison, clerk
4 David Orr, carpenter
2 Thomas Freeman, carpenter

Ellen's Court
OFF NILE STREET.
Six small houses

Elliott's Court
OFF DONEGALL STREET.
6 Thomas Wallace, commission merchant; residence, 3 Ormeau pl.
7 Marshall Brown, & Co., muslin manufacturers; Robert Huston, agent; residence, Sarah street
" George M'Bride, muslin manufacturer; residence, May street
8 Daniel M'Keown & Son, muslin manufacturers; residence, 13 Great George's street
9 Samuel Tierney, muslin manufacturer, agent for Messrs. Chaine and Son, Muckamore, Antrim; residence, Ballymacarrett
11 John Dougherty, painter
The other numbers are either stores (nameless) or unoccupied

Erskine's Court
OFF DURHAM STREET—SOUTH SIDE.
Eleven small houses

Fairy Place
1 John Quin, foreman in *Mercury* office
3 James Parker
5 Wm. M'Clenaghan, mechanic

Falloon's Court
OFF FLEET STREET.
John Murray, stone cutter
James M'Guigan, locksmith
Edward Dawson, plasterer
John Ewins, shipsmith
Patrick Stewart, mariner
Mallice Scullion, foundryman
Charles Bradley, labourer
Frederick Fike, labourer
Samuel Wilson, labourer

Falls Court
FALLS ROAD.
Joseph Waterhouse, mechanic in Combe's Falls foundry

Falls Court
OFF DURHAM STREET.
1 Michael Finlay, labourer
3 Hugh Daly, turner
5 Vacant
7 Thomas M'Cullough, day constable
8 George Savage, cow keeper
6 James Chambers, weaver
4 Mrs Hamill
2 James Mullin, labourer

Falls Road
FROM TOWNSEND STREET.

[Bath place.
James Boomer and Co.'s flax spinning mill; James Boomer's residence, Seafield; James Campbell's residence, 5 College Square North

[Boundary street.
[Hamilton's place.
[Ardmoulin place.
James Alexander and Co., Ardmoulin flour mills; Tobias Porter, manager

Maiden's row.]
Hull, Hart and Co., Flax spinning manufactory; office, 17 Victoria buildings, Waring street
A. W. Craig and Co., flaxspinners and manufacturers; town office, 17 Rosemary street
Samuel Elsler, grocer and haberdasher
John Charters and Co., Falls flax spinning manufactory; J. Charter's residence, Ardmoulin house
J. Combe and Co., Falls foundry and machine shop; J. Combe's residence, 1 Ardmoulin place
Gordon and Co., flax and tow spinners,
Gunning and Campbell's flax and tow spinning manufactory; John Campbell's residence, 5 College square North
James Kennedy and Son, flax and tow spinners, Millvale
M'Connell and Kennedy, flax and tow spinners, Millvale
John Robinson, mill manager

Charters' Buildings.
Henry Boyd, overlooker Falls mill
William Parker, ditto
John Oysten, foreman Falls mill
John Duncan, spirit dealer
James M'Kibbin, grocer and publican
Constabulary station, Constable Baxter
Clonard print works, Lewis Delawney, manager; proprietor, Robert Thompson, 1 Donegall square West, & Holywood
Howie's bleachfield
Springfield works — Stevenson and Co.
DISTRICT LUNATIC ASYLUM, Robt. Stewart, M.D., Physician and Manager
George Milliken, publican
James M'Kavanagh, publican
John Wilson, publican
Robert Milliken, grocer
Richard Carson, publican
Margaret Bush
John Mallin
Henry M'Cance, carding master
Charles M'Quillan, shoemaker
John Stewart, flax dresser
Robert M'Crudden, schoolmaster; James Trimble, asssistant; residence, Conway street
Mrs. White
John M'Cune, engineer
William Douglass, yarn bundler
Maxwell Drennan, labourer
George Ritchie, grocer and muslin warper
Paul Higgins, blacksmith
Edward Crossley, flax dresser
David Robinson, carpenter
Ann Canavan
James Toole, flax dresser
W. M'Quillan, tailor
Hamilton Quin, publican
William Duffy, grocer and publican
David Adams, land surveyor
Thomas Somerset, mechanic
S. Kirkwood, publican
Patrick M'Kenna, publican
James Trainor, publican
Edward Savage, publican
Patrick Maguire, shoemaker
Robert Hanna, gardener and provision shop
John Adair, grocer
John Daniel provision store
Patrick Boyle, provision shop
George Parker, publican
John Burrows, miller
William M'Quillan, Falls road tavern
William Gill, excise office
James M'Cracken, scantling yard

[Devis street.]
47 Ellen M'Caverty, dress maker and milliner
45 James Dougherty, machine master
43 Archibald Magill, weaver

41 James Ireland, labourer
39 Edward Doran, stone mason
37 Margaret O'Hagan, bonnet maker
35 Susan Hagan, dress maker
33 Edward Thomas, mill manager
| *Townsend street.*

Ferguson's Court
OFF SMITHFIELD.
Nine small houses
James Barnett's spirit store

First Street
BETWEEN FALLS ROAD AND SHANK-
HILL ROAD.
Five small houses

Fisherwick Place
COLLEGE SQUARE SOUTH.
1 Misses Whittle's boarding school
3 Wm Home, Captain, half pay, 86th Regt.
5 Mrs Ellen Graham
7 Adam Duffin, of Duffin and Co.'s, flax spinners
9 Rev. George Hutton
11 Adam Hill, sub-treasurer for the Borough of Belfast, and notary public
FISHERWICK-PL. PRESBYTERIAN CHURCH—Rev. Dr Morgan

Fitzwilliam Street
OLD MALONE ROAD.
Charles Bessel, gentleman
Rev. Isaiah Steen
Mrs Duncan
Jas. Elliott, muslin manufacturer, Donegall square east

James Benn, wine merchant
William Benn, general commission merchant; 9, Donegall pl.
Mrs Wardle
Hugh Henry Boyd, land agent; office, Arthur street

Fleet Street
EAST SIDE YORK STREET.
New house building
Enclosed ground
[*Little York street.*
11 Margaret Campbell, boardinghouse
13 William Henry Allen, clerk
15 William Robert Orr, clerk
17 James Clarke, custom house officer

Enclosed ground
[*Collingwood street.*
Aaron Vernon, boiler maker
Robert Millen, book keeper
John Creen, mate
Janet M'Cready
James Ingles, book publisher
Wm. Menarry, mariner
7 Alice Gillespie
5 Thomas Clinton, boiler maker
[*Falloon's court.*
Wm. Cooper, labourer
Daniel Bonner, mariner
John Ewins, labourer
House vacant
Enclosed ground
George Dunbar's yard and side of store
28 Francis O'Neill, labourer
30 Margaret Parker, washerwoman
32 Baptist Trimble, labourer
34 Robert Gibson, labourer
Waste ground
Three new houses building
Collingwood street.]
New house building
Waste ground
Side of David Fulton's (carpenters) workshops and sawpits
Little York street.]
10 Samuel Wallace, clerk
8 Wm. Charnock, drysalter, Corporation square
6 Wm. Todd, book keeper
4 Wm. John Beatty, printer and engraver
2 Mrs Stirling

Forcades' Entry
NORTH SIDE OF BERRY STREET.
Sixteen small houses

Fountain Lane
DONEGALL PLACE TO FOUNTAIN ST.
Side of Bernard Hughes's Railway Bakery
4 Thomas Ford, shirt and shirt collar maker; residence, 11 College street
6 National Infant School; teacher, Miss Lambert
John Praeger & Co., linen and yarn merchants; John Praeger, Austrian and Bremen Vice-Consul; residence, Donegall square south

Two small houses
Side of James Moore's paper warerooms

Fountain Place
OLD DUBLIN ROAD.
18 Vacant
19 Robert M'Bride, muslin manufacturer; Commercial court
20 Miss Dorrian
21 Hugh Rea, of Messrs Sinclair and Boyd's; office, Donegall quay

Fountain Street
CASTLE ST. TO WELLINGTON PLACE.
1 Side of Saml. Kerns' tavern, Castle street
3 Craig, Liddle, and Crymble, piano forte manufacturers; residences: James Liddle's residence, 83 Academy street; Matthew Crymble's residence, 9 Lancaster street
5 William P. Clarke, cabinet and upholstery warerooms
7 Thomas Butler & Son, plumbers; 29 Castle street
9 Law & Co., gasfitters and brassfounders; residence, No. 12
11 Duprey's coach making establishment
13 Alexander Hoy, whitesmith
Donegall Arms Hotel stables
Water Commissioners' yard
15 National Male School; Hugh M. Kelly, teacher
15½ John M'Entire, general and commission merchant; residence, 10 Albion place
17 Surgeon Alexander Harkin
[*College street.*]
19 Rev. Charles Allen, Incumbent, St. Paul's Church
21 Miss Simms
23 Mrs Billsland, glass and china shop, 4 Donegall place
25 Francis Wilson, accountant
27 William Clarke, plain and ornamental painter
29 Side entrance to Mr Barnett's, dentist
[*Wellington place.*]
40 Thomas Bell, provision merchant; office and stores, Queen street

38 Wm. Maxwell, builder and undertaker, Queen street
36 Lyle and Kinahan, wine and spirit merchants; S. Lyle's residence, 2 Victoria place; F. Kinahan's residence, Knockbreda
34 Joseph Magill, commission merchant and Mexican Vice Consul; residence, Marino, Holywood
32 Robert Yeates
24 Hugh Wallace & Co., solicitors; Dublin address, 30 North Gt. George's st., and Downpatrick
12 Mrs A. Law
[*Fountain lane.*]
20 National Female School; Mrs Hayes, teacher
18 Andrew Keatinge, carpenter
16 Thomas Roche
14 Mrs Milne, milliner, Castle place
10 John Reid, car owner
8 John Hill, pillbox manufacturer, 8 Castle street
6 Wm. M'Keown, Fountain Street Tavern
4 Patrick M'Entee, teacher
2 Francis O'Hayer, saddler, 1 Donegall Place Buildings

Fountainville
OLD MALONE ROAD.
1 Wm. Thompson, gentleman
2 Vacant
3 Charles Thompson, gentleman

Fountainville Cottage
Major M'Pherson

Fowl Market
ST. GEORGE'S MARKET.
John Brown, collector

Fox's Row
OFF DURHAM STREET.
Side of Foster Connor's linen factory
Twenty small houses

Francis Street
FROM SMITHFIELD TO MILLFIELD.
John Fisher and Co., flax spinners; residence, Glengall place
Wm. Hicks, weaving factory; residence, 15 Church street
John and J. Herdman & Co.'s flax stores
24 Malcolm Scott, preparing master

22 Rachael Smith, dealer
20 Alex. Stafford, skinner
18 Edward Dougherty, labourer
16 Mathew Johnston, shoemaker
14 Ellen Potts
12 Patrick Hughes, cutler
10, 8 Thos. Hodges, furniture broker
6 Rose Dowd
4 John M'Kibbin, tailor
" Samuel Kennedy, cabinet maker
2 John Hamilton, plumber

Franklin Place

LINEN HALL STREET TO ADELAIDE PLACE.

Side door of the Misses Gillis' preparatory school
1 Robert M'Caw, wholesale grocer, Victoria street
2 William Shannon, grocer in Mathison Brothers, Donegall place
3 Robert T. M'Geagh, woollendraper and haberdasher, Hercules place
4 James P. Corry, timber merchant; Corporation square
5 Samuel Hart, cotton yarn warehouse, 7 Commercial court
6 Andrew Downing, poultry shop, Corn market
7 Samuel Martin, of John Martin and Co., flax spinners and general merchants; 29 Ann street
Side of Mrs Craufurds' day school

Frederick Lane

OFF FREDERICK STREET.

Robert Latham, cooper
Twenty small houses
Side of John Christie's starch and blue works

Frederick Place

OFF FREDERICK STREET.

1 John Harper, clerk
2 Wm. Woods, saddler
3 Robert Shaw, hairdresser
4 Moses Jamieson, constable
5 Daniel Rooney, iron moulder

Frederick Street

YORK STREET TO NORTH QUEEN STREET.

John Hall, grocer and stone cutter
Henry Hunter, clerk
Andrew Redmond, printer
Hugh Fulton, cabinet maker
Samuel Shaw, boot and shoemaker
Ann M'Goughey, washwoman
Industrial and National School; Miss Orr, teacher; Mrs Talbot, matron
GENERAL HOSPITAL AND DISPENSARY
DISPENSARY STATION
SOCIETY OF FRIENDS' MEETING HOUSE
1 Peter Doyle, labourer

[*Frederick lane.*

3 John Christie, starch and blue works
5 William J. Williamson, painter
7 Arthur Adams, clerk

[*Alexander street.*

9 Richard M'Gouran, spirit dealer
11 James Donnelly, pensioner
13 John Maguire, spirit dealer

[*Walker's lane.*

15 James Bond, grocer and spirit dealer
17 William Monair, grocer and Scripture reader
19 Chas. Pullen, gardener and steward
21 R. D. Kirk, wine and spirit dealer

[*North Queen street.*]

Thomas Biggan, pavier
60 Mary Fitzsimmon, boarding house
58 William M'Fall, porter
56 Samuel Scott, labourer
54 John M'Dowell, blacksmith
52 James M'Cance, cooper
50 Daniel M'Keown, custom house officer
48 John Conn, bookbinder
46 Hugh M'Cullough, blacksmith
44 Isaac Nolan, dealer
42 Jane Delany
Frederick place.]
Three small houses
Hugh Reavy, ship carpenter
Three small houses
Thatched House Tavern—John M'Connell, proprietor
24 James M'Bride, labourer
22 George Smyth, pork cutter
20 Andrew Mearn's stables
18 Molyneux and Ferguson's starch works
WESLEYAN METHODIST CHAPEL
16 Rev. William Lupton

14 Rev. Benjamin Bayley
Sarah street.]
12 Alexander Bell, gentleman
10 James Wilson, watchmaker, jeweller, silversmith, and optician; 7 High street
8 Andrew Mearns, paper stainer; 22 Donegall street
Washington street.]
6 Alexander Galt, grocer and spirit dealer
Robert Clements, boarding house
George's court.]
4 James M'Caldin, hat and cap manufacturer; 18 Waring street
2 John Murphy, stone cutter, 12 York street
Side of Giacomo Nannetti's emporium of fine arts

Friendly Street
OFF WELSH STREET.

1 Jane Johnston, dressmaker
3 John Magill, baker
5 James Carr, chandler
7 Hugh Patterson, porter
9 Edward Fitzpatrick, dealer
11 John Smith, stonecutter
13 James M'Knight, gardener
15 William Stewart, tailor
17 William Gilly, mariner
19 James M'Grath, labourer
21 Hugh M'Shane, labourer
23 James M'Ateer, tailor
25 James Davison, constable
27 David Melville, labourer
29 Hugh Burns, sawyer
31 William M'Cullough, lithographic printer
33 Joseph Martin, marble polisher
35 Thomas Erskine, millwright
37 James Price, pensioner
39 Wm Dunn, horse trainer
41 William Touchal, boiler maker
Francis Burden, soda ash manufacturer; residence, 16 Alfred street; Wm. R. Pye, manager; residence, 70 High street
36 Vacant
34½ James Anderson, sawyer
32 Patrick Loughran, brass founder
30½ Michael M'Kenna, brass founder
28½ James Rice, shoemaker
26½ Samuel Dorman, weaver
30 Patrick Denvir, carpenter

32 John Miller, carpenter
30 James Lewis, printer
28 William Fleming, turner
26 Charles Horner, blacksmith
24 James Gooden, labourer
20 James Beatty, butler
18 James Barr, dealer
18 George Caldwell, print cutter
16 Patrick Shanley, printer
14 Patrick M'Cullough, lighterman
12 James Adams, porter
10 Alexander Campbell, porter
8 John Rainey, chandler
6 Thomas Sinclair, shoemaker
4 James Conn, clerk
2 William Gorman, porter
" Mary Smyth, grocer

Fulton's Entry
OFF HERCULES STREET.

A lot of old houses roofless and not tenanted

Gable Street
BOUNDARY ST. TO GREENLAND

1 James Murphy, pensioner
2 Vacant
3 Adams Ellwood, labourer

Galway Court
Five small houses
11 Mary M'Veigh, widow
13 Margaret Woods, widow
15 James Savage, bricklayer
17 Patrick M'Grady, hostler
19 John Downey, pensioner

Galway Street
OFF DURHAM STREET.

1 Andrew Steen, tanner
3 Wm. Mathews, pensioner
5 Patrick Berry, pensioner
7 Richard Gordon, carpenter
9 Robert Donnelly, servant

Gamble Street
CORPORATION STREET TO DONEGALL QUAY.

1 John M'Tear, grocer and spirit dealer
3 Margaret Marriot M'Dowell, boarding house
5 David Monaghan, hairdresser
7 Daniel Murphy, grain merchant
" Daniel Murphy, grocer and spirit dealer

9 Wm. Vint, provision merchant; 4 Dock street
11 Mary Gilles, spirit dealer
13 Samuel Carmichael, grocer and boardinghouse
15 Michael Hall, boarding house
17 Elizabeth Stafford, grocer
19 Arthur Young, Caledonian Hotel
....[*Here Tomb street intersects.*]....
21 Edward Coey, provision merchant; residence, Merville.
23 (Stores) Sinclair and Boyd; 45 Donegall quay
25 Vacant
27 Charles Duffin's flax store (rere entrance)
" William Hughes, corn store; office, 13 North street
29 John Blakley, Crown and Anchor Hotel
34 George C. Pim & Co.'s stores
32 Jane Keys, boarding house
30 Thos. Clay, hotel keeper, Crown Inn
[*Steam Mill lane.*
28, 26 James M'Moreland, spirit dealer
24 Robert Brown, spirit dealer
22 Catherine M'Alister, commercial lodging house
20 John M'Salley, spirit dealer
18 John M'Alister, grocer and spirit dealer
....[*Here Tomb street intersects*]...
16, 14 John Feeney, spirit dealer
12 Patrick Cunningham, seaman
10 Hugh Bailie, ship carpenter
8 Wm. Thomas, butcher
6 James M'Larnon, hairdresser
4 Patrick Fowler, yard and stabling
4 Samuel S. Rankin, wholesale and retail wine and spirit merchant; residence, Ballymacarrett
2½ John Small, writing clerk
2 James M'Kee, sewed muslin manufacturer; residence, 13 Dock street

Garden Place
CROMAC ROAD.

1 Mrs Margaret M'Manus, boarding house
" Wm. M'Roberts, Scripture reader
" John M'Callion, Scripture reader
2 Vacant
3 Henry Magee, proctor

Gardiner Street
PETER'S HILL TO BROWN STREET.

18 James Moorehead, grocer
39 Patrick M'Quillan, pawnbroker
41 Patrick M'Ilroy, grocer and publican
43 Hugh Murphy, grocer
49 J. Duff, grocer and publican
Several smaller houses

Garmoyle Street
NORTH END CORPORATION STREET.

Robinson Welsh, butcher
Sarah Porter, green grocer
Fanny Bonner, clothier
Pilot street.]
Thomas Louden, ship bread baker
John Woods, tailor and grocer
George Strings, tailor
Robert Stevenson, engineer
Charles Butler, sea captain
Robert M'Cready, stonecutter
Enclosed ground
Steam Saw Mills—John Low, proprietor; residence, 71 Ship st.
22 Thomas Vernon, foreman boiler maker
Ship street.]
Yard and office vacant
18 Thomas Wells, boiler maker
16 Wm. Pascoe, sea captain
14 William Coates, clerk
George Dunbar's stores
Fleet street.]
Enclosed ground
Dock street.]
10 James Bradford, block and pump maker
8 Robt. Carmichael, grocer and spirit dealer
Two new houses building
North Thomas street.]
4 Adam Nelson, spirit dealer
2 Thomas Irvine, green grocer
Enclosed ground

George's Court
FREDERICK STREET TO YORK LANE.
Eighteen small houses

George's Lane
FROM MONTGOMERY ST. TO WILLIAM ST. SOUTH.

1 John Dillon, publican
Side of Messrs Waugh and Smyth's coach factory

5 John Cockburn, superintendent of fire engines
7 John Blades, coachmaker
9 William Mulrine, blacksmith
11 Patrick Reilly, clerk, Plough Hotel
13 Mrs M'Cullough piano forte manufacturer
15 J. Brown, horse shoer and farrier
17 Thomas M'Grath's caravansary
Side of Mr Bathurst's coach factory
12 Mary Brown, grocer and publican
10 J. Allen, tailor
8 John Campbell, whitesmith
6 Mr Blackwood's stores and slaughter yard
4 Entrance to Mr Low's spirit store
2 James Crawford, grocer

George's Street, Little
WEST SIDE YORK STREET.

1 James Charley, ship carpenter
3 John Hunter, grocer and publican
[*Molyneaux street.*
5 Eliza Wilson, grocer
7 Michael M'Morran, labourer
9 Margaret Brady
11 Edward Gillis, ship carpenter
[*Southwell street.*
13 Robert Harper, grocer
15 Ann Rooney
17 Mary Gregory
19 James M'Ferran, labourer
21 John Gunning, grocer and publican
23 to 31 Five small houses
33 Joseph Henesey, grocer
[*Economy place.*
35 to 47 Six small houses
49 James Donnelly, publican
34 to 10—Thirteen small houses
Union place.]
Three small houses
Michael street.]
6 John Marr, publican
4 Wm. Savage, seaman
2 Eliza and Jane Wyley, boardinghouse

George's Street, Great
CORPORATION SQUARE TO NORTH QUEEN STREET.

1 Jane Arnold, haberdasher and seaman's outfitter; Post Office Receiving House
3 William Lewis, merchant, of the firm of F. and W. Lewis
" F. and W. Lewis, timber and slate merchants; F. Lewis' residence, Nettlefield, Ballymacarrett
5 John Low, timber and slate merchant; residence, 1 Ship street
5 Daniel Bell, timber merchant
...[*Here Nelson street intersects.*]...
PRESBYTERIAN CHURCH — Rev. Thomas Toye, minister
7 THE MANSE—Rev. Thomas Toye
7½ John Strachan, carpenter and builder
9 Thos. Devlin, druggist and grocer; place of business, North street
11 Rev. William O'Hanlon, Independent minister
[*Here Little York street intersects.*]
13 Rev. Thomas Mills, Methodist minister, new connexion
....[*Here York street intersects.*]....
Cooke & Porter, muslin gas singers; James Cooke's residence, 19 Collingwood street
[*Michael street.*
13 D. M'Keown, manufacturer
15 William Vance, merchant; office, Donegall street
[*Union place.*
17 John Craig, hardware merchant, Bridge street
[*North Queen street.*]
82 James Ford, labourer
80 James Daley, pensioner
78 Ann Montgomery, lodgings
76 Alexander Skinner, painter
74 Jane Johnston, lodgings
72 Mrs Dickson, lodgings
70 James Welsh
Alexander street.]
68 James O'Neill, publican
66 Robert Miller, labourer
64 William Greer, labourer
Magee's lane.]
64½ George Nelson, publican
62 Vacant
60 James Davidson, miller
58 Miss Milford
56 Mrs Grott
Thomas street.]
54 Malcom M'Cracken, bootmaker, Bridge street
52 Mrs Martin
50 Mrs Cooper

48 Samuel Thompson, lodgings
Portland street.]
46 Robert M'Mullan, linen yarn merchant, Rosemary street
44 Mrs Connell
..[*Here York street intersects.*]..
42 Henry M'Monagle, painter and glazier
38 William Johnston, spirit dealer
36 Vacant
34½ John Wilson
34 Michael Smith, spirit dealer
...[*Little York street intersects.*]...
36 William M'Clintock, grocer and provision dealer
32½ Pierce Hayden, spirit dealer
" Samuel Crawford, builder
32 Thomas Byrne, builder
30 James Roden, marble store
28¾ Geo. Pinkerton, passenger agent
28¼ Alexander Kerns, boot and shoemaker
28 Hugh Shaw, stabling yard
28 Hugh Shaw, spirit dealer
....[*Here Nelson street intersects.*]....
24 Robert Lyons, commission agent
22 Hugh Andrews, water inspector
20¾ John Scott, shipowner
20¼ Samuel Taylor, spindle, flyer, and screw bolt maker
20 John Hill, spirit dealer
Caroline street]
18 Shaw and Dickson, provision merchants; residence, 21 Ship st.
16 James & William Pearce, Phœnix foundry; residence, Pebble Cottage
14 Hugh M'Neill, commission mercht.
12 John Lowry, builder
10 Charles Connell
8½ Wm. & J. Campbell, provision merchants; residence, 8 Donegall Square West
8 William Gelston, tobacconist
6 Hugh Wardlow, merchant
4 James Boyle, spirit dealer
2 Miss Margaret M'Cormick
2½ Wm. Hopkins, writing clerk

Gibb's Court
ALEXANDER ST. OFF FREDERICK ST.
Eleven small houses

Glasshouse Street
BOYD STREET TO GARDINER STREET.
Twenty-seven small houses

Glenfield Place
ORMEAU ROAD.
1 John Arnold, woollendraper, High street
2 Joseph Bain, rectifying distiller; office, Seymour street
3 William Douglass, iron and coal agent; office, 20 Waring street
4 Vacant
5 Mrs Vaughan
6 Mrs Caroline Irwin
" James Irwin, wine merchant
7 Andrew Lyle, distiller and brewer; of the firm of A. Mackenzie, Shaw, and Co.
8 Archibald Campbell Colvil, merchant; office, 74 Waring street

Glengall Place
WEST SIDE GREAT VICTORIA STREET.
1 Mrs Mary Murphy
2 John Fisher, of Campbell & Fisher flax spinners, Smithfield
3 Mrs Smith
" Geo. K. Smith, solicitor; office, 3 The Castle
4 Captain John Boyd, flax spinner, Blackstaff mill

Glengall Street
GREAT VICTORIA ST. TO DURHAM ST.
3 Robert Orr's residence
" Robert Orr, linen manufacturer, (office)
Enclosed ground
5 John Scott, woollendraper
7 George Woodhouse, clerk in Northern bank
9 Andrew Mayne, in Wm. Dobbin's, North street
11 Thomas Ridgeway, minister
Constantine S. Cullen, solicitor, in Mr Wallace's (solicitor) office, Victoria street
Side of James Pelan's grocery and spirit store
James Pelan's residence

Glentilt Place
OLD LODGE ROAD.
1 William Wilson, warehouseman
2 James Downey, foreman hackler
3 Thomas M'Nair, writing clerk
4 Joseph Bigger, jun., provision merchant; store, Little Donegall street

5 David Gregg, traveller, for Messrs Lindsay, Brothers
6 John Cochrane, sewed muslin manufacturer; warehouse, Bank lane

---

1 Mary Campbell, milliner
2 William Cunningham, stone mason
3 James Cameron, bricklayer
4 John M'Atamney, stone cutter
5 William Courtenay, stone cutter
6 William Curry, stone cutter
7 Vacant

Gloucester Street
GREAT EDWARD STREET TO MONTGOMERY STREET.

1 James Anderson, grain merchant
.. [*Here Seymour street intersects*]..
3 John Brown, sen., builder
5 Thomas Hume, grain and general commission merchant; residence, Ballynafeigh
7 John Ritchie, salesman
9 James Anderson, grain merchant; store, 1 Gloucester street
11 Hugh White, spirit merchant; Winecellar entry
13 James Ledlie, gentleman
15 Mathew M'Mullan, chandler and soap boiler; Corn market
17 Stewart M'Cleave, writing clerk
19 John Wilson, gentleman
21 Isabella M'Fadden, leather dealer; shop, 74 Ann street
23 Mary Brown, boarding and day school
25 Modesto Silo, carver and gilder; shop, Arthur square
46 Robert Frew, writing clerk
44 Richard Thompson, writing clerk
42 William M'Kenna, veterinary surgeon; offices, 2 May street
40 William Granz, professor of music
38 John Neill, salesman
36 J. P. Branker, salesman
34 Joseph M'Kee, grocer; shop, 69 High street
32 John Worthington, accountant
30 Northern Coach Factory; William Miller, proprietor
28 Ellen Moreland
26 Samuel Rea, surgeon
24 Hugh Hamilton, grocer; shop, Ann street

22 John Robson, posting master; office and stables, 31 Chichester street and Montgomery street
20 John Brown, jun., timber merchant
18 Margaret Galway
16 Hamilton Cherry, gentleman
14 Frances M'Kibbin, boardinghouse
12 Thomas M'Camphill, Belfast Bank
10 William M'Coubrey, carpenter
8 Stewart M'Williams, detective officer
6 Eliza Gamble, schoolmistress
4 Denis Smith, jun., horse dealer
New Market Horse Repository; Denis Smith, proprietor
2 James Barry, entertainment and lodging

Gordon Street
HILL STREET TO CORPORATION ST.

1 Samuel Cochrane, spirit dealer
3, 5 Vacant
7 George Shannon
9 Bruce Gelston, seaman
11 William Kane, butter buyer
13 William M'Guickan, smith
15 John M'Millan, tailor
19 William Ewart's flax store
21 Back entrance to Mr. George Ashs' stores
[*Cotton court.*
27 James M'Mullen, stone cutter
29 John Beattie, emigration agent
NEW CORN EXCHANGE—Side entrance
36 John Beattie, spirit dealer
34½ James Nicholl, soda water, ginger beer, and lemonade manufacturer; residence, 21 Albert square
34 Joseph Brownlee, porter
32 Daniel Montgomery, seaman
30 George Kane, cooper
28 James Allen, coach smith
26 Henry Martin, porter
24 Francis Bailie, groom
22 Mrs Jane Bruce, dress and bonnet maker
20 Robert Scott, cooper
18 William Cleland, cooper
16 William Davison, marine store
14 John Mullen, labourer
12 Wm Gibson, boot and shoemaker
10 Thos. Gibeon, boot and shoemaker
8½ William Oswald

8 Thomas Friel, tobacco spinner and dealer
6 Richard Ferguson, turner
4 Jane Milliken, lodging house
2 John Johnston, nailer

Grace street
HAMILTON ST. TO HENRIETTA ST.
Side of Catherine Dunlop's spirit shop
3 Luke Farrell, carpenter
5 Robert Thistle, coachmaker
7 Ann Kerney
9 Timothy Murphy, blacksmith
" James Smyth, coach painter
11 Patrick M'Cann, car driver
13 John Brown, carpenter
15 Thomas Agnew, carpenter
17 James Nicholl, pork cutter
19 Thomas Gilliland, grocer and spirit dealer
26 Wm. Gregg, gilder
4 John Shields
22 John George, boot and shoemaker
........[*Russell street.*]..........
20 Joshua Campbell, watchman
18 John Donaldson, butler
16 Patrick Devlin, butler
14 George Park, brassfounder
12 James Milbey, stone cutter
10 James M'Kechnie, compositor
8 John Heron, mariner
6 Ellen Hanna, nurse tender
4 Daniel M'Cann, flax merchant
2 John Miller, painter

Graham's Entry
FROM HIGH STREET TO ROSEMARY STREET.
1 Andrew M'Callum, porter
3 Back entrance to James Call's shellfish tavern
5 George Johnston, labourer
7 Andy Downey, labourer
9 Samuel Bogan, labourer
11 Daniel Kain
13 Wm. Bain
15 Patrick Quinn, butler
17 Patrick Mulholland, cooper
19 Dennis Sullivan, porter
21 Wm. M'Gaghey, bricklayer
Side of James Marshall's delph warerooms
12 Hugh Graham & Co., hat manufactory,

Andrew Clendinning, draper; 10 Rosemary street
8 Nicholas Cavanagh, dealer
6, 4, 2 Mary Ann Brady, hotel and tavern

Grattan Court
OFF GRATTAN STREET.
1 Denis Kane
3 Phillip Ross, sailor
5 James Storey, labourer
7 Charles Crawford, cooper
9 Margaret Dickson
11 William Cannon, cooper
13 Patrick Mullan, tailor
15 William Bell, porter
18 John Brown, labourer
16 Edward Ingram, labourer
14 George Clarke, labourer
12 William Steed, painter
10 John M'Kay, carpenter
8 John Connor
6 Alexander M'Kenna, cooper
4 Arthur Malone
2 Vacant

Grattan place
BETWEEN 45 AND 47 GRATTAN ST.
1 Margaret Preston
3 Jane Smith
5 Robert Busley, carpenter
7 John Mateer, clerk
9 Thomas M'Kenna, porter
11 John Hood, shoemaker
14 Thomas Legget, musician
12 James Munce, butcher
10 Wm. Boylan, mason
8 Sarah Loughry
6 Wm. Hawthorn, labourer
4 John Donagan, labourer
2 John Lyons, labourer

Grattan Street
GORDON SREET TO GREEN STREET.
The houses in this street from No. 1 to 37 have been pulled down
Two new houses not numbered
[*Poplar court*
39 Henry Jordan, labourer
41 Jane Haughey, boarding house
43 John Jennings. carpenter
45 John Greer, cooper
[*Grattan place*
47 Jane M'Carroll, boarding house
49 Vacant
51 Richard Galloway, cooper

53 Thomas Ingram, bricklayer
55 Robert M'Quillan, writing clerk
    [*Grattan court.*
57 Mary Mitchell
59 Bernard Smith, cart owner, lodging house
61 Hugh Kernaghan, grocer and spirit dealer
    [*Talbot court.*
63 William Dickson, labourer
65 Rose Ann Mooney, lodgings
67 John Phillips, labourer
69 Joseph Smith, schoolmaster
71 Michael M'Greevy, stone sawyer
73 James Blakely, seaman
75 Mary Livingston, huckster
" James M'Kensey, painter
64 Peter Kearney, wine and spirit dealer
    [*Brady's row.*
62 Elizabeth Mulholland, grocer and spirit dealer
60 John Agnew, provision dealer
58 Edward M'Guigan, labourer
56 James M'Coubrey, seaman
54 Samuel Baird, labourer
52 James Mones, grocer and spirit dealer
Talbot street.]
48, 50 Robert Loughry, spirit dealer
46 Jas. Kennedy, boot and shoemaker
44 Thomas Dyer, nailer
" Matthew Lambert, nailer
42 John Johnston, tailor
40 Elizabeth Collins, green grocer
38 Hugh M'Clean, marine store
36 John Smith, sawyer
34 Daniel Allen, grocer
32 Mary Boyle, grocer
" John M'Anally, canvass weaver
30 J. M'Conkey, labourer
28 Owen M'Mahon, grocer and plasterer
    [*Morrow's entry.*
26 Robert Mitchell, flax and tow dealer
" John Kelly, canvas weaver
24 Hugh Hamill, sailmaker
" Charles Graham, tobacco spinner
22 Agnes M'Anally, bandbox maker
20 Daniel Connor, sawyer
18, 16 James Connor, builder
14 Margaret Fulton, lodging house
12 Daniel Lamp, grocer and lodgings
10 William M'Gawley, porter

8 Alexander Leitch, shoemaker
6 Vacant
4 James Neill, lodging house
2 John Beattie, spirit dealer and emigration agent

Greenland Street
SHANKHILL ROAD TO CARGILL ST.

1 Jeremiah Thompson, fireman
3 Nathaniel Beggs, sawyer
5 James Thompson, labourer
7 James Whiteside, plasterer
9 William Hill, porter
11 John Ewing, grocer and spirit dealer
13 David Shields, flax dresser
15 Sarah Livingston
17 John Thompson, carman
19 William Hinchy, smith
21 John Coleman, smith
23 Daniel O'Neill, blockmaker
25 Sarah Campbell, shoe binder
27 Richard Boyd, smith
29 John Keaton, shoemaker
31 Charles Smith, labourer
33 James Stewart, watchman
35 John Smyth, labourer
37 Michael M'Clarnon, porter
26 Patrick Donaghy, baker
24 Owen O'Neill, publican
22 Margaret Addis, widow
20 John Douglas, engine driver
18 Jeremiah M'Gee, bricklayer
16 Bernard M'Connell, plasterer
14 John Douglas, engineer
12 Thomas Johnston, bookbinder
10 John Gorman, porter
8 William M'Meekan, porter
6 William Fitchie, labourer
4 Matthew Montgomery, spinning master
2 John Cullen, mechanic

Green Street
CORPORATION ST. TO ACADEMY ST.
The south side of the Butter market occupies the space on which were formerly houses up to No. 21

21 Charles M'Clean, pilot
23 Neal M'Loughlan, mariner
25 Edward Murray and John M'Gonigell's cooperage
25½ Courtland Cummings, carpenter
27 James M'Cartan, general jobbing smith

K

27 James M'Cartan's residence
29 Robert Brady, pensioner
31 Charles Kelly, labourer
Green court or Coopers's entry]
33 Francis Rooney, mariner
35 Patrick Smith, salesman
37 Wm. M'Creevy, stone sawyer
39 James M'Blain, mariner
41 Edward Kerr, pensioner
43 Henry Magill, labourer
45 Michael M'Master, labourer
47 Thomas Craig, labourer
49 Andrew Roy, mariner
51 Patrick Gales, porter
53 Samuel Johnston, moulder
55 Charles M'Caffery, sawyer
57 James Smith, pawnbroker
59 Owen Murray, grocer
Lynas' lane.]
61 Henry Murray, grocer
63 John M'Laughlin, porter
65 James Milliken, hatter
67 Matthew Metcalf, dealer
William's lane.]
69 Daniel Dugan, sailmaker
71 Joseph Rea, baker
73 David West, boot and shoemaker
75 Samuel M'Neilly, smith
77 Samuel M'Connell, grocer, and 33 Edward street
........[*Edward street.*]........
79 Chas. and Patrick M'Glade, grocers and spirit dealers, and 34 Edward street
........[*Caxton street.*]........
81 Peter M'Donald, grocer and spirit dealer
83 John Gibson, boot and shoemaker
85 Andrew Dugan, bootcloser
[*Academy street.*]
76 Mathew Cowden, cooper
74 William Maxwell, slater
72 John Brown, grocer and cooper
70 Sarah Marks, dealer
68 John Carland, pensioner
66 James Reany, grocer
64 John Kane, chart reviser
62 William M'Cluney, labourer
60 James Campbell, dealer
58 Margaret Lynn
56 Wm. M'Dermott, tobacco spinner
54 Daniel Gilmore, grocer
 [*Grattan street and Henry square.*
52 William M'Cartney, pilot
50 John Yeates, mariner

48 Thomas Logan, harbour constable
46 Hugh Hamilton, canvas weaver
44 Bernard Hardy, weaver
42 John Canning's cooperage
40 John Canning's residence
38 Wm. Colburn, grocer and dairyman
" Wm. Colburn's stores
36 James Devlin, carman
34 Charles Jones, ticket writer and label maker
32 John Mackwood's residence and cooperage
30 Archer Fitzsimmons, labourer
28 Duncan Murphy, mariner
26 James O'Neill, lumper
24 Jas. Kirkwood, lithographic printer
Building ground

Green's Court or Cooper's Entry
NORTH SIDE OF GREEN STREET.

1 Robert Donnelly, labourer
3 Vacant
5 Steel Laverty, porter
8 John Dixon, carman
6 Patrick Higgins, pensioner
4 John Kearons, labourer
2 Margaret Connor, china mender

Gregg's Lane
WEST STREET TO SAMUEL STREET.
Eleven small houses

Grove Street
NORTH QUEEN ST. TO YORK STREET.

John Flannigan, millwright
Archibald M'Intyre, engineer
John Holings, preparing master
James Johnston, wood turner
1 William Clements, labourer
3 William Graham, blacksmith
5 James Livingstone, machine master
7 Charles Rafferty, labourer
9 William Somerset, millwright
11 John M'Cann, baker
13 Stanley Stewart, moulder
15 Samuel Rushton, moulder
17 Peter Rankin, confectioner
19 John Irvine, mechanic
21 Hugh Ewing, mechanic
23 John Sloan, blacksmith
25 William Alexander, mechanic
27 Solomon Bailey, engineer
29 William Nelson, blacksmith
31 Joseph Adamson, dealer
33 Felix M'Cluskey, brass turner
35 James Hamilton, carpenter

37 Thomas Rusham, metal plainer
39 Simon Steele, stone mason
41 James Marshall, turner
43 William Renwick, labourer
45 William Emerson, mechanic
47 Charles M'Fall, blacksmith
49 Alexander Carr, labourer
51 James Rennick, porter
53 Wm Neilly, spinning master
55 John Hook, brass moulder
57 David M'Turk, iron turner
59 John Lamont, gardener
61 Mary Ferguson
63 Henry Mills, pattern maker
65 Wm Galt, ship joiner
67 Thomas Ferris, spinning master
69 Torrens Robinson, moulder
71 James M'Collough, carpenter

Hagan's Court
14 GRATTAN STREET.
1½ Daniel Lamp, labourer

Hamill Court
OFF HAMILL STREET.
Six small houses

Hamill Street
OFF BARRACK STREET.
1 William Woods, grocer
16 John Elliott, grocer
32 Hugh Dougherty, grocer
Forty-eight small houses

Hamilton's Court
57 HIGH STREET.
Henry Jas. Devlin's bottling house
Rose Canty
John Porter's rent office; residence, Cromac Lodge
James Loughran, printer
John Riddel & Son, successors to Edw. Porter & Co., iron, steel, tinplate, and cast iron merchts.
Musgrave, Brothers' workshops
Mr Lee's hall door

Hamilton Place
OFF STEPHEN STREET.
Eight small houses

Hamilton's Place
OFF BOUNDARY STREET, FALLS ROAD.
1 James Moore, mechanic
3 Archibald Dickson, blacksmith

5 Joseph Crilly, flaxdresser
7 Peter Gartland, fireman
9 Rose Jennings, dealer
11 Michael M'Aleer, engine driver
13 Margaret Robinson, reeler
15 Wm. Taylor, servant
17 Robert Simpson, saw sharper
19 Samuel Hayes, machine maker
21 John Killey, clerk
23 James Coyne, pensioner
25 Widow Smyth
27 John Hamilton, labourer
20 Wm. Clarke, lithographic printer
18 Wm. Smith, plasterer
16 Martha M'Creedy, washerwoman and mangler
14 Robert Arbuthnot, labourer
12 John Branigan, owner of coal carts
10 Mary Armstrong, widow
8 James Young, carpenter
6 Hugh M'Mullan, pensioner
4 Elizabeth Rafferty
2 Wm. John Crawford, linen lapper

Hamilton Street
CROMAC STREET TO JOY STREET.
John Fullerton, grocer and spirit dealer, 17½ Cromac street
1 John Murphy, merchant, residence
3 John Murphy, timber and slate merchant, stores and offices
5 John Freeman, ropemaker, 14 Pottinger's entry
7 Hay Grieve, watchmaker in Mr Gilbert's, High street
9 Thomas Morrison, printer
11 John Russell, clerk
13 Miss Sophia Quaile
15 Miss Elizabeth Benson, dressmaker
17 Mr Frazer
19 Miss Letitia M'Arthur
21 George Kennedy, cloth cutter
23 Mrs Johnston and Miss M'Clune, boarding and day school
25 Mrs Sinclair, boarding house
[Catherine street north.
27 Hugh Hanna, surveyor
29 James Craig, gentleman
31 James Wilson, wholesale and retail spirit merchant, 27 Church lane
33 Robert Wilson, linen merchant, Linen hall
35 James M. Colville, clerk
37 Henry Kingsmill, clerk in Charley and Malcolm's, Donegall quay

34 Mrs Coleman, boarding house
32 Mary Clarke
30 Richard Creeth, commission merchant, Waring street
28 Misses Elizabeth and May Stitt, day school
26 James Anderson, portrait painter
24 Mrs Charles Stewart
Catherine street north.]
22 David Porter, Borough accountant
20 James Sempill, boarding house
18 Mrs Margt. Edgar, boarding house
16 John M'Dowell, wholesale grocer, Victoria street
14 James Agnew, timber merchant, Chichester street
12 Mrs Porter, boarding house
10 Thomas Armour, cashier at John M'Kenzie and Co.'s, Barrack st.
8 John M'Kenzie, clerk in Northern Bank
8¼ John Adams, jeweller, in Mr Gilbert's, High street
6½ Catherine Dunlop, spirit dealer
Grace street.]
6 Borrowes Lucas, perfumer
4 Miss Susanna M'Cormack
2 Mrs Moore

Hammond's Court
CORN MARKET.

Thomas Kane, fruiterer
1 William Annesley, green grocer and fruiterer
3 William Andrews, victualler
5 Edward Colgan, butcher
7 Bernard Meenan, spirit dealer
10 Hugh Dickson and Robt. M'Gredy, fruiterers
8 William Annesley, fruiterer
6 Robert Walls, cheesemonger
4 Richard Thompson, spirit dealer
2 Thomas Kane, fruiterer
Back entrance to Mr Downing's spirit store
Side entrance to John Colgan's, butcher

Hanna's Court
Francis Hanna, spirit dealer
Twelve small houses

Hanna's Lane
PETER'S HILL.
Twenty small houses

Harmony Place
OLD DUBLIN ROAD.
4 Matthew Kennedy, spirit dealer
5 Margaret Kane, in factory
" Robert Higgins, in factory
6 Samuel Fleming, shoemaker
7 Elizabeth Smith
8 Rachael Houston
9 Rebecca M'Neilly, dressmaker
10 Miss Hopkirk, schoolmistress
11 John Stewart, carpenter
12 John Booth, gentleman
13 Nathaniel Wood, draper
14 Alexander Hill, gentleman
15 James Frith, engineer
16 Miss Robinson, dressmaker
Robert Hamill, grocer
Margaret Crawford
John M'Lean, weaver

Harper's Court
OFF CURTIS STREET.
Eight small houses

Henrietta's Court
OFF BOUNDARY STREET.
Nine small houses

Henrietta Street
FROM CROMAC ST. TO JOY ST.
John Jones, grocer and spirit dealer, 47 Cromac street
1 Catherine Robinson
" Catherine Brown, dress maker
3 David Gilmour, designer
5 Eliza M'Clune
[*Grace street.*
7 Moses Brown, dealer
9 Ann Johnston, bonnet maker
11 George Wright, chandler
13 James Luckie, tailor
[*Catherine street North.*
15 Mary Davidson
17 Francis M'Kay, carpenter
19 William Dempster, carpenter
21 John Gribben, carpenter
23 Bridget M'Garry, dealer
25 John Smyth, car driver
[*Joy street.*]
30 Anna Kirker, dress maker
" Sarah Magrath, nurse tender
28 James Smyth, linen lapper
26 Mary Martin, dress maker
24 James Sullivan, clerk
22 Thomas Legg, tailor

STREET DIRECTORY.

20 William Reynolds, carpenter
18 William Irvine, porter
16 George Woods, foreman of a grain store
14 John Welsh, tailor
12 George Campbell, butcher
10 David Kennedy, grocer and spirit dealer
Catherine street.]
8 Samuel Taggart, grocer and spirit dealer
6 Thomas Burns, horse dealer
4 William Watson, builder
2 Mary M'Neill, straw bonnet maker

Henry Square
OFF GREEN STREET.

Sixteen small houses

Henry Street
FROM CORPORATION ST. TO NORTH QUEEN STREET.

1 Gustavus Heyn's residence
3 Gustavus Heyn's office, Prussian Consulate, Consulate for Holland, Ottoman Consulate, Spanish Consul, Consulate for Russia, Consulate for Hamburg, Consulate for Greece, and Consulate for the Two Sicilies; ship broker and general merchant
Gustavus Heyn's stores
5 James Bodel, provision merchant; residence, 14 Henry street
7 Charles Barnett's general stores and office
9 John Campbell, provision merchant; and 8½ Great George's street; residence, Donegall square west
11 Charles Barnett, general merchant
[*Nelson street.*
11 David Grainger, ship owner and general merchant, residence
13 John Dunn, ship owner and general merchant, residence
15 John Dunn's office and stores
Hugh M'Cormick, jeweller
Thomas Tilly, master mariner
15½ James Surplus, grocer and spirit dealer
[*Little York street.*
17 Henry Brown's pawn office
" Henry Brown, pawnbroker

19 Stores of Richardson, Brothers
....[*Here York street intersects.*]....
The York street flax spinning mills and offices; A. Mulholland's residence, Springvale, co. Down; John Mulholland's residence, Craigavad
[*North Queen street.*]
52 James Barber, spirit dealer
Eight small houses
John M'Call, grocer
Seven small houses
42 John Mitton, grocer
Waste ground.
40 Wm Galt, schoolmaster
38 Robert Patrick, pawnbroker
Southwell street.]
36 to 32 Three small houses
30 Letitia Young, grocer and spirit dealer
Molyneaux street.]
Two small houses
William's row.]
24 Arthur Purse, builder, and grocer and spirit dealer
...[*Here York street intersects.*]...
Richard Warren's provision store
Little York street.]
24 Wm. H. Owen, pawnbroker; also, agent for Hill Hamilton, Hill st.
22 William Kennedy, book keeper
20 John Moreland, grocer
Little Berry street.]
20 Miss Young, dressmaker
18 Samuel Walker, house agent, in Hill Hamilton's office, Hill st.
16 Margaret Potts, grocer and spirit dealer
14 James Bodel, general merchant
12 Ralph Green, grocer, Waring street
10 Archd. M'Neilage, captain *Prince of Wales* steamer
8 Mrs. Reid, boarding house
Nelson street.]
Enclosed ground
Stores of Richardson, Brothers, & Co.
6 Vacant
4 J. Faren, of Richardson, Brothers, & Co.

Hercules Place
CASTLE PLACE TO HERCULES STREET.

1, 3 R. T. M'Geagh & Co., woollen and fancy warehouse, drapers and

haberdashers; R. T. M'Geagh's residence, 3 Franklin place
5 Mary Ryans, milliner
7 Alexander Harkin, surgeon and apothecary
9 Miss Maloney, milliner and haberdasher
11 Sarah M'Cormick, dressmaker and baby linen warehouse
13 George Flannigan, picture frame maker and butcher
15 Owen Murray, master tailor
17 Mrs Rose Rice, confectioner
17½ Mrs Hoy, leech importer
19 Hugh Campbell, butcher
21 Mary Ann Montgomery, bonnet maker
23, 25 Joseph Patterson, picture frame manufacturer
25 Edward Lord, manager of Mr M'Cracken's mill
" Miss M. Lord, milliner
27 Miss S. Russell, straw bonnet maker
29 Francis Campbell, clothes dealer
31 James Whisker, butcher
[*Rosemary street.*

Berry Street.]
10 Peter Harkin, clothes dealer
8 Stewart and Cleery, butchers
6 John Bodel, carver and gilder
[*Boyd's court.*
4 Patrick Campbell, clothier
2 Robert James Tennent, M.P.

Hercules Street
FROM HERCULES PLACE TO NORTH STREET.

1 James Close, butcher
3 John Magee, butcher
5 James Morrell, butcher
7 Arthur Hamill, butcher
11 Wm. Watson, wholesale clothier; also, 21 Merchants quay, Dublin; 6 Phil's Building, Houndsditch, London; and 56 Bridgegate street, Glasgow
11 Rose Morrell, butcher
13 James Davy, butcher
15 John Murdock, corkcutter
15¼ Patrick Branagh, butcher
17 David Branagh, butcher
19 Charles Davy, butcher
21 John M'Areavy, butcher
23 James Cooney, butcher
25 Mary Garrett, butcher
27 (Yard James Canning, baker)
29 Vacant
31 James Dugan, butcher
33 John Rice, butcher
37 William Stokesberry, butcher
39 Samuel Shaw, butcher
41 William Davy, butcher
45 James Boston, butcher
47 Thomas Parker, butcher
49 Mary Britton, butcher
51 John M'Sorley, butcher
53 John Burke, butcher and feather dealer [*Round entry.*
55 John Drain, butcher
57 James Burns, butcher
59 Henry Moore, butcher & poulterer
61 John Hennessy, butcher
63 (Yard Thos. Quin, passenger agent)
65 Vacant
67 John Mercer, butcher
69 James Burke, butcher
71 Patrick M'Anally, butcher
73 John M'Mahon, butcher
75 Andrew Morrell, butcher
77 Vacant
79 John Davy, butcher
81 Charles Stokesberry, butcher
83 Hugh Moore, butcher
83½ Simon M'Anally, butcher
85 James Rice, butcher
87 John Davy, butcher
89 Denis Toley, butcher
James Evans, spirit dealer, corner of North street and Hercules st.
[*North street.*]
Adam Duncan, spirit dealer, corner of North street and Hercules st.
86 John Milford, dwelling house
84½ John White, spirit dealer
84 Mackenzie, Shaw, & Co.'s brewery
82 Tate and Bell, soap and candle manufacturers
80 Daniel Shearon, butcher
78 Henry Broe, sawmaker
76 James Roney, butcher
74 Arthur Davy, butcher
72 James Ramsay, butcher
70 Owen O'Hara, foreman baker
68 (Yard, Daniel M'Cann)
66 Thomas Miller, butcher
64 John Gordon, butcher
62 Vacant
Fulton's entry.]
60, 58 Vacant

56 Charles Franklin, butcher
54 John M'Manus, spirit dealer
52 Esther Agnew, grocer
Torrens' market.]
50 John Giles, spirit dealer
48 Thomas Grimes, butcher
46 Vacant
44 Patrick Brannigan, butcher
42 Francis M'Entee, grocer
Torrens's row.]
40 Davidson & Co., grocers and spirit dealers
38 John Morrell, butcher
36 Vacant (yard)
34 David Ferguson, butcher
32 Jane Magee, grocer
30 (Gateway, John Magee)
28 Patrick M'Cann, butcher
26 William Armstrong, green grocer
Law's court.]
24 John Branagh, butcher
22 Thomas Boylan, butcher
20 David Keys, butcher
16 George Scott, butcher
16 Ann Rice, butcher
M'Coubry's entry.]
14 Edward M'Menamy, spirit dealer
12, 10 James Canning, baker
8 William Anderson, grocer
John's court.]
6 Mary Ann Pritchard, lodginghouse keeper
4 William Hamilton, cork manufacturer
2 Peter M'Gouran, spirit dealer

Herdman's Buildings
SHANKHILL ROAD.
Hugh Watson, labourer
Vacant
Edward Greig, shopman in John Arnott and Co.'s, Bridge street
Thomas Jacobs, officer of inland revenue
Samuel Armstrong, ditto
John Wallace, sawyer
Henry Atkinson, brass moulder
James A. Dobbie, draper in J. Young's, Donegall street
John Morrison, clerk
John Boyd, moulder
Henry Taylor, clerk
John Teale, blacksmith
Union Tavern—John N. Hemsley, proprietor
Five small houses in rere

High Street
CASTLE PLACE TO QUEEN'S SQUARE.
1 William M'Comb, bookseller and publisher; and registrar of marriages in Belfast district; residence, 3 Clarence place
3 Forster Green and Co., (Golden Canister tea house) tea and coffee dealers and grocers; residence, 11 Albion place
5 Charles M'Donnell, tobacconist; residence, 1 May street
7 James Wilson, watchmaker and jeweller; residence, 10 Frederick street
" William Crawford, tailor
7½ Glasgow Hotel — Robert Scott, proprietor [*Hodgson's entry.*
9 John Hodgson, bookseller, printseller, stationer, and roompaper warehouse; residence, Holywood
11 Alexander Maguire, old-established boot and shoe warehouse
 [*Quin's entry.*
13 Edward Gribben, watchmaker, jeweller, &c.
15 Wm. Gilbert and Son, silversmiths, jewellers, and watchmakers, wholesale and retail; residence, 36 Upper Arthur street
17 Alex. Munce, tailor and clothier
 [*Crown entry*
19 Greenfield and Harris, haberdashers, hosiers, &c.; residence of Mr Greenfield, 111 York st.; Mr Harris', 89 Joy street
21 Haslett and Frazer, woollen, hat, and Manchester warehouse; residence of Mr Haslett, Anchor Lodge; Mr Frazer's, 17 Hamilton street
23 Neill, Brothers, watch and chronometer makers; jewellers, silversmiths, and opticians
25 Hudson and Co., tea and coffee merchants and general grocers
 [*Wilson's court.*
27, 29 Edward and George Pim, tea dealers, wine importers and general grocers; residences, Ewd. Pim, Royal terrace; Geo. Pim, University square
31 Henry Greer, bookseller, stationer and fancy warehouse
 [*Joy's entry.*
33 Thomas Wheeler, surgeon and apothecary

35, 37 Thomas Hardy, draper, haberdasher, hosier, and silk mercer
39 Mrs Mary Ogston, confectioner
41 Thomas M'Cann, Irish woollen warehouse
43 Edward Gilbert, watchmaker, jeweller, and silversmith
45 John Arnold, (Heimatemporion) woollen draper, clothier, and hatter; residence, Glengall place
49 John Wallace, watchmaker, jeweller, and silversmith
[*Pottinger's entry*
51 George Harrison, bookbinder, stationer, &c.; residence, Holywood
53 Charles Howden, seedsman, nurseryman, florist; residence and nursery, Malone
55 Wm. Trimble, boot and shoe warehouse
[*Hamilton's court*
57 Lee and Son, jewellers to the Queen; watchmakers, silversmiths, and opticians
59 Musgrave, Brothers, ironmongers; residence, 1 Donegall Square South
61 M. Levy & Co., tailors, drapers, clothiers, and hatters
63 James M'Cullough, grocer, tea, and coffee dealer; residence, 36 Nelson street
65 Francis M'Laughlin, tobacco manufacturer and grocer; residence, 2 Donegall Square South
67 John M'Kibbin & Co., engravers and lithographers
67 William Marshall & Co., druggists, apothecaries, and wholesale perfumers; residence, Carrickfergus
69 John and Joseph M'Kee, wholesale and retail grocers and wine merchants
71 Vacant
73 Charles Kelso, hosier
[*Church lane.*
75 Hamilton & M'Cullough, clothiers
ST. GEORGE'S CHURCH
.. [*Here Victoria street intersects.*] ..
[The remaining portion of this street, from the Royal Arch to the quay, is now called Queen's Square]
Wm. Spackman (corner of Victoria street and High street), tailor, draper, and hatter

114 Henry Robinson, chemist and druggist
Stonecutter's entry.]
112 James M'Kee, pawnbroker
110 James and William Greig, cut glass, china, and delf warehouse
108 John Wilkinson, earthenware manufacturer, china and glass warehouse
106 James Blake, boot and shoemaker
104 Francis Glenfield, soap and candle manufacturer
102 Thomas Keenan, rope manufacturer; residence, Lodge Road
100 William Marshall & Co. (Belfast Medical Hall), surgeons, apothecaries, wholesale and retail druggists; residence, Carrickfergus
98 Dr. Samuel Bryson, surgeon
96 Eliza Davis, umbrella, parasol, bonnet, and haberdashery establishment
Skipper street.]
92 James Byrne, boot and shoemaker
90½ William Gibson, boot and shoemaker
88 William Palmer, boot and shoemaker
86 Kennedy Stewart, boot and shoemaker
84 Wm. Bailie, boot and shoemaker
82 Samuel Bullick's academy
Bullock's entry.]
80 Dr. Joseph Stevenson Mulholland, surgeon
78 John Neill, gun maker, fishing tackle warehouse, and bird preserver
76 John Greenfield, wholesale and retail hosiery, haberdashery, and woollen warehouse; residence, Jackson Hall, Holywood
74 James Keegan, tea, wine, and spirit merchant; residence, 4 College square east
72 Hugh Currie, ironmongery and hardware merchant
70 James Wilson, printer and publisher; residence, 10 Frederick street
" William Sinclair, linen lapper
" James Rutherford, room paper manufacturer
68 William Killen, woollen draper, clothier, and hatter; residence, 3 Victoria terrace

STREET DIRECTORY.

66 Patrick M'Guirk, goldsmith, jeweller, and bog oak ornament manufacturer
64 James Chapman, chronometer, watch and clockmaker
62 Catherine Ashenhurst, ready made linen warehouse
60 John and Robert Knox, boot and shoemakers
56 James Harkness, cut glass, china and delf warehouse
Sugarhouse entry]
54 Riddel and Co., ironmongers and hardware merchants; residence Vermont
52 John Riddel, wholesale ironmonger; residence, Vermont
50 John and James Dysart, provincial boot and shoe house; residence, 71 North street
48, 46 John G. M'Gee & Co., (Pantechnetheca) tailors, clothiers, and general outfitters; woollendrapery, and London hat warehouse; residence, Sussex place
44 James Girdwood, carpet, damask, and room paper warehouse; residence, No. 6 Donegall Square West
Bridge street.]
40 Robert and D. J. Patterson, wholesale and retail hardware and house furnishing ironmongery warehouse; residence, 3 College square north
38 Nathaniel Ferguson, woollendraper; residence, 6 Arthur street
36 Mackenzie and Saunders, drapers, silk mercers, and haberdashers; residence, 4 Abbotsford place
34 Alexander Mayne, printer and publisher (late J. Smyth's)
"James Dillon, hat manufacturer
32 Thomas Wilson & Co., hosiery and trimming warehouse
Orr's entry.]
30, 28 Ross, O'Connor, & Co., Ballymacarrett flint glass manufactory warehouse; residence, Holywood; Mr O'Connor, Mount Pottinger
26 Close, Brothers, woollendrapers
Graham's entry.]
24 John Dunlop, boot and shoemaker

22 Robert Boag, Albion Cloth Company; residence, The Cresent
Winecellar entry.]
20 George Moore, family boot and shoe warehouse
18 Henry Murney, East India tea warehouse, and tobacco and snuff manufactory
16, 14 William Gilmore, grocer, tea, wine, fruit, and spirit merchant
12 *Commercial Journal and Family Herald* office, and reading room
10 Mrs Nicholl, gunsmith, fishing tackle warehouse, and bird preserver
Caddell's entry.]
8 James D. Marshall, M.D., apothecary and druggist, Chemist in Ordinary to her Majesty; residence, Holywood
4 William Coffey, music shop; warerooms, 25 Donegall place
2 S. Farrell & Co., nurserymen, seedmen, and florists; nursery, Ballycloughan

Hill Street
FROM WARING ST. TO ROBERT ST.

1, 3 Jane and Eliza Finlay, straw bonnet and millinery establishment
3½ Charles Duffin & Co.'s stores
5 James M'Clure, provision dealer
7 Wm. Cunningham, coach trimmer
9 James Cairnes, porter
11 Thomas Shannon, porter
13 Michl. M'Gennity, provision dealer
15 Isaac Arnott's provision stores
15½ John Henderson, provision dealer
17 Wm. Hodgkinson, provision dealer and hackle maker
19 Alexander Smith, manufacturer
21 Samuel Bradley, provision dealer
23, 25 Hill Hamilton's rent office; residence, Seaview
25 Fortune & Co., plumbers and lead merchants
27 Vacant
29 Samuel Bradley's provision dealer
31 John Hutton, storeman
33 Samuel Cochrane, spirit dealer
[*Gordon street.*
35 Frederick Cowan, master tailor
37 Patrick O'Prey, sawyer
39 John Carlisle, boot closer
41 George Duffin, car driver

43 John Lemon, carpenter
  [*Vinegar court.*
45 Nancy Madden, huckster
  [*Morrow's entry*
47 Arthur Maguire, porter
49 Wm. Rainey, cooper
51 Henry Fegan, boot and shoemaker
53 James M'Cann, brass founder
55 Daniel Weir, tailor and huckster
57 Mary Mitchell, spirit dealer
42 James Thompson, grocer and spirit dealer
40 Francis Campbell, grocer and spirit dealer
38, 36 Hugh M'Call, pawn office
34 Wm. Larmour, (yard)
32½ William Sloan, carter
32, 30 Jas. & Wm. Steen, merchants
28 James Maginnis, porter
26 Wm. Henderson, grocer and carpenter
22 Hugh M'Clelland, yarn and flax merchant
20 Samuel M'Donnell, spirit dealer
18 John Bryson, confectioner
  [*Commercial court*
16 J. T. Kennedy's back entrance to stores
  [*Elliott's court.*
12 Sinclair Ramsay, haberdashery and trimming warehouse
10 Robert Atkinson, commission merchant, general agent, and broker; residence, Holywood
8 William Bryson's (yard)
6 James Maguire, provision dealer
4½ Vacant
4 Bridget Harkin, spirit dealer
2 Margaret Walker

Holmes' Court
OFF VERNER STREET.
Four small houses

Hopes Court
OFF MILLFIELD.
Fourteen small houses

Hope Street
BREDALBANE PLACE
1 Robert Simpson, clerk in Ulster Railway office
2 John Clifford, excise officer
3 Henry Arthur, gentleman

Hopeton Place
OFF SHANKHILL ROAD.
Back entrance to William Bunting's spirit shop
1 Robert Smyth, pensioner
2 Charles Leinster, iron moulder
3 Daniel M'Vey, smith
4 William Pearce, warper
5 Mary Ellison, machine winder
6 John Young, bricklayer
  Eleanor Anderson, widow
  Joseph Hayes, mechanic
  James Connor, gardener
  John Rafferty, smith

Messrs Wallace and Campbell's brickfields
Damask Factory—James Blain, and Co., proprietors; James Blain's residence, Albert place, Donegall pass; John Blain, sen.'s residence, Hopeton place

Houston's Lane
OFF SEYMOUR STREET.
Three small houses

Howard Street
DONEGALL SQUARE SOUTH TO FISHERWICK PLACE.
1 William Carson, wholesale wine merchant and grocer; 14 Corn market
3 Wm. M'Caw, gentleman
5 Geo. C. Hyndman, auctioneer; Castle place
7 Richard Hull, of Hull, Hart & Co., flax spinners, Falls road
9 Dr Frings, professor Queen's Col.
11 George Dundas, gentleman
  [*Upper Queen street.*
13 Rev. James Morgan, D.D.
Side of Fisherwick place Presbyterian Church
COURT HOUSE AND OLD HOUSE OF CORRECTION
College station Dispensary
Brunswick street.]
16 Reuben Simms, poor law auditor
" James Simms, proprietor and editor of *Mercury*
14 Dr J. Ferguson, professor Queen's College
12 Clotworthy Dobbin, brewer; Smithfield

10 William Murphy, of Murphy and Grimshaw, flax spinners; Linfield
8 James Young, collegiate school
6 Charles Peyton, gentleman
4 Wm. Boyd, Vitriol works, Lagan village
2 Wm. D. Henderson, merchant; 42 Waring street

Howard Street North
BETWEEN FALLS ROAD AND SHANKHILL ROAD.
John Stevenson, grocer
Five small houses

Howard Street South
OFF CROMAC ROAD.
Twenty small houses

Hudson's Court
OFF HUDSON'S ENTRY.
Six small houses

Hudson's Entry
OFF NORTH STREET.
4 James M'Kinney, last maker
8 John Jordan, tobacco spinner
10 William Scott, carpenter
12 Robert Best, tobacco spinner
41 Wm M'Dowell, shoemaker
45 Owen M'Sally, boot and shoemaker
56 James Gallagher, boot and shoemaker
58 James Curran, boot and shoemaker
53 Kirkwood Hayney, boot and shoemaker
Forty-one small houses besides

Hunter's Row
NEW LODGE ROAD.
Eleven small houses

Hutchison Street
OFF STANLEY STREET.
Henry Laverty's hall door
Two houses building
1 Francis Patterson, car driver
3 Robert M'Conkey, mechanic
4 Joseph Forsythe, porter
2 Rich. M'Clelland, railway labourer

Improvement Place
LANCASTER STREET.
Two small houses

Institution Place
OFF LETTUCE HILL.
46 Hugh M'Lorinan, grocer and spirit dealer
2 Thomas Welsh, grocer
Thirty-nine small houses

Jacobson's Court
OFF MILL ST.
Nine small houses

James Court
OFF CARRICK HILL.
Nine small houses

James' Place
NELSON ST.
1 Captain James Adams
2 James Davidson, compositor
3 James M'Kee, designer
4 William Barnett

James's Street South
OFF HOWARD STREET.
1 Mrs Amelia Dalton
3 Thomas Russell, writing clerk
5 John Kelly, writing clerk
" D. Holland, editor *Northern Whig*
10 William Allen, civil engineer
8 George Russell, officer of inland revenue
6 Mrs Margaret Calwell
4 Thomas Kirkwood, plasterer
2 Rev. James Glasgow, Presbyterian Minister

Johnny's Entry
TALBOT STREET.
Ten small houses

Johnston's Buildings
SHANKHILL ROAD.
1 Sarah M'Cullough, boarding house
2 William Thomas, toll collector, in butter market
3 Thomas M'Clenaghan
4 Wm. John Barnett, writing clerk
5 Wm. Littlejohn, stereotype founder
6 John A. Dupree, writing clerk
7 John Patrick
8 Charles Lang, first clerk, Inland Revenue office
9 James Wallace, brick manufacturer
10 Robert M'Millan, spirit merchant, Victoria place

11 James M'Cormick, woollendraper; Victoria street.
12 John Kavanagh, writing clerk
13 Thomas Kean, post office clerk

Johnston's Court
OFF GREAT EDWARD STREET.

1 Butter store—Mr Frazer, proprietor
2 Patrick Quinn, carpenter
3 James Mawhinney, coachmaker
4 Wm. Davis, labourer
5 Wm. Stavely, cheesemonger
6 John Black, car driver
7 David Nevin, car driver
8 Patrick Reid, coachmaker
9 Richard Magee, ærated water manufacturer

Johnston's Court
OFF MILLFIELD.

Fourteen small houses

John street
DONEGALL STREET TO NORTH STREET.

1 Paul Henry Mahir, confectioner
3 Matthew Dickson, jeweller
5 Wm M'Ilrea, calico printer
7 Charles Collins, painter and glazier
9 Richard Carroll, shoemaker
11 Mary O'Neill, lodging house keeper
" Bernard Caulfield, tailor
13 Thomas Gribben, painter, glazier, and confectioner
15 John Timbey, shoemaker
17 William John Shaw, watch and clockmaker
19 John M'Garry, spirit dealer
[*Little Donegall st. and Mustard st.*
21 Edward Fegan, spirit dealer
23 Joseph M'Connell, grocer
25 Elizabeth Wilson, boarding house
25¼ Thomas Irvine, spirit store
27 Wm. Bloomfield, tinplate worker
29 Hugh Smith, carrier
31 John Kennnedy, car driver and huckster
[*Kent street.*
33 James Campbell, hairdresser
35 William Boucher, porter
37 Peter Pelling and Co., weaving commission agents; residence, 3 College street
" Alexander Riddel, reed maker; residence, 3 Ship street

37 William Harrison, sewed muslin manufacturer; residence, 11 Hamilton street
" James H. Young & Co., Glasgow, muslin manufacturers — agent, John Jamieson; residence, 2 Reilly's place
" Charles Tennant and Co., of St. Rollox Chemical works, Glasgow, manufacturing chemists, and general merchants
T. and D. Wilson, sewed muslin manufacturers — Jas Adamson, agent

39 John Brown, boot and shoemaker
41 Edw. Bloomfield, tinplate worker
43 William John Taylor, butcher, house painter, &c.
45 William Ritchie, carpenter, haberdasher, milliner, and bonnet maker
47 Joseph Luke, lodgings
49 William Mathews, hairdresser
51 Daniel M'Cann, car owner and spirit dealer
53 John Campbell, labourer
55 William M'Mahon, butcher, North street
56 Arthur Murphy, spirit dealer
54 James Porter, day constable
52 Charles M'Alespie, stokerer and plasterer
50 Hugh Farrell, lodging and eating house
48 Sarah Lyness, lodging and eating house
46 Hugh M'Alister, baker
44 Joseph Bigger, provision merchant; residence, 88 Donegall street
42 Patrick Douris, labourer and eating house keeper
40 Thomas Jefferson, starch maker and eating house keeper
38 John M'Alarry, labourer and eating house keeper
36 Mrs Dorothea Cannavan, spirit dealer and victualling house
34 William Cook, spirit dealer
32 Thomas M'Mahon, butcher
" Robert Brown, spirit dealer
30 John Doody, boot and shoemaker
28 John Fitzpatrick, huckster and eating house keeper
26 John Devlin, writing clerk
24 John M'Auley, musician

STREET DIRECTORY. 121

22 Henry M'Connell, butcher
William street.]
20 Henry Loughran, grocer and spirit dealer
18 Robert Dugan, soap and candle manufacturer
16 James Magee, grocer
14 Jas. Stewart, painter and grocer
12 John Dyer, haberdasher
10 Hugh Dyer, grocer and provision dealer
8 Hugh Dunn, leather cutter
6, 4, 2 Bernard Fitzpatrick, grocer and spirit dealer

Joy's Court
JOY'S ENTRY.

Richard and Joseph Purkis, hacklemakers
James Rodgers, whitesmith

Joy's Entry
OFF HIGH STREET.

1 Henry Greer's residence
3 John Magee's oyster house
9 Wm. Hall, lithographic writer and printer
James Black, spirit dealer
21 Thomas M'Connell, ship carpenter
Twenty-one small houses

Joy's Place
DUBLIN BRIDGE.

8 Denis Joiner, labourer
9 Andrew Cochrane, pensioner
10 Miss M'Credie, boarding house
11 Thomas Henry, compositor

Joy Street
MONTGOMERY ST. TO OLD PAPER MILL

1 Mrs M'Gowan, boarding house
3 Miss Margaret Boyd, milliner
..[*Little May street intersects.*]..
5 Rev. John Oliver, Wesleyan minister, Donegall Square East
7 Robert Donnelly, confectioner &c.;
9 William Mearns, sea captain
[*Sussex place.*
11 Miss I. M'Adam, boarding house
" John Mullan, bookseller
13 Mrs Julia Ann Fetherstonaugh
15 Mrs Crawford
" William John Crawford, Northern Bank
17 Mrs Eliza Russell, boarding house
" Samuel Black, solicitor

19 Mrs Mary Service, boarding house
21 Miss Elizabeth Allen, dressmaker
23 Alexander Smith, builder
25 Miss Letitia Martin, boarding house
27 John Ross, builder
29 John Scott, boarding house
31 Eleanor Dalzell, dressmaker
33 William Ewing, gentleman
35 Wm. M'Millin, cabinet maker
37 Mrs Jane M'Kelvey
39 William M'Coyd, book keeper
41 Robert Wallace, tailor
43 D. Walls, salesman & book keeper
45 Mrs Sarah Palliser, boarding house
47 Henry Reid, salesman, Mr. Riddel's, High street
49 James Maguire, linen merchant
51 Mrs M. A. Davison, boarding house
53 James Oldrin, tailor
55 Charles Swan, salesman
57 James Ross, clerk
59 Robert Nesbitt, superintendant in Arnott & Co.'s, Bridge street
61 William M'Cullough, book keeper
63 Robert Taylor, carpenter
65 Mrs Helen Craig
67 Thomas Carroll, salesman
69 Francis Bunting, foreman tailor
71 Mrs Mary Morgan, dressmaker
73 Henry Mulholland, linen buyer for Richardson Sons and Owden
75 Mrs Ann Jane Dickson
77 John Rose, muslin manufacturer
79 Joseph M'Creedy, clerk
81 John Salters, clerk in Linen hall
83 Arthur Hennan, linen lapper
85 James Hamilton, carpenter and builder
87 Hamilton M'Cay, book keeper
89 Henry Harris, of Greenfield and Harris
91 James Stevelly, commercial agent
93 Mrs Isabella M'Caw
95 Robinson Ireland, clerk
97 John Atkinson, book keeper
99 John Ladley, attorney, Calendar st.
101 Alexander Chambers, builder
[*Old Paper mill.*]
92 John Conland, commission merchant
90 Edward Gibson, draper
88 Edward Gilmore, provision merchant
86 Mrs Mary Gaffikin
84 Mrs Mary Boyce, boarding house

L

82 Martin Downey, excise officer
80 John Beattie, gentleman
78 Bankhead Boyd, builder
76 Alexander Wilson, toy and basket warehouse, 8 Bridge street
74 William Jones, tailor
72 George Mansfield, clerk
70 William Wilson, builder
68 Thomas M'Cann, clerk
66 William Scott, linen lapper
64 Alexander M'Vicker, foreman boot and shoemaker
62 Robert Gray, shopkeeper, Donegall street
60 James Anderson, carpenter and builder
58 James Nesbitt, book keeper
56 William Taylor, builder
54 Mrs Jane Coey
52 Patrick Ellis, commercial traveller
50 Miss E. Phœnix, dressmaker
48 Mrs R. A. Gorman, boarding house
46 John Moore, reporter, *Mercury*
44 Mary Curry, shopwoman, and Jane M'Donnell, shirtmaker
42 Thomas Johnston, bricklayer
Henrietta street.]
40 John Smith, car driver and shop
38 James Bagnell, clerk [keeper
36 Richard Purkis, hackle maker
34 Saml. M'Cutcheon, fancy box maker
32 John Russell, commercial traveller
30 Samuel Haig, foreman bookbinder
Russell street.]
28 M. A. Sutherland, & Co., Alabaster and cement manufacturers
26 D. G. Sutherland, publisher and bookseller
24 Mrs Elizabeth Tannahill, boarding house
22 Miss Dorcas Johnston, dressmaker
20 Richard Carroll, clerk
" John Carroll, professor of music
Hamilton street.]
18 Miss Catherine Lawther, milliner and dressmaker
16 Maria Wetherhead, boarding-house
14 David Duff, Northern Bank
12 John Adam White, book keeper
10 Miss Henrietta Green
8 Mrs Harriet Crawford
6 John Abbott, clerk
Little May street.]
4½ Archibald Simpson, coachmaker
4 Mrs Mary Orr, lodging house

4 Misses Orr, milliners & dressmakers
" Henderson Orr, writing clerk
2¼ Alexander Grant, draper
2 Miss E. Patterson, dress-maker
" William Savage, cloth lapper

Keenan's Court
OFF MILLFIELD.
Four small houses

Kennedy's Court
OFF NORTH STREET.
Eight small houses

Kennedy's Entry
DEVIS STREET.
1 Ann O'Neill
3 Patrick Collins, labourer
5 Ann Duggan
7 Michael M'Quiggan, labourer
12 Catherine Devlin
10 Daniel Ward, bricklayer
8 Joseph Heale, weaver
6 Margaret Loughran
4 Michael Brannigan, labourer
2 George Mann, carpenter

Kennedy's Place
SHANKHILL ROAD.
1 Sophia Stewart, lodging house
2 Hugh Ward, weaver
3 Thomas Kerr, weaver
4 John Haslett, manager of Mr. W. Hick's factory, Francis street
5 James Watson, miller
6 David Corbitt, labourer
7 Mrs Kennedy, huckster
8 Wm. Walker, spirit dealer
9 Thomas Taylor, warper
10 James Brown, house agent
11 Wm. Kirk, mechanic
12 Robert Wardlow, travelling clerk
13 David Nelson, tobacco spinner
14 Wm. Ross, tobacco spinner
15 James Graham, clerk
16 Wm. Watters, rent agent
17 Thomas Scott, clerk
18 Jane Armstrong
19 Arch. Simmington, cabinet maker
20 James Morton's English and mercantile school

Kennedy's Row
OFF SMITHFIELD.
1 Robert Mulryan, auctioneer
3 Edward Kelly, auctioneer

5 Henry Macartney, fish dealer
7 Francis M'Connell, dealer
9 Bernard Monaghan, dealer
11 Arthur Halfpenny, grocer
[*Miller's lane.*
20 Mary Killian, old clothes dealer
18 James Ward, shoemaker
There are eight other small houses occupied by small dealers

Kent Street, Lower
JOHN STREET TO UNION STREET.
6 Francis M'Donald, flax dealer
4 John Stewart and Co., (Kent St. Factory) muslin manufacturers; John Stewart's residence, Silver Stream
25 Saml. Russell, forge bellows-maker
7 John and Jas. M'Connell, muslin manufacturers; residence, 95 Donegall street
Twenty-two small houses

Kent Street, Upper
UNION STREET TO CARRICKHILL.
Wm. M'Canter's, flour store; shop and residence, 23 Carrickhill
8 Robert and Jacob Bell's size works
4 Rodger Lynch, cooper
Twenty-nine small houses
Four small houses not tenanted

Killen Street
OFF COLLEGE STREET.
1 John Beatty, tobacco spinner
3 William Thompson, painter
[*Institution place.*
5 Hugh O'Neill, labourer
7 John Connor, weaver
[*Hamill street.*
6 Richard Christian, night constable and shoemaker
4 Archibald M'Collum, weighbridge keeper, Smithfield
2 Robert Thompson, weaving master
Martin and Hamilton's starch yard; Samuel Martin's residence, 20 Little Donegall street; John Hamilton's residence, 42 Little Donegall street
John M'Cormack, printer
James Ferris, boot closer

King's Court
OFF LANCASTER STREET.
Thirteen small houses

King Street
MILL ST. TO COLLEGE SQUARE EAST.
1 Francis Neeson, spirit dealer
1½ Edward Moore, writing clerk
3 Mrs Mary Montgomery
5 Thomas Roberts, engraver
7 Alex. Mayne, hairdresser
9 James Hanna, apothecary's assistant [*King street court.*
11 Robert Dornan, grocer and spirit dealer
13 Mrs Mary Heron, boarding house
15 Mrs Jane Ainsworth, nurse tender
17 Mrs Sarah Malone
19 John Lowry, chronometer and watch manufacturer
21 Mrs Ellen Ward, of the firm of Marcus Ward & Co., stationers, bookbinders; 6 Corn market
23 Thomas M'Cammon, tanner and corn miller
25 Miss S. Roberts, ladies' seminary
" Richard Ross, M.D., surgeon
27 Mrs Davis
29 Belfast Savings' Bank, John Borthwick, actuary
[*King street Mews.*
33 James Paisley, classical, English, and mercantile seminary
35 Miss Grace Magill
37 Miss Frances Barkley
[*College square North.*
42 George C. Hyndman's timber yard
40 George Stevelly, shopman
38 Miss Mary Ann Magee
36 Mrs S. M'Cammon, dress maker
34 Joseph Scott, manager linen hall
32 Miss Sarah Magee, boarding house
30 William Charles Stancliff, officer of inland revenue
28 Miss Eliza Nettleton, dress maker
26 James Walsh, bricklayer
24 Miss Agnes Lemon, lodgings
22 Miss Alicia Morgan, milliner and dress maker
20 Robert Lynn, house carpenter
18 John Reynolds, boot and shoe maker
MORMONITE MEETING HOUSE
16 Alexander Wilson, town traveller
16 Mrs. Margaret Smith
" James Hanna, stone mason
14 Mrs Rose Ann Reilly, huckster
12 Isaac Goldstein, general dealer
" Mrs Mary Goldstein, dress maker

10 Jane Bradley,
" William Moore, brush maker
8 George F. Stevenson, professor of music
6 John Sinclair, carpenter
4½ John Toman, brass founder, gas fitter, &c.
4 Alexander Boucher, tailor
2 Henry Greer, bookbinder

King Street Court
OFF KING STREET.

1 James Gray, waiter in hotel
2 James M'Govern, labourer
3 Robert Owen, cabinet maker
4 Matthew Heron, upholsterer
5 William Ireland, boot and shoemaker

King Street North
BROWN STREET.

1 Mrs Mary Ann M'Cann, white worker
3 Andrew Edwards, weaver
5, 7 Valentine M'Gibbon, grocer and spirit dealer
[Abbey street.
9 James Smith, boot and shoemaker
11 Samuel Tedford, labourer
13 Patrick M'Quillan, grocer
[Gardiner's street.
16 Mrs Mary Ann Gorman
" James Thorpe, brushmaker
14 James Hare, damask weaver
[Gorman's court.
12 Thomas Stewart, bricklayer
10 Mrs Margaret Magill, millworker
8 Mary Ward, quilter
6 Charles O'Neill, bricklayer
4 William Sands, street sweeper
2 John M'Blain, weaver

Lagan Street
CROMAC STREET.

Thomas Kilmartin, spirit dealer
1 John Brown, tailor
3 John Turney
5 Henry Smyth, tailor
7 Richard Turney, spirit dealer
[Market street.
9 William Lindsay, grocer
11 Mrs M'Cormack
13 Robert Connelly, dealer
[Lagan court.
15 James and John M'Kenna, grocers and spirit dealers

17 Ann M'Gee
19 Michael Heeley, confectioner
20 John M'Connell, omnibus driver
18 Thomas Montgomery, painter
16 Francis Morgan
14 James Barker, shoemaker
12 James Smith
10 John M'Kee, labourer
8 Michael M'Poland, dealer
[Market street.
6, 4 James Clements, pawnbroker
2 Alexander Johnston, spirit dealer

Lagan Street, Upper
EAST END LAGAN ST.

21 Joseph Warnock, carpenter
23 John Johnston, turner
25 Hugh M'Greavy, waterman
27 John Freeman, shoemaker
29 Daniel Killen, car driver
31 Catherine Fenton
33 David Linn, car driver
35 Michael Burns, car driver
37 Charles Murphy, gardener
 Five houses building
 Six new houses, not tenanted
38 William Campbell, shoemaker
36 Cornelius Keenan, packer
34 James M'Grim, car driver
32 Joseph Robinson, sawyer
30 Gilbert Johnston, labourer
28 James Parkinson, labourer
26 Grace Jennings
24 Henry Carson, saddler
22 Henry Smith, shoemaker

Lancaster Street
YORK STREET TO NORTH QUEEN ST.

1 Robert Gibson, brass founder; 5 M'Clennaghan's court
3 Mrs Catherine Gibson
5 John Sloan, carpenter
[Portland street.
7 James Caldwell, pensioner
9 Lucius Crimble, precentor
11 James M'Neill, clothes renovator
13 Wm. M'Cormack cork cutter
15 Abel Hadskins, customhouse officer
17 James Wilson, grocer
[Thomas street.
19 Louisa Barlow, boarding house
21 Hugh Kerr, grocer
23 Charles O'Neill, carpenter
25 Elizabeth Cranston, spirit dealer
27 Charles M'Auley, weaving factory
 residence, 115 York street

29 David Orr, tailor
31 John Martin [*Union place.*
33 Wm. Benson,
35 David Gill, labourer
37 James Savage, cooper
39 John M'Garry, grocer & spirit dealer
    [*King's court.*
41 James Caruth, grocer and spirit dealer
43 Robert Shaw, bundler
45 Wm. Hodge, carman
47 Mary Ann Magee,
49 Alex. Allen, grocer and spirit dealer
51 Hugh Pake, spirit dealer
53 John Thompson, grocer
    [*Alexander street.*
55 Anthony Mullan, grocer and spirit
57 Eliza Devlin, dealer [dealer
59 Mary Hill, dealer
61 James Scott, weaver
63 Wm. Welsh, carpenter
65 Margaret M'Cann, dealer
   Side of Richd. Lavery's spirit store
34 Patrick Haggerty, pensioner
32 Mary Ann Cross
30 James Ritchie, shoemaker
28 Peter Hendron, car driver
26 —— Ellard, labourer
Alexander street.]
24 Eleanor Woods, grocer and spirit
22 Jane Cameron [dealer
20, 18 Isabella Young, pawnbroker
16 Henry Hughes, blacksmith
14 Neill Donnelly, labourer
12 Ellen M'Ilroy, dressmaker
10 Thomas Waugh, muslin manufacturer, 11 Church street
8 John M'Naughten, Constable Board
6 Eliza M'Gaghey [of Health
4 Lawrence May, pensioner
2 Thos. Dugan, boot and shoe maker
   Rere of Frederickst. General hospital

Law's Lane
OFF NORTH STREET
Twelve old houses, not tenanted

Leadbetter Place
OLD LODGE ROAD.
1 James Clendinning, grocer and spirit dealer
2 to 9 Seven small houses
10 Mary Ann Brown, dealer

Leeds Street
CULLINGTREE STREET.
1 Wm. Campbell, baker
3 John Milligan, shoemaker
5 John M'Briar, labourer
7 James Freeburn, labourer
9 Richard Moore, labourer
11 James Brakey, labourer
13 Joseph Patterson, labourer
15 Rebecca White
17 John Potts
19 John Poland, labourer
20 Alexander Rankin, sawyer
18 Jane Campbell, dealer
16 Nancy Rainey
14 Robert Sands, preparing master
12 James Richardson, butler
10 Samuel Moffat, carman
8 Arial Leaky, labourer
6 John Corry, hackler
4 James Kerns, porter
2 Thomas Mitchell, labourer

Legg's Lane
FROM HIGH ST. TO ROSEMARY ST.
Shell Fish Tavern—James Bradley, proprietor
Carter and Martin's tow stores
Side of Post Office—Money Order Office up stairs
10 Vacant
8 James Bradley's oyster house
6 Vacant
4 Edward Foley, spirit dealer
Side of Jas. Cochran's grocer shop

Lemon's Court
SMITHFIELD.
Ten small houses

Lemon's Lane
GREAT EDWARD STREET
1 Wiliam Rice, eating house
3 Samuel Melville, eating house
4 John O'Neill, corn dealer
6 Margaret Gillespie, spirit dealer

Letitia Street
OFF WILSON STREET, MILLFIELD.
1 John Gowdy, plasterer
3 Jacob M'Clenaghan, engineer
5 John Henderson, weaver
7 Thomas Perrie, butler
9 William Harrison, carpente
11 Richard Caughey, butcher

12 Samuel Beck, mechanic
10 Margaret Scott
8 Ellen Jamieson
6 Holmes Scott, plumber
4 James Carr, coach maker
2 James Coey, flax dresser

Lettuce Hill
BARRACK STREET.

50 Samuel Boyd, grocer and spirit dealer
44 John O'Neill, grocer
Sixty small houses

Lewis's Court
BROWN SQUARE.

Seven small houses

Liddy's Court
LITTLE DONEGALL STREET.

Four small houses

Lilliput
OLD CARRICKFERGUS ROAD.

George K. Kennedy, clerk Petty Sessions, and clerk Lord Donegall's office, Lilliput cottage
Thomas George, general merchant, Lilliput house

Lindsay's Place
CROMAC ROAD.

1 Mary Haggerty
3 James Ginn, lamplighter
5 James Murray, labourer
7 Magdalen Church daily Scriptural school, Wm. Black, teacher
9 Wm. Lynass, stokerer

Linen Hall
NORTH SIDE.

John S. Ferguson & Co., linen merchants; residence, 28 Donegall place
William Simms, rent agent and accountant, agent to the London Union Insurance Company; residence, 7 Albion place, Botanic road
LIBRARY—Jas. Stewart, librarian
NEWS-ROOM—W. Simms, treasurer

WEST SIDE.

Jas. Siebert & Co., linen and linen yarn merchants, and commission agents; residence, 3 Breadalbane place

Thomas Ferguson & Son, linen merchants and bleachers; residence, Whiterock
William Gillilan, linen merchant; residence, 15 Wellington place
Saml. Nelson, West India merchant; residence, Glendavis
Foster Connor, linen manufacturer and bleacher; residence, 13 College street South

SOUTH SIDE.

Edward J. Smith & Son, linen merchants
Valentine Whitla, chairman of Harbour Commissioners; residence, Ben Eden
John Conland, commission mercht., &c; residence, 92 Joy street
Storars, Fortescue, & Co., linen merchants
John Cunningham; residence, Macedon
J. & M. Curell & Co., linen merchants; residence, 4 Murray terrace
Fenton, Son, & Co. (late Sadler Fenton & Co.), linen manufacturers and bleachers, and 120 Wood street, London; S. G. Fenton's residence, 9 College square North

EAST SIDE.

Samuel G. Fenton and Co., linen bleachers, linen yarn, and general merchants

Linen hall Street
SOUTH OF LINEN HALL

LINENHALL ST. PRESBYTERIAN CHURCH—Rev. Robert Knox, minister
Vacant ground
Daniel Curell, jun., & Co., linen and cotton manufacturers; Danl. Curell's residence, 8 Royal Terrace
EASTERN REFORMED PRESBYTERIAN MEETING HOUSE—Rev. J. Alexander, D.D., minister, Rev. Robt. Henry, assistant
Tow spinning mill, C. Duffin & Co., proprietors; Town office, 28 Waring street
8 The Misses Gill's preparatory school

7 Richard Waite, book keeper in J. Preston & Co.'s flax stores
6 Adam Macaulay, Belfast Bank
5 Alexander C. Davidson, flax merchant
4 James M'Knight, LL.D., Editor of the *Banner*
3 George Phillips, bookseller, 27 Bridge street
2 Miss Mary Jamison
Back entrance to J. W. Anderson & Co.'s sewed muslin warerooms

Linfield
Conway B. Grimshaw's residence

Linfield Road
LOWER MALONE.
John Murphy & Co., Linfield mill; office in Waring street
Arthur Leonard, guard Ulster Railway
Mrs Moore
Twenty-two small houses

Lisburn Road
MALONE.
BELFAST UNION WORKHOUSE AND HOSPITAL—Wm. Boyce, clerk and returning officer; William Tidd, master
ULSTER DEAF AND DUMB INSTITUTION — Rev. John Martin, principal
John Millar, engineer, Ulsterville
R. T. Usher, gentleman, Mount Prospect
Edward Pretty, landing waiter, Inland Revenue, Mount Prospect
John Lamb, commission agent, Devis View
N. O. Prenter, drysalter, Harryville
Samuel Johnston, tanner, Railway Cottage
Thos. M'Donnell, Q.C., Eglantine
John Owden, linen merchant, Brooklands
Edward H. Clarke, bank director, Elmwood
Royal Terrace.]

Long Lane
FROM CHURCH ST. TO NORTH ST.
1 John Foster, Ulster Servants' Registry Office
5 Neill Ennis, car driver

7 Margaret Noble
9 William John Moore's wine and spirit stores
11 Robert O'Rorke, shoemaker
13 Henry Cregan, butcher
15 John Fulton, provision merchant; residence, 45 Academy street
17 Miss M'Gee
19 Michael M'Gee, labourer
21 Residence of Robert Milliken, saddler, 47 North street
12 Patrick Stewart, marine stores
10 Miss Halliday
8 John Reid, spirit dealer, and proprietor of the Robert Burns' concert rooms
6 Vacant
4 John M'Guigan, lock smith
2 Side of James Shield's spirit store

Lynas's Lane
OFF GREAT PATRICK STREET.
18 James Brown, spirit dealer
Twenty-three small houses

Magee's Lane
GREAT GEORGE'S STREET.
Seventeen small houses

Malone Place
MALONE ROAD.
1 Mrs Rebecca M. Dickey
2 Rev. James Barker
3 George Miller, manager in John Hynd and Sons, Durham street
4 John M'Alister, clerk
5 Mr. Dillon, hatter, High street
6 Mrs Jane Caldwell, boarding house
7 Bartholemew Devine, porter in Queen's College

Malone Road, Lower
BLACKSTAFF BRIDGE TO MALONE
1 Wm. Finnigan, grocer
3 Bernard Quinn, spinning master
5 Samuel Jackson, mechanic
7 John Pentleton, labourer
9 John Shanks, labourer
11 Isabella Gray
13 John Murphy, hackler
15 Robert Millar, dealer
17 Meredith Devlin, weaver & dealer
19 Wm. Ward, labourer
21 Fanny Neill
23 James Bell, weaver

25 Wm. Melville, sawyer
27 John Heron, labourer
29 Margaret M'Tear, dealer
31 Thomas M'Keever, labourer
33 John Graham, carpenter
35 Alexander Stoops
37 John Watt, carpenter
39 James Quigley, labourer
41 Alexander Milligan, labourer
43 Wm. Stewart, labourer
45 Wm. Kinley, labourer
47 Robert Cluloe, labourer
49 James Harbison, labourer
51 Ann M'Mahon
53 Edward Cardoo, weaver
55 Jane Cardwell
57 Catherine M'Adam
59 Wm. Scott, grocer and spirit dealer
      [*Tea lane.*
61, 63 John Crooks, spirit dealer
65 Daniel Morrison, labourer
67 Vacant
69 Robert Downey, labourer
71 James Corry, weaver
73 Wm. Corry, weaver
75 John Corry, weaver
77 Wm. Brady, weaver
79 Wm. Thompson, labourer
 Wm Bell, clerk in Edw. Tucker's starch and glue works
 Edward Tucker's starch and glue works; residence, Donegall sq. south
 Robert Ritchie, clerk in Edward Tucker's starch works
87 Fanny Scullion, whiteworker
89 Lowdy Wick, overseer
91 James Pettigrew, weaver
93 Christie Murphy, painter and glazier
95 Wm M'Kilty, weaver
97 Mary Strain, winder
99 Robert Morrison, brassfounder
101 Robert Lattimer, weaver
103 Richard Curry, spirit dealer
105 John Gardner, weaver
107 Robert Houston, weaver
109 Samuel Hill, weaver
111 James Blakely, rent collector
113 Hugh Crawford, clerk
115 William Cowan, labourer
117 John Rodgers, weaver
119 Samuel Kingsberry, carter
121 James Morrison, warper
123 James M'Gurk, labourer
125 John Parkinson, night constable

127 James Hutchinson, weaver
129 Wm Malcolm, weaver
131 John Adams, weaver
133 Robert Herron, dealer
135 Wm Hunter, pensioner
137 James Logan, engineer
139 John Atkinson, weaver
141 John Nicholsón, carpenter
143 James M'Ilroy
145 Jas. Nixon, boot and shoemaker
147 Ann Bow
149 Wm Orr, sawyer
151 John M'Donald, carpenter
153 John Thompson, labourer
155 Thomas Ward, weaver
157 James M'Connell, carter
159 James Adams, labourer
161 Thomas Moore, brickmaker
 Five new houses not tenanted
      [*Napier street.*
      [*Napier place.*
      [*Renwick place.*
122 James Thompson, brickmaker
120 Charles Campbell, weaver
118 Matthew Campbell, weaver
116 Jane Dodd
114 John Campbell, weaver
112 Samuel M'Ilroy, labourer
110 John Campbell, labourer
108 John Scott,
106 Sarah Pollock, dealer
104 Hugh Hanna, dealer
102 James Watt, night constable
100 Ewd. Mulholland, roving master
98 Wright Brown, weaver
96 Eliza Edmondson
94 John Steel, wood turner
92 James Henderson, tailor
90 Mary Jane Watson, dealer
88 Ann Faulkner
86 William Roulston
84 Flora Murdoch
82 Alexander Kingsberry, porter
80 James M'Kibbin, dealer
78 William Moore, gardener
76 Rachael Veneret
74 Robert Johnston, fireman
72 Eliza M'Ilveen
70 Orr Carland, mechanic
68 Samuel Watson, bricklayer
66 Charles Hill, labourer
64 James Craig, pensioner
62, 58, 56 John Taylor, spirit dealer
54 Wm. Hunter, weaver
52 Robert Gibson, brass founder

STREET DIRECTORY.

50 Ebenezar Dennison, ham curer
48 James Johnston, shoemaker
46 Ellen Hamill, schoolmistress
44 Jos. Johnston, boot and shoemaker
42 Ann Jane Starret
40 James Calvert, labourer
38 Wm. Douglass, rougher
36 James Henry, tailor
34 Robert Fairfield, lamplighter
32 Archibald M'Clelland, labourer
30 John M'Farlane, watchmaker
28 Mary Brown, washerwoman
26 Hugh Napier, shoemaker
24 Henry M'Auley, labourer
22 Wm M'Clure, weaver
20 Robert Foster, weaver
18 Robert Campbell, weaver
16 John Boyd, labourer
14 Edward Mulholland, labourer
12 John Thompson, weaver
10 Wm Whaley, dealer
8 George Smith, in gas works
6 Allen M'Lean, labourer
4 Jacob Bertram, spirit dealer
2 Alexander Agar, porkcutter

Malone Road, Old

12, 14 W. M'Farland, grocer and spirit dealer
10 James M'Mullan, labourer
8 Francis M'Ateer, butcher
6 John Braithwaite, grocer
4 Wm. Madden, haberdasher
2 John Gamble, grocer and publican
   Hugh M'Dowell, bricklayer
   James M'Lean, clerk
   Ann Haslett, dressmaker

Market Street
SOUTH OF MAY'S MARKET.

1 William Quart, labourer
3 Vacant
5 Robert Isles, fruit dealer
7 Edward Armour, corn dealer
9 George Mulligan, labourer
11 John M'Cormick, butcher
13 James Dickie, blacksmith
15 William O'Hare, fruit dealer
17 Margaret Boyle, fruit dealer
19 Mrs Murphy, dealer in poultry
21 Robert Riddell, dealer in poultry
23 Patrick Sheals, labourer
25 John Dunlop, butcher
27 James Brady, dealer in poultry
29 John Baird, shoemaker

31 Mrs Tandy, dealer in poultry
33 Back entrance to Mr Quigley's flour store in Cromao street
        [*Pump entry.*
35 Mrs Banford, dealer in fruit
37 Mrs Magee
39 Andrew M'Larnin, sawyer
41 Hugh M'Veigh, labourer
43 Edward Conway, carter
45 Wallace M'Murray, carpenter
47 Jasper Curry, wood turner
49 James Clements, pawnbroker
        [*Lagan street.*
51 Ann Collins
53 John Chapman, waterman
55 Mary Cunningham
57 Richard Ruddell, cooper
59 H. Savage, grocer and spirit dealer
61 Alice Campbell, lodging house
63 John Doran, shoemaker
65 James M'Bride, fish dealer
67 James Keenan, labourer
69 John Ireland, labourer
71 Robert Irvine, pensioner
73 Rose Mulholland
75 Bernard Travers, huckster
77 James Moore, carpenter
79 Henry Simpson, dealer in poultry
81 Joseph Cunningham, porter
83 William Watson, porter
85, 87 Vacant
89 Robert Wallace, carpenter
86 Hans Martin, ostler
84 William Lenaghan, car owner
Murphy's lane.]
82 Wm. Niblock, grocer and pork cutter
80 John Andrews, newsvender
78 John Chapman, carter
76 William Blair, labourer
74 Henry Magee, labourer
72 Hugh Savage, bricklayer
70 Elizabeth Magee, whiteworker
68 Henry O'Neill, labourer
66 John M'Donnell, fruit dealer
64 Robert M'Veigh, carter
62 John Falloon, bricklayer
60 John Rice, schoolmaster
58 Margt. Moore, dealer in poultry
56 John Carroll, upholsterer
54 David Moore, flax dealer
52 William Burke, muslin warper
50 William Adams, salesman
48 Mary Kenulty
Lagan street.]
46 Catherine Grinan

44 David Walsh, baker
42 Richard Pelan, chandler
Quigley court.]
40 Wm. Lenaghan, labourer
38 James Leonard, waterman
36 Hugh M'Geaghan, dealer
34 John M'Comiskey, rag dealer
32 Mrs Margaret Marner
Verner lane.]
30 Patrick M'Aleer, carpenter
28 Mary Carson, whiteworker
26 Samuel Mulgrave, labourer
24 Michael Reynolds, labourer
" John M'Kinley, nailor
22 Neil Byrne, meal and cow dealer
   David Dinnen, butcher
18 Patrick Kane, dealer in poultry
16 Rosanna Berry, cow keeper
14 David Johnston, nailor
12 Samuel Edgy, waterman
10 Bdgt. M'Donnell, dealer in poultry
8 Margaret Pressick, huckster
Holmes court.]
6 John Stewart, writing clerk
4 John Jamieson, corn dealer
2 James Breen, dealer

Marlborough street
OFF PRINCE'S ST.

3 Patrick M'Creanor, spirit dealer and stabling yard
.. [*Here Prince's street intersects.*]..
5 John Millen's salt store
7 John Carlisle, grocer
9 Samuel Prince, boarding house
11 John Millen, salt merchant
   New house, vacant
   J. W. Stewart's stabling yard
18, 16 John Murdoch, boarding house
.. [*Here Prince's street intersects.*]..
14 James Barry and Co., spirit dealers
12 Thomas Fea, spirit dealer
10 James Wallace's stabling yard
4 Charles M'Call, spirit dealer
   Back gate to L. Clark's malt house
2 Samuel Johnston, whitesmith

Marquis street
FROM MILL ST. TO SMITHFIELD.

1 James Jenkins, pawnbroker
3 Robert Neville, spirit dealer
5 James Calhoun, residence
7 James Calhoun, pawnbroker
   [*M'Clean's entry.*
9 Thomas Magee, boarding house

11 Andrew Taylor, rent agent
13 Patrick Loughran, auctioneer and spirit dealer
15 Edward Quinn, bellows maker
17 Thos. Fenning, grocer and publican
19 Peter Mullen, bookseller; Smithfd.
21 Peter Boyle, spirit dealer
23 Vacant
   [*Smithfield.*]
30 John O'Hagan, clothes dealer
28 Maxwell M'Loughlin, spirit dealer and auctioneer
26 Jas. M'Grade, umbrella and parasol manufacturer
24 Isaac Kelter, carpenter
22 Bernard O'Hagan, clothes dealer
20 James Mullen, clothes dealer
18 Patrick Magee, labourer
16 Mary M'Kenna, boarding house
14 Mary Gartland, lodging house
12 Hugh Cochrane, hairdresser
10 Wm. Moskimmon, tinplate worker
8 James Greenwood, whitesmith
6 George White, carpenter
4 Margaret Raverty
2 James M'Cann, machine maker

Marshall's Lane
LYNAS'S LANE.

Eight small houses

Mary's Market
OFF TOWNSEND STREET.

1 Thomas Peel, shoemaker
2 Archibald Armstrong, carpenter
3 Thomas Reid, smith
4 Joseph Young, soap boiler
5 James Murner, pensioner
6 James Toall, cow keeper
8 Bernard Doyle, baker
9 James Chalmers, cloth lapper
10 Robert Brown, labourer
11 Robert Mitchell, pensioner
12 Henry M'Kay, pensioner
13 Owen M'Neill, spirit dealer
14 Andrew Kerr, labourer
15 Henry Hunt, shoemaker
16 Alexander Hay, whipmaker
17 Robert Hunt, baker
18 John M'Cay, carman
19 Richard Loughran, dealer
20 Wm. Johnston, house carpenter
21 George Carrol, baker
22 Rodger Osborne, labourer
23 Robt. M'Gregor, boot & shoemaker

STREET DIRECTORY.

Mary Street
FROM PARK STREET TO PEEL STREET.
Twenty-six small houses

Massy's Court
OFF DURHAM STREET.
Fourteen small houses

Mawhinney's Court
OFF MELBOURNE STREET.
Five small houses

May street
CLARENCE PLACE TO OXFORD STREET
MAY-ST. PRESBYTERIAN CHURCH, Rev. Henry Cooke, D.D.,LL.D., minister
[*Clarendon place.*
[*Joy street.*
John C. Cramsie, notary public; office, 74 Waring street
William John Coburn, coal merchant, 16 Carrick hill
Wm Moore's stone yard; residence, Crawford street
Wm M'Alister, spirit dealer
Wm M'Alister's yard; front entrance, Little May street
11 James Anderson, builder, yard; residence, 60 Joy street
Anne Kennedy, publican
13 James Crowell, yard and stabling
John F. Murphy, proprietor of Union foundry
17 Wm Clendinning, wholesale haberdasher, 36 North street
Union foundry; proprietor, John F. Murphy
[*Seymour street.*
19 MAY STREET NATIONAL SCHOOL —master, Owen Callan; mistress, Miss Collins
21 John M'Dowell, greengrocer
Jas. Garrett, carpenter and builder
James Garrett's yard and stabling
Alexander Mackenzie, gentleman
John Mackenzie, posting establishment
23 Mackenzie Brothers, brass founders —shop, Regent buildings
George Duncan, spirit dealer—1 Cromac street
[*Cromac street.*
25 Robert Atkinson, spirit dealer—2 Cromac street

William Trimble, boot and shoe shop—55 High street
Two houses vacant
31 William Cowan, grocer and spirit merchant—Church lane
33 Vacant
[*Market street.*
35 Patrick Dogherty, publican
37 William Dogherty, general merchant
39 John Dogherty, fruit merchant
41 George Burns, publican, waste and tow merchant; stores, Oxford st.
43 William Balmer, publican
Flax and fruit market—retail
Flax and fruit market—wholesale
Oxford street.]
Potato, &c., market
16 William Dogherty, fowl store
14 John Leslie, green grocer
Wm. Doherty, fruit stores
MAY'S GRAIN MARKET
John M'Grath, hay and straw dealer; lodging house, &c.
George Huston's yard; shop, Great Edward street
12 Wm. John Rea, hair cutter
Great Edward street.]
10 Daniel Brown, grocer, private entrance; shop, 39 Great Edward street
Daniel Brown's yards
8 Alexander M'Alister, gentleman
Thos. M'Bride, of Thos. and Geo. M'Bride, muslin manufacturers; office, Elliott's court, Donegall street
George M'Bride, ditto
Mrs Maria Collins
.... [*Seymour street intersects.*]....
6½ May Street Iron Foundry—John Scott, proprietor
6 Richardson, Sons, and Owden, linen box manufactory; office, Donegall place
John Neill, linen cloth packer to Richardson, Sons, and Owden.
Shop vacant
4 Samuel M'Auley, tow spinning factory
Wm. M'Auley's residence
2 Horse bazaar and veterinary establishment, proprietor, Wm. M'Kenna, member of the Royal College of Veterinary Surgeons,

London; residence, 42 Gloucester street
Montgomery street.]
   Hugh Morrison, Belfast Undertaking and Posting Establishment; office and stables, 8 Montgomery street
   Back W. Watson's building yard
   BELFAST MUSIC HALL
Arthur street Upper.]

May Street, Little
CROMAC STREET TO ALFRED STREET.
1 David Munce, tailor
3 Patrick Fannin, shoemaker
5 John O'Neill, coach trimmer
7 John M'Crisken, servant
9 Jn. M'Keating, boot & shoe maker
11 Thomas Dover, currier
               [*Seymour street.*
13 Mathew Millar, mechanic
15 James Gorman, labourer
17 Samuel Campbell, seaman
19 John Rea, shoemaker
21 Sarah Coulter, boarding house
23 Alexander M'Alister, spirit dealer and posting establishment
25 Sarah Gillespie, teacher
27 George Stevenson, horse dealer
29 Wm. Bell, check-taker Potato Mkt.
31 William White, night constable
33 William Whitcroft, machine man *Chronicle*
.....[*Here Joy street intersects.*].....
35 Elizabeth Larman, boarding house
37 Elizabeth Tucker, boarding house
39 Mary Cotter, boarding house
41 Charles D. Gordon, professor of music and piano forte tuner
43 Miss Rebecca M'Ferran, dressmaker
45 Girls' school in connexion with May street Presbyterian Church
47 Hugh Crooks, sexton to ditto
               [*Alfred street.*
30 Miss Mary Ann M'Nally, dressmaker
28 Mrs Jane Little, boarding house
26 Mrs Margt. Talbot, boarding house
.....[*Here Joy street in ersects.*]....
24 Ewd. Lennon, billiard-room keeper
22 Timber yard, vacant
20 John Walker, clockmaker
18 James Cousins, pensioner
Catherine street North.]
16 Miss Catherine Murphy, grocer

14 Vacant
12 Wm. Jordan, foreman printer *Banner*
10 Thomas Fletcher, chandler
8 James Jackson, labourer
6 Archibald Moore, carpenter
4 Bernard Burns, flax dealer
2 John Ross, labourer

Meadow Lane
OFF MEADOW STREET.
1 James M'Auley, mariner
2 John Riley, bundling master
3 John M'Kenna, ship carpenter

Meadow Street
OFF YORK ST.
Side entrance to Mr. Hughes's corn mill; residence, 13 North st.
1 Samuel M'Cracken, weigher in mill
2 Joseph M'Roberts, hackle maker
3 John Boyd, travelling clerk
4 John Scott, grocer and block maker; shop, 4 Corporation st.
5 Mary M'Clean
6 Chas. Crossley, hatter, Orr's entry
7 John Douglass
8 William Maclenahen, millwright
9 George Strype, foundry manager
10 Thomas Thompson, millwright
   Samuel Boyle, ship carpenter
   Samuel Hanna, sawyer
   William Creen, ship carpenter
   John Brenton, carpenter
   Vacant

Meek's Court
OFF BARRACK STREET.
Ten small houses

Meetinghouse Lane
OFF WILLIAM STREET.
John Hagan, baker
1 James Hamilton, muslin printer
3 Christie Orrel, labourer
5 Thomas Scully, pensioner
7 John Keenan, labourer
12 David Brown, painter
11 John O'Neill, tanner
10 Patrick Fox, labourer
8 John Russell, porter
6 John M'Kenna, labourer
4 Joseph Whitton, labourer
2 Bernard Mullan, carter

STREET DIRECTORY.

Melbourne Court
OFF MELBOURNE STREET.
Eight small houses

Melbourne Street
BROWN STREET TO TOWNSEND ST.
1,3 Wm Dawson, grocer & spirit dealer
5 Edward Oldham
7 Eleanor Allen
9 William Lynn, manufacturer of cotton yarn
11 James Henry, foreman boot and
13 John Todd, pensioner [shoemaker
15 Robert Hoole, tobacco spinner
17 John Totton, mechanic
19 Thomas Press, carpenter
21 Joseph Greenwood, mechanic
23 Hugh Morrison, wood turner
25 Mary Hull
27 Thomas Mawhinney, plasterer
Hope's place.]
31 John Richardson, provision shop
33 Wm. Horner, boot and shoemaker
35 Mrs Margaret Jordan
37 Rev. John Blackburne, Primitive Methodist Minister
PRIMITIVE METHODIST CHAPEL
[*Mawhinney's court.*
39 Andrew Nimmen, mechanic
[*Townsend street.*]
30 Michael Crossley, stokerer
28 Andrew Doyle, iron moulder
26 James M'Conkey, book canvasser
24 Mrs Renwick
Hanna's place.]
22 Eliza King, grocer
20 Thos. M'Loughlin, painter & glazier
18 Esther M'Loughlin
16 William Coburn, grocer and night
Melbourne court.]   [constable
14 Richard Freckleton, writing clerk
12 Joseph Croft, weigher, Castle mkt.
10 Hugh M'Ilroy, night constable
8 Wm. M'Kenzie, boot & shoemaker
6 Hamilton Flannigan, cattle dealer
4 William Daley, carpenter
2 Thomas Edmondson, head master Brown street School
" Mrs Edmondson's seminary
BROWN STREET MALE AND FEMALE SCHOOLS
[*Brown's square.*

Maxwell's Row
SANDY ROW.
Five small houses

Michael Street
LITTLE GEORGE'S STREET.
1 John Lynass, marble and stone yard, 38 York street
3 Hugh M'Cleery, writing clerk
5 Robert Jamieson, carpenter
7 John M'Mullan, lapper
9 Charles Berry, sea captain
11 Wm. Charley, ship carpenter
13 John Harvey, bricklayer
15 Bernard Marmon, flax buyer
17 Hugh Murray, spinning master
19 John Marrs, spirit dealer
20 C. O'Neill, spirit dealer
18 Thomas M'Mahon, moulder
16 Mary Kane, bonnet maker
14 James Irvine, ship carpenter
12 Andrew Kearney, mariner
10 Hugh Moore, mariner
8 John Johnston, carpenter
6 Michael Woods, jeweller
4 Wm. Hecklin, mechanic
2 Wm. Nelson, printer

Millar's Lane
Nine old houses

Millfield
MILL STREET TO NORTH STREET.
Carson's glass manufactury; and 63 Mill street
1 Henry M'Cleesh, spirit store
[*Anderson's court.*
Arthur M'Laughlin—entrance in court   [*Anderson's row.*
3 Ann Devine, dressmaker
5 John Rawe, chandler
7 David Meek, porter
9 James Bookes, carpenter
11 Peter Quaile, teacher
13 Patrick M'Quaide, cooper
15 Rebecca Yates
17 Henry Fisher, labourer
19 Thomas Hunter
[*Francis street.*
Rere of J. & J. Herdman's flax and tow stores
21 George Arnett
23 Sarah M'Grady
25 Rose M'Keown, dealer
[*M'Grady's court.*
27 Alex. Moore, grocer & spirit dealer
Mrs Havern, cow keeper
Alex. Dornan, green grocer
Rere of Smithfield Brewery

35 Rose M'Cafferty, dealer
37 Solomon Willis, hay and straw dealer, 28 West street
39 Wm. Bradley, barber
41 Robert M'Quaide, publican; and 30 West street

[*West street.*

43 Mary Heron, publican; and 39 West street
45 Wm Miller, dealer and mill worker
47 Charles Burns, marine store
49 Catherine Dalzell, mangler
51 Eliza Madden, dealer
53 Patrick M'Cann, green grocer
55 Thomas Mitchell, pensioner
57 Alex. Finlay, weaver
59 Wm. M'Cullagh, rag store
59½ Nancy Montgomery, green grocer

[*Hope's court.*

61 Margaret M'Conville, mill worker
63 Mary Gordon
65 James Dougal, grocer
67 Thomas M'Kenna, carman
69 Mary Dougall
71 John M'Dowell, cooper
73 Mary Mackan, lodgings
75 John Parkinson, dealer

[*Johnston's court.*

77 Patrick M'Caffry, porter
79 Wm. Kelly, green grocer
81 Daniel Dyer, lodgings
83 John M'Ilvenna, labourer
85 John O'Neill, lodgings
87 Margaret Owens, rag dealer
89 Margaret Tinsley, lodgings
91 John M'Cullagh, marine store
93 Isabella M'Cann, mill worker
95 Ewd. Mullan, publican and grocer

[*Samuel street.*

97 Jane Connolly
99 Henry Lee, pensioner
101 Widow Rice, dealer
103 Hugh Sheals, labourer
105 William M'Cullough, starch manufactory
107 Andrew M'Clure, pensioner
109 Ann Keenan, washerwoman
111 Wm. Abbott, reed maker
113-15 Mary Maginnis, grocer and upholsterer
117 John Harkin, in Mr. M'Adam's, druggist
119 Bernard Magee, lodging house
121, 164 John Martin, hay and straw dealer; and 2½ Great Edward st.

Back entrance to Robt Orr's house, 204 North street
Peter's hill.] [*North street.*
Side entrance to John Loughran's spirit store, 2 Peter's hill
Surgeon James Mawhinney; residence, 8 College square east
Hall door of John Loughran's house, 2 Peter's hill
Gateway of Edw. Tucker's starch works
162 James Magee, labourer
160 Anthony Cappo, optician
158 Thomas M'Greevy, tailor
156 Vacant
154 James Judge, green grocer
152 Andrew Scollan, labourer
150 John M'Anally, pensioner
148 Wm. Burke, dealer in old books
146 Charles M'Afee, dealer
   Edward Tucker's starch works; office, 27 Waring street; residence, 6 Donegall square south
142 Robert M'Williams, labourer
140 Susan Nichol, dealer
138 James Wallace, grocer
136 Robert Swan, labourer
134 James Donnelly, labourer
132 James Moore, carpenter
130 John Henry, grocer and publican
128 John Kelly, teacher
Tate's court.]
126 Patrick Kearney, pensioner
124 James M'Larnon, dealer
122 Margaret Green, lodgings
120 Edward Brophy, bricklayer
118 Rose M'Grath, mill worker
116 Mary Hanna, grocer
Mitchell street.]
114 Hugh M'Gennity, grocer
110 Thomas Wardlow
108 Charles M'Shane, bricklayer
106 John Magowan, hatter
104 Hugh M'Cullagh, blacksmith
102 Patrick Coulter, wireworker and confectioner
100 Thomas Adams, carpenter
98 Wm. Todd, hairdresser
96 George Hope, grocer and publican, Brown street
Brown street.]
94 Elizabeth Scott, 2 Brown street
92 Thomas Kelly, mill worker
90½ Wm. Hunter, bricklayer
90 Thomas Culbert, grocer

88 Hugh M'Donnell, Irish teacher
86 Wm. Hughes, butcher
84 James Warnock, pawnbroker
Rea's court.]
82 Thomas Brown, millwright
78 Jas. Bodel, soda water, lemonade, and gingerale, manufacturer
Keenan's court.]
76 John Keenan, auctioneer
Wilson street]
74 Ellen Hanlon, green grocer
72 Mary Ann Malcomson, lodgings
70 James Murray, grocer and porter
68 Rose Mines, lodging house keeper
66 Wm. Moore, chandler
64 John Lundy, grocer and publican
Tanner's court.]
62 Bern. M'Kay, grocer and publican
60 Mary Forsythe, dealer
M'Master's court.]
   John Mitchel, chimney sweeper, M'Master's court
   Robert Riley, boot and shoemaker
56 Patrick Tasney, grocer
   Three small houses
48 Vacant
   Alexander Crawford, starch works; residence, Mount Charles
Crawford's court]
46 Henry M'Cool, bricklayer
44 Edward Taylor, drayman
42 Wm. Tedd, labourer and dealer
40 Michael Hanlon, tailor
38 Anne Murray
36 Michael Duffy, teacher
34 John Kane, silk dyer and renovator
32 John Doherty, porter
30 Sarah Lavery, lodging house
28 Charles Pollock, bricklayer
26 Wm. Vance, relieving officer
26 Daniel Marrs, spirit dealer
24 Francis M'Donnell, dealer
22 John M'Peake, sawyer
20 Wm. Wilson, publican
18 Isabella Ramsey
16 Mary Dennis, lodging house
14 John Green, grocer and publican
Dam side.]
10 Catherine Sheals, lodging house
8 George Maxwell, labourer
6 Francis Ward, tailor
4 Thomas Morrow, confectioner
2 Isabella Irwin, grocer; shop, 1 Barrack street
Barrack street.]

Mill Street

CASTLE STREET TO BARRACK STREET.
[*Chapel lane.*
1 Ellen & Sarah Dyke, dressmakers
" R. M. Dyke, organist St. Malachi's Roman Catholic Chapel
3 Eliza Blair, dressmaker
5 Daniel Murray, surgeon and licentiate apothecary—medical hall
7 Mrs Jane M'Clean, silk dyer and milliner
9 Jn. Goodman, linen lapper, Messrs. Fenton's office, Linenhall
" Miss Theresa Goodman, dressmaker
11 Edward Mehair, joiner and confectioner
11½ Guy S. Wilson, rectifying distiller; residence, Holywood
13 William Johnston, tanner
" Shop, vacant
15 James M'Alister, slater
17 Eliza Crawford, grocer
19 James Jenkins, pawnbroker; office, Marquis street
[*Marquis street.*
21, 23 James Callender, publican, currier, and leather merchant
25 Wm. Wetherall, tan yard; residence, Holywood
27 Mrs Williams
29, 31 Alexander Rogers, baker, flour, and bran stores
33 Stephen Robert Symmonds, commission merchant; office, 6¼ York street
35 EYE AND EAR DISPENSARY—Attending surgeons, Surg. Browne, R.N., and Surgeon Armstrong
   W. & S. Johnston's tan yard; W. Johnston's residence, No. 13; S. Johnston's residence, Railway Cottage, new Lisburn road
[*Johnston's court.*
37 Messrs Johnston's office and leather store
39 Thomas Stevenson, tailor
41 D. Somerville, boot & shoemaker
43 Doyle and Young, watch and clock makers
" Mrs Doyle, nurse tender
45 Robert M'Kee, plumber
" Mrs M'Kee, bonnet maker
47 Bernard Davy, tobacco spinner
49 Thomas M'Cormac, leather warehouse

49 Robert Greenhill, tanyard; shop and store, 44 Ann street
51 Foster Donaldson, lodging house
53 Wm. Orr, currier
Currier's court.]
53½ Jerem. Popham, suspender maker
55 Patrick Walsh, boot and shoemaker
57 Timothy Farrell, publican
61 Corn Mill, Mackenzie, Shaw, and Co., proprietors
59 Ann Jane Niblock, dealer
63 Lamont Carson, glass manufacturer; office, 1 and 1½ Millfield; residence, 8 Antrim place
[*Millfield.*
72 Thomas Loughran, grocer and spirit dealer
Beattie's entry.]
70 Vacant
68 Terence M'Guirk, green grocer
66 Wm. Johnston, green grocer
64½ Mary Rogers, wine & spirit store,
Burns's court.]
    Henry M'Glade, publican; shop 55 Edward street
62 Joseph Boyle, grocer and publican
Neeson's court.]
60 Pat. Lennon, grocer and publican
58 Hugh Owen, cabinet maker
56 James Barker, lodging house
54 Henry Noon, grocer and publican
52 Waddell Cunningham, gentleman
Cunningham's court.].
50 George Rawlins, grocer
48 Patrick M'Mullan, tanner and leather merchant
46 Mrs Caroline Barnes, lodging house
44 Miss Debora Weldon, milliner and dress maker
42 Surgeon Mawhinney, Medical hall
40 Francis Neeson, grocer and spirit dealer; 1 King street
King street.]
38 William Young, pawnbroker; residence, Bunker's Hill House
36 James Meharg, auctioneer; office, 63 Smithfield
34, 32 Vacant
30 Catherine Kearney, boarding house
28½ Sylvester Maguire, bricklayer
28 William Heyburn, surgeon, accoucheur, &c.
26 Alexander Crawford, manufacturing chemist, drysalter, &c.; residence, Mount Charles, Malone

24 Francis Patterson, chandler and soap boiler
20 William Church, foreman *News-Letter* office
" Mrs Church, confectionary establishment
18 Isabella Hume, spirit dealer
M'CLENAGHAN'S COURT.
16 Reynolds, Brothers, engineers and machine makers; residences: Peter Reynolds, 13 Townsend street; James Reynolds, 10 Cullingtree place
14 William Beattie, scantling yard; residence, Queen's square; office, Arthur square
    Robert Gibson, brass founder, and gas fitter; residence, 3 Lancaster street

12 John Davison, tailor
10 Samuel M'Mullan, tailor
" Ann M'Mullan, stay and corset maker
8 Miss Usher, servants' registry office
" E. Usher, dressmaker
6 Samuel Cunningham, wine and spirit stores; Victoria street
4, 2 John Kearns, grocer, spirit dealer

Millview Place
TOWNSEND STREET.
Nine small houses

Mitchell's Entry
112 HIGH ST.
James M'Kee, pawnbroker
Henry Robinson, druggist

Mitchell Street
OFF GARDINER STREET.
1 Alexander Robinson, labourer
3 John Neill, starch maker
5 Daniel Colville, labourer
7 William Young, miller
9 William Scott, carpenter
11 William Thompson, miller
17 John Black, weaver
19 John Stevenson, labourer
" Hugh Wallace, carpenter
21 James Williamson, weaver
23 John Norris, lime burner
25 John M'Donald, starch maker
27 Mary Harbison, brush maker
29 John Hamilton, pork cutter
31 William Robinson, coppersmith

28 Henry Cullin, labourer
26 James Vallely, labourer
24 Jane Doe
22 Edward Ferguson, shoemaker
20 Robert Chambers, weaver
18 Patrick M'Larnon, bricklayer
16 Rose Ann Sorsby
14 William M'Blain, weaver
12 John Mitchell, plasterer
10 John O'Neill, labourer
8 Robert Allison, pensioner
6 James Starret, car driver
4 Thomas M'Cormack, stone cutter
2 Margaret Smith

Moffet Street
OFF HENRY STREET.

1 William Bell, weaver
3 Edward Hagan, mechanic
5 Sarah Dougherty, dealer
7 Ellen Williamson
9 John Shields, labourer
11 Robert Hagan, stone cutter
13 Robert O'Neill, labourer
15 James M'Glear, labourer
17 Miss M'Ilhatton
19 George Coulter, sawyer
21 Robert Thompson, labourer
23 Henry Barrett, pork cutter
25 John Dunn, cooper
27 Thomas Canning, soap boiler
29 James Bole, ship carpenter
40 Michael Duffy, shoemaker
38 Thomas Brownlee, flax dresser
36 Ann Montgomery, spinner
34 Patrick Gorman, bundler
32 Michael Nelson, labourer
30 Edward M'Laughlin, butler
28 Rose Kelly
26 Patrick M'Mahon, ostler
24 John Galbraith, carman
22 John M'Gee, porter
20 Andrew Alexander, grocer
18 Mrs Miller
16 John Williamson, labourer
14 William Brannagan, labourer
12 Anthony Donnelly, pork cutter
10 Alexander Leeburn, pork cutter
8 James M'Larnon, labourer
6 William M'Gaghey, blacksmith
4 John M'Guigan, yarn carrier
2 Patrick Farnham, linen lapper

Molyneaux Street
LITTLE GEORGE'S STREET.

Twenty small houses

Montgomery Street
CHICHESTER STREET TO MAY STREET.

1 Ulster Coach Factory — John Kennedy, proprietor; residence, 4 Montgomery street
3 Livery Stables and Posting Establishment— John Robson, proprietor; residence, 22 Gloucester street
7 James Carson, boot and shoemaker
11 William Low, marble and stone yard; residence, 24 Chichester street
13 Richard Robson, of John Robson's posting establishment No. 3 [*Joy street.*]
6 Hugh Morrison, tavern; proprietor of posting establishment, May street; Hugh Morrison's posting office and yard
4 John Kennedy, of Ulster coach Factory
2 Coach Factory—vacant

Moore's Place
LOWER MALONE.

1 William M'Ilveen, spirit dealer
" Wm. M'Ilveen's residence
2 James Rogan, pensioner
3 David M'Lean, railway porter
4 John Cooper, forrester
5 Henry Allen, overseer in Ulster Railway

Morrison's Place
POUND STREET.

1 Michael Hughes, tanner
2 Philip M'Cann, labourer
3 James M'Cabe, carter
4 James Dargan, labourer
Four new houses building
William M'Garry
Mary Crawford
Bernard M'Guigan

Morrow's Entry
HILL STREET.

1 Robert Fulton, weighmaster
3 Robert M'Gregor, labourer
5 John Dougall, cooper
7 John Gallagher, lighterman
9 Wm. Harper, carpenter
" Stewart Perry, cooper
11 Thomas M'Auley, basket maker
13 James Neill, labourer

15 John M'Kee, chandler
17 James Fitzpatrick, pork cutter
" Adam Bailey, carpenter
19 Andrew Currell, labourer
21 John Hawthorn, labourer
23 Alexander Hamill, pork cutter
10 James Doolan, labourer
8 Richard Yar, lighterman
6 Alexander Logan, tailor
4 Hugh Markey, lathcutter
" Wm. Stirling, cabinet maker
2 Alexander Parker, labourer

Mount Charles
OLD MALONE ROAD.

Alexander Crawford, starch manufacturer; works, Millfield
Mrs M'Lean
J. Brown, auctioneer, 38 Berry st.

Mountview Terrace
CRUMLIN ROAD.

Two houses not finished
1 John Savage, flax merchant, Skipper street
2 Wm. Ewart, of W. Ewart & Sons, flax spinners, Crumlin road; office, 24 Donegall street
3 Rev. Theophilus Campbell, incumbent of Trinity Church
4 Jackson S. Stevenson, bill and share broker, commercial buildings

Mullan's Lane
TRAFALGAR STREET.

Seven small houses

Murphy's Lane
VERNER STREET.

1 Thomas Jordon, fishmonger
3 John Dougherty, painter
5 Arthur Mason, labourer
7, 9 Wm. Lenaghan, stabling yard
4 Patrick Flinn, labourer
2 James Woods' grain stores; residence, 65 Verner street

Murphy Street
FROM VERNER ST. TO ELIZA ST.

1 James Brown, spirit dealer
3 William Clarke, labourer
" John King, printer
5 Mary Campbell, schoolmistress
Eliza M'Cutcheon, whiteworker
New houses not finished
John Murphy's brick and tile yard; residence, Hamilton street
5 Joseph Campbell, carpenter
7 Archd. Burnett, ornamental painter
9 Richard Stanfield, gentleman
20 Robert Moore, carpenter
18 Hugh Gilmore, baker
16 Robinson Lappan, carpenter
14 James Murray, printer
12 Thomas Bennet, moulder
10 Alex. Thompson, carpenter
8 James M'Crea, plasterer
6 Henry Turney, carpenter
4 John Holland, salesman in H. H. Hanny's, 13 Donegall street
2 William Davey, painter

Murray's Terrace
COLLEGE SQUARE.

1 William Hunter, gentleman
" W. & T. Hunter, merchants; office, Waring street
2 Daniel Brannigan, wine and spirit merchant; store, No. 43 North street
3 Samuel Taylor, book-keeper and cashier in A. & S. Henry & Co.'s, Donegall square North
4 J. Curell, linen merchant, Linenhall
5 Rev. John Porter
6 Robert Neill, gentleman
7 Rev. Dr. Hincks

Mustard Street
JOHN STREET.

1 John Scott, shoemaker
3 Rebecca Phillips
5 Robert Adair, shoemaker
7 Samuel Bailey, painter
9 Hugh Graham, porter
11 Hugh M'Comb, boot & shoemaker
13 Francis Ganston, cooper
15 James Smylie, clerk
17 Samuel Dodd, pensioner
19 John Duffy, labourer
21 Samuel Armor, shoemaker
23 George Strachan, pork cutter
25 Sarah Thompson
Side of John Jackson's spirit store
[*Union street.*
Side of Samuel Patterson's grocery
27 Vacant
29 Samuel Hutchinson, labourer
31 John M'Laughlin, cooper

33 William Downs, pork curer
35 John Shields, pensioner
37 John Regan, dealer
39 David Charters, shoemaker
41 Margaret Campbell, dealer
43 James Boag, weaver
45 Robert M'Cann, labourer
47 John Stewart, horse shoer
49 Margaret Rafferty
51 Job Foster, pensioner
53 Hugh Tilley, shoemaker
55 Charles Liddy, spirit dealer
[*Stephen street.*
57 Michael Kerns, grocer
59 Atchison Cloughley, carpenter
61 James Munro, dealer
63 John Kearney, pensioner
65 John Britton, spirit dealer
74 James M'Auley, brush and bellows maker
72 Patrick Cassidy, shoemaker
70, 68 Vacant
66 James Griffith, nailer
64 Mathew Williamson, comb maker
62 John Stewart, labourer
60 John Stewart, baker
58 John Loughran, labourer
56 James M'Gee, labourer
54 Hugh Harkin, labourer
52 Bernard Laverty, shoemaker
Robert's court.]
50 James M'Laughlin, labourer
48 Jane Black
46 James Kelly, labourer
44 Betsy Dornan, dealer
42 James Kerns, dealer
40 Ellen O'Hara, white worker
38 James M'Keown, labourer
36 Hugh M'Laughlin, coach maker
34 John Harrison, labourer
32 James M'Donald, clerk
Union street.]
30 John Quinn, grocer and publican
28 Patrick M'Cabe, bookbinder
26 William Martin, cooper
24 John M'Caslin, cooper
" Francis Kearns, labourer
22 John Liddy, paver
20 Archibald Reid, tailor
18 Ellen M'Caw
16 James Stewart, porter
14 Robert M'Murray, tailor
12 Mary Ann Toal
10 Mary Nelson
8 Wm. Devanny, blacksmith

6 Daniel O'Neill, dealer
4 R. and J. Bell, yarn and flax store; residence, Whitehouse
2 James Scott, dealer
Side of Edward Fagan's spirit store

M'Adam's Court
CARRICKHILL.
Patrick M'Anally, nailer
Edward Hughes, nailer
John Mullen, nailer
James M'Kenna, nailer
Seven small houses

M'Allen's Place
SHANKHILL.
Nine small houses

M'Auley's Place
M'AULEY ST.
Three small houses

M'Auley Street
OFF CROMAC STREET.
2 John Dunn, shoemaker
4 Samuel Carson, labourer
6 John Doak, sawyer
8 Dennis Vernon, tailor
10 David M'Honey, labourer
[*M'Aulay's court.*
12 Joseph Lavery, labourer
14 Ann Donnelly, dealer
16 Thomas Fairfield, carpenter
18 Catherine Carr
20 William Newell, labourer
22 Samuel M'Bride, labourer
24 William M'Gonigal
26 James Morrison
28 Francis Mulholland, butler
[*Bond street.*
Enclosed ground
New shop vacant
George Firth, ironmoulder
New house vacant

M'Clean's Entry
OFF MARQUIS STREET.
Four small houses

M'Clelland's Lane
PETER'S HILL.
Twenty six small houses

M'Clenaghan's Court
MILL STREET.
James M'Donald, pensioner

James M'Clenaghan, mechanic
Robert Gibson, brass founder and gas fitter; residence, Lancaster street
William Beattie's (rent agent) scantling yard; residence, 9 Queen's square
Reynolds, Brothers, engineers and machine makers; residences; Peter Reynolds, 13 Townsend street; John Reynolds, 13 Cullingtree place

M'Dowell's Court
FORMERLY DAVIDSON'S ENTRY—
DURHAM STREET.
Seventeen small houses

M'Kibbin's Court
155 NORTH STREET.
Twenty-one small houses

M'Master's Row
DURHAM STREET.
6 Robert M'Master, carpenter
8 Joseph Dinley, clerk
Foster Connor's weaving factory; office, Linen Hall; residence, 13 College square south
Eighteen small houses

M'Millen's Place
FALLS ROAD.
2 Felix M'Ilvogue, shoemaker
4 William M'Kaig, labourer
6 Margaret Orr
8 Mark Graham, carpenter
10 Patrick M'Ateer, blacksmith
12 James M'Veigh, labourer
14 John Hunter, mechanic
16 H. Wilkinson, dresser in foundry
18 Terrence Cregan, gateman in distillery
20 James Dougherty, servant
22 Hugh Boyd, copper and tinsmith
24 William M'Auley, pork cutter
26 Samuel Lyons, bricklayer
28 John Scott, bricklayer
30 Hugh Doey, bricklayer
32 Robert M'Caheron, carpenter
34 Elizabeth Lindsay
36 William M'Cracken, carpenter
38 Edward Burns, pensioner

M'Tier's Court
NORTH STREET.
3 Charles Shields, sweep
5 Susan Ross, dealer
" Neill Mullan, sweep
7 Ann Mullan, dealer
9 James Ross, brass founder
11 James Cummerford, sweep
15 Patrick Main, labourer
Mary M'Gregor
Bernard M'Peak, labourer
Nicholas Gallagher, sweep
Four small houses

M'Tiers Street
SHANKHILL.
1 Robert Williamson, millwright
3 James Kennedy, baker
5 John Gamble, printer
Four houses partly built
15 James Jefferson, labourer
17 James Falloon, weaver
19 Margaret Boyd, whiteworker
21 John Clarke, bricklayer
23 Anthony M'Flinn
25 David M'Tier, bookseller
27 John Curry, damask weaver
29 Samuel Perry, porkcutter
31 Daniel M'Cartney, dealer
33 Mary Wilson
James Tilley, muslin manufactory; residence, 2 North Queen street
Elizabeth Gaskin
John Kelly, dealer
Robert Wilkinson, weaver
James Mullen, weaver
37 James Maneely, labourer
39 Francis Whitley, weaver
41 Robert Wilson, labourer
43 James Hillis, shoemaker
45 Alexander Mitchell, bleacher
47 Samuel Weir, stone cutter
49 David Orr, butler
Fifteen houses building
Robert Vance, travelling agent
25 James M'Ginnis, warper
24 Wm. M'Cracken, dealer
23 Thomas Smith, clerk
22 Wm. Johnston, labourer
21 John Scott, labourer
20 James Getty, machine maker
19 Samuel Fulton, ploughman
18 Robert Hood, labourer
17 James Graham, labourer
16 James Scott, pattern maker

15 Elizabeth Morrison, whiteworker
14 James Allen, labourer
13 Robert M'Call, bricklayer
12 Agnes Simmington
11 Jane Ewing
10 James M'Keag, bricklayer
 9 Robert M'Ilroy, book deliverer
 8 Richard Bell, warper
 7 Margaret Anderson
 6 George Bradshaw
 5 John Girvan, warper
 4 John Robinson, teacher
 3 John Watson, porter
 2 John Wright, warper
 1 Samuel Maneely, watchman
48 Robert Vance, publican
46 Mary A. M'Curley, boarding house
44 Wm. Hamilton, weaver
42 Patrick Allen, dealer
40 James Sheerer, labourer
38 John Hannah, dealer
36 James Boyd, labourer
34 James Tracey, labourer
32 Neill M'Keown, labourer
30 Wm. Adams, carter
28 Thomas Tully, hatter
26 Wm. Hemphill, schoolmaster
24 Reynold M'Alister, labourer
22 Wm. Caldwell, pork cutter
20 Wm. Aickin, bookbinder
18 George Murdock, weaver
16 James Mullan
14 Margaret Kennedy
12 Wm. M'Cullough, mechanic
10 Richard Childs, blacksmith
 8 Wm. Gallagher, labourer
 6 David Whitley, labourer
 4 Wm. Milligan, shoemaker
 2 Margaret Waugh

Napier's Place
MALONE ROAD LOWER.

1 Stewart Campbell, cabinet maker, Ann street
2 John Gilmour, muslin agent, with Anderson and Gray, Donegall square South
3 James Calwell, pensioner

Napier Street
OFF MALONE ROAD LOWER.

4 Robert Heron, barber
5 Alexander M'Quillan, engraver
6 Wm. Walker, schoolmaster
7 George Sinclair, clerk
7 Miss Sinclair, milliner & dressmaker
8 Joseph Gray, butler

Neeson's Court
OFF MILL STREET.
Thirty-two small houses

Nelson Court
NELSON STREET.

2 James Bingham, pork cutter
4 Robert M'Cready, carpenter
6 Jane Boyd
8 William Thompson, mariner

Nelson Street
GREAT PATRICK ST. TO EARL ST.

 1 David Thoburn, pawnbroker
 1½ John Teeney, foreign interpreter
 " Andrew Bruce, provision dealer
 3 Ralph Stockman, nail manufacturer
 5 Thomas Derby, cabinet maker
 7 Henry Brankin, grain merchant, 26 Great Patrick street
 9 James M'Minn, warper
 " A. and M. M'Minn, dressmakers
11 John Isdell, ladies' boot maker
13 Hugh Wallace, porter
15 John Robinson, ship carpenter and grocer
17 Andrew Girvan, mechanic
..[*Little Patrick street intersects.*]..
19 W. Weir, jun., & Co., sewed muslin manufacturers; residence, Antrim road
21 Mathew M'Kenzie, designer
23 Mrs Margaret Boyd
25 Mrs Esther M'Ilroy
27 R. & H. Dickson's provision stores
29 Mrs Margaret Whiteside
31 James M'Columb, stone mason
33 Robert Stewart, labourer
35 Thomas Douglass, carpenter
37 Wm. John Kitson, cooper
39 John Bodkin, watchmaker
41 Samuel Park, mate of *Erin's Queen*
43 Robert Kennedy, cabinet maker
45 Adam Corrigan, spirit dealer
47 Mrs Skelton
..[*Great George's street intersects.*]..
Side of John Low's timber yard
 [*Little Corporation street.*
Enclosed ground
.....[*Henry street intersects.*].....
49 George L. Miller, of Miller and Clendinning, North street

51 Mrs Pollock, boarding house
53 William Jackson, pensioner
55 Samuel Owens, gentleman
57 William M'Mahon, sea captain
59 Vacant
61 Robert Brown, professor of music
63 James Turney, sea captain
65 Andrew Park, sea captain
67 Echlin Gordon, relieving officer
69 Matthew Martin, spirit dealer
....[*Trafalgar street intersects.*]....
71 Eliza Johnston, grocer
73 James Black, ship rigger
75 William Graham, sea captain
77 Patrick M'Areavy, lighterman
79 James Johnston, ship carpenter
81 Ellen M'Tear

[*North Ann street.*
83 John Scott, labourer
85 James Kelly, ship carpenter
87 Mary J. Potbury, boarding house
89 Thomas M'Gowan, sailor
91 Thomas Johnston, sergeant of harbour constables
93 James Moorehead, cooper
[*Earl street.*]
98 Wm Bruce, ship smith
96 James Doogan, ship carpenter
94 Samuel Hanna, cooper
92 Thomas Thomson, ship carpenter
90 Hugh Harvey, house carpenter
88 Thomas Shaw, pilot
86 Robert M'Comisky, dealer
84 Rowland Savage, cooper
82 James M'Kenzie, blacksmith
80 Robert Jackson, mariner
78 James Quinn, spirit dealer
Trafalgar street.]
76 John Scott, spirit dealer
74 James M'Cleery, pawnbroker
72 Michael Drenan, clerk
70 Ann Paton
68½ Robert Hoy, spirit dealer
68 Wm. Connell, ship builder
66 Jane Johnston
64 Thomas Owens, provision dealer
.....[*Henry street intersects.*]......
62 James Frazer, muslin manufacturer, 16 Academy street
60 Charles Bailies' scantling yard
58 Charles Bailies, builder—residence
56 Thomas Crossford, agent to John Tallis & Co., London publishers
Nile street.]
54 Kennedy Morrison, clerk

52 William Swan, clerk
50 John Cousins, grocer, 75 North st.
48 Thomas Walker, carpenter
Shipboy street.]
46 James Atkinson
44 John Wallace, sewed muslin manufacturer, 6 Corporation street
Side of Rev. Thomas Toye's meeting house
..[*Great George's street intersects.*]..
42 Mrs Moorcroft's school
40 Eliza Porter
38 John Deering, jeweller
36 Jas. M'Collough, grocer, 63 High street
34 Wm. Dunlop, draper
32 William Millen, schoolmaster
30 Ennis Clarke, butcher
28 James Quirey, spirit merchant, 31 Donegall street
26 Samuel Boyd, clerk
24 Thomas Kirker
22 Francis Johnson, manager in Archer and Sons' engraving establishment, Castle place
20 Mrs Mary Eccles
18 Jane M'Gee
16 Isabella Adair
14 Patrick Hynds, pawnbroker
..[*Little Patrick street intersects.*]..
12 R. Russell, grocer and spirit dealer
10 Wm. Stewart, cooper
8 Samuel M'Clurcan, cooper
6 Edward M'Keating, saddler
4 Francis Lees, schoolmaster
2½ John Arthur, tailor
James place.]
2 James Thompson

New Court
40 TOMB STREET.
Eight small houses

New Lodge Place
LODGE ROAD.
Matthew M'Bride, pensioner
Thomas Moore, carding master
John O'Neill, bundler
John Arthurs, tailor
James Finlay, turner
Ellen Havron
Hutchinson Robinson, mariner
Jane Robinson
James Johnston, bundler
Hugh M'Collough, labourer

Thomas Lindsay, mariner
John Richardson, weighmaster
Margaret Davidson

New Lodge Road
FROM NORTH QUEEN STREET.
New house building
1 James Milligan, porter
2 Hugh Maguire, tailor
3 James Haverl, labourer
4 John Boyes, labourer
5 Isabella Madill, boarding house
6 Charles Mullan, carpenter
1 Daniel M'Namara
3 Ann Dougherty, dealer
5 James Ritchie, carpenter
7 Patrick Kennedy, fishmonger
9 James M'Ilroy, labourer
11 Samuel Gamble, weaver
13 William Forbes, worker in foundry
15 John Heatley, fireman
17 John Johnston, dealer
19 Sarah Haggarty
21 Philip Smith, hackler
23 Eliza Mooney
25 Patrick Daly, dealer
27 James Donnelly, labourer
29 William Hanan, labourer
31 John Douglass, mechanic
[*New Lodge place.*
33 John Hayney, hackler
35 William M'Farell, labourer
37 William Carson, porter
39 John Kane, labourer
41 Jane Finlay
43 Samuel Johnston, dealer
45 Robert Moore, labourer
47 Alice Devine, reeler
49 William M'Kinney, stone mason
51 Isabella Douglass
53 Edward Garner, tailor and spirit dealer
55 Robert Clark, labourer
57 James Guy, spirit dealer
59 Bernard Coyle, coal dealer
61 John Watson, labourer
63 Mary M'Sorley
1 Robert Watson, labourer
2 Charles Johnston, labourer
3 New Lodge Road Spirit Store; Thomas Smyth, proprietor
Entrance gate, Adam J. Macrory, solicitor, Duncairn; office, Rosemary street
1 Hans Wilson, dealer

3 John Rainey
5 Francis Sloan, labourer
7 Wm. John Wye, labourer
9 Margaret Brown
11 Margaret Green, dealer
13 Thomas Killip, butler
15 Owen M'Cann, labourer
Antrim road.]
12 Michael Maloy, labourer
10 Betty Kerr
8 Wm. Holmes, book deliverer
6 Nathaniel Duncan, labourer
4 Daniel M'Cartney, labourer
2 John Roberts, deputy high constable of cess; office, Queen st.
Lodge cotton mill—Messrs. Lepper, proprietors
Wm. Lepper, Laurel Lodge
Mrs Frances Lepper, Trainfield house
72 Malcolm Murray, stonemason
70 Vacant
68 Joseph M'Collough, spirit dealer
66 Robert Lenaghan, labourer
64 Mrs Nelson, dealer
62 James Murray, tailor
60 Wm. M'Stay, grocer
58 John Hunter, dealer
" Wm. James Galway, labourer
56 Allen Cathcart, labourer
54 Michael Cush, labourer
52 George Haslett, labourer
50 Bridget Woods
48 Wm. Gallagher, bricklayer
46 Mary Welsh
44 Neill Hughes, labourer
42 Thomas M'Reynolds, labourer
40 Joseph Shaw, labourer
38 Wm. Duncan
36 Owen Ward, hackler
34 James Dougherty, labourer
32 John M'Kenna, labourer
30 Robert M'Mullan, labourer
28 John O'Neill, dealer
26 Thomas M'Kenna, dealer
24 Joseph Brown, sawyer
22 Hugh Donoho, dealer
20½ Rose Clark, dealer
20 Robert Douglass, labourer
18 Samuel Wright, labourer
16 Owen Hamill, labourer
14 Patrick Ward, dealer
12 Joseph Collier, locksmith
10 Thomas Lynch, dealer
8 Ellen Smith, dealer

6 Daniel M'Ilroy, dealer
Gutter alley.]
4 Margaret M'Keown, dealer
2 Joseph Nevin, labourer
Entrance to Joseph Finlay's spirit store

New Row
BERRY STREET.
Twenty-two small houses

Nile Street
FROM NELSON STREET TO YORK ST.
1, 3 Robert King, grocer and spirit dealer
5 Andrew Armstrong, ship smith
7 Vacant
9 John Smith, stone cutter
11 Samuel Ewing, grocer and spirit dealer
[*Little Henry street.*
13 Ann Bayne, grocer & spirit dealer
15 John O'Leery, customhouse officer
17 Ann Stewart
19 Arthur Walker, grocer and spirit dealer
[*Little York street.*
Side of J. Corduke's provision store
Side of G. and H. M'Kibbin's provision store
Little York street.]
26 Eliza Blair, grocer
24 James Gordon, carpenter
22 Ann Beckett
20 Wm. Eades, joiner
18 Wm. M'Dowell, mechanic
18½ Edward M'Murray, in Rowan's foundry
16 Vacant
James Campbell, sea captain
14½ Archibald Roberts, boat builder
12 John Holmes, millwright
10 John Simmons, sea captain
8 James Dinnen, revenue officer
6 James Adams, ship carpenter
4 James Neill, mechanic
2 Isabella Learmoth

North Ann Street
FROM CORPORATION STREET TO NELSON STREET.
1 Alexander Loughrey, labourer
3 John Knox, quay constable
1 5 Robert Graham, sawyer
7 Wm. M'Cann, labourer

9 Ann Brown
11 David Tumbelty, butler
13 Richd. Loughran, harbour constable
15 Andrew Mahon, clerk in Ballymena Railway office
17 Henry Quinn, customhouse officer
19 Wm. M'Dowell, sea captain
21 Mary Redmond, dressmaker
23 John Quee, painter
25 John Monteith, sailmaker
27 Michael Madden, quay porter
29 Francis M'Cann, pilot
28 Francis Stewart, boarding house
26 Ann Ellington
24 Vacant
22 J. Campbell, customhouse officer
20 Wm. Bickerstaff, boatman
18 James Robinson, stone cutter
16 John M'Cutcheon, pilot
14 Bernard M'Ilveen, watchman
12 Patrick M'Kenna, lumper
18 Wm. Perry, letter carrier
8 Daniel Gribbin, carter
6 Wm. Mullan, labourer
4 James Nelson, cotton spinner
2 Alexander Kerr, spirit dealer

North Boundary Street
OLD LODGE ROAD.
1 Mrs Moffat, boarding house
3 Patrick Darcy, foreman printer
5 Andrew Scully
7 William Lowry, moulder
9 James Cooke, plumber
11 Alexander Stewart, car driver
13 William Young, stone mason
15 Thomas Gillespie, labourer
20 Wm. Moore
18 Wm. Johnston, warper
16 John Smyth, gardener
14 Hugh Montgomery, car driver
12 John Dunlavey, baker
10 Abraham Hill, carpenter
8 John Smylie, mechanic
6 Mary Addy
4 Isaac Waugh, clerk
2 Mrs Campbell, dealer

Northburn Place
OLD LODGE ROAD.
Wm. S. Baird, printer
Wm. Hanna, boiler maker
John Foreman, linen lapper
Three new houses building

Northburn Street
OLD LODGE ROAD.
John Law, farmer
William Watson, warder in jail

North Queen Street
CARRICKHILL TO OLD CARRICK ROAD.
1 Mrs Fawkner, lodging house
3 Hugh O'Neill, green grocer, and boot and shoemaker
[*Frederick street.*
5 R. D. Kirk, wine and spirit shop
7 Isabella M'Comb, white worker
9 Halliday Maltseed, machine smith
11 Vacant
11½ Mrs Eliza Hill
13 Hugh Kelly, spirit store, Bank lane
15 Constabulary Station—Head Constable, William Smith
17 John M'Millan, spirit dealer
19 Miss Noland, boarding house
21 William Delany
23 John Hawkins, cotton spinner
25 Mary Dixon, dealer
27 Denis M'Ginnis, printer
29 Patrick Fitzsimons, labourer
31 William John Leathem, shoemaker
33 Benjamin Gilmore, spirit dealer
[*May's lane.*
35 Martin Rutherford, spirit dealer
37, 39 Robert Maxwell, dealer
41 Richard Lavery, spirit dealer
[*Lancaster street.*
43 James Park, grocer and spirit dealer
45 Thomas Ewart, spirit dealer
47 Patrick Cheevers, grocer & publican
49 William Frame, dealer
51 John Kinny, grocer and publican
53 Christie M'Donald, slater
55 Patrick M'Farley, pensioner
57 Catherine Marson, spirit dealer
59 Ann Hawkes, dealer
61 James Walsh, spirit dealer
63 William Pollock, pensioner
65 Thomas Shaw, spirit dealer
67 Vacant
69 Thomas Montgomery, spirit dealer
[*Great George's street.*
Enclosed ground   [*Henry street.*
71 James Baxter, copper and tinsmith
73 John Campbell, linen lapper
75, 77 John Wilson, baker and forage contractor
79 Jane Gregory, pawnbroker
81 Robert Mooney, editor of *News-Letter*

83 Thomas Price, accountant, Harbour Commissioners' office
85 Vacant
87 Alexander Wilson, grocer
89 Edward Smith, spirit dealer
[*Sussex street.*
91 John Canavan, spirit and provision dealer
93 Vacant
95 Richard Duncan, gardener
97 Wm. Jas. Thompson, grocer
[*Vere street.*
99 Jane Murphy, haberdasher and grocer
101 Miss Margaret Mack
103 Miss Hancock
[*Old Carrickfergus road.*]
Hardinge street—Several houses occupied by millworkers
MARY'S PLACE.
James Holmes, grocer and spirit dealer
John Frazer, mechanic
Bernard Carey, carpenter
North Queen street place.]
James Brown, labourer
Ann M'Crea, whiteworker
New Lodge Road.]
56 Joseph Finlay, grocer, spirit, and provision dealer
54½ Sarah Campbell
54 Patrick Dougherty, dealer
52 Peter Cullin, dealer
50 Wm. Orr, grocer
Artillery street.]
48 James M'Nicholl, green grocer
46 James M'Cann dealer
CAVALRY BARRACKS
44 Thomas M'Gurk, spirit dealer
42 Alexander Burke, tailor
John Wilson's coal & stabling yard
40 Wm. Bryson
38 Alexander Crossett, collector of police rate and haberdasher
36 Mrs Church
34 Mrs Fenwick
32 Mrs M'Kee
30 Edward Smyth, shoemaker
28 Mrs Wightman, dressmaker
26 Thomas Ewart, gentleman
24 Robert Kelso Mathewson, gentleman
22 Mrs Groom, boarding house
20 John Knox, gentleman
18 John Kerr, clerk

STREET DIRECTORY.

16 William Stewart, teller Provincial Bank
INFANTRY BARRACKS
14 Samuel Hunter, manager of Belfast Foundry
12 David Woods, agent for Hill Hamilton
10 Alexander Moncrieff, clerk
8 Wm. Hastings, civil engineer
6 George S. Hill, Sub-Inspector of constabulary
4 John Orr, clerk
" Mrs Orr, servants' registry
2 James Tilley, muslin manufacturer; factory, off Shankhill road
THE OLD POORHOUSE—J. Marshall, house steward

North Queen Street Place
(FORMERLY FINLAY'S COURT.)
Six small houses

North Street
FROM BRIDGE ST. TO PETER'S HILL.
1, 3 John Lytle, wholesale grocer and seed merchant
5 Vacant
7 James H. Smyth and Co., glass, oil, and paint warehouse; residence, 6 Waring street
9 Wm. Lewis, haberdasher
11 James M'Cann, soap and candle manufacturer; residence, 3 Winecellar entry
13 Wm. Hughes, corn merchant and flax spinner
15 William Addison, wholesale grocer and seed merchant
17 Samuel Gelston, wine and spirit merchant; residence, Rosstulla, Whiteabbey
19 Vacant
21 James Boyd, umbrella and parasol maker
[*North street place.*
23 Joseph Lewis, lithographic printer; residence, Carrickfergus
23 John Costley, seedsman
25 Robert Vance, wine and spirit merchant; residence, M'Tier street
27 Wm. Bullock, brush and weavers' utensil warehouse; residence, Bower's hill
[*St. Anne's buildings.*
29 Mrs Robinson's commercial boarding house
31 John and Robert Potts, iron merchants; J. Potts' residence, 25 York street; R. Potts' residence, Rosemount, Antrim road
33,35 Jas. Kavanagh, wholesale grocer, glass, oil, and colour dealer
37,39 Vacant
41 Ann Ievers, grocer and tobacconist
43 Daniel R. Brannigan, wholesale tea, wine, and spirit stores; residence, 2 Murray's terrace
43 Alex. Grant and Co., drapers and silk merchants; A. Grant's residence, 2½ Joy street
45,47 Wm. Dobbin, wholesale grocer, druggist, and drysalter; residence, 102 Donegall street
[*Long lane*
49 Robert Milliken, saddler and harness maker
51 David Rodgers, saddler and harness maker; residence, York street
53 E. and M. Riddell, bonnet makers and haberdashers
55 John Reid, haberdasher
57 Miss Noble, boarding house
59 James Thompson, bakery and flour merchant
61 Osborne Kidd, flour miller; residence, Armagh
63 Nathaniel Dickey, grocer
65 Eliza Jane Duncan, haberdasher
[*Church street.*
67 John Thompson, watch and clock maker, and jeweller
69 Johnston & Kennedy, haberdashers
71 John & James Dysart, boot and shoemakers
73 Isabella Dickson, vender of medicine
75 John & W. R. Cousins, wholesale and retail grocers and cheesemongers; residence, 50 Nelson st.
75 Joseph W. M'Alister, wholesale and retail wine and spirit stores
77 Forster Green & Co., Golden Eagle tea establishment
83 John Milford, corn and flour merchant; residence, 86 Hercules st.
85 William Tate, green hide, leather, and nail stores
87 David Bell, wholesale and retail grocer
89 Robt. Blackburn & Co., wholesale and retail grocers and druggists
[*John street.*
91 Margt. Jane Patrick, haberdasher

STREET DIRECTORY. 147

93 John M'Farlane, clock and watch maker; residence, 30 Sandy row
" Hugh Spence, boot and shoemaker
95 Mrs Hederman, haberdasher; residence, 101 North street
97 Patk. Denvir, baker & flour dealer
99 Mary Hunter, baker & confectioner
101 Mary Moonan, haberdasher
103, 105 Nathaniel Isles, leather merchant, and boot and shoemaker
107 Mary Ann Browne, haberdasher
109 Wm. Campbell, leather merchant
109½ Patrick O'Neill, retail spirit store
111 Pat. O'Neill, boot & shoemaker
113 Jane Crawford, flour store and bakery
115 Thos. Sanders, brazier & tinsmith
117 Catherine Justin, whip manufactory
119 Thomas Frazer, leather mercht.
121 Robt. Mahaffey, boot & shoemaker
123 John Graham, wholesale and retail confectioner
125 Robert Jardin & Co., grocers
127, 129 John Casey, spirit dealer and grocer
131 Vacant   [*Union street.*
133 John Elliot, grocer
135 Wm. Knox, baker & flour dealer
135½ Teressa Maginn, haberdasher
137 W. M'Ilroy, grocer & spirit dealer
" Andrew M'Ilroy's carman's yard
139 James M'Blain, leather merchant
141 James M'Millen's provision store
143 Wm. Moore, currier and leather merchant
145 Allen Martin, grocer and flour merchant
147 James Barry, haberdasher
147½ Robert Guinn, coach maker
" Eliza Guinn, stay maker
[*M'Tier's court.*
149 James Dunlop, whip manufactory
151, 153 Robt. Peel's bakery & flour stores; residence, Shankhill road
[*M'Kibben's court.*
155 George Kerns, saddler and harness maker
157 Hugh Crawford, grocer
159 Lawrence O'Brien, hair dresser & wig maker
161 John Ingram, provision dealer
163 Patrick Toner, provision dealer
165 Mary Wright, dealer
167, 169 Thos. Mullins, provision dealer

171 John Short, baker and flour dealer
173 Margaret Anderson, spirit dealer
[*Hamilton's court.*
175 Michael Kelly, provision dealer
177 Denis Dyer, spirit dealer
179 James Hamill, provision dealer
181 Thos. Boyd, baker and flour dealer
183 Wm. Kealey, provision dealer
185 Rose Ann Adams, confectioner
187 James M'Clements, green grocer
189 John Caruth, grocer, meal, flour, and bran stores
191 Robert Gilmor, pawnbroker
[*Peter's hill.*]
204 Robt. Orr, grocer and spirit dealer
202 Edward Daly, surgeon, North Street Medical Hall
200 John M'Kenna, spirit dealer
198 James Adams, baker
196 Luke M'Cann, dealer
194 John Loughran, butcher
192 John Madden, dealer
190 James M'Peak, pedlar
188 John Halliday, tailor
Law's lane.]
186 Thos. Craig, grocer & spirit dealer
184 Matthew Irvine, spirit dealer & stabling yard
182 James Anderson, provision dealer
180 Thomas Bryson, hardware shop
178 John Smith, looking glass maker
176 John Canavan's timber and coal yard
174 James Wilson, toy shop
172 James Laughlin, confectioner
170 Wm. Patterson, soap and candle manufacturer
168 James A. Cumine, electrical and optical warehouse
166 Thomas Beatty, spirit dealer
164½ Hugh Magee, stabling yard
164 James Ball, spirit dealer
162 James Boyd, baker and flour merchant
160 Samuel Barron, grocer
158 Mary Ann M'Williams, Eagle inn and stabling yard
156 Patrick Henry, dealer
154 John Waugh, bakery and flour dealer
Winetavern street.]
152 Arthur Hunter, leather merchant
150 John Foley, provision dealer and butcher
148 Vacant

146 Patrick Fowler, confectioner
144 Edward Leathem, umbrella maker and bell hanger
142 Michl. M'Avoy, pipe manufactory
140 Jane Wilson, toy shop
138 John Hunter, soap and candle manufactory
136 Dennis Louden, butcher
134 Arthur Alexander, wholesale and retail spirit dealer, coal merchant, and stabling
132 James Waugh, leather warehouse
130 Arthur Crawford's iron stores
128 John Woods Beck, M.D., surgeon and apothecary
126 James Boucher, haberdasher
124 Richard Ware, spirit dealer and stabling yard
122 Arthur Murphy, confectioner
120 John Dougherty, spirit dealer
Hudson's entry.]
118 Henry M'Anally, spirit dealer
116 John M'Ilveen, haberdasher
114 Thomas M'Ateer, grocer and spirit dealer
Ritchie's place.]
112 Richard Colpoy, wholesale flour and grain merchant
110 Hugh Lowe's grocery & flour store
108 Margt. Beattie, boot and shoe shop
108 John S. Dickson, surgeon; residence, Ligoneil villa
106 Wm. Mathews, hairdresser
104 Adam Duncan, carman's inn and stabling yard
Hercules street.]
102 James Evans, spirit dealer
100 James Wilson, tobacconist
98 Patrick Mooney, butcher and spirit dealer
96 Daniel M'Cann, soap & candle manufacturer; residence, 97 York st.
94 Bernard M'Auley, boot and shoemaker
92 John M'Cartin, nail manufactory
90 Bernard M'Auley, boot and shoemaker
88 James Lamb, boot and shoemaker
86 Samuel Elliott, confectioner
84 Margaret Henesay, haberdasher
82 Andrew Kirk, tobacco manufactory
80 Jane Conway, spirit dealer and boarding house
78 Bernard M'Donald, haberdasher & cap manufacturer

76 Thomas Gribbin, bookseller
74 James Dornan, rope and twine manufacturer
72 Jane Caulfield, haberdasher
70 James Marlow, rope and twine manufacturer
68, 66 North Star Inn and Hotel, and posting establishment—George Gordon, proprietor
64 Robert Bunting, confectioner
Round entry.]
62½ Vacant
62 Mary Pollock, bookseller
" Jane Pollock, dressmaker
60 James M'Clarns and Co., curriers, wholesale and retail leather merchants
58½ Joseph M'Alister, soap and candle manufacturer
58 James Torbit, jun., wine merchant and spirit dealer; residence, 9 Albion place
56 William Stewart, brush and trunk maker
54 Jane Greer, soap and candle manufacturer
52 Kirker, Brothers, haberdashers; residence, 24 Nelson street
50 James Stormont, house painter and glazier
48 James Davidson, saddler and harness maker
46 William Riley, haberdasher
44, 42 William Henry Morris, soap and candle manufacturer
40, 38 Mercer and Kerr, wholesale druggists and general merchants
36 Miller, Clindinning, and Co., Manchester and Scotch warehousemen, and manufacturers; residences: Wm. Clindinning, 15 May street; George L. Miller, Henry street
34 Samuel M'Causland, wholesale grocer, tobacco manufacturer, & seed merchant; residence, Lodge Cottage
32, 30, 28 Vacant
26 Samuel D. Robinson, brush, card, and bellows manufacturer; residence, 29 North street
24 Fergus Massy, tobacconist
22 Thomas Gray, wholesale and retail grocer, ship owner, &c.
20, 18 Wm. Dobbin, wholesale and re-

STREET DIRECTORY.

tail grocer and druggist; residence, 102 Donegall street
16, 14 Wm. Sherrie, wholesale and retail brush manufacturer, and gutta percha agent
12 George Massy, tobacco and snuff manufacturer
10 Edward Taylor, seedsman
6 Mrs Magee, wine and spirit store, Derry, Larne, Antrim, and Crumlin mail coach office
4 John M'Donnell, tobacconist and grocer
2 James Skene, spirit dealer, Stag's Head Tavern

O'Haggarty Street
BOUNDARY ST.

1 Thomas M'Kibbin, bundler
3 James Lackey, cabinet maker
5 John M'Kenna, labourer
Side of John Ewing's grocery and spirit store
6 Charles Maken, car driver
4 Daniel Gilliland labourer
2 Tracey Brittain, labourer

Old Lodge Place
OLD LODGE ROAD.
Twelve small houses

Old Lodge Road
FROM PETER'S HILL.
RIGHT SIDE.

1 William Kelly, labourer
3 Peter M'Crory, boot and shoemaker
5 James Henderson, labourer
7 John Black, helper in foundry
9 Leckey Devine, porter
11 Patrick M'Kavanagh, marine store
13 James Suffern, porter
15 Vacant
17 Hugh M'Cann, butcher
19 John Mulgrew, blacking manufacturer
21 Thomas Keenan, rope manufacturer
23 Bernard O'Neill, flaxman
25 George Wilkie, plumber
27 Daniel Magee, grocer
[*Alton street into Wall street.*
29 James Ross, brick manufacturer
31 Catherine Magill, dressmaker
33 John Williamson, whitesmith
35 Owen M'Kee, labourer
37 John Cameron, starch maker
[*Upton street.*
39 Catherine Hannan, boarding house
41 James M'Ilvenna, labourer
43 Arthur M'Gurk, pensioner
45 James O'Hagan, dealer
47 Daniel Dunbar, clerk
[*California street.*
49 Thomas Haggarty, porter
51 George Rice, pensioner
53 James M'Cracken, weaver
55 Andrew Armstrong, chandler
57 John Saunders, labourer
[*Arnon street.*
59 Ezekiel Moore, whitesmith
61 John M'Clusky, salesman
63 Jane Sharpe, widow
65 William Smith grocer
[*Stanhope street.*
67 Henry Harper, carpenter
69 Alexander Davison, baker
71 Joseph Hill, coast guard
Mr Ross's brick field
73 Patrick Burns, weaver
75 Aaron Osborne, weaver
77 Daniel Burns, weaver
79 Richard Johnson, weaver
81 Francis Devlin, weaver
83 Patrick Lyons, dealer
85 Mrs Magee, widow
87 Samuel Kennedy, boot and shoemaker
89 Vacant
[*New street to Crumlin road.*
Two new houses not finished
[*New street to Crumlin road.*
Rere of new Court house
S. M'D. Elliott, Old Lodge House, seneschal and solicitor; office, Arthur street
Arthur Crawford, woollendraper; shop, Waring street
John and Robt. Getty, gentlemen, Beech park
John Hind, flax spinner, The Lodge
Samuel M'Causland, grocer, the Lodge Cottage; shop, North st.
Old Park Print Works—Robert Howie, proprietor

LEFT SIDE.

James M'Tier, gentleman, Vermont Lodge
John Tate, farmer

John Thompson, working bleacher
Crumlin Turnpike.]
Glentilt place.]
Court street.]
John Clarke, commercial traveller
Old Lodge place.]
Small houses—Several vacant
Mary Kirker
Edward Coyle, labourer
Wm. Beatty, grocer & spirit dealer
Conlon street.]
John Quin, grocer and publican
Wm. M'Clenahan, mechanic
James Parker, tailor
Campbell street.]

FLEMING'S PLACE.

1 James Clendining, grocer and publican
2 Robert Campbell, carpenter
3 Wm. Weir, stone cutter
4 Wm. Flanigan, block printer
5 James Lemon, stone cutter
6 Joseph Hamilton, block printer
7 Thomas Collins, print cutter
8 Robert Manson, labourer
8 Wm. Thompson, sawyer
10 Vacant
134 John Magee, bricklayer
132 Hugh Clarke, carpenter
130 John Patterson, carter
128 James M'Auley, brick moulder
126 Mrs Montgomery
124 Mrs Blakely
122 John Fryer, book deliverer
120 Alfred M'Meehan, labourer
118 James Blessington, millworker
116 Ralph Briggs, salesman
114 James Lynch, cooper
112 John R. Darling, grocer
James Gibson, rope maker
108 John Brown, schoolmaster
106 Margaret Campbell, dealer
North Boundary street.]
104 Edward Donnelly, spirit dealer
102 Robert Foster, packer
100 James Beattie, grocer
98 Joseph Quin, labourer
96 Ann M'Cleery
94 James Rogers, porter in bank
92 Wm. Magill, labourer
90 Peter Andrews, Jews' harp maker
88 Samuel Nixon, shoemaker
86 Thomas Ryan, pensioner
84 Thomas Martin, printer
Bernard Gorman, weaver

84½ James Murdoch, weaver
82 James Bruce, pensioner
80 John Hamilton, cooper
78 Joseph Haslett, labourer
76 Ann Houston, sewer
74 John M'Cullogh, painter
M'Clelland's lane.]
From 72 to 48 small houses
46 Patrick Heggarty, bricklayer
44 Bernard Mallon
Arthur's open.]
42 Hugh Bigham, watchman
40 Thomas Lewis, publican
38 James Gallagher, porter
36 Robert Palmer, labourer
34 Archibald Smith, labourer
32 Samuel Hart, lapper
30 Francis Miller, shoemaker
28 Wm. Irvine, porter
26 Sarah M'Williams, widow
From 24 to 2 small houses

Ormeau Place
ORMEAU ROAD.

1 Miss Brown
2 Mrs Greenfield
3 Thos. Wallace, commission agent, Elliot's court
4 Wm. Shaw, in Ulster bank
5 Rev. Edward Johnston
6 John Farrel, gentleman
7 Mrs Monteith
8 Miss M'Naughten
9 Mrs Garrett   [*Ormeau street.*
10 Mrs Magill
11 Mrs Simms
12 James Thomson, linen merchant
13 Major Henry Kean
14 Miss Mary Harrison

Ormeau Road
FROM CROMAC TO BALLYNAFEIGH.
RIGHT SIDE.
            [*Ormeau place.*
            [*Glenfield place.*
Samuel G. Getty, gentleman, Cromac Park
    [*Ormeau bridge.*]
James Bristow, Northern Bank, Prospect
Anna's Cottage, vacant
LEFT SIDE
Ormeau—seat of the Marquis of Donegal
Thomas Verner, D.L., J.P., Ormeau House; office, Castle place

STREET DIRECTORY. 151

The Rev. Henry Cooke, D.D., LL.D.
Hugh C. Clarke, auctioneer and broker, Rosemary street
Henry Garrett, solicitor, Cromac House; office, Castle lane
Miss Moreland, Cromac
William Barlow, Gasfield House, manager of Belfast Gas Works

BALLYNAFEIGH.
RIGHT SIDE.

John Dawson, pensioner
Wm. Hazlett, pensioner
John Mooney
House vacant
Thomas Purvis, commission agent
Charles Grogan, general merchant in wood and iron, and hay exporter, 49 Smithfield
George Emerson, stone cutter
Mary Furlong, dealer
Samuel Martin, porter
Wm. Lawder, labourer
Martha Sinnamend
Thomas Simpson, mill banding, leasing, tambouring, and sewing thread manufacturer
John Newell, schoolmaster
James Gorman, shoemaker
Mary Stewart
Thomas Simpson, cotton twister
David Agnew, bricklayer
Isabella Stewart
James Clark, nail maker and dealer
James Jamieson, gentleman
George Jamieson, boiler maker
George M'Connell, blacksmith
Daniel Stockman, labourer
Hans Wilgar, spirit dealer
Mary Hawkins
Samuel Spence, labourer
John Johnston, labourer
Sarah Jamison, laundress
George Holmes, dealer
John Holmes, plumber
Amy Crossley
Andrew Kilpatrick, labourer
Dr. Charles Hurst, Locust Lodge [*Newtownbreda road.*]

LEFT SIDE.

Francis D. Finlay, proprietor of the *Northern Whig*, Ballynafeigh Cottage
Miss Margery Smith
Thomas Hume, merchant; office, 5 Gloucester street

Thomas Richardson, clerk in Vitriol Works
Charles Blackham, clerk in Ulster Bank
John A. Stewart, clerk
Henry Rodgers, gentleman
Wm. M'Clusky, butler
Elizabeth Fitzpatrick
James M'Larnon, butler
Doctor Alexander
Wm. Kirkwood, saddler and harness maker
John Hill, labourer
John Johnston, labourer
WESLEYAN CHAPEL
Samuel Carnduff, weaver
John Brittan, spirit dealer
William Mullan, shoemaker
James Smith, plasterer
William Morrison, sawyer
Mary M'Burney, washerwoman
Samuel Johnson
Samuel Campbell, labourer
William Dunbar, tailor
James Brittan, weaver
Hamilton Bell, nailer
Rachael Graham
Hugh Johnston
Eliza Gilmore, washerwoman
Eliza M'Cully
Peter Logan, labourer
Henry Hall, ropemaker
William Magill, pensioner
House vacant
Miss Stannus
Miss Heyland
John M'Caldin, gentleman
Dr. Thomas Wilson

Ormeau Street
NEWTONBREDA ROAD.

Mrs M'Murray
James Robinson, sea captain
Mrs Jane Shaw

Orr's Entry
30 HIGH STREET.

1 James Allen, tailor
3 Patrick Kerns, tailor
5 Ross O'Connor and Co.'s stores
7 Edward M'Auley, ostler
8 Charles Crossley, hat manufacturer
6 Susan M'Anulty, boarding house
4 Back entrance to Mrs Brady's hotel

Oxford Street
EAST END MAY STREET.
Cattle market
Side of flax and fruit market
......[*May street intersects.*]......
Two old houses
Side of vegetable market
.....[*Chichester street intersects.*]....
Side of pork market

Pakenham Place
OLD DUBLIN ROAD.
1 J. N. Macartney, jeweller; Donegall place
2 Richard Baxter
3 Robert Dennison, of Post Office
4 Mrs M'Donald
5 John Preston, of John Preston & Co., Calendar Street, flax and yarn merchants
6 Boyd Fleming, gentleman
7 Ledlie Clarke, brewer, Ann street
8 John Carlisle, comptroller of customs
9 Thomas Wann, secretary in Ulster Bank
10 Robt. Workman, of Robert Workman & Co., sewed muslin manufacturers, Upper Arthur st.

Palmer's Place
LOWER MALONE.
Fifteen small houses

Park Street
OFF STANHOPE STREET.
1 David Robinson, warehouseman
3 Mary Ann Montgomery, dealer
4 Mary M'Cammon, grocer
2 Henry Collins, cloth lapper

Patrick's Lane
40 GT. TO 55 LITTLE PATRICK ST.
Ellen Harper, lodging house keeper
4 Daniel Burns, rag store
Thirteen small houses

Patrick Street, Great
YORK STREET TO CORPORATION ST.
1 Henry Loughran, wine and spirit stores; shop, 41 York street
[*Clark's lane.*
3, 5 Vacant [*Corr's lane.*
Samuel Clotworthy, ship owner
James M'Fadden, ship owner and cooperage, 26 Tomb street
13 James Major, sewed muslin manufacturer; office, 10 York street
15 John Douglass, salesman in Mr. Kennedy's muslin warehouse
17 George Pelan, clerk in Messrs. Richardson's, Corporation street
19, 21 William Kernaghan, grocer
[*Academy street.*
23 Wm. Hamilton, delf merchant
25 John Crawford, sewed muslin manufacturer; residence, 7 Adelaide place
27 John Fisher and Co., sewed muslin manufacturers
29 William Miller, sewed muslin agent to Park & Thompson, Glasgow
31 Wm. Wallace, sewed muslin agent to Hay & Bartholomew, Glasgow
33 Richard Foy, pawnbroker
35 James Calwell, delf merchant
37 Samuel Todd, flax and tow merchant and dealer, 54 Edward st.
[*Edward street.*
39 John Taylor, publican
41 James Shaw, chandler; shop, 23 Ann street
43 James M'Alinden, pork buyer for J. & T. Sinclair, Tomb street
45 Samuel M'Kee, sewed muslin manufacturer
47 John Robinson & Sons, Glasgow, sewed muslin manufacturers; William Donald, agent
49 John Anderson, sewed muslin manufacturer
51 Alexander Kilpatrick, book agent for Blackie and Sons, Glasgow; office, Arthur street
[*Lynas's lane.*
53 Andrew Morrow, publican
55 John Johnston's steam marble works, and residence
57 Sinclair Ramsay, draper; shop, 12 Hill street
59 John Coburn, dealer
61 Mrs Lynchey
63 James Hamilton, pipe maker
BUTTER MARKET.
1 James Scott, 5 Queen's square
2,3 John and Thomas Smith; residences: J. Smith's, Meadow street; T. Smith's, Dock street
4 Vacant
5 Peter M'Kinney, 47 Edward st.
6 S. Duffield, Tomb street

STREET DIRECTORY. 153

7 James Frazer; residence, 17 Great Edward street
8 James M'Comb; residence, 20 Cargill street
9 Wm. Ware; residence, James st.
10 Thomas Erwin; lodgings, 36 Nelson street
11 Felix M'Alinden; residence, 43 Great Patrick street
12 Jn. Erwin; residence, 48 Little Patrick street
13 Samuel Moore; residence, 13 Ann street
14 Joseph Bailie; residence, Fleming's place, Old Lodge road
15 Clements Bell; residence, 7 Great Patrick street
16, 17 Vacant
18 Samuel M'Connell; residence, Edward street; provision store, Academy street
Weighmaster—John Harper; residence, 1 Frederick place
Collector of Toll—Wm. Thomas
[*Corporation street.*]

ORMOND MARKET.

1 William Thomas, butcher; residence, Gamble street
2, 4 James Graham, green grocer
3 Joseph Potts, green grocer, egg and fowl merchant; residence, 20 Henry place
5 Hugh M'Roberts, green grocer; residence, Lower Staunton st.
6, 7, 8, 9, 10 Vacant
11 Hugh M'Genarty, green grocer; residence, Great Patrick street
12, 13, 14 Vacant
15 John Austin, green grocer; residence, Little Patrick street
16, 17 Vacant
18, 19 Daniel Dickson, poulterer
20 Vacant
21 Henry Woodcock, poulterer
22, 23 Vacant
24 Robert Watson, weighmaster; residence, 32 Little Donegall street
69 John Sweney, cooperage; residence, 8 Patrick's lane
Entrance to Ormond market
68 Wm. Ware, butter merchant; residence, 23 Corporation street
66 Smyth and M'Millan, bakery
64 Michael Mulholland, lodgings
62 Hugh M'Guigan, grocer and spirit dealer, and butter merchant
60 John Porter, blacksmith
58, 56 Adam M'Farland, cooperage, grocer, and spirit dealer
54 James Rowan, carman's inn
52 Samuel Weir, publican
" Ellen M'Kee, shirt maker
50 James Rowan's stabling and yard
48 James Livingston, lodging house
46 Wm. Heron, grocer and baker
44 William Lee, car owner
42 Patrick M'Clusky, barber
Patrick's lane.]
40 Ellen Harper, lodging house keeper
38 Daniel Mullan, lodgings
36 Andrew Logan, cow keeper
34 Edward Walsh, carter
32 Robert Martin, grocer and publican
30 John Forde, boarding house
28 Willam Rowan, coast guard
David Thoburn, pawnbroker; office, Nelson street
Nelson street.]
26 Clements Bell's butter store; residence, No. 24
" Henry Brankin, grain and flour merchant; residence, 7 Nelson st.
24 Clements Bell, butter merchant;
22 Vacant
22½ William Eakin, medical store; shop, Donegall street
20 David Cooper, joiner and builder
18 Mrs Dobbin
16 Charles Pelling, sewed muslin manufacturer; office, 30 Donegall street
14 John Johnson, soap and candle manufacturer
12 James Adams, flour merchant, and carman's yard
10 James M'Clure, provision dealer; store, 5 Hill street
8 Mary M'Murtry, spirit dealer
Little York street.]
6, 4 Bell and Kirker, flour, grain, and commission merchants; Mr Bell's residence, No. 4; Mr Kirker's residence, 1 Little York st
2 Entrance to Bell & Kirker's stores

Patrick Street, Little
59 YORK ST. TO CORPORATION ST.
House and store vacant
Mary Ann Robinson, dress maker
John Mills, pilot
William Dooary, coachman

Vacant store
..[*Little York street intersects.*]..
5 James Walsh, provision dealer
7 Eliza Grimshaw, provision dealer
9 Elizabeth M'Varnon, white worker
11 Edward O'Neill, shipwright
13 Robert Baird, sawyer
15 James Kelly, ship carpenter
17 Hugh Rankin, ship carpenter
19 John Smith, tallow chandler
19½ D. Cooper's yard, Great Patrick st.
21 Wm. Murphy, grocer and publican
23 William Robinson, butter dealer
25 William Douglass, provision dealer
[*Tennent's court.*]
27, 29 Alex. Rogers, grocer
31 James Hawthorn, car owner
33 Mrs Brown
35 Walter Johnston, baker
37 Mathew Forde, shoemaker
39 Robert Russell, spirit merchant and grocer, 12 Nelson street
.....[*Nelson street intersects.*]......
41 Andrew Girvin, mechanic, and 17 Nelson street
43 Henry Sands, pork cutter
45 Eliza Small, mill worker
47 James Reid, publican
49 Wm. Caulfield, car owner
51 Richard Cherry, iron ship builder and grocer
53 Alexander Ramsey, baker
55 Robert Boyle, boarding house
[*Patrick's lane.*
57, 59 Vacant
61 Henry Murray, grocer and publican
63 Henry Wilcocks, servant
65 Margaret M'Murray
67 Vacant yard
69 John Logan, dealer
71 Patrick Kelly, stoker
73 Thomas Ewen, ship carpenter
75 Richard Coulter, sawyer
[*Covent garden.*
77 Mary Ann Brown, mangler
79 Ellen Harvey, confectioner
81 Charles M'Connell, shoemaker
[*Vance's court.*
83 Miss Esther Vance
85 John Shannon, pork trier
Entrance to Ormond market
87 Andrew Gorman, green grocer, 25 Ormond market
[*Corporation street.*]
Fergus O'Farrell, residence, Corporation street

Fergus O'Farrell's stores
74 Daniel Murray, marine stores
72 Mrs Johnston, lodging house
70 Mrs Susanna M'Murray
68 Joseph Brabazon, captain *Abigail*
66 William Lynass, carter
64 Susan M'Clements, boarding house
62 John Austin, green grocer
60 John Darby, linen & canvas weaver
58 James M'Keever, seaman
56 Sam.Johnston, marine store keeper and rag merchant
Rere of Phœnix foundry, Great George's street
Andrew Wallace, mechanic, Phœnix foundry
50 John Robinson, sail maker
48 Elizabeth Milliken
46 Thomas Mitchel, seaman
Caroline street.]
44 John Agnew, dealer
42 Patrick Walsh
40 James Graham, clothes cleaner
38 Edward Crofton
Unoccupied wareroom
36 Vacant
......[*Nelson street intersects.*]......
34 Patrick Hynds, pawnbroker, and 24 Nelson street
32 Thomas Saunders, carpenter
30½ Patrick Stevens, marine store
Ross Moorehead's cooperage
28, 26 Samuel Carlisle, wine, spirits, porter, and ale dealer, and flour and bran stores
24 Jane Saunders
22 James Dickey, stone cutter
20½ John Clotworthy, barber
20 Wm. Reynolds, labourer
Victoria court.]
16 Henry M'Kee, carman
14 James Logan, publican
12 Alexander O'Neill, teacher
Patterson's place.]
10 James Service, carpenter
8 Robert Moreland, grocer, flour, and meal dealer
...[*Little York street intersects.*]...
6 Mathew Magorian, publican
James Loughran, watchman
4, 2 Vacant

Patterson's Place
LITTLE PATRICK STREET.
Twenty-eight small houses

STREET DIRECTORY. 155

Patterson's Place
OFF DONEGALL SQUARE EAST.
Frederick M'Coy, Professor in Queen's College

Peel's Place
SHANKHILL ROAD.
James Culbert, labourer
John Taylor, mechanic
James Hillis, mechanic
James Ferguson, mechanic
Michael Leonard, pensioner
Wm. Douglass, painter
Thomas Lynass, mechanic
John Keenan, ropemaker

Peter's Hill
NORTH STREET TO SHANKHILL ROAD.
1 William M'Cloy, spirit store and butcher
3 Francis Hale, butcher
[*Lodge road.*]
5 Bernard O'Neill, publican, and 2 Lodge road
7 John M'Quillan, boot and shoemaker
9 Thomas Shields, lodgings
11 John Carlisle, seaman
13 Robert Armstrong, shoemaker
" Mrs Armstrong, bonnet maker
15 Peter Slane, railway labourer
17 John Creeny, coal porter
19 George Megarry, carter
21 John Cunningham, labourer
23 John Morris, labourer
23½ Wm. Minniece, pawnbroker
25 William Minniece's residence
27, 29 Rose Ann Doherty, spirit dealer
31 James M'Laughlin, barber
33 Ann Steed, grocer
35 John Kearney, grocer & publican
37 Thomas Bailie, green grocer
39 Samuel Moore, tailor
[*Allen's court.*]
41 Edward M'Sherry, carter
43 Thomas Reynolds, mill overseer
45 Mrs Sarah Steele
47 Jas. Reid, grocer, oats, meal, and flour dealer
49 Mrs Mary Brown
51 Thomas Rowell, grocer and spirit dealer
53 Archibald M'Crea, builder
55 Michael Smith, bricklayer
57 Mrs Ann Smith

59 John Downey, gas fitter
[*Barnett's court.*]
61 Patrick Kelly, house carpenter
63 George Williamson, labourer
65 John Gernon, labourer
67 Mrs Hannah Walker, grocer
69 Mrs Margaret Bamford
71 John M'Garell, butcher
73 John Lewis, railway engineer
75 John Kerr, carter
77, 79 Agnes Elliott, grocer & publican
[*M'Clelland's entry.*]
81 Hugh Houston, publican
83 James Caughey, green grocer and shoemaker
85 Alex. Dugan, mechanic
87 Israel Milliken, warm, shower, and vapour baths
87¼ Israel Burrows, brass foundry
89 Israel Burrows' residence
" Molyneux and Ferguson's starch works; office, 4 York lane
91 John Whiteside, carter
93 David M'Larnon, timber dealer
95 John Kyle, cow keeper and green grocer
97 Thomas Trotter, mason
99 Henry Price, butcher
101 Alexander Kelso, dealer
103 John Thompson, fireman
105 Sarah Ann Moore, publican
107 Wm. Brady, grocer
[*Shankhill road.*]
Townsend street.]
104 Alexander Dalgleish, grocer
102 Isaac M'Connell, carpenter
100 John Curran, muslin lapper, Elliott's court, Donegall street
98 Alexander Shields, baker
96 Adam Thompson, file cutter; workshop, 19 Little Donegall street
94 Henry Gray, Townsend street foundry
92 James Graham, linen weaver
90 Mary Mullan, lodgings
88 Mary Magee, sewer
86 Catherine Conway, sewer
84 Samuel Temms, pensioner
82 Robert Heaney, bricklayer
80 Andrew Dates, shopman
Brown square.]
76 Stewart Bamford, publican
74 David Savage, shoemaker
Rere of Mr. Herdman's store, Pipe lane

STREET DIRECTORY.

72 Vacant
70 Hugh M'Keown, labourer
68 Edward Donnelly, grocer and spirit dealer
Abbey street.]
66 John M'Connell, pawnbroker
64 Susanna Warnock, grocer
62 Alex. Jones, carter and coal dealer
Entry.]

M'CULLY'S GATE.

1 John Burns, tide waiter
2 Hugh M'Cormick, labourer
3 Thomas M'Cully, carter
4 Henry Harrison, baker
58 John Mallagh, lodgings
56 John M'Cabe, labourer
54 Francis Hale, butcher
52 Patrick M'Anally, shoemaker
50 Robert Nelson, provision dealer
48 Vacant
Gardiner street.]
46 Peter Hughes, grocer and publican
44 Henry Hunter, bricklayer
42 Peter Donnelly, dealer
40 Vacant
38 Wm. M'Neill, linen lapper
36 Patrick Murray, labourer
34 James Lewis, labourer
32 Mary Black, dealer
30 Adam M'Cappin, hay and straw dealer
28 Vacant
26 Ann Jane M'Auley, white worker
24 Wm. Whiteside, night constable
" Jane Whiteside, bonnet maker
22 Robert Percy, tailor
20, 18 Saml. Kerr, grocer & publican
16 John Hanna, grocer & spirit dealer
Boyd street.]
14½ Robert Connor, grocer
14 James Clelland, haberdasher
" Thomas Walker, cabinet maker
12 Frances Cassidy, toy shop
10 John M'Clure, boot and shoemaker
8 Donald Martin, publican
6 John Wilson, grocer
4 Samuel Cinnamond, nail maker
2 John Loughran, grocery and spirit stores

Pilot Street
OFF CORPORATION STREET

1 Arthur Woods, shoemaker
3 Mrs Kennedy
5 Catherine Barker, grocer and publican

7 Joseph Hunter, marine store
[*Barker's place.*
9 Robert Fleming, ship carpenter
11 Richard Graham, sawyer
13 James Peyton, sail maker
15 John Lightbody, mate *Emulous*
17, 19 Thomas Mathews, turner, and block and pump maker
21 John Hogg, ship smith
" Jane Hogg, grocer and publican
23 Robert Byrne, tailor and clothier
25 Alexander Dyer, pilot
27 Francis Finlay, ship chandler
" John Purse, carpenter
Ship Hotel—John Macartney, proprietor
" John Macartney's forge
" Robert Redpath, labourer
29 Hugh Noble, sawyer
31 John Clarke, publican
Coates and Young's Foundry; residence of Mr Coates, Glentoran; Mr Young's, Lagan Village
Two unfinished houses
SEAMAN'S FRIEND CHAPEL, and National School; teacher of male school, Mr James Houston; teacher of female school, Miss Dorrans; various preachers
Mr Grainger's stores
Foot of street not open
Rere of Mr. John Dunn's stores
20 Robt. Agnew, engineering manager in Coates and Young's foundry
18 John Hollewell, engineer
16 James Crangle, sea captain *Independence*
14 Thos. Vance, custom house officer
Vacant yard
14 Thomas Green, ship carpenter
Short street.]
12 John Wilson, publican
10 Alexander M'Cune, ship carpenter
8 Ellen Kennedy
6 Thomas Gillespie, house carpenter
4 Wm. Rankin, labourer
Wm. Herald, blacksmith
Pat. Fitzsimons, foundry labourer
2 Thomas Campbell, barber and hairdresser
Thomas Loudon, grocer

Plunkett's Court
118 CARRICKHILL
Seventeen small houses

STREET DIRECTORY.

Police Place
WILLIAM ST. SOUTH TO POLICE SQ.

William Bathurst, coach factory; residence, 21 William st. south

TOWN HALL—Mayor's office
  Sub-Treasurer's office—Adam Hill, 11 Fisherwick place
  Borough Accountant's office—D. Porter, 22 Hamilton street
  Town Surveyor's office—William Hastings, North Queen street
  Police Rate Collector's office—Alex. Crossett, North Queen st.
  Jas. Pinkerton, Chichester st.
  Inspector of Provisions, and Weights and Measures office

Telfair's entry.]
8 Robert Gray, agricultural implement and machine maker; 11 Telfair's entry
  FIRE ENGINE HOUSE—John Cockburn, superintendent; residence, 5 George's lane
  John Hayes' stable; residence, 12 William street South
  John Gaffikin's stable
2 John Morgan, porter and lodging house

Police Square
VICTORIA STREET TO POLICE PLACE.

Joseph Bell, publican, 1 Victoria st.
Edward M'Donnell, cheese and bacon dealer, Falls Road
Alexander M'Donald's Scrabo stone yard; residence, Newtownards
1 John Smart, labourer
3 John Cotter, nailer
5 David M'Court, drayman
" Castlebellingham Brewery office—Thomas Ranson, agent; house, 33 Little May street
  Store of Messrs. M'Clean
  James Agnew's timber and slate yard
9 Flax store—Cowan & Co., Whiteabbey
11 Samuel M'Dowell, saddler
  Daniel Cramsie, car owner
13 John Ferris, Shell-fish hotel
15 Thomas M'Bride, publican, and carpenter and builder
17 John Mitchell, fireman
19 James Rutherford, carpenter

21 Jacob Hogg, bricklayer & fireman
[*Thomas court.*
23 Henry Liddy, fireman
25 Thomas Macartney, fireman
27 John Hogg, bricklayer & fireman
29 Henry Dogherty, porter & fireman
  POLICE OFFICE—Thomas Lindsay, chief day constable, residence, 4 Wills' place; Wm. Armstrong, chief night constable, residence, 1 Wills' place
  Fire Escape
  FISH MARKET—John Ferris, superintendant
[*Police place.*
8 James Gallagher, labourer
6 John Finlay, jun., flax and tow merchant; residence, 7 Donegall square east
4 Closed yard
  Charles Dickey's forge
  Jas. Somerville's yard and stabling
  Surgeon Corry's chemical & steam ærated water works; medical hall, 13 Victoria street
  Edward Rogers, publican, 11 Upper Church lane

Poplar Court
GRATTAN STREET.

Five small houses

Portland Place
OFF PORTLAND STREET.

1 Arthur Donohoe, carter
3 Edward Jordan, mechanic
5 James Hunter, moulder
" John Henderson, boiler maker
7 Fanny Mallon, boarding house
9 Margaret Parker, boarding house
6 Robert Lees, labourer
4 Wm. Elcock, pensioner
2 John Wardlow, gun maker

Portland Street
ST. GEORGE'S ST. TO LANCASTER ST.

Seventeen small houses

Pottinger's Entry
49 HIGH STREET TO ANN STREET.

1 J. Wallace, watchmaker, hall door
3 John Arnold, clothier, back entrance
5 William Millikin, tailor
7 Robert Mackintosh, upholsterer

O

9 The Pottinger Arms hotel, tavern, and coffee house—Mrs Collins, proprietor
9 Archibald Moorhead, brazier
11 Mary Robinson, boarding house
13 James Bullick, shuttle maker
15, 19 James Simpson, oyster house
21 Edward Kermode, carrier
23 Alexander M'Kee, tailor
25 Susan M'Cann
27 Davidson and Chermside, flax spinners, Drumaness mills, near Ballynahinch
29 Wm. Magee, coachmaker
31, 33 John Gallagher, carrier
35 Alexander Paton, mariner
37 Hugh Cosgrave, dealer

[*Ann street.*]

28 Michael Noel, car driver
26 Hugh Cosgrave's marine store
24 Wm. Robinson, dealer
20 Richard Creen, dealer
18 Mary Denvir
16 Sarah M'Donald, dealer
14 John Quinn, emigration agent
14½ John Wightman, stores & stables
14 John Freeman and Co., rope and twine makers; residence, 5 Hamilton street
" Coates and Shaw, muslin manufacturers; Samuel Shaw's residence, Skipper street; Edward J. Coates's, 8 Ship street
12 George Nelson, tailor & clothier; residence, Newtonbreda
10 Hibernian Tavern and spirit store—Joseph Moody, proprietor
8 Richd. Copeland, tailor & clothier
4½ Edward Lennon's billiard room
4 Henry Devlin's bottling store
2 Patrick Devlin, spirit dealer

Pound Street
BARRACK STREET TO FALLS ROAD.

1 George Martin, carter
3 Daniel Maddin, fireman
5 James Lee, labourer
7 Ann M'Areavey
9 Felix Donohoe, hackler
11 James Hanratty, hackler
13 Patrick Flannagan, mechanic
15 Terence Haughey, gas fitter
17 Michael Crolly, bricklayer
19 William Faren, dealer
21 John Connolly, shoemaker

23 David Murray, lighterman
25 John Conlon, spirit dealer
27 William Jenkins, sawyer
29 James Craig, labourer
31 Mary Crolly
33 Andrew Moreland, dealer
35 Thomas Corner, sailor
37 Margaret Giffin
39 Thomas Carson, labourer
41 Robert Craig, carpenter
43 John Conley, labourer
45 Peter Donnelly, labourer
47 William Brownlee, schoolmaster
49 Thomas Quinn, blacksmith
51 James Conley, labourer
53 John Donnelly, labourer
55 Sarah Murphy
57 John Robinson, labourer
59 Ann Burns
61 Sarah M'Kee, washerwoman
32 Robert Coburn, labourer
30 Edward Quinn, sawyer
28 Patrick M'Call, gardener
26 George M'Laughlin, labourer

[*Whitehall court.*]

24 Edward M'Quillan, shoemaker
22 Margaret Grant, dealer
20 James Skivington, shoemaker
18 Patrick Skivington, labourer
16 David M'Neill, labourer
12 William Bairns, clerk
10 Robert Webb, car driver
Side of Robert Scott's spirit store

Prince's Court
OFF PRINCE'S STREET.

1 Samuel Johnston, whitesmith
3 John Davison's hemp store
George Murray's tobacco stores
E. Blow & Co.'s paper stores
J. H. Nicholson's grocery stores
Thos. Gardner's soap manufactory
W. D. Henderson's grain stores
6 Wm. Barclay's stores
Bernard Smith's cooperage
4 James Rea
2 David M'Vey, lodgings

Prince's Dock
(FORMERLY DUNBAR'S DOCK.)

1 David Grainger, shipowner and general merchant; residence, Henry street
3 Wm. Downing, general smith; residence, 28 Trafalgar street

5 George Mitchell, ship chandler and sail maker
7 Henry Crace, coal merchant; residence, 10 Queen street
9 James Macdonald, ship and insurance broker, and commission and forwarding agent, Prince's dock and 59 Waring street; residence, 20 Dock street
11 Matthew Forrester, Dock tavern
10 Geo. Mitchell, Navy hotel & tavern
4 Geo. Robinson, Shipwrights' Arms hotel and tavern
6 Eleanor Charters, American hotel and tavern
Back entrance to John Low's patent saw mills
2 Grueber & Co., patent asphalte roofing, sheathing, boiler, and railway felt manufactory; R. Grueber's residence, 70 York st.

Prince's Street
QUEEN'S SQUARE TO ANN STREET.
1 Patrick Lennon's spirit store
3 John Ritchie, board and lodgings
5 David M'Donnell, barber, &c.
7 Hugh M'Michael, lodgings
9 James Dinsmore, painter—sexton in St. George's Church
11 Jane Johnston, board and lodgings
[Prince's court.
13 John Sturt, lodgings
15 Solomon Hart, board and lodgings
17 Wm. Allen, customhouse officer
19 Wm. Fleming, grain agent
21 Samuel Johnston, whitesmith
23 Thomas M'Cormick, grocer
25 Ann Millin, publican
.. [Marlborough street intersects.]..
27 John Murdoch, board and lodgings
29 Arch. Bell, board and lodgings
33 Wm. Johnston, publican
35 Jas. M'Cullough, board & lodgings
37 Robert Murray, publican [ling
Entrance to J. M'Cullough's stab-
41 Bernard Smith, cooper & lodgings
43 Vere Scott, board and lodgings
45 Isabella Johnston, boarding house
47 Agnes Sloan, dealer
49 John Wallace, lodgings
51 William Harrison, lodgings
53 Ann Hill, publican, Ann street
[Ann street.]
Ann Webster, grocer, Ann street

42 John M'Cullough, publican
40 Henry Gracey, millwright
38, 36 Robert Ireland, flour and bran store
34, 32 Adam Millin, publican
30 Andrew Jamison, publican
28 Margaret M'Meekan, dealer
26 Andrew O'Brien, lodgings
24 John Fisher, boarding house
22, 20 James Barry and Co., grocers, wine and spirit dealers; Robert Barry's residence, 13 Catherine street
.. [Marlborough street intersects.]..
18 Patrick M'Creanor's yard and stabling
18½ James Fowler, green grocer
16¼ John M'Givern, labourer
16, 10 John Orr, horse shoer & blacksmith
14 Catherine M'Cullough, lodgings
12 James M'Aulay, lodgings
8 Henry Murphy, master mariner
" Ann Delany, lodgings
6 Mary Hampson, rope and twine manufacturer
4 Charles Laverty, spirit dealer
2 Charles Kirkpatrick, grocer, 2 Queen's square

Prospect Terrace
OLD DUBLIN ROAD.
1 Mrs Lester
2 Benjamin A. Gamble, linen merchant, Donegall place
3 Dr. H. Carlile, professor Queen's College
illiam Richardson, of Richardson, Sons, and Owden, Donegall
4 Wplace
5 Michael Ferrar, in Robert Henderson's steam packet office
6 Johnson Haliday, grain merchant, Tomb street
7 Miss Eccles
8 Samuel Thompson, gentleman
9 Henry Horner, in Mr Stevenson's, Calendar street
10 Alexander Andrews, provision merchant, Tomb street
11 Cunningham Mulholland, surgeon

Quigley's Court
CROMAC STREET.
Twelve small houses

Queen's College

MALONE AND BOTANIC ROAD.
Rev. Dr. Henry, president
Dr. Andrews, vice-president

Queen's Island

Thompsons' and Kirwan's ship building yard; Measrs Thompson's residence, Garden hill; D. Kirwan's, 43 Corporation street
The patent slip and engine house
VICTORIA BUILDING—Erected in commemoration of her Majesty's visit to Belfast, 1849
Corporation timber pond
James M'Williams, slip keeper
Mrs M'Williams, confectionary, ginger beer, &c.
Samuel Lowry, gardener

Queen's Square

(FORMERLY FOOT OF HIGH ST.)
HIGH STREET TO DONEGALL QUAY.
87 Thomas Gardner, soap and candle manufacturer
89 Jn. H. Nicholson, wholesale grocer
91 Edwin Blow & Co., wholesale paper manufacturers; mill, Dunadry
93 Geo. Murray, wholesale grocer & tobacconist; residence, Strandtown
95 John Davidson, rope and twine manufacturer
97 Wm. M. Barkley, commission agent, coal merchant, and ship broker
99 Patrick Lennon, spirit dealer
[*Prince's street.*]
1 Charles Kirkpatrick, grocer
3 Ann Quinn, spirit dealer
5 Margaret Stewart, spirit dealer
7 Alexander Patterson, baker
9 Wm. Beattie, rent agent
11 Hugh S. Hind, ship broker
CUSTOM HOUSE
[*Donegall quay.*]
HARBOUR COMMISSIONERS' OFFICE
23 Mrs M'Donald
21 John Johnston, spirit dealer
19 Vine Hotel and Tavern, Alexander Gunn, proprietor
17 John C. Trotter, general outfitting mart
15 James Lemon, ship owner, ship chandler, and rope and twine manufacturer; residence, Donegall quay
13 Coast Guard Office
11 James Hamilton, oil and commission merchant; residence, 72 York street
9 Wm. Newett, ship broker and coal agent; residence, 9 York street
7 Wm. Wilkinson, ship broker, commission and emigration agent
5 James Scott, pork merchant
3 Peter Quinn, sailmaker and clothier; residence, 7 Queen's sq.
1 Hugh S. Hind, ship broker and commission agent; residence, 11 Queen's square
Store lane.]
156 Rose Ann Prey, spirit store
154 Robert & John Meharey, wholesale and retail grocers
152 Vacant
Side of new Northern Bank

Queen Street

CASTLE ST. TO WELLINGTON PLACE.
Side of John Kearns's grocery and spirit stores
1 Samuel Cunningham, wholesale wine and spirit merchant; residence, Victoria street
3 Mrs Smith
5 Alexander Moore, carpenter
7 County Cess office—Robert Goddard, high constable, also inspector of weights and measures; John Roberts, deputy; residence, New Lodge Road
" Westminster Life Insurance office—James Goddard, agent; residence, Easton Lodge, Cliftonville
9 Newry mills bakery—Kidd, Brothers, proprietors
11 Samuel Gelston, cabinet maker
" Miss Gelston, dressmaker
13 John M'Kavanagh, timber mercht.
15 Henry M'Kavanagh, timber mercht.
15½ John and Henry M'Kavanagh's timber yard
17 Mechanic's Institute — Andrew B. Porter, teacher
19 Miss Riddell
21 Miss Hewett
23 Wm. Byrne, gentleman
25 Alexander Mills, clerk
27 Mrs Marshall
.....[*College street intersects.*].....
29 Auguste C. Badier, French master
31 Miss Richey's seminary

STREET DIRECTORY.

33 Henry Campbell, of Gunning and Campbell, flax spinners; office, Donegall place buildings
35 Bernard Hughes, baker and flour merchant; Donegall place and Donegall street
37 Dr. Stevelly, Professor in Queen's College
  [*Wellington place.*]
26 James Hart, muslin manufacturer, Commercial court, and of Hull, Hart & Co., flax spinners, Falls road
24 Mrs B. Lennon, prefessor of music
22 Mrs Cunningham
..... [*College street intersects.*].....
20 Doctor Collins
18 Miss Letitia Kane
16 Hugh Orr, clerk Petty Sessions
14 Wm. Sheil, supervisor Excise
12 Mrs M'Cune
10 Samuel Finlay, chandler, Ann st.
8 Miss Montgomery
6 James Cochran, grocer, wine and spirit merchant, Castle place
4 James Heron, banker, and of W. C. Heron and Co., merchants; office, Albert square
" Vacant
2 Wm. M'Cleery, accountant & rent agent; residence, 28 Castle st.

Queen Street Upper
WELLINGTON PLACE TO HOWARD ST.

1 Charles Lanyon, C.E., county surveyor and architect, offices; residence, Wellington place
2 Captain Alexander Lewis
3 William John Johnston, wholesale grocer and tobacconist, Waring street and Skipper street
4 Miss Black
5 Mrs Quinn
...[*Wellington street intersects.*]...
6 Miss Ferguson, teacher of drawing
7 Major P. Stuart
8 Mrs Barr
9 James Folingsby, gentleman
10 Miss Wightman
  [*Howard street.*]
Fisherwick place Presbyterian Church school house
Wm. Maxwell's carpenter's yard; residence, 38 Fountain street

Quinn's Entry
11 HIGH STREET.

Alex. Maguire, boot & shoemaker; shop, 9 High street
House vacant
Martin Hanna's (jeweller) workshop
Crown Tavern—Chas. Hunter, proprietor
Edward Gribben, watchmaker and jeweller, 13 High street

Raphael Court
OFF RAPHAEL STREET.
Four small houses

Raphael Street
CROMAC ST.

1 Mary Dunbar
3 Andrew Loughran, carter
18 James M'Cullough, porter
16 Joseph Wilson, sawyer
14 Samuel Jamieson, porter
12 James Ireland, tinsmith
10 William Alderdice, carpenter
8 James M'Lean, card fitter
6 William Patterson, painter
4 William Pollin, carpenter
2 John Bell, painter

Renwick Place
MALONE ROAD, LOWER.

1 Thomas Sinclair
2 Edward Cash, tailor
3 Mrs Martin
4 Hugh Moore, porter in Queen's College
5 Ann Ritchie
6 William Caldwell, weaver
7 Bridget M'Gee
9 John Simpson, bricklayer
10 Thomas Newell, marketman
11 Vacant

Riley's Place
OFF CROMAC STREET.

1 Christopher O'Brien, clerk
3 Wm. M'Auley, manager of Steam Saw Mills
5 Robert Matthews, muslin manufacturer, Commercial court
7 James Rice, car driver
9 Kennedy Stewart, boot and shoemaker, 86 High street
11 William Crow, excise officer

Cromac Steam Saw Mills, timber, deal, and scantling yard, John Brown, jun., proprietor; residence, 20 Gloucester street
12 Thos. Shields, lithographic writer
10 Sarah M'Dowell
8 James Heron, schoolmaster
Two new houses
6 Daniel Monaghan, blacksmith
4 Hugh Connor, travelling clerk
2 John Jamieson, muslin manufacturer, John street court
Three new houses

Ritchie's Place
112 NORTH STREET.
1 Thos. M'Tear, spirit dealer
3 John Curran, boarding house
5 Margaret Clarke
7 Joseph Murphy, carpenter
9 James M'Cormack
11 Arthur Dougherty, sizer
13 James Quinn, labourer
19 John M'Kinney, last maker
21 Clara Dempsey
25 Terence M'Anally, labourer
27 Patrick Stewart, bricklayer
29 Richard Bell, tobacco roller
31 Peter Timney, dealer
John Keenan, dealer
15 John Shipton, spirit dealer
20 Ann Smith
18 Catherine M'Clelland, dealer
16 Jeremiah Casey, lodging house
14 Cornelius M'Kinney, last maker
12 James Alexander's grain stores
8 John Corr, scantling yard
6 John Corr, coffin maker
4 Thomas Guyns, lodging house
2 John Gilmore, fowl dealer

River Street
OFF WELSH STREET.
Now called Stanfield street

Robert Court
50 MUSTARD STREET.
1 Daniel Campbell, labourer
2 Joseph Lindsay, labourer
3 Greenfield Greg, potale dealer
4 David Martin, nailer
5 Patrick Rice, labourer
6 Michael Campbell, tinsmith
7 Robert Lewis, shoemaker
8 James Anderson, porter

Robert street
HILL ST. TO 37 ACADEMY STREET.
[*Talbot street.*
William Powell, grocer & publican, side entrance
1 Hugh Love, gun smith
3 Mrs M'Neill
5 Mary Paul, lodgings
7 Alex. Milliken, nailer
9 Hugh M'Cawley, shoemaker
11 John Hart, dealer
13 Hugh M'Avoy, foundryman
15 John Short, grocer
17 Hugh Dornan, musician
[*Edward street.*
John Owens, slater
[*Caxton street.*
19 Thomas M'Gonigill, writing clerk
23 William Nevin, hairdresser
25 John M'Kenna's spirit store
[*Academy street.*]
34 Vacant
32 Jane Storey, lodgings
30 James O'Neill, barber & hairdresser
28 Mary Quinn, dealer
26½ John Brown's scantling yard
26 Cornelius Knox, boot closer
24 Henry Grant, pork cutter
22½ James Noble, haberdasher
22 Richard Crone, writing clerk
20 Wm. O'Neill, pawnbroker
18 John Orr, confectioner and fancy biscuit maker
16 Sarah Hughes, lodgings
14 Wm. Gibson, day constable
12 John Fullerton, brush and bellows maker
10 James Maginnis, stone cutter
8 Wm. Lavery, factory worker
8½ Richard Dargan, spirit store; shop, 18 Talbot street
8 John M'Innes, seaman
4 Matilda Thompson, milliner
2½ Adam Keenan, tailor
2 Charles M'Ateer, stone cutter

Rochfort Place
OFF COLLEGE COURT.
1 James Godwin, tailor
2 Anthony Paul, clothlapper
3 Wm. Wilson, tailor
4 Thomas Macqueen, upholsterer
5 Henry Adams, porter, Plough hotel
6 James Anderson, servant
7 John Boles, tailor

8 John Berwick, baker
9 Wm. Tottenham, watchman
10 John Kerr, baker
11 Abraham Walker, sexton, Donegall place Methodist Chapel
12 Mrs Susan Birney
13 Jas. Conlon, dealer in tow, flax, &c.
14 Mrs Allen
15 Samuel Stewart, mechanic
16 George Booth, watchman
17 John Kingsberry, servant
18 Mrs Margaret Cochrane
19 Mrs Elizabeth Tully

Roseann Place
OLD CARRICKFERGUS ROAD.
1 Bernard Burns, publican
2 Charles Burns, dealer
3 Robert Lockhart, clerk spirit store

Rosemary street
BRIDGE STREET TO HERCULES ST.
1 James Skene, Stag's Head Hotel
3 James Skene's spirit store
5 Hugh C. Clarke, auctioneer, broker, and valuator; residence, Ormeau road
7 George Massy's tobacco and snuff manufactory; shop, 12 North st.
9 John Fisher & Son, West of England Insurance Office; residence, 2 Glengall place
" James Campbell, solicitor; Dublin address, 8 Inns quay; residence, 8 Donegall square west
11 Vacant
13 Edward Walkington, druggist, oil and colour merchant; residence, Snugville
15 Peter M'Pherson & Co., sugar brokers and commission agents; Peter M'Pherson's residence, 15 Wesley place
" Richard Baxter, agent to Sun Fire and Life Insurance Offices; residence, 2 Pakenham place
" Forster Green & Co.'s stores; shop, High street
15 Wm. N. Blow, wholesale paper merchant; residence, Alblon place
17 Carter and Martin's stores, flax & tow merchants; John T. Carter's residence, 1 Victoria place; Mr Martin's residence, 52 Great George's street

17 Rosemary Street Daily School, in connexion with Synod of Ulster—teacher of male school, Rev. James Baird; teacher of female school, Miss Darling; teacher of infant school, Miss Williamson
ROSEMARY STREET PRESBYTERIAN CHURCH—Rev. Dr Hanna and Rev. J. Macnaughtan, ministers; Rev. Dr. Hanna's residence, at Rev. Dr. Denham's, Derry; Rev. J.Macnaughtan's residence, Duncairn house
17½ Lewis Reford, merchant; residence, Beechmount
19 John Bates, solicitor, and Town Clerk; Dublin address, 37 Blessington street; residence, Seapark, Greenisland
" TOWN CLERK'S OFFICE—deputy Town Clerk, Wm. Spotten; residence, No. 22 Rosemary street
" John Crawford, Sergeant at Mace
21 Wm. J. Beattie, lithographer, engraver, and printer
23 Adam J. Macrory, solicitor; Dublin address, 48 Rutland square West; residence, Duncairn
25 Hugh Twigg, clothes dealer
27 Richd. Kirwan, cork manufacturer
ROSEMARY STREET 1ST AND 2ND UNITARIAN CHURCHES — 1st, Rev. Wm. Bruce, The Farm, Antrim road, and Rev. John S. Porter, College square East, ministers; 2nd, Rev. John Porter, 8 Murray Terrace, minister
Barley mill, unoccupied
29 Francis M'Donnell, pawnbroker
31 M. Hill, gun & pistol manufactory
33 Miss Carpenter's school
" Philip Carpenter, provision dealer
35 David Hennesy, cabinet and chair maker
37 Alex. Stephen, wine & spirit dealer
39 Wm. Fulton, saddler and harness maker
41 Henry Barrett, custom house officer
" Thomas Boylan, butcher
43 James Close, butcher, and 1 Hercules street
[*Hercules street.*]
50 James Whisker, victualler and poulterer, and 33 Hercules place
46½ R. Hamilton, cork manufacturer

46¼ Miss Anne Reddings, milliner
44 John Campbell, clothes dealer
42½ William M'Kinney, hardware and timber merchant
40 John R. Vance and Son, muslin manufacturers and merchants
38 Messrs Vance and Son's weaving factory
36 Samuel Keatley, clothes dealer, 11 Chapel lane
Castle Chambers.]
34 Samuel Todd, spirit and ale store
32 Theobald Bushell, general merchant, stock and share broker; residence, Strandtown cottage, county Down
Legg's lane.]
POST OFFICE—Postmaster, O'Donnell Grimshaw; residence, Linfield
30 O'Donnell Grimshaw, solicitor; Dublin address, 8 Inns quay
" Conway B. Grimshaw and Son, Atlas Fire and Life Insurance agents; residence, Linfield
28 James Gowdy, tract depository for Unitarian Association
26 James Griffith, clothes dealer
Caddell's entry.]
24 German, Petty, and Co., flax spinners; mill, Preston; representative in Belfast, T. S. Petty
22 Sarah Spotten, family grocery
20 *Vindicator* office—Charles Lennon, proprietor; residence, Malone
Winecellar entry.]
18 Thomas Greer, Sons, & Co., wholesale woollen drapers, Manchester and Scotch warehouse; Thos. Greer's residence, 4 Donegall square West
16 Joseph Marshall, delf warehouse
Graham's entry.]
12 Bernard and Edward M'Hugh, wholesale & retail haberdashers; residence, 24 Upper Arthur st.
10 Andrew Clendinning, haberdasher and commission agent
8 M'Mullan & Co., linen yarn merchants; Robert M'Mullan's residence, 46 Great George's st.
6, 4 Robt. Smith, spirit dealer, muslin manufacturer, and commission agent
2 Alexander M'Cracken, military and gentlemen's boot maker, 28 Bridge street

Ross street
FALLS ROAD.
1 William Craig, helper
2 Mary M'Cann
3 Patrick Conolly, hackler
William Ross's office and yard
James Sherry, labourer
Christopher Day, stone cutter
James Moore, bricklayer
James Harpur, hackler
Arthur M'Kee, painter
John Gribben, schoolmaster
Edward Lee, pensioner
Wm. Stembridge, hackler
Wm. Duffy, spirit dealer

Round Entry
62½ NORTH ST. TO HERCULES ST.
1 John Barry, labourer
3 Mary Ann Gilmer
5 Rebecca Boyd
7 Nancy Rafferty
9 John Evans, carpenter
11 Bernard M'Laughlin, labourer
13 Eliza Fee
Vacant
15 James Boyle, writing clerk
[*Suffern's entry.*
John Drain's butcher yard; shop, Hercules street
26 John Hillman, weaver
24 Peter Laverty, weaver
22 Robert Eagleson, bread server
20 Ann Boyd, dealer
18 John Canavan, sawyer
16 James Jones, butcher
14 Elizabeth M'Ilroy, lodgings
12 William Connell, chandler
Seven vacant houses

Royal Academical Institution
Thomas Blain and Wm. Evans, head masters

Royal Terrace
LISBURN ROAD.
1 William Trail, gentleman
2 Mrs Hutchinson
3 John Holden, sewed muslin manufacturer, Donegall street
4 Rev. Wm. M'Ilwaine
5 Mrs Thomas Davison
6 Edward Pim, merchant, High street
7 Edward Geoghegan, agent for the Bank of Ireland
8 Daniel Curell, linen merchant, Linenhall street

Roy's Court
ROY ST.

John Cunningham, stokerer
16 George Shannon, chandler
14 James Cunningham, plasterer
12 Michael Short, pensioner
10 Daniel Keely, servant
8 James Pressley, porter
6 John Beatty, car owner
4 Harriett Lowry
2 Jane Copeland

Roy Street
6 STANFIELD STREET.

1 Samuel Hoy, stone mason
3 John Savage, shoemaker
5 John Collins, carpenter
7 John Burns, labourer
9 John Smith, baker
11 James M'Adam, painter and glazier
13 Wm. Dodds, night constable
15 Robert Hogg, paper stainer
17 Robert Hamilton, paper stainer
19 John Burns, labourer
21 Robert Girvin, pork cutter
23 Mrs Susanna M'Dowell
Foot of street not open
18 Hugh Smith, grain dealer
16½ John Hamilton, labourer
14½ Thomas Ferguson, carter
12 Patrick Burns, labourer
10 Hugh Walker, labourer
James Lewis, labourer
Andrew M'Guiggan, labourer
Hugh Cunningham, labourer
Joseph M'Ilveen, carpenter
Robert Dalzell, carpenter

Russell street
CROMAC STREET TO JOY STREET.

1 Patrick Doherty, stokerer
" George Rainey, meal and provision dealer
3 Samuel M'Murray, tailor
......[*Grace street intersects.*]......
7 Wm. M'Laughlin, writing clerk
9 George Jamison, porter & lodgings
11 William Wilson, assistant woollen-draper
13 Mrs Ireland, lodgings
15 Wm. Hyde, linen buyer
[*Catherine street North intersects.*]
17 William Vance, cabinet maker; workshop, 21 Catherine street North
19 Edward Manning, attorney's clerk
21 Samuel Middleton, mail coach guard
23 Alex. M'Cracken, foreman boot and shoemaker
25 Hugh Boyd, bread deliverer
27 John Lally, cabinet maker
29 John M'Kinstry, painter
...........[*Joy street intersects.*]......
Smith and Ross, builders; residences: Mr Smith, 23 Joy st.; Mr Ross, 27 Joy street
ST. MALACHI'S ROMAN CATHOLIC CHAPEL and GROUNDS
Lane to M'Clean's fields.]
34 John Hawkins, hostler in the Royal hotel
32 James Morrison, coach painter
......[*Joy street intersects.*]......
30 James Staunton, paper stainer
28 Patrick Carlin, lithographic printer
26 John Frazer, musician
24 Eliza Bryson, milliner and dress maker
22 Joseph Campbell, wine bottler
20 Hugh M'Alarney, baker
[*Catherine street North intersects.*]
18 Jane Phillips, washerwoman and mangler
16 William Johnston, tailor
14 Samuel M'Dowell, writing clerk
12 David Willocks, brass founder
10 John Somerville, weigh master
8 Mrs Eleanor Smith, milliner
......[*Grace street intersects.*]......
6 James Crilly, boot and shoemaker
4 Robert Harris, joiner
Side of A. Kirker's bakery, 37 Cromac street

Sackville Place
SACKVILLE ST.

1 Wm. Dawson, grocer and publican
2 Sinnamon May, bricklayer
3 Vacant
4 Eliza Hamilton
5 Robert Havern, painter
6 Jane Irvine, white worker
7 Nathaniel Fulton, carpenter
8 Adam Ward, shoemaker
9 Robert Collins, quay porter
10 Michael Hoy, plasterer
11 David Moore

12 Mary Higgins
13 Hugh Woods, plasterer
14 John M'Mullan, iron moulder
15 Bridget M'Kenna
16 Mary Cochrane
17 James Murphy, labourer
18 Daniel M'Peak, labourer
19 Betsy Wright
20 Wm. John Lowry, labourer
21 Michael Hughes, labourer
22 Daniel M'Areavy, weaver
23 John Pollin, mechanic
24 Francis Harvey, labourer
Sackville Street weaving factory, Wm. M'Ilwrath & Co., proprietors; Wm. M'Ilwrath's residence, Ardmoulin place

Sackville street
OFF TOWNSEND STREET.
1 Elizabeth Geery
3 Wm. Ewings, brush maker
5 Thomas Miskimmons, carpenter
7 Mary Henry, spinner
9 John Martin, bundler
11 John Donald, watchman
13 James Toal, tailor
15 James Harrison, painter & glazier
17 James Greer, blacksmith
19 Wm. Sibbins, dealer
21 James Crothers, weaver
23 Margaret M'Murdie, bag sewer
25 Jane M'Collough
10 Jane M'Larnon
8 Daniel Hill, carpenter
6 Hugh Roberts, linen lapper
4 Wm. Wilson, tailor
2 John Savage, labourer

Salter's Court
BARRACK STREET.
Built up

Samuel street
WINETAVERN STREET TO MILLFIELD
1 Mary Kirk, whiteworker
3 James Kerr, labourer
5 Job Townsley, tinsmith
7 Pat Kelly, labourer
9 Peter M'Court, dealer
11 Margaret M'Coull
13 John Weir, shoemaker
17 Eliza Doogan, dealer
19 Margaret Lowry, spirit dealer
[*Law's lane.*

27 Bernard Doran, dealer
29 James M'Gee, weaver
31 Daniel Kelly, whipmaker
33 Mary M'Gookan
35 Eliza Duffy, grocer & spirit dealer
41 James M'Cullough, spirit dealer
44 Edward Mullan, spirit dealer
40 Michael Mullan, labourer
36 Dennis Mawhinney, labourer
34 Francis Heburn, labourer
30 Henry Hart, shoemaker
26 Wm. Smith, shoemaker

Law's lane.]
24 Samuel Cooper, shoemaker
22 John Crawford, shoemaker
20 Samuel Cooper's stabling yard
18 Sarah Smith, dealer
16 John Kennedy, mat maker
14 James M'Guigan, dealer
19 David Millar, labourer
10 Patrick M'Shane, labourer
8 Murtoch Lawler, labourer
6 Anna Arthurs
4 Jane Bairns, whiteworker
Several houses vacant

Sarah Street
FREDERICK ST. TO YORK LANE.
Wesleyan day schools—Robt. Lindsay, superintendent
1 Bridget Harper
3 Thomas Thompson, spirit dealer, 45 North Queen street
5 Miss M'Ginnis, teacher
7 John Edwards, glass manufacturer
9 John Curoe, mechanic
" James M'Courtney, carpenter
11 Robert M'Clung, weighmaster
13 James Spence, tailor
15 Patrick Devlin, plasterer
17 Michael O'Hanlon, hackler
19 Richard Blair, commissariat staff
21 William Reynolds, grocer
22 Vacant
20 Alexander Murdoch, clerk
18 Alice M'Collough
16 George Gilpin, clerk
14 John O'Neill, overseer in mill
12 William M'Keown, butler
10 John Campbell, butler
8 Mrs Barry, dress maker
6 John Burns, coachman
4 James Armstrong
2 John Mills, mechanic

STREET DIRECTORY.

Second Street
NORTH HOWARD STREET.
Six small houses

Seymour Lane
OFF SEYMOUR STREET.
1 Joseph Johnston, bricklayer
3 Dennis Smith, carter
5 Susan Brown, washerwoman
7 Thomas M'Grillin, horse dealer
9 Matthew M'Dermott, horse shoer
11 John Hennety, labourer
13 Samuel Hanna, labourer
15 James Johnston, stone cutter
17 Joseph Campbell, carpenter
12 John Johnston, coachman
10 Wm. Wright, coach painter
8 Alexander Johnston, bricklayer
6 James Anderson's oatmeal and corn stores
4 Joseph Bain, rectifying distiller; residence, 2 Glenfield place
2 John Brown's timber yard
Three small houses

Seymour Street
CHICHESTER ST. TO LITTLE MAY ST.
Side of Lawson Brown's timber and scantling yard
1 Matthew M'Dermott, horse shoer
3 George Gray, coach painter
5 Joseph Johnston, bricklayer
....[Gloucester street intersects.]....
1 Charles M'Donald, tobacconist, High street
3 E. and J. Boyle, bonnet and dress makers
5 Martha Gibson
7 James Brown, mechanic
10 Thomas Mines, clerk
8 John Lackey, carpenter
6 George Simpson, lighterman
4 Hugh Ross, carpenter
ST. PATRICK'S ORPHAN ASYLUM
......[May street intersects.]......
2 Miss Collins
Alexander Phillips, farmer
Eight small houses
Hugh Tailor, painter
Two small houses

Shankhill Road
FROM TOWNSEND STREET.
1 Mary Kiglety, green grocer
3 Mary Rodgers
5 Margaret Johnston, spirit dealer
7 Jane Smyth
9 Hans Beatty, traveller
" S. Beatty, bonnet maker
11, 13, 15 Vacant
17 Robert Kennedy, carpenter
19 Jane Graham, washerwoman
21 Mary Rankin
23 Thomas Tinsley, grocer
25 James Greer, brassfounder and gasfitter
" Wm. Wright, grocer and publican
John Girvan
Thomas Girvan, pawnbroker
Robert Lorimer, carpenter
Two new shops
Four dwelling houses not finished
Victor C. Taylor, spirit dealer
HUDSON'S ROW.
Patrick M'Mahon, tailor
Samuel Rea, labourer
James Anderson, labourer
John Gray, cow keeper
Rodger Casey, cow keeper
19 Hugh Lewis, labourer
20 John M'Keever, butcher
[Hanna's court.
Francis Hanna, spirit dealer
John Roney, bricklayer
George Morris, glass cutter
John Mullen, labourer
John Hill, baker
James Agnew, dealer
Wm. H. Baxter, tailor
Ann Jane Sedgewick, grocer
[M'Teir street.
John Armstrong, blacksmith
James Johnston, rope maker
Andrew Cowan, spirit dealer
Catherine M'Gee, washerwoman
AGNES PLACE.
Alex. Clements, builder
John Kavanagh, clerk
Wm. J. M'Mullan, reporter
James Wilson, clerk
William Bunting, spirit dealer
HOPETON PLACE.
Samuel Johnstone, grocer
Mrs. Lockhart
Henry Greer, tailor
John Blain, jun., clerk
Messrs. Blain's damask manufactory, offices
John Blain, sen., manufacturer
John Blain's weaving factories

STREET DIRECTORY.

[*M'Allen's place.*
James Hazlett, grocer and spirit dealer
John Bailey, boot and shoemaker
Wm. M'Allen, carter
Thomas M'Allen, pawnbroker
Bell Armstrong, dealer
James Harbison, umbrella maker
Patrick Harkin, grocer

[*Spears's court.*
Alexander Harkness, carpenter
John Devlin, dealer
Joseph Young, bricklayer
Margaret Carroll
Martha Porter, cow keeper
Robert Peel, baker, bran store and spirit dealer
John M'Cormack, grocer
William Doran, mechanic
James M'Anally
Terence M'Laughlin, carter
Mary M'Veigh
James Anderson, grocer and spirit dealer
Eliza Bell
Philip Wright, coal merchant
John Quinn
Charles Rodgers
William M'Cartney, boot and shoemaker
James Hannan, spirit dealer
David Lewis, coal dealer
Adam M'Creight, shoemaker
James Kelly, coal dealer
Wm. Elwood, labourer
Betsy Brannagan
Thomas Black, labourer
Henry O'Neill, dealer
Bower's Hill Tavern, and spirit store—Michl. Campbell, proprietor
Wm. Bell, bundler
James Livingston, labourer
Edward Smith, labourer
Dennis M'Ilhayney, carpenter
James M'Ilwaine, labourer
John Willis, labourer
John Fulton, bleacher

[*Herdman's buildings.*
Charles M'Sperren, carter
Henry M'Keown, labourer
Hugh Mallon, grocer
Andrew M'Cabe, labourer
Robert Addis, labourer

Snugville — Edward Walkington, druggist, Rosemary street
Glenwood—John Cunningham, of Glenwood corn mills
Glenwood Corn Mills
Brookfield—Thos. Tripp, merchant
St. Matthew's Church—Rev. H. Teape, Incumbent
Skankhill Burying Ground
Glenwood Tavern and grocery—Patrick Townly, proprietor
Five small houses
James M'Bride, spirit dealer
John Carson, spirit dealer
Tobias Lynass, blacksmith
Hugh Drain, cartwright
William Stewart, carter

nelson's buildings.
John Askin, clerk
John Denvir, clerk
Alexander Gordon, clerk
Edward Haddock, clerk
Christopher Porteus, sewed muslin manufacturer, Church st.
Sugarfield—Rev. Isaac Nelson
Hugh Gorman, spirit dealer
Robert M'Cully, grocer
Conway street.]
Gasometer
Fifteen small houses
J. M'Cullough, cartmaker
Kennedy's place.]
Alexander street South.]
Row of small houses
Johnston's buildings.]
Alexander Steele
William Nelson, grocer
John Moore, weaver
James Bigger, labourer
Alexander Fitzpatrick, labourer
Daniel M'Caulay
James Madill, carter
James Bell
William Curry, linen lapper
Arthur Simpson, carpenter

gavin's buildings.
1 Jon. Moskimmon, mechanic
3 Mary Madill
5 James Ward, painter
7 John M'Caulay, smith
9 Wm. Smyth, compositor
11 John Campbell, linen lapper
13 George Campbell
15 Charles Dargan, clerk

James Riddell, reedmaker
James Mulholland, cabin steward
William Walker, cabinet maker
David Grisholm, hackler
John Fannan, shoemaker
Hugh Wilson, starch maker
John Matthews, hair dresser
Shankbill ropewalk—J. Abbott, of Corporation street, proprietor
Boundary street.]
40 John Savage, grocer and publican
38 Samuel Moffat, labourer
36 John Fitzpatrick, dealer
34 Charles O'Haggerty
32 William Anderson, schoolmaster
Brady's row.]
30 Richard Ramsey, pensioner
28 Vacant
26 Samuel Rea, spirit dealer
Hanna's lane.]
24 Daniel Kerr
22 Mary Kennedy, dealer
20 Richard Wetherhead, clerk
18 David Johnston, ropemaker
16 Mr. Hunter's starch works
14 Wm. White, dealer

CAMPBELL'S BUILDINGS.

12 Jas. Sinclair, street inspector
10 Arch. Price Fettler
8 John Doran, clerk
6 Elizabeth Whitla, dressmaker
4 Noah Longworth, millwright
2 Mary M'Coubry, dressmaker
Hans Peebles, spirit dealer

Sheal's Entry
43 CARRICKHILL.

Five small houses

Shipboy street
NELSON ST. TO LITTLE YORK ST.

1 Robert Stewart, brassfounder and gasfitter
3 Robert Lowry, plasterer
5 John M'Neill, pilot
7 Nathaniel Robinson, ship carpenter
9 Patrick Keenan, carpenter
11 James Sefton
13 Wm. Price, master mariner
15 James Paton, canvass weaver
17 Elizabeth M'Canagher
19 Abel Gamble, stone cutter
Two new houses vacant
28 John M'Laughlin, store keeper
26 Hugh Cromie, cooper
24 John Bennet, carpenter
22 Mary Brown
20 John M'Creavy, carpenter
18 Samuel Campbell, labourer
16 William Lilley, seaman
14 Daniel Johnston, lapper
12 James Shields, joiner
10 John M'Guikan, master mariner
8 John M'Comley, lapper
6 Richard Berry, master mariner
4 John M'Gee, butler
2 Edward Walker, labourer
" E. J. Walker, dressmaker

Ship street
YORK STREET TO GARMOYLE STREET

1 Mrs Jane Rose
3 Alexander Riddell, reed maker
5 Wm. Hammersley, gentleman
7 Stephen Burlase, clerk
9 James Rose, muslin manufacturer
11 Wm. Gilmore, in Northern Bank
13 Joseph Humphreys, sea captain
15 Mary Keown, boarding house
17 Thomas Ashton, flax spinner
[*Little York street.*
Three new houses building
Waste ground
Three new houses
[*Foot of Collingwood street.*
Waste ground
67 David Munce, stone mason
69 Daniel M'Ewen, ship carpenter
71 John Low, proprietor of steam saw mills
[*Garmoyle street at foot.*]
Enclosed ground
60 John Pescoe, jun., sea captain
58 John Bell, tide waiter
56 John Pescoe, retired coast guard officer
Three new houses building
Collingwood street.]
38 Edward Howell, sea captain
36 Samuel Henderson, acting tide surveyor
34 Isaac Gordon, book keeper and cashier
Seven new houses building
18 David Fulton, carpenter & builder
16 James Holden, iron founder
14 Robert Kelly, manager Lord Londonderry's estate
[*Little York street.*
12 Mrs Catherine Stannus

P

10 Alexander Lang, sea steward
8 Edward Coates, sewed muslin manufacturer
6 Robert Salter, sea captain
4 John Kennedy, gentleman
2 William M'Lurcan

Ship Street, Back
BACK OF SHIP ST.
15 William White, carding master
18 David Norwood, lapper
16 William Anderson, carpenter
14 James Porter, porter
12 William Barclay, railway porter
10 John Ritchie, boiler maker
8 Charles Porter, ship carpenter
6 Archd. M'Bride, miniature painter
4 Thomas Russell, railway porter
2 Mrs Mary Ann Anderson

Ship street, Little
FROM DOCK ST. TO POINT FIELDS.
Three stables
David Fulton's scantling yard and sawpits
Arthur M'Kee, tide waiter
Alexander Bailey, carpenter
James Reid, gentleman
[*Ship street.*
House building
12 John Stewart, labourer
" George Bensey, preparing master
10 James Skivington, labourer
" Michael Kelly, railway porter
8 John M'Ewen, mariner
6 John Seed, ship carpenter
Ship street.]
4 James Porter, ship carpenter
2 John M'Cann, iron moulder
Enclosed ground

Short Street
PILOT STREET TO PRINCE'S DOCK.
Side of Navy Hotel
9 Archibald M'Callum, labourer
7 William Reid, ship carpenter
5 George Murray, mariner
10 Thos. M'Anulty, boarding house
11 John M'Cudden, tailor
12 Robert M'Nally, ship agent
13 Thomas Green, spirit dealer and ship carpenter
 ide of John Wilson's spirit shop
2 James Ritchie's bonded warehouse

Skipper Street
FROM HIGH ST. TO WARING ST.
Eliza Davis, straw bonnet, parasol, and millinery warehouse, 96 High street
Mr Wilkinson's store
1 Robert Campbell, bookbinder and stationer
3 William Wilson, cutler and surgical instrument maker
5 John M'Donnell and Co., merchts.
7 Wm. M'Connell, wholesale grocer
9 Jane Coffey, haberdasher
11 James Irvine, house painter
13 William Wardlow, tailor
15 Robert Cleland, spirit dealer
17 William Gelston, merchant and tobacco manufacturer, and 40 Tomb street; residence, 8 Great George's street
Shop vacant
19 William Johnston, lithographer, stationer, &c., and 25 Waring street; residence, 14 Tomb st.
[*Waring street.*]
30 Philip Johnston, merchant, hall door
28 David Mark, wholesale and retail cheese merchant and grocer
26 Vacant
24 Philip Johnston and Co., wholesale tobacconists
22 John Savage, flax and yarn merchant; residence, 3 Mountview terrace
" John Kerr, commission agent
20 Charles Forsythe, nailer
18 William Boyd, house and sign painter
16 John Crookes, saw maker and repairer
14 David Erskine, grocer
12 Thomas Newell, boarding house
10 Anthony Cranagh, hair dresser
8 Catherine Forsyth, spirit dealer
4 John Duffy, tailor
2 James Byrne, boot and shoemaker

Smithfield
FROM BERRY STREET.
EAST SIDE.
1 Maria Kelly, clothes dealer
2 Bunting Gregory, clothes dealer
3 Catherine M'Curry, clothes dealer
4 George Headley, gas fitter

STREET DIRECTORY.

4½ Charles M'Cafferty, hatter
5 Alexander Mackenzie, Stag Tavern
6, 7 David Ruddell, cabinet and hardware warehouse
8, 9 Vacant
10 Mary Smith, clothes dealer
11 Vacant
12 Robt. Wallace, grocer and publican
    [*Kennedy's row.*
13 Peter Mallon, shoemaker
" Rose O'Hare, fruit dealer
14 Royal Hibernian Concert Hall—
    Robert Calvert, proprietor
15 Thomas Cushley, tailor
    TEETOTAL HALL—Patk. M'Shane, superintendent
16 Vacant
17 Wm. Ferguson, ironmonger
18 John Kerr, grocer and publican, & shoe shop   [*Bell's lane.*
19 James Hamilton, hair cutter
20 Patk. Conway, hay & straw dealer
22 Hugh Wilson, pawnbroker
23 Helena Cinnamond, grocer and publican, and green hide dealer
24 Wm. Todd, auctioneer and appraiser for county Antrim
25 Rosanna and Ellen Frew, publicans
26 Henry M'Larnon, spirit dealer
Hudson's entry.]
NORTH SIDE.
27 Isabel. M'Goughey, provision dealer
28 Margt. Hamilton, provision dealer
Lennon's court.]
29 Patrick O'Donnell, publican and coal dealer
30 Samuel Coburn, pawnbroker
31 Patk. O'Neill, grocer and publican
Smithfield court.]
32 Catherine Mooney, earthenware dealer
33 William Sharp, Smithfield bakery
34 Abel George, grocer
35 Patrick Griffith, wine, spirit, tobacco and snuff dealer, 3 Winetavern street
Winetavern street.]
40 J. and J. Herdman's spinning mill; James Herdman's residence, Tudor hall, Holywood; John Herdman's residence, 9 Wellington place
WEST SIDE.
West street.]
41 Edward Heron, publican

42 Henry M'Lorinan, delf, china, and glass warehouse
43 Smithfield Brewery — Clotworthy Dobbin, proprietor; residence, 12 Howard street
44 James Shields, cap maker
44, 45 National Theatre—Thomas Armstrong, proprietor
    Bernard Redmond, rag dealer
45 Samuel Loughran, clothes dealer
    Vacant house
47 Thomas Armstrong, spirit dealer
48 Andrew Doherty, whitesmith
49 John Christie, dealer
    Henry Hagan, clothes dealer
50 Bernard Devlin, general dealer
51 George Hall, hatter
    John Moreland, weaver
    Gilbert Rogers, carpenters' workshop; residence, Ferguson's court
    Peter Aiken, manager, Fisher and Campbell's mill
    Fisher and Campbell's spinning mill, entrance, Francis street; Mr Fisher's residence, Glengall place; Mr Campbell's residence, College square North
Francis street.]
    Gilbert Rogers' sawing yard; residence, Ferguson's court
SOUTH SIDE.
Ferguson's court.]
53 Fisher and Campbell's stores
57 Mathew Bracegirdle, publican
    [*Marquis street.*
58, 59, 60 Waste houses
61, 62 Owen Gregory, furniture dealer
63 James Meharg, auctioneer
64, 65 John Gordon, cabinet maker
66 Cornelius Neville, publican
67, 68 David Ruddell, furniture dealer
69 George Evans, grocer
    John E. Collins, furniture dealer
71 Wm. M'Stay, wine and spirit stores, and grocery
    Sam. M'Cann, publican, 28 Chapel lane   [*Chapel lane.*

SHEDS.
SOUTH SIDE.
2 John Dignan, carpenter, 9 Letitia street
3 William Moore, furniture dealer, Millar's lane

4 Wm. M'Keown, dealer in old books
5 James Stewart, cabinet maker
6 Nicholas Dillon, basket maker, 12 Torrens's market
7 Bernard O'Hagan, clothes dealer, 22 Marquis street
8 John O'Hagan, clothes dealer, 30 Marquis street
9 John Hinds, furniture dealer
10 John Kearney, basket maker, Peter's hill
11 Constantine Donnelly, carpenter, 2 Millar's lane
12 John Gordon, furniture dealer, 64 Smithfield

EAST SIDE.

13 Hiram M'Conkey, tin smith, 9 Charlemont street
14 John Campbell, hardware dealer
15 Peter Mullan, dealer in old books and hardware, 14 Marquis st.
16 Edward Quinn, hardware dealer, & bellows maker, 15 Marquis st.
17 Bernard Campbell, hardware dealer
18 John O'Hagan, hardware and tools dealer, 9 M'Kibbin's court
19 Hugh Mills, tinsmith, 12 Charlemont street
20 Thomas Adams, furniture maker, 100 Millfield
21 Bernard Monaghan, delf shop and broker, 6 Kennedy's row
22 Francis M'Connell, delf and hardware dealer, 7 Kennedy's row
22 Geo. M'Cullough, furniture dealer, 11 Bell's lane
24 Edward Crozier, carpenter, Millfield
25 Wm. Ruddell, furniture and hardware dealer, 61 Gardiner street
26 John Clements, tinsmith, 76 Hercules street
27 Robert Ross & Co., hat and cap manufacturers, 20 Smithfield
28 Hugh M'Ateer, delf dealer, Drummond's court
29 Peter Timmony, stocking dealer, 33 Hudson's entry
30 Hugh Gilmer, tinsmith, Lennon's court
31 Robert M'Cudden, onion dealer, Bell's lane
32 Catherine Mooney, delf dealer

NORTH SIDE.

33 Daniel Montgomery, clothes dealer, 32 Gordon street
34 James M'Mahon, provision dealer, 49 Hudson's entry
35 James M'Kenna, provision dealer
36 John M'Kenna, provision dealer, Hudson's entry
37 Jeremiah Casey, clothes dealer, Ritchie's place
38 James M'Kenna, provision dealer, Hudson's entry
39 William Gardner, green grocer, 22 Barrack street
40 Archibald M'Collum, weighmaster and market inspector, 3 Killen street
41 William Stitt, carpenter and timber dealer

WEST SIDE—INSIDE.

Occupied by old clothes dealers, and hardware stalls

NORTH SIDE—INSIDE.

42 Patrick Rogers, clothes dealer, 32 Rosemary street
43 Thomas M'Aleese, clothes dealer, 3 Torrens's row
44 Susan Sands, clothes dealer
45 Catherine Tosh, delf dealer, 1 Kennedy's row
46 Mary Kingan, clothes dealer, 20 Kennedy's row
47 Wm. Stewart, clothes dealer, Winetavern street

EAST SIDE.

48 Wm. Ferguson, dealer in old iron
49 Edward Cuming, clothes dealer, 48 Lettuce hill
50 Francis Crawford, dealer in old iron, 25 Winetavern street
51 Charles A. Bell, furniture dealer, 10 Eliza street
52 George Burns, furniture and old iron dealer
53 John Doherty, old iron dealer, Round entry
54 Thomas Hodge, dealer in old iron and furniture, 10 Francis street
55 Samuel Thompson, dealer in old iron and furniture, Charlemont street
56, 58 J. M'Cleave, hardware dealer, 5 Charlemont street
57 John Riley, hardware dealer, Berry street
59 Danl. Mulholland, hardware dealer
60 James O'Hagan, dealer in old iron, 18 New row

STREET DIRECTORY. 173

61 Arthur Halfpenny, hardware dealer, 11 Kennedy's row
62 Robert Muntz, furniture dealer, Cunningham's court
SOUTH SIDE.
63 Robert Mulrine, auctioneer, 2 Kennedy's row
64 Patrick M'Shane, auctioneer
65 Thomas Monaghan, auctioneer, 14 Berry street
66 Patrick Loughran, auctioneer, 13 Marquis street
67 Henry Mallaghen, auctioneer, 26 Berry street
68 Edward Kelly, auctioneer, 3 Kennedy's row
John Spence, auctioneer, 29 West street

Smith street
OFF LAGAN STREET.
1 John Harrison, labourer
Samuel M'Gibbon, night constable
Thomas Cummins, foundryman
[Crawford street.
Rere of Mr Staunton's paper staining manufactory
8 Thomas Rooney, labourer
Hughes's entry.]
6 Mrs M'Clean, dealer
4 Wm. Miller, stone cutter
2 John Stapley, print colourer
John Smith, tailor

Southwell street
OFF HENRY STREET.
28 James M'Larnon, spirit dealer
Twenty-seven small houses

Spa Mount
OLD CARRICKFERGUS ROAD.
1 John Jas. Noble, medical student
2 Mrs Cummins
3 Robert Low, foreman, foundry
4 Roger Hillan, salesman
5 Thos. Lancaster, deputy engineer
6 Edward B. Giltenan, house and land agent

Spencer Street
YORK STREET.
1 Norman B. Gifford, clerk in Ulster bank
3 David Hetherington, captain *Sobraon*

7 Edward Wolfenden, book keeper in Mr Charley's office, Steam lane
9 John Rogan, clerk in Halliday and M'Dowell's office, Corporation street
11 Miss Janet Galbraith
13 William Halliday, salesman in Arnott and Co.'s, Bridge street
15 William Service, clerk in Ferguson and Molyneux's, York lane
17 John W. Henry, sewed muslin overseer, in Mr Holden's, Donegall street
[*Street not named.*
23 William F. Downing, clerk in Thos. Greer, Sons, & Co., Rosemary st.
Two unfinished houses
10 Arthur Robertson, lithographer
8 James Graham, engraver
6 Hugh M'Roberts, hackle maker
4 Thos. Frazer, custom house officer
2 John Powell, engineer

Stanfield Court
3 STANFIELD STREET.
1 John Mason, labourer
3 John M'Neill, labourer
5 Patrick Owens, labourer
7 Bernard Kenulty, sawyer
6 Wm. M'Glone, porter
4 Patrick M'Anulty, porter
2 John Robinson, shoemaker

Stanfield Street
72 VERNER STREET TO WELSH ST.
Mrs Simpson
1 David M'Mullan, boot and shoemaker
3 Mary Loughran
[*Stanfield court.*
5 James M'Areavy, shoemaker
7 James M'Gowan, labourer
9 William M'Nicholl, bootmaker
11 Joseph Steed, whitesmith
13 James Aird, porter
15 David M'Kelvey, bookbinder
17 Jane Cochrane
19 Timothy M'Dowell, coach maker
21 John Finlay, in pork store
23 Bernard M'Cann
25 Bernard Doran, fowl dealer
27 William Boyd, ærated water manufacturer
29 John Gray, carpenter

31 John Dobbs, grocer
..... [*Welsh street intersects.*].....
34 Francis Smith, grocer and spirit dealer, Welsh street
32 James Jenkins, sailor
30 Catherine O'Hare, egg dealer
28 Mary Smith
26 Joseph Harrison, writing clerk
24 Henry Hamilton, brick moulder
22 Hugh M'Polin, tailor
20 Sarah M'Alister, lodgings
18 John M'Auley, paper stainer
16 Edward Hanna, labourer
14 Mary M'Veigh, washerwoman
12 Wm. Bell, servant
10 Mary L. Mullan, grocer
Roy street.]
6 Arthur Hughes, shoemaker
4 John Corke, musician
2 Wm. Davy, painter

Stanfield street, Lower
STANFIELD STREET.

Samuel Mathers, dealer, Welsh st.
1 Joseph Loughran, brassfounder
3 James Martin, shoemaker
5 Thomas Savage, bricklayer
7 Daniel Murray, shoemaker
9 Robert Cronan, writing clerk
11½ Wm. M'Ilveen, carpenter
13½ Wm. Erskine, shoemaker
15½ John Johnston, ship carpenter
17 Richard Lynas, riddle maker
11 John Halliday, shoemaker
13 Francis M'Donnell, labourer
15 John O'Hare, bricklayer
17 John Magan, carpenter
19 Thomas M'Mullan, labourer
21 Wm. Gordon, night constable
23 James Burns, servant
25 Edward M'Alinden, carpenter
27 Hugh M'Roberts, dealer
29 John Coburn, night constable
31 Thomas Freeman, carpenter
33 Robert Sloan, night constable
35 James Havern, coal dealer
[*Open ground at Lagan.*]
26 James Downing, police inspector
24 Samuel Saunders, shoemaker
22 James Kearns, night constable
20 James Neale, night constable
18 John Wilson, night constable
16 John H. Bole, labourer
14 Samuel Lynas, day constable
14 James Thompson, grocer, 1 Staunton street

Staunton street.]
12 Emily Galbraith, dealer
10 Wm. Taylor, labourer
8 Wm. Clelland, tailor
6 William Burleigh, cabinet maker
4 Margaret Magee, fowl dealer
2 Mary Taggart, dealer

Stanhope street
OLD LODGE ROAD.

1 Edward M'Gowan, foreman, timber yard
3 Susan Waters
5 Thomas Williams, day constable
7 Samuel Fleming, carpenter
9 John Welsh, engraver
11 James Allen, beef and ham curer
13 Ephraim Brown, carpenter
15 Patrick Gilmore, rag merchant
17 John Beatty, writing clerk
19 Wm. M'Gowan, day constable
21 Andrew Keith, car driver
[*Park street*
23 Jane Bullick
25 Wm. Boomer, pensioner
27 Wm. Walker, pensioner
29 Henry Blackburn, mechanic
" Miss Evans, dressmaker
31 Edward M'Cabe, carpenter
33 Wm. Shanks, machine maker
35 Wm. Shanks, clerk
37 Robert Hill, baker
39 Joseph Cochrane, engineer
41 Wm. Madden, carpenter
43 Jane Ward, boarding house
62 Thomas Maine, millwright
60 Wm. John Currah, mechanic
58 Margaret Beattie
56 James Rankin, shopman
54 Joseph Brown
52 John Hagan, tailor
50 George Watters, bleacher
48 Gawn Dickson, cabinet maker
46 John Crosby, carter
44 Wm. Montgomery, baker
42 George Watters, compositor
40 Margaret Ferris, lodging house
38 James Windrim, baker
36 Elizabeth Bulla
34 Andrew Morton, carpenter
32 Eliza Boyd, dressmaker
30 Mary M'Mullan, boarding house
28 Rev. J. Harvey, Methodist preacher
26 Mary Morrow, teacher
24 Miss M'Mahon, milliner and straw bonnet maker

3 James Stewart, shoemaker
22 John Rice, baker
20 Jane Ewart
18 Thomas Cooper, cooper
16 Wm. Morrison, master mariner
14 Bridget Connell, boarding house
12 Patrick M'Ginnis, custom house officer
10 Wm. Johnston, clerk
8 John Ireland, pattern designer
6 David M'Niece, night constable
4 Mary Johnston, slipper maker
2 Wm. J. Park, tailor

Stanley lane
OFF LITTLE YORK STREET.

1 Margaret Reid, dressmaker
2 Archibald Glass, mariner
3 James Barkley, mariner
4 Andrew Ireland, storekeeper
5 Ellen M'Quitty
6 Margaret Lyons

Stanley Place
OFF LITTLE YORK STREET.

1 Elizabeth Officer, white worker
2 John Duncan, master mariner
3 John Campbell, pattern designer
4 James Williamson, marble carver
5 Wm. Richardson, master mariner
6 William Mulholland, shopman
7 Miss M'Cormack's school
8 Joseph Barron, clerk
9 Arthur Davis, master mariner
10 Miss Eliza M'Gee
   John Magee, coach painter

Stanley Street
OFF ALBERT STREET.

1 Francis Boyd, grocer
3 John Philips, labourer
5 Thomas Ramsay, blacksmith
7 Matthew Hodgen, mill wright
9 Mrs Jane M'Cartney
11 Joseph Johnston, labourer
13 Samuel Russell, labourer
15 Joseph Keating, baker
17 Jane Hall, mill worker
19 Ansley Keown, baker
21 Edward Toal, baker
23 Wm. Burnby, painter and glazier
25 Mrs Susan Madden
27 Alexander Cooke, grocer and meal and flour dealer
[*Wiley's place.*
29 Hugh Gaw, grocer and publican

31 Samuel M'Askey, mechanic
33 Mrs Jane M'Kibbin, lodgings
35 James Nelson, shoemaker
37 James M'Cracken, carpenter
39 Miss Jane Armour, lodging house
41 James Agnew, carpenter
43 Chichester Dargan, writing clerk
45 John Gamble, blacksmith
47 Henry Laverty, grocer and publican
[*Hutcheson street.*
49 John Mills, provision dealer
51 John Callender, porter
Cullingtree street.]
Cullingtree place.]
   Robert M'Gaghey, grocer, 21 Cullingtree place
32 Joshua Jordan, railway labourer
30 Mrs Eliza Hamilton, whiteworker
28 Mrs Ellen Hawthorne, dressmaker
26 Margaret Wilson, whiteworker
24 Ellen Graham, whiteworker
22 John Convery, shoemaker
20 Charles Greenan, labourer
" Mrs Donaldson, dress maker
18 Thomas Morton, carpenter
16 Mrs Greer
14 Samuel Connolly, mechanic
12 John Cunningham, labourer
10 George Elliot, printer
8 Eliza Faulkner
6 John Faulkner, overlooker in mill
4 James Lightbody, rougher in mill
2 Hannah Munro, bonnet maker

St. Anne's Buildings
FROM DONEGALL ST. TO NORTH ST.

1 Francis Plunkett, general commission merchant, and agent to the Royal Insurance Company, Liverpool ; residence, 7 Ingram place
3 William Ewart and Son, weavers and sewers' office
5 ODDFELLOWS' HALL—Ulster lodge
7, 9 Robert Vance, spirit store; residence, M'Tier street
11 Andrew Ewing, muslin manufacturer ; residence, Ballynafeigh
" Campbell & Co., sewed muslin manufacturers ; residence, 3 Stanley place

Staunton street
VERNER STREET.

1 James Thompson, grocer

5 John M'Neely, paper maker
7 David Duff, day constable
9 Wm. Donaldson, labourer
11 Hugh Finlay, labourer
13 Patrick Bannon, pork cutter
15 James Garrett, newspaper carrier
17 Wm. Strain, labourer
19 George Tighe, bricklayer
21 Margaret Sands, whiteworker
16 John M'Laughlin, currier
14 James Maguire, labourer
12 Elizabeth Maguire
10 Robert Campbell, night constable
8 Wm. Watson, draper
6 George Thompson, stone cutter
4 Henry Jamieson, labourer
2 John Smyth, bricklayer

Steam-mill Lane
CORPORATION SQ. TO GAMBLE ST.
1 Ship Water Office—John M'Kelvy, waterman
Five small houses
[Bradford square.
Five small houses
John Charley and Co.'s coal yard
Tobias Lynass, blacksmith
Back entrance to Glasgow and Belfast spirit store
Back entrance to Clay's hotel
Sinclair and Boyd's stores
John Charley and Co.'s coal yard
Side of steam flour mills and stores

Stephen street
OFF LITTLE DONEGALL STREET.
1 James Galley, day constable
" John Tosh, shoemaker
3 Charles Johnston, shoemaker
5 John Campbell, carpenter
7 Elijah Jordan, shoemaker
9 John Hawthorn, soap boiler
11 James Lyons, bricklayer
13 Margaret Wells
15 Wm. Gough, labourer
17 Thomas M'Auley, shoemaker
19 Robert Finlay, labourer
19½ Wm. Lewis's stabling yard
21 John Hawson, slater
23 May Graham, dealer
5 John Tate, labourer
27 Wm. Lewis, spirit dealer
29 Patrick Gill, labourer
33 George Burns, tailor
35 Thomas Burns, tailor

37 Daniel Burns, dealer
39 Charles Hart, shoemaker
41 Edward M'Gowan, shoemaker
43 Wm. M'Call
45 Wm. Prodden, labourer
47 Henry Arthur, cotton spinner
.... [Mustard street intersects.]....
49 Matthew Williamson, comb maker
49 Rose M'Laughlin
51 Samuel Moreland, millwright
53 Thomas Bruce, labourer
30 Wm. Ward, coal dealer
28 Daniel Gough, labourer
26 Charles Spence, labourer
24 Charles Grahams, labourer
.... [Mustard street intersects.]....
22 Charles Liddy, pavier
20 Wm. M'Clusky, blacksmith
18 Joseph Martin, labourer
16 Sarah Hull, dressmaker
14 Henry Duffin, labourer
12 Archibald Hodgson, hackler
Alexander Henderson, grocer and spirit dealer
10 John Hill, weaver
8 Edward M'Collough, porter
6 Julia Rorke, boarding house
4 Edward Burton, labourer

Store lane
QUEEN SQUARE TO ALBERT SQUARE.
1,3 Terence O'Brien, general mercht.; residence, Donegall place
5 James M'Conville, sawyer & dealer
7 James Savage, dealer
9 Madeline Henry, dealer
11 James Ferguson, mariner & dealer
14 Andrew Dool, spirit dealer and boarding house
14½ James Kelly, hairdresser
12 Edward M'Laughlin, mariner
10 Andrew John Barnett, timber merchant; residence, Clarendon place
8 James Savage, marine store
6 Benjamin Alexander, schoolmaster and dealer
4 James Webb, dealer
2 Arthur Carson, mariner and dealer
Back entrance to Rose Ann Pray's spirit store

Stormont Court
DURHAM ST.
Ten small houses

Suffern's Entry
OFF NORTH STREET.
Eight old houses

Sugar House Entry
HIGH STREET TO WARING STREET.
1 James Harkness, glass, china, and delf warehouse, High street
3 Abraham Bambridge's hotel and tavern
Back entrance to Commercial hotel

Sussex Place
ALFRED STREET TO JOY STREET.
1 Mrs Shubridge
2 Mrs Shaw
3 Miss Rowan, Connaught bazaar
" Miss Jamison, Connaught bazaar
4 Mrs Coffey
5 Mrs M'Kee
6 Robert M'Hinch, grocer, 33 Church lane
7 Mrs. Carse
8 John G. M'Gee, of J. G. M'Gee & Co.'s, merchant clothiers, 46 & 48 High street
[*Joy street.*]
Dr. Burden's field, Alfred street

Sussex street
60 YORK STREET.
2 John M'Philips, mariner
4 James Walsh, carpenter
6 Robert Henderson, mariner
8 James Haliday, labourer
10 Francis M'Keown, pensioner
12 James Quinn, labourer
14 John Moore, sawyer
16 Wm. Mackie, on water works
18 Joseph Collins, painter
20 John Porter, pork cutter
22 Michael Kerr, in felt works
24 John Little, labourer
26 John Wilson, carpenter
28 Wm. Stevenson, labourer
30 Thomas Watson, labourer
32 James Lowry, labourer
34 Thomas Elliot, labourer
36 Charles Jones, pork cutter
38 Hugh M'Cann, labourer
40 John O'Neill, sawyer
42 James M'Lurcan, rent collector
44 Alex. Ross, carter
46 Edward Liddy, labourer
48 Mary Gormley
50 Andrew M'Gill, labourer
52 Henry Conway, labourer
54 John Foster, labourer
56 Wm. Smith, labourer
58 Mary Bigger
60 James Graham, labourer
62 John Berry, pensioner
64 Mary M'Mullen
66 John Foster, baker
68 Bridget Kerr
70 Robert Merryfield, labourer
72 Daniel Robson, labourer
74 Mary M'Mullan
76 Wm. Farrel, labourer
78 Daniel Kennedy, hackler
80 Mary Smyth, washerwoman
82 Catherine M'Anally, washerwoman and dealer
Side of York street mills

Talbot Court
GRATTAN STREET.
Three old houses

Talbot street
DONEGALL STREET TO GRATTAN ST.
1 John Byrne's wine and spirit store; residence, 23 Queen street
1 George P. Wood & Co., linen yarn, flax, and commission merchants; residence, Holywood
3 Jas. Steen & Co., general merchants
5 Vacant
7 Vacant
9 Thomas Fullerton, publican
11 Thomas M'Cartney, clerk
13 Wm. Moore, shoemaker
15 Miss Hainen's school
17 John Ellis, turner
19 Vacant
21 John Mooney, shuttle maker
23 Miss Smylie, dressmaker
25 Wm. Vint, painter and glazier
27 John Hewey, tailor
29 John Loughran, butcher
31,33 Jas. Thompson, grocer and spirit dealer
[*Hill street.*
33½ James Dinnen, butcher
35 Peter Armour, pilot
37 David Hutchison, cooper
39 John Barron
41 John Gilland, cooper
43 Charles Macoon, matrass maker
[*Johnny's entry.*
45 John M'Connell, sailcloth weaver

47 Samuel Thorpe, bricklayer
49 Henry Robinson, carpenter
51 John H. Bond, clerk
53 Roderick Frazer, confectioner
55 Mary M'Allister, boarding house
57 Vacant
59 James M'Cann, master mariner
61 John Donaldson, nailer
63 Side of Robert Loughry's spirit store
[*Grattan street.*]
54 Jas. Mones, grocer & spirit dealer
52 Edward Hamill, labourer
50 Terence Fagan, butcher
48 Miss M. Crawford, lodgings
46 Charles Quin, grocer & spirit store
44 Samuel Russell, labourer
42 John Crozier, warper
   J. & T. Kennedy's sizing factory
40 Thomas Finegan, sailor
38 Wm. Maguire, nailer
36 Robert Hall, tailor
36½ Ellen Carlisle, dealer
34 Silvester M'Gartland, coal dealer
32 Hugh M'Keown, painter
30 Mrs Mary Hood
28 Vacant
26 Edward Roden, marine store
24 Wm. Wharton, starch manufacturer
22 Wm. Powell, grocer & spirit dealer
Robert street.]
20 Isaac Maguire, hair cutter
18 Richard Dargan, grocer
16 Henry Fullerton, tailor
14 Robert Parkhill, baker
12 Scully, Shannon, and Holmes, plumbers
10 Wm. Thompson, cabinet maker
8 Miss Smith, dressmaker
6½ Robert Cunningham, shoemaker
6 Commercial Hotel stables
4 Hugh Quinn, caravansary
2½ G. P. Wood's stores and stables
2 Rev. T. F. Miller, Vicar of Belfast

Tanner's Court
62 MILLFIED.
Seventeen small houses

Taylor's Row
CARRICKHILL.
Now called Wall street

Tea Lane
LOWER MALONE.
Sixty-six small houses

Telfair's Entry
25 ANN STREET.
1 James Shaw's soap and candle manufactory; shop, 23 Ann st.
3 Belfast Bottling Company, and manufacturers of ærated water
5 Robert Long, horse dealer
7 Elizabeth M'Kinney, boardinghouse
28 James Burns, labourer
26 Hugh Connor, marine store
24 Robert Gillespie, day constable
22 John Allen, coach smith
20 Duncan M'Millan, blacksmith
18 James Gordon, bookseller
16 Wm. Croft, shoemaker
14 Wm. Harvey, bill poster
12 Martha Cassidy
10 James Boyd, labourer
8 Henry Morgan, bookbinder
6 Ellen Knight, spirit dealer
4 Wm. M'Mullen, warper
2 Vacant

Third street
BETWEEN FALLS ROAD AND SHANK-
HILL ROAD.
Michael Townley, grocer
Twenty-five small houses

Thomas Court
GEORGE'S LANE.
1 John Brown, spirit dealer
3 John Campbell, whitesmith
5 Thomas M'Lean, labourer
7 Charles M'Ilroy, car driver
9 Michl. Flinn, horse clipper & dealer

Thomas Street
FROM LANCASTER STREET TO GREAT
GEORGE'S STREET.
Back entrance to James Wilson's grocer shop
1 Daniel Quinn, clerk
3 Peter M'Auley, carpenter
5 Andrew Rowan, carpenter
7 Mrs. Elizabeth Sherlock
9, 11 Vacant
18 H. Halliday, flour merchant
   Mr. Halliday's store
16 Richard Riddell, stone cutter
14 Archibald Downs, engineer
12 William Yeaman, machine maker
10 Agnes Killen
8 Adam Magee, bookseller
6 Henry Harvey, carpenter

STREET DIRECTORY.

4 Mrs Margaret white
2 Hugh Bothwell, porter
Louisa Barlow

Thomas Street, North
YORK ST. TO CORPORATION ST.

1 Thomas Holden, foreman smith
3 John Anderson, carpenter
5 John M'Cormick, dresser in foundry
7 William Anderson, house carpenter
9 William Boyd, house carpenter
11 John Smyth, mechanic
13 Martin Murphy, millworker
15 George Brackly, railway porter
17 James Willicks, boiler maker
19 Daniel Savage, porter
21 Peter Ferry, carter
23 James Smith, builder and carpenter
25 William Rowley, master mariner
27 Richard M'Greevey, pilot
29 William Mills, pilot
31 William Farley, boat builder
33 William Gubbins, attorney's clerk
33½ William M'Donald's store
Hall door of Charles Frazer's spirit shop
..[*Collingwood street intersects.*]..
35 Thomas Burns, moulder
37 David Bailey, watchman
39 Alexander M'Ilwaine, revenue boatman
41 Wm. M'Cullough, ship carpenter
43 William Hawkins, servant
45 Robert M'Meekan, shoemaker
47 C. M'Clean's grocery
49 Elisha Wilson, boot and shoemaker
51 William Galway, tailor
53 John Simpson, pilot
55 Henry M'Giffen, overseer
57 David Niblock, ship carpenter
59 James M'Comb, ship carpenter
Two new houses not tenanted
54 James Shields, master mariner
52 Richard Nicholl, mariner
50 William Keating, mariner
Dock lane.]
48 Patrick Quee, shipwright
46 Jas. M'Farland, revenue boatman
44 John Adams, carpenter
42 Hugh M'Goukan, boiler maker
40 William Adair, pensioner & dealer
38 James Giles, smith
36 Ellen Dougherty, dealer
34 James M'Kinley, ship carpenter
32 William Anderson, tailor

30 Patrick Morrow's grocery & spirit store
..[*Collingwood street intersects.*]..
28 John Henderson, superannuated officer
26 Miss Higginson
24 Alexander M'Sparron, car owner
22 William Liddy, weaver
18 Owen Murray's grocery and provision stores
16 John Coleman
14 Felix Linn, labourer
12 Alexander M'Tier, master mariner
10 Captain Welsh
8 William Wilson, mechanic
6 Moses Greer, weaver
......[*Earl lane intersects.*]......
4 Joseph Moneypenny, moulder
2 John M'Crory, engine driver

Thompson's Entry
MILLFIELD.

Alexander Crawford's starchworks;
residence, Mount Charles
Seven small houses

Tomb street
WARING ST. TO CORPORATION SQUARE

1 Samuel Swallow, lodgings
3 Margaret Irvin, lodgings
5, 7, 9, 11 John and Thomas Sinclair, general merchants; residences:
John Sinclair, The Grove; Thos. Sinclair, Hopefield
13, 15, 17, 19 Vacant
21 John Barclay, coal merchant
23 Mrs Cunningham
25 Mrs Rachael Anderson, lodgings
27 Cornelius Nolan
29 James Macnamara, merchant
37 Vacant
Provision store vacant
Messrs. Charley's coal yard
37 John Finlay, bricklayer
39 Thomas Kane, tide waiter
41 John Davidson, clerk
43 Bernard Mooney, block and pump maker
45 Robert M'Garry, fisherman
[*Bradford square.*
47 Robert M'Kelvey, shoemaker
49 Eneas M'Elherron, sailor
51 Thomas Barrigan, sailor
53 Vacant
55 S. Duffield, jun., provision mercht.

57 James M'Bride's residence
59 Jas. M'Bride & Co., ship brokers
66 Vacant
64 S. Johnson, marine store
62 Samuel Dunlop, head constable in Ballast office
62 Alexander Dunlop, publican
60 John Toner, nailer
58 James Duncan, jeweller
56 Joseph M'Anally, ship agent
54 Peter Pierce, engineer
52 Henry Finnegan, store keeper
50 James Allen, painter and glazier
" William Finlay, tailor
48 Sarah Cooper
46 Edward O'Neill, cooper
44 John Heron, grocer
New court.]
42 Wm. Taylor, master mariner
40 Wm. Gelston, provision merchant; residence, 8 Great George's street
38, 36 Vacant
34 John Feeny, publican
Gamble street.]
32 Caledonian Hotel—Arthur Young, proprietor
30 A. Andrews, provision merchant
28 Jas. & John M'Connell, wine and spirit merchants, and rectifying distillers
28 Hugh Moore, surgeon
26 Jas. M'Fadden, stave merchant
24 Robert Stewart, pilot
Blakely's lane.]
22 Alexander Lovett, porter
20 Store
18 John Murphy, master mariner
16 Peter Glenn, agent to Jas. Methuen
14 Wm. Johnston
12½ James Methuen, fish curer
12 William Irwin, porter
10 Thomas Thompson, master mariner
8 Haliday and M'Dowell, grain merchants; Johnson Halliday's residence, Prospect Terrace
6 J. & T. Smith, butter and general merchants; residences: T. Smith, 37 Dock street; J. Smith, 13 Brougham street
4 James Garvey, lodgings
2 George Ingram, publican

Torrens's Row

(FORMERLY CROARKAN'S ROW),
OFF HERCULES STREET.

Twenty-one small houses

Torrens's Market

OFF HERCULES STREET.

1 Mrs Agnew's hall door
3 Mrs Dornan
5 Bernard Maguire, baker
7 James M'Avoy, printer
9 Mrs Ann Wilson
11 Nicholas Abbott, printer
13 Mrs Orr
15 Wm. Robinson
17 Wm. Macartney, carpenter
19 John Burns, shoemaker
24 Daniel Molloy, publican
22 William Mullan, sweep
20 James Hogg, weaver
18 Hugh Kelly, tailor
16 John Coates, copper and tinsmith
14 John Irvin, shoemaker
12 Nicholas Dillon, basket maker
10 Mrs Mary Stewart
8 John M'Clinchy, baker
6 Thomas Gribben, tobacco spinner
4 Denis M'Grory, tobacco spinner
2 Wm. Hadskis, turner
Back entrance to J. Giles' spirit store

Townsend Place

OFF TOWNSEND STREET.

1 Wm. Andrews, millwright and engineer
2 Andrew Lee, mechanic
3 David Cochrane, house painter
4 Wm. Richardson, mechanic
5 Wm. Dougherty, cabinet maker
6 James Savage, tailor
7 Hugh Brown, brassmoulder
8 James Meharg, baker
9 James M'Anally, linen lapper
10 Wm. John Blair, grinder
11 Rebecca Fleck
12 Charles O'Neill, carding master
13 Arthur Turner, mechanic
14 James Innes, mechanic

Townsend street

SHANKHILL ROAD TO FALLS ROAD.

1 Alex. Edgar, foreman carpenter
3 David Imery, foreman in wareroom
5 Wm. Grey, clerk
7 Robert Clements, bricklayer
9 Henry Johnston, engraver
11 George Wilson, mechanic
13 George Reynolds, warper
15 Robert Campbell, carpenter
17 James Withers, editor of Belfast *Commercial Chronicle*

19 John Hodgson, shopman
21 James M'Keever, tobacco spinner
23 Jas. Coates, collector of water tax
[*Dayton place.*
25 Henry Lowry, pawnbroker
27 Bernard M'Connell, builder
29 James B. Owen, pawnbroker
[*Marshall's place.*
31 Wm. Moran, spirit dealer
31½ Ulster foundry; T. Forbes, proprietor
35 Trevor Forbes
37 James Reid, porkcutter
39 Michael Goodman, mechanic
41 Alex. Dobbin, grocer
[*Cargill street.*
43 The Manse—Rev. W. Johnston
" TOWNSEND STREET PRESBYTERIAN CHURCH—the Rev. Wm. Johnston, minister
" Townsend street National School, Hugh Hanna, principal; William Hanna, assistant; Miss Reid, female school; Messrs Hanna's residences, 104 Sandy row; Miss Reid's residence, Peter's hill
45 Soho Foundry—Proprietors, MacAdam, Brothers, & Co., engineers; Mr MacAdam's residence, 18 College square East
47 William Ferris, spirit dealer
49 Mary Gordon
51 Ann Kane, washerwoman
" Patrick Kane, compositor
53 Patrick Foy, flax dresser
55 Edward Glennan, coach painter
57 Lorence Aid, tailor
59 Hall door of P. Savage's spirit shop
[*Falls road*]
Side of Thos. Kinker's spirit shop
62 Thomas Carabine, carter
60 James Kerr, store keeper
58 Daniel Cullen, tailor
56 Wm. John Livingston, manager of Public Baths and Wash houses
54 James Campbell, linen lapper
Millview place.]
52½ Wm. Taylor, carpenter
52 James M'Caffrey, bleacher
50½ John M'Fall, porter
50 Patrick Falloon, leather dresser
48 John Drain, cow keeper
46 Wm. Daley, cow keeper
44 George Munce, clerk

42 Thomas Thompson, publican
Coates street.]
40 Edward Birnie, portrait painter, grocer and spirit dealer
38 Wm. M'Clenahan, machine maker
36 John Horricks, hackle maker
34 Joseph Hemersley, mechanic
32 John M'Cullough, clerk
30 John Davidson, excise officer
28 Hugh Murphy
Townsend place.]
26 John Gill, boiler maker
House not tenanted
24 James Mawhinney
22 Henry Mallon, labourer
20 Robert M'Bride, helper in foundry
18 Ann Walker
16 Eliza Brown
14 Grace Hyndman
12 John Edmondson
Melbourne street.]
10 John Hanna, master carter
8 Alexander Gordon, carpenter
6 James M'Gilaway, shoemaker
4 Thomson and Co., iron founders, machine makers, and engineers; Mr Thomson's residence, 10 Castle street
Mary's market.]
2 Metal Foundry—Henry Gray, proprietor; residence, 94 Peter's hill
Side of Alexander Dalglish's grocery and provision store

Trafalgar Street

16 CORPORATION ST. TO YORK ST.
Patrick Rice, publican, 16 Corporation street
1 Thomas Macartney, foreman in *Vindicator* office
3 Edward Lennon, seaman
5 James Melvin, blacksmith
7 John Dickson, mill wright
9 Vacant
[*Mullan's place.*
11 John Magee, builder
13 William White, carpenter
[*Duffy's court.*
17 Jas. Mulholland, in provision store
19 John Faulkner, cooper
21 Thomas Miller, pensioner
23 William Ross, superannuated tide waiter
25 Catherine Draper, lodgings

Q

27 James Anderson, provision dealer
Eliza Johnston, grocer, 7 Nelson street
..... [*Nelson street intersects.*] ......
Jas. Quinn, publican, 78 Nelson st.
[*Trafalgar court.*
29 Watson Comsty, labourer
31 Joseph Mulgrave, dealer
33 William Barklie, boot and shoe manufacturer, 49 Donegall st.
35 John M'Cloy, ship carpenter
37 Alexander Thompson, ship carpenter
41 Eleanor Tennent, lodgings
43 George Coates and Co., provision merchants; Mr Coates's residence, York street
[*Little York street.*]
Robert Henderson's grain stores; office, Donegall quay
47 Benjamin Clayton, custom house officer and pensioner
49 Alexander Culviner, custom house officer
John R. Todd, publican, 103 York street
[*York street.*]
Thomas Fox, publican, 101 York street
Vacant house
Francis Armstrong, pensioner
44 Alexander Davison, ship carpenter
42 Hugh Allen, ship carpenter
40 Stewart Brown's wine and spirit stores
...[*Little York street intersects.*]...
38 Jas. Ferguson, grocer and publican
36 William Maybin, carpenter
34 Patrick Clarke, labourer
32 John Gilmore, ship carpenter
30 Joseph Magee, harbour constable
28 John Downing, of Downing and Son, iron works, Prince's dock
26 Alexander Clarke, of J. and A. Clarke, flour and grain merchants, office, 21 Church lane
24 James Macklin, gentleman
22 Richard Leighton, writing clerk
20 John Benson, pilot
18 James Hill, pilot
Back entrance to James M'Cleery's pawn office, Nelson street
John Scott, publican, 76 Nelson street
..... [*Nelson street intersects.*] .....

Mathew Martin, publican, 69 Nelson street
16½ John Teeling, writing clerk
16 James Fee, pilot
14 John Keenan, labourer
12 Andrew Thompson, in pork store
10 Thomas Graham, bricklayer
Rere of grain and provision stores, Richardson Brothers, Corporation street, and James Bodel, Henry street
6 Alexander M'Ilvenna, revenue officer
4 Henry M'Kittrick, in Mr M'Caldin's cap manufactory, Waring street
2 William Lindsay, mechanic

Trinity street

ANTRIM ROAD TO UNITY STREET.

1 John Kennedy, general cart maker, residence, 3 Antrim road
3 James Carlisle, building and scantling yard; residence, Donegall street
Enclosed ground
Four new houses building
Jas. Wilson, blacksmith; residence Lancaster street
4 William Erwin, cotton spinner
2 Michael Maguire, bricklayer

Union Place

FROM LANCASTER STREET TO LITTLE GEORGE'S STREET.

1 William John Magill, mariner
3 James Murphy, butler
5 John Thompson, tailor
7 Thomas Heeley, sawyer
" James Robinson, boot and shoemaker
9 James M. Herron, baker
11 John M'Dowell, sailor
" John Crow, ship carpenter
[*Union court.*
13 William Harrison, builder and scantling yard
.. [*Great George's street intersects.*]..
Fourteen small houses
Drake's lane.]
14 John M'Clure, bricklayer
12 James M'Garry, labourer
" James Boyle, carpenter
10 John Crummy, labourer
8 Stewart Bradley, sailmaker
" John Hamill moulder

6 Thomas Kane, mechanic
4 Sarah Caird, washerwoman
2 Robert M'Keown, weighmaster

Union Street

DONEGALL STREET TO NORTH ST.

1 Wm. Anderson, pawnbroker
1½ Henry Rice, spirit dealer
3 Charles O'Hagan, sawyer
5 Mrs Cowden, lodgings
7 Thomas M'Clelland, servant
9 Mrs Black, quilter
11 George Chambers, ladies' boot and shoemaker
13 Anabella Morrow, grocer and publican
15 John Barker, dealer
17 John Hunter, publican
...[*Little Donegall street intersects.*]..
19 Patrick Boyle, provision dealer
21 James Magee, grocer and publican
[*Charles's street.*
23 Robert Boyle, publican
25 Charles Vallely, labourer
27 Patrick Layden, plasterer
29 James Campbell, grocer
31 Sam. M'Gladdery, provision dealer
33 Elizabeth O'Neill, provision dealer
35 Hugh Harper, pawnbroker
37 Samuel Patterson, grocer and provision dealer
....[*Mustard street intersects.*]....
39 Daniel Holywood, smith and provision dealer
41 John O'Hara, butcher
43 Edward Hughes, pavier
" Daniel Hughes, barber
45 James Kane, boot and shoemaker
47, 49 Dorothea Owens, marine store
51 Vacant
53 Joseph Henry, wood turner
55 Joseph Armstrong, publican
[*Upper Kent street.*
57 Francis Daly, grocer and publican
59 Henry Todd, hairdresser
61 John Kelter, undertaker
63 Samuel Montgomery, publican
65 Samuel Tunmore, marine store
67 Margaret Magowan, marine store
69 Robert M'Govern, porter
" TEETOTAL HALL
71 John Fitzsimmons, nailer
73 Wm. Neill, nailer
75 Joseph Braithwaite, coffin maker
77 Patrick Higgins, barber

79 Mary M'Cluskie, dealer
81 John Elliott, grocer, &c., 133 North street
[*North street.*]
Vacant house
68 Francis M'Anally, dealer
66 Bartholemew Magee, spectacle and mattrass maker
64, 62 J. Hart, sawyer and undertaker
Vacant house
60 David Robinson, baker
58 James Macartney, baker
56 Edward Kelly, dealer
54 Wm. M'Closkie, dealer
Kent street.]
52 John Kane, dealer
50 Patrick M'Lornan, marine store
48 Patrick M'Kenna, flax scutcher
46 Patrick Conlon, labourer
44 Patrick Maguire, shoemaker
42 Mrs O'Neill
40 David Bradford, provision dealer
38 John Quin, grocery & spirit store
....[*Mustard street intersects.*]....
36 John Jackson, publican
34½ James Simpson, dealer
34 Mrs Hewey, painter and glazier
32 Jane Plunket
Entry.]
30 John M'Kee, confectioner
28 Edward M'Closkie, warper and grocer
26 Charles Condren, pensioner
24 Hugh Blair, carpenter
22 Wm. Doherty, tailor
20 Bernard Brown, pavier
18 Robert Paul, grocer
...[*Little Donegall street intersects.*]...
16, 14 James Irvine, publican, 29 Little Donegall street
12 Anne M'Kee, lodgings
10 Elizabeth Timby, boarding house
8 Henry Madden, sawyer
6 Samuel Johnston, shoemaker
4 Eliza M'Keown, dressmaker and hiteworker

Unity street

OFF TRINITY STREET, ANTRIM ROAD.

TRINITY CHURCH—Rev. Theophilus Campbell, Incumbent; residence, Mountainview
1 William Dempster, linen lapper
3 David M'Mullan, clerk
5 William Dickson, haberdasher

5 John Dickson, sewed muslin manufacturer
7 Thomas Millford, assistant draper
9 Robert M'Gee, fitter up in Belfast Foundry
11 Gordon A. Thomson's office
13 John R. Tinsdale, compositor, *News-Letter* office
15 Robert Newett, coal merchant

University square
OLD MALONE ROAD.

Fourteen new houses building
1 Henry Black, wholesale grocer, Waring street
2 John Wiley, wholesale grocer, Victoria street
" Alex. Dickey, wholesale grocer, and bursar Queen's College
3 Rev. W. D. Killen, D.D.
4 Mrs Killen
5 Rev. James Murphy, D.D.
6 Rev. John Edgar, D.D.
7 George C. Pim, of E. and G. Pim, High street and Donegall quay
8 Rev. George Bellis
9 Mrs Purdon
10 Mrs Knox

Upton Street
WALL ST.

1 Alexander Clarke, clerk
3 William M'Causland, compositor
5 Robert M'Laughlin, mechanic
7 Thomas Gibson, brass moulder
9 James Carrick, dentist
11 Catherine Hanna
13 Nathaniel Pearson, mechanic
15 George Lemon, mechanic
Four new houses building
12 Robert Knott, hatter
10 James M'Nally, book keeper
8 Hannah Armstrong, hat trimmer
6 Sarah Wetherald
4 George Newberry, pensioner
2 Robert Edmondson, moulder

Valentine street
OFF HENRY STREET.

1 Wm. Devenport, mechanic
3 Charles M'Clelland, belt sewer
5 Wm. Sharpe, car driver
7 Daniel Connor, labourer
9 Patrick M'Bride, labourer
11 Henry Connelly, porter

13 Wm. Kane, yarn boiler
15 John Wilson, labourer
17 John M'Cann, flax dresser
19 Elizabeth Bingham, whiteworker
21 David Martin, coachman
23 Wm. Savage, tailor
25 John M'Sorley, in Rowan's foundry
27 Samuel Bailey, lapper
29 John Bead, tailor
31 John Houston, yarn bundler
33 Joseph Thompson, carpenter
35 John Johnston, labourer
37 John Adams, labourer
39 Joseph Heron, labourer
42 Wm. Crawford, butler
40 James Addison, stone cutter
38 Lowry Laird, labourer
36 Wm. Hughes, car driver
34 John Mulholland, dealer
32 Maria Gibbs, whiteworker
30 Hugh Adair, blacksmith
28 Samuel Cooke, labourer
26 James Thompson, mariner
24 Alexander Greer, shoemaker
22 Edmund Lavery, dealer
20 Daniel Lynass, stone cutter
18 Wm. Martin, labourer
16 Robert Robson, butler
14 Alex. Stevenson, machine master
12 James Batty, helper in foundry
10 Hugh Armstrong, weaver
8 Peter Magill, labourer
6 Margaret Davidson
4 James M'Collough, porter
2 John Taggart, spirit dealer

Vere Street
NORTH QUEEN ST. TO YORK STREET.

1 John Stewart, pensioner
3 William John Bailey, clerk
5 William Montgomery, jun., shoemaker
7 William Montgomery, sen., shoemaker
9 Samuel Thompson, butler
11 Francis M'Comb, reeling master
13 Thomas Willis, ship joiner
15 John M'Natt, labourer
17 Robert Ross, porter
19 John Hamill, porter
21 John Hamill, porter
23 William Gillespie, pensioner
25 Laurence Munroe, labourer
27 David Walker, stone cutter
29 Rodger Osborne, ship carpenter

STREET DIRECTORY.

31 Laurence Angell, engineer
33 John Roseman, clerk
35 Alexander Kirkwood, labourer
37 William Jones, labourer
39 Henry M'Donald, car driver
41 William Spear, weaver
...... [*Grove street intersects.*]......
43 Mary Bell, grocer
45 Henry Walker, labourer
47 John Hanna, labourer
49 Edward Quinn, carter
51 Agnes Herdman
53 Edward Dougherty, weaver
55 Ann Donnelly, dealer
57 John Haddock, labourer
59 Margt. M'Quillan, washerwoman
61 Sarah Bingham, spinner
63 James Walker, labourer
65 James Norris, pork cutter
67 James Finlay, labourer
69 Robert Carruthers, shoemaker
71 John Bell, carpenter
73 James Allen, labourer
75 John M'Clune, tailor
77 John Burns, carpenter
79 David M'Neight, labourer
81 George Robinson, foundryman
76 Ann Hunter, grocer and publican
74 Nathaniel Lewis, carpenter
72 John Dickson, carpenter
70 James Ferguson, joiner
68 William Sanderson, mechanic
66 Thomas M'Connell, painter
64 Jane Lawson, upholsterer
62 James Corrigan, sawyer
60 William Irvine, seaman
58 John Walker, labourer
56 John M'Lean, mariner
54 James M'Comb, ship carpenter
52 Archibald Gibbon, weaver
50 Robert Dale, ship carpenter
48 Ellen Service, cloth cap maker
46 Mary M'Curdy
44 John Bell, stone mason
42 Thomas Wiley, sawyer
40 William Graham, carpenter
38 Isaac Whiteside, labourer
36 Mary Symington, dealer
34 Robert Spear, spinning master
32 Jane M'Ilherron, dressmaker
30 Charles Keenan, labourer
28 James M'Cann, weaver
26 Henry Cochrane, pensioner
24 James Kennedy, bleacher
22 James Greenlees, mariner
20 John Smyth, stone mason

18 Thomas Watterson, boiler maker
16 Wm. J. Torbitt, carpenter
14 Joshua Smyth, tide waiter
12 George Inch, boiler maker
10 Samuel Nixon, flax dresser
 8 Alex. Bowden, carpenter
 6 Alex. Wilson, watchman
 4 Richard White, boiler maker
 2 Wm. White, mechanic
   Robert Hoy, painter
   Margaret Hamilton
   Wm. Strip, customhouse officer

Verner's Lane
OFF VERNER STREET.
Nine small houses

Verner Street
OFF CROMAC STREET.
[*Holm's court.*
1 Thomas Murdoch, dealer
3 Edward Daly, dealer
5 Isabella Wallace, dealer
.[*Balmer's court.*
7 Wm. Benson, carpenter
9 Patrick M'Connell, labourer
11 John Hamill, labourer
13 Charles Young, shoemaker
15 Wm. Leslie, dealer
17 Ellen Murphy, dealer
19 Arthur M'Cann, saddler
21 Margaret Balmer, dealer
23 John M'Aree, dealer
[*Verner's lane.*
25 Dougherty Thompson, grocer
27 James Finlay, warehouseman
29 Francis Webb, shoemaker
31 James Duff, cheesemonger
[*Quigley's court.*
33 Alexander Harrison, tailor
35 Thomas Magee, cabinet maker
37 Jas. Campbell, boot & shoemaker
[*Lagan street.*
39 Nathaniel Duncan's store
41 Hugh Watt, labourer
43 Thomas Graham, bricklayer
45 Edward M'Bride, porter
 " Bernard Murphy, clerk
47 John M'Ateer, blacksmith
 " John Miskelly, shoemaker
49 Wm. Clements, grocer
51 Matthew Quinn, tailor
53 James Waterson, spirit dealer
55 Edward Carlin, grocer
57 Margaret M'Keown
59 Hugh M'Mullan, clerk

61 John Mateer
63 Samuel Thompson, paper dealer
65 James Ward, grocer
72 Vacant
70 Henry Hull, porter
68 James Savage, labourer
66 Jane M'Grillan, mangler
64 James Lynass, stonecutter
60 James Davis, labourer
58 David Lennon, labourer
56 John Carroll, butcher
54 Samuel Hall, shoemaker
52 Felix Hamill, labourer
Colin court.]
50 John Lunn, baker
48 James Donaghy, porter
46 James M'Afee, labourer
44 Patrick Riley, sawyer
42 Joseph Warnock, grocer
Lagan street.]
40 Robert Marlin, spirit dealer
38 Patrick Hollin, porter
36 M. M'Carty, coach smith and grocer
34 Terence M'Kenna, sawyer
32 Robert Munce, butcher
30 Thomas Drummond, spirit dealer
East street.]
28, 26 J. Connor, grocer and publican
24 Richard Evans, blacksmith
22 Mary Watson
20 Mary Carlin, dealer
18 Owen Gillan, labourer
Annette street.]
16 John Crosgrove, grocer & publican
14 Archibald Scott, rent agent
12 James White, car driver
10 John Finlay, plasterer
8 Wm. Murray, grocer and publican
6 Thomas Riley, pensioner
4 Eliza Berwick
2 John Meharrey, labourer

Victoria Court
OFF DURHAM STREET.

Eight small houses

Victoria Place
GREAT VICTORIA STREET.

1 John Carter, of Carter & Martin, Rosemary street
2 Samuel Lyle, wine and spirit merchant, Fountain street
3 Vacant
4 Mrs M'Cammon
5 Jas. Strachan, in Provincial Bank
6 John Gaussen, grain merchant, 11 Albert square

6 Chas. Gaussen, in Messrs. Richardson, Brothers, & Co.'s office
7 Mrs Dickson
8 Richard Lewis, gentleman
9 Rev. Thomas Drew, D.D.
10 Smith Bryan
11 A. Wallace, brewer, Hercules st.
12 Peter Keegan, wine and spirit merchant, Calendar street
13 John Maclurcan, haberdasher, Donegall place
14 Mrs Collins
15 John Cameron, linen merchant, Calendar street
16 Frederick Ogle, wine and spirit merchant, 10 Waring street

Victoria street
CORPORATION ST. TO GT. EDWARD ST.

REGENT BUILDINGS.
Caretakers' house, and side of first shop in Gordon street
Four shops
CORN EXCHANGE—Entrance
One shop
M'Kenzie, Brothers, gasfitters and brassfounders; residence, May st.
Wm. O'Neill, draper and clothier; residence, 20 Robert street
.....[*Waring street intersects.*].....
James Reed, printer, bookseller and stationer; residence, 43 Academy street
One shop vacant
Wm. M'Caw, wholesale grocer; residence, 1 Franklin place
Henry Dickson & Co., wholesale wine and spirit merchants; H. Dickson's residence, 6 Albert place
Andw. Kernohan, wholesale grocer
John Wallace, solicitor, and 22 North Earl street, Dublin; residence, Bunker's hill
John Hoy & Co., wholesale wine and spirit merchants; residence, 4 Botanic road
W. Emerson Prenter, agent for Messrs Absolom, Crocker, and Townsend, wholesale tea and coffee merchants, London; residence, Botanic road
Alexander Dickey and Co., wholesale grocers and oil merchants; A. Dickey's residence, University square; J. Wiley's, ditto

STREET DIRECTORY. 187

James Glenn, wholesale grocer
John M'Dowall, wholesale grocer; residence, 16 Hamilton street
George Sibbin, whosesale grocer; residence, 28 York street
Wm. Spackman, tailor, draper, and hatter, and High street
[*High street.*
Four new houses building
Three shops vacant
James M'Cormack & Co., linen drapers and haberdashers; residence, 11 Johnston's buildings, Shankhill road
S. W. Bullick & Co., drapers and hatters; residence, Holywood
Robert Lindsay & Co., sewed muslin manufacturers, Victoria buildings; Robert Lindsay's residence, Cliftonville
Six shops vacant
James Wilson, wholesale wine and spirit merchant, Victoria Buildings; residence, 31 Hamilton st.
Joseph Waugh, wholesale grocer
William Mullan, wholesale grocer; residence, Brookvale
Shop vacant
......[*Ann street intersects.*]......
Five shops not finished
1 Joseph Bell, spirit dealer
Edward Dailey, fruiterer; residence, 3 Verner street
3 Nicholas Virgin, wine and spirit dealer
5 James M'Meckan, marble and stone yard
7,9 Bernard M'Cann, brassfounder and gasfitter
11 Michael Woods, wine and spirit dealer; residence, 13 Galway st.
13 Thomas C. S. Corry, surgeon, Victoria street Medical Hall, and ærated water manufacturer

St. George's Market
Enclosed ground
......[*Ann street intersects*] ......
Enclosed ground
Marlborough street.]
Andw. Harbison, wholesale grocer
Shop vacant
Benjamin Pratt & Co., Wellington boot and shoe warehouse; residence, 62 Great George's street

Miss Ann Hargrave's commercial boarding house and hotel
Enclosed ground
Queen's square.]
NEW NORTHERN BANK (building)
.....[*Waring street intersects.*].....
VICTORIA CHAMBERS.
Wm. Larmour, commission merchant and broker; residence, 6 Apsley place

Victoria Street, Great

James Keyland, spirit dealer
Dublin and Armagh Hotel and livery stables—James Keyland, proprietor
Ulster Railway Hotel and Tavern —T. O'Hanlon, proprietor
[*Hope street.*
[*Breadalbane place.*
[*Belvidere place.*
Botanic road.]
Mrs Smith, Wellwood house
Wellwood place.]
Victoria place.]
Windsor place.]
ULSTER RAILWAY CO.'S STATION-HOUSE, Office and Stores; John Godwin, engineer; J. G. Smith, manager and secretary
2 Vacant

Victoria Street, Little
OFF GREAT VICTORIA STREET.
1 Joseph Orr, seedsman, 5 Castle pl.
2 John Kelly, brush and comb warehouse, Bridge street
3 John Carruthers, gentleman

Walker's Lane
FREDERICK STREET.
Thirty-eight small houses

Wall street
CARRICKHILL TO STANHOPE STREET.
1, 3 Vacant
5 Henry Simms, starch maker
7 Nicholas Pray, ginger ale maker
9 Nancy Carlisle
11 Denis Mullan, labourer
13 Patrick Burns, labourer
15 Patrick Henry, labourer
17 Felix O'Neill, labourer•
" David Grant, shoemaker
19 Catherine M'Cart, veiner

21 Henry M'Laverty, night constable
18 John Daley, upholsterer
16 Patrick Sloan, saddler
14 Robert Mawhinney, clerk
12 John Templeton, master mariner
10 John M'Keown, clerk
8 John Jenkins, cabinet maker
6 Thomas Robinson, clerk
4 Henry M'Laughlin, builder
2 Mary Cairns, boarding house
1 James Maguire, carpenter
3 Patrick Brown, plasterer
5 Arthur Clarke, carpenter
7 Holms Scott, plumber
9 John Fimister, cooper
11 James Reid, linen lapper
13 Henry M'Ilroy, labourer
15 Mrs Gillespie, whiteworker
17 Susan Morgan
19 John Hull, moulder
California street.]
21 Wm. M'Cormack, brass founder
23 Alex. Wisdom, boot & shoemaker
" John Hayney, moulder
25 Michael Owens, carpenter
27 John M'Dowell, carding master
29 Wm. Connor, carpenter
Upton street.]
31 Samuel Boyd, bookbinder
31 Arthur Edmonson, cabinet maker
35 Eliza Gardner, bonnet maker
37 Wm. Roney, carpenter
39 Alex. Dillon, moulder
" Wm. Ferris, moulder
20 Robert Hagan, weaver
18 Thomas Peak, sawyer
16 John M'Cready, chandler
14 Margaret Mullan
12 Robert Armstrong, labourer
10 Ann Kane
" Thomas West, bellows maker
8 Edward Robinson, labourer
6 Thomas Duff, pilot
4 Henry M'Quade, labourer
2 Francis Boyle, weaver

Waring street

COMMERCIAL BUILDINGS TO ALBERT
SQUARE.

3 Browne, Reid & Co., woollen and Manchester warehousemen; residences: Wm. Browne, Crescent; Joseph Reid, Antrim road
3½ M'Connell and Kennedy, flax and tow spinners; residences: James Kennedy, Millvale; Jas. M'Connell, Liverpool
5 Charles & William Finlay, wholesale tea merchants; Chas. Finlay's residence, Albert place; W. Finlay's, Fountainville Terrace
7 ULSTER BANKING Co.'s OFFICES
ULSTER BANK BUILDINGS.
Thos. C. M'Indoe, sewed muslin manufacturer; residence, 8 Albion place
Hugh Halliday's flour stores
11 John Douglass, wholesale and retail grocer, biscuit and lozenge manufacturer
13 Thomas Henry Reilly, stationer, bookbinder, and printer
15,17 Henry Black, wholesale grocer & tobacco manufacturer; residence, University square
19, 21, 23 Philip Johnston, wholesale grocer and tea merchant; residence, Turf Lodge
[*Skipper street.*
25 Wm. Johnston, lithographic printer, stationer and bookbinder
27 Belfast Starch and Glue Works —Edward Tucker, proprietor; residence, Donegall square
29 Hugh M'Neill, commission and general merchant, and sugar broker; residence, 14 Great George's street
" Patrick Kinnear, linen and linen yarn merchant; residence, Harp Hall, Antrim road
31 Wm. Carson, solicitor; residence, 1 Howard street
33 Langtrys and Herdman, steam packet and ship owners, and general merchants; Mr Langtrys' residence, Fortwilliam; Mr Herdman's residence, Cliftonville
35 John Hunter, jun., and Co., general merchants; J. Hunter's residence, Tyne Cottage, Whiteabbey
37 Samuel M'Crea, general emigration agent; residence, 57 James st.
39 Albion Hotel and Tavern—James Rickards, proprietor
41 Josias Cunningham & Co., foreign agents, general brokers and commission merchants; stock and share brokers; J. Cunningham's residence, 37 King street

43 Wm. Gamble & Co., general commission merchants; W. Gamble's residence, 131 York street
J. & W. Wallace, sewed muslin manufacturers; residence, Glasgow; Wm. Jamieson, agent, Riley's pl.
.... [*Victoria street intersects.*]....
57 Thomas Quinn, general emigration agent; residence, 80 North st.
59 Wm. Garrett, butcher
59 John Hughes, green grocer; residence, Gamble street
59 Patrick Smyth, spirit dealer
59 Frazer and Finch, provision, butter, fish, and salt merchants, and ship stores
59 James Macdonald, ship broker, and general emigration office, and Prince's dock; residence, 20 Dock street
61 Robt. M. Carson, sail maker, patent canvas and cord warehouse, and ship chandler; residence, 137 York street
63 Thomas Parker, jun., butcher; residence, Hercules street
[*Albert square.*]
78 George Ingram, spirit dealer
76 John Thomson, spirit dealer
74 John C. Cramsie, wine merchant & notary public; residence, May st.
" Robert Scott, general commission merchant; residence, Holywood
" Colvil, Auld, & Co., ship brokers and general merchants; residences—Arch. Colvil's, Glenfield place; John Auld's, Glasgow
GATEWAY.
74 Ferrie & Campbell, bonded store keepers and general merchants; residence, Holywood
John Montgomery & Sons, flax spinners, Grove mill and Wolf hill, and entrance by Corporation street
72 Edward Shaw and Co., commission merchants; James Shaw's residence, Glenbank, Crumlin road
VICTORIA CHAMBERS.
24 William and Thomas Hunter, cotton yarn agents, and general commission merchants; residence, 1 Murray's terrace
26 Willam Rodgers and Co., general commission merchants

William Rodgers' residence, 7 Apsley place
19 Andrew Mercer
17 Hull, Hart, and Co., flax spinners, Falls road; Richard Hull's residence, Howard st.; Jas. Hart's residence, Queen st.
20, 22 Vacant
.... [*Victoria street intersects.*]....
48 John Hoy, house painter & publican
46 Dennis Kane, spirit & provision store
44 Ballymena Railway parcel office
Waring street place.]
42 William D. Henderson, broker and commission agent; residence, 2 Howard street
" Scottish Amicable Life Insurance Company's office—William D. Henderson, secretary
Cotton court.]
40 George Ash, wholesale grocer, general merchant, and commission agent; residence, Cliftonville
" George Ash, jun., merchant; residence, Cliftonville
38 Isaac Arrott's salt stores
36 CHAMBER OF COMMERCE—Samuel Vance, secretary; residence, 37 Chichester street
" Samuel Vance, public accountant
" COMMERCIAL CLUB—John Giles, caretaker
34 Isaac Arrott, provision and general merchant; residence, 2 Wellington place
32 John Smyth, boot and shoe maker
30 Robert Jardine & Co., wholesale and retail grocers
28 Charles Duffin & Co., flax spinners and general merchants; C. Duffin's residence, 3 Donegall square North
" James Grimshaw & Son, flax spinners; residence, Whitehouse
" Edmund Grimshaw, flax spinner; residence, Mossley
" Monkstown Flax Spinning Co.
26 John Matthews, hat and cap manufacturer
24 Jane and Eliza Finlay, bonnet makers and haberdashers
Hill street.]
22 Universal Parcel Office — J. E. Richards, manager
" J. E. Richards, snuff & tobacco shop

20 John Pim, commission agent; residence, Crumlin Terrace
" Wm. Douglass, Ardrossan and Troon coal office; residence, Glenfield place
18 Arthur Crawford & Co., drapers; residence, Lodge Road
18 James M'Caldin, hat and cap manufacturer, and warehouseman; residence, 4 Frederick street
" Wm. Bryson, muslin and gingham manufacturer; residence, The Crescent
18 Wm. Adamson, agent for J. & W. Broadley, muslin manufacturers, Glasgow
16 Jas. Boomer & Co., flax spinners; residences: J. Boomer, Seaview; Jas. Campbell, 5 College square North
14 Robert Calwell & Co., hardware merchants; residence, 10 Donegall square North
12 Shop vacant
12 Royal Temperance Hotel, Thomas Farrell, proprietor
Warehouse lane.]
10 Frederick Ogle, tea, wine, spirit, and general merchant; residence, 16 Victoria place
" John Ferguson & Co., linen merchts.
8 Joseph Young, woollendraper and hatter
6 Hugh M'Kendry & Co., glass, oil, and colour warehouse
Ulster Advertiser Office, John Wallace, proprietor
4 Ralph Green, grocer and cheese merchant; residence, 12 Henry street
2 Hill Smyth, wholesale stationer, account book manufacturer, and lithographer

Waring Street Place
42½ WARING STREET.

4 John Murphy and Co., flax spinners; Wm. Murphy's residence, Howard street
3 Robert Stewart, linen yarn mercht.
2 W. S. Shaw, tea and general commission agent

Warehouse Lane
12 WARING STREET.

Richard Creeth & Co., commission agents; residence, 30 Hamilton st.

Washington street
FREDERICK ST. TO YORK LANE.

1 Andrew Cochrane, carpenter
2 Saml. M'Millan, dealer in tow, &c.
3 James Coey, mechanic
4 James Armstrong, carpenter
5 William Crozier, overseer
6 Matthew Purkis, hackle maker
7 Henry M'Clelland, lapper
8 Isaac Mawhinney, porter
9 John Craig, clerk
10 Bernard Ranagan, hair dresser
11 Patrick Hughes, dealer
12 John M'Cully, cooper
13 Robert Adrain, salesman
14 Hugh Quinn, cabinet maker and spirit dealer

Waugh's Court
(FORMERLY HUGHES ROW)
132 NORTH STREET.

Patrick Divine, nailer
Samuel Smith, blacksmith
Six small houses

Wellington Court
WELLINGTON ST.

1 James M'Clean, letter carrier
3 William Adams, carpenter
6 David Taylor, carpenter
4 Constantine M'Auley, carpenter
2 William Johnston, upholsterer

Wellington Place
DONEGALL SQUARE TO COLLEGE SQ.

1 Richard Barnett, dentist
" Dr Richard Barnett, dentist
3 Dr Andrew Marshall
5 Dr Thos. Henry Purdon, surgeon
7 Thomas Kennedy, muslin manufacturer, Commercial court
9 John Herdman, flax spinner, of J. and J. Herdman & Co., Winetavern street
11 Dr Robert Stephenson
Enclosed ground
[*Queen street.*
Enclosed ground
13 Wm. Forsyth, gentleman
15 Wm. Gillilan, linen merchant, Linen Hall
17 Mrs Arthur Millar
20 Dr Wm. Moffat, surgeon
18 Wm. Young, woollen merchant, 19 Donegall street

18 Robert Young, civil engineer
16 Dr John Blizard, surgeon
14 Wm. Grogan, linen merchant, Linen Hall
12 Mrs Hancock
CIRCUS ROYAL—vacant
Queen street Upper.]
10 Charles Lanyon, county surveyor and civil engineer, and architect
8 W. J. C. Allen, J.P., Registrar Queen's College
6 Geo. T. Mitchell, Belfast Bank
4 Dr Henry M'Cormac
2 Isaac Arrott, merchant, Waring st.

Wellington Square
FALLS ROAD.

1 Esther M'Dornan
2 Vacant
3 Sarah Kane
4 Isabella M'Alister
5 Peter Cassidy, weaver
6 John Sullivan, flax rougher
7 Bernard Riley, labourer
8 Samuel Watson, bricklayer
9 Mary Best
10 Geo. Crawford, coachman
11 Eliza Thompson
James Kennedy, of Jas. Kennedy & Son, flax spinners, Falls road
James Agnew
Charles Henderson, flax bundler
Wm. Little, reeling master
Stephenson M'Collough, bookkeeper and cashier, Belfast Flour Mills
Side of Geo. Parker's spirit store

Wellington Street
FISHERWICK PLACE TO DONEGALL SQUARE WEST.

Side of Fisherwick place Presbyterian Church School-rooms
..[*Upper Queen street intersects.*]..
1 Mrs Montgomery, boarding house
3 George Robinson, letter carrier
5 Patrick Connor, lapper
7 William Wilson, lapper
9 Thomas Johnston, car driver
11 Joseph Ferris, cabinet maker
13 John M'Clelland, carpenter
15 Sayers Bamford, coach maker
14 Michael M'Mullan's posting establishment
12 Joseph Sproal, labourer
10 Michael M'Mullan
Wellington court.]
8 John Fulton, painter
6 Samuel Clegg, pensioner
4 Stables
2 Margaret Kimmit

Wellwood Place
OFF GREAT VICTORIA STREET.

1 Vacant
2 Daniel John Allen, hatter, Castle buildings, Castle place
3 Mrs Elizabeth Brown

Welsh street
LAGAN STREET TO ELIZA STREET.

Vacant house [*Friendly street.*
1 Sam. Mathers, bricklayer & grocer
[*Stanfield street Lower.*
John M'Dowell, cow keeper
Wm. Patterson, dealer
7 John Blair, car driver
9 Henry Fee, carpenter
11 James Black, carpenter
13 Philip Pharland, labourer
15 John Winnington, brass founder and gas fitter
17 Wm. Tully, tailor
19 William Kelso, bricklayer
21 Mrs Ann Jane White
[*Eliza street.*]
20 Stewart Oliver, porter
18 James M'Cormick, cooper
16 James Kernaghan, carpenter
14 Henry Boyd, painter
12 Mrs Mary M'Dade
10 Hugh Dugan, carpenter
Francis Smith, grocer and publican, 34 Stanfield street
Stanfield street.]
John Dobbs, grocer; shop, Stanfield street
Moses Stauntan's roompaper manufactory; shop, Donegall place; residence, Ballygomartin
8 Arthur M'Comish, drill weaver
6 John M'Grady, car owner
Crawford street.]
James Savage, captain of schooner *Jewess*
Isaac Hanna, paper stainer

Wesley Lane
WESLEY STREET.

1 John Hamilton, stone cutter

2 Hamlet Woods, bricklayer
3 James Stevenson, labourer
4 Robert Brown, gardener
5 Wm. Wallace, house carpenter
6 John Nixon

Wesley Place
BOTANIC ROAD.

1 Cunningham Matier, grocer
3 Jas. W. Donovan, scripture reader
5 Christopher Stewart, confectioner
7 Jane Thompson
9 Wm. Palmer, baker
[*Stable lane.*]
11 John M'Cottery, cabinet maker
13 Thomas Thompson, coach trimmer
15 Hamtn. Wardlow, house carpenter
17 Wm. Gilmore, sawyer
Vacant building ground
19 Wm. Ferrit, tailor
21 Jas. Rogers, meal and flour dealer
23,25 David Brittain, spirit dealer
[*Sandy row*
Renwick place]
14 Wm. Leebody, carpenter
12 John Rea, railway constable
10 Robert Knox, shoemaker
Wesley lane]
8 James M'Moran, linen weaver
6 Wm. M'Farland, warper
4 Arthur Coates, brazier
James F. Burns, English, mercantile, and mathematical school
2 Joseph M'Farland, grocer
Lane]
WESLEYAN METHODIST MEETING HOUSE—ministers: Rev. John Oliver, residence, Joy street; Rev. Thomas Ballard, residence, Pakenham place
Wm. Fawkner, grocer and publican, 1 Bradbury place—hall door

West street
SMITHFIELD TO MILLFIELD.

1, 3 Vacant
5 James Brown, manager of Messrs. Herdman's mill
7 Andrew Ferguson, engineer
9 David Beck, spinning master
11 John Montgomery, dealer
[*Gregg's lane.*
13 Mary M'Cullough, dealer
15 Robert Cunningham, mariner

17 John M'Laughlin, spirit dealer and undertaker
19 John Burke, shoemaker
21 Mary Robinson, dealer
23 James Donnelly, shoemaker
25 James Farrell, coachmaker
27 John M'Mahon, coachmaker
29 Eliza Hanvey, dealer
31 Charles M'Laughlin, cartmaker
33 George M'Court, labourer
35 Ellen Donnelly, dealer
37 Vacant
39 John Wilson, spirit dealer
[*Millfield.*]
30 Robert M'Quade, spirit dealer
28 Solomon Willis, straw and hay dealer
26, 24 John Hill, rasp and file cutter
22 Eliza Donohoe
20 James M'Laughlin, cartmaker and blacksmith
18 Peter Brannan, shoemaker
16 David M'Clure, butcher
14 Hugh Skelton, shoemaker
John M'Laughlin, stabling yard
12 Michael Burke, shoemaker
" Hiram M'Conaghy, copper and tinsmith
10 Charles M'Clelland, shoemaker
8, 6, 4 John Gillespie, forage stores
2 Edward Heron, auctioneer and appraiser, and spirit dealer

William's Lane
67 GREEN ST. TO LITTLE EDWARD ST.

Mathew Metcalfe, side door; shop, Green street
1 Mrs Keating
3 James Devine, labourer
5 George M'Gaughey, bricklayer
7 John Keenan, labourer
9 William John M'Clurg, labourer
11 William Crossley, cooper
13 Patk. Canavan, tailor and lodgings
15 James Hawthorn, grocer
[*Little Edward street.*]
16 Thomas M'Cullough, labourer
14 William Gribben, labourer
12 Michael Mullan, porter
10 Robert Purdy, shoemaker
8 William Rankin, blacksmith
6 Hugh Ferguson, carpenter
4 Robert Crawford, cooper
2 Mary Purdy

STREET DIRECTORY.

Victoria Terrace
OLD MALONE ROAD.
1 William Morgan, gentleman
2 James Wallace, in Ulster Bank
3 William Killen, woollendraper
4 James B. Andrews, book keeper
5 Rev. Thomas Ballard
6 James Rea, book keeper
7 Anthony Farrell, book keeper
William Montgomery, gentleman
Wm. Anderson, in Murray, Greene, and Lloyd's
Mr. Dennison, of Brown, Reid, &Co.
John Gertshaw, sewed muslin manufacturer

Winetavern Street
SMITHFIELD TO NORTH STREET.
1,3 Patrick Griffith, spirit dealer
5 Wm. Cowan, grocer and publican
Henry Adams, stabling & coal yard
7 David Kennedy, recruiting sergeant
9 Patrick M'Cullough, labourer
11 Mary Jane Irvine, lodging house
13 John M'Anally, labourer
15 James Stewart
17 John Hanvey, lodgings
19 Robert Jackson, labourer
21 Robert Magee, nailer
23 Jane Nelson, dealer
25 Francis Crawford, whitesmith
27 Wm. Stewart, blacksmith
29 G. Colpoy, saddler & haberdasher
31 Patk. M'Cluskey, boot & shoe shop
34 Hugh Heanvey, spirit dealer
35 Mary Baxter, spirit dealer
37 Patrick Gilmore, marine store
39 Thos. Hamilton, pipe manufactory
41 Mary Hunter, lodgings
43 Susanna Green, dyer
43 James Greenwood, whitesmith
45 Robert Bogan's spirit store
54 David Ferran, marine store
52 Joseph Gordon, labourer
50 M'William's stabling yard
48 Andrew Brown, spirit dealer
46 Lucinda Hudson
44, 42 James Gibb, spirit dealer
40 David M'Larnon, carpenter
38 James M'Manus, porter
36 James Nelson, whitesmith
34 Rose Ann M'Cambly, dealer
32 Hugh Tigh, nail maker
30 Alicia Thompson, grocer & publican

Winecellar Entry
HIGH STREET TO ROSEMARY STREET.
1 James M'Call, Shell Fish tavern
3, 5 Mary Davey, tavern keeper
7 Neill and White, wholesale wine and spirit merchants
Belfast Mercury Office, James Simms, proprietor; 16 Howard st.

Williams' Place
OFF WELLWOOD PLACE.
Robert Drummond, gentleman
3 Wm. Devlin, clerk in custom house
4 Mrs. Eliza Little
5 Robert M'Intosh, bookkeeper
6 Wm. E. Prenter, wholesale tea and
7 Sarah Williams [coffee agent

Williams' Row
1 LITTLE GEORGE'S ST. TO HENRY ST.
1 William Quirey, coachman
3 Alex. Stevenson, shipping clerk
5 Samuel Adams, porter
7 Archibald Hook, miller
9 Robert Hunter, spinner
31 Samuel Humphries, linen weaver
Thirty other small houses

William street
7 CHURCH STREET TO JOHN STREET.
1 John Craig, market constable
3 Isabella M'Mullan, whiteworker
5 Margaret Moore, lodgings
7 James Hagan, labourer
9 John Hagan, baker
11 Francis M'Culla, grocer & publican
13 Ezekiel Allen, labourer
15 John Fee, carpenter
17 Stewart M'Auley, musician
19 Mary Ann George
21 Wm. Arthurs, shoemaker
23 Patrick Liddy, pavier
25 Sarah Mitchell, mangler
27 Daniel Robinson, shoemaker
29 Archibald M'Gurk, bricklayer
31 Francis Pinkerton's soda water manufactory—27 Edward street
Henry Loughran, grocery, wine & spirit store, 20 John street
24 Henry M'Connell, butcher
22 Samuel Blain, labourer
20 Wm. Adams, shoemaker
18 Robert Bloomer, labourer
16 Wm. M'Cormick, cooper

R

14 James Sykes, labourer
12 George Strickland, porter in store
10, 8 Thomas Bigger, butter store
6 John Kelly, labourer
Richard Thompson's rectifying dis-
4 Town Fire Engine House [tillery
2 John Reid, carpenter

William street south
ARTHUR SQUARE TO POLICE PLACE.
13 Catherine Curran, provision and
15 James Goudy [fruit dealer
17 Henry Smith, glazier
James Gray, carman
John Kane, hostler
19 Robert Morrison, spirit dealer
21 Wm. Bathurst, coach builder
23 Jas. Allen, grocer and publican
Mail coach yard and stables
Daniel Dunlop, painter
16 Edward Mulholland, cooper
14 Wm. Gray, cabinet maker
12 John Hayes, conveyancer

Wills' Place
MAY'S FIELDS.
1 Wm. Armstrong, chief night constable, local police
2 James Coleman, gentleman
3 Captain Leonard Humphreys
4 Thos. Lindsay, chief day constable
Samuel Barry, writing clerk
Jas. Spratt, toll collector in market
William Thompson, linen lapper
John Galbraith, harbour clerk

Wilson Street
74 MILLFIELD TO SACKVILLE ST.
1 James Miller, in Messrs Herdman's
3 Mrs Armour [mill
5 Joseph Keenan, cloth lapper
Mr Harper's coal yard
7 Daniel Jackson, mechanic
9 Jas. Harper, proprietor of machine
works, No. 10
Alexander Crawford, starch manufacturer and flour miller, and 26
Mill street—Mount Charles
11 James Magee, bricklayer
13 Jane Martin
15 James M'Farland, mechanic
17 Wm. Smyth, carpenter
19 John Imbrie, mechanic
21 James Napier, tailor
23 David Hanna, grocer and publican

10 James Harper's machine works
8 Richard Hyde, manager in Mr
Harper's machine works
6 Jas. Harper's machine works
4 John Chesnut, fireman in steamer
2 Catherine Connor, grocer

Windsor Place
OFF GREAT VICTORIA STREET.
1 Robert M'Adam, in A. & S. Henry
& Co.'s warerooms
3 Wm. Nicholas, excise officer
5 Thomas Clarke, tailor
4 Wm. Crozier, gentleman
2 Hamilton Pink, warehouseman

York Lane
WEST SIDE YORK STREET.
1 Major, Brothers—side entrance
3 Mary Trainor
5 R. Henderson, boot and shoemaker
7 Hugh Quinn, cabinet maker and
spirit dealer
9 John Lytle, starch manufacturer;
residence, 1 and 3 North street
11 Margt. Heslop, straw bonnet maker
13 Wm. Gribben, carpenter
15 George Bradshaw, sawyer
17 John Kennedy, miller
19 Thomas Hill, starch maker
21 Molyneux and Ferguson, starch
manufactory
23 Jas. Gardner, starch manufactory
29 James Tague, starch maker
31 James Foster, starch maker
33 John Keenan, starch maker
20 James Taylor, car driver
18 John M'Cullough, wood turner
16 Mary Roney
14 Joseph Gibson, mechanic
10 James Gardner, starch works
8 Francis M'Cracken, cotton spinning
mills; residence, 91 Donegall st.
4 Molyneux and Ferguson's starch
works; residences: W. R. Molyneux, Carrickfergus; James B.
Ferguson, 74 Donegall street
2 John Bell's yard—Ballyclare

York Road
FROM END OF YORK STREET.
1 Thomas Anderson, clerk
2 John B. Young, umbrella maker
3 Frederick W. M'Clelland, clerk
4 Samuel Simmington, clerk

5 Mrs Sarah Wales
6 Bernard M'Lean, clerk
Enclosed ground
BALLYMENA RAILWAY TERMINUS
—Thomas H. Higgin, general manager
Thomas Erskine, flax dresser
Mile Water Spinning Company—John Rowan and Sons, proprietors
Jennymount mill, James A. M'Kee, proprietor
Six small houses for workers

Cave Hill Lime Co.'s lime depot
ST. PAUL'S CHURCH—Rev. Chas. Allen, incumbent
Thomas Getgood, gentleman
William B. Pearce, iron founder
D. Anderson, manager in Grueber and Company's felt works
Belfast and Ballymena Railway Hotel—Ellen Heslop, proprietor
Three houses building

York Street
DONEGALL STREET TO YORK ROAD.
1 John M'Kenna, Queen's tea and Italian warehouse
3 Joseph Franklin, butcher and poulterer
5 Jas. Gordon, professor of dancing
" Charles D. Gordon, professor of music
Back entrance to J. M'Kenna's spirit store, and B. Hughes' bakery
7 Joshua Moffatt, custom house
" Susanna Moffatt, milliner & straw bonnet maker
Cornelius M'Quillan, butcher
Michael Savage, butcher
John Scott, jun., butcher
Shop vacant
7 George Madine, funeral undertaking, livery stables, and posting establishment
" Thomas Gould, cotton yarn agent; residence, Whiteabbey
9 Wm. Newett, coal broker, Queen's
11 Miss M'Kedy   [square
13 M'Reynolds and Knox, gingham & check manufacturers
15 Robert Pelan and John Rankin, basket and toy merchants; shop, 6 Bridge street
17 Wm. Cowan & Co., flax spinners; Whiteabbey
19 James M'Cleery, surgeon
21 Mrs Birnie
23 Hugh M'Call, sewed muslin manufacturer; residence, Lisburn
" Hugh M'Call, jeweller, &c.
       [*Curtis street.*
25 John Potts, of J. and R. Potts, merchants, North street
27 John Coleman, merchant
29 Misses Henderson's boarding and day school
31 Dr. Francis Heeney, surgeon
33 Samuel MaTeer, muslin manufacturer
35 James M'Court, horse shoer
35½ Thomas Morrell, butcher
37 John Connor, carpenter & builder
39 BETH BIREL UNITARIAN CHAPEL—Rev. David Maginnis, minister
41 Henry Loughran, wholesale and retail grocer, tea, wine, & spirit dealer
       [*Great Patrick street.*
43 Alex, Officer, licentiate apothecary and surgeon, York Street Medical Hall
45 John Boyd, architect and surveyor
" Mrs Talbot
47 Dr. John E. Kidley
49 Dr. Andrew Malcolm
" Wm. H. Malcolm, of Charley and Malcolm, Donegall quay
51 Dr. Horatio Stewart, surgeon
53 Wm. J. Duffield, of W. J. and A. Duffield, provision merchants, Corporation street
55 John Bell, jun., and Co., yarn and general merchants; residence, Whitehouse
55 House vacant
Shop vacant
       [*Little Patrick street.*
Shop vacant
61 Lewis Park, sewed muslin manufacturer, 65 York street
63 Mrs Gamble, boarding and day school
65 Lewis and Charles Park, sewed muslin manufacturers
67 New shop vacant
67 Rainey Brown, York street machine works

69 Edward Henesey, accountant in Ulster bank
71 George F. Wales, surgeon
73 John Kirker, spirit dealer

YORK STREET MARKET.

2 George Rodgers, fruiterer and green grocer
3 James Rafferty, poulterer
5 Daniel Crummey, fruiterer and green grocer
6 Samuel Kennedy, confectioner
7 Æneas Clarke, butcher; residence, 30 Nelson street

..[*Great George's street intersects.*]..
SALEM CHAPEL
73 Mrs Hugh H. Graham
75 Mrs Shaw
77 George Hannay, broker
79 Hugh Graham, hat warehouse, Bridge street
81 George Coates, provision merchant, Trafalgar street
83 John Lowry, linen merchant
83 G. and H. M'Kibbin, provision merchant; Hugh M'Kibbin's residence, Corporation street
[*Nile street.*
85 Richard Waring, provision mercht.
85½ John Davis, provision merchant
87 Richard Waring, provision mercht.
89 George Hill, clerk in J. Low's
.....[*Henry street intersects.*].....
Ruth M'Millan, grocer and confectioner
91 Mrs Stephenson
93 James Roney, tracing paper manufacturer
95 James M'Nea, architect and surveyor
97 Daniel M'Cann, chandler, North street and Castle street
99 Samuel Ewart, cooper

PRIMITIVE SECESSION MEETING HOUSE—The Rev. Dr. Bryce, minister

101 Thomas Fox's butcher's shop
" Thomas Fox's green grocer shop
" Thos. Fox's grocery and spirit store
[*Trafalgar street.*
103 John Todd, spirit dealer
105 James Hamilton, solicitor
107 Miss Johnston
109 Mrs Montgomery
111 Thomas Greenfield, haberdasher
113 James M'Cullough, woollendraper

115 Patrick M'Auley
117 Dennis Haughton, clerk
119 Bryan Joseph Henesey, salesman
121 Mrs M'Keown
123 Miss Tait's day school
125 John Gunning, clerk
[*Earl street.*
127 David Rodgers, saddler, 51 North street
129 John Small, gentleman
[*North Thomas street.*
131 Mrs Gamble
133 John Rowan, of York st. foundry
135 John Rowan, jun., of York street foundry
Enclosed ground
[*Dock street.*
137 Robert M. Carson, ship chandler; 61 Waring street
139 Mrs Eagleson
141 John Wm. M'Cracken, notary public, 25 Corporation street
Two new houses building
New shop building
[*Fleet stree .*
[*Abbotsford place.*
[*Ship street.*
[*York road.*]
74 Robert Henderson, merchant, and Willow Bank, Malone
72 Jas. Hamilton, merchant, Queen's square
70 Richd. Grueber, felt manufacturer; Prince's Dock
Meadow street.]
68 William Hughes, butter merchant
66 Wm. Telford, custom house officer
64 Mrs Davis
62 Peter Fife, mechanic
60 York street Foundry—John Rowan & Sons, proprietor
YORK STREET PRESBYTERIAN CHURCH—Rev. D. Hamilton, minister
Kelly and M'Credie, stone yard
Hugh Craig, coal factor, Queen's quay
Sussex street.]
Front of York Steet Mill
Henry street.]
58 Arthur Purse, carpenter & builder
Thomas M'Dowell, carpenter and builder
56 John Cramsey, green grocer
56 William Graham, stone cutter

54½ Vacant yard
Little George's street.]
54 Thomas Hughes, gentleman
52 Robert Workman, muslin manufacturer
50 James Gardner, starch manufacturer, York lane
48 Vacant
46½ John Lowry, builder residence, Great George's street
 Alexander M'Donald, stone cutter, residence, Newtownards
Great George's street.]
46 Robert Anderson, gentleman
44 James Standfield, gentleman
42 Maxwell Saunders, linen merchant in Henry Bragg & Son, bleachers
40 Thomas M'Dowell, carpenter
 William Fee, marble and stone yard; residence, Portland street
38 John Linas; residence, Michael st.
36 Archibald Kent, carpenter and builder
34 Mrs Dougherty
32 Mrs Major
30 Miss Blackham
28 George Sibbin, wholesale grocer, Victoria street
Lancaster street.]
26 James O'Donohoe, cement manufacturer, Newport
 Molyneaux & Ferguson, starch yard
24 John Robinson, stone cutter
22 John Hall, photographic studio
 John Hall, stone cutter
Frederick street.]
20 Giacomo Nannetti, statuary and artificial stone manufacturer
18 John Murphy, marble and stone yard; residence, Frederick st.
16 Dr. Joseph Bryson, surgeon
14 Hugh H. Hannay, cloth warehouse, Donegall street
12 Miss Cullimore's school
10 Major, Brothers, sewed muslin manufactory
York street..]
8 Henry Bragg and Sons, bleachers, Cottonmount
6½ S. R. Symmonds, broker and commission agent; residence, 33 Mill street
6 John Leadbetter and Co., linen manufacturers; works at Bedford street

 Queen's Arms Hotel coach yard
4 Thomas Jackson's flax store; office, 29 Donegall street
4 Wm. Crozier Cunningham, solicitor, & deputy clerk of the peace
2½ D. and J. Macdonald & Co., sewed muslin manufacturers; residence, Glasgow; manager, Wm. Leck; residence, Cranstone place, Antrim road
2 Queen's Arms Hotel — Thomas Cunningham, proprietor

York street, Little
6 GREAT PATRICK ST. TO EARL ST.
1 John Wilson, captain of schooner *Sophia*
" Andrew Shaw, butter buyer
3 Wm. Stevenson, bookbinder
5 Malcolm Robinson, captain schooner *Temperance*
7 John Purse, house carpenter
9 Samuel M'Kinty, coal carrier
11 Daniel Galley, sail maker
13 Samuel Robinson, labourer
15 George Hall, jobbing smith
.. [*Little Patrick street intersects.*]..
 Robert Moreland, grocer, 8 Little Patrick street, side entrance
17 Henry Johnston, ginger ale manufacturer
19 Patrick Cody, labourer
21 Anne English, sewer
23 John Conway, pavier
25 James Evans, seaman
27 George Whitten, labourer
29 Thomas Robinson, linen weaver
31 Thomas Campbell, labourer
33 Fanny Clokey, dealer
35 Robert Murphy, seaman
37 James Kennedy, porter
39 Arthur Boyd, labourer
41 Isabella M'Bride
43 Sarah Dick
45 Sarah Jane Burns, sewer
47 James Gordon, fireman
49 James Riley, slater
51 Thomas Gamble, cooper
53 John Carlisle, pilot
55 Stable
57 William M'Clintock, side door—grocer, 36 Great George's street
.. [*Great George's street intersects.*]..
59 James Wilson, clerk
61 James Close, grocer and publican

William Clarke, jobbing smith
Patrick Manning, moulder
   [*Shipboy street.*
Three yards
...... [*Nile street intersects.*]......
Arthur Walker, grocer, and publican, 19 Nile street, hall door
67 Thomas Reynolds, labourer
69 Wm. J. M'Caghan, in pork store
71 Samuel Thompson, sawyer
   [*Henry lane.*
73 Campbell Adair, cooper
75 Alexander M'Crea, stone cutter
77 John Spence, labourer
79 Joseph Peden, blacksmith
81 Livingston Greer, ship smith
83 David Simpson, porter
85 David Patterson, smith helper's
87 John Feris, ship carpenter
..... [*Henry street intersects.*].....
James Surplus, grocer and publican, 18 Henry street, hall door
Jane Murphy, lodgings
89 Eleanor Mackin
91 Margaret Colvin
93, 95 Eliza Purvis, provision dealer
   [*Culbert's court.*
97 Charles Lilley, copper and tinsmith
Samuel Ewart, seaman
101 William Keddow, labourer
103 Mrs Ewart
James Ferguson, grocer and spirit dealer, 38 Trafalgar st., hall door
....[*Trafalgar street intersects.*]....
Yard and vacant ground
   [*Earl street.*]
50 Hugh White, carpenter
48 Thomas Darragh, labourer
46 William Petticrew, labourer
44 James Williamson, house carpenter
42 Hugh Kelly, ship carpenter
Coronation place.]
Rere of Mr R. Henderson's stores
....[*Trafalgar street intersects.*]....
40 Robert Neill
38 Thomas M'Alister, day constable
36 Oliver Purvis, gardener
34 Henry Doherty, car owner
32 James Kinkaid, cooper
30 William J. Holywood, plumber
28 Vacant
26 John M'Nabb, carpenter
24 Anne Maguire, washerwoman
22 Mary Colvin, lodgings
Henry Brown, pawnbroker, 17 Henry street, hall door
Rere of Richard Waring's provision stores, York street
...... [*Nile street intersects.*]......
Rere of Mr M'Kibbin's provision stores, York street
Stanley lane.]
Stanley place.]
..[*Great George's street intersects.*]..
Michael Smith's spirit store, 34 Great George's street
Rere of Rainey Brown's machine works
16 Henry M'Laughlin, labourer
14 James Morrison, tailor
12 John Doyle, baker
10 Mary Scott
Mathew M'Girvan, publican, 6 Little Patrick street—side door
..[*Little Patrick street intersects.*]..
Rere of John Bell, jun.'s, stores York street
Bell and Kirker's meal and flour stores, 9 Great Patrick street
Messrs Bell and Kirker's hall door

BALLYMACARRETT.

BALLYMACARRETT is immediately connected with Belfast, and is united to it by the Queen's Bridge. It is situate in the County Down side of the river, including an area of 576 acres, and consists of one main street, in the line of the Holywood road, and a number of smaller ones. A large number of the inhabitants are hand-loom weavers, and persons employed in the various factories in the vicinity—viz., the Flint Glass Works, Vitriol Works, Rope Works, Tileries, Mills, &c. Lagan Village is included with it. On account of its immediate proximity and connexion with Belfast, we have included the reference to its streets and inhabitants in the Alphabetical Directory.

Ashley Place
Mr. Kernohan
Rev. Wm. Moffatt
Mrs. Ralston
Rev. William Heron

Rev. John Meneely, Manse
BALLYMACARRETT PRESBYTERIAN CHURCH—Rev. John Meneely, minister

Bridge End
Andrew Sloan and Co., firebrick and tile yard
F. and W. Lewis's timber pond; office, 3 Great George's street
L. and T. Brown's timber pond; office, 41 Chichester street
House and shop building; Henry Moore, proprietor
Ballymacarrett Pottery Works; Francis M'Wade, proprietor
BALLYMACARRETT DISPENSARY
Dr. James Murray, surgeon
Mrs. Montgomery
James Davidson, flour miller
Robert Patterson, lodgings
John Higgins, spirit dealer
Jas. Murray, carpenter and dealer
John Higgins, grocer
Worsted and cocoa fibre rug, mat, and matting manufactory; Geo. Phillips and Co., proprietors
EDWARDS' BUILDINGS.
Constabulary Station; James M'Intyre, head constable
William Agnew, watch glass manufacturer

Samuel Tierney, of George Phillips and Co.'s cocoa fibre works

John Thompson, blacksmith
Jane Longwill, dealer
David Carlile's hay and straw yard
Henry Shannon, tailor
David Carlile's spirit store
James Cooke, tailor
" Elizabeth Cooke, dressmaker
" Miss J. A. Douglass, tuscan and straw bonnet maker
Robert Black, wood turner
James O'Neill, brick burner
Henry Flannigan, horse shoer and jobbing smith
William Green, miller
Hugh Graham, grocer
Wm. Davis, watch glass maker and glass cutter
James Clarke, carpenter and dealer
Hugh M'Aleavy, butcher
Rebecca Boyce, dealer
Geo. Moffatt, guard on Holywood railway
James May, butcher
Thomas M'Aleavy, butcher
Francis M'Kenna, carpenter
" Thomas Doyle, baker
Hugh Murdoch, compositor
Richard Kearney, basket maker
John Kerr, carpenter
William Kearney, basket maker
Alex. Winn, guard on county Down railway
Jane Nimoe
Daniel Daly, board and lodgings
Wm. Downing, wine & spirit stores

Chapel Lane

Thirty-three small houses
ROMAN CATHOLIC CHAPEL—Rev. James Killen, P.P.
NATIONAL SCHOOL—Jas. Magill, teacher

William Huddleston, pawnbroker, Portview House

Gooseberry Corner

Margaret M'Morran, grocer
Thomas Sloan, grocer
Sixty-one small houses
GROVEFIELD.
Andrew Clarke, grocer, Ann street
NETTLEFIELD.
Frederick Lewis, of F. & W. Lewis, Great George's street

Lagan Village

Francis Milligan, spirit dealer
John Canmer, grocer and publican
Andrew Thompson, clerk
William Busby, gentleman
Margt. Crossen, grocer & publican
Howe M'Coppin, pensioner
Matthew Anderson, engineer
Edward Sloan, iron moulder
Hugh Anderson, iron turner
Samuel M'Kelvey, mechanic
Andrew Wilson, iron turner
Alex. M'Alister, pattern maker
Thomas Harpur, mechanic
Henry Savage, fitter
Neill Robinson, turner
Hugh Watt, engineer
David M'Kelvey, pattern maker
James Boomer, fitter
Shamrock Lodge—John Young, of Coates & Young, Lagan foundry
Lagan Foundry co-operative grocer shop; John M'Cready, manager
John M'Kelvey, whitesmith
Robert Dunlop, foreman mechanic
John M'Gowan, clerk
James Sloan, blacksmith
John Jamieson, bookkeeper
William Brown, tailor
Chas. Brown, boot and shoemaker
James Bailie, grocer
Samuel Moore, spirit dealer
James M'Millan, grocer
Osly Mallart, grocer and publican
Mary Burns, spirit dealer

Vitriol Works—Wm. Boyd & Sons, proprietors; Wm. Boyd's residence, 4 Howard street
Robert Davis, cashier in Lagan Foundry
LAGAN FOUNDRY — Coates and Young, engineers, founders in iron and brass, millwrights, and smiths, proprietors; residences: Wm. Coates, J.P., Glentoran; John Young, Shamrock Lodge
Lagan Bridge toll bar—John Canmer, collector

Ravenhill brick and tile works
John Moore, Donegall Arms proprietor

Mount Pottinger

Alex. Moore, painter, Arthur stree
Mrs Orr
Henry Nichol, book keeper
Captain H. Herdmen
Fras. Ritchie, proprietor chemical and felt works
Miss Montgomery
Aime Koch, patent flax works; Cregagh, Castlereagh
Ami Bernard, patent flax mills
Hugh Crawford, clerk
Wm. Druitt, linen merchant, Donegall street
Rev. George Bennett
Stephen Joseph Cantwell, Custom house
Alexander M'Alister, gentleman
Henry Louth, in Custom house
Mrs Ellison
Thomas John Martin, traveller
Wm. Donaldson, salesman
Wm. Hunter, mill manager
Mr. Ross, of Ross, O'Connor, & Co.
John Gilliland, gentleman

Mountpottinger Cottages

John Thomas, book keeper
Alexander M'Cammon, gentleman

BEER'S BRIDGE COTTAGE.
Miss Montgomery
ELMGROVE.
James Montgomery
Elmgrove Mills
ORANGEFIELD.
R. B. B. Houston, D.L., J.P.

STREET DIRECTORY—BALLYMACARRETT.

GREENVILLE.
William Davis, solicitor; office, Arthur street

BEER'S BRIDGE.
Owen-O'Cork Mill Company—Jas. Steen & Co., proprietors
Wm. Malloy, land steward

M'Crory's Row
James Phillips, weaver
Wm. M'Guigan, ropemaker
12 Thos. O'Kane, grocer & spirit dealer
11 Ed. Hanna, ropemaker and dealer
10 John Taylor, glass maker
9 John Connor, glass blower
8 John Wilks, mechanic
7 Emanuel Milliken, master mariner
6 Thomas Kenna, glass blower
5 James Ivory, rope and twine maker
4 Eli Richards, mechanic
3 Mary Davis
2 David Ferguson, cooper
1 Francis M'Hannay, dealer

Margaret Holden, dealer
Wm. Owens, stone mason
Wm. M'Collough, shoemaker
Andrew Tumbleton, shoemaker
James Jones, grocer
John Howard, glass cutter
Thomas Horner, watch glass maker
John Burns, ropemaker
John Kane, dealer
John Starr, ropemaker
Sarah Minteith, grocer
Alex. Stewart, cooper and dealer
Edward Hanna's ropewalk

BEACH FIELD.
Mrs Harpur

CLUAL.
Samuel M. Bryson, gentleman

James M'Wha, basket maker
Joseph Patton, gentleman, Ballymacarret house
PRIMITIVE METHODIST MEETING HOUSE—Rev. Messrs. M'Fann and Wilson, preachers; Alex. Magill, caretaker

BEAVER HALL.
John MacAdam, merchant; office, Donegall street
WESLEYAN METHODIST MEETING HOUSE — Rev. Messrs. Lupton and Bailey, preachers; John Sykes, caretaker
Samuel M'Clure, grocer
Jane Kirkpatrick, grocer
BALLYMACARRETT POST OFFICE —Jeremiah Wilson, postmaster
John Hare, grocer
S. S. Rankin, spirit dealer
James Sturgeon, coast guard
BALLYMACARRETT NATIONAL SCHOOL—David Christie, teacher
Hugh Swain, clerk
Thomas Brockie
Conswater Bridge

BALLYHACKAMORE.
Thomas Morrow, horse shoer
Adam Vance, spirit dealer

Henry Brown, spirit dealer
Margaret Jackson, grocer
John Sloan, grocer and publican
George T. Thompson, spirit dealer
Alex. Caughey, boot & shoemaker
James Cooper, grocer
Campbell Sturgeon, grocer
Jas. Kirkpatrick, grocer and spirit dealer
Four small houses

STRAWBERRY HALL.
Gawn Davison, gentleman

Martin Perry, grocer

CLUB ROW LOANEN.
Margt. A. M'Bride, grocer

Deborah Walker, spirit dealer
Archd. Irwin, spirit dealer

JACKSON HALL.
William Hall, gentleman

Margaret Finlay, bonnet maker
John Robinson, mariner
Charles Forsythe, nailer
Robert Forsythe, nailer

BELVILLE HOUSE.
James Ritchie, merchant, Prince's Dock

ASHLEY HALL.
Not tenanted

PORTVIEW.
John Russell, gentleman

BALLYMACARRETT INFANT SCHOOL —B. Hanley, teacher

STREET DIRECTORY—BALLYMACARRETT.

BALLYMACARRETT ESTABLISED CHURCH—Rev. George Bennett, incumbent; residence, Mount Pottinger
Curds and Cream Gardens—James Court, proprietor
Edward Hampsey's ropewalk
Patrick Hampsey's ropewalk

M'Larnon's Buildings
Edward Magee, commission agent and auctioneer
James Frazer, land surveyor
Short Strand male & female School; John Ritchie, male teacher; Ann Jane Ritchie, female teacher
William Burrows, clerk
Joseph Croft, bricklayer
John Jamieson, shoemaker

New Road
FROM GLASS HOUSE CORNER TO HOLYWOOD ROAD.
Ballymacarrett foundry; John Reid, proprietor
Robert Burns, car driver
Thomas Newton, rope maker
Jas. M'Quade's brick and tile works
Two new houses
Thomas M'Quigan's ropewalk
David Thompson, rope maker
Alex. W. Douglass, rope maker
Francis Ritchie and Sons, chemists and felt manufacturers; Francis Ritchie's residence, Mount Pottinger
Side of James Lemon's ropewalk
JOHNSTON'S PLACE.
1 Mrs Orr
2 James M'Kay, weighmaster in custom house
3 Josiah Hargreave, grocer
4 James Dewer, mechanic
5 James Harris, sawyer
6 Henry Killen, clerk
  Archibald Blayney, grocer and publican
  Archibald Patton, grocer and publican
David Shields, shoemaker
James Dunlop, moulder
John Rainey, pattern maker
ANDERSON'S HOUSES.
Thomas Muldoon, porter
John Owen, civil bill officer
Andrew Skillen, porter
James Hood,
Alex. M'Master, attorney's clerk
Alex. Heslop, master mariner
John Low's coal yard

Portview or M'Cracken's Row
2 James Black, master mariner
4 Robert Quee, painter and glazier
6 Wm. Isles, rope and twine maker
  Wm. Keenan, rope and twine maker
7 John Scott, carpenter
10 Hugh Scanlon, mechanic
12 Wm. Dickson, master mariner
14 James Ferris, in Vitriol Works
  Seven other houses
TRAINVIEW COTTAGE.
16 Henry M'Cracken, grocer and spirit dealer

Pottinger Place
Thomas Battersby, gentleman
Archibald Reynolds, clerk
Robert M'Call, tailor
Wm. Campbell, teacher
James E. Mansfield, gentleman
James Young, Harbour office

Queen's Quay
Wm. Downing, wine & spirit stores
Two shops vacant
Wm. Spencer, Hibernian Pottery
Queen's Quay and Railway Tavern, James Pelan, proprietor
John Cuddy's oil and colour mills
James Coey, jun., grain and flour merchant, and soap boiler
Shop not finished
Wm. Spencer, of the Pottery
Patrick Hammond, Railway Hotel
BELFAST AND CO. DOWN RAILWAY TERMINUS, Thos. Ward, secy.
Corporation goods sheds
Corporation ferry boat stations
COAL OFFICES.
1 John Hanna
2 Malcolm Johnston
3 Thomas Shiel
4 Robert Newett
5 James Garland
6 Thomas George
COAL EXCHANGE.
7 Hugh Craig
8 Patrick Lindsay
9 William Massey

10 Philip Wright
11 Michael Cush
12 Vacant

COAL YARDS.
1 Robert Boyd
2 William Newett
3 James M'Ferren
4 Ruahon and Blenkinsopp—office, 3 Castle Chambers
5, 6 Harbour Commissioners'
7 William Newett [stone yard
8 Robert Henderson
9 Colville, Auld, and Co.
Harbour Commissioners' weigh-bridge; Richard Loughran, weighmaster

Roundhill Cottage
Robert English, grocer
Mrs Havern

Roundhill House — John Evans, landing surveyor in customhouse
Conswater flax spinning mill, Robt. M'Kibbin, proprietor; residence, Avoneil

Saltpan Row
John Hume, manager, locomotive department, Co. Down Railway
Thomas Barrens, engineer
James Connolly, flax waste dealer
Twelve small houses

GREGG'S ROW.
Belfast Vitriol Works, James W. Moncrieff, proprietor
William M'Liesh, manufacturing chemist
Four small houses

Sea View Place
1 John Hutchinson, engineer
2 Henry Fulton, mechanic
3 Thomas Ranson, agent for Castlebellingham Brewery; office, 5 Police square
4 Samuel Shaw, clerk Harbour office
5 Thos. J. Sugars, Revenue officer
6 James Robinson, pensioner

Short Strand
James Lemon's ropewalk and manufactory; offices, Queen's sq.
Ross, O'Connor, and Co.'s glass works; warerooms, High street

J. MacAdam's bone yard; mills, Donegall street
Ballymacarrett Lime Works—Danl. Murray, proprietor, shipowner, &c.; residence, Lagan Village
Richard M'Sherry, master mariner

Sir Henry's Buildings
1 Isabella Mawhinney, spirit dealer
2 John Nugent, pensioner
3 Margaret Anderson
4 James Magill, millwright
5 John Kane, millwright
6 Daniel M'Pherson, engineer
7 James Magill, mechanic
8 John Reid, engineer
9 Robert M'Kellar, brass moulder
10 John Johnston, carpenter
11 George Crawshaw, engine builder
12 Wm. Campbell, timber dealer
13 William Murray, moulder
14 James Phillips, clerk

Wheeler's Place
John Reid, wine and spirit dealer
Thomas M'Cormick, grocer and haberdasher
John Jones, foreman sailmaker
John Hewitt, watch glass maker

Alexander Murphy, grocer
Queen View Tavern
James Davidson, ropemaker
John Woods, fruit dealer
Joseph Elliott, grocer
Joseph Girven, pawnbroker
Andrew Ferguson, dealer
Arthur Thornton, spirit dealer
Samuel Neill, carman
Wm. Stavelly, dealer

KEENAN'S PLACE.
Patrick Keenan, farmer
James Gelston, medical practitioner and surgeon
Thomas Wilmot, glass blower
Patrick M'Cormack, stone mason
James Reynolds, dealer
Elizabeth Curran, grocer & publican
Edw. Heron, grocer and publican
Hugh M'Neill, dealer
James Noble, dealer

Woodstock Place
Hugh M'Kibbin, gentleman
Three houses vacant

ALPHABETICAL LIST

OF THE PRINCIPAL

INHABITANTS OF BELFAST

AND BALLYMACARRETT.

ABBOTT, Joseph, merchant, ship chandler, patent ropemaker, and canvass manufacturer, 9 Corporation street, 42 Shankhill; residence, Holywood
Abbott, John, clerk, 6 Joy street
Abbott, Nicholas, printer, 11 Torrens' market
Abbott, William, reedmaker, 111 Millfield
Acheson, James, flax merchant, 1 Talbot street
Adair, Archibald, carpenter, 16 Boyd street
Adair, Campbell, cooper, 73 Little York street
Adair, Hugh, cashier *News-Letter* office, 9 College street
Adair, Hugh, blacksmith, 30 Valentine street
Adair, Isabella, 16 Nelson street
Adair, John, grocer, Falls road
Adair, Robert, shoemaker, 5 Mustard street
Adair, William, pensioner and dealer, 40 North Thomas street
Adams, Alexander, smith, 5 Albion lane, Donegall pass
Adams, Arthur, clerk, 7 Frederick street
Adams, Captain James, 1 James' place
Adams, Davison, land surveyor, Falls road
Adams, Henry, porter, 5 Rochfort place
Adams, James, flour merchant and carman's yard, 12 Great Patrick street
Adams, James, ship carpenter, 6 Nile street
Adams, James, porter, 12 Friendly street
Adams, James, baker, 198 North street
Adams, John, jeweller, 8½ Hamilton street
Adams, John, painter and glazier, 13¼ Cromac street
Adams, John, carpenter and builder, 44 North Thomas street
Adams, Robert, provision shop, 43 Edward street
Adams, Rose Ann, confectioner, 185 North street
Adams, Samuel, porter, 5 William's row
Adams, Thomas, carpenter, 100 Millfield
Adams, Thomas, furniture maker, 20 Smithfield
Adams, William, carpenter, 3 Wellington court
Adams, William, carowner, 94 Cromac street
Adams, William, boot and shoemaker, 20 William street
Adamson, James, clerk, Cullingwood street
Adamson, Joseph, dealer, 31 Grove street
Adamson, James, agent for T. & D. Wilson, sewed muslin manufacturers, 37 John street
Adamson, Samuel, sailor, 35 Academy street
Adamson, William, manufacturer, and agent for J. & W. Broadley, sewed muslin manufacturers, Waring street, 2 Posnett's place

ALPHABETICAL DIRECTORY.

Adamson, William, hair dresser, 30¼ Castle street
Addison, James, stone cutter, 40 Valentine street
Addison, William, wholesale grocer and seed merchant, 15 North street
Adrain, Robert, salesman, 13 Washington street
Adries, James, shoemaker, 12 Caxton street
Agar, William, butcher, 19 Caddel's entry
Agnew, Esther, grocer, 52 Hercules street
Agnew, Hugh, mechanic, 89 Boundary street
Agnew, James, dealer, Shankhill road
Agnew, James, of Martin and Agnew, timber merchants, 34 Chichester street, residence, 14 Hamilton street
Agnew, James, carpenter, 41 Stanley street
Agnew, J., carpenter, 15 Ann street
Agnew, John, dealer, 44 Little Patrick street
Agnew, John, provision dealer, 60 Grattan street
Agnew, James, Wellington square
Agnew, Mrs., 7 Donegall square North
Agnew, Robert, foreman engineer, 20 Pilot street
Agnew, Thomas, carpenter, 15 Grace street
Agnew, William, solicitor, 4 Aughton terrace
Agnew, William and Gilmore, printers, stationers, bookbinders, &c., Castle lane, Arthur square, and Calendar street
Agnew, Wm., watch glass manufacturer, Bridge end, Ballymacarrett
Aid, Lorence, tailor, 57 Townsend street
Aicken, Richard, architect, 67 Cromac street
Aicken, T. H., apothecary, 38 Ann street
Aickin, John, surgeon, 5 Adelaide place
Aiken, James, merchant, 6 York street; residence, 1 Albert place
Aiken, Peter, mill manager, Smithfield
Ainsworth, Mrs., nursetender, 15 King street
Alcorn, Benjamin, loom and general carpenter, 31 Academy street
Alderdice, David, Victoria tavern, 117 Durham street
Alderdice, William, carpenter, 10 Raphael street
Alderdice, William, civil bill officer, 115 Durham street
Aldritt, William, brassfounder, gasfitter, &c., 23 Castle street
Alexander, Andrew, grocer, 20 Moffat street
Alexander, Arthur, wholesale and retail spirit dealer, coal merchant, and stabling, 134 North street
Alexander, Benjamin, schoolmaster and dealer, 6 Store lane
Alexander, James, gentleman, 17 Donegall place
Alexander, James, grain stores, 12 Ritchie's place
Alexander, J. A., surgeon, 49 Corporation street
Alexander, J., & Co., Belfast flour mills, Falls road
Alexander, Margaret, milliner, 26 Edward street
Alexander, Mr., 2 College street South
Alexander, Rev. John, D.D., Ballynafeigh
Alexander, Robert, linen merchant, vice-consul for Venezuela; residence, Donegall square West
Alexander, Samuel, baker and grocer, Ashmore street, Conway street
Alexander, William, *Mercury* office, 50 Earl street
Alexander, William, mechanic, 25 Grove street
Allen, Alexander, grocer and spirit dealer, 49 Lancaster street
Allen, Daniel J., hat warehouse, 3 Castle buildings; residence, Wellwood place
Allen, Daniel, grocer, 34 Grattan street
Allen, Eleanor, 7 Melbourne street

ALPHABETICAL DIRECTORY.

Allen, Hugh, grocery and spirit store, Malone road
Allen, Hamilton, mechanic, 18 Catherine street
Allen, Hugh, hairdresser, 25 New Durham street
Allen, Hugh, ship carpenter, 42 Trafalgar street
Allen, Henry, overseer in Ulster railway, 5 Moore's place
Allen, James, coach smith, 28 Gordon street
Allen, James, beef and ham curer, 11 Stanhope street
Allen, James, painter, glazier, and paper-hanger, 50 Tomb street
Allen, J., tailor, 10 Georges' lane
Allen, John, haberdasher, 32 Church lane
Allen, James, grocer and spirit dealer, 23 William street South
Allen, James, tailor, 1 Orr's entry
Allen, John, coachsmith, 22 Telfair's entry
Allen, Mrs., 14 Rochfort place
Allen, Miss, 7 College square East
Allen, Miss Elizabeth, dressmaker, 21 Joy street
Allen, Mrs., 57 Upper Arthur street
Allen, Patrick, dealer, 42 M'Tier's street
Allen, Rev. Charles, incumbent St. Paul's Church, 19 Fountain street
Allen, William, customhouse officer, 17 Prince's street
Allen, William, civil engineer, and surveyor to Water Commissioners, 10 James street south
Allen, William Henry, clerk, 13 Fleet street
Allen, W. J. C., J.P., registrar Queen's College, 8 Wellington place
Allison, Robert, pensioner, 8 Mitchell street
Allworthy, Captain, 2 Aughton terrace
Allwright, William, shoemaker, 75 Green street
Anderson and Gray, muslin manufacturers, 9 Donegall square South and Linenhall street
Anderson, Arthur, tailor, 14 Church lane
Anderson, David, manager at Grueber and Co.'s felt works, York road
Anderson, Ellen, widow, Hopeton place
Anderson, E., milliner and dressmaker, 24 Earl street
Anderson, George, sewed muslin manufacturer, 110 Cromac street
Anderson, Hugh, iron turner, Lagan village, Ballymacarrett
Anderson, James, grain merchant, 1 Gloucester street; residence, No. 9
Anderson, James, servant, 6 Rochfort place
Anderson, James, builder, 60 Joy street
Anderson, James, portrait painter, 26 Hamilton street
Anderson, James, builder, 11 May street
Anderson, James, sawyer, 34½ Friendly street
Anderson, James, grocer and publican, Shankhill road
Anderson, James, provision dealer, 182 North street
Anderson, James, grocer, 27 Trafalgar street
Anderson, James, oatmeal and corn stores, 6 Seymour lane
Anderson, John, merchant, 3 Apsley place; office, 19 Donegall street
Anderson, John, carpenter, 3 North Thomas street
Anderson, Joseph, foreman of works Town Council, 96 Cromac street
Anderson, John, sewed muslin manufactory, 49 Great Patrick street
Anderson, J. C., proprietor *Chronicle*; residence, 51 Upper Arthur street
Anderson, J. W. and Co., sewed muslin manufacturers, 9 Donegall sq. South
Anderson, Jane, Ballynahinch & Castlewellan coach office, 25 Gt. Edward st.
Anderson, Jane, boarding house, 6 Caddell's entry
Anderson, Margaret, publican, 173 North street
Anderson, Mrs. Mary, 2 Back Ship street

Anderson, Mrs. Rachael, lodging house, 25 Tomb street
Anderson, Margaret, 3 Sir Henry's buildings, Ballymacarrett
Anderson, Matthew, engineer, Lagan village, Ballymacarrett
Anderson, Robert, sawyer, 1 Cromac road
Anderson, Richard, sawyer, 15 East street
Anderson, Robert, gentleman, 46 York street
Anderson, Samuel, hackler, 30 Boyd street
Anderson, Thomas, writing clerk, 1 York road
Anderson, William, house carpenter, 16 Back Ship street
Anderson, William, house carpenter, 7 North Thomas street
Anderson, William, grocer, 8 Hercules street
Anderson, William, tailor, 32 North Thomas street
Anderson, William, teacher, 32 Shankhill road
Anderson, William, pawnbroker, 1 Union street
Andrews and Smith, solicitors, 46 Donegall street
Andrews, Alex., provision merchant, Tomb st.; residence, 10 Prospect terrace
Andrews, A., provision merchant, 30 Tomb street
Andrews, Dr., vice-president Queen's College
Andrews, Hugh, water inspector, 22 Great George's street
Andrews, John, merchant, Brookfield, Shankhill road
Andrews, James B., book keeper, Fountain lane
Andrews, James, solicitor, 60 Donegall street
Andrews, Mrs., Lower Crescent, Malone road
Andrews, Peter, trump maker, 90 Old Lodge road
Andrews, S. and W., grocers, 43 Ann street
Andrews, W. S., solicitor, 46 Donegall street
Andrews, William, victualler, 3 Hammond's court
Andrews, William, shoemaker, 2 Chichester lane
Andrews, William, millwright and engineer, 1 Townsend place
Angell, Laurence, engineer, 31 Vere street
Annesley, William, green grocer and fruiterer, 1 and 8 Hammond's court
Arbuthnot, Robert, servant, 14 Hamilton's place
Archer & Sons, wholesale stationers, paper manufacturers, rulers and account book binders, engravers, lithographers, and linen ornament manufacturers, 27 and 29 Castle place; residence, Milltown, Ballyclare
Archer, J., comb manufacturer, 34 Church lane
Arlow, William, carman, 37 Boundary street
Armour, Edward, cow dealer, 7 Market street
Armour, Mrs., 3 Wilson street
Armour, Miss Jane, lodging house, 39 Stanley street
Armour, Peter, pilot, 35 Talbot street
Armour, Samuel, shoemaker, 21 Mustard street
Armour, Thomas, cashier Belfast distillery, 10 Hamilton street
Armstrong, Andrew, ship smith, 5 Nile street
Armstrong, Andrew, chandler, Old Lodge road
Armstrong, Bell, dealer, Hopeton place
Armstrong, George, mail guard, 4 Little Victoria street
Armstrong, James, and Co., tea importers and dealers, 5 and 6 Donegall place buildings
Armstrong, Jane, 18 Kennedy's place
Armstrong, James, carpenter, 4 Washington street
Armstrong, James, shoemaker, 73 Carrickhill
Armstrong, John, blacksmith, Shankhill road
Armstrong, John, painter, 43 Academy street
Armstrong, John, surgeon, 17 College street
Armstrong, Joseph, night constable, 1 Duffy's place

Armstrong, Joseph, publican, 55 Union street
Armstrong, Mary, 10 Hamilton's place
Armstrong, Robert, shoemaker, 13 Peter's hill
Armstrong, Samuel, inland revenue officer, Herdman's buildings
Armstrong, Thomas, publican, 47 Smithfield
Armstrong, Thomas, National Theatre, 44 and 45 Smithfield
Armstrong, Thomas, writing master, Belfast Academy; residence, Cliftonville, Antrim road
Armstrong, William, carpenter, 7 Cullingtree place
Armstrong, William, flaxdresser, 11 Duffy's place
Armstrong, William, chief night constable local police, 1 Wills' place
Armstrong, William, green grocer, 26 Hercules street
Arnold, John, woollendraper, clothier, and hatter, 45 High street; residence, 1 Glenfield place
Arnold, Mrs., seamen's clothing establishment, and post-office receiving house, 1 Great George's street
Arnot, George, watchman in Herdman's mill, 21 Millfield
Arnott, John & Co., wholesale and retail woollen drapers, silk mercers, and general warehousemen, 7, 9, 11, 17, and 17½ Bridge street
Arrott, Isaac, provision and general merchant, 34 Waring street; residence, 2 Wellington place
Arthur, Henry, gentleman, 3 Hope street
Arthur, John, tailor, 2 Nelson street
Arthur, John, tailor, New Lodge place
Arthur, Mrs., 4 Belvidere place
Arthur, Robert, solicitor, 24 Donegall place
Arthur, William, shoemaker, 21 William street
Ash, George, wholesale grocer, general merchant, and commission agent, 40 Waring street; residence, Cliftonville, Antrim road
Ash, George, jun., merchant, 40 Waring street; residence, Cliftonville
Ash, James, stoker, 28 Charles street
Ashenhurst, Catherine, gentlemen's ready-made linen establishment, 62 High st.
Ashmore, Mrs., 8 Donegall square East
Ashton, Thomas, flax spinner, 17 Ship street
Askin, John, clerk, Nelson's buildings
Atkins, Hugh, painter, 17 Collingwood street
Atkinson, Arthur, boot and shoemaker, 7 Church lane
Atkinson, Henry, brass moulder, Herdman's buildings, Shankhill road
Atkinson, John, book-keeper, 97 Joy street
Atkinson, James, 46 Nelson street
Atkinson, Mrs., 2 Apsley place
Atkinson, Richard, innkeeper, 2 Cromac street and 25 May street
Atkinson, Robert, commission merchant, general agent, and broker, 10 Hill street; residence, Holywood
Atkinson, Richard, book-keeper, 2 Belvidere place
Auchinleck, Miss, 4 Chichester street
Aughton, Mrs., 7 Aughton terrace
Auld, William, mariner, 24 Little Corporation street
Austin, John, green grocer, 15 Ormond market; 62 Little Patrick street
Austin, Robert, proprietor of Belfast steam flour mills, 63 Corporation square

BADIER, Auguste Charles, French teacher, 29 Queen street
Bagnell, James, clerk, 38 Joy street
Bailey, Adam, carpenter, 17 Morrow's entry
Bailey, Francis, groom, 24 Gordon street

ALPHABETICAL DIRECTORY.

Bailey, Hugh, ship carpenter, 10 Gamble street
Bailey, John, boot and shoemaker, Shankhill road
Bailey, Samuel, painter, 7 Mustard street
Bailey, Solomon, engineer, 27 Grove street
Bailey, Thomas, dealer, 37 Peter's hill
Bailey, William, boot and shoemaker, 84 High street
Bailey, William John, clerk, 3 Vere street
Bailie, Charles, builder, 58 and 60 Nelson street
Bailie, Isaac, shoemaker, 58 Ann street
Bailie, James, grocer, Lagan village, Ballymacarrett
Bailie, Joseph, 14 Butter market, Great Patrick street; residence, Fleming's place, Old Lodge road
Bain, Alexander, boot and shoemaker, 88 Carrick hill
Bain, Amelia, grocer, 70 Ann street
Bain, Joseph, & Co., rectifying distillers, 4 Seymour lane—2 Glenfield place
Bainbrigge, Major General, 5 Donegall square South
Bainbrigge, Captain, A.D.C., 5 Donegall square south
Baird, Robert, sawyer, 13 Little Patrick street
Baird, Rev. James, teacher of school, 17 Rosemary street
Baird, William, bricklayer, 17 Coates street
Baird, William S., printer, Northburn place
Bairns, Jane, whiteworker, 4 Samuel street
Bairns, William, clerk, 12 Pound street
Bakewell, Robert, carpenter, 4 Earl street
Ball, James, spirit dealer, 164 North street
Ball, Mary, green grocer, 14 Boundary street
Ball, Mary, 5 College street
Ballard, Rev. Thomas, Wesleyan Methodist minister, Victoria terrace
Balmer, Margaret, dealer, 21 Verner street
Bambridge, Abraham, hotel and tavern keeper, Sugarhouse entry
Bamford, Mrs. Margaret, 69 Peter's hill
Bamford, Samuel, spirit store, 49 Brown square
Bamford, Stewart, publican, 76 Peter's hill
Bamford, Sayers, coachmaker, 15 Wellington street
Bammer, William, publican, 43 May street
Banks, B., fancy box manufacturer, 8½ Castle place
Banks, Mrs., milliner, 8¼ Castle place
Barber, James, spirit dealer, 52 Henry street
Barclay and Wallace, milliners and dressmakers, 43 Castle street
Barclay, John, & Co., boot and shoemaker, 49 Donegall street
Barclay, John, coal merchant, 21 Tomb street
Barclay, William, boot and shoemaker, 33 Trafalgar street
Barclay, William, railway porter, 12 Back Ship street
Barker, Catherine, grocer and publican, 5 Pilot street
Barker, James, dealer, 56 Mill street
Barker, James, shoemaker, 14 Lagan street
Barker, John, dealer, 15 Union street
Barker, Rev. James, 2 Malone place
Barkley, James, mariner, 3 Stanley lane
Barkley, Miss Frances, 37 King street
Barkley, Thomas, shipwright, 32 Earl street
Barkley, William M., ship broker, coal merchant, and commission agent, 97 Queen's square
Barklie, Miss, milliner and dressmaker, 5 Chichester street
Barlow, Louisa, boarding house, 19 Lancaster street

Barlow, Wm., manager of gas works, Gasfield house, Cromac road
Barnes, James, spirit dealer, 5 and 7 Caddel's entry
Barnes, Mrs., 7 Alexander street
Barnes, Mrs. Caroline, boarding house, 46 Mill street
Barnes, Thomas A., Lower Crescent
Barnett, Andrew J., merchant, 3 Clarendon place
Barnett, Andrew, spirit dealer, 33 Barrack street
Barnett, Andrew John, timber and stave merchant, 10 Store lane ; residence, 3 Clarendon place
Barnett, Charles, merchant, 7 Henry street; residence, 11 Henry street
Barnett, Dr. Richard, dentist, 1 Wellington place
Barnett, Richard, dentist, 1 Wellington place
Barnett, James, spirit dealer, Ferguson's court, off Smithfield
Barnett, William John, writing clerk, 4 Johnston's buildings, Shankhill road
Barniff, Daniel, carpenter, 25 Bond street
Barr, James, dealer, 18 Friendly street
Barr, Mrs., 8 Upper Queen street
Barrens, Thomas, engineer, Saltpan row, Ballymacarrett
Barrett, Eliza, stay warehouse, 11¼ Castle street
Barrett, Henry, pork cutter, 23 Moffett street
Barrett, Henry, customhouse officer, 41 Rosemary street
Barrett, James, customhouse officer, 2 Earl street
Barron, John, 39 Talbot street
Barron, Joseph, clerk, 8 Stanley place
Barron, Mary, 7 Alexander street
Barron, Samuel, grocer, 160 North street
Barry, J., dealer, 36½ Ann street
Barry, James, and Co., wine and spirit dealers, grocers, and nail manufacturers, 20 and 22 Prince's street; residence, 13 Catherine street
Barry, James, entertainment and lodging, 2 Gloucester street
Barry, James, haberdasher, 147 North street
Barry, Mrs., dressmaker, 8 Sarah street
Barry, Samuel, writing clerk, Wills' place
Bates, Andrew, dealer, 80 Peter's hill
Bates, John, solicitor, and town clerk, 19 Rosemary street ; residence, Sea Park, Greenisland
Bathurst, William, coach factory, 28 Chichester street and Police place; residence, 21 William street South
Batt, Rev. William, 7 Donegall place
Batt, Thomas G., banker, Belfast Bank ; residence, Strandmillis
Battersby, Peter, marine store, 4 Barrack street
Battersby, Thomas, gentleman, Pottinger place, Ballymacarrett
Batwell, William Edward, solicitor, Mr. Bates' office, 19 Rosemary street; residence, 19 Donegall place
Baxter, constable, constabulary station, Falls road
Baxter, Hugh, publican, 35 Winetavern street
Baxter, James, copper and tinsmith, 71 North Queen street
Baxter, Mary, spirit dealer, 35 Winetavern street
Baxter, Richard, agent to Sun Fire and Life office, 15 Rosemary street ; residence, 2 Pakenham place
Baxter, William H., tailor, Shankhill road
Bayley, O'Neill, provision merchant, 41 Corporation street
Bayley, Rev. Benjamin, Wesleyan Methodist minister, 14 Frederick street
Bayne, Ann, grocer and spirit dealer, 13 Nile street
Bead, John, tailor, 29 Valentine street

ALPHABETICAL DIRECTORY. 211

Beath, J. and J., commission merchants, 29 Donegall street
Beath, J., commission merchant, Antrim place cottage
Beatham, Francis, carman, 40 Conway street
Beattie, Hans, traveller, 9 Shankhill
Beattie, James, grocer, 100 Old Lodge road
Beattie, John, gentleman, 80 Joy street
Beattie, Margaret, 58 Stanhope street
Beattie, S. J., bonnet maker, 9 Shankhill
Beattie, William, house and rent agent, 3 Arthur place
Beattie, William, rent agent, 9 Queen's square; scantling yard, M'Clenaghan' court, Mill street
Beattie, William John, lithographer, engraver, and printer, 21 Rosemary st.; residence, 4 Fleet street
Beatty, J., tobacco spinner, 1 Killen street
Beatty, James, butler, 20 Friendly street
Beatty, John, writing clerk, 17 Stanhope street
Beatty, John, car owner, 6 Roy's court
Beatty, John, publican and emigration agent, 63 Waring st. & 2 Grattan st.
Beatty, John, blacksmith, 20 Devis street
Beatty, John, spirit dealer, 36 Gordon street
Beatty, Margaret, ladies' boot and shoe warehouse, 108 North street
Beatty, Thomas, publican, 166 North street
Beatty, William, grocer and spirit dealer, Old Lodge road
Beck, David, spinning master, 9 West street
Beck, John W., M.D., surgeon and apothecary, 128 North street
Beck, Samuel, mechanic, 12 Letitia street
Beckett, Ann, 22 Nile street
Beggs, Hugh, miller, 14 Devis street
Beggs, Miss Rice, dressmaker, 14 Devis street
Beggs, Nathaniel, sawyer, 3 Greenland street
Beggs, Robert, pawnbroker, 54 Cromac street
Behan, James, clerk, 6 Dock street
Bell and Kirker, flour and commission merchants, 4 and 6 Gt. Patrick street
Bell, Abraham, ship and commission agent, 3 Abbotsford place
Bell, Alexander, gentleman, 12 Frederick street
Bell, Archibald, board and lodging, 29 Prince's street
Bell, Charles, broker and furniture dealer, 10 Eliza street, and 51 Smithfield
Bell, Charles, cabinet maker, 24 Earl street
Bell, Clements, butter merchant, 46 Edward st., 15, 24, & 26 Great Patrick st.
Bell, Daniel, timber merchant, 5 Great George's street
Bell, David, grocer, 87 North street
Bell, Hamilton, nailer, Ballynafeigh
Bell, James, weaver, 23 Lower Malone road
Bell, James, weaver, 13 Brown square
Bell, John, printer, 58 Boyd street
Bell, John, jun., and Co., yarn and general merchants, 55 York street; residence, Whitehouse
Bell, John, flax bundler, 41 Conway street
Bell, John, customhouse officer, 58 Ship street
Bell, John, painter, 2 Raphael street
Bell, John L., Ballyclare stores, 2 York lane
Bell, Joseph, publican, Police square and 1 Victoria street
Bell, John, stonemason, 44 Vere street
Bell, John, carpenter, 71 Vere street
Bell, Miss, 11 Dock street

T

ALPHABETICAL DIRECTORY.

Bell, Mary, grocer, 43 Vere street
Bell, Miss, upholstress, 94 Donegall street
Bell, Mrs., 16 Collingwood street
Bell, Mrs., lodgings, 22 King street
Bell, Richard, warper, 8 M'Tier street
Bell, Richard and Jacob, and Co., linen and cotton yarn merchants, flax spinners, &c., 4 Mustard street and 23 Little Donegall street, and Whitehouse
Bell, Richard, tobacco roller, 29 Ritchie's place
Bell, Robert, overseer, 45 Conway street
Bell, Thomas, cutler and surgical instrument maker, 15 Corn market
Bell, Timothy, accountant, 20 Cullingtree street
Bell, William servant, 12 Stanfield street
Bell, William, weaver, 1 Moffet street
Bell, William, mechanic, 13 Cargill street
Bell, William, G., 2 Camden terrace, Botanic road
Bell, William, iron merchant, 114 Ann street
Bell, William, check taker, Potato Market, 29 Little May street
Bell, William, London Tavern, 32 Corn market
Bell, William, baker and grocer, 34½ Great Edward street
Bell, William, clerk, Lower Malone road
Bellis, Rev. George, 8 University square
Belshaw, James John, pawnbroker, 29 Devis street
Benn, James, wine merchant; residence, Fitzwilliam street
Benn, William, general commission merchant, 9 Donegall place; residence, 3 Fitzwilliam place
Bennet, Mrs., 26 College street
Bennet, Thomas, moulder, 12 Murphy street
Bennett, John, carpenter, 24 Shipboy street
Bennett, Rev. George, incumbent, Ballymacarrett Church; Mount Pottinger
Benson, John, pilot, 20 Trafalgar street
Benson, Miss, dressmaker, 15 Hamilton street
Benson, Robert Stitt, manager of bleachgreen; residence, 2 Crumlin place
Benson, William, 33 Lancaster street
Benson, William, carpenter, 7 Verner street
Bernard, Ami, patent flax mills, Mount Pottinger, Ballymacarrett
Berry, Charles, sea captain, 9 Michael street
Berry, John, pensioner, 62 Sussex street
Berry, Patrick, pensioner, 5 Galway street
Bertram, Jacob, spirit dealer, 4 Lower Malone
Berwick, Misses, 3 Antrim place
Berwick, John, baker, 8 Rochfort place
Beverley, Alexander, flax dresser, 43 Conway street
Bessel, Charles, gentleman, Fitzwilliam street, Old Malone road
Best, Robert, tobacco spinner, 12 Hudson's entry
Bickerstaff, William, boatman, 20 North Ann street
Biggan, Thomas, pavier, Frederick street
Biggar, George, gentleman, 6 Donegall pass
Biggar, Joseph, provision merchant, 44 John st.; residence, 88 Donegall st.
Biggar, Jos., jun., provision merchant, 5 Little Donegall st.—4 Glentilt place
Biggar, Thomas, butter merchant, 8, 10 William st.—The Dairy, Mallusk
Bigham, Hugh, watchman, 42 Old Lodge Road
Billsland, Jane, glass and china warehouse, 4 Donegall place
Billsland, Mrs., 23 Fountain street
Bingham, Elizabeth, whiteworker, 19 Valentine street
Bingham, Mrs., lodgings, 20 Edward street

ALPHABETICAL DIRECTORY.

Birch, Emily, teacher, Devis street
Birkmyre, C., baker, 134 Ann street
Birnie, Edward, portrait painter; grocer and spirit dealer, 40 Townsend st,
Birnie, Mrs. Susan, 12 Rochfort place
Black, Adam, hotel keeper, 12 Castle lane
Black, Ellen, shop keeper, Conway street
Black, Dr., surgeon, 96 Donegall street
Black, Henry, wholesale grocer, tobacco and snuff manufacturer, 15, 17 Waring street; residence, 1 University square
Black, James, boot and shoemaker, 28, 26 Ann street
Black, James, spirit dealer, Joy's entry
Black, James, carpenter, 11 Welsh street
Black, James, ship rigger, 73 Nelson street
Black, John, gentleman, 111 Donegall street
Black, John, car driver, 6 Johnston's court
Black, John, shipping clerk, 8 California street
Black, John, weaver, 17 Mitchel street
Black, James, provision shop, 29 Edward street
Black, James, chandler, 9 Charles street
Black, James, master mariner, 2 M'Cracken's row, Ballymacarrett
Black, James, painter, 10 Charlemont street
Black, Margaret, lodginghouse, 5 Bradford square
Black, Miss, 4 Upper Queen street
Black, Mrs., quilter, 9 Union street
Black, Robert John, M.D., surgeon, 10 Botanic road
Black, Rose, publican, 5 Chapel lane
Black, Samuel, solicitor, 12 Chichester street; residence, 17 Joy street
Black, Robert, wood turner, Bridge end, Ballymacarrett
Black, W. R., teacher, 6 Arthur place
Blackburn, Henry, mechanic, 29 Stanhope street
Blackburn, Mary, sempstress, 49 Boyd street
Blackburn, Rev. John, Methodist minister, 37 Melbourne street
Blackburn, Robert, grocer and druggist, 89 North street
Blackham, Charles, clerk in Ulster Bank; residence, Ballynafeigh
Blackham, Miss, 30 York street
Blackwood, Charles, victualler and poulterer, by special appointment, to her Majesty, 20 Corn market; residence, 11 Arthur square
Blackwood, John, Northern Bank, 12 Albion place
Blades, John, coachmaker, 7 George's lane
Blain, Hugh, linen damask warehouse, 7 Donegall street
Blain, James, of John Blain and Son, damask manufacturers, 2 Albert place
Blain, John, jun., of John Blain & Son, 2 Hopeton place
Blain, John, sen., of John Blain & Son, damask manufacturers, Hopeton pl.
Blain, Thomas, head master, Royal Academical Institution
Blake, James, boot and shoemaker, 106 High street
Blair, Alexander, draughtsman and designer, 28 Boundary street
Blair, Eliza, grocer, 26 Nile street
Blair, Eliza, dressmaker, 3 Mill street
Blair, Hugh, carpenter, 24 Union street
Blair, John, car driver, 7 Welsh street
Blair, J., tailor, 25 Alexander street
Blair, Mrs., Crumlin road
Blair, Richard, commissariat staff, 19 Sarah street
Blair, Wm. John, grinder, 10 Townsend place
Blakely, James, seaman, 73 Grattan street
Blakely, James, rent collector, 111 Lower Malone

ALPHABETICAL DIRECTORY.

Blakely, Mrs., 124 Old Lodge Road
Blakley, John, proprietor Crown and Anchor Hotel, 41 Donegall quay
Blaney, Neill, boot and shoe shop, 79 Corporation square
Blayney, Archibald, grocer and publican, Johnston's place, Ballymacarrett
Blessington, James, millworker, 118 Old Lodge road
Blizard, Dr. John, surgeon, 16 Wellington place
Bloomfield, Edward, tinplate worker, 41 John street
Bloomfield, Mrs., Fairview Tavern, Falls road
Bloomfield, William, tinplate worker, 27 John street
Blow, Edwin, and Co., wholesale paper manufacturers, 91 Queen's square; mill, Dunadry
Blow, Wm. N., wholesale paper merchant, 15 Rosemary st.—4 Albion place
Boag, Robert, Albion Cloth Company, 22 High street—6 Upper Crescent
Boal William, cabinet maker, 13 Boyd street
Bodel, Jas., soda water, lemonade, and ginger ale manufacturer, 78 Millfield
Bodel, James, provision merchant, 5 Henry street; residence, 14 Henry st.
Bodel, John, carver and gilder, 6 Hercules place
Bodkin, John, watchmaker, 39 Nelson street
Bogan, James, publican, 43 Berry street
Bogan, Robert, wine and spirit dealer, 45 Winetavern street
Bole, James, ship carpenter, 29 Moffet street
Boles, John, tailor, 17 Rochfort place
Bonar, Daniel, sailor, Fleet street
Bond, James, grocer and spirit dealer, 15 Frederick street
Bond, John H., writing clerk, 51 Talbot street
Bonn, Mark, boarding house, 23 Devis street
Bonner, Fanny, clothier, Garmoyle street
Booker, John, coachmaker, 4 New Durham street
Booker, William, merchant, 14 College square East
Bookes, James, carpenter, 9 Millfield
Boomer, George, accountant, 26 Earl street
Boomer, James, and Co., flax spinners, mills Falls road, office, 16 Waring st.
Boomer, James, fitter, Lagan village, Ballymacarrett
Boomer, Michael, spirit dealer, 69 Cromac street
Boomer, Michael, carpenter, 11 Cullingtree place
Boomer, William, pensioner, 25 Stanhope street
Booth, George, watchman, 15 Rochfort place
Booth, John, 12 Harmony place
Borthwick, John, actuary, Belfast Savings Bank, 29 King street
Boston, James, butcher, 45 Hercules street
Bothwell, Hugh, porter, 2 Thomas street
Bottomley, William, woollen merchant, Calender st.,—Fortbreda, co. Down
Boucher, Alexander, tailor, 4 King street
Boucher, James, family grocer, 4 and 6 Castle Buildings
Boucher, James, haberdasher, 126 North street
Boucher, William, porter, 35 John street
Bournes, H. and Sisters, ladies' repository, 43, Donegall street
Bowman, Robert, solicitor, 16 Donegall street, residence, Carrickfergus
Bowden, Alexander, carpenter, 8 Vere street
Boyce, Mrs. Mary, boarding house, 84 Joy street
Boyce, Rebecca, dealer, Bridge end, Ballymacarrett
Boyce, William, clerk of the Union,—5 Ingram place, Donegall pass
Boyce, William, general commission merchant, 3 Castle Chambersr, residence, Laganville, county Down
Boyd, Ann, 1 College square East

ALPHABETICAL DIRECTORY. 215

Boyd, Arthur, ship carpenter, 6 Nelson court
Boyd, Ann, dealer, 20 Round entry
Boyd, Bankhead, builder, 78 Joy street
Boyd, Captain John and Son, proprietors of the flax spinning mill, 161 Durham street, residence, 4 Glengall place
Boyd, Ellen, confectioner, 50 Alexander street
Boyd, Eliza, dressmaker, 32 Stanhope street
Boyd, Francis, grocer, 1 Stanley street
Boyd, Henry, secretary, Commercial Buildings News Room
Boyd, Henry, painter, 14 Welsh street
Boyd, H. H., house and land agent, 21 Arthur st., residence, Fitzwilliam st.
Boyd, Hugh, bread deliverer, 25 Russell street
Boyd, Hugh, copper and tinsmith, 22 M'Millen's place
Boyd, Henry, overlooker, Falls Mill Company, Falls road
Boyd, John, travelling clerk, 3 Meadow street
Boyd, James, starch works, 35 and 37 Boyd street, residence, Beech lodge
Boyd, James, baker and flour merchant, 162 North street
Boyd, James, umbrella and parasol maker, 21 North street
Boyd, James, grocer, 50 Boundary street
Boyd, John, flax dresser, 59 Conway street
Boyd, John, carpenter, 5 Cullingtree place
Boyd, John, moulder, Herdman's buildings
Boyd, John, architect and surveyor, 45 York street
Boyd, Mrs. Margaret, 23 Nelson street
Boyd, Margaret, whiteworker, 19 M'Tier's street
Boyd, Miss Margaret, milliner, 3 Joy street
Boyd, Robert, bleacher, 62 Brown street
Boyd, Robert, Queen's quay, Ballymacarrett
Boyd, Rebecca, 64 Alexander street
Boyd, Richard, smith, 27 Greenland street
Boyd, Sarah, 7 Albert street
Boyd, Samuel, of S. Boyd and Co., 47 Little Donegall street
Boyd, Samuel, publican and grocer, 59 Lettuce hill
Boyd, Samuel, clerk, 26 Nelson street
Boyd, Samuel, bookbinder, 31 Wall street
Boyd, Samuel, proprietor of Belfast Foundry, 110 Donegall street
Boyd, Thomas, baker and flour dealer, 181 North street
Boyd, William, vitriol works, Lagan village, 4 Howard steeet
Boyd, William, house carpenter, 9 North Thomas street
Boyd, William, house and sign painter, 18 Skipper street
Boyd, William, ærated water manufacturer, 27 Stanfield street
Boyd, Wm. and Sons, Vitriol Works, Lagan village, Ballymacarrett; residence, 4 Howard street
Boylan, Thomas, butcher, 22 Hercules street
Boylan, Thomas, butcher, 41 Rosemary street
Boyle, James, carpenter, Union place
Boyle, C., lodgings, 42 Alexander street
Boyle, Eliza, shopkeeper, 7 Durham street
Boyle, E. and J. bonnet and dressmakers, 3 Seymour street
Boyles, Ferrard, coachman, 18 Cullingtree street
Boyle, Joseph, grocer and publican, 52 Mill street
Boyle, Patrick, provision shop, Falls road
Boyle, James, spirit dealer, 4 Great George's street
Boyle, Mary, grocer, 32 Grattan street
Boyle, James, writing clerk, 15 Round entry

Boyle, Robert, publican, 23 Union street
Boyle, Robert, boarding house, 55 Little Patrick street
Boyle, Samuel, ship carpenter, Meadow street
Boyle, Robert, dealer, 2 Alexander street
Boyle, Patrick, provision dealer, 19 Union street
Boyle, Samuel, merchant, 16 Ann street
Boyle, Peter, spirit dealer, 21 Marquis street
Boyle, Toal, lodgings, 60 Alexander street
Brabazon, Joseph Captain, *Abigail*, 68 Little Patrick street
Brackley, George, railway porter, 15 North Thomas street
Bracegirdle, James, writing clerk, 22 Collingwood street
Bracegirdle, Matthew, publican, 57 Smithfield
Braddell, Joseph, gun and pistol manufacturer, fishing tackle warehouse, 17 Castle place; residence, 2 Castle Chambers
Braddell, George William, notary public, insurance office, 3 Castle lane; residence, Blaris Lodge, Lisburn
Bradford, Henry, book keeper 6, Catherine street North
Bradford, James, block and pump maker, 10 Garmoyle street
Bradford, David, provision dealer, 40 Union street
Bradley, Stewart, sailmaker, 8 Union place
Bradley, James, Shell Fish Tavern, Legg's lane
Bradley, Jane, dealer, 10 King street
Bradley, Samuel, provision dealer, 29 Hill street
Bradley, Samuel, provision store, 21 Hill street
Bradley, William, barber, 39 Millfield
Bradley, John, whitesmith, 1 Alexander street
Bradley, Mary, fishmonger, 13 Black's place
Brady, Francis, carpenter, 21 Charles street
Brady, John, sailmaker, 100 Carrick hill
Brady, Bernard, maltsman, 33 Bank lane
Brady, James, butcher, 16 Great Edward street
Brady, Mary Ann, hotel and tavern, 2, 4, & 6 Graham's entry and Orr's entry
Brady, Robert, pensioner, 29 Green street
Brady, James, dealer in poultry, 27 Market street
Brady, William, grocer, 107 Peter's hill
Bragg, Henry, & Son, bleachers, Cottonmount; office, 8 York street
Braithwaite, Joseph, coffin maker, 75 Union street
Braithwaithe, John, grocer & leather cutter, Bradbury place, old Malone road
Branagh, David, butcher, 17 Hercules street
Branagh, John, butcher, 24 Hercules street
Branagh, Patrick, butcher, 15½ Hercules street
Branker, J. P., salesman, 36 Gloucester street
Brankin, Henry, grain merchant, 26 Gt. Patrick street; residence, 7 Nelson st.
Brannigan, Danl., wine and spirit merchant, 43 North st.—2 Murray's terrace
Brannagan, J., carowner, 12 Hamilton place
Brannigan, Patrick, butcher, 44 Hercules street
Breen, James, dealer, 2 Market street
Bremner, James, upholsterer, 5 Ann street
Brannan, Peter, shoemaker, 18 West street
Brennan, James, dealer, 23 Carrick hill
Brennan, Doctor John, M.D., 23 Chichester street
Brennan, James, dealer, 38 Alexander street
Brenton, John, carpenter, Meadow street
Bridge, Miss, 21 College street
Brice, John, spirit dealer, 36 Church lane

ALPHABETICAL DIRECTORY. 217

Briggs, Addison, writing clerk, 1 Cargill street
Briggs, Ralph, salesman, 116 Old Lodge road
Briggs, John, plain and ornamental painter and decorator, 57 Academy street
Briggs, Mrs., 3 Donegall pass
Bristow, Joseph, Bank of Ireland, 38 College street
Bristow, James, Northern Bank, and Prospect, Ormeau road
Britain, Hugh, rag merchant, 30 Alexander street
Britain, David, Rising Sun Tavern, 23 Wesley place
Britain, John, spirit dealer, 65 Mustard street
Britain, John, spirit dealer, Ormeau road
Britton, Alexander, plasterer, 36 Corporation street
Britton, Mary, butcher, 49 Hercules street
Broadley, J. W., muslin manufacturers, 18 Waring street
Brock, John, compositor, 12 Catherine street
Broe, Henry, saw manufacturer, 78 Hercules street
Brooks, John, servant, 38 Bank lane
Brophy, Edward, bricklayer, 120 Millfield
Brough, Colonel, assistant adjutant general, 3 Adelaide place
Brown, Andrew, spirit dealer, 48 Winetavern street
Brown, Bernard, pavier, 20 Union street
Brown, Catherine, dressmaker, 1 Henrietta street
Brown, Charles, boot and shoemaker, Lagan village, Ballymacarrett
Brown, David, hardware merchant and ironmonger, 35 Castle place
Brown, David, painter, 12 Meetinghouse lane
Brown, Edward, revenue officer, 6 Albion lane
Brown, Eliza, 16 Townsend street
Brown, Ephraim, carpenter, 13 Stanhope street
Brown, Henry, pawnbroker, 17 Henry street
Brown, Henry, spirit dealer, Ballymacarrett
Brown, Hugh, cooper, 16 Earl street
Brown, Hugh, brass moulder, 7 Townsend street
Brown, John, spirit dealer, 1 Thomas court
Brown, James, mechanic, 7 Seymour street
Brown, James, spirit dealer, 18 Lynas's lane
Brown, John, boot and shoemaker, 10 Catherine street North
Brown, James, house agent, 10 Kennedy's place
Brown, John and Son, horse shoers and farriers, 15 George's lane
Brown, James, plasterer, 12 Curtis street
Brown, James, land agent, 59¼ Upper Arthur street
Brown, James, manager of J. & J. Herdman's mill, 5 West street
Brown, James, publican, 1 Murphy street
Brown, John, schoolmaster, 108 old Lodge road
Brown, John, grocer and cooper, 72 Green street
Brown, John, ostler, Donegall Arms, 21 Durham street
Brown, John sen., builder, 3 Gloucester street
Brown, John, tailor, 1 Lagan street
Brown, John, scantling yard, 26½ Robert street
Brown, John, carpenter, 13 Grace street
Brown, John, jun., timber yard, 2 Seymour lane
Brown, John, collector, St. George's market
Brown, John, boot and shoemaker, 39 John street
Brown, Joseph, 54 Stanhope street
Brown, Joseph, sawyer, 24 New Lodge road
Brown, James, porter, 18 Annette street

Brown, L. and T., timber and slate merchants, 41 Chichester st. and Queen's bridge, saw mills, 14 Riley's place; residence, 20 Gloucester street
Brown, Lawson, timber yard, Chichester street; residence, 23 College street
Brown, Moses, dealer, 7 Henrietta street
Brown, Mrs. Mary, 49 Peter's hill
Brown, M., grocery and spirit dealer, 12 George's lane
Brown, Mary Ann, dealer, 10 Leadbetter place
Brown, Mary, grocer, 2 Cullingtree street
Brown, Miss Mary Anne, haberdasher, 107 North street
Brown, Miss, teacher of music, 9 College street
Brown, Miss, 1 Ormeau place
Brown, Miss, boarding and day school, 23 Gloucester street
Brown, Mrs. Elizabeth, 3 Wellwood place
Brown, Mary Ann, mangler, 77 Little Patrick street
Brown, Mrs., commercial boarding house, 81 Donegall street
Brown, Mary, 22 Shipboy street
Brown, Mrs., 33 Little Patrick street
Brown, Patrick, stoker, 3 Wall street
Brown, Rainey, machine maker, 67 York street
Brown, Robert, spirit dealer, 32 John street
Brown, Robert, gardener, 4 Welsh street
Brown, Robert, professor of music, 61 Nelson street
Brown, Robert, spirit dealer, 24 Gamble street
Brown, Robert, hotel keeper, Wilson's court
Brown, Robert, boot and shoe shop, 9 Church lane
Brown, Susan, washerwoman, 5 Seymour lane
Brown, Stewart, wine and spirit store, 40 Trafalgar street
Brown, S. R. and T., sewed muslin warerooms, 74 Little Donegall street
Brown, Thomas, sea captain, 12 Corporation street
Brown, Thomas, jeweller, 7 Cromac road
Brown, Thomas, millwright, 82 Millfield
Brown, William, grocer, 6 Church street
Brown, William, grocery and spirit store, 200 North street
Brown, Wright, weaver, 98 Lower Malone
Brown, William, clerk, 24 Catherine street
Brown, William, tailor, Lagan village, Ballymacarrett
Brown, Daniel, grocer, 39 Great Edward street—10 May street
Browne, George, silk dyer, 26 Arthur street—Arthur street district post-office receiving house
Browne, J. H., wholesale grocer, 53 Ann street
Browne, Reid & Co., wholesale woollen & Manchester warehouse, 3 Waring st.
Browne, Samuel, surgeon, R.N., 5 Clarence place
Browne, William, merchant, office Waring street; residence, 7 The Crescent
Brownlee, Joseph, porter, 34 Gordon street
Brownlee, Thomas, flax dresser, 38 Moffet street
Brownlee, William, schoolmaster, 47 Pound street
Brownjess, Alfred, sea captain, 4 Apsley place
Bruce, Andrew, provision dealer, Nelson street
Bruce, Edward, gentleman, 6 Donegall square North
Bruce, George, coal factor, 12 Edward street
Bruce, James, carter, 39 Carrickhill
Bruce, Joseph, brassfounder, 6 Cullingtree place
Bruce, James, pensioner, 82 Old Lodge road
Bruce, Mrs., provision dealer, 50 Academy street
Bruce, Mrs. Thorndale, Antrim road

ALPHABETICAL DIRECTORY. 219

Bruce, Mrs. Jane, dress and bonnet maker, 22 Gordon street
Bruce, Rev. William, The Farm, Antrim road
Bruce, Samuel, solicitor, 33 Donegall street
Bruce, Thomas, gas fitter, 5 Academy street
Bruce, William, ship smith, 98 Nelson street
Bryan, Smith, 10 Victoria place
Bryce, Rev. R. J., L.L.D., principal of the Belfast academy, 63 Donegall st.
Bryce, Robert, M.D., surgeon, 63 Donegall street; surgery, 7 Academy st.
Bryson, Dr. Samuel, 98 High street
Bryson, Eliza, milliner and dressmaker, 24 Russell street
Bryson, John, clerk, Conway street
Bryson, John, confectioner, 18 Hill street
Bryson, Joseph W., M.D., surgeon, 16 York street
Bryson, Thomas, hardware shop, 180 North street
Bryson, Wm., muslin and gingham manufacturer, 118 Waring st—Crescent
Bryson, William, 40 North Queen street
Bruntz, Francis, foreman tailor, 69 Joy street
Budge, A. W., publican, 42 Ann street
Bulla, Elizabeth, 36 Stanfield street
Bullick, James, shuttle maker, 13 Pottinger's entry
Bullick, Mrs. Jane, 23 Stanhope street
Bullick, Samuel, academy, 82 High street—1 Ingram place, Donegall pass
Bullick, S. W., and Co., woollendrapers and hatters, Victoria street
Bullock, Wm., brush & weavers' utensil warehouse, 27 North st.—Bower's hill
Bunting, Clara, green grocer, 40 Boundary street
Bunting, Robert, confectioner, 64 North street
Bunting, William, publican and grocer, Agnes's place, Shankhill road
Bunting, William, market constable, 3 Brown's square
Burden, Francis, soda ash manufacturer, Friendly street—16 Alfred street
Burden, Miss, 14 Alfred street
Burden, William, M.D., 16 Alfred street
Burgess, J. Howard, drawing master, 16 Donegall place
Burgess, John, shoemaker, 3 Albert street place
Burk, William, book dealer, 148 Millfield
Burke, Alexander, tailor, 42 North Queen street
Burke, James, butcher, 69 Hercules street
Burke, John, boot and shoemaker, 19 West street
Burke, John, butcher and feather merchant, 53 Hercules street
Burke, Mary, fruiterer and confectioner, 51 Cromac street
Burke, Michael, shoemaker, 12 West street
Burlease, Stephen, clerk, 57 Ship street
Burleigh, William, cabinet maker, 6 Lower Stanfield street
Burnby, William, painter and glazier, 23 Stanley street
Burnett, Archibald, painter, 7 Murphy street
Burnett, Mrs., boarding house, 21 Earl street
Burns, Bernard, flax dealer, 4 Little May street
Burns, Bernard, publican, 1 Roseann place
Burns, Charles, dealer, 2 Roseann place
Burns, Charles, marine store, 47 Millfield
Burns, Daniel, rag store, 4 Patrick's lane
Burns, Daniel, marine store, 14 William street
Burns, Daniel, dealer, 37 Stephen street
Burns, Edward, pensioner, 38 M'Millen's place
Burns, George, furniture and old iron dealer, 52 Smithfield
Burns, George, publican, waste and tow merchant, 41 May street

Burns, George, tailor, 33 Stephen street
Burns, Hugh, sawyer, 29 Friendly street
Burns, Hugh, 35 Lagan street
Burns, Hugh, grocer, 52 and 54 Alexander street
Burns, John, carpenter, 77 Vere street
Burns, John ropemaker, Ballymacarrett
Burns, John, coachman, 6 Sarah street
Burns, James, butcher, 57 Hercules street
Burns, John, car owner, 16 Charlemont street
Burns, John, tide waiter, Peter's hill
Burns, James F., schoolmaster, Wesley place
Burns, John, shoemaker, 19 Torrens' market
Burns, Mary, spirit dealer, Lagan village, Ballymacarrett
Burns, Michael, car driver, 35 Upper Lagan street
Burns, M., dressmaker, 59 Upper Arthur street
Burns, Philip, iron moulder, 3 Collingwood street
Burns, Philip, hackler, 21 New Durham street
Burns, Robert, car driver, New Road, Ballymacarrett
Burns, Thomas, horse dealer, 6 Henrietta street
Burns, Thomas, tailor, 35 Stephen street
Burns, Thomas, moulder, 35 North Thomas street
Burnside, John, roper, 5 Boundary street
Burnside, Thomas, bricklayer, 40 Brown street
Burrowes, John, miller, Belfast mills, Wellington square—Falls road
Burrows, Israel, brassfounder, 8 and 89 Peter's hill
Burrows, William, clerk, M'Larnon's buildings, Ballymacarrett
Busby, William, gentleman, Lagan village, Ballymacarrett
Bushell, Theobald, wine and spirit merchant, commission and share broker, 32 Rosemary street—residence, Strandtown cottage, county Down
Butler & Son, plumbers, 29 Castle street—residence, 7 Fountain street
Butler, Charles, master mariner, 13 Garmoyle street
Butler, Patrick, coal factor, 19 Black's place
Butler, William, bootcloser, 36 Bank lane
Byrne, Charles, joiner, 5 Duffy's place
Byrne, Cherry, spirit dealer, 33 Donegall quay
Byrne, James, boot and shoemaker, 92 High street and 2 Skipper street
Byrne, John, auctioneer, 38 Berry street—Mount Charles, Malone turnpike
Byrne, John, wine and spirit store, 1 Talbot street; residence, 23 Queen st.
Byrne, Misses, seminary, 26 Castle street
Byrne, Neil, meal and corn dealer, 22 Market street
Byrne, Robert, tailor and clothier, 23 Pilot street
Burns, Samuel, commercial traveller, 1 Antrim place
Byrne, Thomas, builder, 32 Great George's street
Byrne, William, gentleman, 23 Queen street

Cahoon, Walter, pensioner, 11 Brown's square
Cahoon, James, turner, 5 New Durham street
Cahouln, James, pawnbroker, 7 Marquis street
Cahoun, Miss, Eliza street
Caird, Sarah, washerwoman, 4 Union place
Cairncross, William, gentleman, 17 Dock street
Cairnes, James, porter, 9 Hill street
Cairns, Mary, boarding house, 2 Wall street
Cairns, Thomas, of Cairns and Kennedy, High street; residence, Oak street
Calder, Lieut., 5 College street south

ALPHABETICAL DIRECTORY. 221

Caldwell, James, pensioner, 7 Lancaster street
Caldwell, Mrs. Jane, boarding house, 6 Malone place
Caldwell, William, porkcutter, 22 M'Tier's street
Caldwell, William, weaver, 6 Renwick place
Callan, Owen, master May street National school, 19 May street
Callender, James, publican, currier, and leather merchant, 21 and 23 Mill st.
Callwell, Mrs. Margaret, 6 James' street South
Calvert, Robert, proprietor of Royal Hibernian Concert Hall, 14 Smithfield
Calwell, George, print cutter, 18 Friendly street
Calwell, James, delf merchant, 35 Great Patrick street
Calwell, James, pensioner, 3 Napier's place
Calwell, James, muslin manufacturer, 17 Curtis street—28 Academy street
Calwell, Robert, & Co., hardware merchants, &c., 14 Waring street; residence, 10 Donegall square North
Camac, Eliza, grocer, 26 Collingwood street
Cameron, Evan, collector inland revenue, Donegall place Buildings
Cameron, George, goldsmith, 3 Cargill street
Cameron, Henry, sea steward, Little Corporation street
Cameron, John, starchmaker, 37 Old Lodge road
Cameron, James, plumber, lead merchant, &c., 47 Donegall street ; residence, Glentilt lodge, Crumlin road
Cameron, John, linen and ribbon merchant, office 9 Calendar st. ; residence, [15 Victoria place
Cameron, James, bricklayer, 3 Glentilt place
Cameron, Jane, bonnetmaker, 22 Lancaster street
Campbell, Anthony, carpenter, 52 Little Donegall street
Campbell, Agnes, dealer, 43 Little Donegall street
Campbell, Allen, lodging house, 62 Little Donegall street
Campbell, Alexander, porter, 10 Friendly street
Campbell, B. lodgings, 79 Barrack street
Campbell, Bernard, hardware dealer, 17 Smithfield
Campbell, C. bonnetmaker, 8 Brown street
Campbell, Charles, weaver, 120 Lower Malone
Campbell, Duncan, jobbing smith, 1 Little Donegall street
Campbell, David, pig dealer, 69 Barrack street
Campbell, Edward, merchant, 53 Academy street
Campbell, Elizabeth, 2 Downshire place
Campbell, Francis, brick manufacturer, Shankhill road
Campbell, Francis, grocer and spirit dealer, 40 Hill street
Campbell, Francis, grocery and spirit store, 1 Albert square, south side
Campbell, F. grocer, 53 Barrack street
Campbell, Francis, clothes dealer, 29 Hercules place
Campbell, George, butcher, 12 Henrietta street
Campbell, Henry, sawyer, 42 Annette street
Campbell, Hugh, butcher, 19 Hercules place
Campbell, Hugh, linen lapper, California street
Campbell, Henry, of Gunning & Campbell, flax spinners—33 Queen street
Campbell, James, hairdresser, 33 John street
Campbell, James, solicitor, 9 Rosemary street—8 Donegall square west
Campbell, James, dealer, 60 Green street
Campbell, James, gentleman, 8 Donegall square west
Campbell, James T., cabinet maker, 7 Ann street
Campbell, John, sergeant day police, 10 Annette street
Campbell, John, hardware dealer, 14 Smithfield
Campbell, John, provision merchant, 9 Henry street and 8½ Great George's street ; residence, 8 Donegall square West

Campbell, James, joiner, 2 Catherine court
Campbell, Jane, dealer, 18 Leeds street
Campbell, James, sea captain, Nile street
Campbell, J., custom house officer, 22 North Ann street
Campbell, James, boot and shoemaker, 37 Verner street
Campbell, James, cloth lapper, 54 Townsend street
Campbell, James, flax spinner, Falls Mills; residence, 5 College square North
Campbell, James, clerk, 20 College square North
Campbell, John, accountant, 12 Cromac street
Campbell, John, flax spinner, of Gunning & Campbell—5 College sq. North
Campbell, John, publican, 135 Durham street
Campbell, John, publican, 2 Edward street
Campbell, John, whitesmith, 8 George's lane
Campbell, John, weaver, 114 Lower Malone
Campbell, John, pattern drawer, 3 Stanley place
Campbell, Joseph, grocer, 112 Cromac street
Campbell, Joseph, wine bottler, 22 Russell street
Campbell, Joseph, carpenter, 5 Murphy street
Campbell, Joseph, carpenter, 17 Seymour lane
Campbell, Joshua, watchman, 20 Grace street
Campbell, J., linen lapper, 73 North Queen street
Campbell, John, linen lapper, 11 Gavin's buildings, Shankhill road
Campbell, John, carpenter, 5 Stephen's street
Campbell, John, whitesmith, 3 Thomas' court
Campbell, James, grocer, 29 Union street
Campbell, John, clothes dealer, 44 Rosemary street
Campbell, Mrs., 6 Adelaide place
Campbell, Mary, schoolmistress, 5 Murphy street
Campbell, Margaret, boarding house, 11 Fleet street
Campbell, Mary, milliner, 1 Glentilt place
Campbell, Mrs., 9 Donegall square North
Campbell, Matthew, weaver, 118 Lower Malone
Campbell, Mrs., dealer, 2 North Boundary street
Campbell, Margaret, dealer, 41 Mustard street
Campbell, Mrs., dressmaker, 4 King street
Campbell, Michael, tinsmith, 6 Robert court
Campbell, Margaret, dealer, 100 Old Lodge road
Campbell, Michael, proprietor of the Bower's Hill Tavern, Shankhill road
Campbell, Patrick, watchman, 13 Duffy's place
Campbell, Patrick, clothier, 4 Hercules place
Campbell, Patrick, watchman, 1 Conway street
Campbell, Robert, carpenter, 2 Fleming's place, Old Lodge road
Campbell, R., bookbinder, bookseller, and stationer, 1 Skipper street
Campbell, Robert, night constable, 10 Staunton street
Campbell, Robert, baker, 10 Arthur street
Campbell, Robert, carpenter, 15 Townsend street
Campbell, Robert, baker, 10 Arthur street
Campbell, Robert, carpenter, 15 Campbell's buildings, Townsend street
Campbell, Robert, Damside foundry, Millfield
Campbell, Rev. Theophilus, incumbent Trinity church; 3 Mountview terrace
Campbell, Rose, huckster, 3 Caddell's entry
Campbell, Stewart, cabinet maker, 1 Napier's place; Ann street
Campbell, Samuel, grocer, 12 Berry street
Campbell, Sarah, shoe binder, 25 Greenland street
Campbell, Sarah, 54½ North Queen street

ALPHABETICAL DIRECTORY.

Campbell, Samuel, seaman, 17 Little May street
Campbell, Thomas, hairdresser, 2 Pilot street
Campbell, William, baker, 1 Leeds street
Campbell, William, leather merchant, 109 North street
Campbell, William, boot and shoemaker, 38 Lagan street
Campbell, W. & J., provision merchants, 8½ Great George's street
Campbell, William, bookbinder, 6 California street
Campbell, William, timber dealer, 12 Sir Henry's buildings, Ballymacarrett
Campbell, William, teacher, Pottinger place, Ballymacarrett
Canavan, John, sawyer, 18 Round entry
Canavan, John, grocer and publican, 91 North Queen street
Canavan, John, timber and coal yard, 176 North street
Canavan, Mrs. Dorothea, spirit dealer and victualling house, 36 John street
Canavan, Patrick, tailor and lodgings, 13 Williams lane
Canmer, John, grocer and publican, Lagan village, Ballymacarrett
Canning, Jas., proprietor of the Dublin & Belfast Bakery, 8 & 10 Donegall st.
Canning, John, Cooper, 40 and 42 Green street
Canning, James, baker, 10 and 12 Hercules street
Canning, Robert, tailor, 31 Brown street
Canning, Sarah, widow, 134 Carrick hill
Canning, Thomas, soap boiler, 27 Moffet street
Canovan, James, Templepatrick Inn, 36 John street
Cantwell, Stephen Joseph, Custom house; Mount Pottinger, Ballymacarrett
Canty, Rose, Hamilton's court
Cappo, Anthony, optician, 160 Millfield
Cardoo, Edward, weaver, 53 Lower Malone road
Carey, Bernard, carpenter, Mary's place, North Queen street
Carland, James, rent agent, 13 Castle lane—Ballynafeigh
Carland, John, pensioner, 68 Green street
Carland, Orr, mechanic, 70 Lower Malone
Carlin, Edward, grocer, 55 Verner street
Carlin, Mary, dealer, 20 Verner street
Carlin, Peter, engraver and lithographer, 28 Russell street
Carlile, Dr. H., Professor Queen's College, 3 Prospect terrace
Carlile, David, spirit store, hay and straw yard, Bridge end, Ballymacarrett
Carlile, John, comptroller of customs, 8 Pakenham place
Carlisle, Ellen, dealer, 36½ Talbot street
Carlisle, James, builder, mill owner, 85 Donegall street—1 Antrim road
Carlisle, John, grocer, 7 Marlborough street
Carlisle, John, bootcloser, 39 Hill street
Carlisle, John, pilot, 53 Little York street
Carlisle, John, seaman, 11 Peter's hill
Carlisle, Mary, 18 Charles street
Carlisle, Samuel, wine, spirit, flour and bran stores, 26 & 28 Little Patrick st.
Carlisle, William, car driver, 88 Cromac street
Carlisle, William, emigration agent, 37 Corporation street
Carmichael, Arthur, Fox Tavern, 2 Calendar street
Carmichael, John, baker, 89 Carrickhill
Carmichael, Miss, dressmaker, 11 College street
Carmichael, Robert, grocer and spirit dealer, 8 Garmoyle street
Carmichael, Samuel, grocer and lodgings, 13 Gamble street
Carmichael, Thomas, carman, 55 Brown square
Carnduff, Robert, baker, 31 and 33 Brown square
Carnduff, Samuel, weaver, Ballynafeigh
Carnes, Thomas, travelling clerk, 11 Bond street new

Carpenter, Miss, school, 33 Rosemary street
Carpenter, Philip, provision dealer, 33 Rosemary street
Carr, Hugh B., upholstery, venetian, & wire blind establishment, 2 Castle st.
Carr, James, coachmaker, 4 Letitia street
Carr, James, chandler, 5 Friendly street
Carr, Mrs., 5 Brougham street
Carrabine, Thomas, carter, 62 Townsend street
Carraher, M., cowkeeper, 68 Alexander street
Carrick, James, dentist, 9 Upton street
Carroll, George, baker, 21 Mary's market
Carroll, Henry, fancy biscuit manufacturer, 12 Annette street
Carroll, John, butcher, 56 Verner street
Carroll, John, professor of music, 20 Joy street
Carroll, Margaret, Shankhill road
Carroll, Patrick, butcher, 19½ Great Edward street
Carroll, Richard, shoemaker, 9 John street
Carroll, Richard, clerk, 20 Joy street
Carroll, Thomas, salesman, 67 Joy street
Carroll, William, grocer, 78 Ann street
Carruthers, George A., wine and spirit merchant, Corporation street
Carruthers, Hugh, linen ornament printer, 2 Aughton terrace
Carruthers, John, gentleman, 3 Little Victoria street
Carse, Mrs., 7 Sussex place
Carson, Arthur, mariner and dealer, 2 Store lane
Carson, Henry, saddler, 24 Lagan street
Carson, James, boot and shoemaker, 7 Montgomery street
Carson, J. & N., grocers and wine merchants, 53 Donegall street
Carson, John, publican, Shankhill road
Carson, Lamont, glass manufacturer, High street—8 Antrim place
Carson, Richard, publican, Falls road
Carson, R. M., ship chandler and sailmaker, 61 Waring street—137 York st.
Carson, R., grocer and publican, 36 Conway street
Carson, Robert, grocer, 17 Bradbury place
Carson, William, porter, 37 New Lodge road
Carson, William, merchant, 14 Corn market; residence, 1 Howard street
Carson, William, solicitor, 31 Waring street; residence, 1 Howard street
Carswell, Robert, bookbinder, 12 California street
Carter & Martin, flax, tow, and grain merchants, 17 Rosemary street
Carter, John T., of Carter and Martin, 1 Victoria place
Carty, D., coach builder, 18½ Castle street
Caruth, James, grocer, 41 Lancaster street
Caruth, John, grocer, meal, flour, and bran stores, 189 North street
Caruthers, J., boot and shoemaker, 17 Bond street
Caruthers, Robert, shoemaker, 69 Vere street
Casement, Thomas, ship carpenter, 12 Dock street
Casey, Hugh, dealer in hay, 7 Carrickhill
Casey, Jeremiah, lodging house, 37 Smithfield
Casey, John, spirit dealer and grocer, 127 and 129 North street
Casey, Rodger, cow keeper, Hudson's row, Shankhill road
Cash, Edward, tailor, 2 Renwick place
Cassidy, Alfred, solicitor, 9 Donegall place—9 The Crescent
Cassidy, Francis, toy shop, 12 Peter's hill
Cassidy, Miss, and Mrs. Irwin's dancing academy, 27 Chichester street
Cassidy, Mary, 102 Carrickhill
Cassidy, Patrick, shoemaker, 72 Mustard street

ALPHABETICAL DIRECTORY.

Cassidy, Peter, weaver, 5 Wellington square
Cassidy, Robt., solicitor, 9 The Crescent, Botanic road ; office, 9 Donegall pl.
Caughey, Alexander, boot and shoemaker, Ballymacarrett
Caughey, James, shoemaker, and green grocer, 83½ Peter's hill
Caughey, Miss, 14 Albion place
Caughey, Richard, butcher, 11 Letitia street
Caughey, William B., Northern Bank, 3 Castle street
Caulfield, Bernard, tailor, 11 John street
Caulfield, Jane, haberdasher, 72 North street
Caulfield, William, car owner, 49 Little Patrick street
Cavanagh, John, musician and provision dealer, 11 Cromac street
Cavanagh, Nicholas, dealer, 8 Graham's entry
Chalmers, James, cloth lapper, 9 Mary's market
Chambers, Alexander, builder, 101 Joy street
Chambers, George, boot and shoemaker, 11 Union street
Chambers, Jane, lodgings, 6 Great Edward street
Chambers, James, weaver, 6 Falls court, Durham street
Chambers, Robert, weaver, 20 Mitchell street
Chancellor, John, & Co., sewed muslin manufacturers, 6 Curtis street
Chancellor, M., Ladies' day school, 55 Cromac street
Channon, William, garrison librarian, 38 Brown street
Chapman, James, tailor, 17 New Durham street
Chapman, James, chronometer, watch, and clock maker, 64 High street
Chapman, Simon, 28 Earl street
Charley and Malcolm, merchants and general steam-packet agents, 49, 51, 53, and 55 Donegall quay
Charley, Henry, merchant, 8 Alfred street—office, Donegall quay
Charley, James, ship carpenter, 1 Little George's street
Charley, John, of Charley and Malcolm, 8 Donegall square South
Charley, William, ship carpenter, 11 Michael street
Charnock, Brothers, wine & spirit merchants & drysalters, 65 Corporation sq.
Charnock, William, drysalter, 8 Fleet street
Charters, David, shoemaker, 39 Mustard street
Charters, Ellen, publican, 45 Dock street
Charters, Eleanor, American hotel, 6 Prince's dock
Charters, John, & Co., flax spinners, Falls mill—Falls road
Charters, John, of Falls Mill Company, Ardmoulin house, Falls road
Cheevers, Patrick, grocer and publican, 47 North Queen street
Chermside and Davidson, flax spinners, 27 Pottinger's entry
Chermside, Thos., & Co., corn millers, Conway street mills, Falls road
Chermside, Thos., flax merchant, 1 College square North—Pottinger's entry
Cherry, Hamilton, gentleman, 16 Gloucester street
Cherry, Moses, saddler and American trunk manufactory, 9 Donegall street
Cherry, Richard, iron ship builder and grocer, 51 Little Patrick street
Chesnut, John, fireman in steamer, 4 Wilson street
Chignell, Isabella, lodging house, 15 Collingwood street
Childs, Richard, blacksmith, 10 M'Tier street
Christain, Richard, night constable and shoemaker, 6 Killen street
Christle, David, teacher, Ballymacarrett National school
Christie, John, dealer, 49 Smithfield
Christy, Alexander, mariner, 8 Little Corporation street
Christy, John, starch and blue manufacturer, 3 Frederick st.; 5 Alexander st.
Church, Mrs., 36 North Queen street
Church, Mrs., confectionary establishment, 20 Mill street
Church, William, foreman *News-Letter* office, 20 Mill street

Cinnamond, Helena, spirit dealer, and green hide merchant, 23 Smithfield
Cinnamond, Henry, boot & shoe manufacturer, 9 Castle place—5 Arthur st.
Cinnamond, John, boot and shoe warehouse, 9 Castle place ; 5 Arthur street
Cinnamond, Samuel, nail manufacturer, 4 Peter's hill
Clark and Drummond, cotton yarn warehouse, 7 Commercial court
Clark, Alexander, writing clerk, 1 Upton street
Clark, Alex., flour and grain merchant, 21 Church lane—26 Trafalgar street
Clark, Arthur, carpenter, 5 Wall street
Clark, Hugh, and Co., letterpress printers, 24 Corn market
Clark, Isabella, 4 Aughton terrace, Donegall pass
Clark, John, gas fitter, 21 Cromac road
Clark, James, nailmaker and dealer, Ballynafeigh
Clark, Mary, 32 Hamilton street
Clark, Richard, spirit dealer, 18 Corporation street
Clark, Rose, dealer, 20½ New Lodge road
Clark, William, general smith, Little York street
Clarke, Andrew, grocer, Ann street; residence, Grovefield, Ballymacarrett
Clarke, Æneas, butcher, 7 York street market; 39 Nelson street
Clarke, Dr. John, surgeon, 90 Donegall street
Clarke, Edward H., director Belfast Bank, Elmwood, Lisburn road
Clarke, Henry W., solicitor, Castle Chambers; residence, 7 Clarence place
Clarke, Hugh C., auctioneer and valuator, 5 Rosemary street—Ormeau road
Clarke, Hugh, carpenter, 132 Old Lodge road
Clarke, John, bricklayer, 21 M'Tier's street
Clarke, James, dealer, 2 Bond street
Clarke, John, commercial traveller, Old Lodge road
Clarke, John, publican, 31 Peter's hill
Clarke, John A., flour stores, 21 Church lane
Clarke, James, carpenter and dealer, Bridge end, Ballymacarrett
Clarke, James, customhouse officer, 17 Fleet street
Clarke, John, boarding house, 6 Chichester lane
Clarke, John, J.P., 12 College square east
Clarke, John, confectioner, 70 Cromac street
Clarke, Ledlie, brewer, 130½ Ann street; residence, Pakenham place
Clarke, Margaret, 5 Ritchie's place
Clarke, Miss, boarding house, 10 Corporation street
Clarke, Mrs., 58 Barrack street
Clarke, Neal, spirit dealer, 78½ Cromac street
Clarke, Peter, ship chandler, 31 Corporation street
Clarke, Thomas, servant, 32 Durham street
Clarke, Thomas, tailor, 5 Windsor place
Clarke, William, lithographic printer, 20 Hamilton's place
Clarke, William, plain and ornamental painter, 27 Fountain street
Clarke, William P., cabinet and upholstery warerooms, 5 Fountain street
Clarke, Young, grocer, 78 Cromac street
Clay, Samuel, poulterer, Calendar street ; residence, 6 Wellington street
Clay, Thomas, proprietor of Crown Inn, 30 Gamble street
Clayton, B., custom house officer and pensioner, 47 Trafalgar street
Clegg, Samuel, pensioner, 6 Wellington street
Cleland, James, haberdasher, 14 Peter's hill
Cleland, Robert, grocery and spirit store, 15 Skipper street
Cleland, William, cooper, 18 Gordon street
Cleland, Willliam, tailor, 8 Lower Stanfield street
Clements, Alexander, builder, Agnes place, Shankhill road
Clements, H., dressmaker, 61 Academy street

ALPHABETICAL DIRECTORY.

Clements, James, pawnbroker, 49 Market street
Clements, James, slater, 15 Charlemont street
Clements, James, publican, 12 Smithfield
Clements, John, tinsmith, 28 Smithfield
Clements, James, pawnbroker, 4 and 6 Lagan street
Clements, Robert, boarding house, Frederick street
Clements, Robert, builder, 7 Campbell's buildings, Townsend street
Clements, Robert, bricklayer, 7 Townsend street
Clements, Robert, publican, 7 Church street
Clements, Thomas, drayman, Chapel lane
Clements, William, grocer, 49 Verner street
Clendinning, Andw., wholesale & retail Manchester warehouse, 10 Rosemary st.
Clendinning, James, grocer and spirit dealer, 1 Leadbetter place
Clendinning, James, grocer and publican, 1 Fleming's place, Old Lodge road
Clendinning, John, merchant, 2 Arthur place; office, Donegall street place
Clendinning, Mrs., milliner, 14 Arthur street
Clendinning, William, wholesale haberdasher, North street, 17 May street
Clifford, John, excise officer, 2 Hope street
Clinton, Thomas, mechanic, Fleet street
Clokey, Fanny, dealer, 33 Little York street
Close, Brothers, woollendrapers, 26 High street
Close, James, grocer and publican, 61 Little York street
Close, James, butcher, 1 Hercules street and 43 Rosemary street
Close, John, joiner, 10 Earl street
Close, John, grocer, 76 Barrack street
Clotworthy, John, barber, 20¼ Little Patrick street
Clotworthy, Samuel, shipowner, Great Patrick street
Cloughley, Atchison, carpenter, 59 Mustard street
Clugston, Robert, weaver, 83 Durham street
Coates and Young, Lagan Foundry; also, Pilot street; Mr. Coates' residence, Glentoran; Mr. Young's residence, Lagan village
Coates and Shaw, muslin manufacturers, 14 Pottinger's entry
Coates, Arthur, brazier, 4 Wesley place
Coates, Edward J., of Coates and Shaw; residence, 8 Ship street
Coates, Francis, house, sign, and ornamental painter, and stained glass warehouse, 37 and 39 Castle street
Coates, George, provision merchant, 43 Trafalgar street; 81 York street
Coates, John, solicitor, 29 Arthur street
Coates, John, copper and tinsmith, 16 Torrens' market
Coates, James, collector of water tax, 23 Campbell's buildings, Townsend st.
Coates, William, clerk, 14 Garmoyle street
Coates, William, coppersmith and gasfitter, 12 Castle street
Coates, William, publican, Campbell's buildings, Conway street
Coburn, John, night constable, 29 Lower Stanfield street
Coburn, John, dealer, 59 Great Patrick street
Coburn, S., pawnbroker, 30 Smithfield
Coburn, William, grocer and night constable, 16 Melbourne street
Coburn, William John, coal merchant, May street
Cochran, James, tea, wine, and spirit merchant, 1 Castle place—6 Queen st.
Cochrane, Andrew, carpenter, 1 Washington street
Cochrane, Andrew, pensioner, 9 Joy's place
Cochrane, Brothers, & Co., sewed muslin manufacturers, 5 and 7 Bank lane; residence, 6 Glentilt place
Cochrane, David, house painter, 3 Townsend place
Cochrane, Henry, pensioner, 26 Vere street

Cochrane, Hugh, hairdresser, 12 Marquis street
Cochrane, Joseph, engineer, 39 Stanhope street
Cochrane, Mrs., tin worker, 19 Charlemont street
Cochrane, Mrs. Margaret, 18 Rochfort place
Cochrane, Samuel, spirit dealer, 1 Gordon street
Cochrane, Samuel, spirit dealer, 33 Hill street
Cochrane, Thomas, saddler, 38 Cromac street
Cochrane, William, tinsmith, 14 Great Edward street
Cockburn, John, superintendent of fire engines, 5 George's lane
Coey, Edward, provision merchant, 21 Gamble street; residence, Merville
Coey, James, jun., grain and flour merchant, and soap boiler, Queen's quay
Coey, James, boot and shoe warehouse, 12 Donegall place and 3 Calendar st.
Coey, James, mechanic, 3 Washington street
Coey, James, jun., provision merchant, Queen's quay, Ballymacarrett
Coey, James, jun., 35 Upper Queen street
Coey, James, flax dresser, 2 Letitia street
Coey, Mrs. Jane, 54 Joy street
Coffey, Jane, haberdasher, 9 Skipper street
Coffey, Mrs., 4 Sussex place
Coffey, William, music and musical instrument warehouse, 4 High street, and 25 Donegall place
Colburn, William, grocer and dairyman, 38 Green street
Coleman & Dobbin, wine and spirit merchants, 1 Church street
Coleman, James, of Coleman and Dobbin, wine & spirit merchants, 1 Church street; residence, 2 Crumlin terrace
Coleman, James, gentleman, 2 Wills' place
Coleman, John, merchant, 27 York street
Coleman, John, smith, 21 Greenland street
Coleman, Mrs., boarding house, 34 Hamilton street
Coleman, Patrick, spirit merchant, 71 and 73 Academy street
Coleman, Samuel, publican, 66 Barrack street
Colgan, Edward, butcher, 5 Hammond's court
Colgan, John, butcher and poulterer, 1 Corn market
Collier, Joseph, locksmith, 12 New Lodge road
Collier, Samuel, grocer, 41 Durham street
Collins, Bernard, mason, 14 Caxton street
Collins, Charles, painter, glazier, and paper hanger, 7 John street
Collins, Dr., 20 Queen street
Collins, Elizabeth, green grocer, 40 Grattan street
Collins, John, carpenter, 5 Roy street
Collins, John E., furniture dealer, 69 Smithfield
Collins, Joseph, painter, 18 Sussex street
Collins, Mrs., 14 Victoria place
Collins, Henry, cloth lapper, 2 Park street
Collins, Mrs., Pottinger Arms hotel, Pottinger's entry
Collins, Mrs. Maria, May street
Collins, Miss, 2 Seymour street
Collins, Miss, schoolmistress, May street National school, 19 May street
Collins, Robert, quay porter, 9 Sackville place
Collins, Rev. Joshua, Lisburn road
Collins, Thomas, print cutter, 7 Fleming's place, Old Lodge road
Collins, Thomas, sailor, 9 Cotton court
Collins, Wm. M., solicitor, 21 Arthur street; residence, Fitzwilliam place
Collins, William, fishmonger, 15 Black's place
Combe, James, Falls Foundry, 1 Ardmoulin place, Falls road

ALPHABETICAL DIRECTORY.

Combe, J., & Co., Falls foundry and machine manufactory, Falls road
Colvil, Archibald Campbell, merchant, Waring street—Glenfield place
Colvil, Auld, & Co., ship agents, commission & coal merchants, 74 Waring st.
Colvill, John, proprietor Royal Victoria Yacht Tavern, 15 Donegall quay
Colville, Auld, and Co., coal agents, Queen's quay, Ballymacarrett
Colville, James M., clerk, 35 Hamilton street
Colvin, Margaret, 91 Little York street
Colvin, Mary, lodgings, 22 Little York street
Colvin, James, lapper, 17 Catherine street North
Colpoy, Richard, wholesale flour and grain merchant, 112 North street
Colpoys, George, saddler and dealer, 29 Winetavern street
Condren, Charles, pensioner, 26 Union street
Conland, John, commission merchant, 92 Joy street ; office, Linen hall
Conlon, John, spirit dealer, 25 Pound street
Conlon, James, dealer in tow, 13 Rochfort place
Conly, Felix, carman, 74 Barrack street
Conn, James, clerk, 4 Friendly street
Conn, John, bookbinder, 48 Frederick street
Connell, Alexander, & Co., ship builders, Graving dock, Corporation street
Connell, Bridget, boarding house, 14 Stanhope street
Connell, Mrs., 44 Great George's street
Connell, William, land agent, 35 Corporation street
Connell, William, ship builder, 68 Nelson street
Connell, William, chandler, 12 Round entry
Connelly, Robert, dealer, 13 Lagan street
Connery, Dennis, machine master, 8 Conway street
Connery, Richard, commission agent, 15 College square East
Connolly, Henry, porter, 11 Valentine street
Connolly, John, flax, tow, and waste store, 14 Little Donegall street
Connolly, James, flax waste dealer, Saltpan row, Ballymacarrett
Connolly, Jane, 97 Millfield
Connolly, John, shoemaker, 21 Pound street
Connolly, Samuel, mechanic, 14 Stanley street
Connor, Catherine, grocer, 2 Wilson street
Connor, Daniel, sawyer, 20 Grattan street
Connor, David, flax and yarn commission agent, 27½ Ann street—Dundonald
Connor, E., grocer, 2 Boyd street
Connor, Foster, linen manufacturer, Linen Hall ; factory, M'Master's row—13 College street South
Connor, Hugh, marine store, 26 Telfair's entry
Connor, Hugh, salesman and traveller, 4 Riley's place
Connor, James, builder, 16 and 18 Grattan street
Connor, James, gardener, Hopeton place
Connor, James, grocer, 26 Conway street
Connor, James, Ulster Bank, 6 Botanic view
Connor, John, carpenter and builder, 37 York street
Connor, John, grocer, 1 East street
Connor, John, glass blower, 9 M'Crory's row, Ballymacrrett
Connor, Joseph, grocer and publican, 26 and 28 Verner street
Connor, James, pipe maker, 60 Carrickhill
Connor, Margaret, china mender, 2 Green's court
Connor, Robert, grocer, 14½ Peter's hill
Connor, William, carpenter, 29 Wall street
Convery, John, shoemaker, 22 Stanley street
Conville, John, car driver, 23 Edward street

Conway, Jane, spirit dealer and boardinghouse, 80 North street
Conway, John, pavier, 23 Little York street
Conway, Michael, weaver, 21 Brown street
Conway, Mary, 72 Little Donegall street
Conway, Patrick, hay and straw dealer, 20 Smithfield
Cook, Alexander, grocer, 27 Stanley street
Cook, Margaret, green grocer, 9 Devis street
Cooke, Elizabeth, dressmaker, Bridge end, Ballymacarrett
Cooke, James, plumber, 9 North Boundary street
Cooke, James, 19 Collingwood street
Cooke, James, tailor, Bridge end, Ballymacarrett
Cooke, Rev. Henry, D.D., LL.D., Ormeau road
Cooke, William, spirit dealer, 34 John street
Cooney, James, butcher, 23 Hercules street
Cooper, David, joiner and builder, 20 Great Patrick street
Cooper, Hugh, cowkeeper, 34 Alexander street
Cooper, John, forester, 4 Moore's place
Cooper, Joseph, sawyer, 11 Collingwood street
Cooper, James, grocer, Ballymacarrett
Cooper, Mrs., 50 Great George's street
Cooper, Mrs., 9 Botanic view
Cooper, Miss, school, 51 Boyd street
Cooper, Margaret, 9 Duffy's place
Cooper, Samuel, shoemaker, 24 Samuel street
Cooper, Samuel, stabling yard, 20 Samuel street
Cooper, Thomas, cooper, 18 Stanhope street
Cooper, William, merchant, 24 College square North
Cooper, William, carpenter, 56 Boyd street
Copeland, John, carpenter, 68 Cromac street
Copeland, Mrs., 2 Eagleson place
Copeland, R., clothier and tailor, 8 Pottinger's entry
Corbett, William, 14 Cromac street
Corbitt, Jane and Eliza, dressmakers and milliners, 14 Cromac street
Corbitt, Thomas, merchant, 5 Clarendon place
Cordukes, Jonathan, provision merchant, Nile street—Spafield, Holywood
Corke, John, musician, 4 Stanfield street
Corr, John, flax dresser, 1 New Durham street
Corr, John, coffin maker, and scantling yard, 6 and 8 Ritchie's place
Corrigan, Adam, spirit dealer, 45 Nelson street
Corrigan, Andrew, painter, 8 Boyd street
Corrigan, Charlotte, widow, 122 Carrick hill
Corrigan, James, sawyer, 62 Vere street
Corry, James P., and Co., timber and slate merchants, 1 Corporation square
  4 Franklin place
Corry, John, hackler, 6 Leeds street
Corry, Robert, merchant, 10 The Crescent, Botanic road
Corry, T. C. S., surgeon and chemist, 13 Victoria street—34 Chichester st.
Cosgrove, Hugh, dealer and marine store, 26 and 37 Pottinger's entry
Cosgrove, John, grocer and publican, 16 Verner street
Costley, John, seedsman, 23 North street
Cotter, John, nailer, 3 Police square
Cotter, Mrs., boarding house, 39 Little May street
Cotter, Robert, grocer, 21 College square
Coulter, Andrew, grocer and spirit dealer, 29 Durham street
Coulter, George, sawyer, 19 Moffet street

Coulter, Patrick, wireworker and confectioner, 102 Millfield
Coulter, Richard, sawyer, 75 Little Patrick street
Coulter, Sarah, boarding house, 21 Little May street
Court, James, proprietor curds and cream gardens, Ballymacarrett
Courtney, William, stone cutter, 4 Glentilt place, Old Lodge road
Cousins, James, 18 Little May street
Cousins, John and W. H., wholesale and retail grocers and cheesemongers, 75 North street; 50 Nelson street
Cowan, Andrew, J.P., county Down; 9 Chichester street
Cowan, Andrew, spirit dealer, Shankhill road
Cowan, Frederick, tailor, 35 Hill street
Cowan, Jane, boarding house, 18 Little Edward street
Cowan, Samuel, merchant, Cromac lodge; office, 27 Ann street
Cowan, Wm., grocer, wine, and spirit merchant, 19 Church lane—31 May st.
Cowan, Wm. & Co., flax spinners, Whiteabbey, 9 Police square, & 17 York st.
Cowan, William, grocer, and spirit dealer, 5 Winetavern street
Cowden, Jane, lodgings, 5 Union street
Cowden, Matthew, cooper, 76 Green street
Coyle, Bernard, coal dealer, 59 New Lodge road
Coyle, John, grocer and spirit dealer, 13 Cromac road
Coyne, James, pensioner, 23 Hamilton's place
Crace, Henry, coal merchant, 7 Prince's dock; residence, 10 Queen street
Craig, A. W. and Co., flax spinners, Falls road; town office, 17 Rosemary st.
Craig, Hugh, coal factor, Queen's quay; York street
Craig, John, engineer, 26 Cullingtree street
Craig, John, wholesale and retail ironmonger, 15 Bridge st.; residence, 17 Great George's street
Craig, John, clerk, 9 Washington street
Craig, John, market constable, 1 William street
Craig, James, gentleman, 29 Hamilton street
Craig, Liddle, and Crymble, piano forte manufacturers, 3 Fountain street
Craig, Mrs. Jane, 7 William's row
Craig, Miss, 35 Earl street
Craig, Mrs. Helen, 65 Joy street
Craig, Robert, carpenter, 41 Pound street
Craig, Thomas, grocer and spirit dealer, 186 North street
Craig, William, helper, 1 Ross street
Cramsie, Daniel, car owner, Police square
Cramsie, John, green grocer, 56 York street
Cramsie, John C., wine merchant and notary public, 74 Waring st.—May st.
Cranagh, Anthony, hairdresser, 10 Skipper street
Crang, Mr., surgeon, 104 Donegall street
Crangle, James, sea captain, 16 Pilot street
Cranston, Elizabeth, publican, 25 Lancaster street
Cranston, Wm. and Alex. J., solicitors, 33 Arthur street
Craufurd, Mrs., ladies' seminary, 7 Adelaide place
Craw, William, ropemaker, 47 Boundary street
Crawford and Co., ærated water manufacturers, 3 Church street
Crawford and Russell, solicitors, 24 Arthur street
Crawford, Alexander, manufacturing chemist, drysalter, &c., 26 Mill street—Mount Charles, Malone
Crawford, Alexander, starch works, 9 Bradford's entry, off Millfield
Crawford, Arthur, & Co., drapers, 18 Waring street—Old Lodge road
Crawford, Arthur, iron and tin plate merchant, 131 North street
Crawford, Ann, eating house, 55 Alexander street
Crawford, Eliza, grocer, 17 Mill street

Crawford, Francis, whitesmith, 25 Winetavern street—50 Smithfield
Crawford, George, servant, 10 Wellington square
Crawford, Hugh, clerk, 113 Lower Malone
Crawford, Hugh, Wolfhill
Crawford, Hugh, grocer, 157 North street
Crawford, Hugh, clerk, Mount Pottinger, Ballymacarrett
Crawford, James, ship chandler, 13 and 15 Corporation street
Crawford, James, grocer, Cromac street
Crawford, Jas., wine and spirit merchant, 1 Calender street—26 Donegall pl.
Crawford, John, lodging house, 60 Little Donegall street
Crawford, Jane, bakery and flour stores, 113 North street
Crawford, John, sergeant-at-mace, 19 Rosemary street
Crawford, John, sewed muslin manufacturer, 25 Gt. Patrick st.—7 Adelaide pl.
Crawford, John, boot and shoemaker, 22 Samuel street
Crawford, John, jun., grocer and spirit dealer, 25 Berry street
Crawford, Miss M., lodgings, 48 Talbot street
Crawford, Mrs. Arthur, 15 Joy street
Crawford, Robert, clerk, 27 Dock street
Crawford, Samuel, builder, 32 Great George's street
Crawford, Sarah, milliner, 46 Ann street
Crawford, William, tailor, 7 High street
Crawford, William, butler, 42 Valentine street
Crawford, William John, linen lapper, 2 Hamilton place
Crawford, William, builder, Antrim road
Crawford, Wm. John, Northern Bank, 15 Joy street
Crawshaw, George, engine builder, 11 Sir Henry's buildings, Ballymacarrett
Creen, John, mate, Fleet street
Creen, Robert, marine store, &c., 96 Corporation street
Creen, Richard, dealer, 20 Pottinger's entry
Creen, William, ship carpenter, Meadow street
Creeny, John, coal porter, 17 Peter's hill
Creeth, Richard, commission merchant, Waring street—30 Hamilton street
Cregan, Henry, butcher, 13 Long lane
Cregan, Terence, gateman in Distillery, 18 M'Millen's place
Crenard, Daniel, guard on Ballymena railway, 5 Caxton street
Crilley, James, boot and shoemaker, 6 Russell street
Crilly, Joseph, flax dresser, 5 Hamilton's place
Croan, William, brush maker, 11 Economy place
Croft, Joseph, bricklayer, M'Larnon's buildings, Ballymacarrett
Croft, Joseph, weigher in potato market, 12 Melbourne street
Croft, William, shoemaker, 16 Telfair's entry
Crofton, Edward, 38 Little Patrick street
Crolly, Michael, bricklayer, 17 Pound street
Cromie, Hugh, cooper, 26 Shipboy street
Crommelin, N. Delacherois, York st. flax spinning mills; residence, Cliftonville
Cronan, Robert, writing clerk, 9 Lower Standfield street
Crone, Richard, writing clerk, 22 Robert street
Crooks, Hugh, sexton May street Presbyterian Church, 47 Little May street
Crooks, John, saw maker and repairer, 16 Skipper street
Crooks, John, spirit dealer, 61 Lower Malone
Crooks, Robert, grocer, 4 Bond street
Crooks, William, carpenter, 32 Brown street
Crosbie, J., carter, 46 Stanhope street
Cross, Mary Ann, 32 Lancaster street
Crossen, Margaret, grocer and publican, Lagan village, Ballymacarrett

ALPHABETICAL DIRECTORY.

Crossett, Alex., collector of police rate and haberdasher, 38 North Queen st.
Crossford, Thomas, agent to J. Tallis & Co., London publishers, 56 Nelson st.
Crossley, Charles, hat manufacturer, 6 Meadow street—8 Orr's entry
Crossley, Edward, flax dresser, Falls road
Crossley, Michael, plasterer, 30 Melbourne street
Crossley, William, cooper, 11 William's lane
Crothers, James, weaver, 21 Sackville street
Crothers, Mrs., grocer, 60 Cromac street
Crothers, Moses, grocer, 69 Donegall street
Crow, James, 27 Boyd street
Crow, William, carpenter, 14 Charles street
Crowe, John, ship carpenter, 11 Union place
Crowe, William, excise officer, 11 Riley's place
Crowell, James, stabling yard, May street
Crozier, Edward, carpenter, 24 Smithfield
Crozier, James A., gentleman, 6 Ingram place, Donegall pass
Crozier, John, warper, 42 Talbot street
Crozier, William, 5 Washington street, overseer
Crozier, William, gentleman, 4 Windsor place
Cruikshanks, Mrs., school, 101 Donegall street
Crummey, Daniel, green grocer, 5 York street market
Crummey, Mary, sewer, 33 Caxton street
Crymble, J., day constable, 31 Little George's street
Crymble, Lucius, precentor, 9 Lancaster street
Crymble, Matthew, of Craig, Liddle, & Crymble, Fountain st.—9 Lancaster st.
Crymble, Miss, dressmaker, 9 Lancaster street
Crymble, Mrs. Ann, 100 Cromac street
Cuddy, Hugh, spirit store, 36 Ann street
Cuddy, John, merchant and shipowner, 42 Church lane, 9 Upper Church lane, & Queen's quay, Ballymacarrett; residences: Summerhill, co. Down, and 1 Clarendon place
Cuddy, John, spirit store, 59 Academy street
Culbert, Thomas, grocer, 90 Millfield
Cullen, Constantine S., assistant in Mr. Wallace's office, Victoria street
Cullen, Daniel, tailor, 58 Townsend street
Cullen, John, mechanic, 2 Greenland street
Cullimore, Miss, school, 12 York street
Cullin, Peter, dealer, 52 North Queen street
Culloden, Joseph, 9 Arthur street
Culloden, Miss, baby linen warehouse, 9 Arthur street
Culvinor, Alexander, revenue officer, 49 Trafalgar street
Cumine, James A., electrical and optical warehouse, 168 North street
Cuming, J., grocer, wine and spirit merchant, 55 Donegall street
Cummerford, James, sweep, 11 M'Tier's court
Cummin, Mrs., 2 Spamount
Cumming, Brothers, tea dealers, grocers, &c., 83 Corn market
Cumming, Courtland, carpenter, 25 Green street
Cumming, Edward, clothes dealer, 48 Lettuce hill, and 49 Smithfield
Cunningham, J. & T., grain stores, Chapel lane
Cunningham, James, plasterer, 14 Roy's court
Cunningham, John, stokerer, Roy's court
Cunningham, John, Glenwood mills, merchant; residence, Glenwood
Cunningham, Josias, and Co., brokers, agents, and general commission merchants, stock and share brokers, 41 Waring street—37 King street
Cunningham, John, Linen hall and The Castle, Castle Buildings—Macedon

Cunningham, Mrs., 22 Queen street
Cunningham, Mrs., 23 Tomb street
Cunningham, Peter, breweryman, 27 Charlemont street
Cunningham, Patrick, seaman, 12 Gamble street
Cunningham, Robert, boot and shoemaker, 6½ Talbot street
Cunningham, Robert, mariner, 15 West street
Cunningham, Samuel, wine and spirit merchant, 6 Mill st. and Victoria st.
Cunningham, Samuel, general merchant and commission agent, Glenwood
Cunningham, S., wine and spirit merchant, 1½ Queen street—Victoria street
Cunningham, Thomas, lessee Theatre Royal, 1 Arthur street
Cunningham, Thomas, proprietor of the Queen's Arms hotel, 2 York street and
Cunningham, Waddell, gentleman, 52 Mill street   [75 Donegall street
Cunningham, William, coach trimmer, 7 Hill street
Cunningham, William Crozier, solicitor & deputy clerk of the peace, 4 York st.
Cunningham, William, stone mason, 2 Glentilt place, Old Lodge road
Cuppage, John, flax and yarn stores, 9 and 10 Donegall street place—Lurgan
Curran, Bernard, ship carpenter, 9 Economy place
Curran, Catherine, fruit dealer, 12 & 13 Castle market—13 William st. South
Curran, Elizabeth, grocer and spirit dealer, Keenan's place, Ballymacarrett
Curran, James, shoemaker, 58 Hudson's entry
Curran, John, muslin lapper, Elliott's court, 100 Peter's hill
Curran, John, boarding house, 3 Ritchie's place
Curran, Michael, miller, in Belfast mills, 12 Devis street
Curran, Waring, druggist, &c., 22 Bridge street—99 Donegall street
Curran, William John, mechanic, 60 Stanhope street
Curell, Daniel, jun., & Co., Linenhall street factory—8 Royal terrace
Curell, J. & M., & Co., merchants, Linenhall; residence, 4 Murray's terrace
Curoe, John, mechanic, 9 Sarah street
Curoe, Rev. William, 97 Donegall street
Currie, Hugh, hardware and ironmongery warehouse, 72 High street
Currie, William, linen lapper, Shankhill road
Curry, Jasper, wood turner, 47 Market street
Curry, John, damask weaver, 27 M'Tier's street
Curry, Mary, shopwoman, 44 Joy street
Curry, Richard, publican, 103 Lower Malone
Curry, William, stonecutter, 6 Glentilt place, Old Lodge road
Cush, Michael, coal agent, Queen's quay, Ballymacarrett
Cushnahan, E., grocer, 81 Carrickbill
Cushley, Thomas, tailor, 15 Smithfield

Dale, P., Antrim cottage, tailor, 15 Smithfield
Dale, Robert, ship carpenter, 50 Vere street
Dale, William, broker and auctioneer, 4 Donegall st.—109 Donegall st.
Dalgleish, Alexander, grocer, 104 Peter's hill
Dalley, Edward, fruiterer and dealer, Victoria street—3 Verner street
Dalton, Mrs. Amelia, 1 James's street South
Daly, Daniel, board and lodgings, Bridge end, Ballymacarrett
Daly, Edward, surgeon, North Street Medical Hall, 202 North street
Daly, Francis, grocer and publican, 57 Union street
Daly, Hugh, turner, 3 Falls court, Durham street
Daly, John, upholsterer, 18 Wall street
Daly, James, pensioner, 80 Great George's street
Daly, James, ship owner, 23 Earl street
Daly, Patrick, dealer, 25 New Lodge road
Daly, William, joiner, 4 Melbourne street

ALPHABETICAL DIRECTORY.

Daly, William, cowkeeper, 46 Townsend street
Dalzell, Catherine, mangler, 49, Millfield
Dalzell, Miss, dressmaker, 31 Joy street
Dalzell, Robert, carpenter, Roy street
Daniel, Jackson, mechanic, 7 Wilson street
Daniel, John, provision store, Falls road
Darby, John, weaver, 60 Little Patrick street
Darcy, Patrick, foreman printer, 3 North Boundary street
Dargan, Charles, clerk, 15 Shankhill road
Dargan, Chichester, writing clerk, 43 Stanley street
Dargan, James, shoemaker, 8 Caxton street
Dargan, Richard, grocer and spirit store, 8½ Robert street and 18 Talbot st.
Darling, John R., grocer, 112 Old Lodge road
Darragh, William, caretaker, Museum, 7 College square North
Davey, Patrick, spirit dealer, Winecellar entry
Davey, William, painter, 2 Murphy street
Davidson and Co., grocers and spirit dealers, 48 Hercules street
Davidson, Alexander C., flax merchant, 5 Linenhall street
Davidson, Alexander, ship carpenter, 44 Trafalgar street
Davidson, Alexander, baker, 69 Old Lodge road
Davidson, John, excise officer, 30 Townsend street
Davidson, John, iron plainer, Short strand, Ballymacarret
Davidson, John and Co., grocers, 15½ Castle place
Davidson, James, compositor, 2 James's place
Davidson, James, flour miller, Bridge end, Ballymacarrett
Davidson, James, saddler and harness maker, 48 North street
Davidson, James, ropemaker, Wheeler's place, Ballymacarrett
Davidson, Mrs. Thomas, 5 Royal terrace
Davis, Arthur, master mariner, 9 Stanley place
Davis, Chs. N., furrier and shoe warehouse, 24 Castle place—3 Posnett's place,
Davis, Eliza, straw bonnet, millinery, and umbrella warehouse, 96 High st.
Davis, George, proprietor Plough Hotel, 5 to 9 Corn market
Davis, H. cooper, 35 Barrack street
Davis, John, provision merchant, 85½ York street
Davis, Mary, M'Crory's row, Ballymacarrett
Davis, Mrs. 64 York street
Davis, Mrs., 27 King street
Davis, Robert, cashier in Lagan Foundry, Lagan village, Ballymacarrett
Davis, William John, nailer, 34 Brown street
Davis, William, message porter, California street
Davis, Wm., watch glass maker, and glass cutter, Bridge end, Ballymacarrett
Davis, William, solicitor, 23 Arthur st.; residence, Greenville, Ballymacarrett
Davis, William, coach painter, 36 Alexander street
Davis, William, solicitor, Arthur street—Greenville, Ballymacarrett
Davison and Torrens, solicitors, 25 Donegall place
Davison, Gawn, gentleman, Strawberry hall, Ballymacarrett
Davison, John, clerk, 41 Tomb street
Davison, John, block cutter, Conway street
Davison, James, constable, 25 Friendly street
Davison, John, rope and twine manufacturer, 95 Queen's sq. & 3 Prince's ct.
Davison, John, tailor, 12 Mill street
Davison, John, builder, 137 Durham street
Davison, James and George, brassfounders, 15 Henrietta street
Davison, Mrs. M. A., boarding house, 51 Joy street
Davison, Patrick, porter, 32 Boyd street

ALPHABETICAL DIRECTORY.

Davison, William, marine store, 18 Grattan street
Davy, Arthur, butcher, 74 Hercules street
Davy, Bernard, tobacco spinner, 47 Mill street
Davy, Charles, butcher, 19 Hercules street
Davy, John, butcher, 79 Hercules street
Davy, James, butcher, 13 Hercules street
Davy, John, butcher, 87 Hercules, street
Davy, William, butcher, 41 Hercules street
Davy, Wiliam, painter, 2 Stanfield street
Dawson, Edward, plasterer, Falloon's court
Dawson, John, pensioner, Ballynafeigh
Dawson, William, grocer and spirit dealer, 1 and 3 Melbourne street
Day and Bottomley, wholesale woollen merchants, Calender street
Day, Christopher, stone cutter, Ross street
Deering, John, jeweller, 38 Nelson street
Delany, Ann, lodgings, 8 Prince's street
Delany, Jane, 42 Frederick street
Delany, William, 21 North Queen street
Delawney, Lewis, manager, Clonard print works, Falls road
Dempsey, Clara, 21 Ritchie's place
Dempster, William, cloth lapper, 1 Unity street
Dempster, William, carpenter, 19 Henrietta street
Dennis, Mary, lodging house, 16 Millfield
Dennison, Mr., in Browne, Reid and Co.'s, Victoria terrace, Old Malone road
Dennison, Robert, post-office, 3 Pakenham place
Denvir, John, clerk, Nelson's buildings, Shankhill road
Denvir, Mary, 18 Pottinger's entry
Denvir, Patrick, carpenter, 30 Friendly street
Denvir, Patrick, baker and flour dealer, 97 North street
Denvir, Right Rev. Dr., Roman Catholic Bishop, 97 Donegall street
Derby, Thomas, cabinet and cane chair maker, 5 Nelson street
Devanny, William, blacksmith, 8 Mustard street
Devenport, William, mechanic, 1 Valentine street
Devine, Ann, dressmaker, 3 Millfield
Devine, Bartholemew, porter in Queen's College, 7 Malone place
Devine, Leckey, porter, 9 Old Lodge road
Devlin, Bernard, hardware and furniture dealer, 50 Smithfield
Devlin, Charles, stabling yard, 32 Chichester street
Devlin, Eliza, dealer, 30 Lancaster street
Devlin, Francis, weaver, 81 Old Lodge road
Devlin, Henry, bottling store, 4 Pottinger's entry
Devlin, Henry James, bottling house, Hamilton's court
Devlin, John, dealer, Shankhill road
Devlin, James, porter, 38 Edward street
Devlin, James, tailor, 49 Barrack street
Devlin, John, writing clerk, 26 John street
Devlin, John, mechanic, 19 Earl lane
Devlin, James, carman, 36 Green street
Devlin, John, auctioneer, &c., 2 Castle lane and 8½ Donegall place
Devlin, Meredith, weaver and dealer, 17 Lower Malone road
Devlin, Patrick, plasterer, 15 Sarah street
Devlin, Patrick, shoemaker, Conway street
Devlin, Patrick, butler, 16 Grace street
Devlin, Patrick, publican, 2 Pottinger's entry
Devlin, Thomas, druggist and grocer, North street—9 Great George's street

Devlin, William, customhouse clerk, 3 William's place
Dewer, James, mechanic, 1 Johnston's place, Ballymacarrett
Dickey, Adam, poor rate collector, 15 College square North
Dickey, Alexander, bursar Queen's College, University square
Dickey, Alexander and Co., wholesale grocers and oil merchants, Victoria st.
Dickey, James, stone cutter, 22 Little Patrick street
Dickey, Nathaniel, 63 North street and 18 Church street
Dickey, Mrs. Rebecca M., 1 Malone place
Dickey, William, carpenter, 39 Boundary street
Dickie, Charles, forge, 2 Police place
Dickie, Dr., professor of natural history, Queen's College, 4 Botanic view
Dickie, James, blacksmith, 13 Market street
Dickinson, John, & Co., wholesale stationers, 4 Donegall square North
Dickson, Alex., of Farrell & Co., seed merchants, 2 High st.—Ballycloughan
Dickson, Alexander, nurseryman, and fruit dealer, 18 Castle market
Dickson, Arthur, spirit dealer, 67 Corporation square
Dickson, Gawn, cabinet maker, 48 Stanhope street
Dickson, Henry, wine, spirit, flax & corn merchant, Victoria st.—6 Albert place
Dickson, Hugh, fruiterer, 10 Hammond's court
Dickson, John, carpenter, 72 Vere street
Dickson, John, bookbinder, 43 Boyd street
Dickson, John, millwright, 7 Trafalgar street
Dickson, James, publican, 128 Ann street
Dickson, Mathew, jeweller, 3 John street
Dickson, Mrs., lodgings, 4 Bradford square
Dickson, Mrs., medicine warehouse, 73 North street
Dickson, Mrs., 7 Victoria place
Dickson, Mrs. Ann Jane, 75 Joy street
Dickson, Mrs., lodgings, 72 Great George's street
Dickson, R. and H., provision stores, 27 Nelson street
Dickson, Simon, bleacher, 49 Carrickhill
Dickson, William, haberdasher, 5 Unity street
Dickson, William, master mariner, Portview, Ballymacarrett
Dignan, John, carpenter, 2 Smithfield—9 Letitia street
Dill, Dr. R.S., surgeon, 42 Upper Arthur street
Dillon, Ann, lodgings, 19 Devis street, Falls road
Dillon, Alexander, moulder, 39 Wall street
Dillon, Henry, basket maker, 22 Bank lane
Dillon, James, hatter, 34 High street; residence, 5 Malone place
Dillon, John, publican, 1 George's lane
Dillon, Nicholas, basket maker, 6 Smithfield and 12 Torrens' market
Dillon, R. M., solicitor, at Davison and Torrens'; residence, Holywood
Dillon, William, solicitor, 31 Arthur street; residence, Roseville, Whiteabbey
Dinley, Joseph, clerk, 8 M'Master's row
Dinnan, John, solicitor, 18 Arthur street, and 22 Middle Gardner st., Dublin
Dinnen, David, butcher, 5 Castle market
Dinnen, David, butcher, Market street
Dinnen, James, butcher, 33 Talbot street
Dinnen, James, butcher, 3 Castle market
Dinnen, James, revenue officer, 8 Nile street
Dinsmore, James, painter, and sexton in St. George's Church, 9 Prince's st.
Disney, Miss, 28 College street
Dixon, Archibald, blacksmith, 3 Hamilton's place
Dixon, Archibald, carman, 27 Brown street
Dixon, Alexander, millwright, 5 California street

Dixon, Daniel, poulterer, Ormond market
Dixon, James, caretaker Protestant Hall, 80 Donegall street
Dixon, John, carman, 8 Green's court
Dixon, Mary, dealer, 25 North Queen street
Doak, John, sawyer, 6 M'Auley street
Dobbie, James A., draper, in J. Young & Co.'s, Herdman's buildings
Dobbin, Alexander, grocer, 41 Townsend street
Dobbin, Alexander Charles, 14 Castle lane, and 8 Inns quay, Dublin
Dobbin, Clotworthy, brewer, 43 Smithfield ; residence, 12 Howard street
Dobbin, H., of Coleman and Dobbin's, 1 Church street
Dobbin, James Anderson, draper, Herdman's buildings
Dobbin, Mrs., 18 Great Patrick street
Dobbin, Wm., wholesale grocer, druggist, & drysalter, 18,20,45,& 47 North st
Dobbin, William, druggist and general merchant, 102 Donegall street
Dobbs, John, grocer, 31 Stanfield street
Dodd, Jane, 116 Lower Malone
Dodd, Samuel, pensioner, 17 Mustard street
Dodd, William, night constable, 13 Roy street
Dodds, Jane, dealer, Short strand, Ballymacarrett
Dodds, Joseph, ship carpenter, Artillery street
Doey, Hugh, bricklayer, 30 M'Millan's place
Dogherty, Henry, porter, 29 Police square
Dogherty, Hugh, grocer, 32 Hamill street
Dogherty, John, 51 Carrickhill
Dogherty, John, porter, 32 Millfield
Dogherty, John, fruit merchant, 39 May street
Dogherty, James, servant, 20 M'Millan's place
Dogherty, Patrick, plasterer, 1 Russell street
Dogherty, Patrick, dealer, 54 North Queen street
Dogherty, William, fowl and fruit stores, 14 and 16 May street
Dogherty, William, tailor, 22 Union street
Dogherty, William, general merchant, 37 May street
Doherty, Andrew, whitesmith, 48 Smithfield
Doherty, Ann, dealer, 3 New Lodge road
Doherty, Ellen, dealer, 36 North Thomas street
Doherty, Henry, car owner, 34 Little York street
Doherty, John, old iron dealer, 53 Smithfield
Doherty, James, machine master, 45 Falls road, Devis street
Doherty, Rose Ann, spirit dealer, 27 and 29 Peter's hill
Dolan, Matthew, whitesmith, 13 Bank lane
Dolan, Miles, clothes dealer, 8 Berry street
Dolway, William, tobacco spinner, 12 Little Edward street
Donaghy, Ann, 9 New Durham street
Donaghy, Charles, shoemaker, 20 Brown street
Donaghy, James, chandler, 26 Charles street
Donaghy, James, porter, 48 Verner street
Donaghy, Patrick, baker, 26 Greenland street
Donaghy, Robert, lamplighter, 24 Bond street
Donald, John, watchman, 11 Sackville street
Donald, William, agent for J. Robinson & Sons, Glasgow, sewed muslin manufacturers, 47 Great Patrick street
Donaldson, Eliza, lodging house, 20 Curtis street
Donaldson, Foster, lodging house, 51 Mill street
Donaldson, H. W., spirit dealer, 1 Ann street
Donaldson, James, foreman sailmaker, 25 Edward street

Donaldson, John, smith, 24 Cargill street
Donaldson, John, butler, 18 Grace street
Donaldson, John, nailer, 61 Talbot street
Donaldson, Miss, milliner, 8 Arthur square
Donaldson, Mrs., dressmaker, 20 Stanley street
Donaldson, W., horse repository, 33 Chichester street—8 Arthur square
Donaldson, William, salesman, Mountpottinger, Ballymacarrett
Donnelly, Anne, dealer, 14 M'Auley street
Donnelly, Anthony, pork cutter, 12 Moffet street
Donnelly, Bridget, Wellington square
Donnelly, Constantine, carpenter, 11 Smithfield—2 Miller's lane
Donnelly, Edward, engineer, 79 Boundary street
Donnelly, Edward, grocer and publican, 68 Peter's hill
Donnelly, Edward, publican, 104 Old Lodge road
Donnelly, Ellen, dealer, 35 West street
Donnelly, Francis, carpenter, 23 Durham street
Donnelly, Henry, stonemason, 58 Boundary street
Donnelly, James, sawyer, 7 Coates street
Donnelly, James, publican, 49 Little George's street
Donnelly, James, boot and shoemaker, 23 West street
Donnelly, James, pensioner, 11 Frederick street
Donnelly, John, dyer, 31 Bank lane
Donnelly, John, gasfitter, 22 Charlemont street
Donnelly, Peter, dealer, 42 Peter's hill
Donnelly, Peter, spirit dealer, Mustard street
Donnelly, Peter, shoemaker, 17 Winetavern street
Donnelly, Robert, confectioner and cigar dealer, 4 Bridge street—7 Joy street
Donnelly, Robert, servant, 9 Galway street
Donning, James, police inspector, 26 Lower Stanfield street
Donoghue, Hugh, dealer, 22 New Lodge road
Donohoe, Felix, hackler, 9 Pound street
Donovan, James William, Scripture reader, 3 Wesley place
Dooary, William, coachman, 59 Little Patrick street
Doody, John, boot and shoemaker, 30 John street
Doole, Andrew, spirit dealer and boarding house, 14 Store lane
Dooley, James, stonecutter and huckster, 11 Curtis street
Doran, Bernard, fowl dealer, 25 Stanfield street
Doran, Bernard, dealer, 27 Samuel street
Doran, Bernard, cow keeper, 9 Annette street
Doran, Edward, mason, 39 Falls road
Doran, John, manager in foundry, 8 Campbell's buildings, Townsend street
Doran, John, clerk, 8 Campbell's buildings, Shankhill road
Doran, Miss, teacher at the Infant school, Pilot street
Doran, William, mechanic, Shankhill road
Dorman, Samuel, weaver, 26½ Friendly street
Dornan, Alexander, green grocer, 29 Millfield
Dornan, Betsy, dealer, 44 Mustard street
Dornan, Hugh, musician, 1 Edward street
Dornan, James, rope and twine manufactory, 74 North street
Dornan, James, ropemaker, Short strand, Ballymacarrett
Dornan, Mrs., 3 Torrens' market
Dornan, Robert, grocer and spirit dealer, 11 King street
Dorrian, E., surgeon and apothecary, 68 Donegall street
Dorrian, Miss, 20 Fountain place
Dougal, James, grocer, 65 Millfield

Dougal, Mary, 69 Millfield
Dougall, John, cooper, 5 Morrow's entry
Dougan, Eliza, dealer, 17 Samuel street
Dougherty, Arthur, sizer, 11 Ritchie's place
Dougherty, Daniel, mechanic, 77 Boundary street
Dougherty, Edward, weaver, 53 Vere street
Dougherty, John, painter, 11 Elliott's court
Dougherty, John, painter, 3 Murphy's lane
Dougherty, John, spirit dealer, 120 North street
Dougherty, James, tide waiter, 2 Dock lane
Dougherty, Mrs., 34 York street
Dougherty, Patrick, grocer and spirit dealer, 35 May street
Dougherty, Sarah, dealer, 5 Moffett street
Dougherty, William, lapper, 10 East street
Dougherty, William, teacher, 30 Durham street
Dougherty, William, cabinetmaker, 5 Townsend place
Douglas, Alexander, salesman, 1 Brougham street
Douglas, Arthur, house painter, 18 Curtis street
Douglas, John, salesman in Mr. Kennedy's warehouse, 15 Gt. Patrick street
Douglas, John, mechanic, 31 New Lodge road
Douglas, John, engine driver, 20 Greenland street
Douglas, John, wholesale and family grocer, 11 Waring street
Douglas, John, engineer, 14 Greenland street
Douglas, John, 7 Meadow street
Douglas, Samuel, butler, 24 Durham street
Douglas, Samuel, 107 Donegall street
Douglas, Thomas, carpenter, 35 Nelson street
Douglas, William, iron and coal agent, 20 Waring st.—3 Glenfield place
Douglas, William, painter, Peel's place
Douglas, William, flax bundler, Falls road
Douglas, William, yarn bundler, Falls road
Douglas, William, dealer, 25 Little Patrick street
Douglass, Alexander, W., ropemaker, New road, Ballymacarrett
Douglass, Miss J. A., tuscan & straw bonnet maker, Bridge end, Ballymacarrett
Douglass, Samuel, butler, 24 Durham street
Douglass, Wm., provision mercht. & commis. agent, 59,61 & 63 Corporation st.
Douris, Patrick, lodging house, 42 John street
Dover, Thomas, currier, 11 Little May street
Dowds, Patrick, overseer, 53 Conway street
Dowling, Arthur, poulterer & feather mercht., 11 Corn market—Franklin pl.
Dowling, John, writing clerk, Donegall pass
Dowling, Thomas, customhouse officer, Cranston place, Antrim road
Downey, Henry, coach driver, 2 Catherine street
Downey, John, gasfitter, 59 Peter's hill
Downey, John, pensioner, 19 Galway court
Downey, J., clerk *Banner* office, 41 Brown street
Downey, James, foreman hackler, 20 Glentilt place, Old Lodge road
Downey, Martin, excise officer, 82 Joy street
Downey, Thomas, ironmonger, 53 Edward street
Downing, James, provision merchant, 8 Academy street
Downing, Rev. Samuel, Methodist minister, 21 Brougham street
Downing, William, iron works, 3 Prince's dock
Downing, William, Grape Tavern, 3 Corn market
Downing, William, clerk, 23 Spencer street
Downing, William, wine and spirit stores, Queen's Quay, Ballymacarrett

ALPHABETICAL DIRECTORY.

Downs, Archibald, engineer, 14 Thomas street
Downs, William, pork cutter, 33 Mustard street
Doyle and Young, watch and clockmakers, 49 Mill street
Doyle, Andrew, ironmoulder, 28 Melbourne street
Doyle, John, baker, 12 Little York street
Doyle, James, baker, 12 Boyd street
Doyle, Mrs., nurse tender, 43 Mill street
Doyle, Thomas, baker, Bridge end, Ballymacarrett
Drain, Hugh, cartwright, Shankhill road
Drain, John, butcher, 55 Hercules street
Drain, John, cow keeper, 48 Townsend street
Draper, Catherine, lodgings, 25 Trafalgar street
Drennan, Dr. John, 23 Chichester street
Drennan, James, cartwright, Short strand, Ballymacarret
Drennan, Michael, clerk, 72 Nelson street
Drennan, Nevin, carpenter, Ashmore street, Conway street
Drew, Rev. Thomas, D.D., 9 Victoria place
Druitt, George, writing clerk, 1 Crumlin place
Druitt, Wm., linen merchant, Donegall st.—Mountpottinger, Ballymacarrett
Druitt, W. & R., linen merchants, 32 Donegall street—Mount Pottinger
Drummond, Dr. James, 8 College square North
Drummond, John, clothes dealer, 35 Berry street
Drummond, Robert, gentleman, William's place
Drummond, Thomas, spirit dealer, 30 Verner street
Duff, Alexander, bookbinder, 6 Collingwood street
Duff, Benjamin, storekeeper, 15 Earl street
Duff, David, day constable, 7 Staunton street
Duff, David, publican, 14 Joy street
Duff, James, cheesemonger, 31 Verner street
Duff, James, grocer, 49 Gardiner street
Duff, John, porter, 2 Carr's row, Old Malone road
Duff, Isaac, soap boiler, 147 Durham street
Duff, Thomas, pilot, 6 Wall street
Duffin, Adam, merchant, 7 Fisherwick place
Duffin, Charles and Co., merchants, 28 Waring street, mill, Linenhall street
Duffin, Charles, merchant, 3 Donegall square North
Duffin, George, car driver, 41 Hill street
Duffield, S., 6 Great Patrick street, and 55 Tomb street
Duffield, W. J. merchant, 53 York street
Duffield, W. J. and A., provision merchants, 86 Corporation street
Duffy, Eliza, grocer and publican, 35 Samuel street
Duffy, John, tailor, 4 Skipper street
Duffy, John, tailor, 14 Annette street
Duffy, Michael, shoemaker, 40 Moffett street
Duffy, Michael, teacher, 36 Millfield
Duffy, William, spirit dealer, Ross street
Duffy, William, grocer and publican, Falls road
Dugan, Alexander, mechanic, 85 Peter's hill
Dugan, Andrew, bootcloser, 85 Green street
Dugan, Daniel, sailmaker, 69 Green street
Dugan, Henry, car proprietor, 8 Chapel lane
Dugan, Hugh, carpenter, 10 Welsh street
Dugan, James, ship carpenter, 96 Nelson street
Dugan, James, butcher, 31 Hercules street
Dugan, Joseph, weaver, 75 Durham street

Dugan, Robert, soap and candle manufacturer, 18 John street
Dugan, Thomas, boot and shoemaker, 2 Lancaster street
Dunbar, Daniel, clerk, 47 Old Lodge road
Dunbar, William, tailor, Ballynafeigh
Duncan, Adam, publican, and carman's inn, 104 North street, & Hercules st.
Duncan, Eliza Jane, haberdasher, 65 North street
Duncan, George, grocer and publican, 1 Cromac street—27 May street
Duncan, John, spirit dealer, Charter's buildings, Falls road
Duncan, John, master mariner, 28 Stanley place
Duncan, James, jeweller, 58 Tomb street
Duncan, Mrs., Fitzwilliam street, Old Malone road
Duncan, Nathaniel, grocer, wine, spirit, and provision merchant, 28 and 30 Cromac street, and 39 Verner street
Duncan, Richard, gardener, 95 North Queen street
Duncan Robert, bleacher, Falls road
Duncan, William, night constable, 16 Little Donegall street
Dundas, George, gentleman, 11 Howard street
Dunlavey, John, baker, 12 North Boundary street
Dunlop, Alexander, publican, 62 Tomb street
Dunlop, Alex., foreman, *Banner of Ulster* jobbing office, 13 Collingwood st.
Dunlop, Catherine, spirit dealer, 6¼ Hamilton street
Dunlop, David, confectioner, Arthur square
Dunlop, Daniel, painter, William street South
Dunlop, Ellen, boarding house, 102 Cromac street
Dunlop, James, whip manufactory, 149 North street
Dunlop, John, butcher, 11¼ Cromac street
Dunlop, James, moulder, Ballymacarrett
Dunlop, James, grocer, 109 Carrickhill
Dunlop, John, boot and shoemaker, 24 High street
Dunlop, Margaret, nurse tender, 7 Downshire place
Dunlop, Mrs., boarding house, 4 College street
Dunlop, Mrs., 24 Catherine street North
Dunlop, Robert, foreman mechanic, Lagan village, Ballymacarrett
Dunlop, Samuel, head constable in Ballast office, 62 Tomb street
Dunlop, William, draper, 34 Nelson street
Dunn, Hugh, leather cutter, 8 John street
Dunn, James, sailmaker, 5 Dock lane
Dunn, John, cooper, 25 Moffet street
Dunn, John, merchant and ship owner, 13 Henry street; office, 15
Dunn, John, shoemaker, 9 M'Auley street
Dunn, William, horse trainer, 39 Friendly street
Dunville, John, & Co., wholesale, wine, tea, and spirit merchants, 10 Calender street; William Dunville's residence, Richmond Lodge, Co. Down
Dunwiddy, Alexander, carman, 33 Conway street
Duprey, Hastings, coach factory, 11 Fountain street
Duprey, William, writing clerk, 6 Johnston's buildings
Dyer, Alexander, branch pilot, 25 Pilot street
Dyer, Dennis, spirit dealer, 177 North street
Dyer, Daniel, lodgings, 81 Millfield
Dyer, Hugh, grocer and provision dealer, 10 John street
Dyer, John, haberdasher, 12 John street
Dyer, John, Northern servants' registry office, 3½ Arthur street
Dyer, Thomas, nailer, 44 Grattan street
Dyke, E. and S., dressmakers, 1 Mill street
Dyke, R. M., organist, St. Malachi's Roman Catholic Chapel, 1 Mill street
Dysart, John and James, provincial boot and shoe house, 50 High street

ALPHABETICAL DIRECTORY.

Eades, William, joiner, 20 Nile street
Eager, Andrew, writing clerk, 11 Charlotte street
Eagle, Luke, Northern Racket Court and Billiard Room, 35 Chichester st.
Eagleson, Mrs., 139 North street
Eagleson, Robert, bread server, 22 Round entry
Eakin, William, and Co., drug, oil, and colour merchants; stores, 52 and 58 Donegall street; residence, Great Patrick street
Eaton, Joseph, warehouseman, 4 Crumlin place
Eccles, Mrs., 94 Donegall street
Eccles, Mrs. Mary, 20 Nelson street
Eccles, Miss, 7 Prospect terrace
Eccles, Rev. W. S., Baptist minister, 42 Academy street
Echlin, Edward, cabinet maker, 14 Boyd street
Echlin, P., proprietor of the Commercial Hotel, Commercial buildings
Edgar, Alexander, foreman carpenter, 1 Campbell's buildings, Townsend st.
Edgar, Mrs., boarding house, 18 Hamilton street
Edgar, Rev. John, D.D., 6 University square
Edgar, Samuel, woollendraper and haberdasher, 5 Arthur sq.—2 Arthur st.
Edmondson, Arthur, cabinet maker, 31 Wall street
Edmondson, Eliza, 96 Lower Malone
Edmondson, John, turner, 12 Townsend street
Edmondson, John, moulder, 12 Townsend street
Edmondson, John, wood turner, 12 Chapel lane
Edmondson, Mrs., seminary, 77 Donegall street
Edmondson, R., mechanic, 12 Upton street
Edmondson, Thomas, head master Brown Street School, 77 Donegall street
Edwards, John, glass manufacturer, 7 Sarah street
Eid, Anna, milliner and dressmaker, 39 Cromac street
Elcock, Wm., pensioner, 4 Portland place
Elder, Samuel, printer, 10 Cullingtree street
Ellis, Alexander, caretaker grain store, Artillery street
Ellis, John, turner, 17 Talbot street
Ellis, Patrick, commercial traveller, 52 Joy street
Ellis, William, schoolmaster, 3 Bell's lane
Elliott, Agnes, publican and grocer, 77 Peter's hill
Elliott, George, printer, Stanley street
Elliott, H. & J. & Co., general commission merchants, and sewed muslin manufacturers, 1 Donegall square East
Elliott, James, muslin manufacturer, Donegall square East—Fitzwilliam st.
Elliott, John, grocer and flour dealer, 133 North street
Elliott, John, grocer, 16 Hamill street
Elliott, Joseph, grocer, Wheeler's place, Ballymacarrett
Elliott, S. M'Dowell, solicitor, seneschal of Belfast, 12 Arthur street; residence, Old Lodge road
Elliott, Samuel, confectioner, 86 North street
Elliot, Thomas, accountant, 100 Donegall street
Elliott, William John, manager Public Bakery, 16 Church street
Ellison, Mrs., Mountpottinger, Ballymacarrett
Emerson, George, gentleman, 106 Donegall street
Emerson, George, stonecutter, Ballynafeigh
Emerson, William, merchant, 106 Donegall street
Emerson, William, mechanic, 45 Grove street
English, Anne, sewer, 21 Little York street
English, Robert, grocer, Roundhill cottage, Ballymacarrett
Ennis, Neal, car driver, 5 Long lane

Entwisle, James, architect, 18 Eliza street
Erskine, David, grocer, 14 Skipper street
Erskine, Robert, grocer, 159 Durham street
Erskine, Thomas, millwright, 35 Friendly street
Erskine, William, shoemaker, 13½ Lower Stanfield street
Erwin, John, butter merchant, 12 Butter market—48 Little Patrick street
Erwin, Mrs., fruit dealer, 26 Charlemont street
Erwin, Thomas, 10 Butter market—36 Nelson street
Erwin, William, cotton spinner, 4 Trinity street
Esler, Samuel, grocer and haberdasher, Falls road
Evans, George, grocer, 69 Smithfield
Evans, J., landing surveyor in custom house, Roundhill house, Ballymacarrett
Evans, James, seaman, 25 Little York street
Evans, John, carpenter, 9 Round entry
Evans, James, publican, 102 North street
Evans, Miss, dressmaker, 29 Stanhope street
Evans, Richard, blacksmith, 24 Verner street
Evans, Thomas W. Eyre, Ex. S.T.C.D., head master classical school, [Royal Academical Institution
Everett, Mrs., 3 Brougham street
Ewart, James, muslin manufacturer, 8 Botanic road
Ewart, James, architect, 29 Donegall street
Ewart, Rachael, publican, 22 Cromac road
Ewart, Samuel, cooper, 99 York street
Ewart, Thomas, spirit dealer, 45 North Queen street
Ewart, Thomas, gentleman, 26 North Queen street
Ewart, William, and Son, linen, cotton, and muslin manufacturers, and flax and tow spinners,; office, 24 Donegall street—Crumlin road mill
Ewart, William, 2 Mountview terrace
Ewart, William, jun., Wheatfield
Ewing, Andrew, muslin manufacturer, 11 St. Anne's buildings—Ballynafeigh
Ewing, Hugh, mechanic, 19 Grove street
Ewing, John, grocer and spirit dealer, 11 Greenland street
Ewins, John, shipsmith, Falloon's court
Ewing, Samuel, grocer and spirit dealer, 11 Nile street
Ewing, Thomas, ship carpenter, 73 Little Patrick street
Ewing, William, gentleman, 33 Joy street
Ewings, William, brushmaker, 3 Sackville street

FAGAN, Edward, wine and spirit dealer, 21 John street
Fagan, Terence, butcher, 50 Talbot street
Fagan, William, gardener, 61 Conway street
Fairfield, Thomas, carpenter, 16 M'Auley street
Falloon, James, weaver, 17 M'Tier's street
Falloon, Miss, 16 Dock street
Faloon, Patrick, leather dresser, 50 Townsend street
Faloon, Sarah, boardinghouse, 9 Chichester lane
Faloon, William, blacksmith, 4 Campbell's place, Old Lodge road
Falloon, William, blacksmith, Conlon street
Fannan, John, shoemaker, Plunkett's court
Fannin, Patrick, shoemaker, 3 Little May street
Faren, J., of Richardson, Brothers, & Co., 4 Henry street
Faren, William, dealer, 19 Pound street
Farley, Wm., boat builder, 31 North Thomas street
Farnham, Patrick, linen lapper, 2 Moffet street
Farrell, Anthony, book keeper, 7 Victoria terrace, Old Malone road

ALPHABETICAL DIRECTORY. 245

Farrell, Hugh, lodgings and eating house, 50 John street
Farrell, John, gentleman, 6 Ormeau place
Farrell, James, coachmaker, 25 West street
Farrell, Luke, carpenter, 3 Grace street
Farrell, S., & Co., nurserymen, seedsmen, and florists, 2 High street; nursery, Ballycloughan
Farrell, Thomas, Royal Temperance hotel, 12 Waring street
Farren, David, marine store, 54 Winetavern street
Faulkner, Ann, 88 Lower Malone
Faulkner, James, porter, 21 Cullingtree street
Faulkner, John, cooper, 19 Trafalgar street
Fawkner, Mrs., lodging house, 1 North Queen street
Fawkner, William, grocer and spirit dealer, 1 Bradbury place
Fea, John, pensioner, 24 Charlemont street place
Fea, Thomas, spirit dealer, 12 Marlborough street
Fee, David, lighter owner, 130 Ann street
Fee, Henry, carpenter, 9 Welsh street
Fee, James, pilot, 16 Trafalgar street
Fee, Jane, publican, 130 Ann street
Fee, John, pensioner, 24 Charlemont street
Fee, William, marble and stone cutter, York street
Feenan's boarding house, 8 Caddell's entry
Feeney, John, spirit dealer, 14 and 16 Gamble street
Feeny, John, spirit store, 34 Tomb street
Fegan, Henry, boot and shoemaker, 51 Hill street
Fegan, Henry, boot and shoemaker, 8 Castle place; residence, 57 Hill street
Fegan, John, sawyer, 18 Little Corporation street
Fegan, John, 18 Curtis street
Fegan, William, tailor, Chapel lane
Fehrenbach, John, watch & clock maker, and toy merchant, 19 Corn market
Fenning, Thomas, grocer and publican, 17 Marquis street
Fenton, Catherine, 31 Lagan street
Fenton, Son, and Co., linen manufacturers and bleachers, Linen hall
Fenton, S. Græme, J.P., Mayor of Belfast, 9 College square north
Fenton, William, car driver, 21 East street
Fenwick, Mrs., 34 North Queen street
Feran, Patrick, spirit dealer, 16 Alexander street
Ferguson & Molyneaux, starch manufactory, 21 York lane
Ferguson, Andrew, engineer, 7 West street
Ferguson, Archibald, clock manufacturer, 1 Church lane
Ferguson, Andrew, dealer, Wheeler's place, Ballymacarrett
Ferguson, Bernard, provision dealer, 58 Cromac street
Ferguson, D., curator, Royal Botanic Gardens, Botanic road
Ferguson, David, butcher, 34 Hercules street
Ferguson, Dr. J., Professor Queen's College, 14 Howard street
Ferguson, David, butcher and green grocer, 25 and 26 Corn market
Ferguson, David, cooper, 2 M'Crory's row, Ballymacarrett
Ferguson, Elizabeth, 41 Edward street
Ferguson, Hugh, carpenter, 5 William's lane
Ferguson, Dr. Henry, surgeon, 55 Upper Arthur street
Ferguson, James, mariner and dealer, 11 Store lane
Ferguson, James, linen draper, 2 Dock street
Ferguson, John, linen merchant, 10 Waring street—3 Donegall square south
Ferguson, John F., J.P., D.L, linen merchant, 28 Donegall place;
Ferguson, James, joiner, 70 Vere street

ALPHABETICAL DIRECTORY.

Ferguson, James, mechanic, Peel's place
Ferguson, James, master porter, 10 Dock lane
Ferguson, James, grocer and publican, 38 Trafalgar street
Ferguson, James B., starch manufacturer, 79 Donegall street
Ferguson, J. F., & Co., linen merchants, Linen hall
Ferguson, Mary, 61 Grove street
Ferguson, Mrs., 19 Eliza street
Ferguson, Miss, drawing school, 6 Upper Queen street
Ferguson, Miss, 63 Durham street
Ferguson, Mrs., commission agent, 7 Antrim place
Ferguson, Nathaniel, woollendraper, 38 High street—6 Arthur street
Ferguson, Richard, turner, 6 Gordon street
Ferguson, Thos., & Son, linen merchants & bleachers, Linenhall—Whiterock
Ferguson, Thomas, house and rent agent, 31 Castle street
Ferguson, Thomas, carter, 14½ Roy street
Ferguson, William, hardware dealer, 17 Smithfield
Ferguson, William, dealer in old iron, 48 Smithfield
Ferrar, Michael, in Robt. Henderson's steam-packet office—5 Prospect terrace
Ferrie & Campbell, merchants, 74 Waring street; bonded stores, 11 Corporation street; Mr. Ferrie's residence, Holywood
Ferris, John, ship carpenter, 87 Little York street
Ferris, James, in vitriol works, 14 Portview, Ballymacarrett
Ferris, John, superintendent Fish market, Shell Fish hotel, 13 Police square
Ferris, Jos., cabinet maker, 11 Wellington street
Ferris, James, carpenter, 28 Charlemont street
Ferris, James, carpenter, 27 Cromac road
Ferris, James, bootcloser, Killen street
Ferris, Margaret, lodging house, 40 Stanhope street
Ferris, Robert, boot and shoemaker, 18 Ann street
Ferris, Thomas, spinning master, 67 Grove street
Ferris, William, spirit store, 47 Curell place
Ferris, William, spirit dealer, 47 Townsend street
Ferris, William, moulder, 39 Wall street
Ferrit, William, tailor, 19 Wesley place
Festu, Mons. Jules, French master, 45 Upper Arthur street
Fetherston, John spirit dealer, &c., 49 Ann street and 1 Upper Church lane
Fetherstonhaugh, Julia Ann, 13 Joy street
Fettler, Archibald Price, 10 Campbell's buildings
Fiers, Charles, gentleman, 2 Adelaide place
Fife, Peter, mechanic, 62 York street
Fimister, John, cooper, 9 Wall street
Finegan, Thomas, sailor, 40 Talbot street
Finigan, William, grocer, 1 Lower Malone
Finlay, Alexander, weaver, 57 Millfield
Finlay, Charles, tea merchant, 5 Waring street—4 Albert place
Finlay, Charles and Wm., wholesale tea merchants, 5 Waring street
Finlay, Francis, ship chandler, 27 Pilot street
Finlay, F. D., proprietor of the *Northern Whig*, Adelaide place, and Ballynafeigh Cottage; office, 6 Calender street
Finlay, Jn., soap and candle manufacturer, 31 Ann st.—Tudor hall, Holywood
Finlay, John, plasterer, 10 Verner street
Finlay, John, bricklayer, 37 Tomb street
Finlay, James, warehouseman, 27 Verner street
Finlay, Jane & Eliza, straw bonnet & millinery establishment, 24 Waring st.
Finlay, James, turner, New Lodge road

ALPHABETICAL DIRECTORY.

Finlay, John, flax merchant, stores, Police place—7 Donegall square East
Finlay, Joseph, grocer, spirit and provision dealer, 56 North Queen street
Finlay, Margaret, bonnetmaker, Ballymacarrett
Finlay, Samuel, chandler, Ann street—10 Queen street
Finlay, Wm., wholesale tea merchant, 5 Waring st—Fountainville terrace
Finlay, William, linen yarn dealer, 23 Cromac street
Finlay, William, plasterer, 5 East street
Finlay, William, tailor, 50 Tomb street
Finlay, William, Donegall Pass Tavern, 1 Donegall pass
Finnegan, Henry, storekeeper, 52 Tomb street
Firth, George, iron moulder, M'Auley street
Firth, Thomas, Eliza street flax mill—1 Bond street
Fisher, John, & Son, flax spinners, Francis street mills; office, 9 Rosemary street; John Fisher's residence, 2 Glengall place
Fisher, John, & Co., sewed muslin manufacturers, 27 Great Patrick street
Fisher, John, boarding house, 19 Princess street
Fisher, Wm., wholesale and retail grocer, 40 Church lane
Fitzgerald, Mrs., 6 Aughton terrace
Fitzgerald, William, smith, 27 Caxton street
Fitzpatrick, Bernard, wine & spirit merchant, 72 Donegall st. & 19 Albert sq.
Fitzpatrick, Bernard, grocer and spirit dealer, 2, 4, 6 John street
Fitzpatrick, Edward, dealer, 9 Friendly street
Fitzpatrick, John, dealer, Plunket's court
Fitzpatrick, John, lodgings, 28 John street
Fitzpatrick, James, coachman, 35 Bank lane
Fitzpatrick, James, carpenter, 13 and 14 Duffy's place
Fitzpatrick, James, pork cutter, 17 Morrow's entry
Fitzsimons, Ellen, shop keeper, 53 Durham street
Fitzsimons, John, nail manufacturer, 71 Union street
Fitzsimons, Mary, boarding house, 60 Frederick street
Fitzsimons, Nicholas, merchant and ship owner, Lloyd's agent, shipwright surveyor, agent for the Glasgow and Liverpool Underwriters' Association, Corporation street—Dunsona, Whiteabbey
Flanigan, William, block printer, 3 Fleming's place, Old Lodge road
Flannagan, Hamilton, cattle dealer, 6 Melbourne street
Flannagan, John, millwright, Grove street
Flannagan, Patrick, mechanic, 13 Pound street
Flannigan, George, picture frame maker, and butcher, 13 Hercules place
Flannigan, Henry, jobbing smith, Bridge end, Ballymacarrett
Flannigan, Lawrence, pensioner, 85 Carrickhill
Fleck, Rebecca, 11 Townsend place
Fleeton, N., day constable, 68 Brown street
Fleming, Boyd, gentleman, 6 Pakenham place
Fleming, Johnston, grocer, 3 Boundary street
Fleming, Mrs., 9 Antrim place
Fleming, Robert, ship carpenter, 9 Pilot street
Fleming, Robert, tailor, 14 California street
Fleming, Samuel, boot and shoemaker, 6 Harmony place
Fleming, Samuel, carpenter, 7 Stanhope street
Fleming, William, grain agent, 19 Prince's street
Fleming, William, turner, 28 Friendly street
Fletcher, Mrs., 11 Catherine street North
Fletcher, Miss, dressmaker, 11 Cromac road
Fletcher, Thomas, chandler, 10 Little May street
Fletcher, William, silver plater, 66 Cromac street

Y

Flinn, Michael, horse clipper and dealer, 9 Thomas court
Flinn, Patrick, green grocer and flour dealer, 15 Castle market
Flood, John, carpenter, 14 Catherine street North
Foley, Edward, spirit dealer, 4 Legg's lane
Foley, John, provision dealer and butcher, 150 North street
Folie, Michael M., horse shoer at the Donegall street bazaar, Sarah street
Folingsby, James, gentleman, 9 Upper Queen street
Folingsby, T. G., and Co., commission merchants, ship and insurance agents, 15 Albert square—1 Clarence place
Forbes, J., governor new county prison, Crumlin road
Forbes, Mrs., staymaker, 13 Castle street
Forbes, Trevor, Ulster foundry, 31¼ Townsend street
Forbes, Thomas, upholsterer and Venetian blind maker, 13 Castle street
Forbes, William, worker in foundry, 13 New Lodge road
Ford and Godwin, civil engineers, 9 Donegall place
Ford, John, boarding house, 30 Great Patrick street
Ford, Matthew, shoemaker, 37 Little Patrick street
Ford, Thomas, shirt maker, 4 Fountain lane—11 College street
Forde, Arthur K., stamp office, 12 and 13 Donegall place buildings, Castle st.
Fordyce and Mullan, brewers and wholesale spirit merchants, 84 Cromac st.
Fordyce, James M., brewer, Cromac brewery—5 New Bond street
Foreman, John, linen lapper, 3 Northburn place
Forrester, Alexander, of T. G. Folingsby and Co., 51 Corporation street
Forrester, Matthew, Dock Tavern, 11 Prince's dock
Forsyth, Mary, grocer, 60 Millfield
Forsythe, Charles, nailer, Ballymacarrett
Forsythe, Charles, nailer, 20 Skipper street
Forsythe, Catherine, publican, 8 Skipper street
Forsythe, John, land agent, 13 Castle Chambers
Forsythe, Joseph, porter, 4 Hutcheson street
Forsythe, Robert, nailer, Ballymacarrett
Forsythe, William, gentleman, 13 Wellington place
Fortune and Co., plumbers and lead merchants, 25 Hill street
Fortune, Alexander, of A. Fortune & Co., 5 Crumlin place
Foster, Job, pensioner, 51 Mustard street
Foster, John, Ulster servants' registry office, Long lane
Foster, James, starch maker, 31 York lane
Foster, John, baker, 66 Sussex street
Foster, Margaret, boarding house, 10 Caddell's entry
Foster, Robert, packer, Old Lodge road
Fowler, James, green grocer, 18¼ Prince's street
Fowler, Patrick, yard and stabling, 4 Gamble street
Fowler, Patrick, confectioner, 146 North street
Fox, Catherine, 8 College street south
Fox, Patrick, dealer, 17 Bell's lane
Fox, Patrick, flax dresser, 53 Townsend street
Fox, Thomas, butcher, green grocer, and spirit dealer, 101 York street
Fox, William, haberdasher, 12 Church lane
Foy, Richard, pawnbroker, 33 Great Patrick street
Frame, William, dealer, 49 North Queen street
Franklin, Charles, butcher, 56 Hercules street
Franklin, Joseph, butcher, poulterer, and victualler, 3 York street
Fraser and Finch, provision, butter, fish, salt, and ship stores, 59 Waring st.
Fraser, Charles, spirit store, 14 Collingwood street
Fraser, John, musician, 26 Russell street

Fraser, James, butter merchant, Butter market—17 Great Edward street
Fraser, James, muslin manufacturer, 62 Nelson street—16 Academy street
Fraser, James, spirit and provision merchant, 15 and 17 Great Edward street
Fraser, Mr., butter store, 1 Johnston's court
Fraser, T., 53 Corporation street
Fraser, Tanner, and Co., sewed muslin manufacturers, 11 Academy street
Frazer, James, land surveyor, M'Larnon's buildings, Ballymacarrett
Frazer, John, mechanic, Mary's place, North Queen street
Frazer, Mr., 17 Hamilton street
Frazer, Roderick, confectioner, 53 Talbot street
Frazer, Thomas, customhouse officer, 4 Spencer street
Frazer, Thomas, leather merchant, 119 North street
Freckleton, Richard, writing clerk, 14 Melbourne street
Freebairn, William, boot and shoemaker, 3 Coates street
Freeman, John, shoemaker, 27 Upper Lagan street
Freeman, John, and Co., ropemakers, 14 Pottinger's entry—5 Hamilton st.
Freeman, Thomas, carpenter, 31 Lower Stanfield street
Freeman, Thomas, carpenter, 2 Eliza street
Frew, John, publican, 111 Durham street
Frew, Robert, clerk, 46 Gloucester street
Frew, Rosanna and Ellen, publicans, 25 Smithfield
Friel, Thomas, tobacco spinner and dealer, 8 Gordon street
Frings, Dr., professor Queen's college—9 Howard street
Frith, James, engineer, 15 Harmony place
Frith, Thomas, flax spinner, 31 Eliza street; residence, 1 New Bond street
Fryer, Dr., surgeon and apothecary, 39 Donegall street
Fryer, John, book deliverer, 122 Old Lodge road
Frys, Francis, bailiff, 15 Bell's lane
Fullarton, Brothers, grocers and spirit dealers, 17$\frac{1}{2}$ Cromac street
Fullarton, Henry, tailor, 16 Talbot street
Fullarton, John, brush and bellows maker, 12 Robert street
Fullarton, Thomas, spirit dealer, 9 Talbot street
Fulton, Ann Jane, clothes dealer, 20 Berry street
Fulton, David, builder and scantling yard, 18 Ship street
Fulton, George, clothes dealer, 23 Berry street
Fulton, Henry, mechanic, 2 Seaview place, Ballymacarrett
Fulton, Hugh, cabinet maker, Frederick street
Fulton, John, provision merchant, 15 Long lane—45 Academy street
Fulton, John, painter, 8 Wellington street
Fulton, John, bleacher, Shankhill road
Fulton, Matthew, cow keeper, Conlon street
Fulton, Margaret, lodging house, 14 Grattan street
Fulton, Matthew, cow keeper, 5 Campbell's place, Old Lodge road
Fulton, Nathaniel, carpenter, 7 Sackville place
Fulton, Robert, weighmaster, 1 Morrow's entry
Fulton, Robert, carpenter, 21 Earl lane
Fulton, Samuel, ploughman, 19 M'Tier's street
Fulton, William, saddler, 39 Rosemary street
Furlong, Mary, dealer, Ballynafeigh

GAFFIKIN, Arthur, 12 Chichester street
Gaffikin, Arthur C., 26 Catherine street
Gaffikin, Arthur, provision merchant, 35 Dock street
Gaffikin, Mrs. Mary, 86 Joy street
Gaffikin, James D., poulterer, 21 Corn market

Gaffikin, John, butcher, 25 Corn market
Gaffikin, R., carver and gilder, 7 Arthur square—32 Upper Arthur street
Gaffikin, Thomas, butcher, 13 Corn market—1 Apsley place
Gainford, George, custom house officer, 33 Earl street
Galbraith, Emily, dealer, 12 Lower Stanfield street
Galbraith, John, harbour clerk, Wills' place
Galbraith, John, carman, 24 Moffet street
Galbraith, Miss Janet, 11 Spencer street
Galbraith, Robert, hair cutter and wig maker, &c., 8 Arthur street
Gales, Patrick, porter, 51 Green street
Gallagher, John, carrier, 31 and 33 Pottinger's entry
Gallagher, James, porter, 38 Old Lodge road
Gallagher, John, lighterman, 7 Morrow's entry
Gallagher, James, boot and shoemaker, 56 Hudson's entry
Gallagher, Nicholas, sweep, M'Tier's court
Gallagher, Richard, cooper, 51 Grattan street
Gallagher, William, bricklayer, 48 New Lodge road
Galley, Daniel, sailmaker, 11 Little York street
Galley, James, day constable, 11 Stephen street
Gallogly, Rev. John, 97 Donegall street
Galloway, Thomas, painter, 47 Castle street
Galt, Alexander, grocer and spirit dealer, 6 Frederick street
Galt, William, ship joiner, 65 Grove street
Galt, William, schoolmaster, 40 Henry street
Galway, Arthur, gentleman, 26 Durham street
Galway, Margaret, 18 Gloucester street
Galway, William, tailor, 51 North Thomas street
Gamble, Abel, stonecutter, 19 Shipboy street—Antrim road
Gamble, Benjamin A., and Co., linen warehouse, 5 Donegall street place; residence, 2 Prospect terrace
Gamble, David, tinsmith, 4 Cargill street
Gamble, John, blacksmith, 45 Stanley street
Gamble, John, printer, 5 M'Tier street
Gamble, John, publican and grocer, Bradbury place, Old Malone road
Gamble, J. and W., millowners, 26 Academy street
Gamble, Mrs., 131 York street
Gamble, Miss, schoolmistress, 6 Gloucester street
Gamble, Mrs., boarding and day school, 63 York street
Gamble, Orr R., solicitor, Arthur place, 22 Middle Gardener street, Dublin—Trainview, Whiteabbey
Gamble, Robert, merchant, 3 College place North
Gamble, Samuel, weaver, 11 New Lodge road
Gamble, Thomas, cooper, 51 Little York street
Gamble, William, and Co., general commission merchants, 43 Waring street; William Gamble's residence, 131 York street
Gamble, William, general commission agent, 3 Donegall street place
Ganston, Francis, cooper, 13 Mustard street
Gardener, Thos., soap and candle maker, 87 Queen's sq. and Prince's court
Gardner, Eliza, confectioner, 31 Castle place
Gardner, Eliza, bonnet maker, 35 Wall street
Gardner, James, starch works, 10 York lane—50 York street
Gardner, James, starch manufacturer, 23 York lane
Gardner, William, green grocer, 22 Barrack street—39 Smithfield
Garland, James, coal office, 5 Queen's Quay, Ballymacarrett
Garner, Edward, tailor, and spirit dealer, 53 New Lodge road

ALPHABETICAL DIRECTORY. 251

Garrett, H., contracter and builder, 2 College court, College street
Garrett, H. J. and T., solicitors, 16 Castle lane, and 8 Inn's quay, Dublin
Garrett, Henry, solicitor, Cromac house
Garrett, James, carpenter and builder, 21 May street
Garrett, James, newspaper carrier, 15 Staunton street
Garrett, Margaret, washerwoman, 25 Charlemont street
Garrett, Mary, butcher, 25 Hercules street
Garrett, Mrs., 9 Ormeau place
Garrity, Thomas, lodging house, 69 Carrick hill
Gartins, Denis, baker, 59 Boundary street
Gartland, Mary, lodgings, 14 Marquis street
Gartland, Peter, fireman, 7 Hamilton's place
Garvey, James, lodgings, 4 Tomb street
Gaskin, James, painter and glazier, 56 Donegall street
Gaussen, Charles, in Richardson, Brothers, and Co.'s office—6 Victoria place
Gaussen, John, and Co., grain merchants, 11 Albert square—6 Victoria place
Gavin, William, rent and house agent, 24 Castle street
Gaw, Hugh, grocer and publican, 29 Stanley street
Gelston, Hugh, wholesale wine & spirit store, 35 Ann st. & Up. Church lane
Gelston, James, medical practitioner, Keenan's place, Ballymacarrett
Gelston, Miss, dressmaker, 11 Queen street
Gelston, Samuel, cabinet maker, 11 Queen street
Gelston, Samuel, wine & spirit merchт., 17 North st.—Rosstulla, Whiteabbey
Gelston, William, merchant and tobacconist, 40 Tomb st.—8 Gt. George's st.
Geoghegan, Edwd., agent, Bank of Ireland, Donegall place—7 Royal terrace
George, Abel, grocer, 34 Smithfield
George, Mary Ann, 19 William street
George, John, boot and shoemaker, 22 Grace street
George, Thomas, coal office, 6 Queen's Quay, Ballymacarrett
George, Thomas, general merchant, Lilliput house
German, Petty, and Co., flax spinners, Preston, 24 Rosemary street
Gertshaw, John, clerk, Victoria terrace, Old Malone road
Getgood, Thomas, gentleman, York road
Getty, Edmund, secretary Harbour Commissioners, 6 Abbotsford place
Getty, James, machine maker, 20 M'Tier street
Getty, John, gentleman, Beech park, Old Lodge road
Getty, Robert, gentleman, Beech park, Old Lodge road
Getty, Samuel G., gentleman, Cromac park
Gibeon, Thomas, boot and shoemaker, 10 Gordon street
Gibbon, Archibald, weaver, 52 Vere street
Gibbs, James, spirit dealer, 44 Winetavern street
Gibbs, Maria, whiteworker, 32 Valentine street
Gibson, David, chainmaker, 12 Charles street
Gibson, Edward, draper, 90 Joy street
Gibson, Elizabeth, 12 Cullingtree place
Gibson, Emily, 24 Collingwood street
Gibson, George, linen lapper, 14 Cullingtree street
Gibson, Joseph, mechanic, 14 York lane
Gibson, John, boot and shoemaker, 83 Green street
Gibson, John nailer, 28 Little Donegall street
Gibson, James, ropemaker, Old Lodge road
Gibson, Joseph, solicitor, 4 Arthur street, and 103 Capel street, Dublin
Gibson, Mrs. Catherine, 3 Lancaster street
Gibson, Mrs., 8 Coates street
Gibson, Martha, 5 Seymour street

Gibson, Mrs., grocery and seaman's clothing establishment, 38 Corporation st.
Gibson, Mary, eating house, 4 Caddell's entry
Gibson, Robert, brass founder, 52 Lower Malone
Gibson, Robert, haberdashery establishment, 19 Castle street
Gibson, Rev. Wm., Professor of Christian Ethics, Assembly's College, Cliftonville, Antrim road
Gibson, Robert, brassfounder, M'Clenaghan's court, Mill st.—5 Lancaster st.
Gibson, Thomas, brass moulder, 7 Upton street
Gibson, Thomas, travelling clerk, 7 New Bond street
Gibson, William, day constable, 14 Robert street
Gibson, William, boot and shoemaker, 19 High street
Gibson, William, boot and shoemaker, 12 Gordon street
Gifford, Norman B., clerk Ulster Bank, 1 Spencer street
Gilbert, Edward, watchmaker, jeweller, and silversmith, 43 High street
Gilbert, William, aud Son, jewellers, silversmiths, and watchmakers, 15 High street—36 Upper Arthur street
Giles, James, smith, 38 North Thomas street
Giles, John, caretaker Commercial Club, Waring street
Giles, John, publican, 50 Hercules street
Giles, John, shoemaker, 16 Torrens' market
Gilles, Mary, publican, 11 Gamble street
Gill, John, boiler maker, 26 Townsend street
Gill, Misses, school, 8 Linenhall street
Gill, Robert, master of vessel, 10 Caroline street
Gill, William, excise officer, Falls road
Gillan, Roddy, pavier, 24 Little Donegall street
Gilland, John, cooper, 41 Talbot street
Gillespie, Alice, 7 Fleet street
Gillespie, John, hay dealer, 46 West street
Gillespie, Jane, lodging house, 11 Collingwood street
Gillespie, Margaret, publican, 22 Great Edward street
Gillespie, Mrs., whiteworker, 15 Wall street
Gillespie, Robert, day constable, 24 Telfair's entry
Gillespie, Sarah, teacher, 25 Little May street
Gillespie, Thomas, carpenter, 6 Pilot street
Gillespie, W., pensioner, 1 Plunket's place
Gillespie, Wm., pensioner, 23 Vere street
Gilliland, Jane, bonnet maker, 15 Boyd street
Gilliland, John, gentleman, Mountpottinger, Ballymacarrett
Gilliland, Thomas, grocer and spirit dealer, 19 Grace street
Gillilan, William, linen merchant, Linen Hall—15 Wellington place
Gillis, Edward, ship carpenter, Little George's street
Gillis, John, Northern Bank, 2 Bank lane
Gillis, John, grocer and spirit dealer, 98 Corporation street
Gilly, William, mariner, 17 Friendly street
Gilmore, Andrew, gentleman, Albert place, Donegall pass
Gilmore, Brothers, cabinet and upholstery warerooms, 21 Donegall place; timber yard, Fountain street
Gilmore, Benjamin, publican, 33 North Queen street
Gilmore, Daniel, grocer, 54 Green street
Gilmore, Edward, shoemaker, 19 Bank lane
Gilmore, Edward, provision merchant, 88 Joy street
Gilmore, Eliza, washerwoman, Ballynafeigh
Gilmore, Hugh, tinsmith, 30 Smithfield, and Lennon's court
Gilmore, Hugh, baker, 18 Murphy street

ALPHABETICAL DIRECTORY. 253

Gilmore, John, fowl dealer, 2 Ritchie's place
Gilmore, John, shipwright, 32 Trafalgar street
Gilmore, Patrick, rag merchant 15 Stanhope street
Gilmore, Patrick, marine store, 37 Winetavern street
Gilmore, Robert, pawnbroker, 56 Little Donegall street, and 191 North st.; residence, 103 Donegall street
Gilmore, Robert, grocer and spirit dealer, 19 Ann street
Gilmore, Thomas, pawnbroker, 74 Cromac street—17 New Bond street
Gilmore, William, clerk, Northern Bank, 11 Ship street
Gilmore, William, cattle dealer, 39 Durham street
Gilmore, William, sawyer, 17 Wesley place
Gilmore, Wm., grocer, tea, wine, fruit, and spirit mechant, 14 and 16 High street—Antrim place
Gilmour, David, designer, 3 Henrietta street
Gilmour, J., muslin agent, Anderson & Gray's, Donegall sq. S.—2 Napier's pl.
Gilpin, George, clerk, 16 Sarah street
Giltenan, Edward B., house agent and land agent, 6 Spamount
Ginn, James, lamplighter, 3 Lindsay's place
Girdwood, James, carpet, damask, moreen, and room paper warehouse, 44 High street—6 Donegall square West
Girvan, Andrew, mechanic, 17 Nelson street—41 Little Patrick street
Girvan, John, foreman in distillery, 16 Devis street
Girvan, Joseph, pawnbroker, Wheeler's place, Ballymacarrett
Girvan, John, weaver, 5 M'Tier's street
Girvan, James, weaver, 39 Brown street
Girvan, Mrs. Elizabeth, 14 Eliza street
Girvan, Robert, pork cutter, 21 Roy street
Girvan, Thomas, pawnbroker, Shankhill road
Glasgow, Rev. James, Presbyterian minister, 2 James's street South
Glasgow, Mrs., green grocer, 14 Castle market
Glass, Archibald, mariner, 2 Stanley lane
Glass, Hugh, linen lapper, 16 California street
Gladstone, Thomas Nugent, plate iron works, Eliza street
Glen, Alexander, grocer, 71 Durham street
Glen, Peter, agent for James Methuen, 16 Tomb street
Glenfield, Francis, soap and candle manufacturer, 104 High street
Glenn, James, wholesale grocer, Victoria street
Glennan, Edward, coach painter, 55 Townsend street
Goddard, James, gentleman, Easton Lodge
Goddard, Robert T., high constable, county cess office, 7 Queen street—New
Godfrey, Mary, confectioner, 4 Charlemont street [Lodge road
Godwin, James, tailor, 1 Rochfort place
Godwin, John, civil engineer, Ulster Railway, &c.; residence, Woodhouse, Rostrevor, County Down
Goldstein, Isaac, general dealer, 12 King street
Goldstein, Mrs. Mary, dressmaker, 12 King street
Gooden, Dr., 10 Academy street
Goodman, John, linen lapper, Messrs. Fenton's office, Linen Hall—9 Mill st.
Goodman, Michael, mechanic, 39 Townsend street
Goodman, Miss, dressmaker, 9 Mill street
Goodwin, William, shoemaker, 11 Bradbury place
Gordon & Co., flax and tow spinners, Falls road
Gordon & Crawford, agents for the Royal Exchange Assurance office of London, Castle Chambers; R. F. Gordon's residence, Craigdarragh, co. Down
Gordon, Alexander, clerk, Nelson's buildings, Shankhill road

Gordon, Alexander, & Son, wine merchants, Castle chambers
Gordon, Alexander, carpenter, 8 Townsend street
Gordon, A., surgeon, 2 College square East
Gordon, Benjamin, saddler, 33 Great Edward street [and York street
Gordon, C. D., professor of music and piano forte tuner, 41 Little May street
Gordon, Echlin, relieving officer, 67 Nelson street
Gordon, Edward, dealer, 80 Cromac street
Gordon, George, clothes dealer, 7 Berry street
Gordon, G., North Star inn & hotel & posting establishment, 66 & 68 North st.
Gordon, Isaac, book keeper and cashier, 34 Ship street
Gordon, John, spirit dealer, 11 Castle lane
Gordon, James, carpenter, 24 Nile street
Gordon, John, clothes dealer, 10 Berry street
Gordon, Joseph, car driver, 52 Winetavern street
Gordon, James, bookseller, 18 Telfair's entry
Gordon, John, butcher, 64 Hercules street
Gordon, James, professor of dancing, 5 York street
Gordon, James, fireman, 47 Little York street
Gordon, John, cabinet maker, 64 and 65 Smithfield
Gordon, John, furniture dealer, 12 and 64 Smithfield
Gordon, Mary, 49 Townsend street
Gordon, Richard, carpenter, 7 Galway street
Gordon, Robert, tow bundler, 39 Conway street
Gordon, Samuel, cloth lapper, 11 California street
Gordon, William, ship carpenter, 7 Little Corporation street
Gordon, William, night constable, 21 Lower Stanfield street
Gorman, Andrew, green grocer, 27 Ormond market—87 Little Patrick st.
Gorman, Hugh, spirit dealer, Shankhill road
Gorman, James, shoemaker, Ballynafeigh
Gorman, John, porter, 10 Greenland street
Gorman, Mrs., boarding house, 48 Joy street
Gorman, Mrs. Mary Ann, 16 North King street
Gorman, Wm., colporteur, Conway street
Gorman, William, porter, 2 Friendly street
Gossan, E., provision dealer, 2 Arthur square
Gould, Thomas, cotton yarn agent, 7 York street—Whiteabbey
Gourley, Thomas, baker, 46 Little Donegall street
Gowan, Captain John, harbour master, Corporation street
Gowdy, Charles, cabinet maker, 57 Edward street
Gowdy, James, 15 William street South
Gowdy, James, bookseller and agent, 28 Rosemary street
Gowdy, John, plasterer, 1 Letitia street
Gowdy, Wm., spirit dealer, 51¼ Cromac street
Gracey, Henry, millwright, 40 Prince's street
Gracey, Robert, millwright, 10 Curtis street
Gracey, William, oyster house, 11 Crown entry
Graham and Magee, coachmakers, 26 Chichester street; Mr. Graham's residence, 5 Catherine street; Mr. Magee's, Pottinger's entry
Graham, Charles, tobacco spinner, 24 Grattan street
Graham, Edward, clerk, 4 Catherine street
Graham, E., whiteworker, 24 Stanley street
Graham, Hugh, grocer, Bridge end, Ballymacarrett
Graham, Hugh, porter, 9 Mustard street
Graham, Hugh, & Co., hat and cap manufacturers, 28½ Bridge street and 12 Graham's entry—79 York street

ALPHABETICAL DIRECTORY.

Graham, James, barber and hairdresser, 1 Carrickhill
Graham, James, green grocer, Ormond market
Graham, James, engraver, 8 Spencer street
Graham, James, damask weaver, 92 Peter's hill
Graham, John, coachmaker, 5 Catherine street
Graham, James, clerk, 15 Kennedy's place
Graham, J. C., & Co., sewed muslin manufacturers, 89 Donegall street
Graham, John, carpenter, 33 Lower Malone road
Graham, John, confectioner, 123 North street
Graham, John, entertainment and lodgings, 13 Great Edward street
Graham, John, chimney sweep, 5 Academy court
Graham, Robert, linen manufacturer, 106 Cromac street
Graham, J., haircutter, 62 Ann street
Graham, Jane, washerwoman, 19 Shankhill road
Graham, James, clothes cleaner, 40 Little Patrick street
Graham, Moses, boot and shoemaker, 18 Durham street
Graham, Mark, carpenter, 8 M'Millan's place
Graham, Mary, dealer, 23 Stephen street
Graham, Mrs., Longford Arms hotel and tavern, 61 Corporation square
Graham, Mrs. Ellen, 5 Fisherwick place
Graham, Mrs. Hugh H., 73 York street
Graham, Patrick, grocer, 105 Carrickhill
Graham, Patrick, cotton spinner, 107 Carrickhill
Graham, William, marble and stone yard, 56 York street
Graham, Richard, merchant, 77 Barrack street
Graham, Richard, sawyer, 11 Pilot street
Graham, Robert, sawyer, 5 North Ann street
Graham, Thomas, bricklayer, 10 Trafalgar street
Graham, Thomas, bricklayer, 43 Verner street
Graham, Thomas, chimney sweep, 45 Birch street
Graham, William, blacksmith, 3 Grove street
Graham, William, sea captain, 75 Nelson street
Graham, Wm., carpenter, 40 Vere street
Grainger, David, merchant and shipowner, 1 Prince's dock—11 Henry street
Grant, Alex., and Co., drapers and silk merchants, 43 North st.—2½ Joy st.
Grant, Charles, carpenter, 29 Earl street
Grant, David, shoemaker, Wall street
Grant, Henry, porkcutter, 24 Robert street
Grant, James, publican, 30 Upper Church lane
Grant, James, confectioner, 3 Donegall street—Cregagh Cottage, Castlereagh
Grant, Margaret, dealer, 22 Pound street
Grant, P., provision shop, 83 Barrack street
Granz, Wm. professor of music, 40 Gloucester street
Grattan & Co., chemists and apothecaries, 10 and 12 Corn market; ærated water manufactory, 33½ Chichester street—Merview
Grattan, Abraham, shoemaker, 36 Boundary street
Grattan, Crawford, railway guard, 25 Collingwood street
Grattan, Miss, milliner, 41 Upper Arthur street
Grattan, Thomas, dentist, 11 College square East
Gray, Clark, nailer, 59 Durham street
Gray, George, White Linen Hall; residence, Graymount
Gray, George, coach painter, 3 Seymour street
Gray, Henry, Townsend Street Foundry—94 Peter's hill
Gray, James, & Co., firebrick and tile works, 4½ Cromac road and Coalisland
Gray, James, waiter in hotel, 1 King street court

Gray, John, of H. Gray & Son, iron founders, 94 Peter's hill
Gray, John, cow keeper, Shankhill road
Gray, John, carpenter, 29 Stanfield street
Gray, John, watchmaker, jeweller, silversmith, &c., 18 Castle place
Gray, James, carman, William street south
Gray, Joseph, butler, 8 Napier street
Gray, Robert, and Co., woollendrapers and mercers, 15 Donegall street
Gray, Robert, shop keeper, Donegall street—62 Joy street
Gray, Robert, agricultural implement and machine maker, 8 Police place, & 11 Telfair's entry
Gray, Thomas, wholesale and retail grocer and shipowner, 22 North street
Gray, William, cabinetmaker, 14 William street south
Greaves, Miss, 6 Botanic view, Botanic road
Green, Alexander, dyer and grocer, 51 Boundary street
Green, Forster, and Co., tea merchants and grocers, 3 High street; Mr. Green's residence, 11 Albion place
Green, Forster, and Co., golden eagle tea establishment, 72 North street
Green, Francis, night constable, 42 Boundary street
Green, John, grocer and publican, 14 Millfield
Green, Margaret, lodgings, 122 Millfield
Green, Margaret, dealer, 11 New Lodge road
Green, Miss Henrietta, 10 Joy street
Green, Ralph, grocer and cheese merchant, 4 Waring street—12 Henry street
Green, Susannah, blue dyer, 43 Winetavern street
Green, Thomas, street inspector, 14 Dock street
Green, Thomas, ship carpenter, 14 Pilot street
Green, Thomas, spirit dealer and ship carpenter, 13 Short street
Green, William, miller, Bridge end, Ballymacarrett
Greenan, P., sawyer, 2 Annette street
Greene, James, Custom house, 5 The Crescent, Botanic road
Greenfield & Harris, haberdashers, hosiers, &c., 19 High street
Greenfield, John, draper, hosier, haberdasher, and woollen warehouse, 76 High street—Jackson hall, Hollywood
Greenfield, Mrs., 2 Ormeau place
Greenfield, Thomas, haberdasher, 111 York street
Greenhill, R., currier and leather merchant, 44½ Ann street and 49 Mill st.
Greenlees, James, mariner, 22 Vere street
Greenwood, James, whitesmith, 43 Winetavern street
Greenwood, Joseph, mechanic, 21 Melbourne street
Greenwood, James, whitesmith, 8 Marquis street
Greenwood, Joseph, flax dresser, Conway street
Greer & Oakman, woollen merchants, 13¾ Donegall street
Greer, Alexander, shoemaker, 24 Valentine street
Greer, Adam, weighmaster, 5 Cullingtree street
Greer, Edward, proprietor of Dublin coach; office, 15 Castle place—Newry
Greer, Henry, bookbinder, 2 King street
Greer, Henry, bookseller, stationer, and fancy warehouse, 31 High street
Greer, Henry, tailor, 3 Hopeton place
Greer, James, blacksmith, 17 Sackville street
Greer, Jane, soap and candle manufacturer, 54 North street
Greer, John, cooper, 45 Grattan street
Greer, James, brassfounder and gasfitter, 25 Shankhill road
Greer, Livingston, ship smith, 81 Little York street
Greer, Mrs., 16 Stanley street
Greer, Moses, weaver, 6 North Thomas street

Greer, R., merchant, 13 Donegall street—3 Aughton terrace
Greer, Thos., Sons, & Co., merchants, 18 Rosemary st.—4 Donegall sq. West
Greer, William, muslin manufacturer, 80 Donegall street
Gregg, David, traveller for Messrs. Lindsay, Brothers, 5 Glentilt place
Gregg, Greenfield, dealer, 3 Robert court
Gregg, John, buyer to J. Young & Co., woollen drapers, 15 New Bond st.
Gregg, William, gilder, 26 Grace street
Gregory, Bunting, clothes dealer, 2 Smithfield
Gregory, Jane, pawnbroker, 79 North Queen street
Gregory, Owen, furniture dealer, 61 Smithfield
Greig, Edward, shopman J. Arnott & Co.'s, Herdman's buildings
Greig, James & Wm., glass and china merchants, 110 High street
Greig, William, delf merchant, High street—9 New Bond street
Grey, Edward Prior, Shakspeare hotel, 21 Castle lane
Grey, William, clerk, 5 Townsend street
Gribben, Daniel, carter, 8 North Ann street
Gribben, Edward, watchmaker and jeweller, 13 High street
Gribben, Thomas, confectioner, painter, and glazier, 13 John street
Gribben, Thomas, bookseller, 76 North street
Gribben, William, carpenter, 13 York lane
Gribbin, Edward D., surgeon, 23 Great Edward street
Gribbin, John, tailor, 21 Henrietta street
Gribbin, John, schoolmaster, Ross street
Gribbin, Thomas, tobacco spinner, 6 Torrens' market
Grieve, Hay, watchmaker, 7 Hamilton street
Griffith, B., clothes dealer, 41 Berry street
Griffith, Isaac, dealer in hay, 3 Carrick hill
Griffith, J., clothes dealer, 5 Berry street
Griffith, James, clothes dealer, 26 Rosemary street
Griffith, James, clothes dealer, 39 Berry street
Griffith, John, pawnbroker, 30 Great Edward street
Griffith, James, nailer, 66 Mustard street
Griffith, P., wine, spirit, tobacco, & snuff dealer, 35 Smithfield & Winetavern st.
Grimes, M., clothes dealer, 9 Berry street
Grimes, Thomas, butcher, 48 Hercules street
Grimmea, Thomas, grocer, 29 Alexander street
Grimshaw, Conway B., and Son, agents to the Atlas Assnrance Company—Linfield, Lower Malone
Grimshaw, Edmund, flax spinner, 28 Waring street—Mosley
Grimshaw, Eliza, provision dealer, 7 Little Patrick street
Grimshaw, James, & Son, flax spinners, 28 Waring street—Whitehouse
Grimshaw, O'Donnell, post master and solicitor, 30 Rosemary st.—Linfield
Grisholm, David, hackler, Shankhill road
Grogan, Charles, general merchant in wood and iron, and hay exporter, &c., 49 Smithfield—Ballynafeigh
Grogan, John, veterinary surgeon, The Castle yard
Grogan, Mrs., 15 Chichester street
Grogan, Robert, bonded stores and agent, 3 Albert square—19 Dock street
Grogan, William, linen merchant, Linen hall—14 Wellington place
Grogan, Wm., ship carpenter, 43 Little George's street
Groom, Mrs., boarding house, 22 North Queen street
Grott, Mrs., 56 Great George's street
Grubb, Henry, butcher, 87 Hercules street
Grubb, William, mechanic, 31 Durham street
Guinn, Eliza, stay maker, 147½ North street

Guinn, Robert, coachmaker, 147¼ North street
Gunn, Alexander, proprietor of the Vine hotel and tavern, 19 Queen's square
Grueber and Co., asphalte works, Prince's dock—70 York street
Grueber, Thomas, merchant, 3 The Crescent, Botanic road
Gubbins, William, attorney's clerk, 33 North Thomas street
Gunning and Campbell, flax and tow spinners, Falls road
Gunning, John, clerk, 125 York street
Gunning, John, grocer, and publican, 21 Little George's street
Gunning, Robert, 2 The Castle, of Gunning and Campbell's mills, Falls road
Guy, Alexander, publican, 3 Little Donegall street
Guy, James, publican, 57 New Lodge road
Guy, William, poor rate collector, 5 Campbell's buildings, Townsend street
Guyns, Thomas, lodging house, 4 Ritchie's place

HADDOCK, Edward, clerk, Nelson's buildings, Shankhill road
Haddock, Jane, lodging house, 2 Bradford square
Haddock, Thomas, turnkey in jail, Crumlin terrace
Haddock, Wm., publican and grocer, 15 and 17 Ann street
Hadskins, Abel, tailor and customhouse officer, 15 Lancaster street
Hadskis, William, turner, 2 Torrens' market
Haffern, Miss, 21 Cromac street
Haffern, William, linen measurer, Linen Hall—21 Cromac street
Hagan, Ann, grocer, 45 Barrack street
Hagan, Edward, mechanic 3 Moffet street
Hagan, Henry, clothes dealer, 49 Smithfield
Hagan, John, tailor, 52 Stanhope street
Hagan, John, baker, Meeting house lane, 9 William street
Hagan, Miss, dressmaker, 35 Devis street, Falls road
Hagan, Robert, stone cutter, 11 Moffet street
Hagan, Robert, weaver, 20 Wall street
Hagerty, Alice, lodgings, 13 Carrickhill
Haggerty, Patrick, pensioner, 34 Lancaster street
Haggarty, Thomas, porter, 49 Old Lodge road
Haig, Samuel, foreman bookbinder, 30 Joy street
Hainen, Miss, school, 15 Talbot street
Hainey, Hugh, publican, 33 Winetavern street
Hale, Francis, butcher, 54 Peter's hill
Hale, Francis, butcher, 3 Peter's hill
Halfpenny, A., grocer & hardware dealer, 11 Kennedy's place—61 Smithfield
Hall, Daniel, brush manufacturer, 10 Brown square
Hall, Edward, shipsmith, 12 Collingwood street
Hall, George, jobbing smith, 15 Little York street
Hall, George, hatter, 51 Smithfield
Hall, Hugh, porter, 11 Charlemont street
Hall, Henry, ropemaker, Ballynafeigh
Hall, James, porter, 3 Annette street
Hall, James, constable, 5 Boyd street
Hall, John, smith's helper, 12 William's row
Hall, John, photographic studio, 22 York street
Hall, John, lodgings, 141 Durham street
Hall, John, grocer and stonecutter, Frederick street
Hall, Mrs., 3 Botanic view, Botanic road
Hall, Michael, lodgings, 15 Gamble street
Hall, Patrick, flax dresser, 53 Curell's place
Hall, Robert, tailor, 36 Talbot street

ALPHABETICAL DIRECTORY. 259

Hall, Samuel, shoemaker, 54 Verner street
Hall, William, lithographic writer and printer, 9 Joy's entry
Hall, William, in pork store, 30 William's row
Hall, William, gentleman, Jackson's hall, Ballymacarrett
Hall, William, cabinet maker, 46 Boundary street
Hall, William, painter, 35 Brown street
Halleron, Miss, 9 Clarendon place
Halliday & M'Dowell, grain merchants, 8 Tomb street; Johnson Halliday's residence, 6 Prospect terrace
Halliday, Hugh, flour merchant, 18 Thomas street
Halliday, John, shoemaker, 11 Lower Stanfield street
Halliday, Jacob, & Co., hardware warehouse, 35 Castle street—20 Castle st.
Halliday, John H., surgeon, 59 Donegall street
Halliday, John, tailor, 188 North street
Halliday, Mrs., 5 Albion place
Halliday, Miss, 10 Long lane
Halliday, William, salesman, 13 Spencer street
Halpan, Michael, tailor, 12 Boundary street
Hamill, Alexander, pork cutter, 23 Morrow's entry
Hamill, Arthur, butcher, 7 Hercules street
Hamill, Alexander, clothes dealer, 8½ Berry street
Hamill, Henry, marine store, 3 Lettuce hill
Hamill, H., green grocer, 2 Albion lane
Hamill, Hugh, sailmaker, 24 Grattan street
Hamill, Henry, cooper, 12 Economy place
Hamill, James, provision dealer, 179 North street
Hamill, John, moulder, 9 Union place
Hamill, John, stoker, 17 Charles street
Hamill, John, porter, 19 Vere street
Hamill, John, porter, 21 Vere street
Hamill, Mrs., schoolmistress, 46 Lower Malone
Hamill, Robert, grocer, Harmony place
Hamilton & M'Cullough, clothiers, 75 High street
Hamilton, Andrew, starch manufacturer, 18 Mary's market
Hamilton, Hill, rent office, 23 and 25 Hill street—Mount Vernon
Hamilton, Hugh, canvass weaver, 46 Green street
Hamilton, Henry, brickmoulder, 24 Stanfield street
Hamilton, Hugh, wholesale grocer, 35 Ann street—24 Gloucester street
Hamilton, James, muslin printer, 1 Meetinghouse lane
Hamilton, James, oil and commission merchant, 11 Queen's sq.—72 York st.
Hamilton, James, bark and oil stores, 13 Albert square
Hamilton, James, carpenter and builder, 85 Joy street
Hamilton, James, solicitor, 105 York street
Hamilton, James, carpenter, 35 Grove street
Hamilton, James, hair cutter, 19 Smithfield
Hamilton, James, pipemaker, 63 Great Patrick street
Hamilton, John, paper works, 42 Little Donegall street
Hamilton, John, cooper, 80 Old Lodge road
Hamilton, James, rag store, 29 Brown's square
Hamilton, John, plumber, 2 Francis street
Hamilton, John, cork manufacturer, 46¼ Rosemary street
Hamilton, John, pork cutter, 29 Mitchell street
Hamilton, Joseph, block printer, 6 Fleming's place, Old Lodge road
Hamilton, John, stone cutter, 1 Wesley lane

Hamilton, Margaret, provision dealer, 28 Smithfield
Hamilton, Mrs., white worker, 30 Stanley street
Hamilton, Mrs., shirtmaker, 44 Annette street
Hamilton, Rev. David, 10 Dock street
Hamilton, Robert, engraver, 33 Castle street—2 Ardmoulin place
Hamilton, Robert, paper stainer, 17 Roy street
Hamilton, Robert S., hair cutter and wig maker, 14 Ann street
Hamilton, Robert, weaving factory, 1 College court—Hamilton street
Hamilton, Robert, 6 Belvidere place
Hamilton, Thomas, pipe maker, 39 Winetavern street
Hamilton, William, cork manufacturer, 4 Hercules street
Hamilton, William, merchant, Glenfield place, Ormeau road
Hamilton, William, delf merchant, 23 Great Patrick street
Hamilton, Wm., manager in Messrs. Sinclair's, Tomb street—5 Antrim place
Hammersley, William, gentleman, 5 Ship street
Hammond, Betsy, washerwoman, 21 Caddel's entry
Hammond, Patrick, Railway hotel, Queen's quay, Ballymacarrett
Hammond, Robert, weaver, 11 Cullingtree street
Hampsey, Edward, ropewalk, Ballymacarrett
Hampsey, Patrick, ropewalk, Ballymacarrett
Hampson, Mary, rope and twine manufacturer, 6 Prince's street
Hancock, John, & Co., estate agents, 12 Wellington place
Hancock, Miss, 103 North Queen street
Hancock, Mrs., 12 Wellington place
Hancock, W. Neilson, LL.D., barrister-at-law, professor of political economy and jurisprudence in Queen's College, 12 Wellington place
Hanley, B., teacher Ballymacarrett Infant school
Hanley, John, shoemaker, 87 Carrick hill
Hanlon, Ellen, green grocer, 74 Millfield
Hanlon, John, house carpenter, 9 Albert street
Hanlon, John, whitesmith, 15 Durham street
Hanlon, Michael, tailor, 40 Millfield
Hanlon, Michael, boat builder and scantling yard, 7 Corporation square
Hanlon, Mrs., 10 Alfred street
Hanna, Catherine, 11 Upton street
Hanna, Catherine, boarding house, 14 Caldell's entry
Hanna, David, grocer and publican, 23 Wilson street
Hanna, Daniel, assistant county surveyor, 8 College street
Hanna, Ellen, nurse tender, 6 Grace street
Hanna, Edward, ropemaker, M'Rory's row, Ballymacarrett
Hanna, Francis, publican, Hanna's court, Shankhill road
Hanna, Hugh, dealer, 104 Lower Malone
Hanna, Hugh, surveyor, 27 Hamilton street
Hanna, Isaac, paper stainer, Welsh street
Hanna, James, apothecary's assistant, 9 King street
Hanna, James, stone mason, 16 King street
Hanna, John, grocer and spirit dealer, 16 Peter's hill
Hanna, John, master carter, 10 Townsend street
Hanna, John, grocer and publican, 1 Boyd street
Hanna, John, dealer, 38 M'Tier's street
Hanna, Joseph, boot and shoemaker, 21 Edward street
Hanna, John, coal office, 1 Queen's quay, Ballymacarrett
Hanna, Martin, jeweller, Quinn's entry, High street
Hanna, Mary, grocer, 116 Millfield
Hanna, Robert, book keeper, 8 Dock street

ALPHABETICAL DIRECTORY. 261

Hanna, Robert, gardener and provision dealer, Falls road
Hanna, Rev. Hugh, 104 Lower Malone
Hanna, Samuel, military boot maker, 4 Arthur square
Hanna, Samuel, sawyer, Meadow street
Hanna, Samuel, cooper, 94 Nelson street
Hanna, William, boiler maker, Northburn place
Hanna, Wm., assistant Townsend street National school—104 Lower Malone
Hannan, Catherine, boarding house, 39 Old Lodge road
Hannan, James John, attorney's clerk, 65 Cromac street
Hannan, James, spirit dealer, Shankhill road
Hannay, George, broker, 77 York street
Hannay, Hugh H., woollen merchant, 13 Donegall street—14 York street
Hanratty, James, hackler, 11 Pound street
Hanvey, Eliza, dealer, 29 West street
Hanvey, John, entertainment and lodging, 17 Winetavern street
Hanvey, William, publican, 24 Albert square
Harbison, Andrew, wholesale grocer, Victoria street
Harbison, James, umbrella maker, Hopeton place, Shankhill road
Harbison, Mary, brush maker, 27 Mitchell street
Hardy, Bernard, weaver, 44 Green street
Hardy, Thomas, woollendraper, silk mercer, haberdasher, hosier, &c., 35 and 37 High street
Hare, James, damask weaver, 14 North King street
Hare, John, carpenter, 17 Brown's square
Hare, John, grocer, Ballymacarrett
Hargrave, Miss Ann, commercial boarding house and hotel, Victoria street
Hargrave, Josiah, grocer, 3 Johnston's place, Ballymacarrett
Harkin, A., surgeon and apothecary, 7 Hercules place—17 Fountain street
Harkin, John, in Mr. M'Adam's, druggist, 117 Millfield
Harkin, Mrs., spirit store, 4 Hill street
Harkin, Patrick, grocer, Shankhill road
Harkin, Peter, clothes dealer, 2 and 3 Berry street and 10 Hercules place
Harkness, Alexander, carpenter, Shankhill road
Harkness, James, china, delf, and cut glass warehouse, 56 High street and 1 Sugarhouse entry
Harley, John, starch worker, 47 Boyd street
Harper, Bridget, 1 Sarah street
Harper, Ellen, lodging house, 40 Great Patrick street
Harper, Hugh, pawnbroker, 46 Barrack street
Harper, Henry, carpenter, Old Lodge road
Harper, Hugh, pawnbroker, 35 Union street
Harper, John, clerk, 1 Frederick place
Harper, James, machine works, 6, 9, 10 Wilson street
Harper, James, hackler, Ross street
Harper, John, weighmaster, Butter market—1 Frederick lane
Harper, Martin, wholesale grocer, 44 Church lane—22 College street
Harper, Mrs., bleachfield, M'Rory's row, Ballymacarrett
Harper, Robert, grocer, 13 Little George's street
Harper, Thomas, caretaker Masonic Hall, 15 Donegall place
Harper, Thomas, mechanic, Lagan village, Ballymacarrett
Harper, William, carpenter, 9 Morrow's entry
Harper, William, cooper, 8 Earl lane
Harris, Henry, haberdasher and hosier, 89 Joy street
Harris, James, sawyer, 5 Johnston's place, Ballymacarrett
Harris, Robert, joiner, 4 Russell street

ALPHABETICAL DIRECTORY

Harrison, Alexander, tailor, 33 Verner street
Harrison, George, ladies' boot and shoemaker, 46 Donegall street
Harrison, George, stationer, bookbinder, 51 High street—Holywood
Harrison, Henry, baker, 60 Peter's hill
Harrison, Joseph, writing clerk, 26 Stanfield street
Harrison, James, mechanic, 8 Curtis street
Harrison, John, merchant, 1 Albert square—Mertoun Hall, County Down
Harrison, Joseph, writing clerk, 6 Eliza street
Harrison, James, painter and glazier, 15 Sackville street
Harrison, James, clerk, 4 College place North
Harrison, Miss Mary, 14 Ormeau place
Harrison, Mrs., 13 College square East
Harrison, William, lodgings, 51 Prince's street
Harrison, William, sewed muslin manufacturer, 37 John st.—11 Hamilton st.
Harrison, Wm., carpenter, 9 Letitia street
Harrison, Wm., builder and scantling yard, 13 Union place
Harroworth, Thomas, brewer, 6 College street
Harston, Captain, R.N., marine office, 67 Corporation street
Hart, Charles, shoemaker, 39 Stephen street
Hart, Henry, shoemaker, 30 Samuel street
Hart, James, muslin manufacturer, and flax spinner, 6 Commercial court—26 Queen street
Hart, John, professor of music, 6 Arthur square
Hart, John, dealer, 11 Robert street
Hart, John, undertaker and scantling yard, 62 and 64 Union street
Hart, Joseph, piano forte and music warehouse, 14 Castle place
Hart, Samuel, lapper, 32 Old Lodge road
Hart, Solomon, lodgings, 15 Prince's street
Hart, Samuel, manager, Clark and Drummond's—5 Franklin place
Hartley, John, notary public, 1 The Castle, Castle buildings—7 Botanic road
Hartley, William, agent and accountant, 1 The Castle, Castle buildings—25 Chichester street
Hartrick, Rev. E. J., parsonage, Magdalene Episcopal Chapel, Donegall pass
Harvey, Ellen, confectioner, 79 Little Patrick street
Harvey, Francis, dealer, 56 Barrack street
Harvey, Hugh, house carpenter, 90 Nelson street
Harvey, Henry, carpenter, 6 Thomas street
Harvey, James, dyer, 57 Boundary street
Harvey, John, bricklayer, 13 Michael street
Harvey, Rev. James, Methodist minister, 28 Stanhope street
Harvey, Thomas, grocer, 32 Great Edward street
Harvey, William, bill poster, 14 Telfair's entry
Haslett and Fraser, woollendrapers and hatters, 21 High street
Haslett, Anne, dressmaker, Old Malone road
Haslett, John, manager of factory, 4 Kennedy's place
Haslett, James, grocer, Shankhill road
Haslett, Wm. Henry, solicitor, 14 Chichester street
Haslitt, Mrs., milliner and dressmaker, 7 Arthur street
Hassard, Henry, customhouse officer, 18 Dock street
Hastings, Wm., civil engineer, Town Surveyor's office—8 North Queen street
Haughey, Jane, lodging house, 41 Grattan street
Haughey, Terence, gasfitter, 15 Pound street
Haughton, Dennis, clerk, 117 York street
Havern, James, coal dealer, 35 Lower Stanfield street
Havern, Mrs., Roundhill Cottage, Ballymacarrett

ALPHABETICAL DIRECTORY.

Haveron, Mrs., cow keeper, Millfield
Haveron, Robert, painter, 5 Sackville place
Hawkes, Ann, dealer, 39 North Queen street
Hawkins, John, cotton spinner, 23 North Queen street
Hawkins, John, hostler Royal hotel, 34 Russell street
Hawkins, Wm., servant, 43 North Thomas street
Hawson, John, slater, 21 Stephen street
Hawthorne, James, car owner, 31 Little Patrick street
Hawthorne, Mrs. Ellen, dressmaker, 28 Stanley street
Hawthorn, John, soap boiler, 9 Stephen street
Hawthorn, James, grocer, 15 William's lane
Hay, Alexander, whip maker, 16 Mary's market
Hay, Peter, block printer, 55 Conway street
Hay, Wm., confectioner, 20 Church lane
Hayden, Pierce, spirit dealer, 32½ Great George's street
Hayes, Catherine, house keeper, 47 Durham street
Hayes, John, butcher, 11 Barrack street
Hayes, John, conveyancer, 12 William street south
Hayes, Joseph, mechanic, Hopeton place
Hayes, Mrs., teacher National Female School, 20 Fountain street
Hayes, Samuel, mechanic, 19 Hamilton's place
Hayes, Thomas, house painter, 9 Brown street
Haynan, Samuel, brassfounder, 19 Cullingtree place
Hayney, John, moulder, 23 Wall street.
Hayney, Kirkwood, boot and shoemaker, 53 Hudson's entry
Hazard, Henry, customhouse officer, 18 Dock street
Hazelton, M., Haberdasher, 22 Ann street
Hazlett, Wm., pensioner, Ballynafeigh
Headley, George, gasfitter, 4 Smithfield
Heaney, John, hackler, 33 New Lodge road
Heaney, Robert, bricklayer, 82 Peter's hill
Heaney, Thomas, baker, 38 Boyd street
Heatley, John, fireman, 15 New Lodge road
Heburn, Isaac, ropemaker, 28 Brown street
Heburn, Miss, milliner, 56 Ann street
Heburn, Patrick, engraver, 12 Duffy's place
Hecklin, William, mechanic, 4 Michael street
Hector, Edward, bootcloser, 8 Edward street
Hederman, Mrs., haberdasher, 95 North street—residence, 101 North street
Heeley, Thomas, sawyer, 7 Union place
Heely, Michael, confectioner, 19 Lagan street
Heeney, Dr. Francis, surgeon, 31 York street
Heeney, Hugh, spirit dealer, 33 Winetavern street
Heggarty, Patrick, bricklayer, 46 Old Lodge road
Hemersley, Joseph, mechanic, 34 Townsend street
Hemphill, William, schoolmaster, 26 M'Tier's street
Hemsley, John N., Union Tavern, Herdman's buildings, Shankhill road
Henderson, Alexander, grocer and spirit dealer, 30 Charles street
Henderson, Alexander, grocer and spirit dealer, 12 Stephen street
Henderson, Charles, flax bundler, Wellington square
Henderson, John, printer, publisher, and stationer, 13 Castle place
Henderson, John, superannuated officer, 28 North Thomas street
Henderson, Joseph, in the Water Commissioners' office—30 Earl street
Henderson, John, weaver, 5 Letitia street
Henderson, John, provision dealer, 15½ Hill street

ALPHABETICAL DIRECTORY.

Henderson, James Alexander, publisher *News-Letter;* office, 10 Bridge street; residence, Mount Collyer Park
Henderson, John, boiler maker, 5 Portland place
Henderson, John, water tax collector, 13 Harmony place
Henderson, James, tailor, 92 Lower Malone
Henderson, Misses, boarding and day school, 29 York street
Henderson, Mrs., 11 Botanic road
Henderson, Patrick, car driver, 28 Lancaster street
Henderson, Robert, mariner, 6 Sussex street
Henderson, Robert, whitesmith, 11 Ann street
Henderson, Robert, corn factor, commission and general steampacket agent, 23, 25 & 27 Donegall quay—74 York street and Willow Bank, Malone
Henderson, Robert, coal yard, 8 Queen's quay, Ballymacarrett
Henderson, Robert, boot and shoemaker, 5 York lane
Henderson, Serjeant, constabulary station, 69 Durham street
Henderson, Samuel, acting tide surveyor, 35 Ship street
Henderson, William D., grain merchant, broker and commission agent, 42 Waring street; residence, 2 Howard street
Henderson, William, grocer and carpenter, 26 Hill street
Henesey, Bryan Joseph, salesman, 119 York street
Henesey, Joseph, grocer, 33 Little George's street
Henesy, Edward, accountant Ulster bank—69 York street
Hennesey, David, cabinet maker, 35 Rosemary street
Hennesy, John, butcher, 61 Hercules street
Hennesy, Margaret, haberdasher, 84 North street
Hennan, Arthur, linen lapper, 83 Joy street
Hennon, James and John, attorney's clerks, 65 Cromac street
Henry, A. & S., and Co., linen merchants and commission agents, 2 Donegall square north, and 13 Calender street
Henry, James, foreman boot and shoemaker, 11 Melbourne street
Henry, James, weighmaster, 34 Durham street
Henry, James, tailor, 36 Lower Malone
Henry, John, grocer and publican, 130 Millfield
Henry, John W., sewed muslin overseer in Mr. Holden's—Spencer street
Henry, Joseph, wood turner, 53 Union street
Henry, Mary, green grocer, 23 Castle market
Henry, Madeline, dealer, 9 Store lane
Henry, Mrs., milliner, 49 Upper Arthur street
Henry, Martha, confectioner, 15 Boundary street
Henry, Nathaniel, 6 College square east
Henry, Patrick, dealer, 156 North street
Henry, Robert, blacksmith, 30 Dock street
Henry, Rev. Dr., president Queen's College
Henry, Thomas, compositor, 11 Joy's place
Herald, William, blacksmith, 4 Pilot street
Herd, David, linen manufacturer, 8 Donegall square north
Herdman, Captain H., Mount Pottinger, Ballymacarrett
Herdman, Jas., of J. & J. Herdman & Co., flax spinners, Tudor hall, Holywood
Herdman, J. & J., and Co., flax and tow spinners, 40 Smithfield
Herdman, John, of J. & J. Herdman and Co.—9 Wellington place
Herdman, William, of Langtrys and Herdman—Cliftonville, Antrim road
Heron, Edward, grocer and publican, Keenan's place, Ballymacarrett
Heron, Edward, spirit dealer, 41 Smithfield
Heron, James, schoolmaster, 8 Riley's place
Heron, John, mariner, 8 Grace street

Heron, Jas., banker, of W. C. Heron & Co., merchants, Albert sq.—4 Queen st.
Heron, John, grocer, 44 Tomb street
Heron, Mrs., 2 Ingram place, Donegall pass
Heron, Rev. William, Ashley place, Ballymacarrett
Heron, William C., and Co., West India merchants, 13 Albert square—residence, Maryfield, county Down
Heron, William, grocer and baker, 46 Great Patrick street
Herron, Edward, auctioneer, appraiser, and spirit dealer, 2 West street
Herron, James M., baker, 9 Union place
Herron, Mrs. Mary, boarding house, 13 King street
Herron, Matthew, upholsterer, 4 King street court
Herron, Mary, publican, 43 Millfield and 39 West street
Herron, Robert, hair dresser, 12 Ann street
Herron, Robert, dealer, 133 Lower Malone
Herron, Robert, barber, 4 Napier street
Heslop, Alexander, master mariner, Ballymacarrett
Heslop, Ellen, Belfast and Ballymena Railway Hotel, York road
Heslop, Margaret, straw bonnet maker, 11 York lane
Hetherington, Captain David, 3 Spencer street
Hewey, John, tailor, 27 Talbot street
Hewey, Mrs., painter and glazier, 34 Union street
Hewitt, James, manager of sewed muslin warehouse, Herdman's buildings, Shankhill road
Hewitt, John, watch glass maker, Wheeler's place, Ballymacarrett
Hewitt, Miss, 21 Queen street
Heyburn, William, surgeon, 28 Mill street
Heyland, Miss, Ballynafeigh
Heyn, Gustavus, general commission merchant, ship agent and consul, 1 and 3 Henry street
Hicks, William, sewed muslin manufacturer, 15 Church street; weaving factory, Francis street
Higgin, Thos. H., general manager Belfast & Ballymena Railway, York road
Higgin, William, car driver, 10 Edward street
Higgins, John, grocer, Bridge end, Ballymacarrett
Higgins, John, spirit dealer, Bridge end, Ballymacarrett
Higgins, John, shoemaker, 13 Barrack street
Higgins, Paul, blacksmith, Falls road
Higgins, Patrick, barber, 77 Union street
Higgins, Patrick, pensioner, 6 Green's court
Higginson, Miss, 26 North Thomas street
Hill, Abraham, carpenter, 10 North Boundary street
Hill, Adam, sub-treasurer for the Borough of Belfast, and notary public, 11 Fisherwick place
Hill, Alexander, 14 Harmony place
Hill, Anne, publican, 120 Ann street, and 53 Prince's street
Hill, Daniel, carpenter, 8 Sackville street
Hill, George, book keeper, 89 York street
Hill, George S., sub-inspector of constabulary, 6 North Queen street
Hill, George L., engraver, 9 Castle street
Hill, James, pilot, 18 Trafalgar street
Hill, John, rasp and file cutter, 24 and 26 West street
Hill, John, publican, 20 Great George's street
Hill, John, pill box manufacturer, 8 Castle street; residence, 8 Fountain st.
Hill, Joseph, coast guard, 71 Old Lodge road
Hill, James, carpenter, 22 Edward street

ALPHABETICAL DIRECTORY.

Hill, John, weaver, 10 Stephen street
Hill, John, baker, Shankhill road
Hill, Mrs., Donegall pass
Hill, Mrs., 8 Chichester street
Hill, Margaret, dealer, 45 Durham street
Hill, M., gunsmith, 31 Rosemary street
Hill, Mrs. Eliza, 11½ North Queen street
Hill, Miss, milliner, 8 Donegall place buildings, Castle street
Hill, Mary, dealer, 59 Lancaster street
Hill, Rev. George, Botanic cottage
Hill, Robert, baker, 37 Stanhope street
Hill, Thomas, starch maker, 19 York lane
Hill, Thomas, marketman, 10 Charles street
Hill, Thomas, weaver, 33 Brown street
Hill, William, porter, 9 Greenland street
Hillan, Rodger, salesman, 4 Spa mount
Hilland, Charles, grocery and spirit store, 25 Barrack street
Hillis, James, shoemaker, 43 M'Tier's street
Hillis, James, mechanic, Peel's place
Hillman, John, weaver, 26 Round entry
Hinchy, William, smith, 19 Greenland street
Hincks, Rev. Dr., 7 Murray's terrace
Hind, Hugh S., ship broker and commission agent, 1 and 11 Queen's square
Hind, John, jun., of S. K. Mulholland and Co., 11 Chichester street
Hind, John, of S. K. Mulholland & Co., the Lodge, Antrim road
Hinds, Hugh, sawyer, 16 Chapel lane
Hinds, John, furniture dealer, 9 Smithfield
Hinks, William, pensioner, 6 Boyd street
Hitchcock and Black, solicitors, 70 Donegall street
Hodge, T., furniture broker, & dealer in old iron, 54 Smithfield, 10 Francis st.
Hodge, William, carman, 45 Lancaster street
Hodgen, Matthew, mill wright, 7 Stanley street
Hodgens, Mrs., 6 Antrim place
Hodges, Dr., professor of chemistry, 23 Queen street, and 7 Arthur street
Hodges, Thomas, furniture broker, 8 and 10 Francis street
Hodgkinson, William, hackle maker, and provision dealer, 17 Hill street
Hodgson, Archibald, hackler, 12 Stephen street
Hodgson, John, grocer, 19 Campbell's buildings, Townsend street
Hodgson, John, shopman, 19 Townsend street
Hodgson, Robert A., bookseller, printseller, stationer, and room paper warehouse, 9 High street ; residence, Holywood
Hoffmeister, Charles, collector at Custom house—Cliftonville, Antrim road
Hogg, John, bricklayer and fireman, 27 Police place
Hogg, James, weaver, 20 Torrens' market
Hogg, Jacob, bricklayer, 21 Police square
Hogg, Jane, grocer and publican, 21 Pilot street
Hogg, John, ship smith, 21 Pilot street
Hogg, Robert, paper stainer, 15 Roy street
Hogg, William, grocer, 30 Ann street
Hogg, William, shoemaker, 28 Annette street
Holden, John, and Co., sewed muslin manufacturers, 32 Donegall street ; John Holden's residence, 3 Royal terrace
Holden, J., manufacturer, 3 Royal terrace
Holden, James, iron founder, 16 Ship street
Holden, Margaret, dealer, M'Crory's row, Ballymacarrett

ALPHABETICAL DIRECTORY.

Holden, Thomas, foreman smith, Rowan's foundry, 1 North Thomas street
Holings, John, preparing master, Grove street
Holland, D., editor *Northern Whig*, 5 James's street South
Holland, John, salesman, 4 Murphy street
Hollewell, John, engineer, 18 Pilot street
Hollin, Patrick, porter, 38 Verner street
Holmes, George, dealer, Ballynafeigh
Holmes, Geo., Lieut. R.E., 1 Aughton terrace
Holmes, Hugh, blacksmith, 43 Alexander street
Holmes, John, plumber, Ballynafeigh
Holmes, John, millwright, 12 Nile street
Holmes, Jane, lodgings, 33 Bradbury place
Holmes, James, grocer and spirit dealer, Mary's place, North Queen street
Holmes, Mrs., 19 Academy street
Holmes, Valentine, United States consul, 5 and 6 Commercial buildings
Holmes, Wm., book deliverer, 8 New Lodge road
Holywood, Daniel, smith and provision dealer, 39 Union street
Holywood, William J., plumber, 30 Little York street
Home, Captain William, 3 Fisherwick place
Hood, David, publican, 25 Caddell's entry
Hood, J., surgeon, 41 Castle street
Hood, John, Ballymacarrett
Hood, James, cooper, 6 Dock lane
Hood, John, shoemaker, 11 Grattan place
Hood, James, Anderson's houses, Ballymacarrett
Hood, Mrs. Mary, 30 Talbot street
Hook, Archibald, miller, 7 William's row
Hook, John, brass moulder, 55 Grove street
Hooke, Richard, artist, 17 Chichester street
Hoole, Robert, tobacco spinner, 15 Melbourne street
Hope, George, grocery and spirit store, 96 Millfield, and Brown street
Hope, Robert, bookbinder, Antrim road
Hopes, Geo., grocer and spirit dealer, 1 Brown street
Hopkins, Wm., writing clerk, 2½ Great George's street
Hopkirk, Miss, 10 Harmony place
Horner, Charles, blacksmith, 26 Friendly street
Horner, David, mechanic. 10 Conway street
Horner, Henry, linen merchant, 9 Prospect terrace
Horner, James, grocery and spirit store, 10 Durham street
Horner, Thomas, watch glass maker, M'Rory's row, Ballymacarret
Horner, Wm., boot and shoemaker, 33 Melbourne street
Horricks, John, hackle maker, 36 Townsend street
Horswill, Mrs., baby linen establishment, 5 Arthur street
Houston, Anthony, carpenter, 50 Little Donegall street
Houston, Ann, sewer, 76 Old Lodge road
Houston, George, boarding house, 42 Great Edward street
Houston, Hugh, canvass weaver, 16 Little Edward street
Houston, Hugh, publican, 81 Peter's hill
Houston, John, grocer and publican, 21 Devis street, Falls road
Houston, John, yarn bundler, 31 Valentine street
Houston, James, teacher at the Seaman's Chapel School, Pilot street
Houston, Misses, 1 Eagleston place
Houston, Robert, linen lapper, 3 Dublin bridge
Houston, R. B. B., D.L., J.P., Orangefield, Ballymacarrett
Houston, Samuel, ship owner, 39 Dock street

ALPHABETICAL DIRECTORY.

Houston, Stephen, mechanic, 26 Cargill street
Howard, John, glass cutter, M'Rory's row, Ballymacarrett
Howard, William, wire worker, 15 Church lane
Howden, Charles, nursery and seedsman, 52 High st.—nursery, Malone
Howell, Edward, sea captain, 38 Ship street
Howie, Robert, proprietor Old Park print works, Old Lodge road
Hoy, Alexander, whitesmith, 13 Fountain street
Hoy, John, plain and ornamental painter and publican, 48 Waring street
Hoy, John, wine and spirit merchant, Victoria street—4 Botanic road
Hoy, Mrs., leech importer, 17½ Hercules place
Hoy, Michael, plasterer, 10 Sackville place
Hoy, Robert, painter, Vere street
Hoy, Robert, spirit dealer, 68½ Nelson street
Hoy, Samuel, stonemason, Roy street
Huddleston, Wm., pawnbroker, Portview house, Ballymacarrett
Hudson and Co., tea and coffee merchants and grocers, 25 High street
Hudson, J. Percival, inspector of factories, 2 Botanic road
Hudson, Lucinda, widow, 46 Winetavern street
Hughes, Arthur, shoemaker, 6 Stanfield street
Hughes, Bernard, bakery, and flour merchant, 5 Donegall place, and 71 Donegall street; residence, 35 Queen street
Hughes, Daniel, barber, 43 Union street
Hughes, Edward, pavier and green grocer, 43 Union street
Hughes, Edward, nailer, M'Adam's court
Hughes, Henry, blacksmith, 16 Lancaster street
Hughes, James, cork cutter, 7 Charlemont street
Hughes, John, green grocer, 59 Waring street; residence, Gamble street
Hughes, James, eating house, 24 Caddell's entry
Hughes, James, cork cutter, 30 Caddell's entry
Hughes, Margaret, spirit dealer, 13 Donegall quay
Hughes, Mrs., clothes dealer, 49 Berry street
Hughes, Patrick, dealer, 11 Washington street
Hughes, Peter, grocer and publican, 46 Peter's hill
Hughes, Patrick, cutler, 12 Francis street
Hughes, Peter, porter, 1 Caddell's entry
Hughes, Robert, ribbon merchant, 16 Castle street
Hughes, Sarah, lodgings, 16 Robert street
Hughes, Thomas, gentleman, 54 York street
Hughes, Thomas, cabinetmaker, 5 Edward street
Hughes, Wm., car driver, 36 Valentine street
Hughes, Wm., cattle dealer, 57 Barrack street
Hughes, Wm., corn merchant & flax spinner, 13 North st. & 27 Gamble st.
Hughes, Wm., butcher, 86 Millfield
Hughes, Wm., butter merchant, 68 York street
Hull, Francis, of Hull, Wilson, and Co.; mills, Falls road
Hull, Henry, porter, 70 Verner street
Hull, Henry, civil bill officer, 23 Cromac road
Hull, Hart, & Co., flax spinners, Falls road; 17 Victoria buildings, Waring st.
Hull, John, moulder, 19 Wall street
Hull, John, weaver, 43 Durham street
Hull, Mary, 25 Melbourne street
Hull, Richard, of Hull, Hart, and Co., flax spinners, Falls road; office, 17 Waring street; residence, 7 Howard street
Hull, Sarah, dressmaker, 16 Stephen street
Hull, William, grocer and publican, 26 Cromac street

ALPHABETICAL DIRECTORY.

Hume, Isabella, spirit dealer, 18 Mill street
Hume, John, head engineer co. Down railway—Saltpan row, Ballymacarrett
Hume, Mrs., 9 Botanic road
Hume, Thomas, grain merchant, 5 Gloucester street; residence, Ballynafeigh
Humphrey, Robert, house and rent agent, 2 Brown square
Humphrey, Samuel, linen weaver, 31 William street
Humphreys, William, pork cutter, 30 Boundary street
Humphries, Leonard, captain *Princess Alice*, 3 Wills' place
Humphries, Robert, machine maker, Conway street
Humphrys, Captain Joseph, 13 Ship street
Hunt, Henry, shoemaker, 15 Mary's market
Hunt, Robert, baker, 17 Mary's market
Hunter, Alexander, chandler, 138 North street
Hunter, Alexander, warehouseman, Court street, side of New Court House
Hunter, Alexander, confectioner, 23 Donegall street
Hunter, Ann, grocer, and spirit dealer, 76 Vere street
Hunter, Arthur, green hide and leather merchant, 152 North street
Hunter, Charles, proprietor of the Crown Tavern, Quinn's entry, Crown entry
Hunter, E., confectioner, 12 Donegall street
Hunter, Eliza. grocer, 56 Cromac street
Hunter, Elizabeth, grocer, 1 Caroline street
Hunter, Henry, bricklayer, 44 Peter's hill
Hunter, Henry, clerk, Frederick street
Hunter, John, waiter, 1 Coates street
Hunter, John, publican, 17 Union street
Hunter, James, moulder, 5 Portland place
Hunter, John, mechanic, 14 M'Millan's place
Hunter, John, grocer, 3 Little George's street
Hunter, John, dealer, 58 New Lodge road
Hunter, John, jun., and Co., general merchants, 35 Waring street; John Hunter's residence, Tyne cottage, Whiteabbey
Hunter, John, lodging house, 31 Little Donegall street
Hunter, Joseph, marine store, 7 Pilot street
Hunter, Mary, entertainment and lodging, 41 Winetavern street
Hunter, Mary, baker and confectioner, 99 North street
Hunter, Mr., starch works, 16 Shankhill road
Hunter, Robert, in Messrs. Mulholland's mill, William's row
Hunter, Robert, rag store, 2 Caroline street
Hunter, Samuel, manager of Belfast foundry, 14 North Queen street
Hunter, Samuel, physician and surgeon, 9 Clarence place
Hunter, Thomas, 19 Millfield
Hunter, W. and T., leather merchants, 45 Ann street
Hunter, William and Thomas, cotton yarn agents, and general commission merchants, 24 Waring street; residence, 1 Murray's terrace
Hunter, William, gentleman, 1 Murray's terrace
Hunter, William, mill manager, Mount Pottinger, Ballymacarrett
Hunter, William, bricklayer, 90½ Millfield
Hunter, William, pensioner, 135 Lower Malone
Hurst, Chas., M.D., proprietor of Imperial hotel, Donegall pl.—Locust Lodge
Huston, Robert, linen lapper, 3 Carr's row, Old Malone road
Huston, Robert, muslin agent, Sarah street
Hutchinson, David, cooper, 37 Talbot street
Hutchinson, John, engineer, 1 Seaview place, Ballymacarrett
Hutchinson, James, & Co., muslin manufacturers, 16 Academy street
Hutchinson, John, carpenter, 35 Caxton street

Hutchinson, Moses, publican and grocer, 5 Curtis street
Hutchinson, Mrs., 2 Royal terrace
Hutton, James, marble polisher, 45 Carrickhill
Hutton, John, storeman, 31 Hill street
Hutton, Rev. George, 9 Fisherwick place
Hyde, Richard, foreman in Mr. Harper's foundry, 8 Wilson street
Hyde, William, mechanic, 14 Cullingtree place
Hyde, William, linen buyer, 15 Russell street
Hyndman, George C., broker, auctioneer, and commission agent, 7 Castle place—5 Howard street
Hyndman, Grace, 14 Townsend street
Hyndman, Isabella, confectioner, 24 Church lane
Hynds, Patrick, pawnbroker, 34 Little Patrick street and 14 Nelson street

IEVERS, Ann, grocer and tobacconist, 41 North street
Imbrie, John, mechanic, 19 Wilson street
Imray, David, foreman in muslin warehouse, 3 Campbell's buildings
Inch, George, boiler maker, 12 Vere street
Ingle, Ann, straw plait warehouse, 50 Ann street
Ingles, James, book publisher, Fleet street
Ingram, George, publican, 2 Tomb street
Ingram, George, publican, 78 Waring street
Ingram, John, provision dealer, 161 North street
Ingram, Thomas, bricklayer, 53 Grattan street
Innes, James, mechanic, 14 Townsend place
Ireland and M'Neill, house furnishing ironmongers, 17 and 19 Corn market; James Ireland's residence, Clifden, Holywood
Ireland, Andrew, store keeper, 4 Stanley lane
Ireland, George, tinsmith, 8 Cargill street
Ireland, James, tinsmith, 12 Raphael street
Ireland, John, pattern drawer, 8 Stanhope street
Ireland, Mrs., lodgings, 13 Russell street
Ireland, Robinson, clerk, 95 Joy street
Ireland, Robert, flour and bran stores, 36 and 38 Prince's street
Ireland, Wm., boot and shoemaker, 5 King street court
Irvin, John, shoemaker, 14 Torrens' market
Irvin, Margaret, lodgings, 3 Tomb street
Irvine, Archibald, spirit dealer, Ballymacarrett
Irvine, Jane, whiteworker, 6 Sackville place
Irvine, James, house painter, 11 Skipper street
Irvine, John, mechanic, 19 Grove street
Irvine, James, spirit dealer, 29 Little Donegall street and 14 & 16 Union st.
Irvine, Mrs., grocer, 1 Barrack street—2 Millfield
Irvine, Matthew, spirit dealer and stabling yard, 184 North street
Irvine, Thomas, green grocer, 2 Garmoyle street
Irvine, Thomas, spirit store, 25¼ John street
Irvine, Wm., porter, 28 Old Lodge road
Irvine, Wm., porter, 18 Henrietta street
Irvine, Wm., seaman, 60 Vere street
Irwin, James, ship carpenter, 14 Michael street
Irwin, James, merchant, 6 Glenfield place
Irwin, Mrs. Caroline, 6 Glenfield place
Irwin, Mary Jane, lodgings, 11 Winetavern street
Irwin, William, porter, 12 Tomb street
Isdell, John, ladies' bootmaker, 11 Nelson street

ALPHABETICAL DIRECTORY. 271

Isles, Nathaniel, boot and shoe shop and leather merchant, 105 North street
Isles, Robert, fruit dealer, 5 Market street
Isles, William, rope and twine maker, 6 M'Cracken's row, Ballymacarrett
Ivers, Timothy, cabinet maker, 21 Eliza street
Ivory, James, rope and twine maker, 5 M'Rory's row, Ballymacarrett

JACKSON, Alexander, harper, 3 Catherine street North
Jackson, John, publican, 36 Union street and 25 Mustard street
Jackson, James Kennedy, solicitor and Coroner for Belfast, 8 Castle lane
Jackson, Margaret, grocer, Ballyhackamore, Ballymacarret
Jackson, Robert, mariner, 80 Nelson street
Jackson, Robert, confectioner, &c., 19 Winetavern street
Jackson, Samuel, mechanic, 5 Lower Malone road
Jackson, Thomas, linen merchant, 29 Donegall street and 4 York street
Jackson, Thos., architect, 16 Donegall pl.—Cliftonville cottage, Antrim road
Jackson, William, pensioner, 53 Nelson street
Jacobs, Thomas, officer Inland Revenue, Herdman's buildings
Jacobson, Daniel, clothier, 1 Earl street
Jaffa, Brothers, merchants, 4 Fountain lane and 29 Cowgate, Dundee
Jamieson, John, shoemaker, M'Larnan's buildings, Ballymacarrett
Jamison, Andrew, publican, 30 Prince's street
Jamison, Charles, porter, 38 Annette street
Jamison, Grace, quilter, 13 East street
Jamison, George, night constable, 1 Abbey street
Jamison, George, boiler maker, Ballynafeigh
Jamison, George, porter and lodgings, 9 Russell street
Jamison, John, book keeper, Lagan Village, Ballymacarrett
Jamison, James, gentleman, Ormeau road
Jamison, John, grocer, 16 Cullingtree street
Jamison, John, agent for J. H. Young & Co., muslin manufacturers, 37 John st.
Jamison, Miss, Connaught Bazaar, 3 Sussex place
Jamison, Moses, constable, 4 Frederick place
Jamison, Mrs., 3 Albert place
Jamison, Miss Mary, 2 Linenhall street
Jamison, Robert, joiner, 5 Michael street
Jamison, Samuel, porter, 14 Raphael street
Jamison, Samuel, clerk, 12 Earl street
Jamison, Sarah, laundress, Ballynafeigh
Jamison, Thomas, general agent, 4 Donegall street place
Jardin, Robert, & Co., grocers, 125 North street
Jardin, Robert, & Co., wholesale and retail grocers, 30 Waring street
Jefferson, Thomas, starch maker and eating house keeper, 40 John street
Jeffryes, John Reid, Northern Bank
Jenkins, James, pawnbroker, Marquis street—19 Mill street
Jenkins, John, cabinet maker, 8 Wall street
Jenkins, James, sailor, 32 Stanfield street
Jenkins, Wm., sawyer, 27 Pound street
Jennings & Co., iron merchants, 67 Donegall street
Jennings, Grace, 26 Lagan street
Jennings, John, woollendraper, 5 Bridge street
Jennings, John, carpenter, 43 Grattan street
Jennings, Mrs., dealer, 9 Hamilton's place
Jennings, Richard, carpenter, 42 Boyd street
Jobling, Edward W., Lloyd's surveyor, 94 Donegall street
Johnson & Co., wholesale London & Manchester warehousemen, 18 Donegall pl.

2 A

ALPHABETICAL DIRECTORY.

Johnson, Alexander, bricklayer, 8 Seymour lane
Johnson, Alexander, grocer and publican, 34 Cromac street
Johnson, Henry, engraver, 9 Campbell's buildings, Townsend street
Johnson, John, soap and candle manufacturer, 14 Great Patrick street
Johnson, John, clerk, 80 Carrick hill
Johnson, James, stonecutter, 15 Seymour lane
Johnson, James E., of Johnson & Co., 18 Donegall place
Johnson, Mrs., & Miss M'Clune, ladies' boarding & day school, 23 Hamilton st.
Johnson, Richard, weaver, 79 Old Lodge road
Johnson, Richard, linen lapper, 12 Cullingtree street
Johnson, Robert, fireman, 74 Lower Malone
Johnson, Sir W. G., 12 College square North, office, 7 Castle Chambers
Johnson, Thomas B., solicitor, 22 Arthur street
Johnson, William, of Johnson & Co., 18 Donegall place
Johnson, Wilson, clerk, Charlotte street
Johnston and Pelling, sewed muslin manufacturers, 30 Donegall street
Johnston, Alexander, painter, Academy street
Johnston, Alexander, spirit dealer, 2 Lagan street
Johnston, Ann, grocer, 66 Carrickhill
Johnston, Ann, bonnet maker, 9 Henrietta street
Johnston, Cooke, and Co., hat warehouse, 1 Bridge street
Johnston, Charles, shoemaker, 3 Stephen street
Johnston, David, plasterer, 27 Catherine street North
Johnston, Daniel, lapper, 14 Shipboy street
Johnston, David, ropemaker, 18 Shankhill road
Johnston, Eliza, grocer, 71 Nelson street—27 Trafalgar street
Johnston, F., manager S. Archer & Sons' engraving department—22 Nelson st.
Johnston, George, sawyer, 8 Eliza street
Johnston, Henry, ginger ale manufacturer, 17 Little York street
Johnston, Isabella, boarding house, 45 Prince's street
Johnston, John, carpenter, 10 Sir Henry's buildings, Ballymacarrett
Johnston, Joseph, bricklayer, 1 Seymour lane
Johnston, James, wood turner, Grove street
Johnston, John, coachman, 12 Seymour lane
Johnston, Joseph, bricklayer, 5 Seymour street
Johnston, Jane, 66 Nelson street
Johnston, John, proprietor Belfast steam marble works, 55 Great Patrick st.
Johnston, John, grocer, 40 Alexander street
Johnston, John M., land agent, clerk to the trustees of Malone, Falls, and Castlerobin turnpike roads, High Sheriff's office, 6 Castle Chambers
Johnston, John, gardener, 16 Eliza street
Johnston, John, spirit dealer, 21 Queen's square
Johnston, James, 1 Aughton terrace, Donegall pass
Johnston, J. S., baker, 38 Donegall street
Johnston, John, whitesmith, 2 Gordon street
Johnston, John, turner, 23 Upper Lagan street
Johnston, John carpenter, 8 Michael street
Johnston, John, dealer, 17 New Lodge road
Johnston, James, shoemaker, 48 Lower Malone
Johnston, James, bricklayer, Shankhill road
Johnston, James, moulder, 54 Boundary street
Johnston, John, tailor, 42 Grattan street
Johnston, James, bundler, New Lodge road
Johnston, Jane, board and lodgings, 11 Prince's street
Johnston, Jane, lodgings, 74 Great George's street

Johnston, Jane, dressmaker, 1 Friendly street
Johnston, Joseph, boot and shoemaker, 44 Lower Malone
Johnston, James, ship carpenter, 79 Nelson street
Johnston, John, ship carpenter, 15½ Lower Stanfield street
Johnston, John, compositor, 12 Seymour lane
Johnston, Matthew, shoemaker, 16 Francis street
Johnston, Mary, slipper maker, 4 Stanhope street
Johnston, Miss Dorcas, dressmaker, 22 Joy street
Johnston, Miss, dressmaker, 19 College street
Johnston, Miss, 107 York street
Johnston, Mr., writing school, 27 College street
Johnston, Mrs., lodging house, 72 Little Patrick street
Johnston, Margaret, publican, 5 Shankhill road
Johnston, M. and M., bonnet and dressmakers, 51 Great Patrick street
Johnston, Malcolm, coal office, 2 Queen's quay, Ballymacarrett
Johnston, Neill, currier, 110 Carrickhill
Johnston, Philip, and Co., wholesale tobacconists, 24 and 30 Skipper street
Johnston, Philip, wholesale grocer and tea merchant, 19, 21, & 23 Waring st.
Johnston, Rev. Edward, Wesleyan minister, 5 Ormeau place
Johnston, Rev. William; residence, the manse, Townsend street
Johnston, Robert, of William M'Connell and Co., Donegall street
Johnston, Surgeon Henry M., 77 Donegall street
Johnston, Samuel, ropemaker, 7 Boundary street
Johnston, Samuel, marine store keeper & rag merchant, 56 Little Patrick st.
Johnston, Samuel, grocer, 43 New Lodge road
Johnston, Samuel, whitesmith, 21 Prince's street
Johnston, Samuel, whitesmith, 1 Prince's court
Johnston, Samuel, marine stores, 64 and 66 Tomb street
Johnston, Samuel, grocer, 5 Hopeton place, Shankhill road
Johnston, Samuel, whitesmith, 2 Marlborough street
Johnston, Samuel, moulder, 35 Green street
Johnston, Samuel, jun., currier and wholesale leather merchant, 13 Mill st.
Johnston, Samuel, tailor, 52 Edward street
Johnston, S., shoemaker, 6 Union street
Johnston, Thomas, car driver, 9 Wellington street
Johnston, Thomas, bricklayer, 42 Joy street
Johnston, Thomas, carpenter, 7 Bradbury place
Johnston, Thomas, bookbinder, 12 Greenland street
Johnston, Thomas, sergeant of Harbour constables, 91 Nelson street
Johnston, William, carman, 22 Boundary street
Johnston, William, of Wm. M'Connell & Co., Donegall street
Johnston, William, clerk, 10 Stanhope street
Johnston, William, green grocer, 66 Mill street
Johnston, Walter, baker, 35 Little Patrick street
Johnston, Wm. John, wholesale grocer and tobacconist, Waring street and Skipper street—3 Upper Queen street
Johnston, W. and S., tan yard, 37 Mill street; W. Johnston's residence, 13 Mill street
Johnston, William, 14 Tomb street
Johnston, Wm., warper, 18 North Boundary street
Johnston, Wm., surgeon, 33 Corporation street
Johnston, Wm., spirit dealer, 38 Great George's street
Johnston, Wm., cabinet maker, 20 Mary's market
Johnston, Wm., publican, 33 Prince's street
Johnston, Wm., tailor, 16 Russell street

Johnston, Wm., lithographer, bookbinder, and stationer, 25 Waring street &
  19 Skipper street—14 Tomb street
Johnston, Wm., upholsterer, 2 Wellington court
Jones, Alexander, carter and coal dealer, 62 Peter's hill
Jones, Charles, ticket writer and label maker, 34 Green street
Jones, Charles, pork cutter, 36 Sussex street
Jones, James, butcher, 16 Round entry
Jones, John, carpenter, 24 Charles street
Jones, John, grocer and spirit dealer, 47 Cromac street—Henrietta street
Jones, John, stone cutter, 38 Carrickhill
Jones, James, grocer, M'Crory's row, Ballymacarret
Jones, John, foreman sailmaker, Wheeler's place, Ballymacarrett
Jones, Richard, clothes dealer, 6 Berry street
Jones, Thomas, writing clerk, 6 Bond street
Jones, Wm., tailor, 74 Joy street
Jones, William, cloth lapper, 22 Charles street
Jordan, Edward, mechanic, 3 Portland place
Jordan, Elijah, shoemaker, 7 Stephen street
Jordan, John, leather cutter, 42 Cromac street
Jordan, John, tobacco spinner, 8 Hudson's entry
Jordan, Mrs. Margaret, 35 Melbourne street
Jordan, Philip, grocery and spirit store, 136 Ann street
Jordan, Robert, grocery and delf warehouse, 125 North street
Jordan, Thomas, fishmonger, 1 Murphy's lane
Jordan, Wm., foreman, *Banner of Ulster*, 12 Little May street
Joy, Frederick, solicitor, 5 Arthur place
Judge, James, green grocer, 154 Millfield
Junk, James, 22 Corporation street
Justin, Catherine, whipmaker, 117 North street

Kane, Ann, boarding house, 8 Chichester lane
Kane, Ann, washerwoman, 51 Townsend street
Kane, Denis, provision and spirit store, 46 Waring street
Kane, George, cooper, 30 Gordon street
Kane, John, dealer, M'Rory's row, Ballymacarrett
Kane, John, bricklayer, 3 Little Corporation street
Kane, John, chart reviser, 64 Green street
Kane, John, dyer and renovator, 34 Millfield
Kane, John, hostler, 17 William street South
Kane, James, boot and shoemaker, 45 Union street
Kane, John, dealer, 52 Union street
Kane, John, millwright, 5 Sir Henry's buildings, Ballymacarrett
Kane, Major Henry, 13 Ormeau place
Kane, Miss, milliner, 57½ Academy street
Kane, Mrs., dealer, 11 Alexander street
Kane, Mary, bonnet maker, 16 Michael street
Kane, Miss Letitia, 18 Queen street
Kane, Patrick, compositor, 51 Townsend street
Kane, Sarah, 3 Wellington square
Kane, Thomas, green grocer, 2 Hammond's court
Kane, Thomas, mechanic, 6 Union place
Kane, Thomas, Oyster Tavern, Wilson's court
Kane, Thomas, tide waiter, 39 Tomb street
Kane, Wm., butter buyer, 11 Gordon street
Kane, Wm., yarn boiler, 13 Valentine street

ALPHABETICAL DIRECTORY.

Kavanagh, James, grocer, glass, oil, and colour merchant, 33 & 35 North st.
Kavanagh, John, writing clerk, 12 Johnston's buildings
Kavanagh, John, clerk, Agnes place, Shankhill road
Kealey, Wm., provision dealer, 183 North street
Kealy, Daniel, servant, 10 Roy's court
Kean, A., milliner, 38 Academy street
Kean, Francis, carver, 38 Academy street
Kean, Margaret, 9 Durham street
Kean, Thomas, post office clerk, 13 Johnston's buildings
Kearney, Andrew, mariner, 12 Michael street
Kearney, Catherine, boarding house, 30 Mill street
Kearney, Hugh, lodging house, 11 Carrickhill
Kearney, John, pensioner, 63 Mustard street
Kearney, John, publican, grocer, 35 Peter's hill
Kearney, J., basketmaker, Peter's hill and 10 Smithfield
Kearney, Patrick, pensioner, 126 Millfield
Kearney, Peter, spirit dealer, 64 Grattan street
Kearney, Richard, basket maker, Bridge end, Ballymacarrett
Kearney, Wm., basket maker, Ballymacarrett
Kearns, Wm., night constable, 22 Lower Stanfield street
Kearns, John, grocery and spirit store, 2 and 4 Mill street and 1 Queen street
Kearns, Mary, boarding house, 12 Caddell's entry
Keating, Andrew, builder and jobbing carpenter, 18 Fountain street
Keating, Joseph, baker, 15 Stanley street
Keating, William, mariner, 50 North Thomas street
Keatley, Samuel, clothes dealer, 11 Chapel lane and 36 Rosemary street
Keaton, John, shoemaker, 29 Greenland street
Keegan, James, rectifying distiller, 8 Arthur place
Keegan, James, wine merchant, 72 High street—4 College square East
Keegan, Peter, rectifying distiller and wine and spirit merchant, 4 Calender street—12 Victoria place
Keegan, William, gardener, 22 Dock street
Keenan, Ann, washerwoman, 109 Millfield
Keenan, Adam, tailor, 2½ Robert street
Keenan, Cornelius, packer, 36 Lagan street
Keenan, John, ropemaker, 10 Peter's hill
Keenan, John, starch maker, 33 York lane
Keenan, John, auctioneer, 76 Millfield
Keenan, John, dealer, Ritchie's place
Keenan, Joseph, linen lapper, 3 Wilson street
Keenan, John, solicitor, 13 Arthur street
Keenan, Patrick, confectioner, 18 Berry street
Keenan, Patrick, carpenter, 9 Shipboy street
Keenan, Patrick, farmer, Keenan's place, Ballymacarrett
Keenan, Thomas, rope and twine manufacturer 102 High street—21 Old Lodge road
Keenan, Wm., rope and twine maker, Portview, Ballymacarrett
Keir, Wm., gentleman, 34 Earl street
Keith, Andrew, car driver, 21 Stanhope street
Keith, Mrs., milliner and dressmaker, 53 Upper Arthur street
Kelly & M'Credie, stoneyard, 60 York street
Kelly, Daniel, whipmaker, 31 Samuel street
Kelly, Edward, auctioneer, 3 Kennedy's row—68 Smithfield
Kelly, Edward, dealer, 56 Union street
Kelly, Hugh, tailor, 18 Torrens' market

ALPHABETICAL DIRECTORY.

Kelly, Hugh M., teacher National School, 15 Fountain street
Kelly, Hugh, ship carpenter, 42 Little York street
Kelly, Hugh, wine and spirit merchant, 13 North Queen street
Kelly, James, ship carpenter, 85 Nelson street
Kelly, John, brush, comb, & trunk manufacturer, 24 Bridge street—2 Little Victoria street
Kelly, John, writing clerk, 5 James's street South
Kelly, John, canvass weaver, 26 Grattan street
Kelly, John, master mariner, 24 Caroline street
Kelly, John, sawyer, 26 Caroline street
Kelly, John, teacher, 128 Millfield
Kelly, J., & Co., drug and chemical warehouse, Victoria street
Kelly, J., cabinet warerooms, 9 Ann street
Kelly, James, ship carpenter, 15 Little Patrick street
Kelly, James, coal dealer, Shankhill road
Kelly, John, dealer, M'Tier's street
Kelly, James, hair dresser, 14½ Store lane
Kelly, Maria, clothes dealer, 1 Smithfield
Kelly, Michael, railway porter, 10 Little Ship street
Kelly, Michael, provision dealer, 175 North street
Kelly, Michael, pensioner, 12 Conway street
Kelly, Patrick, stokerer, 71 Little Patrick street
Kelly, Patrick, house carpenter, 61 Peter's hill
Kelly, Robert, manager Lord Londonderry's estate, 14 Ship street
Kelly, Rose, 28 Moffet street
Kelly, Rev. Edward, 97 Donegall street
Kelly, Samuel, grocer and commission coal merchant, 43 Cromac street
Kelly, Samuel, spirit dealer, New Durham street
Kelly, Samuel, shoemaker, 10 Alexander street
Kelly, Thomas, mill worker, 92 Millfield
Kelly, Wm., green grocer, 79 Millfield
Kelly, William, butcher, 15 Barrack street
Kelsey, John A., wine and spirit dealer, Gamble street
Kelso, Alexander, dealer, 101 Peter's hill
Kelso, Charles, hosier, 73 High street
Kelso, William, bricklayer, 19 Welsh street
Kelter, Isaac, carpenter, 24 Marquis street
Kelter, John, undertaker and scantling yard, 61 Union street
Kenna, Thomas, glassblower, 6 M'Rory row, Ballymacarrett
Kennedy & Johnston, haberdashers, 69 North street
Kennedy, Anthony, musician, 91 Carrick hill
Kennedy, Anne, publican, May street
Kennedy, Arthur, meal and flour dealer, 6 Castle market
Kennedy, David, gingham manufacturer, 4 Curtis street
Kennedy, Daniel, hackler, 78 Sussex street
Kennedy, David, grocer and spirit dealer, 10 Henrietta street
Kennedy, David, of the East India company's staff, 7 Winetavern street
Kennedy, Ellen, 8 Pilot street
Kennedy, George, cloth cutter, 21 Hamilton street
Kennedy, George K., clerk of petty sessions, Lilliput cottage
Kennedy, John, gentleman, 4 Ship street
Kennedy, John, car driver and huckster, 31 John street
Kennedy, John, house and general agent, conveyancer, &c., 13 Arthur street
Kennedy, John, pork cutter, 5 Durham street
Kennedy, John B., solicitor, 10 Castle lane; residence, Holywood

Kennedy, John, proprietor Ulster coach factory, 1 Montgomery street; residence, 4 Montgomery street
Kennedy, John, sawyer, 12 Little Corporation street
Kennedy, John, cart maker and publican, 3 Antrim road
Kennedy, John, grocer, 31 Alexander street
Kennedy, John, mat maker, 16 Samuel street
Kennedy, James, manufacturer, Commercial court—Rosetta, Ormeau road
Kennedy, James, boot and shoemaker, 46 Grattan street
Kennedy, John, & Co., umbrella and parasol manufacturers, 25 Ann street
Kennedy, John, miller, 17 York lane
Kennedy, James, baker, 3 M'Tier's street
Kennedy, Jas., of J. Kennedy & Son, flax spinners, Wellington sq., Falls road
Kennedy, James, linen inspector, 25 Bradbury place
Kennedy, James, & Son, flax and tow spinners, Millvale, Fall's road—3½ Waring street
Kennedy, J. & T., muslin manufacturers and bleachers, 13 Commercial court and Bedford street; size works, 42 Talbot street
Kennedy, James, porter, 37 Little York street
Kennedy, James, bleacher, 24 Vere street
Kennedy, Mrs., huckster, 7 Kennedy's place
Kennedy, Mrs., 3 Pilot street
Kennedy, Miss, teacher of music, 17 College street
Kennedy, Matthew, publican and grocer, 4 Harmony place
Kennedy, Mary, dealer, 22 Shankhill
Kennedy, Patrick, tanner, 49 Castle street
Kennedy, Patrick, fishmonger, 7 New Lodge road
Kennedy, Russell, merchant, 13 College square North
Kennedy, Robert, spirit store, 37 Bradbury place
Kennedy, Robert, cabinet maker, 43 Nelson street
Kennedy, Robert, boot and shoemaker, 95 Carrickhill
Kennedy, Robert, carpenter, 17 Shankhill road
Kennedy, Robert, branch pilot, 21 Collingwood street
Kennedy, S., carowner, 8 Arthur lane
Kennedy, S., solicitor, 17 Arthur street and 26 Lower Ormond quay, Dublin
Kennedy, Sampson, clerk Post office, 3 Academy street
Kennedy, Samuel, cabinet maker, Francis street
Kennedy, Samuel, confectioner, 6 York street
Kennedy, Samuel, boot and shoemaker, 87 Old Lodge road
Kennedy, Thos., manufacturer, 7 Wellington place—office, Commercial court
Kennedy, William, baker, 23 Church lane
Kennedy, William, book keeper, 22 Henry street
Kent, Archibald, carpenter and builder, 36 York street
Kenulty, Bernard, sawyer, 7 Stanfield court
Keown, Ansley, baker, 19 Stanley street
Keown, Mary, boarding house, 15 Ship street
Kermode, Edward, carrier, 21 Pottinger's entry
Kernaghan, Elizabeth, 15 Carrick hill
Kernaghan, Hugh, grocer and spirit dealer, 61 Grattan street
Kernaghan, James, carpenter, 16 Welsh street
Kernaghan, William, grocer, 19 and 21 Great Patrick street
Kernohan, Andrew, wholesale grocer, Victoria street
Kernohan, Mr., Ashley place, Ballymacarrett
Kerns, Alexander, boot and shoemaker, 28½ Great George's street
Kerns, Charles, Royal hotel and posting establishment, 27 Donegall place
Kerns, George, saddler, 155 North street

Kerns, James, porter, 4 Leeds street
Kerns, James, dealer, 42 Mustard street
Kerns, Michael, grocer, 57 Mustard street
Kerns, Patrick, tailor, 3 Orr's entry
Kerns, Samuel, tavern, 1 Fountain street, and Castle street
Ker, John, provision dealer, 13 Hill street
Kerr and Mercer, wholesale druggists & general merchants, 38 & 40 North st.
Kerr, Andrew, 14 Marquis street
Kerr, Alexander, pensioner, 26 Caddell's entry
Kerr, Alexander, publican, 2 North Ann street
Kerr, Alexander, carpenter, 27 Alexander street
Kerr, Charlotte, Star saloon, 21 Ann street
Kerr, Daniel, 24 Shankhill road
Kerr, Daniel, saddler and harness maker, 12 Castle place
Kerr, Edward, pensioner, 41 Green street
Kerr, Hugh, grocer, 21 Lancaster street
Kerr, Hugh, car driver, 6 Devis street
Kerr, John, commission agent, 22 Skipper street
Kerr, John, clerk, 18 North Queen street
Kerr, John, carter, 75 Peter's hill
Kerr, James, damask weaver, 12 Alexander street south
Kerr, James, storekeeper, 60 Townsend street
Kerr, John, carpenter, Bridge end, Ballymacarrett
Kerr, John, baker, 10 Rochfort place
Kerr, John, grocer and publican, and shoe shop, 18 Smithfield
Kerr, Michael, in felt works, 22 Sussex street
Kerr, Owen, Roman Catholic bookseller, 18 Chapel lane
Kerr, P., boot and shoemaker, 5 Bell's lane
Kerr, Robert, warper, 22 Cullingtree street
Kerr, Samuel, carpenter, 11 East street
Kerr, Samuel, grocer and publican, 18 and 20 Peter's hill
Kerr, William, merchant, 15 Albion place
Keyland, James, Dublin and Armagh hotel, Great Victoria street
Keys, David, butcher, 20 Hercules street
Keys, Jane, boarding house, 32 Gamble street
Kidd, Brothers, proprietors Newry mills bakery, 9 Queen street
Kidd, Osborne, flour miller, 61 North street; residence, Armagh
Kidd, William, carpenter, 5 Economy place
Kidley, Dr. John E., 47 York street
Kiglety, Mary, dealer, 1 Shankhill road
Killen, Agnes, 10 Thomas street
Killen, Bridget, spirit dealer, 47 Carrickhill
Killen, Daniel, car driver, 29 Lagan street
Killen, Henry, clerk, 6 Johnston's place, Ballymacarrett
Killen, Mrs., 4 University square
Killen, Rev. W. D., D.D., 3 University square
Killen, Rev. James, P.P., Chapel lane, Ballymacarrett
Killen, Wm., woollendraper, hosier, & hatter, 68 High st.—3 Victoria terrace
Killey, John, clerk, 21 Hamilton's place
Killian, Mary, old clothes dealer, 20 Kennedy's place—46 Smithfield
Kilmartin, Thomas, writing clerk, and spirit dealer, 36 Cromac street
Kilmartin, Thomas, spirit dealer, Lagan street
Kilpatrick, A., agent for Blackie and Sons, Glasgow, 28 Arthur street
Kimmit, Margaret, 2 Wellington street
Kimpson, Thomas, lapper, 8 Cullingtree place

ALPHABETICAL DIRECTORY.

Kinahan, F., of Lyle and Kinahan, wine and spirit merchants, Fountain st.; residence, Knockbreda
King, Cunningham, cutler, 6 Cromac road
King, Eliza, grocer, 22 Melbourne street
King, John, printer, 3 Murphy street
King, James, veterinary surgeon, proprietor of the Horse bazaar and veterinary establishment, 108 Donegall street
King, Richard, ropemaker, 11 Boundary street
King, Robert, merchant tailor, 21 Donegall street
King, Robert, grocer and spirit dealer, 3 Nile street
King, William, spirit dealer, 51 Durham street
Kinghan, Rev. John, assistant secretary, Ulster Deaf and Dumb Institution
Kingsberry, Alexander, porter, 82 Lower Malone
Kingsberry, John, servant, 17 Rochfort place
Kingsmill, Henry, clerk, 37 Hamilton street
Kinkaid, James, cooper, 32 Little York street
Kinnear, Patrick, linen and yarn merchant, 29 Waring street; residence, Harp hall, Antrim road
Kinney, Felix, grocer and publican, 11 and 13 Durham street
Kinney, John, grocer and publican, 51 North Queen street
Kirk, Andrew, tobacco manufacturer, 82 North street
Kirk, David, in pork store, 15 William's row
Kirk, Miss, 18 Earl street
Kirk, Mary, whiteworker, 1 Samuel street
Kirk, Robert D., wine & spirit dealer, 21 Frederick st. and 5 North Queen st.
Kirk, Wm., mechanic, 11 Kennedy's place
Kirker, Archibald, baker and flour merchant, 37 Cromac street
Kirker, Anna, dressmaker, 30 Henrietta street
Kirker, Brothers, haberdashers, 52 North street—24 Nelson street
Kirker, John, spirit dealer, 73 York street
Kirker, John, tailor, 136 Carrickhill
Kirker, Thomas, 24 Nelson street
Kirker, Thomas, spirit dealer, 77 Durham street
Kirker, Thomas, grocer and publican, Falls district post office, 22 Devis st.
Kirkpatrick, Charles, grocer, 2 Prince's street and 1 Queen's square
Kirkpatrick, William John, blacksmith, 22 Caxton street
Kirkwood, James, lithographic printer, 24 Green street
Kirkwood, Mary, 8 Duffy's place
Kirkwood, S., publican, Falls road
Kirkwood, Thomas, printer, 24 Green street
Kirkwood, Thomas, plasterer, 4 James' street south
Kirkwood, William, saddler, Ballynafeigh
Kirkwood, William, mechanic, 9 Conway street
Kirner, R., watch and clock maker, 18 Church lane
Kirwan, David, of Thompsons and Kirwan, ship builders, 43 Corporation st.
Kirwan, Richard, cork manufacturer, 27 Rosemary street
Kitson, William John, cooper, 37 Nelson street
Knight, Ellen, spirit dealer, 6 Telfair's entry
Knott, Robert, hatter, 12 Upton street
Knowles, Miss, seminary, 30 Upper Arthur street
Knox, Alexander, gentleman, 8 Apsley place
Knox, Cornelius, boot closer, 26 Robert street
Knox, John, manufacturer, 109 Donegall street
Knox, John, gentleman, 20 North Queen street
Knox, Mrs. Alice, 9 College street South

Knox, Mrs., 10 University square
Knox, Robert, boot and shoemaker, 60 High street
Knox, Rev. R., Presbyterian minister, licenser of marriages, Belfast district, 4 Adelaide place
Knox, Robert, shoemaker, 11 Wesley place
Knox, Wm., plumber, 3 California street
Knox, William, baker and flour dealer, 135 North street
Koch, Aime, patent flax works, Mount Pottinger—Cregagh, Castlereagh
Kyle, John, cow keeper and green grocer, 95 Peter's hill
Kyle, Geo. W., hosier, glover, outfitter, &c., 21 Bridge st.—33 Donegall st.

Lackey, James, cabinet maker, 3 O'Haggarty street
Lackey, John, carpenter, 8 Seymour street
Ladley, John, attorney, 16 Calendar street—99 Joy street
Lally, John, cabinet maker, 27 Russell street
Lamb, John, commission agent, Devis view, New Lisburn road
Lamb, James, boot and shoe shop, 88 North street
Lamb, Ann, lodging house, 3 Bradford square
Lamb, Patrick, engineer, 10 Campbell's buildings, Conway street
Lambert, Miss, boarding school, 6 Chichester street
Lambert, Mathew, nailer, 44 Grattan street
Lamont, John, gardener, 59 Grove street
Lamont, Miss, and Miss Rook's school, 38 Upper Arthur street
Lamont, Miss, artist, 3 Castle street
Lamont, Surgeon Æ., 3 Castle street
Lamp, Daniel, grocer and lodgings, 12 Grattan street
Lancaster, Thomas, deputy engineer, 5 Spamount
Lang, Alexander, steward, 10 Ship street
Lang, Charles, 1st clerk, Inland Revenue office—8 Johnston's buildings
Langtrys and Herdman, merchants, 33 Waring street
Lanyon, Charles, civil engineer and county surveyor and architect, &c., 10 Wellington place; office, 1 Upper Queen street
Lanyon, Edward, coach painter, 55 Curell's place
Lappan, Hugh, porter, 4 Bond street
Lappan, J., writing clerk, 11 Alexander street South
Lappan, Robinson, carpenter, 16 Murphy street
Largy, Thomas, butcher, 19 Great Edward street
Larkin, Miss, 2 Charlotte street
Larman, Elizabeth, boarding house, 35 Little May street
Larmour, Hugh, grocer, 23 Bradbury place
Larmour, Hugh, gentleman, 6 Apsley place
Larmour, Wm., flour & grain and commission merchant and broker, Victoria Buildings; residence, 6 Apsley place
Latham, Robert, cooper, Frederick lane
Lattimer, Mrs., publican, 127 and 129 Durham street
Lattimore, Samuel, cabinet maker, 4 Church street
Laughlin, James, confectioner, 172 North street
Laverty, Charles, spirit dealer, 4 Prince's street
Laverty, Henry, grocer and publican, 47 Stanley street
Laverty, Steel, porter, 5 Green's court
Lavery, Bernard, shoemaker, 52 Mustard street
Lavery, Edmund, dealer, 22 Valentine street
Lavery, Richard, publican, 41 North Queen street
Lavery, Sarah, lodgings, 30 Millfield
Lavery, Wm., linen lapper, California street

Law & Co., brassfounders and gasfitters, 9 Fountain street
Law, David, publican, 145 Durham street
Law, David, brassfounder, 30 Cargill street
Law, John, farmer, 1 Northburn street
Law, Mrs., Fairview cottage, New Crumlin road
Law, Mrs. Andrew, 12 Fountain street
Lawson, Jane, upholsterer, 64 Vere street
Lawson, Robert, writing clerk, 7 California street
Lawther, Mrs. Catherine, milliner and dressmaker, 18 Joy street
Layden, Patrick, plasterer, 27 Union street
Leadbetter, J., & Co., linen merchants & manufacturers, 6 York st. & Bedford st.
Learmoth, Isabella, 2 Nile street
Leathem, Blythe, and Leathem, muslin manufacturers, 55 Academy street
Leathem, E., umbrella maker and bell hanger, 144 North street
Leathem, William John, shoemaker, 31 North Queen street
Leck, Wm., of J. & D. Macdonald & Co., York st., Cranston pl., Antrim road
Ledlie, James, gentleman, 13 Gloucester street
Ledgett, Richard, clothes dealer, 31 Berry street
Lee & Son, jewellers to the Queen, watchmakers, silversmiths, and opticians, 57 High street
Lee, Andrew, mechanic, 3 Townsend place
Lee, Edward W., of Lee & Son, jewellers to the Queen, 57 High street
Lee, Francis, schoolmaster, 4 Nelson street
Lee, Henry, pensioner, 99 Millfield
Lee, Wm., car owner, 44 Great Patrick street
Leebody, Wm., carpenter, 14 Wesley place
Leeburn, Alexander, pork cutter, 10 Moffet street
Leeburn, Thomas, clerk, &c., 7 Curtis street
Legg, Thomas, tailor, 22 Henrietta street
Leetch, Alexander, shoemaker, 8 Grattan street
Legget, Thomas, musician, 14 Grattan place
Leggitt, Thomas, sea captain, 31 Earl street
Leighton, Richard, writing clerk, 22 Trafalgar street
Leinster, Archibald, porter, 44 Boundary street
Leinster, Charles, iron moulder, 2 Hopeton place
Lemon, George, mechanic, 15 Upton street
Lemon, James, stonecutter, 5 Old Lodge road
Lemon, James, ship owner, ship chandler, patent rope and canvass manufacturer, 15 Queen's square; residence, 17 Donegall quay
Lemon, James, roper, 87 Boundary street
Lemon, John, carpenter, 43 Hill street
Lemon, Miss, lodgings, 24 King street
Lenaghan, B., pensioner, 15 Albert street
Lenaghan, William, sawyer and provision dealer, 41 Cromac street
Lenaghan, Wm., stabling yard, 7 and 9 Murphy's lane
Lenaghan, William, car owner, 84 Market street
Lennon, Charles, proprietor *Vindicator*, 20 Rosemary street—Malone
Lennon, Edward, seaman, 3 Trafalgar street
Lennon, Edward, billiard room, 4½ Pottinger's entry—24 Little May street
Lennon, John, grocer and baker, 17 Carrickhill
Lennon, J., iron founder, 12 Annette street
Lennon, John, porter, 60 Boyd street
Lennon, Michael, ship carpenter, 2 Little Corporation street
Lennon, Mrs. B., professor of music, 24 Queen street
Lennon, Patrick, spirit store and grocery, 60 Mill street

Lennon, Patrick, spirit store, 1 Prince's street and 99 Queen's square
Lennon, Richard, clothes dealer, 22 Berry street
Leonard, Arthur, station master Ulster railway, Linfield road, Lower Malone
Leonard, Michael, pensioner, Peel's place
Leonard, Michael, mechanic, 75 Boundary street
Lepper, Messrs., cotton spinners, Lodge mills
Lepper, Robert S., cotton spinner, 1 Abbotsford place
Leslie, John, green grocer, 14 May street
Leslie, William, dealer, 15 Verner street
Lester, Mrs., 1 Prospect terrace
Levy, Mier, & Co., drapers and hatters, 61 High street
Lewis, Captain Alexander, 2 Upper Queen street
Lewis, David, coal dealer, Shankhill road
Lewis, Frederick, of F. & W. Lewis, timber merchants, 3 Great George's street—Nettlefield, Ballymacarrett
Lewis, John, railway engineer, 73 Peter's hill
Lewis, Joseph, lithographic printer, 23 North street—Carrickfergus
Lewis, James, printer, 30 Friendly street
Lewis, Nathaniel, carpenter, 74 Vere street
Lewis, Richard, gentleman, 8 Victoria place
Lewis, Thomas, publican, 40 Old Lodge road
Lewis, William, spirit dealer, 27 Stephen street
Lewis, William, haberdasher, 9 North street
Lewis, William Robert, of F. & W. Lewis, merchants, 3 Great George's st.
Liddle, James, piano maker, Fountain street; residence, 83 Academy street
Liddy, Charles, spirit dealer, 55 Mustard street
Lilley, Charles, copper and tinsmith, 97 Little York street
Liddy, Charles, pavier, 22 Stephen street
Liddy, Henry, fireman, 23 Police square
Liddy, Hugh, accountant, 14 Earl street
Liddy, John, pavier, 22 Mustard street
Liddy, Patrick, pavier, 23 William street
Liddy, William, weaver, 22 North Thomas street
Lightbody, James, rougher in mill, 4 Stanley street
Lightbody, John, mariner, 15 Pilot street
Lightbody, William, scutcher, 19 Cullingtree street
Lilley, William, seaman, 16 Shipboy street
Linden, William, confectioner to the Queen, 16 Corn market
Lindsay, Brothers, silkmercers, woollendrapers, and haberdashers, 1 and 3 Donegall place
Lindsay, Elizabeth, 34 M'Millan's place
Lindsay, John, gentleman, 3 Donegall place
Lindsay, James, merchant, 3 Donegall place
Lindsay, Patrick, 8 Coal exchange, Queen's quay, Ballymacarrett
Lindsay, Patrick, grocer, 8 Cromac road
Lindsay, Robert, and Co., sewed muslin manufacturers, Victoria street
Lindsay, Robert, merchant, Cliftonville, Antrim road
Lindsay, Samuel, coal merchant, 10 Cromac road
Lindsay, Thomas, mariner, New Lodge place
Lindsay, Thomas, chief day constable local police, 4 Wills' place
Lindsay, William, grocer and provision dealer, 9 Lagan street
Lindsay, William, mechanic, 2 Trafalgar street
Ling, Wm., professor of music, and organist St. Patrick's Chapel, 15 Ship st.
Linn, David, car driver, 35 Upper Lagan street
Linn, Edward, bootmaker, 26 Boundary street

ALPHABETICAL DIRECTORY. 283

Linn, Henry, engineer, 6 College street south
Linn, Mrs. Margaret, 6 College street South
Lithgow, Robert, boot and shoemaker, 9 Boyd street
Little, George, clerk, 2 College place North
Little, John William, stereotype founder, 5 Johnston's buildings
Little, Mrs. Jane, boarding house, 26 Little May street
Little, Mrs., 4 William's place
Little, William, reeling master, Wellington square
Livingston, James, lodging house, 48 Great Patrick street
Livingston, James, machine master, 5 Grove street
Livingston, Mary, huxter, 75 Grattan street
Livingstone, Moses, weaver, 45 Boundary street
Livingstone, William J., manager baths & wash houses, 56 Townsend st.
Lloyd, Edward, cabinet maker, 18 Catherine street North
Lloyd, Thomas, haberdasher, 2 Cumberland place, Donegall pass
Lockhart, John, smith, 52 Boyd street
Lockhart, Mrs., 4 Hopeton place
Lockhart, Robert, clerk spirit store, 3 Rose Ann place
Logan, Andrew, cow keeper, 36 Great Patrick street
Logan, Alexander, tailor, 6 Morrow's entry
Logan, James, publican, 14 Little Patrick street
Logan, John, dealer, 69 Little Patrick street
Logan, James, engineer, 137 Lower Malone
Logan, Thomas, harbour constable, 48 Green street
Logan, William, coach washer, 10 Arthur lane
Loney, Thomas, mason, 6 Alexander street
Long, Allen R., publican, 116 Ann street
Long, Robert, horse dealer, 5 Telfair's entry
Long, Robert, carpenter, 34 Boyd street
Longwill, Jane, dealer, Ballymacarrett
Longworth, Noah, millwright & engineer, 4 Campbell's buildings, Townsend st.
Lord, Edward, mill manager, 25 Hercules place
Lord, Miss M., milliner, 25 Hercules place
Lorimer, Mrs., grocer, 13 Academy street
Lorimer, Robert, carpenter, 25 Shankhill road
Louden, Dennis, butcher, 136 North street
Louden, Henry, carpenter, 11 Boundary street
Louden, Thomas, grocer and baker, 1 and 3 Garmoyle street
Loudon, Thomas grocer, 2 Pilot street
Lough and Gregg, iron merchants, 37 Ann street
Loughran, Andrew, carter, 3 Raphael street
Loughran, Ann, butcher, 16 Castle market
Loughran, Henry, wholesale and retail grocer, tea, wine, and spirit merchant, 41 York street and 16 Great Patrick street
Loughran, Henry, grocer, wine and spirit stores, 20 John st. and William st.
Loughran, John, butcher, 29 Talbot street
Loughran, Joseph, brass founder, 1 Lower Stanfield street
Loughead, James, clerk, 27 Earl street
Loughran, John, butcher, 194 North street
Loughran, James, watchman, 4 Little Patrick street
Loughran, James, printer, Hamilton's court
Loughran, John, grocer and spirit dealer, 2 Peter's hill and Millfield
Loughran, John, mechanic, 56 Brown street
Loughran, Patrick, brassfounder, 32 Friendly street
Loughran, Patrick, publican & auctioneer, 13 Marquis street & 66 Smithfield

Loughran, Richard, weighmaster Harbour Commissioners, Queen's quay
Loughran, Richard, harbour constable, 13 North Ann street
Loughran, Richard, dealer, Mary's market
Loughran, Samuel, clothes dealer, 45 Smithfield
Loughran, Thomas, grocer and spirit dealer, 72 Mill street
Loughrey, James, sawyer, 16 Little Corporation street
Loughry, Robert, spirit store, 48 & 50 Grattan street
Louth, Henry, in customhouse, Mount Pottinger, Ballymacarrett
Love, Henry, wholesale grocer and commission agent, 21 Church lane
Love, Hugh, gunsmith, 1 Robert street
Lovett, Alexander, porter, 22 Tomb street
Low, James, spirit stores, 24 Chichester street and 4 George's lane
Low, John, timber and slate merchant, proprietor of steam saw mills Garmoyle street, 5 Great George's street—residence, 71 Ship street
Low, Robert, foreman foundry, 5 Spamount
Low, William, commission office, 30 College street
Low, Wm., marble and stone yard, 11 Montgomery st.—24 Chichester street
Lowe, Hugh, grocery and flour stores, 110 North street
Lowry, Henry, pawnbroker, 25 Townsend street
Lowry, John, linen merchant, 83 York street
Lowry, John, builder, Prince's dock ; residence, Great George's street
Lowry, John, watch and chronometer maker, 19 King street
Lowry, James, linen measurer, 11 Catherine street
Lowry, Margaret, spirit dealer, 19 Samuel street
Lowry, Mrs. Ellen, 3 College street South
Lowry, Robert, plasterer, 3 Shipboy street
Lowry, Samuel, gardener, Queen's island
Lowry, T. K., barrister, 1 Arthur place ; residence, Ballytrim, Killyleagh
Lowry, Wm., moulder, 7 North Boundary street
Lowry, Wm., linen merchant, 4 Alfred street
Lucas, Borrowes, perfumer, 6 Hamilton street
Lucas, Patrick, comb maker, 27 Black's place
Luckie, James, tailor, 13 Henrietta street
Luke, Joseph, lodgings, 47 John street
Luke, Mrs., 3 Donegall pass
Lundy, John, grocer and publican, 64 Millfield
Lunn, John, baker, 50 Verner street
Lupton, Rev. William, Wesleyan minister, 16 Frederick street
Lyle and Kinahan, wine and spirit merchants, 36 Fountain street
Lyle, Andrew, of Mackenzie, Shaw, and Co., brewers, &c.—7 Glenfield place
Lyle, Samuel, of Lyle and Kinahan, 2 Victoria place
Lyle, Samuel, porter, 3 Economy place
Lynas, John, marble and stone yard, 38 York street—1 Michael street
Lynas, Richard, riddle maker, 17 Lower Stanfield street
Lynas, Samuel, day constable, 14 Lower Stanfield street
Lynas, Tobias, blacksmith, Steam mill lane
Lynas, Thomas, mechanic, Peel's place
Lynas, Daniel, stonecutter, 20 Valentine street
Lynass, James, stonecutter, 64 Verner street
Lynass, Sarah, lodging and eating house, 48 John street
Lynas, Tobias, blacksmith, Shankhill road
Lynass, William, stokerer, 9 Lindsay's place
Lynass, William, carter, 66 Little Patrick street
Lynch, James, cooper, 114 Old Lodge road
Lynch, Messrs. professors of dancing, 11 Donegall place buildings

Lynch, P., M.D., surgeon, 17 Donegall place
Lynch, Rodger, cooper, 4 Upper Kent street
Lynch, Thomas, dealer, 10 New Lodge road
Lynchey, Mrs., 61 Great Patrick street
Lynn, John, house painter, 54 Ann street
Lynn, Miss, 105 Donegall street
Lynn, Mrs., 58 Green street
Lynn, Robert, carpenter, 20 King street
Lynn, William, manufacturer of cotton yarn, 9 Melbourne street
Lyons, Francis, tailor, 19 Edward street
Lyons, James, clothes dealer, 51 Berry street
Lyons, James, clothes dealer, 26 Chapel lane
Lyons, James, bricklayer, 11 Stephen street
Lyons, Mrs., 25 College street
Lyons, Patrick, dealer, 83 Old Lodge road
Lyons, Robert, commission agent, 24 Great George's street
Lyons, Samuel, bricklayer, 26 M'Millen's place
Lytle, John, wholesale grocer, and starch manufacturer, 1 & 3 North street

MacAdam, and Co., oil and bone mills, 31 Donegall st. and Ballymacarrett
MacAdam, Brothers, and Co., engineers and iron founders, Soho Foundry, Townsend street
MacAdam, John, merchant, Beaver hall, Ballymacarrett
MacAdam, James, of MacAdam, Brothers, & Co., 18 College Square East
MacAdam, James, jun., secretary to the Royal Flax Society, Vice-consul, for Portugal, 7 Commercial buildings—Beaver hall, Ballymacarrett
MacAdam, Robert, of MacAdam, Brothers & Co., 18 College Square East
Macartin, James, whitesmith, 27 Green street
Macartney, Andrew, gilder, 29 Academy street
Macartney, Bernard, dealer, 3 Durham street
Macartney, Henry, fish dealer, 5 Kennedy's place
Macartney, James, baker, 58 Union street
Macartney, John N., watchmaker, jeweller, and optician, 6 Donegall place
Macartney, John, forge and proprietor of Ship Hotel, 27 Pilot street
Macartney, Thomas, fireman, 25 Police place
Macartney, Thomas, foreman *Vindicator* office, 1 Trafalgar street
Macartney, William, carpenter, 17 Torrens' market
Macartney, William M., barrister at law, 40 Upper Arthur street
Macaulay, Adam, of Belfast Bank, 6 Linenhall street
Macaulay, Jasper, & Co., grain merchants, brokers, and commission agents; 9 Albert quay, and 7 Corporation square
Macaulay, Jasper, merchant, 15 College street South.
Macaulay, P., flax and tow spinner and commission agent, 75 Donegall street; residence, Mills, Randalstown
Macauley, George, shoemaker, 55 Durham street
Macauley, Thomas, whitesmith, 53 Brown's square
Macdonald, D. and J. and Co., sewed muslin manufacturers, 2½ York street; residence, Glasgow
Macdonald, James, ship broker, and commission merchant, 59 Waring street and Prince's dock; residence, 20 Dock street
Macdonald, Peter, grocery and spirit store, 81 Green street
MacElheran, W. F., residence, Belfast Bank
Mack, James, dealer, 3 Dayton place
Mack, Miss Margaretta, 101 North Queen street
Mackan, Mary, lodgings, 73 Millfield

Mackay, Arthur, tailor, 29 Bradbury place
Mackay, Mrs., Mount Collyer park
Mackenzie and Saunders, drapery, silk mercers, and haberdashers, 36 High st
Mackenzie, Alexander, Stag tavern, 5 Smithfield
Mackenzie, Alexander, May street
Mackenzie, Brothers, brassfounders, gas fitters, and patent axle manufacturers, 23 May street—shop, Regent buildings, Victoria street
Mackenzie, John, posting establishment, May street
Mackenzie, J. and Co., Belfast distillery, 39 Barrack street
Mackenzie, Robert, draper and haberdasher, 4 Abbotsford place
Mackenzie, Shaw, and Co., brewers, 84 Hercules st., corn mill, 51 Mill st.
Mackeown, George D., solicitor, 55 Donegall street
Mackeral, Peter, grocer, 16 Albert square
Mackey, Mrs., 5 College square east
Mackie, William, water works, 16 Sussex street
Mackin, Ellen, 89 Little York street
Mackin, Thomas, tobacconist and spirit dealer, 27 Corn market
Mackintosh, Robert, upholsterer, 7 Pottinger's entry
Macklin, James, 44 Boyd street
Macklin, James, gentleman, 24 Trafalgar street
Macklin, Thomas, turner, 15 New Durham street
Mackwood, John, cooper, 32 Green street
Macloskie, C. H., travelling clerk, *News-Letter* office—13 Catherine st. North
Macloskie, Paul, classical teacher, 13 Catherine street north
Macloskie, William, flax dresser, 16 Duffy's place
Maclurcan, James, rent office, 42 Sussex street
Maclurcan, John, silk mercer, 2 Donegall place, buildings—13 Victoria place
Macmullan, Surgeon Charles Clarke, medical hall, 48 Donegall street
Macnamara, James, J.P., merchant, 29 Tomb street—residence, Holywood
Macnaughtan, Rev. John, Duncairn house
Macnaughtan, Miss, Cliftonville, Antrim road
Macoon, Charles, matrass maker, 43 Talbot street
Macnish, Jn. O., & Co., cotton yarn agent, 7 Donegall st. pl.—7 Prospect terrace
Macoun, George, furrier, silk mercer, and milliner, 23 and 25 Castle place; residence, 19 College square north
Macpherson, Major, Fountainville cottage, Botanic road
Macqueen, Thomas, upholsterer, 4 Rochfort place
Macrae, Feaquhea, butler, 5 Downshire place
Macrory, Adam J., solicitor, 23 Rosemary street; residence, Duncairn
Madden, Eliza, dealer, 51 Millfield
Madden, Henry, sawyer, 8 Union street
Madden, John, dealer, 192 North street
Madden, Michael, quay porter, 27 North Ann street
Madden, Mrs. Susan, 25 Stanley street
Madden, Nancy, huckster, 47 Hill street
Madden, William, haberdasher, Bradbury place, Old Malone road
Madden, William, carpenter, 41 Stanhope street
Maddox, James, tailor, Eliza street
Madill, Isabella, boarding house, 5 New Lodge road
Madill, James, carter, Shankhill road
Madine, Daniel, fireman, 3 Pound street
Madine, George, funeral undertaking and posting establishment, 7 York st.
Magan, John, carpenter, 17 Lower Stanfield street
Magee, Adam, bookseller, 8 Thomas street
Magee, Bartholomew, optician, and mattrass maker, 66 Union street

Magee, Bernard, entertainment and lodging, 119 Millfield
Magee, Daniel, grocer, 27 Old Lodge road
Magee, Edward, sailor, 27 William's row
Magee, Edw., commis. agent and auctioneer, M'Larnon's buildings, B.carrett
Magee, Henry Bell, proctor, 8 Garden place, Cromac road
Magee, H., stabling, 164½ North street
Magee, John, oyster house, 3 Joy's entry
Magee, James, blacksmith, 7 Antrim road
Magee, James, grocer, 40 Brown's square
Magee, James, grocer, 16 John street
Magee, James, grocer and publican, 21 Union street
Magee, John, builder, 11 Trafalgar street
Magee, James, bricklayer, 11 Wilson street
Magee, John, coach painter, 10 Stanley place
Magee, John, bricklayer, 134 Old Lodge road
Magee, John, plumber, 32 Ann street
Magee, John, butcher, 3 Hercules street
Magee, Joseph, harbour commissioners' constable, 30 Trafalgar street
Magee, John, moulder, Boundary street
Magee, Jane, grocer, 32 Hercules street
Magee, Mary, sewer, 88 Peter's hill
Magee, Mrs., 85 Old Lodge road
Magee, Miss Sarah, 32 King street
Magee, Miss, 47 Lancaster street
Magee, Miss, dealer, 17 Long lane
Magee, Mrs., wine and spirit dealer, Larne, Derry, Antrim, and Crumlin mail coach office, 6 North street
Magee, Margaret, fowl dealer, 4 Lower Stanfield street
Magee, Richard, ærated water manufacturer, 9 Johnston's court
Magee, Robert, clerk, 10 College street south
Magee, Robert, nail manufacturer, 21 Winetavern street
Magee, Robert, spirit dealer, 16 Caddell's entry
Magee, Robert, gentleman, 7 Donegall square west
Magee, Tully, huckster, 50 Cromac street
Magee, Thomas, boarding house, 9 Marquis street
Magee, Thomas, cabinet maker, 35 Verner street
Magee, William, coachmaker, 29 Pottinger's entry
Magennis, John, 1 Economy place
Maghaham, Rev. John, Dean of Seminary, 97 Donegall street
Magill, Archibald, weaver, 43 Devis street, Falls road
Magill, Catherine, dressmaker, 31 Old Lodge road
Magill, George and James, brewers, 25 Bank lane
Magill, Hugh, Linen Hall ; residence, Bellevieu, Malone
Magill, James, bookseller, stationer, and printseller, 2 Castle buildings ; residence, 33 King street
Magill, James, brewer, Bank lane ; residence, 16 College square North
Magill, John, baker, 3 Friendly street
Magill, Joseph, commission merchant, and Mexican consul, 34 Fountain st.; residence, Marino, Holywood
Magill, James, millwright, 4 Sir Henry's buildings, Ballymacarrett
Magill, James, mechanic, 7 Sir Henry's buildings, Ballymacarrett
Magill, James, teacher National school, Bridge end, Ballymacarrett
Magill, Mrs., 10 Ormeau place
Magill, Miss, 14 Queen street
Magill, Miss Grace, 35 King street

Magill, Miss, 14 Victoria place
Magill, Robert, woollendraper and hatter, 1 Castle buildings; residence, 1 Posnett's place, Donegall pass
Magill, Wm., pensioner, Ballynafeigh
Magill, Wm., brewer, Bank lane; residence, 6 Downshire place
Magill, Wm., John, mariner, 1 Union place
Magin, Teresa, haberdasher, 135½ North street
Maginnis, James, stone cutter, 10 Robert street
Maginnis, James, bricklayer, 14, Black's place
Maginnis, James, porter, 28 Hill street
Maginnis, Mary, grocer and upholsteress, 113 and 115 Millfield
Maginnis, Patrick, custom house officer, 12 Stanhope street
Maginnis, Rev. David, 23 Eliza street
Magorian, Matthew, publican, 6 Little Patrick street
Magowan, Margaret, marine store, 67 Union street
Magrath, Mrs., nurse tender, 30 Henrietta street
Magreevy, Hugh, carman, 25 Lagan street
Maguire, Alexander, boot and shoemaker, 11 High street
Maguire, Ann, grocer and publican, 20¼ Chapel lane
Maguire, Arthur, porter, 47 Hill street
Maguire, Anne, washerwoman, 24 Little Patrick street
Maguire, Bernard, baker, 5 Torrens' market
Maguire, G., boot and shoemaker, 28 Church lane
Maguire, Hugh, tailor, 2 New Lodge road
Maguire, Henry, pawnbroker, 20 and 24 Chapel lane
Maguire, Isaac, hair dresser and wig maker, 20 Talbot street
Maguire, John, dyer, 15 Castle street; house, 17 Cromac street
Maguire, John, cooper, 56 Conway street
Maguire, John, spirit store, 13 Frederick street
Maguire, J., dyer, 14 Bank lane
Maguire, James, linen merchant, 49 Joy street
Maguire, James, provision dealer, 6 Hill street
Maguire, James, carpenter, 1 Wall street
Maguire, Michael, bricklayer, 2 Trinity street
Maguire, Patrick, shoemaker, Fall's road
Maguire, Patrick, boot and shoemaker, 44 Union street
Maguire, Sylvester, bricklayer, 28¼ Mill street
Maguire, Thomas, pawnbroker, 17 Cromac street
Maguire, William, boot and shoemaker, 30 Church lane
Maguire, William, nailer, 38 Talbot street
Mahaffey, Robert, boot and shoemaker, 121 North street
Maharg, Arthur, cooper, 21 Bank lane
Mahir, P. H., confectioner, 74 Donegall street
Mahon, Andrew, clerk in Ballymena railway office, 15 North Ann street
Maine, Matthew, engineer, 1 California street
Major, James, flax bundler, 8 College place North
Major, James, sewed muslin manufacturer, 13 Great Patrick street; office 10 York street
Major, Mrs., 32 York street
Major, Thomas, 9 Donegall square West
Major, T. S. & Co., sewed muslin manufacturers, 13¼ Donegall st.—Dunmurry
Maken, Charles, car driver, 6 O'Hagarty street
Makepeace, Wm., excise officer, Cranstone place
Malcolm, Dr. Andrew, 49 York street
Malcolm, William, of Charley and Malcolm, 49 York street

ALPHABETICAL DIRECTORY.

Malcolmson, Mary Anne, boarding house, 72 Millfield
Malcolmson, Margaret, boarding house, 4 Cullingtree street
Mallagh, John, lodgings, 58 Peter's hill
Mallaghen, Henry, auctioneer, 26 Berry street and 67 Smithfield
Mallart, Osly, grocer and publican, Lagan village, Ballymacarrett
Mallon, Bernard, 44 Old Lodge road
Mallon, Felix, carpenter, 82 Carrickhill
Mallon, Fanny, boarding house, 7 Portland place
Mallon, Hugh, grocer, Shankhill road
Mallon, Peter, shoemaker, 13 Smithfield
Mallon, Timothy, pensioner, 126 Carrickhill
Malloy, William, land steward, Beer's bridge, Ballymacarrett
Malone, Eliza, washerwoman, 26 Catherine street North
Malone, Mrs. Sarah, 17 King street
Maloney, Miss, milliner and haberdasher, 9 Hercules place
Maltseed, Halliday, machine smith, 9 North Queen street
Maneely, Samuel, watchman, 1 M'Tier's street
Mann, George, carpenter, 2 Kennedy's entry
Manning, Edward, attorney's clerk, 19 Russell street
Manning, Mrs., 31 Cromac street
Manning, Patrick, moulder, 63 Little York street
Mansfield, George, salesman, 72 Joy street
Mansfield, James E., gentleman, Pottinger place, Ballymacarrett
Mariner, Bernard, lodging house, 81 Academy street
Mariner, Mary, grocer and spirit dealer, 28 Corporation street
Mark, David, cheese merchant and grocer, 28 Skipper street
Mark, Rev. John, Academy, 39 Chichester street
Mark, Sarah, dealer, 70 Green street
Markely, Hugh, lath cutter, 4 Morrow entry
Marley, Joseph, boot and shoemaker, 10 Devis street
Marlour, James, rope and twine manufacturer, 70 North street
Marlin, Robert, publican, 40 Verner street
Marlow, Patrick, mechanic, 78 Carrickhill
Marmon, Bernard, flax buyer, 15 Michael street
Marr, John, publican, 6 Little George's street
Marrs, Daniel, publican, 26 Millfield
Marrs, John, publican, 19 Michael street
Marrs, Lewis, clerk, 3 Cromac road
Marrs, Patrick, coachman, 5 Arthur lane
Marshall, A. & J., hosiers and glovers, 18 Bridge street
Marshall, Brown, and Co., muslin manufacturers, 7 Elliott's court
Marshall, Dr. Andrew, 3 Wellington place
Marshall, James D., chemist in ordinary to her Majesty, apothecary and druggist, 8 High street; residence, Holywood
Marshall, James, turner, 41 Grove street
Marshall, James, clothier and draper, 5 Donegall street; residence, Holywood
Marshall, J., house steward Old Poorhouse, North Queen street
Marshall, Joseph, delf warehouse, 16 Rosemary street
Marshall, Mary, whiteworker, 8 William's row
Marshall, Mrs., 27 Queen street
Marshall, Sturgeon, dealer, 49 Durham street
Marshall, Thomas, shoemaker, 17 Berry street
Marshall, Wm., & Co., Medical Hall, 67 and 100 High street—residence, Carrickfergus
Marson, Catherine, spirit dealer, 57 North Queen street

Martin, Allen, grocer and flour merchant, 145 North street
Martin, Agnes, boarding house, 8 Great Edward street
Martin, Archibald, press and machine man, *News-Letter* office—6 Carrickhill
Martin, Campbell, sizer, 25 Little Donegall street
Martin, Donald, publican, 18 Peter's hill
Martin, David, nailer, 4 Robert court
Martin, David, coachman, 21 Valentine street
Martin, George, carter, 1 Pound street
Martin, Henry, porter, 26 Gordon street
Martin, John and James, and Co., ship owners, 23 Donegall quay; John Martin's residence, Glenview
Martin, James, grocer, 3 Bradbury place
Martin, John, 31 Lancaster street
Martin, John, hay and straw dealer,121, 164 Millfield and 2½ Great Edward st.
Martin, John, and Co., merchants, 29 Ann street
Martin, John, boot and shoemaker, 36 Boyd street
Martin, John, bundler, 9 Sackville street
Martin, Joseph, marble polisher, 33 Friendly street
Martin, J., cotton and flax spinner, Killileagh mills; office, 29 Ann street
Martin, Jane, 13 Wilson street
Martin, James, shoemaker, 3 Lower Stanfield street
Martin, Mrs., 5 Renwick place
Martin, Margaret, dressmaker, 40 Great Edward street
Martin, Mary, dressmaker, 26 Henrietta street
Martin, Matthew, publican, 69 Nelson street
Martin, Miss Letitia, boarding house, 25 Joy street
Martin, Mrs., 5 Belvidere place
Martin, Mrs., 52 Great George's street
Martin, Rev. John, principal Ulster Deaf and Dumb institution, Lisburn road
Martin, Rev. Jas., minister Presbyterian church, Alfred place & Eglinton st.
Martin, Robert, grocer and publican, 32 Great Patrick street
Martin, Robert, publican, 40 Verner street
Martin, Samuel, of John Martin and Co., 29 Ann street—7 Franklin place
Martin, Samuel, spirit store, 20 Little Donegall st.; starch works, No. 29
Martin, Thomas, pensioner, 27 New Durham street
Martin, Thomas, printer, 84 Old Lodge road
Martin, Thomas John, traveller, Mount Pottinger, Ballymacarrett
Martin, William, cooper, 26 Mustard street
Mason, Hugh, grocer, 10 Barrack street
Mason, Miss, 7 College street south
Massey, Mrs., 157 Durham street
Massey, Sarah, lodging house, 6 Bradford square
Massey, William, coal office, Queen's quay, Ballymacarrett
Masson, Edward, professor of Greek, Assembly's College—3 Camden terrace
Massy, Fergus, tobacco and snuff manufacturer, 24 North street
Massy, George, tobacco and snuff manufacturer, 12 North st.—7 Rosemary st.
Mateer, Cunningham, grocer, 1 Wesley place
Mateer, George, Malone toll keeper, 39 Bradbury place
Mateer, John, 61 Verner street
Mateer, John, schoolmaster, 72 Cromac street
Mateer, John, clerk, 7 Grattan place
Mateer, Robert, master mariner, 81 Nelson street
Mateer, Samuel, muslin manufacturer, 33 York street
Mathers, Samuel, bricklayer and grocer, 1 Welsh street
Mathers, Thomas, and Sons, block and pump makers, 17 and 19 Pilot street

ALPHABETICAL DIRECTORY. 291

Mathews, Mrs., 12 Catherine street north
Matthews, Abraham, grain merchant and starch manufacturer, 51¾ Cromac street; residence, 45 Cromac street
Matthews, John, hairdresser, Shankhill road
Matthews, John, writing clerk, 9 Cromac road
Matthews, John, hat and cap manufacturer, 26 Waring street
Matthews, Robert, muslin manufacturer, Commercial court, 5 Riley's place
Matthews, William, pensioner, 3 Galway street
Matthews, William, shoemaker, 9 Chapel lane
Matthews, William, hairdresser and wig maker, 106 North st. & 49 John st.
Matthewson, Robert Kelso, gentleman, 24 North Queen street
Mathison, Brothers, tea and coffee merchants, 3 Donegall place buildings; residence, 1 Brunswick street
Mawhinney, Isaac, porter, 8 Washington street
Mawhinney, Isabella, spirit dealer, 1 Sir Henry's buildings, Ballymacarrett
Mawhinny, J., preparing master, 1 Campbell's buildings, Conway street
Mawhinney, James, surgeon and licentiate apothecary, medical hall, 42 Mill street and 113 Millfield; residence, 8 College square east
Mawhinney, James, coachmaker, 3 Johnston's court
Mawhinney, James, 24 Townsend stseet
Mawhinney, Robert, clerk, 14 Wall street
Mawhinney, Robert, pork cutter, 28 Cargill street
Mawhinney, Thomas, plasterer, 27 Melbourne street
Maxwell, Archibald, carpenter, Conway street
Maxwell, James, cabinet maker, 41 Donegall street
Maxwell, John, dealer, 47 Alexander street
Maxwell, Miss, 21 Chichester street
Maxwell, Robert, dealer, 37 and 39 North Queen street
Maxwell, Wm., slater, 74 Green street
Maxwell, Wm., builder and undertaker, Queen st.; residence, 38 Fountain st.
May, James, butcher, Bridge end, Ballymacarrett
May, James T., professor of music, 59 Upper Arthur street
May, Lawrence, pensioner, 4 Lancaster street
May, Sinnamon, bricklayer, 2 Sackville place
Maybin, Wm., carpenter, 36 Trafalgar street
Mayne, Alexander S., book and tract depository, 1 Donegall square East
Mayne, Andrew, in Wm. Dobbin's, North street; residence, 9 Glengall street
Mayne, Alexander, printer and publisher, 34 High street
Mayne, Alexander, hairdresser, 7 King street
Mayne, Thomas, millwright, 62 Stanhope street
Mearns and Co., room paper manufacturers, 22 Donegall st. and 10 Castle pl.
—manufactory, Low Lodge, Old park, and Indian corn mills
Mearns, Andrew, paper stainer, 22 Donegall st.; residence, 8 Frederick st.
Mearns, Wm., master mariner, 9 Joy street
Meek, David, porter at G. C. Hyndman's, 7 Millfield
Meek, Robert, baker, 5 Barrack street
Meenan, Bernard, fishmonger & publican, 9 Castle market & 7 Hammond's ct.
Meenan, Jane, poulterer, 3½ Castle lane
Meenan, Patrick, dealer, 26 Barrack street
Megarry, George, carter, 19 Peter's hill
Megaw, John O., of W. M'Clure and Son, Corporation st.—12 Alfred street
Meharey, Robert and John, grocers, 154 Queen's square
Meharg, James, auctioneer and appraiser, 63 Smithfield—36 Mill street
Meharg, James, baker, 8 Townsend place
Meharg, Wm. C., clerk, 37 Conway street

Melvin, James, blacksmith, 5 Trafalgar street
Melville, Samuel, eating house, 3 Lemon's lane
Melville, William, sawyer, 25 Lower Malone
Menarry, William, mariner, Fleet street
Meneely, Rev. John, Manse, Ballymacarrett
Mercer, Andrew, 19 Waring street
Mercer, James, linen merchant, 3 Commercial buildings—8 Upper Queen st.
Mercer, John, butcher, 67 Hercules street
Metcalf, Matthew, dealer, 67 Green street
Methuen, James, herring, fish, and salt stores, 12½ Tomb street
Middleton, Samuel, mail coach guard, 21 Russell street
Midgley, John, reed maker, 23 New Durham street
Milbey, James, stone cutter, 12 Grace street
Milford, Henry, solicitor, 29 Donegall street
Milford, John, corn and flour merchant, 83 North st. and 86 Hercules st.
Milford, Miss, 58 Great George's street
Millford, Thomas, assistant draper, 7 Unity street
Millar, James, in Messrs. Herdman's mill, 1 Wilson street
Millar, John, engineer, Ulsterville, New Lisburn road
Millar, Mrs. Arthur, 17 Wellington place
Millen, Alexander, house carpenter, 10 Bond street
Millen, H. & J., wholesale and retail spirit store, 12 Great Edward street
Millen, Hugh, spirit dealer, Downpatrick, Portaferry, Bangor, &c., coach office, 68 Ann street and 46 Church lane
Millen, John, salt merchant, 5 and 11 Marlborough street
Millen, Robert, book keeper, Fleet street
Millen, William, schoolmaster, 32 Nelson street
Millen, William, haberdasher, 21 Castle place—14 Fountain street
Millin, Adam, publican, 32 and 34 Prince's street
Millin, Ann, publican, 25 Prince's street
Miller, Ann, 91 Durham street
Miller, Clendinning, and Co., Manchester & Scotch warehouse, 36 North st.
Miller, Francis, shoemaker, 30 Old Lodge road
Miller, George, manager in J. Hind and Son's mill, 3 Malone place
Miller, G. L., Henry street
Miller, George L., of Miller and Clendinning, North street—49 Nelson st.
Miller, James, night constable, 155 Durham street
Miller, John, painter, 2 Grace street
Miller, J., dressmaker, 65 Academy street
Miller, John, carpenter, 32 Friendly street
Miller, Matthew, mechanic, 13 Little May street
Miller, Mrs., 18 Moffet street
Miller, Mary, dealer, 50 Carrickhill
Miller, Robert, dealer, 15 Lower Malone road
Miller, S. E. W., of Day and Bottomley, Fitzwilliam street
Miller, Rev. Thomas F., Vicar of Belfast; The Vicarage, 2 Talbot street
Miller, Thomas, pensioner, 21 Trafalgar street
Miller, Thomas, butcher, 66 Hercules street
Miller, Wm., stone cutter, 4 Smith street
Miller, Wm., sewed muslin agent to Park and Thompson, 29 Gt. Patrick st.
Miller, Wm., dealer and millworker, 45 Millfield
Miller, Wm., Northern Coach Factory, 30 Gloucester street
Miller, Wm., engraver and linen ornament manufacturer, 22 Castle street
Miller, Wm., of Day and Bottomley, William's place
Milligan, Alexander, nailer, 7 Robert street

ALPHABETICAL DIRECTORY.

Milligan, Francis, spirit dealer, Lagan village, Ballymacarrett
Milligan, James, porter, 1 New Lodge road
Milligan, John, shoemaker, 3 Leed's street
Milligan, Robert, pawnbroker, 41 Barrack street
Milligan, Wm. H., grocer and tobacconist, 33 Ann street
Milligan, William, shoemaker, 4 M'Tier's street
Milliken, Emanuel, master mariner, 7 M'Crory's row, Ballymacarrett
Milliken, Elizabeth, 48 Little Patrick street
Milliken, George, publican, Falls road
Milliken, Israel, warm, vapour, and shower baths, 87 Peter's hill
Milliken, James, hatter, 65 Green street
Milliken, Jane, lodging house, 4 Gordon street
Milliken, James, boot and shoemaker, 44 Cromac street
Milliken, Margaret, dressmaker, 64 Donegall street
Milliken, Robert, grocer, Falls road
Milliken, Robert, saddler, 49 North street and 21 Long lane
Milliken, William, ostler, 11 Little Donegall street
Millikin, William, tailor, 5 Pottinger's entry
Mills, Alexander, clerk, 25 Queen street
Mills, Hugh, tinsmith, 19 Smithfield and 12 Charlemont street
Mills, Henry, pattern maker, 63 Grove street
Mills, John, mechanic, 2 Sarah street
Mills, John, provision dealer, 49 Stanley street
Mills, John, pilot, Little Patrick street
Mills, Matthew, stone cutter, 17 Charlemont street
Mills, Rev. Thomas, Methodist minister, 13 Great George's street
Mills, William, pilot, 29 North Thomas street
Mines, Rose, lodging house, 68 Millfield
Mines, Thomas, accountant, 10 Seymour street
Minniece, William, pawnbroker, 23½ and 25 Peter's hill
Miskelly, John, shoemaker, 47 Verner street
Mitchell, Alexander, bleacher, 45 M'Tier's street
Mitchell, Alexander, civil engineer, 2 Alfred street
Mitchell, Sarah, mangler, 25 William street
Minteith, Sarah, grocer, M'Crory's row, Ballymacarrett
Mitchell, Andrew, blockmaker, 4 Dock lane
Mitchell, George, Navy hotel, 10 Prince's dock
Mitchell, George, ship chandler and sail maker, 5 Prince's dock
Mitchell, G. T., director Belfast Bank, 6 Wellington place
Mitchell, John, plasterer, 12 Mitchell street
Mitchell, John, chimney sweeper, M'Master's court, Millfield
Mitchell, John, fireman, 17 Police square
Mitchell, Mary, spirit dealer, 57 Hill street
Mitchell, Mary, lodgings, 39 Grattan street
Mitchell, Robert, flax and tow dealer, 26 Grattan street
Mitchell, Robert, pensioner, 11 Mary's market
Mitchell, Thomas, mariner, 46 Little Patrick street
Mitchell, Thomas, pensioner, 55 Millfield
Miskimmons, Thomas, carpenter, 5 Sackville street
Mitton, John, grocer, 42 Henry street
Moffatt, George, guard Holywood railway, Bridge end, Ballymacarret
Moffatt, Mrs., boarding house, 1 North Boundary street
Moffatt, Rev. William, Ashley place, Ballymacarrett
Moffat, Samuel, carman, 10 Leed's street
Moffat, Thomas, shoemaker, 31 Boyd street

Moffet, Joshua, customhouse, 7 York street
Moffet, Miss, milliner and straw bonnet maker, 7 York street
Moffett, Dr. William, surgeon, 20 Wellington place
Moffett, John, chandler, 76 Ann street
Moffett, John, grocer, 113 Durham street
Molloy, Daniel, publican, 24 Torrens' market
Molloy, Thomas, flax dresser, 34 Conway street
Molyneux and Ferguson, starch manufacturers, 4 and 21 York lane; W. R. Molyneux's residence, Carrickfergus.
Moody, Joseph, Hibernian Tavern and spirit store, 10 Pottinger's entry
Monaghan, Bernard, delf shop and broker, 21 Smithfield
Monaghan, Bernard, dealer, 9 Kennedy's row
Monaghan, Daniel, blacksmith, 6 Riley's place
Monaghan, David, hairdresser, 5 Gamble street
Monaghan, Luke, 21 Alexander street
Monaghan, Thomas, clothes dealer & auctioneer, 14 Berry st. & 65 Smithfield
Monair, William, grocer and Scripture reader, 17 Frederick street
Moonan, Mary, haberdasher, 101 North street
Moncrieff, Alexander, clerk, 10 North Queen streeet
Moncrieff, James W., vitriol works, Gregg's row, Ballymacarrett
Moncrieff, James, vitriol works, Ballymacarrett—8 Aughton terrace
Mones, James, grocery and spirit store, 52 Grattan street & 54 Talbot street
Mooney, Bernard, block and pump maker, 43 Tomb street & Bradford square
Mooney, Catherine, delf shop, 32 Smithfield
Mooney, John, shuttle maker, 21 Talbot street
Mooney, John, Ballynafeigh
Mooney, Mary, 11 Chichester lane
Mooney, Patrick, butcher and publican, 98 North street
Mooney, Roseann, lodgings, 65 Grattan street
Mooney, Robert, editor of the *News-Letter*, 81 North Queen street
Moneypenny, Joseph, moulder, 4 North Thomas street
Monteague, Thomas, waiter, 62 Cromac street
Monteith, John, sailmaker, 25 North Ann street
Monteith, Mrs., 7 Ormeau place
Montgomery, Ann, lodging house, 78 Great George's street
Montgomery, Charlotte, dressmaker, 4 Cromac street
Montgomery, Daniel, seaman, 32 Gordon street
Montgomery, Daniel, clothes dealer, 33 Smithfield
Montgomery, George, deputy harbour master, 22 Earl street
Montgomery, Hugh, car driver, 14 North Boundary street
Montgomery, James, linen and cotton manufacturer, 34 Durham street
Montgomery, James, shoemaker, 35 Little Donegall street
Montgomery, John, book keeper, 125 Durham street
Montgomery, John, dealer, 11 West street
Montgomery, John, porkcutter, 22 Cargill street
Montgomery, John, and Son, merchants, Elmgrove mills and Wolfhill—office, 11 Corporation street
Montgomery, Mrs., 126 Old Lodge road
Montgomery, Mrs., Bridge end, Ballymacarrett
Montgomery, Miss, dressmaker, 125 Durham street
Montgomery, Mrs., 109 York street
Montgomery, Mary Anne, bonnet maker, 21 Hercules place
Montgomery, Matthew, spinning master, 4 Greenland street
Montgomery, Miss, 8 Queen street
Montgomery, Mrs., 4 Adelaide place

Montgomery, Mrs., boarding house, 1 Wellington street
Montgomery, M., dressmaker, 22 Cargill street
Montgomery, Mary Ann, dealer, 3 Park street
Montgomery, Miss, Mount Pottinger, Ballymacarrett
Montgomery, Mrs. Mary, 3 King street
Montgomery, Nancy, green grocer, 57 Millfield
Montgomery, Samuel, publican, 63 Union street
Montgomery, Thomas, spirit dealer and tavern, 57 North Queen street
Montgomery, Thomas, painter, 18 Lagan street
Montgomery, Thomas, tailor, 9 Edward street
Montgomery, William, baker, 44 Stanhope street
Montgomery, William, sen., shoemaker, 7 Vere street
Montgomery, William, jun., shoemaker, 5 Vere street
Montgomery, William, gentleman, Victoria terrace
Moore, Alex., house painter and decorator, 19 Arthur st.—Mount Pottinger
Moore, Alexander, grocer and spirit dealer, 27 Millfield
Moore, Alexander, carpenter, 5 Queen street
Moore, Archibald, carpenter, 6 Little May street
Moore, David, flax dealer, 54 Market street
Moore, David, writing clerk, 33 Dock street
Moore, David, 11 Sackville place
Moore, Dr. James, surgeon, 7 Chichester street
Moore, Edward, writing clerk, 1½ King street
Moore, Ezekiel, smith, 59 Old Lodge road
Moore, George, family boot and shoe warehouse, 20 High street
Moore, Hugh, porter Queen's College, 4 Renwick place
Moore, Henry, butcher and poulterer, 59 Hercules street
Moore, Hugh, surgeon and licentiate apothecary, 28 Tomb street
Moore, Henry, Bridge end, Ballymacarrett
Moore, Hugh, master mariner, 10 Michael street
Moore, Hugh, butcher, 83 Hercules street
Moore, James, carpenter, 77 Market street
Moore, James, bricklayer, Ross street
Moore, James, carpenter, 132 Millfield
Moore, John, sawyer, 14 Sussex street
Moore, John, Donegall Arms hotel and posting establishment, 11 Castle place
Moore, James, stationer and account book manufacturer, 5 Donegall place
Moore, James, mechanic, 1 Hamilton's place
Moore, James, printer, 1 Castle court, Castle place
Moore, John, reporter *Mercury*, 46 Joy street
Moore, John, weaver, Shankhill road
Moore, Margaret, lodgings, 5 William street
Moore, Mrs. Wm. John, 3 Albion place
Moore, Mrs. F., 20 College square east
Moore, Mrs., Linfield road, Lower Malone
Moore, Mrs., 2 Hamilton street
Moore, Robert, carpenter, 20 Murphy street
Moore, Sarah Ann, publican, 105 Peter's hill
Moore, Samuel, butter merchant, 13 Butter market; residence, Eliza place
Moore, Samuel, overseer, 12 Campbell's buildings, Conway street
Moore, Samuel, solicitor, 25 Arthur street
Moore, Samuel, tailor, 39 Peter's hill
Moore, Samuel, spirit dealer, Lagan village, Ballymacarrett
Moore, Samuel, grocer, 13 Ann street and 13 Great Patrick street
Moore, Thomas, brickmaker, 161 Lower Malone

Moore, Thomas, carding master, New Lodge place
Moore, William, brushmaker, 10 King street
Moore, William, currier and leather merchant, 143 North street
Moore, William, chandler, 66 Millfield
Moore, William John, wine and spirit merchant, 12 Church street
Moore, William, shoemaker, 13 Talbot street
Moore, William, gardener, 18 Lower Malone
Moore, William, architect, 18 Chichester street
Moore, Wm., stone yard, May street; residence, Crawford street
Moore, William, furniture dealer, 3 Smithfield
Moran, William, spirit dealer, 31 Townsend street
Moreland, John, weaver, 51 Smithfield
Moreland, Samuel, millwright, 51 Stephen street
Moorcroft, Mrs., school, 42 Nelson street
Moorehead, James, cooper, 25 Earl street
Moorehead, James, grocer, 18 Gardner street
Moorehead, James, cooper, 93 Nelson street
Moorehead, Ross, cooperage, 30 Little Patrick street
Moreland, Andrew, dealer, 33 Pound street
Moreland, Dr. James, surgeon, 55 Corporation street
Moreland, Ellen, 28 Gloucester street
Moreland, John, grocer, 20 Henry street
Moreland, Miss, Cromac, Ormeau road
Moreland, Mrs., vest maker, 27 Caroline street
Moreland, Robert, grocer, and meal and flour dealer, 8 Little Patrick street
Morgan, Charles, trimming shop, 26 Castle place; residence, 71 Joy street
Morgan, Francis, 16 Lagan street
Morgan, Hiram, butcher, 4 Castle market
Morgan, Henry, bookbinder, 8 Telfair's entry
Morgan, James, general dealer, 11 Charles street
Morgan, John, porter and lodging house, 2 Police place
Morgan, Miss Alicia, milliner and dressmaker, 22 King street
Morgan, Mrs., dressmaker, 71 Joy street
Morgan, Rev. James, D.D., 13 Howard street
Morgan, Susan, 17 Wall street
Morgan, Thomas, salesman, 26 Brown street
Morgan, William, gentleman, 1 Victoria terrace
Morrell, Andrew, butcher, 75 Hercules street
Morrell, John, butcher, 38 Hercules street
Morrell, James, butcher, 5 Hercules street
Morrell, Rose, butcher, 11 Hercules street
Morrell, Thomas, butcher, 35½ York street
Morris, Bridget, clothes dealer, 23 Academy street
Morris, George, glass cutter, Hudson's row
Morris, Roseann, boarding house, 1 Dock lane
Morris, Wm. Henry, chandler, &c., 42 and 44 North street
Morrison, Elizabeth, whiteworker, 15 M'Tier's street
Morrison, Hugh, Belfast tavern and posting establishment, Montgomery st.
Morrison, Hugh, tailor, 12 Academy street
Morrison, Hugh, wood turner, 23 Melbourne street
Morrison, James, milkman, 73 Boundary street
Morrison, James, publican and grocer, 52 Cromac street
Morrison, John, clerk, Herdman's buildings
Morrison, James, tailor, 14 Little York street
Morrison, James, coach painter, 32 Russell street

ALPHABETICAL DIRECTORY.

Morrison, Kennedy, clerk, 54 Nelson street
Morrison, Robert, brush and trunk maker, 1 Cullingtree place
Morrison, Robert, brassfounder, 99 Lower Malone road
Morrison, Robert, porter, 48 Brown street
Morrison, Robert, spirit dealer, 19 William street south
Morrison, Thomas, printer, 9 Hamilton street
Morrison, William, weaver, 12 Cargill street
Morrison, William, master mariner, 16 Stanhope street
Morrison, William, sawyer, Ballynafeigh
Morrow, Andrew, publican, 53 Great Patrick street
Morrow, Hugh, inspector Belfast Bank, 3 Belvidere place
Morrow, John, boot and shoemaker, 48 Edward street
Morrow, John, porter, 34 Annette street
Morrow, Mrs. Anabella, grocer and publican, 13 Union street
Morrow, Mary, teacher, 26 Stanhope street
Morrow, Patrick, publican and grocer, 30 North Thomas street
Morrow, Thomas, horse shoer, Ballyhackamore, Ballymacarrett
Morrow, Thomas, confectioner, 4 Millfield
Mortimer, James, boot and shoemaker, 5 Church lane
Mortimer, John, boot and shoemaker, 4 Church lane
Mortimer, Margaret, lodging house, 9 Little Donegall street
Mortimer, William, boot and shoemaker, 8 Church lane
Morton, Andrew, carpenter, 34 Stanhope street
Morton, James, English and mathematical seminary, 20 Kennedy's place
Morton, Thomas, moulder, 2 Alexander street
Morton, Thomas, sen., overlooker, 2 Alexander street
Morton, Thomas, carpenter, 18 Stanley street
Moskimmon, John, mechanic, 1 Gavin's buildings
Moskimmon, William, tin plate worker, 10 Marquis street
Moyne, Patrick, publican, 22 Albert square
Muckian, Bernard, cooper and grocer, 82 Cromac street
Muir, Speirs, bookbinder, 18 Boundary street
Muirhead, William, ironmonger, 73 Corporation square
Muldoon, Thomas, porter, Anderson's buildings, Ballymacarrett
Mulgrave, Joseph, dealer, 31 Trafalgar street
Mulgrew, John, blacking manufacturer, 19 Old Lodge road
Mulgrew, Patrick, hackler, 92 Carrickhill
Mulholland, Andrew, York street flax spinning mills, 21 Henry st.; residence, Springvale, county Down
Mulholland, Cunningham, surgeon, 11 Prospect terrace
Mulholland, Dr. Joseph S., surgeon, 80 High street
Mulholland Daniel, hardware dealer, 59 Smithfield
Mulholland, Edward, roving master, 100 Lower Malone
Mulholland, Elizabeth, grocer and spirit dealer, 62 Grattan street
Mulholland, Edward, cooper, 16 William street South
Mulholland, Henry, linen buyer, 73 Joy street
Mulholland, James, cabin steward, Shankhill road
Mulholland, John, dealer, 34 Valentine street
Mulholland, James, in provision store, 17 Trafalgar street
Mulholland, John, merchant, 75 Barrack street
Mulholland, James, starch worker, 17 Boyd street
Mulholland, John, York street flax spinning mills; residence, Craigavad
Mulholland, Michael, lodgings, 64 Great Patrick street
Mulholland, S. K., & Hind, proprietors of Durham street mill, Albert street; S. K. Mulholland's residence, Eglantine, Hillsborough

Mulholland, William, shopman, 6 Stanley place
Mullan, Ann, dealer, 7 M'Tier's court
Mullan, Anthony, grocer and publican, 55 Lancaster street
Mullan, Bernard, carter, 2 Meetinghouse lane
Mullan, Charles, carpenter, 6 New Lodge road
Mullan, Daniel, entertainment, 38 Great Patrick street
Mullan, Edward, grocer and spirit dealer, 95 Millfield
Mullan, Edward, spirit dealer, 44 Samuel street
Mullan, Francis, lodging house, 5 Carrickhill
Mullan, Hugh, saddler, 10 Bank lane
Mullan, John, nailer, M'Adam's court
Mullan, James, sawyer, 25 Catherine street north
Mullan, James, 16 M'Tier's street
Mullen, James, clothes dealer, 20 Marquis street
Mullan, James, linen merchant, 6 Cromac street
Mullan, James, weaver, M'Tier's street
Mullan, John, porter, 83 Boundary street
Mullan, John, bookseller, 8 Castle buildings, Donegall place—11 Joy street
Mullan, Mary L., grocer, 10 Stanfield street
Mullan, Michael, porter, 12 William's lane
Mullan, Margaret, 14 Wall street
Mullan, Matthew, of Fordyce and Mullan, brewers—27 Eliza street
Mullan, Mary, lodgings, 90 Peter's hill
Mullan, Neill, sweep, 5 M'Tier's court
Mullan, Patrick, confectionary, Antrim road
Mullen, Peter, bookseller, Smithfield—19 Marquis street
Mullan, Thomas, provision dealer, 167 North street
Mullan, Thomas, boot and shoemaker, 4 Edward street
Mullan, William, shoemaker, Ballynafeigh
Mullan, William, wholesale grocer, Victoria street; residence, Brookvale
Mullan, William, master sweep, 22 Torrens' market
Mulligan, J. & T., wholesale warehouse, 6 Donegall st.—2 Antrim place
Mulligan, Misses, school, 7 College street south
Mulligan, Mrs., 3 Cumberland place, Donegall pass
Mullin, Mrs., 47 Corporation street
Mullins, Thomas, provision dealer, 167 and 169 North street
Mulrine, William, smith, 9 George's lane
Mulryan, Robert, auctioneer, Kennedy's row and 63 Smithfield
Munce, Alexander, tailor and clothier, 17 High street
Munce, David, tailor, 1 Little May street
Munce, David, stone mason, 67 Ship street
Munce, George, clerk, 44 Townsend street
Munce, James, builder, Eliza street
Munce, James, butcher, 12 Grattan place
Munce, Robert, butcher, 32 Verner street
Munro, George, dealer, 58 Carrickhill
Munro, Hannah, bonnet maker, 2 Stanley street
Munro, James, dealer, 61 Mustard street
Munster, P. L., ship broker, commission merchant, Danish, Swedish, and Norwegian consul, Corporation street; residence, Holywood
Muntz, Robert, furniture dealer, 62 Smithfield and Cunningham's court
Murdoch, Hugh, compositor, Bridge end, Ballymacarrett
Murdoch, Mrs., Glenfield place, Ormeau road
Murdoch, Thomas, dealer, 1 Verner street
Murdock, Alexander, writing clerk, 20 Sarah street

Murdock, George, weaver, 18 M'Tier's street
Murdock, H., house agent, 4 Annette street
Murdock, John, boarding house, 16 and 18 Marlborough street
Murdock, John, cork manufacturer, 15 Hercules street
Murdock, James, weaver, 80¼ Old Lodge road
Murdock, John, board and lodgings, 27 Prince's street
Murdock, Thomas, cloth lapper, 15 Coates street
Murnaghan, Hugh, grocer, publican, and engineer, 26 Great Edward street
Murney, Dr. Henry, surgeon, 10 Chichester street
Murney, Edward, fireman, 8 Durham street
Murney, H., tea, wine, & gunpowder mercht., & tobacco manufacturer, 18 High st.
Murney, Patrick, musician, 38 Little Donegall street
Murphy, Alexander, boot and shoemaker, 9 Bradbury place
Murphy, Arthur, confectioner, 122 North street
Murphy, Arthur, publican, 56 John street
Murphy, Alexander, grocer, Wheeler's place, Ballymacarrett
Murphy, Bernard, clerk, 45 Verner street
Murphy, Charles, gardener, 37 Lagan street
Murphy, Christie, painter and glazier, 93 Lower Malone road
Murphy, Dr. Washington, surgeon, 11 Donegall street
Murphy, Daniel, grain merchant, 7 Gamble street
Murphy, Daniel, grocer and publican, 7 Gamble st. & 17 Corporation street
Murphy, Duncan, mariner, 28 Green street
Murphy, Ellen, dealer, 17 Verner street
Murphy, Hugh, 28 Townsend street
Murphy, Henry, master mariner, 8 Prince's street
Murphy, Hugh, grocer, 43 Gardiner street
Murphy, James, working chandler, 18 Black's place
Murphy, John, grain merchant, 4 Catherine street north
Murphy, James, butler, 3 Union place
Murphy, John F., Union foundry, 17 May street
Murphy, Jane, haberdasher and grocer, 99 North Queen street
Murphy, James, pensioner, 1 Gamble street
Murphy, Joseph, carpenter, 7 Ritchie's place
Murphy, John, timber & slate merchant, 3 Hamilton st.; brick and tile yard, Murphy st.; residence, 1 Hamilton street and Martillo, Holywood
Murphy, John, & Co., flax spinners, Linfield mill; office, 4 Waring st. place
Murphy, John, hackler, 13 Lower Malone road
Murphy, John, marble and stone yard, 18 York street—2 Frederick street
Murphy, John, master mariner, 18 Tomb street
Murphy, John, dealer, Artillery street
Murphy, Miss, 36 Earl street
Murphy, Miss Catherine, grocer, 16 Little May street
Murphy, Mrs., 1 Glengall place
Murphy, Nancy, green grocer, 41 Dock street
Murphy, Peter, grocer and spirit dealer, 17 Barrack street
Murphy, Robert, seaman, 35 Little York street
Murphy, Rev. James, D.D., professor, 5 University square
Murphy, Timothy, blacksmith, 9 Grace street
Murphy, Wm., of J. Murphy & Grimshaw, flax spinners, Linfield—10 Howard st.
Murphy, William, grocer and publican, 21 Little Patrick street
Murray, Mrs. Anne, tobacco manufactory, 8 Calender street—15 Arthur street
Murray, Anne, 38 Millfield
Murray, Daniel, surgeon and apothecary, medical hall, 5 Mill street
Murray, Daniel, marine store, 74 Little Patrick street

Murray, David, lighterman, 23 Pound street
Murray, Daniel, shoemaker, 7 Lower Stanfield street
Murray, Dr. James, surgeon, Bridge end, Ballymacarret
Murray, Daniel, lime works, Short strand, Ballymacarrett
Murray, Edward, cooperage, 25 Green street
Murray, George, jun., merchant, 8 Calender street—15 Arthur street
Murray, George, mariner, 5 Short street
Murray, Greene, and Lloyd, silk mercers, haberdashers, &c., 13 Donegall place
Murray, George, wholesale grocer and tobacconist, Queen's sq.—Strandtown
Murray, Henry, grocer and publican, 61 Little Patrick street
Murray, Hugh, millwright, 20 Boyd street
Murray, Henry, painter, 37 Brown street
Murray, Henry, grocery and provision store, 61 Green street
Murray, Hugh, spinning master, 17 Michael street
Murray, James, printer, 14 Murphy street
Murray, John, weaver, 17 Caddell's entry
Murray, John, stone cutter, Falloon's court
Murray, James, carpenter, and dealer, Bridge end, Ballymacarrett
Murray, James, tailor, 62 New Lodge road
Murray, James, grocer and porter, 70 Millfield
Murray, Mrs., 2 Botanic view, Botanic road
Murray, Malcolm, stonemason, 72 New Lodge road
Murray, Michael, carpenter, 5 Collingwood street
Murray, Mrs., 15 Arthur street
Murray, Owen, grocer and provision dealer, 18 North Thomas street
Murray, Owen, grocer, 59 Green street
Murray, Owen, master tailor, 15 Hercules place
Murray, Robert, publican, 37 Prince's street
Murray, Samuel, painter, 43 Boyd street
Murray, William, moulder, 13 Sir Henry's buildings, Ballymacarrett
Murray, William, grocer and publican, 8 Verner street
Murray, William, clerk, 10 Catherine street north
Musgrave, Brothers, ironmongers and hardware merchants, 59 High street
Musgrave, Mrs., 1 Donegall square south
Musgrave, William, barrister at law, 1 Donegall square south

M'Adam, John, cabinet maker, 2 Cargill street
M'Adam, James, painter and glazier, 11 Roy street
M'Adam, Miss J., boarding house, 11 Joy street
M'Adam, Robert, of A. and S. Henry and Co., 1 Windsor place
M'Adorey, John, grocer, 38 Barrack street
M'Afee, Charles, dealer, 146 Millfield
M'Afee, George, boot and shoe shop, 2 Ann street
M'Afee, John, boot and shoemaker, 18 Corn market
M'Alarney, Hugh, baker, 20 Russell street
M'Alavry, John, eating house keeper, 38 John street
M'Aleavy, Hugh, butcher, Ballymacarrett
M'Aleavy, Thomas, butcher, Ballymacarrett
M'Aleece, Elizabeth, boarding house, 4 Chichester lane
M'Aleer, Michael, engine driver, 11 Hamilton's place
M'Aleer, Patrick, carpenter, 30 Market street
M'Aleese, Thomas, clothes dealer, 3 Torrens' row and 43 Smithfield
M'Alespie, Charles, stokerer and plasterer, 52 John street
M'Alister, Alexander, gentleman, 8 May street
M'Alister, Alexander, pattern maker, Lagan village

ALPHABETICAL DIRECTORY. 301

M'Alister, Alex., spirit dealer & posting establishment, 23 Little May street
M'Alister, Catherine, commercial boarding house, 22 Gamble street
M'Alister, Hugh, baker, 46 John street
M'Alister, John, grocer and spirit dealer, 18 Gamble street
M'Alister, Joseph, soap and candle manufacturer, 58½ North street
M'Alister, James, slater, 15 Mill street
M'Alister, Mary, board and lodgings, 55 Talbot street
M'Alister, Sarah, lodgings, 20 Stanfield street
M'Alister, William, spirit dealer and stabling yard, May street
M'Allister, Alexander, gentleman, Mount Pottinger, Ballymacarrett
M'Allister, Isabella, Wellington square
M'Allister, Thomas, day constable, 58 Little York street
M'Alinden, Edward, carpenter, 25 Lower Stanfield street
M'Alinden, Felix, butter merchant, 11 Gt. Patrick st.—43 Gt. Patrick st.
M'Alinden, Jas., pork buyer, for J. & T. Sinclair, Tomb st., 43 Gt. Patrick st.
M'Alinden, Patrick, cow dealer, 7 Durham street
M'Alish, James, carman, 3 Conway street
M'Allen, Thomas, pawnbroker, Shankhill road
M'Allen, William, carter, Shankhill road
M'Alpin, Allen, travelling clerk, 5 Alexander street south
M'Allister, John, clerk, 4 Malone place
M'Allister, Joseph W., wine and spirit stores, 75 North street
M'Anally, Agnes, bandbox maker, 22 Grattan street
M'Anally, B., butcher, 63 Barrack street
M'Anally, Catherine, washerwoman and dealer, 82 Sussex street
M'Anally, Francis, dealer, 68 Union street
M'Anally, Hugh, lodging house, 41 Carrick hill
M'Anally, Henry, spirit dealer, 118 North street
M'Anally, John, lodging house, 12 Winetavern street
M'Anally, James, Shankhill road
M'Anally, James, linen lapper, 9 Townsend place
M'Anally, Joseph, ship agent, 56 Tomb street
M'Anally, John, shoemaker, 25 Boyd street
M'Anally, John, canvass weaver, 32 Grattan street
M'Anally, Patrick, nailer, M'Adam's court, Carrickhill
M'Anally, Patrick, shoemaker, 52 Peter's hill
M'Anally, Patrick, butcher, 71 Hercules street
M'Anally, Simon, butcher, 83½ Hercules street
M'Andrew, Robert, carpenter, 24 Cullingtree street
M'Anulty, Patrick, porter, 4 Stanfield court
M'Anulty, Susan, boarding house, 6 Orr's entry
M'Anulty, Thomas, boarding house, 2 Short street
M'Areavey, John, butcher, 21 Hercules street
M'Areavey, John, grain merchant, 22 Cromac street
M'Areavey, John & James, hay exporters, and provision dealers, East street
M'Areavey, Patrick, lighterman, 77 Nelson street
M'Areavy, Ann, 7 Pound street
M'Areavy, Daniel, weaver, 22 Sackville place
M'Areavy, James, shoemaker, 5 Stanfield street
M'Aree, John, dealer, 23 Verner street
M'Aree, John, car keeper, Chapel lane
M'Arthur, Miss, 19 Hamilton street
M'Atamney, John, stonecutter, 4 Glentilt place, Old Lodge road
M'Ateer, Francis, butcher, 8 Malone road
M'Ateer, Hugh, delf dealer, Drummond's court, 28 Smithfield

M'Ateer, John, blacksmith, 47 Verner street
M'Ateer, James, tailor, 23 Friendly street
M'Ateer, Patrick, grocer and publican, 59 Cromac street
M'Ateer, Patrick, carpenter, 28 Catherine street
M'Ateer, Patrick, blacksmith, 10 M'Millen's place
M'Ateer, Thomas, grocer and publican, 114 North street
M'Ateer, William, carpenter, 15 New Durham street
M'Aulay, Charles, linen and cotton factory, 27 Lancaster st.—115 York st.
M'Aulay, Con., carpenter, 4 Wellington court
M'Aulay, Edward, ostler, 7 Orr's entry
M'Aulay, Joseph, bandbox maker, 26 Alexander street
M'Aulay, John, paper stainer, 18 Stanfield street
M'Aulay, Samuel, flax and tow spinning factory, 4 May street
M'Aulay, William, pork cutter, 24 M'Millan's place
M'Aulay, William, bricklayer, 19 Boyd street
M'Aulay, William, 4 May street
M'Auley, Ann Jane, white worker, 26 Peter's hill
M'Auley, James, lodgings, 12 Prince's street
M'Auley, James, mariner, 1 Meadow lane
M'Auley, John, musician, 24 John street
M'Auley, James, brush and bellows maker, 74 Mustard street
M'Auley, Mrs., 61 Cromac street
M'Auley, Patrick, 115 York street
M'Auley, Peter, carpenter, 3 Thomas street
M'Auley, Robert, carpenter, 11 Bond street
M'Auley, Stewart, musician, 17 William street
M'Auley, Thomas, shoemaker, 17 Stephen street
M'Auley, Thomas, basket maker, 11 Morrow's entry
M'Auley, William, manager of steam saw mills, 3 Riley's place
M'Avoy, Hugh, foundryman, 13 Robert street
M'Avoy, James, printer, 7 Torrens' market
M'Avoy, Michael, pipe manufacturer, 142 North street
M'Blain, James, leather merchant, 139 North street
M'Blain, John, weaver, 2 North King street
M'Blain, James, sailor, 39 Green street
M'Blain, John, currier and leather merchant, 40 Donegall street
M'Blain, William, weaver, 14 Mitchell street
M'Bratney, Alexander, weighmaster, 14 East street
M'Bratney, William, 20 Catherine street north
M'Bride, Archibald, miniature painter, 6 Back Ship street
M'Bride, Edward, porter, 45 Verner street
M'Bride, Captain, 57 Tomb street
M'Bride, George, muslin manufacturer, 7 Elliott's court—May street
M'Bride, Henry, compositor, 22 Catherine street
M'Bride, Isabella, 41 Little York street
M'Bride, James, and Co., ship brokers, 59 and 57 Tomb street
M'Bride, James, spirit dealer, Shankhill road
M'Bride, James, fish dealer, 65 Market street
M'Bride, Joseph, sewed muslin manufacturer, 59½ Academy street
M'Bride, Matthew, pensioner, New Lodge place
M'Bride, Mary Ann, grocer, 23 Boyd street
M'Bride, Margaret A., grocer, Ballymacarrett
M'Bride, Patrick, harbour master, 5 Earl street
M'Bride, Robt., & Co., muslin manufacturers, 4 Commercial court
M'Bride, Robert, muslin manufacturer, 19 Fountain place

ALPHABETICAL DIRECTORY.

M'Bride, Thos., of Thos. & Geo. M'Bride, Elliott's court—May street
M'Bride, Thomas, publican, carpenter and builder, 15 Police square
M'Burney, Mary, washerwoman, Ballynafeigh
M'Cabe, Edward, carpenter. 31 Stanhope street
M'Cabe, James, carter, 3 Morrison's place
M'Cabe, Patrick, grocer, 85 Boundary street
M'Cabe, Peter, bookbinder, 28 Mustard strret
M'Cabe, S., carver and gilder, 15 Academy street
M'Cafferty, Charles, hatter, 4½ Smithfield
M'Caffery, Charles, sawyer, 55 Green street
M'Cafferty, Rose, dealer, 35 Millfield
M'Caffrey, James, bleacher, 52 Townsend street
M'Caffrey, Patrick, porter, 77 Millfield
M'Caghan, William J., in pork store, 69 Little York street
M'Cahan, Robert, grocer, 21 Cullingtree street
M'Cahern, Robert, carpenter, 32 M'Millen's place
M'Cahey, David, starch manufacturer, Boyd st.; residence, 1 College street
M'Caig, Robert, salesman, Eliza street
M'Caldin, James, hat and cap manufacturer, 18 Waring st.—4 Frederick st.
M'Caldin, John, gentleman, 2 Ormeau road
M'Call, Charles, spirit dealer, 4 Marlborough street
M'Call, Elizabeth, whiteworker, 61 Durham street
M'Call, Hugh, sewed muslin manufacturer, 23 York street—Lisburn
M'Call, Hugh, pawnbroker and jeweller, 1 & 3 Curtis st. and 23 York street
M'Call, James, oyster house, Winecellar entry
M'Call, John, grocer, Henry street
M'Call, Margaret, 8 Catherine street North
M'Call, Patrick, gardener, 28 Pound street
M'Call, Robert, tailor, Pottinger place, Ballymacarrett
M'Call, Robert, bricklayer, 13 M'Tier's street
M'Callin, Bernard, 4 Cromac road, agent Gray & Co.'s tile works, Coalisland
M'Callion, John, scripture reader, 25 Cromac road
M'Callum, James, merchant draper, 9 Dock street
M'Camisky, John, marine store, 11¼ Cromac street—34 Market lane
M'Cammon, Alexander, gentleman, Mount Pottinger cottages, Ballymacarrett
M'Cammon, Mrs., 4 Victoria place
M'Cammon, Mary, grocer, 4 Park street
M'Cammon, Misses, Antrim road
M'Cammon, Mrs. S., dressmaker, milliner, &c., 36 King street
M'Cammon, Thomas, tanner and corn miller, 23 King street
M'Camphill, Thomas, Belfast Bank, 12 Gloucester street
M'Cance, Henry, carding master, 2 Falls road
M'Cance, James, cooper, 52 Frederick street
M'Cance, John, 6 Donegall square East
M'Cance, Patrick, engine driver, 45 Conway street
M'Cann, Arthur, saddler, 19 Verner street
M'Cann, Bernard, brassfounder and gasfitter, 7 and 9 Victoria street
M'Cann, Daniel, printer, 20 Russell street
M'Cann, Daniel, chandler, 9 Donegall place buildings—97 York street
M'Cann, Daniel, flax merchant, 4 Grace street
M'Cann, Daniel, car owner and spirit dealer, 51 John street
M'Cann, Francis, pilot, 29 North Ann street
M'Cann, Hugh, butcher, 17 Old Lodge road
M'Cann, Henry, coach driver, 7 Cromac street
M'Cann, James, hairdresser, 18 Great Edward street

M'Cann, John, iron moulder, 2 Little Ship street
M'Cann, John, flax dresser, 17 Valentine street
M'Cann, James, master mariner, 59 Talbot street
M'Cann, James, hairdresser, 15 Castle lane
M'Cann, James, machine maker, 2 Marquis street
M'Cann, James, boot and shoemaker, Conlon street
M'Cann, John, baker, 11 Grove street
M'Cann, James, soap and candle manufacturer, 11 North street
M'Cann, James, dealer, 46 North Queen street
M'Cann, James, brassfounder, 53 Hill street
M'Cann, James, weaver, 28 Vere street
M'Cann, James, master mariner, 59 Talbot street
M'Cann, Luke, dealer, 196 North street
M'Cann, Mary, dealer, Artillery street
M'Cann, Mrs. Mary Ann, whiteworker, 1 North King street
M'Cann, Margaret, dealer, 65 Lancaster street
M'Cann, Patrick, carter, 24 Annette street
M'Cann, Patrick, green grocer, 53 Millfield
M'Cann, Patrick, butcher, 28 Hercules street
M'Cann, Patrick, car driver, 11 Grace street
M'Cann, Patrick, maker of cordials, 49 Little Donegall street
M'Cann, Samuel, spirit dealer, 28 Chapel lane, and 71 Smithfield
M'Cann, Susan, 25 Pottinger's entry
M'Cann, Samuel, Railway and Steamboat Tavern, 6 Castle street
M'Cann, Samuel, baker, 15 Catherine street North
M'Cann, Thomas, writing clerk, 68 Joy street
M'Cann, Thomas, Irish woollen warehouse, 41 High street
M'Cappin, Adam, hay and straw dealer, 30 Peter's hill
M'Carroll, Jane, lodgings, 47 Grattan street
M'Carroll, Rev. Wm., College street South
M'Cartan, James, general jobbing smith, 27 Green street
M'Carten, John, nailer, 92 North street
M'Carten, Joseph, clerk, 27 Castle street
M'Carter, Wm., grocer and baker, 21 and 22 Carrickhill
M'Cartney, Daniel, dealer, 31 M'Tier street
M'Cartney, Francis, linen lapper, 15 Devis street
M'Cartney, John, sailor, 8 Collingwood street
M'Cartney, Mrs. Jane, 9 Stanley street
M'Cartney, Wm., boot and shoemaker, Shankhill road
M'Cartney, Thomas, clerk, 11 Talbot street
M'Cartney, Wm., pilot, 52 Green street
M'Carty, Jane, cow keeper, 14 Charlemont street
M'Carty, M., coach smith and grocer, 36 Verner street
M'Caskey, Samuel, mechanic, 31 Stanley street
M'Caslin, John, cooper, 24 Mustard street
M'Caughtry, Robert, shoemaker, 7 Charles street
M'Cauley, B., boot and shoe shop, 90 and 94 North street
M'Cauley, Hugh, shoemaker, 9 Robert street
M'Cauley, John, smith, 7 Gavin's buildings, Shankhill
M'Cauley, James, brick moulder, 128 Old Lodge road
M'Caull, James, publican, 89 Durham street
M'Causland, Samuel, wholesale grocer, tobacco manufacturer, and seed merchant, 34 North street; residence, Lodge Cottage
M'Causland, Wm., compositor, 3 Upton street
M'Caverty, Ellen, dressmaker and milliner, 47 Devis street

ALPHABETICAL DIRECTORY. 305

M'Caw, James, merchant, 2 College square North
M'Caw, Mrs. Isabella, 93 Joy street
M'Caw, Wm., wholesale grocer, Victoria street ; residence, 1 Franklin place
M'Caw, Wm., 3 Howard street
M'Cay, Hamilton, book keeper, 87 Joy street
M'Cay, John, carman, 18 Mary's market
M'Clarnon, James, carpenter, 50 Boyd street
M'Clarnon, James, carpenter, 20 Eliza street
M'Clarnon, James, dealer, 124 Millfield
M'Clarnon, John, carpenter, 26 Boyd street
M'Clarnon, Michael, porter, 37 Greenland street
M'Claverty, Hanan, dealer, 55 Carrickhill
M'Clean, A. & A. T., gentlemen, 4 Donegall square south
M'Clean, Charles, pilot, 21 Green street
M'Clean, C., grocer, 47 North Thomas street
M'Clean, Henry, mariner, 12 Corporation street
M'Clean, Henry, pilot, 9 Little Corporation street
M'Clean, Hugh, marine store, 38 Grattan street
M'Clean, James, letter carrier, 1 Wellington court
M'Clean, James, solicitor, 3 Arthur street ; residence, 3 Chichester street
M'Clean, John, mariner, 56 Vere street
M'Clean, Laughlin, nailer, 30 Brown street
M'Clean, Mrs. Jane, silk dyer and milliner, 7 Mill street
M'Clean, Mrs., Mount Charles, Malone turnpike
M'Clean, Mary, 5 Meadow street
M'Clean, Mrs., dealer, 6 Smith street
M'Clean, Sarah, clothes dealer, 29 Berry street
M'Clean, Thomas, 20 Alexander street
M'Clearns, James, and Co., curriers and wholesale & retail leather merchants, 60 North street
M'Cleave, J., hardware dealer, 56 and 58 Smithfield—5 Charlemont street
M'Cleave, James, & Son, saddler and harness makers, 6 Castle place
M'Cleave, Mary, 18 Devis street
M'Cleave, S. R., stone seal engraver, 18 Corn market
M'Cleave, Stewart, clerk, 17 Gloucester street
M'Cleery, Hugh, writing clerk, 3 Michael street
M'Cleery, James, pawnbroker, 74 Nelson street
M'Cleery, James, surgeon, 19 York street
M'Cleery, Wm., rent agent and accountant, 28 Castle street and 2 Queen st.
M'Cleesh, Henry, spirit store and scantling yard, 1 Millfield
M'Cleevy, William, weaver, 119 Durham street
M'Cleland, Charles, belt sewer, 3 Valentine street
M'Cleland, Thomas, servant, 7 Union street
M'Clelland, Catherine, dealer, 18 Ritchie's place
M'Clelland, Charles, shoemaker, 10 West street
M'Clelland, Frederick W., clerk, 3 York road
M'Clelland, Henry, linen lapper, 7 Washington street
M'Clelland, Hugh, yarn and flax merchant, 22 Hill street
M'Clelland, John, carpenter, 13 Wellington street
M'Clelland, Mrs., 10 College street
M'Clelland, William, shoemaker, 43 Boundary street
M'Clelland, W. R., grocer, 37 Church lane
M'Clements, Hugh, 29 Cromac street
M'Clements, James, green grocer, 187 North street

M'Clements, John, carpenter, 3 Dock lane
M'Clements, Susan, boarding house, 64 Little Patrick street
M'Clenaghan, James, mechanic, M'Clenaghan's court
M'Clenaghan, Jacob, engineer, 3 Letitia street
M'Clenaghan, Robert, master of *Belfast*, steam tug, Collingwood street
M'Clenaghan, Thomas, 3 Johnston's buildings
M'Clenaghan, Wm., mechanic, Old Lodge road
M'Clenaghan, Wm., mechanic, 5 Fairy place
M'Clenaghan, William, machine maker, 38 Townsend street
M'Clenaghan, Wm., millwright, 8 Meadow street
M'Clinchy, John, baker, 8 Torrens' market
M'Clintock, Wm., grocer and provision dealer, 36 Great George's street
M'Clinton, & Thompson, soap & candle manufacturers, 47 & 49 Academy st.
M'Closkey, Patrick, barber, 42 Great Patrick street
M'Closkey, Wm., grocer, 54 Union street
M'Closkie, Edward, warper and grocer, 28 Union street
M'Cloy, John, painter, 17 Castle street
M'Cloy, James, house and rent agent, 128 Carrickhill
M'Cloy, John, ship carpenter, 35 Trafalgar street
M'Cloy, Wm., publican, 2 Carrickhill
M'Cloy, Wm., spirit store and butcher, 1 Peter's hill
M'Clune, Eliza, 5 Henrietta street
M'Clune, Miss, boarding and day school, 23 Hamilton street
M'Clurcan, Samuel, cooper, 8 Nelson street
M'Clure, Andrew, pensioner, 107 Millfield
M'Clure, David, butcher, 16 West street
M'Clure, James, provision dealer, 10 Great Patrick street; store, 5 Hill st.
M'Clure, John, tailor, 75 Vere street
M'Clure, John, bricklayer, 14 Union place
M'Clure, John, boot and shoemaker, 10 Peter's hill
M'Clure, Joseph, boot and shoemaker, 31 Church lane
M'Clure, Robert, shoemaker, 48 Ann street
M'Clure, Samuel, grocer, Ballymacarrett
M'Clure, Wm. & Son, general merchants, Corporation street—Belmont
M'Clurg, Robert, weighmaster, 11 Sarah street
M'Cluskey, Felix, brass turner, 33 Grove street
M'Cluskey, Michael, foreman flax dresser, 3 Campbell's buildings, Conway st.
M'Cluskey, Mary, dealer, 79 Union street
M'Cluskey, Patrick, dealer, shoemaker, and lodgings, 31 Winetavern street
M'Clusky, John, salesman, 61 Old Lodge road
M'Clusky, Wm., blacksmith, 20 Stephen street
M'Clusky, William, butler, Ballynafeigh
M'Collough, James, porter, 4 Valentine street
M'Collum, Archibald, weighmaster, 40 Smithfield, 4 Killen street
M'Collum, James, pensioner, 130 Carrick hill
M'Collumb, James, stone mason, 31 Nelson street
M'Comb, Francis, reeling master, 11 Vere street
M'Comb, Hugh, boot and shoemaker, 11 Mustard street
M'Comb, Isabella, whiteworker, 7 North Queen street
M'Comb, James, ship carpenter, 54 Vere street
M'Comb, James, butter merchant, 8 butter market—20 Cargill street
M'Comb, James, ship carpenter, 59 North Thomas street
M'Comb, Robert, carpenter, 25 Durham street
M'Comb, Wm., bookseller and publisher, 1 High street—3 Clarence place

ALPHABETICAL DIRECTORY.

M'Comish, Arthur, drill weaver, 8 Welsh street
M'Comish, James, butcher, 17 Cromac road
M'Comisky, John, rag dealer, 34 Market street
M'Comisky, Robert, dealer, 86 Nelson street
M'Comley, John, lapper, 8 Shipboy street
M'Conaghy, Hiram, copper and tinsmith, 12 West street
M'Conagill, Daniel, boiler maker, 45 Boyd street
M'Conagil, James, jeweller and watchmaker, 37 Castle place
M'Conkey, Hiram, tinsmith, 9 Charlemont street and 13 Smithfield
M'Conkey, James, book canvasser, 26 Melbourne street
M'Conkey, James, gentleman, 2 College street South
M'Conkey, John, weaver, 20 Brown square
M'Conkey, Mrs., 4 Ingram place, Donegall pass
M'Conkey, Robert, machine maker, 3 Hutchinson street
M'Connell and Kennedy, flax and tow spinners, Millvale, Falls road
M'Connell, Bernard, builder, 27 Townsend street
M'Connell, Bernard, plasterer, 16 Greenland street
M'Connell, Charles, shoemaker, 81 Little Patrick street
M'Connell, David, merchant office, High street.—Charleville
M'Connell, Francis, delf & hardware dealer, 7 Kennedy's row, & 22 Smithfield
M'Connell, Francis, dealer, 7 Kennedy's place
M'Connell, George, blacksmith, Ballynafeigh
M'Connell, Henry, butcher, 22 John street
M'Connell, Isaac, carpenter, 102 Peter's hill
M'Connell, James and J., wine & spirit merchants, and rectifying distillers,
M'Connell, James, carter, 157 Lower Malone [28 Tomb street
M'Connell, James, commission agent, 7 Corporation street
M'Connell, James, publican and car driver, 5 Eliza street
M'Connell, John, calico printer, Conway street
M'Connell, John, tavern, 26 Frederick street
M'Connell, John, and James, muslin manufacturers, 95 Donegall street
M'Connell, Joseph, grocer, 23 John street
M'Connell, John, weaver, and sail cloth manufacturer, 45 Talbot street
M'Connell, John, pawnbroker, 66 Peter's hill
M'Connell, John, omnibus driver, 20 Lagan street
M'Connell, James, linen lapper, 10 Cromac street
M'Connell, Samuel, grocer, 77 Green street, 33 Edward street
M'Connell, Samuel, grocer, butter and provision merchant, 18 Great Patrick street, 33 Edward street, and 22 and 24 Academy street
M'Connell, Thomas, painter, 66 Vere street
M'Connell, Thomas, ship carpenter, 21 Joy's entry
M'Connell, William, wholesale grocer, 7 Skipper street
M'Connell, William, calico printer, 2 Bath place
M'Connell, Wm., and Co., wholesale woollen merchants, &c., 25 Donegall st.
M'Connell, William, of W. M'Connell & Co., Charleville
M'Conville, James, sawyer and dealer, 5 Store lane
M'Cool, Henry, bricklayer, 46 Millfield
M'Coppin, Howie, pensioner, Lagan village, Ballymacarrett
M'Cord, John, leather dealer, 16 Church lane
M'Cord, Samuel, surveyor, 9 College place north
M'Cormac, Dr. Henry, 4 Wellington place
M'Cormac, Hamilton, gentleman, Royal hotel, Donegall place
M'Cormick, Hugh, jeweller, 15 Henry street
M'Cormack, Hugh, dealer, 13 Curtis street
M'Cormack, John, dresser in foundry, 5 North Thomas street

M'Cormack, James, and Co., linen drapers and haberdashers, Victoria street
M'Cormick, John, butcher, 11 Market street
M'Cormick, James, woollendraper, 11 Johnston's buildings, Victoria street
M'Cormick, John, printer, 3 Killen street
M'Cormick, John, boot and shoemaker, 14 Chapel lane
M'Cormick, John, grocer, Shankhill road
M'Cormick, James, cooper, 18 Welsh street
M'Cormick, Miss Margaret, 2 Great George's street
M'Cormick, Mary, dealer, 9 Barrack street
M'Cormick, Miss Susanna, 4 Hamilton street
M'Cormick, Miss Sarah, dressmaker, &c., 11 Hercules place
M'Cormick, Miss, school, 7 Stanley place
M'Cormick, Mrs., 11 Lagan street
M'Cormick, Patrick, stonemason, Keenan's place, Ballymacarrett
M'Cormick, Patrick, spirit dealer, 25 Donegall quay
M'Cormick, Thomas, leather warehouse, 49 Mill street
M'Cormick, Thomas, stone cutter, 4 Mitchell street
M'Cormick, Thomas, grocer, 23 Prince's street
M'Cormick, Thomas, grocer and haberdasher, Wheeler's place, Ballymacarrett
M'Cormack, William, brassfounder, 21 Wall street
M'Cormick, William, cooper, 16 William street
M'Cormick, Wm., cork cutter, 13 Lancaster street
M'Corry, James, publican, 60 Boundary street
M'Cottery, John, cabinet maker, 11 Wesley place
M'Coubery, James, sailor, 56 Grattan street
M'Coubry, Mary, dressmaker, 2 Campbell's buildings, Shankhill road
M'Coubry, Wm., carpenter, 10 Gloucester street
M'Coulery, M., dressmaker, 6 Campbell's buildings, Townsend street
M'Court, David, drayman, 5 Police square
M'Court, James, horse shoeing establishment, 35 York street
M'Court, John, dealer in old books, 3 Bond street
M'Court, Mary, huckster, 20 Caddell's entry
M'Court, Peter, dealer, 9 Samuel street
M'Courtney, James, carpenter, 9 Sarah street
M'Coy, Frederick, Professor in Queen's College, Patterson's place
M'Coyd, Wm., book keeper, 39 Joy street
M'Cracken, Alexander, foreman boot and shoemaker, 23 Russell street
M'Cracken, A., boot and shoemaker, 28 Bridge street—2 Rosemary street
M'Cracken, Anne Jane, milliner, 3 Crown entry
M'Cracken, Francis, jun., cotton spinner, 8 York lane—91 Donegall street
M'Cracken, Henry, grocer and publican, Trainview cottage, Ballymacarrett
M'Cracken, James, weaver, 53 Old Lodge road
M'Cracken, James, carpenter, 37 Stanley street
M'Cracken, James, scantling yard, Falls road
M'Cracken, James, builder, and grocer, 29 and 31 Barrack street
M'Cracken, John, general dealer, 15 Brown street
M'Cracken, James, bricklayer, 14 Little Edward street
M'Cracken, John W., notary public, 25 Corporation street—141 York street
M'Cracken, Joseph, spirit dealer, 66 Brown street
M'Cracken, Joseph, day constable, 81 Durham street
M'Cracken, Malcolm, boot and shoemaker, 3 Bridge st.—54 Gt. George's st.
M'Cracken, Samuel, weigher in mill, 1 Meadow street
M'Cracken, Samuel, publican, 43 Carrick hill
M'Cracken, Thomas, and Co., engravers, 5 Crown entry
M'Cracken, William, dealer, 24 M'Tier street

ALPHABETICAL DIRECTORY.

M'Cracken, William, of Northern Bank, 93 Donegall street
M'Cracken, William, carpenter, 36 M'Millen's place
M'Crea, Ann, whiteworker, North Queen street place
M'Crea, Archibald, builder, 53 Peter's hill
M'Crea, Alexander, stone cutter, 75 Little York street
M'Crea, James, plasterer, 8 Murphy street
M'Crea, Samuel, emigration agent, 37 Waring st.—57 Corporation st.
M'Crea, Robert, grocer, 76 Cromac street
M'Cready, John, chandler, 16 Wall street
M'Cready, Janet, Fleet street
M'Cready, John, tailor, 15 Caddell's entry
M'Cready, John, manager of Co-operative grocery, Lagan village
M'Cready, Robert, carpenter, 4 Nelson court
M'Creanor, Patrick, spirit dealer and stabling, 3 Marlborough street
M'Creavy, John, carpenter, 20 Shipboy street
M'Credie, Miss, boarding house, 10 Joy's place
M'Credie, Martha, washerwoman and mangler, 16 Hamilton's place
M'Creedy, Joseph, clerk, 79 Joy street
M'Creedy, Robert, stone cutter, Garmoyle street
M'Creedy, William, stone sawyer, 37 Green street
M'Creight, Adam, shoemaker, Shankhill road
M'Creight, Patrick, carman, 23 Charlemont street
M'Crisken, John, servant, Little May street
M'Crory, Charles, porter, 24 Boyd street
M'Crory, Charles, bleacher, Ashmore street, Conway street
M'Crory, John, engine driver, 2 North Thomas street
M'Crory, Peter, boot and shoemaker, 3 Old Lodge road
M'Cruden, Robert, shoemaker, Falls road
M'Cudden, John, tailor, 11 Short street
M'Cudden, Robert, onion dealer, 31 Smithfield and Bell's lane
M'Culla, Francis, grocer and publican, 11 William street
M'Cullagh, Wm., rag store, 59 Millfield
M'Culloch, D., shoemaker, 126 Ann street
M'Culloch, Mrs., dealer, 32 Barrack street
M'Cullough, Catherine, lodgings, 14 Prince's street
M·Cullough, Edward, porter, 8 Stephen street
M'Cullough, George, furniture dealer, 11 Bell's lane and 22 Smithfield
M'Cullough, G., carpenter, 41 Bell's lane
M'Cullough, Hugh, smith, 104 Millfield
M'Cullough, Hugh, blacksmith, 46 Frederick street
M'Cullough, James, copper and tin smith, 1 Albert street
M'Cullough, James, engineer, 49 Boundary street
M'Cullough, James, woollendraper, 113 York street
M'Cullough, James, carpenter, 71 Grove street
M'Cullough, James, grocer, tea & coffee merchant, 63 High st.—36 Nelson st.
M'Cullough, John, marine store, 91 Millfield
M'Cullough, John, painter, 74 Old Lodge road
M'Cullough, John, publican, 42 Prince's street
M'Cullough, J., and Co., solicitors, 44 Donegall street
M'Cullough, John, sea captain, 40 Earl street
M'Cullough, Joseph, publican, 68 New Lodge road
M'Cullough, Joseph, publican and grocer, 79 Durham street
M'Cullough, J., cartmaker, Shankhill road
M'Cullough, John, clerk, 32 Townsend street
M'Cullough, James, board and lodgings, 35 Prince's street

M'Cullough, James, porter, 18 Raphael street
M'Cullough, Jane, 25 Sackville street
M'Cullough, James, spirit dealer, 41 Samuel street
M'Cullough, John, wood turner, 18 York lane
M'Cullough, Mary, dealer, 13 West street
M'Cullough, Matthew, currier, 8 Coates street
M'Cullough, Mrs., piano forte manufacturer, 9 Arthur place—3 George's lane
M'Cullough, Patrick, lighterman, 14 Friendly street
M'Cullongh, Patrick, carpenter, 45 Edward street
M'Cullough, Robert, porter, 30 Annette street
M'Cullough, Robert, Courthouse tavern, Crumlin terrace
M'Cullough, Sarah, boarding house, 1 Johnston's buildings
M'Collough, Stevenson, cashier Belfast flour mills—Wellington square
M'Cullough, Samuel, shoemaker, 93 Carrickhill
M'Cullough, Thomas, publican, 140 Carrickhill
M'Cullough, Thomas, market constable, 7 Falls court, Durham street
M'Cullough, Thos., carman's yard, Antrim road
M'Cullough, William, shipwright, 11 North Thomas street
M'Cullough, William, lithographic printer, 31 Friendly street
M'Cullough, W., starch manufacturer and grain merchant, 105 Millfield
M'Cullough, William, mechanic, 12 M'Tier's street
M'Cullough, William, book keeper, 61 Joy street
M'Cullough, William, shoemaker, M'Crory's row, Ballymacarrett
M'Cully, John, cooper, 12 Washington street
M'Cully, Mrs., boarding house, 10 College square east
M'Cully, Robert, grocer, Shankhill road
M'Cully, Thomas, car owner, 60 Peter's hill
M'Cune, Alexander, shipbuilder, 10 Pilot street
M'Cune, E., milliner, 17 Academy street
M'Cune, Isaac, in Mr. Gelston's spirit store, North st.—3 Ingram place
M'Cune, John, engineer, Falls road
M'Cune, Mrs., 12 Queen street
M'Cune, Richard, spirit dealer, 17 Albert square
M'Cune, William, builder, Castle street
M'Curley, Mary, boarding house, 46 M'Tier's street
M'Curry, Ann, grocer, 4 Carrickhill
M'Curry, Catherine, clothes dealer, 3 Smithfield
M'Curtin and Riley, grocers and flour merchants, 31½ Chichester street
M'Cutcheon, Eliza, whiteworker, Murphy street
M'Cutcheon, John, pilot, 16 North Ann street
M'Cutcheon, Samuel, fancy box maker, 34 Joy street
M'Dade, Mrs. Mary, 12 Welsh street
M'Dermot, Matthew, horse shoer, 9 Seymour lane and 1 Seymour street
M'Dermott, Patrick, dealer, 49 Alexander street
M'Dermott, William, tobacco spinner, 56 Green street
M'Donald, Alexander, Scrabo stone yard, Police square—Newtownards
M'Donald, Alexander, stonecutter, 46 York street; residence, Newtownards
M'Donald, Alexander, clerk Harbour Commissioners' office, Queen's square
M'Donald, Bernard, haberdasher and cap manufacturer, 78 North street
M'Donald, Christie, slater, 53 North Queen street
M'Donald, Francis, flax dealer, 6 Lower Kent street
M'Donald, Henry, cardriver, 39 Vere street
M'Donald, James, ship broker, 20 Dock street
M'Donald, Jas., agent to Fullarton & Sons, publishers, 45 Upper Arthur st.
M'Donald, John, tobacconist, 4 North street and 25 Eliza street

M'Donald, James, clerk, 32 Mustard street
M'Donald, John, starch maker, 25 Mitchell street
M'Donald, John, carpenter, 151 Lower Malone
M'Donald, James, pensioner, M'Clenaghan's court
M'Donald, Mrs., 23 Queen's square
M'Donald, Mrs., 4 Pakenham place
M'Donald, Peter, grocer and spirit dealer, 81 Green street
M'Donald, Samuel, spirit dealer, 20 Hill street
M'Donald, Sarah, dealer, 16 Pottinger's entry
M'Donald, William, store, 33½ North Thomas street
M'Donald, William, clerk Harbour Commissioners' office, Queen's square
M'Donald, William, shoemaker, 17 Alexander street
M'Donnell, Charles, tobacconist, 5 High street; residence, 1 May street
M'Donnell, David, barber, 5 Prince's street
M'Donnell, Francis, dealer, 24 Millfield
M'Donnell, Francis, pawnbroker, 29 Rosemary street
M'Donnell, Hugh, teacher of the Irish language, 88 Millfield
M'Donnell, James, sawyer, 32 Academy street
M'Donnell, James, porter, 44 Cromac street
M'Donnell, Jane, shirt maker, 44 Joy street
M'Donnell, James, cooper, 26 Caxton street
M'Donnell, John, and Co., merchants, 5 Skipper street
M'Donnell, John, butler, 3 Earl street
M'Donnell, John, tea, tobacco and snuff warehouse, 4 North street
M'Donnell, John, green grocer, 17 Castle market
M'Donnell, Mrs., shoemaker, 18 Alexander street
M'Donnell, Mrs., 2 Abbotsford place
M'Donnell, Thomas, Q.C., Eglantine, Lisburn road
M'Donnell, William, publican and boarding house, 5 Upper Church lane
M'Dornan, Esther, 1 Wellington square
M'Dornan, John, pawnbroker, 28 Durham st., and 14 College st. south
M'Donnell, Edward, cheese and bacon dealer, Falls road—Police square
M'Dowell, Hugh, bricklayer, Old Malone road
M'Dowell, John, sailor, 11 Union place
M'Dowell, John, carpenter, 133 Durham street
M'Dowell, John, cow keeper, Welsh street
M'Dowell, John, blacksmith, 54 Frederick street
M'Dowell, John, grocer, wholesale and retail, Victoria st.—16 Hamilton st.
M'Dowell, John, carding master, 27 Wall street
M'Dowell, John, cooper, 71 Millfield
M'Dowell, John, chandler, 37 Little Donegall street
M'Dowell, John, green grocer, 21 May street
M'Dowell, Margaret, lodgings, 3 Gamble street
M'Dowell, Mrs. Susanna, 23 Roy street
M'Dowell, Mrs., 34 Upper Arthur street
M'Dowell, M., haberdasher, 6 Ann street
M'Dowell, Robert, clothes dealer, 45 Berry street
M'Dowell, Samuel, clerk, 14 Russell street
M'Dowell, Samuel, saddler, 11 Police square
M'Dowell, Sarah, 10 Riley's place
M'Dowell, Timothy, coach maker, 19 Stanfield street
M'Dowell, Thomas, builder and scantling yard, 58 York street
M'Dowell, William, shoemaker, 41 Hudson's entry
M'Dowell, William, mechanic, 18 Nile street
M'Dowell, William, sea captain, 19 North Ann street

M'Elherron, Eneas, sailor, 49 Tomb street
M'Entee, Francis, grocer, 42 Hercules street
M'Entee, Patrick, teacher, 4 Fountain street
M'Entire, John A., silk manufacturer, 14 Commercial ct.—Carrickfergus rd.
M'Entire, John, merchant, 15½ Fountain street—10 Albion place
M'Evoy, T., grocer, 34 Barrack street
M'Ewen, Daniel, ship carpenter, 69 Ship street
M'Ewen, John, mariner, 8 Little Ship street
M'Fadden, James, cooper, 20 Charles street
M'Fadden, Jas., stave merchant and ship owner, 26 Tomb st.—Gt. Patrick st.
M'Fadden, Mrs., leather dealer, 74 Ann street—21 Gloucester street
M'Fall, Cornelius, shoemaker, 64 Little Donegall street
M'Fall, Charles, blacksmith, 47 Grove street
M'Fall, John, porter, 50¼ Townsend street
M'Fall, William, porter, 58 Frederick street
M'Farland, Adam, cooper, publican and grocer, 56 and 58 Gt. Patrick street
M'Farland, Joseph, grocer, 2 Wesley place
M'Farland, James, mechanic, 15 Wilson street
M'Farland, James, revenue boatman, 46 North Thomas street
M'Farland, William, grocer and spirit dealer, 12 and 14 Old Malone road
M'Farland, William, warper, 6 Wesley place
M'Farlane, John clock and watchmaker, 93 North street—30 Sandy row
M'Farlane, John, watchmaker, 30 Lower Malone
M'Farley, Patrick, pensioner, 55 North Queen street
M'Ferran, James, coal yard, Queen's quay, Ballymacarrett
M'Ferran, James, ship broker, 39 Corporation street
M'Ferran, Miss, dressmaker, 43 Little May street
M'Ferran, Robert, ship carpenter, 20 Little Corporation street
M'Ferran, William, publican and lodging house, 18 Albert square
M'Gaghey, William, blacksmith, 6 Moffett street
M'Gahan, Robert, grocer, 21 Cullingtree place
M'Gallarty, Daniel, lodging house, 14 Curtis street
M'Garrell, John, butcher, 71 Peter's hill
M'Garry, Bridget, dealer, 25 Henrietta street
M'Garry, John, spirit dealer, 19 John street
M'Garry, John, grocer, and publican, 39 Lancaster street
M'Garry, Robert, fisherman, 45 Tomb street
M'Garry, William, pensioner, 15 Curtis street
M'Gartland, Sylvester, coal dealer, &c., 34 Talbot street
M'Gaughey, George, bricklayer, 5 William's lane
M'Gawley, William, porter, 10 Grattan street
M'Geagh, R. T., woollendraper and haberdasher, Hercules pl.—3 Franklin pl
M'Geaghan, Hugh, dealer, 36 Market street
M'Geary, Thomas, sawyer, 62 Alexander street
M'Gee, Ann, 17 Lagan street
M'Gee, Bridget, 7 Renwick place
M'Gee, Catherine, washerwoman, Shankhill road
M'Gee, John, butler, 4 Shipboy street
M'Gee, J., boot and shoemaker, 23 Church lane
M'Gee, John G., & Co., Pantechnetheca, clothiers and out fitters, 46 and 48 High st.
M'Gee, John G, 8 Sussex place
M'Gee, Jeremiah, bricklayer, 18 Greenland street
M'Gee, John, porter, 22 Moffett street
M'Gee, Jane, 18 Nelson street
M'Gee, James, weaver, 29 Samuel street

M'Gee, Miss Eliza, 10 Stanley place
M'Gee, Robert, in foundry, 9 Unity street
M'Gee, William, M.D., surgeon, R.N., 10 Donegall square east
M'Genarty, Hugh, green grocer, 11 Ormond market—Great Patrick street
M'Gennity, Hugh, grocer, 114 Millfield
M'Gennity, Michael, provision dealer, 13 Hill street
M'Geough, Charles, butcher, 64 Barrack street
M'Geough, M., baker, 62 Barrack street
M'Gibbon, Samuel, night constable, Smith street
M'Gibbon, Valentine, grocer and spirit dealer, 5 and 7 North King street
M'Giffen, Henry, overseer, 55 North Thomas street
M'Gilaway, James, shoemaker, 6 Townsend street
M'Gimpsey, A., publican, 11 Brown street
M'Gimpsey, John, 6 Durham street
M'Ginley, George, clothes dealer, 19, 21 and 34 Berry street
M'Ginnis, Denis, printer, 22 North Queen street
M'Ginnis, James, warper, 25 M'Tier's street
M'Ginniss, Miss, teacher, 5 Sarah street
M'Girvan, Matthew, publican, 6 Little Patrick street
M'Gladdery, James, Post-office, Rosemary street
M'Gladdery, Samuel, provision dealer, 31 Union street
M'Glade, Charles and Patrick, grocery and spirit store, Caxton street, 34 and 36 Edward street and 8 Green street
M'Glade, Henry, spirit store, 55 Edward street—Mill street
M'Glenn, Margaret, lodgings, 12 Black's place
M'Goff, James, pensioner, 65 Carrick hill
M'Glone, William, porter, 6 Stanfield court
M'Gonigal, John, cooper, 25 Green street
M'Gonigal, John, cooper, 40 Edward street
M'Gonigill, Thomas, writing clerk, 19 Robert street
M'Gookin, Mary, lodging house, 54 Carrick hill
M'Goughey, Isabella, provision dealer, 27 Smithfield
M'Gouran, Peter, spirit store, 1 Berry street and 2 Hercules street
M'Gouran, Richard, spirit dealer, 9 Frederick street
M'Govern, James, bleacher, 43 Conway street
M'Govern, Robert, porter, 69 Union street
M'Gowan, Charles, hatter, 106 Millfield
M'Gowan, Edward, shoemaker, 41 Stephen street
M'Gowan, Edward, foreman timber yard, 1 Stanhope street
M'Gowan, James, flax dresser, 31 Conway street
M'Gowan, James, mechanic, 4 Duffy's place
M'Gowan, John, clerk, Lagan village, Ballymacarrett
M'Gowan, Margaret, marine store, 67 Union street
M'Gowan, Mrs., boarding house, 1 Joy street
M'Gowan, Thomas, mariner, 89 Nelson street
M'Gowan, Wm., day constable, 19 Stanhope street
M'Grade, James, umbrella and parasol manufacturer, 26 Marquis street
M'Grady, Patrick, hostler, 17 Galway court
M'Grannell, Neal, shoemaker, 15 Alexander street
M'Grath, John, hay and straw dealer, and lodging house, May street
M'Grath, Thomas, caravansary, 17 George's lane
M'Graw, Hugh, waste dealer, 13 Edward street
M'Graw, Wm., servant, 8 Economy place
M'Grady, John, carowner, 6 Welsh street
M'Gredy, Robert, fruiterer, 10 Hammond's court

M'Greevey, Michael, stone sawyer, 71 Grattan street
M'Greevy, Hugh, waterman, 25 Upper Lagan street
M'Greevy, Richard, pilot, 27 North Thomas street
M'Greevy, Thomas, tailor, 158 Millfield
M'Gregor, Dr., accoucheur, 27 Barrack street
M'Gregor, J. B., surgeon, 34 Upper Arthur street
M'Gregor, Robert, boot and shoemaker, 23 Mary's market
M'Grim, James, car driver, 34 Upper Lagan street
M'Grillan, Jane, mangler, 66 Verner street
M'Grillan, Thomas, horse dealer, 7 Seymour lane
M'Grory, Denis, tobacco spinner, 4 Torrens' market
M'Grotty, John B., & Co., woollendrapers, hatters, & clothiers, 23 Bridge st.
M'Grotty, John B., 26 College street
M'Guickan, Hugh, boiler maker, 42 North Thomas street
M'Guickan, John, master mariner, 10 Shipboy street
M'Guickan, Wm., smith, 13 Gordon street
M'Guigan, Hugh, publican, grocer, and butter merchant, 62 Gt. Patrick st.
M'Guigan, James, lodgings, 65 Barrack street
M'Guigan, James, locksmith, 4 Long lane and Falloon's court
M'Guigan, James, dealer, 14 Samuel street
M'Guigan, John, yarn carrier, 4 Moffet street
M'Guigan, Wm., ropemaker, M'Crory's row, Ballymacarrett
M'Gnirk, Patrick, goldsmith, jeweller, and bog-oak carver, 66 High st.
M'Gurk, Arthur, pensioner, 43 Old Lodge road
M'Gurk, Archibald, bricklayer, 29 William street
M'Gurk, Thomas, publican, 44 North Queen street
M'Gurk, Terence, green grocer, 68 Mill street
M'Hannay, Francis, dealer, 1 M'Crory's row, Ballymacarrett
M'Henry, Daniel, publican, 2 Church street and 50 Donegall street
M'Henry, Paul, civil engineer, 31 Arthur street
M'Hinch, Robert, wholesale and retail grocer, 33 Church lane—6 Sussex pl.
M'Hugh, Bernard and Edward, wholesale and retail Manchester and Glasgow warehouse, 12 Rosemary street; residence, 24 Upper Arthur street
M'Hugh, Edward, hat and cap warehouse, 26 Bridge street
M'Ilhatton, Miss, 17 Moffet street
M'Ilhayney, Dennis, carpenter, Shankhill road
M'Ilheron, Daniel, publican, 1 Durham street
M'Ilherron, Jane, dressmaker, 32 Vere street
M'Ilrea, Wm., pattern printer, 5 John street
M'Ilneel, James, day constable, 5 Annette street
M'Ilroy, Andrew, carman's yard, 137 North street
M'Ilroy, Charles, cardriver, 7 Thomas court
M'Ilroy, Daniel, dealer, 5 New Lodge road
M'Ilroy, Elizabeth, lodgings, 14 Round entry
M'Ilroy, Esther, 25 Nelson street
M'Ilroy, Hugh, night constable, 10 Melbourne street
M'Ilroy, Mrs. E., dressmaker, 12 Lancaster street
M'Ilroy, Patrick, grocer and publican, 41 Gardner street
M'Ilroy, Robert, book deliverer, 9 M'Tier's street
M'Ilroy, Wm., publican and grocer, 137 North street
M'Ilveen, Arthur, cloth lapper, 17 Cullingtree place
M'Ilveen, Bernard, watchman, 14 North Ann street
M'Ilveen, Joseph, carpenter, Roy street
M'Ilveen, John, engineman, 70 Brown street
M'Ilveen, John, haberdasher, 116 North street

ALPHABETICAL DIRECTORY. 315

M'Ilveen, James, mechanic, 20 Boundary street
M'Ilveen, Thomas, nailer, 29 Carrickhill
M'Ilveen, Wm., spirit dealer, 1 Moore's place
M'Ilveen, Wm., carpenter, 11½ Lower Stanfield street
M'Ilvenna, Alexander, revenue officer, 6 Trafalgar street
M'Ilveeny, Thomas, carman, 4 Dayton place
M'Ilvogue, Felix, shoemaker, 2 M'Millen's place
M'Ilwaine, Agnes, 46 Brown street
M'Ilwaine, Alexander, revenue boatman, 39 North Thomas street
M'Ilwaine, Rev. Wm., 4 Royal terrace
M'Ilwaine, Samuel, car owner, 16 Bond street
M'Ilwee, John, printer, 61 Carrickhill
M'Ilwrath, Wm., grocer, 34 Boundary street
M'Ilwrath, Wm., and Co., canvass, sheeting, sacking, damask, &c., manufacturers, 4 Donegall street place—factory, Sackville street
M'Ilwrath, Wm., of Wm. M'Ilwrath & Co., 3 Ardmoulin place
M'Indoe, Thos. C., sewed muslin manufacturer, 7 Waring st.—8 Albion place
M'Innes, John, seaman, 8 Robert street
M'Intosh, Robert, book keeper, 5 William's place
M'Intyre, Archibald, engineer, Grove street
M'Intyre, James, of Simms and M'Intyre, 19 College square East
M'Intyre, James, head constable, Edward's buildings, Ballymacarrett
M'Ivor, Wm., brassfounder, brazier, and gasfitter, 11½ Castle street
M'Kavana, Patrick, marine store, 11 Old Lodge road
M'Kavanagh, Henry, timber merchant, 15 Queen street
M'Kavanagh, James, spirit dealer, Falls road
M'Kavanagh, John, timber merchant, 13 Queen street
M'Kay, Bernard, grocer and publican, 62 Millfield
M'Kay, Francis, carpenter, 17 Henrietta street
M'Kay, Francis, grocer and spirit dealer, 1 Lower Chichester street
M'Kay, Henry, pensioner, 12 Mary's market
M'Kay, James, weighmaster in custom house, 2 Johnston's pl., B.carrett
M'Keag, James, bricklayer, 10 M'Tier's street
M'Kean, David, agent for S. R. and T. Brown of Glasgow—82 Donegall st.
M'Keating, Edward, saddler, 6 Nelson street
M'Keating, John, boot and shoemaker, 9 Little May street
M'Kechnie, James, compositor, 10 Grace street
M'Kedy, Miss, 11 York street
M'Kee, Alexander, tailor, 23 Pottinger's entry
M'Kee, Ann, lodgings, 12 Union street
M'Kee, Arthur, painter, Ross street
M'Kee, Arthur, tide waiter, Little Ship street
M'Kee, Daniel, master of vessel, 12 Caroline street
M'Kee, Ellen, whiteworker, 52 Great Patrick street
M'Kee, Francis, chandler, 7 Black's place
M'Kee, Henry, carman, 16 Little Patrick street
M'Kee, James, designer, 3 James's place
M'Kee, James, pawnbroker, 112 High street
M'Kee, James, sewed muslin manufacturers, 2 Gamble street and 19½ Corporation street; residence, 13 Dock street
M'Kee, James A., of Jennymount flax mill, York road
M'Kee, John, confectioner, 30 Union street
M'Kee, J. and J., wholesale and retail grocers, 69 High st.—34 Gloucester st.
M'Kee, John, chandler, 15 Morrow's entry
M'Kee, Mrs., bonnetmaker, 45 Mill street

ALPHABETICAL DIRECTORY.

M'Kee, Mrs., 32 North Queen street
M'Kee, Mrs., 5 Sussex place
M'Kee, Mary, 9 Cullingtree street
M'Kee, Robert, plumber, 45 Mill street
M'Kee, Samuel, sewed muslin manufacturer, 45 Great Patrick street
M'Kee, Sarah, washerwoman, 61 Pound street
M'Kee, Thomas, cooper, 52 Barrack street
M'Kee, William, bookbinder, Pottinger's entry
M'Keever, James, tobacco spinner, 21 Campbell's buildings, Townsend street
M'Keever, John, gatekeeper in Messrs. Herdman's stores, 65 Brown's sq.
M'Keever, John, butcher, 20 Shankhill road
M'Keever, James, seaman, 58 Little Patrick street
M'Keith, Daniel, bootmaker, 7 Boyd street
M'Keldin, John, clothier, 24 Corporation street
M'Kellar, Robert, brass moulder, 9 Sir Henry's buildings, Ballymacarrett
M'Kelvay, David, bookbinder, 15 Stanfield street
M'Kelvey, David, pattern drawer, Lagan village, Ballymacarrett
M'Kelvey, John, waterman, 1 Steam mill lane
M'Kelvey, John, whitesmith, Lagan village, Ballymacarrett
M'Kelvey, Mrs. Jane, 37 Joy street
M'Kelvey, Robert, shoemaker, 47 Tomb street
M'Kelvey, Samuel, mechanic, Lagan village, Ballymacarrett
M'Kelvey, William, carpenter, Bradbury place
M'Kembly, Rose Ann, dealer, 34 Winetavern street
M'Kendry, Denis, grocer, 98 Carrickhill
M'Kendry, Hugh, and Co., wholesale and retail glass, paint, oil, and colour merchants, 6 Waring street
M'Kenna, Francis, carpenter, Ballymacarrett
M'Kenna, James and John, grocers and spirit dealers, 15 Lagan street
M'Kenna, James, provision dealer, 35 Smithfield
M'Kenna, John, spirit dealer, 200 North street
M'Kenna, John, grocer, foreign fruit, and wine and spirit merchant, &c., 73 Donegall street, and 1 York street—39 and 41 Academy street
M'Kenna, John, draper & haberdasher, sign of the "golden lamb," 20 Bridge st.
M'Kenna, John, ship carpenter, 3 Meadow lane
M'Kenna, John, provision dealer, Hudson's entry and 36 Smithfield
M'Kenna, John, butcher, 31 Edward street
M'Kenna, John, butcher, 3 Albert square south
M'Kenna, James, nailer, M'Adam's court
M'Kenna, Mary, lodgings, 16 Marquis street
M'Kenna, Michael, brassfounder, 30½ Friendly street
M'Kenna, Mrs., dealer in wool, 1 Chapel lane
M'Kenna, Owen, dealer, 19 Durham street
M'Kenna, Patrick, lumper, 12 North Ann street
M'Kenna, Patrick, publican, Falls road
M'Kenna, Patrick James, dealer, 1 Winetavern street
M'Kenna, Patrick, flax scutcher, 48 Union street
M'Kenna, Rev. Francis, 97 Donegall street
M'Kinty, Samuel, coal carrier, 9 Little York street
M'Kenna, Stephen, clothes dealer, 27 Berry street
M'Kenna, Terence, sawyer, 34 Verner street
M'Kenna, Thomas, dealer, 26 New Lodge road
M'Kenna, Thomas, & Co., linen and woollendrapers, 12, 14 & 16 Bridge st.
M'Kenna, Thomas, carman, 67 Millfield
M'Kenna, Wm., horse bazaar, veterinary surgeon, 47 Gloucester st.—2 May st.

M'Kenney, Peter, butter merchant, 47 Edward street
M'Kenny, Tully, solicitor, 3 Arthur street
M'Kenzie, John, clerk Northern Bank—8 Hamilton street
M'Kenzie, James, painter, 75 Grattan street
M'Kenzie, James, blacksmith, 82 Nelson street
M'Kenzie, John, brassfounder, 16 Catherine street
M'Kenzie, Matthew, pattern drawer, &c., 21 Nelson street
M'Kenzie, Shaw, and Co., corn mills, 61 Mill street
M'Kenzie, William, boot and shoemaker, 8 Melbourne street
M'Keown, Daniel, customhouse officer, 50 Frederick street
M'Keown, Daniel, and Son, muslin manufacturers, 8 Elliott's court
M'Keown, Eliza, dressmaker and whiteworker, 4 Union street
M'Keown, Francis, pensioner, 10 Sussex street
M'Keown, Hugh, house painter, 52 Ann street
M'Keown, Hugh, lodging house, 67 Carrickhill
M'Keown, Hugh, painter, 32 Talbot street
M'Keown, John, tailor, 7 Chapel lane
M'Keown, John, clerk, 10 Wall street
M'Keown, James, musician, 33 and 35 Carrickhill
M'Keown, Margaret, 57 Verner street
M'Keown, Mrs., dealer, 99 Carrickhill
M'Keown, Mrs., 121 York street
M'Keown, Michael, hackler, Ashmore street, Conway street
M'Keown, Margaret, dealer, 4 New Lodge road
M'Keown, Margaret, lodging house, 68 Carrickhill
M'Keown, Rose, dealer, 25 Millfield
M'Keown, Robert, weighmaster, 2 Union place
M'Keown, William, dealer in old books, 4 Smithfield
M'Keown, William, butler, 12 Sarah street
M'Keowu, William, Fountain street tavern, 6 Fountain street
M'Key, Francis, grocery and spirit store, 2 Great Edward street
M'Kibbin, A., of Northern Bank, 51 Donegall street
M'Kibbin, Dr. Robert, 13 Chichester street; residence, Avoneil
M'Kibbin, Frances, boarding house, 11 Gloucester street
M'Kibbin, George & Hugh, provision merchants, 83 York street
M'Kibben, Hugh, gentleman, Woodstock place, Ballymacarrett
M'Kibbin, James, dealer, 80 Lower Malone
M'Kibbin, James, reeling master, 6 Campbell's buildings, Conway street
M'Kibbin, John, tailor, 4 Francis street
M'Kibbin, Jane, lodgings, 33 Stanley street
M'Kibbin, James, grocer and publican, Charters' buildings, Falls road
M'Kibbin, John, & Co., engravers and lithographers, 67 High street
M'Kibbin, M. & A., & Co., milliners and dressmakers, 51 Donegall street
M'Kibbin, Robert, Conn's water flax spinning mill, Ballymacarrett—Avoneil
M'Kibbin, Thomas, bundler, 1 O'Hagarty street
M'Kinlay, James, ship carpenter, 34 North Thomas street
M'Kinney, Cornelius, last maker, 14 Ritchie's place
M'Kinney, Elizabeth, boarding house, 7 Telfair's entry
M'Kinney, James, last maker, Hudson's entry
M'Kinney, John, last maker, 19 Ritchie's place
M'Kinney, Peter, butter merchant, 6 Butter market—47 Edward street
M'Kinney, William, hardware and timber merchant, 42½ Rosemary street
M'Kinney, William, stone mason, 49 New Lodge road
M'Kinstry, John, painter, 29 Russell street
M'Kisack, James, 47 Upper Arthur street, office, 10 Corporation street

M'Kittrick, Henry, in Mr. M'Caldin's, Waring street—4 Trafalgar street
M'Knight, James, LL.D., editor of the *Banner*, 4 Linenhall street
M'Laine, Alexander, and Sons, ship builders, Graving dock, Corporation st.
M'Laine, John, weaver, Harmony place
M'Larnin, Andrew, sawyer, 39 Market street
M'Larnon, David, timber dealer, 93 Peter's hill
M'Larnon, David carpenter and dealer, 40 Winetavern street
M'Larnon, Henry, publican, 31 Devis street
M'Larnon, Henry, spirit dealer, 26 Smithfield
M'Larnon, James, spirit dealer, 28 Southwell street
M'Larnon, James, hair dresser, 6 Gamble street
M'Larnon, John, mechanic, Ashmore street, Conway street
M'Larnon, Patrick, bricklayer, 18 Mitchell street
M'Larnon, Patrick, shoemaker, 11 Devis street
M'Laughlin, Arthur, Millfield
M'Laughlin, Charles, cartmaker, 31 West street
M'Laughlin, Edward, mariner, 12 Store lane
M'Laughlin, Esther, 18 Melbourne street
M'Laughlin, Francis, tobacconist & grocer, 65 High st.—2 Donegall square S.
M'Laughlin, Gregory, block printer, Ashmore street—Conway street
M'Laughlin, Henry, builder, 4 Wall street
M'Laughlin, Hugh, coachmaker, 36 Mustard street
M'Laughlin, James, cartmaker and smith, 20 West street
M'Laughlin, John, cooper, 31 Mustard street
M'Laughlin, John, grocery and spirit stores, 1 Brown square &43 Brown st.
M'Laughlin, J., publican, undertaker, hay and straw dealer, 17 West street
M'Laughlin, John, wholesale tobacconist, 4 Donegall street
M'Laughlin, John, storekeeper, 28 Shipboy street
M'Laughlin, James, barber, 31 Peter's hill
M'Laughlin, John, spirit store and grocery, 5 Curtis street
M'Laughlin, J., curds and cream house, Antrim road
M'Laughlin, John, currier, 16 Staunton street
M'Laughlin, Maxwell, publican and auctioneer, 28 Marquis street
M'Laughlin, Neill, mariner, 23 Green street
M'Laughlin, Patrick, bricklayer, 63 Boundary street
M'Laughlin, Robert, mechanic, 5 Upton street
M'Laughlin, Terence, carter, Shankhill road
M'Laughlin, Thomas, painter and glazier, 20 Melbourne street
M'Laughlin, Wm., writing clerk, 7 Russell street
M'Laughlin, William, clothes dealer, 36 Berry street
M'Laughlin, William, mechanic, 91 Boundary street
M'Laughlin, William, smith, 42 Brown street
M'Laverty, Henry, night constable, 21 Wall street
M'Lean, Bernard, clerk, 6 York road
M'Lean, David, railway porter, 3 Moore's place
M'Lean, James, clerk, Old Malone road
M'Lean, James, card fitter, 8 Raphael street
M'Lean, James, copper smith, 13 Cullingtree place
M'Leish, William, manufacturing chemist, Gregg's row, Ballymacarrett
M'Lorinan, Henry, delf, china, and glass warehouse, 42 Smithfield
M'Lorinan, Hugh, grocer, spirit dealer, &c., 46 Institution place
M'Lornan, Patrick, marine store, 50 Union street
M'Lurcan, William, 2 Ship street
M'Mahon, John, butcher, 73 Hercules street
M'Mahon, John, coach maker, 27 West street

ALPHABETICAL DIRECTORY.

M'Mahon, James, provision dealer, 49 Hudson's entry, and 34 Smithfield
M'Mahon, Miss M., milliner and straw bonnet maker, 24 Stanhope street
M'Mahon, Mary A., 7 East street
M'Mahon, Owen, grocer and plasterer, 28 Grattan street
M'Mahon, Patrick, hostler, 26 Moffet street
M'Mahon, Patrick, tailor, Hudson's row
M'Mahon, Thomas, moulder, 18 Michael street
M'Mahon, Thomas, butcher, 82 John street
M'Mahon, William, sea captain, 57 Nelson street
M'Mahon, William, butcher, 55 John street—North street
M'Manamy, Charles, porter in brewery, 2 Chapel lane
M'Manus, Eliza, 14 Charles street
M'Manus, Francis, grocery and spirit shop, 8 Corporation street
M'Manus, James, porter, 38 Winetavern street
M'Manus, John, publican, 54 Hercules street
M'Manus, James, spirit store, 1 Birch street
M'Manus, Mrs., boarding house, 25 Cromac road
M'Master, Alexander, clerk, Anderson's houses, Ballymacarrett
M'Master, A., carpenter, 73 Barrack street
M'Master, Robert, carpenter, M'Master's row
M'Master, Thomas, pork cutter, 34 Little Donegall street
M'Meekan, James, marble and stone yard, 5 Victoria street
M'Meekan, Margaret, grocer, 28 Prince's street
M'Meekan, Robert, shoemaker, 45 North Thomas street
M'Meekan, William, porter, 8 Greenland street
M'Menamy, Edward, spirit dealer, 14 Hercules street
M'Michael, Hugh, lodgings, 7 Prince's street
M'Millan and Smyth, bakery, 66 Great Patrick street
M'Millan, Duncan, blacksmith, 20 Telfair's entry
M'Millan, James, grocer, Lagan village, Ballymacarrett
M'Millan, James, provision store, 150 North street
M'Millan, John, publican, 17 North Queen street
M'Millan, John, saddler, 3 Edward street
M'Millan, John, tailor, 15 Gordon street
M'Millan, Jane, upholstress, 8½ Hercules place
M'Millan, Ruth, grocer, confectioner, and upholstress, 89 York street
M'Millan, Robert, spirit merchant, 10 Johnston's buildings, Victoria place
M'Millan, Samuel, dealer in tow, &c., 2 Washington street
M'Millan, William, cabinetmaker, 35 Joy street
M'Millen, Samuel, tow merchant, 14 Academy street
M'Minn, A. and M., dressmakers, 9 Nelson street
M'Minn, James, warper, 9 Nelson street
M'Minn, Robert, shoemaker, 1 Charles street
M'Moran, James, linen weaver, 8 Wesley place
M'Moran, Margaret, grocer, Gooseberry corner, Ballymacarrett
M'Moreland, James, spirit dealer, 26 and 28 Gamble street
M'Monagle, painter and glazier, 42 Great George's street
M'Mullan and Co., linen merchants, 8 Rosemary st.—46 Gt. George's st.
M'Mullan, Alexander, painter, 11 Castle street
M'Mullan, Andrew, ropemaker, 9 Boundary street
M'Mullan, Ann, stay and corset maker, 10 Mill street
M'Mullan, David, clerk, 3 Unity street
M'Mullan, David, boot and shoemaker, 1 Stanfield street
M'Mullan, David, clerk, 3 Unity street
M'Mullan, Hugh, spirit dealer, 53 Carrick hill

M'Mullan, Hugh, pensioner, 6 Hamilton's place
M'Mullan, Hugh, clerk, 59 Verner street
M'Mullan, Isabella, whiteworker, 3 William street
M'Mullan, John, lapper, 7 Michael street
M'Mullan, John, tailor, 1 Cambridge street
M'Mullan, John, iron moulder, 14 Sackville place
M'Mullan, James, flax dresser, 49 Currel's place
M'Mullan, Mary, boarding house, 30 Stanhope street
M'Mullan, Matthew, chandler and soap boiler, Corn mkt.—15 Gloucester st.
M'Mullan, Michael, posting establishment, 14 Wellington street
M'Mullan, Michael, 10 Wellington street
M'Mullan, Mary, bonnet maker, 3 Charlemont street
M'Mullan, Patrick, tanner and leather merchant, 36 Mill street
M'Mullan, Samuel, tailor, 10 Mill street
M'Mullan, William, sea captain, 44 Earl street
M'Mullan, William John, reporter, Agnes place, Shankhill road
M'Mullen, James, stonecutter, 27 Gordon street
M'Mullen, William, warper, 4 Telfair's entry
M'Murdie, Margaret, bag sewer, 23 Sackville street
M'Murray, Edward, in Rowan's foundry, 18½ Nile street
M'Murray, Hugh, tailor, 5 Coates street
M'Murray, Mrs., Ormeau street
M'Murray, Mrs., 70 Little Patrick street
M'Murray, Margaret, 65 Little Patrick street
M'Murray, Robert, tailor, 14 Mustard street
M'Murray, Samuel, tailor, 3 Russell street
M'Murray, Wallace, carpenter, 45 Market street
M'Murtry, James, provision dealer, 50 Edward street
M'Murtry, Mary, publican, 8 Great Patrick street
M'Nabb, John, carpenter, 26 Little York street
M'Nair, Thomas, writing clerk, 3 Glentilt place, Old Lodge road
M'Nally, Agnes, lodgings, 22 Grattan street
M'Nally, James, book keeper, 10 Upton street
M'Nally, Miss, dressmaker, 30 Little May street
M'Nally, Robert, ship agent, 12 Short street
M'Namara, Daniel, 1 New Lodge road
M'Namara, H., rope, and sail maker, 26 Church lane
M'Namee, John, flax dresser, 3 Duffy's place
M'Namee, Thomas, day constable, 21 Brown's square
M'Naughtan, Miss, 8 Ormeau place
M'Naughtan, Rev. John, Duncairn house
M'Naughten, John, constable, Board of Health, 8 Lancaster street
M'Nea, James, architect and surveyor, 95 York street
M'Neice, Conway, cow keeper, 1 Campbell's place, Old Lodge road
M'Neice, Robert, cabinet maker, 29 Boyd street
M'Neight, James, gardener, 19 Friendly street
M'Neilage, A., Captain of *Prince of Wales*, 10 Henry street
M'Neill, Daniel, dealer, 64 Carrickhill
M'Neill, Hugh, commission agent and sugar broker, 29 Waring street; residence, 14 Great George's street
M'Neill, Hugh, dealer, Keenan's place, Ballymacarrett
M'Neill, James, clothes renovator, 11 Lancaster street
M'Neill, John, pilot, 5 Shipboy street
M'Neill, Mary, straw bonnet maker, 2 Henrietta street
M'Neill, Mrs., 3 Robert street

ALPHABETICAL DIRECTORY.

M'Neill, Neill, bricklayer, 19 Brown street
M'Neill, Owen, publican, 13 Mary's market
M'Neill, Wm., linen lapper, 38 Peter's hill
M'Neill, Wm., hardware merchant, 4 Adelaide place
M'Neilly, John, papermaker, 5 Staunton street
M'Neilly, Rebecca, dressmaker, Harmony place
M'Neilly, Samuel, smith, 75 Green street
M'Nichol, James, dealer, 48 North Queen street
M'Nicholl, William, bootmaker, 9 Stanfield street
M'Niece, W. J., medical hall, 29 Corporation street
M'Peak, Edward, 31 Catherine street North
M'Peak, Eliza, grocer, 30 Charlemont street
M'Peak, James, pedlar, 190 North street
M'Peake, John, sawyer, 22 Millfield
M'Pherson, Daniel, engineer, 6 Sir Henry's buildings, Ballymacarrett
M'Pherson, Major, Fountainville Cottage
M'Pherson, Peter, & Co., sugar brokers & commission agents, 15 Rosemary st.
M'Philips, John, mariner, 2 Sussex street
M'Poland, Michael, dealer, 8 Lagan street
M'Polin, Hugh, dealer, 22 Stanfield street
M'Quade, Tobias, baker, 28 Barrack street
M'Quaide, John, porter, Caxton street
M'Quaide, Patrick, cooper, 13 Millfield
M'Quaide, Robert, spirit dealer, 41 Millfield and 30 West street
M'Quaide, Robert, spirit dealer, 30 West street
M'Quigan, Thomas, ropewalk, New road, Ballymacarrett
M'Quillan, Charles, shoemaker, Falls road
M'Quillan, Cornelius, butcher, 7 York street
M'Quillan, Edward, shoemaker, 24 Pound street
M'Quillan, Hugh, grocer, 3 Barrack street
M'Quillan, Patrick, grocer, 13 North King street
M'Quillan, Patrick, pawnbroker, 39 Gardiner street
M'Quillan, Robert, writing clerk, 55 Grattan street
M'Quilland, Alexander, engraver, 5 Napier's place
M'Quilland, John, boot and shoemaker, 7 Peter's hill
M'Quilland, Margaret, washerwoman, 59 Vere street
M'Quilland, Wm., tailor, Falls road
M'Quilland, Wm., gold printer, &c., Falls road tavern, Devis street
M'Quiston, John and Thomas, painters, 16 Arthur street
M'Quiston, John, house painter, 8 Cullingtree street
M'Quiston, Robert, gentleman, 4 Cumberland place, Donegall pass
M'Quiston, Thomas, painter, 2 Arthur place
M'Quoid, John, caretaker water works, Antrim road
M'Quoid, U., boot and shoemaker, 9 Church lane
M'Reynolds and Knox, gingham and check manufacturers, 13 York street
M'Roberts, George, provision dealer, 25 Cromac street
M'Roberts, Hugh, green grocer, Ormond market—Lower Staunton street
M'Roberts, Hugh, dealer, 27 Lower Stanfield street
M'Roberts, Joseph, hackle maker, 2 Meadow street
M'Roberts, Samuel, publican, Downpatrick and Newtownards coach office, 11 Great Edward street
M'Roberts, Wm., Scripture reader, 1 Garden place, Cromac road
M'Sally, John, spirit dealer, 20 Gamble street
M'Sally, Owen, boot and shoemaker, 45 Hudson's entry
M'Shane, Charles, bricklayer, 108 Millfield

M'Shane, P., lodging house, 75 Carrickhill
M'Shane, Patrick, auctioneer, 64 Smithfield
M'Sherry, Edward, carter, 41 Peter's hill
M'Sherry, Richard, master mariner, Short strand, Ballymacarrett
M'Sorley, John, butcher, 51 Hercules street
M'Sorley, John, in foundry, 25 Valentine street
M'Sparron, Alexander, car owner, 24 North Thomas street
M'Sperren, Charles, carter, Shankhill road
M'Stay, Wm., grocer, 60 New Lodge road
M'Stay, Wm., grocery, wine and spirit stores, 71 Smithfield
M'Tear, Ellen, 81 Nelson street
M'Tear, George, merchant and steam packet agent, 33, 35, and 37, Donegall quay; residence, Hazlebank
M'Tear, John, grocery, spirit, and provision stores, 1 Gamble street
M'Tear, John, grocer, publican, and provision merchant, 19 Corporation st.
M'Tear, Margaret, 29 Lower Malone road
M'Tier, Alex., master mariner, 12 North Thomas street
Nelson, Adam, spirit dealer, 4 Garmoyle street
M'Tier, David, bookseller, 25 M'Tier's street
M'Tier, James, gentleman, Vermont Lodge, Old Lodge road
M'Tier, Thomas, grocery and spirit store, 114 North street
M'Trustery, John, carpenter, 48 Boundary street
M'Turk, David, turner, 57 Grove street
M'Varnon, Elizabeth, whiteworker, 9 Little Patrick street
M'Vea, David, green grocer, Cromac street
M'Vey, Daniel, smith, 3 Hopeton place
M'Vey, David, lodgings, 2 Prince's court
M'Veigh, Brothers, feather merchants, 13 Church lane; factory, 6 Gregg's lane
M'Veigh, Mary, washerwoman, 14 Stanfield street
M'Veigh, Mary, 11 Galway court
M'Vicker, Alexander, foreman boot and shoemaker, 64 Joy street
M'Vicker, John, merchant clothier, 3 Donegall place
M'Vicker, John, constable, 13 Chapel lane
M'Wade, Francis, proprietor of Pottery works, Ballymacarrett
M'Wade, James, brick and tile works, New road, Ballymacarrett
M'Wade, James, grocer, 94 Carrickhill
M'Wade, Patrick, soap boiler, 22 Little Corporation street
M'Wha, James, basket maker, Ballymacarrett
M'William, Mrs., confectionary, &c., Queen's Island
M'Williams, James, slip keeper, Queen's Island
M'Williams, John, watchman, 6 Brown street
M'Williams, Mary Ann, 158 North st., proprietress of the "Eagle" inn
M'Williams, Robert, lodgings, 142 Millfield
M'Williams, Stewart, detective officer, 8 Gloucester street
M'Williams, Sarah, 28 Old Lodge road

NANNETTI, Giacomo, statuary and artificial stone manufacturer, of 16 Brunswick street, Dublin, 20 York street
Napier, Hugh, shoemaker, 26 Lower Malone
Napier, James, tailor, 21 Wilson street
Neeson, Francis, spirit store, 40 Mill street and 1 King street
Neild, James, commission agent, 3 Castle Chambers
Neill, Abraham, night constable, 32 Boundary street
Neill & White, wine and spirit merchants, 7 Winecellar entry
Neill, Brothers, watchmakers, jewellers, silversmiths, & opticians, 23 High st.

Neill, Henry, and Co., grain merchants, 17 Albert square—2 Albion place
Neill, John, gunmaker, fishing tackle warehouse, & bird preserver, 78 High st.
Neill, James, night constable, 20 Lower Stanfield street
Neill, John, salesman, 38 Gloucester street
Neill, John, at Richardson, Sons, and Owden's, 5 Calender st. and 6 May st.
Neill, John, starch maker, 3 Mitchell street
Neill, James, mechanic, 4 Nile street
Neill, James, lodgings, 4 Grattan street
Neill, Mrs., 15 Dock street
Neill, Robert, 40 Little York street
Neill, Robert, jeweller, High street; residence, 2 Albion place
Neill, Robert, gentleman, 6 Murray's terrace
Neill, Samuel, carman, Wheeler's place, Ballymacarrett
Neill, Wm., nailer, 73 Union street
Neill, James, wine and spirit merchant, Winecellar entry—Ballyrobin
Neilly, Wm., spinning master, 53 Grove street
Nelson, Adam, spirit dealer, 4 Garmoyle street
Nelson, Andrew, tobacco spinner, 13 Kennedy's place
Nelson, George, tailor and clothier, 12 Pottinger's entry—Newtonbreda
Nelson, George, publican, 64½ Great George's street
Nelson, James, tailor, 42 Durham street
Nelson, James, shoemaker, 35 Stanley street
Nelson, James, smith and chain maker, 36 Winetavern street
Nelson, Jane, dealer, 23 Winetavern street
Nelson, Mary, 10 Mustard street
Nelson, Mrs., dealer, 64 New Lodge road
Nelson, Rev. Isaac, Presbyterian church, Donegall st.—Sugarfield, Shankhill
Nelson, Robert, provision dealer, 50 Peter's hill
Nelson, Samuel, West India merchant, Linen hall; residence, Glendevis
Nelson, Wm., blacksmith, 9 Grove street
Nelson, Wm., foreman printer, 2 Michael street
Nelson, Wm., grocer, 2 Shankhill road
Nesbit, David, designer and lithographer, 63 Academy street
Nesbit, Joseph, writing clerk, 58 Joy street
Nesbitt, Robert, 59 Joy street
Nettleton, Miss Eliza, dressmaker, 28 King street
Neville, Cornelius, publican, 66 Smithfield
Neville, Robert, publican, 3 Marquis street
Nevin, David, cardriver, 7 Johnston's court
Nevin, Wm., hairdresser, 23 Robert street
Newberry, George, pensioner, 4 Upton street
Newell, John, porter, 81 Boundary street
Newell, John, schoolmaster, Ballynafeigh
Newell, Thomas, marketman, 10 Renwick place
Newell, Thomas, boarding house, 12 Skipper street
Newett, Robert, coal merchant, 15 Unity street
Newett, Robert, coal agent, 4 Queen's square; office, 4 Queen's quay
Newett, Wm., ship chandler, 2 Corporation street—9 Queen's square
Newett, Wm., stoneyard, 9 Queen's quay, Ballymacarrett
Niblock, Ann Jane, dealer, 59 Mill street
Niblock, David, ship carpenter, 57 North Thomas street
Niblock, Robert, mechanic, 70 Brown street
Niblock, Wm., grocer and porkcutter, 82 Market street
Nichol, Daniel, mechanic, 17 Cullingtree street
Nichol, Jas., tavern, 21 Albert sq.; soda water manufactory, 34½ Gordon st.

Nichol, James, baker, 27 Donegall street
Nichol, Susan, dealer, 140 Millfield
Nicholl, James, porkcutter, 17 Grace street
Nicholl, Mrs., fishing tackle and gunsmith warehouse, 10 High street
Nicholl, Richard, mariner, 52 North Thomas street
Nicholl, Samuel, porkcutter, 20 Little Edward street
Nicholis, Wm., excise officer, 3 Windsor place
Nicholson, John, carpenter, 141 Lower Malone
Nicholson, John H., wholesale grocer, 89 Queen's square
Nicol, Henry, book keeper, Mount Pottinger, Ballymacarrett
Nimack, Joseph, cabinetmaker, 12¼ Castle street
Nimack, John, cabinetmaker, Arthur street, and 16 Crown entry
Nimmins, Andrew, millwright, 39 Melbourne street
Nimoe, Jane, Ballymacarrett
Nixon, James, inland revenue officer, Donegall pass
Nixon, James, travelling clerk, Donegall pass
Nixon, James, boot and shoemaker, 145 Lower Malone
Nixon, Samuel, flax dresser, 10 Vere street
Nixon, Samuel, shoemaker, 88 Old Lodge road
Noble, Hugh, sawyer, 29 Pilot street
Noble, James, haberdasher, 22½ Robert street
Noble, John James, medical student, 1 Spamount
Noble, James, dealer, Keenan's place, Ballymacarrett
Noble, Miss, boarding house, 57 North street
Noble, Margaret, 7 Long lane
Nocher, John, linen and damask warehouse, 16 Arthur street
Noel, Michael, car driver, 28 Pottinger's entry
Nolan, Cornelius, servant, 27 Tomb street
Nolan, George, publican, 120 Carrickhill
Nolan, Isaac, dealer, 44 Frederick street
Noland, Miss, boarding house, 19 North Queen street
Noon, Henry, publican and grocer, 54 Mill street
Noon, Patrick, shoemaker, 1 Bell's lane
Norris, James, porkcutter, 65 Vere street
Norris, John, lime burner, 23 Mitchell street
Norwood, David, assistant in lapping room, 18 Back Ship street
Nugent, John, pensioner, 2 Sir Henry's buildings, Ballymacarrett
Nugent, James, baker and grocer, 16 Curtis street
Nugent, Mrs., boarding house, 75 Corporation square
Nursey, Claude, head master School of Design; residence, Lower Crescent

OFFICER, Alexander, surgeon and licentiate apothecary, 43 York street
Officer, Elizabeth, whiteworker, 1 Stanley place
Ogle, Frederick, wine & spirit merchant, 10 Waring street—16 Victoria place
Ogston, Mrs. Mary, confectioner, 39 High street
Oldham, Edward, 5 Melbourne street
Oldrin, James, tailor, 53 Joy street
Oldrin, Mary and Sarah, children's linen warehouse, 20 Castle place
Oliver, Rev. John, Wesleyan minister, 5 Joy street
Oliver, Stewart, grocer and spirit dealer, 26 Eliza street
Orem, Jane, clothes dealer, 25 Black's place
Orr and Montgomery, solicitors, 3 The Castle, Castle buildings ; A. Montgomery's residence, Mount Pottinger, Ballymacarrett
Orr, David, carpenter, 4 Eliza street
Orr, David, tailor, 29 Lancaster street

ALPHABETICAL DIRECTORY.

Orr, David, butler, 49 M'Tier's street
Orr, Henderson, writing clerk, 4 Joy street
Orr, Hugh, sawyer, 7 Eliza street
Orr, Hugh, clerk of petty sessions, 16 Queen street
Orr, John, clerk, 4 North Queen street
Orr, John, horse shoer and blacksmith, 10 and 16 Prince's street
Orr, Joseph, seedsman, 5 Castle place—1 Little Victoria street
Orr, John, confectioner and fancy biscuit maker, 18 Robert street
Orr, Mrs., 13 Torrens' market
Orr, Misses, milliners and dressmakers, 4 Joy street
Orr, Mrs., 1 Johnston's place, New road, Ballymacarrett
Orr, Mrs., Mount Pottinger, Ballymacarrett
Orr, Margaret, lodgings, 6 M'Milian's place
Orr, Matthew, ship carpenter, 14 Little Corporation street
Orr, Mrs., servants' registry office, 1 Academy street—4 North Queen street
Orr, Robert, linen merchant, 1 Glengall street
Orr, Robert, excise officer, 1 Downshire place
Orr, Robert, grocery and spirit store, 204 North street
Orr, William Robert, clerk, Fleet street
Orr, William, grocer, 50 North Queen street
Orr, William, sawyer, 149 Lower Malone
Orr, Wm., & Sons, bleachers, Genalina; office, 3 Glengall street
Orr, William, currier, 53 Mill street
Osborne, Rodger, ship carpenter, 29 Vere street
Osborne, Rodger, watchman, 22 Mary's market
Oswald, William, 8¼ Gordon street
Oulton, Mrs., 36 College street
Oulton, Plato, clerk Water Commissioners, 36 College street
Oulton, Rev. Richard, military chaplain, inspector county gaol, Holywood
Owden, John, of J. N. Richardson & Sons, Brooklands
Owen, Hugh, cabinet maker, 58 Mill street
Owen, James B., pawnbroker, 29 Townsend street
Owen, John, civil bill officer, Anderson's houses, New road, Ballymacarrett
Owen, Robert, cabinet maker, 3 King street court
Owen, Thomas, sawyer, 10 Little Corporation street
Owen, William H., pawnbroker, 24 Henry street
Owens, Dorothea, marine store, 47 and 49 Union street
Owens, J. B., pawnbroker, 19 Barrack street
Owens, John, slater, 17 Robert street
Owens, Michael, carpenter, 25 Wall street
Owens, Mary, washerwoman, 15 Cromac road
Owens, Margaret, marine store, 87 Millfield
Owens, Samuel, gentleman, 55 Nelson street
Owens, Thomas, provision dealer, 64 Nelson street
Owens, William, stone mason, Ballymacarrett
Oysten, John, fireman, Falls mill, Charters' buildings, Falls road
Oyston, Thomas, manager of Falls Mill; residence, 65 Durham street

O'Brie, Thomas, gilder, 10 Catherine street
O'Brien, Andrew, lodgings, 26 Prince's street
O'Brien, Christopher, clerk, 1 Reilly's place
O'Brien, George, 19 Donegall place
O'Brien, Laurence, hairdresser and wig maker, 159 North street
O'Brien, Miss, dressmaker, 3 Catherine street
O'Brien, Terence, general merchant, 1 and 3 Store lane—Donegall place

O'Connor, Anthony, of Ross, O'Connor, & Co., High street—Mount Pottinger
O'Connor, Hugh, teacher, 7 Arthur place
O'Connor, James D., accountant Savings' Bank—1 College place north
O'Connor, Sarah, green grocer, 23 Castle market
O'Donnell, Patrick, publican and coal dealer, 29 Smithfield
O'Donohoe, James, cement manufacturer, Newport—26 York street
O'Farrell, Fergus, spirit store, Little Patrick street—84 Corporation street
O'Flaherty, Francis H., proctor, 13 Arthur street
O'Hagan, Bernard, clothes dealer, 22 Marquis street and 7 Smithfield
O'Hagan, Charles, sawyer, 3 Union street
O'Hagan, John, clothes dealer, 30 Marquis street and 8 Smithfield
O'Hagan, James, dealer, 45 Old Lodge road
O'Hagan, James, dealer in old iron, 18 New row and 60 Smithfield
O'Hagan, John, hardware and tool dealer, 18 Smithfield
O'Hagan, Margaret, bonnet maker, Devis street
O'Hagarty, Charles, publican, 34 Shankhill
O'Hanlon, John, tailor, 45 Castle street
O'Hanlon, Michael, hackler, 17 Sarah street
O'Hanlon, Rev. Wm., Independent minister, 11 Great George's street
O'Hanlon, T., proprietor Ulster Railway tavern, Great Victoria street
O'Hara, Amelia, millworker, 27 Charles street
O'Hara, Ellen, whiteworker, 40 Mustard street
O'Hara, Henry, carman, Conlon street
O'Hara, John, butcher, 41 Union street
O'Hara, Owen, foreman baker, 70 Hercules street
O'Hara, Rose, washerwoman, 13 Earl lane
O'Hara, William, coachman, 5 College place north
O'Hare, Catherine, egg dealer, 30 Stanfield street
O'Hare, John, bricklayer, 15 Lower Stanfield street
O'Hare, Rose, fruit dealer, 13 Smithfield
O'Hare, William, fruit dealer, 15 Market street
O'Hayer, Francis, saddler, 1 Donegall place buildings—2 Fountain street
O'Kane, Thomas, grocer and spirit dealer, M'Rory's row, Ballymacarrett
O'Kean, James, shoe shop, 7 Barrack street
O'Leery, John, custom house officer, 15 Nile street
O'Loughran, Rev. Henry, 97 Donegall street
O'Meely, Timothy, haberdasher, 3 Barrack street
O'Neile, Daniel, dealer, 6 Mustard street
O'Neile, John, dealer, 28 New Lodge road
O'Neill, Alexander, teacher, 12 Little Patrick street
O'Neill, Bernard, blacksmith, 23 Old Lodge road
O'Neill, Bernard, publican, 5 Peter's hill and 2 Lodge road
O'Neill, Charles, bricklayer, 6 North King street
O'Neill, Charles, carpenter, 23 Lancaster street
O'Neill, Con., publican and grocer, 20 Michael street
O'Neill, Charles, carding master, 12 Townsend place
O'Neill, Daniel, blockmaker, 23 Greenland street
O'Neill, Edward, shipwright, 11 Little Patrick street
O'Neill, Elizabeth, provision dealer, 33 Union street
O'Neill, Edward, cooper, 46 Tomb street
O'Neill, Elizabeth, 17 Earl street
O'Neill, Henry, dealer, Shankhill road
O'Neill, Hugh, boot and shoemaker, 3 North Queen street
O'Neill, James, bookseller, stationer, and printer, library, and fancy toy warehouse, 4 Castle place

ALPHABETICAL DIRECTORY.

O'Neill, James, butcher, 50 Barrack street
O'Neill, James, lumper, 26 Green street
O'Neill, James, confectioner, 35 Great Edward street
O'Neill, James, publican, 68 Great George's street
O'Neill, James, barber, 30 Robert street
O'Neill, James, dealer, 24 Barrack street
O'Neill, Jane, lodgings, 26 Little Donegall street
O'Neill, John, dealer, 67 Barrack street
O'Neill, John, tanner, 11 Meetinghouse lane
O'Neill, John, coach trimmer, 5 Little May street
O'Neill, John, corn dealer, 4 Lemon's lane
O'Neill, John, haberdasher, 28 Great Edward street
O'Neill, John, grocer, 44 Lettuce hill
O'Neill, John, carter, 78 Brown street
O'Neill, John, lodgings, 85 Millfield
O'Neill, John, butcher, 7 Devis street
O'Neill, John, overseer in mill, 14 Sarah street
O'Neill, John, bundler, New Lodge place
O'Neill, James, brickburner, Ballymacarrett
O'Neill, John, sawyer, 40 Sussex street
O'Neill, John, plasterer, 5 Devis street
O'Neill, Mary, lodgings, 11 John street
O'Neill, Mrs., 10 College place north
O'Neill, Mrs., 29 William's row
O'Neill, Mrs., 42 Union street
O'Neill, Mrs., lodging house, 17 Little Donegall street
O'Neill, Owen, publican, 24 Greenland street
O'Neill, Patrick, boot and shoe shop, 111 North street
O'Neill, Patrick, publican and grocer, 31 Smithfield
O'Neill, P., carpenter, 51 Barrack street
O'Neill, Patrick, publican, 109½ North street
O'Neill, Wm., draper and clothier, Victoria street—Robert street
O'Neill, William, pawnbroker, 20 Robert street
O'Prey, Patrick, sawyer, 37 Hill street
O'Regan, Simon, engineer, 15 Eliza place
O'Reilly, Thomas, clothes dealer, 4 Berry street
O'Rorke, Alexander & Daniel, solicitors, 14 Donegall street; residences: A. O'Rorke, 4 College square north; D. O'Rorke, Howard street
O'Rorke, Jeremiah, book keeper, 1 College street south
O'Rorke, Robert, shoemaker, 11 Long lane

Pace, Robert, jun., Belfast Plate Iron Works, Eliza street—43 High street
Page, Wm., hair cutter, wig maker, perfumer and chiropodist, 19 Castle place
Paisley, James, classical, English and mercantile seminary, 33 King street
Pake, Hugh, spirit dealer, 51 Lancaster street
Palliser, Mrs. Sarah, boarding house, 45 Joy street
Palmer, H., boot and shoe shop, 2 Church lane
Palmer, Thomas, boot and shoemaker, 6 Church lane
Palmer, William, boot and shoemaker, 3 Church lane & 88 High street
Palmer, William, baker, 9 Wesley place
Park, Andrew, sea captain, 65 Nelson street
Park, George, brass founder, 14 Grace street
Park, James, publican and grocer, 45 North Queen street
Park, Lewis and Charles, sewed muslin manufacturers, 61 York street
Park, Samuel, mate of *Erin's Queen*, 4, Nelson street

Park, Wm. John, tailor, 2 Stanhope street
Parker, Ellen, 15 Charles street
Parker, George, publican, Falls road
Parker, James, tailor, Old Lodge road
Parker, James, butcher, 11½ Cromac street
Parker, James, Fairy place
Parker, Margaret, washerwoman, Fleet street
Parker, Margaret, boarding house, 9 Portland place
Parker, Thomas, butcher, 47 Hercules street
Parker, Thomas, jun., butcher, 63 Waring street—Hercules street
Parker, Wm., overlooker, Falls mill company, Falls road
Parkhill, David, gentleman, 7 Brougham street
Parkhill, Robert, baker, 14 Sussex street
Parkinson, John, night constable, 125 Lower Malone road
Parkinson, John, dealer, 75 Millfield
Pascoe, Captain Wm., 16 Garmoyle street
Patterson, Alexander, baker, 7 Queen's square
Patterson, Doctor James, 4 Donegall square east
Patterson, David, smiths' helper, 85 Little York street
Patterson, Eliza, dressmaker, 30 Church lane
Patterson, Francis, chandler and soap boiler, 24 Mill street
Patterson, Francis, cardriver, 1 Hutchinson street
Patterson, Hugh, porter, 7 Friendly street
Patterson, Jos., picture frame manufacturer, 23 and 25 Hercules place
Patterson, John, stonecutter, 29 Catherine street north
Patterson, John, carter, 130 Old Lodge road
Patterson, Miss E., dressmaker, 2 Joy street
Patterson, Mrs., shoe shop, 30 Church lane
Patterson, Mrs., 2 Breadalbane place
Patterson, Robert, of R. & D. Patterson, hardware merchants, High street—
  College square north
Patterson, Samuel, grocer and provision dealer, 37 Union street
Patterson, Robert, lodgings, Bridge end, Ballymacarrett
Patterson, Thomas, cabinet maker, 54 Brown street
Patterson, William, dealer, Welsh street
Patterson, William, painter, 6 Raphael street
Patterson, William, chandler, 170 North street
Paton, Alexander, mariner, 35 Pottinger's entry
Patton, Archibald, grocer and publican, Ballymacarrett
Patton, Ann, 10 Nelson street
Patton, George, house agent and accountant, 30 Corporation street
Patton, James, carpenter, Earl lane
Patton, Thomas, bleacher, 9 Cullingtree street
Patrick, Jane, dealer, 101 Carrickhill
Patrick, John, porter Queen's College, 27 Bradbury place
Patrick, Margaret Jane, haberdasher, 91 North street
Patrick, Robert, pawnbroker, 38 Henry street
Paul, Anthony, cloth lapper, 2 Rochfort place
Paul, Mary, lodgings, 5 Robert street
Paul, Robert, grocer, 18 Union street
Peacock, John, currier, 41 Boyd street
Peak, Michael, grocer, and publican, 30 Edward street
Peake, B., Commercial lodging house, 24 Ann street
Peake, Thomas, sawyer, 18 Wall street
Pearce, James & William, Phœnix foundry, 16 Gt. George's st.—Pebble lodge

ALPHABETICAL DIRECTORY. 329

Pearce, William, warper, 4 Hopeton place
Pearce, William B., of Phœnix foundry—York road
Pearson, Nathaniel, mechanic, 13 Upton street
Peebles, Hans, spirit dealer, Campbell's buildings, Shankhill
Peden, Joseph, blacksmith, 79 Little York street
Peel, Robert, bakery and flour stores, Shankill road & 151 and 153 North st.
Pelan & M'Mullan, soap and candle manufacturers & window glass merchants, 26 Corn market; George Pelan's residence, Lisburn
Pelan and Rankin, toy and basket merchants, 6 Bridge street
Pelan, George, clerk in Messrs. Richardson's, 17 Great Patrick street
Pelan, James, grocery and spirit store, 36 Durham street
Pelan, James, 5 Glengall street
Pelan, John, hackler, 1 Collingwood street
Pelan, Mrs. Ellen, 3 College street
Pelan, Richard, chandler, 42 Market street
Pelan, Robert, 15 York street
Pelling, Charles, sewed muslin manufacturer, 30 Donegall street; residence, 16 Great Patrick street
Pelling, Peter, & Co., weaving commission agents, 37 John st.—3 College st.
Pentland, Mrs., 1 Belvidere place
Penton, Wm., seedsman, 2 Donegall street; residence, Holywood
Percy, Robert, tailor, 20 Peter's hill
Perry, George, tide waiter, 23 Collingwood street
Perry, John, carpenter, 35 Edward street
Perry, Martin, grocer, Ballymacarrett
Perry, Stewart, cooper, 9 Morrow's entry
Perry, Samuel, pork cutter, 29 M'Tier's street
Perry, Wm., letter carrier, 18 North Ann street
Pescoe, John, retired coastguard officer, 56 Ship street
Pescoe, John, jun., sea captain, 60 Ship street
Pettigrew, Daniel, mill wright, 28 Boyd street
Pettigrew, James, weaver, 91 Lower Malone road
Peyton, Charles, gentleman, 6 Howard street
Peyton, James, sail cloth weaver, 15 Shipboy street
Peyton, James, sail maker, 13 Pilot street
Phillips, Alexander, farmer, Seymour street
Phillips, F., mechanic, 4 Alexander street
Phillips, George, and Co., proprietors cocoa mat manufactory, Ballymacarrett
Phillips, George, bookseller, stationer, and librarian, 27 Bridge street; residence, 3 Linen-hall street
Phillips, John, whitesmith, 30 Carrickhill
Phillips, James, weaver, M'Crory's row, Ballymacarrett
Philips, James, clerk, Sir Henry's buildings, Ballymacarrett
Phillips, Jane, washerwoman and mangler, 18 Russell street
Phillips, Rebecca, 3 Mustard street
Phoenix, Miss E., dressmaker, 50 Joy street
Pierce, Peter, engineer, 54 Tomb street
Pike, Mrs., Crumlin terrace
Pim, Edward and George, tea dealers, wine importers, and general grocers, 27 and 29 High street,
Pim, Edward, merchant, High street; residence, 6 Royal terrrce
Pim, George C., merchant, High st. and Donegall quay—7 University square
Pim, Hamilton, warehouseman, 2 Windsor place
Pim, John, commission merchant, 20 Waring street—Crumlin terrace
Pim, Joshua, of Richardson, Brothers, and Co.—Sans Souci

Pinkerton, Francis, soda water manufactory, 31 William st.—27 Edward st.
Pinkerton, George, passenger agent, 28¾ Great George's street
Pinkerton, James, police rate collector; office, Police place—Chichester st.
Pinkerton, James, boarding house, 24 Carrickhill
Pirrie, Dr. John M., physician and surgeon, 66 Donegall street
Pirrie, Wm., ship owner, 66 Donegall street; residence, Conlig
Pitchoni, Signor, artist, 6 Castle lane
Plunket, James, plasterer and builder, 30 Durham street
Plunket, Jane, 32 Union street
Plunkett, Francis, commission merchant and agent, St. Anne's buildings, Donegall street
Pollin, John, mechanic, 23 Sackville place
Pollin, Wm., carpenter, 4 Raphael street
Pollock, Charles, bricklayer, 28 Millfield
Pollock, Jane, dressmaker, 62 North street
Pollock, Mrs., boarding house, 51 Nelson street
Pollock, Mrs., haberdasher, 66 Ann street
Pollock, Margaret, lodgings, 23 Alexander street
Pollock, Margaret, huckster, 124 Carrickhill
Pollock, Mary, bookseller, 62 North street
Pollock, Sarah, dealer, 106 Lower Malone
Pollock, William, pensioner, 63 North Queen street
Popham, Jeremiah, suspender manufacturer, 53¼ Mill street
Porteous, Christopher, sewed muslin manufacturer, Church street
Porteous, James, of James Porteous & Co., 9 Brougham street
Porteous, J., & Co., sewed muslin manufacturers, 15 Church street
Porter, Andrew B., teacher Mechanics' Institute, 17 Queen street
Porter, Charles, ship carpenter, 8 Back Ship street
Porter, David, borough accountant, 22 Hamilton street
Porter, Eliza, 40 Wilson street
Porter, Edward, & Son, iron stores, Albert square
Porter, Hugh, clerk, 84 Donegall street
Porter, James, ship carpenter, 4 Little Ship street
Porter, James, porter, 14 Back Ship street
Porter, John, rent office, Hamilton's court; residence, Cromac lodge
Porter, James, day constable, 54 John street
Porter, John, smith, 60 Great Patrick street and Covent garden
Porter, John, pork cutter, 20 Sussex street
Porter, Mrs., boarding house, 12 Hamilton street
Porter, Matthew, cow keeper, Shankhill road
Porter, Rev. John Scott, 16 College square east
Porter, Rev. John, 5 Murray's terrace
Porter, Sarah, green grocer, Garmoyle street
Porter, Tobias, manager of Belfast flour mill, 4 Ardmoulin place
Porter, William, & Son, wholesale clothiers & general outfitters, 28 Berry st.
Posnett, Hutcheson, agent for Viscount Dungannon, Rose lodge, Donegall pass
Potbury, Mary Jane, boarding house, 87 Nelson street
Pott, John, 17 Leeds street
Potter, Mrs., Marine hotel and tavern, 69 Corporation square
Potts, Ellen, 14 Francis street
Potts, John, grocer, 112 Carrick hill
Potts, Joseph, green grocer, egg and fowl merchant, 3 Great Patrick street
Potts, John and Robert, iron merchants, 31 North street; residences: John Potts, 25 York street; Robert Potts, Rosemount, Antrim road
Potts, Margaret, grocer and spirit dealer, 16 Henry street
Powell, John, engineer, 2 Spencer street

ALPHABETICAL DIRECTORY.

Powell, Wm., grocer and spirit dealer, 22 Talbot street
Praeger, Francois, of J. Praeger & Co., Fountain street—10 Chichester street
Praeger, John, and Co., linen and yarn merchants, Fountain street
Praeger, John, Austrian & Bremen vice-consul, Fountain st.—7 Donegall sq. so.
Pratt, Benjamin, and Co., Wellington boot and shoe house, Victoria street
Pray, Nicholas, ginger ale maker, 7 Wall street
Prenter, N. A., oil and colour merchant, 8 and 10 Cotton court, Waring street; residence, Harryville, Lisburn road
Prenter, W. Emerson, wholesale tea & coffee agent, Victoria st.—6 William's pl.
Press, Thomas, carpenter, 19 Melbourne street
Pressley, James, porter, 8 Roy's court
Preston, John & Co., linen yarn and flax merchants, 12 Calender street
Preston, John, 5 Pakenham place
Preston, S., dealer, 39 Alexander street
Pretty, Edward, landing waiter, inland revenue, Mount Prospect
Prey, Rose Ann, spirit store, 156 Queen's square
Price, Archibald, ironfounder, 10 Campbell's buildings, Townsend street
Price, Henry, butcher, 99 Peter's hill
Price, James, pensioner, 37 Friendly street
Price, Thos., accountant, Harbour Commissioners' office, 38 North Queen st.
Price, Wm., master mariner, 13 Shipboy street
Prince, Samuel, lodgings, 9 Marlborough street
Pritchard, Mary Ann, lodging house, 16 Hercules street
Pullan, Charles, gardener and steward, 19 Frederick street
Purdon, Dr. C. D., 17 College square East
Purdon, Dr. Henry Thomas, surgeon, 5 Wellington place
Purdon, Mrs., 9 University square
Purdy, Mary, 2 William's lane
Purdy, Robert, shoemaker, 10 William's lane
Purkis, Matthew, hacklemaker, 6 Washington street
Purkis, Richard and Joseph, hackle makers, 36 Joy st.; works, Joy's court
Purse, Arthur, builder, grocer & spirit dealer, 58 York st. and 24 Henry st.
Purse, John, builder, 27 Pilot street
Purse, John, house carpenter, 7 Little York street
Pursely, Thomas, 139 Durham street
Purvis, Eliza, provision dealer, 93 and 95 Little York street
Purvis, Oliver, gardener, 36 Little York street
Purvis, Thomas, commission agent, Ballynafeigh
Pye, W. B., manager soda ash manufactory, Friendly street—70 High street

QUAIL, Matthew, starch maker, 10 Boundary street
Quail, William, cabinet maker, 34 Donegall street
Quaile, Miss, 13 Hamilton street
Quaile, Peter, teacher, 11 Millfield
Quaile, Thomas, reporter, 39 Cromac street
Quart, John, green grocer and mason, 9 Cromac street
Quee, John, painter, 23 North Ann street
Quee, Patrick, shipwright, 48 North Thomas street
Quee, Robert, painter and glazier, 4 M'Cracken's row, Ballymacarrett
Quee, William, butcher, 17 Durham street
Quigley, Samuel, grain merchant, 18 Cromac street
Quigley, Thomas, fruiterer, 10 Great Edward street
Quigley, William, grain merchant, 16 Cromac street
Quin, Daniel, clerk, 1 Thomas street
Quin, Edward, carter, 49 Vere street

2 F

Quin, Edward, sawyer, 30 Pound street
Quin, George, surgeon and apothecary, 16 Castle place
Quin, Hugh, caravansary, 4 Talbot street
Quin, Hugh, publican, and cabinet maker, 14 Washington street
Quin, John, foreman *Mercury* office, Fairy place
Quin, John, grocer and publican, Old Lodge road
Quin, John, grocer and publican, 30 Mustard street, and 38 Union street
Quin, John, emigration agent, 14 Pottinger's entry
Quin, John, Shankhill road
Quin, Mary, dealer, 28 Robert street
Quin, Mrs., 5 Upper Queen street
Quin, T., emigration agent, 57 Waring street—63 Hercules street
Quin, Thomas, blacksmith, 49 Pound street
Quinn, Ann, spirit store, Queen's square
Quinn, Bernard, spinning master, 31 Malone road
Quinn, Bernard, lodgings, 50 John street
Quinn, Bernard, reporter *Mercury*, 57 Cromac street
Quinn, Charles, grocer and spirit store, 46 Talbot street
Quinn, Edwd., hardware dealer & bellows maker, 16 Smithfield—15 Marquis st.
Quinn, Henry, custom house officer, 17 North Ann street
Quinn, Hugh, carman, Conlon street
Quinn, Hamilton, publican, Falls road
Quinn, James, publican, 78 Nelson street
Quinn, James, green grocer, 8 Devis street
Quinn, John, surgeon, 3 Bank lane
Quinn, Matthew, tailor, 51 Verner street
Quinn, Patrick, butler, 15 Graham's entry
Quinn, Peter, sail maker and clothier, 3 and 7 Queen's square
Quinn, Patrick, carpenter, 2 Johnston's court
Quirey, James, and Co., wine and spirit merchants, leather dealer, &c., 33 Donegall street—28 Nelson street
Quirey, M. A., and Co., haberdashers, &c., 24 Donegall street
Quirey, William, coachman, 1 William's row

RAFFERTY, Elizabeth, 4 Hamilton place
Rafferty, George, grocer and publican, 48 Barrack street
Rafferty, Jane, huckster, 22 Caddell's entry
Rafferty, John, smith, Hopeton place
Rafferty, James, poulterer, 3 York street market
Rafferty, Michael, lath cutter, 11 Little Corporation street
Rainey, George, meal and provision dealer, 1 Russell street
Rainey, John, chandler, 8 Friendly street
Rainey, John, pattern drawer, New road, Ballymacarrett
Rainey, Thomas, publican, 40 Ann street
Rainey, William, cooper, 49 Hill street
Ralston, Mrs., Ashley place, Ballymacarrett
Ramsay, Isabella, 18 Millfield
Ramsay, James, grocer, and publican, 29 Charlemont street
Ramsay, James, butcher, 72 Hercules street
Ramsay, Richard, pensioner, 30 Shankhill
Ramsay, Sinclair, haberdasher, 12 Hill street—57 Great Patrick street
Ramsay, Thomas, blacksmith, 5 Stanley street
Ramsey, Alexander, baker, 53 Little Patrick street
Ranahan, Bernard, hair cutter, wig maker, and ornamental hair worker—Castle Chambers—10 Washington street
Rankin, Alexander, sawyer, 20 Leeds street

Rankin, Hugh, ship carpenter, 17 Little Patrick street
Rankin, James, shopman, 56 Stanhope street
Rankin, John, 15 York street
Rankin, Peter, confectioner, 17 Grove street
Rankin, Samuel S., wholesale and retail wine and spirit merchant, 4 Gamble street—Ballymacarrett
Rankin, William, blacksmith, 8 William's lane
Ranson, John, writing clerk, 104 Cromac street
Ranson, Thomas, agent, for Castlebellingham brewery, office, Police square, 33 Little May street, 3 Seaview place
Raw, John, chandler, 5 Millfield
Rawe, Richard, shoemaker, 30 Edward street
Rawling, George, grocer, 50 Mill street
Raymond, Francis, boarding house, 25 Church lane
Rea, Alexander, hair cutter, 11½ Great Edward street
Rea, Francis, clerk of the markets, 98 Donegall street
Rea, Hugh, of Messrs. Sinclair and Boyd's Donegall quay—21 Fountain place
Rea, James, book keeper, 6 Victoria terrace
Rea, John, solicitor, 12 Donegall street
Rea, John, shoemaker, 19 Little May street
Rea, John, railway constable, 12 Wesley place
Rea, Joseph, baker, 71 Green street
Rea, Miss Anna, milliner, 37 Edward street
Rea, Mrs., 37 Edward street
Rea, Samuel, surgeon, 26 Gloucester street
Rea, Samuel, spirit dealer, 36 Shankhill road
Rea, William John, hair cutter, 12 May street
Read, Isabella, dressmaker, 1 Catherine street
Read, Patrick, tobacconist and cigar dealer, 2 Castle place—Crown entry
Read, R. and D., letter-press printers and publishers, Crown entry
Reaney, James, grocer, 36 Green street
Reavey, Hugh, ship carpenter, Frederick street
Reddings, Miss Ann, milliner, 46½ Rosemary street
Reddington, Patrick, servant, 15 Edward street
Redmond, Andrew, printer, Frederick street
Redmond, Bernard, rag dealer, Smithfield
Redmond, Mary, dressmaker, 21 North Ann street
Redpath, William, seaman's boarding house, 32 Corporation street
Reed, Jas., printer, bookseller, and stationer, Victoria street—43 Academy st
Reford, Lewis, merchant, 17½ Rosemary street—Beechmount
Regan, John dealer, 37 Mustard street
Reichel, Rev. Charles, 1 Camden terrace, Botanic road
Reid, Archibald, tailor, 20 Mustard street
Reid, Alexander, musician, Conway street
Read, Dr. Thomas, surgeon, 5 Donegall square West
Reid, Dr. James Seaton, 3 College square east
Reid, Eliza, dealer, 4 Brown street
Reid, Henry, salesman, 47 Joy street
Reid, James, of Messrs. Wm. Browne and Co., Waring street—Cliftonville
Reid, James, linen lapper, 11 Wall street
Reid, James, grocer, 60 Ann Ann street
Reid, James, gentleman, 5 Little Ship street
Reid, James, pork cutter, 37 Townsend street
Reid, James, publican, 47 Little Patrick street
Reid, James, cooper, 41 Little Donegall street

ALPHAPETICAL DIRECTORY.

Reid, James, grocer, meal and flour dealer, 47 Peter's hill
Reid, James, gentleman, 7 Clarendon place
Reid, James, wholesale and retail wine and spirit stores, Cole's alley
Reid, John, Burns' Tavern and Concert Room, 8 Long Lane
Reid, John, car owner, 10 Fountain street
Reid, John, haberdasher, 55 North street
Reid, John, carpenter, 2 William street
Reid, John, engineer, 8 Sir Henry's buildings, Ballymacarrett
Reid, John, wine & spirit dealer, Wheeler's place, Ballymacarrett
Reid, Miss Mary, 4 Downshire place
Reid, Mrs., boarding house, 8 Henry street
Reid, Margaret, 10 Economy place
Reid, Margaret, dressmaker, 1 Stanley lane
Reid, Oswald, blacksmith, California street
Reid, Patrick, coach maker, 8 Johnston's court
Reid, William, haberdasher, 9 Arthur square
Reid, William, piano forte tuner, 1 Chichester street
Reid, Wm., ship carpenter, 7 Short street
Reid, Wm., grocer, 15 Cromac street
Reid, Wm., pensioner, 5 Dayton place
Reimbach, David, second master School of Design, 1 Botanic view
Reilly, B., grocer and provision merchant, 124 Ann street
Reilly, John, clothes dealer, 11 Berry street
Reilly, Mrs. Rose Ann, huckster, 14 King street
Reilly, Patrick, writing clerk, 11 George's lane
Reilly, Rose, staymaker, 40 Great Edward street
Reilly, Thomas, coachmaker, 27 Durham street
Reilly, Thomas, H., printer, bookbinder, and stationer, 13 Waring street
Rennick, James, porter, 51 Grove street
Renton, Hugh, foreman hackler, 2 Cambridge street
Reynolds, Archibald, clerk, Pottinger place, Ballymacarrett
Reynolds, Brothers, engineers and machine makers, 16 Mill street
Reynolds, George, sea captain, Earl lane
Reynolds, George, warper, 13 Townsend street
Reynolds, James, engineer, 16 Mill street; residence, 10 Cullingtree place
Reynolds, J., boot and shoemaker, 18 King street
Reynolds, John, fancy, jewellery and toy warehouse, 45 Donegall street
Reynolds, James, dealer, Keenan's place, Ballymacarrett
Reynolds, Peter, engineer, 16 Mill street; residence, 13 Townsend street
Reynolds, Robert, 13 Campbell's buildings, Townsend street
Reynolds, Thomas, mill overseer, 43 Peter's hill
Reynolds, Wm., grocer, 21 Sarah street
Reynolds, Wm., carpenter, 20 Henrietta street
Rice, Ann, butcher, 16 Hercules street
Rice, George, pensioner, 51 Old Lodge road
Rice, Henry, spirit dealer, 1¼ Union street
Rice, John, baker, 22 Stanhope street
Rice, James, butcher, 85 Hercules street
Rice, James, auctioneer, 33 Cromac street
Rice, James, car driver, 7 Riley's place
Rice, James, shoemaker, 28½ Friendly street
Rice, John, butcher, 23 Hercules street
Rice, John, schoolmaster, 60 Market street
Rice, Mrs., dealer, 101 Millfield
Rice, Patrick, spirit dealer, 16 Corporation street

ALPHABETICAL DIRECTORY.

Rice, Rose, confectioner, 17 Hercules place
Rice, Thomas, meal dealer, 7 Castle market; residence, 3 Bond street New
Rice, Wm., eating house, 1 Lemon's lane
Rice, Wm., shoemaker, 17 Boundary street
Richards, Eli, mechanic, 4 M'Rory's row, Ballymacarrett
Richards, J. E., snuff & tobacco shop, & universal parcel office, 22 Waring st.
Richardson, Brothers, and Co., general merchants, Corporation street
Richardson, J., wine and spirit merchant, Upper Church lane & 35 Ann st.
Richardson, James, butler, 12 Leeds street
Richardson, John, clerk post office, 21 Academy street
Richardson, J. N., Sons and Owden, linen manufacturers and linen bleachers, 14 Donegall pl.; stores, 5 Calendar st.; linen box manufactory, 6 May st.
Richardson, John, provision shop, 31 Melbourne street
Richardson, John, weighmaster, New Lodge place
Richardson, John Grubb, of Richardson, Brothers, & Co., Lisnagarvy, near Lisburn, & Bessbrook, near Newry
Richardson, Thomas, clerk in vitriol works, Ballynafeigh
Richardson, Wm., master mariner, 5 Stanley place
Richardson, Wm., 4 Prospect terrace
Richardson, Wm., mechanic, 4 Townsend place
Richey, Ann, 5 Renwick place
Richey, James, shoemaker, 4 Alexander street
Richey, John, 31 Queen street
Richey, Miss, 73 Corporation street
Richey, Miss, seminary, 31 Queen street
Rickards, J., proprietor of the Albion hotel, 39 Waring street
Riddel and M'Callum, Berlin wool establishment, haberdashers and lacemen, 13 Bridge street
Riddel and Co., ironmongers and hardware merchants, 54 High street
Riddel, John, wholesale ironmonger, 52 High steeet—Vermont, Botanic road
Riddel, James, reedmaker, Shankhill road
Riddel, M., Berlin wool and fancy warehouse, 5 Castle buildings
Riddell, Alexander, reed manufacturer, 37 John st.—3 Ship street
Riddell, E. and M., bonnet makers and haberdashers, 53 North street
Riddell, J., and Son, wholesale iron merchants, 17 Church lane
Riddell, Miss, 19 Queen street
Riddell, Robert, dealer in poultry, 21 Market street
Riddle, Alexander, shoemaker, 10 Cargill street
Riddle, Richard, stone cutter, 16 Thomas street
Ridgway, Mrs., 12 College street south
Ridgway, Rev. Thomas, Wesleyan minister, 8 Glengall street
Ridgway, R., boot and shoemaker, 44 Ann street
Riley, John, bundling master, 2 Meadow lane
Riley, James, slater, 49 Little York street
Riley, John, hardware dealer, 57 Smithfield and Berry street
Riley, James, of M'Curtin and Riley, grain merchants, 31½ Chichester street
Riley, Patrick, sawyer, 44 Verner street
Riley, Robert, boarding house, 29 Great Edward street
Riley, Robert, boot and shoemaker, 60 Millfield
Riley, Thomas, pensioner, 6 Verner street
Riley, Wm., haberdasher, 46 North street
Ring, Edward, doctor, 42 Earl street
Rippingham, Mrs., 4 Charlotte street
Rippit, Henry, cattle dealer, 55 Barrack street
Ritchie, Francis, proprietor chemical & felt works—Mount Pottinger

Ritchie, George, warper and grocer, Falls road
Ritchie, James, bonded warehouse, 2 Short street
Ritchie, James, carpenter, 5 New Lodge road
Ritchie, James, merchant, Prince's dock—Bellville house, Ballymacarrett
Ritchie, John, teacher Short strand school, Ballymacarrett
Ritchie, Jane, teacher Short strand school, Ballymacarrett
Ritchie, John, printer, Crumlin terrace
Ritchie, John, boiler maker, 10 Back Ship street
Ritchie, John, foreman in muslin manufactory, 4 California street
Ritchie, J., boarding house, 3 Prince's street
Ritchie, John, salesman, 7 Gloucester street
Ritchie, James, shoemaker, 30 Lancaster street
Ritchie, Lewis, grocer, 2 Coates street
Ritchie, Mrs., haberdasher, millinery, & bonnet dealer, 45 John street
Ritchie, Robert, clerk, Lower Malone
Ritchie, Wm., carpenter, 45 John street
Ritchie, Wm., mechanic, 4 Coates street
Robb, Alexander, merchant tailor, 6 Arthur street; residence, Ormeau road
Robb, Gawn, sea captain, 77 Academy street
Robb, Gilbert, writing clerk, Eliza street
Roberts, Archibald, ship carpenter, 14½ Nile street
Roberts, Hugh, linen lapper, 6 Sackville street
Roberts, John, deputy high constable, cess office, Queen street; residence, 2 New Lodge road
Roberts, Joseph, spinning master, 4 Economy place
Roberts, Miss, seminary, 25 King street
Roberts, Oswald, boat builder, 43 Dock street
Roberts, Thomas, engraver, 5 King street
Robertson, Arthur, lithographer, 10 Spencer street
Robie, James, reporter, *Banner* office, 3 Crumlin place
Robinson, Alexander, carman, 28 Caddell's entry
Robinson, Catherine, 1 Henrietta street
Robinson, David, carpenter, Falls road
Robinson, David, baker, 60 Union street
Robinson, David, warehouseman, 1 Park street
Robinson, Daniel, boot and shoemaker, 27 William street
Robinson, Edward, warper, 26 Little Corporation street
Robinson, Eliza, milliner, 21 Church street
Robinson, George, shipwrights' arms tavern, 4 Prince's dock
Robinson, George, foundryman, 81 Vere street
Robinson, George, letter carrier, 3 Wellington street
Robinson, Henry, carpenter, 49 Talbot street
Robinson, Hugh, cowkeeper, 4 Durham street
Robinson, Henry, drug and chemical warehouse, 114 High street
Robinson, Hutchinson, mariner, New Lodge place
Robinson, John, marble and stone establishment, 65 and 87 Donegall street
Robinson, James, sea captain, Ormeau street
Robinson, John, stonecutter, 24 York street
Robinson, John, mill manager, Falls road
Robinson, John, ship carpenter and grocer, 15 Nelson street
Robinson, Jane, New Lodge place
Robinson, John, teacher, 4 M'Tier's street
Robinson, John, confectioner, 36 Carrick hill
Robinson, John, sailmaker, 50 Little Patrick street
Robinson, John, mariner, Ballymacarrett

ALPHABETICAL DIRECTORY. 337

Robinson, John, shoemaker, 2 Stanfield court
Roseman, John, clerk, 33 Vere street
Robinson, James, boot and shoemaker, 7 Union place
Robinson, James, pensioner, 6 Seaview place, Ballymacarrett
Robinson, Joseph, sawyer, 32 Upper Lagan street
Robinson, James, stonecutter, 18 North Ann street
Ross, Hugh, carpenter, 4 Seymour street
Robinson, Miss, milliner and dressmaker, 16 Harmony place
Robinson, Mrs., commercial boarding house, 29 North street
Robinson, Mrs., 3 Albion lane
Robinson, Mary, dealer, 21 West street
Robinson, Malcolm, sea captain, 5 Little York street
Robinson, Mary, boarding house, 11 Pottinger's entry
Robinson, Mary Ann, dressmaker, Little Patrick street
Robinson, Mrs., millinery and dress rooms, 62 Donegall street
Robinson, Mr., teacher St. Anne's parochial school, 27 Academy street
Robinson, Nathaniel, ship carpenter, 7 Shipboy street
Robinson, Neill, turner, Lagan village, Ballymacarrett
Robinson, Richard, schoolmaster, 9 California street
Robinson, Richard, agricultural implement and bobbin manufacturer, 13 & 29 Eliza street
Robinson, Robert, bootmaker, 19 Boundary street
Robinson, S., brush, card, and bellows manufactory, and gutta percha depot, 26 North street—29 North street
Robinson, Thomas, grocer and spirit store, 25 Dock street
Robinson, Thomas, linen weaver, 29 Little York street
Robinson, Thomas, clerk, 6 Wall street
Robinson, Torrens, moulder, 69 Grove street
Robinson, William, coppersmith, 31 Mitchell street
Robinson, Wm., 15 Torrens' market
Robinson, William, dealer, 24 Pottinger's entry
Robinson, William, butter dealer, 23 Little Patrick street
Robson, John, livery stables and posting establishment, 31 Chichester street and 5 Montgomery street—22 Gloucester street
Robson, Richard, of John Robson's, 3 Montgomery street
Robson, Robert, butler, 16 Valentine street
Roche, Thomas, posting establishment, 16 Fountain street
Roche, Patrick, grocer and provision store, 48 Cromac street
Roddy, Robert, linen & damask manufacturer & bleacher, 18 Donegall street
Roden, Edward, marine stores, 26 Talbot street
Roden, James, marble store, 30 Great George's street
Rodgers, Alexander, grocer, 27 and 29 Little Patrick street
Rodgers, David, saddler, 51 North street—127 York street
Rodgers, Edward, publican and stabling, 11 Upper Church lane & Police sq.
Rodgers, George, fruiterer and green grocer, 2 York street market
Rodgers, Henry, gentleman, Ballynafeigh
Rodgers, James, whitesmith, Joy's court
Rodgers, James, porter, Belfast bank, 94 Old Lodge road
Rodgers, James, sea captain, 30 Earl street
Rodgers, John, gardener, 13 Bradbury place
Rodgers, Misses, dressmakers and milliners, 7 Downshire place
Rodgers, Patrick, clothes dealer, 32 Rosemary street and 42 Smithfield
Rodgers, Wm., general commission merchant, Victoria buildings—7 Apsley pl.
Rodgers, William, porter, 14 Edward street
Rodgers, William, auctioneer and valuator, 15 Church street

ALPHABETICAL DIRECTORY.

Roe, Misses, school, 16 College street
Rogan, Henry, carter, 138 Carrickhill
Rogan, James, pensioner, 2 Moore's place
Rogan, John, clerk, 9 Spencer srreet
Rogan, Patrick, spirit dealer, 37 Carrickhill
Rogan, Thomas, horse shoer, 53 Cromac street
Rogers, Alex., baker, grain and flour store, 29 and 31 Mill street
Rogers, Gilbert, carpenter, 51 Smithfield; residence, Ferguson's court
Rogers, James, meal and flour dealer, 12 Wesley place
Rogers, Mary, spirit dealer, 64½ Mill street
Rollands, Thomas, carter, 149 Durham street
Rolleston, James, watch and clock maker, 3 Castle place
Rooney, Francis, mariner, 33 Green street
Roney, Daniel, iron moulder, 5 Frederick place
Roney, James, tracing paper manufacturer, 93 York street
Roney, James, butcher, 76 Hercules street
Roney, John, bricklayer, Shankhill road
Roney, Mary, 16 York lane
Roney, William, carpenter, 37 Wall street
Rook, Mrs., 3 Charlotte street, Donegall pass
Rorke, Julia, boarding house, 6 Stephen street
Rorke, William, 8 Cromac street
Rossbotham, William, grocer and spirit dealer, 51 Edward street
Rose, James, muslin manufacturer, 9 Ship street
Rose, John, muslin manufacturer, 77 Joy street
Ross, Alexander, carter, 44 Sussex street
Ross, John, builder, 27 Joy street
Ross, James, clerk, 57 Joy street
Ross, James, brick manufacturer, 29 Old Lodge road
Ross, James, brassfounder, 9 M'Tier's court
Ross, Miss, 13 Albion place
Ross, Mrs. Jane, 1 Ship street
Ross, O'Connor, & Co., glass manufacturers and china warehouse, 28 and 30 High street; glass works, Ballymacarrett
Ross, Robert, and Co., hat and cap manufacturers, 20 and 27 Smithfield
Ross, Robert, dealer, 12 Bank lane
Ross, Richard, M.D., surgeon, 25 King street
Ross, Susan, dealer, 5 M'Tier's court
Ross, Wm., superannuated tide waiter, 23 Trafalgar street
Ross, Wm., of Ross, O'Connor, & Co., glass merchants, Mount Pottinger
Ross, Wm., builder and architect, 25 College square north
Ross, William, tobacco spinner, 14 Kennedy's place
Ross, William, seminary, 9 Academy street
Rowan, Andrew, builder, 5 Thomas street
Rowan, Miss, Connaught bazaar, 3 Sussex place
Rowan, Mrs., lodgings, 54 Carrickhill
Rowan, James, carman's inn, 54 Great Patrick street
Rowan, James, servant, 9 Coates street
Rowan, John, jun., of Rowan & Sons, 135 York street
Rowan, John, sen., of Rowan & Sons, 133 York street
Rowan, John, & Sons, proprietors York street foundry and Mile water mill
Rowan, William, coast guard, 28 Great Patrick street
Rowell, Thomas, grocer and publican, 51 Peter's hill
Rowley, William, master mariner, 25 North Thomas street
Roy, Andrew, mariner, 49 Green street

ALPHABETICAL DIRECTORY.

Roy, William, carpenter, 6 Edward street
Ruddell, David, hardware and general house-furnishing warehouse 6, 7, 67, and 68, Smithfield
Ruddell, Richard, cooper, 57 Market street
Ruddell, Wm., furniture and hardware dealer, 29 Smithfield—61 Gardiner st.
Rusham, Thomas, metal plainer, 37 Grove street
Rushton, Samuel, moulder, 15 Grove street
Rule, A., court keeper New County Courthouse
Russell, George, tailor, 22 Catherine street north
Russel, George, officer of inland revenue, 8 James street south
Russel, John, commercial traveller, 32 Joy street
Russel, James, grocery and spirit store, 9 Cargill street
Russell, John, grocery and spirit store, 39 Barrack street
Russell, John, clerk, 11 Hamilton street
Russell, Mrs., 45 Corporation street
Russell, Miss, straw bonnet maker, 27 Hercules place
Russell, Mrs. Ellen, boarding house, 17 Joy street
Russell, Mrs., huckster, 30 Little Donegall street
Russell, Nelson, publican and grocer, 62 Carrickhill
Russell, Robert, grocer and publican, 12 Nelson st. & 39 Little Patrick st.
Russell, Samuel, forge-bellows maker, 25 Lower Kent street
Russel, Thomas, railway porter, 4 Back Ship street
Russel, Wm., grocer and publican, 40 Cromac street
Russell, Thomas, writing clerk, 3 James' street south
Rutherford, Arch., & Co., sizing establishment, 25 Little Donegall street
Rutherford, Alexander, cabinet maker, 79 Academy street
Rutherford, James, room paper manufacturer, 70 High street
Rutherford, James, carpenter, 19 Police square
Rutherford, James, publican, 34 Corporation street
Rutherford, James, painter, glazier, and paper hanger, 5 Castle street
Rutherford, Martin, publican, 35 North Queen street
Ryan, Stephen, sailor, 34 Academy street
Ryans, Sarah, milliner, 5 Hercules place
Ryans, Thomas, pensioner, 86 Old Lodge road
Ryans, Thomas, pilot, 4 Little Corporation street

SALES, Hugh, night constable, 16 Boundary street
Salters, John, clerk, Linenhall—81 Joy street
Salters, Robert, sea captain, 8 Ship street
Sands, Joseph, grocer, 4 Ann street
Sands, Margaret, whiteworker, 21 Staunton street
Sands, Henry, pork cutter, 43 Little Patrick street
Sands, Robert, preparing master, 14 Leeds street
Sands, Susan, clothes dealer, 44 Smithfield
Sanders, Mrs., 3 Campbell's place, Old Lodge road
Sanders, Thomas, brazier and tinsmith, 115 North street
Sanderson, John, pattern maker, 6 Little Corporation street
Sanderson, Wm., mechanic, 68 Vere street
Saunders, Jane, 24 Little Patrick street
Saunders, John, horse dealer, Conlon street
Saunders, Maxwell, linen merchant, 42 York street
Saunders, Robert, carpenter, 16 Bank lane
Saunders, Samuel, shoemaker, 24 Lower Stanfield street
Saunders, Thomas, carpenter, 32 Little Patrick street
Saunders, Wm., shopman, 19 Catherine street north

Saunders, W. B., of Mackenzie and Saunders, haberdashers, 36 High street
Savage, David, shoemaker, 74 Peter's hill
Savage, Daniel, porter, 19 North Thomas street
Savage, E., grocery and spirit store, 2 Barrack street and Falls road
Savage, H., grocer and spirit dealer, 46 Cromac street and 59 Market street
Savage, Henry, fitter, Lagan village, Ballymacarrett
Savage, John, grocer, 2 Boundary street
Savage, James, cooper, 37 Lancaster street
Savage, James, tailor, 6 Townsend place
Savage, James, sea captain, Walsh street
Savage, James, bricklayer, 15 Galway court
Savage, James, marine store, 8 Store lane
Savage, John, shoemaker, 30 Roy street
Savage, John, grocer and publican, 40 Shankhill road
Savage, John, flax and tow merchant, 22 Skipper st.—Mountview terrace
Savage, James, dealer, 7 Store lane
Savage, Michael, butcher, York street
Savage, Mrs. Col., 4 Camden terrace, Botanic road
Savage, Patrick, Bath tavern, 1 Bath place
Savage, Patrick, solicitor, 4 Arthur street
Savage, Rowland, cooper, 84 Nelson street
Savage, Thomas, bricklayer, 5 Lower Stanfield street
Savage, William, tailor, 23 Valentine street
Savage, Wm., clothlapper, 2 Joy street
Savage, Wm. H., seaman, 4 Little George's street
Scanlon, Hugh, mechanic, 10 M'Cracken's row, Ballymacarrett
Scott, Archibald, house and rent agent, 14 Verner street
Scott, Eliza, dressmaker, 94 Millfield and 2 Brown street
Scott, George, butcher, 16 Hercules street
Scott, Holmes, plumber, 6 Letitia street
Scott, Joseph, commercial traveller, 21 Corporation street
Scott, Jane, lodging house, 16 Edward street
Scott, James, pattern maker, 16 M'Tier's street
Scott, James, provision merchant, 7 Albert square
Scott, James, weaver, 61 Lancaster street
Scott, James, provision merchant, 5 Queen's square
Scott, James, dealer, 2 Mustard street
Scott, John, carpenter, 7 M'Cracken's row, Ballymacarrett
Scott, James, grocer and salesman, 2 California street
Scott, James, 4 Butter market, Great Patrick st.—5 Queen's square
Scott, John, woollendraper, 5 Glengall street
Scott, John, 108 Lower Malone
Scott, John, shoemaker, 1 Mustard street
Scott, John, bricklayer, 28 M'Millan's place
Scott, John, ship chandler, block and pump maker, 4 Corporation street
Scott, John, ship owner, 20¾ Great George's street
Scott, John, boarding house, 29 Joy street
Scott, John, butcher, 20½ Great George's street
Scott, John, jun., butcher, York street
Scott, John, publican, Trafalgar street and 76 Nelson street
Scott, John, watchman, 83 Nelson street
Scott, Joseph, manager Linen hall—34 King street
Scott, John, iron founder, 6¼ May street
Scott, Mrs., Catherine street north
Scott, Matthew, bricklayer, 75 Academy street

Scott, Malcolm, preparing master, 24 Francis street
Scott, Robert, cooper, 20 Gordon street
Scott, Robert, general commission merchant, 74 Waring street—Holywood
Scott, Robert, proprietor Glasgow Hotel, 7½ High street
Scott, Thomas, grocer and publican, 29 New Durham street
Scott, Thomas, gentleman, 4 Crumlin terrace
Scott, Thomas, clerk, 17 Kennedy's place
Scott, Vere, board and lodgings, 43 Prince's street
Scott, William, linen lapper, 66 Joy street
Scott, William, grocer and spirit dealer, 59 Lower Malone
Scott, William, carpenter, 10 Hudson's entry
Scott, William, reed maker, 5 Upton street
Scott, William, carpenter, 9 Mitchell street
Scott, William, publican, 114 Carrickhill
Scott, William, in Dublin mail coach office, 51 Little Donegall street
Scullion, Fanny, whiteworker, 87 Lower Malone road
Scullion, Mallice, foundryman, Falloon's court
Scully, Andrew, 5 North Boundary street
Scully, Simeon, engineer, 2 Cargill street
Scully, Shannon, and Holmes, plumbers, 12 Talbot street
Scully, Thomas, pensioner, 5 Meetinghouse lane
Sedgwick, Ann Jane, grocer, Shankhill road
Seed, John, ship carpenter, 6 Little Ship street
Seeds, Henry & William, solicitors, 18 Castle lane, and Lisburn
Sefton, James, 11 Shipboy street
Sergison, Eliza, furrier, 72 Ann street
Sergison, James, tinsmith, 72 Ann street
Sempill, James, boarding house, 20 Hamilton street
Semple, Paul, shoemaker, 48 Little Donegall street
Service, Ellen, cloth capmaker, 48 Vere street
Service, James, carpenter, 10 Little Patrick street
Service, Mrs. Mary, boarding house, 19 Joy street
Service, William, book keeper, 15 Spencer street
Sessions, Thomas, excise officer, 108 Cromac street
Shane, Joseph, car owner, 42 Durham street
Shankley, Patrick, printer, 16 Friendly street
Shanks, James, millwright, 7 Alexander street South
Shanks, John, sawyer, 4 William's row
Shanks, Thomas, tailor, 44 Durham street
Shanks, Wm., machine maker, 33 Stanhope street
Shanks, William, clerk, 35 Stanhope street
Shannon, George, 7 Gordon street
Shannon, George, chandler, 16 Roy's court
Shannon, Henry, tailor, Bridge end, Ballymacarrett
Shannon, James, spinning master, 6 Economy place
Shannon, John, superintendent, pork market—85 Little Patrick street
Shannon, John B., gentleman, 16 Chichester street
Shannon, Thomas, porter, 11 Hill street
Shannon, Wm., grocer in Mathison, Brothers, Donegall place, 2 Franklin pl.
Sharkey, Miss, dressmaker, 75 Academy street
Sharp, Mrs. Jane, 63 Old Lodge road
Sharp, Thomas M., broker, 17 Donegall street
Sharp, Wm., baker, 32 Smithfield
Sharp, Wm., car driver, 5 Valentine street
Shaw and Dickson, provision merchants, 18 Great George's st.—21 Ship st.

Shaw, Alexander, sawyer, 8 Dock lane
Shaw, Andrew, butter merchant, 1 Little York street
Shaw, Alexander Mackenzie, of A. Mackenzie and Co.—39 Barrack street
Shaw, Ann, boarding house, 1 Chichester lane
Shaw, Andrew, grocer, 72 Brown street
Shaw, Charles W., merchant, 52 Waring street—3 Donegall square west
Shaw, Edward, and Co., commission merchants, 72 Waring street; James Shaw's residence, Glenbauk, Crumlin road
Shaw, Hugh, publican and stabling yard, 28 Great George's street
Shaw, John, car driver, 8 Brown street
Shaw, James, soap and candle manufacturer, 23 Ann st.—41 Great Patrick st
Shaw, Mrs., 2 Sussex place
Shaw, Mrs. Jane, Ormeau street
Shaw, Mrs., 75 Waring street
Shaw, Mrs., 35 Cromac street
Shaw, Rev. George, 1 Alfred street
Shaw, Robert, dealer, 123 Durham street
Shaw, Robert, bundler, 43 Lancaster street
Shaw, Robert Jackson, 4 Renwick place
Shaw, Robert, hairdresser, 3 Frederick place
Shaw, Samuel, clerk Harbour office—4 Seaview place, Ballymacarrett
Shaw, Samuel, butcher, 39 Hercules street
Shaw, Samuel, muslin manufacturer, 14 Pottinger's entry—Skipper street
Shaw, Samuel, boot and shoemaker, Frederick street
Shaw, Samuel, hatter, 38 Church lane
Shaw, Thomas, publican, 65 North Queen street
Shaw, Thomas, pilot, 88 Nelson street
Shaw, Wm. J., watch and clock maker, 17 John street
Shaw, William, board and lodgings, 4 Great Edward street
Shaw, William, in Ulster bank, 4 Ormeau place
Shaw, W. S., tea and general commission agent, 2 Waring street place
Sheals, Alexander, baker, 98 Peter's hill
Sheals, Catherine, lodgings, 10 Millfield
Sheals, James, carpenter, 12 Shipboy street
Sheals, James, cap maker, 44 Smithfield
Sheals, James, spirit store, 8 Church lane
Sheals, Mary, dressmaker, 103 Carrickhill
Shearon, Daniel, butcher, 80 Hercules street
Sheil, Wm., supervisor of excise, 14 Queen street
Sheilds, Robert, boot and shoemaker, 118 Carrickhill
Sheilds, Thomas, lodgings, 9 Peter's hill
Sheils, Charles, boot and shoemaker, 16 Brown street
Sheppard, Wm., mechanic, 1 Cullingtree street
Sherlock, Mrs., 7 Thomas street
Sheridan, Patrick, pensioner, 28 Alexander street
Sherrard, Conolly, house, rent, and law agent, 14 Calendar street; residence, 2 Chichester street
Sherrrie, Wm., brush, card, and bellows manufacturer, 14 and 16 North st.
Sherry, Francis, cattle dealer, 27 Carrickhill
Shiel, Thomas, coal office, 3 Queen's quay, Ballymacarrett
Shields, Charles, sweep, 3 M'Tier's court
Shields, David, shoemaker, New road, Ballymacarrett
Shields, Hugh, carpenter, 6 Duffy's place
Shields, James, master mariner, 54 North Thomas street
Shields, James, flax dresser, 13 Greenland street

ALPHABETICAL DIRECTORY.

Shields, James, grocer, 20 Albert square
Shields, John, 24 Grace street
Shields, John, clothes dealer, 15 Berry street
Shields, John pensioner, 35 Mustard street
Shields, Thomas, lithographic printer, 10 Riley's place
Shields, Thomas, pawnbroker, 46 and 48 Academy street
Shillington, Edward, law messenger, Conlon street
Shipton, John, spirit dealer, 15 Ritchie's place
Short, John, grocer, 15 Robert street
Short, John, proprietor Ulster bakery, 171 North street
Short, Michael, pensioner, 12 Roy's court
Shubridge, Mrs., 1 Sussex place
Sibbald, George, Belfast bank, 5 Camden terrace, Botanic road
Sibbin, George, wholesale grocer, Victoria street—28 York street
Sibbin, George, pawnbroker, 4 Bath place
Sibbins, Wm., dealer, 19 Sackville street
Siebert, James, linen yarn merchant, Linen hall—3 Breadalbane place
Silo, M., carver and gilder, 11 Arthur square—25 Gloucester street
Simmington, Samuel, clerk, 4 York road
Simms and M'Intyre, printers and publishers, 26 Donegall street
Simms, Henry, starch maker, 5 Wall street
Simms, Jane, dealer, 20 Little Patrick street
Simms, Jas., proprietor & editor of *Mercury*, Winecellar entry—16 Howard st.
Simms, Mr., 33 Mill street
Simms, Mrs., 11 Ormeau place
Simms, Miss, boarding school, 29 Chichester street
Simms, Miss, 21 Fountain street
Simms, Robert, of Simms & M'Intyre, Seaview Cottage
Simms, Reuben, poor law auditor, 16 Howard street
Simms, Wm., agent and accountant, Linen hall; residence, 7 Albion place
Simpson, Archibald, coachmaker, 4½ Joy street
Simpson, Arthur, carpenter, Shankhill road
Simpson, David, porter, 83 Little York street
Simpson, George, lighterman, 6 Seymour street
Simpson, James, dealer, 34½ Union street
Simpson, James, oyster house, 15 and 19 Pottinger's entry
Simpson, John, pilot, 53 Talbot street
Simpson, John, bricklayer, 9 Renwick place
Simpson, Martin, car owner, 92 Cromac street
Simpson, Mrs., Stanfield street
Simpson, Robert, clerk Ulster railway—1 Hope street
Simpson, Robert, saw sharper, 17 Hamilton's place
Simpson, Thomas, cotton twister and thread manufacturer, Ballynafeigh
Sinclair and Boyd, West India and general merchants, 45 Donegall quay; stores, 23 Gamble street; R. Boyd's residence, Bloomfield
Sinclair, George, clerk, 7 Napier street
Sinclair, John and Thomas, general merchants, 5, 7, 9 and 11, Tomb street; residences: John Sinclair's, The Grove; Thomas Sinclair's, Hopefield
Sinclair, John, carpenter, 6 King street
Sinclair, James, street inspector, 12 Campbell's buildings, Townsend street
Sinclair, Mrs., boarding house, 25 Hamilton street
Sinclair, Miss, milliner and dressmaker, 7 Napier street
Sinclair, Thomas, gentleman, 1 Renwick place
Sinclair, Thomas, shoemaker, 6 Friendly street
Sinclair, William, linen lapper, 35½ York street—70 High street

Skelton, Hugh, shoemaker, 14 West street
Skelton, Mrs., 47 Nelson street
Skene, Jas., Stag's Head tavern & spirit store, 2 North st. & 3 Rosemary st.
Skillen, Andrew, porter, New road, Ballymacarrett
Skinner, Alexander, painter and glazier, 76 Great George's street
Skivington, James, shoemaker, 20 Pound street
Slane, Henry, coachmaker, 37 Bank lane
Sloan, Agnes, dealer, 47 Prince's street
Sloan, Archibald, cabinet and upholstery warehouse, 33 Castle place
Sloan, Andrew, and Co, fire brick and tile yard, Bridge end, Ballymacarrett
Sloan, Edward, iron moulder, Lagan village, Ballymacarrett
Sloan, James, blacksmith, Lagan village, Ballymacarrett
Sloan, John, grocer and publican, Ballyhackamore
Sloan, James, car proprietor, 15 Bank lane
Sloan, John, carpenter, 5 Lancaster street
Sloan, John, blacksmith, 23 Grove street
Sloan, Mrs., 11 College square north
Sloan, Mrs., 10 College square north
Sloan, Orr, boot and shoemaker, 13 Talbot street
Sloan, Patrick, saddler, 16 Wall street
Sloan, Robert, master mariner, 13 Little Corporation street
Sloan, Robert, night constable, 33 Lower Stanfield street
Sloan, Thomas, grocer, Gooseberry corner, Ballymacarrett
Sloan, W., smith, 3 Boyd street
Sloan, William, carter, 32½ Hill street
Small, Eliza, 45 Little Patrick street
Small, John, gentleman, 129 York street
Small, John, writing clerk, 2½ Gamble street
Smith and Waugh, coach builders, 20 Chichester street—22 Chichester street
Smith and Son, E. and J., linen merchants and bleachers, Linen hall
Smith, Alexander, builder, 23 Joy street
Smith, Alexander, manufacturer, 19 Hill street
Smith, Ann, staymaker, 7 Castle street
Smith, Bernard, cooper and lodgings, 41 Prince's street
Smith, Bernard, carman and lodging house, 59 Grattan street
Smith, Bernard, clerk, 3 East street
Smith, Charlotte, dealer, 13 West street
Smith, Catherine, 73 Cromac street
Smith, David, ticket writer, 20 Earl street
Smith, Dennis, jun., horse dealer, 4 Gloucester street
Smith, Dennis, publican, horse repository and Ballynahinch coach office, 31 Great Edward street
Smith, Dennis, carter, 3 Seymour lane
Smith, Ellen, dealer, 8 New Lodge road
Smith, Edward, spirit dealer, 89 North Queen street
Smith, Francis, publican, and grocer, 31 Stanfield street—Welsh street
Smith, George, in gas works, 8 Lower Malone
Smith, Geo., cashier, at Lindsay, Brothers, 1 Cumberland pl., Donegall pass
Smith, G. K. and F., solicitors, 3 The Castle, Castle buildings—3 Glengall pl.
Smith, George, engineer to Harbour Corporation, Cliftonville, Antrim road
Smith, George, grocer, 116 Carrickhill
Smith, George, dentist in Mr. Barnett's, 3 Downshire place
Smith, George, pork cutter, 22 Frederick street
Smith, Henry, glazier, 17 William street south
Smith, Hugh, grain dealer, 18 Roy street

Smith, Helena, dress and staymaker, 31 Wall street
Smith, Henry, shoemaker, 22 Upper Lagan street
Smith, Henry, tailor, 5 Lagan street
Smith, Hugh, servant, 3 Wellington court
Smith, Hugh, carrier, 29 John street
Smith, Henry N., attorney, 2 College street south
Smith, Hugh, butler, 3 Cullingtree place
Smith, John, teacher, 131 Durham street
Smith, John, car driver, 25 Henrietta street
Smith, John, blacksmith, 33 Boyd street
Smith, John, butter merchant, 13 Brougham street
Smith, James, builder and jobbing carpenter, 23 North Thomas street
Smith, J. and T., engravers, 25 Castle street
Smith, James, cloth lapper, 28 Henrietta street
Smith, James, coach painter, 9 Grace street
Smith, James, pawnbroker, 49 Cromac street
Smith, James, pawnbroker, 37 Green street
Smith, Jane, 7 Shankhill road
Smith, Jeremiah, boot and shoemaker, 4 Boundary street
Smith, James, builder and carpenter, 23 North Thomas street
Smith, John, baker, 9 Roy street
Smith, John, sawyer, 36 Grattan street
Smith, James, plasterer, Ballynafeigh
Smith, John, stonecutter, 11 Friendly street
Smith, John, car driver and shopkeeper, 46 Joy street
Smith, John and Thomas, butter merchants, 2 and 3 Butter market, Great Patrick street; residences: J. Smith, Meadow street; T. Smith, Dock st.
Smith, John, blacksmith, 2 Economy place
Smith, John, tailor, Smith street
Smith, Joseph, teacher, 69 Grattan street
Smith, J. G., manager and secretary Ulster railway Co.—3 Glengall place
Smith, James, boot and shoemaker, 9 North King street
Smith, John, tallow chandler, 19 Little Patrick street
Smith, John, stonecutter, 9 Nile street
Smith, Mrs., Wellwood house
Smith, Miss, dressmaker, 8 Talbot street
Smith, Mrs., 3 Queen street
Smith, Mary, 28 Stanfield street
Smith, Margaret, 2 Mitchell street
Smith, Mary, grocer, Friendly street
Smith, Michael, bricklayer, 55 Peter's hill
Smith, Michael, spirit dealer, 34 Great George's street
Smith, Miss Margery, Ballynafeigh
Smith, Mrs., 3 Glengall place
Smith, Mrs. Ann, 57 Peter's hill
Smith, Mrs. Margaret, 16 King street
Smith, Mrs., 25 Hamilton place
Smith, Mrs. Eleanor, milliner, 8 Russell street
Smith, Patrick, salesman, 35 Green street
Smith, Rachel, dealer, 22 Francis street
Smith, Robert, in distillery, 5 Aughton terrace, Donegall pass
Smith, Robert, publican and muslin manufacturer, 4 & 6 Rosemary street
Smith, Robert, pensioner, 1 Hopeton place
Smith, Samuel, muslin printer, Artillery street
Smith, Surgeon, 18 Arthur street

Smith, Sarah, dealer, 18 Samuel street
Smith, Thomas, clerk, 23 M'Tier street
Smith, William, carpenter, Devis street
Smith, William, grocer, 65 Old Lodge road
Smith, William, plasterer, 18 Hamilton's place
Smith, William, head constable, 15 North Queen street
Smith, Wm., shoemaker, 26 Samuel street
Smith, William, carpenter, 17 Wilson street
Smylie, David, grocer, 11 Edward street
Smylie, John, mechanic, 8 North Boundary street
Smylie, James, tailor, 69 Academy street
Smylie, James, clerk, 15 Mustard street
Smylie, Miss, dressmaker, 23 Talbot street
Smylie, Samuel L., of J. Steen and Co.'s, Talbot street
Smylie, William, and Co., boot and shoe warehouse, 20 Ann street
Smyrl, Adam, writing clerk, 2 Catherine street north
Smyth and M'Millen, bakers, 66 Great Patrick street
Smyth, Edward, shoemaker, 30 North Queen street
Smyth, Hill, stationer, 1 Donegall street, and 2 Waring street
Smyth, Hy., of Smyth and Weir, Donegall pl.—8 Lower Crescent, Malone rd.
Smyth, John, solicitor, 42 Donegall street
Smyth, John, sea captain, 48 Earl street
Smyth, John, bricklayer, 2 Staunton street
Smyth, J. H., and Co., glass, paint, oil, and colour warehouse, 7 North st.
Smyth, James, gentleman, 37 Dock street
Smyth, John, looking glass maker, 178 North street
Smyth, John, mechanic, 11 North Thomas street
Smyth, John, gardener, 16 North Boundary street
Smyth, John, boot and shoemaker, 32 Waring street
Smyth, John, stone mason, 20 Vere street
Smyth, Joshua, tide waiter, 14 Vere street
Smyth, Mary, washerwoman, 80 Sussex street
Smyth, Patrick, spirit dealer, 59 Waring street
Smyth, Surgeon John, apothecary and medical hall, 29 Corn market
Smyth, Thomas, spirit store, 3 New Lodge road
Smyth, William, commercial traveller, 46 Earl street
Snowden, Dr. Samuel, surgeon, 14 Corporation street
Somerset, Thomas, mechanic, Falls road
Somerset, William, millwright, 9 Grove street
Somerville, Daniel, shoemaker, 41 Mill street
Somerville, James, stabling, 4 Police square
Somerville, John, weighmaster, 10 Russell street
Sorsby, Rose Ann, 16 Mitchell street
South, Mrs., dressmaker, 32 Durham street
Spackman, Wm., merchant tailor, draper, and hatter, Victoria st. and High st.
Sparling, Mary, dressmaker, 26 Upper Arthur street
Spear, Robert, spinning master, 34 Vere street
Spear, William, weaver, 41 Vere street
Spence, Alexander, flaxdresser and dealer, 71 Barrack street
Spence, Hugh, boot and shoemaker, 93 North street
Spence, James, tailor, 13 Sarah street
Spence, John, auctioneer, Smithfield—29 West street
Spence, William, nailer, Caxton street
Spence, William, writing clerk, 3 Bath place
Spence, William, provision dealer and publican, 31, 33, and 35 Boundary st.

Spencer, William, Hibernian pottery, Queen's quay, Ballymacarrett
Spiller, Frederick, clerk, Collingwood street
Spiller, Mrs., 25 Cromac street
Spotten, S. & Co., grocers, &c., agents for Cassell's coffee, 22 Rosemary st.
Spotten, William, deputy town clerk, 22 Rosemary street
Spratt, James, toll collector in market, Wills' place
Sproull, Mrs., 32 College street
Sproull, W. H., solicitor, 34 College street
Stafford, Alexander, skinner, 20 Francis street
Stafford, Elizabeth, grocer, 17 Gamble street
Stafford, Sarah, 9 Catherine street
Stancliff, William Charles, officer of inland revenue, 30 King street
Standfield, James, gentleman, 44 York street
Stanfield, Richard, gentleman, 9 Murphy street
Stanley, Harvey, sawyer, 29 Caxton street
Stannus, Miss, 4 Ormeau road
Stannus, Thomas R., distributor of stamps; stamp office, 2 Donegall place buildings; residence, Lisburn
Stapley, John, print colourer, &c., 2 Smith street
Starr, John, ropemaker, Ballymacarrett
Starret, James, car driver, 6 Mitchell street
Starret, Thomas, smith, 1 Cotton court
Staunton, Moses, room-paper, carpet, and damask warehouse, 9 Donegall place; residence, Ballygomartin
Staveley, Margaret, grocer, 57 Durham street
Staveley, Miss, seminary, 20 College street
Stavely, William, cheesemonger, 5 Johnston's court
Stavely, William, dealer, Wheeler's place, Ballymacarrett
Steed, Anne, grocer, 33 Peter's hill
Steed, Jane, grocer and publican, 20 Cromac street
Steed, Joseph, whitesmith, 11 Stanfield street
Steel, John, wood turner, 94 Lower Malone
Steel, Mrs., 45 Peter's hill
Steel, Simon, stone mason, 39 Grove street
Steen, Andrew, tanner, 1 Galway street
Steen, James, and Co., merchants, 3 Talbot street; James Steen's residence, Skeigoneil; William Steen's residence, Greenisland
Steen, James and William, merchants, 30 and 32 Hill street
Steen, John, painter, 52 Brown street
Steen, Rev. Isaiah, Fitzwilliam street, Old Malone road
Steenson, William, weaver, 73 Durham street
Stephen, Alexander, wine and spirit dealer, 37 Rosemary street
Stephenson, Dr. Robert, 11 Wellington place
Stephenson, George, solicitor, 6 Castle Chambers—Lisburn
Stephenson, Mrs., 91 York street
Stevelly, Dr., professor in Queen's College—37 Queen street
Stevelly, George, shopman, 40 King street
Stevelly, James, commercial agent, 91 Joy street
Stevens, Patrick, marine store, 30½ Little Patrick street
Stevens, William, 18 College square north
Stevenson, and Co., bleachers, Springfield works, Falls road
Stevenson, Alexander, shipping clerk, 3 William's row
Stevenson, Alexander, machine maker, 14 Valentine street
Stevenson, George, horse dealer, 27 Little May street
Stevenson, George F., professor of music, 8 King street

ALPHABETICAL DIRECTORY.

Stevenson, Jackson S., bill and share broker, and commission agent, 1 Commercial buildings—4 Mountview terrace
Stevenson, J., spinning master, 27 Conway street
Stevenson, John, caretaker, at Mr. Tilley's, M'Tier street—6 Alexander street
Stevenson, John, grocer, Howard street north
Stevenson, Robert, engineer, Garmoyle street
Stevenson, Robert, grain merchant, 5 Gloucester street—Eliza street
Stevenson, Robert, grocer and carpenter, 1 Dock street
Stevenson, Samuel, tailor, 17 Arthur street
Stevenson, Thomas, tailor, 39 Mill street
Stevenson, Thomas, warper, 3 Alexander street south
Stevenson, Wm., butcher, 3 Charles street
Stevenson, Wm., jun. and Co., general merchants, 9 Calender st.—Dunmurry
Stevenson, Wilshaw, bookbinder, 3 Little York street
Stewart and Cleery, fleshers, 8 Hercules place
Stewart, Andrew, flesher, 20 Great Edward street
Stewart, Alexander, gardener, Bradbury place
Stewart, Alexander, cooper and dealer, Ballymacarrett
Stewart, Ann, 17 Nile street
Stewart, Alexander, car driver, 11 North Boundary street
Stewart, Christopher, confectioner, 5 Wesley place
Stewart, Dr. Horatio, 51 York street
Stewart, Francis, boarding house, 28 North Ann street
Stewart, Henry, tanner, 10 Brown street
Stewart, Isabella, Ballynafeigh
Stewart, James, shoemaker, 3 Stanhope street
Stewart, John, pensioner, 1 Vere street
Stewart, James, cabinet maker, 5 Smithfield
Stewart, John, baker, 60 Mustard street
Stewart, James, porter, 16 Mustard street
Stewart, J. W., stabling yard, Marlborough street
Stewart, John, flax dresser, Falls road
Stewart, James, painter and grocer, 14 John street
Stewart, Jane, whiteworker, 9 East street
Stewart, James, dealer, 15 Winetavern street
Stewart, James, watchman, 33 Greenland street
Stewart, John, night constable, 13 Cullingtree street
Stewart, John, dealer, 121 Durham street
Stewart, John, clothes dealer, 13 Berry street
Stewart, John, shoemaker, 67 Academy street
Stewart, John, horse shoer, 47 Mustard street
Stewart, James, librarian; library, Linen Hall—5 Catherine street
Stewart, J., clothes dealer, 53 Berry street
Stewart, James, theatre tavern, 17 Castle lane—Bryansburn Cottage, Bangor
Stewart, John, lodging house, 71 Carrickhill
Stewart, James, flesher, 5 Cromac street
Stewart, John A., clerk, Ormeau road
Stewart, John, and Co., muslin manufacturers, 4 Lower Kent street; John Stewart's residence, Silver Stream
Stewart, John, writing clerk, 6 Market street
Stewart, James, 15 Winetavern street
Stewart, Kennedy, boot and shoemaker, 86 High street—9 Riley's place
Stewart, Mary, Ballynafeigh
Stewart, Mrs. Mary, 10 Torrens' market
Stewart, Mrs. Charles, 24 Hamilton street

Stewart, Miss, 15 College street
Stewart, Mrs., 14 College square north
Stewart, Mrs., 5 Botanic view, Botanic road
Stewart, Mary, boarding house, 3 Lower Chichester street
Stewart, Margaret, spirit store, 5 Queen's square
Stewart, Patrick, marine store. 12 Long lane
Stewart, Patrick, mariner, Falloon's court
Stewart, Patrick, bricklayer, 27 Ritchie's place
Stewart, Robert, pilot, 24 Tomb street
Stewart, Robert, M.D., resident physician and manager of Belfast district Lunatic Asylum, Falls road
Stewart, Robert, linen yarn merchant, 3 Waring street place
Stewart, Robert, baker, 7 Upper Church lane
Stewart, Robert, brassfounder and gasfitter, 1 Shipboy street
Stewart, Sarah, clothes dealer, 37 Berry street and 1 Charlemont street
Stewart, Sophia, lodging house, 1 Kennedy's place
Stewart, Samuel, mechanic, 15 Rochfort place
Stewart, Stanley, moulder, 13 Grove street
Stewart, Thomas, provision merchant, 29 Castle street
Stewart, Thomas, bricklayer, 12 North King street
Stewart, Wm., blacksmith, 27 Winetavern street
Stewart, William, clothes dealer, 47 Smithfield—Winetavern street
Stewart, Wm., brush and trunk maker, 56 North street
Stewart, Wm., shoemaker, 18 Caddell's entry
Stewart, Wm., carter, &c., Shankhill road
Stewart, Wm., tailor, 15 Friendly street
Stewart, Wm., cooper, 10 Nelson street
Stewart, Wm., horse shoer, 25 Winetavern street
Stewart, Wm., teller Provincial Bank, 16 North Queen street
Stirling, James, gentleman, 2 Clarence place
Stirling, James, mechanic, 10 Alexander street south
Stirling, Mrs., 2 Fleet street
Stirling, Wm., cabinet maker, 4 Morrow's entry
Stirrat, James, sewed muslin manufacturer, 9 Bank lane
Stitt, E., and M., day school, 28 Hamilton street
Stitt, Wm., carpenter and timber dealer, 1 Smithfield
Stockdale, Edward, Victoria Hotel, 80 Ann street
Stockman, Ralph, nail manufacturer, 3 Nelson street
Stokesberry, Charles, butcher, 81 Hercules street
Stokesberry, Wm., butcher, 37 Hercules street
Storars, Fortescue, and Co., linen merchants, Linen hall
Storey, Jane, lodgings, 32 Robert street
Stormont, James, painter and glazier, 50 North street
Stott, Wm., foreman smith, 20 Cromac road
Strachan, George, pork cutter, 23 Mustard street
Strachan, James, in Provincial Bank—5 Victoria place
Strachan, John, carpenter and builder, 2 Great George's street
Strain, Wm., publican, 22 Durham street
Strickland, George, porter, 12 William street
Strings, George, tailor, Garmoyle street
Stripp, Wm., custom house officer, Vere street
Stritch, Edward, haberdasher, 16 Berry street
Strype, George, foundry manager, 9 Meadow street
Stuart, Major, 7 Upper Queen street
Sturgeon, Campbell, grocer, Ballymacarrett

ALPHABETICAL DIRECTORY.

Sturgeon, James, coast guard, Ballymacarrett
Sturt, John, lodgings, 13 Prince's street
Sueter, Misses, stay warehouse, 18 College street
Suffern, James, porter, 13 Old Lodge road
Suffern, John, solicitor, 76 Donegall street; residence, 78 Donegall street
Suffern, Wm., gentleman, 86 Donegall street
Sugars, Thomas J., revenue officer, 5 Seaview place, Ballymacarrett
Sullivan, James, clerk, 24 Henrietta street
Sullivan, John, flax rougher, 6 Wellington square
Sullivan, James, shipowner, 16 Brougham street
Surplus, James, grocer and spirit dealer, 15¼ Henry street
Surplus, Mrs., gentlemen's white worker, 38 Durham street
Sutherland, D. G., bookseller and publisher, 26 Joy street
Sutherland, H. A., and Co., alabaster and cement manufacturers, 28 Joy st.
Sutton, Frederick Henry, of Armstrong, Brothers, Donegall place; residence, 107 Donegall street
Swallow, Samuel, publican, lodgings, 1 Tomb street
Swan, Charles, salesman draper, 55 Joy street
Swan, Wm., clerk, 52 Nelson street
Swain, Hugh, clerk, Ballymacarrett
Sweeny, John, cooperage, 69 Great Patrick street
Sweeny, Wm., mechanic, 10 California street
Symington, Archibald, cabinet maker, 19 Kennedy's place
Symington, Agnes, 12 M'Tier's street
Symington, Daniel, teacher of Salem school; residence, 13 Earl street
Symington, Mary, dealer, 36 Vere street
Symonds, John, master mariner, 10 Nile street
Symmonds, Stephen R., broker & commission agent, 6½ York st.—33 Mill st.

TAGGART, Henry, carpenter, 11 New Durham street
Taggart, John, publican, 2 Valentine street
Taggart, Mary, dealer, 2 Lower Stanfield street
Taggart, Moses, commercial traveller, 1 Bank lane
Taggart, Samuel, grocer and spirit dealer, 8 Henrietta street
Tague, James, starch maker, 21 York lane
Tailor, Hugh, painter, Seymour street
Tait, Miss, day school, 123 York street
Talbot, Mrs., Woodstock place, Ballymacarrett
Talbot, Mrs. Margaret, boarding house, 26 Little May street
Talbot, Mrs., matron of the Industrial and National School, Frederick street
Tallis, John, and Co., London publishers, 56 Nelson st., Thos. Crossford agent
Tandy, Mrs., dealer in poultry, 31 Market street
Tannahill, Mrs. Elizabeth, boarding house, 24 Joy street
Tasney, Patrick, grocer, 56 Millfield
Tate and Bell, soap and candle manufacturers, 82 Hercules street
Tate, Andrew, house agent, 11 Marquis street
Tate, John, farmer, Old Lodge road
Tate, Wm., wholesale and retail leather merchant, 85 North street
Taylor, David, of John Arnott and Co.; residence, 2 Lower Crescent
Taylor, David, carpenter, 6 Wellington court
Taylor, Edward, seedsman, 16 North street
Taylor, Edward, drayman, 44 Millfield
Taylor, Hugh, publican and grocer, 70 Carrickhill
Taylor, Henry, clerk, Herdman's buildings
Taylor, John, grocer and spirit dealer, 13 Cromac road

ALPHABETICAL DIRECTORY.   351

Taylor, John, publican, 39 Great Patrick street
Taylor, John, publican, 56, 58, and 62 Lower Malone
Taylor, John, general manager Ulster bank, 6 College square north
Taylor, John, mechanic, Peel's place
Taylor, James, car driver, 20 York lane
Taylor, John, watch glass maker, 10 M'Crory's row, Ballymacarrett
Taylor, Robert, builder, 63 Joy street
Taylor, Robert, iron moulder, 16 Cargill street
Taylor, Samuel, cashier in A. & S. Henry's, 3 Murray's terrace
Taylor, Susan, 18 Cargill street
Taylor, Samuel, spindle, flyer, and screw bolt maker, 20½ Great George's st
Taylor, Thomas, moulder, 63 Carrickhill
Taylor, Thomas, warper, 9 Kennedy's place
Taylor, Victor C., spirit dealer, Shankhill road
Taylor, William John, butcher and house painter, 43 John street
Taylor, Wm., carpenter, 52½ Townsend street
Taylor, William, builder, 56 Joy street
Taylor, William, servant, 15 Hamilton's place
Taylor, Wm., master mariner, 42 Talbot street
Teale, John, blacksmith, Herdman's buildings
Teape, Rev. H., incumbent of St. Matthew's church, Shankhill road
Tedford, James, ship chandler and provision dealer, 29 Donegall quay; residence, 34 Chichester street
Teeling, John & Francis, solicitors, 6 Castle lane
Teeling, John, writing clerk, 16½ Trafalgar street
Teeney, John, foreign interpreter, 1¼ Nelson street
Telford, Wm., customhouse officer, 66 York street
Templeton, John, master mariner, 12 Wall street
Tennant, Chas., & Co., drysalters, chemists, & general merchants, 37 John st.
Tennent, Eleanor, lodgings, 41 Trafalgar street
Tennent, Robert James, M.P., D.L., 2 Hercules place
Tennus, Samuel, pensioner, 84 Peter's hill
Terrier, George, mechanic, 6 College place north
Tewton, Matthew, carpenter, 143 Durham street
Thacker, Eliza, stationer, 3 Ann street
Thistle, Robert, coachmaker, 5 Grace street
Thoburn, David, pawnbroker, 1 Nelson street
Thomas, Edward, mill manager, 33 Falls road
Thomas, John, book keeper, Mount Pottinger cottages, Ballymacarrett
Thomas, Samuel, bellhanger, 6 Arthur lane
Thomas, William, butcher, 1 Ormond market—8 Gamble street
Thomas, Wm., toll collector in butter market, 2 Johnston's buildings
Thompsons and Kirwan, ship builders, Queen's Island; Messrs. Thompson's residence, Gardenhill
Thompson, Alexander, coachman, 7 College place north
Thompson, Alice, haberdasher, 27 Great Edward street
Thompson, Andrew, pork store, 12 Trafalgar street
Thompson, Andrew, linen lapper, 18 California street
Thompson, Adam, file cutter, 19 Little Donegall street—96 Peter's hill
Thompson, Alexander, carpenter, 10 Murphy street
Thompson, Charles, confectioner, 2 Donegall place
Thompson, Charles, gentleman, 3 Fountainville, Old Malone road
Thompson, Charles, dealer in old iron and furniture, 55 Smithfield
Thompson, Dr. Thomas, R.N., physician and surgeon, 83 Donegall street
Thompson, Dr. James, 7 Botanic view

ALPHAPETICAL DIRECTORY.

Thompson, David, rope maker, New road, Ballymacarrett
Thompson, Dougherty, grocer, 25 Verner street
Thompson, Eliza, 11 Wellington square
Thompson, George, haberdasher, 37 Great Edward street
Thompson, George T., spirit dealer, Ballyhackamore, Ballymacarrett
Thompson, H., publican and grocer, 33 Carrickhill
Thompson, James, letter carrier, 24 Edward street
Thompson, James, cooper, 7 Edward street
Thompson, James, grocery and spirit store, 42 Hill street
Thompson, James, linen merchant, 12 Ormeau place
Thompson, James, grocer and spirit dealer, 31 and 33 Talbot street
Thompson, James, grocer, 14 Lower Staufield street—1 Staunton street
Thompson, Jeremiah, fireman, 1 Greenland street
Thompson, John, grocer, 53 Lancaster street
Thompson, James, 2 Nelson street
Thompson, Joseph, carpenter, 33 Valentine street
Thompson, John, tailor, 5 Union place
Thompson, John, carman, 17 Greenland street
Thompson, John, fireman, 103 Peter's hill
Thompson, Mr., electropist, 92 Donegall street
Thompson, Matilda, milliner, 4 Robert street
Thompson, Mrs. Alicia, grocer and publican, 30 Winetavern street
Thompson, Mrs., grocer, Antrim road
Thompson, Mrs., thread manufacturer, 27 Cromac street
Thompson, Robert, merchant, 1 Donegall square west—Holywood
Thompson, Richard, writing clerk, 44 Gloucester street
Thompson, R., wine & spirit merchant, 17 Church st.—The Mount, near C.fergus
Thompson, Robert, mechanic, Durham street
Thompson, Richard, publican, 4 Hammond's court
Thompson, Robert, weaving master, 2 Killen street
Thompson, Robert, manager in linen office, 18 Castle street
Thompson, Samuel, paper dealer, 63 Verner street
Thompson, Samuel, gentleman, 8 Prospect terrace
Thompson, S. & W., foundry, Brown's square
Thompson, Samuel, merchant, Corporation street—6 Alfred street
Thompson, Samuel, butler, 9 Vere street
Thompson, Samuel, 67 Durham street
Thompson, Sarah, 25 Mustard street
Thompson, Sarah Jane, haberdasher, 38 Great Edward street
Thompson, Samuel, sawyer, 71 Little York street
Thompson, Samuel, dealer, 8 Charlemont street
Thompson, Samuel, lodgings, 48 Great George's street
Thompson, Thomas, spirit dealer, North Queen street—3 Sarah street
Thompson, Thomas, master mariner, 10 Talbot street
Thompson, Thomas, publican, 42 Townsend street
Thompson, Thomas, coach trimmer, 13 Wesley place
Thompson, Thomas, millwright, 10 Meadow street
Thompson, Thomas, shipwright, 92 Nelson court
Thompson, William, miller, 11 Mitchell street
Thompson, William, mariner, 8 Nelson court
Thompson, William, gentleman, 1 Fountainville, Botanic road
Thompson, William James, grocer, 97 North Queen street
Thompson, William, painter, 3 Killen street
Thompson, William, foreman lapper, Wills' place
Thompson, William, stone cutter, 7 Economy place

ALPHABETICAL DIRECTORY.

Thomson and Co., iron founders, machine makers, and engineers, 4 Townsend street; Mr. Thomson's residence, 10 Castle street
Thomson, Andrew, clerk, Lagan village, Ballymacarrett
Thomson, Alexander, ship carpenter, 37 Trafalgar street
Thomson, Elias, of R. and J. Bell's, 4 Antrim place
Thomson, Gordon A., gentleman; office, 11 Unity street; residence, Bedeque house, Crumlin road
Thomson, George, stonecutter, 8 Staunton street
Thomson, Jane, 7 Wesley place
Thomson, James, brickmaker, 122 Lower Malone
Thomson, James, bakery and flour merchant, 59 North street
Thomson, John, watch and clock maker, 67 North street
Thomson, John, blacksmith, Edward's buildings, Ballymacarrett
Thomson, John, publican, 76 Waring street
Thomson, James, mariner, 26 Valentine street
Thomson, John, working bleacher, Old Lodge road
Thomson, John, J.P., director Belfast bank; residence, Lowwood
Thomson, Mary Anne, dressmaker, 16 Little George's street
Thomson, Mrs., 1 Donegall square west
Thomson, Robert, engraver, dye sinker, and copper plate printer, 4 Castle st.
Thomson, William, sawyer, 8 Old Lodge road
Thomson, William, cabinet maker, 10 Talbot street
Thornton, A. H., 22 Robert street
Thornton, Arthur, spirit dealer, Wheeler's place, Ballymacarrett
Thornton, Huggins, and Co., linen merchants, Bedford street
Thorpe, James, brushmaker, 16 North King street
Thorpe, Samuel, bricklayer, 47 Talbot street
Tidd, Wm., master of Union Workhouse, 5 Apsley place
Tierney, Samuel, muslin manufacturer, 9 Elliott's court—Ballymacarrett
Tierney, Samuel, of George Phillips and Co.'s cocoa fibre works—Edwards' buildings, Ballymacarrett
Tigh, Hugh, nailer, 32 Winetavern street—Samuel street
Tighe, George, bricklayer, 19 Staunton street
Tilley, Hugh, shoemaker, 53 Mustard street
Tilley, James, muslin manufactory, 35 M'Tier's street—2 North Queen street
Tilly, Thomas, master mariner, 15 Henry street
Timbey, John, boot and shoemaker, 15 John street
Timby, Elizabeth, boarding house, 10 Union street
Timmony, Peter, stocking dealer, 29 Smithfield—33 Hudson's entry
Timney, Peter, dealer, 31 Ritchie's place
Tinsdale, John R., compositor, *News-Letter* office, 13 Unity street
Tinsley, Margaret, lodgings, 89 Millfield
Tinsley, Thomas, grocer, 23 Shankhill road
Tittle, James, solicitor, 19 Arthur street
Titley, Samuel, spirit store, 20 Church street
Toal, Denis, shoemaker, 77 Carrick hill
Toal, Edward, baker, 21 Stanley street
Toal, James, tailor, 13 Sackville street
Todd, F., umbrella maker, 37 Donegall street
Todd, George, shoemaker, 7 Ann street
Todd, Henry, hairdresser, 59 Union street
Todd, James, farmer, 44 Conway street
Todd, John R., publican, 103 York street
Todd, John, pensioner, 13 Melbourne street
Todd, Samuel, bookbinder, 2 Cullingtree place

Todd, Samuel, smith, 1 Boundary street
Todd, Samuel, spirit and ale stores, 34 Rosemary street
Todd, Samuel, grocer, flax and tow mercht., Edward st. & 37 Gt. Patrick st.
Todd, Wm., auctioneer and appraiser, 24 Smithfield
Todd, Wm., book keeper, 6 Fleet street
Todd, Wm., dealer, 42 Millfield
Todd, Wm., hairdresser, 98 Millfield
Toley, Denis, butcher, 89 Hercules street
Toman, John, grocer, 30½ Ann street
Toman, John, brassfounder, gasfitter, &c., 14½ King street
Tomb, Mrs., 19 Donegall place
Tonchal, Wm., boiler maker, 41 Friendly street
Toner, John, nail manufacturer, 60 Tomb street
Toner, Patrick, provision store, 163 North street
Toole, James, flax dresser, Falls road
Torbett, Miss Ann, 17 College square north
Torbitt, James, wine and spirit merchant, 58 North street—9 Albion place
Torbitt, Wm. J., carpenter, 16 Vere street
Torrens, Hannah, green grocer, 22 Castle market
Torrens, James, of Messrs. Davison and Torrens, 23 Donegall place: residence, Woodbank, Whiteabbey
Tosh, Catherine, delf dealer, 45 Smithfield—1 Kennedy's row
Tosh, John, shoemaker, 1 Stephen street
Tottenham, Wm., watchman, 9 Rochfort place
Totton, John, mechanic, 17 Melbourne street
Toussaint, Henry, foreman tailor M. Levy's, High street—29 Dock street
Townley, Job, tinsmith, 5 Samuel street
Townley, Michael, grocer, Third street
Townly, Patrick, Glenwood tavern and grocery, Shankhill road
Toy, Hugh, nailer, 32 Winetavern street
Toye, Rev. Thomas, 7 Great George's street
Trail, William, gentleman, 1 Royal terrace
Trainer, James, carpenter, 40 Boyd street
Trainor, James, publican, Falls road
Trainor, Mary, 3 York lane
Travers, Bernard, huckster, 75 Market street
Trelford, Hamilton, grocer, 36 Barrack street
Trelford, William, baker, 44 Alexander street
Trevor, Mary, spirit dealer, 4 Castle lane
Trimble, James, assistant schoolmaster, Conway street
Trimble, William, boot and shoemaker, 55 High street, and May street
Tripp, Thomas, merchant, residence, Brookfield, Shankhill road
Trollan, Michael, carter, 37 Alexander street
Trotter, James, mason, 97 Peter's hill
Trotter, James, clothier, 65 Corporation street
Trotter, John C., ship broker and commission agent, 17 Queen's square
Trotter, Robt., manager of Provincial Bank of Ireland; office, 36 Donegall st.
Trueman, John, English baker and fancy biscuit manufacturer, 14 Castle st.
Tucker, Edward, glue and starch manufacturer, 27 Waring st.; works, Lower Malone, York lane, and Millfield; residence, 6 Donegall square south
Tucker, Mrs., boarding house, 37 Little May street
Tully, Mrs. Elizabeth, 19 Rochfort place
Tully, Thomas, hatter, 28 M'Tier street
Tully, Wm., tailor, 17 Welsh street
Tumbleton, Andrew, shoemaker, Ballymacarrett

ALPHABETICAL DIRECTORY.

Tumblety, Charles, tailor, 25 Academy street
Tumbelty, David, butler, 11 North Ann street
Tunmore, Samuel, marine store, 65 Union street
Turnbull, Alexander, gas collector, 21 Castle street; works, Cromac road
Turner, Arthur, mechanic, 13 Townsend street
Turner, Hugh, boot and shoemaker, 17 Nile street
Turner, Samuel, dentist, 13 Chichester street
Turner, Thomas, architect, 8 Donegall place buildings—21 Queen street
Turney, Henry, carpenter, 6 Murphy street
Turney, James, master mariner, 63 Nelson street
Turney, John, 3 Lagan street
Turney, Richard, publican, 7 Lagan street
Tweedy, Robert, painter, 9 Eliza street
Twigs, Hugh, clothes dealer, 25 Rosemary street

USHER, E., dressmaker, 8 Mill street
Usher, John, butler, 6 Cullingtree street
Usher, Miss, servants' registry office, 8 Mill street
Usher, R. T., gentleman, Mount prospect, Lisburn road

VALENTINE, William, of Richardson, Brothers, and Co.—Whiteabbey
Vallely, Bernard, boot & shoemaker, & boarding honse, 7 Chichester lane
Vance, Adam, spirit dealer, Ballyhackamore, Ballymacarrett
Vance, John, gentleman, 15 College square east
Vance, John R. & Son, muslin manufacturers & merchants, 40 Rosemary st.
Vance, Messrs. and Son's weaving factory, 38 Rosemary street
Vance, Miss Esther, 83 Little Patrick street
Vance, Robert, wine and spirit merchant, and travelling agent, 25 North st.
Vance, Robert, publican, 48 M'Tier street
Vance, Samuel, public accountant, secretary of Belfast Chamber of Commerce, 36 Waring street—37 Chichester street
Vance, Thomas, custom house officer, 14 Pilot street
Vance, William, carpenter, 39 Edward street
Vance, William, poor law relieving officer, 26 Millfield
Vance, William, cabinet and upholstery warerooms, 21 Catherine street north; residence, 17 Russell street
Vance, William, merchant, 111 Carrickhill, proprietor of Corn mill; office, 112 Donegall street; residence, 15 Great George's street
Vaughan, Mrs., 5 Glenfield place
Verner, Mary, 71 Cromac street
Verner, Thomas, D.L., J.P., receiver of Marquis of Donegall's rents; office, The Castle, Castle buildings; residence, Ormeau
Vernon, Aaron, boiler maker, Fleet street
Vernon, Dennis, tailor, 8 M'Auley street
Vernon, Thomas, foreman boiler maker, 22 Garmoyle street
Victor, Elizabeth Ann, 9 Earl street
Vincent, Elizabeth, grocer, 109 Durham street
Vint, A., stonecutter, 18 Boyd street
Vint, Jonathan, wine and spirit store, 54 Little Donegall street
Vint, William, provision merchant, 4 Dock street—9 Gamble street
Vint, William, painter and glazier, 25 Talbot street
Virgin, Nicholas, wine, and spirit dealer, 3 Victoria street

WALES, George F., surgeon, 71 York street
Wales, Mrs. Sarah, 5 York road

Walker, Arthur, grocer and spirit dealer, 19 Nile street
Walker, Andrew, carman, 5 Brown square
Walker, Abraham, sexton, Donegall place Methodist Chapel, 11 Rochfort pl.
Walker, Ann, 18 Townsend street
Walker, Deborah, spirit dealer, Ballymacarrett
Walker, David, confectioner and restaurant, 19 Bridge street
Walker, David, fireman, 3 New Durham street
Walker, David, stonecutter, 27 Vere street
Walker, Eliza Jane, dressmaker, 2 Shipboy street
Walker, John, confectioner, 61 Donegall street
Walker, John clock maker, 20 Little May street
Walker, Margaret, 2 Hill street
Walker, Mrs. Hannah, grocer, 67 Peter's hill
Walker, Samuel, house and rent agent, 18 Henry street
Walker, Samuel, grocer, 12 and 14 Alexander street
Walker, Thomas, cabinet maker, 14 Peter's hill
Walker, Thomas, carpenter, 48 Nelson street
Walker, William, pensioner, 27 Stanhope street
Walker, William, publican, 8 Kennedy's place
Walker, William, cabinet maker, Gavin's buildings, Shankhill road
Walker, William, schoolmaster, 6 Napier street
Walkington, Edward, druggist, oil, and colour warehouse, 13 Rosemary st,; residence, Snugvale, Shankhill road
Wallace and Campbell's brick fields, Hopeton place
Wallace, Andrew, mechanic, Phœnix Foundry, Little Patrick street
Wallace, Andrew, brewer, 11 Victoria place
Wallace, Hugh, and Co., solicitors, 24 Fountain street—Downpatrick
Wallace, Hugh, porter, 13 Nelson street
Wallace, Hugh, carpenter, 19 Mitchell street
Wallace, Isabella, dealer, 5 Verner street
Wallace, James, in Ulster Bank—2 Victoria terrace
Wallace, James, brick manufacturer, 9 Johnston's buildings
Wallace, James, stabling, 10 Marlborough street
Wallace, James, grocer, 138 Millfield
Wallace, James, lodgings, 49 Prince's street
Wallace, John, solicitor, Victoria street—Bunker's hill
Wallace, John, proprietor of the *Ulster Advertiser*, 6 Waring street; residence, 53 Cromac street
Wallace, John, watchmaker, jeweller, and silversmith, 49 High street
Wallace, J. and John, sewed muslin manufacturers, 6 Corporation street—44 Nelson street
Wallace, John, sawyer, Herdman's buildings
Wallace, J. and W., sewed muslin manufacturers, 45 Waring street
Wallace, Robert, grocer and publican, 12 Smithfield
Wallace, Robert, tailor, 41 Joy street
Wallace, Rose Ann, sempstress, 12 Conway street
Wallace, Samuel, clerk, 10 Fleet street
Wallace, Thomas, commission merchant, 6 Elliott's court—3 Ormeau place
Wallace, William, sewed muslin agent, 31 Great Patrick street
Wallace, William, house carpenter, 5 Wesley lane
Wallace, Wm., house carpenter, 5 Wesley lane
Walls, Daniel, salesman, 43 Joy street
Walls, James, dealer, 40 William's row
Walls, Robert, cheesemonger, 6 Hammond's court
Walsh, David, baker, 44 Market street

ALPHABETICAL DIRECTORY.

Walsh, Edward, plasterer, 33 Academy street
Walsh, Edward, carter, 34 Great Patrick street
Walsh, James, carpenter, 4 Sussex street
Walsh, James, bricklayer, 26 King street
Walsh, James, publican, 61 North Queen street
Walsh, Patrick, 42 Little Patrick street
Walsh, Patrick, boot and shoemaker, 55 Mill street
Wann, Thomas, Ulster Bank—9 Pakenham place
Ward, Adam, shoemaker, 8 Sackville place
Ward, Arthur, boarding house, 13 Caddell's entry
Ward, Daniel, bricklayer, 16 Kennedy's entry
Ward, Francis, tailor, 6 Millfield
Ward, Hugh, weaver, 2 Kennedy's place
Ward, Hugh, stocking dealer, 55 Berry street
Ward, James, painter, 5 Gavin's buildings, Shankhill road
Ward, James, shoemaker, 18 Kennedy's place
Ward, James, grocer, 65 Verner street
Ward, Jane, boarding house, 43 Stanhope street
Ward, Marcus, and Co., stationers, bookbinders, lithographers, &c., 6 and 8 Corn market
Ward, Mary, quilter, 8 North King street
Ward, Mrs Ellen, of Marquis Ward & Co., stationers, Corn market, 21 King st.
Ward, Owen, hackler, 36 New Lodge road
Ward, Patrick, dealer, 14 New Lodge road
Ward, Thomas, weaver, 155 Lower Malone
Ward, Thomas, secretary county Down railway, sub-stamp office, gunpowder merchant, &c., 25 Bridge street; residence, Cherryhill, Malone
Ward, William, coal dealer, 30 Stephen street
Wardle, Mrs., Fitzwilliam street, Old Malone road
Wardlow, Hamilton, house carpenter, 15 Wesley place
Wardlow, Hugh, merchant, 6 Great George's street
Wardlow, J. and H., and Co., merchants and ship owners, 94 Corporation st.
Wardlow, John, gun maker, 2 Portland place
Wardlow, Robert, travelling clerk, 12 Kennedy's place
Wardlow, Thomas, 110 Mill street
Wardlow, Wm., tailor, 13 Skipper street
Ware, Richard, spirit dealer and stabling yard, 124 North street
Ware, William, butter merchant, 68 Great Patrick st.—28 Corporation st.
Waring, Mrs., dealer, 1 Albion lane
Waring, Robert, woollendraper, 1¼ Donegall street
Waring, Richard, provision merchant, 87 York street
Waring, Richard, provision merchant, Henry street and 85 York street
Warnock, James, pawnbroker, 84 Millfield
Warnock, James, tallow chandler, 36 Great Edward street
Warnock, Joseph, carpenter, 21 Upper Lagan street
Warnock, Joseph, grocer, 42 Verner street
Warnock, Wm., tobacco spinner, 5 Cargill street
Warren, Doctor, 37 Academy street
Warwick, Dr., surgeon, 29 Corporation street
Warwick, Susanna, grocer, 64 Peter's hill
Waste, Richd., book keeper, in J. Preston & Co.'s flax stores, 7 Linenhall st.
Waterhouse, Joseph, mechanic, Falls court, Falls road
Waterson, James, publican, 53 Verner street
Waterson, W. T., and R. S., solicitors, 132½ Ann street; W. T. Waterson's residence, Seville Lodge, Strandtown

ALPHABETICAL DIRECTORY.

Watson, Agnes, dressmaker, 12 Eliza street
Watson, James, publican and grocer, 46 Durham street
Watson, John, porter, 3 M'Tier's street
Watson, James M., 5 Kennedy's place
Watson Mary, 22 Verner street
Watson, Mary Jane, dealer, 90 Lower Malone
Watson, Robt., grocer & weighmaster, 32 Little Donegall st. & Gt. Patrick st.
Watson, Samuel, bricklayer, 8 Wellington square
Watson, Wm., builder, 4 Henrietta street
Watson, Wm., warder, New Bridewell, 2 Northburn street
Watson, Wm., wholesale clothier, 11 Hercules street—2 Donegall sq. east
Watson, William, draper, 8 Staunton street
Watt, David, publican, 45 Little Donegall street
Watt, Hugh, engineer, Lagan village
Watt, James, night constable, 102 Lower Malone
Watt, James, and Co., seedsmen, 11½ Donegall street
Watt, John, carpenter, 37 Lower Malone road
Watters, Allen, baker, 77 Corporation square
Watters, George, compositor. 42 Stanhope street
Watters, George, bleacher, 50 Stanhope street
Watters, Robert, engineer, Corporation docks; residence, 5 Corporation st.
Watters, Susan, 3 Stanhope street
Watters, Thomas, brazier, copper, and tinsmith, 27 Corporation street
Watters, Wm., rent agent, 16 Kennedy's place
Watterson, Thomas, boiler maker, 18 Vere street
Waugh and Smith, coach builders, 9 May street
Waugh, Isaac, clerk, 4 North Boundary street
Waugh, James, leather warehouse, 132 North street
Waugh, John, baker, and flour dealer, 154 North street
Waugh, Joseph, of Waugh and Smith, coachmakers, 22 Chichester street
Waugh, Joseph, wholesale grocer, Victoria street
Waugh, Thos., sewed muslin manufacturer, 11 Church st. & 10 Lancaster st.
Webb, Francis, shoemaker, 29 Verner street
Webb, James, dealer, 4 Store lane
Webb, Robert, car driver, 10 Pound street
Webb, Thomas, machinist, 20 Corporation street
Webster, Ann, grocer, 122 Ann street
Weinberg, J., 10 College square east
Weir, Arthur Collins, merchant, 1 Albion place
Weir, A. C., and Co., woollen Manchester warehouse, 24¼ Bridge street
Weir, Daniel, tailor and huckster, 55 Hill street
Weir, G., muslin manufacturer, Great Patrick street—Lodgeview
Weir, Henry, of Smyth, Weir, and Co., linen merchants, &c., 11 Donegall pl.
Weir, John, shoemaker, 13 Samuel street
Weir, Samuel, publican, 52 Great Patrick street
Weir, Samuel, stone cutter, 47 M'Tier street
Weir, William, stonecutter, 3 Fleming's place, Old Lodge road
Weir, Wm., butter merchant, 23 Corporation street
Weir, Wm., jun., & Co., sewed muslin manufacturers, 19 Nelson street
Weldon, Miss Deborah, milliner, and dressmaker, 44 Mill street
Wells, Thomas, boiler maker, 18 Garmoyle street
Welsh, Abner, printing office, 10 Arthur square
Welsh, Captain, 10 North Thomas street
Welsh, James, provision dealer, 5 Little Patrick street
Welsh, John, tailor, 14 Henrietta street

Welsh, John, engraver, 9 Stanhope street
Welsh, Robinson, butcher, Garmoyle street
Welsh, Robert, fishmonger, 5 Black's place
Welsh, Thomas, grocer, 2 Institution place
Welsh, Wm., carpenter, 63 Lancaster street
West, David, shoemaker, 73 Green street
West, Thomas, bellows maker, 10 West street
Wetheral, Wm., tanner, 25 Mill street—Holywood
Wetherald, Sarah, 6 Upton street
Wetherhead, Maria, boarding house, 16 Joy street
Wetherhead, Richard, clerk, 20 Shankhill road
Whaley, Wm., dealer, 10 Lower Malone
Wharton, Wm., starch manufacturer, 24 Talbot street
Wheeler, Thomas K., surgeon and apothecary, 11 Arthur st. and 33 High st.
Wheeler, Walter, lime works, 16 and 18 Carrickhill
Whisker, James, butcher and victualler, 31 Hercules place and Rosemary st.
Whisker, John, butcher, 8 Boundary street
Whitaker, Joseph, boot and shoemaker, 30 Corn market
Whitcroft, Wm., machine man, *Chronicle*, 33 Little May street
White and Clendinning, commission agents, 2 Donegall street place ; Mr. White's residence, 6 Brunswick street
White, George, carpenter, 10 Boyd street
White, George, carpenter, 6 Marquis street
White, Hugh, carpenter, 50 Little York street
White, Hugh, spirit merchant, Winecellar entry—11 Gloucester street
White, John, spirit dealer, 84½ Hercules street
White, James, car driver, 12 Verner street
White, John, carver, 29 Castle street
White, John A., accountant, 12 Joy street
White, Joseph, mechanic, 14 Cargill street
White, Mrs., 4 Thomas street
White, Mrs. A. J., 21 Welsh street
White, Richard, boiler maker, 4 Vere street
White, Rebecca, 15 Leeds street
White, Robert, confectioner, 17 Edward street
White, William, mechanic, 2 Vere street
White, William, carding master, 15 Back Ship street
White, Wm., carpenter, 13 Trafalgar street
White, Wm., of Law, White, and Co., linen commissioners, 2 Brunswick st.
White, Wm., night constable, 31 Little May street
White, Wm., dealer, 14 Shankhill
Whiteside, Isaac, pork cutter, 18 William street
Whiteside, James, plasterer, 7 Greenland street
Whiteside, Jane, straw bonnet maker, 24 Peter's hill
Whiteside, John, carter, 91 Peter's hill
Whiteside, John, sailmaker, 28 Carrickhill
Whiteside, Mrs. Margaret, 29 Nelson street
Whiteside, Wm., night constable, 24 Peter's hill
Whitford, John, and Neill Johnston, curriers, 110 Carrickhill
Whitla, Elizabeth, dressmaker, 6 Campbell's buildings, Shankhill road
Whitla, Valentine, merchant, Linen hall ; residence, Ben Eden
Whitley, Francis, weaver, 39 M'Tier street
Whittle, Misses, boarding school, 1 Fisherwick place
Wick, Lowry, overseer, 89 Lower Malone road
Wiggins, Robert, blacksmith, 48 Boyd street

Wightman, John, wholesale grocer, 41 Ann street; stores, Pottinger's entry
Wightman, Miss, 10 Upper Queen street
Wightman, Mrs., dressmaker, 28 North Queen street
Wilard, David, painter, 13 Charlemont street
Wilock's, Henry, servant, 63 Little Patrick street
Wild, Margaret, lodgings, 8 Alexander street
Wiley, John, boot and shoemaker, 20 Durham street
Wilgar, Hans, publican, Ormeau road
Wilkie, George, plumber, 25 Old Lodge road
Wilkinson, George, engineer, 95 Boundary street
Wilkinson, John, glass, china, and earthenware house, 108 High street
Wilkinson, Robert, weaver, M'Tier's street
Wilkinson, William, ship broker and commission agent, 7 Queen's square
Wilks, John, mechanic, 8 M'Crory's row, Ballymacarrett
Williams, Mrs., 27 Mill street
Williams, Mrs. Sarah, 7 Williams place
Williams, Robert, dealer, 85 Barrack street
Williams, Thomas, day constable, 5 Stanhope street
Williams, William, builder, 11½ and 19 Cromac street
Williamson, Francis, day constable, 25 Brown square
Williamson, Hugh, dresser in foundry, 6 M'Millen's place
Williamson, James, marble carver, 4 Stanley place
Williamson, James, house carpenter, 44 Little York street
Williamson, John, whitesmith, 33 Old Lodge road
Williamson, James, weaver, 21 Mitchell street
Williamson, John, York road
Williamson, John, carter, Canning street
Williamson, John, dealer, 96 Carrickhill
Williamson, James, clothes dealer, 2 Charlemont street
Williamson, Miss A. J., 28 Upper Arthur street
Williamson, Mr., 6 Catherine street
Williamson, Miss, teacher Rosemary-street Infant School—17 Rosemary st.
Williamson, Matthew, cabinet maker, 64 Mustard street
Williamson, Matthew, comb maker, 49 Staunton street
Williamson, Robert, millwright, 1 M'Tier street
Williamson, Thomas, sea captain, 6 Earl street
Williamson, Wm. J., painter, 5 Frederick street
Willicks, David, brassfounder, 12 Russell street
Willicks, James, boiler maker, 17 North Thomas street
Willis, John, professor of music, 4 College street south
Willis, Solomon, hay and straw dealer, 28 West street and 37 Smithfield
Wills, Mary Ann, shirt maker, 33 Alexander street
Willis, Thomas, ship joiner, 13 Vere street
Wilmot, Thomas, glass blower, Keenan's place, Ballymacarrett
Wilson, Alexander, toy and basket merchant, 76 Joy street
Wilson, Alexander, traveller, 16 King street
Wilson, Alexander, watchman, 6 Vere street
Wilson, Alexander, grocer, 87 North Queen street
Wilson, Alex., basket manufacturer and toy merchant, 8 Bridge street
Wilson, Dennis, publican, Antrim road
Wilson, Dr. Thomas, Ballynafeigh
Wilson, Elisha, shoemaker, 49 North Thomas street
Wilson, Eliza, grocer, 5 Little George's street
Wilson, Eliza, boarding house, 25 John street
Wilson, Eliza, 26 Carrickhill

Wilson, Francis, accountant, 25 Fountain street
Wilson, Francis, forgeman, 15 East street
Wilson, George, mechanic, 11 Townsend street
Wilson, George, mechanic, 11 Campbell's buildings, Townsend street
Wilson, G. S., rectifying distiller, 11½ Mill street—Holywood
Wilson, Hans, dealer, 1 New Lodge road
Wilson, Hugh, starch maker, Shankhill road
Wilson, Hugh, pawnbroker, 22 Smithfield
Wilson, John, sea captain, 21 Little York street
Wilson, Jeremiah, postmaster, Ballymacarrett
Wilson, John, baker, 21 Boyd street
Wilson, James, clerk, 59 Little York street
Wilson, Jane, toy shop, 140 North street
Wilson, James, grocer, 17 Lancaster street
Wilson, James, blacksmith, Trinity street—Lancaster street
Wilson, James, clerk, Agnes's place, Shankhill road
Wilson, James, tobacconist and snuff dealer, 100 North street
Wilson, James, wholesale wine and spirit merchant, Victoria buildings, and 27 and 29 Church lane; residence, 31 Hamilton street
Wilson, Jas., watchmaker, jeweller, & optician, 7 High st.—10 Frederick st.
Wilson, James, printer, 70 High street; residence, 10 Frederick street
Wilson, James, spirit dealer, Cole's alley
Wilson, John, publican, 12 Pilot street
Wilson, John, baker, coal & forage contractor, 75 & 77 North Queen street
Wilson, John, 34½ Great George's street
Wilson, John, gentleman, 19 Gloucester street
Wilson, John, carpenter, 26 Sussex street
Wilson, John, publican, Falls road
Wilson, John, grocer, 6 Peter's hill
Wilson, John, sawyer, 2 William's row
Wilson, John, publican, 39 West street
Wilson, John, night constable, 18 Lower Stanfield street
Wilson, Joseph, sawyer, 16 Raphael street
Wilson, James, toy shop, 174 North street
Wilson, Mary, boarding house, 2½ Great Edward street
Wilson, Mary, 33 M'Tier's street
Wilson, Mrs. Elizabeth, 2 College street
Wilson, Margaret, 20 Catherine street
Wilson, Margaret, whiteworker, 26 Stanley street
Wilson, Mrs., 1 Breadalbane place
Wilson, Mary, linen and damask warehouse, 58 Donegall street
Wilson, Mrs. Ann, 9 Torrens' market
Wilson, Mrs., lodgings, 20 Collingwood street
Wilson, Robert, linen merchant, Linen hall—33 Hamilton street
Wilson, Robert, ship owner, 19 Earl street
Wilson, Rev. Robert, D.D., 6 Albion place
Wilson, Robert, captain, 38 Earl street
Wilson, Robert, weigher at Smithfield weighbridge, 23 Brown street
Wilson, Robert, dealer, 34 William's row
Wilson, S., grocer, 19 Alexander street
Wilson, Thomas, & Co., hosiery and trimming warehouse, 32 High street
Wilson, Thomas & David, sewed muslin manufacturers, 37 John street
Wilson, Thomas, publican, 71 Corporation square
Wilson, Thomas, engineer, 15 Cullingtree place
Wilson, T., cartmaker, Antrim road

ALPHABETICAL DIRECTORY.

Wilson, Wm., tailor, 3 Rochfort place
Wilson, Wm., publican, 20 Millfield
Wilson, Wm., mechanic, 8 North Thomas street
Wilson, William, tailor, 4 Sackville street
Wilson, William, assistant woollendraper, 11 Russell street
Wilson, Wm., lapper, 7 Wellington street
Wilson, William P., professor Queen's college, 2 Upper Crescent
Wilson, William, cutler, 3 Skipper street
Wilson, William, warehouseman, 1 Glentilt place, Old Lodge road
Wilson, William, builder, 70 Joy street
Windrim, James, baker, 38 Stanhope street
Winnington, John, brassfounder and gasfitter, 15 Welsh street
Wisdom, Alexander, shoemaker, 23 Wall street
Withered, George, grocer and publican, 11 Cromac street
Withers, A., grocer and provision dealer, 14 and 16 Barrack street
Withers, James, editor *Chronicle*—17 Campbell's buildings, Townsend street
Withers, John, carman, 58 Brown street
Wolfenden, Edward, book keeper, 7 Spencer street
Woodcock, Henry, poulterer, 21 Great Patrick street
Woodhouse, George, clerk in Northern bank, 7 Glengall street
Wood, George P., and Co., linen yarn, flax, and commission merchants, 1 Talbot street—Holywood
Wood, Nathaniel, draper, 13 Harmony place
Woods, Arthur, baker, 23 Charles street
Woods, Arthur, shoemaker, 1 Pilot street
Woods, Charles, reeling master, 15 Cullingtree street
Woods, David, agent for Hill Hamilton, 12 North Queen street
Woods, Eleanor, publican, 24 Lancaster street
Woods, George, foreman in grain store, 16 Henrietta street
Woods, Hugh, plasterer, 13 Sackville place
Woods, Hamlet, bricklayer, 2 Wesley lane
Woods, John, fruit dealer, Wheeler's place, Ballymacarrett
Woods, James, grain stores, 2 Murphy's lane—65 Verner street
Woods, John, tailor and grocer, 7 Garmoyle street
Woods, James, night constable, 12 Artillery street
Woods, Margaret, 13 Galway court
Woods, Michael, jeweller, 6 Michael street
Woods, Michael, wine and spirit dealer, 11 Victoria street
Woods, Patrick, grocer and publican, 12 Barrack street
Woods, Robert, tailor, 18 Durham street
Woods, William, saddler, 2 Frederick place
Woods, William, grocer, 1 Hamilton street
Woodwark, John, cabinet maker, 26 Black's place
Woolsey, Samuel, flax merchant, 5 Abbotsford place
Workman, John, and Sons, manufacturers, 60 Upper Arthur street
Workman, John, manufacturer, The Crescent, Botanic road
Workman, John, 9 Donegall square east
Workman, John, bootmaker, 11 Eliza street
Workman, Robert, of R. Workman and Co., sewed muslin manufacturer Upper Arthur street; residence, 10 Pakenham place
Workman, Robert, and Co., muslin manufacturers, Corporation street
Workman, R. and J., manufacturers, Bedford street
Workman, Robert, of R. and J. Workman, 52 York street
Worthington, John, accountant, 32 Gloucester street
Wright, George, chandler, 11 Henrietta street

Wright, Hugh, in provision store, 16 William's row
Wright, John, warper, 2 M'Tier street
Wright, James, dealer, 58 Alexander street
Wright, Mary, dealer, 165 North street
Wright, Philip, coal merchant, Shankhill road
Wright, Philip, coal office, 10 Queen's quay, Ballymacarrett
Wright, Robert, publican, 6 Barrack street
Wright, William, coach painter, 10 Seymour lane
Wright, William, grocer and publican, 25 Shankhill road
Wyley, Alexander, cooper, Ashmore street, Conway street
Wyley, E. and J., boarding house, 2 Little George's street
Wylie, John, of A. Dickey & Co., merchants—2 University square
Wylie, William, boot and shoemaker, 22 Annette street

Yar, Richard, lighterman, 8 Morrow's entry
Yeaman, Wm., machine maker, 12 Thomas street
Yeates, John, mariner, 50 Green street
Yeates, Martha, baker, 28 Corn market
Yeates, Rebecca, 15 Millfield
Yeates, Robert, 32 Fountain street
Young, Arthur, proprietor Caledonian Hotel, 32 Tomb street
Young, Andrew, watchman, Mr. Howie's green, 9 Alexander street south
Young, Andrew, commission merchant, Corporation st.—4 Upper Crescent
Young, Charles, shoemaker, 13 Verner street
Young, Hugh, chandler, 64 Cromac street
Young, Isabella, pawnbroker, 20 and 18 Lancaster street
Young, James, carpenter, 8 Hamilton's place
Young, Jas. G., collegiate school, 8 Howard street
Young, James, & Co., wholesale woollen warehouse, 19 Donegall street
Young, James, solicitor, 3 Arthur square; residence, 5 Dock street
Young, John, iron merchant, 7 Dock street
Young, John, ship carpenter, 5 Little Corporation street
Young, John, flax, tow, and yarn dealer, 25 and 27 Devis street
Young, John, bricklayer, 6 Hopeton place
Young, Joseph, chandler, 4 Mary's market
Young, Joseph, woollendraper and hatter, 8 Waring street
Young, J. H., and Co., muslin manufacturers, 37 John street
Young, John B., umbrella and parasol maker, 2 York road
Young, John, of Coates & Young, Lagan foundry—Shamrock Lodge, B.carrett
Young, James, Harbour office—Pottinger place, Ballymacarrett
Young, Joseph, bricklayer, Shankhill road
Young, Letitia, grocer and spirit dealer, 30 Henry street
Young, Miss, dressmaker, 20 Henry street
Young, Robert, civil engineer, 18 Wellington square
Young, William, of J. Young and Co.—18 Wellington place
Young, Wm., stonemason, 13 North Boundary street
Young, Wm., miller, 7 Mitchell street
Young, Wm., proprietor of Belfast Arms, 57 Donegall quay
Young, Wm,, pawnbroker, 38 Mill street—Bunker's hill house
Young, Wm , shoe warehouse, 2½ Arthur street

PROFESSIONS AND TRADES DIRECTORY.

Academies
AND PUBLIC SCHOOLS

Those marked (a) are boarding and day
Royal Belfast Academical Institution; classical master, T. W. E. Evans; mathematical and mercantile, Rev. I. Steen; English, T. Blain, A.M.; French, Auguste Badier; writing, Patrick Johnston; drawing, Joseph Molloy
Belfast Academy, 63 Donegall street; Rev. R. J. Bryce, LL.D., principal; classical master, the Principal; mathematical and mercantile, Thos. M'Clinton; writing, Thomas Armstrong; drawing, Joseph Molloy; English, W. F. Collier; French, Jules Festu
Ballymacarrett Infant school; Miss Hanley, teacher
Ballymacarrett National school, D. Christie, teacher
Bethel school, Pilot street; James Houston, teacher
Black, W. R., 6 Arthur place
Brown street Schools—Thomas Edmondson, teacher
aBrown, Mary, 23 Gloucester street
Bullick, Samuel, Academy, 82 High st.
Burns, James F., Wesley place
Byrne, Misses, 26 Castle street
Campbell, William, Pottinger's place, Ballymacarrett
Carpenter, Miss, 33 Rosemary street
Chancellors, the Misses, 55 Cromac st.
Church Educational Society's school, Ballymacarrett
Christ's Church school, Durham st.
Christ's Church Infant do., Durham st.
aCraufurd, Mrs., 7 Adelaide place
aCruikshank, Mrs., 101 Donegall st.
aCullimore, Miss, 12 York street
Diocesan Seminary, Donegall street
Donegall Street National schools
Dougherty, Wm., 30 Durham street
Duffy, Michael, 36 Millfield
Edmondson, Mrs., 77 Donegall street
Fountain street National school; H. Kelly, teacher
Galt, Wm., 40 Henry street
aGamble, Eliza, 6 Gloucester street
aGamble, Mrs., 63 York street
Gill, Misses, 8 Linen-hall street
Government School of Design, Royal Academical Institution, College sq. north; Claude L. Nursey, principal; D. W. Raimbach, second master
aHainen, Miss, 15 Talbot street
Harrild, Miss, 1 Prospect terrace
aHenderson, Misses, 29 York street
Hopkirk, Miss, 10 Harmony place
aHutton, Rev. Geo., 9 Fisherwick place
Industrial and National schools, Frederick street; Miss Orr, teacher; Mrs. Talbot, matron
aJohnston, Mrs., and Miss M'Clune, 23 Hamilton street
Kelly, John, 128 Millfield
aKnowles, Miss, 30 Upper Arthur st.
aLambert, Miss, 6 Chichester street
Lamont, Miss, 38 Upper Arthur st.
Lee, Mrs. Francis, 4 Nelson street
Lancasterian schools, Frederick street
Macloskie, Paul, 13 Catherine st. north
Mason, Miss, 7 College street south
Mark, Rev. J. academy, 39 Chichester st.
Mateer, John, 72 Cromac street
Millen, H., 32 Nelson street
Moorcroft, Mrs., 42 Nelson street
Morton, James, 20 Kennedy's place
Mulligan, Misses, 7 College st. south
May street National school; Owen Callan, teacher
M'Entee, Patrick, 4 Fountain street

M'Ginnis, Miss, 5 Sarah street
M'Donnell, Hugh, 88 Millfield
National Infant school, Fountain lane ; Miss Lambert, teacher
O'Connor, Hugh, 7 Arthur place
O'Neill, A., 12 Little Patrick street
Pilot street Infant school; Miss S. Dorrans, teacher
Paisley, James, 33 King street
aRichey, Miss, 31 Queen street
aRoberts, Miss S., 25 King street
aRoe, Misses, 16 College street
Ross, Wm., 9 Academy street
Rook, Miss, 38 Upper Arthur street
Rosemary street schools ; Rev. James Baird, teacher
St. George's school, High street
Salem school, York street
Scientific School, Mechanics' Institute, Queen street ; A. B. Porter, teacher
aSims, Miss, 29 Chichester street
Smyth, John, 131 Durham street
aStavely, Miss, 20 College street
aStitt, Misses, 28 Hamilton street
Symington, Daniel, 13 Earl street
Tait, Miss, 123 York street
Trinity Church school, Wall street
Whittle, Misses, 1 Fisherwick place
Young, James, Collegiate School, 8 Howard street

Accountants

Those marked (a) public accountants
Campbell, John, 12 Cromac street
Elliott, Thomas, 100 Donegall street
aHartley, Wm., office, 1 The Castle
O'Connor, J. D., (Savings' Bank) 1 College place North
Patton, George, 30 Corporation st.
Porter, D., (Borough) 22 Hamilton st.
aSimms, Wm., Linen Hall
aVance, Samuel, 36 Waring street
Wilson, Francis, 25 Fountain street
Worthington, John, 32 Gloucester st.

Aerated Water Manufacturers

Bodel, James, 78 Millfield
Carson, Wm., 14 Corn market
Corry, Thos. C. S., 13 Victoria street
Crawford and Co., 3 Church street
Fetherston, John, 49 Ann street
Grattan and Co., 12 Corn market
Hamilton, John, 10 Church street
Harkin, Alex., 7 Hercules place
Magee, Richard, 9 Johnston's court

Millen, Hugh, 46 Church lane
Nicholl, James, 34½ Gordon street
Pinkerton, Francis, 31 William street

Agents

See Book agents, Commission agents, Emigration agents, General agents, House, Rent, and Land agents, Insurance agents, News agents, and Steam Packet agents

Agricultural Implement Makers

Gray, Robert, 8 Police place
Robinson, Richard, 13 Eliza street

Alabaster and Roman Cement Manufacturers

Thus marked (a) are importers only
Cuddy, John, 9 Upper Church lane
aLow, James, 24 Chichester street
aO'Donohoe, James, 26 York street
Sutherland, H. A., and Co., 28 Joy st.

Apothecaries and Surgeons

SEE ALSO PHYSICIANS AND SURGEONS

Thus marked (a) are apothecaries only
aAikin, T. H., 38 Ann street
Alexander, J. A., 49 Corporation st.
Beck, John Wm., M.D., 128 North st.
Belfast Apothecaries' Hall, 33 High st.
Black, Robt. J., M.D., 10 Botanic road
aBryson, Samuel, 98 High street
Corry, Thomas C. S., 13 Victoria st.
Daly, Edward, 202 North street
Dickson, John S., 108 North street
Dorrian, Edward, 68 Donegall street
Fryer, Wm. F., M.D., 39 Donegall st.
Gelston, Jas., Keenan's place, B.carrett
aGrattan & Co., 12 Corn market
Gribben, Edw., 23 Great Edward st.
Harkin, Alex., 7 Hercules place
Heyburn, Wm., 28 Mill street
Hood, John, 41 Castle street
Johnston, Wm., 33 Corporation st.
Lynch, P., M.D., 17 Donegall place
MacMullan, Chas. C., 48 Donegall st.
Marshall, Wm., & Co., 100 High st.
Marshall, Jas. D., M.D., 8 High street
Mawhinney, James, New Durham st.
Mawhinney, James, 42 Mill street
Moore, Hugh, 28 Tomb street
Moreland, H., M.D., 53 Corporation st.
Mulholland, J. S., M.D., 80 High st.
Murphy, W., M.D., 11 Donegall street

Murray, Daniel, 5 Mill street
M'Cleery, James, 19 York street
M'Gregor, Geo. A., 27 Barrack street
Officer, Alexander, 43 York street
Quin, George, 16 Castle place
Rea, Samuel, 26 Gloucester street
aRing, Edward, General Hospital
Smyth, John, 29 Corn market
Snowden, Sam.,M.D.14Corporation st.
Wales, George F., 71 York street
Warwick, Wm., 29 Corporation street
Wheeler, Thos. K., M.D., 11 Arthur st.

Architects
Boyd, James, 45 York street
Ewart, James, 29 Donegall street
Godwin, John, C.E., Ulster Railway
Hastings, Wm., North Queen street
Jackson, Thomas, 16 Donegall place
Lanyon, Chas.,C.E., 1 Upper Queen st.
Moore, Wm., 20 Chichester street
M'Nea, James, 95 York street
Turner, Thos., 8 Donegall pl. buildings

Artists
PORTRAIT AND LANDSCAPE PAINTERS
Anderson, James, 26 Hamilton street
Brown, Charles J., 26 Arthur street
Burgess, J. Howard, 16 Donegall place
Hooke, Richard, 17 Chichester street
Lamont, Miss, 36 Upper Arthur street
Marshall, Miss, 27 Queen street
Newell, Hugh, 10 Renwick place
Nursey, C. L., Lower Crescent
Pitchoni, Signor, 6 Castle lane
Raimbach, D. W., 1 Botanic View
Rook, Miss, 36 Upper Arthur street

Asphalte & Felt Manufacturers
Grueber & Co., 2 Prince's dock
Ritchie, F., & Sons, New road, B.carrett

Assurance Offices
See Insurance offices

Attorneys
See Solicitors

Auctioneers
Byrne, John, 38 Berry street
Devlin, John, 8½ Donegall place
Heron, Edward, 41 Smithfield
Heron, William, 2 West street
Kelly, Edward, 68 Smithfield
Keenan, John, 76 Millfield
Loughran, Patrick, 66 Smithfield
Magee, Edward, M'Larnon's buildings, Ballymacarrett
Mallaghan, Henry, 26 Berry street
Meharg, James, 63 Smithfield
Monaghan, Thomas, 65 Smithfield
Mulryan, Robert, 1 Kennedy's row
Mulrine, Robert, 63 Smithfield
M'Loughlin, M'L., 28 Marquis street
M'Shane, Patrick, 64 Smithfield
Rice, James, 33 Cromac street
Rodgers, William, 12¼ Church street
Spence, John, Smithfield
Todd, William, 24 Smithfield

Auctioneers and Brokers
Clarke, Hugh C., 5 Rosemary street
Dale, William, 4 Donegall street
Hyndman, George C., 7 Castle place
Mathews, Joseph, 31 Waring street

Baby Linen Warehouses
Culloden, Miss, 9 Arthur street
Horswill, Mrs., 5 Arthur street
Milliken, Margaret, 64 Donegall street
M'Cormick, Sarah, 11 Hercules place
Oldrin, Mary and Sarah, 20 Castle pl.

Bakers
Adams, James, 198 North street
Alexander, Samuel, Ashmore street
Belfast Public Bakery, 14 Church st., Wm. J. Elliott, manager
Bell, William, 34 Great Edward street
Birkmyre, Catherine, 134 Ann street
Boyd, Thomas, 181 North street
Boyd, James, 162 North street
Campbell, Robert 10 Arthur street
Canning, James, 10 & 12 Hercules st.
Carroll, Henry, 12 Annette street
Carmichael, John, 89 Carrick hill
Carnduff, Robert, 31 & 33 Brown's sq.
Crawford, Jane, 113 North street
Denvir, Patrick, 97 North street
Dublin Bakery, 8 and 10 Donegall street, James Canning, proprietor
Gilmore, Hugh, 18 Murphy street
Heron, William, 46 Great Patrick st.
Hughes, Bernard, 71 Donegall street, also, Railway Bakery
Hunter, Mary, 99 North street
Johnston, J. S., 38 Donegall street
Johnston, Walter, 35 Little Patrick st.

PROFESSIONS, TRADES, &c. 367

Kirker, Archibald, 37 Cromac street
Knox, William, 135 North street
Lennon, John, 17 Carrick hill
Louden, Thomas, Garmoyle street
Macartney, James, 58 Union street
Meek, Robert, 5 Barrack street
M'Cann, Samuel, 15 Catherine st. N.
M'Carter, Wm., 21 & 22 Carrick hill
M'Geough, Matthew, 62 Barrack st.
Newry Mills Bakery, 9 Queen street, Kidd, Brothers, proprietors
Kennedy, W., 23 Church lane
Nichol, James, 27 Donegall street
Palmer, William, 9 Wesley place
Parkbill, Robert, 14 Talbot street
Patterson, Alex., 7 Queen's square
Peel, Robert, Shankhill road
Peel, Robert, 151 North street
Railway Bakery, 5 Donegall place, Bernard Hughes, proprietor
Rea, Joseph, 71 Green street
Robinson, David, 60 Union street
Rodgers, Alex., 29 and 31 Mill street
Short, John, 171 North street
Smith and M'Millan, 66 Great Patrick street
Smithfield Bakery, 33 Smithfield, W. Sharp, proprietor
Stewart, Robt., 7 Upper Church lane
Trelford, William, 44 Alexander st.
Trueman, John, 14 Castle street
Waters, Allen, 77 Corporation street
Waugh, John, 154 North street
Wilson, John, 75 North Queen st.
Wilson, John, 21 Boyd street
Yeates, Martha, 28 Corn market

Banks

SEE ALSO BANKING COMPANIES.
Bank of Ireland, 22 Donegall place
Belfast Bank, Donegall street
Northern Bank, 1 Castle street—Victoria street (building)
Provincial Bank of Ireland, 36 Donegall street
Savings' Bank, 29 King street
Ulster Bank, 7 Waring street

Barristers-at-Law

Allen, W. J. C., 8 Wellington place
Allen, Wm., 64 Donegall street
Andrews, Robt., Q.C., Donegall street
Close, Arthur, Glenview
Crawford, Arthur S., 16 Arthur street
Dobbin, J. W., 12 Howard street

Faloon, Wm. H., 100 Donegall street
Gibson, James, 4 Chichester street
Gilmore, J. B.,Q.C.,Ravenhill,C.fergus
Hancock, W. N., LL.D., professor Queen's College; 12 Wellington place
Lowry, Thomas K., 1 Arthur place
May, George A., Craigavad
Macartney, Wm., 40 Upper Arthur st.
Macrory, Edmund, Duncairn
Meade, Francis, 1 Fisherwick place
Molyneux, Echlin, professor Queen's college
Musgrave, Wm., 1 Donegall sq. south
M'Donnell, Thos., Q.C., Eglantine hill

Basket Makers

Dillon, Henry, 22 Bank lane
Dillon, Nicholas, 6 (sheds) Smithfield
Kearney, John, 10 (sheds) Smithfield
Kearney, Richd., Bridge end, B.carrett
Kearney, Wm., Bridge end, B.carrett
Pelan, Robert, & Co., 6 Bridge street
Wilson, Alex., 8 Bridge street

Baths

Baths and Wash-houses, Bath place, Falls road—W. J. Livingston, superintendent
Davis, Geo., Plough hotel, Corn market
Hurst, Dr. C., Imperial hotel, 10 Donegall place
Moore, Jn., Donegall Arms, 11 Castle place
Milliken, Israel, 87 Peter's hill

Bell Hangers

Ireland & M'Neill, Corn market
Leathem, Edward, 144 North street
Thomas, Samuel, 6 Arthur lane

Bleachers

Andrews, Michael, Kilroot ; Ardoyne
Bell, J. L., Ballyclare; York lane
Bragg, Henry, and Sons,Cottonmount; 8 York street
Charley, J. W., and Co., Seymourhill
Curell, J. and M., and Co., Linen hall
Fenton, Son, and Co., Falls bleach green; Linen Hall
Ferguson and Co., Falls bleach green ; Waring street
Ferguson, John S., & Co., Ballysillan; Linen hall
Ferguson, Thos., and Sons,Whiterock ; Linen hall

2 I

PROFESSIONS, TRADES, &c.

Ferguson, Jas., & Son, Newforge green
Gray, Wm., and Sons, Graymount
Howie, Robert (printer and dyer), Old Lodge road
Hunter, Alexander, Dunmurry
Hunter, Wm., jun., Dunmurry
Kennedy, J. and T., Woodburn, Carrickfergus; Commercial court
M'Cance, John Wm., & Co., Suffolk
Orr, Wm., and Sons, Glennalina
Richardson & Co., Lambeg & Lisburn
Richardson, J. N., Sons, and Owden, Glenmore; 14 Donegall place
Roberts and Derbyshire, Colin
Smyth, Weir, and Co., Milltown, Banbridge; 11 Donegall place

Block, Pump, and Mast Makers
Bradford, James, 10 Garmoyle street
Mathers, Thomas, 17 and 19 Pilot st.
Mooney, Bernard, 1 Bradford square
Scott, John, 4 Corporation street

Bobbin Manufacturers
Low, John, patent saw mills, Garmoyle street
Robinson, Richard, saw mills, 13 Eliza street

Bookbinders
Agnew, W. & G., Arthur square
Archer and Sons, 27, 29 Castle place
Campbell, Robert, 1 Skipper street
Haig, Samuel, 9 Donegall place
Harrison, George, 51 High street
Johnston, Wm., 25 Waring street
M'Kee, Wm., Pottinger's entry
Reilly, T. H., 13 Waring street
Smyth, Hill, 1 Donegall street
Ward, Marcus, & Co., 6 Corn market

Booksellers and Stationers
SEE ALSO STATIONERS AND ACCOUNT BOOK MANUFACTURERS.
Those marked (*a*) are only booksellers
Agnew, W. & G., Arthur square
Campbell, Robert, 13 Skipper street
*a*Gowdy, James, 28 Rosemary street
Greer, Henry, 31 High street
Gribbin, Thomas, 76 North street
Henderson, John, 13 Castle place
Hodgson, Robert, 9 High street
Johnston, Wm., 19 Skipper street
Kerr, Owen, 18 Chapel lane
Magill, James, 2 Castle buildings
Mayne, Alex., 1 Donegall square east
*a*Mullan, John, 8 Castle buildings
M'Comb, William, 1 High street
O'Neill, James, 4 Castle place
Phillips, George, 27 Bridge street
Pollock, Mary, 62 North street
Reed, James, Victoria street
Reilly, Thos. H., 13 Waring street
*a*Sutherland, D. G., 26 Joy street
Thacker, Eliza, 3 Ann street
Tract Depository — Alex. Mayne, 1 Donegall square east
Unitarian Tract Depository, 28 Rosemary street—James Gowdy, agent

Book Agents
Croxford, Thomas, for Tallis and Co., London—56 Nelson street
Maitland, J. H., for Blackie and Son, Glasgow & Edinburgh; 28 Arthur st.
M'Donald, James, for A. Fullarton & Co., of Glasgow and Edinburgh—45 Upper Arthur street
Magee, Adam, for G. Virtue, & others, London—8 Thomas street

Boot and Shoe Shops
Atkinson, Arthur, 7 Church lane
Bailie, William, 84 High street
Bailie, Isaac, 58 Ann street
Barclay, John, & Co., 49 Donegall st.
Beatty, Margaret, 108 North street
Black, James, 26 Ann street
Blaney, Neill, 79 Corporation square
Blake, James, 106 High street
Brown, Robert, 9 Church lane
Brown, John, 39 John street
Byrne, James, 92 High street
Cinnamond, John, 9 Castle place
Coey, James, 12 Donegall place
Davis, Chas. N., 24 Castle place
Doody, John, 30 John street
Dunlop, John, 24 High street
Dysart, John and James, 50 High st.
Fegan, Henry, 8 Castle place
Feris, Robert, 18 Ann street
Gibson, William, 90½ High street
Harrison, George, 46 Donegall street
Isles, Nathaniel, 105 North street
Knox, John and Robert, 60 High st.
Lamb, James, 88 North street
Maguire, William, 30 Church lane
Maguire, G., 28 Church lane
Maguire, Alexander, 11 High street
Mahaffey, Robert, 121 North street

PROFESSIONS, TRADES, &c.

Milliken, James, 44 Cromac street
Mortimer, James, 5 Church lane
Mortimer, William, 8 Church lane
Mortimer, John, 4 Church lane
Moore, George, 20 High street
M'Afee, John, 18 Corn market
M'Afee, John, 2 Ann street
M'Auley, Bernard, 90 and 94 North street
M'Clure, Joseph, 31 Church lane
M'Clure, Robert, 48 Ann street
M'Cormick, John, 14 Chapel lane
M'Cracken, Malcolm, 3 Bridge st.
M'Cracken, A., 28 Bridge street
M'Gee, J., 22 Church lane
M'Quoid, J., 11 Church lane
M'Quillan, John, 7 Peter's hill
O'Kane, James, 7 Barrack street
O'Neill, Hugh, 3 North Queen street
O'Neill, Patrick, 111 North street
Palmer, William, 3 Church lane
Palmer, Thomas, 6 Church lane
Palmer, H., 2 Church lane
Palmer, William, 88 High street
Reynolds, John, 18 King street
Smyth, John, 32 Waring street
Somerville, D., 41 Mill street
Spence, Hugh, 93 North street
Stewart, Kennedy, 86 High street
Trimble, William, 55 High street
Wellington boot and shoe warehouse, Victoria street, J. B. Pratt and Co.
Whittaker, Joseph, 30 Corn market

Brassfounders and Gasfitters
Those marked (a) are also lead merchants

Aldritt, Wm., 23 Castle street
Bruce, Thomas, 5 Academy street
Burrowes, Israel, 87½ Peter's hill
aCameron, James, 47 Donegall street
Coates, William, 12 Castle street
Coates & Young, Lagan foundry
Combe, James, & Co., Falls foundry
aFortune & Co., 25 Hill street
Gibson, Robert, M'Clenaghan's court, Mill street
Ireland & M'Neill, Corn market
Law and Co., 9 Fountain street
M'Cann, Bernard, 7 and 9 Victoria st.
M'Cann, James, 53 Hill street
M'Ivor, William, 11½ Castle street
M'Kenzie, Brothers, Regent buildings, Victoria street

Brewers
Castlebellingham Brewery—office, 5 Police square—T. Ranson, agent
Clarke, Ledlie, 130½ Ann street
Dobbin, Clotworthy, 43 Smithfield
Fordyce & Mullen, 84 Cromac street
Mackenzie, Shaw, & Co., 84 Hercules street
Magill, Geo. & Jas., 25 Bank lane

Brick and Tile Makers
Campbell, F., Bower's hill, Shankhill
Campbell, M., Bower's hill, Shankhill
Carlisle and Murphy, near Orangefield, county Down
Chambers, Alex., Malone
Gray, James, & Co., 4 Cromac road
Gregg, Cranston, Malone
Houston, John, Ravenhill, B.carrett
Morrison, Charles, Shankhill road
Morrison, Chas., jun., Shankhill road
Moore, John, Ravenhill, Ballymacarrett
Murphy, John, 3 Hamilton street and Ulsterville
M'Cracken, James, 29 Barrack street
M'Wade, Fras., Bridge end, B.carrett
O'Neill, James, Ravenhill, B.carrett
O'Neill, Con., Ravenhill, B.carrett
Ross, James, 29 Old Lodge road
Ross, William, Falls road
Sloan, Andrew, and Co., Bridge end, Ballymacarrett
Smith & Ross, Malone
Wallace, Jas., 9 Johnston's buildings, Shankhill road
Wallace, John, Shankhill road
Wallace, Martin, Shankhill road

Bricklayers (Masters)
Agnew, David, Ballynafeigh
Baird, Wm., 17 Coates street
Clements, Robert, 7 Townsend street
Finlay, John, 37 Tomb street
Harvey, John, 13 Michael street
Hunter, Henry, 44 Peter's hill
Ingram, Thos., 53 Grattan street
Johnston, Thomas, 42 Joy street
Johnston, Joseph, 5 Seymour street
Kane, John, 3 Little Corporation st.
Magee, James, 11 Wilson street
Maguire, Silvester, 28½ Mill street
M'Cracken, Wm., 36 M'Millen's place
M'Cracken, Jas., 14 Little Edward st.
M'Dowell, Hugh, Old Malone road
M·Larnon, P., 18 Mitchell street

PROFESSIONS, TRADES, &c.

M'Shane, Charles, 108 Millfield
O'Neill, Charles, 6 North King street
Scott, Matthew, 75 Academy street
Scott, John, 28 M'Millen's place
Simpson, John, 9 Renwick place
Smith, Michael, 57 Peter's hill
Stewart, Thomas, 12 North King st.
Walsh, James, 26 King street

Brush Makers
Those marked (a) are also trunk makers
Bullock, Wm., 27 North street
Hall, Daniel, 10 Brown's square
aKelly, John, 24 Bridge street
Robinson, Samuel D., 26 North street
Sherrie, Wm., and gutta percha agent, 14 and 16 North street
aStewart, Wm., 56 North street

Builders and Carpenters
Adams, John, 44 North Thomas st.
Anderson, James, 11 May street
Bailie, Charles, 60 Nelson street
Boyd, Bankhead, 78 Joy street
Boyd, William, 9 North Thomas st.
Brown, John, jun., & Co., Riley's place
Brown, John, sen., 3 Gloucester street
Byrne, Thomas, 32 Great George's st.
Carlisle, James, 85 Donegall street
Chambers, Alex., 101 Joy street
Clements, R., 7 Campbell's buildings
Crawford, Saml., 32½ Gt. George's st.
Crawford, William, 6 Antrim road
Clements, Alex., Shankhill road
Connor, Jas., 16 & 18 Grattan street
Connor, John, 37 York street
Cooper, David, 20 Great Patrick st.
Davison, John, 137 Durham street
Entwisle, James, 18 Eliza street
Fulton, David, 18 Ship street
Garrett, James, 21 May street
Garrett, Henry, 2 College court
Gregg, Cranston, Malone
Hamilton, James, 85 Joy street
Kent, Archibald, 36 York street
Lowry, John, 46½ York street
Magee, John, 11 Trafalgar street
Maxwell, Wm., 38 Fountain street
M'Ateer, Patrick, 59 Cromac street
M'Bride, Thomas, 15 Police square
M'Connell, Bernard, 27 Townsend st.
M'Cracken, Jas., 29 & 31 Barrack st.
M'Crea, Archibald, 53 Peter's hill
M'Cune, William, 12½ Castle street

M'Dowell, Thomas, 40 York street
M'Laughlin, Henry, 4 Wall street
M'Lorinan, Hugh, 46 Institution place
Munce, James, Eliza street
Neeson, Francis, 1 King street
Plunkett, James, Durham street
Purse, Arthur, 58 York street
Purse, John, 27 Pilot street
Ross, John, 27 Joy street
Ross, Wm., Ross street, Falls road
Rowan, Andrew, 5 Thomas street
Smith and Ross, Russell street
Smith, Alexander, 23 Joy street
Smith, James, 23 North Thomas st.
Smith William, Devis street
Strachan, John, 7½ Gt. George's st.
Taylor, Robert, 63 Joy street
Taylor, William, 56 Joy street
Wilson, William, 70 Joy street
Williams, William, 11½ Cromac street

Butchers
Those marked (a) sell poultry & game
Adams, Robert, 43 Edward street
aAndrews, Wm., 3 Hammond's court
aBlackwood, Charles, 20 Corn market
Boston, James, 45 Hercules street
Brady, James, 16 Edward street
Branagh, Patrick, 15¼ Hercules street
Branagh, David, 17 Hercules street
Branagh, John, 24 Hercules street
Brannigan, Patrick, 44 Hercules st.
Britton, Mary, 49 Hercules street
Boylan, Thomas, 22 Hercules street
Burke, John, 53 Hercules street
Burke, James, 69 Hercules street
Burns, James, 57 Hercules street
Campbell, George, 12 Henrietta street
Campbell, Hugh, 19 Hercules street
Carroll, Patrick, 19¼ Great Edward st.
Clarke, Aeneas, 7 York street market
Clay, Samuel, Calender street
Close, James, 43 Rosemary street
Colgan, Edward, 5 Hammond's court
aColgan, John, 1 Corn market
Cooney, James, 23 Hercules street
Davy, Charles, 19 Hercules street
Davy, James, 13 Hercules street
Davy, William, 41 Hercules street
Davy, John, 79 Hercules street
Davy, John, 87 Hercules street
Davy, Arthur, 74 Hercules street
Dinnen, David, 5 Castle market
Dinnen, James, 3 Castle market
Dinnen, James, 33½ Talbot street

PROFESSIONS, TRADES, &c.

aDowling, Arthur, 11 Corn market
Drain, John, 55 Hercules street
Dugan, James, 31 Hercules street
Dunlop, John, 11¼ Cromac street
Fagan, Terence, 50 Talbot street
Ferguson, David, 1 Castle market
Ferguson, David, 34 Hercules street
Flannigan, George, 13 Hercules place
Fox, Thomas, 101 York street
Franklin, Charles, 56 Hercules street
aFranklin, Joseph, 3 York street
Gaffikin, Thomas, 13 Corn market
aGaffikin, James D., 21 Corn market
aGaffikin, John, 25 Corn market
Garrett, Mary, 25 Hercules street
Garrett, William, 59 Waring street
Gordon, John, 64 Hercules street
Grimes, Thomas, 48 Hercules street
Hayes, John, 11 Barrack street
Hennesey, John, 61 Hercules street
Hamill, Arthur, 7 Hercules street
Hughes, William, 86 Millfield
aHunter, Alex., 23 Donegall street
Kelly, William, 15 Barrack street
Keys, David, 20 Hercules street
Largy, Thomas, 19 Great Edward st.
Louden, Dennis, 136 North street
Loughran, Ann, 16 Castle market
Loughran, John, 194 North street
Loughran, John, 29 Talbot street
Magee, John, 3 Hercules street
May, James, Bridge end, B.carrett
Mercer, John, 67 Hercules street
Miller, Thomas, 66 Hercules street
Moore, Hugh, 83 Hercules street
Moore, Henry, 59 Hercules street
Morrell, Rose, 11 Hercules street
Morrell, James, 5 Hercules street
Morrell, Andrew, 75 Hercules street
Morrell, John, 38 Hercules street
Morrell, Thomas, 35½ York street
Morgan, Hiram, 4 Castle market
M'Aleavy, Hugh, Bridge end, B.carrett
M'Aleavy, Thos., Bridge end, B.carrett
M'Anally, Bernard, 63 Barrack street
M'Anally, Patrick, 71 Hercules street
M'Anally, Simon, 83½ Hercules street
M'Areavy, John, 21 Hercules street
M'Cann, Patrick, 28 Hercules street
M'Comish, James, 17 Cromac road
M'Connell, Henry, 22 John street
M'Geough, Charles, 64 Barrack st.
M'Garell, John, 71 Peter's hill
M'Kenna, John, 31 Edward street
M'Kenna, J., 3 (south side) Albert sq.
M'Mahon, Thomas, 32 John street

M'Mahon, John, 73 Hercules street
M'Quilan, Cornelius, 3 York street
M'Sorley, John, 51 Hercules street
O'Neill, James, 50 Barrack street
O'Neill, John, 7 Devis street
Parker, James, 11¼ Cromac street
Parker, Thomas, 47 Hercules street
Parker, Thos., jun., 63 Waring street
Price, Henry, 99 Peter's hill
Quee, William, 17 Durham street
Ramsay, James, 72 Hercules street
Rice, John, 33 Hercules street
Rice, James, 85 Hercules street
Rice, Ann, 16 Hercules street
Roney, James, 76 Hercules street
Savage, Michael, 7 York street
Scott, John, 21 Great Edward street
Scott, George, 16 Hercules street
Scott, John, jun., York street
Shaw, Samuel, 39 Hercules street
Shearon, Daniel, 80 Hercules street
Stewart, Andrew, 20 Great Edward st.
Stewart & Cleery, 8 Hercules place
Stokesberry, Wm., 37 Hercules street
Stokesberry, Charles, 81 Hercules st.
Taylor, Wm. John, 43 John street
Thomas, Wm., 8 Gamble street and 1 Ormond market
Toley, Denis, 89 Hercules street
Welsh, Robinson, Garmoyle street
Whisker, James, 31 Hercules place & 50 Rosemary street

Butter Merchants

Bell, Clements, 46 Edward street, Gt. Patrick street, & 15 Butter market
Bailie, Joseph, 14 Butter market
Biggar, Thomas, 8 and 10 William st.
Biggar, Joseph, 44 John street
Duffield, S., 6 Butter market
Erwin, Thomas, 10 Butter market
Erwin, John, 12 Butter market
Frazer, Mr., 1 Johnston's court
Frazer, James, 7 Butter market
Gelston, William, 40 Tomb street
Hughes, William, 68 York street
Moore, Samuel, 13 Butter market
M'Alinden, Felix, 11 Butter market
M'Comb, James, 8 Butter market
M'Connell, Samuel, 22 & 24 Academy street and 18 Butter market
M'Guigan, Hugh, 62 Great Patrick st.
M'Kinney, Peter, 5 Butter market
M'Kenney, Peter, 47 Edward street
Scott, James, 1 Butter market

Smith, John and Thomas, 6 Tomb st.
Smith, John, 13 Brougham street
Ware, William, 68 Great Patrick street

Button Blue Manufacturers
Christie, John, 3 Frederick street
Craig, John, 9 Washington street

Cabinet Makers
Thus marked (a) are also upholsterers.
Campbell, James, 7 Ann street
aClarke, William P., 5 Fountain street
Derby, Thomas, 5 Nelson street
aGilmore, Brothers, 21 Donegall place
Gordon, John, 64 and 65 Smithfield
Gowdy, Charles, 57 Edward street
Gray, Wm., 14 William street south
Hennesy, David, 35 Rosemary street
Hughes, Thomas, 5 Edward street
Ivers, Timothy, 10 Donegall place buildings
Kelly, John, 9 Ann street
Lattimore, Samuel, 4 Church street
Maxwell, James, 41 Donegall street
Nimack, Joseph, 12½ Castle street
Quaile, William, 34 Donegall street
Ruddell, David, 68 Smithfield
aSloan, Archibald, 33 Castle place
Thompson, William, 10 Talbot street
Vauce, Wm., 21 Catherine st. north

Canvass Manufacturers
Abbott, Joseph, Corporation street; Shankhill road
Lemon, James, Queen's square; Ballymacarrett

Carpenters
SEE BUILDERS AND CARPENTERS.

Carpet and Damask Warerooms
Girdwood, James, 44 High street
Hardy, Thomas, 35 and 37 High st.
Staunton, Moses, 9 Donegall place

Carriers Quarters
Adams, James, 12 Great Patrick st.
Allen, James, 23 William street south
Ball, James, 164 North street
Duncan, Adam, 104 North street
Fowler, Patrick, 4 Gamble street
Irwin, Mathew, 184 North street
Murphy, Peter, 17 Barrack street
M'Roberts, Samuel, 11 Gt. Edward st.
Quinn, Hugh, 4 Talbot street

Rodgers, E., 11 Upper Church lane
Rowan, James, 54 Great Patrick st.
Stewart, J. W., 10 Marlborough street
Wallace, James, 10 Marlborough st.

Carvers, Gilders, and Picture Frame Makers
Bodel, John, 6 Hercules place
Flannigan, George, 13 Hercules place
Gaffikin, Robert, 7 Arthur square
Kean, Francis, (carver) 38 Academy st
M'Cabe, S., 15 Academy street
Patterson, Joseph, 23 Hercules place
Silo, Modesto, 11 Arthur square

Cheesemongers
Green, Ralph (& grocer), 4 Waring st.
Mark, David (& grocer), 28 Skipper st.
M'Dowell, Edward, Police square
Stavely, William, 5 Johnston's court
Walls, Robert, 6 Hammond's court

Chemists, Manufacturing
Crawford, Alexander, 26 Mill street
Vitriol Works, Gregg's row, Ballymacarrett, James W. Moncrieff, proprietor; William M'Leish, manufacturing chemist
Vitriol Works, Lagan village, Ballymacarrett, William Boyd and Sons, proprietors

Chimney Sweepers
Cunningham, Jas., 11 M'Tier's court
Gallagher, Nicholas, M'Tier's court
Graham, John, 5 Academy court
Graham, Thomas, 45 Birch street
Mitchell, John, 58 Millfield
Mullan, Neill, 5 M'Tier's court
Shields, Charles, 3 M'Tier's court

China, Glass & Delf Warehouses
Those marked (a) are glass only
Billsland, Jane, 4 Donegall place
Calwell, James, 35 Great Patrick st.
Greig, James and Wm., 110 High st.
Harkness, Mrs., 56 High street
aHarrison, Eliza, 10 Castle buildings
Marshall, Joseph, 16 Rosemary street
aRoss, O'Connor, & Co., 28, 30 High st.
Wilkinson, J., 108 High street

Civil Engineers and Land Surveyors
Allen, Wm., 10 James street south

PROFESSIONS, TRADES, &c.

Firth, James, 15 Harmony place
Frazer, James (surveyor), M'Larnon's buildings, Ballymacarrett
Godwin, John, Ulster Railway
Hanna, Daniel, 8 College street
Hastings, William (town surveyor), 8 North Queen street
Lanyon, Charles, 1 Upper Queen st.
Moore, Wm., 18 Chichester street
M'Henry, Paul, 31 Arthur street
M'Nea, James, 95 York street
Robinson, George, 16 Harmony place
Smith, George (Harbour office), Cliftonville

Clock and Watchmakers

SEE ALSO JEWELLERS & SILVERSMITHS

Chapman, James, 64 High street
Dickson, Matthew, 3 John street
Fehrenbach, John, 19 Corn market
Ferguson, A., 1 Church lane
Gilbert, Wm., and Son, 15 High st.
Gilbert, Edward, 43 High street
Gray, John, 18 Castle place
Gribben, Edward, 13 High street
Kirner, R., 18 Church lane
Lee and Son, 57 High street
Lowry, John, 19 King street
Macartney, J. N., 6 Donegall place
M'Conagill, James, 37 Castle place
M'Farlane, John, 93 North street
Neill, Brothers, 23 High street
Rolleston, James, 3 Castle place
Shaw, Wm. John, 17 John street
Thompson, John, 67 North street
Wallace, John, 49 High street
Wilson, James, 7 High street

Clothes Dealers

Boomer, Fanny, Garmoyle street
Campbell, Francis, 29 Hercules place
Campbell, Patrick, 4 Hercules place
Campbell, John, 44 Rosemary street
Casey, Jeremiah, 37 Smithfield
Cuming, Edward, 49 Smithfield
Dolan, Miles, 8 Berry street
Drummond, John, 35 Berry street
Fulton, George, 23 Berry street
Fulton, Ann Jane, 20 Berry street
Gibson, Jane, 38 Corporation street
Gordon, John, 10 Berry street
Gordon, George, 7 Berry street
Gregory, Bunting, 2 Smithfield
Griffith, James, 39 Berry street
Griffith, Elizabeth, 41 Berry street
Griffith, James, 5 Berry street
Griffith, James, 26 Berry street
Grimes, Michael, 9 Berry street
Hagan, Henry, Smithfield
Hamill, Alexander, 8½ Berry street
Harkin, Peter, 2 and 3 Berry street
Harkin, Peter, 10 Hercules street
Hughes, Allen, 49 Berry street
Jones, Richard, 6 Berry street
Keatley, Samuel, 11 Chapel lane and 36 Rosemary street
Kelly, Maria, 1 Smithfield
Killian, Mary, 20 Kennedy's row
Kingan, Mary, 46 Smithfield
Ledgett, Richard, 31 Berry street
Lennon, Richard, 22 Berry street
Loughran, Samuel, 45 Smithfield
Lyons, James, 51 Berry street
Lyons, James, 26 Chapel lane
Mallaghan, Henry, 26 Berry street
Monaghan, Thomas, 4 Berry street
Montgomery, Daniel, 33 Smithfield
Morris, Bridgett, 23 Academy street
Mullen, James, 20 Marquis street
M'Aleese, Thomas, 43 Smithfield
M'Clean, Sarah, 29 Berry street
M'Curry, Catherine, 3 Smithfield
M'Dowell, Robert, 45 Berry street
M'Ginley, George, 34 Berry street
M'Keldin, John, 24 Corporation street
M'Kenna, Stephen, 27 Berry street
M'Laughlin, William, 36 Berry street
Orem, Jane, 25 Black's place
Porter, William, and Son, 28 Berry st.
O'Hagan, Bernard, 22 Marquis street
O'Hagan, Bernard, 7 Smithfield
O'Hagan, John, 8 Smithfield
O'Reilly, Thomas, 4 Berry street
Quinn, Peter, 3 Queen's square
Reilly, John, 11 Berry street
Rodgers, Patrick, 42 Smithfield
Sands, Susan, 44 Smithfield
Sheals, John, 15 Berry street
Smith, Mary, 10 Smithfield
Stewart, John, 13 Berry street
Stewart, Sarah, 37 Berry street
Stewart, James, 53 Berry street
Stewart, William, 47 Berry street
Trotter, James, 65 Corporation street
Trotter, John C., 17 Queen's square
Twigg, Hugh, 25 Rosemary street
Watson, William (wholesale), 11 Hercules street

Clothes Renovators

Graham, James, 40 Little Patrick st.
M'Neill, James, 11 Lancaster street
Kane, John, 34 Millfield

PROFESSIONS, TRADES, &c.

Clothiers

Albion Cloth Company, 22 High st.
Arnold, John (Heimatemporian), 45 High street
Hamilton & M'Cullough, 75 High st.
Killen, William, 68 High street
King, Robert, 21 Donegall street
Levy, Mier, and Co., 61 High street
Marshall, James, 5 Donegall street
Munce, Alexander, 17 High street
M'Gee, John G., and Co. (Pantechnetheca), 46 and 48 High street
M'Grotty, John B. & Co., 23 Bridge street
M'Vicker, John, 3 Donegall place
O'Neill, William, Regent buildings, Victoria street
Spackman, William, corner Victoria street and High street
Stevenson, Samuel, 17 Arthur street

Coach Factories

Bathurst, Wm., Police place and 28 Chichester street
Carty, David, 18¼ Castle street
Duprey, H., 11 Fountain street
Graham and Magee, 26 Chichester st.
Kennedy, John, 1 Montgomery street
Miller, Wm., 30 Gloucester street
Smith and Waugh, 20 Chichester st.

Coach Offices

Ballynahinch & Castlewellan, 25 Great Edward st.; Jane Anderson, agent
Ballynahinch, 31 & 31½ Great Edward street; D. Smith, agent
Derry, Larne, Antrim, and Crumlin, 6 North street; Mrs. Magee
Downpatrick, Portaferry, and Bangor, 68 Ann street; Hugh Millen, agent
Downpatrick and Portaferry, 49 Ann street; John Featherston, agent
Dublin & Enniskillen (mail), 15 Castle place; Edward Greer, proprietor

Coal Merchants

Alexander, Arthur, 134 Nort street
Barclay, John, 21 Tomb street
Barkley, Wm. M., 97 Queen's square
Bell, William, 114 Ann street
Canavan, John, 176 North street
Charley, John, & Co., Prince's Steammill lane
Crace, Henry, 7 Prince's dock
Craig, Hugh, 7 Queen's quay
Cush, Michael, 11 Queen's quay
Douglas, William, 20 Waring street
Garland, James, 5 Queen's quay
George, Thomas, 6 Queen's quay
Hanna, John, 1 Queen's quay
Johnston, Malcolm, 2 Queen's quay
Kelly, Samuel, 43 Cromac street
Lindsay, Samuel, 10 Cromac road
Lindsay, Patrick, 8 Queen's quay
Massey, William, 9 Queen's quay
M'Cune, Richard, 17 Albert square
M'Tear, George, 33 Donegall quay
Newett, William, 9 Queen's square
Newett, Robert, 4 Queen's quay
Ruabon and Blenkinsopp Company, 3 Castle Chambers
Shiel, Thomas, 3 Queen's quay
Wilson, John, 40¼ North Queen st.
Wright, Philip, 10 Queen's quay

Commission Merchants and Agents

Alexander, Robert, 2 Donegall square West
Atkinson, Robert, 10 Hill street
Beath, J. and J., 29 Donegall street
Bell, R. & J., & Co., 4 Mustard street
Bell & Kirker, 4 & 6 Gt. Patrick st.
Benn, William, 9 Donegall place
Boyce, William, 3 Castle Chambers
Boyle, Samuel, 16 Ann street
Burden, F., 29 Waring street
Clendinning, Andw., 10 Rosemary st.
Colvil, Auld, and Co., 74 Waring st.
Conland, John, Linen hall
Connor, David, 27½ Ann street
Cramsie, John C., 74 Waring street
Creeth, Richard, and Co., 12 Warehouse lane
Cunningham, Josias, and Co., 41 Waring street
Elliott, A. and J., and Co., 1 Donegall square east
Ferrie & Campbell, 11 Corporation st.
Folingsby, T. G., & Co., 15 Albert sq.
Gamble, William, 43 Waring street
Hamilton, James, 11 Queen's square
Henderson, Wm. D., 42 Waring st.
Henderson, R., 23, 25 Donegall quay
Heyn, Gustavus, 1 Henry street
Hume, Thomas, 5 Gloucester street
Hunter, John, jun., and Co., 35 Waring street
Hunter, Wm. and Thos., 24 Victoria Chambers
Hunter, Thomas, 5 Gloucester street

Kerr, John, 22 Skipper street
Larmour, Wm., Victoria buildings, Victoria street
Lyons, Robert, 24 Great Edward st.
Macauley, Jasper, and Co., Albert sq.
Magill, Joseph, 34 Fountain street
Mercer, J. M., Victoria buildings
Munster, Paul L., Corporoation street
M'Connell, James, 7 Corporation st.
M'Clure, W., & Son, Corporation st.
M'Donnell, John, & Co., Skipper st.
M'Entire, John, 15½ Fountain street
M'Ilwrath & Co., 4 Donegall st. place
M'Neill, Hugh, 29 Waring street
M'Pherson, Peter, and Co., 15 Rosemary street
Neild, James, 3 Castle Chambers
Pelling, P., & Co. (weaving), 37 John st.
Pim, Geo. C., & Co., 43 Donegall quay
Pim, John. 20 Waring street
Plunkett, Francis, 1 St. Anne's buildings
Praeger, John, & Co., Fountain street
Richardson, Brothers, and Co., Corporation street
Rodgers, Wm., and Co., 26 Victoria chambers
Scott, Robert, 74 Waring street
Sharp, Thomas M. (general broker), 17 Donegall street
Shaw, W. S., 2 Waring street place
Shaw, Ed., & Co., Victoria chambers
Smith, Robert, 4, 6 Rosemary street
Stevenson, J. S., 1 Commercial buildings
Symmonds, Stephen R., 33 Mill street, and 6½ York street
Vance, Samuel, 36 Waring street
Wallace, Thos., 6 Elliott's court
White and Clendinning, 2 Donegall street place
Wood, Geo. P., & Co., 1 Talbot st.

Confectioners

Adams, Rose Ann, 185 North street
Bunting, Robert, 64 North street
Church, Mrs., 20 Mill street
Clarke, John, 70 Cromac street
Cochrane, Thomas, 38 Cromac street
Donnelly, Robert, 4 Bridge street
Dunlop, David, 1 Arthur square
Elliott, Samuel, 86 North street
Fowler, Patrick, 146 North street
Frazer, Roderick, 53 Talbot street
Gardner, Mrs. Eliza, 31 Castle place
Graham, John, 123 North street
Grant, James, 3 Donegall street
Gribben, Thomas, 13 John street
Godfrey, Mary, 4 Charlemont street
Hay, William, 20 Church lane
Hunter, Mary, 99 North street
Hyndman, Isabella, 24 Church lane
Jackson, Robert, 19 Winetavern st.
Kennedy, Samuel, 6 York st. market
Laughlin, James, 172 North street
Linden, William, 16 Corn market
Mahir, P. H., 74 Donegall street and 1 John street
Mehair, Edward, 11 Mill street
Murphy, Arthur, 122 North street
M'Kee, John, 30 Union street
M'Millan, Ruth, York street
Ogston, Mrs. Mary, 39 High street
Orr, John, 18 Robert street
Rice, Rose, 17 Hercules place
Thompson, Charles, 2 Donegall place
Walker, John, 61 Donegall street
Walker, David, 19 Bridge street

Consuls and Vice-Consuls
OF FOREIGN POWERS.

Austria—John Praeger, Fountain st.
Belgium—John Hind, jun., Abbey st.
Denmark and Sweden—Paul L. Munster, Corporation street
France—A. Duffin, 28 Waring street
Greece—Gustavus Heyn, 1 Henry st.
Hamburg—Gustavus Heyn, 1 Henry st.
Holland—Gustavus Heyn, 1 Henry st.
Mexico—Joseph Magill, Fountain st.
Portugal—Jas. MacAdam, jun., 7 Commercial buildings
Prussia—Gustavus Heyn, 1 Henry st.
Russia—Gustavus Heyn, 1 Henry st.
Spain—Gustavus Heyn, 1 Henry st.
Turkey—Gustavus Heyn, 1 Henry st.
Two Sicilies—Gust. Heyn, 1 Henry st.
United States—Valentine Holmes, 5 and 6 Commercial buildings
Venezuela—Robert Alexander, 2 Donegall square west

Copper and Tinplate Workers

Baxter, James, 71 North Queen st.
Bloomfield, Wm., 27 John street
Bloomfield, Edward, 41 John street
Clements, John, 26 (sheds) Smithfield
Coates, Wm., 12 Castle street
Coates, John, 16 Torrens' market
Cochran, Wm., 14 Great Edward st.
Gamble, David, 4 Cargill street

Gilmer, Hugh, 30 (sheds) Smithfield
Ireland, George, 8 Cargill street
Ireland and M'Neill, 17 Corn market
Mills, Hugh, 19 (sheds) Smithfield
Moorehead, Archd., 9 Pottinger's entry
M'Collough, James, 1 Chester st.
M'Conkey, Hiram, 13 (sheds) Smithfield
Sanders, Thomas, 115 North street
Sergison, James, 72 Ann street
Waters, Thomas, 27 Corporation st.

Coopers

Canning, John, 42 Green street
Cannon, Wm., 11 Grattan court
Cleland, William, 18 Gordon street
Crawford, Charles, 7 Grattan court
Cromie, Hugh, 26 Shipboy street
Davis, Henry, 35 Barrack street
Dunn, John, 25 Moffet street
Ewart, Samuel, 99 York street
Galloway, Richard, 51 Grattan street
Ganston, Francis, 13 Mustard street
Gilland, John, 41 Talbot street
Greer, John, 45 Grattan street
Harper, William, 8 Earl street
Mackwood, John, 32 Green street
Martin, William, 26 Mustard street
Moorehead, James, 25 Earl street
Moorehead, Ross, 30 Little Patrick st.
Montgomery, S., 63 Union street
Mulholland, E., 16 William st. south
Murray, Edward, 25 Green street
M'Caslin, John, 24 Mustard street
M'Fadden, James, 26 Tomb street
M·Farland, A., 56 & 58 Great Patrick street
M'Gonigal, John, 40 Edward street
M'Quaide, Patrick, 13 Millfield
Savage, James, 37 Lancaster street
Savage, Rowland, 84 Nelson street
Scott, Robert, 20 Gordon street
Smith, Bernard, Prince's court
Stewart, William, 10 Nelson street
Sweney, John, 69 Great Patrick street
Thomson, James, 7 Edward street
Wyley, Alexander, Ashmore street

Cork Cutters

Hamilton, William, 4 Hercules street
Hamilton, R., 46½ Rosemary street
Hughes, James, 7 Charlemont street
Kirwan, Richard, 27 Rosemary street
Murdock, John, 15 Hercules street

Cotton Spinners

Cochrane, James, Bangor; High street
Gamble, Jas., Ballynure; 26 Academy st.
Gamble, J. & W., Woodburn; 26 Academy street
Lepper, Messrs., New Lodge road
M'Cracken, Francis, 8 York lane

Cotton Yarn Merchants

Clarke and Drummond, 7 Commercial court; S. Hart, representative
Gould, Thos. (agent), 7 York street
Hunter, John, jun., & Co., 35 Waring st.
Macnish, J.O., & Co., 7 Donegall st. pl.

Cutlers and Surgical Instrument Makers

Bell, Thomas, 15 Corn market
Hughes, Patrick, 12 Francis street
King, Cunningham, 6 Cromac road
Wilson, William, 3 Skipper street

Damask Manufacturers

Andrews, Michael, Royal Damask Factory, Ardoyne
Blain, Messrs., Shankhill road
Roddy, Robert, 18 Donegall street

Dentists

Barnett, Richard, 1 Wellington place
Barnett, Richard, M.D., 1 Wellington place
Davis, Charles, 22 Arthur street
Grattan, Thos., 11 College square east
Turner, James, 13 Chichester street

Designers

Agar, Alexander O., Charlotte street
Ashcroft, Joshua, 9 Henrietta street
Blair, Alexander, 28 Boundary street
Campbell, John, 3 Stanley place
Gilmour, David, 3 Henrietta street
Ireland, John, 8 Stanfield street
M'Kee, James, 3 James's place
M'Kenzie, Matthew, 21 Nelson street
Nesbit, David, 63 Academy street

Distillers

SEE RECTIFYING DISTILLERS.
Mackenzie, Shaw, & Co., 37 and 39 Barrack street

Dressmakers

SEE MILLINERS AND DRESSMAKERS

PROFESSIONS, TRADES, &c.

Druggists and Chemists
Blackburn, Robt., & Co., 89 North st.
Corry, Thos. C. S., 13 Victoria street
Curran, Waring, 22 Bridge street
Dickson, Isabella, 73 North street
Dobbin, William, 18, 20, 45 and 47 North street
Eakin, William, and Co., 52 Donegall street
Grattan and Co., 12 Corn market
Kelly, J., and Co., Victoria street
Mercer and Kerr, 38 and 40 North st.
Marshall, William, and Co., 67 and 100 High street
Marshall, James D., 8 High street
Robinson, Henry, 114 High street
Walkington, Edwd., 13 Rosemary st.
Wheeler, Thos. K., 11 Arthur street

Drysalters, Oil and Colour Merchants
Charnock, Brothers, 65 Corporation sq.
Crawford, Alexander, 26 Mill street
Cuddy, John, 42 Church lane
Curran, Waring, 22 Bridge street
Dobbin, William, 18, 20, 45 and 47 North street
Eakin, Wm., and Co., 52 Donegall st.
Kavanagh, Jas., 33 and 35 North st.
MacAdam and Co., 31 Donegall st.
M'Kendry, H., and Co., 6 Waring st.
Pelan and M'Mullan, 26 Corn market
Prenter, N. A., 8 and 10 Cotton court
Smyth, James H., and Co., 7 North st.
Tennant, Chas., and Co., 37 John st.

Dyers
Browne, George (silk), 26 Arthur st.
Donnelly, John, 31 Bank lane
Green, Alexander, 51 Boundary street
Harvey, James, 57 Boundary street
Kane, John (silk), 34 Millfield
Maguire, John, 14 Bank lane
Maguire, John, 15 Castle street
M'Clean, Mrs. Jane (silk), 7 Mill st.

Earthenware and Glass Dealers
SEE ALSO CHINA AND GLASS WAREHOUSES.

Monaghan, B., 21 (sheds) Smithfield
Mooney, C., 32 Smithfield
M'Ateer, Hugh, 28 (sheds) Smithfield
M'Connell, Frs., 22 (sheds) Smithfield
M'Lorinan, Henry, 42 Smithfield
Tosh, Catherine, 45 (sheds) Smithfield

Electrical and Optical Manufacturer
Cumine, James A., 168 North street

Emigration Agents
Beattie, John, 2 Grattan street
Carlisle, Wm., 57 Corporation street
Douglass, Wm., 59 Corporation street
M'Crea, Samuel, 37 Waring street
Macdonald, James, 59 Waring street and Prince's dock
Quinn, John, 14 Pottinger's entry
Quinn, Thomas, 57 Waring street
Wilkinson, Wm., Queen's square

Engravers, Lithographers, and Copperplate Printers
Agnew, W. and G., Arthur square
Archer and Sons, 27 and 29 Castle pl.
Beattie, Wm. J., 21 Rosemary street
Hamilton, Robert, 33 Castle street
Hill, George L., 9 Castle street
Johnston, Wm., 25 Waring street
Lewis, Joseph, North street place
Miller, Wm., 25 Castle street
M'Cracken, Thos., & Co., 5 Crown entry
M'Kibbin, John, and Co., 67 High st.
Roberts, Thomas, 5 King street
Smith, J. and T., 25 Castle street
Thompson, Robert, 4 Castle street
Ward, Marcus, & Co., 6 Corn market

Farriers
SEE HORSE SHOERS.

Feather Merchants
Burke, John, 53 Hercules street
Dowling, A., 11 Corn market
MacVeigh, Brothers, 13 Church lane

File Cutters
Hill, John, 24 and 26 West street
Thompson, Adam, 19 Little Donegall st.

Fish (Dried) Merchants
Arrott, Isaac, 34 Waring street
Crawford, Jas., 13, 15 Corporation st.
Frazer and Finch, 59 Waring street
M'Garry, Robert, 45 Tomb street
Methuen, James, 12½ Tomb street

Fishmongers
AND SHELL FISH DEALERS.

Bradley, James, 8 Legg's lane
Fish market, Police square

PROFESSIONS, TRADES, &c.

Ferris, John, Police square
Kane, Thomas, Wilson's court
Magee, John, 3 Joy's entry
Meenan, Bernard, 9 Castle market
M'Bride, James, 65 Market street
Simpson, Jas., 15, 19 Pottinger's entry

Flax and Tow Merchants

Carter and Martin, 17 Rosemary st.
Cunningham, J., & Co., 41 Waring st.
Cuppage, John, and Co., 9 and 10 Donegall street place
Duffin, Charles, & Co., 28 Waring st.
Finlay, John, jun., 6 Police square
Gamble, Wm., 43 Waring street
Hunter, John, jun., 35 Waring street
M'Clelland, Hugh, 22 Hill street
Preston, John and Co., 12 Calender st.
Richardson, Brothers, and Co., Corporation street
Savage, John, 22 Skipper street
Ure, James and Co., Grattan street
Wood, George P., and Co., 1 Talbot st.

Flax Spinners

Bells & Calvert, Whitehouse; 4 Mustard street
Boyd, J., & Son, Pound Mill, Durham st.
Boomer, J., & Co., Falls road; Waring st.
Charters, John, and Co., Falls road; Bridge street place
Cowan, Wm., and Co., Whiteabbey; 17 York street
Craig, A. W., & Co., Falls road
Cuppage, John, and Co., Lurgan; 9 & 10 Donegall street place
Davidson and Chermside, Drumaness mill; 27 Pottinger's entry
Duffin, Chas., & Co., 28 Waring street
Dunmurry Spinning Co., Dunmurry
Emerson, John, Ballysillan
Ewart, Wm., and Son, Crumlin road; Donegall street
Firth, Thomas, 29 Eliza street
Fisher John, & Co., Francis street
German, Petty, and Co., Preston; 24 Rosemary street
Gordon and Co., Falls road
Grimshaw, James, and Son, Whitehouse; 28 Waring street
Grimshaw, E., Mossley; 28 Waring st.
Gunning and Campbell, Falls road
Herdman, J. and J., & Co., 40 Smithfield, and Sion mills, Strabane
Hind, John, and Sons, Durham street

Hughes, William, 13 North street
Hull, Hart, & Co., Falls road; Victoria buildings
Johnston and Carlisle, Crumlin road
Kennedy, James, and Son, Falls road; Waring street
Martin, John, Killyleagh; co. Down, 29 Ann street
Monkstown Spinning Co., 28 Waring st.
Montgomery, John, and Sons, Elmgrove; 11 Corporation street
Moreland, Cowan & Co., Ballymacarrett
Murphy, John, and Co., Linfield mill
M'Auley, Samuel (tow), 4 May street
Macaulay, P., Randalstown; 75 Donegall street
M'Connell and Kennedy, Falls road
M'Kee, James, Jennymount, York road
M'Kibbin, Robert, Conswater mill, Ballymacarrett
Owen-o'Cork Spinning Company, Beer's bridge; Talbot street
Richardson, J. N., Sons, and Owden, Bessbrook, Newry; 14 Donegall place
Rowan, John, and Sons, Milewater mill; York road
Shaw, Joseph, Celbridge; Victoria st.
Shaw & Houghton, Celbridge; Victoria street
Stevenson, James, Doagh
Thompson, Robert, Wolfhill; 1 Donegall square west
York street Spinning Company

Flour Merchants

Adams, James, 12 Great Patrick street
Bell & Kirker, 4 & 6 Great Patrick st.
Boyd, James, 162 North street
Brankin, Henry, 26 Great Patrick st.
Caruth, John, 189 North street
Clarke, John A., 21 Church lane
Coey, Jas., jun., Queen's quay, B.carrett
Colpoy, Richard, 112 North street
Crawford, Jane, 113 North street
Crawford, Alexander, 26 Mill street
Davidson, James, Bridge end, B.carrett
Flinn, Patrick, 15 Castle market
Halliday, Hugh, Waring street place
Henderson, Robt., 23 Donegall quay
Henderson, Wm. D., 42 Waring street
Hughes, Bernard, Donegall place and 71 Donegall street
Hume, Thomas, 5 Gloucester street
Ireland, Robert, 36 & 38 Prince's st.
Kennedy, A., 6 Castle market

PROFESSIONS, TRADES, &c. 379

Kirker, Archibald, 37 Cromac street
Larmour, William, 9 Albert square
Lowe, Hugh, 110 North street
Murphy, John, 4 Catherine st. north
Martin, Allen, 145 North street
Milford, John, 83 North street
M'Curtin & Riley, 31½ Chichester st.
Peel, Robert, 151 & 153 North street
Quigley, William, 16 Cromac street
Rice, Thomas, 7 Castle market
Thompson, James, 59 North street

Fruiterers and Green Grocers

Annesley, Wm., 1, 8 Hammond's court
Armstrong, Wm., 26 Hercules street
Austin, John, 15 Ormond market
Bamford, Mrs., 35 Market street
Boyle, Margaret, 17 Market street
Burke, Mary, 51 Cromac street
Cramsey, John, 56 York street
Crummey, Daniel, 5 York st. market
Curran, C., 12 and 13 Castle market
Dickson, Alexander, 18 Castle market
Dickson & M'Gredy, 10 Hammond's ct.
Erwin, Mrs., 26 Charlemont street
Ferguson, David, 25, 26 Castle market
Fox, Thomas, 101 York street
Glasgow, Mrs., 14 Castle market
Graham, James, 24 Ormond market
Henry, Mary, 24 Castle market
Hughes, John, 59 Waring street
Isles, Robert, 5 Market street
Johnston, Wm., 66 Mill street
Kane, Thomas, 2 Hammond's court
Murphy, Ann, 41 Dock street
M'Clements, James, 187 North street
M'Donnell, John, 17 Castle market
M'Donnell, John, 66 Market street
M'Ganarty, Hugh, 11 Ormond market
M'Gurk, Terence, 68 Mill street
M'Roberts, Hugh, 5 Ormond market
M'Vea, David, Cromac street
O'Connor, Sarah, 23 Castle market
O'Hare, Wm., 15 Market street
O'Hare, Rose, 13 Smithfield
O'Neill, Hugh, 3 North Queen street
Potts, J., (&poulterer) 3 Ormond market
Rodgers, George, 2 York street market

Furniture Brokers

Adams, Thomas, 20 (sheds) Smithfield
Bell, Chas. A., 51 (sheds) Smithfield
Burns, George, 52 (sheds) Smithfield
Collins, John E., Smithfield
Gordon, John, 12 (sheds) Smithfield
Gregory, Owen, 61 and 62 Smithfield
Hinds, John, 9 (sheds) Smithfield
Moore, Wm., 3 (sheds) Smithfield
Muntz, Robert, 62 (sheds) Smithfield
M'Cullough, G , 22 (sheds) Smithfield
Ruddell, David, 6 and 7 Smithfield
Ruddell, Wm., 25 (sheds) Smithfield
Stewart, James, 5 (sheds) Smithfield
Thompson, Saml.,55(sheds) Smithfield

Furriers

Davis, Charles N., 24 Castle place
Macoun, George, 23 and 25 Castle pl.
Sergison, Eliza, 72 Ann street

Gingham Manufacturers
SEE MUSLIN MANUFACTURERS.

Glass Manufacturers

Carson, Lamont, 1 Millfield
Ross, O'Connor, and Co., Short strand, Ballymacarrett; 28 & 30 High st.

Glue Manufacturers

Johnston, S. and W., 37 Mill street
Tucker, Edward, 27 Waring street

Grain Merchants

Anderson, James, 1 Gloucester street
Barnett, James, Smithfield
Bell & Kirker, 4 & 6 Gt. Patrick st.
Brankin, Henry, 26 Gt. Patrick st.
Gaussen, John, & Co., 11 Albert sq.
Haliday & M'Dowell, 8 Tomb street
Henderson, Robert, 23 Donegall quay
Henderson, Wm. D., 42 Waring st.
Heyn, Gustavus, 1 Henry street
Hughes, William, (corn) 13 North st.
Hughes, Bernard, 5 Donegall place
Hume, Thomas, 5 Gloucester street
Hunter, Jn, jun., & Co., 35 Waring st.
Larmour, William, 9 Albert square
Macaulay, Jasper, & Co., 9 Albert sq.
Mathews, Abraham, 51½ Cromac st.
Milford, John, 83 North street
Murphy, Daniel, 7 Gamble street
M'Areavy, John, 22 Cromac street
M'Entire, Jn., & Co., 15½ Fountain st.
M'Clure, Wm., & Son, Corporation st.
M'Curtin & Riley, 31½ Chichester st.
M'Kenzie, J., & Co., 37 Barrack st.
O'Neill, John, Lennon's lane
Pim, John, 20 Waring street
Quigley, William, Police square

2 K

Quigley, Samuel, 18 Police square
Richardson, Brothers, and Co., Corporation street

Grocers, Retail

SEE ALSO WHOLESALE GROCERS.

Those marked (*a*) are also spirit dealers

Adair, John, Falls road
Agnew, Esther, 52 Hercules street
Alexander, Andrew, 20 Moffet street
Alexander, Samuel, Ashmore st., Falls
*a*Allen, Alexander, 49 Lancaster st.
Allen, Daniel, 34 Grattan street
*a*Allen, James, 23 William st. south
*a*Anderson, James, Shankhill road
Anderson, William, 8 Hercules street
Bailie, James, Lagan village
Bain, Amelia, 70 Ann street
*a*Barker, Catherine, 5 Pilot street
Barron, Samuel, 160 North street
*a*Barry, Jas., & Co., 20, 22 Prince's st.
*a*Bayne, Ann, 13 Nile street
Bell, David, 87 North street
Bell, Timothy, 26 Corporation street
Bell, Mary, 43 Vere street
Bell, William, 34 Great Edward street
Beattie, James, 100 Old Lodge road
*a*Beatty, William, Old Lodge road
Blair, Eliza, 26 Nile street
*a*Blayney, Archd., Johnston's place, Ballymacarrett
*a*Bond, James, 15 Frederick street
*a*Boyd, Samuel, 59 Lettuce hill
*a*Boyle, Joseph, 62 Mill street
Boyle, Mary, 32 Grattan street
Brady, William 107 Peter's hill
Braithwaite, John, 6 Old Malone road
*a*Brown, Daniel, 39 Great Edward st.
Brown, John, 72 Green street
Brown, Mary, 2 Cullingtree street
*a*Brown, Mary, 12 George's lane
Brown, William, 6 Church street
Burns, Hugh, 52, 54 Alexander street
Camac, Eliza, 26 Collingwood street
Campbell, Francis, 53 Barrack street
*a*Campbell, Francis, 40 Hill street
Campbell, James, 29 Union street
Campbell, Joseph, 112 Cromac street
Campbell, Samuel, 12 Berry street
*a*Canmer, John, Lagan village
Carlin, Edward, 55 Verner street
Carlisle, John, 7 Marlborough street
*a*Carmichael, Samuel, 13 Gamble st.
Carmichael, Robert, 8 Garmoyle st.
*a*Carson, R., 36 Ashmore street, Falls

*a*Caruth, James, 41 Lancaster street
Caruth, John, 189 North street
*a*Casey, John, 127 & 129 North st.
Cherry, Richard, 51 Little Patrick st.
*a*Cinnamond, H., 23 Smithfield
*a*Clarke, Andrew, 47 Ann street
Clarke, Young, 78 Cromac street
*a*Clendinning, Jas., 1 Leadbetter place
*a*Clendinning, Jas., 1 Fleming's place
Close, James, 61 Little Patrick street
Close, John, 76 Barrack street
Colburn, William, 38 Green street
Coleman, Samuel, 66 Barrack street
Collier, S., 41 Durham street
Connor, Catherine, 2 Wilson street
Connor, James, Conway street
Connor, John, 1 East street
*a*Connor, J., 26, 28 Verner street
Connor, Robert, 14½ Peter's hill
Cooper, James, Ballymacarrett
Cotter, Robert, Durham street
*a*Coulter, Alexander, 29 Durham st.
Cousins, John, 50 Nelson street
Cousins, J. and W. R., 75 North st.
*a*Coyle, John, 13 Cromac road
*a*Craig, Thomas, 186 North street
Crawford, Eliza, 17 Mill street
Crawford, Hugh, 157 North street
*a*Crawford, John, jun., 25 Berry st.
Crawford, James, Cromac street
*a*Crosgrove, John, 16 Verner street
*a*Crossen, Margaret, Lagan village
Crothers, Moses, 69 Donegall street
Crothers, Mary A., 60 Cromac street
Culbert, Thomas, 90 Millfield
*a*Curran, Elizabeth, Keenan's place, Ballymacarrett
Cushnahan, E., 81 Carrick hill
*a*Daly, Francis, 57 Union street
Dalgleish, Alexander, 104 Peter's hill
Dargan, Richard, 18 Talbot street
Darling, John R., 112 Old Lodge road
Davidson, John, & Co., 15½ Castle pl.
*a*Davidson & Co., 40 Hercules street
*a*Dawson, William, 1 Sackville place
Dobbin, Alexander, 41 Townsend st.
Dobbs, John, 31 Stanfield street
*a*Dornan, Robert, 11 King street
Dougal, James, 65 Millfield
Dougherty, Hugh, 32 Hamill street
*a*Duff, J., 49 Gardiner street
*a*Duffy, William, Falls road
*a*Duncan, Nathaniel, 28, 30 Cromac st.
*a*Duncan, G., 1 Cromac street
Dunlop, James, 109 Carrick hill

PROFESSIONS, TRADES, &c.

aElliott, Agnes, 77 and 79 Peter's hill
Elliott, John, 16 Hamill street
Elliott, John, 133 North street
Elliott, John, 81 Union street
Elliott, John, Ballymacarrett
Elsler, Samuel, Falls road
Erskine, David, 14 Skipper street
Erskine, Robert, 159 Durham street
Erwin, Isabella, 1 Barrack street
Evans, George, 69 Smithfield
aEwart, Rachael, 22 Cromac road
aEwing, John, 11 Greenland street
aEwing, Samuel, 11 Mill street
aFawkner, Wm., 1 Bradbury place
aFenning, Thomas, 17 Marquis street
aFerguson, James, 38 Trafalgar street
aFinlay, Joseph, 56 North Queen street
aFitzpatrick, Bernard, 72 Donegall st.
Fleming, Johnston, Boundary street
aFox, Thomas, 101 York street
aFullerton, John, Hamilton street
Fullerton, Brothers, 17½ Cromac street
aGalt, Alexander, 6 Frederick street
Gamble, John, 2 Old Malone road
aGaw, Hugh, 29 Stanley street
George, Abel, 34 Smithfield
aGillis, John, 98 Corporation street
aGilliland, Thomas, 19 Grace street
Gilmore, Daniel, 54 Green street
aGilmore, Robert, 19 Ann street
Glenn, Alexander, 71 Durham street
Graham, Patrick, 105 Carrickhill
Graham, Hugh, Bridge end, B.carrett
Grant, Patrick, 68 Barrack street
aGreen, John, 14 Millfield
Grimmea, Thomas, 29 Alexander st.
aGunning, John, 21 Little George's st.
aHaddock, Wm., 15 and 17 Ann st.
Hagan, Ann, 45 Barrack street
aHanna, David, 23 Wilson street
aHanna, John, 16 Peter's hill
aHanna, John, 1 Boyd street
Hanna, Mary, 116 Millfield
Hare, John, Ballymacarrett
Harkin, Patrick, Shankhill road
Harper, Robert, 13 Little George's st.
Harvey, Thos., 32 Great Edward street
aHazlett, J., 8bankhill road
aHenderson, Alex., 30 Charles street
Henderson, William, 26 Hill street
Henesey, Joseph, 33 Little Donegall st.
aHeron, E., Keenan's place, B.carrett
Heron, Wm., 46 Great Patrick street
Higgins, John, Bridge end, B.carrett
aHilland, Chas., 23 and 25 Barrack st.

aHogg, Jane, 21 Pilot street
Hogg, William, 30 Ann street
aHolmes, James, North Queen street
aHope, George, 96 Millfield
aHull, William, 26 Cromac street
aHunter, John, 3 Little George's st.
Hunter, Eliza, 56 Cromac street
Ievers, Ann, 41 North street
Jackson, Margaret, Ballymacarrett
Jamison, John, 16 Cullingtree street
Johnston, Samuel, Shankhill road
Johnston, Eliza, 71 Nelson street
aJohnston, Alexander, 34 Cromac st.
Johnston, John, 20 Alexander street
Johnston, Ann, 66 Carrickhill
aJones, James, 54 Talbot street
aJones, John, 47 Cromac street
aKearney, John, 35 Peter's hill
aKearns, John, 24 Mill street
Kearns, Michael, 57 Mustard street
Kelly, Samuel, 43 Cromac street
aKennedy, David, 10 Henrietta street
Kennedy, John, 31 Alexander street
Kernohan, Hugh, 61 Grattan street
Kerr, Hugh, 21 Lancaster street
aKerr, John, 18 Smithfield
aKerr, Samuel, 18 and 20 Peter's hill
aKing, Robert, 1 and 3 Mill street
aKinney, Felix, 11 and 13 Durham st.
aKinney, John, 51 North Queen street
aKirker, Thomas, 22 Devis street
Kirkpatrick, Charles, 1 Queen's square
Kirkpatrick, Jane, Ballymacarrett
aKirkpatrick, James, Ballymacarrett
Lamp, Daniel, 12 Grattan street
Larmour, Hugh, 23 Bradbury place
Lennon, John, 17 Carrickhill
aLennon, Patrick, 60 Mill street
Lorimer, Mrs., 13 Academy street
Loudon, Thomas, Pilot street
aLoughran, Thomas, 75 Mill street
aLoughran, John, 2 Peter's hill
Lowe, Hugh, 110 North street
aLundy, John, 64 Millfield
Magee, James, 32 Hercules street
Magee, James, 16 John street
Magee, Daniel, 27 Old Lodge road
aMagee, James, 21 Union street
uMaguire, Ann, 20½ Chapel lane
aMaginnis, Mary, 113 Millfield
aMallart, Osly, Lagan village
Mark, David, 28 Skipper street
aMartin, Allen, 145 North street
aMartin, Robert, 32 Great Patrick st.
aMartin, James, 3 Bradbury place

PROFESSIONS, TRADES, &c.

Mateer, C., 1 Wesley place
Meharey, R. and J., 154 Queen's sq.
Milliken, Robert, Falls road
Mitton, John, 42 Henry street
Moffett, John, 113 Durham street
Monaghan, H., 26 Edward street
Monair, Wm., 17 Frederick street
aMones, James, 52 Grattan street
Moore, Samuel, 13 Ann street
Moorehead, James, 18 Gardiner street
Moreland, John, 20 Henry street
Moreland, Robert, 8 Little Patrick st.
aMorrison, James, 52 Cromac street
Morrow, Patrick, 30 North Queen st.
Muckian, Bernard, 82 Cromac street
aMulholland, Elizabeth, 62 Grattan st.
aMullan, Anthony, 55 Lancaster st.
aMullan, Edward, 95 Millfield
aMurphy, Wm., 21 Little Patrick st.
Murphy, Alexander, Ballymacarrett
aMurphy, P., 17 Barrack street
aMurphy, Daniel, 17 Corporation st.
  and 7 Gamble street
Murphy, Hugh, 43 Gardiner street
Murphy, Jane, 99 North Queen street
Murray, Owen, 59 Green street
Murray, Henry, 61 Green street
aMurray, Henry, 61 Little Patrick st.
Murray, Owen, 18 North Thomas st.
Murray, Wm., 8 Verner street
M‘Adorey, John, 38 Barrack street
aM‘Alister, John, 18 Gamble street
aM‘Ateer, Thomas, 114 North street
M‘Cahan, Robert, 21 Cullingtree pl.
M‘Call, John, Henry street
M‘Carter, Wm., 21 and 22 Carrickhill
M‘Clean, C., 47 North Thomas street
M‘Clelland, W. R., 37 Church lane
M‘Closkie, Edward, 28 Union street
M‘Clure, Samuel, Ballymacarrett
M‘Connell, Samuel, 33 Edward street
M‘Connell, Joseph, 23 John street
M‘Connell, Samuel, 77 Green street
M‘Cormick, T., Wheeler's pl., B.carrett
M‘Cormick, Thomas, 23 Prince's st.
M‘Cormack, John, Shankhill road
aM‘Cracken, Henry, Ballymacarrett
M‘Cracken, Jas., 29, 31 Barrack st.
M‘Crea, Robert, 76 Cromac street
M‘Cready, John, Lagan village
M‘Cullough, James, 63 High street
aM‘Cullough, Joseph, 79 Durham st.
aM‘Culla, Francis, 11 William street
M‘Curry, Ann, 4 Carrickhill
aM‘Donald, Peter, 81 Green street

M‘Entee, Francis, 42 Hercules street
M‘Evoy, Thomas, 34 Barrack street
aM‘Farland, W., 12, 14 Old Malone road
aM‘Farland, Adam, 56, 58 Gt. Patrick st.
aM‘Garry, John, 39 Lancaster street
aM‘Gibbon, V., 5, 7 North King st.
aM‘Glade, Charles and Patrick, 34
  Edward street and 79 Green street
aM‘Guigan, Hugh, 62 Gt. Patrick st.
aM‘Ilroy, W., 137 North street
aM‘Ilroy, Patrick, 41 Gardiner street
aM‘Kay, Bernard, 62 Millfield
aM‘Kay, Francis, 1 Lower Chichester st.
M‘Kendry, Denis, 98 Carrickhill
aM‘Kenna, Jos. and John, 15 Lagan st.
aM‘Kibbin, James, Falls road
aM‘Laughlin, John, 45 Brown street
aM‘Laughlin, John, 5 Curtis street
M‘Clintock, Wm., 36 Gt. George's st.
M‘Mahon, Owen, 28 Grattan street
aM‘Mannus, Francis, 8 Corporation st.
M‘Millan, Ruth, York street
M‘Millan, James, Lagan village
M‘Morran, Margt., Gooseberry corner,
  Ballymacarrett
M‘Quillan, Hugh, 8 Barrack street
aM‘Stay, Wm., 71 Smithfield
aM‘Tear, John, 19 Corporation street
M‘Wade, James, 94 Carrickhill
Nelson, Wm., Shankhill road
Niblock, Wm., 82 Market street
aNoon, Henry, 54 Mill street
aOliver, Stewart, 24 Eliza street
Orr, Wm., 50 North Queen street
aOrr, Robert, 204 North street
aO'Kane. T., M‘Rory's row, B.carrett
O'Neill, John, 44 Lettuce hill
O'Neill, John, 65 Barrack street
aO'Neill, Patrick, 31 Smithfield
Park, James, 53 North Queen street
Patterson, Samuel, 37 Union street
aPatton, Archibald, Ballymacarrett
Paul, Robert, 18 Union street
aPelan, James, 36 Durham street
Potts, John, 112 Carrickhill
aPotts, Margaret, 16 Henry street
aPowell, Wm., 22 Talbot street
aPurse, Arthur, 24 Henry street
aQuinn, John, 30 Mustard street
aQuin, John, Old Lodge road
aQuin, Charles, 46 Talbot street
aQuin, John, 38 Union street
aRafferty, S., 48 Barrack street
aRamsey, James, 29 Charlemont st.
Rawlins, George, 50 Mill street

PROFESSIONS, TRADES, &c. 383

Reany, James, 66 Green street
Reid, James, 47 Peter's hill
Reid, Wm., 15 Cromac street
aReid, James, 60 Ann street
Reilly, Bernard, 124 Ann street
Ritchie, George, Falls road
aRobinson, Thomas, 25 Dock street
Roche, Patrick, 48 Cromac street
Rogers, Alex., 27, 29 Little Patrick st.
aRosbotham, Wm., 51 Edward street
aRowell, Thomas, 51 Peter's hill
aRussell, N., 62 Carrickhill
Russell, R., 12 Nelson street
aRussell, Wm., 40 Cromac street
aRussell, James, 9 Cargill street
Russell, John, 39 Barrack street
aRussell, Robt., 39 Little Patrick st.
Sands, Joseph, 4 Ann street
Savage, Elizabeth, 2 Barrack street
aSavage, Henry, 46 Cromac street and 59 Market street
aSavage, John, Shankhill road
Scott, James, 2 California street
aScott, Thomas, 29 New Durham st.
aScott, Wm., 59 Lower Malone road
Sedgewick, Jane, Shankhill road
Shaw, Edward, 72 Brown street
Shields, James, 20 Albert square
Short, John, 15 Robert street
Sloan, T., Gooseberry corner, B.carrett
Sloan, John, Ballymacarrett
Smith, Geo., 116 Carrickhill
aSmith, Francis, 34 Stanfield street
Smith, Wm., 65 Old Lodge road
Smyth, Mary, 2 Friendly street
Smylie, David, 11 Edward street
Spotten, Sarah, 22 Rosemary street
Stafford, Elizabeth, 17 Gamble street
Stavely, Margaret, 57 Durham street
Steed, Ann, 33 Peter's hill
aSteed, Jane, 20 Cromac street
aStevenson, Robert, 1 Dock street
Stevenson, John, Howard street north
Stewart, James, 14 Dock street
Sturgeon, C., Ballymacarrett
aSurplus, James, 15½ Henry street
aTaggart, Samuel, 8 Henrietta street
Tasney, Patrick, 56 Millfield
aTaylor, Hugh, 72 Carrickhill
Thompson, Wm. J., 97 North Queen st.
Thompson, John, 53 Lancaster street
aThompson, James, 42 Hill street
aThompson, H., 38 Carrickhill
aThompson, James, 31, 33 Talbot st.
Thompson, Dougherty, 25 Verner st.
Thompson, Margaret, Antrim road

Todd, Samuel, 54 Edward street
Toman, John, 30½ Ann street
aTrelford, H., 36 Barrack street
Walker, Samuel, 12, 14 Alexander st.
aWalker, Arthur, 19 Mill street
Walker, Hannah, 67 Peter's hill
aWallace, Robert, 12 Smithfield
Wallace, James, 138 Millfield
Ward, James, 65 Union street
Warnock, Susanna, 64 Peter's hill
Warnock, Joseph, 42 Verner street
aWatson, James, 46 Durham street
Watson, Robert, 32 Little Donegall st.
Williams, Robert, 85, 87 Barrack st.
Wilson, Eliza, 5 Little George's street
Wilson, John, 6 Peter's hill
Wilson, James, 17 Lancaster street
Wilson, Alex., 87 North Queen street
aWitherhead, Geo., 11½ Cromac st.
Withers, Alex., 14 and 16 Barrack st.
Woods, Patrick, 10 Barrack street
Woods, John, Garmoyle street
Woods, Wm., 1 Hamill street
Woods, Eleanor, 24 Lancaster street
aWright, Wm., 25 Shankhill road

Grocers, Wholesale

Those marked (a) are also retail
Andrews, S. and W., Victoria street
Addison, William, 15 North street
aArmstrong, James, and Co., 5 and 6 Donegall place buildings
Ash, George, 40 Waring street
aBell, David, 87 North street
Black, Henry, 15 and 17 Waring street
aBlackburn, Robt., & Co., 89 North st
aBoucher, Jas., 4 & 6 Castle buildings
aBrown, John H., 53 Ann street
aCarson, William, 14 Corn market
Clarke, Andrew, and Sons, Ann street
aCarroll, William, 78 Ann street
aCarson, J. and N., 53 Donegall st.
aCochran, James, 1 Castle place
Cowan, William, Church lane
Cuming, Brothers, 23 Corn market
aCuming, J., 55 Donegall street
aDickey, Nathaniel, North street
aDobbin, William, 18, 20, 45 and 47 North street
Dickey, Alex., and Co., Victoria street
aDickey, Nathaniel, 18 Church street and 63 North street
Douglass, John, 11 Waring street
Finlay, C. and W., 5 Waring street
aFisher, William, 40 Church lane
aGilmore, Wm, 14 and 16 High street

384 PROFESSIONS, TRADES, &c.

Glenn, James, Victoria street
aGray, Thomas, 22 North street
aGreen, Forster, and Co., 3 High street and 77 North street
aGreen, Ralph, 4 Waring street
Hamilton, Hugh, and Co., 35 Ann st.
Harbison, Andrew, Victoria street
Harper, Martin, 44 Church lane
Johnston, Philip, 21 & 23 Waring st.
aJardine, Robert, and Co., 30 Waring street and 125 North street
Kavanagh, James, 33, 35 North st.
Kernohan, Andrew, Victoria street
aLoughran, Henry, 41 York street and 20 John street
Love, Henry, 21 Church lane
Lytle, John, 1 and 3 North street
aMathison, Brothers, 13 Donegall place buildings
aMilligan, William H., 33 Ann street
Mullan, William, Victoria street
Meharey, R. and J., High street
Murray, George, 93 Queen's square
M'Caw, William, Victoria street
M'Donnell, John, & Co., Skipper st.
M'Connell, William, 7 Skipper street
aM'Causland, Samuel, 34 North street
M'Dowall, John, Victoria street
M'Hinch, Robert, 33 Church lane
aM'Kee, John and Joseph, 69 High st.
aM'Kenna, John, 1 York street, 73 Donegall st., and 39, 41 Academy st.
M'Laughlin, Francis, High street
Nicholson, John H., 89 Queen's square
aPim, E. and G., High street
Sibbin, George, Victoria street
Waugh, Joseph, Victoria street
aWightman, John, 41 Ann street

Gun and Pistol Manufacturers
Those marked (*a*) are also bird stuffers.
Braddell, Joseph, 17 Castle place
Hill, M., 31 Rosemary street
aNeill, John, 78 High street
aNicholl, Mrs., 10 High street

Haberdashers
Allen, John, 32 Church lane
Arnold, Jane, 1 Great George's street
Arnott, John, and Co., 7, 9 Bridge st.
Barry, James, 147 North street
Boucher, James, 126 North street
Browne, Mary Ann, 107 North street
Bullick, S. W., and Co., Victoria st.
Caulfield, Jane, 72 North street
Clelland, James, 14 Peter's hill
Clendinning, A. (wholesale), 10 Rosemary street
Coffey, Jane, 9 Skipper street
Crossett, Alex., 38 North Queen st.
Davis, Eliza, 96 High street
Duncan, Eliza Jane, 65 North street
Dyer, John, 12 John street
Edgar, Samuel, 5 Arthur square
Finlay, Jane and Eliza, 24 Waring st.
Fox, William, 12 Church lane
Gibson, Robert, 19 Castle street
Greenfield, John, 76 High street
Greenfield and Harris, 19 High st.
Hardy, Thomas, 35 & 37 High street
Hazlett and Frazer, 21 High street
Hazleton, Mrs., 22 Ann street
Hederman, Mrs., 95 North street
Hennesey, Margaret, 84 North street
Hepburn, Jane, 56 Ann street
Johnston and Kennedy, 69 North st.
Kirker, Brothers, 52 North street
Lewis, William, 9 North street
Lindsay, Brothers, 1 Donegall place
Lindsay, Brothers (wholesale), 3 Donegall place
Maloney, Miss, 9 Hercules place
Macoun, George, 23, 25 Castle place
Madden, William, 4 Old Malone road
Maginn, Teressa, 135½ North street
Millen, William, 21 Castle place
Moonan, Mary, 101 North street
Murray, Greene, and Lloyd, 13 Donegall place
Murphy, Jane, 99 North Queen street
M'Cormack, Jas., & Co., Victoria st.
M'Donald, Bernard, 78 North street
M'Dowell, Matilda, 6 Ann street
M'Geagh, R. T., and Co., (wholesale) 1 and 3 Hercules place
M'Hugh, B. and E., 12 Rosemary st.
M'Ilveen, John, 116 North street
aM'Kee, John and Joseph, 69 High st.
M'Kenna, John, 20 Bridge street
M'Kenna, Thomas, and Co., 12, 14 and 16 Bridge street
M'Kenzie and Saunders, 36 High st.
Noble, James, 22½ Robert street
O'Meely, Timothy, 3 Barrack street
O'Neill, John, 28 Edward street
Patrick, Margaret Jane, 91 North st.
Pollock, Mrs., 66 Ann street
Pollock, M., 39 Church street
Quirey, M. A., & Co., 24 Donegall st.
Ramsay, Sinclair, 12 Hill street
Reid, John, 55 North street

PROFESSIONS, TRADES, &c.

Reid, William, 9 Arthur square
Riddel and M'Callum, 13 Bridge st
Riddell, E. and M., 53 North street
Riley, William, 46 North street
Ritchie, William, 45 John street
Stritch, Edward, 16 Berry street
Thompson, Alice, 27 Gt. Edward st.
Thompson, Geo., 37 Great Edward st.
Thompson, Sarah J., 38 Gt. Edward st.
Wilson, T., and Co., 32 High street

Hackle and Gill Makers
Hodgkinson, Wm., 17 Hill street
Horricks, John, 36 Townsend street
M'Roberts, Hugh, 6 Spencer street
M'Roberts, Joseph, 2 Meadow street
Purkis, Richard & Joseph, Joy's court

Hairdressers
Those marked (a) are also wig makers and perfumers.
Adamson, Wm., 30½ Castle street
Allen, Hugh, 25 New Durham street
Campbell, Thomas, 2 Pilot street
Clotworthy, Jn., 20½ Little Patrick st.
Cochrane, Hugh, 12 Marquis street
aGalbraith, Robert, 8 Arthur street
Graham, John, 62 Ann street
Graham, James, 1 Carrick hill
Hamilton, James, 19 Smithfield
Hamilton, Robert, 14 Ann street
Heron, Robert, 12 Ann street
Maguire, Isaac, 20 Talbot street
Mathews, William, 106 North street
aMonaghan, David, 5 Gamble street
M'Cann, James, 15 Castle lane
M'Cann, J., 18 Great Edward street
M'Larnon, James, 6 Gamble street
aO'Brien, Lawrence, 153 North street
aPage, William, 19 Castle place
aRanagan, Bernd., 1 Castle Chambers
Rea, William John, 12 May street
Todd, William, 98 Millfield

Harbour Master
Gowan, Capt. John, 69 Corporation st.

Hardware Dealers
Campbell, Jn., 14 (sheds) Smithfield
Campbell, B., 17 (sheds) Smithfield
Halfpenny, A., 61 (sheds) Smithfield
Mullen, Peter, 15 (sheds) Smithfield
Mulholland, D., 59 (sheds) Smithfield
M'Cleave, J., 56, 58 (sheds) Smithfield
O'Hagan, John, 18 (sheds) Smithfield
Quinn, Edward, 16 (sheds) Smithfield
Riley, John, 57 (sheds) Smithfield
Ruddell, David, 6 and 7 Smithfield

Hardware Merchants and Iron-mongers
Brown, David, 35 Castle place
Bryson, Thomas, 180 North street
Craig, John, 15 Bridge street
Calwell, Robert, & Co., 14 Waring st.
Currie, Hugh, 72 High street
Halliday, Jacob, & Co., 35 Castle st.
Ireland & M'Neill, 17, 19 Corn mkt.
Ferguson, William, 17 Smithfield
Jennings and Co., 67 Donegall street
Musgrave, Brothers, 59 High street
M'Kinney, William, 42½ Rosemary st.
Patterson, R. & D. J., 40 High street
Riddell and Co., 54 High street

Hatters, &c.
Those marked (a) are manufacturers
Allen, Daniel J., 3 Castle buildings
Arnold, John, 45 High street
Arnott, John, and Co., 17 Bridge st.
Bullick, S. W., and Co., Victoria st.
Cooke, Johnston, & Co., 1 Bridge st.
aCrossley, Charles, 77 North street
aDillon, James, 34 High street
aGraham, H., and Co., 28½ Bridge st.
Hazlett and Frazer, 21 High street
King, Robert, 21 Donegall street
Killen, William, 68 High street
Levy, Mier, and Co., 61 High street
Magill, Robert, 1 Castle buildings
Marshall, James, 5 Donegall street
aMatthews, John, 26 Waring street
aMulligan, J. & T. (cap), 6 Donegall st.
aM'Caldin, James (hat and cap), 18 Waring street
M'Cann, Thos., 41 High st.
M'Gee, John G., and Co., 46 and 48 High street
M'Grotty, J. B., & Co., 23 Bridge st.
M'Hugh, Edward, 26 Bridge street
aRoss, Robert, and Co., 27 (sheds) Smithfield
Shaw, Samuel, 38 Church lane
Spackman, Wm., corner of High st. and Victoria street

Hide Merchants
SEE LEATHER MERCHANTS — ALSO TANNERS.

Horse Bazaars

Donaldson, Wm., 33 Chichester street
Grogan, John, Castle yard, Castle lane
King, James, 108 Donegall street
Long, Robert, 5 Telfair's entry
M'Kenna, William, 2 May street
Smyth, Dennis, 31 Great Edward st.

Horse Dealers

Burns, Thomas, 6 Henrietta street
Cahoon, James, Marquis street
Fenning, Thomas, Marquis street
Long, Robert, 5 Telfair's entry
O'Neill, James, May street
O'Rourke, William, May's market
Ruby, Robert, May's market
Saunders, John, Conlon street
Smyth, Denis, 4 Gloucester street
Stevenson, Geo., 27 Little May street
Rice, Ambrose, Mustard street

Horse Shoers and Farriers

Adams, Alexander, 15 Albion lane
Allen, James, 28 Gordon street
Beatty, John, 20 Devis street
Berkley, Thomas, 32 Earl street
Boyd, Richard, 27 Greenland street
Campbell, Duncan, 1 Little Donegall st.
Clarke, Wm., Little York street
Coleman, John, 21 Greenland street
Devlin, John, Earl lane
Dickson, Archibald, 3 Hamilton pl.
Dickey, Charles, Police square
Donaldson, John, 24 Cargill street
Downing, Wm., 3 Prince's dock
Ewins, John, Falloon's court
Falloon, Wm., 4 Campbell's place
Falloon, Wm., Conlon street
Flannigan, Hy., Bridge end, B.carret
Folie, M., 108 Donegall street
Hogg, John, 21 Pilot street
Herald, Wm., Pilot street
Kirkpatrick, Wm. John, 22 Caxton st.
Lynass, Tobias, Steam-mill lane
Mulrine, Wm., 9 George's lane
M'Cartin, James, 27 Green street
M'Connell, George, Ballynafeigh
M'Court, James, 35 York street
M'Neilly, Samuel, 75 Green street
Orr, John, 10 and 16 Prince's street
Rogan, Thomas, 53½ Cromac street
Thompson, J., Bridge end, B.carrett
Wilson, James, Trinity street

Hosiers and Glovers

Greenfield, John, 76 High street
Greenfield and Harris, 19 High street
Hardy, Thomas, 35 and 37 High st.
Kelso, Charles, 73 High street
Kyle, George W., 21 Bridge street
Marshall, A. and J., 18 Bridge street
M'Kenna, Thos., & Co., 12, 14 and 16 Bridge street
M'Kenna, John, 20 Bridge street
Riddell & M'Callum, 13 Bridge street
Timmony, Peter (dealer), 29 (sheds) Smithfield
Wilson, Thomas, and Co., 32 High st.

Hotels, &c.

Bambridge, A., 3 Sugarhouse entry
Black, Adam, 12 Castle lane
Blakely, J., Crown and Anchor Hotel and Tavern, 41 Donegall quay
Brown, Mrs., commercial boarding house, 81 Donegall street
Charters, Eleanor, American Hotel, 6 Prince's dock
Clay, T., Crown Hotel, 30 Gamble st.
Collins, Mrs., Pottinger Arms, Pottinger's entry
Cunningham, Thomas, Queen's Arms, 2 York street
Davis, George, Plough Hotel, 7 Corn market
Dunlop, David, Thistle Hotel, 1 Arthur square
Echlin, P., Commercial Hotel, Commercial buildings
Farrell, Thomas, Royal Temperance Hotel, 12 Waring street
Graham, Mrs., Longford Arms, 61 Donegall quay
Grey, Edward P., Shakspeare Hotel, 21 Castle lane
Gunn, Alex., Vine Hotel and Tavern, 19 Queen's square
Hammond, Patrick, Railway Hotel, Queen's quay, Ballymacarrett
Hargraves, Miss A., Commercial boarding house and Hotel, Victoria street
Heslop, Ellen, Belfast and Ballymena Railway Hotel, York road
Hurst, Dr. C., Imperial Hotel, 10 Donegall place
Kearns, Charles, Royal Hotel, 27 Donegall place
Keyland, James, Dublin and Armagh Hotel, Great Victoria street

PROFESSIONS, TRADES, &c.

Macartney, John, Ship Hotel, 27 Pilot street
Mitchell, George, Navy Hotel and Tavern, 10 Prince's dock
Moore, John, Donegall Arms, 11 Castle place
O'Hanlon, T., Ulster Railway Hotel and Tavern, Great Victoria street
Potter, Mrs., Marine Hotel, 69 Corporation square
Rickards, James, Albion Hotel and Tavern, 39 Waring street
Robinson, George, Shipwrights' Arms Hotel and Tavern, 4 Prince's dock
Robinson, Mrs., Commercial boarding house, 29 North street
Scott, Robert, Glasgow Hotel, 7½ High street
Stockdale, Edward, Victoria Hotel, 80 Ann street
Young, William, Belfast Arms, 57 Donegall quay
Young, Arthur, Caledonian Hotel, 32 Tomb street

House, Rent, and Land Agents

Beattie, William (house and rent), 3 Arthur place
Boyd, Hugh H. (land), 21 Arthur st.
Brown, James (house), 10 Kennedy's place
Brown, J. (land), 59½ Upper Arthur st.
Carland, James (rent), 13 Castle lane
Connell, Wm. (land), 35 Corporation st.
Connery, Richard, 15 College sq. east
Ferguson, Thomas (house and rent), 31 Castle street
Forsythe, J. (land), 13 Castle chambers
Gavin, W. (house and rent), 24 Castle st.
Giltenan, Edward B. (house and land), 6 Spamount
Glenn, Peter, 16 Tomb street
Humphreys, Robert (house and rent), 2 Brown's square
Johnston, John M. (land), 6 Castle chambers
Kennedy, John (house and general), 13 Arthur street
Kinney, John, 21 Hamilton place
Murdock, Hugh (house), 4 Annette st.
M'Cleery, Wm. (rent), 28 Castle st.
M'Cloy, James (house and rent), 128 Carrickhill
Patton, G. (house), 30 Corporation st.
Posnett, H (land), Rose Lodge
Scott, Archibald, (rent), 14 Verner st.
Sherrard, Connolly (house and land), 14 Calender street
Simms, Wm. (rent), Linen hall
Taylor, Andrew, (rent), 11 Marquis st.
Tierney, Samuel, 9 Elliott's court
Vance, Saml. (rent), 36 Waring street
Walker, Samuel, 18 Henry street
Watters, Wm., (rent), 16 Kennedy's pl.
Woods, David, 12 North Queen st.

Insurance Agents

SEE ALSO INSURANCE COMPANIES' OFFICES.

Abbott, Joseph, 9 Corporation street—Aberdeen Fire and Life
Atkinson, Robert, Hill st.—Patriotic Fire and Life
Baxter, Richard, 15 Rosemary street—Sun Fire and Life
Beath, J. and J., 29 Donegall street—Monarch Fire and Life
Borthwick, John, 29 King street—United Mutual Life, and Railway Passengers'
Bottomley, Wm., 7 Calender street—Edinburgh Life
Boyd, H. H., 21 Arthur street—Medical Invalid Life
Braddell, George W., 3 Castle lane—Scottish Widows' Fund Life
Charley and Malcolm, Donegall quay—Royal Insurance Fire and Life
Connor, D., 27½ Ann street—London Corporation Fire and Life
Cowan, Wm., and Co., 55 York st.—North British Fire and Life
Cranston, Wm. and Alex. J., 33 Arthur street—Clerical and Medical Life
Creeth, Richard, and Co., Warehouse lane—Equitable Fire, and Accidental Death
Coates, John, 29 Arthur st.—Albion Life
Curell, J. and M., and Co., Linen hall—Liverpool Fire and Life
Druitt, William, 32 Donegall street—Gresham Life
Emerson, George, 106 Donegall st.—Liverpool and London Fire & Life
Faren, Joseph, at Richardson, Brothers, and Co., Corporation street—North of England Fire and Life
Fisher, John, and Son, 9 Rosemary st.—West of England Fire and Life

PROFESSIONS, TRADES, &c.

Folingsby, T. G., 15 Albert square—Marine and Scottish Underwriters', and Imperial Fire and Life
Garrett, Messrs., 16 Castle lane—Alfred Life
Goddard, James, 7 Queen street—Sun Fire and Westminster Life
Gordon and Crawford, Castle Chambers—Royal Exchange Fire and Life
Grimshaw, Conway B., 30 Rosemary street—Atlas Fire and Life
Harrison, John, 1 Albert square—National (Ireland) Fire and Life
Harper, Martin, 44 Church lane—British Empire Mutual Fire and Life
Henderson, Wm. D., 42 Waring st.—Scottish Amicable Life, and Northern Assurance Fire
Henderson, Robt., 25 Donegall quay—Scottish Equitable Life
Heyn, Gustavus, 1 Henry street—Alliance Fire and Life
Hyndman, Geo. C., 7 Castle place—Manchester Fire, and Pelican Life
Lamb, John, 10 Hill street—Patriotic Fire and Life
Macaulay, Jasper, 9 Albert square—North British Fire and Life
Martin, J., and Co., 29 Ann street—County Fire, Provident, and Life
M'Cammon, Thomas, 23 King street—United Kingdom Life
M'Cracken, John W., 25 Corporation street—General Commission Life, and Phœnix Fire
M'Tear, George, 33 Donegall quay—Scottish Provident Life
O'Connor, Jas. D.,1 College place north—Family Endowment Life
O'Rorke, Daniel, 14 Donegall street—City of London Life
Phillips, Geo., 27 Bridge st.—Church of England Life
Pim, Edward and George, 27 and 29 High street—Britannia Fire & Life
Pim, John, 20 Waring st.—Imperial Fire and Life
Plunkett, F., 1 St. Anne's buildings—Royal Insurance Fire and Life
Rea, Hugh, at Sinclair and Boyd's, 45 Donegall quay—British Fire & Life
Ritchie, John, 7 Gloucester street—National Mercantile Fire and Life
Rodgers, Wm., & Co., Victoria chambers—Waterloo Fire, &c.
Stevenson, J. S., Commercial buildings—Promoter Life and Annuity
Simms, William, Linen hall—London Union Fire and Life
Taylor, John, 16 Donegall place—Standard Life, and British Guarantee Association
Teeling, John F., 6 Castle lane—Mitre Life and Annuity
Vance, Samuel, 36 Waring street—Globe Fire and Life
Ward, Thomas, 25 Bridge street—Norwich Union Fire and Life

Insurance Companies' Offices
SEE ALSO INSURANCE AGENTS.

Aberdeen—J. Abbott, 9 Corporation st.
Accidental Death—R. Creeth and Co., Warehouse lane
Albion—John Coates, 29 Arthur st.
Alfred Home and Foreign—Messrs. Garrett, 16 Castle lane
Alliance—G. Heyn, 1 Henry st., & R. Trotter, Provincial Bank, Donegall st.
Atlas—C. B. Grimshaw, 30 Rosemary st.
Britannia—Edward & Geo. Pim, 27 & 29 High street
British Empire Mutual—M. Harper, 44 Church lane
British Guarantee Association—John Taylor, 16 Donegall place
British—Hugh Rea, at Sinclair and Boyd's, Donegall quay
Church of England—George Phillips, 27 Bridge street
City of London—Daniel O'Rorke, 14 Donegall street
Clerical and Medical—Wm. and Alex. J. Cranston, 33 Arthur street
County Fire, Provident—J. Martin & Co., 29 Ann street
Edinburgh—William Bottomley, 7 Calender street
Equitable—Richard Creeth and Co., Warehouse lane
Family Endowment—Jas. D. O'Connor, 1 College place north
General Commission—John W. M'Cracken, 25 Corporation street
Globe—Samuel Vance, 36 Waring st.
Gresham—W. Druitt, 32 Donegall st.
Imperial—John Pim, 20 Waring st., & T. G. Folingsby and Co., Albert sq.
Liverpool—J. and M. Curell and Co., Linen hall
London Union—W. Simms, Linenhall

PROFESSIONS, TRADES, &c.

Liverpool and London—G. Emerson, 106 Donegall street
London Assurance Corporation—D. Connor, 27½ Ann street
Manchester—George C. Hyndman, 7 Castle place
Marine and Scottish Underwriters'—T. G. Folingsby & Co., 15 Albert sq.
Medical Invalid—Hugh H. Boyd, 21 Arthur street
Mitre Life and Annuity Association—John F. Teeling, 6 Castle lane
Monarch—J. and J. Beath, 29 Donegall street
National Mercantile—John Ritchie, 7 Gloucester street
Norwich Union—Thomas Ward, 25 Bridge street
North British—Wm. Cowan & Co., 55 York street, and Jasper Macaulay, 9 Albert square
National (Ireland)—John Harrison, 1 Albert square
Northern—William D. Henderson, 42 Waring street
North of England — J. Faren, at Richardson, Brothers, & Co., Corporation street
Patriotic—R. Atkinson & John Lamb, 10 Hill street
Pelican—G. C. Hyndman, 7 Castle pl.
Phœnix — John W. M'Cracken, 25 Corporation street
Professional — T. B. Johnson, 27 Arthur street
Promoter, Life, and Annuity—J. S. Stevenson, Commercial buildings
Railway Passengers' Assurance—John Borthwick, 29 King street
Royal Exchange—R. F. Gordon & W. S. Crawford, 1 Castle chambers
Royal Insurance of Liverpool—Charley & Malcolm, Donegall quay, and F. Plunkett, 1 St. Anne's buildings
Scottish Widows' Fund—George W. Braddell, 3 Castle lane
Scottish Amicable— William D. Henderson, 42 Waring street
Scottish Provident—George M'Tear, 33 Donegall quay
Scottish Equitable—Robert Henderson, 25 Donegall quay
Scottish Union—Gustavus Heyn, 1 Henry street
Standard—J. Taylor, 16 Donegall place
Sun—R. Baxter, 15 Rosemary street, and James Goddard, 7 Queen street
United Guarantee—Richard Creeth & Co., Warehouse lane
United Kingdom—Thomas M'Cammon, 23 King street
United Mutual—John Borthwick, 29 King street
Waterloo—William Rodgers and Co., Victoria chambers
West of England— John Fisher & Sons, 9 Rosemary street
Westminster—J. Goddard, 7 Queen st.

Iron and Brassfounders

Boyd, Samuel, Belfast Foundry, 110 Donegall street
Campbell, Robert, Damside Foundry, 15, 17 Damside, Millfield
Coates and Young, Lagan Foundry, and Pilot street
Combe, J., and Co., Falls Foundry, Falls road
Forbes, T., Ulster Foundry, 31½ Townsend street
Gray, Henry, 2 Townsend street
Murphy, J. F., Union Foundry, May st.
MacAdam, Brothers, and Co., Soho Foundry, 45 Townsend street
Pearce, James and William, Phœnix Foundry, 16 Great George's street
Reid, John, Ballymacarrett Foundry, New road, Ballymacarrett
Rowan, John, and Sons, York Street Foundry, 60 York street
Scott, John, 6 May street
Thompson and Co., 4 Townsend st.
Thompson, S. and W., 20, 22, 24, 26 Brown's square

Iron and Tinplate Merchants

Bell, Wm., 114 Ann street
Crawford, Arthur, 130 North street
Jennings and Co., 67 Donegall street
Lough and Gregg, 30 Ann street
Musgrave, Brothers, 59 High street
Potts, John and Robert, 31 North st.
Riddell, John, 52 High street
Riddell, J., and Sons, 17 Church lane

Iron Works

The Belfast Iron Works, Eliza street Robert Pace, jun., and Thomas N. Gladstone managers

PROFESSIONS, TRADES, &c.

Ironmongers
SEE HARDWARE MERCHANTS AND IRONMONGERS.

Jewellers
GOLD AND SILVERSMITHS, AND OPTICIANS.

Chapman, James, 64 High street
Gilbert, Edward, 43 High street
Gilbert, and Son, 15 High street
Gray, John, 18 Castle place
Gribben, Edward, 13 High street
Lee and Son, 57 High street
Macartney, J. N., 6 Donegall place
Neill, Brothers, 23 High street
Wallace, John, 49 High street
Wilson, James, 7 High street

Last and Boot Tree Makers
M'Kinney, John, 19 Ritchie's place
M'Kinney, Cornelius, 14 Ritchie's pl.

Leather and Hide Merchants
Black, James, 26 Ann street
Cinnamond, Helena, 23 Smithfield
Callender, James, 21 and 23 Mill st.
Campbell, Wm., 109 North street
Dunn, Hugh, 8 John street
Frazer, Thomas, 119 North street
Greenhill, Robert, 44½ Ann street
Hunter, Arthur, 152 North street
Hunter, W. and T., 45 Ann street
Isles, Nathaniel, 103 North street
Johnston, W. and S., 37 Mill street
Moore, Wm., 143 North street
M'Blain, James, 139 North street
M'Blain, John, 40 Donegall street
M'Cammon, Thomas, 23 King street
M'Clarns, James, and Co., 60 North st.
M'Cord, John, 16 Church lane
M'Cormac, Thomas, 49 Mill street
M'Fadden, Mrs., 74 Ann street
Quirey, Jas., and Co., 33 Donegall st.
Tate, Wm., 85 North street
Waugh, James, 132 North street

Limeburners
Belfast Gas Company, Ormeau road
Green, Mr., Whitewell
Murray, Danl., Short strand, B.carrett
M'Cullough, Thos., M'Clelland's court
M'Cullough, Thomas, Whiterock
M'Ferran, Mr., Whitewell
Wheeler, Walter, 16 Carrickhill

Linen and Cotton Printers and Dyers
Bragg, Henry, & Sons, Cottonmount ; York street
Delauney, L., Clonard Print Works, Falls road
Howie, Robt., Old Park Print Works
Walker, R., Whitehouse

Linen and Damask Warehouses
Ashenhurst, C. (ready made linen), 62 High street
Blain, Hugh, 7 Donegall street
M'Cormack, Jas. and Co., Victoria st.
Nocher, John, 20 Arthur street
Roddy, R., 18 Donegall street
Wilson, M., 58 Donegall street

Linen Manufacturers and Merchants
Alexander, Robt., 1¼ Donegall sq. west
Andrews, Michael, Ardoyne
Cameron, J., 9 Calender street
Connor, Foster, Linenhall
Curell, J. and M., and Co., Linenhall
Curell, Daniel, jun.,&Co.,Linenhall st.
Druitt, W. & R., 32 Donegall street
Ewart, Wm., & Sons, 24 Donegall st.
Fenton, Son, & Co. (late Sadler Fenton and Co.), Linenhall
Ferguson, John S., & Co., Linenhall
Ferguson and Co., Falls bleach green; 10 Waring street
Gamble and Co., 5 Donegall st. place
Gillilan, William, Linenhall
Hamilton, Robert, 1 College court
Henry, A. S., & Co., 1 and 2 Donegall square north
Herd, David, 8 Donegall square north
Jackson, Thomas, 29 Donegall street
Leadbetter, John, and Co., York street and Bedford street
Magill, Joseph, Fountain street
Mercer, J. M., 3 Commercial buildings
M'Auley, Charles, 27 Lancaster street
M'Ilwrath & Co., 4 Donegall st. place; sacking, &c., Sackville st. factory
M'Mullan and Co., 8 Rosemary street
Orr, William, and Co., 3 Glengall st.
Praeger, John, and Co., Fountain st.
Preston, John, & Co., 12 Calender st.
Richardson, Brothers, and Co., Corporation street
Richardson, J. N., Sons, and Owden, 14 Donegall place

Roddy, Robert, 18 Donegall street
Saulter, Ross, 29 Ann street
Siebert, James, and Co., Linen hall
Smyth, Weir, & Co., 11 Donegall pl.
Smyth, Edward J., & Son, Linen hall
Stevenson, William, jun., and Co., 9 Calender street
Storars, Fortescue, and Co., Linen hall, Herbert Dale, representative
Thornton, Huggins, & Co., Bedford st.

Linen Ornament Manufacturers

Those marked (a) are also fancy paper box makers.

Archer and Sons, Castle place
Banks, Benjamin, Castle place
aDickinson, John, and Co., Donegall square north
Hamilton, Robert, Castle street
Miller, Wm., Castle street
M'Cracken, Thomas, Crown entry
Smyth, Thomas, Castle street
Thompson, Robert, Castle street

Linen Thread Manufacturers

Thompson, Ann, 27 Cromac street
M'Ilwrath and Co., Sackville street and Donegall street place

Linen Yarn Merchants

Bell, R. and J., 4 Mustard street
Connor, David, 27½ Ann street
Cuppage, John, and Co., 8 and 10 Donegall street place
Duffin, Charles, and Co., 28 Waring st.
Ewart, Wm., and Sons, 24 Donegall st.
Fenton, S. G., and Co., Linen hall
German, Petty, & Co., 24 Rosemary st.
Kinnear, Patrick, 29 Waring street
Martin, John, and Co., 29 Ann street
Montgomery, J., & Sons, Corporation st
M'Mullan and Co., 8 Rosemary st.
Praeger, John, and Co., Fountain st.
Preston, John, & Co., 12 Calender st.
Richardson, Brothers, and Co., Corporation street
Shaw, E., and Co., Victoria chambers
Siebert, James, and Co., Linen hall
Stewart, Robert, 3 Waring st. place
Woods, George P., & Co., 1 Talbot st.

Livery Stable Keepers

Brown, James, 9½ Castle place
Davis, George, Plough Hotel, Corn market
Donaldson, William, 33 Chichester st.
Donegall Arms, 9¼ Castle place
Echlin, Peter, Commercial Hotel, Commercial buildings
Grogan, John, Vet. S., Castle lane
Hurst, Dr. C., Imperial Hotel, 10 Donegall place
Kerns, Chas., Royal Hotel, 27 Donegall place
King, Jas., Vet. S., 108 Donegall st.
Madine, George, 7 York street
M'Kenna, William, Vet. S., 2 May st.
Smyth, Denis, 31 Gt. Edward street

Lloyd's Agent

Fitzsimmons, N., Corporation street

Lloyd's Surveyor

Jobling, Edward W., 94 Donegall st.

Looking Glass Maker

Smith, John, 178 North street

Machine Makers

Boyd, Samuel, Belfast foundry, 110 Donegall street
Brown, Rainey, 67 York street
Campbell, Robert, Damside Foundry, Millfield
Coates and Young, Lagan Foundry Lagan village
Combe, J., and Co., Falls Foundry, Falls road
Forbes, T., Ulster Foundry, 31½ Townsend street
Gray, Robert, 8 Police place
Harper, James, 10 Wilson street
Murphy, John F., Union Foundry, May street
MacAdam, Brothers, and Co., Soho Foundry, Townsend street
Pearce, Jas. & W., Phœnix Foundry, 16 Great George's street
Reynold, Brothers, M'Clenaghan's court, Mill street
Rowan, John, and Sons, York Street Foundry, 60 York street
Scrimgeour, James, Albert street
Thomson and Co., 4 Townsend street

Maltsters

Clarke, Ledlie, 130½ Ann street
Dobbin, Clotworthy, 43 Smithfield
Fordyce and Mullan, 84 Cromac st.
Mackenzie, Shaw, and Co., 84 Hercules street
Mackenzie, J., & Co., 39 Barrack st.

PROFESSIONS, TRADES, &c.

Marble and Stone Cutters

Those marked (a) are stonecutters only.

Fee, Wm., 38 York street
aGamble, Abel, Antrim road
aGraham, Wm., 56 York street
aHall, John, 22 York street
Johnston, John, steam marble works, 55 Great Patrick street
Linas, John, 38 York street
Low, Wm., 11 Montgomery street
Murphy, John, 18 York street
aM'Donald, Alexander, York street
M'Meckan, James, 5 Victoria street
Robinson, John (late Robinson and Kelly), 65 and 87 Donegall street and 24 York street

Masters in Chancery

AND COMMISSIONERS FOR TAKING AFFIDAVITS AND SPECIAL BAIL.

Ch., Chancery; Q.B., Queen's Bench; C.P., Common Pleas; Ex., Exchequer; F.C., Four Courts.

Armstrong, William, Q.B., C.P., Ex., and Special Bail, Police Office and 1 Wills' place
Bates, John, solicitor, 19 Rosemary street, F.C., and master extraordinary in Chancery in Ireland, for taking affidavits, pleas and answers, in Chancery, &c., for the English Court of Chancery
Cramsie, Jn. C., 74 Waring st., Q.B., C.P. and Ex.
Cunningham, Thomas, 2 York street, F.C., and Commissioner for taking acknowledgments of deeds by married women in Ireland
Cunningham, W. C., solicitor, 4 York street, commissioner for taking acknowledgments of deeds by married women
Cranston, Wm., solicitor, 33 Arthur street, commissioner for taking acknowledgments of deeds by married women
Davison, Richard, solicitor, 23 Donegall place, commissioner for taking acknowledgments of deeds by married women
Davis, Wm., solicitor, 25 Arthur st., Ch., perpetual commissioner for taking acknowledgments of married women, master extraordinary for taking affidavits, pleas, &c., in Chancery for England, commissioner of High Court of Admiralty for Down and Antrim
Foster, Wm., Special Bail and Q.B.
Hartley, John, Castle Office, Ch.
Jackson, James K., solicitor, 8 Castle lane, F.C. and Special Bail, and commissioner for taking acknowledgments of deeds by married women
Johnston, J. M., F.C., 6 Castle Chambers and 17 Arthur street
Kennedy, John, 13 Arthur street, Ch., C.P., Q.B. and Ex., and commissioner for taking affidavits
Macrory, A. J., solicitor, 23 Rosemary street, commissioner for taking acknowledgments of deeds by married women
M'Cleery, Wm., 28 Castle street, Ch., Q.B., and Ex.
M'Loughlin, F., Victoria street, Ch. and Common Law Courts
Posnett, Hutchinson, Rose lodge, Ch., Q.B., and Ex.
Simms, Wm., Linenhall, Ch., Q.B., C.P. and Ex.
Simpson, Daniel P., Belfast and Larne, Ch. and Common Law Courts
Smith, George K., 3 The Castle, master extraordinary for taking affidavits, pleas and answers in Chancery, and affidavits in Bankruptcy, for English Court of Chancery
Spotten, William, 22 Rosemary street, Ch., Q.B., C.P. and Ex.
Suffern, John, jun., solicitor, 76 Donegall street, master extraordinary for taking affidavits, pleas, and answers in Chancery, and affidavits in Bankruptcy, for English Court of Ch.
Tierney, Samuel, 9 Elliott's court, off Donegall street, F.C.
Torrens, James, solicitor, 23 Donegall place, F.C. and Special Bail,
Wallace, John, solicitor, Victoria street, Ch. and Common Law Courts
Walkington, E., 13 Rosemary street, F.C. and Special Bail

Matress Makers

Macoun, Charles, 43 Talbot street
Magee, Bartholemew, 66 Union st.

PROFESSIONS, TRADES, &c.

Matting Manufactory

Worsted and cocoa fibre rug, mat, and matting manufactory, Bridge end, Ballymacarrett; Phillips and Co., proprietors

Merchants

Abbott, Joseph, Corporation street
Ash, George, 40 Waring street
Barnett, A. J., 10 Store lane
Barnett, Charles, 7 Henry st.
Barnett, James, Ferguson's court, Smithfield
Bell, John, jun., & Co., 55 York street
Bushell, Theobald, 32 Rosemary street
Coey, Edward, 21 Gamble street
Colvil, Auld, and Co., 74 Waring street
Corry, James, 1 Corporation square
Cuddy, John, 42 Church lane
Cunningham, John, Linen hall
Duffin, Charles, and Co., 28 Waring st.
Dunn, John, 15 Henry street
Ferrie & Campbell, 11 Corporation st.
Fenton, Samuel G., and Co., Linen hall
Fitzsimmons, Nicholas, Corporation st.
Gaussen, John, and Co., 11 Albert sq.
Grainger, David, 1 Prince's dock
Haliday and M'Dowell, 8 Tomb street
Hamilton, James, 11 Queen's square
Harrison, John, 1 Albert square
Henderson, Robert, Donegall quay
Henderson, Wm. D., Waring street
Heron, Wm. C., & Co., 13 Albert sq.
Heyn, Gustavus, 1 Henry street
Houston, Samuel, 39 Dock street
Hunter, John, jun., 35 Warng street
Langtrys and Herdman, 33 Waring st.
Lemon, James, Queen's square
Macaulay, Jasper, & Co., 9 Albert sq.
Martin, John, and Co., 29 Ann street
M'Clure, Wm., and Son, Corporation street
M'Donnell, John, & Co., 5 Skipper st.
M'Tear, George, Donegall quay
Nelson, Samuel (West India), Linen hall
Reford, Lewis, 17½ Rosemary street
Richardson, Brothers, and Co., Corporation street
O'Brien, T., 1, 3 Store lane
Sinclair & Boyd (West India), Donegall quay
Sinclair, John and Thos., Tomb street
Smith, J. and T., 6 Tomb street
Steen, Jas. and Wm., 30, 32 Hill st.
Steen, James, and Co. 3 Talbot street
Stevenson, William, jun., and Co., 9 Calender street
Thomson, Samuel, 1, 3 Corporation st.
Thompson, Robt., 1 Donegall sq. west
Whitla, Valentine, Linen hall

Mill Banding and Leasing Manufacturer

Simpson, Thomas, Ballynafeigh

Millers

Andrews, James, and Son, Comber
Alexander, J., and Co., Ardmoulin Mills, Falls road
Austin, Robert, 63 Corporation square
Boyd and M'Naughten, Moyallen
Cunningham, John, Glenwood
Cuddy, John, (Indian corn) Queen's quay, Ballymacarrett
Dawson, John, Glenavy
Hughes, William, (Indian corn) 1 Meadow street
Hunter, Wm., and Son, Dunmurry
Kennedy, R. and T., Lisburn Mills
Kidd, Osborne (Armagh), 61 North st.
Langtry, W., and Co., Portadown
Macaulay, R., and Son (Crumlin and Glenend Mills), 9 Albert square
Mackenzie, Shaw, and Co., 61 Mill st,
M'Cammon, Thos., (corn) 23 King st.
Neeson, Mr., (Indian corn), Oldpark
Russell, F. and H., Edenderry
Simpson, D. P., Larne
Steen, Henry, Hill street
Tripp, Thomas, Shankhill
Vance, William, (Indian corn) 112 Donegall street

Milliners and Dressmakers

Those marked (*m*) milliners only.
Those marked (*d*) dressmakers only.
*m*Alexander, Margaret, 26 Edward st.
*d*Allen, Elizabeth, 21 Joy street
*m*Armstrong, Mrs., 13 Peter's hill
*m*Banks, Mary, 8¼ Castle place
Barclay and Wallace, 43 Castle street
Barklie, Miss, 5 Chichester street
*d*Barry, Mrs., 8 Sarah street
*m*Beatty, S., 9 Shankhill road
*d*Beggs, Rice, 14 Devis street
*d*Benson, E., 15 Hamilton street
*d*Blair, Eliza, 3 Mill street
*m*Bourns, H., & Sisters, 43 Donegall st.
Boyd, M., 3 Joy street

*d*Boyd, Eliza, 52 Stanhope street
Boyle, E. and J., 3 Seymour street
*d*Brown, Catherine, 1 Henrietta street
Bruce, Jane, 22 Gordon street
Bryson, Eliza, 24 Russell street
*m*Campbell, Mary, 1 Glentilt place
*d*Carmichael, Eliza, 11 College street
*d*Carr, Mrs., 3 Vere street
*d*Clements, H., 61 Academy street
*m*Clendinning, Mrs., 14 Arthur street
Corbett, Jane and Eliza, 14 Cromac st.
*d*Cooke, Eliza, Bridge end, B.carrett
*m*Crawford, Sarah, 46 Ann street
*d*Dalzell, Eleanor, 31 Joy street
*m*Davis, Eliza, 96 High street
*d*Devine, Ann, 3 Millfield
*m*Donaldson, Miss, 8 Arthur square
*d*Donaldson, Mrs., 20 Stanley street
*d*Dyke, Ellen & Sarah, 1 Mill st.
Eid, Anna, 39 Cromac street
*d*Evans, Miss, 29 Stanhope street
*d*Fletcher, Miss, 11 Cromac road
*d*Gelston, Miss, 11 Queen street
*d*Goldstein, Mary, 12 King st.
*d*Goodman, Theresa, 9 Mill street
*m*Grattan, Miss, 41 Upper Arthur st.
Haffern, Margaret, 21 Cromac street
*d*Hagan, Susan, 35 Devis street
Haslett, J., 7 Arthur street
*d*Haslett, Ann, Old Malone road
*d*Hawthorne, E., 28 Stanley street
*m*Henry, Mrs., 49 Upper Arthur st.
*m*Hill, Miss, 8 Donegall pl. buildings
*d*Hull, Sarah, 16 Stephen street
*d*Johnston, Miss, 19 College street
*d*Johnston, Miss Dorcas, 22 Joy street
Johnston, Jane, 1 Friendly street
*m*Johnston, Ann, 9 Henrietta street
*m*Kane, Miss, 57½ Academy street
*m*Kean, A., 38 Academy street
Keith, Mrs., 53 Upper Arthur street
*d*Kirker, Anna, 30 Henrietta street
Lawther, Catherine, 18 Joy street
*m*Lord, M., 25 Hercules place
*d*Magill, Catherine, 31 Old Lodge road
*m*Maloney, Miss, 9 Hercules place
*d*Martin, Margaret, 40 Gt. Edward st.
*d*Martin, Mary, 26 Henrietta street
*d*Miller, J., 65 Academy street
*m*Milne, Mrs., 21 Castle place
*m*Moffatt, Misses, 7 York street
*d*Montgomery, Miss, 125 Durham st.
*d*Montgomery, M., 22 Cargill street
*d*Montgomery, Charlotte, 4 Cromac st.
*m*Montgomery, Mary A., 21 Hercules pl.
*d*Morgan, Mary, 71 Joy street
Morgan, A., 22 King street
*d*M'Cannnon, Mrs., 36 King street
M'Caverty, Ellen, 47 Devis street
*m*M'Clean, Jane, 7 Mill street
*d*M'Cormick, Sarah, 11 Hercules place
*d*M'Coubrey, M., 2 Campbell's buildgs
*m*M'Cracken, Ann Jane, 3 Crown entry
*m*M'Cune, E., 17 Academy street
*d*M'Ferran, Rebecca, 43 Little May st.
*d*M'Ilroy, Ellen, 12 Lancaster street
*d*M'Keown, Eliza, 4 Union street
*m*M'Kee, Mrs., 45 Mill street
M'Kibben, M. and A., and Co., 51 Donegall street
*m*M'Mahon, Miss, 24 Stanhope street
*d*M'Minn, A. and M., 9 Nelson street
*d*M'Nally, Mary Anne, 30 L. May st.
*d*M'Neilly, Rebecca, 9 Harmony place
*d*Nettleton, Eliza, 28 King street
Orr, Misses, 4 Joy street
*d*O'Brien, Mary, 3 Catherine street
*d*Patterson, E., 2 Joy street
*d*Patterson, Eliza, 30 Church lane
*d*Phœnix, E., 50 Joy street
*d*Pollock, Jane, 62 North street
*d*Read, Isabella, 1 Catherine street
*m*Rea, Anna, 37 Edward street
*d*Redmond, Mary, 21 North Ann st.
*m*Reddings, Ann, 46¾ Rosemary st.
*d*Reid, Margaret, 1 Stanley lane
Robinson, Mrs., 62 Donegall street
*d*Robinson, Miss, 16 Harmony place
*m*Robinson, Eliza, 21 Church street
*d*Robinson, Mary Ann, Little Patrick st.
Rodgers, Misses, 7 Downshire place
*m*Ryans, Sarah, 5 Hercules place
*d*Scott, Eliza, 2 Brown street
*d*Sharkey, Miss, 75 Academy street
*d*Sheals, Mary, 103 Carrickhill
Sinclair, Miss, 7 Napier street
*m*Smith, Eleanor, 8 Russell street
*d*Smith, Miss, 8 Talbot street
*d*Smylie, Miss, 23 Talbot street
*d*South, Mrs., 32 Durham street
*d*Sparling, Mary, 26 Upper Arthur st.
*m*Thompson, Matilda, 4 Robert street
*d*Usher, E., 8 Mill street
Walker, E. J., 2 Shipboy street
*d*Watson, Agnes, 12 Eliza street
Weldon, Deborah, 44 Mill street
*d*Wightman, Mrs., 28 North Queen s
*d*Whitla, E., 6 Campbell's buildings
*d*Whiteside, Jane, 24 Peter's hill
*d*Young, Miss, 20 Henry street

Music Sellers
AND MUSICAL INSTRUMENT WAREHOUSES.

Those marked (a) only music sellers
Coffey, William, music shop, 4 High street, and piano-forte warehouse, 25 Donegall place
Hart, John, 6 Arthur square
Hart, Joseph, 14 Castle place
aHenderson, John, 13 Castle place
aMagill, James, 2 Castle buildings
aMullan, John, Donegall place

Muslin Gas Singers

Cooke and Porter, Great George's st.

Muslin Manufacturers

Those marked (a) are also sewing agents.

aAnderson, J. W., and Co., 9 Donegall square south
aAnderson & Gray, 9 Donegall sq. south
aAnderson, John, 49 Great Patrick st.
Broadley, J. W., and Co. (of Glasgow), 18 Waring st.—W. Adamson, agent
aBrown, S. R. and T., 82 Donegall st. —D. M'Kean, agent
Bryson, Wm. (gingham), 18 Waring st.
aCaldwell, James, 28 Academy street
aCampbell and Co., 11 St. Anne's buildings
aChancellor, John, & Co., 6 Curtis st.
Coates and Shaw, 14 Pottinger's entry
aCochrane, Brothers, and Co., 5 and 7 Bank lane
aCrawford, John, 25 Great Patrick st.
aElliott, A. and J. & Co., 1 Donegall square east
aEwart, Wm., and Sons, 3 St. Anne's buildings
Ewing, Andw., 11 St. Anne's buildings
aFisher, John, & Co., 27 Gt. Patrick st.
Fraser, Tanner, & Co., 11 Academy st.
Frazer, James, 62 Nelson street
aGraham, J. C., & Co., 89 Donegall st.
Greer, Wm., 80 Donegall street
aHarrison, Wm., 37 Donegall street
Hart, James, 6 Commercial court
aHicks, Wm., 13 Church street
aHolden, John, & Co., 32 Donegall st.
aHutchinson, J., & Co., 16 Academy st
aJohnston and Pelling, 30 Donegall st.
Kennedy, J. and T. (hand and power loom), Commercial court & Bedford street—Donegall square south
Kennedy, Danl. (gingham), 4 Curtis st.
aLetham, Blyth, and Letham, 55 Academy street
aLindsay, Robert, and Co., Victoria buildings, Victoria street
MaTeer, Samuel, 33 York street
Marshall, Brown, & Co., 7 Elliott's ct.
aMacdonald, J. and D., and Co. (of Glasgow), 2½ York st.—W. Leck, manager
Major, Brothers, 10 York street
aMajor, T. S., and Co., 3½ Donegall st.
aMiller, Wm., 29 Great Patrick st.
aM'Bride, Joseph, Academy street
M'Bride, R., & Co., 4 Commercial ct.
aM'Call, Hugh, 23 York street
M'Connell, J. and J., 7 Lower Kent st.
M'Bride, Geo., 7, Elliott's Court
aM'Indoe, Thos. C., Waring street
M'Keown, D., & Son, 8 Elliott's court
aM'Kee, James, 2 Gamble street
M'Kee, James, 19½ Corporation street
M'Kee, Samuel, 45 Great Patrick st.
M'Reynolds and Knox (gingham), 13 York street
Park, L. and C., 65 York street
Pelling, Peter, and Co., 37 John street
aPorteus, James, and Co., 15 Church st.
aRobinson, J., & Sons, 47 Great Patrick street
Smith, Robt., 4, 6, Rosemary street
Stewart, J., and Co., 4 Lower Kent st.
aStirrat, James, 9 Bank lane
Tierney, Samuel, 9 Elliott's court
Tilley, James, M'Tier street
Vance, J. R. & Sons, 40 Rosemary st.
aWallace, John, 44 Nelson street
aWallace, Wm., 31 Gt. Patrick street
aWallace, J. and W. (of Glasgow) 43 Waring st.—W. Jamieson, agent
aWallace, J. and J., 6 Corporation st.
aWaugh, Thomas, 11 Church street
Weir, W., jun., & Co., 19 Nelson st.
aWorkman, R.,& Co., Corporation st.
Workman, J., & Sons, (also gingham), 60 Upper Arthur street and Bedford street
aWilson, T. & D., John street
Young, James, II., & Co., 37 John st.

Nail Manufacturers

Cinnamond, Samuel, 4 Peter's hill
Dyer, Thomas, 44 Grattan street
Forsythe, Charles, 20 Skipper street
Gibson, John, 28 Little Donegall st.

PROFESSIONS, TRADES, &c.

Gray, Clark, 59 Durham street
Hughes, Edward, M'Adam's court
Johnston, John, 2 Gordon street
Lambert, Matthew, 44 Grattan street
Mullen, John, M'Adam's court
M'Anally, Patrick, M'Adam's court
M'Cartin, John, 92 North street
M'Ilveen, Thomas, 29 Carrickhill
M'Kenna, James, M'Adam's court
Spence, Wm., 10 Caxton street
Stockman, Ralph, 3 Nelson street

News Agents

Boyd, Henry, Commercial buildings, for Charles Willmer, Liverpool
Henderson, John, 13 Castle place
O'Neill, James, 4 Castle place

Newspapers

Banner of Ulster (established 1842), 35 Donegall st. (Tuesday & Friday); publisher, J. F. M'Cormick, Glenfield place; editor, James M'Knight, LL.D., Linenhall street
Belfast Commercial Chronicle (estd. 1805), 6 Arthur street (Monday, Wednesday, & Saturday); publisher, C. Anderson, Upper Arthur st.; editor, James Withers, 17 Campbell's buildings, Townsend street
Belfast Mercantile Register (estd. 1822), Tuesday; publisher, John C. Cramsie, 74 Waring street
Belfast Mercury (estd. 1851), Winecellar entry (Tuesday, Thursday, & Saturday) ; publisher and editor, J. Simms, 16 Howard street
Belfast News-Letter (estd. 1737), 10 Bridge street; (Monday, Wednesday, and Friday); publisher, J. A. Henderson, Mount Collyer Park; editor, R. Mooney, A.B., T.C.D., 81 North Queen street
Commercial Journal & Family Herald 12 High st. (Saturday); published in Dublin by H. Shaw
Northern Whig (estd. 1824), Calender street (Tuesday, Thursday, and Saturday); publisher, F. D. Finlay, 1 Adelaide place ; editor, D. Holland, 5 James's street south
Ulster General Advertiser (estd. 1842), 6 Waring st. (Saturday); publisher, John Wallace, 53 Cromac street

Weekly Vindicator (estd. 1839), 20 Rosemary street (Saturday); publisher, James M'Convery, 20 Rosemary st. ; editor, C. Lennon, Malone

Nautical Instrument Makers

Lee and Son, High street
Neill, Brothers, 23 High street

Notaries Public

Braddell, George Wm., 3 Castle lane
Cramsie, John C., 74 Waring street
Hartley, John, office, 1 The Castle Hill, Adam, 11 Fisherwick place
M'Cracken, J. W., 11 Corporation st.

Nursery, Seedsmen, & Florists

Addison, Wm. (seed merchant), 15 North street
Costley, John, 23 North street
Farrell, S. and Co., 2 High street
Howden, &c., 53 High street
Lytle, J. (seed mercht.), 1, 3 North st.
M'Causland, Samuel (seed merchant), 34 North street
Orr, Joseph, 5 Castle place
Penton, Wm., 2 Donegall street
Taylor, E. (seed mercht.), 10 North st.
Watt, Jas., and Co., 11½ Donegall st.

Nurse Tenders

Allen, Mrs., at C. Lavery's, near Victoria place
Ainsworth, Mrs. Jane, 15 King street
Barber, Catherine, 11 Queen street
Bilford, Mary, 24 Catherine st. south
Conn, Mrs., Stormont's court
Creighton, Mrs.
Doyle, Mrs., 43 Mill street
Hanna, Mrs., Trafalgar street
Hanna, Ellen, 6 Grace street
Magrath, Sarah, 30 Henrietta street
Montgomery, Mrs., 17 Ann street
M'Collum, Charlotte, 5 Berry street
Paton, Mrs., Shankhill
Pettigrew, Anne, King street
Thompson, Mrs., 8 Greenland st., fever
White, Mrs., Fountain st., at Black's upholstery

Oil Merchants

Cuddy, John, Queen's quay, Ballymacarrett, and 42 Church lane
Dickey, Alexander, & Co., Victoria st.
Hamilton, James, 11 Queen's square
MacAdam and Co., 31 Donegall street
Prenter, N. A., 8 and 10 Cotton court

Painters and Glaziers

Adams, John, 13½ Cromac street
Allen, James, 50 Tomb street
Armstrong, John, 43 Academy street
Boyd, William, 18 Skipper street
Briggs, John, 57 Academy street
Clarke, William, 27 Fountain street
Coates, Francis, 37 and 39 Castle st.
Collins, Charles, 7 John street
Douglass, Arthur, 18 Curtis street
Dunlop, Daniel, William street south
Galloway, Thomas, 47 Castle street
Gaskin, James, 56 Donegall street
Gribben, Thomas, 13 John street
Hewey, Mrs., 34 Union street
Hoy, John, 48 Waring street
Irvine, James, 11 Skipper street
Johnston, Alexander, 40 Academy st.
Lynn, John, 54 Ann street
Moore, Alexander, 19 Arthur street
M'Cloy, John, 17 Castle street
M'Kendry, Hugh, & Co., 6 Waring st.
M'Kensey, James, 75 Grattan street
M'Keown, H., 52 Ann street
M'Kinstry, John, 29 Russell street
M'Loughlin, Thos., 20 Melbourne st.
M'Mullan, Alex., 11 Castle street
M'Monagle, Hy., 42 Gt. George's st.
M'Quiston, Thos., 16 Arthur street
Rutherford, James, 5 Castle street
Shaw, William John, 17 John street
Skinner, Alexander, 76 Gt. George's st.
Stewart, James, 14 John street
Stormont, James, 50 North street
Vint, William, 25 Talbot street
Williamson, Wm. J., 5 Frederick st.

Paper Makers and Merchants

Archer and Sons, Ballyclare paper mill; 27 and 29 Castle place
Blow, Edwin, & Co., Dunadry paper mill; 91 Queen's square
Blow, Wm. N., 15 Rosemary street

Patent Saw Mills

Brown, John, jun., Cromac street saw mills, Riley's place
Low, John, patent saw mills, Garmoyle street

Pawnbrokers

Anderson, Wm., 1 Union street
Beggs, Robert, 54 Cromac street
Belshaw, Jas. John, 29 Devis street
Brown, Henry, 17 Henry street
Calhoun, James, 7 Marquis street
Clements, James, 49 Market street
Clements, James, 4 and 6 Lagan street
Coburn, Samuel, 30 Smithfield
Foy, Richard, 33 Great Patrick street
Gilmer, Robert, 56 Little Donegall st.
Gilmore, Robert, 191 North street
Gilmore, Thomas, 74 Cromac street
Girvan, Thomas, Shankhill road
Girven, Joseph, Ballymacarrett
Gregory, Jane, 79 North Queen street
Griffith, John, 30 Great Edward street
Harper, Hugh, 46 Barrack street
Harper, Hugh, 35 Union street
Hynds, Patrick, 14 Nelson street and 34 Little Patrick street
Huddleston, Wm., Portview House, Ballymacarrett
Jenkins, James, 19 Mill street and Marquis street
Lowry, Henry, 25 Townsend street
Maguire, Henry, 20, 24 Chapel lane
Maguire, Thomas, 17 Cromac street
Milligan, Robert, 41 Barrack street
Minniece, Wm., 23½ Peter's hill
M'Allen, Thomas, Shankhill road
M'Call, Hugh, 1 Curtis street, and 36, 38 Hill street
M'Cleery, James, 74 Nelson street
M'Connell, John, 66 Peter's hill
M'Donnell, Francis, 29 Rosemary st.
M'Dornan, John, 28 Durham street
M'Kee, James, 112 High street
M'Quillan, Pat., 39 Gardiner st.
O'Neill, Wm., 20 Robert street
Owen, Jas. B., 19 Barrack street and 29 Townsend street
Owen, Wm. H., 24 Henry street
Patrick, Robert, 38 Henry street
Shields, Thomas, 46, 48 Academy st.
Sibbin, George, 4 Bath place
Smith, James, 49 Cromac street
Smith, James, 57 Green street
Thoburn, David, 1 Nelson street
Warnock, James, 84 Millfield
Wilson, Hugh, 22 Smithfield
Young, Isabella, 18, 20 Lancaster st.
Young, Wm., 38 Mill street

Pipe Makers

Connor, James, 60 Carrick hill
M'Avoy, Michael, 142 North street

Picture Frame Makers

SEE CARVERS AND GILDERS

PROFESSIONS, TRADES, &c.

Physicians and Surgeons
SEE ALSO APOTHECARIES AND SURGEONS.
Aickin, John, 5 Adelaide place
Armstrong, John, 17 College street
Andrews, Thomas, Queen's College
Barnett, Richard, 1 Wellington place
Black, C., 96 Donegall street
Blizard, John, 16 Wellington place
Breakey, John, General Hospital
Browne, Samuel, R.N., 5 Clarence pl.
Bryce, Robert, 63 Donegall street
Bryson, Joseph, 16 York street
Burden, William, 16 Alfred street
Clarke, John, 90 Donegall street
Collins, R., 20 Queen street
Carlisle, Hugh, professor of anatomy, Queen's College
Crang, Frederick, 104 Donegall street
Dill, R. S., 42 Upper Arthur street
Dickie, G., 4 Botanic view
Drennan, John, 23 Chichester street
Drummond, James, 8 College sq. north
Ferguson, Henry, 55 Upper Arthur st.
Ferguson, J. C., 14 Howard street
Gordon, Alexander, 2 College sq. east
Halliday, John H., 59 Donegall street
Hurst, Charles, 10 Donegall place
Hunter, Samuel, 9 Clarence place
Heeney, Francis, 31 York street
Johnston, Henry M., 77 Donegall st.
Kidley, John E., 47 York street
Lamont, Æ., 3 Castle street
Malcolm, A. G., 49 York street
Marshall, Andrew, 3 Wellington place
Mawhinney, Jas., 8 College sq. east
Moffatt, William, 20 Wellington place
Moore, James, 7 Chichester street
Mulholland, C., 11 Prospect terrace
Murray, James, 41 Arthur street
Murney, Henry, 10 Chichester street
M'Cormac, Henry, 4 Wellington place
M'Gee, Wm., R.N., 10 Donegall sq. east
M'Gregor, J. B., 34 Upper Arthur st.
M'Kibbin, Robt., 13 Chichester street and Avoneil
Patterson, James, 4 Donegall sq. east
Pirrie, John M., 66 Donegall street
Posnett, John B., Workhouse
Purdon, Wm., University square
Purdon, Chas. D., 17 College sq. east
Purdon, Thos. H., 5 Wellington place
Quinn, John, 3 Bank lane
Read, Thomas, 5 Donegall sq. west
Reid, James S., 3 College square east
Ross, Richard, 25 King street
Smith, J. W., 18 Arthur street
Stephenson, Robert, 11 Wellington pl.
Stewart, Horatio, 51 York street
Stewart, R., Lunatic Asylum
Thompson, Thos., R.N., 83 Donegall st.
Thompson, James, 7 Botanic view

Pianoforte Makers, Tuners, and Repairers
SEE ALSO PIANOFORTE WAREHOUSES.
Those marked (a) are manufacturers.
Coffey, William, 25 Donegall place & 4 High street
aCraig, Liddle, and Crymble, 3 Fountain street
Hart, Joseph, 14 Castle place
aM'Cullough, Mrs., 9 Arthur place & 13 George's lane

Plasterers, Masters
Ash, James, 28 Charles street
Bole, Hugh, 25 Caroline street
Britten, Alex., 36 Corporation street
Brown, James, 12 Curtis street
Brown, Patrick, 3 Wall street
Crow, James, 27 Boyd street
Cunningham, John, Roy's court
Cunningham, James, 14 Roy's court
Dawson, Edward, Falloon's court
Doherty, Patrick, 1 Russell street
Finlay, William, 5 East street
Gowdy, John, 1 Letitia street
Johnston, David, 27 Catherine st. north
Kelly, Patrick, 71 Little Patrick street
Lowry, Robert, 3 Shipboy street
Mitchell, John, 12 Mitchell street
M'Crea, James, 8 Murphy street
M'Mahon, Owen, 28 Grattan street
O'Neill, John, 5 Devis street
Overend, Peter, 52 Carrick hill
Plunkett, James, Durham street
Smith, William, 18 Grove street
Smith, James, Ballynafeigh
Walsh, Edward, 33 Academy street
Whiteside, James, 7 Greenland street

Plumbers, &c.
Butler, Thomas, & Son, 7 Fountain st.
Cameron, James, 47 Donegall street
Fortune and Co., 25 Hill street
Hamilton, John, 2 Francis street
Mackenzie, Brothers, Regent buildings, Victoria street
Magee, John, 32 Ann street
Scully, Shannon, and Holmes, 12 Talbot street

Posting Establishments
Brown, James, 9½ Castle place

PROFESSIONS, TRADES, &c.

Davis, George, Plough Hotel, Corn market
Donegall Arms, 9½ Castle place
Echlin, Peter, Commercial Hotel, Commercial buildings
Hurst, Dr. C., Imperial Hotel, 10 Donegall place
Kerns, Chas., Royal Hotel, 27 Donegall place
Madine, George, 7 York street
Morrison, Hugh, 8 Montgomery street
Robson, John, 31 Chichester street and 2 Montgomery street

Post Offices

General Post Office, Rosemary street, O'Donnell Grimshaw, Postmaster
Receiving Office, 26 Arthur street
Receiving Office, 1 Gt. George's street
Receiving Office, 22 Devis street
Receiving Office, Lying-in-Hospital, Antrim road
Ballymacarrett Post Office, Jeremiah Wilson, Postmaster

Potteries

Ballymacarrett Pottery Works, Bridge end, Ballymacarrett, Fras. M'Wade, proprietor
Hibernian Pottery, Queen's quay, Ballymacarrett, William Spencer, proprietor

Poulterers

SEE ALSO BUTCHERS

Dickson, Daniel, 18 and 19 Ormond market
Kane, Patrick, 18 Market street
Moore, Margaret, 58 Market street
M'Donnell, Bridget, 10 Market street
Rafferty, James, 3 York street market
Simpson, Henry, 79 Market street
Tandy, Mrs., 31 Market street
Woodcock, Henry, 21 Ormond market

Printers

Agnew, W. & G., Calender street
Anderson, J. C., *Commercial Chronicle*, 6½ Arthur street
Clarke, Hugh, & Co., 24 Corn market
Finlay, Francis D., *Northern Whig*, 6 Calender street
Henderson, Jas. Alex., *News-Letter*, 10 Bridge street
Henderson, John, 13 Castle place

Mayne, Alexander, 34 High street
Moore, James, 1 Castle court
O'Neill, James, 4 Castle place
Read, R. and D., Crown entry
Reed, James, Victoria street
Reilly, Thomas Henry, 13 Waring st.
Simms, James, *Mercury*, Winecellar entry
Simms and M'Intyre, 26 & 28 Donegall street
Wallace, J., *Ulster General Advertiser*, 6 Waring street
Welsh, A., 10 Arthur square
Wilson, James, 70 High street

Provision Dealers

Agnew, John, 60 Grattan street
Anderson, James, 27 Trafalgar street
Anderson, James, 182 North street
Black, James, 29 Edward street
Boyle, Patrick, Falls road
Bradford, David, 40 Union street
Bradley, Samuel, 21 and 29 Hill st.
Bruce, Andrew, 1½ Nelson street
Bruce, Mrs., 50 Academy street
Carpenter, P., 33 Rosemary street
Cavanagh, John, 11¼ Cromac street
Curran, Catherine, 13 William st. S.
Daniel, John, Falls road
Douglass, Wm., 25 Little Patrick st.
Ferguson, Bernard, 58 Cromac street
Foley, John, 150 North street
Gossan, Eliza, 2 Arthur square
Grimshaw, Eliza, 7 Little Patrick st.
Hanna, Robert, Falls road
Hamill, James, 179 North street
Hamilton, Margaret, 28 Smithfield
Henderson, John, 15½ Hill street
Holywood, Daniel, 39 Union street
Hodgkinson, William, 17 Hill street
Ingram, John, 161 North street
Kane, Dennis, 46 Waring street
Kelly, Michael, 175 North street
Lenaghan, William, 41 Cromac street
Maguire, James, 6 Hill street
Mullins, Thomas, 167, 169 North st.
M'Clure, James, 10 Gt. Patrick street
M'Clure, James, 5 Hill street
M'Gennity, Michael, 13 Hill street
M'Gladdery, Samuel, 31 Union street
M'Goughey, Isabella, 27 Smithfield
M'Kenna, James, 35 & 38 Smithfield
M'Kenna, John, 36 Smithfield
M'Millen, James, 141 North street
M'Murtry, James, 50 Edward street

M'Roberts, George, 25 Cromac street
Nelson, Robert, 50 Peter's hill
O'Neill, Elizabeth, 33 Union street
Owens, Thomas, 64 Nelson street
Rainey, George, 1 Russell street
Richardson, John, 31 Melbourne st.
Roche, Patrick, 48 Cromac street
Spence, William, 31, 33 and 35 Boundary street
Stewart, Thomas, 29 Castle street
Toner, Patrick, 163 North street
Welsh, James, 5 Little Patrick street
Wright, Mary, 165 North street

Provision Merchants

Andrews, A., 30 Tomb street
Arrott, Isaac, 34 Waring street
Bayley, O'Neill, 41 Corporation street
Bigger, Jos., jun., 5 Little Donegall st.
Bigger, Joseph, 44 John street
Bodel, James, 5 Henry street
Campbell, John, 9 Henry street
Campbell, William and J., 8½ Great George's street
Coates, Geo., and Co., 43 Trafalgar st.
Coey, Edward, 21 Gamble street
Davis, John, 85½ York street
Dickson, R. and H., 27 Nelson street
Douglass, Wm., 63 Corporation street
Duffield, William J. and A., 86 Corporation street
Frazer and Finch, 59 Waring street
Fulton, John, 15 Long lane
Gelston, Wm., 40 Tomb street
M'Connell, Saml., 22, 24 Academy st.
M'Kibbin, G. and H., 83 York street
Scott, James, 7 Albert square
Shaw and Dickson, 18 Gt. George's st.
Sinclair, John and Thomas, 5, 7, 9, 11 Tomb street
Waring, Richard, 87 York street

Publishers

Henderson, Jas. Alex., 19 Bridge st.
Henderson, John, 13 Castle place
Mayne, Alexander, 34 High street
M'Comb, William, 1 High street
O'Neill, James, 4 Castle place
Read, R. and D., Crown entry
Simms and M'Intyre, 26 & 28 Donegall street

Railway Companies

Belfast and Ballymena Railway, York road, Thomas H. Higgin, general manager
Belfast and County Down Railway, Queen's quay, Ballymacarret, Thos. Ward, secretary
Ulster Railway, Great Victoria street, J. G. Smith, secretary

Reading Rooms and Libraries

Commercial News Room, Commercial Buildings, Henry Boyd, secretary
"Commercial Journal & Family Herald" Reading Room, 12 High street
Corn Exchange News Room, Victoria street
Linenhall Library, Linenhall
News room, Linenhall
Peoples' Reading, Newspaper, and Library Room, 4 Castle chambers

Rectifying Distillers

Bain, Joseph, 4 Seymour lane
Keegan, James, 8 Arthur place
Keegan, Peter, 4 Calender street
M'Connell, Jas. & John, 28 Tomb st.
Thompson, Robert, 17 Church street
Wilson, Guy S., 11¼ Mill street

Reed Makers

Midgley, John, 23 New Durham st.
Riddel, Alexander, 37 John street
Riddell, James, Gavin's buildings, Shankhill road
Riddell, Alexander, 3 Ship street

Restaurants

Clarendon Rooms, Victoria street
Dunlop, David, 1 Arthur square
Hurst, Dr. C. (Imperial Hotel), 1 Castle lane
Walker, David, 19 Bridge street

Room Paper Warehouses

Those marked (a) are manufacturers
Hodgson, Robert, 9 High street
Girdwood, James, 44 High street
aMearns and Co., 10 Castle place and 22 Donegall street
Rutherford, James, 70 High street
aStaunton, Moses, 9 Donegall place

Rope and Twine Makers.

Abbott, Joseph, 9 Corporation street
Carson, Robt. M., 61 Waring street
Davidson, John, 95 Queen's square
Dornan, James, 74 North street
Freeman, J. & Co., 14 Pottinger's entry

PROFESSIONS, TRADES, &c.

Hanna, Edward, 11 M'Crory's row, Ballymacarrett
Hampsey, Edward, Ballymacarrett
Hampsey, Patrick, Ballymacarrett
Hampson, Mary, 6 Prince's street
Ivory, James, 5 M'Crory's row, Ballymacarrett
Johnston, James, Shankhill
Johnston, David, 18 Shankhill
Keenan, Thomas, 102 High street
Lemon, James, 15 Queen's square
Marlow, James, 70 North street
M'Namara, Henry, 26 Church lane

Saddlers and Harness Makers

Cherry, Moses (and American trunk manufactory), 9 Donegall street
Davidson, James, 48 North street
Ferguson, David, 22 Boyd street
Fulton, Wm., 39 Rosemary street
Gordon, Benjamin, 33 Gt. Edward st.
Kerr, Daniel, 12 Castle place
Kerns, George, 155 North street
Milliken, Robert, 49 North street
Mullan, Hugh, 10 Bank lane
M'Cleave, J., and Son, 6 Castle place
O'Hayer, F.,1 Donegall place buildings
Rodgers, David, 51 North street
Woods, Wm., Frederick place

Saloons

Clarendon, Regent Buildings, Thomas Linden, proprietor
Hibernian, 14 Smithfield, R. Calvert, proprietor
Robert Burns, 8 Long lane, John Reid, proprietor
Shakspeare, 21 Castle lane, E. P. Grey, proprietor
Star, 21 Ann street, Charlotte Kerr, proprietor

Salt Merchants

Arrott, Isaac, 36 Waring street
Crawford, James, 13 and 15 Corporation street
Harper, Martin, 44 Church lane

Saw Makers and Sharpers

Broe, Henry, 78 Hercules street
Crookes, John, 16 Skipper street
Simpson, Robert, 17 Hamilton place

Seal Engraver

M'Cleave, S. R., 18 Corn Market

Servants' Registry Offices

Dyer, John, 3½ Arthur street
Foster, John, 1 Long lane
Orr, Mrs,, 1 Academy street
Usher, Miss, 8 Mill street

Ship Brokers.

Barkley, Wm. M., 97 Queen's square
Bell, Abraham, 3 Abbotsford place
Colvil, Auld, & Co., 74 Waring street
Folingsby, T. G., & Co., 15 Albert sq.
Hind, Hugh S., 11 Queen's square
Hind, Joseph, & Sons, 1 Queen's sq.
Heyn, Gustavus, 1 Henry street
Henderson, Robt., 23 Donegall Quay
Macdonald, James, 59 Waring street and 8 Prince's dock
Munster, Paul L., Corporation street
M'Bride, James, & Co., 59 Tomb st.
M'Ferran, James, 39 Corporation st.
M'Nally, Joseph, 56 Tomb street
M'Nally, Robert, 12 Short street
Newett, Wm., 9 Queen's square
Reid and Forrest, 10 Albert square
Trotter, J. C., 17 Queen's square
Wilkinson, Wm., 7 Queen's square

Ship Builders

Coates and Young (iron), Lagan foundry and Pilot street
Connell, Alex., and Co. (late Charles Connell and Sons), Graving dock, Corporation st.
M'Laine, Alexander, & Sons, Graving dock, Corporation street
Thompsons & Kirwan, Queen's island

Ship Chandlers

Abbott, Joseph, 9 Corporation street
Carson, Robert M., 61 Waring street
Clarke, Peter, 31 Corporation street
Crawford, Jas., 13, 15 Corporation st.
Finlay, Francis, 27 Pilot street
Lemon, James, 15 Queen's square
Mitchell, George, 5 Prince's dock
Newett, William, 2 Corporation street
Scott, J., 4 Corporation street
Tedford, James, 29 Donegall quay

Ship Owners

Abbott, Joseph, 9 Corporation street
Alexander, Arthur, 134 North street
Arrott, Isaac, 34 Waring street
Barlow, Wm., Gasfield House
Bell, Jacob, 4 Mustard street

PROFESSIONS, TRADES, &c.

Bell, Richard, 4 Mustard street
Boag, Neil, Consbrook
Boyd, Robert, Bloomfield
Boyd, James, Beech lodge
Boyle, Samuel, 16 Ann street
Bradford, James, 10 Garmoyle street
Brown, Henry, 17 Henry street
Carson, R. M., 61 Waring street
Charley, John, 53 Donegall quay
Coates, William, Glentoran
Coates and Young, Lagan village
Coleman, John, 27 York street
Colvil, Auld, and Co., 74 Waring st.
Corry, Robert, 10 The Crescent
Corry, James P., 4 Franklin place
Crawford, Henry Sharman, Castle pl.
Craig, Hugh, York street
Cuddy, John, 42 Church lane
Dunn, John, 13 Henry street
Entwistle, James, 18 Eliza street
Ewing, Samuel, 11 Nile street
Feeney, John, Welsh's Glen, C.fergus
Ferrie and Campbell, 74 Waring st.
Fitzsimmons, Nicholas, Corporation st.
George, Thomas, Lilliput house
Gaussen, John, and Co., 11 Albert sq.
Glenfield, Francis, 104 High street
Grainger, David, Prince's dock
Grainger, David, jun., Prince's dock
Gray, Thomas, 22 North street
Gregg, Cranston, Malone
Greenfield, John, 76 High street
Hamilton, Wm., Ann street
Harrison, John, 1 Albert square
Harper, Martin, 44 Church lane
Henderson, Robert, 23 Donegall quay
Heron, Wm. C., & Co., 13 Albert sq.
Heron, James, of W. C. Heron & Co., 13 Albert square
Herdman, William (of Langtrys and Herdman), Cliftonville
Heyn, Gustavus, 1 Henry street
Houston, Samuel, 39 Dock street
Hughes, Bernard, 5 Donegall place
Ireland, Jas. (of Ireland and M'Neill), 17 Corn market
Johnston, Robert, 25 Donegall street
Johnston, Wm., 25 Donegall street
Keenan, Thomas, 102 High street
Langtry, Charles (of Langtrys and Herdman), 33 Waring street
Langtry, Richard (of Langtrys and Herdman), 33 Waring street
Langtrys and Herdman, 33 Waring st.
Lemon, James, 15 Queen's square
Lepper, Robert S., 1 Abbotsford place
Lewis, Frederick (of F. & W. Lewis), 3 Great George's street
Lewis, F. & W., 3 Great George's st.
Low, John, 71 Ship street
Macnamara, James, 29 Tomb street
Martin, John, and Co., 29 Ann street
Martin, Samuel (of John Martin and Co.), 29 Ann street
Meenan, Bernard, 7 Hammond's court
Massey, Sarah, Durham street
Millen, John, 5, 11 Marlborough st.
Morrow, Patrick, 30 North Thomas st.
Morrison, Hugh, Montgomery street
Murphy, John, 3 Hamilton street
Murray, Dan., Short strand, B.carrett
Murray, Owen, 18 North Thomas st.
M'Causland, Samuel, 34 North street
M'Clure, Wm., & Son, Corporation st.
M'Connell, David, High street
M'Fadden, James, Tomb street
M'Ferran, Wm., 18 Albert square
M'Ferran, Jas., Queen's quay, B.carrett
M'Millan, Ruth, 89 York street
M'Tear, George, 35 Donegall quay
Nelson, Samuel, Linen hall
Newett, Wm., Queen's square
Owens, Thomas, 64 Nelson street
Pascoe, Wm., 16 Garmoyle street
Pirrie, Wm., 66 Donegall street
Potts, John and Robert, 31 North st.
Robinson, James, Ormeau street
Sands, Joseph, 4 Ann street
Sinclair, John and Thos., 5 Tomb st.
Steen, James (of Jas. Steen and Co.), 3 Talbot street
Stewart, William, 10 Nelson street
Suffern, John, 76 Donegall street
Sullivan, James, 16 Brougham street
Tedford, James, 29 Donegall quay
Thomson, Samuel, 1 Corporation st.
Tucker, Edward, 27 Waring street
Wardlow, Hugh, 6 Great George's st.
Wilson, Robert, 19 Earl street
Wright, P., 10 Queen's quay, B.carrett
Young, James, 3 Arthur square

Shirt Makers
Blackburn, Mary, 49 Boyd street
Curry, Mary, 44 Joy street
Ford, Thos. (& collar), 4 Fountain lane
Hamilton, Mrs., 44 Annette street
M'Kee, Ellen, 52 Great Patrick street
M'Roberts, Agnes, 13 Cromac street
Surplus, Mrs., 38 Durham street

PROFESSIONS, TRADES, &c.

Shuttlemakers
Bullock, William, 27 North street
Mooney, John, 21 Talbot street

Silk Manufacturers
Lindsay, Brothers, & Co., Eliza street

Silk Mercers
Arnott, John, and Co., 7, 9, 11, 17 and 17½ Bridge street
Hardy, Thomas, 35 and 37 High st.
Johnsons & Co., 18 Donegall place
Lindsay, Brothers, 1, 3 Donegall place
Mackenzie and Saunders, 36 High st.
Maclurcan, John, 2 Donegall place buildings
Murray, Greene and Lloyd, 13 Donegall place
M'Kibbin, M. & A., & Co., 51 Donegall street
Robinson, Mrs., 62 Donegall street

Sizing Factories
Bell, Richard and Jacob, 8 Upper Kent street
Kennedy, J. and T., Talbot street
Rutherford, A., 25 Little Donegall st.

Soap and Candle Makers
Dugan, Robert, 18 John street
Finlay, John, 31 Ann street
Fletcher, Thomas, 10 Little May st.
Gardner, Thomas, 87 Queen's square
Glenfield, Francis, 104 High street
Greer, Jane, 54 North street
Hunter, John, 138 North street
Johnson, John, 14 Great Patrick st.
Moffet, John, 76 Ann street
Morris, Wm. Henry, 42 & 44 North st.
M'Alister, Joseph, 58½ North street
M'Cann, James, 11 North street
M'Cann, Daniel, 96 North street
M'Cann, Daniel, 9 Donegall place buildings [Academy street
M'Clinton and Thomson, 47 and 49
Patterson, Francis, 24 Mill street
Patterson, William, 170 North street
Pelan and M'Mullan, 26 Corn market
Shaw, James, 23 Ann street
Tate and Bell, 82 Hercules street
Warnock, James, 36 Gt. Edward st.

Soda Ash Manufacturers
Burden, Francis, Friendly st. & Eliza street; Wm. R. Pye, manager

Solicitors and Attorneys.
Agnew, Wm., 4 Aughton Terrace
Andrews, James, 60 Donegall street and 103 Capel street, Dublin
Andrews & Smith, 46 Donegall street and 103 Capel street, Dublin
Arthur, Robt., 24 Donegall place and 18 Belvidere place, Dublin
Bates, John (Town Clerk), 19 Rosemary st, and 37 Blessington street, Dublin
Black, Samuel, 12, Chichester st. and 54 Upper Dorset street, Dublin
Bowman, Robert, 16 Donegall st. 8 Inns Quay, Dublin & Carrickfergus
Bruce, Samuel, 33 Donegall street and 19 Upper Ormond Quay, Dublin
Cassidy, R. and A., 9 Donegall pl. and 19 Upper Ormond quay, Dublin
Coates, John, 29 Arthur street, 25 Upper Mecklenburg street, Dublin, and Newtownards
Campbell, James, 9 Rosemary st. and 8 Inns Quay, Dublin
Carson, Wm., 31 Waring street and 37 Blessington street, Dublin
Cinnamond, Thos., 30 Donegall street and 48 Rutland square, Dublin
Collins, W. M., 21 Arthur street and 103 Capel street, Dublin
Cranston, Wm. and Alexander J., 33 Arthur st., and 29 Upper Ormond Quay, Dublin
Crawford and Russell, 24 Arthur st. and 46 Lower Gardiner st., Dublin
Cunningham, W. C. (and Deputy Clerk of the Peace), 4 York street and 29 Upper Ormond Quay, Dublin
Davis, Wm., 23 Arthur street and 185 Great Brunswick street, Dublin
Davison & Torrens, 23 Donegall place and 65 Lower Gardiner st., Dublin
Dillon, Wm., 31 Arthur street and 22 Middle Gardiner street, Dublin
Dinnen, John, 18 Arthur street and 22 Middle Gardiner street, Dublin
Dobbin, Alexander C., 14 Castle lane and 8 Inns Quay, Dublin
Elliott, S. M'Dowell (and Seneschal of Belfast), 12 Arthur street, and 15 Lower Ormond Quay, Dublin
Gamble, O. R., 2 Arthur place, and 22 Middle Gardiner street, Dublin
Garrett, Henry J. R. and Thos., 16 Castle lane and 8 Inns Quay, Dublin

PROFESSIONS, TRADES, &c.

Gibson, Joseph, 4 Arthur street and 103 Capel street, Dublin
Grimshaw, O'Donnell, 30 Rosemary st. and 8 Inns Quay, Dublin
Hamilton, James, 105 York street
Haslett, W. H., 14 Chichester street
Higginson, J. M. (and Deputy Registrar Consistorial Court, Down and Connor), 35 Upper Arthur street
Hitchcock & Black, 70 Donegall st.
Jackson, J. K. (and coroner for the district of Belfast, and Deputy Clerk of the Crown for Antrim), 8 Castle lane, and 37 Blessington street, Dublin
Joy, Frederick, 5 Arthur place
Johnson, Thomas B., 27 Arthur st. and 103 Capel street, Dublin
Kennedy, John B., 10 Castle lane and 5 Summerhill, Dublin
Kennedy, Samuel, 17 Arthur st. and 26 Lower Ormond Quay, Dublin
Keenan, John, 13 Arthur street and 18 Fleet street, Dublin
Ladley, John, 16 Calender street, and 74 Dame street, Dublin
Macrory, Adam J., 23 Rosemary st. and 48 Rutland square west, Dublin
Macrory, Robert, 23 Rosemary street and Rutland square west, Dublin
Mackeown, Geo. F., 55 Donegall st. and 26 Lower Ormond Quay, Dublin
Milford, Henry, 29 Donegall st., and 26 Lower Ormond Quay, Dublin
Moore, Samuel, 25 Arthur street and 19 Upper Ormond Quay, Dublin
M'Clean, James, 3 Arthur street, and 43 Dame st. and Leinster Chambers, Dublin
M'Clean, James, 3 Chichester street
M'Cullough, J., & Co., 44 Donegall st.
M'Kenny, Tully, 3 Arthur street and 107 Capel street, Dublin
Orr and Montgomery, 3 The Castle
O'Rorke, Alex. and Daniel, 14 Donegall st. & 39 Eccles st., Dublin.
Rea, John, 12 Donegall street and 22 Middle Gardiner street, Dublin
Savage, Patrick, 2½ Arthur street and 52 Jervis street, Dublin
Seeds, H. and W., 18 Castle lane, 54 Upper Dorset street, Dublin, and Railway street, Lisburn
Smyth, John, 42 Donegall street and 43 Dame street, Dublin

Smith, Geo. K. and F., 3 The Castle and 35 North Cumberland street, Dublin
Sproull, W. H., 34 College street and 19 Upper Ormond Quay, Dublin
Suffern. John, 76 Donegall street and 12 Upper Temple street, Dublin
Stephenson, G., 6 Castle Chambers, and Lisburn
Teeling, John and Fras., 6 Castle lane
Tittle, James H. 19 Arthur street and 19 Upper Ormond Quay, Dublin
Wallace, John, Victoria street, and 22 North Earl Street, Dublin
Waterson, W. T. & R. S. 132½ Ann street, and 26 Lower Ormond Quay, Dublin
Wallace, Hugh and Co., 24 Fountain street, and 30 North Great George's street, Dublin, and Downpatrick
Young, James, 3 Arthur square and 51 Camden street, Dublin

Spirit Dealers
SEE ALSO GROCERS AND SPIRIT DEALERS.

Adams, James, 12 Gt. Patrick street
Alexander, Arthur (and stabling), 134 North street
Anderson, Margaret, 173 North st.
Armstrong, Thos., 47 Smithfield
Armstrong, Joseph, 55 Union street
Atkinson, Richard, 2 Cromac street
Ball, James, 164 North street
Bammer, Wm., 43 May street
Barry, J., & Co., 14 Marlborough st
Barber, James, 52 Henry street
Barnes, James, 5, 7 Caddell's entry
Barnett, Andrew, 33 Barrack street
Barnett, James, Ferguson's court
Baxter, H., 35 Winetavern street
Beattie, John, 2 Grattan street
Beatty, Thomas, 166 North street
Bell, Joseph, 1 Victoria street
Bertram, Jacob, 4 Lower Malone
Boomer, Michael, 69 Cromac street
Black, James, Joy's entry
Black, Rose, 5 Chapel lane
Boyd, Robert, Brittain Mount, Carrickfergus road
Boyle, James, 4 Gt. George's street
Blakely, John, 41 Donegall quay
Boyle, Peter, 21 Marquis street
Brice, John, 36 Church lane
Britain, John, 65 Mustard street
Britain, David, 23 Wesley place

PROFESSIONS, TRADES, &c.

Brittain, John, Ballynafeigh
Bracegirdle, Matthew, 57 Smithfield
Brown, Stewart, 40 Trafalgar street
Brown Henry, Ballymacarrett
Brown, James, 1 Murphy street
Brown, Robert, 24 Gamble street
Brown, Robert, 32 John street
Budge, A. W., 42 Ann street
Burns, Bernard, 1 Roseann place
Burns, George, 41 May street
Burns, Mary, Lagan Village, B.carrett
Byrne, Cherry, 33 Donegall quay
Callender, James, 21, 23 Mill street
Campbell, John, 135 Durham street
Campbell, John, 2 Edward street
Campbell, Francis, 1 Albert square
Canavan, John, 91 North Queen st.
Cannavan, Dorothea, 36 John street
Carlisle, S., 26, 28 Little Patrick st.
Carson, John, Shankhill road
Carson, Richard, Falls road
Clark, Richard, 18 Corporation street
Clarke, Neal, 78¼ Cromac street
Clarke, John, 31 Pilot street
Clements, James, 12 Smithfield
Clements, Robt., 7 Church street
Cleland, Robert, 15 Skipper street
Coates, Wm., Conway street
Cochrane, Samuel, 1 Gordon street
Conway, Jane, 80 North street
Coleman, Patrick, 71, 73 Academy st.
Corrigan, Adam, 45 Nelson street
Coleman, Samuel, 66 Barrack street
Cowan, Andrew, Shankhill road
Cuddy, John, 59 Academy street
Cranston, Elizabeth, 25 Lancaster st.
Cuddy, Hugh, 36 Ann street
Curry, Richard, 103 Lower Malone
Dickson, Arthur, 67 Corporation sq.
Dickson, James, 128 Ann street
Dillon, John, 1 George's lane
Dogherty, Patrick, 35 May street
Donaldson, H. W., 1 Ann street
Donnelly, Edwd., 104 Old Lodge road
Donnelly, James, 49 Little George's st.
Dougherty, John, 120 North street
Dougherty, Rose Ann, 27 Peter's hill
Downing, Wm., Bridge end, B.carrett
Duncan, John, Falls road
Duncan, Adam, 104 North street
Dunlop, Catherine, 6¼ Hamilton st.
Dunlop, Alexander, 62 Tomb street
Dyer, Denis, 177 North street
Evans, James, 102 North street
Ewart, Rachael, 22 Cromac road

Ewart, Thomas, 45 North Queen st.
Farrell, Timothy, 57 Mill street
Fee, Jane, 130 Ann street
Fea, Thos., 12 Marlborough street
Ferran, Patrick, 16 Alexander street
Feeney, John, 14, 16 Gamble street
Ferris, Wm., 47 Currell's place
Fetherston, J., 1 Upper Church lane
Fetherston, John, 49 Ann street
Fitzpatrick, Bernard, 19 Albert square
Foley, Edward, 4 Legg's lane
Forsythe, Catherine, 8 Skipper street
Frazer, James, 17 Great Edward st.
Frazer, Charles, 14 Collingwood street
Frew, John, 111 Durham street
Frew, R. and E., 25 Smithfield
Fullarton, Thomas, 9 Talbot street
Garner, Edward, 53 New Lodge road
Giles, John, 50 Hercules street
Gilles, Mary, 11 Gamble street
Gillespie, Margaret, 22 Gt. Edward st.
Gilmore, Benjamin, 33 North Queen st.
Gordon, John, 11 Castle lane
Goudy, William, 51¼ Cromac street
Grant, James, 3 Upper Church lane
Green, Thos., 13 Short street
Griffith, Patrick, 35 Smithfield
Guy, James, 57 New Lodge road
Guy, Alex., 3 Little Donegall street
Hanna, Francis, Shankhill road
Hanna, Francis, Hammond's court
Hanvey, Wm., 20 Albert square
Hainey, Hugh, 33 Winetavern st.
Harkins, Mrs., 4 Hill street
Hayden, Pierce, 32½ Gt. George's st.
Heron, Edward, 41 Smithfield
Hill, John, 20 Great George's street
Hill, Ann, 120 Ann street
Horner, James, 10 Durham street
Houston, John, 21 Devis street
Hoy, Robert, 68½ Nelson street
Hoy, John, 48 Waring street
Hood, David, 25 Caddell's entry
Hughes, Mary, 13 Donegall quay
Hume, Isabella, 18 Mill street
Hunter, James, Antrim road
Ingram, George, 78 Waring street
Irvine, James, 29 Little Donegall st.
Irvine, Thomas, 25½ John street
Irvine, Matthew, 184 North street
Irwin, Archibald, Ballymacarrett
Johnston, Wm., 38 Great George's st.
Johnston, Margaret, 5 Shankhill road
Johnston, John, 21 Queen's square
Jordan, Philip, 136 Ann street

PROFESSIONS, TRADES, &c.

Kane, Denis, 46 Waring street
Kearney, Peter, 64 Grattan street
Kelly, Samuel, New Durham street
Kennedy, John, 3 Antrim road
Kelsey, John A., Gamble street
Kennedy, Robert, 37 Bradbury place
Kennedy, Matthew, 4 Harmony place
Kerr, Alex., 2 North Ann street
Kerr, Charlotte, Star Saloon, 21 Ann street
Keyland, James, Great Victoria street
Killen, Bridget, 47 Carrick hill
Kilmartin, Thos., 36 Cromac street
King, William, 51 Durham street
Kirk, R. D., 21 Frederick street, and 5 North Queen street
Kirker, Thomas, 77 Durham street
Kirker, John, 73 York street
Kirkwood, S., Falls road
Lavery, Richard, 41 North Queen st.
Law, David, 145 Durham street
Lewis, Thomas, 40 Old Lodge road
Lemon, Patrick, 99 Queen's square
Logan, James, 15 Little Patrick st.
Long, Allan R., 116 Ann street
Loughry, Patrick, 48, 50 Grattan st.
Loughran, Patrick, 13 Marquis street
Loughran, Henry, 1 Gt. Patrick st.
Low, Mr., 4 George's lane
Low, James, 24 Chichester street
Mackin, Thos., 27 Corn market
Magee, Mrs., 6 North street
Magee, Robert, 16 Caddell's entry
Magouran, Peter, 1 Berry street
Magorian, M., 6 Little Patrick street
Mawhinney, I., Sir Henry's buildings, Ballymacarrett
Maguire, John, 13 Frederick street
Marson, Catherine, 57 North Queen st.
Marr, John, 6 Little George's street
Marrs, John, 19 Michael street
Marrs, Daniel, 26 Millfield
Martin, Samuel, 20 Little Donegall st.
Martin, Matthew, 69 Nelson street
Martin, Robert, 40 Verner street
Melville, Samuel, 3 Lemon's lane
Meenan, Bernard, 7 Hammond's ct.
Millen, H. & J., 12 Gt. Edward st.
Millen, Hugh, 68 Ann street
Millikin, George, Falls road
Montgomery, T., 69 North Queen st.
Montgomery, Samuel, 63 Union street
Mitchell, Mary, 57 Hill street
Morrow, Andrew, 53 Gt. Patrick st.
Mooney, Patrick, 98 North street
Moore, W. J., 9 Long lane
Morrison, R., 19 William st. south
Moynes, Patrick, 22 Albert square
Murney, Patrick, 38 Little Donegall st.
Murphy, Arthur, 56 John street
M'Caull, James, 89 Durham street
M'Ateer, Patrick, 59 Cromac street
M'Call, Chas., 4 Marlborough street
M'Bride, Thomas, 15 Police square
M'Cann, Samuel, 28 Chapel lane
M'Cloy, Wm., 2 Carrickhill
M'Cullough, J., 68 New Lodge road
M'Cormick, Patrick, 25 Donegall quay
M'Cracken, Joseph, 66 Brown street
M'Anally, Henry, 118 North street
M'Cracken, Saml., 43 Carrick hill
M'Cullough, Thos., 140 Carrick hill
M'Cune, Richard, 17 Albert square
M'Creanor, Patk., 3 Marlborough st.
M'Donald, Samuel, 20 Hill street
M'Ferran, Wm., 18 Albert square
M'Gibbon, Valentine, 2 Abbey street
M'Gimpsey, Andrew, 11 Brown street
M'Glade, Henry, 55 Edward street
M'Gladery, William, Antrim road
M'Gouran, Peter, 2 Hercules street
M'Gouran, Richard, 9 Frederick street
M'Gurk, Thos., 44 North Queen street
M'Henry, Daniel, 50 Donegall street
M'Ilherron, Daniel, 1 Durham street
M'Ilroy, Andrew, 137 North street
M'Kavanagh, James, Falls road
M'Kenna, Patrick, Falls road
M'Kenna, John, 200 North street
M'Kenna, John, 25 Robert street
M'Keys, Francis, 2 Great Edward st.
M'Larnon, Henry, 26 Smithfield
M'Larnon, Henry, 31 Devis street
M'Laughlin, John, 1 Brown square
M'Mannus, John, 54 Hercules street
M'Menamy, Edward, 14 Hercules st.
M'Millan, John, 17 North Queen st.
M'Moreland, James, 26, 28 Gamble st.
M'Millan, Hugh, 53 Carrick hill
M'Murtry, Mary, 8 Great Patrick st.
M'Neill, Owen, 13 Mary's market
M'Quaide, Robert, 41 Millfield
M'Roberts, Samuel, 11 Gt. Edward st.
M'Sally, John, 20 Gamble street
Nelson, George, 64½ Great George's st.
Nelson, Adam, 4 Garmoyle street
Neville, Robert, 3 Marquis street
Neville, Cornelius, 66 Smithfield
Nolan, George, 120 Carrick hill
O'Donnell, Patrick, 29 Smithfield

O'Farrel, Fergus, 84 Corporation st.
O'Haggerty, Charles, 34 Shankhill
O'Neill, James, 11 Cromac street
O'Neill, James, 68 Great George's st.
O'Neill, C., Michael street
O'Neill, Patrick, 109½ North street
O'Neill, Bernard, 5 Peter's hill
O'Neill, Owen, 24 Greenland street
Peake, Hugh, 51 Lancaster street
Parker, George, Falls road
Peak, Bernard, 24 Ann street
Peak, Michael, 32 Edward street
Prey, Rose Ann, 156 Queen's square
Quinn, James, 78 Nelson street
Quinn, Ann, 3 Queen's square
Quinn, Hugh, 7 York lane
Quinn, Hugh, 14 Washington street
Rainey, Thomas, 40 Ann street
Rankin, Samuel S., 4 Gamble street
Rankin, S. S., Ballymacarrett
Reid, John, Robert Burn's concert room, 8 Long lane
Reid, James, 47 Little Patrick street
Reid, John, Wheeler's pl., B.macarrett
Rice, Patrick, 16 Corporation street
Rice, William, 1 Lemon's lane
Rice, Henry, 1¼ Union street
Rodgers, E., 11 Upper Church lane
Rodgers, Mary, 64¼, Mill street
Rogan, Patrick, 37 Carrick hill
Rowan, James, 54 Gt. Patrick street
Rutherford, James, 34 Corporation st.
Rutherford, M., 35 North Queen street
Savage, Edward, Falls road
Scott, John, 76 Nelson street
Scott, William, 114 Carrick hill
Shaw, Hugh, 28 Great George's st.
Shaw, Thomas, 65 North Queen street
Shiels, James, 8 Church street
Smith, Edward, 89 North Queen st.
Smith, Michael, 34 Great George's st.
Smith, Robert, 4 & 6 Rosemary street
Smyth, Thomas, 3 New Lodge road
Smyth, Patrick, 59 Waring street
Smyth, Denis, Great Edward street
Strain, William, 22 Durham street
Spence, William, 35 Boundary street
Stewart, Margaret, 5 Queen's square
Stephen, Alexander, 37 Rosemary st.
Taylor, John, 39 Great Patrick street
Thomson, John, 76 Waring street
Thornton, Arthur, Ballymacarrett
Thompson, Richard, 4 Hammond's ct.
Thompson, George T., Ballymacarrett
Titley, Samuel, 20 Church street

Todd, Samuel, 34 Rosemary street
Todd, John, 103 York street
Trainor, James, Falls road
Taylor, Victor C., Shankhill road
Trevor, Mary, 4 Castle lane
Taylor, John, 62 Lower Malone
Thompson, George T., Ballyhackamore, Ballymacarrett
Vance, Robert, 48 M'Tier's street
Vance, Adam, Ballyhackamore, Ballymacarrett
Vint, Jonathan, 54 Little Donegall st.
Virgin, Nicholas, 3 Victoria street
Walker, Deborah, Ballymacarrett
Walsh, James, 61 North Queen street
Ware, Richard, 124 North street
Waterson, James, 53 Verner street
Watt, David, 45 Little Donegall street
Walker, William, 8 Kennedy's place
Weir, Samuel, 52 Great Patrick street
White, John, 84½ Hercules street
Wilson, John, Falls road
Wilson, Wm., 20 Millfield
Wilson, Dennis, Antrim road
Wilson, Thomas, 71 Corporation sq.
Wilson, John, 12 Pilot street
Wilson, James, Cole's alley
Woods, Eleanor, 24 Lancaster street
Woods, Michael, 11 Victoria street
Wright, Robert, 6 Barrack street

Starch Manufacturers

Boyd, James, 35, 37 Boyd street
Christie, John, 3 Frederick street
Crawford, Alexander, 26 Mill street
Gardner, James, 10 and 23 York lane
Hunter, Mr., 16 Shankill road
Lytle, John, 9 York lane
Martin, Samuel, 20 Little Donegall st.
Martin and Hamilton, Killen street
Molyneaux and Ferguson, 18 Frederick street and York lane
M'Cullough, William, 105 Millfield
Tucker, Edward (and glue), 27 Waring street
Vance, William, 112 Donegall street
Wharton, William, 24 Talbot street

Stationers and Account Book Manufacturers

Archer & Sons, 27 Castle place
Dickinson, John, and Co., (wholesale) and box makers, 4 Donegall sq. north
Harrison, George, 51 High street
Moore, James, 5 Donegall place

Smyth, Hill, 1 Donegall street
Ward, M., & Co., 6 and 8 Corn market

Stay and Corset Makers

Forbes, Mrs., 13 Castle street
Guinn, Eliza, 147½ North street
M'Mullan, Ann, 10 Mill street
Reilly, Rose, 40 Great Edward street
Smith, Ann, 7 Castle street
Sueter, Miss (Paris and London House), 18 College street

Steam Packet Agents

Charley & Malcolm, 49 Donegall quay
Henderson, Robert, 23 Donegall quay
Langtrys & Herdman, 33 Waring st.
M'Tear, George, 33 Donegall quay

Stock and Share Brokers

Bushell, T., 32 Rosemary street
Connor, David, 27½ Ann street
Cunningham, J., & Co., 41 Waring st.
Hunter, John, jun., & Co., 35 Waring street
Steen, J. and W., 30, 32 Hill street
Stevenson, Jackson S., Piazza, Commercial buildings

Straw Bonnet Makers

Armstrong, Mrs., 13 Peter's hill
Beatty, S., 9 Shankhill
Browne, Miss M. A., 107 North st.
Cameron, Jane, 22 Lancaster street
Davis, Eliza, 96 High street
Douglass, J. A., Bridge end, Ballymacarrett
Finlay, Jane and Eliza, 24 Waring st.
Finlay, Margaret, Ballymacarrett
Gardner, Eliza, 35 Wall street
Gilliland, Jane, 15 Boyd street
Heslop, Margaret, 11 York lane
Ingle, Anne, 50 Ann street
Johnston, Ann, 9 Henrietta street
Kane, Mary, 16 Michael street
Macoun, George, 23, 25 Castle place
Moffatt, Miss, 7 York street
Montgomery, Mary Ann, 21 Hercules place
M'Kee, Mrs., 45 Mill street
M'Mahon, Miss, 24 Stanfield street
M'Mullan, Mary, 3 Charlemont st.
M'Neill, Mary, 2 Henrietta street
O'Hagan, Margaret, 37 Devis street
Patrick, Margaret, 91 North street
Russell, S., 27 Hercules place
Whiteside, Jane, 24 Peter's hill

Tailors

SEE ALSO CLOTHIERS.

Allen, J., 10 George's lane
Allen, James, 1 Orr's entry
Anderson, A., 14 Church lane
Anderson, Wm., 32 North Thomas st.
Arthur, John, 2¼ Nelson street
Baxter, William H., Shankhill
Blair, Joseph, 25 Alexander street
Boucher, Alexander, 4 King street
Burke, Alex., 42 North Queen street
Bunting, Francis, 69 Joy street
Byrne, Robert, 23 Pilot street
Cash, Edward, 2 Renwick place
Caulfield, Bernard, 11 John street
Chapman, James, 17 New Durham st.
Copeland, Richard (and clothier), 8 Pottinger's entry
Cowan, Frederick, 35 Hill street
Crawford, William, 7 High street
Davison, John, 12 Mill street
Devlin, James, 49 Barrack street
Duffy, John, 4 Skipper street
Ferrit, William, 19 Wesley place
Fegan, William, Chapel lane
Finlay, William, 50 Tomb street
Fleming, Robert, 14 California street
Garner, Edward, 53 New Lodge road
Greer, Henry, Shankhill
Gribben, John, 21 Henrietta street
Halliday, John, 188 North street
Johnston, Samuel, 52 Edward street
Johnston, William, 16 Russeell street
Jones, William, 74 Joy street
Kerns, Patrick, 3 Orr's entry
Kirker, John, 136 Carrickhill
Legg, Thomas, 22 Henrietta street
Luckie, James, 13 Henrietta street
Lyons, Francis, 19 Edward street
Maddox, James, Eliza street
Milliken, William, 5 Pottinger's entry
Montgomery, Thomas, 9 Edward st.
Morrison, H., 12 Academy street
Murray, Owen, 15 Hercules place
M'Ateer, James, 23 Friendly street
M'Keown, John, 7 Chapel lane
M'Kee, Alex., 23 Pottinger's entry
M'Kibbin, John, 4 Francis street
M'Mahon, Patrick, Shankhill
M'Millan, John, 1 Cambridge street
M'Millan, John, 15 Gordon street
M'Muaray, Hugh, 5 Coates street
M'Mullan, Samuel, 10 Mill street
M'Murray, Robert, 14 Mustard street
M'Quilian, W., Falls road

PROFESSIONS, TRADES, &c.

George Nelson, (and clothier), 12 Pottinger's entry
Nelson, James, 40 Durham street
Oldrin, James, 53 Joy street
Orr, David, 29 Lancaster street
O'Hanlon, John, 45 Castle street
Reid, Archibald, 20 Mustard street
Robb, Alexander, 6 Arthur street
Russell, G., 22 Catherine street north
Shanks, Thomas, 44 Durham street
Smylie, James, 69 Academy street
Stevenson, Samuel, 17 Arthur st.
Stevenson, Thomas, 39 Mill street
Stewart, William, 15 Friendly street
Strings, George, Garmoyle street
Tousseant, Henry, 29 Dock street
Tumblety, Charles, 25 Academy st.
Wallace, Robert, 41 Joy street
Ward, Francis, 6 Millfield
Wardlow, William, 13 Skipper street
Welsh, John, 14 Henrietta street
Wood, Robert, 28 Durham street

Tanners and Curriers

Greenhill, Robert, 49 Mill street
Johnston, William, 13 Mill street
Johnston, W., and S., 37 Mill street
Kennedy, Patrick, 49 Castle street
M'Blain, Jn., 108½ Carrickhill
M'Cammon, Thomas, 23 King street
M'Mullan, Patrick, 48 Mill street
Wetherall, William, 25 Mill street

Taverns and Coffee Houses

Alderdice, David, Victoria tavern, 117 Durham street
Bell, Wm., London tavern, 32 Corn market
Bradley, James, Shell Fish Tavern, Legg's lane
Campbell, Michael, Bower's Hill tavern, Shankhill
Carmichael, Arthur, Fox tavern, 2 Calender street
Colvill, John, Royal Yacht tavern, 15 Donegall quay
Downing, William, Grape tavern, 3 Corn market
Duncan, Adam (and stabling), 104 North street
Ferris, John, Shell Fish Tavern, 13 Police square
Finlay, William, Donegall Pass tavern, 1 Donegall pass
Forrester, Matthew, Dock tavern, 11 Prince's dock
Gordon, George, North Star inn, hotel, and posting establishment, 66 and 68 North street
Hemsley, John N., Union tavern, Shankhill
Hunter, Chas., Crown tavern, Crown entry
Jordan, Philip, Queen's Bridge tavern, 35 Donegall quay
Mackenzie, Alexander, Stag tavern, 5 Smithfield
Moody, Joseph, Hibernian tavern, 10 Pottinger's entry
Morrison, Hugh, 6 Montgomery street
M'Alister, Cath., Commercial lodging house, 22 Gamble street
M'Cann, Samuel, Railway and Steampacket tavern, 6 Castle street
M'Collough, Robt., Courthouse tavern, Crumlin road
M'Connell, John, Thatched House tavern, Frederick street
M'Keown, William, Fountain Street tavern, 6 Fountain street
M'Quillan, Wm., Falls Road tavern, Falls road
M'Williams, Mary A., Eagle inn (and stabling), 158 North street
Nichol, James, 21 Albert square
Pelan, James, Queen's quay; and Railtavern, Queen's quay, Ballymacarrett
Potter, Mrs., Marine hotel and tavern, 69 Corporation square
Savage, Pat., Bath-house tavern, Falls
Skene, James, Stag's Head tavern, 2 North street
Stewart, James, Theatre tavern, 17 Castle lane
Townly, Patrick, Glenwood tavern, Shankhill

Teachers of

DANCING.

Cassidy, Miss, 27 Chichester street
Gordon, James, 5 York street
Irwin, Mrs., 27 Chichester street
Lowe, Robert, 11 George's lane
Lynch, Messrs., 11 Donegall place buildings

DRAWING.

Burgess, John H., 16 Donegall place
Cinnamond, Miss, 5 Arthur street
Ferguson, Miss, 6 Upper Queen street
Molloy, Joseph, Academical Institution
Nursey, Claude L. (School of Design), Lower Crescent, Old Malone

Reimbach, David (School of Design), 1 Botanic view

FRENCH.
Badier, Auguste C., 29 Queen street
Festu, Jules, 45 Upper Arthur street

MUSIC.
Barry, Wm. V., 49 Upper Arthur st.
Brown, Miss, 9 College street
Brown, Robert, 61 Nelson street
Carroll, John, 20 Joy street
Cavanagh, John, 11¼ Cromac street
Dyke, R. M., 1 Mill street
Gordon, Charles D., 41 Little May st. and 5 York street
Granz, Wm., 40 Gloucester street
Hart, John, 6 Arthur square
Jackson, Alex., 3 Catherine st. south
Lennon, Mrs. B., 24 Queen street
Ling, William, 15 Ship street
May, James T., 59 Upper Arthur st.
M'Cann, Mrs., 123 York street
Stevenson, George F., 8 King street
Willis, John, 4 College street south

WRITING.
Armstrong, Thomas, Cliftonville
Johnston, P., 27 College street

Tea Merchants, Wholesale
SEE ALSO WHOLESALE GROCERS.
Armstrong, J., and Co., 5, 6 Donegall place, buildings
Ash, George, 40 Waring street
Brannigan, Daniel R., 43 North street
Dunville, Jn., & Co., 10 Calender st.
Finlay, Chas. and Wm., 5 Waring st.
Johnston, Philip, Waring street
Keegan, James, 74 High street
Mathison, Brothers, 3 Donegall place buildings
Mullan, William, Victoria street
Murray, Henry, 18 High street
M'Clure, William, and Son, Corporation street
M'Laughlin, F., High street
Ogle, Frederick, 10 Waring street
Prenter, W. E., Victoria street, agent for Absolom, Crocker and Townsend, tea & coffee merchts., London
Thompson, Richard, 17 Church street
Wilson, James, Victoria street

Timber Merchants
Agnew, James, 34 Chichester street
Barnett, Andrew J., 10 Store lane
Brown, John, jun., 20 Gloucester st.
Brown, L. and T., 41 Chichester st
Cavanagh, John, 176 North street
Corry, James P., and Co., 1 Corporation square
Lewis, F. and W., 3 Gt. George's st.
Low, John, 5 Great George's street
Murphy, John, 3 Hamilton street
M'Kavanagh, John and Henry, 15½ Queen street
Wardlow, J. and H., and Co., 94 Corporation street

Tobacco and Snuff Dealers
Those marked (*a*) are manufacturers.
*a*Black, Henry, 15, 17 Waring street
*a*Gelston, William, 17 Skipper street
*a*Harper, Martin, 44 Church lane
Ievers, Ann, 41 North street
*a*Johnston, Philip, and Co., 24 Skipper street
*a*Kirk, Andrew, 82 North street
Love, Henry, Church lane
Mackin, Thomas, 27 Corn market
*a*Massy, Fergus, 24 North street
*a*Massy, George, 12 North street
*a*Milligan, W. H., 33 Ann street
*a*Murney, Henry, 18 High street
*a*Murray, George, 93 Queen's square
*a*Murray, Mrs. Anne, 8 Calender st.
*a*M'Causland, Samuel, 34 North st.
M'Donnell, Charles, 5 High street
M'Donnell, John, 4 North street
*a*M'Laughlin, Francis, 65 High street
*a*M'Laughlin, John, 4 Donegall street
Read, Patrick, 2 Castle place
Wilson, James, 100 North street

Toy Shops
Pelan, Robert, and Co. (Prince of Wales'), 6 Bridge street
Reynolds, John (fancy warehouse), 45 Donegall street
Wilson, Alexander, 8 Bridge street
Wilson, James, 174 North street
Wilson, Jane, 140 North street

Trimming Warehouses
Greenfield, John, 76 High street
Morgan, Charles, 26 Castle place
Riddel and M'Callum (late Brown's), 13 Bridge street
Riddel, M., 5 Castle buildings
Wilson, Thos., and Co., 32 High st.

PROFESSIONS, TRADES, &c. 411

Umbrella Makers
Boyd, James, 21 North street
Davis, Eliza, 96 High street
Kennedy, John, and Co., 25 Ann st.
Leathem, Edward, 144 North street
Todd, F., 37 Donegall street

Undertakers
Madine, George, 7 York street
Maxwell, William, 38 Fountain street
Morrison, Hugh, 6 Montgomery street
M'Laughlin, John, 17 West street
Robson, John, 3 Montgomery street

Universal Parcels Office
Richards, J. E., 22 Waring street

Upholsterers
SEE ALSO CABINET MAKERS AND UPHOLSTERERS.
Bell, Miss, 94 Donegall street
Bremner, James, 5 Ann street
Carr, Hugh B., 2 Castle street
Forbes, Thomas, 13 Castle street
Mackintosh, R., 7 Pottinger's entry
Macqueen, Thomas, 4 Rochfort place
M'Millen, Jane, 8½ Hercules place

Venetian Blind Makers
Carr, Hugh B., 2 Castle street
Forbes, Thomas, 13 Castle street

Veterinary Surgeons
Grogan, John, the Castle yard
King, James, 108 Donegall street
M'Kenna, William, 2 May street

Watch Glass Manufacturers
Agnew, W., Bridge end, B.carrett
Davis, W., Bridge end, B.carrett
Hewitt, J., Wheeler's place, B.carrett
Horner, Thomas, Ballymacarrett

Whip and Thong Makers
Dunlop, James, 149 North street
Justin, Catherine, 117 North street

Whitesmiths
Bradley, John, 1 Alexander street
Campbell, John, 8 George's lane
Campbell, John, 3 Thomas court
Doherty, Andrew, 48 Smithfield
Doland, Matthew, 13 Bank lane
Greenwood, J., 8 Marquis street
Hanlon, John, 15 Durham street

Henderson, Robert 11, Ann street
Henderson, Robert, 43 Cooney's ct.
Hoy, Alexander, 13 Fountain street
Johnston, Samuel, 1 Prince's court
Macauley, James, 53 Brown's square
Moore, Ezekiel, 59 Old Lodge road
M'Guigan, James, Falloon's court
M'Gloughlen, W., 42 Brown street
Phillips, John, 30 Carrick hill
Porter, John, Covent Garden, Little Patrick street
Rodgers, James, Joy's court
Williamson, John, 33 Old Lodge road

Wholesale London, Manchester and Scotch Warehouses
Browne, Reid, & Co., 3 Waring street
Clendinning, A., 10 Rosemary street
Day and Bottomley, Calender street
Greer, T., Sons, & Co., 18 Rosemary street
Greer & Oakman, 13¾ Donegall st.
Hannay, Hugh H., 13 Donegall st.
Johnsons, and Co., 18 Donegall place
Lindsay, J. & D., & Co., 3 Donegall place
Miller, Clendinning, and Co., 36 North street
Mulligan, J. and T., 6 Donegall st.
M'Connell, Wm., and Co., 25 Donegall street
M'Hugh, B. aud E., 12 Rosemary st.
Weir, A. C., and Co., 24½ Bridge st.
Young, James, and Co., 19 Donegall st.

Wholesale Printed Calico and Trimming Warehouses
Arnott, John, & Co., 7, 9 Bridge st.
Browne, Reid, and Co., 3 Waring st.
Clendinning, A., 10 Rosemary street
Day and Bottomley, 7 Calender street
Greer and Oakman, 13¾ Donegall st.
Greer, T., Sons, and Co., 18 Rosemary street
Johnsons and Co., 18 Donegall place
Lindsay, J. and D., 3 Donegall place
Miller, Clendinning, and Co., 36 North street
Mulligan, J. and T., 6 Donegall street
M'Caldin, James, and Co., 18 Waring street
M'Connell, Wm., and Co., 25 Donegall street
M'Hugh, B. & E., 12 Rosemary street
Young, J., and Co., 19 Donegall street

PROFESSIONS, TRADES, &c.

Wholesale Wine and Spirit Merchants

Those marked (a) are also retail
Boyle, Samuel, 16 Ann street
Brannigan, Daniel R., 43 North st.
Bushell, Theobald, 32 Rosemary st.
Carruthers, George A., Corporation st.
Charnock, Brothers, 65 Corporation square
Cowan, William, 19 Church lane
Coleman and Dobbin, 1 Church st.
aColeman, Patk., 71, 73 Academy st.
Crawford, James, 1 Calender street
Cramsie, John C., 74 Waring street
Cunningham, Samuel, 1 Queen street
Cunningham, Thos. 2 York street
Dobbin, Clotworthy, 43 Smithfield
Dunville, John, & Co., 10 Calender st.
Dickson, Henry, and Co., Victoria st.
aFitzpatrick, Bernard, 72 Donegall st.
Fordyce and Mullan, 84 Cromac st.
Gelston, Hugh, Upper Church lane
Gelston, Samuel, 17 North street
Gordon, Alexander, and Son, 17 Castle Chambers
Gilmore, William, 14 High street
Hoy, John, and Co., Victoria street
Keegan, Peter, 4 Calender street
Keegan, James, 74 High street
Kelly, Hugh, 36 Bank lane
aLoughran, Henry, 41 York street
Lyle and Kinahan, 36 Fountain street
Mackenzie, Shaw, and Co., 37 and 39 Barrack street
Moore, William John, 12 Church st.
aM'Alister, Joseph W., 75 North st.
M'Connell, Jas. & John, 28 Tomb st.
M'Kee, John and Joseph, 69 High st.
M'Kenna, John, 1 York street and Academy street
Neill and White, Winecellar entry
Ogle, Frederick, 10 Waring street
Pim, E. & G. 27 & 29 High street
Quirey, Jas., and Co., 33 Donegall st.
aReid, James, Cole's alley
aRichardson, J., Upper Church lane
Thompson, Richard, 17 Church lane
Torbit, James, jun., 58 North street and 92 Donegall street
Vint, Jonathan, 54 Little Donegall st.
Wilson, James, Victoria buildings, Victoria street

Wire Cloth Manufacturers

Howard, William, 15 Church lane

Woollendrapers

Albion Cloth Company, 22 High street
Arnott, John, & Co., 17 Bridge street
Arnold John, (Heimatemporion), 45 High street
Bullick, S. W., and Co., Victoria st.
Close, Brothers, 26 High street
Crawford, Arthur, and Co., 18 Waring street
Edgar, Samuel, 5 Arthur square
Ferguson, Nathaniel, 38 High street
Grant, Alex., and Co., 43 North st.
Gray, Robt., and Co., 15 Donegall st.
Hardy, Thomas, 35 and 37 High st.
Hazlett and Frazer, 21 High street
Jennings, John, 5 Bridge street
Killen, William, 68 High street
King, Robert, 21 Donegall street
Levy, Mier, and Co., 61 High street
Lindsay, Brothers, 3 Donegall place
Mackenzie and Saunders, 36 High st.
Magill, Robert, 1 Castle buildings
Marshall, James, 5 Donegall street
M'Cann, Thomas, 41 High street
M'Gee, John G., and Co. (Pantechnetheca), 46 and 48 High street
M'Geagh, R. T., and Co., 1 and 3 Hercules place
M'Grotty, John B., and Co., 23 Bridge street
M'Kenna, Thos., & Co., 16 Bridge st.
M'Vicker, John, 3 Donegall place
O'Neill, William, Regent buildings, Victoria street
Waring, Robert, 1 Donegall street
Weir, A. C., and Co., 24½ Bridge st.
Young, Joseph, 8 Waring street

ALPHABETICAL LIST

OF

COUNTRY RESIDENTS

IN THE VICINITY OF BELFAST.

Abbott, Jos., Tudor house, Holywood
Alexander, Rev. Dr., Ballynafeigh
Allan, J. G., Collin, Ballyclare
Andrews, Michael, Ardoyne
Archer, Samuel, Milltown, Ballyclare
Ash, Miss, Holywood
Ash, George, Cliftonville, Antrim road

Barlow, Rev. Robert Burrows, Newtonbreda
Barlow, William, Gasfield house
Bates, John, Seapark, Greenisland
Bateson, Sir Robert, bart., Belvoir park, county Down
Batt, Robert, Purdysburn
Batt, Thos. G., Strandmillis, Malone
Beath, J., Antrim place cottage
Bell, Jacob, Glenbracken, Whiteabbey
Bell, Richard, Lucyville, Whiteabbey
Bell, Richard, Clearstream cottage
Bennett, Rev. Geo., Mount Pottinger
Bernard, Ami, Mount Pottinger
Black, Rev. T. F., Whitehouse
Blair, Mrs., Crumlin road
Bland, Rev. R. W., J.P., Abbeyville, Whiteabbey
Blizzard, David, Larkfield, Dunmurry
Boag, Neal, Connsbrook
Boomer, James, Seaview, Carrick road
Bottomley, John, Fortbreda
Bottomley, William, Fortbreda
Boyce, William, Laganville
Boyd, James, Beech lodge
Boyd, Robert, Bloomfield
Braddell, Geo. W., Camp lodge, Blaris
Bragg, Henry, Coltonmount
Branagh, D., Everton cottage, Ardoyne
Bristow, Jas., Prospect, Ballynafeigh
Bryson, Jas., The Castle, Whiteabbey
Bryson, Samuel, Clual, co. Down
Bruce, Mrs., Thorndale
Bruce, Rev. Wm., The Farm
Bushell, Theobald, Strandtown cottage

Calwell, George, Lismoyne
Cameron, James, Glentilt
Cantwell, S. J., Mount Pottinger
Carruthers, J., Glencregagh, N.breda
Carson, Mrs., Dundonald cottage
Carson, Matthew, Rosevale
Carson, Samuel, Glenvale
Charley, John, Finaghy, Dunmurry
Charley, Miss, Lennoxvale
Charley, Wm., Seymourhill, Dunmurry
Charters, John, Ardmoulin house
Clarke, Andrew, Grovefield, B.carrett
Clarke, E. H., Elmwood
Cleland, Mrs., Stormount, Dundonald
Cleland, Rev. Andrew, Dundonald
Coates, William, J.P., Glentoran
Coey, Edward, Merville, Greencastle
Connell, Alex., Rifle Lodge, Whiteabbey
Connor, David, The Cottage, Dundonald
Cooper, Miss, Seaview
Cordner, Rev. E. J., Derramore
Cordukes, Jonathan, Spafield, H.wood
Coulter, Rev. Dr., Gilnahirk
Cowan, Samuel, Cromac lodge
Cowan, William, Whiteabbey house
Crawford, Arthur, Old Lodge road
Crawford, Alexander, Mount Charles
Crawford, Rev. Andrew, Manse, Ballynafeigh
Crawford, William Sharman, M.P., Crawfordsburn
Crawford, William, Dalchoolin, Holywood
Crommelin, N. D., New Lodge road
Cunningham, John, Glenwood
Cunningham, John, Macedon, Whitehouse
Cunningham, Mrs., Meadow bank, Whitehouse
Curell, Miss, Abbeyhill, Whiteabbey
Cuddy, John, Summerhill, Co. Down

COUNTRY RESIDENTS.

Darbishire, James, Collin grove, Dunmurry
Darbishire, Mrs., Woodburn, Dunmurry
Davis, William, Greenville, Co. Down
Davison, Gawn, Strawberryhill
Davison, Richard, The Abbey, Whiteabbey
Dickson, Alexander, Ballycloughan nurseries, Co. Down.
Dillon, Mrs., Alleybrook house, Dundonald
Dillon, William, Roseville, W.abbey,
Dinnen, John, Cabinhill, Dundonald
Dobbs, C. R., D.L., J.P., Castle Dobbs, Carrickfergus
Druitt, William, Mount Pottinger, Co. Down
Duffield, Samuel, Summerhill
Dunlop, C., Edenderry
Dunville, William, Richmond lodge, Holywood

Elliott, Saml. M'Dowell, Old Lodge
Emerson, John, Ballysillan
English, Robert, Roundhill cottage,
Ewart, William, jun., Wheatfield
Ewing, P., Bankmore
Evans, John, Roundhill house, Co. Down

Fall, Mrs., Greencastle
Ferguson, James, New Forge
Ferguson, D., Botanic garden
Ferguson, Thomas, Whiterock
Finlay, F. D., Ballynafeigh cottage
Finlay, John, Tudor hall, Holywood
Fitzsimons, N., Dunsona, Whiteabbey

Galloway, William, Millmount
Gamble, Orr R., Trainview, Whiteabbey
Garner, Captain, Garnerville
Garrett, Henry, Cromac house
Gelston, Saml., Rostulla, Whiteabbey
George, Thomas, Lilliput house
Getty, John, Beech park
Getty, Robert, Beech park
Getty, Samuel G., Cromac park
Gibson, Rev. William, Cliftonville
Goddard, James, Easton lodge, Cliftonville
Gordon, Robert Francis, J.P., Craigdarragh, Holywood
Gordon, Robert, J.P., Florida Manor, Killinchy

Gordon, Robert A., J.P., Summerfield
Grant, James, Cregagh, Castlereagh
Grattan, John, Merview
Gray, William, Graymount house
Greenfield, John, Jackson hall, Holywood
Greer, Mrs., Frogmore, Whitehouse
Greg, Thomas, J.P., Ballymenoch, Holywood
Grimshaw, Robert, D.L., Whitehouse
Gunning, Robert, Craigavad

Hall, William, Jackson hall
Halliday, Alex. Henry, Clifton
Hamilton, Hill, Mount Vernon
Hamilton, The Misses, Mount Vernon
Hargrave, Jas., Maryvale, Holywood
Harper, Mrs., Bleachfield, B.carrett
Harrison, John, Merton, Holywood
Harrison, Henry, Holywood house
Haslett, Rev. Henry, Castlereagh
Henderson, J. A., Mount Collyer park
Henderson, Rev. Henry, Glenside, Holywood
Henderson, Robt,, Willowbank, Malone
Herdman, Jas., Tudor hall, Holywood
Herdman, William, Cliftonville
Heron, John, Maryfield, Holywood
Heron, Wm., Ashley place, B.carrett
Hill, Rev. George, Botanic cottage
Hind, John, The Lodge, New Lodge road
Hoffmeister, Charles, Forton lodge, Cliftonville
Houston, R. B. B., D.L., J.P., Orangefield, County Down
Howden, Charles, Malone Nursery
Howie, Robert, Old Park
Hudson, Rev. Teape, Lisnabreen house
Hume, Thomas, Ballynafeigh
Hunter, Aiex., The Green, Dunmurry
Hunter, John, Tyne cottage, Whiteabbey
Hunter, James, Beech lawn, Dunmurry
Hunter, Miss, Dunmurry cottage
Hunter, William, Dunmurry house
Hunter, William, Huntley, Dunmurry
Hurst, Dr. C., Locust lodge, Ballynafeigh

Ireland, James, Clifden, Holywood

Jackson, Thomas, Cliftonville
Johnston, Mrs. John, Albion place

COUNTRY RESIDENTS. 415

Johnston Philip, Turf Lodge
Johnston, S., Railway cottage, Malone
Joyce, John, Thornhill, Dundonald

Kelso, Mrs., Bellview
Kennedy, George K., Lilliput cottage
Kennedy, H., J.P., Cultra
Kennedy, Jas., Rosetta, Ballynafeigh
Kennedy, James, Millvale, Falls
Kennedy, John, Knocknagoney
Kinahan, Rev. John, Knockbreda
Kinnear, Pat., Harphall, Antrim road
Knox, Right Rev. Dr., Lord Bishop of Down, &c., the Palace, Holywood
Koch, Ami, Mount Pottinger

Lamb, John, Devis view, Malone
Langtry, Richard, Fortwilliam
Law, Mrs., Fairview cottage, Crumlin road
Legge, Wm. W., D.L., Malone house
Lepper, Wm. Laurel lodge, Antrim road
Lepper, Mrs. F., Trainfield, Antrim road
Lewis, Francis, Nettlefield, B.carrett
Lewson, Wm., Willowdale, Dunmurry
Lindsay, Robert, Cliftonville
Lyle, Rev. John, Whiteabbey
Lyons, Miss, Old park

Mackay, Mrs., Mount Collyer park
Macnaughtan, Miss, Cliftonville, Antrim road
Macnaughtan, Rev. John, Duncairn house
Macrory, A. J., Duncairn
Magill, Captain, Whitehouse
Magill, Joseph, Marino, Holywood
Major, Thomas S., Dunmurry
Martin, James, Knock, County Down
Martin, John, Glenview
Millar, Mrs., Laurel lodge, Lodge road
Millar, John, Ulsterville
Miskelly, Mrs., Bunkershill, Co. Down
Moffatt, Rev. W., Ashley place, Ballymacarrret
Montgomery, Alex., Mount Pottinger
Montgomery, Hugh, Ballydrain
Montgomery, John, Elmgrove
Montgomery, Mr., Mount Pottinger
Montgomery, Miss, Deer's bridge cottage
Montgomery, Rev. Dr. H., Dunmurry
Montgomery, Robert, Sandymount
Moreland, Miss, Cromac
Mullaghan, Mr., Warrenview, Dunmurry

Mullan, William, Brookvale, New Lodge road
Mulholland, Mrs., Mount Collyer
Mulholland, Andrew, J.P., Springvale, County Down
Mulholland, John, J.P., Craigavad, Holywood
Mulholland, S. K., J.P., Eglantine, Hillsborough
Munster, Paul L., Spafield, Holywood
Murray, George, Bunker's hill
MacAdam, James, jun., Beaver hall, Ballymacarrett
MacAdam, John, Beaver hall, Ballymacarrett
M'Calmont, Mrs., Abbeylands, Whiteabbey
M'Cance, J. W. S., Glenville, Dunmurry
M'Cance, Wm., Suffolk, Dunmurry
M'Causland, Samuel, Lodge cottage
M'Clelland, Henry, Ligoneil
M'Clure, Thomas, Belmont
M'Connell, William, Charleville, Castlereagh
M'Cullagh, Rev. W. C., Ballysillan
M'Cutcheon, Hugh, Ballybeen, Dundonald
M'Dowell, Charles, Ballybeen, ditto
M'Donnell, Alex., Annadale, co. Down
M'Donnell, Thos., Q.C., Eglantine
M'Ilwaine, Willliam, Millbank, ditto
M'Kenzie, Rev. Joseph, Malone
M'Kenzie, William, Rockfort
M'Kibbin, R. D., Farmhill, Dunmurry
M'Kibbin, Dr. Robert, Avoneil, Ballymacarrett
M'Kittrick, William, Ashfield
M'Lorinan, Daniel, Knock house, Co Down
M'Master, Mrs., Rose lodge
M'Mechan, Dr., Whitehouse
M'Minn, Dr., Dunlady, Dundonald
M'Namara, James, J.P., Victoria terrace, Holywood
M'Neale, John, jun., Rushpark
M'Neile, John, D.L., J.P., Parkmount
M'Neile, Robert, Mossvale, D.murry
M'Pherson, Major, Fountainville cottage
M'Roberts, W., Dundonald
M'Tear, George, Hazlebank, Greencastle
M'Tear, The Misses, Abbotscroft
M'Teir, Jas., Vermont lodge, Lodge road

2 N

COUNTRY RESIDENTS.

Nash, Andrew, Cavehill
Nelson, Rev. I., Sugarfield, Shankhill
Nelson, Samuel, Glendavis

Orr, James, M.D., Ballylesson
Orr, Rev. William, Woodbank
Orr, Wm., Glennalina
Ostend, Mr. (engineer), Britainmount
Oulton, Rev. Richard, Holywood
Owden, John, Brooklands
Owens, Mrs., Maryfield

Patterson, John, Whitehouse
Pearce, J., Pebble Lodge, Antrim rd.
Pim, Joshua, Sans souci
Pirrie, Wm., Conlig house, co. Down
Potts, Robert, Rosemount, Antrim rd.
Prenter, N. O., Harryville
Pretty, Edward, Mount prospect
Price, Francis, Lodge house

Rea, Hugh, Killeen
Reford, Lewis, Beechmount
Reid, James, Cliftonville, Antrim rd.
Reid, Richard, Whiteabbey
Richardson, Jonathan, Lambeg
Richardson, J., Glenmore, Lisburn
Richardson, J. G., Lisnegarvey, do.
Riddel, John, Vermont
Riddel, John, jun., Vermont
Ritchie, Francis, Mount Pottinger
Ritchie, James, Bellville house
Robb, Alexander, Ballybeen, D.donald
Roberts, John, Collin
Robinson, David, Ballyorn, D.donald
Russell, Frederick, Edenderry
Russell, Houston, Edenderry
Russell, John, Portview

Sanders, Capt., Bunker's hill
Shaw, Captain, Whitehouse
Shaw, James, Glenbank
Shaw, John, Ballysillan house
Simms, John, Ballykeel, Holywood
Simms, Hugh, Bellview, Holywood
Simms, Mrs., Seaview cottage
Sinclair, John, The Grove, York road
Sinclair, Wm., Milltown lodge, Falls
Sinclair, Thomas, Hopefield
Smith, Geo., Cliftonville, Antrim road
Smyth, Edward James, Abbeyville
Sneyd, Richard M., Cherryvale
Starke, Lieutenant, Ardoyne
Steen, James, Skiegoniel
Steen, William, Ashfield house

Stevenson, John, Springfield
Stevenson, Wm., jun., Phœnix lodge
Stewart, Dr. R., Asylum, Falls road
Stewart, John, Silver stream
Stewart, James, Greencastle
Stewart, Robert, Ashfield

Trape, Rev. Hudson, Shankhill
Tennent, James Thompson, Hazlebank
Thomson, Robert, J.P., Castleton
Thomson, John, J.P., Lowwood
Thomson, Gordon, Bedeque house
Thomson, William, Fountainville, Botanic road
Thomson, Charles, Fountainville, Botanic road
Thompson, Robt., Tudor house, Holywood
Thompson, Richard, The Mount, Carrickfergus
Thompson, J. G., Garden hill
Torrens, James, Woodbank, W.abbey
Tracy, William S., R.M., Ravenhill
Tripp, Thomas, Brookfield
Turnley, Francis, Richmond lodge
Tyrrell, Rev. G. W., Drumbeg rectory

Usher, R. T., Mount prospect

Valentine, William, Harmony hill, Whiteabbey
Verner, Thomas, D.L., J.P., Ormeau
Verner, William, J.P., Loughview, Carrickfergus

Walkington, E., Snugville, Shankhill
Wallace, John, Edenderry house
Wallace, John, Henryville, Bunker's hill
Ward, Thomas, Cherryhill, Malone
Waterson, Wm. Thos., Seville lodge Strandtown
Wetherall, William, Holywood
Weir, Gilbert, Lodgeview
Whitla, Valentine, Ben Eden
Wiley, Alex., Ross lodge, Dunmurry
Wilson, G. S., Victoria terrace, Holywood
Wilson, Mrs., Victoria terrace, Holywood
Wilson, A., Maryville
Wrixon, Rev. Mr., Malone

Young, William, Bunker's hill house
Young, John, Shamrock lodge

VILLAGE DIRECTORY.

ARDOYNE, BALLYSILLAN, &c.

RESIDENTS IN VICINITY.

Andrews, Michael, Ardoyne Royal Damask Manufactory
Bell, Richard, Clearstream cottage
Branagh, David, Averton cottage
Dickson, Dr. S., Ballysillan Dispensary
Emerson, John, The Mountain
Ewart, William, jun., Wheatfield
Ferguson, Thomas, Greenville
M'Clelland, Henry, Ligoniel
M'Cullagh, Rev. W. C., Ballysillan Presbyterian Church Manse
Shaw, James, Glenbank
Shaw, John, Ballysillan house
Starke, Lieutenant, Ardoyne cottage
Stevenson, John, Springfield
Teape, Rev. H., Shankhill Church

MANUFACTURERS AND TRADERS.

Ardoyne Royal Damask Manufactory
Campbell, Mic., Bower's hill tavern
Carson, John, publican
Emerson, John, flax spinner
Ewart and Sons, flax spinners
Ferguson, Jn. S., & Co., bleach green
Hemsley, John, publican
Johnston and Carlisle, flax spinners
Ligoniel Flax Spinning Mill
Townley, J., Glenwood tavern

DUNDONALD.

Four miles from Belfast, Co. Down.

Established Church and School
Presbyterian Church
Gilnahirk Presbyterian Church
National School—W. Gowdy, teacher
Dispensary (closed)
Post Office—J. Wallace, postmaster
Constabulary Station—Const. Hicks

RESIDENTS IN VICINITY.

Blackwood, Mr., Castlekennedy
Carson, Mrs., Dundonald cottage
Carson, Samuel, Glenvale
Carson, Matthew, Rosevale
Dillon, Mrs., Alleybrook house
Dinnen, John, Cabinhill
Cleland, Mrs., Rosepark and Stormont
Cleland, Rev. Andrew, rector
Connor, David, The Cottage
Cooper, Miss, Seaview
Coulter, Rev. Dr., Gilnahirk
Cuddy, John, Summerhill
Farrel, Mr., Rockfield
Galloway, William, Millmount
Gordon, Robert, J.P., Summerfield
Joyce, John, Thornhill
Martin, Rev. E. T., Presbyterian min.
M'Cutcheon, Hugh, Ballybeen
M'Dowell, Charles, ditto
M'Ilwaine, William, Millban
M'Kenzie, William, Rockfort
M'Minn, Dr., Dunlady
M'Roberts, William
Quee, Doctor
Rea, Hugh, Killeen
Robb, Alexander, Ballybeen
Robinson, David, Ballyorn
Sinclair, John, Henryvale

TRADERS.

Long, Mrs., publican
Moody, A., grocer and haberdasher
M'Creight, J., publican
M'Crea, John, grocer and publican
Shannon, John, publican
Wallace, John, innkeeper

DUNMURRY.

Four miles from Belfast.

Unitarian Presbyterian Meeting house
Roman C. Chapel—Rev. Mr. M'Carten
National School—Misses Burrows and M'Conkey, teachers
Post Office—Miss Burrows

RESIDENTS.

Blizzard, David, Larchfield
Callwell, George, Lismoyne
Charley, William, Seymour hill
Close, Arthur, barrister, Glenview
Darbishire, James, Colin grove
Darbishire, Mrs., Woodburn
Darbishire, Herbert, Woodburn
Duffield, Samuel, Summer hill
Hunter, Miss, Dunmurry cottage
Hunter, James, Beechlawn
Hunter, Wm., Dunmurry house
Hunter, Alexander, The Green
Hunter, William, Huntley
Lewson, Wm., Willowdale
Major, Thomas S.
Montgomery, Rev. Dr. H.
Mulligan, Baldwin, Warrenview
M'Cance, William, Suffolk
M'Cance, J. W. S., Glenville

VILLAGE DIRECTORY.

M'Kibbin, Ross Dickson, Farmhill
Neill, Robert, Mossvale
Paine, Dr. Thomas
Roberts, John, Colin
Stevenson, Wm., jun., Phœnix lodge
Wiley, Alexander, Rose lodge

MANUFACTURERS, TRADERS, &C.

Carmichael, James, publican
Carmichael, Mrs., grocer
Charley, Messrs., linen manufacturers
Craig, Edward, linen merchant
Hall, John, grocer
Hunter and Moat, flax spinners
Hunter, Wm., and Sons, Dunmurry Flour mills
Hunter, William, jun., linen merchant
M'Kittrick, Mr., grocer
Roberts, William, linen merchant
Simpson, John, publican
Stewart, Isaac, grocer

GREENCASTLE.

Roman Catholic Chapel
Railway Station (Ballymena line)

RESIDENTS.

Connor, Mrs. O.
Gray, Wm., Graymount house
Stewart, James, gentleman

TRADERS.

Cavanagh, James, grocer and publican
Clements, John, grocer
Lavery, William, grocer
Mearns, Gilbert, tavern
M'Carthy, Edward, Greencastle tavern
M'Kinstry, Wm., saddler
Stephen, Mary, grocer
Stewart, Matthew, publican

HOLYWOOD.

Four and a quarter miles from Belfast.

INSTITUTIONS.

Established Church
Presbyterian Church
Primitive Wesleyan Meetinghouse
Unitarian Meetinghouse
Roman Catholic Chapel
National School—Mr and Mrs Joyce
Dispensary
Post Office—James Greenfield
Constabulary Station—Constable Fitzpatrick
Court House and Assembly Rooms
Loan Fund
Railway Station—Alex. Long, clerk

CLERGY AND PROFESSIONAL.

Cosgrave, Hugh, surgeon
Dillon, Roger, solicitor
Flood, Rev. J. C., Incumbent
Garrett, James, solicitor
Gabbey, J., surgeon
Henderson, Rev. Henry, Presbyterian minister, Glenside
Kelly, Dr., M.R.I.A., Decca lodge
Kennedy, John B., solicitor
M'Alester, Rev. C. J., Pres. min.
Oulton, Rev. Richard
Young, Dr. G. H., F.R.C.S., Dispensary

RESIDENTS.

Abbott, Joseph, Tudor house
Armstrong, Hugh, Shore street
Ash, Miss
Atkinson, Robert, Main street
Bain, John, Church street
Bain, Mrs., Shore street
Bankhead, William, Hillbrook
Batt, Miss, Crescent
Blackwell, Robert, The Prairie
Bullick, S. W.
Cairns, Mrs.
Charnock, James
Craik, Professor, Queen's college, Belfast
Cordukes, Jonathan, Spafield
Crawford, William, Dalchoolin
Dawson, Misses, Hillbrook
Dillon, Mrs.
Dunville, William, Richmond lodge
Ferrie, John, Marine parade
Finlay, John, Tudor hall
Forsythe, Robert, Shore street
Forsythe, John
Foster, William
Garner, Captain, Garnerville
Gordon, R. F., J.P., Craigdarragh
Greenfield, John, Jackson hall
Greg, Thomas, J.P., Ballymenoch
Greer, Robert, Church street
Harrison, John, J.P., Mertoun hall
Hardy, Thomas
Harrison, Henry, Holywood house
Harrison, George Howard, Mertoun
Herdman, James, Tudor hall
Heron, John, Maryfield
Hodgson, John
Ireland, James, Clifden
Jones, Mr., Shore street
Kerr, The Misses
Kirkpatrick, Robert, Spafield
Kelsey, Mrs., Bellevue
Kennedy, H., J.P., Cultra

VILLAGE DIRECTORY.

Knox, Right Rev. Dr., Lord Bishop of Down and Connor
Leadbetter, Mr.
Magill, Joseph, Marino
Marshall, Dr. James
May, Mrs., Rockport
Mulholland, John, J.P., Craigavad
Munster, Paul L., Spafield
Murphy, John, Myrtello
M'Cutcheon, Mrs.
M'Ilroy, Mrs., Shore street
M'Ilveen, Mrs.
M'Namara, Jas., J.P., Victoria terrace
M'Neill, H.
Neill, James
Patton, Captain, High street
Ross, William
Ross, Mrs., Farmhill
Ross, Mrs. Colonel
Rounds, Mrs.
Rowley, Miss
Simms, Hugh, Bellevue
Simms, John, Ballykeel
Simms, John, Hillbrook
Stewart, Hugh
Stitt, Mr., Glenside place
Suffern, Mrs., Churchfield
Thompson, Robert, J.P., Tudor house
Ward, William H., Stewart's place
Wetherall, William
Wilson, Guy S., Victoria terrace
Wilson, Mrs., Victoria terrace
Wood, George P., Marine parade
Wood, Mrs. J.
Young, Lieut.-Colonel, Farmhill

TRADERS.

Anderson, Wm., Bangor hotel
Anderson, John, publican
Bankhead, Mrs., ladies' seminary
Bellew, Miss, teacher
Boyd, Misses, grocers
Byres, Francis, cartmaker
Carson, Rowley, grocer
Cavan, Mrs., haberdasher
Connelly, Archd., grocer and painter
Cooper, Eliza, grocer
Davison, W., nailmaker
Gill, W., grocer
Johnston, James, grocer
Johnston, James, loan fund clerk
Kennedy, Miss, ladies' school, Shore st.
Killips, John, publican
Killips, Mrs., grocer
Kincade, Wm., Railway hotel
Langridge, James, grocer
Lennon, David, publican
Lennon, Mrs., lodgings
Lennox, David, publican
Logan, James, publican
Magee, James, builder
Marshall, Thos., Liverpool tea house
Moffatt, Thomas, grocer, Shore street
Moore, Mrs., lodgings
Murray, J., spirit dealer
M'Cutcheon, Hugh, watchmaker
M'Dowell, Mrs., lodgings
M'G. Wilson, provision store
M'Kinnon, Mr., Academy
M'Knight, Margaret, green grocer
Patton, Mrs., lodgings
Power, John, Belfast hotel
Rodgers, Alex., baker and flour dealer
Sanders, John, butcher
Sedgewick, Mr., valuator
Shepherd, John, smith
Simms, Miss, grocer
Sloan, Hugh, grocer
Spence, John, butcher
Thompson, Mrs., lodgings
Tolerton, James, boot and shoemaker

NEWTOWNBREDA,
Three miles from Belfast.

MISCELLANEOUS INSTITUTIONS.

Newtownbreda Established Church
Parochial School—Gawn Yeates and Elizabeth Dorman, teachers
Newtownbreda Female School
Dispensary
Library—Gawn Yeates, librarian
Bible Depository—Ditto
Post-office—Ditto, postmaster
Constabulary Station—Gore Mervyn, sergeant

RESIDENTS IN VICINITY.

Barlow, Rev. Robert Burrows, curate
Bateson, Sir Robt., Bart., Belvoir Park
Bottomley, John, Fortbreda
Bottomley, William, ditto
Carruthers, J., Glencregagh
Hamilton, Dr. Thomas William
Kinahan, Rev. John, The Glebe
M'Donnell, Alexander, Annadale
Sneyd, Richard M., Cherryvale

TRADERS, ETC.

Burns, Edward, publican
Hunter, Eliza, grocer
M'Clean, Samuel (late coach guard)
M'Keown, Joseph, baker

THE KNOCK.
Two and a-half miles from Belfast.

The Old Burying Ground
Railway Station (two calls in the day)
—Henry Campbell, clerk of do.
National School (50 scholars)—Wm. Burke, teacher

RESIDENTS IN VICINITY.

Boyd, James, Beech lodge
Cox & Co's Flax works
Hazlett, Rev. Henry
Lewis Reford's Logwood mill
Martin, James, Knock
M'Lorinan, Daniel, Knock house
M'Kee, John, Craigah
S. Farrell & Co.'s Nursery

WHITEHOUSE,
AND LOWER WHITEHOUSE,
Three miles from Belfast.

MISCELLANEOUS INSTITUTIONS.

St. John's Episcopal Church—Rev. T. F. Black, incumbent
St. John's Church School—Thomas and Margaret M'Quitty, teachers
National School—John M'Crickard,
Dispensary (Monday and Thursday)—Dr John M'Mechan
Court House (Petty Sessions)—James Johnston, clerk
Constabulary Station—Const. Lawler
Post Office—Thomas M'Clean
Revenue Station—Lieut. J. G. Morgan
General Provision and Goods Store—David Ritchie, proprietor

RESIDENTS IN VICINITY.

Bell, Jacob, Glenbracken
Bell, Richard, Lucieville
Black, Rev. T. F., Parsonage
Calvert, Joseph, flax spinner
Coey, Edward, Merville
Cunningham, Mrs., Meadowbank
Cunningham, John, Macedon
Curell, Miss, Abbeyhill
Grimshaw, Robt., D.L , J.P., Longwood
Grimshaw, James, Whitehouse
Grimshaw, Thomas, Whitehouse
Greer, Mrs., Frogmore
Magill, Captain
M'Calmont, Mrs., Abbeylands
M'Neale, John, jun., Rushpark
M'Tear, George, Hazelbank
M'Tear, Misses, Abbotscroft
Owens, Mrs., Maryfield
Patterson, Dr., Greenisland
Patterson, John (of A. and J. Henry)
Shaw, Captain
Wolfenden, Edward

MANUFACTURERS AND TRADERS.

Anderson, Francis, grocer
Bells & Calverts' flax spinning mill
Daly, William, grocer
Ellis, Henry, grocer
Giffin, John, tailor
Gray, Wm., & Sons' bleach green
Grimshaw and Sons' spinning mills
Gregg, M., grocer
Hamill, Charles and Conn, butchers
Kelly, John, grocer
Murphy, William, smith
M'Carrol, Hugh, carpenter
M'Carthy, John, grocer
M'Connell, Sarah, grocer
M'Millen, Robert, provision dealer
Shaw, Martha, publican
Strickland, William, grocer
Walker, Robert, dyer and bleacher

WHITEABBEY.
Four miles from Belfast.

Presbyterian Church—Rev. John Lyle
National School—Thomas Wallace
Post Office—Mrs. Foster
Railway Station

RESIDENTS IN VICINITY.

Bland, Rev. R. W., J.P., Abbeyville
Bryson, James, The Castle
Connell, Alexander, Rifle Lodge
Cowan, William, Whiteabbey house
Davison, Richard, The Abbey
Dillon, William, solicitor, Roseville
Fitzsimons, N., Dunsona
Gamble, Orr, solicitor, Trainview
Gelston, Samuel, Rosstulla
Hunter, John, Tyne cottage
Hunter, Charles
M'Ilveen, Mrs.
Owens, Mrs., Marykeld cottage
Reid, Richard
Smyth, Edward J., Abbeyvilla
Torrens, James, Woodbank
Valentine, Wm., Harmony hill
Tennent, Jas. Thompson, Hazlebank

TRADERS.

Boyd, John, Belfast hotel
Cowan & Reid, flax spinners
Hendren, Robert, grocer
Millikin, Robert, publican
Smith, Wm., Whiteabbey tavern
Smith, James, cabinet maker
Stewart, Mr., railway clerk

ULSTER RAILWAY.

From Belfast to Armagh, calling at all the stations, at 7 10, 8 45, 10 15, a.m. 12 40, 2 15, 2 45, 5 15, and 6 30. p.m. To Lisburn only, at 10 15, am., 12 40, and 6 30, p.m. On Sundays, at 9 a.m., 3 and 6 p.m.; to Lisburn only at 3 p.m.

To Belfast from Armagh, calling at all the stations, at 7 and 9 20, a.m., 2 30, 2 50, , and 6 25 p.m. On Sundays at 9 a.m., and 6 p.m.

Lisburn to Belfast, 9 25, 10 33, a.m., and 1 30, 4 55, 4 6 (mail), 7 5, 7 38 p.m. On Sundays, at 10 18 a.m., 4 30, and 7 18 p.m.

Goods' Trains, with 3rd class passengers, leave Belfast at 7 morn., and 2 45 afternoon.

An extra train for Lisburn, on Market days, leaves Belfast at 8 45 a.m., returns 12 noon.

FARES.—Belfast to Dunmurry, 8d., 6d., 4d.; to Lisburn, 1s., 9d., 4d.; to Moira, 2s., 1s. 6d., 8d.; to Lurgan, 3s. 0d., 2s. 3d., 1s.; to Portadown, 4s. 0d., 3s. 0d., 1s. 4d.; to Richhill, 5s. 0d., 3s. 9d., 1s. 8d.; to Armagh, 5s., 4s. 6d., 2s.

BELFAST AND BALLYMENA RAILWAY.

Belfast to Ballymena, calling at all the stations, with branches to Carrickfergus and Randalstown, at 6 a.m., mail; 10 5 a.m., 12 45, 4 35, and 6 20, p.m. On Sundays, at 6 and 9 a.m., and 4 35 p.m.

Ballymena to Belfast, at 4 50, 7 35, 10 5 a.m., 12 30 and 5 15 p.m. From Carrickfergus, at 6, 8 42, 10 55, a.m., 2 10, 6 8, p.m. On Sundays, 9 15, a.m., 6 8, and 8 5, p.m.

On Wednesdays and Fridays, the Belfast 4 35 o'clock train will stop at Templepatrick to set down passengers. On the same days, the second Ballymena train will stop at Templepatrick. On Saturdays, an extra train will leave Belfast at 8, a.m., for Ballymena, and return at 7 5, p.m.

FARES.—Belfast to Greencastle, 6d., 4d., 2d.; to Whiteabbey, 6d., 5d., 3d.; to Carrickfergus Junction, 9d., 7d., 4d.; to Carrickfergus, 1s., 8d., 4d.; to Ballypallady, 1s. 7d., 1s. 2d., 6d.; to Dunadry, 2s. 3d., 1s. 8d., 9d.; to Antrim, 2s. 6d., 1s. 9d., 10d.; to Drumsough Junction, 3s., 2s., 1s.; to Randalstown, 3s. 6d., 2s. 6d., 1s. 3d.; to Ballymena, 4s., 3s., 1s. 6d.

BELFAST AND COUNTY DOWN RAILWAY.

Belfast to Holywood, 8, 9, 10, 11, a.m., 1, 3, 4, 5, 6, 7 30, and 8 30, p.m. Holywood to Belfast, 8 30, 9 30, 10 30, 11 30, a.m., 1 30, 3 30, 4 30, 5 30, 6 30, 8, and 9, p.m. On Sundays, from Belfast, at 10, a.m., 1, 2, 3, 4, 5. 8, p.m. From Holywood, 10 30, a.m., 1 30, 2 30, 3 30, 4 30, 5 30, 8 30, p.m.

FARES.—First class, 6d.; second class, 4d.

From Belfast to Newtownards, calling at Dundonald and Comber, at 7 45 and 9 45, a.m., 1 45, 4 15, 7, p.m. Sundays, at 9 45, a.m., 2 15, 7, p.m. Leaves Newtownards, at 8 45, 10 45, a.m., 3 15, 5 15, 8, p.m. Sundays, at 10 30, a.m., 3 15, 8, p.m.

FARES.—Belfast to Newtownards, First 1s., Second, 8d. To Comber, First, 9d., Second, 6d. To Knock, First, 6d. second, 4d. Young persons between the ages of six and fifteen, at half-rates.

DUNDALK AND ENNISKILLEN RAILWAY.

Dublin to Castleblayney, * 10, a.m., 4, and 7¼, p.m. Castleblayney to Dublin, 1 5, 7 45, 11 40, 5. p.m. Sundays, from Dublin to Castleblayney, 7 15, a.m. From Castleblayney to Dublin, 1 5, p.m.

FARES.—First, 12s.; second, 9s. 7d.; third, 5s.

* This train is the only one which brings passengers on to Belfast.

DUBLIN AND BELFAST JUNCTION RAILWAY.

Dublin to Belfast, *via* Portadown, 10 a.m. Belfast to Dublin, *via* Portadown, 7½, a.m., and 12½, p.m.

FARES.—First, 18s. 4d.; second, 14s. 6d.; third, 8s. 6d.
Dublin to Newry, 7½, 10, a.m., and 4, p.m. Newry to Dublin, 8½, a.m., and 12¼, 5 55, p.m.

MAIL AND STAGE COACHES, CARAVANS, &c., FROM BELFAST.

ANTRIM.—A coach starts from Mrs. Magee's, No. 6, North Street, every evening (Sunday excepted), at 2 o'clock, and arrives in Antrim at 4 o'clock. Leaves Antrim every day at 4½ o'clock, A.M , and arrives in Belfast at 6½ o'clock, A.M.

BALLYNAHINCH.—The "Victoria" leaves Dennis Smyth's, 31, Great Edward Street, every evening (Sunday excepted), at a quarter-past 4 o'clock; and leaves Patrick Mulvanney's, Ballynahinch, every morning at 7 o'clock.

BALLYNAHINCH AND CASTLEWELLAN.—The "Lark" leaves Mrs. Anderson's, 25, Great Edward Street, every evening (Sunday excepted), at half-past 4 o'clock, and arrives in Castlewellan at 9 o'clock. Leaves John Meharg's, Castlewellan, every morning (Sunday excepted), and arrives in Belfast at 9 o'clock.

BANGOR AND HOLYWOOD.—A mail car starts from Millen's, No. 32, Prince's Street, every morning at 7 o'clock; arrives in Holywood ten minutes before 8, and in Bangor at 9. Leaves Bangor at a quarter to 4, and arrive in Belfast at a quarter-past 6 evening. Cars leave Belfast at a quarter-past 4, and arrives in Bangor at a quarter-past 6 evening. Leave Bangor at half-past 8 morning, and arrives in Belfast at 10½.

CARRICKFERGUS.—Cars start from M'Henry's, Donegall Street, every evening, at 4 o'clock, and return next morning, at half-past 10 o'clock, and cars constantly from York Street throughout the day.

CARRICKMANNON.—The Farmer, a one horse conveyance, leaves Patrick M'Creanor's, 18, Prince's Street, every Monday, Wednesday, Friday, and Saturday evening, at 4 o'clock; runs through Monyrea. Leaves A. Clelland's, Carrickmannon, at 7 o'clock on the mornings of the same days, and arrives in Belfast at 10.

CRUMLIN.—A conveyance leaves Mrs. Magee's, No. 6, North Street, every Monday, Wednesday, and Friday, at 4 o'clock, P.M. — Leaves the Packenham Arms, Crumlin, at seven o'clock, morning, of the same days, and arrives in Belfast at nine.

DOWNPATRICK.—Mail conveyance leaves the Post-office every day at ten minutes past two, and arrives at six evening. —Leaves the Post-office, Downpatrick, every morning, at 20 minutes past 6 o'clock, and arrives in Belfast at a quarter past 10.

Two Downpatrick coaches leave J. Fetherston's, 49, and Millen's, 68, Ann Street, every evening, at 4 o'clock, and arrive at 7.—Leave Down every morning at 7, and arrive in Belfast at 10.

DUBLIN.—Night mail starts from No. 15, Castle Place, every evening, at 40 minutes past 8 o'clock, and arrives in Dublin at a quarter past 5 next morning.

ENNISKILLEN.—Mail starts every evening from the office, No. 15, Castle Place, at 40 minutes past 4 o'clock, and arrives in Enniskillen next morning, at half-past 5 o'clock. Leaves Enniskillen every evening at a quarter before 7, and arrives in Belfast next morning, at 25 minutes past 7.

LARNE.—A coach leaves Mrs. Magee's, No. 6, North Street, every evening (Sunday excepted) at 4 o'clock, and arrives in Larne at 7½ o'clock. Leaves Stewart's, Larne, every morning (Sunday excepted) at 6 o'clock, and arrives in Belfast at 9½ o'clock.

PORTAFERRY.—Mail car leaves the Post-office at a quarter past 7 morning, and arrives in Portaferry a quarter past 12. Leaves Portaferry at 2, and arrives in Belfast at 6 o'clock evening. Seats are taken at Hugh Millen's, 68, Ann Street.

BOROUGH OF BELFAST.

PARLIAMENTARY REPRESENTATIVES.

Lord JOHN L. CHICHESTER, D.L., 8, St. George's-place, Hyde Park Corner, London.

ROBERT JAMES TENNENT, Esq., D.L., Hercules-place, Belfast, and Reform Club, London.

Corporation of Belfast.

The Municipal Act came into operation, in this Borough, on the 1st of November, 1842.

MAYORS from 1842 to 1851:

GEORGE DUNBAR, Esq., . 1842-3	JOHN HARRISON, Esq., . 1847
JOHN CLARKE, Esq., . 1844	GEORGE SUFFERN, Esq.,(dead)1848
ANDREW MULHOLLAND, Esq., 1845	Sir WM. G. JOHNSON, Kt. 1849
JOHN KANE, Esq., (dead) 1846	JAMES STIRLING, Esq., 1850-1

MAYOR FOR 1852:
SAMUEL GRÆME FENTON, Esq., J.P.

ALDERMEN AND TOWN COUNCILLORS FOR 1852:

DOCK WARD.

ALDERMEN.
John Harrison, Albert-square,
Samuel Thomson, Corporation-st.

COUNCILLORS.
Gordon A. Thomson, Bedeque House
David Grainger, 11, Henry-street,
John Coleman, York-street,
Fred. H. Lewis, 3, Gt. George's-st.,
Robert S. Lepper, Abbotsford-place
William Valentine, Corporation-st.

SMITHFIELD WARD.

ALDERMEN.
Samuel Nelson, Linen Hall,
Robert Magee, 7, Donegall-sq. West.

COUNCILLORS.
Wm. Forsythe, 13, Wellington-pl.
Samuel M'Causland, 34, North-st.
Thomas H. Purdon, M.D., 5, Wellington-place,
James Hart, 26, Queen-street,
William Gillilan, 15, Wellington-pl.,
John Suffern, 76, Donegall-street.

SAINT ANNE'S WARD.

ALDERMEN.
John Potts, 25, York-street,
James Stirling, 2, Clarence-place.

COUNCILLORS.
William Ewart, Jun., Donegall-st.,
John Black, 111, Donegall-street,
Joseph Young, 8, Waring-street,
Hill Hamilton, Mount Vernon,
James Coleman, Church-street,
John Lytle, 1, North-street.

SAINT GEORGE'S WARD.

ALDERMEN.
James Crawford, 26, Donegall-place,
William Hamilton, 35, Ann-street.

COUNCILLORS.
Philip Johnston, 21, Waring-street,
John Cuddy, Church-lane,
William Carson, 1, Howard-street,
David M'Connell, 68, High-street,
W. M'Gee, M.D., 10, Donegall-sq. E.,
Ledlie Clarke, Ann-street.

CROMAC WARD.

ALDERMEN.
Sir Wm. G. Johnson, Kt., 12, College-square North,
Samuel G. Fenton, 9, College-square North.

COUNCILLORS.
John Holden, Donegall-street,
James Patterson, M.D., Donegall-square East,
Robert Lindsay, Donegall-place,
Thomas Major, 9, Donegall-square West,
James Kennedy, Commercial-court
Hutcheson Posnett, Rose Lodge,

LIST OF THE COMMITTEES OF THE TOWN COUNCIL OF BELFAST FOR 1852, WITH THE DAYS, HOURS, AND PLACES OF MEETING.

COMMITTEE ON POLICE AFFAIRS.

JOHN POTTS, Chairman.

John Potts,	John Black,	Gordon A. Thomson,
Sir W. G. Johnson	Joseph Young,	Thomas Major,
James Stirling,	William Hamilton,	William Carson,
Robert S. Lepper,	Robert Magee,	John Cuddy,
Samuel Nelson,		

This Committee meets, every Tuesday, at Twelve o'clock, in the Town Hall, Police Buildings.

TOWN IMPROVEMENT COMMITTEE.

JAMES STIRLING, Chairman.

James Stirling,	Robert Lindsay,	William Ewart, Jun.,
Robert S. Lepper,	William Carson,	John Holden,
Hutcheson Posnett,	Sir W. G. Johnson,	Thomas Major,
James Hart,	Samuel Nelson,	William Valentine.
John Potts,		

This Committee meets, occasionally, at the Town Clerk's Office, Rosemary-street.

MARKET COMMITTEE.

JOSEPH YOUNG, Chairman.

James Stirling,	William Carson,	Ledlie Clarke,
James Hart,	Robert S. Lepper,	John Black,
Joseph Young,	Sir W. G. Johnson,	James Patterson,
John Potts,	Samuel Nelson.	John Coleman,

This Committee meets every Saturday, at Twelve o'clock, in the Office of the Clerk of the Markets, Castle Lane.

FINANCE COMMITTEE.

SAMUEL NELSON, Chairman.

Samuel Thomson,	Thomas Major,	Frederick H. Lewis,
Samuel Nelson,	Samuel G. Fenton,	John Coleman,
William Forsythe,	Robert S. Lepper,	David M'Connell,
John Harrison,	James Crawford,	James Kennedy.

This Committee meets every month, at the Town Clerk's Office, Rosemary-street.

GRAND JURY COMMITTEE.

THOMAS HENRY PURDON, Chairman.

Samuel G. Fenton,	Hutcheson Posnett,	Thomas Major,
John Harrison,	Robert Lindsay,	Ledlie Clarke,
William M'Gee,	Sir W. G. Johnson,	John Suffern,
Robert S. Lepper,	Thomas H. Purdon,	James Patterson,

This Committee meets occasionally at the Town Clerk's Office, Rosemary-street.

HARBOUR COMMISSIONERS, &c.

In addition to these Committees are the following: The Custom-house—The Mail and Mail Packets—The Appeal—The Bye-Law—The General Purposes—and The Audit.

Treasurer, ... John Thomson, (Belfast Bank.)
Sub-Treasurer, ... Adam Hill.
Town-clerk and Solicitor, ... John Bates.
Surveyor of Works, ... William Hastings.
Assessors for the Borough, { The Mayor, Geo. K. Smith, and James Lindsay.

WARD ASSESSORS.—Hugh Wardlow and J. Rowan, *Dock Ward*; R. Greer and R. Roddy, *St. Anne's Ward*; Martin Harper and T. Chernside, *Smithfield Ward*; John G. M'Gee and James Close, *St. George's Ward*; Charles Finlay and J. Crawford, *Cromac Ward*.

Auditors, ... { John Preston, 5, Pakenham-place, Robert Roddy, 18, Donegall-street.

Accountant, David Porter, Police Buildings.

Clerk of the Markets, Francis Rea.

Inspector of provisions, cars, carriages, and gunpowder, Arthur Gaffikin, Police Buildings.

Chief Constables, Thomas Lindsay; William Armstrong.

Sergeants-at-Mace, ... { John Crawford, Rosemary-street, William Harpur, Cromac-street.

PUBLIC OFFICERS.

Seneschal, Samuel M'Dowell Elliott.
Coroner, J. K. Jackson, Castle-lane.
High Constable for Upper Half Barony of Belfast, Robt. T. Goddard.

Churchwardens, W. Carson, Corn Market, and John G. M'Gee, High-street.
Overseer of Deserted Children, Dr. Stevelly.

PUBLIC WEIGH-HOUSES.

Smithfield—Great George's-street—and May's Market.

Belfast Harbour Commissioners.

Incorporated in 1785, by the Act 25th George III., cap. 64, for the improvement of the port and harbour, meet at the Harbour Office, Queen's-square, every second Tuesday, at Twelve o'clock.

MEMBERS.

The Marquis of Donegall, as Lord of the Castle.
The Honble. and Very Rev. Lord Edwd. Chichester.
The Mayor of Belfast.

Vacate Feb. 1853.	*Vacate, Feb.* 1854.	*Vacate, Feb.* 1855.
Nicholas Fitzsimons,	James Heron,	William Mullan,
William Pirrie,	John Dunn,	William Valentine,
Hugh Magill,	John Clarke,	Gustavus Heyn,
Valentine Whitla,	George M'Tear,	William Bottomley.
Chairman.	Samuel Thomson.	John Harrison.
David Grainger.		

CHAMBER OF COMMERCE, &c.

HARBOUR COMMISSIONERS' OFFICERS:

Secretary, Edmund Getty.—*Accountant*, Thomas Price.—*Auditors*, W. Hartley and Robt. Alexander.—*Chief Clerk*, W. E. Young.—*Clerks*, George M'Clean and William M'Donald.—*Dock and Harbour Master*, Captain John Gowan.—*Deputy Harbour Masters*, Alexander Craig, George Montgomery, Patrick M'Bride.—*Pilot Masters*, Samuel Irvine, Daniel M'Cullagh, and Henry M'Lean.—*Clerk of Delivery*, Samuel Shaw.—*Clerk of Dunbar's Dock*, William Thomson.—*Engineer*, George Smith.—*Assistant Engineer*, James Hewitson.—*Consulting Engineers*, Walker and Burgess, London.—*Law Agent*, Richd. Davison.—*Treasurer*, George Thomas Mitchell.

Agent for Lloyd's ... ... N. Fitzsimons, Corporation-St.,
Surveyor for Lloyd's ... ... E. W. Jobling, 74, Donegall-St.,

Belfast Water Commissioners.

Established by Act of Parliament, in the year 1840, to supply the Town of Belfast with spring water. The water works are situate on the Antrim Road. The Commissioners sit every Thursday, for the despatch of business, at 10½ o'clock, at the Commissioners' Board-Room, Commercial Buildings.

Professor Stevelly,	Hugh Wardlow,	John Potts,
James Cameron,	Robert Lindsay,	John Murphy,
Charles Finlay,	George C. Pim,	Dr. M'Gee.
Adam Hill,		

William Allen, *Engineer.*—Plato Oulton, *Secretary and Clerk.*—Hugh Andrews, *Inspector.*—John Henderson and James Coates, *Collectors.*

Chamber of Commerce.

OFFICE, 36, WARING STREET.

First established in 1783, and remodelled in 1848, for the advancement of Commerce and Manufactures in Belfast and its neighbourhood; the protection of the trading interests of the community, and the arbitration of commercial matters in dispute.

OFFICERS FOR 1852.

President: WILLIAM COATES, J.P.

Vice-Presidents, WILLIAM VALENTINE, and JAMES BRISTOW.

COUNCIL:

Retire in 1856;	Retire in 1855;	Retire in 1854:
James Kennedy,	*J.F.Ferguson, D.L., J.P.	Robert S. Lepper,
Gustavus Heyn,	Robert Henderson,	George Ash,
John Thomson, J.P.,	James Steen,	Charles Duffin,
Theobald Bushell,	Robert Boyd,	John Mulholland, J.P.,
William Bottomley,	S. G. Fenton, J.P.,	Edward Geoghegan,
	Edward Coey,	

Retire in 1853.

Thomas M'Clure,	James Heron,	James Hamilton.
Richard Hull,	John Herdman,	

*Ex-officio member of Council, being the President for the past year.

Treasurer: EDWARD COEY.

Secretary: SAMUEL VANCE.

BANKING COMPANIES.

Belfast Banking Company.

CAPITAL, £500,000.

HEAD OFFICE—DONEGALL-STREET.

Formed in 1827, by the merging of two private banks. Its capital is £500,000, in 5,000 shares of £100 each, all of which have been issued. £125,000 were paid in three calls, making £25 per share paid up. There was a bonus of £10,000 declared in 1830, £10,000 in 1834, £5,000 in 1847, £5,000 in 1850, and £5,000 in 1851. The fixed issue of the bank is £281,611. The notes are payable at the place of issue. Interest is allowed on deposits for a term of three months. The rates of annual dividend to the shareholders have been—

5 p c, from 1st Aug., 1827, till 1st Feb., 1835. | 7 p. c. from 1st Feb., 1836, till 1st Feb. 1846.
6 p. c., from 1st Feb., 1835, till 1st Feb., 1836. | 8 p. c. from 1st Feb., 1846, till 1st Aug. 1851.

DIRECTORS.

John Thomson, Esq.,
Thomas G. Batt, Esq.,
George T. Mitchell, Esq.,
E. H. Clarke, Esq.

BOARD OF SUPERINTENDENCE.

Robert Batt,
John Harrison,
Andrew Mullholland,
S. G. Fenton,
Wm. Herdman,
Richard Hull, and
N. Fitzsimons, Esqrs.

BRANCHES AND MANAGERS.

Armagh, Thomas Kidd,
Ballymena, John Patrick, jr.
Ballymoney, James Thomson,
Castleblaney, Andrew M'Math,
Coleraine, James M'Farland,
Cookstown, Thomas A. Vesey,
Drogheda, W. C. Joyce,
Dundalk, R. O. Blackader,
Dungannon, W. J. Mines,
Enniskillen, Massy H. Morphy,
Larne, Frederick M'Kinstry,
Letterkenny, Thomas Patterson,
Londonderry, William Haslett,
Magherafelt, J. Walker & Sons,
Monaghan, N. Greer,
Navan, J. Roberts,
Newry, William Kinkead,
Newtownards, W. Parr,
Newtonlimavady, Thomas Moody,
Portadown, George Kinkead,
Strabane, William Smith,
Tandragee, Charles A. Creery.

CORRESPONDENTS.

London, Union Bank of London,
Dublin, Bank of Ireland,
Edinburgh, National Bank of Scotland and Branches,
Glasgow, Union Bank of Scotland and Branches,
Liverpool, Union Bank,
Manchester, Loyd, Entwisle & Co.
Birmingham, Midland Bank.
Bristol, Bath, Gloucester, &c. National Provincl. Bank of England and Branches,
Preston, Pedder & Co.
Aberdeen, Banking Co. & Branches,
Sheffield, Sheffield & Rotherham,
Leeds, Beckett & Co.
Greenock, Banking Company,
Carlisle, Newcastle, and Cockermouth, Carlisle City and District Banking Company.
Whitehaven, Bank of Whitehaven,
Workington, Maryport, Cockermouth, Keswick, Wigton, Penrith, Cumberland Union Bank.
Newcastle and Sunderland, Lambton and Company.

The Notes of this Company are paid in Dublin by the Bank of Ireland.

Northern Banking Company, Belfast.

CAPITAL, £500,000.

Formed in 1825 on a private bank, and was the first joint-stock bank in actual operation in Ireland. The capital is £500,000, in 5,000 shares, of £100 each. On the share capital £125,000 was paid up; and a bonus of £5 per share was added to the capital in 1839—making a total of £150,000. The fixed circulation is £243,440. The rest was £55,254 7s in 1851. The bank allows interest on deposits. The dividends and bonus have been as follow:

1826 to 1827 5 per cent Dividend, and in 1827 Bonus to make up 10 per cent to that date.
1827 to 1834, 5 per cent. Dividend, and in 1832 Bonus 4*l*. per Share,
1835, 6 per cent, | 1837, 8 per cent, | 1839 to 1851, 10 per cent.
1836, 7 per cent, | 1838, 9 per cent, |

DIRECTORS.

John M'Neile, Esq. | James Bristow, Esq.
Hugh Montgomery, Esq. | John M'Neile, jr., Esq.

COMMITTEE.

William Coates, Esq., *Chairman*.

Charles Murland, | John F. Ferguson,
Jacob Bell, | Alexander M. Shaw,
Daniel Blair, | Isaac Andrews, Esqrs.

Adam Hill, *Notary*.

BRANCHES AND MANAGERS.

Armagh, John R. Jeffreys, | *Lisburn*, Henry J. Manly,
Ballymena, James Young & Co., | *Londonderry*, E. H. Smyth,
Carrickfergus, Alexander Johns, | *Lurgan*, Thomas Hall,
Clones, John Brady, | *Magherafelt*, Gaussen & Duncan,
Coleraine, J. H. Macauley, | *Newtownlimavady*, Wm. Cather.
Downpatrick, Hugh Wallace, |

CORRESPONDENTS.

Dublin, Bank of Ireland, | *Sheffield*, Sheffield Banking Co.,
London, { H. & J. Johnston & Co. | *Bristol*, Miles, Harford, & Co.,
{ Glynn & Co., | *Whitehaven*, Whitehaven Bg. Co.,
Liverpool, Liverpool Borough Bk., | *Preston*, Pedder, Fleetwood & Co.,
Manchester, Manchester and Liverpool District Bank. | *Workington*, ⎫
Birmingham, B.ham Banking Co., | *Cockermouth*, ⎬
Leeds, W. Williams, Brown, & Co., | *Maryport*, ⎬ The Cumberland
Edinburgh, Glasgow, &c., { Commercial Bank of Scotland and Branches, | *Wigton*, ⎬ Union Bank.
| *Carlisle*, ⎬
| *Penrith*, ⎭

Ulster Banking Company, Waring-Street, Belfast.

Capital, £1,000,000, in 10,000 Shares, of £10 each.
25 Per Cent. paid up.

Commenced business in July, 1837. Its capital is £1,000,000, in 100,000 shares of £10 each, on which £187,000 has been paid up in two calls. The fixed issue is £311,079. The notes are payable at each branch where issued, and also at the Royal Bank in Dublin. Interest is paid on deposits, and on balances. The dividend to the shareholders is 5 per cent per annum.

DIRECTORS—Robert Grimshaw, and James Heron, Esqrs.

BANKING COMPANIES. 42

COMMITTEE.

Thomas Corbitt,
William J. C. Allen,
Joseph Bigger,
Thomas Greer,

Charles Duffin,
Robert Roddy,
Wm. J. Duffield, Esqrs.

John Taylor, *General Manager.*—Thomas Wann, *Secretary.*

BRANCHES AND MANAGERS.

Antrim, William Crawford,
Armagh, A. J. Mulligan,
Aughnacloy, Thos. Montgomery,
Ballymena, William Hogg,
Ballymoney, James Boyle,
Banbridge, R. P. M'Kee,
Cavan, William Thomson,
Cookstown, Robert Stark,
Cootehill, James Jamieson,
Donegal, John Jackson,
Downpatrick, Hugh Cleland,
Enniskillen, Samuel Clarke,
Londonderry, Thomas Davison,
Lurgan, Thomas Ringland,
Monaghan, R. G. Warren,
Omagh, N. M. Montgomery,
Portadown, Thomas H. Carleton.

CORRESPONDENTS.

Dublin, Royal Bank of Ireland,
London, Prescott, Grote, Ames, &Co.
Liverpool, Bank of Ireland,
Birmingham, Taylor & Lloyd,
Manchester, Union Bank of Manch.
Rochdale, Blackburn, Stockport, &c., } Manchester and Liverpool District Bank,
Leeds, Leeds Banking Company,
Leeds, Huddersfield, Bradford, &c., } Yorkshire Banking Company,
Preston, Roskell, Arrowsmith, & Co.
Glasgow, City Bank, Western Bank and Clydesdale Bank,
Bristol, Baillie, Baillie, & Co.,
New-York, Bird and Gillilan,
Philadelphia, A. J. Catherwood,
Edinburgh, Glasgow, Dundee, Paisley, &c., } The Western Bank of Scotland and Branches,
Carlisle, Carlisle and Cumberland Bank,
Newcastle-on-Tyne, Northumberland and Durham District Bank.

Bank of Ireland Branch Office,
DONEGALL-PLACE.

AGENT, Ed. Geoghegan, Esq.,—**SUB-AGENT,** J. Bristow, Esq.,—**NOTARY,** G. W. Braddell.

Originally established in 1783, with a capital of £600,000, enlarged at various times, and, on the renewal of the charter in 1821, was increased to £3,000,000, of which £1,615,384 was lent to Government at 4 per cent., and £1,015,384 at 5 per cent.—total, £2,630,769. The yearly dividends of the bank have been at no time less than 5½ per cent, except in 1783-4, when they were 5, and in 1792-3, 2⅜. From 1800 to 1814, they were 7, 7¼, and 7½; and from 1814 to 1829, 10 per cent, excepting two years; and since 1829 the rates have been 9, 8½, and 8 per cent. Besides these dividends, the proprietors at different times since 1793 have received bonuses amounting to £665,000 Irish.

BRANCHES.

TOWNS.	AGENTS.	TOWNS.	AGENTS.
Armagh	Thomas Dobbin,	Kilkenny	Richard Cully,
Ballinasloe	Michael E. Murphy,	Maryboro'	Hugh Law,
Carlow	Thomas Whelan,	Newry	Samuel Parsons,
Cork	John Craig,	New Ross	John M'Conkey,
Clonmel	Thomas Roberts	Sligo	James Duncan,
Derry	James Mackey,	Tralee	Chas. K. Magrath,
Drogheda	Robert Roberts,	Tullamore	Oliver N. Birney,
Dundalk	Wm. Edmundson,	Wexford	Richard Hore,
Galway	J. C. M'Dowell,	Westport	Rt. M'Ilree,
Limerick	William Frazer,	Waterford	H. D'Olier Grant,
Longford	William Woolseley,	Youghall	Thomas John

THIS BRANCH DRAWS ON

The Bank of Ireland and Branches,
The Bank of England and Branches,
The Royal Bank of Scotland and Branches,
The British Linen Company and Branches,
The Bank of Scotland and Branches,

Tip. Joint Stock Banking Company and Branches,
The West of England, and S. District Bank,
Whitehaven Joint Stock Bank,
Williams & Co. Bankers,
Bangor, Carnarvon and Chester.

Provincial Bank of Ireland,

BROAD-STREET, LONDON.—CAPITAL, TWO MILLIONS.
BELFAST BRANCH, 36, DONEGALL-STREET.

Established in 1825, and is managed by a board in London, assisted in the transactions at the branches by a local manager and one or more directors of 10 shares and upwards. The paid up capital of the bank is £540,000, and its fixed issue is £927,667.

Local Director,—Samuel Thomson, Esq.

Robert Trotter, Esq., *Manager.*—John Raphael, *Accountant.*—A. Hill, *Notary.*—William Emerson, *Teller.*

BRANCHES AND MANAGERS.

Armagh, James Bowman,
Athlone, William Hay,
Ballina, Joseph S. Joyner,
Ballymena, Charless Ross Munro,
Ballyshannon, Wm. Allingham,
Banbridge, Robert M'Tier,
Bandon, John J. Thomson,
Cavan, William Anderson,
Clonmel, William Sibbald,
Coleraine, William N. Rowan,
Cootehill, William Leslie,
Cork, Richard Purcell,
Drogheda, Walter Lucas,
Dungannon, James Guthrie,
Dungarvan, William Crosbie,
Enniscorthy, William Freeman,
Enniskillen, George Stewart,
Ennis, James Menzies,
Fermoy, James M'Creery,
Galway, Robert Fisher,
Kilkenny, Andrew M'Kean,
Kilrush, George Hickson,
Limerick, William Franklin,
Londonderry, David Webster,
Mallow, Frederick Abrahall,
Monaghan, James Syme,
Newry, William M'Cullough,
Omagh, J. F. Alexander,
Parsonstown, William White,
Skibbereen, John William Clerke,
Sligo, Richard Gordon,
Strabane, James Crosbie,
Tralee, Thomas Stewart,
Waterford, Richard Harris,
Wexford, Samuel Johnston,
Youghal, James Gray.

DUBLIN BRANCH.—Robert Murray, *Chief Officer.*—A. T. Macfarlane, *Sub-Agent.*

Correspondents on whom the Bank draws—Spooner, Attwoods, and Co., London; and all the leading towns in England and in Scotland.

Belfast Savings' Bank,
KING-STREET.

Instituted January, 1816, for the receipt and accumulation of the savings of the industrious classes. Deposits are taken so low as 1s. at a time, and not more than £30 in one year from any depositor; nor can any account be allowed to exceed £150 in all, exclusive of interest.

James Bristow, Esq., Treasurer; Michael Andrews, Esq., Secretary; John Borthwick, Chief Clerk, and James D. O'Conner, Assistant Clerk.

RAILWAY COMPANIES. 431

Abstract of Balance, as per annual statement, furnished to the Commissioners for the Reduction of the National Debt, 20th November, 1851.

Dr. Balances due to 4,885 Depositors,................£106,460 4 7
" Reserved Fund, towards Payment of Expenses, ... 65 17 10

Cr. Lodged with the Commissioners £106,526 2 5
for Reduction of National Debt,
as per their acknowledgment
in the hands of the Treasurer,
JAMES BRISTOW, Esq., Nor-
thern Bank £104,993 2 4
" Balance of Cash in Treasurer's
hands 1,533 0 1
                                                    £106,526 2 5

James Moore, } Managers   James Bristow, Treasurer.
Robert Roddy,   Michael Andrews, Secretary.

I have extracted the 4,885 Balances as above, from the Ledgers of this Bank, and hereby certify the same to be correct, in every respect.

JOHN HARTLEY, Notary Public, Auditor.

The Bank is open every Tuesday and Friday—to take notices for repayment, from 9 till 11 o'clock, in the forenoon; to make repayments, from 1 till 3 o'clock, in the afternoon; and to receive deposits, from 6 till 7 o'clock, in the evening.

Belfast and Ballymena Railway,

Opened 11th April, 1851.

CAPITAL, £385,000, IN £50 SHARES.

Act of incorporation, passed 21st July, 1845. Share capital authorized, £385,000 and loans, £128,300—together, £513,300. The arrears of calls amount to £3,965; and 352 shares have been forfeited. £128,300 has been borrowed on debentures. The length of the line authorized by the act is 37¾ miles, of which 33 form the main line from Belfast to Ballymena, in the county of Antrim, 2¾ miles the Carrickfergus, and 2 miles the Randalstown branch; the entire being opened for traffic with a single line of rails, on the 11th of April, 1848.

DIRECTORS.

Chairman, Hon. Geo. Handcock.
Deputy Chairman, J. M'Neile, Parkmount.

Thos. Greg, Ballymenoch, Holywood,
John Harrison, Merton Hall,
S. K. Mulholland, Eglantine,
William Chaine, Ballycraigy,
John Herdman, Belfast,
John White, Broughshane,
Robert Langtry, Fortwilliam,
Robert Grimshaw, Longwood,
G. J. Clarke, Steeple, Antrim,
Edward Walkington, Belfast,
John Jackson, Manchester,
Thomas Verner, Ormeau,
Benjamin Clements Adair, Loughanmorne,

Solicitors, Messrs. R. Davison and Torrens, Belfast.—*Engineer,* Charles Lanyon, C.E.—*General Manager.*—Thos. H. H. Higgin.
Office, York Road, York-Street.

Ulster Railway, from Belfast to Armagh.
OFFICE, GREAT VICTORIA-STREET.

Capital, £600,000, in 12,000 Shares, of £50 Each.

This Railway runs from Belfast to Portadown and Armagh. The Dublin and Belfast Junction now joins the line at Portadown. The act of incorporation was passed on the 19th of May 1836, and a further act for the extension from Portadown to Armagh was obtained on the 21st July, 1845. The former authorized the company to raise capital to the amount of £600,000 and to borrow £200,000—together, £800,000. No additional capital was authorized by the extension act. The share capital consists of 12,000 shares, of £50 each, £49 called; 11,994 of which have been issued, 1,689 having been allotted to the directors.

The Railway from Belfast to Lisburn, 7½ miles, was opened in August, 1839, from Lisburn to Portadown, 17¾ miles, in 1842; and from Portadown to Armagh, 10½ miles, on the 1st of March, 1848. The total length is 35¾ miles, and the cost about £19,900 per mile.

DIRECTORS.

Chairman, James Goddard, Belfast.—*Deputy Chairman*, W. J. C. Allen, Belfast.

Robert Grimshaw, Belfast, D.L., J.P.	Dr. Thomson, Lisburn,
Andrew Mulholland, Belfast, J.P.	James M'Caw, Belfast.
Thomas Bouch, Liverpool,	S. K. Mulholland, J.P.
William Steen, Belfast,	Edward Walkington,
Robt. H. Dolling, J.P., Magheralin,	George Scott, Armagh,
George Greer Lurgan, J.P.	William Gregg, Lisburn, J.P.
John Smyth, Whitepark,	George Pim, Dublin,
J. Macnamara, J.P., Belfast,	Joseph Boyd, Lurgan,
Samuel Murland, Castlewellan,	William Cairnes, Drogheda.
William H. Malcolm, Belfast,	

Auditors, G. Bell, Gilford, and Thomas Wann, Belfast.—*Secretary to the Company*, John G. Smith....*Bankers*, Northern Banking Company....*Solicitor*, Hugh Wallace....*Engineer*, John Godwin.

Belfast and County Down Railway Company.

OFFICE, Queen's Quay, at the Station.

Act of incorporation, passed 26th June, 1846. Capital authorized—shares, £500,000; loans, £166,666—total, £666,666. Subscription capital, 10,000 shares, of £50 each, of which £42 10s has been called.

The length of line authorized is 45 miles 32 chains. The branch from Belfast to Holywood, 4 miles and 35 chains, was opened on the 2nd August, 1848; and the main line to Newtownards, 12¼ miles, on the 6th May, 1850.

DIRECTORS.

Chairman, Guy Stone, J.P., Barnhill, Comber,
Vice Chairman, James Macnamara, J.P.

James Boomer, Seaview, Belfast,	John Harrison, J.P., Merton Hall,
R. H. Dolling, J.P. Magheralin.	Hugh Wallace, Downpatrick,
William Pirrie, Conlig House, Newtownards,	Edward Walkington, Snugville, Belfast,

Secretary, Thomas Ward, Belfast.—*Solicitor*, William Wallace, Belfast and Downpatrick.—*Engineer*, John Godwin.—*Bankers*, The Northern Banking Company, Belfast; The Bank of Ireland, Dublin; Glyn & Co., London.

CUSTOMS AND INLAND REVENUE.

Custom-House, Queen's-Square.

Attendance every day, Sunday and the following Holidays excepted:— the birth-day of the King and Queen, for the time being; Christmas day; Good Friday, and any general fast. The gross produce of the Customs duties in 1838, was 315,774*l*; in 1843, 439,980*l*; for the year ending October, 1848, 335,074*l*. 9s. 10d.; for the year ending 10th October, 1849, 345,532*l*. 4s. 1d.; for the year ending 10th October, 1850, 348,033*l*. 16s.; and for the year ending 10th October, 1851, 368,922*l*. 19s. 3d.

Charles W. Hoffmeister, Collector.
John Carlile, Comptroller.
James Greene, 1st Clerk.
Joshua Moffett, 2nd do.
S. J. Cantwell, 3rd do.
James Moore, 4th do.
John L. Henry, 5th do.
Henry Joy M'Cracken, 6th do.
Henry Brigs, 7th do.
William Devlin, 8th do.
James Campbell, 9th do.
John Evans, Landing Surveyor.
E. J. Pretty, Registrar.

T M'Ewen,
Edward Brown,
Wm. T. Tripp, } Landingwaiters
Adam Hill,
Thos. W. Dowley,
Henry Lowth, Superintendent of Lockers, &c.
Fras. M'Keown,
Robert Joynt, } Tide Surveyors.
James Dawson,
Daniel Sheriff, Principal Coast Officer, &c., at Larne creek.
Henry G. Victor, Principal Coast Officer, &c., Donaghadee creek.

COAST-GUARD OFFICE, 13, QUEEN'S QUAY.

Capt. H. Blair, R.N., Inspecting Commander, Carrickfergus.
R. Studdert, R.N., Inspecting Commander, Donaghadee.
Lieutenant Samuel Lloyd, R.M., Chief Officer of the Belfast Station.

INLAND REVENUE OFFICE, 6, DONEGALL-PLACE BUILDINGS.

Collector, Evan Cameron, Esq.

Charles Lang, 1st Clerk. | Thomas Rhodes, 2nd. Clerk.
W. C. Stancliffe, Supernumerary.

Wm Sheil, *Supervisor Belfast Dist.*
Robert Ord, Officer, Belfast
Martin Downey, do
William Gillan, do
Samuel Armstrong, do
John Clifford, do
*Thomas Sessions do
*James L Nixon, do
Thos J Sugars, Ride Officer, Bfast
Gabriel W Wright Assistant do
James Vasey do do
Wm M Crowe, Permit Writer, do
Geo Russell, *Supervisor Belfast 2d District*
Wm Makepiece, Warehouse keeper
Robert Pugh, do
William Nicholas do
Thomas Jacobs, do

HILLSBOROUGH DISTRICT.
Edward Best Hill, *Supervisor*
Robt Hamilton, Officer, Glenavy

Joshua Fox, Officer, Hillsboro'
Joseph D Griffiths, do do
John Glass do Dromore
Edmund Lovel, do Lisburn
Alex Claghorne do Glenavey

CARRICKFERGUS DISTRICT.
John Farquharson, *Supervisor*
John Prickett, Officer, Cfergus
John G Browne do Larne
John G Thornley do Ballyclare
John R Davis, do do

COMBER DISTRICT.
William Armour, *Supervisor*
William Reid Officer, Comber
James Robinson do do
George Kent do do
John Griffiths do Newtonards
William Lewis do Kirkcubbin
William E Carter } Assistants
Edmund Tomes }

Those marked thus * are export officers.

Belfast Poor-Law Union.

The Belfast Union is partly in the County of Antrim, and partly in the County of Down; it contains an area of 47,702 statute acres, and a population of about 82,512. There are 12 Electoral Divisions, represented by 22 elected, and 22 *ex-officio* Guardians. The Workhouse was built for the accommodation of 1,000 paupers; since which time an extensive Fever Hospital is erected, capable of containing 600 patients. In connexion with the establishment is a School-house, to accommodate 1,000 children. The house was opened on the 11th May, 1841. The Board of Guardians meet at the Workhouse, Malone, every Wednesday, at Eleven o'clock. Attendance at the Office, from Ten till Four each day.

Poor Law Inspector, Edward Senior, Esq.

EX-OFFICIO GUARDIANS.

Robert Thomson, Castleton,
John F. Ferguson, Belfast
William Coates, Glentoran
Robert Jas. Tennent, M.P., Belfast
John Harrison, Merton-hall,
Sir William G. Johnson
Thomas Greg, Ballymenoch
Andrew Mulholland, Springvale

John Thomson, Low-wood
R. B. B. Houston, Orangefield, *Chairman*
John Clarke, Belfast
Robert Thomson, Clonard
John Mulholland, Craigavad
John M'Neile, Parkmount.
Samuel G. Fenton, Belfast

ELECTED GUARDIANS.

Electoral Division of Belfast.
Smithfield Ward.. Thos. Chermside
    W. M'Gee, M.D.
St. Ann's Ward.. William Watson
    Hutcheson Posnett
St. George's and ⎫ Henry Murney
Cromac Ward ⎬
West,........ ⎭ James Stirling
Dock Ward .... John E. Kidley, M.D.
    John Holden
Country Ward .. Robert Magee
    Robert S. Lepper

Electoral Division of
Ballyhackamore.. Samuel Boyle
Castlereagh ...... Robt. M'Connell
Greencastle ...... Arthur Aiken
Ballysillan...... Thomas Bigger
Ballymurphy .... J.W.S. M'Cance, V.C.
Whitehouse .... Jacob Bell
Carnmoney...... Samuel Giffen
Ballygomartin ....Samuel Nelson
Holywood ...... John Greenfield
Dundonald ...... Samuel Carson
Ballymacarrett....E. H. Clarke
    Robert Carlisle

NAMES OF THE SEVERAL OFFICERS.

Protestant Chaplain, Rev. H. Teape.
Presbyterian do., Rev. J. M'Kenzie
Roman Catholic do., Rev. John M'Grahan
Clerk, William Boyce
Assistant Clerk, William F. Boyce
Master, William Tidd
Assistant Master, John C. Owens
Matron, Margaret Galway
Assistant Matron, M. Lourimer
Schoolmaster, David Edgar
Assistant do., John Adrain
Supt. Indl. Training, Jos. Watt
Schoolmistress, Elizabeth Stewart
Assistant do., Jane Gowdy,
Medical Officer, Jas. S. Reid, M.D.
Assistant do., Cunningham Mulhulland, Surgeon, &c.
Surgeon Apothecary, J.B. Posnett,

Agricultural Overseer, S. Anderson
Head Nurse, Hospital, E. Hamilton,
Valuators, George Smart and A. Wyley
Auditor, Geo. B. Braddell, Esq.

Relieving Officers.
Belfast District, William Vance,
County Antrim, Echlin Gordon
County Down, John Ferguson

Rate collector.
Adam Dickie, 15, College-sq. North.

Vaccinators.
Belfast, Jas. Mawhinney, surgeon
Ballaghagan, James Mawhinney
Ballymacarrett, T. W. Hamilton,
Whitehouse, J. M'Mechan, M.D.
Dundonald, Robert Quee, surgeon,

MEDICAL INSTITUTIONS.

BELFAST UNION DISPENSARIES,

Commenced January, 1852, under the Act 14 and 15 Victoria, Cap. 68, being an Act to provide for the better distribution, support, and management of medical charities. Supported by the Poor Rates.

Medical Inspector for Ulster, DR. KNOX, Strangford.

BELFAST DISTRICT MEDICAL ATTENDANTS.

Christopher S. Black, M.D.	J. W. T. Smith, Surgeon, &c.
John H. Halliday, M.D.	Richard Ross, M.D.
T. C. S. Corry, Surgeon, &c.	John S. Armstrong, M.D.

RESIDENT APOTHECARIES.

North Station—Dispensary, Frederick-street, Edward Ring.
South Station—Dispensary, Old Barracks, Saml. Rea, Surgeon, &c.

BALLYMACARRETT DISTRICT.
Medical Attendant, Thomas William Hamilton, M.D.

BALLYGOMARTIN DISTRICT.
Medical Attendant, John Steele Dickson, Surgeon, &c.

CARNMONEY DISTRICT.
Medical Attendant, John Dundee, M.D.

HOLLYWOOD DISTRICT.
Medical Attendant, George Henry Young, M.D.

WHITEHOUSE DISTRICT.
Medical Attendant, John M'Mechan, M.D.

BELFAST MEDICAL SOCIETY.

Established in 1822, for the mutual advancement of Medical Knowledge, and social Professional intercourse. Meets the first Monday in every month, at 7 o'clock evening, in the General Hospital, when a paper upon some interesting case is usually read and discussed. The Office-bearers are elected annually in May. The society possesses a well-selected Medical Library, of above 2,000 volumes, and a valuable Pathological Museum.

President—Robert Stephenson, M.D.; *Vice-Presidents*—Wm. M'Gee, M.D., and A. G. Malcolm, M.D.

COUNCIL.

Samuel Browne, R.N.	J. M. Pirrie, M.D.
William Moffat, M.D.	Henry Murney, M.D.
J. C. Ferguson, M.D.	Alexander Gordon, M.D.

Treasurer, J. Patterson, M.D.; *Secretaries*—Æ. Lamont, F.R.C.S. J. S. Drennan, M.D.

MEDICAL BENEVOLENT FUND SOCIETY OF IRELAND.
BELFAST BRANCH.

Established in 1842, for the purpose of creating a fund, by donations and subscriptions, for the relief of medical men (physicians and surgeons) under severe and urgent distress occasioned by sickness, accident, or any other calamity; also, to relieve the widow or family of a professional man, who may have been deprived of the support and protection of a husband or parent.

Contributions are received from all persons friendly to the objects of the Society, though not belonging to the profession. The payment of £10 constitutes a life subscriber; and of one guinea annually, an annual subscriber; but any contributions, however small, will be thankfully received and acknowledged.

The following are the officers and committee of the Belfast Branch of the Society, established in 1843, and embracing the counties of Antrim and Down, who meet quarterly, in the Library Rooms of the Medical Society, at the General Hospital, Frederick Street.

Permanent President—Dr. Stephenson. Treasurer—Dr. Gordon (Queen's College). Hon. Secretary—Dr. Stewart (Hospital for the Insane).

Committee—Thos. Thompson, M.D.; T. H. Purdon, M.D.; Thos. Read, M.D.; J. M. Pirrie, M.D.; J. C. Ferguson, M.D., Queen's College; Wm. Black, Surgeon, Ballymena; J. M'Gowan, M.D., Carrickfergus; James Patterson, M.D.; W. M'Gee, M.D.; Surgeon Getty, Donaghadee; W. P. Deverall, M.D., Dromore.

BELFAST GENERAL HOSPITAL, FREDERICK-STREET.

Opened in 1817, and supported by Voluntary Contributions.

PRESIDENT—THE MOST NOBLE THE MARQUIS OF DONEGALL.

VICE-PRESIDENTS.

Mayor of Belfast	A. Mulholland, Esq., J.P.
Lord Bishop of Down and Connor	S. K. Mulholland, Esq., J.P.
Roman Catholic Bishop	Moderator of Belfast Presbytery
Lord John Chichester M.P.	Moderator of Antrim Presbytery
R. J. Tennent, Esq., M. P.	Senior Preacher of the Wesleyan Methodists, and President of the Queen's College
T. H. Purdon, Esq., M.D.	
Thomas Ferguson, Esq.	

LIFE-GOVERNORS.

Viscount Massereene	Alexander Shaw, Esq.
Sir Robert Bateson, Bart.	John Hind, Esq.
R. B. B. Houston, Esq., J.P.	Alexander M'Donnell, Esq.
Richard Davison, Esq.	John Clarke, Esq.
S. G. Fenton, Esq., J.P.	Robert Langtry, Esq.
J. G. Richardson, Esq.	John Turnley, Esq.

COMMITTEE OF MANAGEMENT.

Lord Bishop of Down	Rev. William Bruce
Right Rev. Dr. Denvir	Dr. Thomas Read
Samuel Archer, Esq	Alexander Brennan, Esq.
Henry Murney, Esq.	Andrew Mulholland, Esq., J.P.
G. Thompson, Esq.	A. J. Macrory, Esq.
Robert Boag, Esq.	John Clarke, Esq., J.P.
J. S. Stevelly, Esq., LL.D.	Rev. John Porter
Dr. Andrews	Gustavus Heyn, Esq.
Robert Roddy, Esq.	William Mullan, Esq.
Samuel Boyd, Esq.	Rev. Dr. Morgan
Colonel Brough	

Treasurer, Gustavus Heyn, Esq., 1, Henry Street.

MEDICAL OFFICERS.

Consulting Physicians—Doctors Stephenson, M'Cormac, Andrews, T. Thompson, S. Reid, and Matear.—*Consulting Surgeon*, Dr. Andrew Marshall—*Attending Physicians*, Drs. Moffatt, Malcolm, Pirrie, and Lynch—*Attending Surgeons*, Doctors Moore, Stewart, Messrs. Lamont, and Browne—*House Surgeon*, Mr. J. Breakey—*Assistant House Surgeon*, Mr. Robert M'Kibbin—*Apothecary*, Mr. Edward Ring.

EXTERN DEPARTMENT.

Patients affected with wounds, ulcers, and cutaneous diseases, generally attend three times weekly, and are dressed and treated under the superintendence of one of the attending medical staff. Days of attendance—Monday, Wednesday, and Friday, at 11 o'clock, forenoon.

Committee meet every Saturday at 11 o'clock, for admission of patients and transaction of business, but accidents and urgent cases are taken in at all times.

MEDICAL INSTITUTIONS, &c.

BELFAST DISTRICT HOSPITAL FOR THE INSANE POOR,
FALLS-ROAD.

Established in 1829, for the relief of the Insane Poor, pursuant to Act of Parliament. The district comprehends the counties of Antrim and Down, and the county of the town of Carrickfergus. The Board of Governors meets the first Monday of every month. No patient can be received without a medical certificate of insanity, and an affidavit of inability to meet the expenses of a private asylum. Printed forms may be had at the Hospital, where all communications are to be addressed, (post-paid) to the resident physician.

Board of Governors appointed by the Lord Lieutenant and Privy Council of Ireland.

Marquis of Donegall	William M'Cance, J.P.	Very Rev. the Dean of Ross
Marquis of Downshire	Robt. J. Tennent, M.P.	Rev. Dr. Cooke, LL.D.
Mayor of Belfast	John Sinclaire, Esq.	J. M'Neile, J.P., D.L.
The Lord Bishop of Down and Connor and Dromore	Edward Bruce, J.P.	C. B. Grimshaw, Esq.
	Rev. J. S. B. Monsell	John Clarke, J.P.
Rev. Thomas Hincks	Right Rev. Bishop Denvir, D.D.	Robert Batt, J.P., D.L.
R. B. Blackiston Houston, J.P.	Rev. Dr. Montgomery, LL.D.	Robert Gordon, J.P.
Sir Robt. Bateson, bart.	Rev. Dr. Edgar, D.D.	John S. Crawford, J.P.
		Wm. Dunville, Esq.

Resident Physician, Robert Stewart, M.D.—*Visiting Physician*, H. M'Cormac, M.D.—*Surgeon-Apothecary*, J. S. Mulholland, M.D.

Number of patients in Asylum, 1st November, 1850, 282. Admitted from ditto, till 1st Nov., 1851, 120. Discharged, &c., during same period, 131. Remaining in Asylum 1st November, 1851, 271. Total admissions since Asylum was opened, 2405. Total Discharges—2134.

BELFAST OPHTHALMIC INSTITUTION,

No. 35, Mill-Street (opposite King-Street), supported by voluntary contributions.

This institution was opened 9th April, 1844. Attendance—Mondays, Wednesdays, and Fridays, at 11 o'clock; Operation-day, Saturday, at 11. During the last twelve months upwards of 1,348 cases have been treated; making a total of 8,000 since its commencement. Diseases of the Ear are also prescribed for.

Surgeon, Samuel Browne, Esq., R.N., 5 Clarence-place.
Assistant, Mr. Armstrong.

OFFICERS OF HEALTH.

For the Parish of Belfast, for 1851-52—Old House of Correction—Appointed at Vestry Parish Meeting, under 59 Geo. 3, chap. 41, which empowers to take up and remove Beggars from the Parish, and cleanse infected Houses, and remove nuisances. Additional powers for the latter purpose have been given by a recent Act, 11 and 12 Vict:, chap. 123. whereby the expenses can be recovered by summary process from offenders.

Rev. T. F. Millar, Vicar	William Carson
Samuel Browne, R.N,	Robert Boag
John Holden	

ROYAL SOCIETY FOR THE PROMOTION AND IMPROVEMENT OF THE GROWTH OF FLAX IN IRELAND.

OFFICE:—COMMERCIAL BUILDINGS.

THIS Society was founded in 1841, to introduce in Ireland the most approved continental systems of Flax cultivation, and to extend the growth of the plant to those districts in which it had not hitherto been cultivated. Its chief means of attaining these ends is through the practical teachings of a staff of twenty-four Instructors, who have been trained in Belgium, and who are located in the different Flax-growing districts of Ireland, in the sowing and pulling seasons. The funds of the Society are supported by annual subscriptions from landed proprietors, flax-spinners, and linen merchants. It has also had, since 1848, an annual grant of £1000 from Government, from the Irish Reproduction Loan Fund. The expenditure of the latter is restricted to certain counties of the South and West. The exertions of the Society have been highly successful, the growth of Fax in Ireland having increased from 53,863 acres, in 1848, to 138,619, in 1851.

PATRONS;
Her most Gracious Majesty, THE QUEEN; H.R.H. PRINCE ALBERT.

VICE-PATRON;
His Excellency the EARL OF CLARENDON, Lord Lieut. of Ireland.

PRESIDENT;
The MARQUIS OF DOWNSHIRE.

VICE-PRESIDENTS;

The Marquis of Waterford,
The Marquis of Hertford,
The Earl of Ranfurley,
The Earl of Roden,
The Earl of Erne,
The Earl of Caledon,
The Earl of Enniskillen,
Viscount Dungannon,
Viscount Bernard, M.P.
Lord Rossmore,
The Lord Bishop of Down, &c.

Sir R. A. O'Donnell, Bart.
Sir J. M. Stronge, Bart.
Sir Robert Bateson, Bart.
Sir William Verner, Bart, M.P.
Sir Robert Kane
W. S. Crawford, Esq., M.P.
A. Shafto Adair, Esq., M.P.
Thomas Conolly, Esq., M.P.
Colonel A. Knox Gore
The Very Rev. the Dean of Ross
E. M'Donnell, Esq., D.L.,J.P.

COMMITTEE:

Andrews, W. G.
Bankhead, J. B.
Blakely, Rev. F.
Borthwick, John
Campbell, James
Charters, John
Crawford, John S., J.P.
Dargan, William
Fenton, S. G., J.P.
Filgate, Fitzherbert, J.P.
Green, George, J.P.
Grimshaw, James, jun.
Hancock, John, J.P.

Herdman, John
Mulholland, Andrew, J.P.
Mulholland, S. K., J.P.
M'Kibbin, Robert, M.D.
M'Master, John
Niven, Richard
Preston, John
Reilly, J. T., D.L.,J.P.
Richardson, Jonathan J.
Skinner, Captain, J.P.
Valentine, William
Walker, Richard

TREASURERS:
The Belfast Banking Company.

AUDITORS: John Charters and James Campbell.

SECRETARY: James MacAdam, jun.

SOCIETIES.

CHEMICO-AGRICULTURAL SOCIETY OF ULSTER.

Instituted in 1845, for the dissemination of practical knowledge, on the connection of chemistry with agriculture, and for the analyses of soils and manures, &c.

OFFICERS FOR THE YEAR.

PATRON:
His Excellency the Earl of Clarendon, Lord Lieutenant of Ireland.

PRESIDENT:
The Most Noble the Marquis of Downshire.

VICE-PRESIDENTS:

Marquis of Hertford,	R. J. Tennent, Esq., M.P.,
Earl of Antrim,	David S. Ker, Esq., D.L,,
Earl of Erne,	Edmund M'Donnell, Esq., D.L.,
Earl Annesley,	John M'Neile, Esq., D.L.,
Lord Dufferin and Claneboy,	T. Fortescue, Esq., D.,L.,
Viscount Massareene and Ferrard,	James Price, Esq., D.,L.,
Viscount Templeton.	James Agnew, Esq., J.,P.,
Lord George Hill,	Thomas Greg, Esq., J.,P.,
Sir Robert Bateson, Bart., *Belvoir Park*,	A. Mulholland, Esq., J.,P.,
	William Agnew, Esq., J.,P.,
Lord Bishop of Down,	Professor Andrews, M.D.,
Rt. Rev. Doctor Denvir,	Thomas Kirkpatrick, Esq., M.D.

HONORARY MEMBERS:

Baron Von Liebig, *Giessen University*,   Professor Johnston, *Durham University*

COUNCIL:

John Andrews, J P. *Comber*,	John Hanson, *Doagh*,
Rev F Blakely, *Moneyrea*,	D Lindsay, J P *Ashfield, Dromore*,
Rev W Bruce, *Belfast*,	James MacAdam, Sen. *Belfast*.
Thos Bateson, J P *Templepatrick*,	Richard Nevin, *Chrome Hill*,
George J Clarke, J P *Antrim*,	Robert Neill, *Dunmurry*,
Andrew Cowan, J P *Belfast*,	W B Price, J P *Saintfield*,
A Dickson, *Belfast*,	R O Pringle, *Saintfield*
D Ferguson, *Belfast*	Richard Robinson, *Belfast*,
Fitz. Filgate, J P *Hillsborough*,	William Simms, *Belfast*,
John Hancock, J P *Lurgan*,	Rev I Steen, *Belfast*,
P M'Henry, C E *Belfast*,	J Walker, *Larne*,
A H Montgomery, J P *Tyrella*,	Lieut Col Young, *Holywood*

TREASURER:
GUY STONE, J.P., *Barnhill, Comber*.

SECRETARIES:
JAMES ORR, M.D.,   W. B. RITCHIE.

CHEMIST:
PROFESSOR HODGES, M.D.

Laboratory and Assembly Room, 7, Arthur-Street.

ODD-FELLOWS' SOCIETIES.

ULSTER LODGE.—Established 10th November, 1840. Meets in St. Anne's Buildings, North-street, every alternate Wednesday; conducted by a President, Vice-President, and Secretary, elected half-yearly. Dr. Clarke, Surgeon of the Lodge, Donegall-street.

MARQUIS OF DONEGALL LODGE.—Established 10th October, 1841. Meets in Montgomery-street every alternate Tuesday; conducted by a President, &c., elected half-yearly.—Dr. Mulholland, Surgeon of the Lodge, 68, High-street.

BELFAST LODGE.—Established 22nd January, 1845, and conducted in the same manner as the others.—Dr. J. W. Beck, Surgeon of the Lodge, 128, North-street. Meets in the Salem School-Room, York-street.

NATURAL HISTORY AND PHILOSOPHICAL SOCIETY.

This Society was formed in 1821, for the cultivation of Natural History, and the investigation of the Topography, Statistics, and Antiquities of Ireland. Subsequently, the range of subjects became more extensive, it being agreed to receive communications on all branches of physical science and their applications. The meetings (private and public) for the reading of papers, are held on alternate Wednesday evenings, during the winter months, at the Museum, College-square North. The Museum was founded in 1830, and is open daily (Sundays excepted) from twelve till four o'clock. The internal arrangements are under the care of the Council for the time being.

COUNCIL FOR 1851-2.

Thomas Andrews, MD, M R I A
Edmund Getty, M R I A
John Grattan
James R Garrett
W N Hancock, LL D
James MacAdam, F G S
Robert S MacAdam
James MacAdam, jun.
George C Hyndman
Robert Patterson
Rev I Steen
John Stevelly, LL D
William Thomson
A O D Taylor

OFFICERS.

President, William Thompson
Honorary Vice-President, Rev. Thos Hincks, LL D, F G S, M R I A
Vice-Presidents, Thomas Andrews, M D, M R I A; John Stevelly, LL D, Robert Patterson; Robert S MacAdam

Secretaries, James MacAdam, FGS and A O'D Taylor
Corresponding Secretary, James MacAdam, jun.
Treasurer, John Grattan
Librarian, Rev. I. Steen

BELFAST LIBRARY AND SOCIETY FOR PROMOTING KNOWLEDGE.

This Society was instituted in 1788, and meets in the centre building of the Linen-Hall, Donegall-square, under the direction of a President, Vice-President, and Committee, annually elected. It now possesses upwards of 8,500 volumes on history, biography, voyages, travels, political economy, encyclopedias, French and English; with books on natural philosophy, chemistry, &c.; dictionaries, maps, charts, reviews, magazines, philosophical journals, &c. The Library contains an almost complete file of the *Belfast NewsLetter* from 1737 to the present date. Terms, one guinea entrance, and one guinea per annum. A register of the weather is kept by the Librarian, viz., barometer, thermometer, and quantity of rain. The Committee meet the first and third Thursday of every month, at 10 o'clock, A.M.; the Society at half-past 10.

President, Rev. William Bruce.—*Vice-President*, William Thompson. *Secretary*, Dr. Kidley.—*Treasurer*, Wm. Bottomley.—*Librarian*, James Stewart.

COMMITTEE.

William Suffern,
Dr. Drennan,
William Ferguson,
Dr. M'Gee,
Rev. Dr. Bryce,
Dr. Hodges,
William Simms,
Thomas Chermside,
James MacAdam,
Professor Craik,
Robert Gray.

SOCIETIES. 441

ROYAL BOTANICAL AND HORTICULTURAL SOCIETY.

Patroness, Her Most Gracious Majesty the Queen.
Patron, His Royal Highness Prince Albert.
President, The most noble the Marquis of Donegall.
Vice-presidents, The Marquis of Hertford, the Marquis of Downshire, and Lord O'Neill.
Trustees, Wm. Thompson, Valentine Whitla, and J. F. Ferguson esqrs.
Corresponding Secretaries, Rev. Dr. Hincks and Francis Whitla, esq.
Treasurers, The Northern Banking Company.
Secretary, Thomas Sinclaire, esq.—*Curator,* Mr. D. Ferguson.

John F. Ferguson	Dr. Kidley	Charles Lanyon
John Clarke	Samuel Lyle	William Bottomley
Richard Davison	William Forsythe	Edward H. Clarke
William Stevenson	Rev. W. Bruce	John Grattan
William Gillilan	Samuel G. Fenton	Thomas Chermside
John Owden	Charles Langtry	John Curell
George C. Hyndman	John Herdman	

BELFAST PUBLIC BATHS AND WASH-HOUSES.

Corner of Townsend-street, Falls-Road.
Erected by voluntary Subscriptions—Opened 22nd May, 1847.

This Establishment has recently been considerably improved, and the commodation extended for all classes. Report for year ending Aug, 1851

Number of Bathers—Males...9,894
Do. Females 1,437

Number of bathers previous year..............—Males....8,384
Do. do. —Females 1,401

Total, 11,331
Total, 9,785

Increase on last year, 2,010—No. of articles washed by the Poor, 57,715.
Private Washing Department.—Number of articles washed and finished, 43,661, being an increase of 4,001 over previous year.
Superintendent and Secretary, W. J. Livingston.

BELFAST WORKING CLASSES' ASSOCIATION FOR THE PROMOTION OF GENERAL IMPROVEMENT.

FORMED 1845—ROOMS, 4, CASTLE CHAMBERS.
President, Doctor Malcolm.
Vice-presidents, J. Scott, and J. Hartrick.
Treasurer, Mr. H. Pink.—*Hon. Secretary,* Abner Walsh.—*Librarian,* James Long.

Lectures have been delivered, under the auspices of the association, by several eminent gentlemen. The money raised by all lectures, delivered in connexion with the association, is used in improving and extending the Library.

The People's News-Room, opened 22nd June, 1846, at 4, Castle Chambers, is supplied regularly with the leading Irish, English, Scotch, and American journals, newspapers, and periodicals. It is open daily, from 7, a.m., till 10, p.m. Terms, to the working-classes, 1s. 6d. per quarter to all others, 2s. 6d. Visitors admitted at the charge of one penny.

The People's Circulating Library, opened 8th July, 1847—consists of one thousand three hundred volumes. It is open daily from 2 till 3, and from 7 till 8. p.m. Terms. to the working classes, 1s. 6d. per quarter—if subscribers to the News-room, 1s. To others, 2s. and 1s. 6d. respectively.

The Committee meet every Thursday evening. The general meetings of the Association are held on the first Thursday of January and July.

EDUCATIONAL INSTITUTIONS.

QUEEN'S COLLEGE, BELFAST.
MALONE ROAD, OPENED OCT., 1842.

President,	Rev. P. Shuldham Henry, D.D.
Vice-President,	Thomas Andrews, M.D., F.R.S., M.R.I.A.

PROFESSORS.

Faculty of Arts.—Division of Literature.

The Greek Language	C. Macdouall, A M
The Latin Language	Rev C. P. Reichel¹, A M
History and English Literature..	G. L. Craik, A M
Modern Languages	M. I. Frings, Ph. D
The Celtic Languages	John O'Donovan, M R I A

Division of Science.

Mathematics	{ W. Parkinson Wilson, M A, Fellow Saint John's, Cambridge
Natural Philosophy,	John Stevelly, LL D
Chemistry..	T. Andrews, M D, F R S, M R I A
Logic and Metaphysics,..	Rev James M'Cosh, A M, LL D
Natural History..	George Dickie, M D
Mineralogy and Geology	F. M'Coy, Esq
Civil Engineering	John Godwin, C E
Agriculture	John F. Hodges, M D

Faculty of Medicine.

Anatomy and Physiology	{ Hugh Carlile, A M, M D
Practical Anatomy	
Practice of Medicine	John C. Ferguson, A M, M B
Practice of Surgery	Alexander Gordon, M D
Midwifery	William Burden, M D
Materia Medica ...	Horatio Stewart, M D

Faculty of Law.

English Law,	E. Molyneux, A M
Jurisprudence and Political Economy	{ W. N. Hancock, LL D

DEAN OF RESIDENCES.

Church of England, Rev H. Murphy—*Presb. Church,* Rev H. Cooke, D D, LL D—*Association of Non-Subscribing Presbyterians,* Rev John Porter—*Wesleyan Methodists,* Rev William Lupton.

OFFICERS.

Registrar, W. J. C. Allen—*Librarian,* Rev G. Hill—*Bursar,* A. Dickey.

The subjects of the matriculation or entrance examination for students in the Faculties of Arts, Medicine, and Law, are English Grammar and Composition; in the Greek Language, any two of the following authors the candidate may select, viz.:—Homer's Iliad, the first four books—Xenophon's Anabasis, the first three books—Walker's Lucian; in the Latin Language, any two of the following authors the candidate may select, viz.:—Virgil's Æneid, the four first books—Livy, the first two books; all Sallust; Cæsar, the 5th and 6th books of the Gallic War; retranslation of Cæsar's Commentaries from English into Latin; Arithmetic, Fractions, vulgar and decimal, Practice, Proportion, Interest, Discount, and the Square Root; Algebra, to the end of Simple Equations; Euclid's Elements, the first two books; Grecian History, to the death of Alexander the Great; Roman History, to the accession of Augustus; Outlines of Ancient and Modern Geography. The entrance course for Engineering and Agricultural students is the same as the preceding, with the exclusion of the Greek and Latin Languages.

EDUCATIONAL INSTITUTIONS. 443

Thirty junior scholarships, of £24 each, are awarded in each of the Colleges; ten to undergraduate students of the 1st, 2nd, and 3rd years respectively, of the Faculty of Arts, exclusive of Civil Engineering and Agriculture; six junior scholarships of £20 each, to undergraduate students of the 1st, 2nd, and 3rd years respectively, of the Faculty of Medicine; three junior scholarships, of £20 each, to undergraduate students of the 1st, 2nd, and 3rd years respectively, of the classes of the Faculty of Law. Two scholarships, of £20 each, are to be awarded to students of Civil Engineering; and four, of £15 each, to those of Agriculture, to be distributed in each case equally for the 1st and 2nd years. The thirty junior scholarships of Arts are to be divided into two classes, the Literary and the Scientific. Five of the ten junior scholarships of each year to be appropriated to each class, exclusive of Civil Engineering and Agriculture. All the junior scholarships are tenable for one year only; but the students of each year are not be disqualified from becoming candidates for scholarships of the succeeding year in their several departments. The examinations for junior scholarships of the first year are to take place immediately after the matriculation or entrance examination, and to be open to all students who have passed that examination. The subjects of examination for the junior scholarships are published annually in the Belfast Queen's College Calendar.

Ten senior scholarships, of £20 each, are to be awarded to students in the three faculties, in the following proportions, viz.:—seven to the most distinguished students who have proceeded to the degree of Bachelor of Arts—one for proficiency in each of the following departments:—in Greek, Latin, and Ancient History; in Modern Languages and History; in Mathematics; in Natural Philosophy; in Metaphysics and Economical Science; in Chemistry, and Natural History;—two to students who have completed the three years' course prescribed for candidates for the degree of Doctor of Medicine, viz., one for Anatomy and Physiology, and one for Therapeutics and Pathology;—one to the pupils who have proceeded to the degree of Bachelor of Arts, and have completed the course of legal studies prescribed for candidates for the degree of Bachelor of Law. The student first on the list of candidates, both in the Literary and Science divisions, at the examination for junior scholarships in Arts, shall be entitled to a scholarship in each division; but in no other case are two scholarships to be held by the same student.

BELFAST COLLEGE TERMS, 1852.

JANUARY TERM, (Session 1851-52)—begins Wednesday, January 7; ends Tuesday, April 6

MAY TERM—begins Tuesday, May 20; ends, (Session 1851-52) Saturday, June 12

NOVEMBER TERM, (Session 1852-53)—begins Tuesday, October 19; ends Tuesday, December 21

GENERAL ASSEMBLY'S COLLEGE, BELFAST.

President of Faculty, Rev. H. Cooke, D.D., LL.D.—*Secretary of Faculty*, Rev. Robert Wilson, D.D.

PROFESSORS.

Systematic Divinity, Rev. Samuel Hanna, D.D., Rev. John Edgar, D.D.

Ecclesiastical History and Pastoral Theology, Rev. W. D. Killen, D.D.

Sacred Criticism and Interpretation, Rev. Robert Wilson, D.D.—*Biblical and Ecclesiastical Greek*, Mr. E. Masson.

Oriental Languages, Rev. James Murphy, LL.D.

Moral Philosophy, Rev. William Gibson.—*Sacred Rhetoric*, Rev. H. Cooke, D.D. LL.D.

The Classes in this College open on the first Tuesday of November, and close the last week in April.

EDUCATIONAL INSTITUTIONS.

GOVERNMENT SCHOOL OF DESIGN,

North wing, Royal Academical Institution, College-Square, North.

Established in 1850, in connexion with the Parent School of Design, in London, for the promotion of the arts of Design and Decoration.

President—Lord Dufferin and Claneboy.

Vice-Presidents—William Thompson, Charles Lanyon, C.E.

GENERAL COMMITTEE.

A. S. Adair, M.P.
J. F. Ferguson,
M. J. Anketell, Monaghan
William M'Gee, M.D.
S. K. Mulholland,
David Lindsay, Ashfield
Francis M Cracken,
John Henning, Waringstown
John Holden,
John Herdman,
Samuel Archer, jun.
William Valentine,
John Owden,
James MacAdam,
J. R. Neill,
Francis Coates,
Robert Corry,

R. J. Tennent, M.P.
Rowley Miller, Moneymore
W J. C. Allen,
Thomas Andrews, M.D.
William Bottomley,
James Gibson,
Robert MacAdam,
John M'Master, Gilford
William Dunville,
S. G. Fenton,
John Godwin, C.E.
James Brown, Donacloney
Robert Roddy,
John Simms,
Moses Staunton,
Alexander Moore,
John Mulholland.

MANAGING COMMITTEE.

William M'Gee, M.D.
John Holden,
Francis M'Cracken,

John Herdman,
William Bottomley,
Robert MacAdam.

John Godwin, C.E.

Treasurer—W. J. C. Allen.

Hon. Secretary, Jas. MacAdam, jun.; Assistant Secretary, S. Vance.

Head Master, C. L. Nursey; Second Master, D. Reimbach.

Terms: Evening Classes for Males, five nights in the week; time 7 to 9½—per month, 1s. 6d.

Evening Classes for Females, five nights in the week; time a quarter from 7 to 9—per month, 9d.

Private Classes for Ladies and Gentlemen twice in the week—One Guinea per Quarter.

ROYAL BELFAST ACADEMICAL INSTITUTION.

(Incorporated by Act of Parliament, 1810.)

President—Marquis of DONEGALL.

Vice-Presidents, R. B. B. Houston, esq., G. T. Mitchell, esq., and W. S. Crawford, esq., M.P. There are also 20 managers, and eight visitors, elected by the Proprietors, and 13 ex-officio visitors appointed by Act of Parliament.

Secretary, W. J. C. Allen.—Treasurer, John Gillis.

Classical Master, T. W. Evans, ex-schol. T.C D.—*Mathematical and Mercantile*, Rev. Isaiah Steen.—*English*, T. Blain, A.M.—*French*, Monsieur Badler.—*Writing*, Patrick Johnston.—*Drawing*, Joseph Molloy.

The Institution is empowered to issue Certificates to candidates for Degrees in Art and Law, to be granted, on examination by the University of London.

BELFAST ACADEMY.—INSTITUTED 25TH JANUARY, 1786.

The Academy is under the superintendence of a Principal; and its general affairs are managed by a Committee of the subscribers, conjointly with the Principal and Masters.

Trustee for Subscribers, J. Cunningham, esq.—Trustee for the Masters, The Principal.

Principal, Rev. R. J. Bryce, LL.D.

MASTERS.—*Classical School*, the Principal; *Mathematical and Mercantile School*, Thomas M'Clinton; *Writing School*, T. Armstrong; *Drawing School*, Joseph Molloy; *English School*, W. F. Collier; *French*, Jules Festu.

There are also classes for Logic, Belles Lettres, Natural Philosophy, and Natural History; and for the German, Italian, Spanish, and Oriental languages.

EDUCATIONAL INSTITUTIONS. 445

LADIES' INDUSTRIAL SCHOOL FOR GIRLS, FREDERICK-STREET.
Established 1849.

Under the management of a committee of 50. There are at present 100 children fed, clothed, and educated in the building designated as the "Lancasterian School-house." These children have been selected after careful scrutiny, from the most destitute of our population; they are taught Reading, Writing, Arithmetic, Geography, Plain Sewing, Mending, Darning, Knitting, Washing and Ironing, and Housemaids' work.—Patroness, Mrs. Knox, the Palace, Holywood; President, Mrs. Thomson, Castleton; Vice-President, Mrs. Thomson, Low-wood; Treasurer, Mrs. Bruce, Thorndale; Recording Secretaries, Miss Smyth, Glengall-Place, and Miss Hardcastle; Corresponding Secretary, Miss Ireland, Royal College; Teacher, Miss Orr; Patron, Mrs. Todd.

In another apartment of the same building an Infant School is conducted, the arrangements of which are entirely different. The average attendance of pupils in this apartment is from 100 to 150. Teacher, Miss Anderson; Assistant Teacher, Miss Ferguson; managing Committee, the same as that of the Industrial School.

During the past year, a Lace School has been established in the same building.

ST. MALACHY'S DIOCESAN SEMINARY.

DONEGALL-STREET,

Under the patronage and superintendence of Right Rev. Dr. Denvir.

Dean, Rev. John M'Grahan; Professor of Classics, Belles Lettres, and Mathematics, Rev. Edward Kelly; Head Master in the Mercantile department, Mr. Thomas Duignan.

The course comprises the Greek, Latin, and French Languages, Algebra, Geometry, Trigonometry, plane and spherical; Conic Sections, Mensuration, Navigation, Use of the Globes, Book-keeping, together with all the various branches of an English and Mercantile education. Music, Drawing, Dancing, &c., are also taught by competent Professors. The boarding-house, Vicinage, is situated on the Antrim Road.

Terms for the Academical year—Board, Washing, and Medical Attendance, £14 5s per annum.

Tuition in the Classical and Mathematical departments, £4 per annum; English, stationery included, from £1 to 12s 9d per quarter, in proportion to the subjects taught, and the length of time daily devoted to them.

French, which is taught by a native of Paris, six shillings per quarter.

Music, Drawing, Dancing, &c., as per agreement with the Professors.

During extra hours, and free of expense to the Pupils, Lectures on Natural Philosophy are delivered and experimentally illustrated, the Diocesan Seminary being for this purpose provided with perfect Chemical and Philosophical Apparatus.

DONEGALL-STREET NATIONAL SCHOOL.
Established in 1829.

Since that period the names of 23,000 children have been received upon its books in the male school, and nearly an equal number in the female school—the weekly average number in actual attendance is 600. Teachers, Michael Doyle and John Lawler in the male—Miss Ann Maginness and Miss S. M'Cann in the female department.

NORTHERN SUNDAY SCHOOL ASSOCIATION.

Established May, 1839, for the purpose of supplying Sunday Schools with Bibles, Testaments, and other books and requisites. The Committee meet at their Depository in Rosemary-street, on the first Thursday of every month, at half-past 6, p.m.

COMMITTEE.

Rev. J. Scott Porter	Robert Patterson	W. H. Greer
— John Porter	William Spackman	S. M'Millen
— David Maginnis	Lennox Drennan	William M'Caw, jun.
— Hugh Moore	Thomas O'Gorman	John Kennedy

BROWN-STREET SUNDAY AND DAILY SCHOOL,
Established in 1810,

For the purpose of supplying the children of the poor with Scriptural and Literary Education. Nearly 500 children are taught in the Sunday Schools, and upwards of 550 receive instruction in the Daily Schools.

Richard Hull, Esq. *Treasurer*; Archibald Rutherford and R. T. M'Geagh, *Secretaries*; Thomas Edmondson, *Master*; Miss Stevenson, *Mistress*. There is an infant School connected with this establishment, Miss Tate, *Mistress*.

THE BELFAST PAROCHIAL SUNDAY AND DAY SCHOOLS,
ACADEMY-STREET.
Established in 1830.

Upwards of 300 children are taught; and in the daily school department, upwards of 300 receive instruction in spelling, reading, writing, arithmetic, grammar, book-keeping, geography, etymology, mensuration, and navigation. The females are taught needle-work also. Mr. Robinson, and Mrs. Morrow, Teachers.

GEORGE'S CHURCH DAILY SCHOOLS.
Opened January, 1834.

On books of male school, 56; female school, 146, who are taught spelling, reading, writing, English Grammar, geography, mensuration, and an explanation of the Scriptures. Teacher of male school, Dr. Walker; of female school, Mr. Anglesey. SUNDAY SCHOOL, held in the School-rooms at 9 o'clock, morning; numerously attended by male and female children.

CHRIST CHURCH DAILY SCHOOLS.
Opened November, 1836.

On books of male School, 500; female School, 315; infant School, 214; total, 1029.—Teacher of male school, Mr. Dogherty; of female School, Miss Stewart; of infant school, Miss Wheeler.

CHRIST CHURCH SUNDAY SCHOOLS.

The schools, male and female, held in Christ's Church School-rooms, at a quarter past 9, A.M., and 4, P.M; average attendance 400, and 50 teachers. Total on Books of Sunday Schools, 1000—Adult Schools, 50.

Suburban Schools contain upwards of 200 children.—Luther Sunday and Daily Schools, containing 70 children; and Huss Sunday Schools, containing about 80 children, are held in connexion with Christ's Church.

EDUCATIONAL INSTITUTIONS. 447

ULSTER INSTITUTION FOR PROMOTING THE EDUCATION OF THE DEAF AND DUMB AND THE BLIND.

Lisburn Road—Office, 4, Commercial Buildings.

Opened, 1845.—The objects of this Society are to afford to Deaf and Dumb and to Blind Children, whose parents reside in the Province of Ulster, a religious and literary education, in accordance with the standard doctrines of the Churches of England and Scotland, and to prepare them for learning some useful trade, by which they may be enabled to earn their livelihood. The Society consists of members for life, and annual members. Every donor of £10 at one time is a life member, and every contributor of £1, or collector of £3, per annum, an annual member of the Society. The charge to day scholars for instruction in the schools is two guineas per annum for each pupil. The charge for Deaf and Dumb boarders in the Institution does not exceed the sum of £18 per annum; for which they are provided with suitable food, clothing and education.

Treasurer—James Bristow, Esq. Hon. Secretaries—James Shaw, Esq., and Rev. Richard Oulton. Assistant-Secretary—Rev. Mr. Kinghan. Principal—Rev. John Martin. Physician—Dr. H. Purdon. Matron—Miss Warner.

ST. PATRICK'S ORPHAN SOCIETY,

May Street and Seymour Street, established February 1840; and supported by voluntary contributions. The objects of the Society are to afford the means of support to destitute orphans; to bestow on them a religious education. There is a school-house adjoining the society's establishment, for educating the poor of the neighbourhood. Patron—Right Rev. Dr. Denvir. The Committee is formed of ladies.

ULSTER FEMALE PENITENTIARY.—Brunswick-Street.

Established 1st Nov., 1839.

This noble institution receives penitent victims of seduction, and encourages them to work for their own support within the walls of the institution, where there are the most extensive and appropriate facilities for washing, drying, mangling, &c. The institution offers a refuge to all proper objects, without distinction of sect or party—no suitable applicant has yet been refused.

Secretary—Rev. G. Shaw. Treasurer—Dr. Edgar.

MAGDALENE ASYLUM,

Donegall Pass, for the reception of erring and repentant females. There is a Chapel of Ease connected with this building.

Chaplain—Rev. E. J. Hartrick.

LYING-IN HOSPITAL.

Instituted in 1794, is situated at the upper end of Donegall-street, on the Antrim Road, where a commodious building was erected in the year 1830, for the reception and recovery of indigent females.

Patroness, the Marchioness of Donegall—Vice-Patroness, Mrs. Cunningham. It is managed by a Committee of Ladies, appointed by subscribers annually in February. Treasurer, Mrs. Smith; Secretary, Mrs. Bruce; Medical Attendant, Dr. Burden; Matron, Mrs. Todd; House-keeper, Miss Henry.

CHARITABLE SOCIETY.

Incorporated by Act of Parliament, for the maintenance and instruction of poor children, and support of the aged and infirm poor. On 25th November, 1851, it contained 205 old persons and children. It is supported by annual subscriptions, bequests, donations, and the sum of 800*l*. per annum, applotted on the inhabitants of the town as water tax, in consideration of a large capital expended by the Charitable Society on the water works for the supply of the town. Poor-house and Infirmary, North Queen-street.

John Thomson, *Treasurer*.

COMMITTEE.

Rev. W. Bruce	Rt. Rev. Dr. Denvir	John Owden
Robert Magee	John Clarke	Rev. William Gibson
John Knox	Rev. Dr. Cooke	Rev. T. F. Millar
John Getty	Edward H. Clarke	The Bishop of Down,
Adam J. Macrory	Dr. Charles Purdon	Connor, & Dromore.
Professor Stevelly	Edward Pim	Rev. J. Macnaughtan
John Lindsay	Rev. R. Oulton	Gordon A. Thomson
James Standfield		

Dr. Charles Purdon, *Attending Physician*.—Dr. M'Cleery, *Surgeon*.
J. Marshall, *Steward*.

SOCIETY FOR RELIEF OF THE DESTITUTE SICK.
ESTABLISHED 1826.

This Society directs its benevolence exclusively to cases where sickness and poverty are united. Since its commencement, it has given relief in articles of food and nourishment to 17,829 sick persons, and has expended £6,320 6s. 9d. It is supported by donations and subscriptions, and is under the management of a committee and visitors, who personally investigate every case.

Treasurer—S. G. Fenton, Esq. Secretary—Mr. H. Horner.

THE LADIES' BELFAST CLOTHING SOCIETY.

Supported by annual Subscriptions.—*Treasurer*, Mrs. Mateer, Murray's Terrace.—*Secretary*, Miss Stevenson, Adelaide-Place.

SOCIETY FOR THE PREVENTION OF CRUELTY TO ANIMALS.

Established in 1836, after the example of the London Society for the same purpose.

Treasurer—E. Pim, High Street. Secretaries—Rev. I. Steen, and F. A. Calder. Constable—Wm. K'Kechnie, 22 Carrick hill.

BELFAST AUXILIARY TO THE BRITISH AND FOREIGN ANTI-SLAVERY SOCIETY.

Treasurer—Robert Workman. Honorary Secretaries—James Stanfield, and Lieut. F. A. Calder.

BELFAST AUXILIARY TO THE SOCIETY FOR PROMOTING CHRISTIANITY AMONG THE JEWS.

This Auxiliary of the above Society has been established for several years, and has extended its branches to several towns in the province of Ulster—as Carrickfergus, Lisburn, Downpatrick, Bangor, Newtownards, Kirkcubbin, &c. Dr. T. H. Purdon, Wellington Place, Secretary. Meeting in October in each year.

LAW COURTS, &c.

QUARTER SESSIONS.
Held in the Court-House, Crumlin Road, four times each year.
ASSISTANT BARRISTER—John Gibson, Esq.

MAGISTRATES.
Allen, W. J. C., Wellington Place,
Belfast, Earl of, D.L., Ormeau,
Belfast, The Mayor of, for the time being,
Bland, Rev. R. W., Abbeyville,
Clarke, John, College Square,
Coates, William, Glentoran,
Cowan, Andrew, (County Down) Chichester Street,
Crommelin, N. Delacherois, jun.
Curell, John, sen.,
Fenton, Samuel G., College Square,
Ferguson, J. F., D.L., Donegall Pl.,
Ferguson, Thomas, Greenville,
Grimshaw, Edmund, Mossley,
Grimshaw, Robert, D.L., White-house,
Houston, R. B. B., Orangefield,
Johnson, Sir W. G., D.L., College Square,
M'Cance, James L., Glenville,
M'Cance, William, Suffolk,
M'Namara, James,
M'Neile, John, D.L., Parkmount,
Stevenson, William,
Tennent, James Thompson,
Tennent, Robt. James, M.P., D.L., Hercules Place,
Tennent, Sir J. E., M.P., (Lisburn) London,
Thompson, Robt., Donegall Square West,
Thomson, John, Lowwood,
Thomson, Robert, Castleton,
Tracy, W. S., R.M.,
Verner, Thos. D.L., Ormeau.

GENERAL QUARTER SESSIONS FOR 1852,
Will be held at the following places and times, viz.:—

HILARY.	SUMMER.
Ballymena, 30th December, 1851	Ballymena, 17th June, 1852
Antrim, 5th January, 1852	Antrim, 23rd June, "
Belfast, 8th January, "	Belfast, 26th June, "
Carrickfergus, 16th January, "	Carrickfergus, 3rd July, "
EASTER.	OCTOBER.
Ballymoney, 26th March, 1852.	Ballymoney, 12th October, 1852.
Ballymena, 30th March, "	Ballymena, 15th " "
Antrim, 5th April, "	Antrim, 21st " "
Belfast, 8th April, "	Belfast, 25th " "

PETTY SESSIONS
Is held in the Court-House, Howard Street, every day, at half-past ten o'clock. W. S. Tracy, Esq., Resident Magistrate. Clerks—H. Orr and G. K. Kennedy.

POLICE-OFFICE.
Police Square.
Superintendent Magistrate—The Mayor of Belfast. Thos. Lindsay and Wm. Armstrong, Chief-Constables. John Kane and Stewart M'Williams, Detective Officers.

CONSTABULARY OFFICERS.
County Inspector—E. S. Flinter, Esq., Ballymena.

SUB-INSPECTORS' STATIONS.
Belfast—Geo. S. Hill, 6, North Queen Street.
Antrim—S. B. Studdert.
Ballymena—William Henry.
Ballymoney—R. W. Bagley.
Carrickfergus—John H. Daly.
Glenarm—C. J. Gernon.

CONSISTORIAL COURT, AND REGISTRY OF DOWN AND CONNOR.

OFFICE:—35, UPPER ARTHUR STREET.

Vicar-General—Charles George Knox, Esq., LL.D.
Surrogate—Rev. Thomas Knox, A.M.
Registrars—Rev. James Alexander, D.D., Ferbane, King's County; H. T. Higginson, Esq., A.M., J.P., Lisburn.
Deputy Registrar — John M. Higginson, Esq., Solicitor, 35, Upper Arthur Street, Belfast.

This Court will (until further notice) sit to hear causes in the late Grand Jury Room, Court House, Howard Street, Belfast, every second Monday in the month, at Twelve o'clock Noon. The Registry Office and Vicar-Generals' Chambers are at No. 35, Upper Arthur Street (corner of Chichester Street), where there will be attendance every day (save Sunday) from Ten to Four o'clock.

The Consistorial Court has exclusive jurisdiction to grant Probates of the Wills, and Administration to the effects, of persons dying without leaving property in any other Diocese, and has also concurrent jurisdiction with the Court of Chancery to enforce the payment of legacies to any amount bequeathed by the wills and the distribution of the effects of persons so dying.

The following are the names and addresses, in Belfast, of the Gentlemen who practise as Proctors:—John Pennington, 132, Ann Street; Hugh Wallace, Fountain Street; John Wallace, Victoria Street; H. B. Magee, Ormeau Road; George Stephenson, 6, Castle Chambers; William Dillon, 31, Arthur Street; Francis H. O'Flaherty, 13, Arthur Street; Henry Seeds, 18, Castle Lane; John Birney, 16, Castle Chambers. *Apparitor*—Arch. M'Afee.

MANOR COURT OF BELFAST.

Seneschal—S. M'Dowell Elliot, Esq. Registrar—Robt. M'Master.

The Court has jurisdiction for the recovery of all sums not exceeding £20, by civil bill process. Decrees affect the person or the goods of the defendant. The following townlands and denominations are included in the Manor of Belfast:—Altegarron, Ballyaghagan, Ballycullo, Ballydownfine, Ballygammon, Ballygomartin, Ballymagarry, Ballymoney, Ballymurphy, Ballysillan (Lower), Ballysillan (Upper), Ballynafeigh, Belfast, Blackmountain, Ballyfinaghey, Carntall, Carnmoney, Devis, Dunmurry, Edenderry, Englishtown, Greencastle, Hannahstown, Ligoneil, Lowwood, Malone (Lower), Malone (Upper), Oldpark, Oldforge, Skeigoneil.

The Court sits at 10 o'clock each day. All processes must be entered with the Registrar before 6, P.M., on the evening previous to each Court day.

COURT DAYS FOR 1852.

Thursday, 22nd January	Thursday, 29th July
... 12th February	... 19th August
... 4th March	... 9th September
... 25th March	... 30th September
... 15th April	... 21st October
... 6th May	... 11th November
... 27th May	... 2nd December
... 17th June	... 23rd December
... 8th July	

Manor Court Officers—David Evans, 12, Charlotte Street; William Alderdice, 115, Durham Street; James M'Neill, Joy's Dam; Thomas Johnson, 14, Castle Lane; Reeves Hagan, 12, Galway's Entry; Danl. Ritchie, 6, Institution Place; Stephen Leigh, 19, Frederick Street; James M'Crea, Carnmoney.

COURT-HOUSE AND GAOL. 451

THE COUNTY COURT HOUSE.

This noble structure, which is admitted to be the most elegant and commodious building of its kind in Ireland, stands opposite the New Jail, on the Crumlin Road. In addition to the Crown and Nisi Prius Courts, and a superb common hall for the use of the public, it contains ample accommodation for the grand jury and the county officers. It is in the Corinthian order of architecture, with a spacious portico and pedement, supported by eight columns. It was opened at the Summer Assizes of 1850.

COUNTY OFFICERS.

High-Sheriff—Robert Smyth, Esq.

Clerk of the Crown—Walter Bourne, Esq., 17, Fitzwilliam Square West, Dublin.

Clerk of the Peace—George A. H. Chichester, Esq.

Deputy Clerk of the Peace—William C. Cunningham, Solicitor, 4, York Street, Belfast.

Crown Solicitor—Maxwell Hamilton, Esq.; office, 5, Kildare Street, Dublin.

Crown Solicitor at Quarter Sessions—Neil John O'Neil, Esq., 9, Lower Gloucester Street, Dublin.

Treasurer—Alexander Miller, Esq., Ballycastle.

Secretary to the Grand Jury—John Coates, Esq., Carrickfergus.

County Surveyor—Charles Lanyon, Esq., Belfast.

Sub-Sheriff—Robert Clark, Esq.; office, 6, Castle Chambers.

Court-House Keeper—Alexander Rule.

THE NEW JAIL

Stands in a very elevated and healthy situation, outside the town, on an area of ten acres, designed after the great model prison of Pentonville, London. Hammocks are used in the cells, which are suitably furnished; combs, brushes, towels to each, with Bible and Prayer Books, tools and working materials, and a bell in each cell to call the warder when required.

Board of Superintendence—John M'Neile, Esq., D.L., Parkmount; Robert Thomson, Esq., Jennymount; Thomas Montgomery, Esq., Birchhill, Antrim; John Clarke, Esq.; Thomas Verner, Esq.; C. R. Dobbs, Esq., D.L., Castle Dobbs, Carrickfergus; Samuel G. Fenton, Esq.; Rev. R. W. Bland; Charles O'Hara, Esq., O'Hara-Brook, Ballymoney; James E. Leslie, Esq., Leslie Hill, Ballymoney; George J. Clarke, Esq., Steeple, Antrim; John R. Dickey, Esq., Ballymena.

Inspector—Rev. R. Oulton.

Chaplain—Rev. C. Allen.

Presbyterian Chaplain, Rev. Geo. Shaw.

Roman Catholic Chaplain—Rev. H. O'Loughlen.

Surgeon—Thomas H. Purdon, M.D.

Apothecary—James Moore, M.D.

Governor—John Forbes.

DISTRICT MILITARY STAFF.

Major-General—Philip Bainbrigge, C.B.

Aide-de-Camp—Lieut. Bainbrigge, R.E.

Assistant Adjutant-General—Lieut.-Colonel R. W. Brough.

Commanding Officer of Artillery—Colonel Crawford.

Commanding Officer of Engineers—Lieut.-Colonel Wright.

ESSAYISTS' CLUB.—ESTABLISHED 7th MARCH, 1831.

This club consists of a number of professional gentlemen, merchants, and others, associated for the purpose of mutual instruction. The members meet on the last Friday evening in each month, at Mrs. Gardner's, Castle Place, when an essay on some subject, of which notice has been previously given, is read by one of the members, and a discussion afterwards takes place. Members are admitted by ballot.

Secretary - Samuel Vance, Esq.

BELFAST SOCIAL INQUIRY SOCIETY.

This Society was established in December, 1851, for the purpose of promoting the scientific investigation of social questions of general interest, including inquiries in the sciences of statistics, political economy, and jurisprudence. The meetings are held once in each month, from December till April, inclusive, at 8 P.M.

Members of Council—Rev. John Edgar, D.D.; James Garrett, Chas. B. Hancock, John Hancock, Jas. MacAdam, jun., Wm. M'Gee, M.D., Andrew G. Malcolm, M.D., John Mulholland, Joseph John Murphy, John Owden, James Shaw, and John Taylor, Esqrs.

Secretaries—Professor Hancock, LL.D., 12, Wellington Place; James M'Intyre, Esq., 19, College Square East.

Treasurer—William Bottomley, Esq., 7, Calender Street.

LITERARY SOCIETY.

Instituted 1801, meets once in each month, on Monday evening, from October till May, inclusive, in the houses of the members. It has for its object literature, science, and the arts; and solicits information respecting the history, antiquities, and present state of Ireland. A paper, confined to the subjects announced, is read every night of meeting by the members in succession.

President—Professor Craik.   *Secretary*—J. J. Murphy.

QUEEN'S COLLEGE LITERARY AND SCIENTIFIC SOCIETY,

Founded Feb., 1850.   *Patron.*—The President of the Queen's College.

This Society, which was established for the purpose of affording to Students of the Queen's College, and others, an opportunity of improving themselves by writing papers on Literary and Scientific subjects, and reading them at the Meetings of the Society, now numbers upwards of 80 members. It is managed by the members themselves, under the care, and with the sanction of the College Authorities. Meets every alternate Thursday during the College Terms, in the Queen's College; Annual Subscription—5s.

President—Robert Taylor. Vice-Presidents—Charles Brownlow Hancock and Joseph John Murphy. Treasurer—Alexander Montgomery. Secretary—Alexander C. Dobbin, 14, Castle Lane.

SOCIETY FOR THE PROMOTION OF THE FINE ARTS.
FIRST EXHIBITION IN BELFAST, 1850.

President—The Lord Dufferin and Claneboye. Vice-Presidents—Lord John Chichester, M.P.; Robert James Tennent, Esq., M.P.; Sir James Emerson Tennent ; James Stirling, Esq.. Mayor of Belfast ; Richard Blackiston B. Houston, Esq.; Sir Robert Bateson, Bart. Committee—G. T. Mitchell, Treasurer; C. L. Nursey, Honorary Secretary; S. G. Fenton, Charles Lanyon, W. M'Gee, M.D.; Robert Boag, James Moore, M.D.; Robert Gaffikin, Francis M'Cracken, William Coffey, W. H. Malcolm, Richard Davison, Robert Henderson, Robert J. T. Macrory, John Godwin, James M'Caw.

MASONIC INSTITUTIONS. 453

THE PROVINCIAL GRAND LODGE OF BELFAST AND NORTH DOWN

Meets on the second Wednesday in March, June, September, and December, at High Noon, in the Freemason's Hall, Donegall Place, Belfast.

OFFICERS FOR 1852:—

R.W.P.G.M.—The Ven. Archdeacon Mant.
R.W.D.P.G.M.—Samuel G. Getty, P.M.
R.W.P.G.S.W.—Houston Russell, P.M.
R.W.P.G.J.W.—James A. Henderson, P.M.
V.W.P.G. Chaplain—Rev. H. M'Sorley.
V.W.P.G.S. Deacon—Wm. Young, W.M.
V.W.P.G.J. Deacon—Ledlie Clark, W.M.
V.W.P.G. Treasurer—Chas. Duffin, P.M.
V.W.P.G. Director of Ceremonies—W. S. Tracy, P.M.
V.W.P.G. Secretary—George A. Carruthers.
P.G. Steward—Henry Murney.
    Do.   John Moore, P.M.
P.G. Superintendent of Works—John Johnston, P.M.
P.G. Marshal—J. G. M'Gee, P.M.
P.G. Organist—B. May.
P.G. Swordbearer—B. M'Fall.
P.G. Pursuivant—James Pelan.
P.G. Tyler—Thomas Harper.

MASONIC LODGES IN THE TOWN OF BELFAST.

No.	Name.	Place of Meeting.	Time.
10.	The Ark,	Donegall Place,	2nd Wednesday, at 4.
22.	Truth,	74, Waring Street,	1st Monday, at 8.
40.	L. of Concord,	Donegall Place,	1st Thursday, at 4½.
51.	Temple Lodge,	Castle Lane,	1st Wednesday, at 7.
58.	St. George's L.,	Castle Lane,	2nd Monday, at 8.
59.	Alfred's L.,	Castle Lane,	2nd Tuesday.
88.	St. John's,	Castle Lane,	1st Monday, at 8.
97.	Hiram's Lodge,	Cromac Street,	1st Monday, at 8.
111.	L. of Harmony,	11½, Cromac Street,	1st Monday, at 8.
154.	Prince of Wales's,	Donegall Place,	1st Tuesday, at 7.
272.	True Blue Lodge,	Castle Lane,	2nd Monday, at 7.
309.		Cromac Street,	1st Tuesday af. full m.
550.	St. Paul's L.,	19, John Street,	1st Wednesday, at 8.

FREEMASONS' CLUB.

Masonic Hall—Donegall Place.

ESTABLISHED 1ST NOVEMBER, 1851.

COMMITTEE.

(Original Members.)

W. S. Tracy, Lodge 10	G. A. Carruthers, Lodge 40
Charles Duffin, 10	Wm. Mullan, 154
J. M. Pirrie (Hon. Sec.), 40	F. Ogle, 154

and, also, the Worshipful Masters and Wardens of Lodges 10, 40, and 154, if subscribing Members to the Club.

Steward—Thomas Harper.

ANTRIM MILITIA STAFF.

Colonel—Marquis of Donegall.
Lieutenant-Colonel—Thomas Verner.
Majors—George Ferguson, Frederick Seymour.
Adjutant—Captain C. B. Carrothers.

CLUBS AND NEWS-ROOMS.

UNION CLUB.
Castle Buildings, Donegall Place.

COMMITTEE.

James Boomer, Theobald Bushell, Samuel Thomson, C. Duffin, John Charters.

J. F. M'Caw, Treasurer. George K. Smith, Secretary.

BELFAST COMMERCIAL CLUB.
Waring Street.

President—John Campbell. Secretary—Samuel Vance. Treasurer—William Cowan.

BELFAST RIFLE CLUB.
COMMITTEE.

Wm. Hunter, jun., Wm. E. Young, J. G. M'Gee, Wm. Cowan. Alex. Connell, Secretary.

COMMERCIAL BUILDINGS

Were built by a joint stock company, which has been brought under the protection of an Act of Parliament. The building, &c., cost about 20,000*l*, which is divided into 200 shares. The business is managed by a Committee, chosen annually, the 2nd Thursday in January, from among the proprietors; Mr. Henry Boyd, Secretary. The public apartments consist of a spacious subscription News-room, liberally supplied with the principal daily and other periodical publications, and furnished with a valuable assortment of books and maps. A hotel, together with various offices, and rooms adapted for public meetings, festivities, and exhibitions, are attached to the buildings. In the interior is a quadrangle, sheltered by a piazza; 'Change is held in the buildings on Mondays, Wednesdays, and Fridays, from two to three o'clock. The facade, fronting Donegall-street, is of the Ionic order, of classical proportions, substantially erected in stone, and forms one of the principal architectural features of Belfast.

COMMITTEE FOR 1852.

George Ash	Robert Getty	Charles Duffin
Theobald Bushell	Edward Walkington	H. H. Boyd
Thomas Corbitt	Nicholas Oakman	James Boomer
William Suffern	Henry Murney	William Pirrie

THE CORN EXCHANGE.

This institution was established in the year 1851, by the Corn Merchants of Belfast. The building, which is situate at the Northern extremity of Victoria Street, at its junction with Corporation Street, was completed in February, 1852, at a cost of £3,500, in 120 shares. It is a substantial structure, in the best Scotch stone, and is regarded as one of the most elegant specimens of architecture in the town. The basement storey is occupied by an entrance hall, and four handsome shops. The Corn Exchange hall occupies the upper storey, and is approached by a very spacious flight of stone stairs. It is very elaborately decorated with classic mouldings, and is lighted by eight lofty windows, and a lantern in the roof. Besides the principal use for which it is intended, it also serves as a news-room, amply supplied with the leading journals and periodicals. The business is managed by the following Committee:—

William Valentine,	Johnston Halliday,
Thomas M'Clure,	James Hamilton,
Edward Coey,	Tobias Porter, Esqrs.
Robert Henderson,	

W. D. Henderson, Esq., Secretary.

BELFAST ANACREONTIC SOCIETY,

Instituted in 1814 for the cultivation of Instrumental and Vocal Music. The Society meets for practice every Thursday evening, during the Winter six months, at Eight o'clock, in the Music Hall (erected by the Members at an expense of more than £3,000), when admission may be obtained by Tickets from Members. Occasional Concerts are given.

President—James Bristow, Esq. Vice-Presidents—Theobald Bushell, James Cameron, and James Campbell. Secretary and Treasurer—W. H. Malcolm. Assistant Secretary—R. W. Dyke. Leader of the Instrumental Band—Herr Granz. Conductor of the Vocal Department—Mr. May.

Committee—J. R. Musgrave, John Crawford, Edward W. Lee, W. Galgey, James F. M'Caw, W. S. Tracy.

BELFAST CLASSICAL HARMONIST SOCIETY.

This Society was established in 1851, for the Study of Classical Music only: it is also intended to produce, at annual concerts, complete works of the great masters, particularly Bach, Beethoven, Mendelssohn, Mozart, and others. The society meets for practice on Tuesday and Friday evenings, from Eight till half-past Nine o'clock, and it is managed by a President, Vice-President, Secretary and Treasurer, Musical Director, and a Committee of eight members. The Society consists of practical members only who, are elected by ballot.

President—The Right Honourable the Earl of Belfast. Vice-President—Mr. B. Pratt. Secretary and Treasurer—Mr. H. Cinnamond.

SINGING CLASSES (ON THE MAINZER SYSTEM),

For the Young Men and Females engaged in business in Belfast and its Neighbourhood, under the superintendence of Mr. Willis. The Classes meet every Tuesday and Friday evening, at the Wellington hall, Montgomery Street.

PROVIDENT BUILDING SOCIETIES.

Registered in conformity to the law and to the provisions of the statutes in force relating to Benefit Building Societies.

The *first* Society was established September 4, 1850, and has on its books 160 members, holding 356 shares. The *second* was established October, 2, 1850, and has 136 members, holding 253 shares. Both Societies hold their weekly meetings together, to receive subscriptons, in the Odd-Fellows' Hall, Donegall-street, on every Monday evening, from half-past 7 till half-past 9, p.m. A single share is *Five pence* per week, and members can hold any amount of shares. When the subscriptions amount to £100, that sum is allotted (free of interest) to some member, who repays it at the rate of £10 per year.

The Society is conducted by three Trustees, a Treasurer, and a Secretary (all under approved security, according to the Act 10 Geo. IV. cap. 56, sec. 11), and 10 of a committee. WM. NELSON, Secretary.

TOTAL ABSTINENCE ASSOCIATION.
ESTABLISHED IN 1836.

For the suppression of intemperance, by abstaining entirely from the ordinary use of all intoxicating drinks.

John Scott, President; John Fitzsimons, Vice-President; Charles Pelling, Secretary; Alexander Riddell, Treasurer.

Meetings are held at the Beth Birei Chapel, York Street, every Tuesday evening, at eight o'clock.

LOCAL MARINE BOARD,

Appointed under the Mercantile Marine Act, 1850, for the examination of Masters and Mates, and the shipping and discharging of Crews.—Board-Room and Shipping Office, 67, Corporation-street.

MEMBERS OF THE BOARD.

Ex-Officio Members, Mayor of Belfast and W. S. Tracy, Esq., Resident Magistrate.

Nominees of the Board of Trade, Sir W. G. Johnson, James Steen, John M'Neale, jun., and James Grimshaw, esqrs.

Members elected by the Ship-Owners, David Grainger, John Martin, John Harrison, Robert Corry, Nicholas Fitzsimons, and Hugh Wardlow, esqrs.

Examiner in Navigation and Seamanship, and Shipping Master, Commander Henry C. Harston, R.N.

Medical Inspector, Dr. J. M. Pirrie, 66, Donegall-street.

Deputy Shipping Masters, James Campbell and William Falkner.

BELFAST SHIPOWNERS' ASSOCIATION.

OFFICE, 15, ALBERT SQUARE.

Committee—John Harrison, Esq., Chairman; John Dunn, David Grainger, John Martin, James Lemon, Esqrs.

Secretaries—Thomas G. Folingsby & Co.

MASTER MARINERS' ASSOCIATION.—ESTABLISHED 1816.

The object of this Society is to secure certain annuities to the Widows and Families of members, allowances to members in time of sickness, and in cases of shipwreck, &c. It is supported by entrance fees, monthly subscriptions, and fines, together with the interest of a considerable accumulated fund. Though this society consists chiefly of master mariners, several ship-owners, and other respectable landsmen are members of it. Meetings are held every month for transaction of the general business

COMMITTEE.

President, John Gowan, Harbour Master.

Charles Peyton,	James Bradford,	Edward Hennesey,
Thomas Wann,	Joseph Braddell,	Samuel Shaw.
John Dunn,	John W. M'Cracken,	

Treasurer, Thomas Wann—*Secretary*, James Moore.

SEAMAN'S FRIEND SOCIETY, PILOT-STREET.

The object of this Society is to provide preaching, and promote Scriptural and religious instruction among the seamen visiting this port. A Chapel has been erected in Pilot-street, in which flourishing Sunday, Infant, and Day-schools have been established. Treasurer, Edward Coey; Secretary, Thomas Sinclair.

TRUSTEES OF THE FUND FOR RELIEF AND SUPPORT OF SICK, MAIMED, AND DISABLED SEAMEN,

And the Widows and Children of those killed, slain, or drowned in the Merchant Service.

Under Act of Parliament, 4 and 5 Wm. IV., chap. 52.

William Pirrie, sen., Robert Boyd, David Grainger, Hugh Wardlow, William Newett, John Potts, James Lemon, John Dunn, Alexander M'Laine, Nicholas Fitzsimons, S. D. Stuart, Wm. C. Heron, Thomas Sinclair, John Martin, Esqrs.

Receiver—Charles W. Hoffmeister, Esq., Office, at the Custom-House.

Medical Officer—Dr. Pirrie, 66, Donegall Street.

MISCELLANEOUS.

BELFAST STEAM SHIP COMPANY.

Established, 1852. To provide additional steam communication between this port and Liverpool. Capital, £50,000, in 1,000 shares of £50 each. Provisional Committee:—S. G. Fenton, J. F. Ferguson, J. Mulholland, W. Ewart, jun., P. Johnston, T. G. Lindsay, J. Magill, J. Lemon, S. Martin, S. Bristow, R. S. Lepper, W. Valentine, J. Kennedy, J. Cordukes, W. Mullan, D. Grainger, J. Hind, jun., J. Bell, G. Murney, G. M'Tear. Bankers—The Northern Banking Company. Solicitor—John Bates. Secretary—George M'Tear, Donegall quay.

LAGAN NAVIGATION COMPANY.

Office, 2, Queen Street, Belfast. Managed by a Board of Directors. Secretary and Engineer—Wm. M'Cleery.

EMIGRATION AGENT—Belfast—Lieutenant Starke, R.N.

Medical Inspector of Emigrants—Dr. James Moore, 7, Chichester St.

BELFAST MARKETS.

Market	Goods	Days
May's Market, May Street, and Lower Chichester Street,	Grain and Meal,	Daily.
George's Market, Lower Chichester Street,	Butchers' Meat, Poultry, Fresh Butter, Cheese, Eggs,	Daily. Principal days—Tuesday and Friday.
Grass Market, Lower Chichester Street,	Grass, Bogwood, and Turf,	Daily.
Flax and Fruit Market, May Street,	Flax and Fruit,	Daily.
Cattle Market, Oxford Street,	Veal Calves, Monday — Fat Cattle, Wednesday—Cattle, Sheep, and Goats,	Friday.
Pork Market, Lower Chichester Street,	Pork,	Daily.
Butter Market, Great Patrick Street,	Butter in Firkins, Crocks, or Lumps,	Daily.
Smithfield Market,	Hides, Hay and Straw, Pedlars' Goods, Furniture (old and new), old Iron, Marine Stores, and old Clothes,	Daily.
Potato and Vegetable Market, May Street,	Potatoes, and Vegetables, wholesale,	Daily.
Castle Market, Castle Lane,	Fruit, Potatoes, Vegetables, Butchers' Meat, and Fish, by retail,	Daily.
Ormond Market, Great Patrick Street,	Fruit, Potatoes, Vegetables, Butchers' Meat,	Daily.
Brown Linen Hall, Donegall Street,	Brown Linen, 4-4ths Cloth, and Coarse Sacking,	Friday.

BELFAST MONTHLY FAIR.

Fair at the Cattle Market and Fair Green, May's Fields, on first Wednesday of every Month, for the sale of Horses, Black Cattle, Sheep, Pigs, and Goats.

RELIGIOUS INSTITUTIONS.

Houses of Public Worship.

Houses.	Situations.	Ministers.	Times of Service.
Parish Church, (St. Anne's	Donegall-st.	Miller, T.F. A M. *Vicar* Mathews, G F. A.B. Waldo, J.P.	Sunday, hf-p. 11 & 7, Wednesday & Friday, half-past 11.
Chapel of ease, (St. George's)	High-street	M'Ilwaine, Wm. A.M. M'Sorley, H. A.B.	Sunday, hf-p. 11 & 7; Thursday, hf-p. 8
Christ's Church	College-Sq. N.	Drew, T. D.D., L.L.D.	Sunday, hf-p. 11 & 7; Wednesday, qr. to 7
St. Mathew's Chapel	Shankhill	Teape, Hudson, A.B.	Sunday, half past 11
Magdelene Asylum Chapel	Donegall Pass.	Hartrick, E. J.	Sunday, hf-p. 11 & 7; Friday, hf-p. 7
Trinity Church	Antrim Road	Campbell, Theo.	Sunday, hf-p. 11 & 7
St. John's Church	Malone	Wrixon, J., A.B.	
St. Paul's Church	York-street	Allen, Charles	Sunday, hf-p. 11 & 7
Parish Church (B. macarrett)	Ballymacarrett	Bennett, George, A.M.	Sunday,h-p.11&h-p6
First Presbyterian Church	Rosemary-st.	Hanna, Samuel, D.D. MacNaughtan, John	Sunday, 11 & h-p. 1
Second do do do	Donegall-st.	Nelson, Isaac	Sunday, h-p. 11, & 7
Third do do do	Fisherwick.pl.	Morgan, James D.D.,	Sunday, 11 & hf-p.1
Fourth do do do	May-street	Cooke, H., D D., L L.D.	Sunday, h-p. 11 & 7
Fifth do do do	Townsend-st.	Johnson, William	Sunday, h-p. 11 & 7,
Sixth do do do	York-street	Hamilton, David	Sunday, h-p. 11, & 7
Seventh do do do	Berry-street		
Eighth do do do	Ballysillan	M'Cullagh, W. C.	Sunday, 11½ and 5
Ninth do do do	Linenhall-st.	Knox, Robert A.M.	Sunday, 11 and h-p. 1
Tenth do do do	Alfred-street	Shaw, George	Sunday, 11 and h-p.1
Eleventh do do do	Alfred-place	Martin, James	Sunday,h-p. 11 and 7
Twelfth do do do	Gt Georges-st.	Toye, Thomas	Sunday h-p. 11 and 7
Thirteenth do do do	Ballymacarrett	Meneely, J.	Sunday, 11 and 7
Fourteenth do do do	Malone	M'Kenzie, Joseph	Sunday, 12
Fifteenth do do do	Newtonbreda.	Crawford, Andrew	Sunday, 11
Sixteenth do do do	College-sq. W.	Collins, Joshua W.	Sunday, 11 and h-p.1
First Presbyterrian Meeting-house (Unitarian)	Rosemary-st	Bruce, William Porter, J. Scott	Sunday, 11 and 1
Second do do do	Rosemary-st.	Porter, John	Sunday, 11 and 1
Third do do do	York-street	Magennis, David	Sunday, 12 & hf-p. 6
Primitive Seceding Congregn.	York-street	Bryce, R. J., L.L.D.	Sunday, 11 and 3
Covenanting Meeting-house	Dublin Road	Alexander, J. D.D.	Sunday,11 h-p.1, &7
Do do do	College-st. S.	Henry, Robt.	Sunday, 11 × hp. 1
Independent Meeting-house	Donegall-st	O'Hanlon, W. M.	Sunday,11,7,M.&T 8
Old Catholic Chapel	Chapel-lane	Denvir, Rt. Rev Dr. O'Loughlan, Henry M'Kenna, Fras.	Sunday, 9 & 10
St. Patrick's Catholic Chapel	Donegall-st.		Sunday, 8 10 & 12
St. Malachy's Catholic Chapel	M'Clean's fields	Gallogly, John Curoe, Wm.	Sunday, 10 & 12
Roman Catholic Chapel	Ballymacarrett	Killen, James	Sunday, One
Friends' Meeting-house	Frederick-st.	Various	Sunday, 10 and 2
Methodist House (Wesleyan)	Donegall-sq.	Ballard, T.	Sunday, 11 and 7
Do do	Wesley-place	Oliver, J.	Sunday, 11 and 7
Do do	Balymacarret	Lupton, W.	Sunday, 11 and 7
Do do	Frederick-st.	Bayley, Benj.	Sunday, 11 and 7
Do (New Connexion)	York-street	Mills, Thomas	Sunday, 11 and 7
Do (Primitive Wesleyan)	Donegall-pl.	M'Fann, Thomas	Sunday 10 and 7
Do do	Balymacarett	Wilson, John	Sunday. 10 and 7
Do (Primitive)	Melbourne-st	Blackburn, J.	Snnday, 11 and 7
Baptist Meeting house	Academy-st.	Eccles, W. S.	Sunday, 11 and 7
Apostolic Chapel	Queen-street	Various	Sunday, 11 and 7
Seamen's Chapel	Pilot-street	Wilson, Robert	Sunday, 11 and 7

BELFAST TOWN MISSION.

The object of this mission is, to employ licentiates of the General Assembly who are to visit the poor from house to house, distribute tracts, hold prayer-meetings, and preach the gospel in places suited for collecting numbers together. Twelve agents are now employed, Revs. Dr. Edgar, and Dr. Morgan, *Honorary Secretaries*; Rev. Robert Knox, *Secretary;* H. H. Boyd, *Treasurer.*

POST-OFFICE, ROSEMARY STREET.
O'Donnell Grimshaw, Esq., Postmaster.

James M'Gladery, Chief Clerk; Robert Dennison, Second Clerk; Edward Walsh, John Richardson, John H. Pelan, Sampson C. Kennedy, John Fox, James Birch, Nathaniel D. Avern.

The letter-box at this office is closed at the periods hereunder specified, in order to allow time to prepare the mails for despatch.

TABLE EXHIBITING THE HOURS OF CLOSING THE LETTER-BOX.

For what Mail closed.	Time of Closing Box.	Received with postage paid by stamps, and one additional stamp as late fee, until	Time of Despatch.
	H. M.	H. M.	H. M.
Newry Day Car, ...	4 45 a.m.	5 5 a.m.	5 15 a.m.
Derry, Larne, &c.,	4 45 a.m.	5 5 a.m.	5 50 a.m.
Donaghadee, Portaferry, & Newtownards,	6 15 a.m.	6 35 a.m.	7 15 a.m.
Holywood, Bangor,	6 15 a.m.	6 30 a.m.	7 0 a.m.
Dublin Day and Armagh...	8 0 a.m.	8 20 a.m.	8 30 a.m.
Down, ...	1 30 p.m.	1 45 p.m.	2 10 p.m.
Enniskillen, Armagh, Derry,	4 0 p.m.	4 20 p.m.	4 40 p.m.
Scotland and North of England,...	7 0 p.m.	7 20 p.m.	7 50 p.m.
Dublin, Newry, England, &c.,	7 50 p.m.	8 10 p.m.	8 40 p.m.

Letters not intended to be forwarded by the mail, then being made up, should be deposited in the "Late Letter Box."

Letters for England, marked "Private Ship," and put into the receiving box three-quarters of an hour before the advertised hour of sailing of the Fleetwood steamers, on Mondays, Wednesdays, and Fridays; and on Tuesdays, Thursdays, and Saturdays, by the Liverpool steamers, will be forwarded. Newspapers, if marked in the same way, are also taken, but are subject to 1d. of postage. Letters will not be in time, if posted after nine o'clock, P.M., when the above vessels sail after that hour.

ARRIVAL OF MAILS.

	Due at	Window delivery com. at	Carriers' delivery com. at
	H. M.	H. M.	H. M.
Dublin Night Mail, Newry, English, and Scotch ...	3 45 a.m.	7 0 a.m.	7 0 a.m.
Enniskillen Night Mail, including Sligo, Armagh, and Derry ...	7 30 a.m.	8 0 a.m.	11 0 a.m.
Downpatrick Day Car	10 15 a.m.	10 40 a.m.	11 0 a.m.
Dublin Day Mail and Armagh, including English and Foreign...	4 30 p.m.	5 0 p.m.	5 0 p.m.
Bangor Day Car	6 40 p.m.	6 50 p.m.	7 30 p.m.
Portaferry Day Car, including Donaghadee and Newtownards	6 45 p.m.	6 50 p.m.	7 30 p.m.
Derry Day Mail, including Larne, Carrickfergus, &c. ...	7 0 p.m.	7 30 p.m.	7 30 p.m.
Newry Day Car	7 30 p.m.	7 35 p.m.	7 35 p.m.

Receiving Offices—Mr. Brown's, Arthur Street; Mrs. Arnold's, Gt. George's Street; Lying-in Hospital, Antrim Road; Mr. Mateer's, Malone; Mr. Kirker's, Falls Road.

STEAMERS FROM AND TO BELFAST.

Belfast to Dublin, every Thursday; fares, cabin, 12s.; deck, 5s.
Belfast to Fleetwood, every Monday, Wednesday, Thursday, and Friday ; fares, saloon, 12s. 6d.; deck, 3s.
Belfast to Glasgow, via Ardrossan, every Tuesday, Thursday, and Saturday; fares to Ardrossan, 8s. and 2s.; to Glasgow, 10s. 6d., and 2s. 6d.
Belfast to Greenock and Glasgow, daily, (Sundays excepted); fares, 10s. 6d., and 2s. 6d.
Belfast to Liverpool, every Tuesday, Thursday, and Saturday; fares, 15s., and 4s.
Belfast to Stranraer, every Saturday; fares, 5s. and 2s.
Belfast to Whitehaven, every Friday; fares, 10s. and 3s.
Belfast to London, direct, (screw steamers) weekly.
Belfast to Londonderry, every Wednesday; fares, 6s. and 2s. 6d.
Belfast to Morecambe, every Saturday; fares, 10s. and 2s. 6d.
Dublin to Belfast, every Tuesday; fares, 12s. and 5s.
From Kingstown, Dublin, to Holyhead, twice a-day.

COACHES, JAUNTING CARS, CABS, &c.
AUTHORISED FARES.

One-Horse Carriages with 2 Wheels, Licensed to carry 6 passengers.

BY DISTANCE, PER MILE.
For 1 or 2 passengers, ... 0s 6d
3 ... ... 0s 9d
4 ... ... 1s 0d
5 ... ... 1s 3d
6 ... ... 1s 6d

BY TIME, PER HOUR.
For 1 or 2 passengers, not exceeding 1 hour, ... 1s 0d
3 passengers, ... 1s 6d
4 ... ... 2s 0d
5 ... ... 2s 6d
6 ... ... 3s 0d
For every additional half-hour, 0s 4d
For every additional hour, ... 0s 8d
BY THE DAY, 8s.

One Horse Carriages with Four Wheels.

BY DISTANCE, PER MILE.
For 1 or 2 passengers, not exceeding 1 mile, ... 0s 8d

For 3 passengers, ... 1s 0d
4 ... ... 1s 4d
5 ... ... 1s 8d
6 ... ... 2s 0d
Every additional half-mile, ... 0s 4d

BY TIME, PER HOUR.
For 1 or 2 passengers, not exceeding 1 hour, ... 1s 4d
3 passengers, ... 2s 0d
4 ... ... 2s 8d
5 ... ... 3s 4d
6 ... ... 4s 0d
Every additional half-hour, ... 0s 6d
Every additional hour, ... 1s 0d
BY THE DAY, 10s 3d.

Two-Horse Carriages.

BY DISTANCE, PER MILE.
For 1, 2, 3, or 4 passengers, 1s 0d

BY TIME.
For 1, 2, 3, or 4 passengers, per hour 1s 8d
BY THE DAY, 13s. 4d.

LUGGAGE PORTERS.

	s	d
For carrying Boxes, Trunks, &c., not exceeding 56lbs., to any part within the Lamps, ...	0	6
For carrying the same beyond the Lights, but within the Turnpikes and Ormeau Bridge, ...	1	0
For carrying Trunks, Boxes, &c., above 56lbs., and not more than 140lbs. weight, to any part within the Lights, ...	1	0
For carrying same beyond the Lights, &c.	2	0
For so much Luggage as may require a handcart, if above 140lbs.,	1	6
For carrying same beyond the Lights, &c., ...	2	0

PROVINCE OF ULSTER.

ULSTER, the Northern province of Ireland, is bounded on the North and West by the Atlantic ocean, on the East by the North channel, on the South-east by the province of Leinster, and on the South-west by the province of Connaught. It is nearly 130 miles in its greatest length, and 110 in its greatest breadth. It consists of nine counties, viz., Antrim, Down, Londonderry, Donegal, Tyrone, Armagh, Cavan, Fermanagh, and Monaghan, exclusive of the county of the town of Carrickfergus. These are subdivided into 79 baronies, and these again into 391 parishes. The province contains 5,475,438 acres, of which 3,407,539 are arable, 1,764,370 uncultivated, 79,738 plantation, 8,790 included in towns, and 214,956 under water. Its population, in 1821, was 1,998,404; in 1831, 2,286,622; in 1841, 2,386,373; and in 1851, it was 2,004,298, there being a decrease, during the last decennial period, of 406,436 souls, or sixteen per cent. The number of houses was, in 1851, 373,159. The area of the province is 8,555 square miles, giving, in 1851, to each square mile 234 persons, a decrease of 44 to each square mile since 1841. The annual amount of property in the province, according to Griffith's valuation, including that exempted from local taxation, is £2,533,281. The poor law valuation is £3,248,650. The value of live stock, in 1841, was £5,417,956—the value for 1851 is not yet ascertained. Ulster has the advantage, to a large extent, of railway communication. The following lines are, for the most part, completed within the province, viz.—The Ulster Railway, from Belfast to Armagh; Belfast and Ballymena, with branches to Carrickfergus and Randalstown; Belfast and County Down, for the present terminating at Newtownards, with a branch to Holywood; Londonderry and Enniskillen, completed to Newtownstewart; Dundalk and Enniskillen, open to Castleblayney; Dublin and Belfast Junction, from Dundalk to Portadown; Newry and Warrenpoint; and Londonderry and Coleraine, rapidly advancing to completion. Other railways are in contemplation, to open up the whole inland district, and connect the larger towns. The metropolis of Ulster is Belfast: other important cities and towns in the province are Armagh (the metropolitan see), Londonderry, Newry, Enniskillen, Ballymena, Ballymoney, Larne, Carrickfergus, Dungannon, Omagh, Downpatrick, Newtownlimavady, Cookstown, and Strabane. Ulster also participates largely in the advantage of inland navigation. The Ulster Canal commences at Charlemont, on the Blackwater, by which it is connected with Lough Neagh, and proceeding South-west by Monaghan and Clones, enters Upper Lough Erne at its Eastern extremity, its total length being forty-eight miles. The Newry navigation proceeds from that town to Portadown, where it joins the Tyrone navigation. The Lagan navigation proceeds from Belfast, by Lisburn and Moira, to Lough Neagh. The Foyle, the Blackwater, and the Bann, are all navigable rivers, wholly or in part. Ulster is the great seat of Irish flax cultivation and manufacture. In 1851, there were 123,726 acres under flax cultivation, or one acre in every forty-four. In the county Donegal alone, in 1851, the immense quantity of 20,955 acres was sown with flax. Ulster is rich in mineral productions. It possesses three coal fields—those of Coalisland, near Dungannon; Ballycastle, in the Northern extremity of Antrim; and the third in Monaghan; but these, from the narrowness of their seams, are comparatively useless. There are strong indications of the existence of coal at Carrickfergus, on the property of the Marquis of Downshire, in boring for which, an immense field of salt rock, of a very valuable description, has recently been discovered. Lignite, or wood-coal, is found in the dense stratifications encompassing the Southern half of Lough Neagh. There are lead mines in the clay-slate formations at Conlig and Newtownards, county Down; lead is also found in the county Armagh, near Newry, and at Castleblayney, in the county Monaghan. Large tracts of old red and yellow sandstone are found in Fermanagh and Tyrone, from Lough Erne to Cookstown. It is also found in patches in Antrim, Derry, and Tyrone. Crystallised gypsum occurs in Derry and Antrim, and selenite at Benburb. Uncrystallised gypsum is raised in large quantities at Carrickmacross. The basalt is confined almost exclusively to the North-east portion of the province, forming the substratum of the county Antrim, and of some portions of Derry and Armagh, and appearing in magnificent crystallised columns at Fair Head and the Giant's Causeway. Two of the six judicial circuits almost wholly proceed through Ulster, viz.—the North-east and the North-west. The former commences at Louth, and proceeds, successively, to Monaghan, Armagh, Downpatrick, and Belfast; the North-West circuit proceeds from Longford to Cavan, Enniskillen, Omagh, Lifford, and Londonderry. Ulster sends six representative peers to the House of Lords, and 29 members to the House of Commons. The peaceable and law-respecting character of its people, notwithstanding the great diversity of religious and political creeds, and the dense population of its manufacturing towns, may be judged of from the fact, that since 1841, inclusive, there have been only five executions. The gross produce of the sales of property in Ulster, in the Encumbered Estates Court, since the opening of the Commission in October, 1849, to the 25th of October, 1851, inclusive, was £854,960 12s. 4d.

STATISTICAL SUMMARY OF ULSTER.

COUNTIES.	AREA IN STATUTE ACRES.	INHABITANTS.		TOTAL.	FAMILIES	HOUSES
		MALES.	FEMALES.			
ANTRIM.......	743881	120516	129839	250355	47274	46694
BELFAST.......	1872	46443	53217	99660	20553	15100
CARRICKFERGUS	16700	3746	4742	8488	1688	1679
ARMAGH.......	328076	96341	100079	196420	37409	37406
CAVAN........	477360	86835	87468	174303	32088	31612
DONEGAL	1193443	124919	129369	254288	46679	46799
DOWN.........	611919	151582	166196	317778	62471	62363
FERMANAGH ...	457195	56731	59247	115978	22127	21393
LONDONDERRY	518595	93123	98621	191744	35869	35610
MONAGHAN....	319757	69584	73826	143410	27557	27346
TYRONE.......	806640	124415	127450	251865	47016	47157
TOTAL......	5475438	974235	1030054	2004289	380731	373159

☞ The DIRECTORY having extended so much beyond the space intended, we have been obliged to omit several of the smaller towns in this portion of the work; but in our next edition, these will be all included, and equally full information given with regard to them as to the other towns.

PROVINCIAL DIRECTORY.

COUNTY OF ANTRIM.

A MARITIME county. Greatest length, N. and S., 56 miles; greatest breadth, E. and W., 30½ miles; comprising an area of 1,164 square miles, or 745,177 acres, of which 503,288 are arable, 176,335 uncultivated, 10,358 in plantations, 1,908 in towns, and 53,288 under water, including a portion of Lough Neagh. On the Maiden Rocks, off Larne Bay, are two Lighthouses, showing fixed lights. The principal bays are Belfast Lough and Lough Larne. The subsoil is basalt or trap, forming the celebrated Giant's Causeway on the N. coast, clay-slate and limestone: there is coal at Ballycastle. One-third of the county is mountain, not rising more than 1,600 feet above high sea level, and declining from the sea-coast towards Lough Neagh in the S.W. The river Bann forms the W., and the Lagan the S. boundary of the county. The Lagan canal connects Lough Neagh with Belfast Lough. The great staple commodity of this county is the spinning of linen and cotton yarn, and linen and cotton weaving, in which the great bulk of the population are engaged. The fishery districts are Ballycastle and Carrickfergus, comprising 121 miles of maritime boundaries, which in 1850 had 1,025 registered fishing vessels, employing 3,115 men and boys. The population in 1841 was 276,188, of which 256,352 is in the rural, and 19,836 in the civic district, exclusive of the towns of Belfast and Carrickfergus. According to the census of 1851, the total population of the same district was 250,355, being a decrease of 25,833. The county is divided into fourteen baronies—Antrim Lower and Upper, Belfast Lower and Upper, Carey, Dunluce Lower and Upper, Glenarm Lower and Upper, Kilconway, Massereene Lower and Upper, Toome Lower and Upper, and contains seventy-five parishes and parts of parishes. It is in the diocese of Connor. Belfast is the head-quarters of the military district of that name; and there are Barracks there and in Carrickfergus; and at Belfast the staff of the County Militia is stationed. The head-quarters of the Constabulary force, consisting of 229 men, officers included, are at Ballymena; those of the six districts, comprising thirty-eight stations, at Ballymena, Belfast, Ballymoney, Carrickfergus, Cushendall, and Antrim. There are Resident Magistrates at Belfast and Ballymena, a Revenue Police station at Ballymoney, and twenty-three Coast Guard stations through the county, consisting of 16 officers and 129 men.

Lieutenant and Custos Rotulorum—The Most Noble George Hamilton Chichester, Marquis of Donegall, Ormeau, Belfast

High-Sheriff (1852-3)—Robt. Smyth, Esq., of Gaybrook, Mullingar

Members for the County—Nathaniel Alexander, Portglenone House, Portglenone, and Long's Hotel, London; Sir Edmund Charles Workman Macnaghten, Bart., D.L., Dundarave, Bushmills, in this co., 42 Upper Brook street, and Carlton Club, London

DEPUTY LIEUTENANTS.

Adair, Robert Shafto, M.P., Farm Lodge, Ballymena
Antrim, Earl of, Eaton place, London
Belfast, Earl of, Ormeau, Belfast
Chichester, Lord John, M.P.
Crommelin, N. D., Newton Crommelin

COUNTY OF ANTRIM.

Dobbs, Conway Richard, Castle Dobbs, Carrickfergus
Dunbar, George, Donaghadee
Ferguson, John Francis, Belfast
Grimshaw, Robt., Whitehouse, Belfast
Kirk, Peter, Thornfield, Carrickfergus
Legge, William Wallace, Malone House, Belfast
M'Donnell, Edmund, Glenarm Castle
M'Neile, John, Parkmount, Belfast
Macartney, George, Lissanore Castle, Ballymoney
Macnaghten, Sir E. C. W., M.P., Dundarave, Bushmills
Magennis, Richard, Harrold Hall, Bedfordshire
Massereene and Ferrard, Viscount, Antrim Castle, and Oriel Temple, county Louth
Montgomery, John, Benvardin, Ballymoney
Moore, James Stewart, Ballydivitty, Dervock
Pakenham, Edward, Langford Lodge, Crumlin
Tennent, Robert James, M.P., Belfast
Verner, Thomas, Ormeau

ASSISTANT BARRISTER.

John Gibson, 11 Fitzwilliam st. Upper, Dublin

MAGISTRATES.

Adair, R. S., M.P.,D.L., Farm Lodge, Ballymena
Adair, T. B., Loughanmore, Antrim
Agnew, James, Larne
Agnew, W., Kilwaughter Castle, Larne
Alexander, N., M.P., Portglenone house
Allen, W. J. C., Belfast
Antrim, Earl of
Armstrong, Charles W., Cherryvalley, Crumlin
Bankhead, John B., Glenarm
Belfast, the Earl of, D.L., Ormeau
Belfast, the Mayor of, for time being
Bennett, Thomas, Coleraine
Birnie, Thomas M., Carrickfergus
Bland, Rev. Robert W., Abbeyville
Boyd, John, M.P., Dundoan House, Coleraine
Boyd, John Augustus Hugh, Drumawillen House, Ballycastle
Bruce, Edward, Belfast
Bruce, Henry S. B., Bellaghy
Burnett, John J., Ayrshire, Scotland
Casement, Edmund M'G., Invermore
Casement, T., Balee House, B.mena
Clarke, George J., Steeple, Antrim
Clarke, John, College square, Belfast
Cloncurry, Lord, Maretimo, Blackrock, Dublin
Coates, William, Glentoran, Belfast
Coulson, D. R., Omagh, co. Tyrone
Courtenay, J., Glenburn, Portglenone
Crommelin, N. D., D.L., Carradore Castle, county Down
Crommelin, N. D., jun., Belfast
Cuppage, Adam, Glen Bank, B.castle
Cuppage, Edmund F., Mount Edwards, Cushendall
Currel, John, sen., Belfast
Davison, Alex., Knockboy, Ballymena
Dickey, John, Leighenmore, B.mena
Dobbs, Conway Richard, D.L., Castle Dobbs, Carrickfergus
Douglas, Charles, Dervock
Downshire, Marquis of, Hillsborough
Dunbar, George, D.L., Woodburn, Donaghadee
Fenton, Samuel G., Belfast
Ferguson, John Francis, D.L., Belfast
Ferguson, Thomas, Greenville, Belfast
Gage, Rev. Robert, Rathlin Island, Ballycastle
Gihon, Wm., Hillhead, Ballymena
Gordon, Robert Francis, Holywood
Greg, Thos., Ballymenock, Holywood
Gregg, William, Lisburn
Grimshaw, Edmund, Mossley, Belfast
Grimshaw, Robert, D.L., Whitehouse, Belfast
Haliday, Alex. H., Clifden, Holywood
Hancock, John, Lurgan
Handcock, Hon. George, Dublin
Heyland, L., Glendarragh, Crumlin
Higginson, Henry T., Lisburn
Hill, John, Bellaghy
Holland, John, Grange, Ballymoney
Houston, R. B. B., Orangefield, Belfast
Hunter, William, Dunmurry
Johnson, Sir Wm. G., knight, Belfast
Jones, Thomas M. H., Moneyglass, Toomebridge
Ker, David S., Montalto, Ballynahinch
Kirk, Peter, D.L., Thornfield, Carrickfergus
Lanktree, John, Glenarm
Lecky, Hugh, Beardiville, Coleraine
Leslie, Jas. E., Leslie hill, Ballymoney

COUNTY OF ANTRIM. 465

Lyle, James Acheson, Knockintera, Coleraine
M'Cance, Jas. Law, Glenville, Belfast
M'Cance, William, Suffolk, Belfast
M'Clintock, H. S., Randalstown
M'Donnell, Edmund, D.L., Glenarm Castle, Glenarm
M'Garel, Charles, Magheramourne House, Larne
M'Garel, Peter, Larne
M'Gildowny, John, Clare Park, Ballycastle
M'Namara, James, Belfast
M'Neile, John, D.L., Parkmount, Belfast
M'Neill, Edmund Alex., Cushendall
Macartney, George, D.L., Lowther Lodge, Balbriggan
MacNaghton, Bartholomew, Ballyboggy, Col raine
Macnaghten, Sir E. C. W., Bart., M.P., D.L., Dundarave, Bushmills
Magennis, Richard, D.L., Harrold Hall, Bedford, England
Massereene and Ferrard, Viscount, D.L., Antrim Castle
Miller, Ro ley, Portna House, Moneymore
Montgomery, John, D.L., Benvarden, Ballymoney
Montgomery, Thomas, Birch Hill, Antrim
Moore, James Stewart, D.L., Ballydivitty, Dervock
Moore, John Stewart, Moyarget Lodge, Dervock
Moore, William, Moore Fort
Mulholland, Andrew, Spring Vale, Greyabbey
O'Hara, Charles, O'Hara Brook, Ballymoney
O'Hara, Henry Hutchinson, Crebilly House, Ballymena
O'Rorke, Ambrose, Ahoghill
Owens, John, Holestone, Ballyclare
Pakenham, Edward, D.L., Langford Lodge, Crumlin
Richardson, William P., Portrush
Rowan, John, Mount Davis, Portglenone
Rowan, Rev. R. W., Mount Davis, Ahoghill
Smyth, John, Whitepark, Ballyclare
Smyth, Roger Johnson, Lisburn
Smyth, Thomas Johnson, Lisburn
Stevenson, William, Belfast
Stewart, Major William, Drumnagessan, Bushmills
Stuart, Charles George, Ballybibbistock, Dervock
Tennent, James Thompson, Belfast
Tennent, Robert James, M.P., D.L., Belfast
Tennent, Sir James E., knt., M.P., London
Thompson, Robert, Clonard, Belfast
Thomson, John, Lowwood, Belfast
Thomson, Robert, Castletown, Belfast
Verner, Thomas, D.L., Ormeau
Verner, William, Donegall place, Belfast
Whitla, George, Larne
Whitla, James, Gobrana, Glenavy
Wray, Geo. A., Blackrock, Bushmills

RESIDENT MAGISTRATES.
Tracy, William Samuel, Belfast
Goold, George J., Antrim

COUNTY OFFICERS.
Clerk of the Crown—Walter Bourne, Dublin
Clerk of the Peace—George A. H. Chichester
Deputy Clerk of the Peace—W. C. Cunningham, solicitor, 5 York st., Belfast
Crown Solicitor—Maxwell Hamilton, 42 Upper Sackville street, Dublin
Crown Solicitor at Quarter Sessions—Neil John O'Neil, 9 Lower Gloucester street, Dublin
Treasurer—Alexander Miller, Ballycastle
Secretary to the Grand Jury—John Coates, Carrickfergus
County Surveyor—Charles Lanyon, Belfast
Sub-Sheriff—Robert Clark, 6 Castle Chambers, Belfast
Sheriff's Returning Officers—Messrs. Davison and Torrens
Coroners—James Kennedy Jackson, Belfast; Alexander Markham, Randalstown; John Jellett, Ballymena; Robert Clarke, Ballycastle

STAMP DISTRIBUTOR.
Head Distributor for the county—Thomas Robert Stannus, Belfast

INSPECTORS OF WEIGHTS AND MEASURES.	COAST-GUARD STATIONS.
Belfast District—R.T.Goddard, Belfast	Ardclinis; Ballintoy, Ballycastle; Ballygally, Belfast; Blackhead; Carrickfergus; Causeway Head; Cushendall; Cushendun; Curran; Dunseverick; Garron Point; Glenarm; Kilroot; Murlough; Pattensfall; Portballintray; Portrush; Portmuck; Rathlin Island; Torrhead; Whitehouse
Ballymena District—Jas. Greer, Ballymena	
Ballymoney District—David Reid, Ballymoney	
Larne District—George H. M'Neill, Larne	

ANTRIM.

ANTRIM, a market town (formerly a parliamentary borough), in the county of Antrim—13 miles from Belfast, 93 from Dublin, 8 from Ballymena, and 4 from Randalstown; situated on the banks of the Sixmile Water river, on the great road from Belfast to Londonderry. This town, which is seated in one of the most beautiful and fertile valleys in the county, was anciently called *Entrium*, or *Entrum Neagh*, signifying, according to some authorities, " the habitation upon the waters." In 1649 the town was burned by General Monroe; and during the disturbances of 1798 it was the principal scene of hostilities which occurred in the county, and here the insurgents were defeated with great slaughter. Near the town is one of those round towers so often met with in Ireland; it is 95 feet in height and 49 in circumference, is of four stories, and its summit surmounted by a cone. Closely contiguous to the town is Antrim Castle, an elegant, spacious, and stately building, the ancient residence of the Earls of Massareene, now the property of Viscount Massareene and Ferrard, who is also proprietor of the town. Shane's Castle is situated about two miles west of the town. The castle itself is in ruins, having been burned down, by accident, in the year 1814. By extensive and costly additions, however, to a pile of buildings on the demesne (formerly the office-houses), a very commodious mansion, where the present viscount generally resides, has been constructed. The parks and grounds (which are extensive), are kept in the highest state of order by their noble proprietor, and are generously thrown open to the public, who, during the summer months visit them in large numbers. The manufacture of paper has been carried on here for many years, and there are flour and meal mills of considerable power. General Sessions of the Peace are held four times a year, and Petty Sessions once a month. The courthouse, situated near the centre of the town, is a commodious building. The Belfast and Ballymena railway passes at an inconsiderable distance north of the town. Lough Neagh approaches within half a mile of town.

The church is a neat edifice, with a square embattled tower, surmounted by a finely proportioned octagonal spire; there is one Presbyterian church (and another about to be erected), one Unitarian, two Methodist chapels, and one for the Society of Friends; the Roman Catholic chapel is spacious. A public Dispensary, and free schools, including one for infants, comprise the principal charities. The market days are Tuesday and Thursday. Fairs—January 1, May 12, and November 12. The parish of Antrim contained, in 1841, 4,312 inhabitants, and the town 2,645 of that number.

PLACES OF WORSHIP.
Established Church; Rev. William Greene, vicar
Presbyterian, No. 1; Rev. C. Morrison
Do. No. 2; Rev. John H. Orr
Unitarian; Rev. James Carley
Methodist (Primitive); Geo. Hamilton
Do. (Wesleyan); Rev. J. Feely
Roman Catholic Chapel; Rev. Daniel Curoe, P.P.

ANTRIM.

PUBLIC INSTITUTIONS, ETC.

Manor Court; seneschal, Samuel M'-Dowell Elliot, Belfast

Antrim Poor Law Union, estab. 1840; chairman, George J. Clarke, J.P., Steeple; vice-chairman, Thos. Montgomery, J.P., Birchhill; deputy vice-chairman, Chas. W. Armstrong, J.P., Cherryvalley; clerk and returning officer, Henry C. Scott; medical officer, Thos. S. M'Combe; master of workhouse, Wm. Steen; matron, Anna Stavely; relieving officers, H. Campbell & J. M'Quitty

Police Station—S. B. Studdart, sub-inspector

Bridewell Keeper—John M'Lorinan

Ulster Bank Branch; Wm. Crawford, manager; Charles Thompson, accountant

Loan Fund Society—treasurer, Rev. James Carley; manager, John Kirk

Kildare-place Society School—patron, Lord Visc. Massereene; patroness, Lady Massereene; teachers, John Lamont and Miss Kempston

Infant School—patroness, Miss Clarke, Steeple; teacher, Miss M'Gee

Registrar of Marriages—Dr. A. Bruce

Dispensary Officer—Geo. Nixon, M.D.

NOBILITY AND GENTRY.

Adair, Thomas B., J.P., Loughermore
Agnew, Miss, Main street
Bryson, Misses, Main street
Chaine, Wm., sen., Ballycraigy
Chaine, Wm., jun., Moylinny
Chaine, Stafford, Spring farm
Clarke, George J., J.P., Steeple
Gilmore, Colonel, Boghead
Goold, George J., R.M., Main street
Hughes, Thomas, Bush
Massereene and Ferrard, Lord Visc., D.L., J.P., Antrim castle
Montgomery, Thomas, J.P., Birchhill
Montgomery, Alexander, Potterswalls
Montgomery, Misses, Birchhill
O'Neill, Lord Viscount, Shane's castle
Studdart, S. B., sub-inspector of constabulary, Main street
Wall, Henry H., J.P., Wilderness lodge

CLERGY AND PROFESSIONAL.

Bruce, Alex., surgeon, Main street
Carley, Rev. J., Pres. minister, Main st.
Curoe, Rev. Daniel, P.P., Antrim and Randalstown
Greene, Rev. W., vicar, Dunsilly house
Ferguson, John, solicitor, Main street
Gwynn, Wm. J., solicitor, Main street
Hitchcock, John, solicitor, Mill row
Hall, Francis E., surgeon, Mill row
Malone, Edmund, solicitor, Main st.
Morrison, Rev. Charles, Presbyterian minister, Ashville
M'Combe, Thos. S., surgeon, Main st.
M'Greevy, Neil, apothecary, Main st.
Nixon, George, M.D., Mill row
Orr, John H., Pres. min., Main street

TRADERS, ETC.

Anderson, Henry, publican, Main st.
Armstrong, J., railway clerk, Bow lane
Agnew, William, publican, Main st.
Birnie, Samuel, pawnbroker, Bow lane
Brown, Wm., innkeeper, Main street
Bruce, Misses, haberdashers, Main st.
Brennan, Wm., painter, Main street
Cussack, Jn., baker & grocer, Main st.
Clugston, Wm., grocer, Main street
Crawford, Wm., manager of Ulster Bank, Mill row
Crawford, Taggart, & Co., woollendrapers, Main street
Craig, Wm., grocer and linendraper, Main street
Craig, John, publican, Main street
Crowe, Mrs., grocer, Main street
Cuddy, Misses, haberdashers, Main st.
Crawford, John, builder, Main street
Dickson, Edmund, builder, Main st.
Diamond, Margt., innkeeper, Bow lane
Davis, P. R., clerk of Petty Sessions, Main street
Gibson, Mathew, boot and shoemaker, Main street
George, Thomas, publican, Main st.
Goold, George, postmaster, Main st.
Gray, Jas., sen., publican, Massereene
Gray, Jas., jun., pawnbroker, Main st.
Hamilton, Miss, haberdasher, Main st.
Johnson, Alexander, grocer, woollendraper, baker, &c., Main street
Johnson, William, grocer, Main street
Lavery, John, publican and tailor, Main street
Kirk, John, manager of Loan Fund, Massereene
Kelso, Edw., watch and clock maker, Main street

Kerr, Wm., auctioneer, Main street
Moore, John, grocer & leather cutter, Main street
Moore, John, publican, Massereene
Morwood, Arthur, saddler, Main st.
Miliken, Henry, grocer, Main street
M'Gee, James, builder, Main street
M'Quillan, James, innkeeper and mail coach proprietor, Main street
M'Quillan, John, victualler, Main st.
M'Quillan, Mrs., innkeeper, Main st.
M'Nally, Mrs, Massereene Arms hotel, Main street
M'Connell, Langford, grocer, Main st.
M'Cormick, John H., woollendraper, Main street
M'Lorinan, Joseph, Main street
Neeson, Horace, saddler, Main street
Neeson; Daniel, innkeeper, Main st.
Neill, Wm., publican, Main street
O'Neill, Jas., boot & shoemaker, Main street
Prenter, Thomas, Antrim paper mills
Reid, Wm., grocer, Main street
Richey, David, grocer, Main street
Scott, Robert, & Son, cabinet makers, upholsterers & undertakers, Main st.
Scott, Henry C., clerk of Union, & agent Scottish Amicable Insurance Company, Main street
Scott, Henry, spirit merchant, & posting establishment, Main street
Scott, James, publican, Main street
Syrrel, W., supervisor excise, Main st.
Smyth, Ann, grocer, Main street
Suffern, John, grocer, Bow lane
Taggart, J., spirit merchant, Main st.
Thompson, S., inn-keeper, Main st.
Todd, John, excise officer, Main street
Vance, Wm., builder, Bow lane
Vance, Wm., grocer, Main street
Williamson, Wm., sen., delf merchant, and farmer, Main street
Williamson, W., jun., clerk & grocer, Main street
Wallace, H., sewed muslin agent, Main st

POST-OFFICE—GEORGE GOOLD, POSTMASTER.

TIME OF CLOSING BOX.	FOR WHAT MAIL CLOSED.	DESPATCH.
7-30 A.M.	Kells	8-45 A.M.
5-10 P.M.	Belfast and Scotch Mail	5-30 P.M.
5-20 P.M.	Dublin and Lurgan Mail	5-30 P.M.
9-30 P.M. 10- 0 P.M.	Dublin Day and early Morning Mails to Belfast	4- 0 A.M.
7-30 A.M.	Magherafelt, &c.	7-45 A.M.

ARDGLASS.

A MARITIME town in the County Down, and one of the watering places, 23 miles distant from Belfast, 5 from Downpatrick. It was formerly of much commercial importance. There is abundant fishery, which affords employment for a great portion of the working classes.

Post Office—Mrs. Kearns
Petty Sessions and Manor Court—Bath street
Coast Guard Station—Lieut. Carrol
Constabulary Station—Wm. Hamilton, Head Constable
Harbour Master—Bernard Hughes
Light House — Hugh Cunningham, keeper
Church of England — Rev. Charles Campbell
Primitive Wesleyan Chapel
Presbyterian Church—Rev. Thomas M'Afee
Roman Catholic Chapel—Rev. Wm. M'Mullin
Protestant School—James Caldwell, master
Ladies' Seminary and Boarding school, Castle street—Miss Morris, principal
Female School—Ann Calwell, mistress
Infant School—Mrs. Johnston, mistress
Dispensary—John Harrison
Public Baths—Bath street

GENTRY AND CLERGY.

Auchinleck, John, Castle street
Beauclerk, John, Castle
Beauclerk, Captain, Bam Castle
Brabazon, Henry, Castle street
Brown, P. R. M., J.P., Castle place
Cottingham, Mrs., The Crescent
M'Grath, Rev. F. F., The Crescent
M'Kitrick, Mrs., The Crescent
Saul, Thomas M., The Crescent
Savage, Henry, The Cresent
Thellison, Ernest, Seneschal, and agent to Major Beauclerk
Wilson, ——, Linner, The Crescent
Young, Rev. Charles, Castle place

TRADERS, ETC.

Allen, Robert, steward and agriculturist, Cottage
Blaney, Daniel, corn and butter merchant, and baker, Castle street
Brown, Mrs., tavern, Shore road
Curran, Thomas, trader and shipowner, Castle street
Cunningham, Miss, dressmaker and haberdasher, Castle street
Clarke, Richard, grocer, &c., Castle st.
Dowie, Arthur, ship carpenter, Bath street
Hughes, James, baker, Bath street
Hughes, John, grocer, &c., Bath st.
Hunter, Thos., general trader, Castle st.
Johnston, Chas., grocer, Bath street
Kearns, Richard, contractor & builder, Castle street
Kearns, Mrs., grocer, milliner, and haberdasher, Castle street
Lloyd, John, hotel keeper, Castle st.
Martin, James, grocer and publican, Bath street
M'Kinney, Robert, master tailor, Castle street
M'Nally, Simon, butcher, Castle street
M'Mahon, Wm., publican, Bath street
M'Nown, John and Richard, Ringford Cottage
Norris, James, grocer and haberdasher, Castle street
Rooney, Margaret, tavern keeper, Castle street
Towney, William, grocer, Hill street
Wheeler, John, publican, &c., Bath st.

COUNTY OF ARMAGH.

ARMAGH is an inland county. Greatest length, N. and S., 32 miles; greatest breadth, E. and W., 20 miles; comprising an area of 512½ square miles, or 328,076 acres, of which 265,243 are arable, 35,117 uncultivated, 8,996 in plantations, 778 in towns, and 17,942 under water. The Newry canal skirts the county on the East. The Ulster railroad is extended from Belfast to Armagh. The population in 1841 was 232,393—211,893 in the rural and 20,500 in the civic district. According to the census of 1851, the total population of the county was 196,420, being a decrease of 35,973.

Lieutenant and Custos Rotulorum—Lieut.-Col. James Molyneux Caulfield, M.P., Hockley
High Sheriff (1852-3)—Marcus Synnott, jun., Ballymoyer house, Newtownhamilton
Members for the County—Colonel Sir William Verner, Bart., Churchhill, Moy, and 86 Eaton square, London; Lieut.-Col. James Molyneux Caulfield, Hockley, and Brookes' Club, London
Assistant-Barrister—Edward Tickell, Q.C., 10 Clare street, Dublin

DEPUTY LIEUTENANTS.

Bacon, Edmund, Richhill
Blacker, Col. Wm., Carrick, Portadown
Charlemont, Earl of, K.St.P., Roxborough Castle, Moy
Close, Col. Maxwell, Drumbanagher Castle, Newry
Close, M., jun., Drumbanagher, Newry
Cope, Robert Wright, Loughgall
De Salis, Count, Tandragee
Eastwood, Jas., Castletown, Dundalk
Fox, Charles, Keady
Gosford, Earl of, Gosford Castle, Markethill

COUNTY OF ARMAGH.

Harden, Jas., Harrybrook, Tandragee
Manchester, Duke of, Tandragee Castle
Robinson, George, Abbey st., Armagh
Stronge, Sir James Matthew, Bart., Tynan Abbey
Stronge, Jas. Matthew, Tynan Abbey
Wilson, Thomas, Lisnadill and Dublin

MAGISTRATES.

Alexander, Robert Quin, Acton, Poyntzpass
Atkinson, Joseph, Crowhill, Loughgall
Bacon, Edmund, D.L., Richhill
Bernard, Major Arthur, Crossmaglen
Blacker, Col. William, D.L., Carrick, Portadown
Bond, Edward Wellington, Bondville, Tynan
Boyd, James Brown, Balleer, Keady
Boyd, John, Newry
Campbell, Rev. James, LL.D., Forkhill
Chambre, Meredith, Hawthorn Hill, Flurrybridge
Charlemont, Earl of, D.L., Roxborough Castle, Moy
Clermont, Lord, Ravensdale, Flurrybridge
Cloncurry, Lord, Maretimo, Blackrock, Dublin
Close, Col. Maxwell, D.L., Drumbanagher Castle, Newry
Cope, Robert Wright, Loughgall
Corry, Isaac, Abbey-yard, Newry
Crawford, Lieutenant-Colonel Adam White, R.A.
Cross, Maxwell, Dartan, Armagh
Cuppage, John, Lurgan
De Salis, Count, D.L., Tandragee
Dobbin, Thomas, Scotch st., Armagh
Dobbs, Conway Richard, Castle Dobbs, Carrickfergus
Eastwood, James, D.L., Castletown, Dundalk
Eyre, John, Maydown, Benburb
Foxall, John, Forkhill house, Forkhill
Foxall, Powell, Killevy Castle, Flurrybridge
Greer, George, Lurgan
Greer, Joseph, The Grange, Moy
Hall, Roger, Narrow-water Castle, Newry
Hamilton, Thomas Claude, Hampton Hall, Balbriggan, county Dublin

Hancock, John, Lurgan
Harden, James, D.L., Harrybrook, Tandragee
Harris, John Porter, Ashfort, Tynan
Henry, Thomas Gibson, Mill street, Newry
Irwin, John Robert, Carnagh House, Keady
Jones, Thos. Morris Hamilton, Moneyglass House, Toome
Kidd, Thomas, English street, Armagh
Kilmorey, Earl of
Kirk, William, Annvale, Keady
Lucas, Rt. Hon. E., Castle Shane, Monaghan
Loftie, John Henry, Loughbrickland House, Tandragee
M'Kee, Joseph, Markethill
M'Kinstry, Lee, Dublin
M'Watty, James, Castleblayney
Manchester, Duke of, D.L., Tandragee Castle
Nicholson, Joseph, Cranagill House, Loughgall
O'Callaghan, Hugh, Culloville, Crossmaglen
O'Callaghan, Jas., Culloville, Dundalk
Olpherts, Wm., Dartry, Blackwatertown
Paton, William, Charlemont place, Armagh
Prentice, Henry Leslie, Caledon
Quinn, Peter, Acton Lodge, Poyntzpass
Reid, John, Rahens, Carrickmacross
Reid, Wm., Ballymoyer, Newry
Reilly, John Temple, Scarva House, Loughbrickland
Robinson, George, D.L., Abbey street, Armagh
Stronge, Sir James Matthew, Bart., D.L., Tynan Abbey
Stronge, James Matthew, D.L., Tynan Abbey
Stronge, John Calvert, Tynan Abbey
Synnot, Marcus, Ballymoyer, Newtownhamilton
Tenison, Thos. Joseph, Port Nelligan, Tynan
Thompson, Wm. Needham, Newry
Verner, Col. Sir William, Bart., M.P., Churchhill, Verner's bridge, Moy
Verner, William, jun., Churchhill, Verner's bridge, Moy
Waring, Major Henry, Newry

White, John, Divernagh, Newry
Wilson, Thomas, D.L., Lisnadill

RESIDENT MAGISTRATES.
Miller, Wm. M., Loughgall
Singleton, M., Newtownhamilton

COUNTY OFFICERS.
Clerk of the Crown and Clerk of the Peace—Leonard Dobbin, English street, Armagh, and 27 Gardiner's place, Dublin
Crown Solicitor—Maxwell Hamilton, 5 Kildare street, Dublin
Crown Solicitor at Quarter Sessions—John M'Kinstry, jun., Armagh
Treasurer—Acheson St.George,Woodpark, Tynan
Secretary to the Grand Jury—John Gervais Winder, English street
County Surveyor—Henry Davison, Gosford place
Sub-Sheriff—Wm. Hardy, Loughgall
Coroners—Joshua Michael Magee, Newry; George Henry, Glenburn, Keady; Edw. D. Atkinson, Church street and Tandragee

STAMP DISTRIBUTORS.
Head Distributor for the County—T. A. Prentice, Scotch st., Armagh
Keady—Thomas Small
Lurgan—W. B. Morris
Markethill—Wm. Woodhouse
Newtownhamilton—Alexander Stitt
Portadown—George Kinkead
Tandragee—Robert Trotter

MILITIA STAFF.
Colonel—Earl of Gosford, Gosford Castle
Lieut.-Colonel—Wm. Blacker, Carrick

CONSTABULARY OFFICERS.
County Inspector—Louis Anderson, Armagh
SUB-INSPECTORS' STATIONS.
Armagh—William Kelly
Ballybot, Newry—S. P. Crawford
Crossmaglen—Gordon Holmes
Newtownhamilton—Thos. Armstrong
Portadown—William Little

PETTY SESSIONS COURT.
Armagh—Thursday, W. Barnes, clerk

COUNTY GAOL, ARMAGH.
Board of Superintendence — John Hancock, Acheson St. George, Wm. Paton, Henry L. Prentice, Maxwell Cross, George Robinson, Thomas A. Prentice, Thomas Dobbin, James Harden, D.L., Stewart Maxwell, R. W. Cope, Joseph Atkinson
Inspector—John M'Kinstry
Protestant Chaplain—Rev. Benjamin Wade, A.B.
Presbyterian Chaplain — Rev. Wm. Henderson
R. C. Chaplain—Rev. A. Rogers, P.P.
Surgeon—Alexander Robinson, A.M., M.B., F.&L.R.C.S.I.
Apothecary — Meredith Armstrong, M.R.C.S.E.
Governor—John M'Cutcheon

ARMAGH.

ARMAGH, an inland city and parliamentary borough, 30 miles distant from Belfast, comprising within its ancient boundary an area of 1,147 acres, and within its present municipal boundary 269 acres. It is the seat of the archiepiscopal see of the Primate of all Ireland, whose ecclesiastical province comprises six consolidated dioceses: 1. Armagh and Clogher; 2. Tuam, Ardagh, Killala, and Achonry; 3. Derry and Raphoe; 4. Down, Connor, and Dromore; 5. Kilmore and Elphin; 6. Meath. The town stands on the acclivities of a hill, of which the cathedral, repaired and beautified, chiefly at the expense of the present primate, tops the summit; there are also a Protestant Chapel of Ease, 3 Presbyterian churches, a Roman Catholic chapel (a cathedral is being built), 2 places of worship for Methodists, and 1 for Independents. The other public buildings are the County Courthouse, Prison, and Infirmary, the District Lunatic Asylum for Armagh, Cavan, Fermanagh, and Monaghan counties (which maintains 134 patients), the Royal School, a Public Library built and endowed by Primate Robinson in 1741, and lately rebuilt and improved—(it contains about 14,000 volumes, some of them considered very scarce, and open to the public from twelve to three o'clock)—a Fever Hospital, built by the present Primate, a Market House, erected by the late Primate Stewart, a Linen Hall, a Yarn Hall, Music Hall, and Tontine Buildings (in which is a large public assembly room, and a spacious News room), a National, a Sunday School, and a School for the Choristers, which is maintained by the Vicars Choral. Near the city is the archiepiscopal palace, with a domestic Chapel; an Observatory, with a very superior astronomical apparatus; and Barracks for 200 men. In or near the city are 2 distilleries, not now worked, a brewery, and several tanneries and flour mills. The Callen, a branch of the Blackwater, passes near the town, and the Ulster Canal within 4 miles. The Ulster Railway now connects the town with Belfast; and that from Newry to Enniskillen, when completed, will be of great benefit to it and the surrounding neighbourhood. The Corporation, which was styled "The Sovereign, Free Burgesses, and Commonalty of the Borough of Armagh," was abolished by the provisions of the Municipal Reform Bill. The Borough returns 1 member to Parliament; constituency on 1st January, 1851, 697. The lighting, cleansing, and watching the streets is vested in Commissioners, under 9th Geo. IV., c. 82. Markets are held on Tuesdays, for general purposes, and on Wednesdays and Saturdays for grain. The tolls have been bought up by the inhabitants, for the improvement of the town. Water is supplied by pipes, the management of which is vested in the Police Commissioners; and the streets and interior of many of the houses are lighted with gas. There are branches of the Bank of Ireland, Belfast Banking Co., Northern Banking Co., Ulster Banking Co., and Provincial Bank of Ireland. The Savings' Bank was established in 1818. The Union Workhouse was opened in 1842. Two newspapers are published in Armagh, the *Armagh Guardian* and the *Armagh Gazette*.

Post Office, Robert Birch, master—Arrivals—Enniskillen, 2 30 a.m.; Dublin Night, 3 45 a.m.; Dublin Day, 5 15 p.m.; Keady, 7 0 p.m.; Loughgall, 6 30 p.m.; Richhill, 6 30 p.m.; Monaghan Day, 7 5 p.m.; Coleraine, 8 45 p.m.; Belfast, 9 50 p.m. Despatches—Belfast, 2 30 p.m.; Coleraine, 3 45 a.m.; Monaghan Day, Keady, Loughgall and Richhill 5 15 a.m.; Dublin Day, 8 0 a.m.; Dublin Night, 8 45; Enniskillen, 9 50 p.m.

Tontine Rooms, English street, containing Public News-room, Sub-Sheriffs' office, handsome Assembly and other rooms; Robert Cochrane, secretary; Kingsberry Smith, keeper

Music Hall, for the use of the Choral School, Vicar's hill

Depository for the Church Education Society, and for the Association for Promoting Christian Knowledge; Rev. John Chomber, secretary; J. T. Leslie, keeper, Abbey st.

Member for the City—Colonel John D. Rawdon, 3 Great Stanhope street, London

Thomas Charles Anderson, Scotch street, Inspector of weights and measures

Gas Works, Callan street, M. R. Bell, secretary; J. Gibbs, manager

ECCLESIASTICAL.

Armagh Cathedral, Abbey street

St Mark's Church, the Mall

Primate of all Ireland, Right Hon. and most Rev. Lord John George Beresford, The Palace

Dean, Rev. Brabazon William Disney

Archdeacon, Rev. J. W. Stoker

Precentor, Rev. Richard Allott, A.M.

Chancellor, Rev. James Jones

Rector, Principal Surrogate, and Private Secretary to the Archbishop, Rev. Alexander Irwin

Treasurer, Rev. Wm. Barlow

Vicar-General, Joseph Ratcliff, LL.D

ARMAGH. 473

Curates, Rev. Benjamin Wade, Rev. John Sharkey, Rev. James Hogan, Rev. J. M. Strangways

Organist of Cathedral, Robert Turle

Organist of St. Marks, Charles Edmondson

Cathedral Choir, George Scott, Neal M'Neal Edmondson, Edward Rogers, George Allen, W. J. Cordner, Geo. D. Hughes, Charles Edmondson, Jas. Lee, and J. T. Leslie

Consistorial Court—Registrar, George Scott, office, Vicar's hill; Deputy Registrar, Robert Riddal, English street; Clerk, J. P. Hughes, Vicar's hill

First Presbyterian Church, Abbey street—Rev. John Hall, minister

Second Presbyterian Church, Lower English street—Rev. William Henderson, minister

Third Presbyterian Church, The Mall —Rev. J. R. M'Alister, minister

Roman Catholic Cathedral (in course of erection), Sandy hill

Roman Catholic Chapel, Chapel lane.

Roman Catholic Primate—The Right Rev. Dr. Paul Cullen, Abbey street; Rev. A. Rodgers, P.P., Abbey street

Independent Chapel, College street— Rev. Henry Martin, minister

Wesleyan Methodist House, Abbey street, Rev. Messrs. Lindsay and Hazleton, ministers

Primitive Methodist House, Abbey street, Rev. T. Maguire, minister

Registrar of Marriages—Alexander J. Dobbin, Scotch street

LEGAL.

Court House, Mall, Assizes twice a-year, Quarter Sessions four times, Petty Sessions every Thursday, and Manor Court every Third Monday

Town Commissioners whose term of Office ends 31st July, 1854— Thomas Kidd, chairman; George Robinson, John S. Riggs, George Scott, James Close, Richard C. Vogan, William Barker, Thomas A. Prentice, John Stanley, John M'Kinstry, Fras. M'Kee, Wm. Gardner, Robert Riddal, James Wiltshire, James Bennett, Hugh Treanor, Andrew Boyd, John Hughes, Robt. Fulton, Thomas M'Cann, Matthew Bell; Samuel Gardner, treasurer; Robert Cochran, clerk; William Morrison, collector

LITERARY AND SCIENTIFIC.

Natural History and Philosophical Society, Lord Primate, patron; Dr. T. R. Robinson, president; B. P. Davidson, Secretary; Thos. Smith, Assistant Secretary

Royal School, Rev. W. H. Guillemard, Principal

Public Library, Rev. James Hogan, librarian, Edward Rodgers, deputy

Observatory, Rev. Dr. T. Romney Robinson, Principal Astronomer; Neal M'Neal Edmonson, Assistant ditto

St. Patrick's College,

National School, School of Choristers, &c. &c.

Newspapers, *Armagh Guardian* (Saturday), English street, John Thomson, proprietor; *Armagh Gazette*, (Saturday), Scotch street, Mathew Small, proprietor

COMMERCIAL.

Market-house, containing Corn Market, large Assembly and Commissioners' Rooms; Crane Master, Chas. Keys; Keeper of Room, Jane Hughes, Market street

Linen Hall, under Toll Commissioners, keeper, E. Cullen, Linen Hall street

Bank of Ireland, Thomas Dobbin, agent; Mr. Francis Horner, manager

Provincial Bank, Wm. Paton, agent; James Bowman, manager

Belfast Bank, Thos. Kidd, J.P., manager

Northern Bank, John Jeffreys, Market street, manager

Ulster Bank, Angus J. Mulligan, Esq., manager

Savings' Bank, Rev. Richard Allott, secretary, Wm. Paton, treasurer, Wm. Christian, actuary

Shambles, Lower English street, open every Tuesday, Wednesday, and Saturday

ARMAGH.

CHARITABLE.

County Infirmary, Abbey street, Alex. Robinson, A.M., M.B., surgeon ; R. Riddal, treasurer
Fever Hospital, Caledon road, John Colvan,M.D.,Surgeon,&c.,physician
Dispensary, Scotch street, Jas. Leslie, M.D., surgeon
District Lunatic Asylum, Thos. Jackson, manager; Thomas Cuming, M.D., physician
Workhouse—Thos. Archer, master ; Malcolm M'N. Johnston, clerk
Nunnery, The Pavilion—Madam Croft, abbess

NOBILITY, GENTRY, ETC.

Beresford, The Right Hon. and Most Rev. John George, Archbishop of Armagh and Primate of all Ireland, The Palace
Barnes, Major, Market street
Bell, Mrs. J., Melbourne terrace
Bennet, James, Lower English street
Bingham, George E., Dobbin street
Boyle, Hugh, Beresford row
Bowman, James, Abbey street
Butler, Mrs., 5 College street
Carson, Mrs., Palace row
Christian, William, Victoria street
Cochran, Robert, English street
Craig, Mrs. S., Palace row
Davison, Henry, County surveyor, Gosford place
Davidson, J. W., Charlemont place ; office, Dobbin street
Dobbin, Thomas, J.P., Scotch street
Dobbin, Alexander J., Scotch street
Farmar, Major, Beresford row
Flack, Captain, Palace row
Gunning, Miss, Abbey street
Hardy, Mrs., Charlemont place
Hardy, Mrs. R. C., Beresford row
Heeney, Miss, Melbourne terrace
James, Mrs. M. A., Palace row
Johnston, Mrs. Catherine, Beresford row
Kane, Mrs. J., Upper English street
Kidd, Thomas, J.P., Upper English st.
Kidd, Mrs., Charlemont place
Kidd, Osborne, Thomas street
Kidd, Joseph, Ballina house
Mauleverer, Mrs. Mary, Beresford row
Maxwell, Stewart, Melbourne terrace
Magill, Miss, Melbourne terrace
Millar, George, English street
Moore, Mrs., English street
Mulligan, Angus, Ulster Bank, English street
M'Geough, Miss, Drumsill
M'Kane, William, Meredith place
M'Kinstry, John, Beresford row
M'Kinstry, Mrs., Beresford row
M'Kinstry, John, Charlemont place
Noble, Miss, Dobbin street
Noble, Joshua Thomas, Beresford row
Orr, Mrs., College hill
Paton, Wm., J.P., Charlemont place
Pooler, Miss Ann, College street
Pooler, Mrs., College street
Prentice, Alexander, Ardmore cottage
Robinson, George, J.P., Abbey street
Robinson, Lieutenant, College street
Scott, George, Vicar's hill
Sloan, Mrs., English street
Stanley, John, Beresford row
Smith, Mrs., Abbey street
Winder, John Gervais, English street

CLERGY AND PROFESSIONAL.

Armstrong, Rev. W., English street
Armstrong, M. & J., surgeons, English street
Allott, Rev. Richard, Vicar's hill
Barrett, Jacob, solicitor and proctor, English Street
Barker, Wm., solicitor, Abbey street
Bell, J. Trueman, solicitor, English st.
Briggs, James, M.D.
Bryce, Alex., apothecary, English st.
Colvan, John, M.D., surgeon, English st.
Cullen, Paul, Rev. Dr., R.C. Primate, Abbey street
Cuming, Thos., M.D., Beresford row
Davidson, John, Master in Chancery, &c., Abbey street
Fullerton, Wm., architect, Palace row
Grattan, Thos., dentist, Scotch street
Hardy, Rev. James, Charlemont place and Kildartin
Hazleton, Robert, surgeon and dentist, Russell street
Hall, Rev. John, Abbey street
Henderson, Rev. Wm., Abbey street
Hogan, Rev. James, Abbey street
Irwin, Rev. Alex., Charlemont place
Jenkinson, Joseph, solicitor, Abbey street
King, Rev. Robert, Abbey street
Lavery, Phillip, surgeon, English street
Lindsay, Rev. Robt. Hill, Abbey street

ARMAGH. 475

Leslie, James, surgeon and licentiate apothecary, Scotch street
Martin, Rev. H., Ballycrummie
M'Alister, Rev. John R., Abbey street
M'Causland, Rev. J. C., Gosford place
M'Kee, John, solicitor, College street and Markethill
M'Kinstry, John, Crown solicitor
Quinn, John, solicitor, Castle street
Riggs, J. L., surgeon
Robinson, Alexander, B.M., surgeon, Abbey street
Robinson, Rev. T. Romney, D.D., Observatory
Rogers, Rev. Mr., Abbey street
Savage, Marc Anthony, surgeon and apothecary, English street
Sharkey, Rev. John, Abbey street
Stanley, John, solicitor and proctor, Beresford row and College street
Strangways, Rev. Jas., Abbey street
Vogan, John, solicitor, College street
Wade, Rev. Benjamin, Victoria terrace
Wilson, W. Thomas, M.D., M.R.C.E., Thomas street

TRADERS, ETC.

Adams, John Clarke, woollen and hat warehouse, English street
Adams, William, publican, Scotch st.
Allen, E. and J., haberdashers and milliners, English street
Allen, T., school & residence, Abbey st.
Armstrong, M. and J., apothecaries, English street
Armstrong, Geo., meal and flour store, Market street
Armstrong, James, and Co., hardware merchants & grocers, Scotch street
Anderson, Eliza, toy shop, Scotch st.
Andrews, William, Commercial hotel, Scotch street
Andrews, John, sewed muslin warehouse, Abbey street
Arnold, John, sewed muslin warehouse, Abbey street
Allen, James, boot and shoemaker, Barrack street
Allen, Robt, cabinetmaker, Barrack st.
Albin, W. and R., plumbers, tin and coppersmiths, Scotch street
Barnes, G., provision store, Market st.
Barnes, Robert, tanner, &c., Scotch st.
Barnes, William, clerk of Petty Sessions, Scotch street

Baker, Charles, china and glass shop, Scotch street
Bell, Matthew Robert, auctioneer and valuator, Russell street
Bell, Matthew, seedsman and miller, English street
Begley, Francis, butcher, Scotch st.
Brown, Messrs. (of Glasgow), sewed muslin warehouse, Market street
Boyd, William, and Co., grocers and seedsmen, Thomas street
Boyd, Wm., jun., grocer and spirit dealer, Thomas street
Boyd, A. & F., grocers, iron, and coal merchants, Dobbin street
Boyd, J. B., flax store, Dobbin street
Bloomfield, Thomas, leather store, Thomas street
Burns, Bernard, lodgings, and posting establishment, Thomas street
Burns, Hugh, publican, English street
Burns, Samuel, watchmaker and jeweller, English street
Carpenter, Henry, ironmonger, English street
Carr, John, baker, Lower English st.
Cardwell, W. F., flour and meal store, English street
Campbell, Wm., family grocer, confectioner, and publican, English st.
Campbell, John (of Keady), posting establishment, English street
Campbell, Henry, publican & grocer, English street
Caldwell, Eliza, publican and grocer, Lower English street
Caldwell, Miss, Temperance hotel and reading room, Lower English st.
Campbell, Jane, grocer, Scotch street
Carolan, Hugh, publican, Lower English street
Collins, John, saddler, Lower English street
Cole, James, and Co., woollendrapers, &c., Market street
Cole, Robert, grocer and flax mercht., Barrack street
Caulfield, Samuel, forwarding agent, Thomas street
Conry, John, grocer and spirit dealer, Market street
Conry, Richard, grocer & spirit dealer, Thomas street
Cordner, William, teacher of music, Vicar's hill

2 s

ARMAGH.

Corrigan, John, linen merchant, Dobbin street
Close, Jas., woollendraper, Scotch st.
Cochran, Mary Ann, umbrella maker, Scotch street
Crummy, Edw., baker and flax dealer, Lower English street
Davison, Martha, coal, iron, & leather dealer, Thomas street
Davison, Wm., grocer & haberdasher, 20 and 62 Thomas street
Davidson, Wm., haberdasher, Thomas street
Darvey, Patrick, leather and spirit dealer, Thomas street
Deacon, John, grocery, wine & spirit dealer, Barrack street
Devlin, Thomas, chandler, Barrack st.
Devlin, Owen, grocer and publican, Lower English street
Devlin, Patrick, White Cross Inn and posting establishment, Lower English street
Donnelly, Jas., innkeeper, English st.
Donnelly, Margt., publican, Scotch st.
Donnelly, Peter, stone cutter, Ogle st.
Donnelly, Hugh, tailor, Ogle street
Donohoe, Wm., grocer and publican, Lower English street
Donohoe, James, family grocer and baker, Lower English street
Dobbin, Robert, publican, Thomas st.
Douglas, A., tailor, Scotch street
Dundas, M., haberdasher, English st.; residence, Russell street
Eager, Thomas, publican, Market st.
Farr, John, carpenter and builder, the Mall
Fagan, Wm., baker, Thomas street
Ferris, Wm. Robert, hardware merchant and general grocer, Market and English street
Foster, Charles, tea, coffee, and spirit shop, Scotch street
Frizell, A., cabinet maker, English st.
Fulton, Robert, druggist, grocer, and timber merchant, English street
Fulton, M. and M. J., Berlin wool, fancy haberdashery, and perfumery warehouse, English street
Fullerton, Wm., architect, Palace row
Foster, Mrs., English street
Gardner, James, woollen merchant, English street
Gardner, Wm., tan yard, Dobbin st.
Gardner, Samuel, Sun Fire agent, English street
Gardner, S. and E., iron and brass founders, and machine makers, Dobbin street
Gillespie, David, grocer, English st.
Gibson, Alex., pawnbroker, Chapel lane
Gillespie, David, rope and twine manufacturer, Scotch street
Gibson, John, yarn store, Dobbin st.
Gribben, Mary, grocer and publican, Thomas street
Graham, Henry, woollen and linen draper, English street
Greacen, N., printer and stationer, Market street
Gray, John, grocer, &c., Scotch street
Gough, Thomas, boot and shoemaker, Thomas street
Gordon, Medley, smith and farrier, Dobbin street
Grimley, Mary, milliner, Thomas st.
Greer, James, & Co., linen yarn store, Dobbin street
Hall, James, painter, Lower English st.
Hazleton, Hamilton, watch maker and jeweller, English street
Hazleton, Mrs., confectioner, English street
Hamilton, John, painter, Abbey street
Hagan, Bernard, publican, Thomas st.
Hamill, Patrick, baker, Ogle street
Hazleton, John, pawnbroker, Ogle st.
Harrison, Wm., grocer, &c., Thomas st.
Hardy, Thos., leather store, Thomas st.
Hart, James, publican, Scotch street
Heaney, Hiram, butcher, English st.
Henry, W. H., upholsterer and cabinet maker, Scotch street
Henry, Ann, confectioner, Scotch st.
Hinchey, Patrick, coachmaker, The Mall
Hughes, John, spirit store, Lower English street
Hughes, John, Charlemont Arms, Lower English street
Hughes, George P., clerk Metropolitan Registry office
Hughes, Francis, Plough inn, Lower English street
Hughes, Wm., & Co., boot and shoemaker, Scotch street
Hughes, Mrs. Ann, delf and glass shop, Scotch street
Hughes, Arthur, publican, Thomas st

ARMAGH.

Hughes, Charles, publican, Thomas st.
Hughes, Felix, publican, Mill street
Hughes, Thos., baker, &c., Thomas st.
Hughes, Henry, baker, &c., Thomas st.
Hughes, A. & G., linen drapers and haberdashers, Thomas street
Hodgens, Wm., boot and shoemaker, Thomas street
Jackson, Robt., spirit shop, Thomas st.
Johnston, Robert James, boot maker, English street
Johnston, Robt., boot maker, Thomas street
Johnston, Jas., stationer and school, Ogle street
Johnston, Malcolm M'N., clerk, Ogle st.
Johnston, Eliza Jane, haberdasher, Ogle street
Kearney, John, publican, Scotch street
Kennedy, John, New Armagh coach factory; residence, Victoria street
Kelly, Patrick, furniture mart, M'Crum's court
Keenan, Judith, Royal hotel & spirit store, Scotch street and Dobbin st.
Kidd, Brothers, flour and oatmeal millers, bread and biscuit bakers, English street
Kingston, John, boot and shoemaker, Scotch street
Kidd, Osborne, store & office, Thomas street
Lamb, Henry, grocer and publican, Barrack street
Lawson, William, spirit shop, Thomas street
Lavery, Phillip, apothecary, English st.
Leathem, Wm. H., agent for Castlebellingham brewry, English street
Lowden, William, baker and grocer, English street
Lowden, Jas., baker and flour dealer, Lower English street
Lee, James, piano-forte warehouse, College street
Loughran, Lawrence, boot and shoe shop, Thomas street
Loughran, Bridget, oats & meal shop, Ogle street
Loughran, Owen, meal store, Dobbin st.
Lyle, Jane, bakery, Scotch street
Maxwell, J., painter, &c., The Mall
Matchett, James, Albert hotel, English street
Maglone, Bernard, dealer, English st.

Magowan, Samuel, tailor, Thomas st.
Mathews, Joseph, auctioneer and valuator, English street
Marshall, Jas., provision store, Scotch street
Mallew, Peter, traveller's home, Ogle st.
Moore, Ann, grocer, English street
Moore, James, wine and spirit merchant, Market street
Moore, A., publican, Barrack street
Moore, Robert, hosier and haberberdasher, Scotch street
Morrow, Samuel, butcher, English st.
Morrison, Adam, bran, flour, grocery, and spirit shop, Scotch street
Morrison, Thomas, publican, Scotch st.
Morrison, Wm., publican and grocer, Scotch street
Morton, Chas., haberdasher, Thomas st.
Moffett, Mary, flour shop, Thomas st.
Morgan, James, flax buyer, Dobbin st.
Murray, James, publican and tailor, Scotch street
Murray, John, haberdasher, Thomas st.
M'Arthur, Samuel, boot and shoemaker, Thomas street
M'Bride, E. G., land surveyor, English street
M'Alevey, grocer, publican, & bakery, Ogle street
M'Connell, Mr., farming implement maker, The Mall
M'Crum, Mr., Milford mill wheat stores, English street
M'Cann, Thomas, family grocer and fruit warehouse, English street
M'Court, Patrick C., bookseller and stationer, English street
M'Culla, Robert, family grocer and spirit dealer, Market street
M'Connell, Mr., grocer and publican, Barrack street
M'Cully, John & James, haberdashers, Scotch street
M'Cullough, Mr., wine and spirit store, Thomas street
M'Carten, E., tailor, Ogle street
M'Cullough, David, marble and stone works, Dobbin street
M'Farland, Patrick, saddler, English street
M'Ganty, Rose, publican, Barrack st.
M'Glone, James, publican, Scotch st.
M'Gowan, R., tailor, Thomas street
M'Kay, Mrs., Dobbin street

ARMAGH.

M'Kean, Sons, & Co., spinners, yarn store, Dobbin street
M'Kinlay, Mr., yarn store, Dobbin st.
M'Kenzie, Alex., wholesale spirit store, English street
M'Kenna, James, saddler, Thomas st.
M'Kee, Thos., bakery, Thomas street
M'Knight, James, sewed muslin agent, Ogle street
M'Kee, Francis, grocer and publican, Ogle street
M'Kean, Wm., yarn merchant, Dobbin street
K'Kenna, Patrick, publican, Thomas st.
M'Keavney, Railway Arms hotel, at Railway terminus
M'Lorinan, Patrick, linen draper, &c., shop, Scotch street
M'Laughlin, Mr., glass, delf, and toy Ogle street
M'Linden, George, publican, English st.
M'Neilly, Alex., watchmaker, Scotch st.
M'Nally, John, furniture dealer, English street
M'Mahon, James, grocer, English st.
M'Parland, Owen, baker, English st.
M'Parland, John, jun., Whitehorse inn, Barrack street
M'Parland, Arthur, grocer, Ogle street
M'Waters, John, bookseller, printer, &c., English street
O'Callaghan, Owen, grocer and spirit dealer, Thomas street
O'Neill, Bernard, butcher, English st.
O'Neill, Charles, butcher, English st.
O'Neill, Robt., haberdasher, Thomas st.
Orr, Thomas, baker, Barrack street
O'Toole, Catherine, millinery shop, Thomas street
Penton, Eliza, seed warehouse, Thomas street and Scotch street
Park, L. and C., sewed muslin office, Thomas street
Quin, Francis, grocer, and boot and shoemaker, Lower English street
Quin, Margaret, haberdasher, Thomas street
Quin, John, boot and shoemaker, Ogle street
Rea, James, servants' registry office, Court-house
Ray, R. G., pawnbroker, Ogle street
Reid, Robert, chandler and grocer, Lower English street
Reilly, J., pawnbroker, Abbey street
Reilly, Henry, pawnbroker, Lower English street
Riggs, R. & S., family grocers, wine and spirit merchants, English street
Riddall, Robt., & Co., flour and corn millers and bakers, English street
Riddal, Mrs., girls' school, Abbey st.
Ross, Thomas, builder, English street
Ross, Mrs., Armagh delf and china warehouse, English street
Rose, Arthur, sewed muslin agent, Market street
Roddy, Charles, woollendraper, &c., Scotch street
Robertson and Sons, sewed muslin warehouse, Dobbin street
Ryan, Samuel, Harp hotel, Lower English street
Savage, Henry, spirit dealer, Ogle st.
Shaw & Co., flax store, Dobbin street
Sherry, Laurence, pawnbroker, Ogle st.
Sheppard, A. P., pawnbroker, Scotch st.
Shillington, Henry, grocer, Scotch st.
Sling, W. H., hairdresser, Scotch st.
Sling, John, barber and hairdresser, Ogle street
Sloan, Mary Ann, drug and perfumery shop, English street
Simpson, John, flour and meal store, Market street
Simpson, William, grocer and spirit dealer, Market street
Smith, Thomas, grocer, Scotch street
Small, Mathew, veterinary surgeon, horse bazaar, & publisher, Scotch st.
Smith, Wm., vet. surgeon, Scotch st.
Stut, Robt., upholsterer, Abbey street
Taylor, Jas., coach factory, Abbey st.
Taylor, Robt., publican, Lower Hill st.
Thompson, John, bookseller, stationer, and publisher, English street
Thompson, John, haberdasher, Scotch street
Thompson, Alexander, linen yarn and commission agent, Dobbin street
Tippin, Joshua, publican, English st.
Trainer, Hugh, grocer, English street
Turle, Robt., organist, Vicar's hill
Twyford, Thomas, butcher, English st.
Unger, W. H., professor of modern languages, College street
Vogan, R. C., grocer, wine and spirit merchant, and chandler, English st.
Vallely, John, & Co., drapers, &c., Scotch street

Vint, John, room paper, glass, oil, and colour merchant, Market street
Ward, Constantine, butcher, English street
Warmoll, Robt., butcher, &c., English st.
Wallace, A., sewed muslin agent, English street
White, Samuel, bookseller and bookbinder, Dobbin street
Wilson, Robert, woollendraper, &c., Market street
White, Robert, publican, Barrack st.
Wheelan, Mr., builder, Dobbin street
Williams, John, English street
Williams, M. A., silk mercer and milliner, English street
Wilson, B. D., haberdasher, English st.
Wiltshire, J., Beresford Arms Hotel, English street
Wilton, Thos., confectioner, Thomas street
Wilson, Thomas, grocer and spirit store, Thomas street

Wilson, Wm. T., apothecary, Thomas street
Wright, Mrs., milliner, College street

CONVEYANCES.

Dublin *via* Castleblayney, on the arrival of the 8-45 o'clock train from Belfast
Newry, from Keenan's, van, at 8 a.m. and 4 p.m., one horse; Newry from Post-office, 9 p.m., one horse
Monaghan, from Hughes' Charlemont Arms, 10¼ a.m.
Clones, from Hughes' Charlemont Arms, 10¼ a.m
Enniskillen by Omagh, from Wiltshire's, 9¾ p.m.; Enniskillen by Aughnacloy, coach and van, 9 p.m
Dungannon mail from Wiltshire's, 4½ o'clock a.m.; Dungannon, from Keenan's, every evening, at half-past 6 o'clock

AUGHNACLOY.

A MARKET town, in the county of Tyrone, 41 miles from Belfast. The town consists of one long street, and several diverging subordinate streets and lanes; its appearance is clean and neat, and of late a good deal improved. Its trade is good, and at the markets and fairs, a considerable amount of business is transacted. A constabulary police station has been established, and Petty Sessions are held every alternate Monday. The Parish Church, erected by Acheson Moore, Esq., is a spacious and handsome structure, with a spire, containing a good clock. The other places of public worship are a large Presbyterian Church, a Roman Catholic Chapel, a Chapel for Independents, and two for Wesleyan Methodists. The market is on Wednesday, and the fairs are held on the first Wednesday monthly.

Post Office — David Campbell, postmaster—Letters from Dublin arrive every morning at half-past two, and are despatched every night at a-quarter to ten o'clock; letters from Londonderry arrive every night at twenty minutes to ten, and are despatched every morning at twenty minutes to three o'clock
Constabulary Station—T. S. Barnes, sub-inspector
Bank (Ulster Banking Co.'s branch)— Thomas Montgomery, jun., manager
Established Church, the Ven. Archdeacon Stokes, rector
Presbyterian Church—Rev. Wm. M'Ilwain, minister

Wesleyan Methodist Chapel—various ministers
Primitive Wesleyan Chapel—various
Roman Catholic Chapel
Church Education Society's School— Wm. Lett, master; Infant School, Sarah Harvieson, mistress
National School—J. M'Kenna, master

GENTRY AND CLERGY.

Anketell, Thomas, Dungilleck
Betty, Rowland
Crossley, Henry, J.P., Annahoe House
Davis, Mrs., Armagh house
Falls, Mrs.
Fleming, Rev. Horace Townsend
Horner, Rev. R. N., Killeshill Glebe

AUGHNACLOY.

Hurst, Rev. Francis, Errigle Glebe
Johnston, Wardlaw, J.P., Casgha Moan
Montgomery, Vaughan, Crilly House
Mayne, Nathaniel, Rehaghey
Montgomery, James, Garvey
Moutray, John Corry, Favour Royal House
Moutray, Rev. J. Jas., Richmond Glen
Moore, Acheson, Cauldrum
Moore, Edward, J.P., Bawn House
Moore, Cecil, solicitor
Moore, Cecil, Cottage Hill
Mullan, Rev. John, C.C.
M'Ilwain, Rev. Wm.
O'Brien, Rev. Charles, P.P.
Olpherts, Capt. George, Springmount
Richardson, Misses, Armagh House
Scott, William, M.D.
Simpson, Hugh, solicitor
Sproull, Thomas W.
Simpson, Miss Mary Ann
Spear, William
Stewart, Capt. Mervyn, Martry House
Stokes, Rev. Archdeacon, Bellmont
Waller, Edward, J.P., Lisnadavy
William, Happer

TRADERS, ETC.

Anderson, John, grocer
Barnes, Samuel, spirit dealer
Best, Wm., earthenware dealer
Bridge and Montgomery, linen and woollendrapers, &c.
Bridge, Thomas M., linen and woollendraper and hatter
Burn, John, spirit dealer
Burns, Thomas, spirit dealer
Busby, John, grocer
Busby, John, baker
Campbell, David, and Co., merchants
Campbell, Catherine, spirit dealer
Campbell, David, and Co., grocers
Campbell, John, Queen's Arms hotel and posting establishment
Carroll, William, spirit dealer
Carroll, John, spirit dealer
Chapman, Robert, earthenware dealer
Chapman, Robert, grocer
Corbltt, William, No Surrender hotel
Corbet, John, spirit dealer
Corbet, William, spirit dealer
Coote, James, spirit dealer
Coyle, Patrick, tailor
Curran, John, spirit dealer
Devlin, Daniel, spirit dealer
Ellison, William, saddler
Early, John, spirit dealer
Farrell, John, haberdasher and cotton manufacturer
Fiddes, Simpson, and Co., merchants
Fulton, Joseph, watch & clock maker
Graham, Samuel A., linen and woollendraper
Hatton, Arthur, clothes dealer
Hardy, William, apothecary
Horner, Elizabeth, grocer
Kellett, Eleanor, haberdasher
Keenan, James, blacksmith
Keenan, John, blacksmith
Kingston, Mary, straw bonnet maker
Little, Francis, and Co., grocers, bakers, ironmongers, &c.
Little, Richard, spirit dealer
Loughead, Timothy, baker, grocer, &c.
Montgomery, Cairns, and Co., grocers and bakers
Montgomery, Cairns, & Co., merchants
Montgomery, Cairns, and Co., tallow chandlers
Murdock, Joseph, tailor
Murray, Patrick, tailor
M'Carron, James, spirit dealer
M'Cully, Ann, haberdasher
M'Daniel, Thomas, spirit dealer
M'Dowell, John, saddler
M'Elmeel, John, spirit dealer
M'Elmeel, Anne, spirit dealer
M'Gee, Andrew, spirit dealer
M'Genaty, Thomas, grocer
M'Kenna, William, grocer
M'Kenna, William, baker
M'Kenna, Hugh, baker
M'Kenna, Peter, grocer
M'Kenna, Peter, iron, timber and coal merchant
M'Kenna, Owen, spirit dealer
M'Kenna, Peter, spirit dealer
O'Brien, Dennis, linen and woollendraper
Robinson, William, tailor
Simpson, James, and Co., linen and woollendrapers and general warehousemen
Sherrard, Edward F., Imperial hotel
Slowey, Bernard, baker
Soraghan Peter, baker
Traynor, Ann, clothes dealer
Walker, James, grocer
Woods, John, hotel keeper

BALLIBAY.

A MARKET town in the county of Monaghan. Is fifty-two miles distant from Belfast, and eight miles from the county town Monaghan; is situate on the direct line of road from Dundalk to Enniskillen, and the Dundalk and Enniskillen line of Railway is laid off to pass through the Northern end of the town, and will leave it within reach of the latter town in a few hours, being thirty miles distant. Its markets are held on Saturday, and its fairs on the third Saturday in each month. It has obtained great celebrity for the quality and quantity of flax shown in its markets. The description brought to market is more particularly confined to hand flax, but a fair supply of milled is also shown. Its fair is celebrated for a choice supply of horses and black cattle. A market for the sale of grain is also held on Tuesdays and Fridays, but is principally confined to oats. Where bleach greens formerly stood, there is now very extensive concerns for the preparation of flax, under Schenck's patent, owned by the Messrs. Shaw, of Belfast and Celbridge. A vast supply of superior water-power and extensive buildings still remain unoccupied; but it is generally believed will sooner or later be converted into spinning concerns. Lying between the town and Carrickmacross, distant about five miles, are spinning mills belonging to Mrs. M'Kean, of Keady, and adjacent to which stands a tower, the seat of David Leslie, Esq., Laragh. Within one mile of the town are very extensive corn mills, the property of Mr. William Jackson of Cremorne, and Mr. George Brown of Drumfalda, and in which a very extensive trade is carried on for the home and English markets; also, about five miles distant, at Deragooney, mills belonging to R. A. Minnett, Esq., J.P., worked very extensively for the English markets; there are also several smaller mills in the neighbourhood, and particularly that of Donraymond and Corfadd, owned by Thomas and James M'Cullagh, Esqrs., and of vast benefit to the country. Rather more than central of the town, stands a plain but useful and substantial Market-house, lately erected by the owner of the estate, Mrs. Leslie. Petty Sessions are held every alternate Monday, in the Old Petty Sessions Room. There is an Established Church and Presbyterian Meeting-house in the town; and in the adjacent localities are one Established and five Presbyterian Churches, one Covenanting House, and the Roman Catholic Chapel of Tullycorbitt and Balintra

Post Office — Postmaster, William Gray—Letters arrive at ten minutes past seven morning, and despatched thirty-five minutes past six evening

Constabulary Station—Mark Bloxham, sub-inspector, Castleblayney; A. Trimble, head constable, Ballibay

Established Church—Rev. Jn. Dunbar

Ditto Tullycorbitt—Rev. John Hare; curate, Rev. James Fields

First Presbyterian Church, Derryvalley—Rev. J. G. Smith

Second Presbyterian Church, Ballibay —Rev. John H. Morell

Derryvalley Presbyterian Church— Rev. David Bell

Crieve Presbyterian Church—Rev. Martin M'Dowell

Cahan's Presbyterian Church—Rev. Mathew M'Auley

Lough Morne Presbyterian Church— Rev. John Dougan

Mountain Meeting-House (Covenanters)—Rev. Thomas Cathcart

Roman Catholic Priest of the parishes of Ballibay and Tullycorbitt, Rev. John Goodwin; curate, Rev. Edward Goodwin

GENTRY, ETC.

French, Robert, Ballibay house

French, Miss, Ballibay house

Hazlett, Mrs. Captain

Jackson, John, Cremorne, secretary to the Grand Jury

Johnston, Miss, Crieve

BALLIBAY.

Kerr, Wm. A.W., J.P., Mount Carmell
Leslie, Mrs. Emily, Ballibay house
Lucas, Thomas, agent to the Ballibay estate
Montgomery, Arthur, Crieve house
M'Cullagh, James, J.P., Corfadd house
M'Cullagh, Thomas, J.P., Derryvally and Donraymond
Oulton, John, Crieve

CLERGY AND PROFESSIONAL.

Bell, Rev. David, Bridge house
Brannen, Rev. Phillip, P.P., Tatty Brack
Callan, Rev., C.C.
Cathcart, Rev. Thomas, Covenating minister
Cathcart, James, apothecary and surgeon
Corrie, Rev. Samuel, Derryvally
Donigan, Rev. Phillip, C.C.
Donaldson, Robert, L.R.C.S.I.
Doogan, Rev. John, Lough Mourne Manse
Dunbar, Rev. John, Rectory
Fields, Rev. James
Goodwin, Rev. John, P.P.
Goodwin, Rev. Edward, C.C.
Hare, Rev. John, Tullycorbitt
Leslie, Rev. Charles, Ballibay house
Morell, Rev. John Harris, Comery Lodge
M'Auley, Rev. Mathew
M'Clean, William, M.D.
M'Dowell, Rev. Martin, Rockmount
M'Mahon, Richard, solicitor
Robinson, Joseph, L.K.Q.C.P. & R.C.S., &c., attendant to the Ballibay Dispensary in the Castleblayney Union
Rowley, Rev. Jas., Rockmullen house
Smith, Rev. John G.

TRADERS, ETC.

Anderson, James, spirit dealer
Bradshaw, James, linen manufacturer
Barnes, Charles, tailor
Bartley, James, linen and woollendraper
Boyle, Timothy, glass and delf warehouse
Boyle, Bernard, grocer and publican
Boyd, Alexander, tanner and publican
Boyd, William, grocer, baker, & letter carrier
Breakey, John, Petty Sessions clerk and grocer
Breakey, John, Drumakell
Brown, George, miller and corn dealer
Brady, John, spirit dealer
Brown, Benjamin, baker, grocer, hardware and general merchant
Boyd, Francis, schoolmaster (Church Education Society's school) & clerk to the Established Church
Branon, Patrick, spirit dealer
Burgoyne, Margaret, haberdasher and china warehouse
Carson, David, Moniarton
Carson, James
Charles, Joseph, spirit dealer
Cunningham, John, boot & shoemaker
Conolly, Mr., woollendraper & publican
Cole, James, pawnbroker & auctioneer
Dixon, Elizabeth, linen & haberdashery
Dixon, Samuel and Robert, woollendrapers and spirit dealers
Donaldson, George, spirit dealer
Donohoe, Edward, spirit dealer
Drury, George, grocer, wine and spirit dealer, hardware & general mercht.
Duffy, James, baker and grocer
Duffy, Patrick, baker and grocer
Daily, Thomas, spirit dealer
Francis, Samuel, spirit dealer
Francis, Susan, dressmaker
Glenny, Wm., spirit dealer & carpenter
Gray, Rebecca, Leslie Arms hotel
Gray, James, haberdasher and spirit dealer
Gray, S. and E. W., York hotel
Graham, Henry, process server and boot maker
Hagan, Mrs., dressmaker
Hagan, John, publican & confectioner
Hanna, William, spirit dealer
Hazlett, Miss, ladies' school
Hoy, Andrew, reed maker
Hughes, John James, woollendraper and spirit dealer
Johnston, James, haberdasher
Johnston, John, blacksmith
King, Hugh, harness maker & saddler
Logan, James, grocer and dealer
Mateer, Daniel, corn dealer and miller
Marron, James, baker, grocer and spirit dealer
Martin, James, grocer, publican, and provision merchant
Moore, Robert, haberdasher, baker, grocer, wine and spirit dealer
Murray, Edward, grocer and publican

Murphy, Michael, spirit dealer
Miller, John, boot and shoemaker
Miller, Jane, lodging and entertainment
Mullin, John, Comey
M'Adam, Terence, baker, grocer and spirit dealer
M'Cabe, James, grocer, ironmonger, and general merchant
M'Carten, Joseph, baker and grocer
M'Caffry, Mathew, spirit dealer
M'Cleave, Mr., Ballinagarry
M'Cleave, Miss and Master, Ballinagarry
M'Cormick, A., watch and clock maker
M'Creery, Robert, grocer, baker and spirit dealer
M'Cullagh, Elizabeth, spirit dealer
M'Donald, Michael, blacksmith
M'Ginniss, John, leather cutter
M'Gurk, James, old clothes dealer
M'Ivor, John, tailor
M'Kelvey, William, leather cutter and boot and shoe merchant
M'Murray, Thomas and James, woollendrapers
M'Mahan, Bernard, grocer and leather cutter
M'Mahan, Francis, flax & spirit dealer
M'Manus, Patrick, spirit dealer
Quin, F., lodging house and dealer
Riddle, Gordon, corn dealer
Reid, William, grocer, spirit dealer, and stamp office
Rutherford, John, spirit dealer
Rutledge, John, tailor and publican
Sloan, David, Corfadd
Somerville, John, butcher
Somerville, Francis, butcher
Thompson, Mary, haberdasher
Wilson, Thomas, Aghayert
Wilson, Miss, Aghayert

CONVEYANCES.

A car every morning, at 5 o'clock, for Castleblayney, to catch the 6 o'clock mail for Armagh, and first trains for Belfast and Dundalk, and 6 o'clock mail car for Newry; returns from Castleblayney at 8 p.m., on the return of the Armagh and Newry cars, and 8 o'clock Dundalk train

The Cootehill and Castleblayney day car passes every day from the former town at 10 morning, to reach the latter for the half-past 11 train for Dublin; leaves the latter town on arrival of the half-past 10 train from Dublin, passes at 3 o'clock on its way to Cootehill

The Enniskillen coach passes every Monday, Wednesday, and Friday, at 10 a.m., to catch the half-past 11 o'clock train at Castleblayney for Dublin; and every Tuesday, Thursday, and Saturday, at a quarter to 4 p.m., to catch the 5 o'clock train at Castleblayney for Dublin; returns from Castleblayney, every day, on arrival of the train from Dublin at half-past 1 o'clock p.m., and passes at a quarter to 3 o'clock for Enniskillen

The mail car leaves Castleblayney, and passes at 10 minutes past 7 a.m., *via* Rockcorry, to Cootehill; leaves Cootehill at half-past 4 p.m., and passes at 6-35 for Castleblayney

BALLYCASTLE.

A SEA-PORT and market town, in the county of Antrim, 42 miles N.N.W. from Belfast. The name of this place *Ballycashlin*, signifying, in the Irish language, "Castletown," is derived from a castle, built here in 1609, by Randolph, Earl of Antrim, of which there are still some remains. North-east of Ballycastle lies the island of Rathlin. Ballycastle owes its origin to Hugh Boyd, Esq., to whom a lease of the estate was granted, by the Earl of Antrim, in 1736. This gentleman obtained a grant from Parliament of £20,000, and upwards, for the purpose of erecting a pier to protect the shipping frequenting this part of the coast; in consequence, however, of the transfer of the property upon the decease of Mr. Boyd, to other parties, who took little interest in the place as a harbour, the accumulation of sand, and the injury done to the pier by high tides, its value as a haven of refuge is not now recongnized. The place consists of the upper and the lower town, lying about a quarter of a mile asunder, and connected by a beautiful avenue of lofty trees. The lower town is called the Quay, separated from which, by a small channel, stands the Glass-house, fallen to ruin since the decline of the local trade; likewise a building once used as a Custom-house, but now occupied as a Barrack. The upper town is the larger and more important section, and contains the places of worship, several neat villas, and the principal inns—these, the Antrim Arms and Mr. Nelson's Royal Hotel, are well conducted establishments, and are both posting-houses. Its advantages for sea-bathing have rendered Ballycastle attractive in the summer. A station of the constabulary police and of the coast are established here.

A handsome church, in the Grecian style of architecture, with a finely-proportioned octagonal spire, was erected, in 1756, at the sole expense of Mr. Boyd, who was interred within its walls on the day of its consecration. The Parish Church of Ramoan is a short distance from the town. The other places of worship are for Presbyterians, Roman Catholics, and Methodists. The charities comprise a dispensary and fever hospital, alms-houses, founded and endowed by Mr. Boyd, and a Union workhouse. In the neighbourhood are two chalybeate springs; some remains of the ancient castle, from which the town obtained its name, and the ruins of Bona-Margs monastery, founded for monks of the Franciscan order. The chapel of this establishment, which is the burial place of the Antrim family, is in a more perfect state than the other remains. The weekly general market is held on Saturday, and for grain on Thursday; there is also a market for yarn, &c., held every third Tuesday. Fairs—1st January, the last Tuesday in May, July 26th, and the last Tuesday in the months of August, October, and guard November, for cattle, pigs, &c.

Post Office — Archibald M'Donnell, post master—Letters from Belfast, Antrim, Ballymoney, Ballymena, Coleraine, and Londonderry arrive every afternoon at half-past one, and are despatched every morning at eleven o'clock; letters from Belfast, Carrickfergus, Larne, Glenarm, and Cushendall arrive every evening at half-past seven o'clock, and are despatched every morning at half-past eight

Cars—To Ballymena, from James Laverty's, every Tuesday and Saturday, at five morning

Union Workhouse—Master, George Butler; matron, Mary Butler

Constabulary Station—C. J. Gernon, sub-inspector

GENTRY, CLERGY, ETC.

Abbott, Captain, R.N., Ballycastle
Black, James, Ballycastle
Boyd, Misses, Ballycastle
Boyd, Captain Francis
Boyd, Augustus, Lieutenant R.N., Willmount
Blois, Captain John, R.N., Ballycastle
Brooke, Basil G., Moyaver
Campbell, John, Ballyverdagh
Carter, Rev. H., D.D., Ballintoy
Clark, Robert, Breen
Courtney, Rev. Charles S., Ballynaglough house
Cuppage, Adam, J.P., Glenbank
Dunlop, Mrs., Ballycastle
D'Evelyn, Rev. W., Glebe, Armoy
Gage, Rev. Robt., J.P., Rathlin Island
Graham, Rev. Jackson, Armoy
Hamill, James Clarke, M.D., Ballycastle
Hunter, Rev. Stevenson, Turnarobert
Kerney, Rev. R., P.P., Ballyvoy
Kirkpatrick, Charles, Whitehall
Lyle, Rev. Samuel, Ballycastle
Miller, Alexander, treasurer county Antrim, Ballycastle
Micklethwait, Henry S. N., Lieutenant R.N., Ballintoy
Moore, John Stewart, J.P., Moyarget Lodge
Moore, Miss Mary, Ballycastle
Monsell, Rev. J. S. B., Ramoan rectory
M'Gildowney, John, J.P., Clare park
M'Neill, Edmund, Ballycastle
M'Neill, Hugh, Annaville

BALLYCASTLE.

M'Glennon, Rev. James, P.P., Ballycastle
O'Connor, George Mathew, surgeon, Ballycastle
Simms, Rev. John, Toraloskin
Stewart, Alexander, surgeon
Wrightson, Rev. Thomas Richard, Ballycastle

TRADERS, ETC.

Archer, Hugh, carpenter
Black, Archibald, leather seller
Black, Dennis, tailor and haberdasher
Boyle, Henry, civil bill officer
Brady, Ellen, dressmaker
Cameron, John, blacksmith
Coyle, Archibald, butcher
Crossman, John, excise officer
Duncan, Daniel, spirit dealer
Donnelly, Edward, butcher
Douglass, George, carpenter
Happer, John T., apothecary
Hollywood, John, linen merchant
Jolly, Mary, dressmaker
Jolly, Miller, grocer
Jolly, Ann, grocer
Jolly, John, linen and woollendraper
Keown, A., boot and shoemaker
Kerr, Christy, blacksmith
Kelly, Mrs., dressmaker
Kelly, John, spirit dealer
Keenan, James, haberdasher
Kinnaird, The Misses, straw bonnet makers
Laverty, James, butcher
Laverty, Mary, straw bonnet maker
Laverty, Ann, dressmaker
Mathers, Samuel, clock and watchmaker
Mathers, Mary Ann, grocer
Moore, W., saddler
M'Alister, Rose, straw bonnet maker
M'Alister, Samuel, clerk of Petty Sessions
M'Cambridge, Edward, spirit dealer
M'Conaghy, John, linen and woollendraper
M'Curdy, M., tailor
M'Donnell, Archibald, Antrim Arms hotel and posting establishment
M'Donnell, Catherine, grocer
M'Donnell, Alexander, spirit dealer
M'Dougall, Charles, boot and shoemaker
M'Guile, James, carpenter
M'Googan, Neal, spirit dealer
M'Quigg, Henry, baker, grocer, ironmonger, and hardware merchant
M'Kenzie, Hugh, baker
M'Kinley, Mary, dressmaker
M'Kernon, John, wheelwright
M'Neill, Neal, carpenter, painter, and glazier
M'Michael, Hugh, leather seller
M'Lean, Alexander, painter, glazier and spirit dealer
M'Kiernan, Bernard, butcher
Neilly, James, grocer
Nelson, William, Royal hotel and posting establishment
Reynolds, William, clerk to the board of guardians
Robinson, George, wheelwright
Robinson, Miss E., linen and woollendraper
Robinson, George, grocer
Ross, John, tailor
Saunders, Robert, boot and shoemaker
Scallion, Henry, blacksmith
Scally, William, boot and shoemaker
Sergeant, Miss E., organist and pianist
Smith, James, blacksmith
Stewart, John, boot and shoemaker
Sharp, John, spirit dealer
Sharp, Andrew, ironmonger and hardware merchant
Sharp, Andrew, grocer
Sharp, Andrew, registrar of marriages
Thompson, John, linen and woollendraper
Thompson, John, leather seller
Thompson, John, grocer
Thompson, John, baker
Thompson, John, haberdasher
Thompson, John, tanner, &c.
White, Hugh, grocer
White, Hugh, ironmonger and hardware merchant
Wilson, Elizabeth, grocer
Woods, Michael, master extraordinary C.C. and commmissioner for taking affidavits, Q.B., &c.

BALLYMENA.

BALLYMENA is a stirring, business, and thronged market inland town, in the County of Antrim; 21 miles N.W. from Belfast, 21 S.E. by S. from Colene, and 8 N.N.W. from Antrim; pleasantly situated, two miles above the confluence of the Braid and the Main Waters, and on the high road from Belfast to Londonderry and Coleraine. Large quantities of linen cloth are made in the neighbourhood, and brought to the Ballymena bleach-greens, of which there are many in the vicinity of the town, where the water is abundant and pure. General Sessions of the Peace are held four times a year, and Petty Sessions every fortnight. Courts-leet are held on the last Friday in the months of April and October, and Manorial Courts on the last Friday of each month, before the seneschal. The town, which is the property of Sir Robert Shafto Adair, bart., within the last few years has been greatly improved. The principal street is new, wide, well-built, and gas-lighted, as are the chief shops; many of the houses are of a respectable class and appearance. The market-house, near the centre of the town, is a large and convenient edifice, surmounted by a steeple, 96 feet in height. A court-house has lately been erected by the county, and a large hotel, which is now occupied by Mr. Greer, by the owner of the town.

The management of the town is vested in twenty-one commissioners, elected every three years. The monetary establishments of Ballymena are a branch of the Belfast Banking Company, of the Northern Banking Company, of the Ulster Banking Company, and of the Provincial Bank. A news-room, well supplied with the Irish, Scotch, and English newspapers, and the best periodicals, is well conducted, and thrown open to strangers. The Belfast and Ballymena Railway has a terminus at the end of the town. The Parish Church of Kirkinriola is a small, plain edifice, with an embattled tower, crowned with pinnacles. The other places of worship are four Presbyterian churches, a Roman Catholic chapel, and one for Methodists. There are three weekly markets—namely, on Tuesday, for pork and butter; on Wednesday, for grain; but the principal one is on Saturday, and is a large linen market. Fairs—July 26th and October 21st.

Post Office, Church street—George Dugan, postmaster. Ballymoney, Coleraine, and Derry mail, 8-15 a.m.; Belfast, Dublin, and England, 5-15 p.m.

Railway—Five trains to and from Belfast daily, and three on Sundays

Conveyances—Coleraine coach leaves Railway station every evening at 6½ o'clock; Portglenone and Kilrea cars at same hour; Derry mail, every morning at 8¼ o'clock

Court-house, Ballymoney road—Thos. Pattison, keeper

Manor Court—Last Friday in each month, Wm. Gihon, seneschal

Bridewell—behind the Court-house—contains seven cells and one solitary, one male and one female day room; Thomas Pattison, governor; Rev. Dr. Reeves, local inspector

Constabulary Barrack (head quarters for the County), High street—E. S. Flinter, county inspector; William Henry, sub-inspector

Union Workhouse, Cushendall road—Thomas H. Jones, J.P., Moneyglass house, chairman to Poor-law guardians; John Raphael, Galgorm, vice-chairman; Captain Harrison, Hugomount, deputy vice-chairman; and Frederick Albert Mathews, clerk to Board; medical attendant, Dr. Kidd

Dispensary—Dr. Ross, medical officer

Market-house, corner of Bridge st.—Undergoing an alteration and improvement, to fit it for an armoury for local pensioners; Sergeant Borland to have charge. John Nelson, clerk to markets, and collector of tolls for Sir R. Shafto Adair

Cattle Market—Hugh Devenie, clerk

BALLYMENA.

Magistrates—Wm. Gihon, Hillhead; John Dickey, Lehinmohr; George J. Goold, R.M., Antrim; Henry Hutchinson Hamilton O'Hara, Crebilly; Thomas Casement, Ballee house; John O'Neill Higginson, Springmount; Alexander Davison, Knockboy; Ambrose O'Rorke, Ballybobbin; Shafto Adair, Farm lodge

Town Commissioners — William B. Taylor, chairman; George Dugan, George Tomb, Patrick M'Vicar, Hugh Rea, Hugh Davidson, John Jellett, Robt. Chesney, John Baird, Bristow Miniss, William Black, Charles Ross Munro, Archibald Christie, David Syme, Andrew T. Dickey, John Strachan, Luke Jacobson, John Gardner, John Callaghan, Alexander Patterson, James Kinnear; George Ballentine, clerk—office, High street

Seneschal for manors of Mulloughgane, Cashel, Buckna, and Edenduffcarrick—Wm. Orr; office, Bridge st.

Coroner—John Jellett

Clerk to Petty Sessions and to Manor court—George Ballentine, Master in Chancery and Commissioner for taking Affidavits for all Courts, Church street

Stamp distributor, inspector of weights and measures, district registrar of marriages — James Greer, agent for the Northern Fire and Life Assurance Company, Bridge street

Notary Public—Geo. White, Church st.

Banks—Belfast Bank, Bridge street, John Patrick, jun., manager; Northern Bank, Shamble street, James and Robt. Young, managers; Ulster Bank, Wellington street, William Hogg, manager; Provincial Bank, Wellington street, Chas. R. Munro, manager

Episcopal Church—Rev. Wm. Reeves, D.D., rector

First Presbyterian Church, Castle st.—Rev. H. J. Dobbin, D.D., minister

Second ditto, High street—Rev. Wm. Campbell, minister

Third ditto, Wellington street—Rev. S. J. Moore, minister

Unitarian Meeting-house, High street—Rev. James M'Ferran, minister

Wesleyan Methodist Chapel, Castle street—Rev. John Feeley, minister

R. C. Chapel—Rev. J. Lynch, P.P.

Do. Crebilly— Ditto

Diocesan School—Rev. Wm. Reeves, D.D., head master

Parochial School—J. Madden, master

Guy's Free School, Wellington st.—James Andrews, master

Industrial National School, Wellington street—John Boyd, master; Elizabeth Boyd, mistress

Ballymena Library and News-room, Wellington street—Wm. A. Young, secretary; J. Craig, keeper

Circulating Library, Church street—George Dugan, proprietor

GENTRY, CLERGY, ETC.

Adair, A. Shafto, M.P., D.L., J.P., Farm Lodge
Adair, Miss, Church street
Black, Wm., surgeon, Church street
Bloxam, Mrs., High street
Campbell, Rev. William. High street
Casement, Thos., J.P., Ballee house
Casement, Rev. Robert, Harryville
Caruth, Alexander, solicitor, Church st.
Christie, Robert, solicitor, Mill street
Cobain, Rev. Edward, Albert place
Curell, Andrew, Ballygarvey
Davison, Alexander, J.P., Knockboy
Dickey, John, J.P., Leighenmohr
Dickey, Andrew, Brookville
Diamond, Patrick, surgeon, Mill street
Disney, Charles, architect, Wellington street
Dunseath, William, Wellington street
Ferguson, George, solicitor, High st.
Fleming, Rev. James, Albert place
Gihon, William, J.P., Hillhead
Gihon, Andrew, Clonavon
Harrison, Robert, High street
Hay, P. R., M.D. and surgeon, Mill st.
Jackson, Luke, Fountain cottage
Kidd, Abraham, M.D. and surgeon, Wellington street
Miller, David, High street
Moore, Misses, Wellington street
Moore, Rev. S. J., Broughshane street
M'Gee, Edward, land surveyor, Fountain place
M'Neale, Stephen Wilson, solicitor, High street
M'Ferran, Rev. James, High street

BALLYMENA.

M'Sayers, Duffin, solicitor, Mill street
M'Killip, John, Ballygarvey
Newell, Frederick Wm., A.M., Inspector of National schools, Wellington street
Ormond, Mrs., Mill street
O'Hara, H. H. H., J.P., Craigbilly
O'Rorke, Alexander and Daniel, solicitors, High street
Orr, William, solicitor, Bridge street; residence, Harryville
O'Neill, John, M.D. and licentiate in midwifery, Bridge street
Patrick, J., surgeon, Bridge street
Raphael, John, Galgorm
Ross, Arthur, M.D. and surgeon, Church street
Reeves, Rev. Wm., D.D., Church st.
Skelly, Mrs., Fountain place
Smyth, Andrew, M.D., surgeon and apothecary, Church street
Smyth, Rev. John, Rector, Ballyclug, High street
Stoney, Captain, Albert place
Taylor, Robert, Church street
Taylor, William B., Church street
Taylor, Mark P., solicitor, Church st.
Wallace, Dr., Wellington street
Young, Wm., M.D., Galgorm Castle

MERCHANTS, TRADERS, ETC.

Anderson, William, cloth and yarn merchant
Anderson and Co., sewed muslin agents, High street
Atkinson, John, and Son, hardware, delf, glass and china warehouse, Mill street
Baird and Hardy, woollendrapers and haberdashers
Barr, William, posting establishment, Wellington street
Ballentine, R. J., grocery, bakery, and spirit store, Bridge street
Ballentine, J., leather cutter, Wellington street
Ballentine, Robert, grocer, Harryville
Balfour, Miss, boarding school, Wellington street
Beggs, Francis, linen merchant, Albert place; residence, Lisnafillen
Beattie, Robert, publican, Broughshane street
Black, Robert, publican, Wellington street
Black, Robert, yarn store, Rridge st.
Boyle, James, woollendraper, &c., Mill street
Brown, J., publican, Shamble street
Brown, S. and T., sewed muslin agents, High street
Bowman, W. H., sewed muslin agent, High street
Brown, Jane, family grocer and spirit dealer, Mill street
Bradshaw, James, grocer, Mill street
Brownlee, James, publican, Church street
Brownlee, J., saddler, Rallymoney st.
Brangan, Ann, hotel, Church street
Burk, Wm., grocer, Broughshane st.
Buchanan, John, publican, Wellington street
Cameron, The Misses, teachers, High street
Carson, Henry, publican, Bridge street
Carson, Ellen, spirit and leather shop
Callaghan, John, publican, High st.
Charters, Wm., publican, Bridge st.
Christie, Archibald, cabinet maker, Mill street
Colville, Hugh, spirit dealer, Mill st.
Cosbie, Andrew, saddler, Wellington street
Compton, Thomas, publican, High st.
Craig, Alexander, grocer, Church st.
Craig, Alexander, saddler, Church street
Craig, Joseph, grocer, delf and china house, Church street
Craig, John, flour and meal store, Church street
Cunningham, Thomas, publican, Bridge street
Curell, J. and D., linen merchants, Ballygarvey
Cobain, Miss, ladies' school, Albert place
Cowan, Eliza, ladies' school, High st.
Davidson, William, reed maker, Church street
Davison, William, grocer, Harryville
Davison, Hugh, rope and twine maker, Bridge street
Davison, A. and J., yarn stores, Wellington street
Dempsey, Gordon, grocer, Galgorm st.
Dickey, John, publican, Church st.
Dickey, John and Andrew, bleachers, Leighenmohr

BALLYMENA.

Dickson, John, yarn merchant, High street
Diamond, Margaret, publican, Galgorm street
Dugan, George, printer, bookseller, and stationer, Church street
Dunseath, William and Hugh, linen merchants, Galgorm street
Duffin, John, spirit dealer, Bryan st.
Eager, Robert, clothes broker, Mill st.
Elliott, John, saddler, Church street
Farrell, Thomas, publican, Shamble st.
Fleck, James, grocer, Broughshane st.
Fowler, Joseph, boot and shoemaker, Wellington street
Gardner, John, hardware and delf shop, Church street
Getty, James, publican, Mill street
Getty, Matthew, grocer, Springwell st.
Given, Thomas, yarn merchaut, Church street
Given, James, watchmaker, Church st.
Gilmour, Wm, publican, Church street
Gihon, William, and Sons, bleachers, Lisnafillen and Ballymena
Gordon, Robert, publican, Bridge st.
Graham, John, ironmonger and leather dealer, Bridge street
Greene, T., publican, Wellington st.
Greene and Sinclair, linen and woollendrapers, and silk merchants, Mill street
Greer, Alexander, family grocer
Greer, James, Adair Arms new hotel
Hamill, M., linen mercht., Church st.
Hamill, George, publican, Bridge st.
Hanna, William, leather merchant, Bridge street
Hanna, Wilson, publican, Church st.
Houlihan, C., grocer, Bridge street
Houston, William, fishing tackle shop, Church street
Irwin, Ruth, milliner, Church street
Irwin, William, boot and shoemaker, Church street
Jack, Maria, publican, Church street
Jack, Eliza, haberdasher, Mill street
Jellett, John, hotel, Albert place
Johnston, S., Railway tavern, Harryville
Kane, Wm., publican, Bridge street
Kennedy, John, Broughshane street
Kennedy, Eliza, hotel and coach office, Bridge street
Kennedy, Wm., publican, Bridge st.

Kennedy, J., sewed muslin agent, Wellington street
Kernohan, Andrew, publican, Bridge st.
Killen, J. B., woollendraper & haberdasher, Church street
Kilpatrick, Elizabeth, spirit dealer, Mill street
Knowles, James, haberdasher, Mill st.
Knowles, Robert and Wm., grocers and spirit dealers, Shamble street
Kyle, John, grocer, Galgorm street
Lavery, John, publican, Church street
Larkin, David, grocer and publican, Galgorm street
Lindsay, Matthew, haberdasher, Mill street
Lindsay, D., clothes dealer, Mill st.
Lindsay, John & Thos., clothes dealers, Mill street
Liggett, Alexander, spirit store, Harryville
Linn, David, publican, Church street
Magill, Geo., classical school, Broughshane street
Mackey, John, boot and shoemaker, Church street
Maguire, Felix, oyster house, Church street
Martin, Andrew, grocer and chandler, wine and spirit merchant, Church st.
Martin, Daniel, publican, Bridge st.
Mehan, William, publican, Church st.
Mills, John, grocer, Springwell street
Miniss, Bristow, grocer, wine & spirit store, Church street
Mitchell, John, glazier, Church st.
Millar, James, publican, Church st.
Montgomery, Matthew, coach maker, Church street
Montgomery, Wm., carpenter, Church street
Montgomery, John, and Son, linen-yarn merchants, High street
Montgomery, Jane, publican, Church street
Moore, H. C., woollendraper, Mill st.
Moore, W. and R., builders, Wellington street
Molloy, Neal, publican, Church street
Morton, Robert, wholesale and retail grocery, &c., Church street
Mullan, Hugh, spirit store, Church st.
M'Adam, Thos., spirit shop, Bryan st.
M'Aulay, James, publican, Bridge st.
M'Aulay, James, haberdasher, Mill st.

BALLYMENA.

M'Auley and Steele, coach makers and house builders, Mill street and George's street
M'Aleese, Daniel, grocer and publican, Broughshane street
M'Afee, Robt., haberdasher, Church st.
M'Callion, J., grocer, Bridewell row
M'Camphill, S., leather seller, Church st.
M'Cann, Patrick, clothes dealer, Mill st.
M'Cleery, Wm., butcher, Shamble st.
M'Connell, A., clothes broker, Mill st.
M'Curdy, John, publican, Bridge st.
M'Clarnon, H., publican, Wellington st.
M'Dowell, John, publican, Mill street
M'Erlean, G., painter, Broughshane st.
M'Elheran, Archd., Broughshane st.
M'Elwain, J., pawnbroker, Shamble st.
M'Fall, D., grocer & publican, Mill st.
M'Gerill, Richard, grocer, Harryville
M'Gee, Wm., plumber, Shamble st.
M'Gaughey, J., publican, Wellington st.
M'Harg, James, grocer, baker, and spirit dealer, Bridge street
M'Harg, Jas., spirit store, Bridge st.
M'Naughten, M., grocer, Harryville
M'Neill, Hugh, grocer, Bridge street
M'Nees, Henry, reedmaker, Mill st.
M'Kendry, Jas., publican, Church st.
M'Kee, James, grocer, Harryville
M'Kinlay, J., publican, Wellington st.
M'Vicker, Patrick, woollen and linen draper, Church street
Nesbitt, John, publican, Mill street
Nicholl, David, saddler and harness maker, Mill street
O'Rawe, Bernard, flour and meal dealer, High street
O'Neill, Jas., watchmaker, Castle st.
O'Neill, C., classical school, Castle st.
Patterson, A., family grocer, High st.
Park, L. and C., sewed muslin warehouse, Wellington street
Patrick, John, and Son, linen merchants, Bridge street
Quinn, Mathew, smith, Galgorm st.
Rainey, Hugh, grocer, Church street
Rea, Hugh, Railway hotel, Harryville
Rea, Aaron, grocer, wine and spirit store, Bridge street
Reilly, James, clothes broker, Mill st.
Reid, R. G., grocer and ironmonger, Church street
Ross, John, grocer, Bridge street
Robinson, Alexander, woollen and Manchester house, Mill street
Sands, John, publican, Shamble st.
Sanderson, Arthur, publican, Bridge st.
Smyth, Jas., leather dealer, Broughshane street
Smyth, Robert, publican, Church st.
Smyth, Alexander, boot and shoemaker, Church street
Small, Andrew, auctioneer and clothes shop, Church street
Smith, The Misses, haberdashers, Bridge street
Smith, John, publican, Bridge street
Smith, Robt., publican, Wellington st.
Steele, Adam, grocer, baker, wine and spirit dealer, Mill street
Strahan, John, grocer and chandler, Church street
Stewart, Joseph, bakery, Bridge st.
Stevenson and Lyle, yarn store, Wellington street
Suter, Robert, publican, Church st.
Swan, William, publican, Bridge st.
Taylor, Archibald, grocer, wine and spirit merchant, Mill street
Taylor, James, grocery, bakery, wine and spirit stores, Church street
Taylor, William, cloth merchant, Church street
Telford, Alexander, boot and shoemaker, Mill street
Tomb, Geo., woollendraper, Church st.
Thompson, Shepherd, and Co., linen merchants, High street
Tumblety, Hugh, Farmer's inn, Mill st.
Wasson, John, smith, George's street
Watson, John, woollendraper, Church street
Walkingshaw, Mary, delf and china shop, Bridge street
Walkingshaw, John, cabinet maker, Wellington street
White, George, printer, bookseller and stationer, Church street
White, Catherine, publican, Bridge st.
White, James, grocer, Wellington st.
White, Daniel, blacksmith, Wellington street
Wilson, W., woollendraper, Church st.
Young, J. and R., bleachers and linen merchants, Shamble street
Young, Alexander, pawnbroker, Shamble street
Young, Alex., pawnbroker, Castle st.
Young, William, watchmaker, Castle street

BALLYMONEY.

A MARKET town and parish, partly in the liberties of Coleraine, county of Londonderry, and partly in the barony of Kilconway, but chiefly in that of Upper Dunluce, county of Antrim, 35m. 6f. N.N.W. from Belfast, 14m. 4f. N.N.W. from Ballymena, seated on a small tributary water of the Bann, about two and a-half miles from its confluence with that river. The town lies over an area extending from Milltown, on the Rasharkin road, to Rawdon foot. It was originally irregularly built, but, in 1845, the inhabitants placed it under the Act " for lighting and cleansing, &c.," since which time there is no town of the same size in the North of Ireland so much improved, partly by the inhabitants, who, however, were liberally assisted by their noble landlord, the Earl of Antrim, since he came to reside on his property. The benefits of a resident landlord are very visibly observed by any one visiting this town who has not been in it for the last ten years; neat and clean footpaths are in every street, the old Town-hall has been remodelled, and now stands a beautiful and commodious building, a monument to the liberality of the noble owner, who also granted to the Ballymoney Gas Company a lease of the ground on which their works stand, free of rent, and gave one-eight of the whole cost of the erection of the works as a donation to the improvement of the town. It is the capital of the two baronies of Dunluce, and the largest seat of their population and trade. The linen manufacture prevails in the neighbourhood.

A branch of the Belfast Bank, and of the Ulster Bank, are established here. General Sessions of the peace are held alternately with Ballymena; Petty Sessions once a fortnight, and a Manorial Court, for the barony of Dunluce, on every third Wednesday. The Court-house, a convenient building, wherein the courts are held, is situated in Charlotte street, and the Bridewell is attached to it.

The church, a large, plain edifice, with a tower and cupola, was erected in 1782, near the site of an ancient church, of which some fragments still remain. The other places of worship are for Presbyterians, Roman Catholics, Unitarians, and Covenanters. The trustees of Erasmus Smyth's fund established a school in 1813. A linen market is held on the first and third Thursday in each month, and a weekly market for the usual domestic commodities on Thursday. Fairs—May 5th, July 10th, and October 6th. Ballymoney contained, in 1851, 2,678 inhabitants.

Post Office, Church street—Mrs. Jane Hamilton, post-mistress

Coaches—Mails from Antrim Arms every day at 2-40 p.m. for Belfast; the Fair Trader from Commercial Hotel or Queen's Arms every morning at 7-20 for Ballymena, in time for 10 o'clock train

Carriers—William Knox, to Belfast, from Linen-hall street, every Tuesday and Saturday; Bernard Laverty, from Castle st., Tuesday and Saturday

Excise Office, Charlotte street—Joseph Pinche, chief officer

Constabulary Station, Cameron place—R. W. Bagley, sub-inspector

Dispensary, Main street — William Moore, surgeon

Clerk of Petty Sessions—Robt. Steele, Main street

Baronial Surveyor—Henry Johnson, Charles street

High Constable for Upper Dunluce—Henry West Hamilton, Church st.

Commissioner for taking acknowledgments of married women, and affidavits in the Court of Queen's Bench—James Cramsie, High st.

Belfast Banking Company (branch), Church street (drawn on Denison, Heywood, & Co., London)—James Thompson, manager

BALLYMONEY.

Established Church, Church street—Rev. James Russell Phillot, rector; Rev. Thos. Ferguson Creary, curate
First Presbyterian Church, Meetinghouse street—Rev. Robert Parke, minister
Second Presbyterian Church, Townhead street—Rev. James Usher, minister
Third Presbyterian Church, Rawdonfoot—Rev. J. L. Rentoul, minister
Eastern Reformed Presbyterian Church —Rev. John Paul Marcus, minister
Covenanters' Meeting-house, Charlotte street—Rev. Wm. John Stavely, minister
Unitarian Meeting-house, Charles st. —Rev. Joseph M'Fadden, minister
R.C. Chapel—Rev. John Heggarty, P.P.
National School, Castle street—Wm. Johnston, master
Free School, Church street—John M'Farland, master

GENTRY, CLERGY, ETC.

Anderson, Henry, Ballynacre
Barclay, Alexander, Mullamore
Barclay, George, Mullamore
Boyle, James, Charlotte street
Cramsie, James, solicitor, High street
Creary, Rev. T. Ferguson, Main st.
Greene, Mrs. Elizabeth, Charlotte st.
Greene, William Francis, solicitor, Charlotte street
Heggarty, Rev. John, P.P., Chapel house
Lamadge, William, S.L., Main street
Leatham, William Thomas, M.D.
Leslie, James Edmund, Leslie hill
Leslie, James, J.P., D.L., Leslie hill
Mitchell, Joseph, solicitor, Church st.
Mitchell, Miss Sarah, Main street
Montgomery, John, J.P., D.L., Benvarden
Moore, William, J.P., Moorefort
Moore, Mrs. Mary, Main street
Moore, Hugh, Larchfield
Moore, William, M.B.
Moore, Quintin, M.D.
M'Afee, John, Agivey
M'Fadden, Rev. Joseph, Charles st.
O'Hara, Charles, J.P., O'Hara brook
Park, Rev. Robert, Charlotte street
Phillott, Rev. James Russell, Glebe
Rentoul, Rev. James, Landhead
Stavely, Rev. William John, Ballyboyland
Stirling, Captain, Moneycarrie
Thomson, Adam, M.D., Main street
Thomson, James, Charlotte street
Usher, Rev. James, Main street
Walker, Roger, Linenhall street

TRADERS, ETC.

Adams, Robert, shuttle maker, Linenhall street
Adams, Robert, wheelwright, Linenhall street
Adair, Thomas, earthenware dealer, Church street
Anderson, John, baker, High street
Aikin, Margaret, straw bonnet maker, Main street
Barr, William, tailor, Linenhall st.
Barr, Gabriel, grocer, Main street
Boyd, Hugh, wine and spirit merchant, Main street
Boyd, Hugh, grocer, Main street
Caldwell, Sarah, straw bonnet maker, Church street
Caldwell, Sarah, dress maker, Church street
Caldwell, Alexander, boot and shoemaker, Church street
Cameron, Archd., carpenter, Church street
Casey, John, butcher, Charles street
Cameron, Daniel, earthenware dealer, Church street
Cameron, Daniel, grocer, Church st.
Cameron, James, painter and glazier, Cameron place
Cameron, James, linen yarn merchant, Cameron's place
Campbell, Jane, baker, High street
Canning, James, baker, Main street
Cowan and Reid, yarn spinners, Liscolman
Clarke, John, woollendraper and haberdasher, Main street
Canning, James, grocer, Main street
Cochran, Wm., haberdasher, High st.
Coffey, William, grocer, Main street
Coffey, William, wine and spirit merchant, Main street
Cochran, David, publican, Main street
Cramsie, Edward, boot and shoemaker, Charlotte street
Cramsie, Isabella, spirit dealer, Main street

BALLYMONEY.

Crozier, William, spirit dealer, Charles street
Culbert, Robert, baker, High street
Doherty, John, and Co., flax, grain and provision merchants, High st.
Dillon, Patrick, publican, Main street
Farrell, Samuel, publican, Main st.
Galloway, James, woollendraper and haberdasher, Main street
Gamble, Alexander, painter, &c., Townhead street
Gardner, Jn., clothes broker, Main st.
Gault, Henry, emigration agent, High street
Getty, William, watch and clock maker, Main street
Givin, James, publican, Church street
Gray, John, publican, Linenhall st.
Gray, John, cooper, Linenhall street
Gilmour, Brice, publican, Church st.
Gilmour, Brice, grocer, Church street
Gordon, Jas., watch and clock maker, Main street
Griffith, John, leather seller, Main st.
Griffith, John, bookseller, Main st.
Haltridge, Jane, grocer, Main street
Hamil, Charles, boot and shoemaker, Charlotte street
Hamil, Joseph, boot and shoemaker, Linenhall street
Hamil, Stewart, boot and shoemaker, Charlotte street
Hamilton, M'Curdy, woollendraper and haberdasher, Church street
Hamilton, Richard, ironmonger and hardware merchant, Church street
Hamilton, Richard, bookseller, &c., Church street
Hopkins, William, linen yarn merchant, Main street
Henry, Alexander, publican, Main st.
Jordan, Robert, carpenter, Main st.
Kennedy, Michael, blacksmith, Rawdon-foot
Kelly, Hugh, saddler and harness maker, Church street
Knox, William, publican, Linenhall street
Lilley, James, publican, Cameron place
Lilley, James, grocer, Cameron place
Lithgow, James W., bookseller, &c., High street
Loughry, John, tailor, Main street
Macdonald, Ann, straw bonnet maker, Main street

Matthews, William, leather seller, Church street
Meekan, John, rope and twine maker, Castle street
Moody, John, blacksmith, Castle st.
Moore, William, miller, Glenstall
Moore, Archibald and Hugh, soap and candle manufacturers, tanners and curriers, Main street
Moore, Archibald and Hugh, tobacco manufacturers and grocers, Main st.
Moore, William, distiller, Bann Distillery
Mulholland, Joseph, grocer, Castle st.
M'Afee, William, publican, Church st.
M'Afee, Samuel, tailor, Church street
M'Caughern, John, painter and glazier, Castle street
M'Cook, Daniel, publican, Church st.
M'Caw, James, wheelwright, Townhead street
M'Dowell, David, carpenter, Townhead street
M'Intyre, William, architect, Charlotte street
M'Intyre, Miss, teacher, Charlotte st.
M'Keown, Francis, publican, Main st.
M'Kenna, John, butcher, Charles st.
M'Keag, Benjamin, saddle and harness maker, Main street
M'Master, Alexander, tailor, Charlotte street
M'Millan, John, grocer and hardware merchant, Linenhall street
Neill, Hannah, Antrim Arms hotel and posting establishment, High st.
M'Naul, Robt., apothecary & surgeon
Nickle, Bernard, blacksmith, Meetinghouse street
Nickel, George, boot and shoemaker, Castle street
Orr, William, & Co., linen and woollendrapers and haberdashers, High st.
O'Bryan, James, brewer, Main street
O'Bryan, James, baker, Main street
O'Brian, James, wine and spirit merchant, Main street
O'Kane, Daniel, cabinet maker, Church street
Perry, Samuel, & Son, vitriol, bleaching liquid, soda ash, and bleaching powder manufacturers, Charles st.
Pollock, James, grocer, High street
Pollock, James, ironmonger and hardware merchant, High street

Read, Patrick, cooper, Main street
Read, Matilda, dressmaker, Main st.
Reid, David, Queen's Arms hotel and posting establishment, Church street
Reany, Archibald, publican, High st.
Robinson, Charles, blacksmith, Linenhall street
Ross, Margaret, linen and woollendraper and haberdasher, Church st.
Rowan, Robert, wine and spirit merchant, Main street
Scott, Hugh, grocer, High street
Scullion, Henry, spirit dealer, Linenhall street
Sloan, Richard, wheelwright, Coldale
Spier, Mrs., dressmaker, Main street
Stavely, Robert, and Co., linen and woollendrapers and haberdashers, Church street
Steele, Eliza, & Co., linen and woollendrapers and haberdashers, Main st.
Stuart, Hugh, pawnbroker, Main st.
Snodgrass, Robert, grocer and clothes dealer, Main street
Telford, Sarah A., earthenware dealer and haberdasher, Church street
Thomson, James, yarn spinner, Balnamore
Thomson, Adam, leather seller, Church street
Thomson, James, miller, Balnamore
Thomson, James R., apothecary and surgeon, Church street
Torrens, Wm., leather seller, Main st.
Wallace, James, grocer, Charlotte st.
Warnock, Wm., tailor, Charlotte st.
Warwick, John, grocer, Meetinghouse street
Wilson, David, tanner and currier, Charlotte street
Williamson, William, cooper, Townhead street
Young, Mary, earthenware dealer, Charlotte street
Young, William, blacksmith, Charlotte street
Young, Wm., carpenter, Charlotte st.
Young, James, grocer, Main street

BALLYNAHINCH.

A SMALL market town in the county of Down, 13 miles from Belfast. The manor on which the town stands was granted by Charles II. to Sir George Rawdon, the ancestor of the present Marquis of Hastings, and it continued in the possession of the family of Moira, until the year 1810, when it became the property of David Ker, Esq. Montalto House, adjoining the town, was formerly the chief seat of the Earls of Moira, and has lately been rebuilt in the most costly style by the present owner, D. S. Ker, Esq., D.L., J.P. It was at Ballynahinch that the insurgents, in 1798, met with a complete overthrow, by the troops under General Nugent, when the former sustained a loss of one hundred-and-fifty men, and the Royal troops forty. The Spa is about two miles S.W. of the town, and the wells have been put in the best order by the proprietor. A very commodious news-room has also been erected by Mr. Ker. The places of worship are a very neat church, a Roman Catholic chapel of similar character, and one each for Presbyterians, Unitarians, and Seceders. The market-house is a very commodious one; the market is held on Thursday. Fairs, the first Thursday in January, February 12th, March 6th, May 12th, July 10th, and the first Thursdays in August and November (old style).

Post-office, Market square—Rebecca Smith, postmistress. Letters from Belfast, Dublin, and various places, arrive every morning at seven, and are despatched every evening at half-past five. Letters from Comber and Saintfield arrive every afternoon at half-past five, and are despatched every morning at seven

Conveyances—To Belfast, at 7 a.m.; Castlewellan, 7 p.m.; Dromore, 7 p.m.; Saintfield & Comber, 4½ a.m.
Market-House—Market square
Police Station—William Stafford, sub-inspector
Established Church, Main Road—Rev. Charles Boyd, vicar
Presbyterian Church—Rev. D. Edgar

Presbyterian Church—Rev. J. Shaw
Presbyterian Church—Rev. J. Davis
Roman Catholic Chapel, Main Street—Rev. Daniel Sharkey, P.P.
National School—Mr. Shaw's Meeting house
National School—Mr. Edgar's Meeting house, John Holmes, teacher
Dispensary, Main Street—William White, M.D., surgeon

GENTRY, CLERGY, ETC.

Boyd, Rev. Charles, Magheradrool
Crozier, Rev. William, Main street
Edgar, Rev. David, Ballyene
Ker, David, D.L., J.P., Montalto House
M'Cully, William, Drumna hall
Ryans, Rev. Thomas, Main street
Sharkey, Rev. Daniel, Main street
Shaw, Rev. John, Main street

TRADERS, ETC.

Bain, William, publican, Main street
Black, Henry, woollendraper and haberdasher, Market square
Black, Samuel, publican, Dromore st.
Baillie, John, linen and woollendraper, and haberdasher, Main street
Baillie, Robert, grocer and spirit dealer, Market square
Baillie, John, grocer, Market square
Baillie, Sarah, grocer, Market square
Barr, Robert, grocer, Market square
Bell, Ephraim, publican, Market sq.
Black, Samuel, grocer, Dromore st.
Brown, Edward, grocer, Market sq.
Brown, Alexander, baker, grocer, &c., Dromore street
Campbell, Hugh, butter merchant and grocer, Market square
Carlins, James, grocer and haberdasher, Main street
Cleland, Moses, woollendraper, haberdasher, and spirit dealer, Dromore street
Croskerry, Johnston, grocer and spirit dealer, Main street
Darvey, Alexander, blacksmith, Meeting-house street
Graham, John, chandler, Market sq.
Hanna, John, reed maker and linen manufacturer, Main street
Johnston, John, publican, Main street
Kenmaire, William, watch and clock maker, Main street
Logan, Michael, blacksmith, Main st.
M'Alinden, Patrick, publican, Main st.
M'Calla, James, grocer, Market square
Magill, Wm., leather cutter, Market square
M'Calla, James, publican, Market sq.
M'Creevy, John, grocer, Dromore st.
M'Comb, Catherine, publican, Market square
M'Creevy, James, grocer, Main street
M'Kee, Alex., grocer, Main street
M'Kee, Wm., publican, Dromore street
M'Ilvenna, Patrick, grocer, Market sq.
M'Calla, Margt., haberdasher, Main st.
M'Cauley, saddler, Market square
M'Clelland, Ann and Margaret, haberdashers, Main street
Maguire, Thomas, painter, Main st.
Mulveny, Patrick, publican, Main st.
O'Neill, John, publican, Main street
Rankin, John, earthenware and hardware dealer, grocer, spirit and butter merchant, Main street
Robinson, Robert, leather seller and grocer, Main street
Robinson, James, grocer and butter merchant, Main street
Scott, James, watch and clock maker, Main street
Scott, Jane, haberdasher, Main street
Scott, Sarah, bonnet maker, Main st.
Stewart, Maria, linen & woollendraper, and haberdasher, Main street
Wilson, Wm., grocer, Main street
Wilson, Hugh, grocer and publican, Market square

BANBRIDGE.

A FLOURISHING market town, in the county of Down, twenty miles S.S.W. from Belfast, lying on the mail road from Belfast to Dublin, and on the left bank of the Bann, from which river, and the bridge (at the foot of the town) by which it is crossed, the name of the place originated. The principal street, which commences at the bridge, is straight and spacious, and forms part of the great thoroughfare between Belfast and Dublin. There is a considerable weekly market for linen, and one for flax; in addition to which the proximity of the town to the river is very advantageous to the numerous surrounding bleach-works. The general aspect of the town is neat. The market-house, erected at the cost of the Marquis of Downshire, is a handsome building. The spacious apartments over it are occupied as news and reading rooms, and afford also accommodation to the magistrates, who assemble here in Petty Sessions every alternate Thursday. The Parish Church, situated in Church Street, close to the Bann, is a chaste and elegant structure, in the Elizabethian or Tudor style—cruciform, with a tower surmounted by a spire. The other places of worship are Presbyterian and Unitarian Churches, and a neat Roman Catholic Chapel. The town is now lighted with gas. The market days are Monday, Tuesday, and Thursday—the first named being the most important one. Fairs, January 12th (a large one for horses), June 9th, and August 26th. There is also a fair (or large market) held on the first Monday in every month.

Post-Office, Newry Street—Margaret Mitchell, postmistress

Conveyances—To Dublin, the Royal mail (car) every morning at 9 o'clock, and Royal mail (coach) every night at half-past 11 o'clock; to Belfast, every morning at 2 o'clock, and every evening at 4 o'clock; to Lurgan, a car every morning at half-past 8 o'clock; to Newry, a car every morning at 9 and every evening at half-past 7 o'clock

Constabulary station, Church street—B. Plummer, sub-inspector

Provincial Bank, Bridge street—R. M'Tier, manager

Ulster Bank, Bridge street—R. P. M'Kee, manager

Corn Market and Sessions House, Bridge street

Dispensary, Rathfriland street—Geo. Tyrrell, M.D., medical officer

Union Workhouse—Thos. Sherridan, master; Mrs. Sherridan, matron

Registrar of Marriages—John Scott, Bridge street

Seapatrick Established Church, Church street—Rev. D. Dickenson, rector; Rev. Mr. Metge, curate

Presbyterian Church, Scarva street—Rev. R. Anderson, minister

Unitarian Church, Bridge street—Rev. John Montgomery, minister

Unitarian Church, Dromore street—Rev. D. Gordon, minister

Wesleyan Chapel, Rathfriland street—ministers various

Primitive Wesleyan Chapel, Scarva st.—ministers various

Baptist Chapel, Newry street—Rev. Mr. Bean, minister

R. C. Chapel, Dromore street—Rev. J. Mooney, P.P.

National School, Church st.—A. Glass, master; E. Glass, mistress

Church Education Society's School, Church street

English & Classical Academy, Library street—Andrew Mullen, principal

English & Classical Academy, Church st.—Rev. John Ashwood, principal

Ladies' Boarding School, Dromore st.—Misses Godfrey

GENTRY, CLERGY, ETC.

Anderson, Rev. Robert, Church street
Bean, Rev. Mr., Rathfriland street
Bowen, George, solicitor, Newry street
Brownlow, Nathaniel, physician and surgeon, Rathfriland street
Crawford, Thos., Ballyvally, Banbridge
Chain, Robert, surgeon, Bridge street

BANBRIDGE.

Crozier, Thomas, solicitor, Dromore st.
Dickenson, Rev. Daniel, Glebe house
Evans, Wm., Ballyvalley, Banbridge
Frazer, S. L., solicitor, Newry street
Gordon, Rev. David, Newry street
Hawthorne, Wm., surgeon, Newry st.
Law, George Wm., solicitor, Newry st.
Leonard, D., solicitor, Dromore street
Malcolmson, R., surgeon, Newry street
Metge, Rev. Wm., Rathfriland street
Montgomery, Rev. John, Dromore st.
Mooney, Rev. John, Dromore street
M'Clelland, Thos., solicitor, Bridge st.
M'Clelland, Robert, physician and surgeon, Newry street
Plummer, B., Church street, Banbridge
Rutherford, Rev. John, Ballyvalley
Smyth, G. K. & F., solicitors, Bridge street
Tyrrell, George, M.D., coroner, Dromore street
Tyrrell, George G., solicitor, Bridge st.
Welsh, John, Chinaully, Banbridge

TRADERS, ETC.

Ardery, Margaret, milliner and dressmaker, Bridge street
Anderson, M., confectioner, Bridge st.
Ardery, James, publican, Church st.
Bambrich, Wm. and John, saddlers, Newry street
Baxter, Nathaniel, tinsmith and plumber, Rathfriland street
Beck, Alexander, spirit dealer, Rathfriland street
Bell, James, publican, Bridge street
Bell, Robert, grocer and publican, Newry street
Bittle, Wm., grocer and baker, Dromore street
Bell, Robinson, and Co., linen merchants, Ballydown
Brown, Ann, dressmaker, Dromore st.
Carson, James, and Co., linen manufacturers, Church street
Crothers, A., haberdasher, Bridge st.
Crothers, Archibald, cabinet maker
Chapman, George, cabinet maker, Dromore street
Clibbon, Hill, and Co., flour millers and linen merchants, Bridge street
Cathcart, Robert, woollendraper, Bridge street
Crawford and Lindsays, linen merchants, Ballydown
Coyle, Jas., coach maker, Newry st.
Craig, Stewart, weighmaster, Church street
Card, James, coach maker, &c., Dromore street
Card, James, grocer and timber merchant, Newry street
Darragh, John, shuttle maker, Scarva street
Dickson, John, grocer, &c., Newry st.
Dickson, J. and W., haberdashers, Bridge street
Davidson, Joseph, spirit dealer, Rathfriland street
Eward, William, spirit dealer, Dromore street
Ervine, Thomas, woollendraper, Bridge street
Finlay, John, baker and grocer, Bridge street
Finlay, William, baker and grocer, Bridge street
Finlay, James, baker and grocer, Newry street
Ferguson, Thomas, linen manufacturer, Bridge street
Gray, John, ropemaker, Scarva street
Gordon, James, spirit dealer, Dromore street
Glass, Samuel, publican, Dromore st.
Gracey, William, spirit dealer, Dromore street
Geoaghan, James, spirit dealer and butcher, Dromore street
Halliday, Jacob, grocer and hardware merchant, Bridge street
Hamilton, Robert, grocer, Newry st.
Hughes, Patrick, blacksmith, Newry st.
Hutchinson, Jas., ironmonger, Bridge street
Hutchinson, Thomas, haberdasher, Bridge street
Hayes, Frederick, linen manufacturer and flax spinner, Seapatrick
Hayes, Wm., and Son, linen merchants, Millmount
Harriss, Russell, spirit dealer, Rathfriland street
Hargraves, David, spirit dealer, Dromore street
Hamilton, James, baker, Bridge street
Kerr, Jonathan, publican, Dromore st.
Kinley, Samuel, butcher, Bridge street
Kinley, John, butcher, Bridge street
Leckey, Mary, spirit dealer, Bridge st.

BANBRIDGE.

Leetch, William, Downshire Arms hotel, Newry street
Linn, George, provision merchant, Newry street
Love, John, grocer and haberdasher, Bridge street
Love, Robert, grocer, Bridge street
Lindsay, Samuel, tailor, Dromore st.
Mercer, Robert, butcher, Bridge st.
Moore, David, grocer, Rathfriland st.
Moore, Hamilton, grocer and baker, Newry street
Main, John, woollendraper, Newry st.
Magaw, Hugh, woollendraper, Newry street
Main, Alex., haberdasher, Bridge st.
Morton, Joseph, and Son, provision merchants, Newry street
Morton, George, grocer and publican, Bridge street
Matchet, Jonathan, grocer and spirit dealer, Scarva street
Megarry, Sarah, haberdasher, Rathfriland street
Mulligan, E., haberdasher, Bridge st.
Morton, Joseph, spirit dealer, Rathfriland street
Macklen, Mary, haberdasher, Bridge street
Morrow, John, farming implement maker and grocer
M'Clelland, Andrew, and Sons, linen merchants, Bellmount
M'Caw, John, tailor, Newry street
M'Clelland, James, & Co., linen merchants, Banville
M'Combish, Mr., painter and glazier, Newry street
M'Cormick, John, clerk of Petty Sessions, Church street
M'Cullough, John, pawnbroker, Newry street
M'Dowell, Robert, grocer, Bridge st.
M'Guinness, N., chandler, Bridge st.
M'Grath, Henry, boot and shoemaker, Bridge street
M'Mahon, Patk., chandler, Bridge st.
M'Mullen, Hugh, coach builder, &c., Dromore street
M'Teer, Robert, haberdasher, Bridge street
M'Tier, Robert, nailer, Dromore st.
M'Williams, M., haberdasher, Bridge st.
M'Williams, William, pawnbroker, Scarva street
M'Williams, Mr., Victoria hotel, Newry street
O'Flagherty, F., grocery and seed house, Newry street
O'Callaghan, John, spirit dealer, Newry street
O'Neil, James, saddler, Bridge street
Prenter, John, saddler, Scarva street
Preston, Thomas, tailor, Church st.
Powers, Thomas, tailor, Newry street
Robinson, George, spirit dealer, Newry street
Robinson, William, linen manufacturer, Rock view
Russell, Samuel, spirit dealer, Rathfriland street
Rodgers, David, painter and glazier, Newry street
Reilly, W. H., printer, Newry street
Scott, John, woollendraper, Bridge st.
Strong, Robt., and Co., haberdashers, Bridge street
Shekelton, J., publican, Bridge street
Shekelton, Thomas, spirit dealer and grocer, Bridge street
Sterling, Robt., cabinet maker, Newry street
Scott, S., dressmaker, Dromore street
Sheeren, Joseph, civil bill officer, Newry street
Stevenson, Hugh, Albert hotel, Newry street
Smyth, Joseph, boot and shoemaker, Newry street
Smart, Samuel, haberdasher, Bridge st.
Sprott, Hans, publican, Bridge street
Templeton, Robt., baker and grocer, Bridge street
Templeton, Wm., baker and grocer, Bridge street
Thompson, James, grocer, Newry st.
Urey, Robert, grocer & leather dealer, Rathfriland street
Wallace, J., publican, Rathfriland st.
Waugh, Wm., linen merchant, Dromore street
Woods, John, woollendraper, Newry street
Woods, Samuel, woollendraper, Newry street
Woods, John, grocer, Newry street
Woods, Moses, grocer, Scarva street
Willas, Jas., blacksmith, Scarva st.
Willas, George, spirit dealer, Newry st.
White, John, publican, Scarva street

BALLYCLARE.

BALLYCLARE is a flourishing little market town, in the County of Antrim, 10 miles from Belfast. Near the town, which is neatly built, are the the extensive bleach works of Messrs. Bell and Co., and Messrs. Archer and Sons' paper mill; and linen is manufactured by other establishments in the vicinity. A Manor court is held every third week by the Seneschal, for the recovery of debts under £20.

The places of worship are the Established Church at Ballyeaston, and Presbyterian, Unitarian, Methodist, and Roman Catholic Chapels. Within the parishes of Ballynure and Doagh-Grange are schools for the gratuitous education of the poor. The markets, which are chiefly for cattle, are held on the third Wednesday monthly; and the fairs in the months of January, May, July, and November—the May fair is one of the largest in the province of Ulster.

Post-office—James Cunningham, postmaster.— Letters from all parts arrive from Belfast every morning at nine, and are despatched every afternoon at half-past three p.m.

Conveyances—Cars from Samuel Milliken's, Ballyclare, to meet the various trains to and from Belfast and Ballymena Railway at the Ballypallady station, daily, and to Belfast, every Wednesday and Friday

Established Church, Ballyeaston—Rev. William Campbell
Established Church, Ballynure—Rev. Francis H. Allen
Presbyterian Church, 1st Ballyeaston—Rev. Wm. James Raphael
Presbyterian Church, 2nd Ballyeaston—Rev. Alexander Pollock
Presbyterian Church, Ballynure—Rev. S. A. Hamilton
Presbyterian Church, Kilbride—Rev. William Orr
Presbyterian Church, Ballybinney—Rev. Isaac Adams
Unitarian Church—Rev. John Hall
Covenanters' Church—Rev. W. Russell
Wesleyan Chapel—Rev. Hugh Moore
Methodist (new connection) Chapel—Rev. William Sorsby
R. C. Chapel—Ministers, various

GENTRY, CLERGY, ETC.

Agnew, Robert S.
Allen, John G., high constable, Collin
Archer, Samuel, Milltown
Allen, Rev. Francis H., Ballynure
Adams, Rev. Isaac, Ballylinney
Alexander, James, Sizehill
Alexander, James R., Le Ballyclare
Bain, Rev. James, Straid
Campbell, Rev. William, Doagh
Cunningham, James, surgeon
Ferguson, Mrs. Rachael, Tildarg
Ferguson, William John, Tildarg
Gamble, James, Ballynure
Gardner, Mrs. Robert, Bruslee
Gillis, The Misses, Craigs
Hall, Rev. John
Hill, Mr. Edward
Hamilton, Rev. S. A., Ballynure
Kirkpatrick, John J., Henryfield
Langtry, Charles, Drumadarragh
Ledlie, George, Cogry
Magill, John, solicitor
Moore, Rev. Hugh M.
Montgomery, Rev. John, Glenwherry
M'Keown, David, surgeon
Nelson, Rev. Joseph, Springvale
Owens, John, J.P., Holestone
Orr, Rev. William, Kilbride
Park, Alexander, Ballynure
Peden, James, surgeon
Pollock, Rev. Alexander, Ballyeaston
Raphael, Rev. Wm. Jas., Ballyeaston
Russell, Rev. William
Smyth, John, J.P., Whitepark
Simpson, William
Sorsby, Rev. William
Stevenson, Hans, Cogry
Wilson, Hugh G., Rashee
Wilson, John, Rashee
Wilson, John, Cogry
Woodside, Alexander, surgeon

TRADERS, ETC.

Archer and Sons, paper manufacturers
Bayne, George, baker

BALLYCLARE.

Bayne, George, publican
Beatty, R., woollendraper, Ballynure
Beck, Henderson, baker
Beck, Henderson, publican
Boyd, David, publican, Ballynure
Boyd, James, publican, Straid
Baird, John, publican
Bell, John and George L., bleachers
Bragg, Henry, and Sons, bleachers, Doagh
Cannon, John
Corry, Samuel, bookbinder
Dempsey, James
Dickey, John, publican
Eagleson, John, woollendraper
Ewing, Robert, blacksmith
Forsythe, Samuel, publican, Ballynure
Forsyth, Andrew, publican
Galt, Alexander, woollendraper, Doagh
Gordon, Robert T., woollendraper
Gamble, James, cotton spinner, Ballynure
Hamilton, Robert, publican
Houston, Wm. John G., publican
Hill, David, publican, Ballynure
Hill, John, publican, Ballynure
Hill, Edward, commissioner for taking affidavits for the superior courts of common law
Kerr, William, Ballynure
Kirk, Sarah, Ballynure
Kennedy, David, publican
Knox, Samuel, publican
Lawson, William, woollendraper
Lindsay, Joseph
Lamb, Samuel, constable of police
Lyle and Stevenson, flax spinners, Brookfield
Magee, Francis, painter and glazier
Millar, David, publican
Murdoch, Eliza, stamp distributor
Milliken, Samuel, jaunting car proprietor
Moon, William, flax spinner, Cogry
M'Crea, Samuel, civil bill officer
M'Cullough, Adam, saddler
M'Cullough, William, builder
M'Cune, David John, teacher of national school
M'Kinstry, Thomas, Ballynure
M'Muckin, William, leather seller
M'Cune, William, publican
M'Clelland, David, publican, Doagh
Nesbitt, James
Park, William, miller, Ballynure
Percy, Thomas, publican and cooper
Stewart, James, publican
Smyth, John, bleacher, Whitepark
Stewart, William, sewed muslin agent
Stevenson, James, flax spinner, Doagh
Wasson, Jane, teacher of female national school
Whiteside, John, publican, Doagh
Valentine, James
Walmsley, James

BANGOR.

A SMALL sea-port town in the County of Down, 10 miles distant from Belfast. The terminus of the County Down Railway at Newtownards is within 3 miles of Bangor. The town is very ancient. It is stated that Saint Comgall founded an Abbey about the middle of the sixth century, which was burned in 674, and rebuilt in 1125, by Malachy O'Morgair, then abbott; he also added an oratory or chapel, of white stone, from which the place derived the name of *Beauchoir*, now Bangor, signifying the "White Church," or "Fair Choir." Part of the abbey ruins still exist, and the traces of the foundations show it to have been of great extent. The town has greatly improved within the last few years; the harbour is good and commodious—there is a neat and useful pier and fine beach, well adapted for bathing. Near the beach are many neat furnished houses and villas, built for the accommodation of parties visiting this favourite bathing shore during the summer season. The principal hotel—Mr. Henry M'Fall's—is in a most agreeable position, exactly facing the sea, and commanding a beautiful view of the Lough, and of the county Antrim on the other side. These conveniences and attractions, together with hot and cold baths, render this one of the most agreeable localities for the summer season. The vicinity is enriched with several elegant seats. R. E. Ward, Esq., part proprietor of the town, has just finished his splendid new castle, in the Elizabethian style of architecture, costing upwards of £20,000. It is a superb building, and well worth notice. The old castle, built sometime in the year 1600, is still standing, but is to be pulled down when Mr. Ward removes into the new one. The castle is surrounded by an extensive demesne, tastefully planted, and is contiguous to the town. Crawfordsburn is the residence of Sharman Crawford, Esq., M.P.; and the splendid seat of Lord Dufferin is within two miles of the town. Two cotton mills are constantly at work, and the sewed muslin business is carried on to a very great extent, giving employment to thousands of females through the country and town. Bangor was incorporated by charter of James I., and previous to the union, the corporation returned two members to the Irish Parliament, since which period the borough has ceased to be represented. A court of Petty Sessions is held by the magistrates of the county occasionally, a court-leet annually, by the seneschal, for appointing constables to the several townlands of the manor, and a local court, before the same official, every third Thursday. The church is a beautiful edifice, with a lofty spire; there are two Presbyterian churches, one of which is very handsome. The Wesleyan Methodists have one place of worship. A parochial school, an infant school, and a dispensary are the established charities. Fairs—January 12, May 12, and November 22.

Post Office, Postmaster, William Pritchard—Letters from Dublin, Belfast, Scotland, and North of England, arrive every morning at nine o'clock, and are despatched at 20 minutes to five. The mail car starts from Mr. M'Fall's hotel, at half-past four o'clock daily

Cars—To Belfast every morning (Sunday excepted), at eight o'clock, from M'Wha's, Main street; Whannell's, Kinnegar; Drennan's, Ballymagee street; Neill's, Fisher hill. To Newtownards Railway, from Keenan's, Main street, at 9 o'clock morning and 1 o'clock afternoon

Market House, Petty Sessions, and Manor Court, Main street—Seneschal of Manor Court, Thomas Stott M'Cullough

Coast Guard—Chief officer, William Burt, R.N., the Parade

Constabulary Station, Main street—Sub-Inspector, John Kelly

Dispensary—Under Medical Charities Act, Catherine place, Philip Crampton Russell, surgeon; Committee of management meet at the Dispensary, on the first and third Monday of the month. Chairman of committee, Robert E. Ward, D.L., J.P.; vice-chairman, John Sharman Crawford, J.P.; honorary secretary, R. Percival Maxwell, J.P.; honorary assistant secretary, H. M'Fall

Established Church—Rector, Rev. Richard Binney; curate, Rev. J. C. Devylyn

First Presbyterian Church—Rev. H. Woods

Second Presbyterian Church—Rev. William Patterson

Methodist Chapel—Rev. W. Argue

Roman Catholic Chapel

NOBILITY, GENTRY, ETC.

Bell, Robert J., Ballywooley
Brownrigg, Thomas, Castle street
Burt, William, R.N., the Parade
Cleland, James D. Rose, Rathgael House
Crawford, William Sharman, M.P., Crawfordsburn
Dufferin, Dowager Lady, Glenghand
Dufferin, Lord, Clandeboye
Dunlop, Mrs., Ballymagee street
Fulton, Colonel K. H., Catherine place
Hart, Miss, Currazon House
Jackson, Captain, Catherine place
Kelly, John S. J.
Kennedy, James, Ballysallagh
Maxwell, R. Percival, J.P., Groomsport House

Malcolm, Samuel, Sandy row
Moore, W. H., Ballyvernon
M'Culloch, Thomas Stott, Rathgael
Nicholson, R. Steele, J.P., Ballow
Pirrie, Wm., Conlig House
Sinclair, Richard, Sandy row
Ward, Robert, Edward, D.L., J.P., Castle

CLERGY AND PROFESSIONAL.

Argue, Rev. James, Catherine place
Binney, Rev. Richard, rector and J.P., Parsonage
Develyn, Rev. J. C., curate, Sandy row
M'Cartney, James, surgeon, Main st.
Patterson, Rev. W., Sandy row
Ritchey, Wm., surgeon, Main street
Russell, Philip Crampton, M.D., Dispensary surgeon, Main street ;
Sheil, Robert G., surgeon, Main street
Wilson, John, surgeon, R.S.D.M., Main street
Woods, Wm., surgeon, Main street
Woods, Rev. Hugh, Woodville

TRADERS, ETC.

Agnew, John, carpenter, Main street
Andrews, Robert, sewed muslin agent, Catherine place
Barr, David, publican, Ballymagee st.
Barr, John, saddler, Main street
Bowman, John, butcher, Main street
Bowman, Robert, butcher, Market-house square
Brown, J. and R., and Co., woollen-drapers and grocers, Ballymagee st.
Brown, J. & R., & Co., sewed muslin manufacturers, M'William street
Brown, Alexander, chandler, Castle st.
Brown, Jane, grocer, Ballymagee st.
Buchanan, John, town sergeant, Main street
Campbell, Hugh, grocer, Main street
Campbell, Mr., watchmaker, Main st.
Campbell, James, tailor, Main street
Campbell, Hugh, carpenter, Main st.
Campbell, Jas., carpenter, Fisher hill
Cochran, James, cotton spinner
Crosby, Miss, dressmaker, Sandy row
Davidson, John, grocer and leather cutter, Main street
Davis, John, manager of new mill
Diamond, Miss, infant school, Main st.
Dines, Wm., publican, Quay street
Edgar, Robert, baker, Main street
Fee, Mrs., Lodge school, Lodge house
Feay, Arthur, grocer and spirit dealer, Church quarter
Finlay, Miss, grocer, Main street
Fitzpatrick, D., blacksmith, Church quarter
Furry, Hugh, grocer and spirit dealer, Main street
Ferguson, H., car owner, Main street
Francis and Russell, grocers, &c., Ballymagee street
Gibson, James, butcher, Quay street
Gibson, Alexander, butcher, Main st.
Graham, Mrs., grocer & baker, Main street
Gray, Mr., teacher, Market house
Gray, Jas., painter & glazier, Sandy row
Halliday, Mary, publican, Castle street
Hayes, Samuel, grocer, Main street
Heany, Mrs., confectioner, Main st.
Hill, Robert, shoemaker, Quay street
Hughes, John, publican, Quay street
Hughes, R., grocer, Ballymagee street
Iyen, Mrs., dressmaker, Main street
Jamieson, Alex., painter and glazier, Main street
Jamieson, John, painter and glazier, Castle street
Johnston, Alex., grocer, Church street
Johnston, John, saddler, Quay street
Kelly, James, sewed muslin agent, Sandy row
Kelly, James, grocer, Sandy row
Kennedy, Arch., carpenter, Fisher hill
Kennedy, James, harbour master
Lamont, Alex., sewed muslin agent, Main street
Leonard, Miss, dressmaker, Main st.
Lowry, Jas., corn and flax merchant, Ballymaconnell
Manderson, James, grocer, Fisher hill
Manson, Hugh, grocer and publican, Quay street
Martin, Henry, grocer, Main street
Martin, Mrs., grocer, Sandy row
Martin, Mrs., dressmaker, Fisher hill
Mathews, John, grocer and publican, Main street
Miller, A., pawnbroker, Sooter's row
Miller, Alex., carpenter, Main street
Mone, G. L., teacher, Church quarter
Montgomery, Henry, merchant tailor, Main street
Morgan, Robert, grocer, Sandy row
Muir, Miss, drawing school, Main st.

Murray, James, publican, Church st.
M'Briar, Robert, grocer, Castle street
M'Cune, William, grocer, Church st.
M'Cune, Mrs., bakery, Ballymagee st.
M'Fall, Henry, Royal hotel and livery stables, The Parade
M'Feeley, Mrs., green grocer, Main st.
M'Gilvery, Miss, national school, Church quarter
M'Gowan, Hans, publican, Ballymagee street
M'Kane, William, sewed muslin agent, Catherine place
M'Kane, Alex., sewed muslin agent, Main street
M'Kee, Mrs., bonnet maker, Front st.
M'Kee, William, sewed muslin agent, Croft place
M'Kee, William, grocer, Church quarter
M'Kee, John, ship owner and coal merchant
M'Kee, James, tailor, Sandy row
M'Kee, James, tailor, Main street
M'Kerrall, James, grocer and publican, Main street
M'Master, James, academy, Main st.
M'Math, Miss, dressmaker, Fisher hill
M'Murray, Samuel, corn miller
M'Murray, Robert, hardware shop, Main street
M'Nab, John, manager of Old Mill
M'Wha, William, car owner, Main st.
Neill, Robert, ship owner and coal merchant, Sandy row
Neill, Robert, boot and shoemaker, Main street
Neill, Mrs., boot and shoe shop, Church street
Neill, Robert, lime burner, Lime kilns
Neill, John, car owner, Fisher hill
Neill, Robert, carpenter, Sandy row
Oliver, James, grocer, Church quarter
O'Mealy, Michael, grocer, Main st.
Petticrew, John, publican, Quay st.
Pritchard, William, postmaster, clerk of Petty Sessions, and house agent
Reid, Alexander O., haberdasher, Main street
Rippett, Captain, carpenter, Fisher hill
Ritchie, Allan, muslin manufacturer, Castle street
Ritchie, F., currier, Ballymagee street
Ritchie, Henry, grocer, Ballymagee st.
Russell, Robert, woollendraper and grocer, Main street
Russell, James, grocer and spirit dealer, Main street
Russell, John, publican, Sandy row
Seay, Arthur, ship owner and lime burner, Church quarter
Small, Hugh, bog oak carver, Ballymagee street
Smith, Bryce, publican, Church street
Stevenson, James, blacksmith, Main street
Wallace and M'Nab, cotton spinners
Whannell, Thos., car owner, Kinnegar
White, John N., and Son, Ballyhome Flour Mills

BLACKWATERTOWN.

A POST-TOWN in the parish of Clonfeacle, county Armagh, 39 English miles S.W. from Belfast. It is situated on the Northern bank of the Blackwater, from which stream the town derives its name. The ancient cemetry of Clonfeacle is on the western side of the river. The Ulster Canal lies near it; and sloops of fifty tons burthen can deliver their cargoes at the quay, which gives it local facilities for trade. A Constabulary Station, a Dispensary, and National School, are the only public establishments.

Post-Office—Postmistress, M. A. Magarry. Letters arrive every morning at seven o'clock, and are despatched every afternoon at a quarter past five o'clock
Constabulary Station, Blackwatertown —James Cowan, constable
Dispensary—Dr. T. Martin, surgeon
Clonfeacle Parish Church, Benburb— Rev. Henry Griffin, rector; Rev. W. C. Maunsell, curate; Benjamin Beatty, clerk
Roman Catholic Chapel, Clonfeacle— Rev. Michael Coyne, P.P., Rev. J. Breslan, curate

GENTRY, CLERGY, ETC.

Cross, Richard, Carrickaness
Griffin, Rev. H., D.D., Clonfeacle rectory
Jackson, James Eyre, J.P., Tullydoey
Keating, Rev. John, P.P., Ardress
Martin, Thomas, M.D. and surgeon
Maunsell, Rev. W. C., Benburb
M'Keogh, James, classical academy
M'Keogh, James, national school, Clonfeacle
Olpherts, William, J.P., Dartry Lodge
Wilson, Mrs. Maria

TRADERS, ETC.

Branigan, Denis, shoemaker
Cowan, Mrs. Anna, infant school
Crumy, John, publican
Crothers, Alexander and John, timber and coal merchants
Dailey, William, publican
Dickson, Benjamin, saddler
Dooney, Thomas, carpenter, Clonfeacle
Fox, Hugh, shoemaker
Fullon, Peter, tailor
Hagan, John, carpenter
Malone, John, spirit dealer, Clonfeacle
M'Cann, John, blacksmith
M'Cann, Michael, blacksmith
M'Clean, John, grocer
M'Guigan, John, shoemaker
Queen, John, blacksmith
Thomson, William, draper, Clonfeacle
Watson, John, grocer

CARRICKFERGUS.

CARRICKFERGUS, an ancient market town, and maritime county of a town, and a parliamentary borough, situate on the N. shore of Carrickfergus Bay or Belfast Lough, and enclosed on all other sides by Antrim county, is 8 miles from Belfast. The County of the Town comprises an area of 16,700 acres, of which 12,483 are arable, 4,088 uncultivated, and 129 in the town. The surface is hilly; Lough Mourne, a lake of about 90 acres, is 556 feet above high sea level. In 1851 the population was 8,488. The town was formerly a place of great strength, and is rendered memorable by the landing of King William in 1690, previous to the battle of the Boyne; is divided into two sections—namely, Irish Quarter on the west, and Scotch Quarter on the East. The first-named, obtained its present appellation after the year 1677, when the then lord lieutenant, the Duke of Ormond, issued a proclamation commanding all Roman Catholics resident in cities, corporate towns and forts, to remove beyond the walls. The Scotch Quarter is occupied chiefly by fishermen, and had its name from a Scotch colony, who arrived about the year 1665 from Galloway and Argyleshire, and pursued the same occupation as their descendants do now. The castle, supposed to have been built by Hugh de Lacy, in 1778, is a noble structure, boldly situated on a rock projecting into the sea; the inner yard, containing the barrack and different stores, is large and extensive, the walls are of an immense thickness, and the platform is furnished with a battery of twenty-two long twelve-pounders; the magazine in the main building is bomb proof, and the different apartments upwards are occupied as stores for arms and other implements of war. The view from the top is singularly extensive and beautiful. The liberties of the town and county of the town of Carrickfergus extend four miles in all directions from the castle, distinct from, but locally in, the County of Antrim. The landing pier has been much improved, and vessels of one hundred tons and upwards can now discharge at it. The imports consist of coal, timber, slate, barley, and salt; and the exports of cattle and grain. The parish Church of Saint Nicholas possesses a few monumental memorials, the most remarkable and worthy of notice, being one of the Chichester family. Its public buildings are the Town Hall, Market Place, Parish Church, Dis-

CARRICKFERGUS.

senting and Methodist Meeting-houses, Roman Catholic Chapel, Court-House, and Gaol. The Corporation, which was styled "The Mayor, Sheriffs, Burgesses, and Commonalty of the Town of Carrickfergus," under the provisions of the Municipal Reform Act, was dissolved, and a board of Municipal Commissioners constituted, in whom is vested the corporate property, valued at £330 per annum. The borough returns 1 member to Parliament; constituency, under 13 & 14 Vic., c. 69, in 1851, 720. The borough income, derived chiefly from rents, tolls, and dues, amounted in 1847, to £393 16s. 1½d., of which £46 12s. 11d. was applied to public works, repairs, paving, and cleansing, and £100 14s. 1d. in salaries and allowances to municipal officers. There is a Court of Record for the recovery of debts. The town has some trade and manufactures, and extensive fisheries, the district of which comprises 61 miles of maritime boundaries, and had, in 1850, 433 registered vessels, employing 1,307 men and boys. The oysters taken off the coast are prized for their size and flavour. The Customs' duties, having been purchased up in 1637, and the Custom-house transferred to Belfast, its value as a shipping port has ceased. The Northern Bank has a branch in the town. It is the headquarters of a Coast-Guard station, as also of a Constabulary district, comprising the stations of Carrickfergus, Ballyclare, Larne, and Whitehouse. A branch of the Belfast and Ballymena railway terminates near the town.

Post office—Geo. Erskine, postmaster

Conveyances—The mail car starts from the Junction to Larne, at 35 minutes past 6 am., stopping a few minutes in Carrickfergus, and returns at 23 minutes past 6 p.m., to the Railway at the Carrickfergus Branch Junction. Two omnibuses start daily for Belfast, and also a van

Member for the Borough—The Hon. Wellington Henry Stapleton Cotton, (eldest son of Lord Combermere,) Carlton Club, London.

High Sheriff, (1852-53,) Wm. Kirk Martin, Esq., M.D.

Magistrates—Peter Kirk, D.L., Thornfield; William Burleigh; Marriot Dalway, Bellahill; Stewart Dunn, Farmhill; Wm. K. Martin; John Legg, Glynn park; Jas. Barnett

Borough Commissioners—Stephen R. Rice, chairman; Marquis of Downshire; Wm. Burleigh; William K. Martin; Peter Kirk; Jas. Barnett; Charles A. W. Stewart; Samuel D. Stuart; John Legg; John Borthwick; James Alexander; William Gamble; Paul Logan; Russell K. Bowman; V. W. Magill; Wm. Walker; Matthew Nelson; George Forsythe; David Legg, town clerk; James Wilson, treasurer; Edward Rowan & Jas. Alexander, auditors

Coroner—James K. Jackson

Inspector of Weights and Measures— John Smythe

Harbour Committee—S. D. Stuart, Paul Logan, R. K. Bowman

Harbour Master—James Stannus

Ballast Master—Alexander Jones

Inspecting Commander of Coast-Guard—Captain Horatio Blair, R.N.

Sub-distributor of Stamps — S. D. Stuart

Court-House, High street—John M. Eccleston, secretary to the Grand Jury; George Spear, treasurer; Walter Bourne, clerk to the Crown

Town-Hall, Main street—David Legg, clerk of the peace

Constabulary Station, Irish quarter, South — Sub-inspector, John H. Daly; head constable, John Sloane

Excise-office—Irish quarter, South

News-room—Town Hall

Law Courts—Quarter Sessions, now held in Belfast; Petty Sessions held by the magistrates of the borough every fortnight

Court of Record held first Monday of every alternate month

Banks — Branch of the Northern Banking Company, manager, Alex. Johns; accountant, David Pasley; agents in Dublin, the Bank of Ireland; Savings' Bank, High st., A. Johns, manager

CARRICKFERGUS.

Established Church, Church street—
—The Very Rev. John Chaine,
dean of Connor, rector; Rev.
Franklin Bewley, curate
Presbyterian Church, North street—
Rev. James White, minister
Presbyterian Church (new)—Rev. Mr.
Warwick
Unitarian Meeting-house, Joymount
bank—Rev. Jas. N. Porter, minister
Independent Chapel, Irish quarter
South—ministers various
Methodist Chapel, West st.—ministers
various
R. C. Chapel, Carrickfergus road
Church Education Society's School,
Back lane—Mr. Dunlop, master;
Sarah Gorman, mistress
Infants' School, Lancaster street—
Mary Ann Laverty, mistress
National School, Lancaster street—
Mr. Stevenson, master; Elizabeth
M'Ferran, mistress
Private Schools — Ann Jane Hay,
Church street; Mary Shannon,
Irish quarter south; Jane Sloan,
Church street; Isabella Black,
Castle street; William Larmour,
Joymount bank; Wm. Robert Orr,
West st. —

GENTRY, CLERGY, PROFESSIONAL, ETC.
Battersby, Richard, Oakfield
Battersby, Thomas, Oakfield
Battersby, Rev. J. C., A.M., rector
and vicar of Carnmoney, Glebe
house, Coole glebe, Carnmoney;
residence, Oakfield
Bewley, Rev. E., curate, Irish quarter
Birnie, Thos. M., J.P., Joymount bank
Black, Isabella, Castle street
Bowman, Robert, attorney, High street
Burleigh, William, Scotch quarter
Curry, Capt. Thomas, Church street
Chaine, Very Rev. Dean, Glebe
Close, Rev. Mr., High street
Coates, John
Cunningham, Miss, High street
Dalway, Marriott, J.P., Bellahill
Daly, John H., S.I., Irish quarter south
Dobbs, C. R., D.L., J.P., Castle Dobbs
Dobbs, Mrs. Ellen, Market square
Duggan, Rev. James, Independent
minister, Irish quarter
Duncan, Catherine, Scotch quarter
Dunn, Stewart, Farmhill

Erskine, James, jun., attorney, Antrim
street
Feeney, Capt. John, Welsh's glen
Fletcher, Philip, Bellemont
Forsyth, George, physician & surgeon,
High street
Goddard, Robert T., Rocklands
Goldsmith, Capt. R. A., Castle street
Gwynne, Mrs., Rosebrook
Hanson, James, St. Catherine's
Horseborough, Jane, Church street
Johns, Alex., manager of Northern
and Savings' banks, High street
Kidley, Sarah, Castle street
Kirk, Peter, J.P., Thornfield
Legg, John, J.P., Glynn park
Legg, David, solicitor, Scotch quarter;
office, Town hall
Lynar, Rev. William, High street
Martin, William, physician, Scotch
Quarter
Macauley, Hannah
Magill, Valentine Wm., Market square
Molony, Wm., LL.D., boarding school,
Governor's walk
Moore, Margaret, High street
M'Gowan, John, physician, High st.
Ogilvie, Margaret, Castle street
Paine, Rev. George, Castle street
Pickering, Exuperius, C.E., Prospect
Porter, Rev. James Nixon
Rice, Stephen Richard, Scotch quarter
Robinson, Mrs., North lodge
Robinson, James, Burleigh hill
Rowan, Capt. Edward, R.N., High st.
Sinott, Mrs. Agnes
Smyth, John, attorney, North street
Spear, George, High street
Stephens, Lieut., R.N.
Stewart, William, physician and sur-
geon, Castle street
Thompson, James, Orlands
Thompson, Elizabeth, North street
Verner, William, J.P., Lough view
Warwick, Rev. Mr.
White, Rev. James, Irish quarter south
Wilson, Jane, High street
Wilson, James, Eden

TRADERS, ETC.
Agnew, Agnes, milliner, High street
Alexander, Robert, coal dealer
Andrews, Michael, bleacher, Kilroot
Barnett, James, maltster and distiller,
Irish quarter, south

CARRICKFERGUS.

Baxter, Isaac, tinplate worker, West st.
Birnie, Mary Grace, boarding school, Joymount bank
Bishop, William, publican, West street
Black, Mr., blacksmith, Irish quarter
Blair, Daniel, & Co., grocers, spirit dealers, and haberdashers, High st.
Bowman, Isabella, grocer, West street
Bowman, Russell Ker, ironmonger, Market square
Bowman, Johnston, bookseller and stationer, West street
Burrows, George, publican, West st.
Byrtt, James, boot and shoemaker, West street
Campbell, Wm., publican, Irish gate
Carey, Mary, straw bonnet maker & milliner, High street
Cowan & Co., flaxspinners, Duncrew mills
Cox, John, boot & shoemaker, North street
Craig, William, publican, North st.
Cunningham & Co., grocers, wine and spirit merchants, High street
Dobson, John, flaxspinner, Woodlawn
English, James, publican, North st.
Erskine, Samuel, hotel, High street
Gamble, Wm., cotton spinner, Woodlawn mill
Grey, Mr., saddler, North street
Giffin, James, publican, Irish Quarter, South
Gray, David, grocer, North street
Hamilton, Mrs., coal dealer, Joymount bank
Hamilton, John, grocer, Joymount bank
Hamilton, Wm., publican, North st.
Hamilton, Edward, gunsmith, Market square
Hamilton, Joseph, turner, Market sq.
Hamilton, William, blacksmith, Back lane
Hamilton, Mary Anne, milliner, North street
Hamilton & Burrows, milliners and dressmakers, West street
Harrison, George, carpenter, North st.
Hamilton, Joseph, baker, West street
Hay, Samuel, butcher, North street
Hay, James, carpenter, Irish Quarter
Hovell, Thos., Victoria hotel, High st.
Hutcheson, Francis, publican, North street

Larmour, John, tailor, Scotch Quarter
Lawe, Mary, grocer, West street
Lennon, Daniel, blacksmith, North st.
Lewis, Mr., bookseller and stationer, North street
Lockhart, William, saddler, West st.
Moore, James, butcher, North street
Miscampbell, James, tailor, North st.
Morrison, James, publican, West st.
Mogey, Daniel, coal dealer, West st.
Moore, Thomas, saddler, West street
Morrison, James, tailor, Market sq.
Mullan, John, grocer, North street
M'Comb, Samuel, leather seller, West street
M'Creevy, Robert, watchmaker, Market square
M'Ilvoy, John, butcher, North street
M'Atamney, James, butcher, Irish quarter
M'Ferran, James, tailor, West street
M'Dowell, Sarah, milliner, North st.
M'Alpin, Eliza, grocer, North street
Nelson, Mathew, woollendraper, &c., West street
Norris, Samuel, tinplate worker, West street
Parkhill, George, carpenter, North st.
Paul, Ellen and Mary Ann, milliners, North street
Robinson, Thos., butcher and grocer, Joymount bank
Robertson, J., and Sons, sewed muslin manufacturers, Castle street— R. Manners, agent
Rowan, John, grocer, West street
Stevenson, James, miller, Kilroot
Stevens, Mrs., publican, West street
Stannus, Anthony, glazier, Castle st.
Stannus, James, builder and harbour master, High street
Stuart, Samuel, timber merchant and distributor of stamps, Victoria place
Stuart, Brothers, grocers, wine and spirit merchants, &c., Victoria place
Hutcheson, Francis, butcher, Joymount bank
Ingram, James, public baths, Joymount bank
Jenkins, Peter, publican, Castle street
Jones, Robert, grocer, Castle street
Jones, Alexander, publican, Castle street
Kerr, Robert, carpenter, Joymount bank

Stuart, Brothers, ironmongers, High street
Stuart, George, leather seller, Castle place
Stewart, C., pawnbroker, Chester st.
Thom, John, pawnbroker, West street
Thomas, Mary, milliner, Church st.
Thompson, Thomas, grain merchant, North street
Turnbull and Co., sewed muslin manufacturers, Lancaster street—J. Kain, agent
Vint, William, baker, Irish quarter, West
Walker, William, flax spinner, Scotch quarter
Woods, James, flax spinner
Watson, George, butcher, North street
Woods, Mr., cotton spinner, Glenfield
Wallace, Sharp, and Co., sewed muslin manufacturers, West street
Wetherup, James, tailor, West street

CASTLEBLAYNEY.

Is a market town, in the county of Monaghan, pleasantly situated on the road from Londonderry, in the centre of a well cultivated country. The town derives its name from the family of *Blayney*, and the *castle*, which was erected here by Sir Edward Blayney, in the reign of James I., who created him Baron Blayney of Monaghan. In the centre of the town, on an elevated spot, stands the Market-house, a neat and ornamental building, with a spacious room on the second storey, and above the roof a neat bell turret, with a clock. The Sessions-house, a County Bridewell, a Union Poor-house, and a Dispensary, are the other public buildings. General Sessions of the Peace are held four times in the year, and Petty Sessions every alternate week. The Dundalk and Enniskillen Railway passes close to the town. The principal inn here, the King's Arms, is a well conducted house. The Parish Church of Mucknoe is very neat, with a handsome spire; the interior comfortably and neatly fitted up by Lord Blayney. The other places of worship are two Presbyterian Churches, one for Wesleyan Methodists, and a Roman Catholic Chapel. The market days are Tuesday, Wednesday, and Friday, the first and last for grain, the other for general commodities. Fairs on the first Wednesday, monthly.

Post-office, West street—John Smith, post-master
Conveyances—To Dublin, per railway. To Armagh—a day coach passes through Keady. To Ballibay—a mail car, from Mooney's hotel, at 6 o'clock a.m. To Cootehill—a car from the Post-office, goes through Ballibay and Rockferry. To Drogheda—the mail (from Derry) every night at 10½ o'clock, and day coach (from Omagh) every day at 5 o'clock p.m. To Monaghan—a mail car, every evening at 7½ o'clock. To Londonderry—the mail (from Drogheda) every morning at 10½ o'clock. To Newry—a mail car, from West street, every morning at 6 o'clock. To Omagh—a conveyance (from Drogheda) from Smith's, West street.
Bridewell, York street—Richard Mitchell, keeper
Constabulary Station—Sub-inspector, Mark Bloxham; head-constable, J. Kean
Dispensary, West street—Wm. Irwin, M.D., surgeon
Union Workhouse, New street—Wm. Twibill, master; William Irwin, M.D., surgeon; Protestant chaplain, Rev. A. Hurst; Presbyterian chaplain, Rev. Thomas Boyd; Roman Catholic chaplain, Rev. James M'Meille
Parish Church of Mucknoe, Church street—Rev. A. Hurst, incumbent, Glebe house; Rev. T. B. Annesley, curate
Presbyterian Church, Lakeview—Rev. Thomas Boyd, minister

CASTLEBLAYNEY.

Presbyterian Church, Broomfield—
Rev. S. B. Shaw, minister
Presbyterian Church, Frankford—
Rev. George B. Coulter, minister
Wesleyan Methodist Chapel, Church
street—Rev. Jas. Donald, minister
Roman Catholic Chapel, Church street
—Rev. James M'Meille, P.P.; Rev.
Patrick Smith, curate
Lady Blayney's School, Church street
—Catherine Lee, mistress
National Schools, Church street—
Phillip M'Kenna, master; Catherine
M'Kenna, mistress

NOBILITY AND GENTRY.

Blayney, Right Hon. Lord, The Castle
Boyd, Henry, West street
Golding, Edward, J.P., West street
Harpur, Mary, Castle place
M'Burney, James, Milltown cottage
M'Math, Hamilton, J.P., Thornford house
M'Watty, James, J.P., West street
M'Watty, Parker
Mandsley, John, Laurelhill
Swanzy, John, Rockfield house

CLERGY AND PROFESSIONAL.

Boyd, Rev. Thomas, Lakeview cottage
Coulter, Rev. George B., Killicard
Cuming, Benjamin V., surgeon, Market square
Duffy, Rev. James, P.P., Broomfield
Irwin, William, surgeon, M.D., West street
M'Auley, Rev. M.
M'Burney, John, surgeon, Market square
M'Eveigh, Rev. Francis, Broomfield
M'Mahon, Rev. Ross, Monagor cottage
M'Meille, Rev. James, P.P., Drumcrew cottage
O'Callaghan, Jas., surveyor, West st.
O'Callan, Bernard B., surgeon, Market square
Parker, William, attorney, West street
Rooney, Rev. Patrick, Currytanty cottage Glebe
Russell, The Venerable Archdeacon, Clontibret glebe
Shaw, Rev. Mr.
Smith, Rev. Patrick, Drumcrew cottage
Swanzy, Hugh, attorney, Market sq.

TRADERS, ETC.

Ansley, Isabella, milliner and dressmaker, York street
Bell, John, tailor, West street
Brennan, James, miller, Cromartin
Baillie, Ann, haberdasher and delf shop, West street
Birch, James, baker, Market square
Brown, William, carpenter, Market st.
Burns, William, whitesmith, York st.
Boyd, Francis, spirit dealer, West st.
Callan, Mrs., baker, West street
Cooke, John, boot and shoemaker, West street
Comeskey, Joseph, iron, coal, leather and spirit dealer, Henry street
Crosier, George, miller, Liskeenan
Curley, John, miller, Recullis
Clark, Charles, painter and glazier, Henry street
Connell, John, saddler, West street
Casey, Henry, publican, Broomfield
Casey, Terence, tailor, Noble street
Casey, William, tailor, West street
Daly, John, leather seller, West street
Devlin, James, iron, coal, and earthenware dealer, Noble street
Dickson, David, draper, West street
Duffy, Phillip, wheelwright, West st.
Devine, James, pawnbroker
Farlow, Thomas, miller, Darnaglug
Fanning, M., miller, Mullaghanic
Fee, Michael, ironmonger, West street
Flinn, Patrick, butcher, West street
Fitzpatrick, Mary, miller, Toam
Finnagan, Thomas, publican, Broomfield
Flanaghan, Mathew, baker, West st.
Gass, William, wheelwright, Noble st.
Graham, Thos., wheelwright, West st.
Gillen, Mary, West street
Gillen, Thomas, smith and farrier, York street
Grimes, Edward, publican, Seven Houses
Green, Peter, tailor, West street
Henan, James, butcher, West street
Hamilton, Wm., earthenware dealer, Noble street
Herron, Samuel, draper, Market sq.
Hunter, Edward, grocer, Market sq.
Hunter, Ellen, draper, West street
Hagan, Robert, publican, West street
Harvey, Margaret, publican, Henry st.
Henry, John, publican, Market square

Hunter, Henry, publican, Noble st.
Johnston, Wm., whitesmith, Noble st.
Kirk, James, boot and shoemaker and leather dealer, Henry street
Kearns, Catherine, milliner and dressmaker, West street
Kirk, James, publican, Henry street
Levett, Ellen, milliner and dressmaker, New street
Lowey, Robert, draper, West street
Lewers, Mary, spirit, oil and colour dealer, West street
Liggett, John, publican, Lurganmore
Lowey, James, tanner, West street
Mathews, John, chandler, Noble st.
Martin, James, miller, Lurganmore
Maguire, James, boot and shoemaker, Church street
Molloy, William, iron and coal dealer, West street
Mullagan, Catherine, iron, coal and spirit dealer, West street
Molloy, James, grocer, West street
Morris, Ulysses, painter and glazier, West street
Mooney, James, publican, West st.
Millar, William, tailor, Henry street
M'Eneany, Owen, whitesmith, West street
M'Learney, Peter, whitesmith, New street
M'Mahon, Jas., whitesmith, York st.
M'Donald, Felix, butcher, New street
M'Learney, Edward, butcher, West st.
M'Tavey, Owen, carpenter, Henry st.
M'Learney, Michael, grocer, West st.
M'Math, Henry, leather seller, Market square
M'Ardle, John, miller, Laka
M'Math, Hamilton, miller, Thornford
M'Watty, Parker, miller, Drumleck
M'Ardle, James, spirit dealer, Seven Houses
M'Eneany, Owen, publican, West st.
M'Learny, James, publican, West st.
M'Math, William, wholesale spirit dealer and chandler, Market sq.
M'Math, James, tanner, Market sq.
M'Math, William and Henry, tanners, Noble street
M'Namara, Stephen, shoemaker
M'Mahon, Patrick, grocer
M'Kean, Mrs., and Sons, bleachers, Laragh
Nugent, Richard, grocer
O'Callaghan, James, grocer, West st.
O'Callaghan, Michael, grocer, West st.
Parkes, Jane, milliner and dressmaker, Castle place
Quigley, John, baker and grocer, West street
Quin, David, publican, West street
Ralston, John, baker and grocer, Noble street
Ross, John, butcher, New street
Rule, Eleanor, King's Arms hotel, West street
Shiell, John, draper and ironmonger, West street
Thompson, Thomas, draper, West st.
Thompson, Thos., publican, West st.
Watters, John, publican, Donhamlet
Whitby, M., draper, Market square
Whitby, Jessie, milliner and dressmaker, Market square
Wilson, William, wheelwright, Noble street
Ward, William, shoemaker

CASTLEDAWSON.

CASTLEDAWSON is a flourishing little market town, in the county of Londonderry, about 24 miles from Belfast, thirty-eight S. E. from Londonderry, and between two and three N. E. by N. from Magherafelt; delightfully situated on both sides of the Mayola river, on the road from Magherafelt to Ahoghill, and rather more than two miles N. W. of the North-Western extremity of Lough Neagh. The river is crossed by a stone bridge, of one arch, supposed the largest span in Ireland, erected by the Dawson family, and hence its former name of *Dawson's Bridge*. Its present apellation is derived from its proprietor, Joshua Dawson, Esq., who, in 1710, was Chief Secretary for Ireland, and erected, in 1713, a castle, of which only the ruins remain. The present seat of the family, and residence of the Right Hon. G. R. Dawson,

CASTLEDAWSON.

Castledawson, is nearly adjoining to the town, situated in a beautiful demesne, through which passes an ancient avenue, three miles in length, opening to a magnificent view of Lough Neagh, to which it extends.

The town consists of two principal and a few smaller streets, some of the houses composing which are large, and well-built of stone. The manufacture of cotton prevails in the town and neighbouring district, and the making of coarse earthenware and bricks is carried on most extensively. The Church, which stands on the Western side of the river, in the parish of Ballyscullion, was erected by the Right Hon. R. G. Dawson, and by him beautifully ornamented; among other embellishments, its elegant stained glass window is much admired. The other places of worship are for Presbyterians and Wesleyan Methodists. Small market held on Saturdays.

Post-Office—Ann Oliver, postmistress.
Letters from Dublin and the South of Ireland, likewise from England, arrive at eleven a.m., and are despatched at one p.m.; from Belfast and Scotland, at 11-25 a.m., and despatched at 1 p.m.; from Londonderry, Ballymena, &c., at 9 a.m., and despatched at 11½ a.m.

Conveyances—To Antrim, at 3 p.m.; to Ballymena, at 1-20 p.m.; to Randalstown, 5½ a.m.; to Magherafelt, at 7½ a.m. and 6 p.m.

Chapel of Ease—Rev. H. S. Stevenson
Presbyterian Church—Rev. Robert Gamble, minister
National School—Andrew M'Cluskey, master

GENTRY, CLERGY, ETC.

Crawford, Hugh
Dawson, Right Hon. George Robert
Godfrey, Lieut. Whiteside, Leitrim house
Godfrey, Mitchell, physician, &c., Toome bridge
Gordon, R. H., M.D.
Gore, Mrs., Mayola park
Graves, William, J.P., Gravesend villa
Henry, Robert, Fairview house
Johnston, Robert, M.D.
Mann, Alexander
M'Donald, Rev. Mr., R.C.C.
M'Arthur, George
M'Kee, Rev. James, Rossgarn
M'Manus, Mrs. Helen, Toome house
M'Mullen, John, M.D.
Ottley, Charles S., district engineer
Smyth, John, M.D.
Stevenson, Rev. Henry S.

TRADERS, ETC.

Barclay, Thomas, tailor
Bigby, Wiseman, and Co., cotton manufacturers (of Glasgow)
Cassidy, Bernard, haberdasher
Churchman, Wm., hotel keeper and posting establishment
Devlin, Bernard, blacksmith
Dixon, Peter, and Sons (of Carlisle), check and gingham manufacturers —John Boyd, agent
Dogherty, Cornelius, tailor
Ellis, James, brickmaker
Evans, Henry, blacksmith
Ferguson, John, and Co. (of Carlisle), check and gingham manufacturers
Hamersley, Thomas, grocer
Hillman, Thomas, grocer, corn merchant, spirit dealer, and ironmonger
Hunter, Henry, spirit dealer
Hunter, Henry, haberdasher
Huston, Alexander, boot and shoemaker
Johnston, Mrs., grocer and spirit dealer
Kane, Felix, carrier (to Belfast)
Keenan, Ann, milliner and dressmaker
Keenan, Richard, nurseryman, Leitrim
Macauley, Patrick, linen manufacturer and bleacher
Mawhinney, William, linen manufacturer and earthenware dealer, Hill head
Miller, Hugh, linen manufacturer, Green hill
Miller, Thomas, linen manufacturer, Green hill
Morrow, James, woollendraper and haberdasher
M'Callion, James, blacksmith

2 x

CASTLEDAWSON.

M'Cluskey, James, boot and shoe- maker
M'Gucken, Benjamin, linen manufacturer
M'Henry, James, grocer, Hill head
M'Mullen, The Misses, grocers and milliners
M'Veagh, Edward
Oliver, Adam, grocer, spirit dealer, and ironmonger
Oliver, Adam, Three Tuns hotel, and posting establishment
O'Hara, O., spirit dealer
Rice, Margaret, milliner and dress-maker
Sheil, John, spirit dealer, Creagh
Thompson, John, blacksmith
Tipping, Thomas, carpenter
Wallax, James, earthenware dealer, Leitrim

COUNTY OF CAVAN.

CAVAN, an inland county in Ulster province, comprising an area of 746 square miles, or 477,360 acres, of which 375,473 are arable, 71,918 uncultivated, 7,325 in plantations, 502 in towns, and 22,142 under water. The surface is undulating, with mountainous ranges in the North. There are indications of coal, iron, copper, and lead, and numerous mineral springs. The soil is light and poor, except along the courses of the rivers. Lakes are numerous—many highly picturesque. According to the census of 1851, the population of the county was 174,303, being a decrease of 68,855 since 1841. The occupations are chiefly agricultural. The linen trade was carried on here extensively, and there are still many bleach-greens. The principal towns are Cavan, Cootehill, and Belturbet. The county returns two members to Parliament; constituency, under 13 and 14 Vic., c. 69, in 1851, 3,850. The Assizes are held at Cavan, where the County Prison is. There are Bridewells at Bailieborough, Ballyconnell, and Cootehill; Quarter Sessions are held there, as also in Cavan. The County Infirmary is in Cavan; and the District Lunatic Asylum, to which the county is entitled to send 33 patients, is at Armagh. There are Fever Hospitals at Bailieborough, Cavan, Cootehill, and Virginia; and 22 Dispensaries in the county. At Cavan there are branches of the Provincial Bank and the Ulster Banking Company. A Savings' Bank is established at Cavan. The Union Workhouses are at Cavan, Bailieborough, Cootehill, and Bawnboy. There are Barracks in Cavan and Belturbet, the former being within the military district of Belfast, where also the Staff of the County Militia and the Staff Officer of Pensioners are stationed. The head-quarters of the Constabulary force, consisting of 419 men, officers included, are at Cavan; those of the 8 districts, comprising 39 stations, at Cavan, Arva, Ballyjamesduff, Bailieborough, Cootehill, Belturbet, Swanlinbar, and Killeshandra. There are Resident Magistrates at Killeshandra, Enniskillen, and Kingscourt, and Revenue Police stations at Belturbet and Bailieborough. One newspaper, the *Anglo Celt*, is published in Cavan, on Thursdays.

Lieutenant and Custos Rotulorum— The Marquis of Headfort, K.ST.P., Virginia Park, in this county, and Headfort, Kells, county Meath
Vice-Lieutenant—Sir J. Young, Bart., M.P., Bailieborough
High-Sheriff (1852-53)—Saml. Winter, Esq., Agher, Summerhill
Members for the County—Sir J. Young, Bart., D.L., Bailieborough Castle, and 19, Chesham-place, Belgrave square, London; Captain the Hon. J. P. Maxwell, Farnham, 46, Duke street, St. James's, and Carlton Club, London
Assistant-Barrister—P. M. Murphy, 9, Lower Pembroke st., Dublin

COUNTY OF CAVAN.

DEPUTY-LIEUTENANTS.

Burrowes, R., Stradone House, Stradone
Dease, G., Turbotstown, Castlepollard, county Westmeath
Enery, W. H., Ballyconnell House, Ballyconnell
Farnham, Lord, K.St.P., Farnham, Cavan
Humphreys, W., Ballyhaise house, Ballyhaise
Maxwell, Hon. S. R., Arley cottage, Mount Nugent
Morton, Pierce
Nesbitt, J., Lismore, Crossdoney, and London
O'Reilly, A., Baltrasna, Oldcastle
Quin, Lord G., Headfort, Kells
Saunderson, Col. A., Castle Saunderson, Belturbet
Young, Sir J., Bart., M.P., Bailieboro' Castle

MAGISTRATES.

Adams, C. J., Shinan House, Shercock
Adams, Very Rev. S., Dean of Cashel, Northlands, Shercock
Armstrong, J., Woodfort, Kingscourt
Bailie, Major J., Ardloher, Belturbet
Baker, J., Ashgrove, Belturbet
Bell, Andrew William
Benison, J., Mountpleasant, Ballyconnell.
Boyle, M. J., Cootehill
Brush, A., Drumbar, Cavan
Burrowes, R., D.L., Stradone House
Butler, Hon. H.C., Lanesboro' Lodge, Belturbet
Clements, H. T., Ashfield, Cootehill
Clements, T. Lucas, Rakenny House, Cootehill
Clifford, Capt. R., Carn cottage, Belturbet
Cloncurry, Lord, Maretimo, Blackrock, Dublin
Coote, Eyre, Ballyjamesduff
Coote, Thos., Branedrum, Monaghan
Cullen, F. M., Corry, Drumkeeran, county Leitrim
Dare, Robert, Westby hall
Dease, G., D.L., Turbotstown, Castlepollard
Dickson, Joseph, Bailieborough
Dickson, R. S., Bailieborough

Enery, W. H., D.L., Ballyconnell House
Enniskillen, Earl of, Florence Court
Erskine, Robert, Cavan
Farnham, Lord, D.L., K.St.P., Farnham, Cavan
Finlay, George, Corville, Ballyconnell
Finlay, John, Brackley, Ballyconnell
Finlay, Sir Thomas, Knt.
Fitzpatrick, Rev. F., Bailieborough
Fleming, John, Slyan House, Lenamore, county Longford
Fox, R., Aghabane, Killeshandra
Godley, J., Killegar House (county Leitrim), Killeshandra
Gumley, John, Belturbet
Hamilton, J., Castlehamilton, Killeshandra
Hassard, F., Rockwood, Swanlinbar
Hughes, H. G., Cornadrung, Granard
Humphreys, Wm., D.L., Ballyhaise house
Johnston, Captain J., Swanlinbar
Johnston, T., The Lodge, Redhills
Kilbée, H. T., Drumkeen house, Cavan
Knipe, G. M., Erne Hill, Belturbet
L'Estrange, G. Henry, Lisnamandra, Crossdoney
Lynch, J. R., Mount Nugent
Maxwell, Hon. S. R., D.L., Arley Cottage, Mount Nugent
Maxwell, Hon. R., Newtownbarry, co. Wexford
Mayne, Richard, Newbliss
Mortimer, C., Lakeview, Mullagh, Moynalty
Morton, Pierce, D.L.
Nesbitt, J., D.L., Lismore Lodge, Crossdoney
Nesbitt, J. R., Killycar, Belturbet
Nixon, A., Lurgan Lodge, Virginia
Nugent, C. E. J., Farrenconnell house, Mount Nugent
Nugent, Richard, Farrenconnell House, Mount Nugent
O'Reilly, Anthony, D.L., Baltrasna, Oldcastle
Philips, Michael, Glenview, Belturbet
Pratt, Colonel, Cabra Castle, Kingscourt
Ruxton, W., Ardee House, Ardee
Sargent, Henry, Eighter, Virginia
Saunderson, Colonel A., D.L., Castle Saunderson, Belturbet
Scott, R., Fort Frederick, Virginia

Shaw, G., Castlewellan, co. Down
Smith, S., Cherrymount, Moynalty
Smith, W., Drumheel House, Cavan
Story, James, Lockington, Belturbet
Story, J. H., Derryallen house, Ballinagh
Tatlow, J. C., 20 Richmond hill, Dublin
Thompson, J., Killabandrick, Belturbet
Thompson, T., Cavan
Thompson, W., Ross, Mount Nugent
Thornton, P., Greenville, Belturbet
Trench, Charles Le Poer
Vernon, J. E., Castlecosby, Crossdoney
Vesey, G. W., Derrabard house, Omagh
Young, Sir J., Bart., M.P., D.L., Bailieborough Castle

RESIDENT MAGISTRATES.
Holmes, B. H., Enniskillen
M'Cullagh, John, Killeshandra
Willcocks, John, Kingscourt

COUNTY OFFICERS.
Clerk of Crown—S. Swanzy, Cavan
Clerk of Peace—G. T. Dalton, Cavan
Deputy-Clerk of Peace—P. Caffry, Cavan
Crown-Solicitor—Sir E. Tierney, Bart., 44 Lower Mount street, Dublin
Crown-Solicitor at Quarter Sessions—B. Armstrong, Kingscourt
Treasurer—Samuel Moore, Cavan
Secretary to Grand Jury—Edward E. Mayne; office, Cavan
County Surveyor—Alex. Armstrong, C.E.L., Cavan
Coroners—J. M'Fadden, M.D., Cootehill; Thomas Berry, Rockfield, Killeshandra; Wm. Pollock, Ballinagh
Head Stamp Distributor for County—S. Whittaker, Enniskillen

MILITIA STAFF.
Colonel—Alex. Saunderson, Castle Saunderson, Belturbet
Lieut.-Colonel—Joseph Pratt, Cabra Castle, Kingscourt
Major—H. Pratt De Montmorency
Adjutant—Capt. N. Gosselin, Cavan
Surgeon—Charles Halpin, M.D., L.K., and Q.C.P.I.

CONSTABULARY OFFICERS.
County Inspector—D. Patton, Cavan
Arva—G. F. H. M'Clintock
Bailieborough—James L. Bailey
Killeshandra—James Griffin
Ballyjamesduff—Lee M'Kinstry
Cavan—Edward S. Corry
Cootehill—J. F. Fortescue
Belturbet—Joseph H. Phillips
Swanlinbar—James Roe

CAVAN.

A MARKET and post town, the capital of the county of its name, formerly a Parliamentary borough, is 66 miles from Belfast, and is situated on the road from Dublin to Enniskillen. The town consists of two parallel streets, with a few smaller ones branching from them. The places of worship are the Church—a handsome structure, a Presbyterian Church, and Wesleyan and Primitive Methodist Chapels, and a Roman Catholic Chapel. About a quarter of a mile from the town is a classical school chartered by Charles I., and its management, by a late act of Parliament, transferred to a board of commissioners of education, the master being appointed by the Lord Lieutenant. The school-house, re-erected in 1819, in a beautiful situation, is a spacious building, calculated for the reception of one hundred pupils. The market is held on Tuesday. Fairs—February 1st, May 14th, June 30th, Aug. 14th, September 25th, and November 12th.

Post-office, Main st.—James Parker, postmaster. Letters from Dublin and all parts of the South of Ireland, also from England, arrive every morning at half-past three, and are despatched every night at nine; letters from Belturbet and all parts of the North of Ireland, also from Scotland, arrive every morning at nine, and are despatched every afternoon at half-past four o'clock

CAVAN.

Conveyances—To Mullingar, a day coach, every Monday, Wednesday, and Friday; to Belturbet, a car every day at 3½ o'clock; to Dublin and Drogheda, a coach leaves every morning at 8 o'clock to catch the train; to Enniskillen, night mail leaves at 3½ o'clock, every morning; to Scrabby, car every morning at 6 o'clock; to Armagh *via* Clones, a car at 6 o'clock every morning; to Killeshandra, a car every morning (Sunday excepted) at 5 o'clock

Union Workhouse—James Mulligan, master; Mrs. Spinks, matron; Bernard Coyne, M.D., surgeon; Rev. Thomas O'Reilly, Protestant chaplain; Rev. G. Carson, Presbyterian chaplain; Blayney Grier, clerk to house

Infirmary, Main street—Rev. William Wilkins, treasurer and registrar; George Roe, M.D., surgeon; Miss Johnson, house keeper; Mrs. M'-Glone, head nurse

Fever Hospital—L. Halpin, surgeon; Mrs. Maguire, house keeper

Dispensary, Main street — Bernard Coyne, M.D., surgeon

Gaol, Farnham street—Geo. Galogly, governor; George Roe, M.D., surgeon; T. Thompson, local inspector

Military Barrack—Captain H. Bowen, barrack master

Staff Officer—Major James Bales

Constabulary Station, College street—J. Patten, county inspector; J. Curry, sub-inspector; John Moore, head constable

Stamp-office, Main street — James Parker, sub-distributor

Banks—Provincial, Farnham street, Wm. Anderson, manager; Ulster, Main street, William Thomson, manager; Savings' Bank, Main street, open every Saturday, C. Stewart, actuary

Established Church, Farnham street—Rev. Thomas Carson, LL.D., vicar; Rev. Wm. M. Wilkins, and Rev. Mr. Stone, curates

Presbyterian Church, Farnham street—Rev. T. Carson, minister

Primitive Methodist Chapel, Wesley street—Rev. Robt. Wilson, minister

Wesleyan Methodist Chapel, Bridge street—Rev. Robert Bell, minister

Roman Catholic Chapel, Farnham street—Right Rev. James Brown, D.D., bishop; Rev. T. Mulvaney, and Rev. Thomas O'Reilly, curates

Registrar for the Diocese of Kilmore—Capt. Robt. Erskine, Main street

Royal School—Rev. William Prior Moore, A.M., master

Farnham School, Farnham street—Henry Fleming, master; Jane Fleming, mistress

Academy, Bridge street—John Brady, teacher

Roman Catholic School, Farnham street—Rev. John O'Reilly, Rev. N. Connaty, and Patrick Curran, masters

Bible Depository, Main street—Wm. Johnston, agent

Newspaper—*Anglo Celt*, Main street, Z. Wallace, proprietor; and J. H. Darragh, editor

NOBILITY AND GENTRY.

Anderson, William, Farnham road
Bell, William, sub-sheriff
Black, William, Farnham street
Brady, Mrs., Drumbar cottage
Brush, A., J.P., Drumbar house
Burrows, Robt., J.P., Stradone house
Burrows, Miss, Farnham street
Elliott, Mrs. Jane, Farnham street
Erskine, Captain Robert, Main street
Farnham, Right Hon. Lord, Farnham house
Foster, Miss, Main street
Humphreys, Wm., J.P., Ballyhaise castle
Killbee, Henry T., J.P., Drumkeen
L'Estrange, Edmund, Lower Kilmore and Dublin castle
L'Estrange, George, Lisnamandra
Maxwell, Hon. James P., M.P., Farnham house
Maxwell, Hon. Richard, J.P., Farnham house
Moore, Samuel, Kilnacrot
Moore, Mrs., Waterloo cottage
Moore, Wm. Armitage, J.P., Drumelis house
Stafford, John, Tully
Swanzey, The Misses, Wesley street
Thompson, Theophilus, B.A.L.

Veitch, Mrs. Rose Ann, Wesley st.
Vernon, John E., J.P., Castlecosby

CLERGY AND PROFESSIONAL.

Armstrong, James, attorney, Farnham street
Babington, Michael (commissioner for taking affidavits), Brookvale
Babington, William, M.D., Fortview
Brice, Wm. M., apothecary, Main st.
Brown, Right Rev. James, D.D., Roman Catholic Bishop, Farnham street
Caffery, Patrick, deputy clerk of the Peace, Main street
Carson, Rev. T., LL.D., Cullie's house
Carson, John, surgeon and apothecary, Main street
Darragh, J., editor *Anglo Celt*
Dickson, Rev. James Lowry, Lavey
Coyne, Bernard, M.D., Farnham st.
Erskine, Captain Robert, registrar for the diocese of Kilmore, Main st.
Farrell, Martin, C.E., Farnham street
Hamilton, W., attorney, Wesley st.
Halpin, Charles, M.D., Farnham st.
Jackson, Rev. T., Drumard
Leslie, Rev. Charles, Kilmore
Leslie, Right Rev. John, D.D., Lord Bishop of Kilmore, Elphin, and Ardagh, Kilmore palace
Mease, Andrew, M.D., Farnham st.
Moore, Rev. William Prior, A.M., Cavan college
M'Gauran, Edwd., attorney, Main st.
O'Connor, Thos., apothecary, Main st.
O'Reilly, Rev. Thomas, Wesley street
Roe, George, M.D., Main street
Swanzey, Samuel, attorney, Farnham st.
Tully, Matthew, attorney, Main street
Wilkins, Rev. William, Main street

TRADERS, ETC.

Anderson, William, Alliance Fire and Life Assurance agent, Farnham st.
Anderson, Samuel, tin-plate worker, New road
Bannon, Mrs., baker, grocer, and spirit dealer, Main street
Benson, William, painter and glazier, Main street
Brady, Catherine, baker, grocer, and publican, Main street
Brady, John, baker and spirit dealer, Main street
Brady, Peter, jun., Cock and Punch Bowl tavern, Main street
Brady, Stephen, saddler, Main street
Bride, Patrick, publican, Main street
Chadwick, George, auctioneer, Barrack hill
Connor, Edward, boot and shoemaker, Bridge street
Clinton, Francis, grocer and draper, Main street
Clemenger, John, coach builder, College street
Carty, Mrs., seller of flesh meat, Bridge street
Connell, Mary Anne, milliner and dressmaker, Bridge street
Davies, Robert, earthenware dealer and grocer, Bridge street
Downey, John, draper, Main street
Davis, John, painter and glazier, Main street
Devitt, Mrs., clothes broker, Main st.
Devitt, Miles, clothes broker, Main st.
Dougherty, Mrs., milliner and dressmaker, Market square
Ellis, Arthur, baker and grocer, Bridge street
Fitzpatrick, John, boot and shoemaker, Church lane
Farrelly, Catherine, milliner and dressmaker, Wesley street
Farrelly, John, grocer, Main street
Flood, John, tailor, Bridge street
Fegan, James, watch and clock maker, Main street
Fay, James, tobacco manufacturer, Main street
Fagan, Edwd., auctioneer, Barrackhill
Fay, Patrick, tallow chandler, Main st.
Gallaghan, Pat., blacksmith, Main st.
Glancey, Patrick, cooper, Broad road.
Gallagher, Patk., publican, Bridge st.
Hinds, William, butcher, Main st.
Hague, William, jun., hardware and timber merchant, Market square
Higgins, William, stone mason, College street
Johnston, William, bookseller and stationer, and agent for Medical Invalid Assurance Company, Main street
Kay, James, draper, Main street
Kennedy, Edward, baker, grocer, publican, timber merchant, and ironmonger, Main street

Kinnear, James, boot and shoemaker, Market square
Kettyle, Alexander, draper, Main st.
Keogan, Edward, publican, Main st.
Lough, Mathew, grocer, and ironmonger, Main street
Leckey, James, wheelwright, Main st.
Louden, Adam, butcher, Half acre
Lyons, Miss, milliner and dressmaker, Main street
Maguire, William, boot and shoemaker, Half acre
Murray, Michael, boot and shoemaker, Half acre
Matthews, T. W., grocer, earthenware dealer, painter and glazier, Main street
Morrow, Martha, earthenware dealer, Main street
Mervyn, Jones, grocer and leather seller, Main street
Moore, William, draper, Main street
Morris, John, tinplate worker, Half acre
Murray, John, watch and clock maker, Main street
Maguire, Daniel, cabinet maker, Wesley street
Masterson, William, hair dresser, Bridge street
Magennis, John, baker and grocer, Main street
Montgomery, John, grocer and publican, Main street
Magennis, J. and W., spirit dealers, Main street
Masterson, Thomas, spirit dealer, Main street
M‘Cabe, Francis, grocer, chandler, woollen merchant, & leather seller, Main street
M‘Cann, Peter, grocer and tanner, Main street
M‘Gauran, Jas., Globe hotel, Main st.
M‘Arvoy, Michael, tailor, Barrackhill
M‘Manus, Mr., woollendraper, Main street
Noble, John, boot and shoemaker, College street
O'Brien, James, bookseller and stationer, Main street
O'Reilly, Mary, publican, Bridge st.
O'Reilly, Mrs., publican, Main street
Parr, Ann Eliza and Rose, grocers, Bridge street
Parker, Wm., draper and tea agent, Main street
Prior, Miss, publican, Main street
Pepper, Jn., clothes broker, Bridge st.
Reilly, John, boot and shoemaker, Barrackhill
Reilly, Mrs., publican, Main street
Reilly, Bernard, tailor, Half acre
Reilly, James, Farnham Arms hotel and posting house, Main street
Ruxton Thomas, baker, Main street
Rourke, George, publican, Main st.
Smith, Patrick, baker, Main street
Sheridan, John, blacksmith, Main st.
Sheridan, Thos., blacksmith, Bridge street
Smyth, Mathew, butcher, Half acre
Smith, Patrick, grocer, Main street
Smith, Elizabeth, milliner and dressmaker, Wesley street
Simons, James, saddler, Main street
Smith, Abigail, publican, Bridge st.
Smith, James, auctioneer, Main st.
Smith, James, publican, Main street
Sheridan, J., publican, Main street
Somerville, Wm., publican, Main st.
Talbot, John, boot and shoemaker, New road
Thompson, George, boot and shoemaker, Barrackhill
Vertue, Mrs., straw bonnet maker, Main street
Walls, Bernard, butcher, Main street
Wallace, Z., printer and publisher, Main street

CLONES.

CLONES is a market town, in the county of Monaghan, 53 miles from Belfast, 12¼ S.S.W. from Monaghan. The town consists chiefly of five streets, which converge towards the market place, a spacious triangular area, called the Diamond, on the West side of which stands the Market-house. The market is held on Thursday, and the fairs on the last Thursday in every month.

CLONES.

Post-office, Fermanagh street—Benjamin Thompson, postmaster. Letters from Dublin and South of Ireland, also from England, arrive every morning at seven, and are despatched every evening at half-past five; letters from Belfast and the North of Ireland, also from Scotland, arrive every morning at four, and are despatched every evening at half-past eight; letters from Enniskillen and the West of Ireland arrive every evening at half-past eight, and are despatched every morning at four

Union Workhouse—William Montgomery, master; Ann Montgomery, matron

Northern Bank (branch office), Diamond—John Brady, manager

Parish Church, Market place—Rev. Thomas Hand, A.M., rector; Rev. Thomas Howe, curate

Primitive Methodist Chapel—Whitehall street

Wesleyan Methodist Chapel—Cara st.

Roman Catholic Chapel—Rev. James Smyth, P.P.; Rev. John Smith, curate

Church Education Society's School, Cara street—Jones Peace, master; Miss Faulds, mistress

National School, Pound hill—Thomas Cosgrove, master; Catherine Cosgrove, mistress

Classical Academy, Whitehall street—Rev. William White, principal

NOBILITY AND GENTRY.

Brady, John, Diamond
Cochrane, Miss Ann, Whitehall st.
Cochrane, William, Drumard
Crowe, Charles, J.P., Farmhill
Crumly, Miss, Diamond
Crozier, John, Gorta
Ellis, Nicholas, Lisnarow
Fitzgerald, Mrs. Eliza, Whitehall st.
Foster, William, Ballynare
George, Miss Mary, Cara street
Hamilton, John P., J.P., Oakfield
Jackson, James, Clincorn
M'Murray, Mrs. Jane, Whitehall st.
Madden, Mrs., Hilton
Madden, Captain John, J.P., Springgrove
Maginnis, John, Clonkeen cottage
Murray, Andrew A., J.P., Looghoona
Parr, John George, Diamond
Phillips, Thomas, J.P., Aughafin
Shegog, George, Munelly
Smith, David, J.P., Lakeview

CLERGY AND PROFESSIONAL.

Clarke, Rev. James, Newtonbutler
Dudgeon, Alexander, attorney, Whitehall street
Fitzgerald, Thomas, land surveyor, Whitehall street
Hoskins, Joshua Thomas, surgeon and apothecary, Diamond
Hughes, Rev. John, Newtonbutler
Lough, Jas., land surveyor, Diamond
M'Anally, Rev. Thos., Newtonbutler
Richardson, Rev. John, Summerhill
Scott, Ralph and Richard, attorneys, Whitehall street
Smith, Philip, land surveyor, Swift's row
Welsh, Rev. Charles, Eliza lodge
White, Rev. William, Granshaw

TRADERS, ETC.

Alleby, John, boot and shoemaker, Fermanagh street
Annesley, John, grocer and publican, Diamond
Averall, Theophilus, grocer, Fermanagh street
Andrews, David, gunsmith, Cara st.
Boyle, John, tailor, Swift's row
Benson, Samuel, agricultural implement maker, Stone bridge
Brady, William, baker and leather dealer, Fermanagh street
Brady, John, agent for Patriotic Fire Assurance Company
Broagan, John, butcher, Analore st.
Boyle, Johnston, cooper, Fermanagh street
Brady, John, agent for Standard Life Assurance Company, master extraordinary in Chancery, and commissioner for taking affidavits in the Four Courts, Dublin, Diamond
Brady, William, grocer and draper, Fermanagh street
Burnside, Archibald, grocer, Fermanagh street
Clerkin, John, baker, Analore street

CLONES.

Clarke, Andrew, corn merchant and ironmonger, Whitehall street
Clarke, James, flour, meal and corn merchant, Whitehall street
Clarke, Andrew, draper and grocer, Whitehall street
Courtney, James, draper, grocer, and publican, Diamond
Cosgrove, Catherine, publican, Fermanagh street
Cosgrove, S., straw bonnet maker, Fermanagh street
Donnelly, Peter, baker, grocer, and woollendraper, Diamond
Duffy, Phillip, saddler, Cara street
Devany, Hugh, tailor, Whitehall st.
Elliott, George, grocer and draper, Cara street
Farquhar, Robert, draper, Diamond
Farquhar, Robert, watch and clock maker, Diamond
Gillespie, Mrs., publican, Fermanagh street
Graham, Francis, painter and glazier, Fermanagh street
Gallagher, Francis, carpenter, Analore street
Gallagher, Henry, boot and shoemaker, Cara street
Graydon, James, baker, Fermanagh st.
Gray, Johnston, cooper, Poundhill
Graydon, Amina, milliner and dressmaker, Fermanagh street
Harrington, William, blacksmith, Monaghan street
Higgin, Winfield, agent to Ulster Canal Carrying Company, Cara st.
Hand, Patrick, carpenter, Swift's row
Hetherington, James, painter and glazier, Cara street
Irwin, Robert, publican, Fermanagh st.
Jordan, Robert, carpenter, Analore st.
Keenan, James, grocer, publican, and leather dealer, Fermanagh street
Kerr, Richard, Dacre Arms hotel, Diamond
Leghorn, John, butcher and tanner, Analore street
Lynch, Bernard, blacksmith, Analore street
Magood, John, butcher, Fermanagh street
Monaghan, William, blacksmith, Whitehall street
Morrison, Jeremiah, baker, Diamond
Miller, Joseph, boot and shoemaker, Cara street
Morgan, Robert, boot and shoemaker, Cara street
Monaghan, Patrick, butcher, Analore street
Morris, Patrick, butcher, Analore st.
Moore, M. and E., corn merchants, Analore street
M'Aveney, Pat., cooper, Fermanagh st.
M'Donald, John, baker, Analore st.
M'Guiness, Thomas, baker, Diamond
M'Keany, John, baker and publican, Analore street
M'Cabe, P., blacksmith, Abbey lane
M'Ilroy, Wm., butcher, Analore st.
M'Mahon, H., carpenter, Abbey lane
Morrison, J., grocer, Diamond
M'Elroy, J., woollendraper, Diamond
M'Connell, Wm., publican, Analore st.
Murray, L., publican, Analore street
Martin, John, tailor, Cara street
Owens, Michael, butcher, Analore st.
O'Connor, Owen, grocer, Diamond
Porter, Joseph, boot and shoemaker, Cara street
Robinson, Joseph, watch and clockmaker, Diamond
Reynolds, T., publican, Cara st.
Rennick, Andrew, butter dealer and provision merchant, Drumcrew
Robinson, Mary Ann, milliner and dressmaker
Shiels, Francis, boot and shoemaker, Analore street
Shields, Hugh, King's Arms hotel, Diamond
Shegog, Mary Ann, draper, Diamond
Shiel, Edward, woollendraper, Fermanagh street
Stinson, James, saddler, Diamond
Story, Richard, publican, Cara street
Smith, John, coachmaker, Cara street
Sweeney, Francis, pawnbroker, Pound hill
Syme, James, brewer, Analore street
Thompson, William, baker, grocer, and earthenware dealer, Fermanagh st.
Thompson, Andrew, draper, Diamond
Turner, Jas., butter dealer, Pound hill
Wilson, James, printer, Whitehall st.
White, Daniel, tin-plate worker, Cara street

COLERAINE.

Is a Parliamentary borough, in the county of Londonderry, 44 miles N. of Belfast. It is a manufacturing and commercial town, and is situated on the river Bann. The more modern, business, and stirring part of the town is on the west of the river, and the more ancient and now less important part on the east, connected by a substantial stone bridge. This town has been long remarkable for the fineness of its linen cloth, the excellence of its salmon fishery, and the beauty of its rural scenery. It returns one member to Parliament. Borough Representative—The Right Hon. Lord Naas.

Conveyances—To Londonderry, mail coach every day at half-past 11 o'clock, from Davock's hotel; one horse car every morning at 7 o'clock, from Robert M'Kay's, Diamond; one horse car every morning at 7 o'clock, from Miss Mooney's, Swan hotel, Bridge st. To Ballymoney and Ballymena, mail daily, from Davock's, at half past one; the Fair Trader, a four horse coach, every morning (Sunday excepted) at 6 o'clock, from Adam M'Kay's, Diamond, arriving in time for the Belfast train, which leaves Ballymena at 10 o'clock. To Ballycastle, a van every Saturday, at 4 o'clock a.m., from Gillespie's, Church st. One horse cars daily to Portstewart, Portrush, &c.

Gas Works, Bann side—Property of the town, vested in the Commissioners; John Boyd, treasurer; D. Magonigal, secretary; John Robinson, manager

Magistrates—Lord Robert Montague, Cromore; John Boyd, Dundoon; John Cromie, D.L., Cromore; Andrew Orr, Milburne; Charles J. Knox, Jackson hall; William Wilson Campbell, The Castle, Portstewart; Sir H. H. Bruce, bart., D.L., Downhill; Thomas Bennett, jun., Castleroe; Samuel Laurence, Bannfield

Coroner—Daniel Gailey, Diamond

Town Commissioners—Hugh Bellas, chairman; Robert Sharpe, Archd. M'Elwain, Thomas Davock, James Moore, Thomas H. Babington, James Barr, Daniel Taylor, Daniel Gaily, William Warke, Robert Nevin, Patrick M'Laughlin, A. J. H. Moody, Joseph Orr, John Matthews, John Glenn, Robert M'Kay, John Getty, John M'Curdy, Samuel Eccles, James Steen.—Treasurer and agent, John Boyd, Dundoon, Coleraine; Daniel M'Gonigal, clerk; Samuel W. Knox, town clerk

Corporation or Market house, centre of the Diamond—Used for courts of Quarter & Petty Sessions, & by the Town Commissioners; contains the Coleraine Library, Savings' Bank, Night Guard room, and large Public Assembly room, and is let for concerts, balls, &c.—Daniel M'Gonigal, caretaker

Quarter Sessions—Wm. Armstrong, Esq., assistant-barrister; William Gregg, clerk of the Peace for town and county; Jas. W. Gregg, deputy clerk of the Peace

Petty Sessions, every alternate Friday—clerk, John Taggart, Hanover place

Constabulary Barrack, Cross lane—J. R. Gibbons, sub-inspector, New row; Robert Jenkins, head constable

Bridewell, near Beresford place—Jas. Rodgers, superintendent of night watch

Custom-House, Hanover place—Robt. Hunter, collector; John Gordon, comptroller

Excise-office, Newmarket street

Harbour, under Portrush Harbour Commissioners—agent at Coleraine, John Taggart

Markets—Monday, Wednesday, and Friday, corn, &c.; Saturday, the principal market day

Shambles, Meetinghouse Street—Contains eighteen stalls, open every lawful day for the sale of meat and fish; present proprietor, Hugh Kane

COLERAINE.

Banks—Northern Bank, Diamond, J. H. M'Auley, manager; Belfast Bank, Diamond, James M'Farland, manager; Provincial Bank, Hanover place, W. N. Rowan, manager; Savings' Bank, Market-house, John Canning, actuary

Notary Public—John Taggart, Hanover place

Poor-Law Union Workhouse, Mountsandal road—To accommodate 860; John Cromie, chairman of Board of Guardians; Andrew Orr, vice-chairman; H. Lecky, deputy chairman; William Mellon, master; Isabella Hemphill, matron. Chaplains—Rev. Jas. O'Hara, Episcopal; Rev. John Martin, Presbyterian; Rev. Richard Killen, P. P., Roman Catholic.— Treasurer, Belfast Bank; clerk, J. V. Fleming; relieving officer, Wm. Simpson, Cross lane

Fever Hospital, to accommodate sixty, contiguous to Workhouse—Dr. H T. Babington, medical attendant

Dispensary, near Hanover place— Open Tuesday and Friday, from nine till twelve, Dr. J. J. Macaldin, medical attendant

Loan Fund, Market-House—James Cowan, clerk

Coleraine Parish Church, Church st. —Rev. James O'Hara, rector; Rev. Richard Young, curate

Killowen Parish Church, Killowen st. —Rev. Wm. Wharton Sillito, rector

First Presbyterian Church, Meetinghouse place—Rev. Wm. Ritchie

Second Presbyterian Church, New row —Rev. James Alfred Canning

Third Presbyterian Church, Terrace row—Rev. Joseph M'Donnell

Independent Congregational Meetinghouse, New row—Rev. T. Pullar

Baptist Chapel, Meetinghouse place— Rev. J. Brown

Wesleyan Methodist Chapel, Meetinghouse lane—Rev. Wallace M'Mullan, Rev. Joseph M'Kee

St. Malachi's R. C. Chapel, Square commons—Rev. Richd. Killen, P.P.

St. John's R. C. Chapel, Killowen— Rev. Charles Flannigan, P.P.

Coleraine Library, Market-House— Robert Given, secretary

District National Model School, Upper Captain street—Average attendance, males fifty, females fifty-four, infants fifty; principal master, John Johnston—6 assistants; principal mistress, Eliza Smyth—four assistants; principal of infant school, M. L. Hellings—one assistant

Mechanics' Institute, Market-house— James Coyle, secretary

The Irish Society's Male and Female School, Beresford place—John and Mrs. Canning, teachers; Mrs. Ellen Brooks, assistant

Irish Society's Female School, Killowen—Mrs. Long, mistress

Killowen Roman Catholic National Male and Female School—James M'Laughlin and Jane Loughrey, teachers

Coleraine Roman Catholic National School—James M'Grotty and Eliza Gillen, teachers

Infant School, Lowerstone row—Mrs. Brown, mistress

Public News-Room, Meetinghouse Street—James Coyle, proprietor

Coleraine Chronicle, every Saturday; H. B. Mackay, proprietor; Robert Huey, publisher; office, Meetinghouse street

---

NOBILITY AND GENTRY.

Babington, Major, Ballysally house
Bennett, Thomas, jun., Castleroe
Bellas, Thomas, The Cottage
Bellas, Hugh
Boyd, John, Dundoon
Boyce, James, Brookhall
Boyle, Joseph
Black, Thomas, Cabinhill
Brownlow, James, Greenfield
Bruce, Sir H. H., bart., Downhill
Bruce, James, Mountsandal
Cromie, John, Culbreene
Dalrymple, Captain,
Dunlop, Mrs. J., Rothesay house
Galt, Griffen Charles, Mountsandal
Harvey, Mrs. and Miss, Northbrook
Hunter, Robert, Meetinghouse street
Knox, Charles James, Jackson hall
Kyle, Henry, Laurel hill
Lang, Captain, Bannview
Laurence, Mrs., Hanover place
Laurence, Samuel, Banefield House

Laurence, Samuel, Banefield House
Lyle, Hugh, Knocktarne
Lyle, James A., Knocktern
Montague, Lord Robt., Cromore house
Orr, Andrew, Milburne house
Orr, Samuel, Flowerfield
Richardson, Lady Emily, Somerset
Richardson, Mrs., Ballyness
Shaw, Captain R. A., Chapel field
Smith, H., Lodge
Smith, Miss, Hanover place
Tyttle, John M., Farmhill

CLERGY, PROFESSIONAL, ETC.

Babington, Thos. H., M.D., F.R.C.S.I.
Barr, James, surgeon & apothecary, New row
Brown, Rev. J., Meeting house place
Cavin, Wm., M.D., Ferry quay st.
Carson, J. C. L., M.D., & licentiate apothecary, Diamond
Canning, Rev. J. A., New row
Clarke, Andrew, surgeon & licentiate apothecary, Diamond
Craig, Rev. George, Macosquin
Flanaghan, Rev. Chas., P.P., Killowen
Gwynne, Rev. Stephen, Agherton Rectory, near Portstewart
Hayden, Very Rev. Archdeacon, Articlave
Houston, Robert, sen., surgeon and apothecary, Church street
Killen, Rev. Richard, P.P., Square Commons
Knox, Samuel W., solicitor, New row
Lyle, Rev. John, Knocktarne
Mackay, Hugh Boyde, solicitor, Hanover place
Martin, Rev. John, Castleroe
Macaldin, J. J., M.D., F.R.C.S.I., Meetinghouse place
M'Donnell, Rev. Joseph
M'Gonigal, Daniel, solicitor, Bridge st.
M'Gonigal, David, solicitor, Master in Chancery, and commissioner for taking affidavids for all law courts, Gaol street
M'Keag, William, M.D., & licentiate apothecary, Water side
M'Kee, Rev. J., Wesleyan minister
M'Mullan, Rev. Wallace, Wesleyan minister
Neill, Alex., surgeon R.N., New row
O'Hara, Rev. James, The Rectory
Pullan, Rev. T., Independent minister
Ritchie, Rev. William
Sillito, Rev. Wm., Wharton, Killowen Glebe

TRADERS, ETC.

Archibald, Robert, publican, New Market street
Baxter, Warren, sen., house painter, paper hanger, &c., Preachinghouse lane
Barber, James, baker, Killowen
Bellas, H. & T., ironmongers, Church street
Bellas, H. and T., timber yard, near Beresford place
Black, Edward, grocer and publican, Meetinghouse street
Boyd, Charles, classical seminary, Hanover place
Boyd, Robert, builder, New row
Boyland, M., publican, Church street
Burrell, Mrs., confectioner, Meetinghouse street
Caldwell, Mrs. grocer, Waterside
Caldwell, Eliza Ann, grocer, oil and colour shop, Waterside
Caldwell, James, saddler and harness maker, Preachinghouse lane
Canning, John, boot and shoemaker, Diamond
Cathcart, William, and Co., silk mercers and haberdashers, New row
Campbell, A., baker, Church street
Christy, Daniel, marble and stone works, Meetinghouse street
Christy, Alexander, grain merchant, Church street
Church, John, boot and shoemaker, Church street
Clarke, James, grocer, druggist, and passage broker, Bridge street
Clark, Robt., confectioner, Church st.
Cowan, James, bookseller & stationer, Church street
Cochrane, Catherine, silk mercer, haberdasher, &c., Diamond
Coyle, James, builder, King's gate
Crowe, J., grocer and haberdasher, Killowen
Curry, Arthur, grocer, Church street
Curriston, J., pawnbroker, Church st
Cunningham, James, pawnbroker, Meetinghouse street
Cuthbert, Alexander, tan yard; residence, Northbrook
Darragh, J., woollendraper, Diamond

Davock, Thomas, Clothworkers' Arms hotel, Waterside
Daly, Charles, seedsman, Bridge st.
Darragh, Neal, grocer and publican, Newmarket street
Dempsey, James, publican, Captain st.
Dempsey, Patrick, general dealer, Lowerstone row
Dillon, James, pawnbroker, Church st.
Dornan, Constantine, publican and builder, Captain street
Doherty, Chas., cabinetmaker, auction and commission mart, Bridge st.
Dougherty, H., spirit dealer, Longcommons
Dunlop, David, silk mercer, New row
Eccles, Samuel, bookseller, stationer, letter-press & copper-plate printer, and room-paper warehouse, &c.
Ellis, Wm., family grocer, Bridge st.
Ferris, Robert, publican, Church st.
Fleming, John, grocer, meal and flour dealer, Waterside
Gage, Mathew, coach builder, Killowen
Gaw, Thos., bookseller and stationer, Bridge street
Geary and Gray, pawnbrokers, Church street
Getty, John, wine and spirit merchant, Church street
Given, Mrs, grocer and publican, Bridge street
Given and Co., wine merchants, Church street
Given, Jn., wholesale grocer, Hanover place
Given and Co., iron and timber merchants, Diamond
Gilmour, Jas., watchmaker, jeweller, &c., Diamond
Gilmour, M., publican, Newmarket st.
Gillespie, James, publican, Church st.
Glenn, John, publican, Killowen
Glenn, John, publican, Diamond
Glenn, John, publican, Newmarket st.
Gordon, Thomas, family grocer, tea and wine merchant, Bridge street
Gowdy, Robert T., classical seminary, Meetinghouse street
Gribben, Edward, and Son, woollendrapers and haberdashers, Waterside
Gribben, Edward, and Son, linen manufacturers and yarn merchants, Killowen

Groves, William, boot and shoemaker, Diamond
Greaves, James, nail manufacturer, Lowerstone row
Haddock, Misses, boarding and day school, Castleview
Haltridge, John, coach builder, New row
Hall, John, auctioneer, New row
Hamilton, John, haberdasher, Church street
Harkin, John, music and dancing academy, Stone row
Hart, Thomas, baker, New row
Henry, Thomas, grocer, Waterside
Horner, J., hardware merchant, Meetinghouse street
Houston, John, grocer, Church street
Hunter, Stewart, general grocer, Bridge street
Hurley and Magowan, tailors, Hanover place
Hunter, James, saddler and harness maker, Diamond
Hughes, John, butcher, Meetinghouse street and Killowen
Hynd, William, silk mercer and haberdasher, New row
Hyndman, Thomas, hardware and house furnishing shop, Bridge st.
Jenkins, J., publican, Newmarket st.
Kane, Hugh, auctioneer and appraiser, Meetinghouse street
Kane, Daniel, cabinet maker, Meetinghouse street
Kane, Ann, grocer, Killowen
Kane, John, grocer and publican, Killowen
Kennedy, David, grocer, &c., Waterside
Kennedy, Hugh, iron and brass founder, Terrace row
Kennedy, John, publican, Brook st.
Keith, James, confectioner, Meetinghouse street
Kelly, James, painter and glazier, New row
Kirkpatrick, Samuel, architect, Stone row
Lithgow, Robert, publican, Brook st.
Loughrey, Archibald, Agricultural inn, Church street
Loughery, John, grocer and publican, Captain street
Lusk, John, baker, Church street

COLERAINE.

Lyons, Adam, grocer and general hardware shop, Newmarket street
Lyons, Jas., publican, Newmarket st.
Lyons, Adam, meal and salt store, New row
Lyons, John, boot and shoemaker, Church street
Lynn, William, grocer, Church street
Magowan, Patrick, cabinet maker, Bridge street
Matthews, John and James, woollendrapers, haberdashers, &c., Bridge street
Martin, Peter, grocer, Waterside
Magilligan, Michael, auctioneer and clothes broker, Meetinghouse st.
Magowan & Hurley, tailors, Hanover place
Mathers, Adam, watchmaker, Church street
May, Mrs. Elizabeth, Oak hotel, Meetinghouse street
Mehan, James, Derry Waterside distillery; spirit store, Bridge street
Miller, David, whitesmith, Killowen
Milligan, Robt., publican, Newmarket street
Moore, James, Coleraine distillery, Newmarket street
Moore, William, Glenstall mills flour store, Church street
Mooney, Sarah, Swan hotel, Bridge street
Moody, A. J. H., family grocer, wine and spirit dealer, Bridge street
Montgomery, Charles, bootmaker, Diamond
Morrison, Robert, sewed muslin agent, Lowerstone row
M'Alister, Æneas, saddler and harness maker, Church street
M'Afee, Hugh, grocer, Church street
M'Carter, Joseph, tanner, New row
M'Candless, John, grocer, Church st.
M'Caughey & Taylor, coach builders, New row
M'Curdy, James, corn dealer, coal, timber, and ironmonger, Killowen
M,Cormick, John, bookseller and stationer, Diamond
M'Conville, Edwd., auctioneer, Lowerstone row
M'Curdy, John, family grocer and spirit merchant, Diamond & Church street

M'Divett, Bernard, publican & grocer, Killowen
M'Divett, Neal, auctioneer & clothes broker, Bridge street
M'Elwain, Archibald, woollen hall and carpet warehouse, Bridge street
M'Elwain, Robert, baker, Church st.
M'Fetridge, James, spirit shop, Church street
M'Fetridge, Daniel, baker, Church st.
M'Gee, Robert, merchant tailor, New row
M'Gee, W. and J., tailors, Preachinghouse lane
M'Gill, John, grocer and provision shop, New row
M'Grotty, John, Corporation Arms hotel, Diamond
M'Grotty, James, butcher, Cross lane
M'Grotty, William, butcher, Long Commons
M'Intyre, Wm., hardware merchant, Diamond
M'Kay, Adam, innkeeper, and proprietor of Ballymena coach, Diamond
M'Kay, Robert, innkeeper, Diamond
M'Kinlay, E., delf and china shop, Diamond
M'Kitterick, Miss, silk mercer and haberdasher, New row
M'Laughlin, Patrick, wine and spirit merchant, Waterside
M'Laughlin, John, spirit store, Preachinghouse lane
M'Mullan, A., publican, Church street
M'Nabb, R., saddler, Church street
M'Neill, J., publican, Church street
M'Neill, Mrs., teacher of music and drawing, Stone row
M'Williams, Mary, publican, Church street
Nevin, Robert, grocer, Church street
Norris, S., grocer, Brook street
Nicholson, J., grocer and posting house, Meetinghouse street
Orr, Joseph, Queen's Arms hotel, Bridge street
Orr, Wm., haberdasher, Church street
Paul, James, publican, Captain street
Patterson, C., publican, Brook street
Pollock, Hannah, innkeeper, Killowen
Robinson, James, woollendraper and haberdasher, Bridge street
Robb, the Misses, haberdashers, Church street

Scobey, Rachael, delf and china shop, Bridge street
Self, John, shirt factory, Lowerstone row
Sharpe, Robert, soap and candle manufacturer, Church street
Small, Robert, tea warehouse, family grocer, &c., Church street
Stirling, Robert, marble and stone works, Preachinghouse lane
Taylor, D. and R., family grocers and seed merchants, Church street
Templeton, Robert, butcher, Long Commons
Thompson, Robert, haberdasher and silk mercer, Diamond
Thompson, Sarah, milliner, New row
Tomb, Wm., publican and saddler, Killowen street
Volatti, Miss, teacher of music, New row
Warke, Wm., ironmonger and timber merchant, Diamond
Warke, Wm., timber yard and bond stores, Bridge street
Weir, Misses, boarding & day school, New row
Weir, Robert, watchmaker & jeweller, Bridge street
Wilson, Richard, spirit shop, Brook street
Wilson, J. and R., grain merchants and general commission agents, Diamond
Wilson, John, Farmers' tavern, Rosemary lane
Woods, J., sewed muslin agent, New row
Young, John, yarn store, Bridge st.

COMBER.

COMBER or Cumber, is a market town and parish, in the co. of Down, 14 miles from Downpatrick, 7 E. S. E. from Belfast, situated on the road from Belfast to Downpatrick. It is tolerably well built, and formed of four main streets, which intersect each other at right angles, and terminate in a handsome square, in the centre of which is a Masonic monument to General Gillespie, erected by subscription. The river Comber, upon whose banks the town is situated, and from which its name is derived, runs into Strangford Lough, on the East side of the parish, and the tide flows to within a short distance of the town. The principal fuel consumed here is turf, which is supplied from an extensive bog in the neighbourhood, called Moneyreagh or the *Royal bog*, from which great quantities are also sent to Belfast and other places. There are two extensive distilleries here, the same number of large corn mills, two respectable hotels, and a large bleach-green. A manorial court is held every third Thursday for the manor of Comber, for recovery of debts not exceeding £10. The Church is a small handsome building. There are places of worship for Presbyterians, Unitarians, and Wesleyan Methodists. The educational institutions are a schoo', founded by Viscountess Castlereagh, in 1813, one under Erasmus Smith's charity, and congregational and national schools. The market is held on Tuesday. Fairs, April 5th, June 28th, and October 19th.

Post-office, Square—Joseph Shean, postmaster. Letters from Dublin and all parts of the South of Ireland, also from England, arrive every morning at eight, and are despatched every afternoon at five; letters from Belfast and all parts of the North of Ireland, arrive every afternoon at twenty minutes past three, and are despatched every morning at nine; letters from Downpatrick and intermediate places, arrive every morning at nine, and are despatched every afternoon at half-past three

Conveyances—To Belfast, a mail car (from Downpatrick) calls at Barry's hotel every morning at 9 o'clock, and a coach (from Killyleagh) calls at James Millings every morning (Sunday excepted), at eight. To Downpatrick—a mail car (from

Belfast) calls at Barry's hotel, every afternoon at twenty minutes past three, goes through Killyleagh. To Dromore—a mail car, calls at Barry's hotel, every afternoon at five o'clock. To Killyleagh—a coach (from Belfast) calls at Milling's hotel, every afternoon (Sunday excepted) at a quarter to five, and by mail car to Downpatrick, at half-past three

Parish Church, Square—Rev. W. D. Crommelin, rector
Presbyterian Church, Downpatrick street—Rev. John Rogers, minister
Presbyterian Church, Cow lane—Rev. James M'Millen, minister
Unitarian Church, Mill street—Rev. John Orr, minister
Wesleyan Methodist Chapel, Bridge street—Ministers various
Erasmus Smith's School, Square—Samuel Mills, master
Infant School, Square—Betty Gilmore, mistress
Constabulary Station, Bridge street—William Gilmore, constable

GENTRY, CLERGY, PROFESSIONAL, ETC.

Allen, John, surgeon, Square
Andrews, John, J.P., Mill street
Birch, James, Ballybeen
Birch, The Misses Mary and Margaret, Bridge street
Crommelin, Miss, Glebe house
Crommelin, Rev. Wm D., Glebe house
Douglass, William, Camperdown
Frame, James, surgeon, Square
Gordon, Robert, D.L., J.P., Florida Manor
Hardy, Freeman, Ballyrainey house
Kennedy, Wm., surgeon, Bridge st.
Killen, Rev. James, Cow lane
Miller, John
M'Cance, The Misses Isabella and Jane, Bridge street
M'Ilwrath, Capt. Thos., J.P., Killynether
Orr, Rev. John, Square
Orr & Montgomery, solicitors, Square
Riddle, Mrs. Jane, Mill street
Rogers, Rev. John, Mill street
Stone, Guy, J.P., Barnhill

TRADERS, ETC.

Andrews, James, and Sons, millers and linen merchants, Mill street
Allen, George, tanner, Square
Barry's Hotel, Square
Bowman, Hugh, saddler, Cow lane
Canning, Henry, tailor, Mill street
Commercial Hotel, Square
Corbett, John, watchmaker, Mill st.
Carse, Maria, straw bonnet maker, do.
Crea, George, miller, Maxwell's court
Duncan, Frances, grocer, &c., Cow lane
Duncan, Agnes, publican, Cow lane
Douglass, Robert, painter and glazier, Mill street
Gibson, Thomas, saddler, Bridge st.
Hamilton, John, carpenter, Bridge st.
Harris, Jane, publican, Mill street
Hamilton, John, grocer, &c., Bridge street
Halliday, Wm., grocer, &c., Cow lane
Hamilton, Mary Jane, dressmaker, Bridge street
Heaney, Robert, grocer, &c., Square
Jeffrey, James, publican, Square
Johnston, Daniel, grocer, Mill street
Lindsay, James, grocer, Cow lane
Lindsay, Wm. John, publican, Mill st.
Lindsay, Robert, and Co., sewed muslin manufacturers, Cow lane—John M'Donnell, agent
Macdonald, D., and J. (of Glasgow), sewed muslin manufacturers, Mill street—J. Robertson, agent
Miller, John, maltster and distiller, Downpatrick street and Bridge st.
Milling, James, publican, Square
Munn, James, blacksmith, Cow lane
Munn, Matthew, blacksmith, Cow lane
Murray, William, grocer, Bridge st.
M'Caw, William, boot and shoemaker, Cow lane
M'Gowan, David, carpenter and spirit dealer, Mill street
M'Keag, William, carpenter, Square
M'Morran, George, grocer, Square
M'Ilwrath, John, blacksmith, Mill st.
M'Briar, J., draper, &c., Mill street
M'Quoid, Samuel, Railway Tavern, Mill street
Mullen, George, grocer, Bridge street
Riddle, Henry, tallow chandler, Cow lane
Riddle, James, grocer, Mill street

Ritchey, Henry D., publican, Mill street
Robb, William, wheelwright, Mill st.
Robb, Gawn, tailor, Mill street
Robb, Susannah, dressmaker, Mill street
Robinson, James, Bradshaw Arms hotel, Bridge street
Robinson, William, publican, Downpatrick street
Shean, Joseph, woollendraper an haberdasher, Square
Simpson, Robert, publican, Downpatrick street
Taylor, W., and J., woollendrapers, haberdashers, &c., Square
Weir, Messrs., sewed muslin manufacturers, Square—William Napier, agent
Wilson, Daniel, grocer, Mill street

COOKSTOWN.

COOKSTOWN is a flourishing and respectable market town, in the county of Tyrone, 35 miles W. from Belfast; very pleasantly seated on the Kildress rivulet, and on the great North road from Armagh, at the point where it communicates with the roads leading respectively towards Londonderry and Coleraine. Its main street, or chief thoroughfare, is spacious, and ornamented with fine lofty trees on either side. This principal street, with its trees, presents the appearance of a mall, and is so intimately connected with the adjacent finely-wooded demesne of Killymoon, as to possess a delightfully rural character. The mansion or castle of Killymoon is a superb edifice, in the Saxon style, built from designs by Nash, at a reputed cost of £80,000. The staple of Cookstown may be considered its linen trade, in which many respectable merchants are embarked; and there are several extensive bleach-greens, flax mills, corn and meal mills, and seed merchants. Petty Sessions are held, by the local Magistrates, once a fortnight, and a Manorial Court, by Robert Evans, Esq., the Seneschal, monthly.

The Parish Church of Derryloran is a neat stone structure, with an elegant and lofty spire; the other places of worship are three Presbyterian Churches, two Methodist Meeting-houses, and a Roman Catholic Chapel. There are several educational and other charitable institutions—the former comprise national and ragged schools, supported by public subscription.

The market days are Tuesday and Saturday, the latter for farming produce, which is brought in abundance; the former for grain. Fairs—first Saturday of each month.

Post-Office, William street—Margaret Patteson, post-mistress. Letters from Dublin and all parts of the South of Ireland, also from England and Scotland, arrive every morning at 8, and are despatched every afternoon at 4-40; from Coleraine and various places, arrive every afternoon at 4-40, and are despatched every morning at 8
Conveyances—To Coleraine, the Royal mail car (from Dungannon), every morning at 8, goes through Moneymore, Magherafelt, Tubbermore, Maghera, and Garvagh; to Dungannon, a mail car (from Coleraine) every afternoon at 4-40, goes through Stewartstown, in time for the coach to Dublin
Carriers—To Belfast, Charles Mooney and James Mooney, once a-week, go through Moneymore, Magherafelt, and Antrim; to Randalstown, John Riely and Robert Hamilton, every day
Constabulary Station, James street—John H. Ridge, Sub-inspector
Stamp Office, William street—Joseph Rodgers, Sub-distributor
Union Workhouse—Francis Murphy master; Wm. Ballantyne, clerk
Belfast Banking Co. (branch of), James street—Thomas A. Vesey, manager; Thomas Leckey, accountant
Ulster Banking Company (branch), William st.—Robt. Stark, manager; John Paul, accountant

COOKSTOWN.

Savings' Bank, James st.—William Ballintine, actuary
Loan Fund, James street—Silas E. Weir, treasurer; John M'Cormick, secretary
Parish Church, Gortlowry—Rev. A. Moloney, rector; Rev. Thomas G. Stokes, curate
Presbyterian Church, 1st—Rev. H. B. Wilson, minister
Presbyterian Church, 2nd—Rev. T. Millar, minister
Presbyterian Church, 3rd—Rev. John Knox Leslie, minister
Wesleyan Methodist Chapel, James street—ministers various
Primitive Methodist Chapel, James street—ministers various
Roman Catholic Chapel, Gortlowry—Rev. Wm. M'Conville, P.P.; Rev. Patrick Campbell and Rev. James M'Kenna, curates
Church Education School, Gortlowry
National School, Gortlowry—Michael Lappin, master
Ragged School—William M'Cormick, master

GENTRY, ETC.

Adair, T., Killymoon.
Agnew, Margaret
Akin, Mary
Allen, Elizabeth
Bailie, Mrs., Turneskea
Brady, Major W. S. R, D.L., J.P., Oaklands
Croker, Richard
Custer, Elizabeth
Fulton, Adam, Gortlowry
Gibson, Mary
Greer, Thomas, J.P., Tullylagan
Griffith, Henry, Killycolpy
Gunning, James, Wellbrook
Knox, Edward C., J.P., Desertcreight
Lavens, John, Clare
Lindsay, F. L.
Linn, Jane, Waterloo place
Magill, Mary
Magill, S. R., J.P., Creene
Newton, Henry, Gortlowry
Nicholson, Anna, Rock lodge
Powell, J. B., William street
Richardson, Elizabeth, Loy
Smyth, Mary
Stafford, Alicia, William street
Staples, Sir Thomas, Q.C., Lissan
Stark, Robert, William street
Tener, John Kinley, J.P., Moree Rock
Vesey, T. A.
Wilford, John, Grouse lodge

CLERGY AND PROFESSIONAL.

Campbell, Rev. Patrick, Loy
Charles, D. H., M.D., James street
Charles, Henry R., M.D. and surgeon, William street
Dickson, Thomas, surgeon, Loy
Ferguson, Rev. William, Tievenagh
Geddes, Rev. Joseph, Sandholes
Graves, Henry, M.D., James street
Holmes, R. W., attorney, William st.
Hamilton, D. J., surgeon, James st.
Heron, William, surgeon, William st.
Hutchinson, Hicks, surgeon, Muff
Irvine, Rev. W. J., Muff
Leslie, Rev. John Knox, William st.
M'Conville, Rev. William, Loy
M'Gowan, Rev. John G., Orritor
M'Kenna, Rev. James, Gortacar
Millar, Rev. Thomas, James street
Miller, Franks, and Miller, attorneys, William street
Molony, Rev. Arthur, Derryloran Glebe
Murray, John, M.D., James street
Newton, A. J., attorney, James street
Porter, Rev. T. H., D.D.
Sloan, George, surgeon, William street
Stewart, Rev. Richard, Drumshambo Glebe

TRADERS, ETC.

Adair, Thomas, and Co., bleachers, Greenvale
Atcheson, James, boot and shoemaker Orritor street
Adair & Gunning, spinners, Greenvale
Allen, William, grocer and publican William street
Aston, William, grocer, William street
Atcheson, Robert, grocer
Anderson, David, baker and grocer William street
Allen, John, blacksmith, Gortlowry
Allen, William, blacksmith, Orritor
Anderson, George, flax merchant, Tullywigan
Anderson, D. W., earthenware dealer
Anderson, James, flax merchant, Tullywigan
Atcheson, M., dressmaker, Orritor st.
Anderson, James, saddler, James st.

COOKSTOWN.

Anderson, James, publican
Ballantyne, James, spirit dealer, James street
Buchanan, Andrew, whitesmith, Gortlowry
Black, John, grocer, ironmonger, and leather seller, William street
Bell, John, grocer, William street
Bole, Jane, grocer, William street
Branigan, John, reedmaker, Gortlowry
Brown, John, watchmaker
Beatty, Thomas, miller
Black, William, flax miller, Corkhill
Black, John, steam corn mill, William street
Carlton, Jas., boot & shoemaker, Loy
Carlton, John, boot & shoemaker, Loy
Cluff, James, cabinetmaker, James st.
Campbell, A., confectioner, James st.
Chambers, J., dressmaker, Gortlowry
Charles, Wm., watchmaker, William street
Campbell, Thos., publican, William st.
Charles, Stuart, publican, William st.
Charles, H. and R., flax millers
Cowan, John, flax miller
Devlin, John, boot and shoemaker, Coagh street
Donnelly, John, clothes broker, William street
Devlin, Mark, cooper, James street
Donnelly, Bernard, clothes broker, James street
Duncan, Isabella, confectioner
Dobson, Samuel, grocer and seedsman
Devlin, James, grocer and publican
Dickson, Robert, corn merchant
Devlin, Mary, dressmaker, Coagh st.
Duncan, A., dressmaker, William st.
Dillon, John, reedmaker, Orritor st.
Dunseith, Robert, tailor, William st.
Dickson, Andrew, flax and corn miller
Eagleson, David, baker, William st.
Eccles, John, flax merchant and spirit dealer, Kildress
Ferguson, Joseph, boot and shoemaker, William street
Ferguson, A. F., baker, William street
Ferguson, E., dressmaker, William st.
Ferguson, Alex., watchmaker, Artrea
Ferguson, Peter, whitesmith, Loy
Farrelly, Michael, flax miller
Gunning and Moore, bleachers, Wellbrook
Gunning, James, bleacher, Wellbrook
Gillespie, Wm., boot and shoemaker, William street
Glasgow, Robert, flax spinner, Draper's field
Gourley, John, grocer & ironmonger, James street
Graham, Charles, grocer
Glasgow, Ben., baker, William street
Galway, James, butcher, William st.
Galway, John, carpenter, William st.
Glasgow, Wm., draper, William street
Graham, Peter, tailor
Graves, John G., publican, William st.
Hughes, William, boot and shoemaker, William street
Harbison, John, spirit dealer, grocer, baker, and seedsman, William st.
Harbison, Francis, Imperial hotel, William street
Hagan, John, blacksmith, Orritor st.
Hunter, John, draper, William street
Henderson, M., and Son, linen manufacturers, Sherrygroom
Hughes, Margt., dressmaker, Coagh st.
Harbison, Francis, saddler, William st.
Harbison, Francis, wine & spirit dealer
Halliday, Jane, teacher, William st.
Johnston, Joseph, builder, James st
Johnston, Wm., earthenware dealer, Orritor street
Johnston, Benjamin, grocer
Kane, Jn., blacksmith and carpenter, Gortlowry
Kane, Richard, boot and shoemaker, Gortlowry
Kyle, Jas., clothes broker, William st.
Kighelty, John, flax merchant and publican, Coagh street
Kelly, Wm., flax merchant, Coagh st.
Kyle, Jemima, dressmaker, William st.
Langford, Bernard, boot and shoemaker, Loy
Lindsay, Frederick, flax merchant, Rock lodge
Leslie, John, tailor, James street
Lynd, Robert, tailor, James street
Lynd, Alex., publican, William street
Little, William, publican, William st.
Milligan, Patrick, blacksmith, Gortlowry
Molloy, Patrick, Stewart's Arms hotel, James street
Molloy, Patrick, publican
Mooney, Michael, blacksmith, Gortlowry

COOKSTOWN.

Mulgrew, David, blacksmith, Orritor street
Moore, James, bleacher, Wellbrook
Molloy, Rbt., boot and shoemaker, Loy
Miller, Rbt, boot and shoemaker, Loy
Molloy, Hugh, butcher, James st.
Mitchell, James, carpenter, Coagh st.
Mayne, John, cooper, Orritor street
Mackenzie, Henry, grocer and earthenware dealer, William street
Mooney, Chas., hide merchant, grocer and flour merchant, James street
Mulligan, James, grocer
Millar, William, baker, Loy
Murray, John, blacksmith, Orritor st.
Moore, Joseph, clothes broker, William street
Millar, Margaret, draper, William st.
Moore, James, linen merchant, Wellbrook
Magill, William, corn merchant, Dunmore
Morgan, William, oatmeal merchant, William street
Mackenzie, Andrew, publican, William street
Murray, John, publican
Morgan, William, wholesale tea dealer, James street
M'Gaghan, Bernard, blacksmith, Gortlowry
M'Cord, Wm., boot and shoemaker, and leather dealer, Gortlowry
M'Nally, Hugh, boot and shoemaker, William street
M'Guigan, Michael, clothes broker, and publican, James street
M'Loughlin, Bernard, cooper and turner
M'Loughlin, Hugh, cooper, Gortlowry
M'Elhatton, Cornelius, flax merchant, Loy
M'Alister, Thomas, grocer and seedsman, James street
M'Cormick, John, grocer, James st.
M'Cormick, Joseph, publican
M'Geagh, John, grocer and linen manufacturer, William street
M'Nally, Charles, baker, Loy
M'Kenzie, Andrew, baker, William st.
M'Dowell, John, builder, William st.
M'Iver, Rbt., flax merchant, Coagh st.
M'Niece, Wm., flax merctht., Coagh st.
M'Aleer, Hugh, publican, Coagh st.
M'Geagh, James, grocer
M'Cudden, Jas., reedmaker, Coagh st.
M'Guoan, James, saddler, James st.
M'Entyre, Jas., publican, William st.
M'Guckian, John, publican, Coagh st.
M'Entee, E. and P., tailors, Gortlowry
M'Gaghey, Robt., linen manufacturer
M'Alister, Robert, flax miller
Magill, Samuel, flax miller, Green lodge
Neeson, Edwd., publican, William st.
O'Farrel, Joseph, clothes broker, James street
Owen, Daniel
O'Farrell, John, publican, James st.
Patterson, William, grocer, oil and colourman, and ironmonger, William street
Paul, Wiliam, linen merchant, William street
Porter, William, publican, William st.
Quin, Ewd., clothes broker, James st.
Quin, John, grocer, William street
Rankin, Robert, boot and shoemaker, Orritor street
Ramsay, Charles, carpenter, Loy
Rodgers, E. & S., drapers, William st.
Roberts, William, publican, painter, and glazier, William street
Rutherford, G , publican, Gortlowry
Rickard, John, woollendraper, William street
Simpaon, John, clothes broker, William street
Shaw, Thomas, publican, Coagh street
Shaw, G., & Co., linen manufacturers, Greenvale
Sheppard, John, grocer, ironmonger, leather, and glass dealer, William st.
Smith, John A., academy, James st.
Stark, Robert, agent for the West of England Fire Insurance Company, William street.
Storey, Jane, grocer, James street
Sloan, John, linen manufacturer Tullyweary
Smith, E., dressmaker, William street
Smith, John, painter and glazier, William street
Stirling & M'Geagh, woollendrapers, William street
Taylor, Alfred, flax merchant, Coagh street
Vance, John, flax and corn merchant, Gortlowry

Weir, Silas E., agent for the Standard Life Assurance Company
Weir, Silas E., bookseller, draper, & silk mercer, James street
White, James, clothes broker, William street
White, Wm., pawnbroker, William st.
White, James, grocer
Wilson, J., linen merchant, William st.
Wilson, Amelia, staymaker, William st.
White, William, straw bonnet maker, William street
Weir, Jas., publican, Gortlowry
Weir, William, linen manufacturer
Wilford, Thos., flax miller, Grouselodge

DONAGHADEE.

DONAGHADEE is a market town and sea-port in the county of Down, fourteen miles from Belfast, and six from Newtownards; situated on the shore of the Irish channel: it is the nearest port to Scotland, being 24 miles from Portpatrick, the passage to which can be made in three hours by steam vessels. The town consists of several streets, which are wide and well kept. That part of the town next the shore is built in the form of a crescent, and the shape, with the whiteness of the houses, gives the place a very pleasing appearance. Donaghadee possesses all the advantages connected with a pleasant bathing place, having a fine beach, good lodging houses, baths, and other requisites for the comfort and accommodation of visitors. It is a creek to the port of Belfast. The principal imports are coal and timber, and its exports consist chiefly of live cattle and pigs. In the town and neighbourhood many industrious females are employed in embroidering muslin. Petty Sessions are held in the Court-house every Wednesday; a Manor court before the Seneschal occasionally, for debts to the amount of 40s.; and a court leet annually in May. The Church is a large cruciform structure, with a lofty tower at its Western end. The other places of worship are two Churches for Presbyterians, and a Wesleyan Methodist Chapel. At the Northern end of the town is a Danish rath—a mount of considerable height, from the summit of which a beautiful prospect of the town and surrounding country, with a distant view of the Scotch coast and the Copeland Isles, is commanded. The market is held on Wednesday. Fairs—June 9th, July 5th, August 16th, October 11th, and the first Wednesday in December.

Post-office, Shore st.—C. C. Curtis, postmaster. Letters from England, Scotland, Ireland, &c., arrive at 10¾ a.m., and are despatched at 3½ p.m.
Conveyances—A car or cars start from Belfast every morning at seven and nine o'clock, and the mail car every day at half-past three p.m.
Coast Guard—Captain Richard, inspecting commander; Lieutenant Edward G. B. Clarke, chief officer
Custom-house — Henry E. Victor, custom officer and harbour master
Constabulary Station—John Kelly, sub-inspector, Newtownards
Endowed School, Sandy row—Ninian M'Kay, master
Wesleyan School, Main street—Wm. Morrison, teacher
National School, Hunter's lane—Jas. Thompson, master; Jane Spencer, mistress

GENTRY, ETC.

Alexander, Nathaniel, Main street
Blackwood, John O'Reilly, Shore st.
Clarke, Edward G. B., lieutenant and chief officer of Coast Guard
Crommelin, Samuel Delacherois, J.P., Carrowdore castle
Delacherois, Mrs., Main street
Delacherois, Nicholas, J.P., Back st.
Getty, Duncan C., J.P., William st.
Leslie, Mrs. George, Main street
Leslie, Edward F., J.P., Main street
Leslie, Martha, Rosebank
M'Minn, Alexander, J.P., Herds town house
M'Minn, John H., Main street

Patton, Mrs. Robert, Main street
Poe, William T., barrister-at-law, Ballywilliam cottage
Sloan, James, Shore street
Smith, Norman H., New road
Studdart, Captain Richard J. C., coast guard, Erin lodge
Thompson, John G., Main street
Thorn, Sarah, New road

CLERGY AND PROFESSIONAL.

Catherwood, William, M.D., Shore st.
Getty, Thomas, surgeon, New street
Hill, Rev. John, Rectory house
M'Auley, Rev. John, Main street
Skelly, Rev. William, Shore street
Stewart, Samuel, surgeon, New street

TRADERS, ETC.

Arthur, William, Arthur's hotel, Shore street
Boomer, Henry, blacksmith
Brown, John, grocer, Sandy row
Brown, Robt., cabinet maker, Main st.
Brown, Robert, carpenter, Main st.
Balnaves, Henry (of Glasgow), sewed muslin manufacturer, Main street —John Robertson, agent
Brown, Samuel and Thomas (of Glasgow), sewed muslin manufacturers —David Nevin, agent
Boyce, Arthur, spirit dealer, Main st.
Catherwood, David, baker, &c., New st.
Campbell, Oliver, cabinet maker, New street
Champion, John, painter, Main street
Catherwood, David, woollendraper, &c., New street
Caughey, Margaret, straw bonnet maker, New street
Conolly, John, grocer and publican, Main street
Claney, William, car owner, Shore st.
Conkey, John, carpenter, Moat st.
Conkey, Robert, carpenter, Back st.
Cooper, David, woollendraper, &c., New street
Cooper, John, woollendraper, &c., Shore street
Ferris, James, publican, Main street
Fraser, Turner, and Co. (of Glasgow), sewed muslin manufacturers, Main street—John Macgavern, agent
Durvors, Sarah, straw bonnet maker, Back street
Gibson, Alexander, butcher, Moat st.
Gibson, Alexander, butcher, Main st.
Gibson, Matthew, butcher, Main st.
Gibson, Ann, grocer, Shore street
Gibson, David, publican, New street
Gray, Robert, carpenter, Bow lane
Hennan, Jane, earthenware dealer, Bow lane
Hasket, John, grocer, Main street
Hunter, William, grocer, Main street
Hudson, John, woollendraper, &c., Shore street
Hurst, Charles, ironmonger, &c., Shore street
Holden, John, and Co., sewed muslin manufacturers, Shore street— Sarah Smith, agent
Hunter, William, haberdasher, &c., Main street
Kelly, John, publican, Main street
Lindsay, David, blacksmith, Main st.
Lindsay, Robt., blacksmith, Bow lane
Lindsay, Alex., earthenware dealer, Back lane
Lowry, Thomas, baker, &c., Bow lane
Lyons, James, publican, Shore street
Macdonald, James, sewed muslin manufacturer—James Allen, agent
Magill, Alexander, tailor, Shore street
Maxwell, Samuel, car owner, Sandy row
Miskelly, William H., earthenware dealer, New street
M'Cance, John, publican, Shore st.
M'Cappin, Hugh, boot and shoemaker, Main street
M'Connel, Martha, straw bonnet maker, New street
M'Cracken, William, car owner, Bow lane
M'Cracken, John, boot and shoemaker, Sandy row
M'Cready, George, grocer, Main st.
M'Kee, Margt., haberdasher, Main st.
M'Keigon, John, grocer, Main street
M'Meekan, Mary A., publican, Main street
M'Meekan, David, earthenware dealer, Main street
M'Meekan, David, grocer, Main st.
M'Meekan, Hugh, grocer, Bow lane
M'Quoid, Geo., coal dealer, Shore st.
Nicholson, Samuel, publican, Main st.
Norwell, Hugh, boot and shoemaker, New street

Norwell, Hugh, grocer, New street
Orr, Jas., Commercial hotel, Shore st.
Park, L. and C., sewed muslin manufacturers, Shore street—Maria Rea, agent
Patton, Robert, grocer, New street
Patton, Robert, coal dealer, New st.
Patterson, John, painter and glazier, New street
Pentland, Thomas, baker, Main st.
Pink, Alexander, publican, Sandy row
Robinson, John, boot and shoemaker, Main street
Robertson, Michael, grocer, &c., Main street
Ross, Alexander, publican, Main st.
Saunders, John, butcher, Moat st.
Saunders, William, butcher, Back st.
Sharpe, Wm., and Co., sewed muslin manufacturers—Mrs. Martin, agent
Smith, Hugh, boot and shoemaker, Back street
Stevenson, James, boot and shoemaker, New street
Smith, Thomas, grocer, Main street
Tedford, Mary, grocer, New street
Tonner, Robert, baker, Main street
Vint, Samuel, painter and glazier, Main street
Walker, Robert, coal dealer, &c., New street
Walker, Robert, ironmonger, New st.
Wallace, James, tailor Main street
Wallace, J. and J. (of Glasgow), sewed muslin manufacturers, Shore street—Samuel Horner, agent
Weir, William, jun., and Co., sewed muslin manufacturers, Main street—William Brown, agent
Wilson, Barr, car owner, Shore st.

COUNTY OF DONEGAL.

DONEGAL, a maritime county in Ulster province. Greatest length, N.E. and S.W., eighty-five miles; greatest breadth, S.E. and N.W., forty-one miles; comprising an area of 1,865 square miles, or 1,193,443 acres, of which 393,191 are arable, 769,587 uncultivated, 7,079 in plantations, 479 in towns, and 23,107 under water The islands are numerous; seventeen are inhabited; the principal are, Innistrahul, North Arran, and Tory. On Innistrahul there is a lighthouse, showing a light revolving every two minutes; there are other lighthouses, showing fixed lights, on Tory Island, at Fannet Point, W. of Lough Swilly, and at St. John's Point, Killybegs. The surface is mountainous and boggy. The lakes are numerous, but small; the most remarkable is Lough Derg, 3,214 acres, having in it St. Patrick's Purgatory, a celebrated place of pilgrimage. The population in 1841 was 296,448, ; 290,022 in the rural, and 6,426 in the civic district. According to the Census of 1851, the total population of the county was 254,288, being a decrease of 42,160. The occupations are chiefly agricultural; the linen manufacture is now declining; but that of woollen stockings is increasing; the inhabitants near the coast are much occupied in the fisheries. The county contains Raphoe diocese, and parts of those of Derry and Clogher, consisting of fifty-one parishes. The principal towns are, Ballyshannon, population in 1841, 3,513; Letterkenny, 2,161; and Ramelton, Donegal, and Killybegs, which are seaports, and carry on a considerable trade. The county returns two members to Parliament: constituency, in 1851, 3,748. The Assizes are held at Lifford, where the County Prison is. There are Bridewells there, and at Donegal, Buncrana, Letterkenny, and Glenties. Quarter Sessions are held at Buncrana, Donegal, Glenties, Letterkenny, and Lifford. The County Infirmary is at Lifford; the District Lunatic Asylum, to which it sends eighty-five patients, at Londonderry. There are Union Workhouses at Ballyshannon, Donegal, Dunfanaghy, Glenties, Inishowen, Letterkenny, Milford, and Stranorlar. The county is within the military district of Belfast, and there are artillery stations at the forts of Rathmullen, Knockalla, Macomish, Dunree,

COUNTY OF DONEGAL.

Inch, Ned's Point, and Greencastle, also on Loughs Swilly and Foyle; and barracks for infantry at Ballyshannon and Lifford, and the staff of the county Militia is stationed at Ballyshannon. The head-quarters of the Constabulary force, consisting of 275 men, officers included, are at Letterkenny; those of the eight districts, comprising forty-eight stations, at Rathmelton, Raphoe, Buncrana, Ballyshannon, Killybegs, Glenties, Dunfanaghy, and Carndonagh. There are thirty-two Coast-Guard stations, having a force of 6 officers and 123 men; and eighteen stations of the Revenue Police, consistiing of 19 officers and 206 men. One newspaper, the *Ballyshannon Herald*, is published there on Fridays.

Lieutenant—The Marquis of Abercorn, Baron's Court
Vice-Lieutenant — Sir J. Stewart, Bart., Fort-Stewart, Ramelton
Custos-Rotulorum—The Earl of Leitrim, Manorhamilton, co. Leitrim
High-Sheriff (1852-3)—Thos. Alexander, Ahilly, Buncrana
Members for the County—Sir E. S. Hayes, Bart., D.L., Drumbo Castle, Stranorlar, and Hanover square, London; Thomas Conolly, D.L., Cliff, Ballyshannon, and 52 Jermyn street, London
Assistant-Barrister—Jonathan Henn, Q.C., Upper Merrion street, Dublin

DEPUTY LIEUTENANTS.

Boyd, J. R., Ballymacool house, Letterkenny
Brooke, T., Lough Esk house, Donegal
Chichester, Lord H. F.
Conolly, T., M.P., Cliff, Ballyshannon
Conyngham, Marquis of, K.St.P., Mount Charles
Denison, Lord Albert
Ferguson, A., Burt house, Derry
Ferguson, Sir R. A., Bart., M.P., Derry
Folliott, J., Woodbrook, Boyle
Hamilton, J., St. Ernan's, Donegal
Hart, G. V., Kilderry, Londonderry
Harvey, J., Malin hall, Carndonagh
Hayes, Sir E. S., Bart., M.P., Drumboe, Stranorlar
M'Clintock, R., Dunmore house, Derry
Montgomery, R. G., Convoy house, Raphoe
Olphert, W., Ballyconnell house, Dunfanaghy
Sinclair, J., Holyhill, Strabane
Stewart, Sir J., D.L., Bart., Fort-Stewart, Ramelton
Style, Sir T. C., Bart., Cloghan lodge, Stranorlar
Stewart, J. V., Rock hill, Letterkenny
Todd, Daniel, London
Young, G., Culdaff house, Malin

MAGISTRATES.

Allingham, E., Stonewold, Ballyshannon
Anderson, J., Lisnacloon, Castlederg
Ashe, W. H., Ashbrook, Derry
Atkinson, T. J., Cavan Garden, Ballyshannon
Barton, F. W., Pettigo, Kish
Barton, H. W., Waterford, Kish
Batt, Thomas, jun., Rathmullen
Beers, J., Leslie Hill, Manor Cunningham
Boyd, J. R., D.L., Ballymacool house, Letterkenny
Brooke, T., D.L., Lough Esk house, Donegal
Cary, G., White Castle, Moville
Cary, L., Redcastle Cottage, Moville
Chambers, Daniel
Chambers, J. F., Letterkenny
Charley, John S.
Clements, Hon. C. S., M.P., Milford, Ramelton
Cloncurry, Lord, Maretimo, Dublin
Cochran, J., Edenmore, Stranorlar
Conolly, T., M.P., D.L., Cliff, Ballyshannon
Cunningham, John, Pettigo
Darley, Arthur, R.N., Dublin
Dogherty, J. S., Redcastle, Derry
Donegal, Marquis of, Ormeau
Fenwick, W., Greenhill, Raphoe
Ferguson, A., D.L., Burt house, Derry
Ferguson, J., Castle Forward, Derry
Ferguson, Sir R. A., Bart., M.P., D.L., The Farm, Derry
Fletcher, Edward, London
Forster, F., Roshine Lodge, Dungloe
Hamilton, A., Coxtown, Ballyshannon
Hamilton, G., Eden, Narin

COUNTY OF DONEGAL

Hamilton, J. D.L.,St.Ernan's,Donegal
Hamilton, J., jun., St.Ernan's,Donegal
Hamilton, Rev. E., Brown hall, Ballyshannon
Hamilton, R., Fintra house, Killybegs
Hart, G. V., D.L., Kilderry, Derry
Harvey, John, D.L., Malin hall, Carndonagh
Hastings, Rev. A., Lurgvale, Letterkenny
Hay, Captain R., R.N.
Hayes, Sir E. S., Bart., M.P., D.L., Drumboe, Stranorlar
Heard, R., Rutland, Dungloe
Hewitt, Hon. J., Meenglass, Stranorlar
Heyland, Major J. R., Fahan House, Fahan, Londonderry
Humfrey, B. G., Cavanacor, Strabane
Humphreys, J., Milltown house, Strabane
Humphreys, W. D., Milltown house, Strabane
Johnston, C., Tullybrook, Donegal
Johnston, J., Kinlough house, Bundoran
Johnston, J., Woodlands, Stranorlar
Kennedy, Major J. P., East Indies
Kennedy, John
Knox, A. F., Urney house, Strabane
Knox, Rev. W., Conleigh, Strabane
Leathem, Henry, Ramelton
Londonderry, Mayor of City
M'Clintock, R., D.L., Dunmore house, Derry
Maxwell, Rev. P. B., Birdstown, Derry
Metcalf, Captain Thomas L., Dresden, Carndonagh
Miller, J., Leinsfort house, Buncrana
Montgomery, Robt. G., D.L., Convoy house, Raphoe
Moss, Lieut. Charles, R.N.
Nixon, Rev. A. B., Heathfield, Dunfanaghy
Olpherts, W., D.L., Ballyconnell house, Dunfanaghy
Patterson, T., Gortlee house, Letterkenny
Pratt, Col., Cabra Castle, Kingscourt
Rankin, S., Tirnaleague, Carndonagh
Roberts, Capt. J. C., Cashel
Shiel, Simon, M.D., Ballyshannon
Sinclair, W., Broomfield, Lifford
Sproule, John, Ramelton
Staples, Rev. J. M., Church hill, Moville

Stewart, A. J. R., Ards house, Letterkenny
Stewart, J. V., D.L., Rock hill, Letterkenny
Stewart, Rev. C., Hornhead house, Dunfanaghy
Stewart, Sir J., Bart., Fort Stewart, Ramelton
Style, Sir T. C., Bart., D.L., Cloghan Lodge, Stranorlar
Todd, Daniel, D.L., London
Tredennick, J., Camlin, Ballyshannon
Tuthill, Rev. J. B., Belleck Glebe, Ballyshannon
Welsh, Rev. J., Killaghtee, Donegal
Wilson, G. V., White house, Killybegs
Wood, G. J., Castlegrove, Letterkenny
Wray, G. C. G., Milford, Ramelton
Wray, W., Oak Park, Letterkenny
Young, G., D.L., Culdaff house, Malin
Young, W., Mount hall, Killygordon

RESIDENT MAGISTRATES.

Fleming, John, Buncrana
Montgomery, A. C., Donegal

COUNTY OFFICERS.

Clerk of the Crown—J. Joyce, Strabane
Clerk of the Peace—J. Cochran, Crohan House, Lifford
Deputy-Clerk of the Peace—J. Walwood, Stranorlar
Crown-Solicitor at Quarter Sessions—W. Barrett, Riverstown, Ardara, and 105 Lower Gardiner st., Dublin
Treasurer—Francis Mansfield, Ardrumman, Letterkenny
Secretary to Grand Jury—S. Sproule, Ramelton
County Surveyor—N.R., H. Smyth, C.E., Letterkenny; S.R., William Haste, C.E., Donegal
Sub-Sheriff—Samuel J. Crookshank, Buncrana
Coroners—C. H. Swiney, Ramelton; J. G. Long, M.D., Newtowncunningham; Wm. O'Donnell, Buncrana; Samuel Crawford, Ballyshannon
Head Stamp Distributor for County—H. E. Peoples, Letterkenny

MILITIA STAFF.

Colonel—The Earl of Leitrim
Lieut.-Col.—Earl of Mount-charles
Major—Sir J. Stewart, Bart.
Adjutant—Samuel Searle

CONSTABULARY OFFICERS.

County Inspector—Henry Townsend, Letterkenny
Ballyshannon—Robert Simpson
Buncrana—Thomas Smith
Carndonagh—George Blakeney
Dunfanaghy—W. Meredith
Glenties—John S. Stuart
Killybegs—J. F. Johnson
Ramelton—J. F. Studdert
Raphoe—Henry Kirwan

COUNTY GAOL, LIFFORD.

Board of Superintendence—Sir E. S. Hayes, Bart., M.P.; Sir J. Stewart, Bart.; Rev. Wm. Knox; W. Fenwick; B. G. Humfrey; J. Johnston; F. Mansfield; J. V. Stewart; Wm. Sinclair; R. G. Montgomery; A. J. R. Stewart; John Ferguson
Inspector and Chaplain—Rev. E. M. Clarke
Presbyterian Chaplain — Rev. W. M'Crea
R. C. Chaplain—Rev. Wm. Brown
Physician—R. Little, M.D., Lifford
Apothecary—Mr. Gillespey
Governor—A. Grant, Lifford

COUNTY OF DOWN.

Down, a maritime county in Ulster province. Greatest length, N.E. and S.W., fifty-one miles; greatest breadth, N.W. and S.E., thirty-eight miles; comprising an area of 967 square miles, or 612,495 acres, of which 514,180 are arable, 78,317 uncultivated, 14,355 in plantations, 2,211 in towns, and 3,432 under water. On the coast are, Carrickfergus Bay, Strangford Lough, or Lough Cone, Killough, Dundrum, and Carlingford Bays; and at a short distance from it are the Copeland Islands, on the lesser of which is a lighthouse showing a fixed light; there are also four others, viz.:—at Hawlbowling Rock, off Carlingford Bay, showing a fixed light; on the South rock, off the Ardes, with a light revolving every minute and a-half; at Ardglass Harbour; and one revolving light at St. John's Point. The surface is hilly, rising into mountains in the South; the highest, Slieve-Donard, being 2,809 feet above high sea level. The fishery districts are Donaghadee and Newcastle, together comprising 139 miles of maritime boundaries, which had in 1850, 1,700 registered fishing vessels, employing 5,493 men and boys. The population in 1841 amounted to 361,446; of which 323,807 were in the rural, and 37,639 in the civic district. According to the Census of 1851, the total population of the county was 317,778, being a decrease of 43,668. The county is divided into eleven baronies—Ards Lower and Upper, Castlereagh Lower and Upper, Dufferin, Iveagh Lower and Upper, Kinelarty, Lecale, Mourne, and Newry Lordship, and contains seventy parishes, &c. It is in the dioceses of Down and Dromore, with a small portion in that of Connor. The county returns two members to Parliament; constituency, in 1851, 10,028. The Assizes are held at Downpatrick, where the County Prison is. There are Bridewells at Newry and Newtownards. Quarter Sessions are held at Downpatrick, Hillsborough, Newtownards, and Newry; Petty Sessions in twenty-four places. The County Infirmary is in Downpatrick; and the District Lunatic Asylum, to which the county can send 124 patients, is at Belfast. The Union Workhouses are at Downpatrick, Banbridge, Kilkeel, Newry, and Newtownards. The county is within the military district of Belfast; and the Staff of the North Down Militia is stationed at Newtownards, and of the South Down at Hillsborough. A Resident Magistrate is stationed at Ballynahinch. The head-quarters of the Constabulary force, consisting of 241 men, officers included, are at Hillsborough; those of

COUNTY OF DOWN.

the six districts, comprising forty-one stations, at Newtownards, Downpatrick, Rathfriland, Newcastle, Banbridge, and Ballynahinch. There are twenty-four Coast Guard Stations, consisting of 17 officers and 149 men. Two newspapers are published in the county, the *Newry Telegraph* (three times a week) Tuesday, Thursday, and Saturday; and the *Downpatrick Recorder*, on Saturdays.

Lieutenant—Viscount Castlereagh, M.P., Chesham place, London

Custos Rotulorum—The Marquis of Londonderry, Mountstewart, and Holderness House, Hertford street, May Fair, London

High-Sheriff, 1852-53—Nicholas D. Crommelin, Carrowdore Castle

Members for the County—Viscount Castlereagh, Chesham place, London; Lord Edwin Hill, 21 Hanover square, London

Assistant Barrister — Theophilus Jones, 18 Harcourt street, Dublin

DEPUTY LIEUTENANTS.

Annesley, The Earl of, The Cottage, Castlewellan
Bailie, J., Ringdufferin, Killyleagh
Bateson, Sir R., bart., Belvoir Park, Belfast
Batt, R., Purdysburn, Belfast
Brown, Captain P., Ardglass
Corry, Isaac, Newry
Crawford, W. S., M.P., Crawfordsburn
Crommelin, S. A. D., Carrowdore Castle, Donaghadee
Douglass, Charles, Gracehall, Lurgan
Dufferin and Claneboye, Lord, Claneboye, Holywood
Gordon, R., Florida Manor, Killinchy
Hall, Roger, Narrow-water Castle
Johnson, Sir W. G., Belfast
Ker, D. S., Montalto, Ballynahinch
Maxwell, J. W., Finnebrogue, Downpatrick
Montgomery, A. H., Tyrella House, Clough
Mussenden, W., Larchfield, Lisburn
Nugent, Major A., Castleward, Strangford
Price, J., Saintfield House
Reilly, J. T., Scarva House, Scarva
Roden, Earl of, K. St. P., Tollymore Park
Smyth, T. J., Lisburn
Stewart, A., Ards House, Dunfanaghy
Stewart, Alex. Robert
Thompson, W. N., Newry
Ward, R., Bangor Castle, Bangor

MAGISTRATES.

Allen, J. R., Mountpanther, Clough
Allen, Wm. J. C., Belfast
Andrews, John, Comber
Anketell, W. R., Ballynahinch
Annesley, Rev. W., Ardilea, Clough
Baillie, J., D.L., Ringdufferin, Killyleagh
Bangor, Viscount, Castleward, Strangford
Barron, W. N., Kinghill House, Rathfriland
Bateson, Sir R., Bart., D.L., Belvoir Park, Belfast
Bateson, T., M.P., Belvoir Park, Belfast
Batt, R., D.L., Purdysburn, Belfast
Binney, Rev. R., Bangor
Birney, J., Oakley, Downpatrick
Boyd, John, Newry
Boyd, Rev. H. E., Dromara
Bowen, Captain G., R.N., Laurencetown House, Banbridge
Bradshaw, H., Culcavey Cottage, Hillsborough
Browne, Captain P., D.L., Ardglass
Bruce, E., Scoutbush, Carrickfergus
Cloncurry, Lord, Maretimo
Coates, James, Eastwood, Kilkeel
Coates, William, Glentoran, Ballymacarrett
Corry, Isaac, D.L., Newry
Corry, Smithson, Rostrevor
Coulson, Robert, R.M., Omagh
Cowan, Andrew, Belfast
Crawford, J. S., Redemon, Crossgar
Crawford, J. S., Crawfordsburn
Crawford, T., Ballydown, Banbridge
Crawford, W. S., M.P., D.L., Crawfordsburn
Crommelin, Nicholas D., Carrowdore Castle, Donaghadee
Crommelin, S. A. D., D.L., Carrowdore Castle, Donaghadee
Delacherois, Nicholas, Donaghadee
Despard, Captain P. H., Killough
Dobbs, C. R., Castle Dobbs, Carrickfergus
Dolling, R., Holback, Magheralin, Lurgan

COUNTY OF DOWN.

Douglass, Charles, D.L., Gracehall, Lurgan
Downshire, Marquis of, Hillsborough Castle
Dunbar, George, Donaghadee
Dungannon, Viscount
Echlin, Rev. J. R., Kircubbin
Fenton, S. G., Belfast
Ferguson, T., Greenville House, Belfast
Filgate, Fitzherbert, Hillsborough
Forde, W. B., jun., Seaford, Clough
Getty, D. C., Donaghadee
Gordon, Rev. J. C., Delamont, Downpatrick
Gordon, R. F., Holywood
Gordon, R., D.L., Florida Manor, Killinchy
Gordon, R. A., Summerfield, Dundonald
Greer, George, Lurgan
Greer, William, Portaferry
Greg, Thomas, Ballymenoch, Belfast
Gregg, William, Lisburn
Grimshaw, Robert, Belfast
Hall, Major, Warrenpoint
Hall, Roger, D.L., Narrow-water, Warrenpoint
Hall, W. D., Fairburn, Rostrevor
Hamilton, Archibald R., Killyleagh
Hancock, John, Lurgan
Harrison, John, Merton Hall, Belfast
Hayes, R., Millmount, Banbridge
Henry, T. G., Newry
Heron, R., Ardigon, Killyleagh
Higginson, H. T., Lisburn
Hill, Lord Edwin, M.P.
Hill, W. S., Bryansford, Castlewellan
Houston, R. B. B., Orangefield, Belfast
Howe, J. H., Killyleagh
Hunter, William, Dunmurry
Jocelyn, Viscount, Tollymore Park
Johnson, Sir W. G., D.L., Belfast
Johnston, H. T., Hollypark, Killinchy
Johnston, Rev. G. H. J. M'D., Ballywillwill, Castlewellan
Jones, T. M. H., Moneyglass, Toome
Kennedy, Henry, Cultra, Holywood
Kennedy, Robert, Cultra, Holywood
Keown, W., Ballydugan House, Downpatrick
Ker, D. S., D.L., Montalto, Ballynahinch
Kilmorey, Earl of
Leslie, E. F., Donaghadee
Lindsay, D., Ashfield, Dromore
Lindsay, J., Tullyhenan, Banbridge
Loftie, J. H., Loughbrickland
Londonderry, Marquis of, Mountstewart, Newtownards
M'Leroth, Thomas, Newtownards
M'Minn, A., Herdstown, Donaghadee
M'Namara, James, Belfast
M'Neil, John, Parkmount, Belfast
Magee, Charles, Rhone Hill, Moy
Magenis, Roger, Ballele, Dromore
Maxwell, J. W., D.L., Finnebrogue, Downpatrick
Maxwell, Robert P., Groomsport, Donaghadee
Miller, Alexander, Downpatrick
Moore, J. S., Shannon Grove, Kilkeel
Moore, Wm., Newcastle, Castlewellan
Montgomery, A. H., D.L., Tyrella House, Clough
Montgomery, Francis, Newtownards
Montgomery, Hugh, Rosemount, Greyabbey
Mulholland, A., Springvale, Kircubbin
Mulholland, Jn., Craigavad, Holywood
Mulholland, St. Clair K., Eglantine House, Hillsborough
Murland, S., Woodlawn, Castlewellan
Mussenden, Wm., D.L., Larchfield, Lisburn
Nicholson, R. H., Stramore House, Gilford
Nicholson, R., Ballow, Bangor
Nugent, Major A., D.L., Castleward, Strangford
Nugent, Lieut-Col., Portaferry House
Potter, R., Ardview, Killinchy
Powell, J. K., Newtownards
Price, James, D.L., Saintfield House
Price, Wm. Blackwood, Tonaghnieve, Saintfield
Quinn, John H., Dromore House, Dromore
Ranfurly, Earl of, Dungannon Park
Reid, A. H., County Tipperary
Reilly, J. T., D.L., Scarva House
Riky, Robert Alexander, Moira
Robinson, James, Lisburn
Ross, David (of Bladensburg), Rostrevor
Rowan, Hill Wilson, Kingstown
Scott, Thomas, Rathfriland
Senior, Lieut.-Col. H., Glass Drummond, Anna Long, Kilkeel

COUNTY OF DOWN.

Shaw, George, Castlewellan
Skinner, C. G. M'G.
Smith, R. J., Lisburn
Smyth, Thos. J., D.L., Lisburn
Stewart, A., Ballyedmond, Rostrevor
Stewart, A., D.L., Ards House, Dunfanaghy
Stewart, Alex. J. R., Laurencetown House
Stone, Guy, Barnhill, Comber
Tennent, J. T., Belfast
Tennent, R. J., M.P., Belfast
Tennent, Sir J. E., Knt., M.P.
Thompson, Robert, Holywood
Thompson, W. N., D.L., Newry
Thompson, John, Lowwood, Belfast
Tighe, T. J., Rathfriland
Trotter, Clifford, Charleville Cottage, Enniskerry
Verner, Thomas, jun., Belfast
Walsh, John, Chenawley, Banbridge
Ward, John R., Bangor
Ward, R., D.L., Bangor Castle
Waring, Henry, Newry
White, John, Divernagh, Newry

RESIDENT MAGISTRATE.
M'Cance, James Law, Ballynahinch

COUNTY OFFICERS.
Clerk of the Crown—Clotworthy Macartney, 38 Upper Gloucester st., Dublin
Clerk of the Peace—Rowland Craig, Downpatrick
Crown Solicitor at Quarter Sessions—C. W. Ruthven, Downpatrick
Treasurer—A. H. Montgomery, Tyrella, Clough
Secretary to Grand Jury—Robert Gordon, Downpatrick
County Surveyor—J. Fraser, C.E., Downpatrick
Sub-Sheriff—S. H. Rowan, Downpatrick
Coroners—George Tyrell, M.D., Banbridge; and John A. Ward, Downpatrick
Agent for Lloyds—Leonard Watson, Warrenpoint
Head Stamp Distributor at Downpatrick—C. Knox
Head Stamp Distributor at Newry—J. Williams

MILITIA STAFF, ROYAL NORTH DOWN.
Colonel—Viscount Castlereagh, M.P.
Lieut.-Colonel—J. P. Nugent
Major—William Read

MILITIA STAFF, ROYAL SOUTH DOWN.
Colonel—The Marquis of Downshire
Lieut.-Col.—Lord A. E. Hill, M.P.
Major—J. Bailie, Carrighill, Belturbet
Adjutant—Captain J. A. Hodgson

CONSTABULARY OFFICERS.
County Inspector—S. H. Decluzeau, Hillsborough
Sub-Inspectors' Stations—Banbridge, B. Plummer; Ballynahinch, Augustus W. Stafford; Downpatrick, George Dickson; Newcastle, Castlewellan, F. W. Janns; Newtownards, John Kelly; Rathfriland, Wm. Wray

COUNTY GAOL, DOWNPATRICK.
Board of Superintendence—Meet on the first Tuesday in every month: J. W. Maxwell, A. H. Montgomery, P. R. M. Brown, James Birnie, Alexander Miller, Major Nugent, Rev. W. B. Forde, Rev. J. F. Gordon, R. Heron, Rev. J. C. Gordon, W. Keown, P. H. Despard, J. S. Crawford, J. Andrews, F. O. Montgomery
Governor—George F. Echlin
Deputy-Governor—John Waterworth
Chaplain—Rev. James Forde
Presbyterian Chaplain—Rev. William White
Roman Catholic Chaplain—Rev. B. Macauley
Physician—Philip E. Brabazon, F.R.C.S.I.
Apothecary—S. Parkinson

BRIDEWELLS AND KEEPERS.
Newry—Thomas Guy
Newtownards—Isaac Munn

COUNTY INFIRMARY, DOWNPATRICK.
Treasurer—John Johnston
Surgeon—Philip E. Brabazon

DISTRICT LUNATIC ASYLUM AT BELFAST.
Manager—Robert Stewart, M.D.
Physician—H. M'Cormac, M.D.

DOWNPATRICK.

DOWNPATRICK is a market town and a Parliamentary borough, the seat of Down diocess, and the Assize and principal town in that county, 22 miles S.E. from Belfast. This respectable and ancient town is built upon a group of hills on the south shore of the western branch of Lough Cone, whose waters communicate with those of Strangford Lough, flow up to near the town, and there receive the Ballynahinch river, which enters by those gates, and, in flood water, close against the tide. The ruins of Inch Abbey are near the town. Downpatrick is celebrated as the burial place of Saint Patrick, and claims, according to some antiquaries, to be the oldest town in Ireland. Before the time of this celebrated saint, it is alleged to have been successively called *Aras-Keltair*, *Rath-Keltair-Mich-Duach*, *Dun-da-Leth-Glass* and *Dunum* or *Down*. On the north-west side of the town stands a conical rath, sixty feet high—enclosed by two ramparts, one of which is thirty feet broad, and the whole circuit of the works is three-quarters of a mile. It is supposed to have been the site of the palace of the kings of Ulidia or Down. The town is composed of four main streets, converging to a centre, and intersected by smaller ones and lanes. In 1846, an act was obtained to light the town with gas. The Court-house is an extensive and handsome building, standing upon an eminence in English street: its interior affords all the facilities for the transaction of public business, whilst its architectural appearance without renders it an ornamental object. The County Goal, situated at a convenient distance, was completed in 1820, at a cost of £60,000 to the county. A large building, called the County Rooms, adjoining the Court-house, is occupied as reception rooms for the gentlemen of the county and the Grand Jury, and, in addition, there is a ball room of good size. The house steward is Mr. Nicholas Coates.

The Down sessions are held twice a year, viz., in March and October, and Petty Sessions on alternate Thursdays. A Manor Court is held every third Tuesday, and a Court-leet is held by the Seneschal twice a year, in Spring and Michaelmas.

The borough returned two members to the Irish Parliament so early as 1585, and exercised that privilege until the Union, since which the borough has sent one only to the Imperial Parliament; the present representative is the Hon. C. S. Hardinge, son of Lord Viscount Hardinge, Stanhope street, Park lane, London, and South Park, Penshurst, Kent.

Quoile Quay is the port of the town, and admits vessels of 100 tons. The exports consist principally of agricultural produce, and imports are chiefly timber, iron, slates, coal, and salt. Brewing, tanning, soap making, &c., are carried on here. The County Down Railway, when completed, will connect the town with Belfast. Branches of the Northern Bank and the Ulster Bank, with a Savings' Bank, are the monetary establishments. The town is the head-quarters of a constabulary district, comprising the stations of Downpatrick, Ardglass, Killough, Killyleagh, Portaferry, and Strangford. The press of the town publishes a newspaper weekly, the *Downpatrick Recorder* (Saturday), conducted and edited by C. Pilson, Esq., the proprietor.

Downpatrick was erected into a bishop's see by Saint Fergus. The remains of St. Patrick were interred in the abbey of the Canons Regular, founded in 493, now the Cathedral. The see was united to that of Connor, and subsequently to that of Dromore—the latter being one of the ten suppressed bishoprics under the Whig Administration. The Cathedral, a stately embattled edifice, is situated on an eminence at the top of English street. It is chiefly built with unhewn stone, supported externally by buttresses, and comprises a nave, choir, and aisles, with a lofty tower at the west end, surmounted

DOWNPATRICK.

by pinnacles, and smaller square towers at each corner of the east gable. It is furnished with a good organ, and the choir is handsomely fitted up with stalls for the dignitaries. The Parish Church, which stands about the centre of the town, is a capacious and well-finished edifice. The other places of worship are two Presbyterian Churches, three Methodist Chapels, and a neat Roman Catholic Chapel. The Diocesan School of Down and Dromore Diocese is in active operation here, and there is also a Blue-coat school.

Within a mile of the town is the celebrated race-course: the meetings are mainly supported by the society of horse breeders, incorporated by charter of James II. The Market-house, in the centre of the town, is a convenient, well-arranged building. Fairs—First Saturday in each month; markets—Tuesday and Saturday. Population in 1851, town district, 3,802; rural, 211; total, 4,013, inhabiting 765 houses.

Post Office, Saul street—Benjamin M'Ivor, postmaster. Letters from Dublin, Newry, and all parts of the south of Ireland, also from England, arrive every morning at 20 minutes past 6, and are despatched every evening at 6. Letters from Belfast and all parts of the North of Ireland, also from Scotland, arrive every evening at 6, and are despatched every morning at 25 minutes past 6. Letters from Portaferry, Strangford, and Crossgar, arrive every evening at 20 minutes before 6, and are despatched every morning at 25 minutes past 6

Conveyances—Two four horse coaches daily (Sunday excepted), from Foster's, Irish street, for Belfast, at 7 morning, returning at 4 afternoon. One four-horse coach, same hour, from Jenning's hotel. Mail car, every morning, from Foster's, for Belfast, and every evening, from Denvir's, for Newry

Town Commissioners — Chairman, Hunter Shaw; James Reid, Edward M'Lester, John Tate, Jas. Murland, Jas. M'Mullan, John M'Henry, John Lloyd, Robert Hutton, Geo. M'Ilroy, James M'Nown, John M'Mullen, Charles M'Creedy, Hugh M'Kee, Hugh Porter, Charles W. Ruthven, Hugh Martin, John Moore, John Jennings.

Fever Hospital—Philip E. Brabazon, surgeon; Miss White, matron

County Infirmary, Pound lane—Philip E. Brabazon, surgeon; Miss E. M'Namara, matron

Banks—Northern, English st., James Stevenson, manager; Ulster, Irish street, Hugh Cleland, manager

Manor Court, every third Tuesday—Hugh Wallace, seneschal

Petty Sessions Court, every alternate Thursday—S. K. Forde, clerk

Military Barracks, English street—Patrick O'Connor, barrack master

Police Barracks, Scotch street—Geo. Dickson, sub-inspector

Stamp Office, Saul street—Charles Knox, distributor

The Cathedral, English st.—Bishop, Right Rev. Robert Knox, D.D.; Dean, Very Rev. T. Blakeley, A.M.; Reader, Rev. Horatio Moffat; Archdeacon, The Ven. Walter Bishop Mant, A.M.; Precentor, Rev. H. S. Cuming, A.M.; Chancellor, Rev. J. L. M. Scott, A.M.; Treasurer, Rev. G. H. M'D. Johnston, A.B.; Organist, Robert M'Cune

Parish Church, Church lane—Rev. Jas. Forde, curate; J. Heron, clerk

Presbyterian Church, Infirmary lane—Rev. William White, minister

Unitarian Church, Stream street—Rev. S. C. Nelson, minister

Wesleyan Methodist Chapel, Scotch street—Revs. Robert Devers and Robert Collier

Primitive Methodist Chapel, Church lane—Rev. Mr. Thompson

Roman Catholic Chapel, Stream st.—Rev. Bernard M'Auley, P.P.

National School, Infirmary lane—John Bell, master; Mrs. Bell, mistress

Diocesan School, Saul street—Rev. Joseph Cooper, master

Infant School, Infirmary lane—Mary Wallace, mistress

Lancaster School, Saul street—Saml. Nicholson, master

Endowed Hospital for old men and women, and Charity School, English

street—John Leer, master; Grace Quade, mistress
County Down Masonic Lodge—Reading & Billiard Rooms, Church lane
Mechanics' Institute, Irish street—D. Harrel, president; M'Henry Montgomery, secretary
News-Room, at Denvir's Hotel, English street

GENTRY, ETC.

Anderson, Misses, Stream street
Beauclerk, Major Aubrey William, Ardglass castle
Birney, James, J.P., Oakley
Brown, Peter, R.M., D.L., Jonville
Cleland, Hugh, Irish street
Curran, Miss, Eliza street
Fleming, Miss, Saul street
Forde, Lady Dowager Harriet, Hollymount
Gracey, James, English street
Hanna, Miss, Irish street
Harrel, David, Quoile road
Johnston, John B., Ballykilbeg
Johnston, Mrs., English street
Keown, William, Ballydugan
M'Kittrick, Mrs., Irish street
Maxwell, John W., J.P., Finnebrogue
Miller, Alexander, J.P., English street
Perry, Captain Joseph, Quoile
Pilson, Aynsworth, Bridge street
Quail, Mrs., Saul street
Stevenson, James, English street
Wallace, Miss Amelia
Ward, John A. (coroner)

CLERGY AND PROFESSIONAL.

Alder, Rev. Samuel, Saul street
Archbold, Rev. Charles, Rathmullan
Brabazon, P. E., physician and surgeon, Infirmary
Caldwell, George, surgeon, English st.
Campbell, Rev. Charles, Ardglass
Cooper, Rev. Joseph, Saul street
Craig, Rowland, attorney, and Clerk of the Peace, Irish street
Craig, Rowland and John, attorneys, County Court-house
Falloon, Rev. J. M., English street
Fraser, John, county surveyor, Down Demesne
Forde, Robert, M.D., Saul street
Forde, Stewart King, attorney and commissioner for taking acknowledgments of deeds by married women, Saul street
Forde, Rev. James, English street
Graham, Wm., attorney, Bridge street
Killen, Hector, M.D., Saul street
Moffat, Rev. Horatio
Milligan, Rev. James, Irish street
Murland & Nelson, attorneys, Saul st.
Murphy, Edward, attorney, Irish st.
M'Auley, Rev. Bernard, Stream street
M'Ewen, Andrew, surgeon, Irish st.
M'Mullan, J. M., surgeon, English st.
Nelson, Rev. S. Craig, Infirmary lane
Ruthven, Charles, attorney, and crown solicitor for the county Down, English street
Wallace, Hugh, of H. Wallace & Co., attorneys, English street
Wallace, W. N., attorney, English st.
Ward, James Auchinleck, attorney, and clerk to the Board of Guardians, Irish street
Warnock, John, attorney, English st.
White, Rev. William, Saul street

TRADERS, ETC.

Archer, Thomas, painter and glazier, Saul street
Agners, Samuel, publican, John street
Blair, William, copper and tinsmith, Irish street
Bell, James grocer, Infirmary lane
Brown, George, grocer and publican, Scotch street
Bailie, William, grocer, Irish street
Bell, John Rowan, linen and woollendraper, Scotch street
Boyd and Little, woollendrapers, English street
Brazier, Ann, milliner and dressmaker, Irish street
Baggs, Richard, publican, Quoile quay
Brown, George, publican, Scotch st.
Bailie, James, watchmaker, Saul street
Caldwell, Geo., apothecary, English st.
Crickard, Francis, blacksmith, Scotch street
Coulter, Thos., blacksmith, Church st.
Cochran, James, boot and shoemaker, Pound lane
Carr, John, butcher, Scotch street
Coriston, Edward, butcher, Irish st.
Casement, James, carpenter, Scotch st.
Crauston, Alexander, corn merchant, Church street

DOWNPATRICK.

Croskery, Hugh, coal dealer, Irish st.
Clelland, Hugh, Standard Life Assurance Office, Irish street
Croskery, Hugh, grocer & ironmonger, Scotch street
Curran, Henry, grocer, Irish street
Carty, Stephen, hairdresser, Irish st.
Croskery, Thos., leather dealer, Irish street
Coulter, Mary Jane, milliner & dressmaker, Irish street
Coulter, George, painter and glazier, Saul street
Coulter, George, pawnbroker, Saul st.
Croskery, Hugh, publican, Scotch st.
Croskery, Thomas, publican, Irish st.
Cochran, John, tailor, Pound lane
Crawford, James, wheelwright, Infirmary lane
Creilly, Robert, wheelwright, Quoile bridge
Creilly, Wm., wheelwright, Mary st.
Croskery, Hugh, wine and spirit merchant, Market street
Darbey, John, baker, Scotch street
Denvir, Robert, Head Inn, English st.
Dougherty, John, leather dealer, Saul street
Dunn, James, and Co., sewed muslin manufacturers, Scotch street
Dougherty, Owen, saddler and harness maker, John street
Darbey, John, publican, Saul street
Dougherty, Isabella, straw bonnet maker, Saul street
Ferguson, John, turner, Irish street
Forsyth, John, painter and glazier, Scotch street
Fowler, Patrick, baker, Scotch street
Foster, James, publican, Irish street
Gilchrist, Hugh, grocer, and wine and spirit dealer, English street
Graham, George, hat manufacturer, Irish street
Gilchrist, Hugh, linen and woollendraper, English street
Graham, James, linen and woollendraper, Scotch street
Gilchrist, Hugh, publican, Irish street
Gray, William, publican, Bridge street
Greer, Thos., publican, Scotch street
Gordon, Mary Ann, straw bonnet maker, Irish street
Hastings, Samuel, marble and stone mason, Saul street
Haffey, James, blacksmith, Bridge st.
Hanna, Thomas, baker, haberdasher, &c., Irish street
Hurst, Wm. G., boot and shoemaker, Irish street
Hutton, Joseph, boot and shoemaker, Scotch street
Hudson, John, builder and carpenter, Stream street
Henry, Thomas, corn and flour miller, Irish street
Hastings, J., corn merchant, Irish st.
Heron, Edward, saddler, Scotch street
Hanna, John, spirit dealer, Scotch st.
Hunter, Jane, bonnet maker, Demesne
Hutton, Robert, chandler, Irish street
Jervis, John, baker, Irish street
Jordan, Wm., builder and carpenter, Scotch street
Johnston, Arthur, grocer and coal dealer, English street
Jennings, John, Victoria hotel, Irish st.
Johnston, Arthur, wine and spirit dealer and ironmonger, English st.
Jennings, Fras., spirit dealer, Demesne
Johnston, James, tailor, Irish street
Johnston, Thomas, tailor, Irish street
Johnston, Arthur, timber merchant, English street
Jordan, Wm., timber merchant, &c., Scotch street
Killen, Hector, apothecary, Saul street
Kennedy, M., blacksmith, Mary street
Kelly, John, grocer, Scotch street
Keown, Wm., grocer and spirit dealer, Scotch street
Kearns, John, ironmonger, Irish street
Kearney, Hugh, tailor, Saul street
Kelly, Arthur, tailor, Stream street
Lennon, Patrick, tailor, Stream street
Lloyd, William, butcher, Saul street
Lloyd, William, jun., butcher, Irish st.
Lloyd, John, cabinet maker, Irish st.
Lennon, James, carpenter, Scotch st.
Lithgow, Robert Thos., coach builder
Little, John, grocer, Irish street
Lloyd, John, ironmonger, Irish street
Lowry, John, woollendraper, Scotch st.
Lowry, Ellen, milliner and dressmaker, Saul street
Little, John, reedmaker, Irish street
Lindsay, Rebecca, publican, Irish st.
Lavery, Fanny, bonnet maker, Irish st.
Martin, John, auctioneer, Scotch st.
Murray, John, auctioneer, Irish street

Moore, John, baker and confectioner, Irish street
Magilton, Hugh, blacksmith, Stream street
Magennis, Hugh, boot and shoemaker, Stream street
Magennis, James, boot and shoemaker, Stream street
Martin, Hugh, builder and carpenter, Church street
Morrison, James, butcher, Stream street
Morrison, Thos., butcher, John street
Martin, John, cabinet maker, Scotch street
Martin, Robert, grocer, Church street
Menowen, James, grocer and spirit dealer, Scotch street
Miller, James, grocer, Bridge street
Martin, Elizabeth, Commercial hotel, Irish street
Martin, John, woollendraper, Irish st.
Miller, Alexander, painter and glazier, Shamble street
Miller, James, reedmaker, Bridge st.
Morrison, Thomas, publican, Church street
Murnin, John, publican, Irish street
Maguire, Henry, tanner, Church street
Martin, Hugh, timber merchant, Church street
Macdonald, D. and J., sewed muslin manufacturers, Scotch street
M'Cune, Matilda, boarding house, English street
M'Dade, Wm., baker, Bridge street
M'Mullan, Chas. C., baker, Irish street
M'Henry, John, boot and shoemaker, Scotch street
M'Cracken, William, boot and shoemaker, Scotch street
M'Neagh, Alexander, boot and shoemaker, Irish street
M'Comisky, Robert, butcher, John st.
M'Cleery, Charles, butcher, English st.
M'Cullagh, Wm., carpenter, Saul st.
M'Call, Alexander, cooper, Bridge st.
M'Call, Alex., jun., cooper, Saul street
M'Bride, Wm. G., grocer and spirit dealer, Irish street
M'Dade, Wm., grocer, Bridge street
M'Ilroy, George, grocer, Scotch street
M'Henry, John, leather seller, Scotch street
M'Cann, Arthur, Scotch street
M'Ganity, Patrick, rope and twine maker, Stream street
M'Cullagh, Sarah, milliner and dressmaker, Saul street
M'Namara, H., pawnbroker, Scotch st.
M'Callister, Jane, publican, Scotch st.
M'Carty, Martha, publican, Stream st.
M'Clean, John, spirit dealer, Demesne
M'Clurg, Mathew, publican, Irish st.
M'Creedy, Chas., publican, Scotch st.
M'Ilheron, John, publican, Irish street
M'Ilroy, George, publican, Scotch st.
M'Kee, Hugh, publican, Church st.
M'Lester, Edward, chandler, Irish st.
Nesbitt, John, carpenter, John street
Nesbitt, James, cooper, Scotch street
Nesbitt, Richard, cooper, Scotch st.
Neill, Thomas, plumber and coppersmith, Irish street
Nesbitt, William, painter and glazier, Irish street
Newell, William, whitesmith, Scotch street
Orr, Jane, milliner and dressmaker
O'Neill, Ann, straw bonnet maker Stream street
Pilson, Conway, bookseller, stationer, and printer, Irish street
Petticrew, Wm., gunsmith, John st.
Porter, Hugh, woollendraper, Irish st.
Quail, James, cabinet maker, Irish st.
Quail, G., woollendraper, &c., Irish st.
Quail, Henry, saddler, &c., Irish st.
Quinn, C., bonnet maker, Stream st.
Reid, Samuel, Turner, Irish street
Russell, John, tobacconist, Irish st.
Ryan, Is., bonnet maker, Stream st.
Roney, Patrick, delph shop, Irish st.
Reid, Samuel, gunsmith, Scotch st.
Reid, Alex., woollendraper, Irish st.
Rowan, Thos., woollendraper, Irish st.
Robinson, E., pawnbroker, Infirmary lane
Reid, S., shuttle maker, Scotch street
Rea, James, saddler, &c., Bridge st.
Reid, James, spirit dealer, Irish street
Reid, James, grocer, Irish street
Stockdale, George, builder, Church st.
Shaw, H., delph & china shop, Irish st.
Steele, Jas., corn merchant, Bridge st.
Saul, Thos. M., grocer and wine and spirit merchant, and agent for Star Life As. Office, Scotch street
Savage, Daniel, grocer, Scotch street
Steele, James, grocer, Bridge street

Savage, Daniel, hairdresser, Scotch st.
Sharrock, Jn., woollendraper, Irish st.
Smyth, Hy., coach builder, Church st.
Steele, James, publican, Bridge st.
Stewart, Thomas, publican, Stream st.
Smyth, Ann, bonnet maker, Scotch st.
Skillen, Mathew and Thomas, tailors, Scotch street
Starkey, William, tanner, Irish street
Shaw, Hunter, watchmaker, Irish st.
Tate, John, boot and shoemaker, English street
Tate, Essy, ironmonger, Irish street
Tate, James, leather seller, Irish st.
Todd, John, draper, Scotch street
Townley, Ann, draper, Irish street
Wilson, The Misses, ladies' boarding and day school
Wallace, Hugh, and Co., Northern Life and Fire Assurance office
Warring, Mr., publican, Church st.
Welshman, Wm., publican, Irish st.
Woods, Honora, publican, John st.

DROMORE.

A MARKET town, and seat of a diocess, in the County of Down, 14 miles distant from Belfast, seated on the river Lagan, and on the road from Dublin to Belfast. The name *Druin mor*, corrupted into Dromore, signifies the great back of a hill, and is significant of the town's position on the side of a rising ground. Its ecclesiastical see is said to have been founded in the sixth century; the records, however, in this particular are not to be relied upon. The town, or city, for in fact it is properly entitled to the latter appellative distinction, consists of a square and a few streets, neither long nor wide, radiating from it; neither is the square spacious. The town is clean and well kept. Its staple trade is linen cloth, of which considerable quantities are brought for sale on the market and fair days. Over the Market-house, a neat building, erected on arches, is a large apartment, used for public meetings and occasional assemblies.

The Parish Church is a comparatively small and unpretending structure, and derives most of its peculiar interest from having been built by the celebrated Jeremy Taylor, and containing his remains, as well as those of other bishops of the see. The episcopal residence, adjoining the town, was built in the time of Bishop Bernard; and the woods around it planted by Bishop Percy. The other places of worship in Dromore are three Presbyterian churches, the same number of Methodist chapels, and one for Covenanters, and a Roman Catholic chapel. The market is held on Saturday. Fairs, February 2d, May 12th, July 28th, August 1st, and October 10th, chiefly for cattle, pigs, &c.

Post Office, Market square—Michael Bodel, postmaster. Letters from Belfast, the north of Ireland, and from Scotland, arrive and are despatched every morning at 8, and every evening at 10½. Letters from Dublin, the south of Ireland, and England, arrive every morning at 2, and afternoon at 5, and despatched every morning at 8, and evening at half-past 10. Letters from Comber, Ballygowan, Saintfield, Ballynahineh, and Dromara, arrive every evening at 9, and are despatched every morning at 3

Conveyances—To Dublin, the royal mail, from the Post office, every morning at 8, and evening at half-past 10. To Belfast, the royal mail, from the Post office, every morning at 2, and evening at 5. To Lisburn, two cars, from M'Gready's, every morning at a quarter before 8; also, two from Edward M'Cartney's, at the same hour

The Cathedral—The Right Rev. Robt. Knox, D.D., bishop; Rev. Edward Kent, rector; Revs. Richard Agar and George A. Patton, curates; Very Rev. D. Bagot (Newry) dean;

DROMORE.

Rev. James Saurin, A.M., archdeacon; Rev. B. W. Dolling, A.M., precentor; Rev. Edward Richards, chancellor; Rev. Edw. Leslie, B.D., treasurer; Rev. Hugh S. Hamilton, vicar-general; M. A. Saurin, registrar; H. Stewart, deputy registrar; Francis H. O. Flaherty, proctor of office; John Bradshaw, apparitor; Rev. H. E. Boyd, A.M., prebendary
Presbyterian Church—Rev. J. Collins
Presbyterian Church—Rev. J. M'Kee
Unitarian Chapel—Rev.W. B. Minniss
Wesleyan Methodist Chapel, Gallows street—Rev. Wm. M'Garvey
Primitive Methodist Chapel and Ebenezer (new connection), Gallows st. —ministers various
Covenanters' Chapel—minis. various
Roman Catholic Chapel, Gallows st.— Rev. John Sharkey, parish priest; Rev. Charles Kinner, curate

GENTRY, CLERGY, ETC.

Agar, Rev. Richard, Dromore square
Bodel, Michael, Mount street
Collins, Rev. James, Park row
Gillmer, James B., Mayfield
Heron, Misses, Bridge street
Kent, Rev. Edward, Rectory
Kinney, Rev. Charles, Gallows hill
Lindsay, David, Ashfield
M'Kee, Rev. John, Banview
M'Garvey, Rev. Wm., Gallows hill
Minniss, Rev. W. B., Mossville
Patton, Rev. George Augustus, Dromore square
Quinn, John H., J.P., Dromore palace
Quinn, James, Dromore palace
Sharkey, Rev. John, Gallows street
Stewart, Hugh, Prince's street
Vaughan, George, Qually
Waddell, James George, Island Derry

TRADERS, ETC.

Austin, Patrick, teacher of National school, Gallows street
Andrews, Samuel, ironmonger and hardware merchant
Abernethy, David, spirit dealer
Ardery, William, tailor
Bennet, Thomas, weaving utensil maker
Bigham, Elizabeth, milliner and dressmaker
Bullick, Charles, woollendraper
Brush, Richard Crane, land agent
Beggs, Mary, spirit and porter dealer
Brennan, Bernard, spirit and porter dealer
Boyce, William John, spirit & porter dealer
Clarke, Robert, teacher of National school
Curry, Samuel, ironmonger & grocer
Cromey, Wm., linen & woollendraper
Clarke, Mrs., teacher of National school
Darry, Richard, boot and shoemaker and leather seller
Drake, John, spirit and porter dealer
Deverell, Ponsonby Wm., surgeon
Donnelly, William, dyer
Dickson, Joseph, attorney
English, James, blacksmith
English, Samuel, blacksmith
English, Eliza, milliner & dressmaker
Frazer, Robert, boot and shoemaker, leather seller, and grocer
Frazer, Hugh, carpenter
Frazer, Robert, carpenter
Fegan, John, grocer, and commissioner for taking affidavits
Frackleton, John, grocer and haberdasher
Ferris, John, spirit and porter dealer
Graham, Henry, surgeon
Gibson, Henry, grocer
Harrison, William, butcher
Hall, John, carpenter
Hawkins, James, carpenter
Harrison, Robert, grocer, tanner, and tallow chandler
Hewitt, John, grocer
Hammond, Joseph, linen and woollendraper, &c.
Hammond, Mark, pawnbroker
Herron, Henry, grocer
Jamieson, George, grocer and haberdasher
Jardine, Mrs., pawnbroker
Jelly, Andrew, spirit and porter dealer
Jardine, John, spirit and porter dealer
Lyttle, Richard, grocer
Lilburn, Samuel, grocer & spirit dealer
Lindsay, David, linen merchant and bleacher
Leebody, Henry, saddler and harness maker
Lyons, William, spirit & porter dealer

Menarry, Alex., spirit & porter dealer
Magee, Cath., straw bonnet maker
Moore, George, tailor
Mahon, Robert, grocer
Miller, Wm., spirit and porter dealer
Morrow, James, spirit & porter dealer
Morrow, Miss, milliner and dressmaker
Magee, Daniel, saddler and harness maker
Mercer, James, ironmonger and hardware merchant
Miller, William, carpenter
Mercer, George, boot and shoemaker and leather seller
M'Dade, Wm., baker, boot and shoemaker, leather seller, &c.
M'Grady, Felix, blacksmith
M'Dade, Henry, boot and shoemaker and leather seller, Bridge street
M'Dade, John, grocer and haberdasher, Bridge street
M'Evoy, Hugh, butcher
M'Cartney, Edward, grocer
M'Caw, Thomas, linen merchant and bleacher
M'Murray, Wm., & Co., linen merchants and bleachers
M'Evoy, John, spirit & porter dealer
M'Grady, John, spirit and porter dealer
M'Whinney, Alexander, spirit and porter dealer
M'Cloughan, Mrs., straw bonnet maker
M'Ilduff, John, spirit & porter dealer
M'Ewan, John, tailor
M'Dowell, James, tailor
M'Kelvey, John, whitesmith
M'Murray, William, wheelwright
Munro, John, hotel keeper
M'Tier, James and Richard, turners
Martin, Mrs., grocer
Megarrell, Richard, painter and glazier
Martin, Jane, milliner and dressmaker
Napier, Henry, blacksmith
Neilson, Mrs., milliner and dressmaker
Neilson, John, pawnbroker
Nelson, Joseph, watch and clockmaker
O'Neill, John, baker, and corn and flour factor
Oswald, Usher, butcher, grocer, and provision dealer
Oswald, Eliza, milliner & dressmaker
O'Neill, RoseAnn, straw bonnet maker
Oswald, James, butcher
Parsnip, M., milliner and dressmaker
Reynolds, George, spirit dealer
Roden, James, tailor
Saul, William, haberdasher
Stewart, Hugh, Stamp and Registry office
Thompson, George, tailor
Thompson, William, carpenter
Watson, William, spirit dealer
Ward, Ruth, spirit dealer
Welsh, Alexander Colvill, painter and glazier
Weir, James, pawnbroker
Walker, John, spirit dealer

DUNGANNON.

DUNGANNON is a Parliamentary borough, market, and post town, of somewhat handsome appearance, in the parish of Drumglass, barony of Dungannon, and county of Tyrone, situated about 5 miles East of the Southern shore of Lough Neagh, 76 miles N. by W. from Dublin, and 32 miles W. by S. from Belfast. It was the seat of the O'Neills from its earliest days; and, on a hill, crowning the town, formerly stood a castle, erected by those powerful chiefs. This castle was surrendered to Gerard, ninth Earl of Kildare, and by him condemned to the flames. In 1782, the delegates of the Irish Volunteers assembled here to declare the independence of the Irish Parliament. Dungannon confers the title of Viscount on the family of Trevor, of Brynkinalt, near Churk, in the county of Denbigh, North Wales. The town consists of a square and four principal, with several smaller, streets. Improvements upon an extensive scale have been made within these few years; handsome houses and public buildings having been erected within and around the town. Gas Works were erected at an expense of £2,400, and the town lighted on the evening of the 25th September, 1835.

Courts of Quarter and Petty Sessions are regularly held, and a Manor Court, every three weeks, by the Seneschal, Robert Wray, Esq., J.P. A new Court-house has been erected, at the back of which is a Bridewell.

The original Parish Church of Drumglass was destroyed in the commotions during the reign of Elizabeth, and a new one erected by Sir Arthur Chichester, in the town of Dungannon, in 1619. This building shared the fate of its predecessor in 1641, was restored in 1672, and rebuilt in 1799, since which time it has been considerably enlarged and improved, and, as it now stands, is a handsome edifice. The other places of worship are 2 Presbyterian Churches, 2 Methodist Chapels, and a Roman Catholic Chapel.

The principal charities consist of free schools, by which the children of the poor are benefited; a fever hospital, a dispensary, and union workhouse.

The College or Royal School, one of the five regal endowments, was founded by Charles I., in 1628, as a free grammar school, and largely endowed. The present building, which was erected in 1786, by Primate Robinson, is situated on the east side of the town, and comprises a centre and two deeply receding wings, erected at an expense of upwards of £4,500, of which a large sum was contributed by the Primate, who also gave the ground upon which it is built. The present Principal is the Rev. F. H. Ringwood, a distinguished scholar of Trinity College. A news-room, with a library, is well supported, and a great acquisition to the town; the books, which form an admirable selection, were the gift of Viscount Northland, at that time M.P. for the borough—a portrait of his lordship adorns the reading-room. The present representative of the borough is the Hon. Mr. Knox, brother of Lord Northland. In 1846, the Dungannon Literary Society was founded.

Drumglass Collieries, rather more than a mile from town, are very extensive; they are now the property of Samuel Hughes, Esq., and, under his management, prove a great acquisition to the town.

The trade in linen and grain is, perhaps, the most important here, but other considerable branches occupy attention There are large dye and bleach-works; the leather trade is of some importance, and paper, earthenware, bricks, and tiles, are manufactured in the vicinity. The merchants embarked in the grain, flax, and coal trades are many and respectable. There are several corn mills actively at work.

The monetary establishments comprise branches of the Belfast Banking Company and Provincial Bank of Ireland, and a Savings' Bank.

The market days are Monday and Thursday, the first for corn and the other for the usual commodities. Fairs—First Thursday in each month.

The present population of the borough is 3,836.

Post-office—Samuel Hughes, postmaster. Letters from Dublin and all parts of the South, also from England and Scotland, arrive at 5-30 a.m. and are despatched at 7 p.m.; from the North, 6.35 p.m. and are despatched at 6-10 a.m.; from the West, by Armagh, mails arrive at 6 p.m. and are despatched at 6-20 a.m.

Conveyances—To Armagh, a car, from Feeney's, Market square, every morning (Sunday excepted) at 4-15; another from Seignor's, Market square, at 6; and a caravan, from Lilburn's, every Tuesday, at 8 a.m. To Coleraine, a caravan, from Lilburn's, at 6-20 a.m. To Drogheda, the Royal mail, from the Post-office, at 6-20 p.m.; and the Fair Trader, from Hughes', every Monday, Wednesday, and Friday, at 7-30. To Omagh, a mail car, from the Post-office, at 7 a.m., and a caravan, from Lilburn's, every Tuesday, Thursday, and Saturday, at 3 p.m. To Portadown, a caravan, from Lilburn's, every morning (Sunday excepted)

Carriers—To Dublin, James Valely, once a fortnight; Belfast, John Quinn and Henry Neill, once a week; Newry, James M'Govern, once a week

DUNGANNON.

Stamp Office, Church street—Thomas Agnew, sub-distributor
Constabulary Station, Market square
Dispensary, Perry street — James Hamilton, surgeon
Gas Works, Washingford row
Union Workhouse—George Moon, clerk to guardians
Belfast Banking Company (branch), Market sq.—W. J. Mines, manager
Provincial Bank of Ireland (branch), Scotch st.—Jas. Guthrie, manager
Savings' Bank, George's st.—Arthur Fullan, actuary
Provident Loan Society, Coalisland—John Lynass, clerk
Parish Church, Church street—Rev. William Quain, rector and surrogate; Rev. T. Twigg, curate
Presbyterian Church—Rev. Andrew Wilson, minister
Presbyterian Church—Rev. Charles L. Morell, minister
Independent Chapel, Donaghmore—Rev. James Hanson, minister
Wesleyan Methodist Chapel, Perry st.—Ministers various
Primitive Methodist Chapel, Shamble lane—Ministers various
Friends' Meeting House, Grange
R. C. Chapel, Northland row—Rev. F. Stane, P.P.; Rev. Mr. Harbison, curate
R. C. Chapel, Donaghmore—Rev. D. Hughes, curate
Royal College, Northland row—Rev. F. H. Ringwood, principal
Church Society's School, Donaghmore—D. J. Pece, master; Mary C. Pece, mistress
Church Society's School, Castlecaulfield—Harcourt Lee, master; Mrs. Frazer, mistress
Church Society's Schools, Newmills—John Hart, master
Church Society's School, Coalisland—John Lynass, master
Earl of Ranfurly's School, William st.—G. De Winter, master
Erasmus Smith's School—Mr. Gilpin, master; Isabella Betty, mistress
Infants' School, Ranfurly terrace
Infants' School (Mrs. Lyle's), Donaghmore—Sophia Ann Wardlaw, mistress
National School, Coalisland—Patrick Larkin, master; Sarah Hopkins, mistress
National School, Donaghmore—Stephen Porter, master
National School, Northland row—James Stuart, master
News-Room and Public Library, Scotch street—William M'Clelland, treasurer; Wm. Holmes, secretary

NOBILITY AND GENTRY.

Barclay, Sir Robert, Northland row
Barclay, Mrs., Northland row
Brown, James, Northland place and Beech valley
Burges, Lady Caroline, Parkanaur
Burges, Jn. Ynyr, D.L., J.P., Parkanaur
Burrows, Eliza and Ellen, George's st.
Cochran, Major, Grange
Cranston, John, Cranebrook
Cranston, Margaret, Anne street
Dickson, Colonel, Northland row
Evans, Edward, Gortmerron
Evans, Edward, jun., Gortmerron
Evans, Robert, Gortmerron
Falls, William, Milltown
Forster, Robert, Springfield
Greer, Thomas, Tullylagan
Greer, Joseph, Grange
Goff, Joseph, Northland house
Irwin, Margaret, Northland row
Irwin, Captain James M., Tullycullion
King, Henry, Castlecaulfield
Kinley, Thomas, Union place
Knox, Hon. Mrs., Bernagh
Lowry, William, Drumreagh
Lyle, Alex. Mackenzie, Donaghmore
Matthew, William, Northland row
M'Avoy, John M., Perry street
M'Niece, James, Mulnagore lodge
Murray, John S., Furchal
Northland, Viscount, Madeira
O'Neill, John, William street
Pike, Jonathan, Beech grove
Pike, Richard, Torren hill
Ranfurly, Right Hon. Earl, Dungannon park
Robinson, William, Coalisland
Shiel, James, barrister, Killymeal
Slevin, George, Beech valley
Stanley, Charles, Roughan house
Smyth, Frances J., Northland row
Stuart, George E., Northland row
Stuart, Mrs., Perry street

Stuart, Miss, Northland row
Thompson, Miss, Northland row
Ward, Thomas, Mount Hamilton
Wilcock, Joshua, Beech valley
Williamson, Richard, Northland row
Wray, Robert, J.P., seneschal, Northland row
Young, James, Annaguinea

CLERGY AND PROFESSIONAL.

Acheson, Rev. Robert, Killiles
Atwell, Rev. William, Clone Glebe
Carpendale, Rev. Thomas, Mulnamore glebe
Cather, Rev. William, Perry street
Davidson, Samuel, attorney, Union place
Dickson, Benjamin, physician and surgeon, R.M., Union place
Disney, Rev. James, Killyman glebe
Hamilton, James, physician and surgeon, Northland row
Hamilton, Thomas, physician and surgeon, Market square
Hanson, Rev. James, Donaghmore
Holmes, William, solicitor, Market sq.
Hughes, Rev. Daniel, Donaghmore
Kearney, Rev. M., Tullynure lodge
Kingsmore, Rev. Robert, Coalisland
Lyle, Robert, attorney, Donaghmore
M'Donald, Rev. John, Durna cottage
M'Guckian, Rev. Neal, Donaghmore
Morell, Rev. Charles L., Market sq.
Neville, William, M.D., Perry street
Newton, Andrew & Courtenay, solicitors, Northland row
Peebles, Wm., solicitor, Market square
Porter, Rev. Thomas H., D.D., Ballymully glebe
Quain, Rev. William, Glebe hill
Ringwood, Rev. F. H., College
Weaney, Rev. Bernard, Durna cottage

TRADERS, ETC.

Atwell, John, baker, Irish street
Anderson, William, grocer, Scotch st.
Agnew, Thomas, grocer and seedsman, Church street
Anderson, Thos., haberdasher, Castlecaulfield
Agnew, Thomas, pawnbroker, Church street
Brown, David, and Son, bakers, Donaghmore
Brown, John, baker, Irish street
Bloomer, Michael, carpenter, Scotch street
Brady, John, carpenter, Milltown
Boardman, Eliza, confectioner, Perry street
Burns, James, earthenware manufacturer, Corr
Burns, Wm., earthenware manufacturer, Ballinakelly
Barecroft, Joseph, flax merchant, Strangmore
Bloomer, Michael, grocer, Scotch st.
Brown, John, grocer, Irish street
Breen, Wm., spirit dealer, George's st.
Bloomer, Michael, leather seller, Scotch street
Barcroft, Wm. J., miller, Redford
Barcroft, John Pim, linen merchant, Strangmore
Beavers, Caroline, milliner and dressmaker, Anne street
Bell, William, painter and glazier, Scotch street
Bell, M., & Co., seedsmen, Church st.
Bates, Wm., publican, Scotch street
Birnie, Hugh, tailor, Irish street
Blair, Wm., tailor, Park road
Brown, David, & Son, chandlers, Donaghmore
Barton, Wm., watchmaker, Church st.
Bradley, Wm., whitesmith, Ann st.
Black, Robert, haberdasher, Market square
Bryars, James, leatherseller, Scotch street
Courtney, Abraham, baker, Scotch st.
Crossin, Denis, blacksmith, Coalisland
Cullan, Maurice, butcher, Shamble lane
Carpmill, James, carpenter, Castlecaulfield
Corr, James, carpenter, Milltown
Campbell, Henry, clothes dealer, Irish street
Caulfield, Staples, & Co., coal proprietors, Coalisland
Courtenay, Mary Ann, confectioner, Perry street
Cavanagh, Bernard, cooper, Perry st.
Campbell, Wm., earthenware manufacturer, Creenagh
Cardwell, Robert, earthenware manufacturer, Creenagh
Cunningham, Jno., hairdresser, Church street

DUNGANNON.

Carrol, Wm., hatter, Scotch street
Corr, Charles, publican, Coalisland
Craig, John, publican, Castlecaulfield
Coulter, Thomas, tailor, Irish street
Creagh, James, merchant tailor and habit maker
Creagh, James, tailor, Market square
Devlin, Patrick, auctioneer, Eskra
Dickson, James, baker, &c., Scotch street
Daily, Wm., blacksmith, Castlecaulfield
Doris, Denis, blacksmith, Newmills
Douglas, Wm., printer, bookseller, & stationer, Market square
Douglas, Alexander, boot and shoemaker, Perry street
Daily, Felix, carpenter, Newmills
Devlin, Patrick, cooper, Coalisland
Duncan, James, insurance agent, Perry street
Dickson, James, grocer, Scotch st.
Dunlop, Alexander, hatter
Duncan, Mary, dressmaker, Perry st.
Donnelly, Bernard, publican, Donaghmore
Ewing, John, grocer, Scotch street
Eccles, John, publican and miller, Coalisland
Frizell, John, cabinetmaker, Scotch st.
Fullin, Thomas, earthenware dealer, Coalisland
Fowler, Enoch, earthenware manufacturer, Derryboy
Falls, Wm., insurance agent, Market square
Frizzell, Jane, grocer, Scotch street
Farmer, Bryan, ironmonger, Irish st.
Fee, Henry, publican, Scotch street
Feeney, Rebecca, publican, Market sq.
Foules, Peter, whitesmith, Perry st.
Frizell, Mrs., leatherseller, Scotch st.
Gallogly, Patrick, carpenter, Donaghmore
Gattens, Patrick, carpenter, William st.
Gillon, John, carpenter, Donaghmore
Grimes, Bridget, earthenware dealer, Coalisland
Gray, James, & Co., brick and tile manufacturers, Coalisland
Gorman, John, publican, Scotch st.
Gaffney, James, tailor, Coalisland
Greene, Geo., whitesmith, Church st.
Hagan, John, baker, Irish street
Hall, Jas., blacksmith, Castlecaulfield

Hamilton, James, boot & shoemaker, Anne street
Hughes, Jane, spirit dealer, Market square
Hughes, Mr., spirit dealer, Irish st.
Hughes, Jane, hotel, Market square
Hughes, Samuel, Drumglass colliery
Hughes, John, earthenware manufacturer, Gortgonis
Hughes, John, earthenware manufacturer, Brocagh
Hughes, John, & Co., brick and tile manufacturers, Coalisland
Hughes, Thomas, grocer, George's st.
Hurson, Edward, grocer, Scotch st.
Hurson, Edwd., spirit dealer, Scotch st
Hughes, Jane, grocer, Market square
Hubbard, Eliza, haberdasher, Market square
Hughes, Thos., spirit dealer, George's st.
Hughes, John, leatherseller, Irish st.
Hazleton, Dawson, linen manufacturer, Bogbawn
Hughes, David, painter and glazier, Scotch street
Hancock, Thomas, saddler, Church st.
Harvey, Hamilton, publican, William street
Henry, Margaret, publican, Newmills
Hurson, Michl., publican, Donaghmore
Hughes, B., tailor, Coalisland
Irwin, Margt., confectioner, Perry st.
Irwin, Joseph, grocer and saddler, Irish street
Irwin, Robert, painter and glazier, Perry street
Irwin, M. A., haberdasher, Irish st.
Kilpatrick, John, earthenware manufacturer, Conannan
Kerr, John, flax merchant, Tullyaran
Kerr & Sinnamon, linen merchants, Parkmount
King, Robert, miller, Coalisland
Lowry, John, paper maker, Perry st.
Kelly, James, tailor, Irish street
Lindsay, Alex., watchmaker, Perry st.
Lilburn, John, architect and builder, Eskra
Lilburn, Thomas, architect & builder, George's street
Loughran, John, carpenter, Donaghmore
Loughran, Patrick, clothes dealer, Irish street
Lowry, John, grocer, Perry street

Loughran, Edward, woollendraper, Market square
Lecky, Stewart, oil and colour, slate, coal, herring, and salt merchant, spade and shovel manufacturer, Coalisland
Leslie, Dickson, haberdasher and umbrella maker, Church street
Lilburn, Thomas, Ranfurley Arms hotel, George's street
Lilburn, Wm., publican, Anne street
Manson, David, blacksmith, Donaghmore
Marshall, Geo., blacksmith, Market sq.
Maars, David, boot and shoemaker, Church street
Monahan, Thomas, boot & shoemaker, Market square
Mulholland, James, boot & shoemaker, Coalisland
Mackenzie, Alexander, & Co., brewers, Donaghmore
Milling, James, builder, Coalisland
Morrison, Ferdinand, butcher, Shamble lane
Morrison, Ferdinand, jun., butcher, Shamble lane
Morrison, Patrick, butcher, Scotch st.
Mullan, Alex., butcher, Scotch street
Millin, James, carpenter, Coalisland
Maddin, Michl., clothes dealer, Irish st.
Mullan, Michl., clothes dealer, Irish st.
Moore, Joseph, draper, Market square
Mackenzie, Alexander, & Co., maltsters, Scotch street
Mackenzie, Alexander, & Co., millers, Donaghmore
Monaghan, Frances, milliner, Market square
Mullan, M. A. and E., dressmakers, Market square
Mooney, Felix, pawnbroker, Irish st.
Mooney, Bernard, publican, Irish st.
Murphy, Thos., publican, Coalisland
Morton, Wm., tinplate worker, Irish street
Murphy, Hugh, watch & clockmaker, Irish street
Macshane, James, merchant tailor and habit maker
Mullan, John, wheelwright, Anne st.
Maxwell, James, haberdasher, Scotch street
M'Clelland, John, baker and leather seller, Irish street

M'Anally, Henry, boot and shoemaker, Donaghmore
M'Ilkenny, Patrick, blacksmith, Sloan street
M'Guffin, Robert, boot and shoemaker, William street
M'Ilhone, Felix, butcher, Irish street
M'Geough, Peter, butcher, Sloan st.
M'Mullan, James, butcher, Irish st.
M'Mullan, John, butcher, Scotch st.
M'Clintock, Mr., Church street
M'Ilkenny, John, carpenter, Sloan st.
M'Shane, Pat., carpenter, Sloan street
M'Shane, Peter, carpenter, Anne st.
M'Clean, Robert, coach builder, Market square
M'Cann, Patrick, cooper, Sloan street
M'Shane, Margaret, china & earthenware dealer, Market square
M'Caughey, James, flax merchant, Anne street
M'Caughey, John, flax merchant, Anne street
M'Gladrizan, Joseph, flax merchant, Annaguinea
M'Kittrick, John, flax merchant, Anne street
M'Clelland, John, grocer and seedsman, Irish street
M'Clelland, Wm., grocer and seedsman, Church street
M'Elhone, John, grocer, Irish street
M'Shane, Margt., grocer, Market sq.
M'Ilroy, R., draper, Market square
M'Kell, Margt., milliner and draper, Church street
M'Avoy, John, linen manufacturer, Bealemount
M'Clelland, Thomas, linen manufacturer, Mullaghmore
M'Cluskey, John, linen manufacturer, Coalisland
M'Donald, John, linen manufacturer, Conannon
M'Niece, James, linen manufacturer, Cavenett
M'Clean, John, miller, Coalisland
M'Clean, Archibald, spade maker, Mullaghatague
M'Clean, John, spade maker, Coalisland
M'Causland, John, publican, Donaghmore
M'Elone, James, publican, Irish street
M'Gerr, Edward, publican, Anne st.

DUNGANNON.

M'Guckian, Hugh and Andrew, blacksmiths, Market square
M'Gill, James, publican, Perry street
M'Guckian, James, publican, Perry st.
M'Neese, James, publican, Church st.
M'Nickle, Felix, publican, Scotch st.
M'Shane, M., publican, Market square
M'Donald, M., staymaker, Perry street
M'Niece, James, land surveyor, Mulnagore
M'Alister, Isaac, haberdasher, Market square
Newton, Robert, miller, Coalisland
O'Neill, Constantine, baker, Irish st.
O'Connor, Bernard, boot and shoemaker, Donaghmore
O'Neill, H., carpenter, Donaghmore
Orr, James, linen and flax merchant, Strangmore
Orr, Wm., grocer and leather seller, Market square
O'Neill, H., linen manufacturer, Coash
O'Neill, Hugh, publican, Donaghmore
Patterson, D., grocer and haberdasher, Market square
Patterson, Dickson, linen and woollendraper, Market square
Patterson, D., spirit dealer, Market sq.
Pike, J., & Son, linen manufacturers, Beech grove
Pearce, John, tailor, Perry street
Quinn, James, baker, Irish street
Quinn, Cornel., blacksmith, Sloan st.
Quinn, Owen, clothes dealer, Irish st.
Quinn, James, publican and chandler, Anne street
Quin, Hugh, flax merchant, Irish st.
Quin, Daniel, publican, Coalisland
Quinn, Hughes, publican, George's st.
Rocks, Mary, baker and publican, Perry street
Richardson, John, boot and shoemaker, Perry street
Richardson, J., boot and shoemaker, Church street
Robinson, Isaiah, tinplate worker, Barrack street
Robinson, Mary, earthenware dealer, Corr
Rodgers, William, grocer, Scotch st.
Roberts, Eliza, staymaker, Perry st.
Rodgers, Thomas, tailor, Market sq.
Sloan, George, baker, Coalisland
Steele, James, butcher, Shamble lane
Stewart, Patrick, butcher, Scotch st.

Smith, Margaret, dyer, Anne street
Speer, Henry, linen & woollen draper and insurance agent, Market square
Stevenson, Joseph and William, flax merchants, Roan mills
Stevenson, Robert, flax merchant, New mills
Sharkey, William, grocer, Scotch st.
Sloan, George, miller, Coalisland
Stevenson, John, grocer, ironmonger, and timber merchant, Church street
Stewart, Mary, grocer, Perry street
Simpson, Robt., spirit dealer, Market sq.
Simpson, Robert, grocer, Market sq.
Spence, John, haberdasher, Scotch st.
Smith, James, linen manufacturer, Scotch street
Steenson, Eliza, milliner, George's st.
Stewart, John, saddler, Scotch street
Swan, Mary, haberdasher, Irish street
Thompson, T. H., auctioneer, Market square
Tener, Richard, baker, grocer, and ironmonger, Perry street
Thornberry, John, boot & shoemaker, Donaghmore
Thompson, Joseph, cabinet maker, Market square
Taggart, James, carpenter, Washingford row
Taylor, George, carpenter, Milltown
Thomson, Eliza, confectioner, Market square
Teasey, Robert, cooper, Carr's row
Timony, Patrick, grocer, Donaghmore
Tullan, Arthur, Master in Chancery
Tener, Richard, oil and colour merchant, Church street
Tener, T., publican, Castlecaulfield
Turner, J., linen merchant, Market sq.
Tague, William, tailor, Scotch street
Vallely & Kelly, linen and woollendrapers, Scotch street
Wilcocks, George, land agent and timber merchant, Coalisland
Woods, Charles, linen merchant, Moygashel
Wiley, James, publican, Scotch street
Wilson, James, publican, Scotch st.
Walpole, Thomas, haberdasher, Market square
Walker, Wm., haberdasher, Market sq.
Walker, Wm., linen & woollendraper, Market square
Wright, Jno., spirit dealer, George's st.

ENNISKILLEN.

ENNISKILLEN is an inland market town and parliamentary borough—the principal town in the county Fermanagh. It stands about 100 miles N.W. by N. from Dublin, and 93 W. by S. from Belfast. The Assizes for the county are held here, Quarter Sessions, and a borough court, every Thursday, are also held at the Court-house. Enniskillen, since the union, returns one member to Parliament. Present representative—James Whiteside, Esq., Solicitor-General for Ireland. Fairs are held on the 10th of every month, on 26th May, and 26th October; markets, toll free, on Thursdays.

Post Office, Townhall street—Richard Ball, postmaster. Letters from the south, including Dublin, also from England, arrive at 45 minutes past 6 a.m., and are despatched at 45 minutes past 5 p.m. Letters from the north, including Belfast and Scotland, arrive at 5-30 a.m., and are despatched at 6-45 p.m. From Sligo, Manorhamilton, and Blacklion, at 5 p.m., and are despatched at 7-35 a.m. From Ballyshannon and Belleek, at 5-15 p.m., and are despatched at 7-25 a.m. From Omagh, Fintona, and Trillick, arrive at 10-45 a.m., and despatched at 1-45 p.m. From Pettigo, Kesh, Ederney, and Lowtherstown, at 4-45 p.m., and are despatched at 7-45 a.m.

Conveyances—To Dublin, a four-horse coach, every morning (Sunday excepted), from the Imperial hotel, on Monday, Wednesday, and Friday, at 5-30, the alternate days at 10-30; passes through Maguiresbridge, Lisnaskea, Newtownbutler, Clones, and Ballibay, to Castleblayney, and by railway to Dublin; returns every evening at 8. The royal mail, from the Imperial hotel, every evening, at 5-45; passes through Maguiresbridge, Lisnaskea, Newtownbutler, Cavan, Virginia, Kells, and Navan, to Dublin; returns every morning at 6-45.—To Belfast, a four-horse coach, from the Imperial hotel, every morning (Sunday excepted), at 7; passes through Maguiresbridge, Brookborough, Fivemiletown, Clogher, Augher, Aughnacloy, and Caledon, to Armagh, and by railway to Belfast; returning every evening at 6. The royal mail coach, from the Imperial hotel, every evening at 6-45, goes through Maguiresbridge, Lisnaskea, Newtownbutler, Clones, Monaghan, Armagh, Portadown, Lurgan, Moira, and Lisburn; returns every morning at 5-30.—To Ballyshannon and Bundoran, the royal mail, from the Imperial hotel, every morning at 7-30; returns every evening at 5.—To Sliga, Ballina, and Castlebar, the royal mail, from the Imperial hotel, every morning at 7-30; goes through Blacklion and Manorhamilton, Sligo, Ballina, and Castlebar; returns every evening at 5.—To Pettigo, a mail car, from the Imperial hotel, every morning at 7-45; goes through Lowtherstown and Kish; returns every evening at 4-45.—To Omagh, a mail car, from the Imperial hotel, every day at 1-45; goes through Ballinamallard, Trillick, and Fintona; returns every morning at 11.—To Longford and Mullingar, a car, from the Imperial hotel, every Tuesday, Thursday, and Saturday; goes through Swanlinbar, Mohill, and Longford, to Mullingar, and by railway, same evening, to Dublin; returns the alternate days at 9

Carriers—To Dublin, Peter Cosgrove, Eden lane; John Chittick, Drumlion—once a week. To Londonderry, Michael Owens, Main street; Michael Keenan, Belmore street. To Belfast, by canal, once a week

Town Commissioners—Wm. Robert Armstrong, David Barry, Robert Beatty, James Baker, Jas. Creden, James Coutts, Hugh Copeland, James Graham, Terence Ingoldsby, John Kerr, Patrick Kerr, John Maguire, John Mihary, James Macartney, Peter M'Bride. Chairman, Wm. Muldoon; secretary, Robert Clegg. Meet on the first Monday in each month

Gaol, Fairview—Jas. Jeffers, governor; H. Morrison, deputy governor; M. Morrison, matron; William Corry, local inspector; George A. Nixon, M.D., surgeon; George Mahood, apothecary; Hon. and Rev. J. C. Maude, Protestant chaplain; Rev. E. Stephenson, Presbyterian chaplain; Very Rev. Mr Boylan, Roman Catholic chaplain

Union Workhouse—Earl of Enniskillen, chairman of Board; Edward Archdall, vice-chairman; Paul Dane, deputy vice-chairman; Alex. Price, master; Rebecca Carson, matron

Barracks—Infantry Barrack, Queen street; Artillery Barrack, Castle st.; Redoubt Barrack, Windmillhill.— Barrack master, Mr. Pringle; Armourer, and Ordnance store keeper, Hill Parkinson

Constabulary—Wade Foot, county inspector; John D. M'Neil, sub do.; John O'Hara, head constable

Infirmary—George A. Nixon, M.D., surgeon; George Mahood, apothecary; Mrs. Johnston, matron; Hon. and Rev. J. C. Maude, treasurer; Stewart Whittaker, secretary

Corn and Butter Market, Boston lane —William Corry, weighmaster

Banks—Belfast Bank, Townhall st., M. H. Morphy, manager. Provincial Bank of Ireland, Darling street, George Stewart, manager. Ulster Bank, Samuel Clarke, manager. Savings' Bank, Townhall street, S. Frith, secretary and treasurer

Freeman's Charitable Club, Townhall —For distributing loans to distressed tradesmen

Parish Church, Hollow—The Hon. and Rev. J. C. Maude, Chanter-hill, rector; the Rev. Mr. Bradshaw, and Rev. Mr. Mathlas, curates

Presbyterian Church, Main street— Rev. A. C. Maclatchy, minister

Wesleyan Methodist Chapel, Preaching lane—ministers various

Primitive Methodist Chapel, Main st.

Roman Catholic Chapel, Darling-street—The very Rev. Mr. Boylan, Parish Priest; Rev. P. Traynor, Rev. Mr. Gartlan

Royal School, Portora — Principal, Rev. John Graham, LL.D.

Church Education Society—Rev. H. A. Burke, secretary; Rev. M. Whittaker, treasurer

Church Education Society's School, Forthill—Nicholas Wilson, master; Ann Wilson, mistress

National School, Darling street—Mr. M'Iver, master; Mary M'Iver, mistress

Ladies' Seminary & Boarding School, Darling-street—Miss Clegg

Ladies' Boarding and Day School, Darling-street—Miss Stoddard

Ladies' Day School, Wellington place —Miss Nesbitt

Ladies' Day School, Wellington place —Miss Patterson

Bible Society's Depository, Darling street—Mr. M'Mullen

North-west Library, Townhall street— John Hamilton, librarian

Newspapers—*Fermanagh Mail*, every Thursday, T. R. J. Polson, proprietor. *Fermanagh Reporter*, every Thursday, Wm. Trimble, proprietor

NOBILITY AND GENTY.

Archdall, Hy. Grey, J.P., Derryargan
Archdall, Henry Mervyn, M.P., Riversdale
Archdall, Nicholas Mervyn, Riversdale
Archdall, Robert, Riverstown
Armstrong, Mrs., Willoughby place
Armstrong, Jardine, Innishmore Island
Armstrong, Montgomery, Innishmore Island
Armstrong, Philip, Enniskillen
Armstrong, William, Lara
Beaufoy, Major, Willoughby place
Bell, Alexander, Willoughby place
Bell, Capt. W. F., Willoughby place
Belmore, Countess of, Castlecoole
Betty, William, Cappy
Brien, John, Castletown
Clarke, Samuel, Darling street
Cole, Hon. Henry A., Florence court
Cole, Hon. John, Florence court
Collum, Archibald, Fanhousewater
Corry, Capt. Wm., J.P., Wellington pl.

Dane, Paul, J.P., Killyhevlin
Drummond, Miss, Darling street
Ely, Most Noble the Marquis of, Ely Lodge
Enniskillen, Right Hon. the Earl of, Florence court
Faussett, Charles, Lisbofin
Fitzgerald, Martha, Fairview
Foot, Wade, Willoughby place
Frith, B. Gamble, J.P., Darling street
Frith, James, Cross
Frith, William, Cross
Gamble, Baptist, Graan
Gamble, Hanna
Graham, Miss, Fort hill
Graham, George, Brook street
Graham, Christopher, Goblusk
Irvine, George, East Bridge street
Irwin, Thomas, Bara
Johnston, Mrs., Drumkeen
Johnston, Mrs., East Bridge street
Jones, Charles John, Rushen
Jones, Lewis, Eden
Jones, William, Lisgoole abbey
Lindsay, Robert, Wellington place
Loftus, Hon. Lord Agustus, Ely Lodge
Loftus, Hon. Lord George, Ely Lodge
Loftus, Hon. Lord Henry, Ely Lodge
Loftus, Hon. Lord Viscount, Ely Lodge
M'Donald, John, Wellington place
Maude, Morice, J.P., Chanterhill
Montgomery, Hugh, Crocklean
Montgomery, James, Oakfield
Moore, George, Innishmore Island
Morony, Captain, Belmore street
Nixon, Alexander, J.P., Henry street
Noble, Elizabeth, Wellington place
Owen, John, Barr
Rankin, Dorothy, Willoughby place
Redmond, Isabella, Fairview
Richardson, Henry Mervyn, Rosfad
Teavan, Alexander, Raceview
Thomson, Ruth, Willoughby place
Weir, John, Hall craig
Weir, Robert, J.P., Hall craig
West, John, R.N., Darling street
Whittaker, Stewart, Darling street
Wilkin, James, Carracreagh
Willis, George Paul, Lakeview
Wood, George, Willoughby place
Wilson, Daniel, Thomastown
Younger, George, Ann street

CLERGY AND PROFESSIONAL.
Acheson, H., surgeon, East Bridge st.
Armstrong, Wm., attorney, Wesley st.
Bradshaw, Rev. William
Bell, Rodney, attorney, Willoughby pl.
Betty, Hazlett, attorney, Main street
Boylan, Very Rev. Mr., P.P.
Beatty, James, M.D., and surgeon, Daily street
Chittick, James, attorney, Darling st.
Clarke, Rev. John S., Enniskillen
Collum, Archd., attorney, Main street
Collum, John, attorney, Bellview
Crummer, William, attorney, Wellington place
Dane, William Auchinleck, attorney, Townhall street
Faussett, Charles, attorney, Castle st.
Frith, B. G., M.D. and surgeon, Darling street
Graham, John, attorney, Darling st.
Greham, Rev. J., LL.D., Portora house
Jones, A., attorney, Darling street
Keys, Robert, attorney, Fortlodge
Kiernan, J., M.D. and surgeon, Darling street
Maclatchy, Rev. Alex. Cooper, M.A., Wellington place
Mathias, Rev. John, Willoughby pl.
Maude, Hon. and Rev. J. C., Chanterhill
Nixon, F., attorney, Willoughby pl.
Nixon, A., surgeon, Willoughby pl.
Nixon, G., M.D. and surgeon, Darling street
O'Donnell, John, surgeon, High st.
Ovenden, William, M.D. and surgeon, Darling street
Read, Rev. L. G., J.P., Levelly Glebe
Rodgers, Robt., surgeon, Ann street
Stevenson, Rev. E., Wellington place
Sweeny, Rev. John, Belnaleck
Teavan, Johnston, attorney, Darling st.
Treanor, Rev. P., C.C., Wellington pl.
Watkins, William, attorney, Brookview Cottage
Weir, Rev. Christopher
West, John, R.N., surgeon, Darling st.
Whittaker, Rev. Mark, Willoughby pl.
Wilson, Rev. John, Derrybrusk
Young, Rev. Walter, Lisbellaw

TRADERS, ETC.
Annon, E., butcher, Diamond
Armstrong, Adam, wine & spirit merchant, Darling street
Allen, Jane, dressmaker, High street

ENNISKILLEN.

Armstrong, Wm., grocer & druggist, High street
Arthur, Wm., grocer and ironmonger, High street
Allen, Alex., haberdasher, Hollow
Armstrong, Wm. Robert, Imperial hotel, Townhall street
Armstrong, William, pawnbroker, Church street
Armstrong, John, publican, Main st.
Ball, John, apothecary, Townhall st.
Bowlan, Andrew, blacksmith, Brooke street
Burley, George, blacksmith, Brooke street
Bushby, Joseph, blacksmith, Tonystick
Bond, Samuel, boot and shoemaker, Barrack street
Bleakley, John, butcher, Darling st.
Berry and Reddington, cabinetmakers, Tonystick
Ball, John, carpenter, Tonystick
Brown, James, clothes broker, Main street
Brennan, James, clothes broker, Main street
Brennan, Thomas, clothes broker, Main street
Ball, Richard, earthenware dealer, Townhall street
Ball, Richard, grocer, Main street
Black, George, grocer and seedsman, High street
Bland, John, Enniskillen hotel, Darling street
Baker, James, draper, High street
Bigham, David, pawnbroker, East Bridge street
Betty, Robert, saddle and harness maker, East Bridge street
Bleakly, Robert, saddle and harness maker, Townhall street
Beatty, Samuel, publican, East Bridge street
Brennan, Ellen, publican, Tonystick
Beatty, Mrs., bonnetmaker, Darling st.
Bigham, Mary, bonnetmaker, East Bridge street
Bleakley, Ellen, bonnetmaker, Castle street
Betty, Richard, tailor, Darling street
Bradshaw, Hugh, timber merchant, East Bridge street
Bradford, Nathaniel, watchmaker, East Bridge street

Clegg, Robert, builder, Darling street
Creden, James, builder, Darling street
Coalter, Wm., baker and confectioner, Main street
Coalter, James, baker and confectioner, Hollow
Carroll, Edward, boot and shoemaker, Strand street
Crooke, Thomas, boot and shoemaker, Darling street
Corrigan, Patrick, butcher
Costello, James, butcher, Eden lane
Crooks, George, commissioner for taking affidavits, Church street
Cox, Mark, cooper, Tonystick
Clegg, Ann, earthenware dealer, High street
Clarke, Samuel, British Commercial Life Insurance office, Darling street
Clegg, Ann, grocer, Hollow
Clegg, Robert, grocer and ironmonger, High street
Coalter, James, grocer, Hollow
Coalter, Wm., grocer, Main street
Creden, James, grocer and ironmonger, Barrack street
Creden, John, grocer and ironmonger, Windmill hill
Creden, Hugh, grocer and ironmonger, Barrack lane
Crooke, George, grocer & ironmonger, Church street
Carson, Wm., haberdasher, High st.
Coutts, James, haberdasher, Townhall street
Copeland, Ralph, draper, Townhall street
Coutts, Jas., draper, Townhall street
Carson, Mary, milliner, High street
Crowe, Thomas, painter, Darling st.
Conigle, Daniel, painter and glazier, Tympinville
Creden, Wm., publican, Windmill hill
Crowe, Mary Ann, straw bonnet maker, Darling street
Caffery, J., tailor, Townhall street
Campbell, James, tailor, Darling st.
Crooke, Thomas, chandler, Main st.
Creden, James, timber merchant, Barrack lane
Creden, John, timber merchant, Windmill hill
Durnian, Michael, boot and shoemaker, Schoolhouse lane
Donnelly, Daniel, butcher, Eden lane

Donnelly, Patrick, butcher, High st.
Donnelly, Thomas, draper, Townhall street
Drennan, James, spirit and porter dealer, Darling street
Drumin, James, spirit and porter dealer, Tonystick
Davis, A. J., straw bonnetmaker, Castle street
Davis, James, watchmaker, East Bridge street
Frith, John Henry, builder, Tonystick
Frith, Wm., builder, Tonystick
Fair, Robert, baker, Hollow
Feely, George, blacksmith, Brooke st.
Faulkner, Wm., boot and shoemaker, Darling street
Fairis, Patrick, butcher
Ferguson, John, coachbuilder, Willoughby place
Falls, James, confectioner, Main st.
Frith, Alex., fishing tackle dealer, Main street
Frith, Alex., grocer, East Bridge st.
Frith, Samuel, draper, Townhall st.
Frith, Mr., miller, Millview
Frith, Ann, dressmaker, Belmore st.
Forster, Archibald, spirit and porter dealer, Townhall street
Gray, Hugh, whitesmith, Tonystick
Gamble, Christopher, apothecary, Wellington place
Gamble, C., registrar of marriages
Grant, Alex., bookseller, Castle street
Gallogly, Thomas, boot and shoemaker, Darling street
Gibson, R., boot & shoemaker, Main st.
Gallagher, John, butcher, Tonystick
Gunning, J., cabinetmaker, Darling st.
Gonnigle, Hugh, carpenter, Main st.
Gunning, John, druggist, Darling st.
Gamble, Samuel, grocer, Ann street
Gordon, Robert, grocer & ironmonger, High street
Graham, James, grocer & ironmonger, Darling street
Goddard, J., hairdresser, Townhall st.
Gamble, Mary, publican, Barrack st.
Gibbons, Mr., publican, Main street
Glenn, Robt., publican, East Bridge st.
Gibson, F., straw bonnetmaker, Courthouse yard
Hall, J., baker & grocer, Townhall
Hughes, Thomas, baker, Darling st.
Halfpenny, John, butcher, Church st.
Harrison, James, butcher, High st.
Henderson, Robt., butcher, Eden lane
Harman, Patrick, coach builder, Belmore street
Hurles, R., cutler, East Bridge street
Hall, Wm., grocer, High street
Hill, Alexander, grocer, Tonystick
Halliday, John, miller, Ballycassidy
Hall, Wm., publican, Boston lane
Hall, William, wine and spirit merchant, High street
Hoey, Wm., tailor, Belmore st.
Irvine, John, gunsmith, Main street
Ingoldsby, Terence, draper, High st.
Innis, Edward, publican, Church st.
Innis, Edward H., wine & spirit merchant, Church street
Johnston, John, publican, Hollow
Johnston, Wm., tobacco and snuff manufacturer, Ann street
Kidney, Mrs., baker, Church street
Kirkpatrick, Mary, earthenware dealer, Church street
Kirkpatrick, Margaret, earthenware dealer, High street
Kernan, Edward, grocer, Belmore st.
Kelly, George, tailor, Barrack street
Kerr, John, grocer and haberdasher, Hollow
Kerr, Patrick, grocer, &c., Townhall st.
Kittson, Christian, wine & spirit merchant, Church street
Kittson, George, draper, Townhall st.
Kernan, E., seedsman, East Bridge st.
Kyle, Thomas, publican, Barrack lane
Kerr, Patrick, draper, High street
Kettyle, Wm., draper, High street
Leith, Wm., auctioneer, Eden street
Lemon, John, baker, East Bridge st.
Lemon, John, wine & spirit merchant, East Bridge street
Lucy, Mervyn, publican, Tonystick
Lyons, Jane, publican, Mill street
Leonard, Henry, tailor, Eden lane
Lowry, Thomas, tanner, Tonystick
Lemon, John, timber merchant, East Bridge street
Law, Andrew, publican, Boston lane
Lemon, John, earthenware dealer, Townhall street
Lemon, John, grocer, Main street
Lemon, John, ironmonger, Bridge st.
Leonard, E., cabinetmaker, Darling st.
Leonard, John, boot and shoemaker, Hollow

Little, Nemia, publican, Church st.
Love, Terence, boot and shoemaker, Shamble square
Lucy, Andrew, publican, Boston lane
Mahood, George, apothecary, Main st.
Morrison, Caleb, baker, Darling st.
Morrison, Edward, baker, Hollow
Morrison, John, baker & confectioner, Darling street
Mihar, J., butcher, Galbraith's row
Magovern, Hugh, butcher, Brook st.
Mihan, Terence, butcher, Linenhall st.
Martin, Patrick, cooper, Cole's row
Magahy, John, earthenware dealer, Eden lane
Molyneaux, John, fishing tackle dealer, Hollow
Macartney, James, grocer and leather seller, Townhall street
Maguire, Mary, grocer, Hollow
Mihar, John, grocer and ironmonger, Hollow
Mulldoon, Wm., grocer & ironmonger, Bridge street
Molyneaux, John, ironmonger and jeweller, High street
Maguire, John, publican, Main street
Maguire, John, whitesmith, Paget's lane
Macartney, James, publican, Main st.
Martin, John, publican, Main street
Murphy, Joseph, publican, Water lane
Murphy, D., whitesmith, Brook st.
Mulhern, Thomas, tailor, Brook street
Mulneux, John, watchmaker, High st.
M'Brien, Patrick, boot and shoemaker, Barrack lane
M'Keagen, Chas., boot & shoemaker, Shamble square
M'Donald, Mathew, clothes broker, East Bridge street
M'Mannus, Patrick, cooper, Brook st.
M'Bride, Peter, Commercial Hotel, Townhall street
M'Garaghan, M., publican, Boston lane
M'Neilly, Catherine, bonnetmaker, Darling street
Nolan, E., auctioneer, Windmill hill
Nelson, R., painter & glazier, Main st.
O'Brien, John, grocer and leather seller, Main street

O'Brien, Francis, publican, Darling st
O'Donnell, Wm., publican, Coleshill
Parkinson, M. A., plumber, Townhall street
Polson, T. R. J., printer, Darling street
Quinton, Alex., saddler, Townhall st.
Quinton, William, wine and spirit merchant, Darling street
Rankin, T., cooper, Schoolhouse lane
Robinson, Jas., carpenter, Darling st.
Richardson, Miss, haberdasher, Church street
Robinson, James, draper, High street
Reilly, James, publican, Hollow
Rexter, Jane, publican, Tonystick
Sharkey, Daniel, butcher, Tonystick
Scollan, Patrick, carpenter, Commons
Scollan, H., pawnbroker, Darling st.
Smith, Richard, gunsmith, Main st.
Scott, Jane, leather seller, Belmore st.
Stevenson, T., printer, East Bridge st.
Thompson, W., butcher, Queen street
Trimble, Wm., bookseller and printer, Main street
Thomson, Arthur, master extraordinary in Chancery, and commissioner for taking affidavits, Willoughby place
Tickel, Jos., plumber, East Bridge st.
Vance, Thomas, grocer, Main street
Watt, Wm., carpenter, Diamond
West, John, baker, Townhall street
Whitley, Thomas, baker, High street
Whitley, Thomas, grocer, Hollow
Willoughby, Edward, baker & grocer, Darling street
Willoughby, Henry, baker, High st.
Willoughby, Henry, grocer, Hollow
West, John, confectioner, Townhall st.
Whitley, Thos., confectioner, High st.
White, Wm., veterinary surgeon
Wood, J., fishing tackle dealer, Hollow
Wilkin, James, grocer, Hollow
Wilkin, James, wine and spirit merchant, Church street
Willis, Mary Ann, White Hart Hotel, Sarah street
Wood, John, ironmonger & seedsman, Church street
Wilson, Margt., dressmaker, Castle st.
Wilkin, James, publican, Church st.

COUNTY OF FERMANAGH.

FERMANAGH, an inland county in Ulster province. Greatest length, N.W. and S.E., 45 miles; greatest breadth, N.E. and S.W., 29 miles; comprising an area of 714 square miles, or 457,195 acres, of which 289,228 are arable, 114,847 uncultivated, 6,155 in plantations, 210 in towns, and 46,755 under water. Lough Erne, its most attractive feature, extends from one extremity to the other, for 45 miles, in a N.W. direction; it bisects the county, and is divided into Upper and Lower—the Upper extends from Wattle-bridge to Enniskillen; the Lower from Enniskillen to Rosscor, where its waters are contracted, and form the river Erne, which extends to the county Donegal, and falls into the sea at Ballyshannon. It is navigable through its whole extent to the fall at Belleek, within three miles of Ballyshannon; and a steamer of 20 horse power plies between Enniskillen and the Ulster canal at Wattle-bridge, and another from Lisnaskea to the same point. The soil is variable, heavy, and retentive of moisture, light and friable, and moorish. Coal and iron ore are found in small quantities, and there is sand and limestone in abundance. The trade in butter is considerable; and the linen manufacture, of a coarse description, chiefly for domestic use, is carried on to a small extent. The population in 1841 was 156,481; 150,795 in the rural, and 5,686 in the civic district. According to the Census of 1851, the total population of the county was 115,978, being a decrease of 40,503. It is chiefly in Clogher diocese, with a small portion in that of Kilmore. The only large town is Enniskillen. The county returns 3 members to Paliament—2 for the county; constituency, in 1851, 3,497; and 1 for Enniskillen borough, constituency, 172. The Assizes are held in Enniskillen, where the County Prison is. Quarter Sessions are held at Enniskillen and Newtownbutler; Petty Sessions in 12 places. The County Infirmary is in Enniskillen, and the District Lunatic Asylum, to which the county is entitled to send 21 patients, is in Armagh. The Union Workhouses are at Enniskillen, Lisnaskea, and Lowtherstown; the net annual value of property rated to the poor in this county is £175,319; and the amount of property valued under 6 & 7 Wm. IV., cap. 84, £170,668. The county is within the military district of Belfast; and there are barrack stations at Enniskillen and Belleek, in the former of which the staff of the County Militia is stationed. The head-quarters of the Constabulary force, consisting of 191 men, officers included, are at Enniskillen; those of the 5 districts, comprising 25 stations, are at Enniskillen, Derrygonnelly, Lisnaskea, Lowtherstown, and Skea. A Resident Magistrate is stationed at Enniskillen. There are stations of Revenue Police at Brookborough, Kesh, and Belcoo.

Lieutenant and Custos Rotulorum—
 The Earl of Erne, Crom Castle, Lisnaskea
High-Sheriff, (1852-53,) John G. Irvine, Rockfield, Enniskillen
Members for the County—Capt. M. Archdall Riversdale, Enniskillen; Sir A. B. Brooke, bart., Colebrooke House, Brookborough, and 63 St. James's, London
Assistant Barrister—Georges Hamilton, 68 Lower Leeson street, Dublin

DEPUTY LIEUTENANTS.
Archdall, Capt. M., M.P.
Archdall, E., Riversdale, Enniskillen
Barton, F. W., Clonelly, Kesh
Barton, H. W., Waterfoot, Pettigo
Bloomfield, John C., Castlecaldwell, Belleek
Brien, John, Castletown, Enniskillen
Brooke, G. F., Ashbrook, Brookborough
Butler, Theophilus B., Cavan
Crawford, Alexander Fitzgerald
Crichton, Hon. S., Knockballymore, Clones
D'Arcy, W., Necarn Castle, Lowtherstown
Enniskillen, Earl of, Florence Court
Irvine, Major J., Rockfield, Enniskillen

COUNTY OF FERMANAGH.

Johnston, J., Magherameena, Belleek
Jones, Michael, Cregg, Sligo
Lendrum, J., Cork-hill, Enniskillen
Madden, J., Rosslea Manor, Rosslea
Nixon, A., Carneyhill, Enniskillen
Perceval, Philip, Sligo
Porter, J. G. V., Belleisle, Lisbellaw
Richardson, H. M., Rossfad, Enniskillen
Tennent, Sir J. E., M.P., Tempo House

MAGISTRATES.

Archdall, Capt. M., M.P., D.L.
Archdall, E., D.L.
Archdall, H. G., Ballinamallard
Archdall, R., Riverstown, Lowtherstown
Archdall, W. H., Dromard, Kesh
Armstrong, S., Hollymount, Manorhamilton
Atthill, Edward, Ardvarney, Kesh
Bailey, Thomas, R.M., Buttevant
Barton, F. W., D.L., Clonelly, Kesh
Barton, H. W., D.L., Waterfoot, Kesh
Bloomfield, J. C., D.L., Castlecaldwell, Belleek
Bloomfield, John C., jun.; Castlecaldwell, Belleek
Brady, John, Clones
Brien, J., D.L., Castletown, Enniskillen
Brooke, G. F., D.L., Ashbrook
Brooke, Sir A. B., bart., M.P.
Bunbury, Capt. Wm. B. M'C., M.P.
Butler, Hon. H. Cavendish
Cloncurry, Lord
Cole, Hon. John, Florence Court
Corry, William, Enniskillen
Crichton, Hon. H., Knockballymore, Clones
Crowe, Charles, Farm Hill, Clones
Crozier, J., Gortra, Newtownbutler
Cunningham, John, Pettigo, Donegal
Dane, Paul, Killyhevlin, Enniskillen
D'Arcy, H., Necarn Castle, Lowtherstown
D'Arcy, W., D.L., Necarn Castle, Lowtherstown
Denny, A., Derryvollen, Enniskillen
Echlin, Henry, Enniskillen
Ely, Marquis of, Ely Lodge, Enniskillen
Enniskillen, Earl of, D.L., Florence Court, Enniskillen
Enery, Wm. H., Ballyconnell House
Evatt, S. R. B., Mount Louise, Monaghan
Faussett, C., Lisbofin, Enniskillen
Fleming, J., Slyan House, Lenamore
Frith, B. G., M.D., Enniskillen
Hall, R., Innismore Hall, Lisbellaw
Hamilton, J. P., Oakfield, Clones
Irvine, C. C., Johnstown, Clones
Irvine, J. G., Rockfield, Enniskillen
Irvine, Major J., D.L., Rockfield, Enniskillen
Irvine, Rev. A., Kilskeery, Trillick
Johnston, J., D.L., Magherameena, Belleek
Johnston, John, Swanlinbar
Jones, T. H., Moneyglass house
Jones, W. C., Lisgoole Abbey, Enniskillen
Knipe, G. M., Ernehill, Belturbet
Lendrum, J., D.L., Cork hill, Trillick
Leslie, B., Forfey, Lisnaskea
Loftus, Rev. Lord A., Ardress Glebe
Madden, J., D.L., Rosslea Manor, Rosslea
Nixon, A., D.L., Carneyhill, Enniskillen
Nixon, T., Dunbar, Enniskillen
Ovendon, C., Whitepark, Brookboro'
Patterson, W., Gortmore, Fivemiletown
Perceval, Lieut.-Colonel A., Temple House, Coollooney
Porter, J. G. Vesey, D.L.
Porter, Rev. J. G., Kilskerry, Trillick
Reade, Rev. L. G., Levally, Enniskillen
Richardson, H. M., D.L., Rossfad, Enniskillen
Richardson, Rev. J., Summerhill, Clones
Saunderson, A., Castle Saunderson, Belturbet
Shegog, G., Monelly, Clones, county Monaghan
Skelton, F., Donagh House, Lisnaskea
Smith, D., Lakeview, co. Monaghan
Taylor, J. E., Cranbrook, Fivemiletown
Tipping, G., Rosferry, Lisnaskea
Tredennick, J., Camlin, Ballyshannon
Trench, Captain C. Le Poer
Tuthill, Rev. J. B., Glebe, Belleek
Weld, Joseph, Newtownbutler
Weir, R., Hall Craig, Enniskillen
Whitsitt, J., Salvo House, Rosslea

RESIDENT MAGISTRATE.

Holmes, Benjamin H., Enniskillen

COUNTY OF FERMANAGH.

COUNTY OFFICERS.
Clerk of the Crown—Vesey Daly, 51 Blessington street, Dublin
Clerk of the Peace—Richard Hamilton, Enniskillen
Crown Solicitor at Quarter Sessions—Thomas Macken, Brookborough
Treasurer—R. D'Arcy, Necarn Castle, Lowtherstown
Secretary to the Grand Jury—Wm. A. Dane, Rutland square, Dublin
Surveyor—R. Gray, Enniskillen
Coroners—C. Faussett, J.P., Enniskillen; J. Armstrong, Brookborough
Head Stamp Distributor — Stewart Whittaker, Enniskillen

MILITIA STAFF.
Colonel—The Earl of Enniskillen
Lieut.-Colonel—Hon. Henry A. Cole, Florence Court
Major—Hon. Henry Crichton, Crom Castle, Lisnaskea
Adjutant—Capt. W. Corry, Enniskillen

CONSTABULARY OFFICERS.
Co. Inspector—W. Foot, Enniskillen
Derrygonnelly—E. N. Burgess
Enniskillen—John D. M'Neale
Lisnaskea—T. D. Maxwell
Lowtherstown—Thomas Ross
Skea, Florence Court—E. Dunsterville

COUNTY GAOL, ENNISKILLEN.
Board of Superintendence meet on the last Saturday in every month—Wm. D'Arcy, H. M. Richardson, Esqs.; Hon. and Rev. J. C. Maude; C. Ovendon, W. Archdall, Esqs.; Capt. E. Morony; Rev. J. G. Porter; Earl of Enniskillen; Paul Dane, G. Brooke, J. Lendrum, R. Archdall, Esqrs.
Inspector—Wm. Corry, Enniskillen
Chaplain—Hon. and Rev. J. C. Maude
Presbyterian do.—Rev. E. Stevenson
Roman Catholic do.—Rev. D. Boylan
Surgeon—G. A. Nixon, M.D.
Governor—James Jeffers

HILLSBOROUGH.

A MARKET town (formerly a Parliamentary borough) in the county of Down, 10 miles from Belfast, on the road from Dublin to Belfast. This town is built on the slope of a hill, and there is so much neatness in its construction, and it joins so harmoniously to the fine demesne of the Marquis of Downshire, that it may be called one of the most agreeable small towns in Ireland. There is a brewery in the town, and an extensive distillery near to it. The Corporation Arms hotel is a respectable and comfortable house. General Sessions of the Peace are held here twice a year, Petty Sessions every second Saturday, and Courts-leet and Baron every three weeks, by the representative of the Downshire family. The Court-house, a handsome building of freestone, in the centre of the market-place, was erected by the late Marquis, to whose memory a monument has been erected near Hillsborough, by public subscription. The parish church is a very elegant building, consisting of a nave and cross aisles; the tower, which is upwards of one hundred feet high, and the steeple one hundred more, form together a beautiful and conspicuous object at a considerable distance; there are also two smaller towers at the sides. The interior corresponds with the exterior in neatness, is furnished with a good organ, and every window is adorned with stained glass. A monument by Nollekens, to the memory of Archdeacon Leslie, erected by the Marquis of Downshire, is worth notice; as, also, a beautiful monument erected to the memory of the late Marquis. There is also a second church of the Establishment, and there is one Presbyterian church. The charitable institutions are a dispensary, a school for children of both sexes, conducted on the modern system of education, founded by the late marquis, and a Sunday school, patronised by the family of that nobleman. The Downshire demesne is contiguous to the town—the mansion, garden, and lawn being on

HILLSBOROUGH.

the west side of it. Hillsborough castle, now a ruin on the demesne, was built in the reign of Charles I., and was afterwards constituted a royal fort, of which the hereditary constableship is held by the present marquis. Hillsborough gives the inferior titles of earl and viscount to the Marquis of Downshire. The market is held on Wednesday; fairs, 16th February, 17th May, 16th August, 15th November. Population in 1851—Town, 1298; rural part of townland, 92; total, 1390.

Post Office—Sarah Lutton, postmistress. Letters from Belfast, the north of Ireland, and Scotland, arrive at 7 a.m., 5-25 and 10-5 p.m., and are despatched at 2-30 a.m. and 5-25 p.m. From Dublin, the south, and various other parts of Ireland, also from England, arrive at 2-30 a.m. and 5-25 p.m., and are despatched at 7 a.m. and 10-5 p.m.

Conveyances—To Dublin, the royal mail, every evening at 10-5. To Belfast, the royal mail, every morning at 2-30. Jas. Eagleson, agent

Dispensary, Ballynahinch st.—George Croker, physician

Market and Session House, Market sq.

Police Station, Main street—Henry S. Decluzeau, county inspector

Savings' Bank, Ballynahinch street—Open on Wednesdays

Established Church—Hon. Walter B. Mant, archdeacon of Down, rector; Rev. James G. Pooler, curate

St. John's Established Church—Rev. Howard B. St. George

Presbyterian Church, Lisburn street—Rev. Samuel Marcus Dill, minister

Hillsborough Schools, Main street—James M'Carthy, master; Susan Yeates and Maria Asherhurst, mistresses

NOBILITY, GENTRY, ETC.

Bradshaw, H., J.P., Culcavy Cottage
Bullock, Mrs., Main street
Corry, Mrs., Main street
Downshire, Most Noble the Marquis of, Hillsborough Castle
Decluzeau, S. H., C.I., Main street
Filgate, F., J.P., Ballynahinch street
Green, John, Orrfield
Harpur, Edward B., Main street
Henderson, James, Hillsborough
Hill, Edward B., Main street
Hopkins, Captain John, Wellington Lodge
Long, William, Main street

Magill, Daniel, Main street
Mitchell, John, Ballynahinch street
Moreland, James L., Carnbane
Morris, Mrs., Lisburn street
Mulholland, S. R., J.P., Eglantine
Murray, Henry, Main street
Murray, Richard, Lisadian
M'Conkey, John, Lion hill
M'Clughan, John, Newforge
M'Donald, Alexander, Square
Nash, Charles F., Newforge
Sands, William, Square
Scott, Edward, Main street
Teague, Wm. Edward, Main street
Wardhaugh, Mark, Park street

CLERGY AND PROFESSIONAL.

Croker, George, M.D., Hillsborough
Dill, Rev. Samuel M., Blundel hill
Mant, Ven. Archdeacon W. B., Archdeaconry
Pooler, Rev. James G., Main street
St. George, Rev. H. B., St. John's Parsonage

TRADERS, ETC.

Blythe, Wm., spirit dealer, Square
Blythe, Mark, spirit dealer, Main st.
Creagan, C., spirit dealer, Main street
Crozier, Thomas, watchmaker, Main st.
Crozier, J., Sergeant-Major, Park st.
Cunningham, J., spirit dealer, Main st.
Davis, Lennox, nursery and seedsman, Ogles Grove
Ellis, V., grocer & spirit dealer, Main st.
Ellis, Wm., grocer, Lisburn street
Galley, David, blacksmith, Lisburn st.
Galley, Thos., spirit dealer, Lisburn st.
Godfrey, Geo., saddler, Lisburn street
Green, Anne, haberdasher, Square
Halliday, Frank, Square
Hamilton, Abel, blacksmith, Ballynahinch street
Higginson, John, spirit dealer, Main st.
Holland, Thomas, Hillsborough park
Ingram, Thomas, boot and shoemaker, Lisburn street
Irwin, Sam., spirit dealer, Lisburn st.
Jefferson, Miss, draper, Lisburn street

Johnston, Joseph, builder, Main st.
King, Patrick, spirit dealer, Square
Lamb, Sarah, haberdasher, Lisburn st.
Loughlin, Thos., spirit dealer, Square
Mercer, John, grocer, Square
Mulligan, John, merchant and grocer, Lisburn street
Murray, Daniel, spirit dealer, Main st.
M'Caw, Mr., spirit dealer, Lisburn st.
M'Quiggan, John, grocer, Square
M'Gowan, Roger, tailor, Lisburn st.
M'Cullen, Joseph, Royal Corporation Arms, Square
O'Hagan, John, tailor, Lisburn street
Parker, Anne, Square
Patterson, H., grocer, Ballynahinch st.
Patterson, I., spirit dealer, Lisburn st.
Patterson, Sam., haberdasher, Main st.
Payne, George, Square
Reid, John, spirit and provision dealer, Lisburn street
Scott, T., baker and grocer, Main st.
Stafford, Thomas, Lisburn street
Tate, Moses, Main street
Turner, Ann, spirit dealer, Lisburn st.
Welsh, Ralph, spirit dealer, Main st.

LARNE.

A MARKET town and sea-port, in the county of Antrim, is 17 miles from Belfast, 9 miles north from Carrickfergus, lying on the road from Glenarm to Belfast, at the head of Lough Larne, on the coast of the North Channel, in the Irish Sea. The town, which was originally called *Inver*, is divided into the old and new towns; the latter consisting chiefly of one long and regular street, the houses of which are of stone and well built; but the streets of the other section are neither so spacious or so well paved. On a peninsula, called the Curran, stand the ruins of Oldfleet Castle; and on the road to it are the remains of a little chapel called Drumalas. The castle is supposed to have been erected by one of the Bissetts, a powerful Scotch family, in the time of Henry III. At this spot Edward Bruce landed in 1315, with the design of making himself King of Ireland; causing much bloodshed, and producing many dreadful calamities to the English settlers in this part of the kingdom. The port possessed at one time a comparatively high importance, but it has suffered a serious diminution of its consequence by the rise and rapid progress of the trade of Belfast. The largest shipments, perhaps, from the harbour are of lime; but these have little influence on the town. There are some good quays on both sides of the lough, about a mile from the town, the water not being of sufficient depth to float vessels further up. The linen and bleaching business is carried on; but here again Belfast steps in, and is continually diminishing this branch of commerce. The neighbourhood is pleasant, and the land of the district fertile. In the summer season, Larne receives many visitants, attracted by its advantages as a salubrious retreat and well adapted bathing place. Petty Sessions are held every alternate week. The church was repaired and much altered in 1819, previous to which it had some interesting specimens of ancient architecture. The other places of worship are three Presbyterian churches, and a Roman Catholic chapel, erected in 1832; and the town was first lighted with gas in 1851. The weekly provision market is held on Wednesday, and for yarn, flax, and cattle on the 2nd Thursday in each month. Fairs, July 31st and Dec. 1st.

Post Office— Jas. Coech, postmaster. The down mail arrives here every morning at 9-15 from Dublin and Belfast, bringing the general mail, Foreign and Colonial, English, Scotch, and Irish letters. At 9-45 a mail conveyance starts from the Post office, for Glenarm, Cushendall, and Ballycastle, and returns in the evening (after delivering the mail to another car), in time for the up mail, which leaves at 3-45 p.m.

Conveyances—A three horse car leaves Larne every morning (Sunday excepted), at 6, and arrives again at 8 in the evening

LARNE.

Custom House, Newtown — Daniel Sheriff, sub-collector

Union Workhouse—J. M. M'Cormick, clerk and returning officer; John Miller, master; Mrs. Dufferon, matron; John White, schoolmaster; Miss Wylie, mistress; S. Smiley, relieving officer

Fever Hospital—Charles Ferris, attending surgeon

Belfast Banking Company (branch)— Frederick M'Kinstry, manager; Mr M'Clinton, clerk

Established Church—Rev. H. Martin, rector; Rev. F. Dobbs, curate

Presbyterian Church—Rev. Dr. H. W. Molyneaux, minister

Presbyterian (Unitarian) Church—Rev. Classon Porter, minister

Presbyterian (Seceding) Church—Rev. Archibald Kennedy, minister

Methodist Chapel—ministers various

Roman Catholic Chapel — Rev. H. O'Loughlin, parish priest

Larne Model, Agricultural, and National School—J. M'Donnell, teacher

Female National School—Miss Starkie

Infant National School—Miss Huston

Congregational School—T. H. Carlisle

Parochial School—James Hamilton and Miss Honor, teachers

NOBILITY AND GENTRY.

Agnew, James, J.P., Cairncastle
Agnew, Wm., J.P., Kilwaughter Castle
Agnew, Misses
Apsley, Misses
Agnew, R. S., Seaview
Barklie, A., Inver
Barklie, Thomas, Inver
Barklie, James, Inver
Burke, Alexander
Bailie, J. M'N., Hillmount
Blair, Misses
Casement, E. M'G., J.P., Inver
Chichester, Samuel, Ballysnodd
Darcus, S., Gardenmore
Hill, Mary
Johnston, George B., Glynn
Kilpatrick, A.H.
M'Garel, P., J.P.
Macauley, Robert
M'Cormick, James M., Ardmore
M'Kinstry, Frederick
Sloan, W.

Whitla, George, J.P., Inver
Whitla, George A.
Walker, James, Curran

CLERGY AND PROFESSIONAL.

Atkinson, W. D., attorney
Campbell, Rev. William
Chambers, Robert, attorney
Cunningham, John, surgeon and apothecary
Dobbs, Rev. F., curate
Ferris, Charles, surgeon & apothecary
Kennedy, Rev. Archibald, Presbyterian minister
Magowan, Rev. O., Presbyterian minister
Martin, Rev. Henry, rector
Molyneaux, Rev. Henry William, D.D., Presbyterian minister
M'Comb, Hugh, surgeon and apothecary
M'Neill, Geo. H. and John, attorneys
Nash, Rev. Mr., Methodist minister
O'Loughlin, Rev. H., P.P.
Porter, Rev. Classon
Porter, Rev. David, Presbyterian minister, Islandmagee
Smiley, Alex., surgeon and apothecary
Waterson, Rev. F., Glynn
Ward, Rev. R., rector, Cairncastle
Ward, Rev. C., Cairncastle
Whiteford, Rev. James, Raloo

TRADERS, ETC.

Agnew, James, tile, brick, and earthenware manufacturer
Alexander, Samuel, grocer
Alexander, Samuel, hardware and ironmonger
Atkinson, Miles, linen and woollendraper, &c.
Abernethy, James, lodging house
Alexander, James, spirit dealer
Barklie, John and A., linen merchants
Burns, John, boot and shoemaker
Berry, Mary, confectioner
Boyd, Jane, earthenware dealer
Brown, Mrs., grocer
Baine, George, grocer and miller, Glynn mills
Boyd, J. T. & Co., linen and woollendrapers and straw bonnet manufacturers
Beggs and Nelson, spirit dealers

Bailie, Robert, spirit dealer
Blair, Robert, teacher
Blair, John, publican
Boyd, Robert, publican
Bell, Edward, painter and glazier
Beggs, Hugh, painter and glazier
Cunningham, David, cooper
Cooch, James, weighmaster and woollendraper
Caldwell, William, baker
Caldwell, John, bookseller & stationer
Chambers, John, butcher
Carson, William, grocer
Cowan, Mrs., grocer
Craig, William, grocer
Cowan, Miss, milliner & dressmaker
Cowan, Agnes, straw bonnetmaker
Carson, Wm., lodging-house keeper
Craig, Mrs., spirit dealer
Cooke, Mary, publican
Cunningham, Thomas, publican
Dixon & M'Cambridge, timber merchants and ironmongers
Darragh, John, earthenware dealer
Dollars, Miss, milliner and dressmaker
Elliot, John, plumber
Eccles, Thomas, accountant, agent for Court-house
English, John, baker
English, John, tailor
Fitzsimons & Henry, rope & canvass manufacturers
Fitzsimons, M., adjuster and stamper of weights and measures
Fitzsimons, Mrs., milliner and dressmaker
Foster, Joseph, publican
Ferris, Charles, plasterer
Ferguson, Wm., saddler and harness maker
Gawn, John, teacher
Gifford, Geo. B., boot and shoemaker
Girvin, James, grocer
Girvin, the Misses, linen and woollendrapers and bonnetmakers
Graham, Gawn, saddler and harness maker
Graham, Miss, day school
Hamilton, John, grain and butter merchant and miller
Hamilton, William, nailer
Hunter, Robert, boot and shoemaker and leather seller
Hamilton, Wm., earthenware dealer
Hamilton, John, grocer

Hamill, Miss, straw bonnet manufacturer
Harvey, Mrs., grocer
Higgin, William, spirit dealer
Hunter, Robert, spirit dealer
Hunter, James, spirit dealer
Hamilton, Alexander, publican
Hutton, Sarah, straw bonnetmaker
Jackson, Mrs., victualler
Jordan, Thomas, grocer
Jackson, Mrs., grocer
Jackson, Mrs., hardware and ironmongery
Johnston, Mrs., milliner & dressmaker
Kennedy, Patrick, mechanic and general smith
Kane, Mrs., linen and woollendraper and milliner
Kennedy, John, lodging-house keeper
Kilpatrick, S., publican
Kilshaw and Cowan, Misses, boarding and day school
Laughton, Val. R., watch and clockmaker
Legg, William, butcher
M'Conley and Son, grain merchants and millers, Inver mills
M'Master and Nairn, grain, butter, and pork merchants
M'Gavock, John, grain, butter, and kelp merchant, and spirit dealer
M'Garel, John, linen works, Magheramorne
M'Ferran, William, flax spinner
M'Neil, George, inspector of weights and measures
M'Comb, Hugh, ship agent
M'Alister, Robert, stamp distributor and registrar of marriages
M'Kissock, John and James, boat builders
M'Calmont, William, printer
M'Alister, Randal, tin plate worker and bell hanger
M'Gregor, Peter, manager of gas work
M'Calmont, John, Petty Sessions clerk
M'Mukain, Mr., nailer
M'Givern, Felix, baker
Martin, William, baker
M'Alister, R., grocer
M'Dowell, Miss, grocer
Mulvenna, John, grocer and publican
Miller, John, grocer
M'Quillan, Thomas, grocer
M'Afferty, Alexander, grocer

Moore, Sarah, grocer
M'Master, James, grocer
M'Allister, R., grocer
M'Loy, D., grocer and leather seller
Meharg, Samuel, ironmonger
M'Keown, Daniel, leather seller and spirit dealer
M'Knight, Mrs., dressmaker
M'Elherron, David, tailor
M'Carthy, Charles, tailor
M'Neill, Catherine, publican
M'Cready, A., publican
M'Gonnell, Daniel, publican
M'Adorey, Rose, publican
Nicol, Malcolm, boot and shoemaker, and leather seller
Nelson, S. and H., linen and woollen-drapers
Orr, John, boot and shoemaker, and leather seller
O'Fay, Mrs., grocer
Owens, Alexander, plasterer
Petrie, W., butcher
Patton, Mrs., victualler
Pool, John, publican
Richey, John, baker
Reid, James, bookseller
Rogan, James, grocer
Reid, Edward, grocer
Reid, James, grocer, and lodgings
Rogers, Miss, milliner and dressmaker
Russell, John, tailor
Saunderson, Margaret, grocer
Simpson, Daniel P., grain merchant and miller, Larne mills
Smiley, John, agent for Lloyd's
Smiley, John, grain and coal mercht
Sloan, William, agent for Tennent & Co's chemical works
Sheriff, D., sub-collector of customs
Simpson, D. P., collector of co. cess
Small, Daniel, cabinet maker
Smith, James, tallow chandler
Simpson, D. P., Master in Chancery
Smyth, Adam, boot and shoemaker, and leather seller
Smyth, Joseph, butcher
Smyth, John, grocer
Stewart, Mr., Antrim Arms hotel
Stewart, Rose, publican
Thompson, John, timber merchant
Thompson, Wm., linen and woollen-draper
Turner, Miss, milliner and dressmaker
Thompson, Mrs., private school
Thompson, Mrs., straw bonnetmaker
Turner, James, watch & clockmaker
Walker, J., saddler and harness maker
Wyles, Francis, baker
Wylie, Mrs., grocer
Wiles, Francis, grocer
Wallace, Arthur, grocer
Workman, Robert, grocer
Young, James, butcher

LISBURN.

LISBURN is a market town and Parliamentary borough, partly in the county of Antrim, 7 miles south-west by south from Belfast. This place, which, in the reign of James I., and long subsequent, was called *Lisnegarvey*, was raised from obscurity chiefly by Edward Viscount Conway, to whom Charles granted the manor of Killultagh, and this nobleman built a castle, which became the head of the manor. Soon after the erection of the castle, some English and Welsh families were induced by the proprietor to settle here, and thus the foundation was laid of a town which has subsequently become one of large population, and considerable manufacturing consequence. The spinning of flax, and the manufacture of linen and linen thread, and muslins, together with bleaching, is carried on extensively in the town and its neighbourhood, particularly at Lambeg. Near the middle of the main street is rather a spacious triangular area, in the centre of which stands the market house. The Castle gardens are kept in fine order, at the expense of the Marquis of Hertford, as a public promenade for the inhabitants. Altogether Lisburn may be pronounced one of the handsomest and cleanest towns in Ireland, and its inhabitants most respectable. The borough returns one member to the Imperial Parliament—the present representative is Sir J. E. Tennent, 66 Warwick square, Belgrave road, London. The seneschal of the manor of Killultagh, William Gregg, Esq., is the returning officer. The same gentleman holds a court for the manor, which has jurisdiction to £20, every third Wednesday, and courts-leet twice a year. Petty Sessions are held in a large handsome courthouse every Tuesday. The parish church is a spacious and handsome building, with a tower, to which an octagonal spire was added in 1807, at the expense of the Marquis of Hertford, and a fine organ has been presented to it by the same nobleman. It is the cathedral church of the united dioceses of Down, Connor, and Dromore, and contains a few interesting monuments, amongst which is one to the memory of the celebrated Dr. Jeremy Taylor, who died here in 1667. There is also a new church in the New Road. The other places of worship are a Presbyterian Church, a Roman Catholic Chapel, a meetinghouse for the Society of Friends, Wesleyan and Primitive Methodist Chapels, and a Salem Chapel. Lisburn confers the titles of earl and viscount on the family of Vaughan. The principal market day is Tuesday. The fairs, which are large, are held on the 21st of July and 5th of October.

Post Office, Castle street — Mary Burns, postmistress. Letters from Dublin arrive at 3 a.m. and 4-15 p.m., and are despatched at 9 a.m. and 9-40 p.m. Letters from Enniskillen arrive at 6-30 a.m., and are despatched at 5-35 p.m. Letters from Belfast arrive at 9-30 a.m., 5-35 and 9-40 p.m., and are despatched at 3-55 p.m.

Conveyances—By coach: To Dublin, first royal mail, every morning at 8, and the second every evening at 7½. To Belfast, the first royal mail every morning at 4-45, the second at 5, and the third every evening at 6. To Enniskillen, the royal mail, every evening at 7¾, goes through Armagh. By railway: Between Belfast, Lisburn, Moira, Lurgan, and Portadown, several times a day

Town Commissioners—Wm. Gregg, J.P., Wm. Caldbeck, Wm. Whitla, Lucas Waring, George Duncan, Hugh M'Call, David Mack, Michael Linn, Thomas Mussen, Thomas M'Creight, Robert Stewart, and Dr. Campbell. Chairman, Thomas J. Smith, J.P.

Town Clerk—John Pennington, Railway street

Workhouse—Chairman of Guardians, Marquis of Downshire; vice-chairman, Thomas J. Smyth; deputy-vice chairman, Capt. Bolton; clerk, Thomas Hunter; master, G. M. M'Kee; matron, E. M'Kee; schoolmaster, Thomas Hanny; mistress, Rebecca Reid; nurse of fever hospital, Sarah Clendinnen. Board day, Tuesday

County Infirmary, Castle street—Wm Thompson, M.D., acting surgeon

Constabulary Station, Railway street —Charles Morgan, sergeant

Distributor of Stamps—Miss Garrett

Gas Works, Bridge street—Secretary and treasurer, John Millar; manager, S. Neill

Banks—Northern Bank, H. J. Manly, manager; G. Wilson, accountant. Savings' Bank, H. J. Manly, secretary; Northern Bank, treasurer; James Coates, clerk

The Cathedral, Market square—Very Rev. Dean Stannus, rector; Rev. E. L. Fitzgerald, curate

Free Church—Rev. H. Hodson, curate

Presbyterian Church, Market lane— Rev. Alex. Henderson, minister

Wesleyan Methodist Chapel, Market street

Primitive Methodist Chapel, Hillsborough road

Salem Chapel, Linenhall street

Quaker Meetinghouse, Railway street

Roman Catholic Chapel, Chapel hill— Rev. J. M'Kenna, P.P.

Free Schools—Hillsborough road

National Schools, male and female, Chapel hill—Patrick Mulholland and Miss Murphy, teachers

Female free School, Seymour street— Miss Herbert, teacher

Infant School, Seymour street—Miss Joyce, teacher

Society of Friends' School, Prospect hill

LISBURN.

Infant School—established and endowed by Miss Stewart, Longstone; Miss Connor, teacher

Lisburn News-room, established 1836—A general supply of London, Dublin, and the local newspapers, regularly taken; also, a few of the leading periodicals and reviews of the day. Secretary, Mr. Waring M. Seeds; treasurer, Dr. Macartney

Literary Society—President of council, George Stephenson; secretaries, Dr. Kelso and John Miller; treasurer, David Beatty; librarian, Dr. Macartney

NOBILITY AND GENTRY.

Barbour, William, Hilden
Bolton, James, R.N., Castle street
Carleton, Edward, Blaris
Carleton, Mrs., Rosevale
Clarke, Misses, Castle street
Clibborn, Mrs., Lisnagarvey
Cupples, Mrs., Railway street
Coulson, William, Market square
Coulson, James, Market square
Campbell, John, M.D. and surgeon, Market square
Garrett, Henry J., Grove
Garrett, Mrs., Chapel hill
Gregg, Wm., seneschal, Derryvolgie, Lambeg
Greig, Mrs. Mary Ann, Castle street
Ensor, Charles
Hunter, William, Plantation
Johnston, Mrs. Mary, Ballymacash
Hawkshaw, Miss, Seymour street
Houghton, Richard R., Springfield cottage
Higginson, Henry T., J.P., Bow street
Higginson, Miss Maria
Hogg, Mrs. Mary, Castle street
Kennedy, Thomas, Castle street
Kennedy, Robert, Mills
Laurence, Mr., Blaris lodge
Malcolmson, Miss, Lisnagarvey House
Manly, Henry J., Castle street
Moore, Miss, Warren Cottage
M'Call, Robert, Chapel hill
Mulholland, Henry, Castle street
Mussen, Matthew, Market square
Mussenden, Daniel, Larchfield House
Nicholson, Mrs., Castle street
Richardson, Jonathan, Lambeg House
Richardson, Joshua P., Aberdelgey
Richardson, Mrs. Mary, Bow street
Richardson, Jonathan, Glenmore House
Richardson, J. N., Lissue
Richardson, Wm., Castle street
Richardson, Jonathan James, The Island
Richardson, John, Castle street
Stannus, Thomas R., Castle street
Stannus, Walter, Castle street
Stewart, Robert, Bow street
Smith, Roger J., J.P., Castle street
Smith, Thomas J., J.P., Castle street
Stott, Edward, Railway street
Wakefield, J. W., Brookhill
Ward, James, Strawberry hill
Whitla, William, Seymour street
Wilson, Robt., Lagan Lodge, Lambeg

CLERGY AND PROFESSIONAL.

Birney, John, attorney, Castle street
Cupples, Rev. Edward, Castle street
Fitzgerald, Rev. Mr., Castle street
Hodson, Rev. Hartley, incumbent
Henderson, Rev. Alexander, Presbyterian minister, Plantation
Kelso, John J., surgeon and apothecary, Market square
M'Harg, Michael, surgeon and apothecary, Market square
M'Kenna, Rev. John, P.P.
Macartney, John, surgeon and apothecary, Market square
Musgrave, Saml., surgeon and apothecary, Castle street
O'Flagherty, Francis H., proctor, Market square
O'Toole, Rev. A., C.C.
Orr, Rev. Alexander, Lambeg glebe
Orr, James, physician, Ballylesson
Pennington, John, proctor, Bow st.
Stephenson, Geo., solicitor, Castle st.
Smith, Mathew Johnston, solicitor, Castle street
Seeds, H. and W., solicitors, Railway street
Seymour, Rev. Mr., Methodist minister, Longstone street
Stannus, The Very Rev. Dean, Castle street
Smyth, Mathew J., attorney, Castle st.
Thompson, Wm., physician, Castle st.
Wallace, Rev. Mr., Methodist minister, Chapel hill
Waring, Lucas, attorney, Castle st.

LISBURN.

TRADERS, ETC.

Armstrong, John, Railway hotel, Railway street
Arnold, Mary, spirit store, Bow street
Anderson, John, sewed muslin manufacturer, Market square
Abbott, Thomas, reedmaker, Linenhall street
Agnew, William, publican, Railway st.
Barbour, Wm., flax spinner, thread manufacturer and bleacher, Hillden
Bloomer, John, publican, Bow street
Boyd, James, boot and shoemaker, Market square
Balmer, Joseph, grocer, Bridge street
Brownlee, Mr., umbrella maker, Castle street
Bell, Henry, grocer and publican, Smithfield
Bell, Archibald, plumber, Railway st.
Bell, Robert, grocer and publican, Chapel hill
Boomer, Rainey, publican, Chapel hill
Belshaw, John, publican, Bow street
Brown, John, grocer, Bow street
Battersby, Sarah, bonnet maker and milliner, Market square
Banister, Jacob, grocer and publican, Market square
Bloomer, Edward, boot and shoemaker, Market square
Bell, Geo., woollendraper and haberdasher, Bridge street
Bell, Henry, publican and grocer, Bridge street
Beatty, John, grocer, Bridge street
Boomer, Mary J., grocer, Antrim st.
Brownlee, William, miller
Cairns, James, shoemaker and leather dealer
Clarke, Mary Ann, haberdasher, Market square
Chapman, John, publican and grocer, Market square
Clarke, Charles, publican, Bridge st.
Carlisle, Wilson, boot and shoemaker, Bridge street
Cordner, Robert, grocer, Bridge st.
Coulson, William, and Sons, damask manufacturers
Coulson, James, damask manufacturer
Dunwoody, Wm., publican, Bridge st.
Davis, Ann, publican, Bow street
Dawson, Eliza, grocer and publican, Bow street
Dawson, William, publican, Bow st.
Duncan, Geo., woollendraper, Market square
Dornan, Robt., whitesmith, Bridge st.
Dawson, Thomas, whitesmith, Linenhall street
Edgar, Eliza, haberdasher, Bow st.
Fawett, Thomas, and Son, linen and cambric manufacturers, Laurel hill
Finlay, John, hardware dealer and grocer, Bow street
Fletcher, John, grocer, Bridge street
Ferguson, Alexander, grocer, Haslem's lane
Foote, Richard, grocer, Bridge street
Ferris, John, grocer, Bridge street
Gilbreath, Armstrong, tailor, Bow st.
Greer, Eliza, grocer, Bow street
Gawley, Richard, grocer, Market sq.
Gallens, Thomas, publican, Smithfield
Gardner, Richd., publican, Chapel hill
Gawley, Richd., haberdasher, Bow st.
Gardner, John, publican, Bow street
Gallery, James, grocer, Linenhall st.
Graham, William, brewer
Green, M. S., milliner and confectioner, Railway street
Hanna, William, grocer, Chapel hill
Harlin, Ann, haberdasher and grocer, Bow street
Hanna, James, grocer, Bow street
Higginson, Edward, grocer, publican, and leather cutter, Bow street
Hodgen, George, grocer, Bow street
Harvey, William John, grocer and leather dealer, Market square
Harvey, Hugh, publican, Bridge st.
Herron, John, cabinetmaker, Smithfield
Hermon, John, grocer, Long stone
Harvey, Thomas, publican, Bow st.
Hagan, Eliza, publican, Market sq.
Halliday, James, grocer, Bridge st.
Hawthorn, Adam, publican, Bridge st.
Hall, William, grocer, Railway street
Irwin, David, baker, Bow street
Irwin, Robert, boot and shoemaker, Bridge street
Jack, Jn., spirit store, Bridgeend hill
Johnston, Sam., whitesmith, Castle st.
Jefferson, George, grocer, Long stone
Jefferson, Redmond, grocer, leather, hardware, and timber merchant, Bow street

LISBURN.

Jefferson, John, woollendraper, Bow street
Johnston, M. J., haberdasher, Market square
Johnston, William, grocer and shuttle maker, Bridge street
Kenmuir, William, and Sons, watchmakers and jewellers, Market sq.
Knox, John, cutler, Castle street
Kain, Agnes, publican, Smithfield
Kenmuir, Alexander, watch and clockmaker, Bow street
Kelso, John, apothecary, Market sq.
Kennedy, R. and T., flour and starch manufacturers
Lennon, Edmund, Hertford Arms hotel, Market sq. and Railway st.
Lavery, John, grocer, Smithfield
Larmour, John, posting establishment, Railway street
Larmour, Mary, publican, Long stone
Laurence, Connolly, publican, Long stone
Lynass, Robert, grocer, Bow street
Loughlin, Timothy, saddler, Bow st.
Lindsay, James, pawnbroker, Bow st.
Linn, Michael, grocer, Bow st.
Lennon, William, provision dealer, Bridge street
Murray, Jas., confectioner and tailor, Bow street
Major, George, muslin manufacturer, Bow street
Magee, W. J., damask manufacturer
Millar, John, baker, flour and coal merchant, Market square
Millar, John, secretary Gas Company
Millar, John, agent for Standard Life Assurance Co., Market square
Mussen, Thomas, spirit store, Market square
M'Afee, A. J., grocer, Smithfield
Murray, J., grocer, Haslem's lane
Maxwell, Stewart, grocer, Bow st.
Murphy, Patrick, grocer and publican, Bow street
Moore, Alex., hair dresser, Bow street
Murray, James, saddler, Bow street
Mitchell, Robert, grocer and spirit dealer, Bow street
Murdoch, Mary Ann, milliner, Bow st.
Macartney, Arthur, baker, Bow st.
Mack, David, woollendraper, Market square
Major, George, publican, Market sq.
Morgan, George, weaver, Bridge st.
Mussen, Robert, publican, Market sq.
Mussen, Edward C., chandler, Market square
Mussen, Jas., woollendraper, Market square
Murray, Richd., hair dresser, Castle st.
M'Lernan, Daniel, spirit store, Bow st.
M'Connell, John, jun., grocer, Bow st.
M'Call, Hugh, pawnbroker, Bow st.
M'Connell, John, grocer, Market sq.
M'Clure, Adam, bakery and spirit shop, Market square
M'Intyre, Agnes, haberdasher, Market square
M'Connell, Mary, grocer, Market sq.
M'Kee, Samuel, sewed muslin manufacturer, Bridge street
M'Donald, Mrs., druggist, Bridge st.
M'Connell, John, grocer, Castle st.
M'Calister, Thomas, tailor, Castle st.
M'Laughlin, Mary, publican, Antrim street
M'Key, J., carpenter, Railway street
M'Cready, Joseph, grocer and baker, Bow street
M'Crea, Michael, grocer and spirit dealer, Bow street
M'Bride, Thomas, butcher, Bow st.
M'Connell, Saml., grocer, Market sq.
M'Creight, Thos., Queen's Arms hotel
M'Cloy, M. and J., painters and glaziers, Castle street
M'Connell, Arthur, clothes dealer, Market square
M'Murray, D., general dealer, Bridge street
M'Keavney, Henry, provision dealer, Bridge street
M'Keaveney, Mark, grocer and publican, Chapel hill
M'Kee, Samuel, sewed muslin warehouse, Bridge street
M'Intyre, John, cabinetmaker, Castle street
Neill, S., manager Gas Company
Neely, Erskine, pawnbroker, Market square
Neely, Wm., teacher, Castle street
Newburn, Thos., publican, Bridge st.
O'Flagherty, Mrs., haberdasher and milliner, Market square
O'Flagherty, Francis, public notary, Market square
Philips, Jas., spirit dealer, Market st.

572 LISBURN.

Pelan, George, chandler, oil, colour, and glass shop, Market square
Priestly, Wm., publican, Bow street
Patterson, John, boot and shoemaker, Bridge street
Richardson, Jonathan J., flax spinner
Richardson and Co., linen manufacturers and bleachers, Lambeg
Richardson, Sons, and Owden, linen manufacturers and bleachers, Millbrook and Glenmore
Reilly, James, printer and bookseller, Bow street
Russel, Eliza, grocery, glass, and delf shop, Bow street
Reilly, Mrs., stationer and bookseller, Market square
Reid, John, spirit dealer, Market sq.
Reid, Wm., grocer, Castle street
Robb, Mr., painter, Railway street
Riddel, Alex., reedmaker, Railway st.
Savage, Edwd., publican, Smithfield
Savage, Jane, publican, Market sq.
Stevenson, Wm., publican, Bow st.
Sloan, M'Alister, and Alister, sewed muslin agents
Smith, Henry, grocer, Market square
Singleton, William, haberdasher, Marker square
Stevenson, J., professor of music, Railway street
Sefton, Geo. H., publican, Bow st.
Sands, Joseph, provision dealer, Market square
Sharpe, Thomas, grocer and spirit dealer, Market square
Savage, Thomas, pork dealer, Haslem's lane
Sheals, Charles, grocer

Stewart, Wm., confectioner, Railway street
Stewart, Robert, and Sons, flax spinners and thread manufacturers
Tenton, James, flour and meal dealer, Bow street
Thompson, George, leather dealer, boot and shoemaker, Bow street
Thompson, Edward, boot and shoemaker, Bow street
Titterington, Alex., watchmaker and jeweller, Market square
Turkington, Mr., manager of Subscription Bakery, Castle street
Turtle, James, bakery, Castle street
Turner, Mary, grocer, Seymour street
Trainor, John, tailor, Castle street
Tumelty, M. A., publican and grocer, Castle street
Vaughan, Wm. John, grocer, Bow st.
Ward, James, agent for Sun Fire and Life Assurance Co., Strawberry hill
Wilson, George, shoemaker, Bow st.
Woods, John, haberdasher, Market sq.
Woods, Patrick, clothier, Market sq.
Wheeler, Owen, grocer and haberdasher, Market square
Woods, Michael, baker and confectioner, Bridge street
Watson, John, spirit store, Bridge st
Wilson, Thomas, boot and shoemaker, Castle street
Wheeler, E., publican, Smithfield
Walsh, Peter, grocer, Bridge street
Wilson, James, baker, Castle street
Yates, Brown, and Howat, sewed muslin agents, Railway street
Young, Wm. and L., spirit dealers and grocers, Market square

COUNTY OF LONDONDERRY.

LONDONDERRY, a maritime county in Ulster province. Greatest length, N. and S., 40 miles; greatest breadth, E. and W., 34 miles; comprising an area of 810 square miles, or 518,595 acres, of which 318,282 are arable, 180,709 uncultivated, 7,718 in plantations, 1,559 in towns, and 10,327 under water. The surface is hilly and rugged, with fertile tracts along the rivers. The rivers are the Bann (part of) on its E., the Foyle (part of) on its W. boundary, and the Faughan, Roe, and Moyola, with their numerous feeders, in the intermediate tracts. The subsoil is mica-slate, sandstone, and floetz-trap; clay-slate basalt and limestone are found in each district. According to the Census of 1851, the total population of the county was 191,744. The greatest part of the county is held by lease under the Irish Society and the 12 London companies. The chief crops are oats, barley, potatoes, and flax, with some wheat. The staple manufacture is linen. The county is chiefly in Derry diocese, with portions in Armagh and Connor. The principal towns are, Londonderry city, Coleraine, and Newtownlimavady. It returns 4 members to Parliament; 2 for the county at large, constituency, 4,305; 1 each for Londonderry and Coleraine, constituencies, 724, and 222. The Assizes are held at Londonderry; Quarter Sessions there and at Coleraine, Magherafelt, and Newtownlimavady; in all which towns there are Bridewells; Petty Sessions in 12 places. The County Prison and County Infirmary are in Londonderry, as is the District Lunatic Asylum for Donegal, Londonderry, and Tyrone counties, which maintains 214 patients, at an annual expense of £3,036, average £14 3s. 9d. each, and to which this county is entitled to send 69 patients. The Union Workhouses are at Londonderry, Coleraine, Magherafelt, and Newtownlimavady; the net annual value of property rated to the poor in this county is £332,269, and the amount of property valued under the Act of 6 & 7 Wm. IV., c. 84, £220,430. The county is within the military district of Belfast, and there are Barracks in Londonderry, where also the staff of the County Militia is stationed. The head-quarters of the Constabulary force, consisting of 152 men, officers included, are at Coleraine; those of the 4 districts, comprising 20 stations, at Coleraine, Londonderry, Magherafelt, and Newtownlimavady. There are 2 stations of the Coast Guard, at Down Hill and Port Stewart, and 2 of the Revenue Police in the county, at Draperstown and Learmont.

Lieutenant, Sir R. A. Ferguson, Bart., M.P., The Farm, Derry
Custos Rotulorum, The Marquis of Londonderry
High-Sheriff, (1852-53), Leslie Alexander, jun., Esq., Foyle Park, Derry
Members for the County—Thomas Bateson, Esq., D.L., Junior Lord of the Treasury, C. 3 Albany, and Carlton Club, London; Captain T. Jones, R.N., 30 Charles-street, St. James's, London
Assistant Barrister—W. Armstrong, Esq., Q.C., 38 Upper Gloucester-street, Dublin

DEPUTY LIEUTENANTS.

Alexander, L., Foyle Park, Londonderry
Alexander, N., M.P., Portglenone House
Ash, W. H., Ashbrook, Londonderry
Bateson, Thomas, M.P.
Bruce, Sir H. H., Bart., Downhill
Bruce, S. C., Coleraine
Conyngham, W. L., Springhill, Moneymore
Cromie, J., Cromore, Portstewart, Coleraine
Dawson, R. P., Moyola Park, Castledawson
Hunter, R., Straid Arran, Feeny
Lecky, C. M'C., Londonderry
Lyle, A., Oaks, Londonderry
M'Causland, M., Fruit Hill, Newtownlimavady
M'Naghten, Sir E., Bart., Bushmills
Miller, Rowley, Moneymore
Ogilby, J., Pellipar House, Dungiven
Scott, T., Willsboro', Muff, Derry
Skipton, Connolly, Londonderry
Stevenson, J., Fortwilliam, Tobbermore
Strafford, General the Earl of, Grosvenor street, London

MAGISTRATES.

Alexander, L., D.L., Foyle Park, Derry
Alexander, L., jun., Newtownlimavady
Alexander, N., M.P., D.L., Portaferry
Anderson, H., Ballymacree House, Ballymoney
Ash, W. H., D.L., Ashbrook, Londonderry
Bateson, T., M.P., D.L.
Bennet, T., Ballydevitt, Coleraine
Bennett, T., Castleroe, Coleraine
Beresford, J. B., Learmount
Bicknell, G., Manor House, Kilrea
Boyd, J., Dundoan House, Coleraine
Boyd, W., Recorder of Londonderry
Browne, T. R., Cumber, Claudy
Bruce, Capt. W. H., Upper Castleroe Coleraine
Bruce, H. B. S., Bellaghy

Bruce, Sir H. H., Bart., D.L., Downhill
Bruce, S. C., D.L., Coleraine
Campbell, W. W., The Castle, Portstewart
Clarke, J. J., Maghera
Cloncurry, Lord
Colthurst, Rev. J., Bovevagh, Dungiven
Conyngham, Wm. L., D.L., Springhill, Moneymore
Courtenay, J., Glenburne, Portglenone
Cromie, J., D.L., Cromore, Portstewart
Dawson, R. Peel, D.L., Moyola Park, Castledawson
De Blaquiere, G., The Belt, Londonderry
Douglass, C., Dervock, Antrim
Ellis, H., Innisrush, Portglenone
Ferguson, A., Burt, Londonderry
Ferguson, J., Castleforward, Newtowncunningham
Gage, W. C., Ballyrena, Newtownlimavady
Gaussen, David, Lakeview, Ballyronan
Gillespie, Joshua, Tullamore
Gilmour, P., The Grove, Londonderry
Given, J., Farloe, Newtownlimavady
Graves, W., Gravesend, Castledawson
Greene, W., Londonderry
Hamilton, A. W. C., Gortin, Omagh
Hannyngton, J. C., Donoghenderry, Stewartstown
Hazlett, Robert, Bovagh
Heyland, Langford Rowley, Crumlin
Hill, John, Castle, Bellaghy
Humphrey, Alderman John, M.P., Southwark
Hunter, J. C. F., Straid Arran, Feeny
Hunter, R., D.L., Straid Arran, Feeny
Jones, Thomas M. H., Moneyglass, Toome
Knox, C. J., Cranagh, Coleraine
Knox, R., Rushbrook, Coleraine
Lancey, J., Gorten, Garvagh
Lawrence, S., Banfield House, Coleraine
Lecky, C. M'C., D.L., Londonderry
L'Estrange, T. F., Lynn, Mullingar, Westmeath
Londonderry, Marquis of
Londonderry, Mayor of
Lyle, Acheson, D.L., Oaks, Londonderry
M'Causland, M., D.L., Fruit Hill, Newtownlimavady
M'Clintock, R., Dunmore, Carrigans, Derry
M'Naghten, B., Ballyboggy, Coleraine
M'Naghten, Sir E., Bart., D.L., Bushmills
Magill, S. Rankin, Cookstown
Maxwell, Rev. P. B., Birdstown, Londonderry
Miller, J. R., Moneymore
Miller, R., D.L., Moneymore
Montagu, Lord R., Portstewart
Nicholson, H., Riverview, Londonderry
Ogilby, R. L., Dungiven
Ogilby, W., Kilcatton, Claudy
Orr, Andrew, Millburn, Coleraine
Sampson, A., Dromond, Ballykelly
Scott, T., D.L., Willsboro', Muff, Derry
Spotswood, A., Millbrook, Magherafelt
Staples, Sir T., Bart., Q.C., Lissan, Cookstown
Stevenson, J., Ashpark, Dungiven
Stevenson, J., D.L., Fortwilliam, Tobbermore
Stewart, A. J. R., Ards House, Creslough, Letterkenny
Stirling, G. C. B., Moneycarrie, Ballymoney
Strafford, General Earl, D.L.
Stuart, Hon. C., Castledawson
Tomkins, G., Caw House, Londonderry
Tyler, H., Newtownlimavady
Wiggins, H., Muff, Derry
Young, R., Coolkeeragh, Muff, Londonderry

COUNTY OFFICERS.

Clerk of the Crown, John Martin, Esq., Newtownlimavady
Clerk of the Peace, Wm. Gregg, Esq., Londonderry
Deputy Clerk of the Peace, James W. Gregg, Esq., Londonderry; and 75 Talbot-street, Dublin
Crown Solicitor at Quarter Sessions, John Martin, Esq., Newtownlimavady; and 1 Hardwicke-street, Dublin
Treasurer, Jas. A. Lyle, Esq., Knockintern, Coleraine
Secretary to the Grand Jury, J. T. Gregg, Esq., Londonderry

County Surveyor, Stewart Gordon, Esq., Londonderry
Coroners, Daniel Gaily, Esq., Coleraine; William Lane, Esq., Newtownlimavady; Minchin Lloyd, Esq., Summerhill, Londonderry
Agents for Lloyds, John A. Smyth & Co., Londonderry; John MacDonnell, Esq., Coleraine
Head Stamp Distributor for the County, Anthony Babington, Esq., Londonderry

MILITIA STAFF.
Colonel, Sir R. A. Ferguson, Bart., M.P.
Lieutenant-Colonel, W. F. Lenox Conyngham
Major, Rowley Miller

CONSTABULARY OFFICERS.
County Inspector, John S. Rich, Esq., Coleraine

Sub-Inspectors' Stations—Coleraine, J. R. Gibbons
Londonderry, John W. S. Cole
Magherafelt, * * *
Newtownlimavady, W. E. Crofton

COUNTY GAOL, LONDONDERRY.
Board of Superintendence meet on the second Monday in every month: the Mayor of Derry; Sir R. A. Ferguson, Bart.; Sir R. Bateson, Bart.; T. Scott, W. H. Ash, W. Greene, A. Babington, J. Dysart, M. M'Causland, H. Nicholson, J. Murray, J. B. Beresford, Esqrs.
Inspector, Alexander Skipton, M.D.
Chaplain, Rev. Robt. Higginbotham
Presbyterian, Rev. W. M'Clure
R. C. Chaplain, Rev. H. Nugent
Physician & Surgeon, F. Rogan, M.D.
Governor, Mr. Samuel Kitchen
Deputy Governor, Mr. Thos. Lecky

CITY OF LONDONDERRY.

LONDONDERRY, a maritime city and Parliamentary borough, in county Londonderry, and Ulster province, 69 miles N.W. by W., from Belfast, comprising an area of 497 acres within its present municipal boundary. The city is situate on a hill, 119 feet above high water, projecting into the western side of the river Foyle, and is surrounded by an ancient rampart, a mile in circumference, with six gates, beyond which the buildings have been considerably extended; a square in the centre, from which the four principal streets diverge is called the Diamond. As a business and manufacturing city it is of considerable importance, and the fisheries of the Foyle give employment to a vast number of people. The original name Doire, or place of Oaks, was first anglicised Derry; and the prefix of London was added by charter of James I., 1613, on the incorporation of the Irish Society. In 1689, it successfully sustained a desperate siege, protracted for 105 days, against the army of James II. The guns used on this memorable occasion are preserved, and the principal one, "Roaring Meg," 11 feet long, 4 feet 6 in circumference, is still to be seen on the walls. These walls, well known to the inhabitants of Ulster, remain almost as perfect as when built, more than two centuries ago. The public buildings, and, as the seat of a Bishop's see, the ecclesiastical edifices, the Walker testimonial monument, and its situation being "a city on a hill," gives Londonderry a most effectively picturesque appearance. The river is crossed by a wooden bridge, 1,068 feet long, connecting the city with the village of Waterside, on its E. shore. The public buildings are, the Cathedral of the see of Derry, and two other Protestant Churches, four Presbyterian Churches, two Roman Catholic Chapels, an Independent and two Methodist meeting-houses; the Episcopal Palace, Foyle College, Gwyn's Charitable Institution, the County and City Court-house, Prison, and Infirmary, Corporation Hall, the Custom-House, the District Lunatic Asylum, Workhouse, and a Barrack. In one of the city bastions there is a pillar erected in memory of the Rev. George Walker, governor of the city during the siege in 1689. There are two flax spinning-mills, and several flour mills, three distilleries, two breweries, two large rope walks, and several smaller, two foundries, and five tan-yards. The city returns one member to Parliament; constituency in 1851, 724. The Municipal Government is vested in the Mayor, elected by the Corporation, six Aldermen, and eighteen Councillors, seven Borough Magistrates, appointed by the Lord Lieutenant, and the Magistrates for the county, whose jurisdiction extends over the city. The Mayor is also a Magistrate for the county during his mayoralty; a Court of Record with pleas to an unlimited amount, and a Court of Conscience for pleas under 40s. Irish currency, held by the Mayor. The Recorder holds Quarter Sessions. The Fairs are on 17th June, 4th Sept., and 17th Oct.; Markets on Wednesdays and Saturdays for butchers' meat, fish, pork, vegetables, eggs and poultry, fruit, butter, meal, potatoes; flax market-day, Thursday; also, cattle, horse, and two grain markets. The Bank of Ireland, and the Provincial, Belfast, Ulster, and Northern Banks, have branches here. The Savings' Bank was established in 1815. The Lunatic Asylum for Londonderry, Donegal, and Tyrone counties, erected at an expense of £25,678, maintains 214 patients. The Union Workhouse was opened 10th November, 1840. The city is the head-quarters of a Constabulary district, comprising the three stations of Londonderry, Claudy, and Muff, and a force of twenty-two city police for day and night duty. The port is formed by the river Foyle, which here expands into a spacious and navigable estuary, possessing great natural advantages. It is under the jurisdiction of the Irish Society, who appoint a Vice-Admiral over it, and the lough, and adjacent coast. It is also in charge of a board of Ballast Commissioners. There are eight steamers belonging to the port, which ply to Liverpool, Glasgow, Greenock, and Campbelton. The coasting trade is considerable; an extensive emigration takes place, chiefly to the United States, Canada, and New Brunswick. There is a building-yard on the strand, at which several ships for the East India trade were built, and two steamers, one for the Liverpool and the other for foreign trade.

Post-Office, Lienhall street—Postmaster, Mr. John Bond Peoples; Deputy Postmaster, Mr. James Cherry

Londonderry and Enniskillen railway (open to Strabane.) Four Trains run daily to Strabane, and four Return Trains to Derry. On Sundays, two Up and two Down Trains

Steam Packets.—Liverpool: The Maiden City sails between Derry and Liverpool every Tuesday; average passage, 18 hours—Agent, Mr. John Munn. Glasgow: The Thistle, every Monday and Thursday; the Rover, every Tuesday; the Fenella, every Monday; the Glow-worm, to Ardrossan, every Monday and Thursday—Agent, Mr. John Lyon. Belfast: The Rover, every Saturday. Fleetwood: The Fenella, every Thursday

Conveyances—For Belfast, the mail coach, from Commercial hotel, every morning at 9-30, catching Ballymena train at 5-15 p.m., arriving in Belfast at 7. For Coleraine, one-horse cars, from Foyle street, every afternoon at 4. For Letterkenny, one-horse cars, from Foyle street, every afternoon at 4. For Moville, vans daily

Member for the borough—Sir R. A. Ferguson, bart.

Governor of Derry and Culmore Fort—Lieut.-General the Right Hon. the Earl of Strafford, G.C.B.

Borough Magistrates—J. E. Miller, M.D., C. M'C. Lecky, G. Tomkins, H. Nicholson, J. Dysart, J. Murray, D. Baird, W. Haslett, Sir R. Bateson, baronet, Sir R. A. Ferguson, bart., M.P.

Recorder—William Boyd, Q.C.

Corporation—Mayor, George Foster. Aldermen—North Ward, G. Foster and B. M'Corkell. East Ward, A. Lindsay and J. Leathem. South

LONDONDERRY.

Ward, S. Gilliland & W. M'Arthur. Town Councillors—North Ward, R. Forster, J. Croscadden, W. Coppin, R. Allen, J. Cooke, W. Thompson. East Ward, J. Thompson, A. Skipton, M.D., J. Allen, J. H. Rowe, J. E. Miller, I. Colquhoun. South Ward, S. Smith, W. D. Porter, J. Greer, H. Darcus, W. Huffington, T.Wallace, J. Hayden. Town Clerk, James W. Gregg. Ballast Master, A. Stewart. Harbour Master, F. Hamilton. Town Surveyor, Stewart Gordon

Custom-house, Ship quay—Collector, John Crampton; Comptroller and Surveyor of Warehouses, Robert Staines; First Clerk, Mr. William Scott; Landing Waiter, Mr. A. Dysart; Tide Surveyor, Mr. Thos. Doulon

Excise Office, Shipquay street—Collector, Golding Bird; Supervisor, Mr. Burgess

Stamp Office, Meetinghouse row—Distributor, Anthony Babington

Ordnance Survey Office, St. Columb's court, Bishop street—Capt. Leitch, master; Sergeant John Carrington, deputy

Consuls for Foreign Powers—Denmark, G. Foster; France, J. Morrison; Russia, Turkey, and the Two Sicilies, Samuel Morrison; Holland, William Davenport; Sweden, Norway, and Prussia, Abraham H. Stewart; United States, James Corscaden

Government Emigration Officer, Edwin A. Smith, R.N.

Superintendent of Out-pensioners, Major J. Stuart

Coroner, Minchin Lloyd, Summerhill,

Union Workhouse, east side of Foyle, to accommodate 1100 inmates— Sir R. A. Ferguson, bart., M.P., chairman; Thos. Scott, vice-chairman; Patrick Gilmour, deputy vice-chairman; Samuel Kennedy, clerk; William Rodgers, master; M. M'Candlas, matron. Chaplains—Rev. Dr. Babington, Established; Rev. Henry Carson, Presbyterian; Rev. A. J. M'Carron, Roman Catholic. Dr. White, medical attendant

General Dispensary, Bishop street— Open Tuesday, Thursday, and Saturday. Medical attendant, Alex. Skipton, M.D.

County and City Infirmary and Fever Hospital, Edenballymore—Francis Rogan, M.D., physician & surgeon; John Thompson, M.D., house surgeon; Rev. Wm. M'Clure, treasurer and secretary; John Kennedy, house steward and manager

Lunatic Asylum, for Derry, Donegal, and Tyrone, built to accommodate 200 patients—D. Cluff, manager; Francis Rogan, M.D., physician

Banks—Bank of Ireland, office, Shipquay street—Agent, Jas. Thompson Mackey; Belfast Banking Company, office, Shipquay street— Manager, Wm. Hazlett; Northern Banking Company, office, Magazine street—Managers, Edward Smith and R. Hanna; Provincial Bank, office, Shipquay street—Manager, David Webster; Ulster Banking Company, office, Foyle street— Manager, Thomas Davison

Loan Fund, Castle street—John S. Davison, secretary; James Gilmour, treasurer

Notaries Public—Mr. William Scott, Custom-house; Mr. Thos. Wallace, Great James's street

Agent for Lloyd's, John A. Smith & Co.

Registry Office for Servants, Linenhall street

Registrar of Marriages for the district —Thomas M'Carter, Pump street

Commissioner for Receiving Affidavits —Thomas M'Carter

Masonic Hall, Magazine street—S. Ormsly, caretaker

The Cathedral, Bishop street, founded by the London Corporation 1628— The Hon. and Right Rev. Richard Ponsonby, Lord Bishop of Londonderry and Raphoe; the Very Rev. Thomas Danbury Gough, Dean of Londonderry and Raphoe. The Rev. John Hayden Dunboe, archdeacon; Revs. George Smith, Mr. Higinbotham, and Chas. Seymour, curates; Mr. Welsh, organist; Mr Stafford, first singer in the choir

LONDONDERRY.

Chapel of Ease, the West wall—Rev. Robert H. Burgh

Free Churh, Great James street—Rev. Mervyn Wilson; Rev. B. B. Gough, first chaplain to the bishop

First Presbyterian Church, Meetinghouse row—Revs. William M'Clure and Rev. Thomas Wallace, pastors

Second Presbyterian Church, off Fountain street—Revs. James Crawford and Matthew Wilson, pastors

Third Presbyterian Church, Great James st.—Rev. J. Denham, D.D.

Fourth Presbyterian Church, Widow's row—Rev. Robert Ross

Covenanter's Meetinghouse, Fountain street—Rev. Robert Niven

Reformed Presbyterian Meetinghouse, Waterside—Rev. Jacob Alexander

Independent Chapel, Mall wall—Rev. John Kay

Primitive Methodist Chapel, Magazine street—Rev. Mr. Jones, minister

Wesleyan Methodist Chapel, East wall—Revs. John Dwyer and G. M'Millin, pastors

Roman Catholic Chapel, Long tower—Right Rev. Francis Kelly, D.D., bishop; Revs. Hugh Nugent Aden, John M'Laughlin, and E. M'Bride, curates

St. Columb's Chapel, Waterside—Ven. Archdeacon A. J. M'Carron, P.P.; Revs. Wm. M'Laughlin and Charles M'Cauley, curates

Sisters of Mercy Convent, Pump st.—Mrs. Locke, superioress

Londonderry Bible Society—Revs. W. M'Clure and Mervyn Wilson, secretaries; Patrick Gilmour, treasurer

Derry Diocesan School (usually called Foyle College)—A Grammar School, with accommodation for eighty boarders. Patron, The Lord Bishop of Derry; Trustees, The Dean and and Chapter of Derry; Head Master, Rev. Robert Henderson

Endowed School, in connection with the Reformed Presbyterian Church, Waterside—Wm. John Snowden, teacher

Irish Society Infant School, in connection with the Independent Meetinghouse, Bridge street—Miss M. Adams, teacher

Gwyn Charitable Institution—Established in 1833, for the maintenance and education of male orphan children, who have been resident in the city and liberties of Londonderry. The institution was established by the late Mr. John Gwyn, a merchant belonging to the city of Derry, who bequeathed a large sum for that purpose. The children are taken into the establishment at the age of from 8 to 12, and maintained, clothed, educated, and apprenticed out of it. There are at present 120 boys in the house. The institution is managed by a board of 21 trustees.—Treasurer, Peachill Irwin; Secretary, Pitt Skipton; Medical Attendant, Alex. Skipton, M.D.; Head Master and Resident Superintendent, Mr. M. Philson

Templemoyle Agricultural Seminary, five miles from Londonderry—Established in 1827, for giving a more suitable education to the sons of farmers and persons intended for agricultural pursuits. Attached to the building, which is capable of accommodating eighty boarders, is a farm containing 172 acres, cultivated in accordance with the most recent discoveries and improvements in agriculture. There are at present seventy-five pupils in the establishment. The institution is governed by a committee of management chosen from the subscribers and patrons. Chairman, Sir Robert A. Ferguson, Bart., M.P.; Treasurer, the Ulster Bank; Hon. Secretary, Pitt Skipton; Head Farmer, Mr. John Campbell; Head Master, Mr. R. Maxwell

Londonderry Library Association and Public News-room, Shipquay st.—Established 1824; the property of 120 shareholders, vested in seven trustees, and managed by a committee of ten proprietors. John Little, secretary; Robert Hanna, treasurer; John Thompson, resident librarian and manager. Admission by ballot; terms, 30s. per annum.

LONDONDERRY.

Londonderry Library and News-room—Librarian, Mr. John Thompson
Londonderry General Subscription Library, Mall Wall—Librarian, Mr. J. G. Leathem
Londonderry Literary Association—W. Boyd, secretary
Ladies' Penny Society, on the Wall—For the relief of destitute room-keepers. Miss Baldrick, secretary
Newspapers—*Londonderry Journal*, Wednesday; Mr. James Cruise, printer and publisher; Arthur M'Corkell, registered proprietor. *Londonderry Sentinel*, Friday; Mrs. Wallen, proprietor and publisher; Mr. G. A. O'Driscoll, editor. *Londonderry Standard*, Thursday; Messrs. James Macpherson and Thomas M'Carter, proprietors and publishers; Mr. James Godkin, editor

NOBILITY AND GENTRY.

Alexander, Mrs., Strand
Bateson, Sir Robert, bart., D.L., J.P., Castruse
Babington, Mrs., East wall
Baird, Daniel
Baldrick, Miss Ann, Magazine street
Bond, Miss M., Meetinghouse row
Bond, Miss Mary, Bishop street
Bogg, Misses, Bishop street
Boyd, Mrs. Ann, Shipquay street
Brown, Misses, East wall
Brown, Mrs., Shipquay street
Blackall, Captain, Great James street
Boyle, James, James street
Cary, Miss Charlotte, East wall
Chatham, Col. John, Waterloo place
Corbett, Hugh, Castle street, and Ravenscliff, Moville
Crampton, Misses, Waterloo place
Crawford, Mrs., Great James street
Darcus, Mrs., Pump street
Denham, Miss, Queen street
Dysart, John, J.P., Meetinghouse row
Ellis, Miss Sarah, Mall wall
Fairley, Miss, Shipquay place
Ferguson, Sir R. A., bart., M.P., The Farm
Foster, George, Strand
Gamble, Miss, Strand
Gilmour, Patrick, Great James street
Graham, Miss Eliza, Pump street
Grant, Mrs., Strand
Gregg, Mrs. Ann, Pump street
Harvey, William, Artillery lane
Hamilton, Mrs. Ann, William street
Hay, Mrs. Elizabeth, Shipquay street
Hazlett, William, Belfast Bank
Hogshaw, Misses, Great James street
Horner, Miss Jane, William street
Huffington, Mrs., Strand road
Inch, Mrs. J., Pump street
Leslie, Captain E., Great James street
Lecky, Conolly M'Causland
Morrison, John, William street
Motherwell, Mrs., Queen street
Moore, Miss Eliza, James street
Munn, John, Shipquay street
M'Auley, Misses, Great James street
M'Causland, Marcus, East wall
M'Causland, Captain, Great James st.
M'Clure, John, Pump street
M'Donagh, Mr., Bridge street
Nicholson, Harvey, J.P., Shipquay st.
Osborne, James, William street
Patterson, Mrs., James street
Ponsonby, Hon. & Right Rev. Richard, Lord Bishop of Derry, The Palace, Bishop street
Renwick, Miss, Bishop street
Shaw, Matthew, Diamond
Skipton, Captain, Pump street
Smyth, Major, Sackville street
Stanes, Robert, Bishop street
Steele, Mrs. Letitia, Waterloo place
Steele, Mrs., Queen street
Stewart, Miss, Bishop street
Stewart, Miss Jane, The Mall
Thompson, Mrs. Ann, Magazine street
Woods, Mrs., Queen street
Young, Miss Ann, Queen street

CLERGY AND PROFESSIONAL.

Alexander, Rev. Jacob, Waterside
Bradley, William George, solicitor, Ferryquay street
Browne, Wm., M.D., Pump street
Burgh, Rev. Robert, Pump street
Cass, N. B., dentist, Sackville street
Corbett, Thomas, surgeon and licentiate apothecary, Shipquay street
Chambers, Thomas, solicitor and sub-sheriff, London street
Colhoun and Knox, solicitors and land agents, Shipquay street
Crawford, A., solicitor, Linenhall st.
Crawford, Rev. James

Denham, Rev. James, D.D., Great James street
Duddy, George, surgeon and druggist, Ferryquay street
Eames, W. J., surgeon and licentiate apothecary
Ferguson, Rev. Samuel
Franks, G. & G., solicitors, London st. and Pump street
Gough, Very Rev. Thomas B., The Deanery, Bishop street
Greene, H., civil engineer, Queen st.
Hamilton, Andrew, M.D. and surgeon, Sackville street
Hagerty, Wm., architect, Strand road
Hall, Thomas, professor of Latin and Greek, Foyle College, William st.
Henderson, Rev. Robert
Higinbotham, Rev. Robert, Mall wall
Huffington, Wm., solicitor, Waterloo place
Jackman, Samuel, architect, Diamond
Johnston, David, civil engineer, Great James street
Kelly, Frederick, solicitor, Market st. and Richmond street
Kinder, George T., solicitor, and agent for the London Mutual Life and Guarantee Society, Pump street
Knox, Robt., solicitor, Great James st.
Lane, M. B., solicitor, Bishop street
Leitch, Capt. Geo., Master of Ordnance Survey; office, St. Columb court
Logan, Henry, professor of music, East wall
Maxwell, Joseph, M.D. and surgeon, Pump street
Millar, Joseph E., M.D. and surgeon, Pump street
Millar, John, engineer and architect, North quay
Morton, Charles, M.D. and surgeon, and licentiate apothecary, Diamond
M'Corkell, Arthur, solicitor, agent for Church of England Fire and Life Assurance Company, Shipquay st.
M'Clure, Rev. Wm., Sackville street
M'Farland, A., artist, Strand road
M'Intire, John, solicitor, London st.
M'Laughlin, William, M.D., surgeon and licentiate apothecary
M'Millen, Rev. George
Nesbitt, James E., solicitor, Castle st.
Nevin, Rev. Robert
Orr, Moore, solicitor, East wall
Orr, W. E., engineer and architect Richmond street
Ponsonby, Hon. & Right Rev. Richd., The Palace, Bishop street
Reid, Forest, attorney, Richmond st.
Rogan, Francis, M.D. and surgeon, Bishop street
Rogan, William F., M.D. and surgeon, Pump street
Ross, Rev. Robert
Rone, John Henry, surgeon and apothecary, Ferryquay street
Skipton, Henry, M.D. and surgeon, Diamond
Skipton, Alex., M.D. and surgeon, Diamond
Sloan, Robert, civil engineer, Great James street
Smith, Rev. George, Mall wall
Staunton, Thomas, drawing master in Foyle College, Great James street
Stevenson, Messrs., solicitors, Richmond street
Thompson, Dr., surgeon and licentiate apothecary, Strand road
Wallace, Rev. T.
White, Barnewell, M.D. and surgeon, Pump street
Wilson, Rev. Mervyn, Great James st.
Wilson, Rev. Matthew

TRADERS, ETC.

Adams, A. & J., grocers, Butcher st.
Aicken, William, butter merchant, Strand
Aitken, Thomas, sailmaker, William street
Allen, James, hardware, clock and fancy warehouse, Shipquay street
Allen, John, wine merchant, Linenhall street
Allen, Robt., & Co., wholesale grocery, oil, colour, glass, and seed warehouse, Shipquay place
Allen, Robert, agent for Life Association, Scotland, Shipquay place; residence, Gt. James's street
Allen, Andrew, publican and grocer, Waterside
Allen, Thomas, delf and leather dealer, Waterside
Alexander, Mathew James, bread & biscuit baker and confectioner, Ferryquay street

LONDONDERRY.

Alexander, J. R. and J., corn millers, Waterside and Foyle street
Anderson, John, family grocer and baker, William street
Andrews, William, watchmaker and jeweller, Foyle street
Ashton, William, & Co., tailors and hat manufacturers, Bishop street
Atkins, Thomas, sailmaker, Shipquay
Baxter, A., plumber and gasfitter, William street
Baxter, A., plumber and gasfitter, Shipquay place
Barr, Thomas, grocer, baker, and spirit dealer, Rossville street
Barber, Joseph, grocer, Waterside
Barber, James, publican, Waterside
Ballantine, T. and S., Clooney and Ardlough flour, oatmeal, and Indian corn mills, Waterside; office, Foyle street—residence, Waterside
Baird, Daniel, & Co., general merchants and shipowners, Strand
Babington, Barbara, family grocer, Diamond
Beagley, Robt., publican, Artillery lane
Beagley, John, tailor, Ferryquay st.
Bigger, William, provision store, Foyle street
Birkmyre, John, baker, Foyle street
Black, Alexander, & Co., wine and spirit merchants, Waterloo place
Blackie and Sons, publishers, Orchard street
Blair, Elizabeth, publican, Society st.
Boyd, Hamilton, printer, Castle st.
Bond, Robert, wholesale grocer, oil, and colour merchant, Shipquay st.
Boardman, Wm., publican, Waterside
Bradley, Patk., pawnbroker, Society st
Bradley, J. and C., cabinetmakers, Bridge street
Bradley, Mary, publican, Strand
Bredin, Thomas, hardware merchant, Ferryquay street
Brigan, Jane, lodging-house, Bridge st.
Brogan, Patk., baker, Bishop street
Bryson, James, publican, Bridge st.
Bryson, Joseph, publican, Waterside
Burnett, Jane and Mary, silk mercers and haberdashers, Pump street
Buchanan, H., general printer, Richmond street
Byrn, Patrick H., chiropidist and perfumer, Artillery lane

Cairns, James, American packet agent, Foyle street
Campbell, Robert, cabinetmaker, &c., Bishop street and London street
Campbell, Robert, saddler and harness maker, Bishop street
Campbell, Michael, clothes broker, Cowbog street
Campbell and Gilmour, grain and commission merchants, Foyle street
Cameron, M., clothes broker, Cowbog street
Carson, Charles, & Co., brewers, maltsters, and millers, William st.
Carson, B., engraver, Artillery lane
Carter, Robt., publican, Linenhall st.
Cary, M'Clelland, & Co., grain merchants and bleachers, Foyle street
Caskey, Samuel, teacher, Bridge st.
Casey, J., ship bread baker & grocer, Foyle street
Casey, J., publican, Foyle street
Caulfield, W. H., watchmaker and jeweller, Ferryquay st. & Diamond
Caulfield, Wm., leather cutter, Diamond
Cherry, J. D., woollen and linendraper and hatter, Diamond
Christie, John, steam flour and grain mills, Foyle street
Christie, John, flour store, Shipquay place
Christie, Claudius, general merchant and emigration agent, Foyle street
Christie, W. & H., general merchants and emigration agents, Foyle street
Christie, W. and H., Globe Insurance office, Foyle street
Clarke, Eliza, milliner and silk mercer, Ferryquay street
Clark, Richard, cutler, Butcher st.
Clarke, Joseph, woollendraper and haberdasher, Waterside
Clements, David, American packet office, Foyle street
Cochrane, Mrs. Joseph, milliner, Castle street
Colhoun, George, publican, Waterside
Colhoun, M., watchmaker & jeweller, Shipquay street
Colhoun, Andrew, woollendraper, Shipquay street
Collins, Anthony, cooper, William st.
Connor, Dennis, clothes broker, Cowbog street
Connor, Andw., Strand tavern, Strand

Cooke, Joseph and John, shipowners and timber merchants, Strand
Cooke, Robt., general grocer, Butcher street
Cooper, Margaret, haberdasher, Shipquay street
Corscaden, James, grain merchant, Shipquay street
Corscaden, James, Northern Fire and Life and Caledonian Life Assurance office, Shipquay place
Coppin, Captain Wm., ship builder and ironfounder, Strand road
Cowan, Jane Ann, boarding-house, East wall
Crawford, Muir, grocer, Waterloo place
Crawford, David, grocer, Waterside
Crockett, A. and J., milliners, Bishop street
Culleton, Andw., auctioneer, Diamond
Cunningham, John, grocer, Bishop st.
Cunningham, Jane, haberdasher, Bishop street
Cunningham, Robert, steam oatmeal mill, Foyle street
Cunningham, Oliver, grocer, Rossville street
Cunningham, S., grocer, Foyle street
Cunningham, James, woollendraper, haberdasher, and leather dealer, Waterside
Cuthbert, Hugh, baker and publican, Foyle street
Cuthbert, Hugh, boot and shoemaker and grocer, Ferryquay street
Davenport, Edward, tanner and bark merchant, William street
Darcus, Henry, land agent, Great James's street
Devlin, John, skinner and publican, Bridge street
Devlin, J., publican, Artillery lane
Devlin, John, grocer, wine and spirit merchant, Foyle street
Dickson, James, grocer, Bridge street
Doak, James, cabinetmaker, Linenhall street
Donaghy, John, tavern, Foyle street
Donaghy, Patrick, City delf, china, and glass house, Diamond
Dougherty, William, wholesale and retail woollendraper, Diamond
Dougherty, Charity, hardware and jewellery shop, Shipquay street
Dougherty, John, Shipquay street

Doughterty, John, cutler, Bridge st.
Dougherty, Daniel, publican, Cowbog street
Dougherty, Chas., publican, Abbey st.
Dougherty, Ann, publican, Strand
Dougherty, James, grocer and publican, Strand
Dougherty, William, publican, Shipquay place
Dougherty, James, publican, Foyle st.
Dougal, John, chandler, Bridge street
Douglas, James, saddler and harness maker, Foyle street
Downey, Charlotte, milliner and haberdasher, Ferryquay street
Duddy, George, oil and colour shop, Ferryquay street
Duddy, James, publican, Foyle street
Dunn, Robert, miller, provision dealer, and grocer, Waterside
Dugall, George, grocer, Bishop street
Dugall, James, soap and candle manufacturer, Bridge street
Duffy, James, clothier, Butcher street
Dunlop, John, grocer, Bishop street
Dunlop, Hugh, plumber, tin, and coppersmith, Richmond street
Eakin and Craig, grocers, Butcher st.
Ewing, John, saddler and harness maker, Waterloo place
Farrel, Thomas, agent for Blackie and Son, Orchard street
Ferris, Joseph, grocer and emigrant agent, Foyle street
Ferris, Wm., grocer, publican, and baker, Bishop street
Fisher, Robert, grocer and emigration agent, Foyle street
Flanaghan, Edward, teacher of dancing, Orchard street
Fleming, John, publican and grocer, William street
Fleming, Charles, tailor, Castle street
Floyd, A., pianoforte tuner, Diamond
Forde, Lewis, flax, tow, and general commission merchant, Foyle street
Forde, Arthur W., railway manager, Queen street
Foster and Co., tanners and bark merchants, Strand
Foster and Co., wholesale grocers and tobacconists, Waterloo place
Foy, Hugh, coach factory, Meetinghouse row
Foyle Ropewalk Co., Shipquay place

Friel, Wm., cabinetmaker, Society st.
Friel, Thomas, cabinetmaker, Shipquay street
Friel, Patrick, tailor, Society street
Friel, Edward, clothier and broker, Cowbog street
Gallagher, Patrick, furniture mart, Bishop street
Gallagher, Mary, publican, Butcher st.
Gallagher, John, butcher, Linenhall st.
Gallagher, Patk., butcher, Richmond st.
Gallagher, J., grocer, William street
Gallagher, William, publican, Shipquay place
Gallagher, Elizabeth, hotel, Waterside
Gallagher, Rebecca, Hibernian tavern, Ship quay
Gardner, Wm., commission and tea merchant, Foyle street
Gaston, the Misses, ladies' school, Butcher street
Gilliland, Samuel, flour miller, grocer, wine and spirit merchant, Bishop st.
Gilliland, Edward, saddler & harness maker, Diamond
Gilliland, Martha, milliner, Shipquay street
Gill, Mrs., milliner and dressmaker, Diamond
Gillespie, Jas., pawnbroker, Bridge st.
Gillespie, Loughlin, spirit dealer, Bishop street
Gilkey, John, cabinetmaker, Bishop st.
Gilmour, James, & Co., wholesale haberdashers, Artillery lane
Gilmour, John R., veterinary surgeon, Bishop street
Gilmour, Patrick, flax and general corn merchant, Foyle street
Glen, Mrs., ladies' school, Saint Columb's court
Gourlay, Wm., publican, Diamond
Gorman, Mathew, skinner, Bridge st.
Graham, John, grocer, Bridge street
Graham & M'Crea, wholesale grocers, Ferryquay street
Greer, James, family grocer, tobacco and snuff manufacturer, Ferryquay street
Greer, Benjamin, Imperial hotel, Bishop street
Green, George, steam-boat agent, Foyle street
Green, Adam, baker, Bridge street
Green, John, publican, Orchard street

Greenslead, Wm., hardware merchant and nailer, Cowbog street
Greenslead, Adam, ironmonger, Waterloo place
Gresham, James, baker, Ferryquay st.
Gribben, James, tobacco and snuff shop, Ferryquay street
Griffin, Wm., gunmaker, Ferryquay st.
Hagan, Daniel, publican, Linenhall st.
Hamilton, David, wholesale grocer, oil and colour merchant, Shipquay place
Hamilton, Robert, grocer and general merchant, Foyle street
Hamilton, John, hardware merchant, Waterloo place
Hamilton, M., grocer, Bishop street
Hamilton, Robt., haberdasher, Bishop street
Hamilton, Jane Ann, ladies' boarding school, Mall wall
Handcock, John, grocer, and clerk to butter market, Bridge street
Handcock, Danl., merchant, and agent for Atlas Fire and Life Assurance Co., Strand
Hanlon, Margt., haberdasher, Ferryquay street
Hannigan, Dennis, pawnbroker, Bishop street
Harvey, Matilda, wine store, Magazine street
Hart, Henry, clothes broker, Cowbog street
Harkness, James, grocer, Foyle street
Hegarty, James, woollendraper and haberdasher, Bishop street
Hegarty, Ann, Foyle tavern, Foyle st.
Heggarty, Thomas, provision shop, William street
Hempton, John, bookseller, stationer, and piano-forte agent, Diamond
Hempton, Mathew, bookseller, printer, and stationer, Ferryquay street
Heming, F. H., proprietor of tolls on Derry bridge
Henderson & Dunn, wholesale grocers, Shipquay place
Henry, Andrew, delf, glass, and provision shop, Waterside
Hislop, Mrs. and Miss, ladies' school, Bishop street
Hoffmeyer, Bernard, German clockmaker, Diamond
Holt, Jas., grocer & publican, Bishop st.

3 D

Hughes, John, chandler, Bishop st.
Hughes, George, military bootmaker, Ferryquay street
Hunter, Mrs., dressmaker, Artillery lane
Hunter, John, woollen hall, Diamond
Hyndman, Samuel, hardware merchant, Diamond
Irvine, Pechell, wholesale grocer, Linenhall street
Jackson, Thomas, grocer and leather dealer, Ferryquay street
Johnston, the Misses, boarding and day seminary, Gt. James's street
Johnston, James, city brewery, Magazine street
Kerr, John, saddler, Diamond
Kearney, Daniel, publican and grocer, William street
Kelly, Edwin, publican, Bridge street
Kelly, Thomas, publican and grocer, Bishop street
Kelly, John, slate and salt dealer, Foyle street
Kelly, Oliver, family grocer, Waterside
Kennedy and Henry, haberdashers, Bishop street
Kirkpatrick, James, spade manufacturer, Kildrum—store, Bishop st.
Kyle, John C., family grocer, Shipquay street
Laughlin, Samuel, baker and grocer, Bishop street
Laughlin, Samuel, baker and grocer, Waterloo place
Leathem, John, and Co., spinning factory, Foyle street
Leathem, John G., teacher, Mall wall
Leitch, Ann, milliner, Ferryquay st.
Linch, Edward, grocer and publican
Little, John, and Co., hardware merchants, Waterloo place
Lindsay, Alex., Son, & Co., wholesale and retail woollendrapers and silk mercers, Bishop street
Lindsay and Little, haberdashers and drapers, Bishop street
Lindsay, Mary, proprietress of lime works, Waterside
Lloyd, M., general agency office, London street
Logue, Mary, grocer and publican, Bishop street
Lyon, John, steamboat agent, Foyle st.
Macpherson, F., blockmaker, Shipquay

Mackay, J. T., agent for Royal Exchange Assurance Corporation
Magowan, William, baker and grocer, Ferryquay street
Manson, Æneas, publican, Foyle st.
Mailley, John, butcher, Linenhall st.
Martin, Hugh, publican, Bridge street
Mathewson, John, grocer, iron, and salt dealer, Waterside
Mehan, James, hairdresser, Bridge st.
Mehan, John, Waterside & Innishowen distilleries
Methueris, Jas., herring store, Waterside
Menan, James, wine and spirit store, Foyle street
Milligan, Samuel, printer, Diamond
Milligan, Samuel, Queen's Arms inn, Market street
Millar, David, tailor, Society street
Miles, Thomas, grocer, Waterloo place
Minniece, James, watchmaker, Market street
Molseed, Ann, publican, Bishop street
Montgomery, John, whitesmith, Great James street
Mooney, Wm., flour and meal store, Foyle street
Moran, Mary, milliner, Diamond
Morrison, Samuel, ship broker, Middle quay
Mullan, William, bookseller and stationer, Shipquay street
Mullan, James, grocer and publican, Great James street
Mulholland, Wm., wholesale and retail woollen and linendraper, and haberdasher, Bishop street
Munn, John, flax spinner and general merchant, Foyle street
Murray, John, Agricultural Inn, grocery and delf shop, Bishop street
Murphy, Francis, publican, Shipquay place
M‘Adoo, John, family grocer, Shipquay street
M‘Adam, Wm., corn factor and grocer, Butcher street
M‘Arthur, Wm., and Co., wholesale woollen, linen, and Manchester house, Ferryquay street
M‘Auley, John, & Co., confectioners, Bishop street
M‘Avoy, Dennis, pipe manufacturer, Fahan street

M'Bride, Patrick, grocer and publican, William street
M'Bride, James, flax merchant, Foyle street
M'Candless, William, tanner and leather cutter, Diamond
M'Carter, Mr., builder, Foyle street
M'Carter, William, leather dealer, Waterside
M'Carter, Geo., leather house, Foyle st.
M'Carter, Thos., printer & publisher, Pump street
M'Causland, John, butcher, Butcher st.
M'Causland, Frederick, wine merchant and agent for Guardian Assurance Company, Richmond street
M'Causland, Patrick, butcher, Ferryquay street
M'Cay, Archibald, hairdresser, Richmond street
M'Colley, Wm., bookseller and stationer, Diamond
M'Colley, Mrs., proprietress of tanyard, Long tower; residence, Bridge st.
M'Conlan, Catherine, clothes broker, Cowbog street
M'Corkell, William, and Co., timber merchants, Strand
M'Cormick, John, merchant tailor, Ferryquay street
M'Cormick, Alexander, Commercial Hotel, Shipquay place
M'Cormick, Wm., publican, Foyle st.
M'Cord, Charles, painter and glazier, Shipquay place
M'Clelland, James, family grocer, oil and colour merchant, Diamond
M'Clelland, Mathew, builder and architect; agent for Garnkirk Coal Company, Orchard street
M'Clean, Isabella, haberdasher, Butcher street
M'Closkey, Jno., pawnbroker, New gate
M'Closkey, Joseph, clothes broker, Cowbog street
M'Culley, Mr., delf, china, and glass warehouse, Diamond
M'Clure, James, & Co., coach factory, Foyle street
M'Crea, James, general merchant, Foyle street
M'Dade, B., butcher, Bridge street
M'Dermott, R., tailor, Richmond st.
M'Dermott, John, clothes broker, Cowbog street

M'Donagh, Ann, green grocer, Richmond street
M'Divett, Edward, lodging-house, Bridge street
M'Feeley, Philip, grocer and publican, Ferryquay street
M'Feeley, Bernard, grocer & publican, William street
M'Feeley, Michael, grocer & publican, Foyle street
M'Gee, George, grocer, Bishop street
M'Govern, Phillip, City hotel, Foyle street
M'Gihon, Edwd., pilot, Magazine st.
M'Ginley, Patrick, clothier & draper, Shipquay street
M'Gra, B., Ship tavern, Middle quay
M'Intyre, Phillip, publican, Waterside
M'Intyre, Archd., tavern, Foyle st.
M'Intyre, Edward, woollendraper, Butcher street
M'Ilwee, Wm., carpenter and builder, Foyle street and Bishop street
M'Ilwee, J., publican, Bishop street
M'Iver, Hugh, grocer, spirit dealer, and clothes broker, Cowbog street
M'Laughlin, James, grocer and publican, Fahan street
M'Laughlin, S., publican, Foyle st.
M'Laughlin, John, provision shop, Waterside
M'Laughlin, James, bookbinder and stationer, Castle street
M'Laughlin, John, cork cutter, Butcher street
M'Laughlin, Margt., milliner, Butcher street
M'Laughlin, Sarah, confectioner, Ferryquay street
M'Laughlin, John, bootmaker, Linenhall street
M'Menemy, Wm., publican & grocer, Foyle street
M'Monagh, Patrick, proprietor of Moville vans
M'Monagle, Patrick, baker, Bishop st.
M'Munn, John, City Spinning Mills, Queen street
M'Murray, William, auctioneer, appraiser, and haberdasher, Butcher street
M'Neely, John, silk mercer and haberdasher, Bishop street
M'Neely, James S., general grocer, Ferryquay street

M'Peake, James, tavern, Foyle street
M'Quilken, Samuel, boarding and day school, Mall wall
M'Reynolds, S., grocer, Foyle street
M'Vicar, Robert and Alexander, merchant tailors, Diamond
Nash, William, house furnishing warehouse, Butcher street
Neills and Minniece, watchmakers, jewellers, and opticians, Shipquay street
Nelis, James H., bookseller, binder, and stationer, Ferryquay street
Nolan, The Misses, ladies' boarding and day school, Linenhall street
Nugent, Margaret, publican, Foyle st.
O'Donnell, Thomas, grocer and provision store, Cowbog street
O'Donnell, M., clothes broker, Cowbog street
O'Donnell, Rooney, baker, Butcher st.
O'Flagherty, James, publican, William street
O'Flynn, John, publican, Bridge st.
O'Kane, Patrick, publican, Strand
O'Kane, Patrick, Foyle street
O'Neill, Henry, grocer, wine and spirit merchant, Butcher street
O'Neill, John, and Co., general merchants, and agents for the Royal Assurance Company, Foyle street
O'Neill, Francis, bookseller and stationer, Foyle street
O'Neill, William, publican and shoemaker, Bridge street
Orr, James, and Co., ship brokers, Shipquay place
Orr, James, assistant to county surveyor, Bridge street
Osborne and Patton, family grocers and Italian warehouse, Shipquay street
Osborne, William, grocer and publican, Bishop street
Osborne, The Misses, ladies' school, William street
Osborne, Allen, and Co., general merchants, Sackville street
Patteson, B., woollen, linen, hat, and room-paper warehouse, Ferryquay street
Patterson, William, and Co., family grocers, Ferryquay street
Pegley, Samuel, painter and glazier, Richmond street
Pearson, James, printer, Bridge st.
Phillips, James, publican, Bridge st.
Pinkerton, John, baker and grocer, Waterside
Porter, James, egg and butter merchant, Bishop street
Porter, John (of the firm of Watt and Co.), Shipquay street
Porter, David, and Co., tobacco and snuff manufacturers, Magazine st.
Pollock, Margaret, boarding-house, East wall
Power, J., horse shoer and farrier, Bishop street
Pressdee, Joseph, tin and coppersmith, Ferryquay street
Quigley, T., publican and tailor, Castle street
Quigley, Geo., publican, Fahan street
Rankin, Mrs., milliner and dressmaker, Sackville street
Reavy, Hugh, grocer and publican, Cowbog street
Reid, James, nursery and seedsman, Bishop street
Reid, Irvine, & Co., wholesale grocers, Richmond and Linenhall street
Rodgers, Francis, gunmaker and fishing tackle warehouse, Bridge st.
Rodgers, John, publican and boarding-house, Shipquay place
Rodgers, Charles, wine and spirit store and billiard room, Foyle st.
Roddy, Michael, George and Dragon inn, Society street
Robinson, Samuel, publican & grocer, Cowbog street
Robinson, John H., shirt factory, Foyle street
Ross, Robert, grocer, Castle gate
Roulston, Martha, registry office for servants, Linenhall street
Roulston, Alexander, shipowner and general merchant, Middle quay
Rowan, Wm., ginger beer maker, Artillery lane
Ritchie, John, shirt factory, Foyle st.
Russel, James, provision and spirit shop, Bishop street
Russel, Jas., grain merchant, Foyle st.
Sawers, Wm., china and glass warehouse, Bishop street
Simpson, Wm. and Robert, classical and mathematical seminary, Society street

Silo, Andw., carver & gilder, Pump st.
Skipton, Pitt, general agent, West of England Fire and Life Assurance office, Foyle street
Smyth, Wm. D., grain store, North quay
Smith, Richard, auctioneer, valuator, and stationer, Ferryquay street
Smyth, Frederick, upholsterer and valuator, Society street
Shaw, Sarah, haberdasher, Bishop st.
Sherrard, Jas., grocer, leather dealer, &c., Bishop street
Sherwood, Wm., publican, keeper of billiard table, racket court, shooting gallery, &c., Bridge street
Sheil, Rose, woollendraper, Diamond
Shannon, James, painter, Orchard st.
Sharmon, Elizabeth, Neptune Hotel, Ship Quay
Smyth and Co., W.D., millers, general merchants, Waterloo place
Smith, Jeremiah, builder, East wall
Smith, Samuel, flax merchant, Shipquay gate
Smith and Osborne, agents for Imperial Fire and Imperial Life Assurance Company, Sackville street
Smyth, John A., and Co., general merchants & agents for Lloyds, Waterloo place
Staines, Robt., jun., Government emigration agent, Custom-house
Steen, Thomas, bread & biscuit baker, and family grocer, Ferryquay street
Stevenson, David, baker and confectioner, Diamond and Rossville street
Stevenson, Hugh, bread and biscuit baker, William st. and Waterloo pl.
Stevenson, John, grocer and publican, Waterside
Stewart, Henry, boot and shoemaker, Ferryquay street
Stirling, John, marble & stone works, Foyle street
Stirling, Patrick, painter and glazier, Bridge street
Stilley, Andrew, baker, Diamond
Stirling, Wm., plate glass warehouse, painter, glazier, &c., Artillery lane

Swan, Moses, grocer, Bishop street
Sweeney, John, grocer, Bishop street
Thompson, James, soap and candle manufacturer, Ferryquay street
Thompson and Crawford, wholesale grocers, &c., Waterloo place
Thompson, James, general merchant, Foyle street
Tillie and Henderson, shirt factory, Foyle street
Toland, John, publican and grocer, Foyle street
Todd, John, grocer, Fahan street
Toy, Daniel, publican, boot and shoemaker, Butcher street
Toy, E., publican, Strand
Waddy, Edwd., publican, Middle quay
Watson, Anne, ladies' boarding school, Bishop street
Watson, Daniel, hair dresser, Shipquay place
Watt and Co., distillery, Abbey street
Watt and Co., wine and spirit store, Shipquay street
Watt, Rebecca, haberdasher, Diamond
Watt, Robt., ropemaker, Shipquay st.
Walker, Geo., salt and lime works, Foyle street
Walker, Henry, seed merchant, Diamond
Wallace, Thomas, flax merchant, Shipquay street
Watters, George, auctioneer and general commission agent, Shipquay st.
Williams, Wm. John, gasfitter, &c., Foyle street
Williams, Joseph, watchmaker, Shipquay street
Wilson, J. and R., corn and general merchants, and agents for Standard Life Assurance Company, Foyle st.
Wilson, William, Ulster Arms hotel, Foyle street
Wylie, William A., general grocer, Bishop street
Young and Nichol, Mesdames, ladies' seminary, Bishop street
Young, Thos., coach factory, Foyle st.
Young, Charles, general iron merchant, Foyle street

LURGAN.

LURGAN is a thriving market town, in the county of Armagh, 17 miles S.W from Belfast, and near the line of the Ulster railway, for which the town is a station. The principal part of the town extends, for nearly a mile, along the Belfast and Armagh road, and is spacious, airy, well-built, and remarkably clean. That which may be considered the suburban part of Lurgan is extensive. Lurgan Castle demesne, the seat of Lord Lurgan, proprietor of the town, extends along the whole of the north-east of it, and the entrance is by an elegant lodge from near the centre of the street. The mansion was some years ago rebuilt, in the Elizabethian style, with beautiful free-stone brought from Scotland. The grounds, which are generously thrown open to the public, are richly embellished with thriving plantations, reflected in a fine sheet of water, and is encompassed by a well-kept gravel walk. The court-house is a stone building, and the Diaper hall is a spacious building, erected in 1825. The linen and cambric manufacture is the staple of Lurgan, and in producing the variety of fabrics, as lawns, diapers, damasks, &c., a large proportion of the population of the town and its vicinity are employed; while some of the establishments of the yarn and linen merchants are extensive. Two noted breweries, and the hotels, are the other principal establishments—among the latter, Irwin's Commercial and Family hotel, in Main street, is one of the most comfortable inns in the county. The Belfast Banking Company, the Northern Banking Company, and the Ulster Bank, have each a branch in operation here. A facility of intercourse with Belfast is afforded by Lough Neagh and the Lagan navigation. The General Quarter Sessions of the county are held in Lurgan, and Petty Sessions every alternate Tuesday. A section of the constabulary police is stationed in the town.

The parish church of Shankill is a handsome structure, with a finely proportioned octagonal spire, containing a good clock: the interior of the church is neatly fitted up, and furnished with a fine-toned organ. There are places of worship for Presbyterians, the Society of Friends, and Wesleyan, Primitive, and the New Connexion of Methodists. The Roman Catholic parochial chapel is a Gothic building. The free educational establishments are a subscription school, one for infants, and one of the Church Society's schools. The other charities are a dispensary and a Union workhouse. The market, which is held on Thursday, is abundantly supplied with provisions, and is, besides, a considerable one for the manufactures of the town and district. Fairs, 5th August and 22d November.

Post Office, Main street—William B. Morris, postmaster. Letters from Dublin, the south of Ireland, and England, arrive every morning at 5, and are despatched every evening at 7-20. Letters from Belfast, the north of Ireland, and Scotland, arrive every evening at 7-40, and are despatched every morning at 3. Letters from Antrim, and other parts of the north, arrive every evening at 8-40, and are despatched every morning at 5. Letters from Enniskillen, and the west, arrive every morning at 3, and are despatched every evening at 7-40

Conveyances—To Antrim, a mail car from Post office, every morning at 3-30. To Banbridge, a mail car, from Post office, every evening at 9. To Belfast, the royal mail (from Enniskillen) calls at Post office, every morning at 4. To Enniskillen, the royal mail (from Belfast) calls at the Post office every evening at 7-40. To Newry, a coach, from Ellen Byrne's, Mall, every evening

Courthouse, Church square—Jane Ferguson, keeper

Bridewell, William street—William Neill, keeper

LURGAN.

Union Workhouse—William Bullick, master; Harriet M'Closkie, mistress. Clerk and returning officer, Thomas Pentland

Constabulary Station—Neal M'Carron, head constable

Dispensary, Main street—Robert S. Hanny, surgeon

Stamp Office, Main street—W. B. Morris, sub-distributor

Banks—Belfast Banking Company, Main street; Henry Greer, agent.—Northern Banking Company, Main street; Thomas Hall, manager.—Ulster Banking Company, Main st.; Thomas Ringland, manager

Railway Station, lower end of William street—John Wilkinson, head clerk

Gas Works, William street—Patrick Cosgrove, manager

Parish Church—Rev. Thomas Knox, rector; Revs. W. P. Oulton and Charles Falloon, curates

Presbyterian Church, Main street—Rev. Thomas Millar, minister

Wesleyan Methodist Chapel, Main street—Rev. James Hughes, superintendent, and Rev. R. G. Cather, A.M.

Primitive Methodist Chapel, Castle lane—William Craig, minister

Methodist (New Connection) Chapel, Ballyblough—Rev. John Service

Friends' Meetinghouse, Ballyblough

Roman Catholic Chapel, Back lane—Rev. William O'Brien, parish priest; Rev. James Denvir, curate

Mechanics' Institute—Dr. Hanny, president; Mat. Wells, vice-president; William Brennian, treasurer; Joseph Matthews, librarian

Lurgan Literary Institute—Dr. Maclaughlin, president; Edward Armstrong, treasurer; Surgeon Shaw, secretary

Public Subscription Library, in Newsroom—P. Carroll, librarian

Reading Room, over Market-house—D. Shaw, secretary

Friendly Society, established 1845—Rev. Thos. Knox, president; Rev. W. P. Oulton and Rev. T. Millar, trustees; James Armstrong, treasurer; Patrick Carroll, secretary

NOBILITY, GENTRY, ETC.

Boyd, Mrs. M., Main street
Boyd, Joseph Hall, Church square
Cuppage, Thomas, Silverwood
Cuppage, John, J.P., official surrogate, Main street
Douglass, Charles, D.L., J.P., Gracehall
Fleming, James, Main street
Forde, Francis, Raughlin
Greer, George, J.P., Woodvale
Greer, Henry, Back lane
Hancock, John, J.P.
Hazlett, Miss D., Church sq. or Mall
Lurgan, Right Hon. Lord, Brownlow House
Mercer, Henry, Laurel Vale
Macoun, John, Kilmore
Macoun, John, Moyraverty
Overend, Miss, Mall
Stevenson, Thomas, Clanrolla
Turtle, James, Tanaghmore Lodge
Waring, Thomas, Waringfield
Watson, Francis, Lakeview
Watson, Hugh, Beechpark

CLERGY AND PROFESSIONAL.

Bell, Robert, surgeon, Main street
Cather, Rev. R. G.
Craig, Rev. Wm.
Denvir, Rev. Jas., C.C., Chapel house
Faloon, Rev. Chas., Armsborough house
Girdwood, Wm., attorney, Main st.
Gilbert, Jonathan, surgeon and apothecary, Church square
Greer, Henry, attorney, Main street
Hanny, R. Strickland, surgeon, Main st.
Hazlett, John, attorney, Mall
Hughes, Rev. James
Knox, Rev. Thomas, Glebe house
M'Laughlin, W. R., surgeon and apothecary, Main street
M'Master, Charles, surgeon and apothecary, Main street
Miller, Rev. Thomas
Morris, Robert, attorney, Main street
O'Brien, Rev. Wm., P.P., Chapel house
Oulton, Rev. Wm. P., deputy surrogate, Main street
Rodger, Samuel, surgeon, Church sq.
Shaw, Wm., surgeon and apothecary, Main street
Service, Rev. John, Ballyblough

TRADERS, ETC.

Anderson, James, insurance agent, &c.

LURGAN.

Anderson, John, seedsman, Main st.
Anderson, Wm., wheelwright & cartmaker, Bridewell place
Anderson, Wm., cabinet maker, Back lane
Armstrong, Robert, grocer, provision dealer, and ironmonger, Main street
Alderdice, Wm., builder, William st.
Armstrong, W., and Son, grocers, timber merchants, woollendrapers, and ironmongers, Main street
Berwick, James, baker, Ballyblough
Black, John, boot & shoemaker, Mall
Bingham, Clements, shoemaker, Watson's row
Byrne, Eleanor, grocer, Mall
Byrne, Ellen, publican, Church square
Burns, Charles, publican, Mall
Blaney, James, publican, Mall
Black, Jonathan, publican and confectioner, Main street
Brown, Mr., publican, Main street
Burns, Ellen, publican, Middle row
Burns, Robert, tailor, Back lane
Byrne, Ellen, tallow chandler, Middle row
Bell, J. and T., and Co., linen manufacturers, Bellview
Chapman, John, blacksmith, Main st.
Cherry, Jos., cabinetmaker, Main st.
Colvan, Henry, builder, Castle lane
Colvan, James, carpenter, Back lane
Campbell, John, corn mercht., Main st.
Conn, Joseph, grocer and provision dealer, Main street
Corry, James, grocer, Main street
Camphill, J. Æ., leatherseller, Main st.
Capper, John, linen yarn merchant, Main street
Cooey, Mary, dressmaker, Main street
Carmichael, Marmion, reed maker, Ballyblough
Cooper, John, shuttle & templemaker, Main street
Cherry, Samuel, publican, Main street
Campbell, Jn., publican, Watson's row
Caddel, Samuel, publican, Pond river
Conley, John, publican, Middle row
Cooper, Robert, publican, Main street
Cherry, Andrew, jeweller, watch and clock maker, Main street
Chapman, John, wheelright and cartmaker, Main street
Cooper, Mary, staymaker, Main street
Cooey, James, butter merchant

Duffy, James, baker, Castle lane
Dickie, Wm., blacksmith, Main street
Downie, John, blacksmith, Main street
Donnelly, Arthur, grocer and spirit dealer, Mall
Donnelly, Wm., carpenter, Main street
Donnelly, Arthur, provision dealer, Main street
Douglas, John, publican, Main street
Doran, John, tailor, Castle lane
Dougan, James, replevinger for county Armagh
Douglas, John, linen manufacturer, Main street
Douglas, G. D., linen manufacturer, Main street
Evans, R. J., printer and stationer
Elliott, John, linen yarn mercht., Mall
Ellis, William, publican, Mall
Emerson, John, publican, Pond river
Emerson, Thomas, publican, Church square
Faloon, John, earthenware dealer, tallow chandler, & grocer, Main st.
Faloon, Mary, publican, Castle lane
Fullerton, Edward, publican, Main street
French, John, tinsmith, Main street
Gray, James, baker and confectioner, Main street
Gallagher, Mr., blacksmith, Main st.
Greer, W. and F., corn merchants, millers, and distillers, Woodvale
Gilbert, John, grocer and earthenware dealer, Main street
Gilbert, Thomas, grocer and provision dealer, Main street
Gaddis, Andrew, publican, Main st.
Gaskin, John, publican, Main street
Gaffrey, Peter, tailor, Main street
Greer, Saml., inspector of weights, &c.
Gilbert, John, linen manufacturer, Main street
Hussian, Patk., blacksmith, Church sq.
Hamilton, Jas., butcher, Ballyblough
Harper, James, cabinetmaker, Main st.
Higgins, William, woollendraper and haberdasher, Main street
Hazleton, John, pawnbroker, Main st.
Hannay, R. S., surgeon and apothecary, Main street
Henry, James, saddler, Main street
Harbinson, W., publican, Middle row
Hughes, Samuel, tailor, Main street
Halfpenny, Hugh, tinsmith, Castle lane

LURGAN.

Hunter, A., linen manufacturer
Irvin, Robert, hotel keeper, Brownlow Arms
Johnston, John, brewer, tobacco and snuff manufacturer, Main street
Johnston, Edward, cabinet maker, Main street
Johnston, Lucinda, dress maker, William street
Kennedy, James, baker and grocer, Main street
Kinkead, E., haberdasher, milliner and dressmaker, Main street
Kero, A. T., tallow chandler, Main st.
Lear, William, insurance agent, auctioneer, and surveyor, &c.
Lockhart, J. and H., linen yarn merchants and manufacturers, Main st.
Lavery, Hugh, publican, Ballyblough
Lavery, Charles, publican, Pond river
Langtry, Eliza, bonnetmaker, Main st.
Lockhart, George, linen manufacturer
Lavery, Thomas, linen manufacturer, Ballyblough
Mathews, Wm., baker, Main street
Magee, Charles, butcher, Main street
Mercer, Sinton, butcher, Ballyblough
Mullan, Jn., earthenware dealer, Mall
Maginnis, Catherine, earthenware dealer, Mall
Moore, Dunlop, tavern keeper, Main st.
Macoun, Wm., linen yarn merchant and manufacturer, Main street
Murphy, Joseph, linen yarn merchant, Main street
Moore, Dunlop, saddler and pawnbroker, Main street
Mercer, Henry, publican
Magee, Charles, publican, Main street
Murray, Wm., publican, Main street
Murchie, Archd., tailor, Middle row
Mullan, John, tinsmith, Main street
May, George, watch and clockmaker, Main street
Montgomery, Wm., wheelwright and cartmaker, Main street
Murray, Wm., butter merchant
Malcolm, James, linen manufacturer, Main street
M'Whinney, Jn., blacksmith, Main st.
M'Haffey, James, shoemaker, Main st.
M'Kernan, Hugh, butcher, Main st.
M'Kernan, Hugh, jun., butcher, Main street
M'Kernan, Richard, butcher, Main st.

M'Geown, Patrick, carpenter, Church lane
M'Clure, Wm., grocer, Main street
M'Keown, Hugh, grocer and leather seller, Main street
M'Keown, Hugh, jun., grocer, Mall
M'Kee, Mr., leather seller, Main st.
M'Ginn, Elizabeth, dressmaker, Castle lane
M'Corry, James, provision merchant
Midgely, J., reed maker, Ballyblough
M'Cabe, Henry, spirit dealer, Back lane
M'Geown, Patk., publican, Church sq.
M'Keown, H., publican, Church sq.
M'Clooney, Jas., publican, Church sq.
M'Connell, Wm., publican, Main st.
M'Stea, John, publican, Main street
M'Corry, John, publican, Main street
M'Comb, John, publican, Middle row
M'Corry, John, publican, Main street
M'Givern, Mary, publican, Main st.
M'Geown, John, publican, Pond river
M'Linden, Arthur, publican, Middle row
M'Rory, Jane, bonnet maker, Castle lane
M'Donnell, E., bonnet maker, Main st.
M'Nally, M., bonnet maker, Ballyblough
M'Corry, James, tallow chandler, Mall
M'Cannon, M., staymaker
M'Caul, Charles, plumber
Nicholson, Thomas, grocer and provision dealer, Main street
Nicholson, Robert, grocer, Mall
Nicholson, Robt., publican, Church sq.
Neill, Wm., inspector of butter and pork market
O'Hara, Francis, publican, Ballyblough
Pelan, James, builder and timber merchant, Main street
Paul & Co., woollendrapers & haberdashers, Main street
Reilly, Henry W., bookseller and registrar of marriages
Ruddell, George, butcher and saddler, Main street
Reilly, Patrick, butcher, Ballyblough
Ringland, Thomas, insurance agent
Russell, George, grocer, Church sq.
Ross, John, linen yarn merchant, Main street
Robinson, John, painter and glazier, Main street
Rogers, Saml., surgeon & apothecary

Ross, Wm., publican, Ballyblough
Roney, John, tallow chandler, Main st.
Shannon, James, baker, Mall
Starkey, Charles, saddler, Main street
Summerville, Samuel, publican, Castle lane
Smyth, John, publican, Main street
Smyth, Wm., publican, Main street
Taaffe, Wm., cabinet maker, Main st.
Taylor, Elizabeth, dressmaker, Main street
Thompson, John, reedmaker, Church square
Thompson, Thos., reedmaker, Church square
Taylor, Jonathan, shuttlemaker, Main street
Vance, John, Star inn
Vance, Joseph, tailor, Castle lane
Wills, M., haberdasher and pawnbroker, Main street
Wilson, Joseph, and Co., linen yarn merchants, Church square
White, Samuel, shuttlemaker, Ballyblough
Waite, John, publican, Main street
Wright, Charles, publican, Main st.
Watson, Robt., and Sons, linen manufacturers
Watson, Armstrong, & Co., linen manufacturers, Main street
Wilson, Joseph, linen manufacturer
Wells, Matthew, linen manufacturer
Young, S. and W., grocers, Main st.
Young, James, painter and glazier, Main street
Younge, S. and W., publicans, Castle lane

MAGHERA.

MAGHERA, a market town and parish, in the barony of Loughnisholin, county of Londonderry; is 101 miles N. by W. from Dublin, and 36 N. by W. from Belfast. The town consists of one long and spacious street, from which several smaller ones branch off; the houses, which are chiefly built of stone, and are modern buildings, have a respectable appearance. It is a place of considerable thoroughfare, which occasions a certain amount of local traffic. Linen cloth is the staple trade. Petty Sessions are held on alternate Saturdays; and a Manorial Court monthly, in which debts under £4 14s. are recoverable. A constabulary station is established in the town. The market days are Tuesday and Friday—the latter for corn. Fairs, 12th Jan., 16th March, 26th April, 12th June, 17th August, 12th October, 16th November. The parish of Maghera contained, in 1851, 11,457 inhabitants, and the town 1172 of that number.

Post Office—M. Thompson, postmistress. Letters from Dublin, the south of Ireland, and England, arrive every forenoon at 11, and are despatched every afternoon at 2. Letters from Coleraine arrive every afternoon at 2, and are despatched at 11

Conveyances—To Coleraine, a mail car (from Dungannon), every forenoon at 11; passes through Garvagh. To Dungannon, a mail car (from Coleraine), every afternoon at 2

Carriers—To Belfast, every Wednesday; Thomas Taylor and John M'Nichol. To Coleraine, every Friday; J. Taylor. To Londonderry, every Thursday; Robert Campbell

Market and Sessions House

Constabulary Station—John Wilson, head constable

Excise Office—James Collier, officer

Sub-distributor of Stamps—Margaret Thompson

Dispensary—Dr. Robert Barr

Parish Church—Rev. S. Knox, rector; Rev. Elias J. Stubbs, curate

Presbyterian Church—Rev. Thomas Witherow, minister

Roman Catholic Chapel—Rev. James Donnelly, P.P.; Revs. J. Donnelly and Michael M'Geogeghan, curates

Church Educational Society's School—H. M'Henry, teacher

Maghera National School—Michael M'Kenna, teacher

Tullyheron National School—Patricia Shiels, teacher

MAGHERA.

NOBILITY AND GENTRY.
Clarke, James J., Lurgantocher
Clarke, Alexander, Upperlands
Henderson, Clotworthy, Tubbermore
Mauleverer, B., Tanneymullen
Mee, John, Music hall
Stevenson, John, Fortwilliam
Torrens, Hon. Judge, Derrynoid

CLERGY AND PROFESSIONAL.
Barr, Robert, surgeon
Brown, Rev. Wm., Blackhill
Cassiday, John B., surgeon
Carson, Rev. Robert, Solitude
Collins, Rev. James, Moninenea
Donnelly, Rev. James, Ballynock
Hamilton, Rev. Richard, Killelagh
Hamilton, Rev. Mr., Kilcronoghan
Henry, Alexander, solicitor
Kennedy, Rev. Charles
Knox, Rev. J. Spencer
M'Kenna, Rev. James, Tennoneeny
M'Namee, Rev. James, Whitewater
Mason, Rev. John, Knockeloghrin
Montgomery, Rev. S. L., Ballymascreen
Mooney, Rev. Daniel, Lavey
M'Cullagh, David G., surgeon
O'Loughlin, Rev. P., Ballinascreen
Smyth, Rev. Samuel, Sixtowns
Stubbs, Rev. Elias
Torrens, Rev. Robert, Gortade
Witherow, Rev. Thomas
Wright, Rev. James, Sixtowns

TRADERS, ETC.
Barr, Rose, toy warehouse
Barkley, James, woollendraper
Begley, Bernard, nailer
Brown, Hugh, shoemaker
Ballagh, John, linen manufacturer
Cassiday, Hugh, coach builder
Connor, John, carpenter
Cassiday, Mary, grocer
Crockett, James, publican
Clarke, Robert, shoemaker
Clarke, John, shoemaker
Clark, Wm., linen manufacturer
Clark, Messrs., linen manufacturers
Connor, John, flax merchant
Davidson, Mr., sewed muslin agent
Dickson, E. and M., haberdashers
Dempsey, Patrick, grocer and earthenware dealer
Daly, Patrick, tailor
Donaghey, John, flax merchant
Flanigan, Michael, publican
Gamble, James, carpenter
Greer, James, whitesmith
Gregg, James, carpenter
Gregg, Sarah, dressmaker
Greer, James, grocer
Henry, John, carpenter
Higgison, Alexander, carpenter
Hasson, Arthur, painter
Hill, Jane, bonnetmaker
Harkin, John, grocer and earthenware dealer
Harkin, Mary, publican
Henry, George, publican
Hughes, James, shoemaker
Hamilton, Allan, sewed muslin agent
Hill, Neill, sewed muslin agent
Hannah, John, bookbinder
Hughes, James, chandler
Irwine, James, tailor
Jenkins, Joseph, Maghera hotel
Kelly, John, blacksmith
Kane, Wm., painter
Kane, A. and M., dressmakers
Kerr, Jas., grocer & hardware dealer
Kelly, Francis, publican
Kennedy, Henry, tailor
Kane, Wm., cooper
Logue, James, nailer
Lytle, Matthew, grocer and hardware merchant
Lytle, J., & J., grocer & leather sellers
Lytle, James, grocer and leather seller
Lagan, Michael, publican
Malone, Bernard, blacksmith
Mean, Hugh, carpenter
Milling, Thomas, draper
Marks, James, grocer & pawnbroker
Mooney, John, publican
Mooney, Edward, Victoria Hotel
Martha, George, shoemaker
Mitchell, John, shoemaker
Mullen, James, saddler
M'Ateer, John, blacksmith
M'Laughlin, Hugh, blacksmith
M'Elhone, Hugh, carpenter
M'Elone, John, carpenter
M'Millan, H. & J., drapers
M'Afee, Rebecca, dressmaker
M'Mullin, Catherine, bonnetmaker
M'Henry, James, grocer and earthenware dealer
M'Clelland, James, grocer and draper
M'Kenna, Patrick, grocer

M'Kenna, Matthew, publican
M'Kinney, Jane, publican
M'Cormick, Patrick, publican
M'Gurk, John, shoemaker
M'Gurk, T. and P., shoemakers
M'Guigan, John, shoemaker
M'Guigan, Charles, tailor
M'Guigan, Neil, tailor
M'Cool, Thomas, provision dealer
M'Rainey, Hugh, provision dealer
M'Clelland, Hugh, baker
M'Eneeny, John, baker
M'Lemon, John, baker
M'Lary, Bernard, saddler
M'Keown, Thomas, watchmaker
M'Eldowney, Patrick, reedmaker
Noon, Robert, provision dealer
O'Neill, Francis, turner
O'Neill, Charles, turner and glazier
O'Rorke, John, shoemaker
Porter, James, nailer
Pettigrew, Ann, publican
Rowan, Henry, builder
Rainey, Sarah, bonnetmaker
Swaney, Patrick, blacksmith
Stewart, James, publican
Shannon, James, sewed muslin agent
Stars, James, dealer in cutlery
Thompson, D. and J., grocers & stationers
Taylor, Thomas, rag and bone store
Wilson, Robert, millwright
Wilson, Wm., sawyer
York, Henry, provision dealer

COUNTY OF MONAGHAN.

MONAGHAN, an inland county in Ulster province. Greatest length, N. and S., 37 miles; greatest breadth, E. and W., 23 miles; comprising an area of 500 square miles, or 319,757 acres, of which 285,885 are arable, 21,585 uncultivated, 5,816 in plantations, 304 in towns, and 6,167 under water. The general surface is hilly, and mountainous in the N.; the highest point of the Slievebeagh range is 1,034 feet above high sea level. The soil is of every variety; that in the more level portion, which forms the N. part of the great central limestone plain of Ireland, is very fertile. The lakes and rivers are numerous, but small; the N. Blackwater, which falls into Lough Neagh, forms a part of the E. boundary. The Ulster Canal passes through the county. The population, in 1841, was 200,442; 191,301 in the rural, and 9,141 in the civic district. According to the Census, of 1851, the total population of the county was 143,410, being a decrease of 57,032. The occupations are almost wholly agricultural. The linen manufacture, however, is reviving. It is wholly in the archdiocese of Armagh. The principal towns are Ballibay, Monaghan, Clones, Castleblayney, and Carrickmacross. It returns two members to Parliament; constituency, in 1851, 4,119. The County Prison is in Monaghan, where the Assizes are held. Quarter Sessions there, and at Castleblayney, Carrickmacross, and Clones. The County Infirmary is in Monaghan; and there are Bridewells at Carrickmacross, Castleblayney, and Clones. The District Lunatic Asylum, to which the county is entitled to send 31 patients, is in Armagh. A Savings' Bank is established at Monaghan. The Union Workhouses are at Carrickmacross, Castleblayney, Clones, and Monaghan; the annual amount of property valued for poor-rate is £260,489; that of property, under the Act of 6 and 7 Wm. IV., cap. 84, £203,347. The county is within the military district of Belfast; and there is a Barrack station at Monaghan, where also the Militia Staff is stationed. The headquarters of the Constabulary, consisting of 208 men, officers included, are at Monaghan; those of the four districts, comprising twenty-four stations, at Castleblayney, Clones, Carrickmacross, and Monaghan. There are Resident Magistrates at Ballibay, and at Kingscourt, Cavan county; and Revenue Police stations at Newbliss and Castleblayney.

COUNTY MONAGHAN.

Lieutenant and Custos Rotulorum, Lord Rossmore, Rossmore Park
Vice-Lieutenant, Lord Cremorne, Dartree, Rockcorry
High-Sheriff, (1852-53,) Capel St. George, Esq., of Dromore, Omagh, County Tyrone
Members for the County—Lieut.-Col. C. P. Leslie, D.L., Glasslough; 48 Berkeley square, London — The Hon. Capt. T. V. Dawson
Assistant Barrister, James Major, Esq., Q.C., 13 Mountjoy square, North, Dublin

DEPUTY LIEUTENANTS.

Anketell, M. J., Anketell Grove, Emyvale
Blayney, Lord, Castleblayney
Bond, E. W., Bondville, Middletown
Brownlow, William
Cole, O. B., Creeve
Coote, T., Branedrum, Monaghan
Cremorne, Lord, V.L., Dartree, Rockcorry
Evatt, S. R. B., Mount Louise, Monaghan
Forster, Sir G., Bart., Coolderry, Carrickmacross
Forster, William, Ballynure
Leslie, Lieut.-Col. C. P., M.P., Glasslough
Lewis, Lieut.-Col. A. G., 10 Fitzwilliam square west, Dublin
Lucas, Edward William, Castleshane
Rowley, Henry, Cordoolough
Shirley, E. P., Loughfea, Carrickmacross
Shirley, E. J., M.P., ditto, and Eatington Park, Warwick
Singleton, Thomas, Fort Singleton
Westenra, Colonel Henry, Camlavale

MAGISTRATES.

Adams, Very Rev. S., Dean of Cashel, Northlands, Kingscourt
Anketell, M. J., D.L., Anketell Grove, Emyvale
Anketell, T., Dungillick, Emyvale
Bashford, J., Donamoine, Carrickmacross
Bellingham, A. O'B., Dunany House, county Louth
Blayney, Lord, D.L., Castleblayney
Bond, E. W., D.L., Bondville, Middletown
Boyle, C., Tannagh, Cootehill
Brady, John, Clones
Cambie, C., Castletown, Borrisokane, Tipperary
Cloncurry, Lord
Coote, T., D.L., Branedrum, Monaghan
Cremorne, Lord, V.L., D.L.
Cunningham, S., Crieve, Ballibay
Evatt, S. R. B., D.L., Mount Louise, Monaghan
Fawcett, J., Drumaconnor, Monaghan
Filgate, W., Lisrenny, Ardee
Forster, Sir G., Bart., D.L.
Forster, Wm., D.L., Ballynure, Clones
Golding, E., Castleblayney
Hamilton, J., Cornacassa, Monaghan
Hatchell, J., Bessmount, Monaghan
Johnstone, J. W., Cassaugh Monne, Aughnacloy
Johnson, J., Thornhill, Monaghan
Kelly, Nicholas, Ballinamore
Kennedy, Henry Alexander
Kenny, W. H., Rocksavage, Carrickmacross
Kernan, J. B., Cabera Lodge, Carrickmacross
Ker, W. A. W., Mount Carmel, Cootehill
Leslie, Lieut.-Col. C. P., M.P., D.L.
Lewis, Lieut.-Col. A. G., D.L.
Lloyd, H., Rossmore Park, Monaghan
Lucas, E. W., D.L., Castleshane, Monaghan
Lucas, Right Hon. E., Castleshane, Monaghan
M'Cullagh, James, Corfadd, Ballibay
M'Cullagh, T., Dunraymond, Ballibay
M'Math, H., Thorn Ford, Castleblayney
M'Watty, James, Castleblayney
Mayne, Richard, Newbliss
Minnett, R. A., Derrygooney, Castleblayney
Moorehead, J., M.D., Anaghmakerry, Newbliss
Moorehead, Samuel, Clones
Morant, G., Shirley House, Carrickmacross
Moutray, J. C., Favor Royal, Aughnacloy
Murray, Andre A., Loughoona

3 E

COUNTY MONAGHAN.

Pendleton, H. L., Trim, co. Meath
Phillips, T., Dumbrain House, Clones
Rawdon, Lieut.-Colonel J. D., M.P.
Reed, J. M., Carrickmacross
Rothwell, T., Chantona, Carrickmacross
Shegog, George, Munilly, Clones
Shirley, E. P., D.L.
Singleton, T., D.L.
Smith, David, Clonowney, Clones
Stopford, Captain T., Newbliss
Thomson, Rev. John
Thompson, R., Scarvagh, Clones
Trench, W. S., Carrickmacross
Wall, C. E., M.D., Clones
Whitsitt, Joseph, Saloo, Monaghan
Resident Magistrate—P. C. Howley, Carrickmacross

COUNTY OFFICERS.

Clerk of the Crown, Thos. D. Bourne, Esq., 17 Harcourt street, Dublin
Clerk of the Peace, Robert Smith, Esq., 10 Mountjoy square, west, Dublin; and Monaghan
Deputy Clerk of the Peace, John Mitchell, Esq., Monaghan
Crown Solicitor at Quarter Sessions, A. Dudgeon, Esq., 86 Talbot street, Dublin; and Sterling Lodge, Clones
Treasurer, Thomas Montgomery, Esq., Monaghan
Secretary to the Grand Jury, John Jackson, Esq., Cremorne
County Surveyor, John Walker, Esq., Monaghan
Coroners, C. Waddell, Esq., Lisnavane, Ballibay, and Hugh Swanzy, Esq., Castleblayney
Head Stamp Distributor, John Lewers, Esq., Diamond, Monaghan

MILITIA STAFF.

Colonel, Lord Rossmore
Lieut.-Col., A. G. Lewis, D.L., Rossmore Park
Major, John Cronin, Bath

CONSTABULARY OFFICERS.

County Inspector, J. J. Saunderson, Esq., Monaghan
Carrickmacross, Thomas R. Barry
Castleblayney, Mark Bloxham
Clones, Robert Fausset
Monaghan, Charles M'Kelvey

COUNTY GAOL, MONAGHAN.

Board of Superintendence meet on the first Monday in every month; Right Hon. E. Lucas, J. Johnson, Lieut.-Colonel A. G. Lewis, H. Mitchell, R. B. Evatt, J. Hamilton, J. Hatchell, E. Golding, J. Jackson, J. Whitsitt, G. Morant, H. Lloyd
Inspector and Chaplain, Rev. Henry Moffatt
Presbyterian Chaplain, Rev. John Bleckley
R.C. Chaplain, Rev. Peter M'Kenna, C.C.
Physician and Surgeon, John S. M'Dowell, M.D.
Apothecary, James G. Lepper
Governor, Thomas L. Mayne

MONAGHAN.

MONAGHAN is a market town (formerly a parliamentary borough) and a parish; the head of a barony, and capital of its county; 60 miles N.N.W. from Dublin, and 43 S.W. by W. from Belfast. The town consists of one principal square, in the centre, called the Diamond (in which is the Linen hall), of another spacious area (in which is the market house), and of three streets diverging from the principal square in a triangular direction. The market days are Monday and Saturday—the first for the usual articles of consumption, the latter for corn. Fairs, the first Monday in every month.

Post Office, Diamond—Thos. Wright, postmaster
Conveyances—To Dublin, by the conveyances to Castleblayney, and thence by railway. To Armagh, at 4 p.m. and at 6 and 11 a.m. To Belfast, at 12-15 p.m. To Clones, at 2 p.m. To Castleblayney, at 11-45 p.m. To Enniskillen, at 12-5 a.m. To Londonderry, at 12-45 a.m. To Newry, at 3 a.m. To Omagh, at 4 p.m.

MONAGHAN. 597

Conveyance by Water—To Belfast, every Tuesday, Thursday, and Saturday morning. To Belturbet, every Tuesday morning. To Clones, every Thursday morning. To Enniskillen, every Friday evening. To Newry, Middleton, Caledon, Charlemont, and Blackwatertown, every Tuesday, Thursday, and Saturday morning

Carriers—To Dublin, Thos. Brannigan and William Hughes, once a week. To Belfast, William Kennedy and Thomas Maguire, every Tuesday

Constabulary Station, Glasslough st.—John James Saunderson, county inspector

Court House, Church square

Excise Office, at the Westenra Arms hotel, Diamond

Stamp Office, Diamond—John Lewis, sub-distributor

County Gaol, Hill street—Governor, John Rowland; matron, Jane Lindsay; local inspector, Rev. H. Moffatt

Union Workhouse, Kilnacloy—Master, John Temple; matron, Rebecca Williams; surgeon, Wm. Temple, M.D. Chaplain, Rev. J. Bleckley, A.M.; schoolmaster, John M'Donnell; mistress, Mary M'Donnell

Infirmary—Registrar, Robert Little; surgeon, Andrew K. Young, M.D.; apothecary, James George Lepper; housekeeper, Sally Little

Fever Hospital—Treasurer, R. G. Warren; surgeon, William Temple, M.D.; apothecary, John L. Robinson; housekeeper, Jane Blair; head nurse, Mary Goodwin

Dispensary, Mill street

Banks—Belfast Banking Company, Dublin street; N. Greer, manager.—Provincial Bank of Ireland, North street; William Slate, manager.—Ulster Banking Company; R. G. Warren, manager.—Savings' Bank, Hill street; Henry Rogers, manager

Loan Fund Office, Dublin street

Parish Church, Church square—Rev. Henry Moffatt

Presbyterian Church, Meetinghouse square—Rev. John Bleckley, A.M.

Wesleyan Methodist Chapel, Market street—ministers various

Primitive Methodist Chapel, New road —ministers various

Roman Catholic Chapel—Rev. Francis Maguire

Bible Society's Depository, Diamond —Richard Robinson, depositary

NOBILITY AND GENTRY.

Anketell, Wm., J.P., Anketell grove
Evatt, James B., J.P., Mount Lewes
Filgate, Fitzherbert, Castleshane
Hamilton, James, J.P., Cornecassa
Hatchell, John, J.P., Bessmount park
Johnston, H. G., Fort-Johnston
Johnston, John, Dublin street
Johnston, John, J.P., Thornhill
Johnston, W. J., Brookvale
Kirk, Lieutenant William, Coolkill
Lewes, A. G., J.P., Ballyleck
Lucas, Edward, J.P., Castleshane
M'Cullagh, Thomas, Dunraymond
Mitchell, Henry, Drumreaske
Mitchell, Richard, Hill street
Mitchell, Samuel, Rosefield
Murray, Andre A., Loughoona
Richardson, Mrs., Poplar vale
Rossmore, Right Hon. Lord, Rossmore park
Slate, William, North street
Waddell, W. C., Lisnavane house
Warren, R. G., Diamond
Whitsitt, Joseph, J.P., Saloo house

CLERGY AND PROFESSIONAL.

Allcock, Rev. A. H., Glasslough st.
Bellew, The Very Rev. Patk., Chapel house
Burnell, Maurice, attorney, notary and registrar for the diocese of Clogher
Bleckley, Rev. John, A.M., Hill st.
Fleming, Alexander, land surveyor, Galena
Hackett, Rev. Cuthbert, Killycorrigan
Jebb, William, proctor, Mill street
Mitchell, John, proctor and deputy clerk of the peace, Hill street
Mitchell, Richard, jun., attorney, Hill street
M'Ally, Rev. Mathew, Corvoam
M'Kenna, Rev. Peter, North street
M'Donnell, Rev. James, North street
Moffatt, Rev. Henry, Park street
Maguire, Rev. Francis, North street
Mooney, Rev. Thomas, The Hill

MONAGHAN.

Morphy, E. P., attorney, Hill st.
M'Dowell, John S., M.D., Townview
M'Dowell, Samuel, M.D., Townview
Murray, Robert, M.D., and county coroner, Beech hill
Nunn, Jeremiah, attorney, Hill street
Rankin, Rev. John, Drumcaw
Robinson, J. L., apothecary, Diamond
Reilly, Thomas, attorney, Hill street
Temple, William, M.D., Hill street
Wright, T. E., attorney, Mill street
Young, Andrew K., M.D., North st.

TRADERS, ETC.

Adams, Francis, woollendraper, Market street
Adams, Francis, miller, Mill street
Brothers, John, blacksmith, Rooskey
Boylan, Bartholemew, cooper, Glasslough street
Beckingham, Charles, publican and leather seller, Park street
Blakely, Richard, haberdasher, Diamond
Blackburn, Edw., publican, Dublin st.
Bond, Richard, publican, Dublin st.
Bell, George, tailor, Dublin street
Baxter, John, watch and clock maker, Market street
Carrol, William, whitesmith, Mill st.
Curry, James, Meeting-house square
Connelly, James, boot and shoemaker, Glasslough street
Cummiskey, Patk., butcher, Dublin st.
Cunningham, Mary, grocer, Park st.
Campbell, E., Stag hotel, Dublin st.
Clarke, Jas., leather seller, Dublin st.
Campbell, Michl., painter and glazier, Market street
Carroll, Catherine, publican, Glasslough street
Corrigan, Mary, publican, Meetinghouse square
Cooper, Mary, bonnet maker, Glasslough street
Donaldson, John, baker, Dublin st.
Duffy, James, boot and shoemaker, High street
Duffy, John, boot and shoemaker, Rooskey
Donaldson, Jas., nailmaker, Rooskey
Duffy, William, nailmaker, Market st.
Duffy, James, painter and glazier, High street
Dailey, Owen, Mill street
Deighan, Peter, publican, Diamond
Fisher, Elizabeth, dyer, Dublin street
Fleming, Francis, grocer, Dublin st.
Fallon, Patrick, draper and tailor, Mill street
Fanning, John, publican, Market st.
Forsythe, S., milliner, Market street
Foster, M. A., milliner, Glasslough st.
Fleming, Francis, chandler, Dublin st.
Graham, Robt., ironmonger, Diamond
Graham, John, flax merchant, Hill st.
Graham, James, nailmaker, New road
Graham, Francis, painter and glazier, Glasslough street
Gromley, James, publican, Dublin st.
Holmes, Mr., agent, Hill street
Hoy, Catherine, baker, Dublin street
Hewitt, John, boot and shoemaker, Glasslough street
Hughes, George, boot and shoemaker, Glasslough street
Hughes, Michael, boot and shoemaker, Glasslough street
Hanlon, James, dyer, Market street
Hallis, M. A., milliner, Glasslough st.
Holmes, John, proprietor of *Northern Standard*, and printer, Mill street
Hollis, Robert, painter and glazier, Glasslough street
Hunt, James, painter and glazier, Market street
Houston, Henry, publican, Dublin st.
Hughes, Margaret, bonnet maker, Glasslough street
Hughes, M. A., bonnet maker, Glasslough street
Irwin, John, publican, Market street
James, Patrick, blacksmith, Glasslough street
Johnston, Thomas, boot and shoemaker, Glasslough street
Jones, John E., cabinetmaker, Mill st.
Jennings, Peter, tailor, Meetinghouse square
Kiernan, Philip, baker, Park street
Kelly, Patrick, baker, Dublin street
King, Alex., baker, Dublin street
Kiernan, Philip, blacksmith, New road
Keenan, Owen, boot and shoemaker, Mill street
Kerr, Thomas, cabinetmaker, Glasslough street
Keiran, Philip, grocer, Park street
Kenna, John, painter and glazier, Glasslough street

MONAGHAN.

Kelly, Thomas, publican, Market st.
Logan, Mary, publican, Glasslough st.
Lepper, J. G., apothecary, Diamond
Lennon, Henry P., grocer, Mill st.
Lewers, John, grocer and ironmonger, Diamond
Little, Robt., woollendraper, Diamond
Lyttle, Susan, milliner, Hill street
Lochead, Jas., nailmaker, Glasslough street
Lennon, H. P., chandler, Mill street
Maguire, Patrick, blacksmith, Park st.
Mahon, Owen, butcher, Dublin street
Murdock, Ann, earthenware dealer, Glasslough street
Milligan, Edward, grocer and leather dealer, Market street
Mitchell, Mr., grocer and leather dealer, Market street
Murdoch, Samuel, grocer and leather dealer, Glasslough street
Murray, John, ironmonger, Church sq.
Moyne, J., woollendraper, Church st.
Maguire, Patrick, nailmaker, Meetinghouse square
Mitchell, Robt., saddler, Glasslough st.
Mitchell, John, publican, Market sq.
Moan, Sarah, publican, Market street
Murphy, Michael, publican, Market st.
Martin, E. and M., bonnetmakers, Park street
Murphy, Mathew, tin worker, Dublin street
M'Carren, John, baker, Dublin street
M'Crudden, Patrick, baker, Market st.
M'Gronan, Patk., baker, Glasslough st.
M'Clelland, John, whitesmith, Meetinghouse square
M'Cormick, John, blacksmith, Glasslough street
M'Entee, Francis, blacksmith, Park st.
M'Entee, Philip, blacksmith, Canal st.
M'Cormack, John, boot & shoemaker, Glasslough street
M'Kenna, John, boot and shoemaker, Glasslough street
M'Keon, John, butcher, Dublin st.
M'Glone, Robert, carpenter & turner, Meetinghouse square
M'Cullough, John Peter, timber and coal dealer, Market street
M'Ginnis, James, flax dresser, Market square
M'Carren, John, grocer, Dublin street
M'Cosker, John, grocer, Dublin street
M'Ginnis, Wm., flax dresser, Market square
M'Cullough, Peter, grocer and ironmonger, Market street
M'Gennis, Wm., grocer & ironmonger, Market street
M'Philips, Peter, excise officer and Westenra arms hotel, Diamond
M'Knight, James, woollendraper, Diamond
M'Quaide, Peter, woollendraper, Church square
M'Phillips, Peter, linen merchant, Diamond
M'Gee, Mary A., milliner, Dublin st.
M'Manus, Eliza, milliner, Dublin st.
M'Ardle, Henry, nailmaker, Glasslough street
M'Donald, Charles, nailmaker, Glasslough street
M'Carren, John, pawnbroker, Meetinghouse square
M'Carren, Andrew, pawnbroker, Dublin street
M'Canna, Catharine, publican, Dublin street
M'Carren, Wm., publican, Meetinghouse square
M'Clelland, John, publican, Meetinghouse square
M'Cullough, Peter, publican, Market st.
M'Enally, Bernard, publican, Market st.
M'Endow, James, publican, Meetinghouse square
M'Ginnis, Wm., publican, Market st.
M'Kenna, Jas., publican, Glasslough street
M'Ardle, Thomas, tailor, Mill street
M'Coy and Peter, tinplate workers, plumbers, and brassfounders, Dublin street
M'Donnell, Randal, tinplate worker, Glasslough street
M'Connell, Wm., wheelwright, Park st.
Owens, Archd., butcher, Dublin st.
O'Hanlon, John, coal dealer, grocer, ironmonger, and timber merchant, Diamond
Owens, Mary, milliner, Market street
Rodgers, Henry, land agent, Hill st.
Richardson, Samuel, baker & grocer, Market street
Robinson, Joseph, bookseller, Diamond
Rodgers, Henry, Life Assurance office, Hill street

Reilly, Daniel, cooper, Park street
Ross, J. A., grocer, ironmonger, leather dealer, & timber merchant, Church square
Robinson, Richard, printer, Diamond
Rush, James, wheelwright, Glasslough street
Slowey, Chas, baker, Market street
Smith, Thomas, baker, Park street
Shaw, Thomas, blacksmith, Rooskey
Stewart, John, carpenter, Glasslough street
Skelton, Richard, gunsmith, Market sq.
Slevin, John, publican and leather seller, Park street
Slowey, Thomas, publican, leather seller, and timber merchant, Meetinghouse square
Sherry, Patrick, saddler and publican, Park street
Sheils, John, publican, Market street
Smyth, Mathew Michael, publican, Dublin street
Soraghan, Felix, publican, Park street
Taggart, Edwd., blacksmith, Park st.
Tighe, John, clothes broker, Dublin st.
Turtle, Isabella, confectioner, Diamond
Turner, Jane, publican, Glasslough st.
Vallely, Ellen, milliner, Market st.
Warren, Mr., brewer, Park street
Woods, John, clothes broker and hosier, Dublin street
Warner, James, earthenware dealer and grocer, Church square
Wright, James, grocer, Glasslough st.
Watson, Wm., haberdasher, Diamond
Wright, Robt., miller, Ballynoda mills
Wilson, William, nailmaker, Market street
Whittle, Robt., pawnbroker, Diamond
Wallace, Samuel, saddler, Market st.
Wilson, Mary, publican, Dublin st.

MONEYMORE.

MONEYMORE is a market town, partly in the parish of Desertlyn, but chiefly in that of Ardtred, barony of Looghinsholin, county of Londonderry; 89 miles N. by W. from Dublin, and 68 W.N.W. from Belfast. The town, and a large tract of the adjacent country, are the property of the Drapers' Company, London, who have greatly improved the town and district. Petty Sessions are held on alternate Tuesdays, and a court for the manor monthly—the latter, which is coextensive, with the whole estates belonging to the company, so often mentioned, comprises 64 townlands. The parish church of Desertlyn, adjoining the town, is a very elegant structure in the Norman style, erected in 1832, at an expense of £6,000, wholly defrayed by the Drapers' Company. The weekly market is held on Friday, and there is a general market or fair on the 21st of each month.

Post Office, High st.—David Ritchie, postmaster
Conveyances—To Coleraine, a mail car (from Dungannon) every morning at 9; goes through Magherafelt, Tubbermore, and Maghera. To Dungannon, a mail car (from Coleraine) every afternoon at 3-20; passes through Cookstown and Stewartstown. Mail cars arrive from Dublin at 9 a.m. and from Coleraine at 4 p.m.
Stamp Office—John Scott, distributor
Northern Banking Company—R. and J. R. Miller, managers
Parish Church—The Hon. and Rev P. Hewitt, rector
Presbyterian Church—Rev. John Barnett, D.D., minister
Presbyterian Church, Coagh—Rev. R. Holmes, minister
Primitive Methodist Chapel—Various ministers
Roman Catholic Chapel
Church Education Society's School
Endowed School—Andrew Harton, teacher
Infants' School—Mary Carmichael, mistress
Infants' School, Coagh—Sarah Taylor, mistress

MONEYMORE.

NOBILITY AND GENTRY.
Aikin, John, Coagh
Bryan, Mrs. Mary Ann, Circular road
Clarke, Miss Mary, Springvale
Conyngham, Wm. L., D.L., Springhill
Conyngham, Lieut.-Col., Springhill
Hamilton, Mrs. Eliza, Coagh
Hewitt, Hon. and Rev. John P., Crossnared
Miller, John R., Moneymore
Miller, Mrs. Mary Ann, Moneymore
Miller, Rowley, J.P., Moneymore
M'Donnell, John, Moneymore
Newton, Mrs. Alicia, Coagh
Patchell, John, R.N., Burboy cottage
Quinn, Michael, Monaghan
Quinn, James, Carndaisey
Smyth, Mrs Frances, Desartlyn cottage
Wright, Mrs. Gertrude, Circular road

CLERGY AND PROFESSIONAL.
Bailie, Rev. Kennedy, D.D., Antred
Blair, Bryce, M.D., Moneymore
Burnett, Rev. J., D.D., Circular road
Carpendale, Rev. M., Tamlaght Glebe
Evans, Rev. Mr., Silver hill
Evans, Rev. John, Ballygonney
Henry, Rev. Jos., curate, Moneymore
Herron, Rev. Thomas, Coagh
Herron, Rev. Thomas, Springbank
Holmes, Rev. John, Coagh
Holmes, Rev. Robert, Fairview
Macool, Rev. Thomas, Ballygrooby
Maxwell, Z., surgeon, Moneymore
O'Brien, Rev. Charles, Loop
Ottersin, Michael, surgeon, Moneymore
Patchell, John, surgeon, R.N., Burboy
Sinclair, Rev. Robert, Rushfield
Quinn, Patrick, P.P., Moneymore
Quinn, James, C.C., Moneymore
Thomson, David, surgeon, Moneymore
Usher, Rev. Henry, Ballinderry

TRADERS, ETC.
Allen, David, Blacksmith
Agnew, Alexander, painter and glazier
Agnew, Lindsay, butcher
Akin, James, grocer, Coagh
Banks, Robert, shoemaker
Boyle, James, corn miller
Bell, Edmund, grocer, Coagh
Brown, Hamilton, reed maker
Caldwell, Wm., woollendraper and haberdasher
Cowden, Alex., shoemaker, Coagh
Campbell, Margaret, grocer
Campbell, Margaret, haberdasher
Duff, Thos., flax spinner, Coagh
Donnelly, Daniel, flax and linen merchant, Cove lodge
Downing, Wm., linen merchant, Coagh
Devlin, John, spirit dealer, Killygonlan
Devlin, Daniel, reed maker, Coagh
Diver, Joseph, clerk of Petty Sessions
Duff, Walter, Conyngham arms, Coagh
Ferguson, Wm., spirit dealer, Coagh
Graham, James, blacksmith
Galway, John, butcher
Ford, William, shoemaker, Coagh
Hamilton, Thomas, grocer, Coagh
Harbison, Wm., grocer
Magee, Daniel, grocer
Magee, Daniel, tailor
Miller, Rowley, agent to the Alliance fire and life insurance company
Mellon, Owen, linen manufacturer, Derrychrin
Mewha, James, spirit dealer
Mulholland, James, butcher
M'Clean, Thomas, boot and shoemaker, Coagh
M'Entire, William, publican, Coagh
M'Corry, Robert, Drapers' arms and livery stables
Pattleton, Richard, grocer
Quin, John, spirit dealer, Ballymurphy
Reid, William, shoemaker
Richey, David, grocer
Richey, Samuel, grocer
Robson, John, spirit dealer
Scott, John, grocer and seed merchant
Scott, John, timber merchant and ironmonger
Scott, John, woollendraper
Sherry, Patrick, shoemaker, Coagh
Simpson, John, grocer
Sterrett, Margaret, dressmaker
Simpson, John, grocer
Sloss, James, grocer, Coagh
Sloan, Thomas, linen manufacturer, Ballydawley
Sloss, James, hardware merchant, Coagh
Story, Duncan, corn mills, Coagh
Simpson, John, hardware dealer
Treanor, C., linen manufacturer, Sessia
Underwood, Walter, forrester to the Drapers' Company
Wilson, Archibald, carpenter

MOY AND CHARLEMONT.

Moy is a small market town, partly in the county of Armagh, but chiefly in the county of Tyrone, 49 miles S.W. from Belfast; situated on the river Blackwater, on the road from Armagh to Coleraine. It was designed, in the year 1764, by the late Earl of Charlemont, the proprietor, after the plan of Marengo, in Italy. Two quays, on the river, were erected by the Charlemont family, with extensive stores; and the Blackwater being navigable from Lough Neagh for lighters of 60 tons burthen, an immediate communication is formed with Belfast and Newry by the Lagan and Newry canals, and with Lough Erne by the Ulster canal. A handsome market place, with courthouse and news-room, was erected by the Earl of Charlemont in 1828. Petty Sessions are held every Monday fortnight, and a court for the Manor of Charlemont in May and November. A constabulary barrack adjoins the market place. In the immediate neighbourhood of the town and of Charlemont are several extensive linen manufacturers. The church is in the early English style, with a handsome square tower, and was built at the cost of £1569. There are places of worship for Presbyterians, Independents, and Wesleyan and Primitive Methodists. The Roman Catholic chapel has a Doric front. On an adjacent hill is Roxborough House, the beautiful residence of Lord Charlemont, originally commenced in 1774, by his uncle, the Hon. Francis Caulfield. The fine plantations, tastefully laid out grounds, and elegant entrance, greatly enhance the general appearance of the town, while a handsome tower to the east is a picturesque feature in its beauty. On the first Friday of every month is held one of the best attended horse fairs in the north of Ireland.

CHARLEMONT, a market and garrison town, and a district parish, in the barony and county of Armagh, divided from Moy by the Blackwater river, over which is a neat stone bridge of five arches, built about 1766. The castle here was built in 1602, by Charles Lord Mountjoy (afterwards Earl of Devonshire), to guard the pass over the Blackwater, and who called it after his own Christian name and title. It was taken by the parliamentary forces under the command of Sir Charles Coote; and on the 13th April, 1664, the castle, town, and fort were sold by William, the first Viscount Charlemont, to Charles II., for £3500. In 1690 the garrison was besieged by Colonel Caillemotte, a French officer (under Marshal Schomberg), from the adjacent height of Legar hill, where the intrenchments are still visible. From that period until 1832, the governorship was held either by the Lords Charlemont, or some old and highly distinguished officer; and in August of that year, the office was abolished, and the lands became vested in the commissioners of woods and forests, and the castle is now the ordnance depot for the north of Ireland. The town is well situated for trade, it participates with Moy in the linen manufacture, and in this branch there are some respectable establishments. A new church was erected in 1833, on ground given by Lord Charlemont; it is a handsome structure, resembling in front one of the grand altars of York Minster. The celebrated and pious John Wesley frequently preached in Charlemont, and occasionally in the fort. The charter conferred the right of holding markets and fairs, but they have fallen into disuse.

Post Office, Charlemont square, Moy—Joseph Patterson, postmaster. Letters from Dublin, the south of Ireland, England, and Scotland, arrive every morning at 4-30, and are despatched every evening at 7-40.

Letters from Coleraine arrive every evening at 7-40, and are despatched every morning at 4-30

Conveyances—To Dublin, the royal mail (from Dungannon) every evening at 7-40, and a car every morning at 8. To Armagh, two cars (from Dungannon) every morning at 7-30. To Dungannon, the royal mail (from Dublin) every morning at 4-30. Two cars (from Armagh) every evening at 8, and a caravan (from Portadown) at the same hour

Conveyance by Canal — The Ulster Canal Steam Carrying Company, Charlemont street, John Richey, manager. Goods forwarded to and from Belfast and Newry, and the following places:—Blackwatertown, Caledon, Charlemont, Clones, Enniskillen, Lisnaskea, Monaghan, Moy, Portadown, Templetate, and Wattlebridge, twice a week

Constabulary Station, Charlemont sq. —James Comsty, head constable

Ordnance Office and Military Station, Charlemont — Gordon Thompson, barrack master and store keeper

Episcopal Church, Moy—Rev. Richard Wrightson, curate

Episcopal Church, Charlemont—Rev. Abraham Nixon, curate

Presbyterian Church—Rev. Thomas Johnston, minister

Independent Chapel, Moy

Primitive Methodist Chapel, Moy— Ministers various

Wesleyan Methodist Chapel, Moy— Ministers various

Roman Catholic Chapel, Moy—Rev. Michael Coyne, P.P.; Rev. James Bracelan, curate

Church Society School, Moy—John Jamieson, master

News-Room, Charlemont square—R. Crothers, M.D., secretary; James Sloan, treasurer

NOBILITY AND GENTRY.

Bond, Walter M., J.P., Argory
Bradley, Major, Charlemont
Charlemont, Right Hon. Earl of, Roxborough
Eyre, John, J.P., Moydown
Greer, Joseph, J.P., Grange house
Goodlatte, D. R., Salem lodge
Greer, Misses, Fort
Harper, Thomas H., Gorestown
Heather, Mrs. Anne
Hore, Walter, J.P., Benburb
Jackson, James E., J.P., Tullydory
Lawson, Mrs. Elizabeth, Charlemont
Lloyd, Jackson, Brookfield
Lloyd, Richard, Tamnamore
M'Clelland, Mrs. Mary
Molesworth, Mrs. Harriet
Olpherts, Wm., J.P., Dartry lodge
Rawlings, Mrs. Frances
Richardson, Jas. G., Trew cottage
Thompson, Gordon, Charlemont
Verner, Lieut. General Sir Wm., M.P., Church hill

CLERGY AND PROFESSIONAL.

Crothers, Robt., M.D., Charlemont sq.
Coyne, Rev. Michael
Davidson, C. C., attorney
Disney, Rev. James, Killyman glebe
Griffen, Rev. Henry, Clonefeacle glebe
Hazelton, Rev. Edward
Johnston, Rev. Thomas
King, James, M.D., Charlemont sq.
Lawson, Jas. A., attorney, Clover hill
Montgomery, Rev. James, Benburb
Nixon, Rev. Abraham
Wrightson, Rev. Richard

TRADERS, ETC.

Alderdice, David, grocer, haberdasher, &c., Charlemont
Barry, Robt., carpenter, Charlemont st.
Best, Jas., hotel keeper, Charlemont sq.
Barry, Robt., grocer, haberdasher and corn merchant, Killyman street
Bennett, Jas., publican, Charlemont
Brown, Joseph, tailor, Dungannon st.
Byrnes, John, tailor, Charlemont st.
Bell, Edwd., publican, Killyman street
Bell, John, watch and clockmaker, Charlemont square
Carson, Alexander, boot & shoemaker, Charlemont
Carson, Robert, boot and shoemaker and letter carrier, Dungannon st.
Conley, Mary Anne, milliner & dressmaker, Charlemont street
Carlisle, Jas., carpenter, Dungannon st.
Clarke, Robert, grocer, linen & woollendraper, Charlemont
Clarke, John, linen manufacturer, Charlemont
Corrigan, Robert, linen manufacturer, Moss spring
Croan, Robert, linen manufacturer, Derryean

MOY AND CHARLEMONT.

Campbell, John, watch & clockmaker, Charlemont street
Dailey, Bernard, baker, Killyman st.
Davidson, Ann, straw bonnet maker, Benburb road
Forrest, Wm., hotel, Charlemont sq.
Gray, G. M., pawnbroker, Charlemont square
Glenn, Wm., clothier, Charlemont st.
Henry, Jas., blacksmith, Charlemont
Hughes, Peter, carpenter, Charlemont
Henderson, Wm., grocer, Charlemont
Hobson, E., & Co., haberdashers and earthenware merchants, Charlemont square
Hobson, Wm., haberdasher & earthenware merchant, Charlemont square
Hunter, Mr., linen manufacturer and merchant, Drumkee
Heather, John, saddler, Charlemont
Hughes, Neill, tailor, Charlemont st.
Hughes, Thos., publican, Charlemont street
Johnston, Margaret, leather seller, linen yarn buyer, ironmonger, grocer, linen and woollendraper, Killyman street
Joyce, Francis W., publican, Charlemont square
Kingsmill, John, blacksmith, Charlemont
Kearney, Patk., publican, Charlemont
Lemon, Henry, publican, Dungannon street
Lowry, Jane, publican, Charlemont sq.
Lutton, Joshua, saddler, Charlemont sq.
Louden, Sarah, publican, Charlemont st.
Moore, Wm., boot and shoemaker, Charlemont
Moreland, Eliza, grocer, Charlemont
Martin, Maria, timber, slate, coal merchant, & shipowner, Charlemont st.
Miles, Elizabeth, publican, Killyman st.
Moore, Wm., publican, Charlemont st.
M'Keown, Wm., corn merchant, Dungannon street
M'Keown, Ellen, milliner and dressmaker, Dungannon street
M'Kell, Samuel, leather seller, baker, and grocer, Charlemont street
M'Kell, Thomas, leather seller, baker and chandler, Dungannon street
M'Mullin, John, blacksmith, Charlemont street
M'Keown, Alex., boot and shoemaker, Charlemont street
M'Neice, Thos., carpenter, Killyman st.
M'Clinton, Samuel, linen yarn buyer, linen and woollendraper, and grocer, Charlemont street
M'Court, Sarah, milliner and dressmaker, Charlemont street
Neely, Margaret, dressmaker, Charlemont street
Nelson, John, blacksmith, Killyman st.
Orr, James, publican, Charlemont
O'Neill, Daniel, wood turner, Killyman street
Patterson, Joseph, baker, grocer, post master, linen yarn and woollendraper, corn merchant, hotel, &c., Charlemont square
Peebles, Nathaniel, boot and shoemaker, Charlemont street
Reid, James, carpenter, Charlemont
Reid, Wm., haberdasher, Charlemont square
Rolston, James, linen manufacturer, Aughinlig
Sheils, John, boot and shoemaker, Dungannon street
Smart, E. & M., & Co., haberdashers, milliners, and dressmakers, Charlemont square
Sloan, James, grocer, linen and woollendraper, ironmonger and ship owner, Charlemont street
Sheppard, John, reedmaker, Charlemont street
Tomney, J., publican, Killyman street
Tomney, Francis, reedmaker, Dungannon street
Tomney, J., reedmaker, Killyman st.
Taylor, George, publican, Charlemont
Warburton, P., publican, Charlemont
Walker, John, publican, Charlemont
Watson, Robert, wood turner, Killyman street
Woods, Susan, publican, Charlemont
Young, Francis, grocer, Charlemont

NEWRY.

NEWRY is an important sea-port, an extensive market town, and parliamentary borough, in Down and Armagh counties, 50 miles N. from Dublin, and 30 from Belfast; comprising, within the parliamentary boundary, 2,543 acres, of which 629 are in the town, and 1,914 in the rural district; population in 1841, of the former portion, 11,972, and of the latter, 1,255; total, 13,227, inhabiting 2,137 houses; average, 6 persons to a house. It is situate near the mouth of the Newry Water, which discharges itself into Carlingford Bay, five miles from the town; there are eight bridges, four of which are stone, and cross the river, which separates the counties of Armagh and Down; the others are drawbridges over the canal.

Newry is a very ancient town, and formerly enjoyed, perhaps, more privileges than any other town in the kingdom—some of them being of a very singular description. In 1175 Maurice M'Loughlin, King of Ireland, founded an abbey here, to which great immunities and endowments were granted, and afterwards confirmed by Hugh de Lacy, Earl of Ulster, in 1237. The abbot exercised episcopal jurisdiction over the lordships of Newry and Mourne, which authority is now enjoyed by the lay proprietor, who, among other privileges, grants marriage licenses, probates of wills, letters of administration, letters of tutelage, and transacts the usual business of an ecclesiastical court, with as plenary and indisputable powers as any other ecclesiastical court in Ireland. He appoints a vicar to discharge the ministerial duties; and as by virtue of his patent he enjoys all episcopal powers, which can be possibly vested in a layman, the vicar is responsible for his conduct to him alone, and is not amenable to either bishop or primate. No writs can be served by the sheriff within the limits of his jurisdiction without his concurrence. The present proprietors are the trustees of the Earl of Kilmorey, who, by virtue of this patent, are entitled to the tithes of the lordship of Newry, and have the right of presentation to the rectory of Mourne. In 1543 the abbey was converted into a collegiate church for secular priests by Henry VIII., but it was totally dissolved by Edward VI., and all its appurtenances granted to Sir Nicholas Bagnal, marshall of Ireland, who converted the abbey into a private residence, built some strong castles, repaired the town, and thus laid the foundation of its subsequent increase. The abbey territory, as it existed at the dissolution, and formed the grant to the marshall, included not only the lordship of Newry, but also the manor of Mourne (or Morne), and it was long enjoyed by the descendants of Sir Nicholas Bagnal, but at length became the joint property of two ladies, the one of whom carried the lordship of Newry to the family of Needham, and the other the manor of Mourne to the ancestor of the Marquis of Anglesey. A celebrated rath, with a large platform formed on its summit, marks the mutual boundaries of the two properties, about a mile from Newry; and it is said to have been erected as a place of single combat between two princes who were competitors for a royal territory. In 1689 the Duke of Berwick, to secure his retreat to Dundalk from the English forces, under the command of the Duke of Schomberg, set fire to Newry, and left it in a very destitute and ruinous condition. The northern entrance of the town is adorned with a chaste and elegant obelisk of chisseled granite, erected in honour of the late, highly respected, and generally lamented Trevor Corry, Esq. The Corry arms, beautifully executed on Portland stone, appear on the north and south recesses, and eulogistic inscriptions on black marble, are executed on the west and east sides of the monument.

The public buildings are, two Protestant Churches, four Presbyterian Churches, three Méthodist Chapels, one Independent Meeting-house, and two Roman Catholic Chapels, a Convent, Court-house, two Bridewells Custom

House, Union Workhouse, National Model School, Hospital, Savings' Bank, and spacious Barracks. The town is handsome and well built of stone, the streets regular and compact, and the shops neatly fitted up, and lighted with gas. Extensive water works have recently been erected. Along the quays are large and well-built warehouses; there are several corn and flour mills, two breweries, ten tan yards, one distillery, three coach and car manufactories, iron and brass foundries, and spade and shovel manufactories. The other manufactures are, linen, yarn, cotton, salt, iron, glass, cordage, &c. The Lordship, extending over 17,054 acres, is an exempt jurisdiction, both ecclesiastical and civil. The Seneschal of the Lord of the Manor holds a Court of Pleas of debt to £60, and a minor Court of Pleas of debt to £3 6s. 8d. Irish. Quarter and Petty Sessions are also held here, as also in Ballybot for a portion of the county Armagh. The paving, lighting, and cleansing of the streets are vested in twenty-one Commissioners, under the Act of 9 Geo. IV., cap. 82; number of houses of the annual value of £5 and under £10, rated at 6d. in the pound, 512; of those of £10 and under £20, rated at 9d., 344; of £20 and upwards, rated at 1s., 458; total value of property rated, £25,917; total amount of annual rate, £1,154. The Fairs are on 24th April and 29th October; and there is a fair on the first Monday, monthly, in that portion of the town in the county of Armagh, called Ballybot; markets on Tuesdays, Thursdays, and Saturdays; all toll free. The Borough returns one member to Parliament; constituency, under 13 and 14 Vic., cap. 69, in 1851, 517. The Bank of Ireland, the Belfast Banking Company, and the Provincial Bank, have branches here. There is also a Savings' Bank, which was established in 1821. The Union Workhouse was opened on 16th December, 1841. There are two constabulary stations, the county Down side belonging to the Rathfriland district, and the Armagh side to Ballybot. "The port of Newry," as stated by the Tidal Harbour Commissioners, in their second report, "lying as it does within Carlingford Lough, at a moderate outlay, might be made a harbour of refuge, which would prove an inestimable boon on this part of the coast." The lough is navigable for six miles by vessels of the greatest burden at all times, and the port admits vessels of 1,000 tons to Warrenpoint, five miles from the town; where the larger vessels remain, but those drawing fifteen feet of water can go up by the ship canal to the Albert basin, Newry. Barges ply by the Newry Canal Navigation to Lough Neagh, thirty-two miles distant inland. The Newry Navigation Company have the management of the port and canal, the latter of which extends along the West side of the river, and is just completed. Steam-boats regularly sail twice a week to Liverpool. The income of the port, in 1850, amounted to £5,000, arising from canal dues, on tonnage—1s. per ton inwards, and 1d. outwards. The Belfast junction railway passes near the town, and thus the communication by railway between Newry and Belfast is complete. The Newry, Warrenpoint, and Rostrevor railway is completed to Warrenpoint. The principal exports are grain, provisions, cattle, eggs, and butter. The number and tonnage of sailing vessels registered as belonging to the port in 1850, was, 103 under 50 tons, and 43 of 50 tons and upwards; their aggregate tonnage 8,965; steamers, two of 603 tons.

Post Office, Hill street—Jas. Wilson, postmaster. Letters from Dublin, the south of Ireland, and England, arrive every night at 11-35, and afternoon at 1-30; and despatched every forenoon at 11-30, and morning at 12-55. Letters from Belfast, the north of Ireland, and Scotland, arrive every forenoon at 11-30, and morning at 12-55; and despatched every night at 11-25, and afternoon at 1-25. Letters from Armagh arrive every morning at 11, and are despatched every afternoon at 2-15. Letters from Down arrive every night at 10-50, and are despatched every morning at 12-35. Letters from Dungannon arrive every night at 11-10, and are despatched every morning at 1-15. Letters from Castleblayney arrive every morning at 9-30, and are despatched every afternoon at 3-15. Letters from Carlingford arrive every night at 9-30, and from Kilkeel at 10-30, and are despatched to both places every morning at 4. Letters from Camlough arrive every evening at 7-20, and are despatched every morning at 7 in Summer, and 7-30 in Winter

Member for the Borough—Edmund Gilling Hallewell, Esq., 6 Royal Crescent, Cheltenham

Consuls—The Netherlands, H. Dalzell; Sweden and Norway, George Guy

Town Commissioners—Jas. Twigge, Richard Liddy, Peter Murphy, Wm. Kirkpatrick, Joseph Loughran, John Moore, Robt. Greer, John Best, Joseph Lupton, James Henderson, Rowan M'Naghten, David Gillis, Robert Stewart, Dr. Savage, Thos. A. Kidd, Henry Murdock. Chairman, Wm. M'Culla

Seneschal of the Manor—J. Boyd, J.P.

County Down Bridewell, Kilmorey street—Thomas Guy, governor

County Armagh (Ballybot) Bridewell —James Craig, governor

Sessions' House, Trevor hill—Isaac Parsons, clerk of Petty Sessions

Constabulary Barracks—County Armagh side, Monaghan street; Down side, Hyde terrace—S. P. Crawford, sub-inspector

Military Barracks, Canal quay—Barrack master, Major M'Queen

Recruiting District and Staff—Nich. Maunsell, district paymaster; Major Sampson, paymaster of out-pensioners; Lieut. Thomas Shields, adjutant; Lieut. Robson, 3d Foot, superintending officer

Customhouse, Merchant Quay—E. N. Brown, collector; E. Watters, comptroller; J. Q. Henry, first clerk; Samuel Ellis, landing waiter; David Blair, port surveyor, Warrenpoint

Stamp Office, Marcus square—James Williams, distributor for the county

Excise Office, Canal street—J. Terry, collector; Thos. Hinds, supervisor; John Warren, clerk; Jas. Quinlan and John Logan, officers

Gas and Water Works, Kilmorey st.— George Seaton, manager

Navigation Office, Needham bridge— W. B. Glenny, secretary

Banks—Bank of Ireland, Trevor hill, Samuel Parsons, agent. Belfast Bank, Trevor hill, William Kinkead, manager. Provincial Bank of Ireland, Hill street, Wm. M'Cullough, manager. Savings' Bank, Sugar Island, Rev. Henry Alexander, secretary, and Robert Medill, actuary

Union Workhouse, Monaghan road— Mr. Bell, master; Mrs. Bell, matron; Michael Smith, clerk. Guardians meet every Saturday

Fever Hospital, Windsor hill—Medical attendant, Dr. Morrison; assistant, Dr. Molloy

St. Mary's Parish Church, Hill st.— Very Rev. D. Bagot, Dean of Dromore, and Vicar-General of Newry and Morne, vicar; Rev. W. R. Williams, curate

St. Patrick's Church, High street— Rev. A. M. Pollock, chaplain

First Presbyterian (Unitarian) Church, High street—Rev. H. Alexander

Second Presbyterian Church, Sandy's street—Rev. John Moran, minister

Third Presbyterian Church, Downshire road—Rev. John Dodd, minister

Covenanters' Meetinghouse, High st. —Rev. Robert Wallace, minister

Independent Chapel, Trevor hill

Wesleyan Chapel, Sandy's street

Primitive Wesleyan Methodist Chapel, Kilmorey street—Rev. A. L. Dobbin

Roman Catholic (St. Patrick's) Cathedral, Hill street—Right Rev. Dr. Michael Blake, bishop; Rev. John O'Neill, parish priest

Convent of St. Clare, High street

Newry School, Hill street—Henry Rihton, master

Newry Academy, Downshire road— Samuel Hall, master

National Model School, Catherine st. —John Brady, master; Misses Gumerson and Fitzgerald, mistresses

NEWRY.

Infant School, High st.—Mrs. Sheffield, mistress
Public News, Reading, and Assembly Rooms, Hill street
Newry Institute, Savings' Bank, Sugar Island—Charles C. Jennings, secretary
Newry Commercial Telegraph—on Tuesday, Thursday, and Saturday, price 4½d.; James Henderson, proprietor; George Henderson, editor
Newry Examiner (printed in Dundalk)—Wednesday and Saturday, 4½d.; Patrick Dowdall, proprietor

PORT OF NEWRY.

The following is a comparative statement of trade for the years 1850 and 1851:—

Receipts.
Year ended 5th Jan. 1851.. £35,107
"   "   1852.. 37,021
                            ———
Increase in 1851....   £1,914

VESSELS, FOREIGN, WITH CARGOES.

	British.	Tonnage.	Foreign.	Ton.
1850..	23	5387	12	2150
1851..	32	6599	41	7146
Inc. 1851	9	1212	29	4996
			9	1212
Total increase 1851..			38	6108

GENTRY, ETC.

Atkins, Mrs. Elizabeth, Canal street
Bailie, Major, Canal street
Bennie, George
Benson, Richard, Fathom
Boyd, John, J.P., seneschal
Boyle, Captain, Trevor hill
Brabazon, W. P., Parkstone lodge
Brady, Dennis C., Bridge street
Brown, E. N., collector of customs
Brown, Mrs., Marcus square
Corbitt, John, Downshire road
C awford, S. P., sub-inspector of constabulary
Campbell, Misses A. and E., Hill street
Carter, Misses Mary and Charlotte, Barrack street
Chambre, Hunt W., J.P., Hawthorn hill
Close, Colonel, Drumbanagher castle
Corry, Isaac, D.L., J.P., Abbey yard
Corry, Isaac W., Ivy lodge
Crozier, Miss Eliza, Canal street
Ellis, John, Crieve
Ellis, Samuel, Bridge street
Fleming, Thomas, Windsor hill
Foxall, Powell, J.P., Killevy castle
Glenny, Mrs. Isaac W., Kilmorey st.
Glenny, Mrs. Joseph, Marcus square
Glenny, Wm. B., Littleton
Gordon, Alexander, Sheepbridge
Gordon, John, Sheepbridge
Greer, Mrs. Mary, Kilmorey street
Gray, George, Eden
Gordon, Mrs. George, Maryvale
Hamilton, Robert, Downshire road
Henderson, James, Hill street
Henderson, George, Emyville
Henry, Thomas H., J.P., Mill street
Heron, Miss Mary, New street
Irvine, Hill, Drumalane
Jefferson, Miss Dorothea, Canal street
Johnston, John, Traymount
Kinkead, William, Trevor hill
Maguire, Dennis, Bridge street
Maunsell, Capt. Nicholas, Trevor hill
Martin, James, Loughorne
Mitchell, Mrs. Allan, Abbey yard
M'Mullan, Mrs., M'Alister's terrace
Maxwell, Mrs. Letitia, Trevor hill
Mollan, Mrs. Elizabeth, New street
Moore, Miss Margaret, Canal street
M'Cullough, Wm., Hill street
Newell, Mrs., Downshire road
O'Farrell, Mrs., Hill street
Ogle, Henry, Ashton
Parsons, Samuel, Trevor hill
Parsons, Wm., J.P., Trevor hill
Parker, Robert, Mountkearney
Peacock, Mrs., 9 Hill street
Quinn, Peter, J.P., Acton house
Robson, Lieutenant
Seaver, Thomas, Heath hall
Seymour, Captain, Hill street
Sampson, Major, Belmont terrace
Speer, Misses, Downshire road
Shields, Adjutant Thomas, Cecil st.
Smith, Lieut., Bridge street
Stevenson, Hugh, New street
Thompson, Miss Jane S., Canal street
Thompson, Wm. N., D.L., J.P., Collector's open
Thompson, Mrs. Ross, Greenwood park
Thompson, Henry, Downshire house
Todd, Mrs. Martha, Windsor hill

Turner, Edward
Twigge, Captain
Waring, Henry, J.P., Trevor hill
Waring, Richard, Trevor hill
White, John, J.P., Divernagh
Wilson, Mrs. Anne, Sugarhouse quay
Williams, James, Hill street
Watters, E., comptroller of customs

CLERGY AND PROFESSIONAL.

Alexander, Rev. Henry, The Manse
Bagot, Very Rev. Daniel, dean of Dromore, &c., Downshire road
Blake, Right Rev. Dr., Violet hill
Black, Thomas H., surgeon and apothecary, Hill street
Browne, R. J., attorney, Needham pl.
Carroll, Rev. John, M'Alister's terrace
Connor, Patrick, physician and apothecary, 39 Hill street
Dodd, Rev. John, Windsor hill
Denvir, M. jun., attorney, Hill street
Davis, Wm. A., surgeon and apothecary, Sugar island
Glenny, Matthew, attorney, Marcus square
Erskine, Archibald, physician, Downshire road
Frazer, Samuel L., attorney, Downshire road and Turner hill
Johnston, Robert, surgeon and apothecary, Kildare street
Magee, Joshua M., attorney and coroner, Hill street
Molloy, Charles, surgeon and apothecary, Upper North street
Moran, Rev. John, Sandy's place
M'Blaine, F. W., barrister-at-law
Morrison, John, physician, Marcus sq.
O'Neill, Rev. John, Hill street
Ogle, Wm. H., attorney, Marcus sq.
Parsons, Isaac, attorney, Hill street
Pollock, Rev. Alexander M., Downshire road
Ribton, Henry, T.C.D., Newry school, Hill street
Reid, Samuel, attorney, Canal street
Savage, Mark, attorney, Hill street
Savage, John, surgeon and apothecary, Hill street
Sharkey, John, attorney, Mall
Starkey, Wm., physician, 85 Hill st.
Taylor, Edward, surgeon, William st.
Todd, Robt. Ross, attorney, Trevor hill
Wallace, Rev. Mr.
Williams, Rev. W. R., Hill street
Waddell, Alexander and Wm., surgeons & apothecaries, Upper North street

TRADERS, ETC.

Arbuthnot & Co., grocers, spirit merchants and seedsmen, 54 Hill street
Anderson, Robt., pawnbroker, High st
Allen, Richard, printer and stationer, Water street
Anderson, John, grocer and spirit dealer, 38 Water street
Aylmer, Patrick, slater and plasterer, 29 Castle street
Acres, P., publican, 65 Castle street
Brannagan, James, butcher, Castle st.
Boyd and Daly, oil and colour merchants, 2 Margaret street
Bennie, John, and Son, iron and brassfounders, Edward street
Barre, W. J., architect, 2 Marcus sq.
Black, James, baker, grocer, and publican, Water street
Blackham, George, watch and clockmaker, 25 Hill street
Byrne, Wm., carpenter and builder, Kilmorey street
Bailie, Samuel, bookseller and binder, 20 Hill street
Butterfield, Mary, publican, Monaghan street
Brown, Wm., publican and grocer, Water street
Best, John, grocer and spirit merchant, Sugar island
Byrne, Wm., publican, Kilmorey st.
Byrne, E., publican, Merchants' quay
Byrne, Bernd., publican, 34 King st.
Byrne, James, publican and grocer, 11 William street
Byrne, James, publican, Edward st.
Byrne, Michael, publican, Lower Water street
Beggs, John and Robt., stone and marble manufacturers, 42 Queen st.
Byrne, Patrick, butter merchant, King street
Bryden, James, cabinet maker, 6 Basin walk
Brown, R., corn dealer, Merchants' quay
Bell, Mrs., haberdasher, &c., 24 Hill st.
Brown and Co., muslin manufacturers, office, Kilmorey street

Bloxham, Mary, publican, 28 Water st.
Boyle, Michael, plumber, Kilmorey st.
Burns, Ann, provision dealer, 8 Market street
Brown, S., slater & plasterer, Chapel st.
Byrne, E., tanner and currier, Boat st.
Campbell, Archd., butcher, Water st.
Clarke, Alex. A., auctioneer, Corn market
Collins, Henry, pawnbroker and chandler, Castle street
Collins, Thos., printer and stationer, 29 Hill street
Campbell, F., publican, 116 Canal st.
Connor, Fras., publican, Bridge street
Cannavan, James, publican and grocer, Sugar island
Cowan, James, grocer and spirit merchant, 39 Water street
Cordner, W. H., watchmaker and jeweller, 46 Hill street
Connolly, Thos., blacksmith, 9 Canal st.
Coulter, Richard, bleacher, Carnmeen
Campbell, Owen, butcher, 30 Market st
Collins, Robert, butcher, 12 Castle st.
Collins, Wm., butcher, Castle street
Crilly, Jas., butcher, 14 Castle street
Crawford, Patk., butcher, 6 Castle st.
Cardwell and Holden, corn merchants, Edward street
Callaghan, Patrick, hairdresser, 50 Mill street
Carvill, F., iron and timber merchant and shipowner, Merchants' quay
Cathcart, Joseph, iron merchant, Upper North street
Conlon, M., leather seller, 41 Mill st.
Cramer, Charles A., music teacher, 40 Kilmorey street
Collins, Arthur, provision dealer, 25 Market street
Connolly, Patrick, slater and plasterer, Shamble yard
Coleman, Bernard, tallow chandler and soap boiler, Castle street
Collins, Michael, tallow chandler, 46 Water street
Cunningham, John, boot & shoemaker, 40 Upper North street
Cunningham, Michael, tanner and currier, Needham place
Donaghy, Thos., boot and shoemaker, 50 Upper North street
Daly & Co., seedsmen, 38 Hill st.
Doyle, John, seedsman, 50 Castle st.
Doyle, Patrick, boot and shoemaker, 60 Hill street
Dempsey, Pat., baker, 17 Sugar island
Darcy, Matthew, wine and spirit merchant, Merchants' quay
Dickson, Henry, wine and spirit merchant, 3 Canal street
Dinsmore, Richardson, bookbinder, Margaret square
Dransfield, J. A., hotel keeper, 37 Hill street
Dalzell, Hugh, merchant, grocer, spirit dealer, salt manufacturer, &c., 8 Sugar island
Daly, Dominic, publican and grocer, Mill street
Daly, Francis, publican, 54 Water st.
Donnelly, Rose, publican, 14 Sugar island
Downey, Richard, publican & grocer, 10 Market street
Doran, Hugh, publican and grocer. Lower North street
Downey, John, grocer, 17 Market st.
Duncan, Wm., haberdasher, 30 Upper North street
Donnelly, Peter, provision dealer, Boat street
Davidson, Wm., ropemaker, 19 Sugar island
Doyle, John, trimming dealer, 2 Upper North street
Denvir, Michael, and Co., woollen-drapers, &c., 52, 53 Hill street
Elliott, James, boot and shoemaker, 15 Upper North street
Edgar, Jos., ropemaker, 47 Water st.
Fairfield, James, boot and shoemaker, Water street
Fleming, John, brazier and tinplate worker, 38 North street
Fletcher, Thomas H., auctioneer and cabinetmaker, 78 Hill street
Fearon, James, hairdresser, 5 Water st.
Flanagan, Edward, publican, Boat st.
Farrell, Alexander, tailor, Mall
Flannigan, John L., cabinet maker, Kilmorey street
Fowler, Joseph, coach builder, William street
Ferguson, Jas., merchant tanner and currier, 38 Merchants' quay
Farmer, Peter, provision dealer, 56 Mill street
Farrell, J., provision dealer, 32 Boat st.

Forrest, Wm., tanner, Downshire road
Finlay, Thomas, 1 Lower North st.
Griffin, George, oil and colour merchant, &c., 21 Sugar island
Guy, George, general merchant, Merchants' quay
Guy, George, jun., spirit dealer, ship broker, and sail maker, Merchants' quay
Grant, Edward, boot and shoemaker, 45 Upper North street
Gass, Robert, wine and spirit mercht., Water street
Glenny, Joseph, pawnbroker, Lower North street
Grandy, Joseph, pawnbroker, Warrenpoint road
Grant, James, baker, 17 Market street
Glenny, I., pawnbroker, 146 High st.
Greer, James, Victoria hotel, Hill st.
Greer, Robert, bookseller, &c., agent for Royal Assurance Fire and Life Assurance Company, Margaret sq.
Graham, John, publican, Hyde terrace
Grant, Eliza, publican, Mill street
Grant, Margaret, publican, Monaghan street
Greacen, George, publican, 22 King st.
Guy, Geo., publican, Lower Mill st.
Griffin, Philip, publican, 2 Queen st.
Grant, Patrick, earthenware dealer, 3 Lower North street
Glenny, Robert, corn and meal merchant, Kildare street
Greer & Co., corn buyers, Merchants' quay
Gillis, David, woollendraper, &c., 40 Hill street
Hill, Edward, boot and shoemaker, 36 Upper North street
Halyday, James, agent for Sun Assurance Company, Hill street
Henderson, James, publisher and printer, *Telegraph* office, agent for the Scottish Amicable Life Assurance Society, and North of Scotland Fire and Life Assurance Company, Hill street
Henderson, John, pawnbroker, Canal street
Henry, Thos., carpenter and builder, 28 Canal street
Henry, Mathew, carpenter & builder, grocer and publican, Kilmorey st.
Hunter, David, publican, 45 Canal st.

Hanratty, James, publican and grocer, King street
Halsall, John, publican and grocer, 3 Queen street
Hawkins, H., haberdasher, North st.
Hopper, John, publican, Canal street
Hunter, Moses, publican, blockmaker, and grocer, Monaghan street
Hancock, R., harness maker and saddler, 27 Hill street
Hancock, William, and Son, wholesale grocers and spirit merchants, agents for Patriotic Assurance Company of Ireland, Sugar Island
Hamilton, Joseph, spirit dealer and grocer, 1 Canal street
Henderson, Wm., spirit dealer and grocer, Lower Mill street
Hughes, Thomas, spirit dealer and grocer, Merchants' quay
Hudson, W., bleacher, Mount Caulfield
Hunter, James, turner & blockmaker, 10 Canal street
Hunter, Eliza, publican, 5 Canal st.
Henning and Co., corn, coal, & butter merchants, Merchants' quay
Harold, Wm., haberdasher, 20 Market street
Halton, Jas., leather seller, 8 Mill st.
Holmes, Nathaniel, provision dealer, 26 Market street
Holywood, John, whitesmith, King st.
Halyday, James T., woollendraper & carpet warehouse, 63 Hill street
Howard and Co., woollendrapers, 22 and 23 Hill street
Henry, William, brewer and maltster, Queen street
Hooks, Michl, haberdasher & cotton manufacturer, 46 Upper North st.
Ivors, David, stationer and bookbinder, 44 Hill street
Irvine, Thomas, grocer and spirit merchant, 30 Hill street
Irvine, James, grocer, &c., 16 Mill st.
Irvine, Wm., grocer and spirit merchant, 53 Water street
Irvine, Robert, grocer and spirit merchant, High street
Jennings, John, wine and spirit merchant, Merchants' quay
Jennings, M. & Son, spirit merchants, 12 Mill street
Jourdan, Mrs., publican and grocer, William street

NEWRY.

Jennings, Charles, coal, iron, and timber merchant, 30 Merchants' quay
Jennings, Andrew, iron merchant, North street
Jamison, S., ropemaker, 26 High st.
Kernahan, Adam, boot and shoemaker, 33 Upper North street
Kidd, Robert, baker, Hill street
Kearney, John, grocer and publican, 1 Castle street
Kirkpatrick, W., haberdasher, Hill st.
Kerr, Patrick, grocer and publican, Lower North street
Keenan, H., tailor, 1 Hill street
Kean, John, cork cutter, 45 Water st.
Kidd, Brothers, corn, meal, flour merchants, millers, and bakers, Mill st.
Kidd, Thomas A., steam-packet agent, Canal quay
Keating. Mary, dyer, Mill street
Kennedy, David, linendraper and haberdasher, 19 Market street
King, Thomas, merchant, Kildare st.
Lucas, Richard, and Son, plumbers, iron & brassfounders, Sugar island
Laing, Thos., pawnbroker, Market sq.
Ledlie, Anna, corn dealer, grocer, and spirit merchant, 4 Canal street
Lowry, James, publican, Castle street
Lawson, Charles, coachbuilder, Hill st.
Lupton, J., corn merchant, Bridge st.
Latimer, James, hairdresser, Hill st.
Liddy, Richard, ironmonger, Upper North street
Loughlin, T., leather seller, 20 Mill st.
Loughran, Joseph, woollendraper, 40 Hill street
Mahood, John, painter and glazier, Margaret street
Madine, John, baker, 38 Castle street
Magennis, Edward A., baker and flour merchant, 8 North street
Murdoch, Henry, grocer, wine, and spirit merchant, 21 Sugar island
Magee, Robert, carpenter and builder, Chapel street
Marron, P., publican and provision dealer, 18 Market street
Marron, Thos., publican and provision dealer, 3 Mill street
Marshall, William, grocer and spirit merchant, High street
Moffet, Esther, publican and grocer, 7 Canal street
Markey, Eliza, publican, Canal st.

Marshall, Thos., grocer and gunpowder merchant, 18 Sugar island
Marshall, John, watch & clockmaker, 1 Sugar island
Magill, Mrs., White Cross hotel, Margaret street
Magennis, D., provision dealer, grocer, and spirit dealer, 8 Canal street
Massy, John, provision dealer and grocer, Monaghan street
Mathers, Francis, 13 Upper North st.
Moore, John, grocer and spirit merchant, 41 Hill street
Murphy, Michl., publican, 28 King st.
Myers, Mr., publican, Canal quay
Markey, Mr., saddler, 54 Water street
Marron, Dennis, stone and marble cutter, Kilmorey street
MacMahon, James, stone and marble cutter, timber and coal merchant, 44 Merchants' quay
Maguire, O., blacksmith, Margaret st.
Mooney, John, blacksmith, 97 Hill st.
Monaghan, Bernard, butcher, Castle st.
Mulholland, Charles, butter merchant, King street
Medill, Robt., grocer, 19 Sugar island
Macdonald, Alexander, herring merchant, Canal quay
Morgan, Mrs., milliner, 45 Hill street
Murphy, Peter, tanner and currier, Marcus square
Maginnis, Edward, engraver and copperplate printer, Hill street
Mackay, Donald, agent for West of England Assurance Co., Newry and Warrenpoint
M'Bride, Misses, boarding and day school, Trevor hill
M'Culla, Mrs., boarding and day school, Kildare street
M'Grath, Wm., whitesmith, 22 Mill st.
M'Grath, James, sheet iron, copper, and tin worker, 44 Canal street
M'Neill, John, watch and clockmaker, Margaret street
M'Guiggan, J. butcher 55 North st.
M'All, John, butcher, 20 North street
M'Mahon, Hugh, grocer, publican, sailmaker, & ship broker, 3 King st.
M'Clelland, Mrs., grocer and seed dealer, 59 Hill street
M'Blain, Robert, and Co., grocers, wine and spirit merchants, and seedsmen, 32 Hill street

NEWRY. 613

M'Cracken, Robt, steam-packet agent, 27 Merchants' quay
M'Donald, Patrick, grocer, spirit dealer, and baker, Canal street
M'Carroll, S. and R., pawnbrokers, Castle street
M'Givern, John, publican, carpenter, and builder, Canal street
M'Kenna, Jas., hairdresser, 5 Mill st.
M'Avoy, D., hairdresser, 2 Water st.
M'Allister, Mr., publican, Lower North street
M'Cann, J., publican, Merchants' quay
M'Culla, Wm., grocer and spirit merchant, 2 Lower North street
M'Kee, Sam., publican, Monaghan st.
M'Cann, T., publican, 13 Water street
M'Cracken, George, grocer and spirit merchant, 2 Canal street
M'Ginnis, Matthew, publican and grocer, 64 Lower North street
M'Naghten, Rowan, wholesale grocer, wine, and spirit merchant, and salt manufacturer, 51 Water street
M'Nally, Anthony, publican and chandler, Hill street
M'Kevitt, B., provision dealer, chandler and publican, 1 Market street
M'Clelland, R., tailor, New buildings, 36 Hill street
M'Alpin, R., mercht. tailor, 71 Hill st.
M'Loughlin, Thomas, tanner and currier, 40 Mill street
M'Grath, Robert, butcher, Margaret street
M'Guiggan, Thos., butcher, 8 Castle street
M'Arevey, John, cabinet maker, 87 Hill street
M'Keown, John, coach builder, 95 Hill street
M'Kenna, Wm., cork cutter, 58 Lower North street
M'Elroy, P., and Co., ironmongers, North street
M'George, James, haberdasher, 4 Lower North street
M'Donald, D. and J., sewed muslin manufacturers, River street
M'Ginnis, Patrick, provision dealer, 27 Market street
M'Minn, Robert, chandler and soap boiler, 22 Sugar island
M'Kenna, James, tanner and currier, 24 Mill street
M'Grath, John, confectioner, 2 Sugar island
M'Alinden, William, confectioner, 11 Hill street
M'Alinden, Henry, confectioner and provision dealer, 17 North street
M'Grath, James, brazier and tinplate worker, Canal street
M'Nally, J. and J. D., publicans, grocers, and bakers, 7 Kildare street
M'Cann, T. & J., bakers, 20 Castle street and Victoria mills
M'Cormick, Mr., tailor, 14 Canal street
Nesbitt, Joseph, butter merchant, 6 Edward street
O'Hair, John, baker, 11 Market street
O'Hare, Owen, publican, Hill street
Osborne, Mrs., confectioner, 56 Hill st.
O'Rorke, Robt., haberdasher, 6 Upper North street
O'Hare, John, wheelwright, Needham street
O'Hagan, John, and Son, woollen-drapers, 13 & 14 Upper North st.
Peatt, Edward, boot and shoemaker, Hill street
Paton, Mrs., confectioner, High street
Pattison, William, brazier and tinplate worker, 1 Margaret street
Polin, Thomas, publican, 16 Castle st.
Postley, Alex., rope and sail maker, Ballybot bridge
Parsons, Wm. and James, corn and flour merchants & millers, 1 Trevor hill and Templegowran mills
Peden, Mary Anne, haberdasher, 43 Hill street
Peacock, Misses, boarding and day school, 9 Hill street
Quigley, Misses, boarding and day school, 80 Hill street
Quinn, Patrick, & Co., bakers, Lower North street
Quin, M. A., publican and grocer, Queen street
Quin and Co., publicans and grocers, Lower North street
Quin, Thomas, publican, Boat street
Quin, Edward, ironmonger, 34 Upper North street
Reside, Henry, painter and glazier, Talbot street
Radcliffe, John, iron & brassfounder, Canal street
Rogan, Mr., publican, 4 Water street

Rogers, Samuel, and Co., bakers, 30 Castle street
Rice, Pat., pawnbroker, 17 Castle st.
Reynolds, James, bookseller and stationer, 5 North street
Rooney, Henry, grocer and publican, 90 Hill street
Rogan, Pat., publican, 29 Water street
Ruddy, Stephen, grocer and publican, 23 Market street
Russell, M. A., publican, Hyde market
Ryan, Anne, grocer and publican, Boat street
Res, Arthur, saddler, 11 Lower Water street
Rice, Mr., saddler, Hill street
Radcliffe, James, tailor, Margaret sq.
Rankin, D., tailor, Sugar island
Reilly, Philip, butcher, Upper North street
Ryan, Michael S., tanner and currier, 60 Kilmorey street
Ryan, Peter, trimming dealer, 7 Upper North street
Scott, Benjamin, publican and grocer, 4 King street
Sturgeon, Wm., publican, 35 Canal st.
Small, John, grocer and publican, Margaret street
Savage, Patrick, tailor, Mall
Savage, Jas., china, glass, and earthenware merchant, 23 Upper North st.
Sinclair, William, corn and meal merchant and miller, Sugar island
Scott, George, wholesale and family grocer and gunpowder merchant, agent for Atlas Assurance Company, New buildings, 35 Hill street
Stewart, James, herring merchant, Merchant's quay
Smith, John, provision dealer, Lower North street
Sturgeon, Wm., wheelwright, Canal st.
Stewart, Robert, woollendraper, 47 Hill street
Small, Matthew, veterinary surgeon, Margaret square
Smith, Michael, clerk to Board of Guardians, Bridge street
Todd, R. R., agent for Scottish Equitable Assurance Co., Trevor hill
Todd, David, and Co., wholesale grocers, agents for Royal Exchange Fire and Life Assurance Company, 118 Canal street
Thompson, J., painter and glazier, 10 Hill street
Thompson, James, grocer, and baker 23 Market street
Thomson, Henry, wine and spirit merchant, Kildare street
Torley, James, boot and shoemaker, Upper North street
Trenor, Patrick, trimming dealer, 29 Market street
Treanor, John, clerk to town commissioners, Canal street
Thompson, John, gunsmith, 25 Lower North street
Williams, James, publican and grocer, Merchants' quay
Wiggins, Thomas, cabinetmaker, Hide market
Wiseman, James, cabinet maker, and servants' registry office, 92 Hill st.
Wallace, H. J., corn and meal merchant, Merchants' quay
Weir, Samuel, whitesmith, 3 Basin walk
Wallace, Henry W., agent for Alliance Fire and Life Assurance Company, Hill street
Williams, James, agent for United Kingdom Fire and Life Assurance Company, Marcus square
Weir, Samuel, painter and glazier, 15 Hill street
Warburton, Henry, boot and shoemaker, 4 Upper North street
Waddell, Miss, confectioner, North street
White, Francis, brazier and tinplate worker, Margaret street
White, Christopher, auctioneer, 4 Mall
West, Mary, baker, 20 Sugar island
Wallace, John H., and Co., wine and spirit merchants, 66 Hill street
Woods, James, wine and spirit merchant, 86 Hill street
Watson, Susan, publican, 1 Kiln st.
Wright, Wm., publican and grocer, 51 Upper North street

NEWTOWNARDS.

NEWTOWNARDS is a market town (formerly a parliamentary borough), in the county of Down, 8 miles east from Belfast, situated near the northern extremity of Lough Strangford, well sheltered on the north and west by contiguous hills. This place has been celebrated from a very early period for the number of religious foundations in its immediate neighbourhood. In 1244, Walter de Burgh, Earl of Ulster, founded a monastery here for Dominican friars, but no vestige of the building now remains. On the north side of the town was the cell of Kiltonga, which has been supposed to have originally given name to the parish; and within five miles were the abbeys of Bangor, Holywood, Moville, Greyabbey, Comber, and the Black Priory. James I., after the forfeiture of the surrounding territory by O'Nial's rebellion, granted lands and the neighbouring monasteries to Sir James Hamilton and Sir Hugh Montgomery, from whom they passed to the Mount-Alexander family, and from them by exchange into that of Londonderry, and the present Marquis is now the proprietor of Newtownards, and a large extent of country round. The town consists of one spacious square, with several wide streets leading from it, and others of inferior note diverging from the principal ones in different directions. In the square, a handsome rectangular area, stands the Townhall, a large and rather elegant structure, in the Grecian-Doric style, erected in 1770, by the first Marquis of Londonderry; it contains an elegant suite of assembly rooms, and other apartments, and beneath is the market offices, shambles, &c. Nearly in the centre of the town stands the lofty and beautiful pedestal of an ancient cross, erected in 1636, ornamented with armorial sculptures, defaced by the rebels in 1653, and restored by the inhabitants in 1666. Mount-Stewart, the magnificent seat of the Marquis of Londonderry, is within three miles of it.

The weaving of muslin employs a large number of the male population, and the embroidering of muslin, for the manufacturers of Belfast and Glasgow, a considerable number of females. About a mile from the town, convenient to the road leading to Bangor, are two extensive lead mines, held on lease from the Marquis by two spirited companies; the ore, which is very rich, is shipped at Bangor, for Flint in North Wales, where it is smelted. There are likewise in the neighbourhood, several prolific quarries, producing stone little inferior to that of Portland. A Manor Court is held before a seneschal appointed by the Marquis of Londonderry, every third Saturday, for the recovery of debts not exceeding £10, and a Court-leet annually, at which various officers are appointed for the manor, and a peace constable for the borough. The General Sessions for the county are held here, and Petty Sessions on the first and third Saturdays in every month, in a very handsome court-house, lately erected at the expense of the county. An ancient church, erected by Sir Hugh Montgomery, was some years ago converted into a court-house by the Marquis, but being insufficient, the new court-house was erected. The Parish church, built in 1817, is an elegant cruciform edifice, with a lofty and finely proportioned spire. The Presbyterian churches, of which there are three, are convenient and neat edifices. The other places of worship are chapels for Unitarians, the Wesleyan and New Connexion of Methodists, a Covenanters' meeting-house, and a Roman Catholic chapel. The principal benevolent institutions are a fever hospital and dispensary, a house of industry, a Union workhouse, and public schools; among the latter is a large one for children of both sexes, supported by the Londonderry family. The market, which is held on Saturday, is abundantly supplied with provisions of all kinds. The annual fairs are held on the 23rd January, 14th May, and 23rd September. The County Down Railway has a station at Newtownards, and trains run daily between it and Belfast.

Post Office, Francis street—S. White, postmistress. Letters from Dublin and Belfast, and from England, arrive every morning at 8-50, and are despatched every afternoon at 4-50. Letters from Donaghadee arrive every morning at 4-30, and are despatched at 9. Letters from Portaferry, and all intermediate places, arrive and are despatched at same hours

Conveyances—Railway trains to Belfast; and to the other towns, mail cars, same hours as the despatch of the mails

Railway Station, foot of Church st.— William Hill, manager

Constabulary Station, Francis street— John Kelly, sub-inspector

Court House, Court street

Stamp Office, High street—Thomas Rogers, sub-distributor

Union Workhouse, off Church st.— John Gordon, master; Miss Quinn, matron; Robert Brown, clerk of Union; John Richie, schoolmaster; Margaret Thompson, schoolmistress; Miss Bowman, head nurse, fever hospital; W. S. Crawford, M.P., chairman of Board of Guardians

Parish Church, Church street—Rev. T. B. Price, incumbent; Rev. Mr. Cuppage, curate

Presbyterian Church, Francis street— Rev. Julius M'Cullough, minister

Presbyterian Church, Mary street— Rev. D. Maxwell, minister

Presbyterian Church, Regent street— Rev. Thomas Watters, minister

Unitarian Meetinghouse, Francis st.— Rev. Hugh Moore, minister

Covenanters' Meetinghouse, Ann st.— Rev. John M'Vickers, minister

Wesleyan Chapel, Regent street—Rev. Mr. Black and Rev. Mr. Howie, ministers

Wesleyan Chapel (New Connexion), Zion place

Roman Catholic Chapel, Ann street— Rev. Wm. M'Lea, parish priest

Erasmus Smith's School, Francis st.— Arthur Bell, master; Miss Bingham, mistress

National School, George's street— Edward Darley, master

National School, East street—Wm. Thompson, master

National School, Mark street—James Charles, master

Academy, West street—Mr. Douglas, master; Miss Olive, mistress

GENTRY, ETC.

Bradshaw, Robert, Milecross lodge
Cassidy, R., seneschal
Dundas, George, Regent street
Dobson, Peter, Derry hall
Evans, Silas, manager of lead mines, Francis street
Kennedy, David, East court
Londonderry, most noble Marquis of, Mount Stewart
Montgomery, Major Fras. O., D.L., J.P., Regent street
Montgomery, Hugh, Rosemount
M'Leroth, Captain
Pirrie, Wm., Conlig
Powell, John K., J.P., High street
Quaile, Capt., Regent street

CLERGY AND PROFESSIONAL.

Black, Rev. Mr., Wesleyan min., High st.
Cuppage, Rev. Mr., curate, Francis st.
Howie, Rev. Mr., Wesleyan minister, Court street
Jamison, David, M.D., Francis street
Johnston, John, M.D., High street
Martin, James, surgeon, High street
M'Vicker, Rev. John, Covenanting minister, Francis street
M'Cullough, Rev. Julius, Presbyterian minister, Church street
M'Lea, Rev. Wm., Ann street
Maxwell, Rev. David, East street
Moore, Rev. Hugh, Church street
Martin, Robt., surgeon, High street
Parr, Mr., Belfast Bank
Price, Rev. Townley B., incumbent, Parsonage
Simpson, Wm., surgeon, R.N., Conway square
Watters, Rev. Thos., High street
Whitlaw, Henry E., surgeon, Francis st.

TRADERS, ETC.

Adams, Wm., grocer, Little Francis st.
Andrews, Jas., cabinetmaker, High st.
Arnott, Alex., grocer and publican, Movilla street
Alexander, Peter, reedmaker, South st.

NEWTOWNARDS.

Anderson, James, baker and confectioner, High street
Alexander, Jane, woollendraper, High street
Alexander, Eleanor, grocer and delf-dealer, Castle place
Brydone, Samuel, lodging house keeper, Francis street
Bashford, Jane, dressmaker, Francis street
Brown, Hugh, grocer, George's street
Bell, Jas., provision dealer, Zion place
Blackstock, James, grocer, Ann street
Bain, James, grocer, North street
Bennett, Wm., baker, North street
Brown, John C., baker, Francis st.
Brown, Robert, clerk to union
Boyd, Robert, spirit dealer, Francis st.
Bennett, Joseph, grocer, Regent st.
Black, Andw., boot and shoemaker, Regent street
Black, S., woollendraper, Conway sq.
Beck, Margaret, grocer, Conway sq.
Boyd, Mary, grocer, Conway square
Boyle, Jane, bonnet maker, Conway square
Baird, Wm., woollendraper, Conway square
Boak, Anne Jane, grocer, Conway sq.
Braine, Mary, publican, Conway sq.
Boyle, Wm., grocer, Greenwell street
Boomer, Robt. and Thos., grocers, druggists, and hardware merchants, High street
Boyle, James, corn merchant, grocer, publican, provision and hardware merchant, Castle place
Brennan, Jeremiah, publican, Mill st.
Bennett, James, grocer, Frederick st.
Bartley, R., grocer, Church street
Brown, John, provision dealer, Church street
Beatty, George, registrar of marriages, Regent street
Collins, John, printer, bookseller and stationer, Francis street
Carr, George, grocer, Little Francis st.
Crawford, Thos., grocer, Francis st.
Conley, James, publican, Francis st.
Cooper, Gawn, delf merchant, grocer, & timber merchant, Regent st.
Caughey, Francis, painter, Regent st.
Cairns, Hugh, grocer, Regent street
Craig, James, watch and clockmaker, Regent street
Campbell, Archibald, carpenter, High street
Campbell, John, woollendraper, High street
Croft, James, baker, Castle place
Crawford, Samuel, publican, Frederick street
Clarke, John, publican, William st.
Campbell, Jane, grocer, West street
Cork, Robert, rope and twine spinner, High street
Dalzell, Andrew, inn keeper, Francis street
Ditty, Wm., grocer, Francis street
Drysdale, Thomas, boot and shoemaker, High street
Dickson, Alexander, seed merchant, High street
Davison, David, shoemaker, Movilla street
Dalzell, Wm., cooper, Movilla street
Davidson, Margaret, milliner, High st.
Davidson, James, chandler, High st.
Dickson, James, boot and shoemaker, Mill street
Dalzell, Robert, cooper, Mill street
Davison, Mrs., milliner & dressmaker, Frederick street
Dobbin, Richard, muslin agent, East street
Dobbin, Wm., muslin agent, East st.
Duggan, Joseph, freestone quarry proprietor, Scrabo
Edgar, Mrs., grocer, William street
Frederick, Margaret, spirit dealer, Francis street
Freeman, Robert, grocer, North street
Finlay, Isaac, corn merchant, publican and grocer, Movilla street and Castle place
Finlay, Wm., publican and leather seller, Greenwell street
Finlay, James, grocer and publican, Court street
Frederick, John, Railway Hotel, Church street
Finlay, Wm., corn merchant, Court st.
Finlay, Samuel, tailor, Greenwell st.
Fleming, Mary A, and Agnes J., embroiderers, East street
Gaw, Wm., inn keeper, Francis street
Gordon, James, tailor, Regent street
Gibson, Wm., hardware dealer, High st.
Gilmore, Patrick, tinsmith and gas-fitter, High street

NEWTOWNARDS.

Grant, Jane, provision dealer, Mill st.
Gilfillan, Thomas, grocer, and muslin agent, West street
Hanna, Hugh, clothes dealer, Francis street
Hayes, Charles, confectioner, Francis street
Henry, Jane, grocer, Little Francis st.
Halliday, Robert, woollendraper, Conway square
Heron, Alex., watchmaker, Mill street
Harrison, Anne, publican, Mill street
Hamilton, Alexander, sewed muslin agent, Little Francis street
Harrison, George, miller, Manor mills and Francis street
Iveston, John, grocer, Little Francis st.
Jackson, Mary, provision dealer, Little Francis street
Johnston, John, grocer, Little Francis street
Jamison, James, woollen and linen draper, Francis street
Johnston, Mary, bonnet maker, Conway square
Jeffrey, James, auctioneer, Conway sq.
Jamison, Wm., deal and timber yard, Castle place
Jelly, Robert, publican, High street
Jones, J., grocer, Church street
Johnston, Sam., muslin agent, East st.
Johnston, John, brewer, Regent st.
Jordan, James, clogger, Little Francis street
Keenan, James, spirit dealer, Regent street
Kennedy, Hugh, woollendraper and haberdasher, Conway square
Kirker, Agnes, grocer, Mill street
Kennedy, Wm. J., grocer and publican, Mill street
Kennedy, Hugh, tailor, Mill street
Kirk, Wm., grocer, Mark street
Lowry, Jane, grocer, Regent street
Long, Letitia, publican, Mill street
Ledgewood, W., boot and shoemaker, Frederick street
Moore, Hugh, delf merchant, Little Francis street
Montgomery, Alexander, blacksmith, Little Francis street
Martin, Dorothea, publican, Zion pl.
Montgomery, George, pawnbroker, Francis street
Magill, James, butcher, Conway sq.
Mayne, Wm., grocer, High street
Montgomery, David, spirit dealer, Francis street
Morrison, James, publican, Regent st.
Murphy, William, hardware dealer, Francis street
Mallon, Mathew, publican, Conway sq.
Murdock, John, cabinet maker, High street
Moore, James, corn merchant, publican and grocer, Movilla street
Muir, John, and Co., gingham manufacturers, Court street
Mena, Elizabeth, grocer and haberdasher, High street
Moore, Andrew, grocer, High street
Moore, John, grocer, High street
Moore, Margaret, milliner and dressmaker, High street
Murphy, Wm., grocer, Mill street
Murray, Wm., publican, Mill street
Moore, John, shoemaker, Mary street
Moore, Wm., cutler, East street
Martin, Alexander, grocer, Church st.
Malone, Edward, publican, Church st.
Munce, Robert, corn merchant, Mill street
M'Donnell, Alex., freestone quarry proprietor, Scrabo.
M'Mahon, Wm., tailor, East street
M'Mahon, James, tailor, West street
M'Kean, David, sewed muslin agent, Little Francis street
M'Vane, John, sewed muslin agent, Francis street
M'Cormick, John, sewed muslin agent, Francis street
M'Cance, Sarah, bonnet maker, Francis street
M'Grattan, David, boot & shoemaker, Little Francis street
M'Jilton, Martha, grocer, George's st.
M'Culla, Elizabeth, grocer, Zion place
M'Whinney, Hugh, grocer, Little Francis street
M'Alpin, Margaret, clothes dealer, Little Francis street
M'William, David, baker, Francis st.
M'Auley, Wm., boot and shoemaker, Francis street
M'Mahon, Wm., blacksmith, North street
M'Bride, Mary, grocer and delf dealer, Regent street
M'Bride, James, grocer, Movilla st.

NEWTOWNARDS.

M'Williams, Wm., grocer and publican, Regent street
M'Loughlin, John, grocer and publican, Regent street
M'Kittrick, John, woollendraper, Conway square
M'Kee, John, spirit dealer and saddler, Conway square and High street
M'Clure, Nessy, spirit dealer, Conway square
M'Bride, Wm. H., boot & shoemaker, High street
M'Cracken, Elizabeth, milliner, High street
M'Cracken, Wm., woollendraper, High street
M'Cully, James, grocer, Movilla st.
M'Ferran, Robert, grocer, Greenwell street
M'Kee, John, publican and corn merchant, Castle place
M'Keown, Francis, and Co., woollendrapers, High street
M'Cutcheon, Andrew, saddler, High st.
M'Ilvenna, James, pawnbroker, High street
M'Cutcheon, Thomas, grocer, Mill st.
M'Donnell, Alexander, grocer, Mill st.
M'Whinney, Kenneth, publican, Frederick street
M'Wha, Jane, provision dealer, Mill street
M'Laughlin, Bernard, grocer, West st.
M'Candless, Andrew, barber, East st.
M'Alpin, James, tailor, Church street
M'Allister, Mr., muslin agent, West st.
Nelson, Charles, pawnbroker, Regent street
Neill, James, car owner, Church st.
Orr, Thomas, publican, George's st.
O'Neill, Edward, grocer, Francis st.
O'Neill, John, grocer, Mill street
Parr, Wm., manager of Belfast bank, Regent street
Patton, James, watch and clockmaker, Francis street
Potter, John, saddler, Francis street
Patterson, Thomas, spirit dealer, Regent street
Platt, David, boot and shoemaker, Conway square
Patterson, Mary, haberdasher and stationer, High street
Patton, Wm., blacksmith and publican, Castle place
Patterson, Alexander, grain merchant, Court street
Patterson, Maria, grocer, High street
Purse, Hans, publican, Castle place
Patton, James, grocer, Frederick st.
Powell, Thomas, provision dealer, William street
Patterson, John, grocer and publican, Mark street
Price, John, corn and butter mercht., Francis street
Rea, James, spirit dealer, Russell pl.
Robinson, Isabella, spirit dealer, Francis street
Rea, John, spirit dealer, Francis st.
Russell, Robert, tailor, Regent street
Russell, Robert, grocer, Conway sq.
Rogers, Thomas, grocer and stamp office, High street
Russell, Samuel, grocer, High street
Robinson, John, grocer and delf merchant, High street
Rea, James, painter & glazier, Mill st.
Stitt, Agnes, bonnet maker, Francis st.
Savage, Isabella, dressmaker, Little Francis street
Stewart, Martha, publican, Zion pl.
Small, David, sewed muslin agent, Francis street
Stewart, Michael and Wm., grocers, Francis street
Simmons, Ezekiel, grocer, North st.
Shaw, James, grocer, North street
Stewart, Robert, spirit dealer, Regent street
Shaw, Wm., publican, Conway square
Simpson, Robt., publican, Castle place
Smith, James, grocer, South street
Saunderson, Wm., hotel keeper, High street and Railway station
Smith, John, grocer, High street
Skilling, Stephen, grocer, Mill street
Scott, Thomas, muslin agent, Greenwell street
Towell, Wm., publican, George's st. and Castle place
Thompson, Hugh, boot & shoemaker, Zion place
Taylor, Nathaniel, publican and corn merchant, Castle place
Tummelty, Wm., publican, Castle pl.
Taylor, John, corn merchant, grocer, and woollendraper, High street
Thompson, John, surveyor, Frederick street

3 G

Vance, Margaret and Jane, haberdashers, High street
Vance, John, muslin manufacturer, High street
Wallace, Joseph, grocer and publican, Francis street
Wallace, John, grocer and corn merchant, High street
Wallace, James, corn merchant, High street
Waugh, Wm., grocer and corn merchant, High street
Waugh, Francis, woollendraper and haberdasher, Francis street
Waugh, Thomas, publican, Francis st.
White, Mrs., grocer, Frederick street
White, James, corn merchant and flour dealer, North street
Wilson, John, boot and shoemaker, Mill street
Wilson, Margaret, sewed muslin agent, Francis street
Worrell, James, miller, Glen mills
Wright, Hugh, grocer, Mark street

PORTADOWN.

PORTADOWN, a market town, in the county of Armagh, 21 miles S.W. by W. from Belfast, eligibly situated on the river Bann, over which is a stone bridge of seven arches. The Newry canal joins the river about a mile above the town, and the latter falls into Lough Neagh at its southern side, and issuing at the opposite side, loses itself in the sea below Coleraine, thus forming, in connection with the canal, a water communication between that place and Newry. This town is a station of the Ulster Railway, which is here joined by the Dublin and Belfast Junction line. The ancient name of this place was *Port-ne-doon*, signifying the " port of the fortified eminence," from a castle of the M'Canns, who occupied this important station, commanding the pass of the river Bann. In the reign of Charles I., Portadown consisted of no more than three or four small houses, and was granted by that monarch, with the estate, to J. P. Obyns, Esq. It now consists of a well-built principal street, and several smaller streets branching from it in various directions. In 1780 a general grain market was established by the late Major Obyns and George Woodhouse, Esq., and of late years the weekly sales of corn have greatly increased. The trade in other agricultural produce, and in pork and cattle, is also great. The manufacture of linen, lawn-cambric, and sheeting is carried on extensively in the town and neighbourhood, and the weaving of cotton goods also affords employment to a considerable number of persons. There are two branch banking establishments. Petty Sessions are held every Saturday. The Parish church of Drumcree, situated about a mile from the town, is a handsome edifice in the early English style, with a tower at the eastern end. A Chapel of Ease, a neat structure, with a square tower, stands in the town; as do also a Presbyterian church, and chapels respectively for Primitive and Wesleyan Methodists. The Roman Catholic Chapel is situated near the Parish Church. The market is held on Saturday, which, besides being a good one for the usual commodities, is likewise for linen and yarn. Fairs, the third Saturday in every month, also on Easter Monday, Whit Monday, and November 12.

Post Office, High street—Richard Edgar, postmaster

GENTRY.

Atkinson, Joseph, J.P., Crowhill, Loughgall
Atkinson, Woolsey, Eden Villa
Boyd, Samuel, Clonnagh
Blacker, Lieut.-Col. William, D.L., J.P., Carrick
Carleton, Cornelius
Druit, Joseph, Corcrain
De Salis, Hon. Peter John, Fane court
Hutchinson, Mrs., Woodside
Henry, James, William street
Little, Wm., sub-inspector constabulary, Woodside
Little, Mr., Devon Lodge
Langtry, William

PORTADOWN.

Miller, William Moore, R.M., Posttown, Loughgall
Nicholson, Joseph, J.P., Crannagill
Nicholson, Rawdon, J.P., Stramore house
Pepper, Richmond, Ballyworkan house
Pepper, George J., Ballyworkan house
Shillington, Thos. A., Tevanagh house
Shillington, John, High street
Trotter, Wm., Drumcree cottage
Woodhouse, John Obins, seneschal
Wakefield, Charles Frederick, Corcrain villa
Wakefield, Thomas C., Moyallen
Waddell, Thomas, Drumcree
Woolsey, Joseph G., Clonnagh house

CLERGY AND PROFESSIONAL.

Annesley, Wm., surgeon, High street
Alexander, Rev. Charles, rector of Drumcree
Annesley, James, M.D.
Bredon, Alexander, M.D., High st.
Best, Rev. Edward, Wesleyan minister
Crawford, Rev. Francis, incumbent
Carleton, Thomas, solicitor, High st.
Crolly, Rev. Eugene, P.P., Drumcree
Carlisle, J. P., Wesleyan minister
Elliott, Rev. L. D., Presbyterian minister, Manse, Edenderry
Hunt, Rev. George, Drumgoon cottage
Leebody, Wm., M.D., Church street
Morrison, Thomas, Bridge street
Massaroon, Rev. Robert, Wesleyan minister
M'Loughlin, P., surgeon, High street
O'Toole, Rev. D., C.C., Drumcree
Proctor, Rev. H. P., curate
Pepper, George J., attorney, High st.
Saurin, Ven. James, archdeacon of Dromore, Seagoe glebe
Searight, James, solicitor, Church st.
Woolesley, Rev. Capel
Woodhouse, John O., solicitor, High street

TRADERS, ETC.

Alexander, John, blacksmith
Armstrong, M., haberdasher, High st.
Annesley, William, grocer, Obins st.
Allen, John, blacksmith, West street
Albion, Alex., carpenter, West street
Adams, Edward, shoemaker, John st.
Bready, George, painter
Bright, David, innkeeper, Bridge st.
Bassier, E., publican, Church street
Barris, Isaac, driver maker, Church st.
Bechan, James, linen manufacturer, Bridge street
Bunting, Eleanor, milliner, Church st.
Brown, Matthew, blacking manufacturer, Woodhouse street
Burns, Daniel, publican, High street
Bulla, Daniel, publican, Church street
Bunting, Jane, milliner, Church st.
Boals, Samuel, shoemaker, Church st.
Boyd, James, publican, Bridge street
Barrett, Walter, carpenter, Woodhouse street
Boyd, Samuel, reedmaker, Obins st.
Burns, John, butcher, Obins street
Bunting, Edward, publican and grocer, West street
Bowman, Richard, shoemaker, West st.
Ballard, Misses, boarding school, &c., Thomas street
Brown, James, shoemaker, John st.
Carleton, Thos. H., manager of Ulster Bank
Cosgrove, John, cooper, Thomas st.
Cox, Mary Anne, milliner, Church st.
Cochran, John, tinsmith, West street
Casey, John, saddler, Woodhouse st.
Carroll, Patrick, baker, High street
Coyle, Edward, publican, and boot and shoemaker, High street
Cullin, Edw., farrier and blacksmith, Thomas street
Cochran, Robert, shoemaker, West st.
Coulter, Mr., clerk, High street
Cowdy, Anthony, boot and shoemaker, High street
Carter, William, delf and glass merchant, Bridge street
Carleton, Cornelius, insurance agent, Bridge street
Carter, John, butcher, Bridge street
Cunningham, Edward, wheelwright, Obins street
Conn, William, publican and grocer, West street
Clarke, James, mechanic, West street
Cunningham, John, loom maker, West street
Chambers, James, linen manufacturer and grocer, Thomas street
Cowdy, Anthony, linen manufacturer, Thomas street
Carroll, William, shoemaker, John st.
Dines, Valentine, butcher

PORTADOWN.

Darragh, R., temple maker, Thomas street
Devlin, Owen, Harp hotel, High st.
Dawson, Wm. J., publican, High st.
Duffy, Bernard, publican, Church st.
Dyer, Mr., manager gas works, Bridge street
Dynes, Henry, tailor, Bridge street
Devlin, John, publican, Woodhouse street
Donnelly, John, publican, Woodhouse street
Downing, Thomas, provision dealer, Woodhouse street
Downing, Mary Jane, bonnet maker, Woodhouse street
Dowie, Robert, shoemaker, John st.
Donnelly, William, teacher, John st.
Edgar, Richard, postmaster, seed merchant, Mandeville Arms, High st.
Fergus, Samuel, nailer and publican, Bridge street
Fowler, Henry, tinsmith, Church st.
Flavell, Wilson, pawnbroker, Church street
Fulton, John, grocer and publican, Church street
Ferguson, David, linen manufacturer, Obins street
Frazer, Thomas, mechanic, Thomas st.
Grew, James, tailor, High street
Grimason, David, tailor, Church st.
Gibson, John, carpenter, William st.
Gibson, John, boot and shoemaker, William street
Greenleigh, Matthew, cart maker and sawyer, John street
Gallagher, Chas., blacksmith, Bridge street
Grew, James, Queen's Arms hotel, High street
Gillespie, John, publican, Church st.
Grey, Thomas, teacher, Church street
Grant, Patrick, publican, Church st.
Gilbert, James, grocer, Castle street
Grimes, Patrick, publican, Woodhouse street
Geatings, Patrick, carpenter, Thomas street
Hollywood, Robert, boot and shoemaker, Obins street
Hollywood, John, boot and shoemaker, Bridge street
Hughes, Edward, butcher, Church st.
Henry, Thomas, baker, Woodhouse st.
Henry, Patrick, publican, High street
Holmes, John, Farmer's inn, High st.
Hennan, Bernard, publican, Bridge st.
Hamilton, Robert, linen manufacturer, Bridge street
Hall, William, publican, Woodhouse street
Hollywood, James, boot and shoemaker, Obins street
Hoy, James, butcher, West street
Hoy, Wm., butcher, West street
Hill, James, carpenter, John street
Irwin, J. & J., linen yarn spinners
Joyce, Wm., woollendraper, High st.
Jelly, Henry, woollendraper, High st.
Johnston, John, builder and pawnbroker, Church street
Jenkinson, Thos., shoemaker, Bridge street
Jelly, Seth, grocer and leather dealer, Castle street
Jennet, Thomas, boot and shoemaker, Woodhouse street
Jennet, James, boot and shoemaker, William street
Kinkead, George, bank, High street
Kernahan, John, boot and shoe warehouse, High street
Kinkead, Joseph, roper, Bridge street
Kilpatrick, James, publican, Woodhouse street
Kelly, Francis, shuttle maker, West st.
Kinney, Edward, wheelwright, West st.
Kennedy, Robt., reed maker, John st.
Logan, John, carpenter, Church street
Lock, George, blacksmith, Woodhouse street
Loughran, Michael, butcher, Church street
Lappin, John, cartmaker, Woodhouse street
Lamb, James, marine store, High st.
Langtry, William, miller and grain merchant
Leany, John, publican, Woodhouse st.
Lavery, Pat., chandler, Woodhouse st.
Leyers, Samuel, delf dealer, Obins st.
Lewis, John, shoemaker, Obins street
Lowland, John, blacking manufacturer, William street
Lappin, John, brick maker, John st.
Laverty, Wm., reed maker, John st.
Macoun, Thomas, grocer, and weavers' warehouse, John street
Mooney, Edward, blacksmith, Obins st.

PORTADOWN.

Morrison, Robert, tailor, Castle street
Mathews, Robert, painter and glazier, Church street
May, Wm., watch and clockmaker, Bridge street
May, David, watch and clockmaker, High street
Mitchell, John, boot and shoemaker, Woodhouse street
Mathews, David, chandler, West st.
Munro, Stewart, grocer, High street
Morgan, John, publican and grocer, High street
Martin, Thomas, publican and grocer, High street
Morrison, Edward, publican and grocer, High street
Morrison, Isaac, publican and grocer, High street
May, Thomas, hardware merchant, High street
May, Ellen, grocer, High street
Mathews, Wm., grocer, High street
Moore, Robert, linen draper, Church street
Madden, James, publican, Church st.
Marley, John J., merchant, Bridge st.
Montgomery, John, merchant, Bridge street
Morrison, Misses, seminary, Bridge st.
Morrison, Robert, tailor, Bridge st.
Montgomery, Hartford, grocer and baker, Woodhouse street
Morrison, Robert, pawnbroker, Woodhouse street
Maginnis, John, sawyer, Woodhouse street
Magee, Robert, sawyer, Obins street
Magee, Robert, blacksmith, Obins st.
Mallagh, John, publican and linen manufacturer, Obins street
Medcalf, John, wheelwright, Obins st.
Mulholland, Michael, butcher, West st.
Matchett, Wm., town sergeant, William street
Murray, Patrick, hairdresser, William street
Magee, James, sawyer, Thomas st.
Mahaffey, James, boot and shoemaker, Thomas street
M'Clelland, Thomas, blacksmith
M'Cullen, Patrick, boot & shoemaker, Woodhouse street
M'Namara, Richard, mason, William street
M'Kinley, James, saddler, Woodhouse street
M'Shane, Charles, nailer, William st.
M'Night, Robert, nailer, West street
M'Cardle, John, slater, Woodhouse st.
M'Gee, Charles, blacksmith, Obins st.
M'Gee, James, sawyer, Thomas street
M'Gee, Robert, sawyer, Obins street
M'Curry, Hugh, butcher, Church st.
M'Fadden, Sarah, milliner, Thomas st.
M'Mannus, Eliza, milliner, High st.
M'Ilveen, Samuel, baker and grocer, High street
M'Connell, James, grocer, Church st.
M'Cutcheon, Hugh, carpenter, Bridge street
M'Gurk, John, shoemaker, Bridge st.
M'Gowan, Robert, grain and spirit merchant, Bridge street
M'Gladdery, John, butcher
M'Caughey, Joseph, tanner
M'Cullough, Samuel, Railway Hotel, Woodhouse street
M'Cann, Owen, publican, Woodhouse street
M'Dowell, Wm., marine store, Obins street
M'Gee, Edward, sawyer, Obins street
M'Convill, Edward, mason, Obins st.
M'Cormick, Charles, merchant, Obins street
M'Eldoon, John, shoemaker, West st.
M'Cusker, John, cooper, Thomas st.
M'Gowan, Mr., tailor, John street
M'Cart, Wm., shoemaker, Thomas st.
M'Logan, John, dealer in foreign clocks, Thomas street
M'Mullan, James, cooper, John street
M'Gregor, John, engineer, John st.
M'Kenna, Terence, butcher, John st.
Nelson, Charles, shuttle maker, High street
Neal, James, shoemaker, Church st.
Neill, Edward, shoemaker, Church st.
Norton, Thomas, tailor, Thomas st.
O'Hanlon, John, sen., mason, West st.
O'Hanlon, John, jun., mason, Castle st.
O'Hanlon, Felix, publican, High st.
O'Hanlon, James, grocery and hardware, High street
Porter, Robert, cooper and publican, Woodhouse street
Potterton, Mr., teacher, High street
Paul, W., & Son, woollen drapers, High street

Pauley, John, linen manufacturer, Bridge street
Porter, Samuel, bricklayer, West st.
Patton, John, gardener, John street
Rooney, Mathew, carpenter & builder, Bridge street
Rooney, James, cooper, Castle street
Rooney, Sarah, milliner, Bridge street
Ruddell, John, linen manufacturer, Bridge street
Robb, Benjamin, grocer
Ruddell, J., spirit store, Castle street
Rooney, James, publican, Castle st.
Renshaw, James, delf and glass warehouse, Woodhouse street
Rice, Bernard, publican, Woodhouse street
Rowland, John, carpenter, Obins st.
Reavy, John, shoemaker, William st.
Rice, John, reed maker, John street
Sitherwood, Wm., watch and clockmaker, West street
Sweney, Jas, whitesmith, Thomas st.
Sweney, Patrick, whitesmith, Thomas street
Shilcock, Hugh, shoemaker, Bridge st.
Saunderson, Henry, painter & glazier, Woodhouse street
Saunderson, Robert, painter & glazier, West street
Stothers, Joseph, carpenter, Church st.
Sheppard, Elizabeth, haberdasher, High street
Shillington, Averel, woollendraper, High street
Stanley, John, grocer, High street
Sinclair, John, grocer, High street
Sinnamon, Thomas W., haberdasher, and publican, High street
Shillington, John, chandler, High st.
Sutton, John, publican, Church street
Stewart, Wm., dealer, Church street
Saunderson, Francis, clothes dealer, Woodhouse street
Stewart, Dawson, grocer, Woodhouse street
Sloan, James, upholsterer, Woodhouse street
Shillington, Thomas A., slate, coal, iron, and timber yard, Woodhouse street
Summerville, John, shoemaker, West street
Smart, Henry, fowl and butter merchant, Thomas street
Sweeney, Patrick, whitesmith, Thomas street
Tedford, George, auctioneer, High st.
Taylor, John, publican, Church street
Totten, Wm., butcher, Church street
Twinem, John, grocer & spirit dealer, Woodhouse street
Totten, Wm., shoemaker, John street
Vaughan, John, coach agent, Bridge street
Vallely, John, blacking manufacturer, Bridge street
Woolsey, John, engineer, Castle street
Wright, Joseph, painter and glazier, Woodhouse street
Wilson, George, printer and stationer, Bridge street
Wilson, Mary Anne, milliner, Church street
Wright, Joseph, cabinetmaker, Woodhouse street
Williamson, Wm., publican, High st.
Waugh, David W., grocer, High street
Wentworth, Catherine, haberdasher, High street
Wilson, Ludovick C., publican, Church street
Wright, James, publican, Church st.
Weir, Hugh, grocer, publican, and leather seller, Church street
Wilson, John F., publican and posting establishment, Church street
Walker, Robert, manager Ulster railway, Bridge street
Watson, John, hotel keeper, Bridge st.
Woodhouse, Wm., publican, Woodhouse street
Wilson, John, publican, Obins street
Wilson, Thomas, brewer, Obins street
Wright, Joseph, pawnbroker, Woodhouse street

RANDALSTOWN.

RANDALSTOWN, a market town (formerly a parliamentary borough), is in the parish of Drummaul, barony of Upper Toome, county of Antrim ; 97 miles N. from Dublin, 17 N.W. by W. from Belfast ; seated on the river Maine, on the roads respectively from Banbridge to Coleraine, and from Belfast to Londonderry, and two miles north from the nearest part of Lough Neagh. The Maine is crossed, at the entrance to the town, by a stone bridge of nine arches, from whence it pursues its course to Lough Neagh, through Shane's Castle Park. This magnificent park (one of the largest in the United Kingdom), where stand the interesting ruins of that once majestic Castle " Edenduffcarrick," for ages the seat of the princely house of O'Neill, is close to the town, and extends from it southwards for upwards of 5 miles through a richly wooded demesne, on " Lough Neagh's Banks," constituting a most attractive feature in the scenery of the neighbourhood, and affording recreation to the inhabitants of the surrounding country, for whose amusement it is kindly thrown open by its noble, indulgent, and hospitable proprietor. The town, in ancient times, was called " Muilleanniarann" (" Iron Mills,") from a mill for smelting iron, which stood at its entrance—the relics of which are still found in the locality ; but Rose O'Neill, sole heiress of the great family estates, having, about the year 1678, married Randal, first Marquis of Antrim, in compliment to her husband, changed it to the much more agreeable name of Randalstown. On the banks of the Maine, adjoining the town, stand the extensive corn, flax, beetling, and linen yarn spinning mills of Patrick Macaulay, Esq., which afford constant employment to 350 persons, both male and female. Charles II. constituted Randalstown a free borough, and gave the inhabitants the privilege of sending two members to the Irish Parliament; but it does not appear that the corporation was ever embodied, and, at the Union, the borough was disfranchised. Petty Sessions are held once in every three weeks, and a manor court once a-month. The Parish Church, a handsome structure, in the Gothic style, is situated in a commanding position close to the town. The rectorial tithes of the parish are lay impropriate, the property of the Marquis of Donegall, who has also the right of presentation —the vicarial tithes (now rent-charge) belong to the vicar, or incumbent. There are also three Presbyterian Churches, a Wesleyan Methodist Chapel, and a Roman Catholic Chapel, a National School, and one established and maintained by the Lord Viscount O'Neill, for the benefit of the children of his Lordship's tenants in the locality. The dispensary for the district, under the Medical Charities Act, is held in the town. There is an extensive weekly market every Wednesday, for grain, butter, meat, poultry, eggs, &c.; and, on the first Wednesday in each month, a great general market. There are two fairs held here in the year, on the 16th of July and 1st of November. The town, under its present noble proprietor, has undergone many changes for the better ; and owing to the large sums of money expended upon it by his Lordship, both in building and fitting up a commodious and elegant hotel, and various improvements, and the liberal encouragement given by him to the people in leases, and other accommodations, in addition to its pleasant site, it now has a handsome and thriving appearance. It contains, according to the census taken in 1851, about 1050 inhabitants.

Post Office—Alex. M'Dowell, postmaster. Letters from Dublin, Belfast, and Antrim, arrive every evening at 8-20, when the mail for Toome-bridge, Castledawson, and Magherafelt is immediately despatched. The mail from the latter places arrives in Randalstown at 4-30, and is despatched for Belfast, Dublin, &c., at 4-40 p.m.

Conveyances—A coach and car from Cookstown, passing through Moneymore, Magherafelt, Castledawson, and Toomebridge, in time for the train at 7-35 a.m. for Belfast, each leaving Randalstown on the arrival of the 4-35 train from Belfast

NOBILITY AND GENTRY.

Alexander, Miss, Shane lodge
Houghton, Captain, Clermont
Kennedy, Lieut.-Col., Hollybrook
Larmour, Robert, Park cottage
Macaulay, Patrick, Neill's brook
Markham, Alexander, county coroner, Duneden lodge
M'Clintock, Henry Stanley, J.P., Mill mount
O'Neill, Right Hon. Lord Viscount, Shane's Castle

CLERGY AND PROFESSIONAL.

Crawford, Rev. Alex., Maine mount
Curoe, Rev. Daniel, P.P.
Denham, Rev. Wm., Craigmore
Hogg, Rev. Robert, LL.D., vicar of Drummaul
Marr, Rev. Robert, Drumminaway
M'Aulay, Rev. N. J., C.C.
M'Kee, James, M.D.
M'Donnell, Michael, surgeon and apothecary
M'Dowell, Alexander, surgeon and apothecary
Neeson, Horace, surgeon
Neeson, Andrew, surgeon
O'Neill, John, surgeon and apothecary
Smythe, Rev. Hugh, Craigmore

TRADERS, ETC.

Adams, Hugh, baker and grocer
Butler, John, haberdasher and draper
Cashell, John, O'Neill Arms Hotel
Craig, J., linen merchant, Craigstown
Crawford, Alexander, grocer, spirit dealer, and ironmonger
Conway, Rose Anne, haberdasher
Corry, James, assistant county surveyor
French, Samuel, baker and grocer
French, Thomas, publican
French, Anne, Publican
Gaine, James, publican
Hart, Charles, grocer & leather cutter
Howard, Whiteside, spirit dealer
Hannan, Mrs., publican
Johnston, Thomas, builder, grocer & provision merchant
Kelly, James, boot and shoemaker
Kerr, Jane, milliner and haberdasher
Laughlin, Alexander, woollendraper
Macaulay, Patrick, mill owner and linen merchant
Moore, Samuel, saddler and harness maker
Moore, Andrew, grocer
M'Cann, Rose, publican
M'Cartney, Wm. John, publican
M'Cleary, John, boot and shoemaker
M'Ewen, Margaret, grocer
M'Aulay, Bernard, inn keeper
Neeson, Peter, painter and glazier and grocer
Nesbitt, Sarah, milliner & haberdasher
O'Kane, John, grocer
Robinson, Edward, grocer, tobacconist, ironmonger, and timber merchant
Swan, Thomas, grocer & weigh master
Swan, Thomas, watch and clockmaker
Scott, John, publican
Scott, Mrs., grocer and earthenware dealer
Stevenson, John, grocer and haberdasher
Wallis, Thomas, railway station master and parish clerk
Wright, Robert, grocer

SAINTFIELD.

SAINTFIELD, or Tonoughnieve, is a small market town, and a parish, in the barony of Upper Castlereagh, county of Down, 78 English miles N.N.E. from Dublin, 9 S.S.E. from Belfast, and 9 N.W. from Downpatrick; situated at the intersection of the roads branching respectively to Belfast, Downpatrick, Ballynahinch, and Comber. Tonoughnieve, the Irish name of the town, means the "Hill of the Saint," or "Saint Hill," translated freely, if not improperly, into Saintfield. On the 9th June, 1798, a brisk skirmish occurred here, between a party of the yeomanry and the insurgents, when the latter obtained the advantage, and the temporary possession of the place. The town is indebted for its present neat appearance, and prosperous condition, to the late Nicholas Price, Esq., the proprietor and lord of the manor, who, in 1802, improved the town in several respects, and erected a market-house and hotel, and gave ground in perpetuity, and £50 of a donation, towards the building of a very handsome school-house. The late seat of this gentleman (now that of his successor, James Price, Esq.), is situated in a beautiful demesne, about a mile north of the town. The weaving of linens, and other fabrics, give employment to a number of persons in the neighbourhood. Petty Sessions are held on alternate Tuesdays, and a Manorial Court every third Saturday. The Parish church is a large, and rather elegant, structure, in the early English style, with a square tower. The Presbyterians have two churches, and the Roman Catholics a chapel. The market is on Monday, and the fairs on the last Wednesday of every month. The parish contained, in 1841, 7,156 inhabitants, including 909 residents in the town; and in the Census of 1851, the town contained 501 males, and 603 females.

Post Office, Main street—J. F. Lowry, postmaster. Letters from Dublin, &c. arrive and are despatched at 6-30 p.m. Letters from Belfast, &c., arrive and are despatched at 5-30 a.m.

Conveyances—To Belfast, a coach, from Bradley's hotel, every morning at 8 and 8-30; and one from Barry's, Main street, at 8-30. To Downpatrick, a coach, from Bradley's hotel, every evening at 5 and 5-30; and one from Barry's at 5-30. A mail car arrives from Dromore at 5-30, and takes passengers to Ballygowan and Comber, by which they can catch the first train to Belfast and Newtownards

Established Church, Main street—
Rev. George Edmonson, vicar
Presbyterian Church, Ballynahinch road—Rev. John Mecredy, minister
Presbyterian Church, Main street—
Rev. Robert M'Ewen, minister
Roman Catholic Chapel, Main street—
Rev. Rowland Magill, P.P.

GENTRY.

Hawkins, Francis, Model farm
Price, Jas., D.L., J.P., Saintfield house
Price, Wm. B., J.P., Tonaghnieve
Price, James C. B., Saintfield house
Walker, Richard, Tullygirvin house
Ward, Francis, The Cottage

CLERGY AND PROFESSIONAL.

Bindon, John V., surgeon of Dispensary, Millview
Edmonson, Rev. George, Glebe house
Gordon, Alex., surgeon and apothecary, Main street
Gordon, William, surgeon and apothecary, Main street
M'Ewen, Rev. Robert, Main street
Mecredy, Rev. John, Lisdalgin
M'Caw, Rev. John, Ravarra
Magill, Rev. Rowland, P.P., Main st.
Reid, Samuel, surgeon and apothecary, New street

TRADERS, ETC.

Bailey, Alex., bailiff for Petty Sessions and Manor Court
Barry, John, hotel keeper, Main street
Bradley, Alex., hotel keeper, Main st.
Bell, James, publican and woollendraper, Main street
Bell, George, grocer, Downpatrick st.
Coyle, George, teacher Church Educational School, Comber road
Clark, Hugh, publican, Main street
Craig, Thomas, publican, Main street
Colhoun, Jane, publican, Main street
Craig, Jane, provision dealer, Main st.
Dick, Eliza, bonnet maker, Main st.
Duff, Samuel, baker, Main street
Dumfy, Bernard, butcher, Market
Gibson, Wm., shoemaker and sewed muslin agent, Main street
Hynds, Arthur, publican, Main street
Holmes, Robert, publican, Main street
Jennings, Henry, woollendraper and haberdasher, Main street
Lowry, J. F., land surveyor, Main st.
Lowry, Jos., teacher National school
Lane, Joseph, publican, Main street

Lowry, Jas., carpenter, Crossgar road
Linas, Wm., grocer and sewed muslin agent
Massey, John, publican, Main street
Murray, Felix, publican, Main street
Murray, Peter, publican, Main street
Murray, Pat., publican, Main street
Munce, Andrew, butcher, Main street
Miller, Adam, saddler, Main street
Miller, Edward, saddler, Main street
Moody, George, woollendraper and haberdasher, Main street
M'Roberts, A., hotel keeper, Main st.
M'Burney, Alex., miller, Killinchy road
M'Dade, Robert, baker and grocer, Main street
Newell, Mr., publican, Main street
Oswald, Andrew, woollendraper and ironmonger, Down street
Priestly, Wm., woollendraper, Down street
Quinn, Isabella, dressmaker, Main st.
Ross, James, civil bill officer
Savage, James, publican, Main street
Stewart, Robert, publican and grocer, Main street
Shaw, Eliza, grocer, Main street
Spratt, Wm., watch and clockmaker, Main street
Thompson, Wm., publican and leather seller, Main street
Thompson, Jas., woollendraper, Main street
Thompson, John, grocer and ironmonger, Main street
White, James, carpenter, Main street
Wilson, Andrew, woollendraper and petty sessions clerk, Main street

COUNTY OF TYRONE.

TYRONE, an inland county in Ulster province. Greatest length N. and S., 46 miles; greatest breadth E. and W., 60 miles; comprising an area of 1,260 square miles, or 806,295 acres, of which 450,286 are arable, 311,867 uncultivated, 11,981 in plantations, 710 in towns, and 31,796 under water. The surface is hilly, rising into mountains in the N. and S., and declining to a level towards Lough Neagh; the soil in the lower districts is fertile, and watered by numerous branches of the Foyle and Blackwater rivers. Coal, fit for domestic purposes, is raised near Lough Neagh, and indication of lead, coal, and iron, are frequent in the hilly districts. The population in 1841 was 312,956; 298,498 in the rural, and 14,458 in the civic district. According to the Census of 1851, the total population of the county was 251,865, being a decrease of 61,091. The manufactures are linens, coarse woollens, blankets, whiskey, beer, flour, meal, and coarse earthenware. It is in Armagh and Derry dioceses, with a small portion in that of Clogher. The principal towns are Strabane, Dungannon, Cookstown, and Omagh. It returns three members to Parliament—two for the county, constituency in 1851, 5,692; and one for Dungannon, constituency 158. The County Prison is at Omagh, where the Assizes are held. Quarter Sessions there, and at Clogher, Dungannon, and Strabane, in each of which towns there is a bridewell. The present District Lunatic Asylum, to which the county is entitled to send 62 patients, is in Londonderry; but there is a new asylum nearly completed at Omagh; and there are fever hospitals at Aughnacloy, Strabane, and Omagh; and 22 dispensaries in the county. Savings' Banks are established in Clogher, Cookstown, Dungannon, and Strabane. The Union Workhouses are at Castlederg, Clogher, Cookstown, Dungannon, Gortin, Omagh, and Strabane. The net annual value of property rated to the poor in the county is £384,299, and the amount of property valued under the Act 6 and 7 Wm. 4, cap. 84, £277,552. The county is within the military district of Belfast, and there is a barrack station at Omagh, and the staff of the County Militia is stationed at Caledon. The head-quarters of the constabulary, consisting of 177 men, officers included, are at Omagh; those of the six districts, comprising 29 stations, at Omagh, Dungannon, Clogher, Cookstown, Fintona, and Strabane.

COUNTY TYRONE.

Lieutenant and Custos Rotulorum—
The Earl of Charlemont, K.St.P., Roxborough Castle, Moy
High-Sheriff (1852-53)—William L. Ogilby, Tirkeenaghan, Donemany
Members for the County—Right Hon. H. T. L. Corry, Castlecoole, county Fermanagh, and 35 Hill st., London.
Lord C. Hamilton, D.L., 19 Eaton square, London
Assistant Barrister—Richard Nunn, Q.C., Upper Fitzwilliam st., Dublin

DEPUTY LIEUTENANTS.

Abercorn, Marquis of, K.G., Baron's Court
Brady, W. S. R., Oaklands, Cookstown
Burgess, J. Y., Parkanour, Dungannon
Castle-Stuart, Earl of, Stuart Hall, Stewartstown
Caulfield, E.H., Drumcairne, Stewartstown
Ferguson, Sir R. A., bart., M.P.
Hamilton, A. W. C., Beltrim
Hamilton, Lord C., M.P.
Lindesay, Frederick, Loughry
Lowry, R. W., Pomeroy House
M'Mahon, Sir B. B., bart., Fecarry Lodge, Mountfield
Moore, R. M., Storm Hill
Moutray, J. C., Favor Royal
Northland, Viscount
Ranfurly, Earl of, Dungannon Park
Sinclair, James, Holly Hill
Staples, Sir T., bart., Q.C., Lissan
Stewart, Sir H., bt., Ballygawley house
Stronge, Sir J. M., bart., Tynan Abbey
Stuart, Hon. A. G., Crevenagh, Omagh
Verner, Wm., Verner's bridge, Moy
Vesey, S., Derrybard House, Fintona

MAGISTRATES.

Abercorn, Marquis of, K.G., D.L.
Anderson, J., Lisnacloon, Castlederg
Archdall, E., jun., Riversdale, E.killen
Archdall, W. H., Riversdale, E.killen
Ashe, W. H., Ashebrook, Londonderry
Boyle, C., Tannagh, Cootehill
Brackenridge, G. C., Ashfield Park, Clogher
Brady, Wm. S. R., D.L.
Brooke, Sir A., bart., Colebrooke, Brookboro'
Browne, T. R., Aughentaine, Fivemiletown
Burgess, J. Y., D.L.
Caledon, Earl of, Caledon Hall
Castle-Stuart, Earl of, D.L.
Caulfield, E. H., D.L.
Cloncurry, Lord
Conyngham,W.L., Spring hill, Moneymore
Cranfield, G. D., Enniskerry
Cranston, J., Cranebrook, Coal island
Crawford, A. W., Lieut.-Col. R.A.
Crossle, J., Anahoe, Ballygawley
D'Arcy, H., Necarn Castle, Lowtherstown
D'Arcy, W. J., Necarn castle, Lowtherstown
Disney, T., 68 Lower Gardiner street, Dublin
Eccles, C., Ecclesville, Fintona
Ellis, F., Fecarry house, Omagh
Evans, R., Gortmerron house, Dungannon
Eyre, John, Benburb
Ferguson, Sir R. A., bart, M.P., D.L.
Galbraith, S., Clanabogan, Omagh
Gardiner, C. J., Corrick lodge, Newtownstewart
Gervais, F. J., Cecil, Augher
Gledstanes, A. U., Fardross, Clogher
Greer, J., The Grange, Moy
Greer, T., Tullylagan, Dungannon
Hamilton, A. W. C., D.L.
Hamilton, Lord Claude, M.P., D.L.
Hannyngton, J. C. D.
Hassard, R., Cookstown
Hill, G., Lislimnahan, Omagh
Holmes, J., Stranabrosny, Dunamanagh
Hore, Walter, Benburb
Houston, Thos., Coneywarren house, Omagh
Humfrey, B. G., Cavanacor, Strabane
Humphreys, John, Strabane
Humphreys, W. D., Milltown house, Strabane
Irvine, Major J., Rockfield, Enniskillen
Irvine, Rev. A., Trillick
Jackson, J. E., Tullydoey, Moy
Knox, A. F., Strabane
Knox, E. C., Desertcrete, Cookstown
Knox, Hon. John J., Northland house
Knox, Hon. William Stuart, M.P., Northland house
Knox, Rev. W., Clonleagh, Strabane
Lendrum, G., Jamestown, Trillick
Lendrum, J., Corkhill lodge, E.killen

Lindesay, F., D.L.
Litton, E. T., Altmore lodge, Dungannon
Londonderry, the Mayor of
Lowry, R. W., D.L.
Lowry, Robert W., jun., Pomeroy house, Dungannon
Lowry, Rev. J., Somerset, Beragh
M'Causland, A., Drumnakelly, Omagh
M'Clintock, Samuel, Seskinore lodge, Fintona
M'Mahon, Sir B. B., bart., D.L.
Magill, S. R., Crieve, Cookstown
Mauleverer, B., Cookstown
Maxwell, R. W., Killyfaddy, Clogher
Miller, J. R., Moneymore
Miller, R., Moneymore
Moore, E., Bawn, Aughnacloy
Moore, R. M., D.L.
Moutray, J. C., D.L.
Moutray, W., Killibrick, Aughnacloy
Northland, Viscount, D.L.
Ogilby, W., Lisclean, Dunamanagh
Patterson, Wm., Gortmore, Fivemiletown
Porter, Rev. J. G., Kilskeery house, Trillick
Prentice, Henry Leslie, Caledon
Ranfurly, Earl of, D.L.
Read, James Montgomery
Richardson, H. M., Rossfad, Enniskillen
Rogers, J., Glennock, Newtownstewart
Sampson, A., Drummona, Ballykelly
Scott, C. R., Straughroy, Omagh
Shaw, W. J. Alexander, Caledon
Spear, J. L., Clonally, Ballygawley
Sproule, E., Spamont, Castlederg
Sproule, T., Bridge hill, Castlederg
Stack, Rev. T., Omagh
Staples, Sir T., bart, D.L.
Stephenson, R., Ard hill, Londonderry
Stewart, M., Martree, Ballygawley
Stewart, Sir Hugh, bart., D.L.
St. George, H. L., Carrickmore, Ballygawley
Stuart, Visc., Stuart hall, Stewartstown
Story, J. H., Derryallen house, Ballinagh
Stronge, J. C., Tynan Abbey
Stronge, Sir J. M., bart., D.L.
Taylor, J. E., Cranbrook, Fivemiletown
Tener, J. K., Moree, Dungannon
Tottenham, Capt., Palace, Clogher
Verner, Lieut.-Col. Sir W., bart., M.P.
Verner, W., D.L.
Vesey, Samuel, D.L.
Waller, E., Lissenderry, Aughnacloy
White, D., Lissonally, Omagh
Willcocks, St. G. L., Coal island
Wray, R., Northland row, Dungannon
Resident Magistrate—R. D. Coulson, Omagh

COUNTY OFFICERS.

Clerk of the Crown—Terence T. Dolan, 47 Dame street, Dublin
Clerk of the Peace—Jn. C. Stronge, Omagh
Crown Solicitor at Quarter Sessions—W. Holmes, Barn hill, Stewartstown, and 18 Upper Dorset street, Dublin
Treasurer—Hon. A. G. Stuart, Crevenagh, Omagh
Secretary to Grand Jury—Burleigh Stuart, Omagh
County Surveyors—A. Gahan and R. Williamson
Coroners—William Orr, Omagh; Jas. Hamilton, M.D., Strabane; H. King, Castlecaulfield; J. Buchanan, Fintona
Head Stamp Distributors—George Buchannan, Omagh; Jos. Rogers, Cookstown

MILITIA ROYAL REGIMENT.

Colonel—The Earl of Caledon
Lieutenant-Col.—J. M. Caulfeild, M.P.
Major—John Irvine
Adjutant—Captain W. Lundie

CONSTABULARY OFFICERS.

County Inspector—H. W. Wray, Mill Bank cottage, Omagh
Clogher—Robert Gore
Cookstown—J. H. Ridge
Dungannon—William H. Matthew
Fintona—James Campbell
Omagh—George A. Molony
Strabane—J. R. Lynch

COUNTY GAOL, OMAGH.

Board of Superintendence meet on the first Thursday in every month: A. W. C. Hamilton, S. Vesey, F. Ellis, J. Anderson, G. Hill, T. Houston, R. Evans, R. Wray, D. White, F. J. Gervais, C. Scott. Inspector—G. A. Rogers. Governor—Alex. Campbell

ADVERTISEMENTS. 1

THE BELFAST NEWS-LETTER,
(ESTABLISHED A.D. 1737,)
THE OLDEST PAPER IN IRELAND,
PUBLISHED EVERY MONDAY, WEDNESDAY, & FRIDAY.
OFFICE, No. 10, BRIDGE STREET, BELFAST.

(FROM MITCHELL'S PRESS DIRECTORY.)

"BELFAST NEWS-LETTER.—Monday, Wednesday, and Friday.—Price of a Single Paper, 4d.

"CONSERVATIVE—Established, September, 1737.

"Circulates in EVERY TOWN in the Counties of Antrim and Down; generally through the other counties in Ulster; and partially in England and Scotland. Is the County Advertiser for Antrim, and one of the County Advertisers for Down.

"Advocates agriculture, commerce, and manufactures; is not a violent partisan, either in religious or political questions, but always anxious to support every measure which tends to the promotion of Christian principles.

"The parent of the Irish Press is the BELFAST NEWS-LETTER, published WITHOUT INTERMISSION since 1737.

"PRINTER AND PUBLISHER—JAMES ALEXANDER HENDERSON."

Terms of Subscription—£2. 10s. 0d. per annum.
ADVERTISING TERMS MODERATE.

THE "NEWS-LETTER" PRINTING OFFICE,

Being furnished with a varied and extensive stock of PLAIN and ORNAMENTAL TYPES, of the most modern character, every kind of LETTER-PRESS PRINTING, EXECUTED WITH RAPIDITY, ELEGANCE AND CORRECTNESS, AND AT MODERATE CHARGES.

The following comprise a few of the articles for the execution of which this Establishment possesses every advantage:—

Bookwork, of every description.	Ticket Books.
Pamphlets.	Check Books of every variety.
Auctioneers' Bills.	Business Cards.
Custom-House Forms.	Address do.
Business Addresses.	Forms for Public Institutions.
Invoice Heads.	Shopkeepers' Delivery Bills.
Receipt Books.	Shop and House Window Bills, &c.

POSTING BILLS of any size, and HANDBILLS, Printed and Posted on the Shortest Notice. ORNAMENTAL PRINTING, in Gold and Fancy Coloured Inks, for Show Bills, Announcements, Labels, &c., in the most approved Styles.

A BIOGRAPHICALM MEMOIR OF THE
LATE JAMES WATSON, ESQ., OF BROOKHILL,
WITH A FULL-LENGTH EQUESTRIAN PORTRAIT.

In medium 12mo, elegantly bound in boards, price Two Shillings and Sixpence

PUBLISHED BY JAMES ALEX. HENDERSON.

For sale at the *News-Letter* Office, 10, Bridge Street, Belfast, and may be ordered from any Bookseller in town or country. Copies will be forwarded, post free, on the receipt of three shillings' worth of postage stamps, sent to the *News-Letter* Office.

JAMES WATT & Co.,
SEED MERCHANTS,
No. 11, DONEGALL STREET,
BELFAST.

THOMAS M'KENNA & CO.,
Linen and Woollen Drapers, Silk Mercers,
HOSIERS, GLOVERS AND HABERDASHERS,
VICTORIA HOUSE,
12, 14, & 16, BRIDGE STREET, BELFAST.

This Establishment is conducted solely on Cash principles. No goods kept but what can be recommended with confidence.

System:—One Price, and all goods marked in plain figures.

UNIVERSAL
FORWARDING AND AGENCY OFFICE.
NORTH OF IRELAND BRANCH,
22, WARING STREET, BELFAST.

GOODS, PARCELS, AND LUGGAGE, FORWARDED DAILY to all parts of the World.

AGENT TO

Messrs. G. W. WHEATLEY & CO. (late WAGHORN & Co.), Oriental and Overland conveyance to India, China, &c.

LONDON—CROUCH'S Universal Parcels' Conveyance, Tudor Street, Blackfriars.

LIVERPOOL—KIMPTON'S Universal Parcels' Conveyance, Royal Bank Buildings, Dale Street.

GLASGOW—Parcels' Delivery Company, 13, Miller Street.

DUBLIN—Parcel Office, 31, Eden Quay.

This is the most extensively connected, cheapest, safest, and most expeditious conveyance of any in the kingdom, having been established in England for many years, and having Agents in all the principal towns.

Rates of carriage, and every information given, by applying, either personally or by letter, to

J. E. RICHARDS, 22, WARING STREET, BELFAST.

N.B.—Every attention paid to the careful Shipping and Forwarding of Goods which is undertaken by Contract (if preferred).

IRELAND & M'NEILL

17 and 19, CORN MARKET,

ARE ALWAYS SUPPLIED WITH AN EXTENSIVE ASSORTMENT of the following and other Goods, purchased in the best Markets, the Patterns and Workmanship of which they can recommend with confidence:—

Gas Chandeliers;
Hall and Lobby Lamps;
Fire-Irons in great variety;
Register, Half-Register, and Common Grates;
Kitchen Ranges;
Hot Air and other Stoves;
London Bronze Tea Urns;
Britannia Metal Tea and Coffee Pots;

Bronze and Berlin Black Fenders;
British Plate Spoons, Forks, &c.;
Patent Tin Dish Covers;
Ivory, Bone, and Horn Handle Knives and Forks;
Pen Knives, Scissors, &c.;
Brushes, in great variety;
Portable Shower and other Baths;
Grocers' Beams, Scales, Canisters, Weights, &c.

IRELAND & M'NEILL have added to the Manufacturing Department of their business that of BRASS FOUNDERS, and have engaged competent Workmen for this branch. They are now ready to receive orders for

BRASS CASTINGS,

Gas and Steam Fittings of Every Description,

WHICH, WITH A GENERAL STOCK OF

House Furnishings, Ironmongery, Copper, Tin, Sheet-Iron, and Brass Goods

Of their own Manufacture, they are enabled to offer on reasonable terms.

THEY ARE WELL SUPPLIED WITH

Iron, Copper, and Brass Tubing, Sheet Copper, Sheet Brass, and Sheet Zinc, Block Tin, Bolt Copper, Spelter, Metal Piping, Eave Spouting, &c., &c.

WALKER'S PATENT STOVES, FOR CHURCHES & HALLS.

Church Gas-Fittings of every Description.

Gas-Fitting and Bell-Hanging by Careful Workmen.

WHOLESALE & RETAIL BRUSH, COMB, TRUNK & PORTMANTEAU MANUFACTORY, 24 BRIDGE ST. BELFAST. JOHN KELLY.

B EGS TO INFORM HIS FRIENDS AND THE PUBLIC THAT HE IS WELL ASSORTED WITH A Large Stock of the following Goods, in their different varieties and best qualities, which he is selling much Cheaper than any other House in the Trade:—

Hair Brushes in White, Black, and Unbleached Hair, of a superior make.
Clothes and Hat Brushes.
Tooth and Nail Brushes.
Shoe and Black Lead Brushes.
Whitewash and Paint Brushes.
Sweeping, Hearth, and Banister do.
Horse, Spoke, Plate, and Crumb do.
Carpet Whisks, Sponges, Chamois.
Marrow Oil and Perfumery.

TRUNKS.
Black Leather Trunks.
Calfskin Hair Trunks.
Ladies' Dress and Bonnet Boxes.
Solid Leather Portmanteaus.
Solid Leather Coat Cases.
Solid Leather Hat Cases.
Brussels Carpet Bags.
Venetian Carpet Bags.
Patent Leather Bags.

COMBS.
French and German Side-combs.
Tortoise-shell Side-combs.
Back Combs.
Dressing Combs.
Pocket Combs.
Fine-tooth Combs.
Comb Cleaners.
Cleaver's Honey Soap.
Windsor Soap.

PLEASE OBSERVE—THE TRUNK AND PORTMANTEAU DEPOT,

24, BRIDGE STREET, BELFAST.

IMPERIAL LIFE INSURANCE COMPANY.

1, OLD BROAD STREET, LONDON.

Directors:

*Charles Cave, Esq., Chairman.
Thomas Newman Hunt, Esq., Deputy-Chairman.

James C. C. Bell, Esq.	*Daniel Mildred, Esq.
*Chas. Francis Cobb, Esq.	*J. Gordon Murdoch, Esq.
*Andrew Colvile, Esq.	Henry Pearse, Esq.
Henry Davidson, Esq.	Henry J. Prescott, Esq.
George Field, Esq.	Joseph Reid, Esq.
*George Hibbert, Esq.	Martin T. Smith, Esq., M.P.
Samuel Hibbert, Esq.	Newman Smith, Esq.

A NEW SCALE OF PREMIUMS ON INSURANCES FOR THE whole term of life has recently been adopted, by which a material reduction has been made at all ages below 50 years.

FOUR-FIFTHS, or 80 per cent. of the Profits, are assigned to Policies *every fifth year;* and may be applied to increase the sum insured; to an immediate payment in Cash; or to the reduction and ultimate extinction of future Premiums.

The following will show the effect of the Bonus on Policies of 30 years' duration, on the 31st of January, 1851.

Age when Insured.	Sum Insured.	Annual Premium.	Addition to Sum payable at death.	Value of Addition in Cash.	Or Premium extinguished & Cash Paid.
	£	£ s. d.	£	£	£
21	1000	22 5 0	560	276	5
26	2000	49 1 8	1120	617	93
31	3000	81 17 6	1680	1027	282
36	4000	122 13 4	2240	1505	582
41	5000	174 7 6	2800	2043	992

ONE-THIRD of the Premium on Insurances of £500 and upwards, for the whole term of life, may remain as a debt upon the Policy, to be paid off at convenience; by which means £1,500 may be insured for the present outlay otherwise required for £1,000.

LOANS.—The Directors will lend Sums of £50, and upwards, on the security of Policies effected with this Company for the whole term of life, when they have acquired an adequate value.

SECURITY.—Those who effect insurances with this Company are protected by its Large Subscribed Capital from the risk incurred by Members of Mutual Societies.

INSURANCES, without participation in profits, may be effected at reduced rates.

SAMUEL INGALL, *Actuary.*

AGENT FOR BELFAST,

JOHN PIM, 20, Waring Street.

JOHN PIM is also Agent for the Imperial Fire Insurance Company of London.

SCOTTISH AMICABLE
LIFE ASSURANCE SOCIETY.

INCORPORATED BY ACT OF PARLIAMENT.

Head Office, 141, BUCHANAN-STREET, GLASGOW.
Office in Belfast, 42, WARING STREET.

OFFICE BEARERS.
PRESIDENT—THE MARQUIS OF DALHOUSIE.
VICE-PRESIDENTS—JOHN C. COLQUHOUN, Esq., of Killermont;
The DUKE OF BUCCLEUGH; The DUKE OF ATHOL.
MANAGER—WILLIAM SPENS, Esq.

BOARD FOR ULSTER.
Rev. Dr. MORGAN, Chairman.

WILLIAM VALENTINE, Esq.	A. B. FILSON, Esq., M.D., Portaferry.
JAMES SHAW, Esq.	W. LANGTRY, Esq., Portadown.
JAMES CAMPBELL, Esq.	Rev. H. J. DOBBIN, D.D., Ballymena.
JAMES A. HENDERSON, Esq.	

The Office-bearers are all insured in the Society.

THE liberal arrangements of this Society, and the large additions made to the sums assured, secure to the holders of its policies the utmost benefits of Life Assurance.

Additions were declared at last septennial investigation, as at 31st December, 1846, at the rate of Two per cent. per annum upon the amount of the policies and previous additions.

AGENTS.

Lisburn	Robert Stewart, jun., Esq.
Lurgan	James Anderson, Esq.
Portadown	C. Carlton, Esq.
Armagh	James Gardner, Esq.
Monaghan	J. G. Lewers, Esq.
Enniskillen	John Lemon, Esq.
Castleblayney	John Sheil, Esq.
Newry	J. Henderson, Esq.
Antrim	Henry C. Scott, Esq.
Ballymena	R. Brown, jun., Esq.
Coleraine	John Horner, Esq.
Londonderry	Thomas Stevenson, Esq.
Strabane	G. Gordon, Esq.
Omagh	William Elliott, Esq.
Cookstown	William Morgan, Esq.
Moy	William Glenn, Esq.
Saintfield	A. Wilson, Esq.
Banbridge	William Smyth, Esq.
Downpatrick	Sydney H. Rowan, Esq.
Newtownards	J. Jamieson, Esq.
Portaferry	John Lawson, Esq.
Dundalk	R. O. Blackader, Esq.

Forms of proposal, and every information, may be obtained from any of the Agents, or from

WILLIAM D. HENDERSON,
Secretary to the Board for Ulster.

ADVERTISEMENTS.

THE
NORTHERN ASSURANCE COMPANY.

INCORPORATED BY ACT OF PARLIAMENT.
Instituted 1836.

CAPITAL, ONE MILLION STERLING.

Head Offices.

ABERDEEN, 3, King Street.	GLASGOW, 19, St. Vincent Place.
EDINBURGH, 20, St. Andrew Sq.	LONDON, 1, Moorgate Street.

Office for Ulster, 42, Waring Street, Belfast.

THIS INSTITUTION WAS ESTABLISHED IN 1836, SINCE which period its business has been extensively prosecuted throughout Scotland, England, and Ireland, with marked success.

Fire Department.

The Company insures Dwelling-houses, Rents, Furniture, Goods, and Merchandise; Farming Stock (live or dead), Shipping, in Port or in Dock, and while Building or Repairing, and other property, from loss or damage by Fire; and losses by Fire from lightning are made good.

The rates of Annual Premiums on the three Ordinary Classes of Insurance—

Common, ...1s. 6d. to 2s. per cent.	Doubly Hazardous, 4s. 6d. to 5s. per cent.
Hazardous, 2s. 6d. to 3s. ,,	(Except in Special Cases.)

The rates for all Insurances, not coming under the above heads, are fixed by special agreement.

FARMING STOCK Insured at *Four Shillings* per cent., without the average clause, and *free of Government duty*.

Life Department.

Life Assurances effected, and Annuities (present or deferred) sold.

The number of Life Policies issued exceeds THREE THOUSAND SEVEN HUNDRED, covering Assurances to the extent of One Million and a-Half Sterling.

Prospectuses, and all information, furnished at the Head Offices and Agencies.

Agencies in the North of Ireland.

Antrim, Henry C. Scott, Esq.	*L.derry*, Messrs. Jas. Corscaden & Co
Armagh, James Gardner, Esq.	*Lurgan*, James Anderson, Esq.
Ballymena, James Greer, Esq.	*Monaghan*, J. G. Lewers, Esq.
Banbridge, William Smith, Esq.	*Moy*, William Glenn, Esq.
Castleblayney, John Sheil, Esq.	*Newry*, J. Henderson, Esq.
Coleraine, H. B. Mackay, Esq.	*Newtownards*, J. Jamieson, Esq.
Cookstown, William Morgan, Esq.	*Omagh*, William Elliot, Esq.
Downpatrick, Hugh Wallace, Esq.	*Portadown*, C. Carlton, Esq.
Dundalk, R. O. Blackader, Esq.	*Portaferry*, John Lawson, Esq.
Enniskillen, John Lemon, Esq.	*Saintfield*, A. Wilson, Esq.
Lisburn, Robert Stewart, jun., Esq.	*Strabane*, G. Gordon, Esq.

W. D. HENDERSON, Esq., Belfast,
Superintendent for Ulster.

WM. CHALMERS, General Manager.
H. AMBROSE SMITH, Secretary.

EDWARD GILBERT,

Watchmaker, Jeweller, and Silversmith,

43, HIGH STREET,

RESPECTFULLY INTIMATES THAT HE HAS ADDED TO his present Stock a large Assortment of

WATCHES, PLATE, AND JEWELLERY,

Which will be disposed of at extremely moderate prices, for

CASH PAYMENTS.

Ladies' Gold Watches, in price, from	£6 0 0	to £18 0 0
Gentlemen's Gold Watches, in price, from	8 0 0	to 25 0 0
Silver Lever Watches,	4 0 0	to 10 0 0
Silver Geneva Watches,	3 0 0	to 6 0 0
A Silver Lever Watch, warranted for three years (particularly recommended),		6 0 0
A Silver Lever Watch, warranted for one year (an accurate time-keeper),		5 0 0

A few Second-hand Gold and Silver Watches, from 20s. upwards.

JEWELLERY.

In Rich Gold Bracelets; Coloured and Bright Gold Brooches; Lockets; Guard Chains; Albert and Drop Chains; Seals and Keys; Enamelled and Gold Studs; Diamond, Ruby, Pearl, and Turquoise Set Rings and Pins; Gold and Silver Pencil Cases; Gold Curb Guard Chains (weight 1¼ sovereigns), for 30s.; 1½ sovereigns weight for 35s.; 2 sovereigns weight for 40s.; 3 sovereigns weight for 60s.; and so on, equal weight of Gold for Sovereigns.

WEDDING RINGS AND KEEPERS,

Irish Bog Oak Brooches, Pins, Bracelets, &c., &c., &c.

PLATE,

In Tea and Coffee Services; Egg and Cruet Stands; Toast Racks; Cake and Fruit Baskets; Salvers; Coasters; Chamber and Table Candlesticks; Tea, Dessert, Table Spoons and Forks; Fish Carvers and Forks, in cases, &c.

French Sixteen-day Clocks, in Shades; Office, Hall, &c.

Marine and House Barometers, Thermometers, Sextants, Quadrants, and Telescopes.

Gold, Silver, Shell, and Steel Spectacles, Eye-Glasses, &c., from 1s. up to 40s.

DIAMONDS, JEWELLERY, WATCHES, AND OLD PLATE

BOUGHT, OR TAKEN IN EXCHANGE.

The utmost attention given to the R E P A I R I N G of English and Foreign WATCHES.

☞ JEWELLERY MADE TO ORDER AND REPAIRED.

11, HIGH STREET.

THE OLDEST BOOT & SHOE WAREHOUSE

IN THE NORTH OF IRELAND.

ALEXANDER MAGUIRE,

IN ANNOUNCING HIS RETURN FROM HIS PERIODICAL VISIT TO LONDON AND DUBLIN, begs to inform his numerous friends, and the public in general, that he has renewed his extensive Stock with a large importation of

PARISIAN AND ENGLISH LEATHER,

Particularly adapted to every branch of the Trade.

In returning thanks to those who have patronised his Establishment, he takes the liberty of stating, that his Stock now embraces every kind of Leather suitable for the present and ensuing season, for

LADIES' AND GENTLEMEN'S

DRESS AND WALKING BOOTS AND SHOES;

BLACK, WHITE, AND BRONZE KID;

BLACK AND WHITE SATIN;

BOOT LEGS, AND THE NEW TOP

FOR GENTLEMEN'S HUNTING BOOTS.

Leather particularly dressed for Sea and Waterproof Boots, &c.

The proprietor respectfully submits this large assortment to the inspection of his friends, with the utmost confidence that it cannot be exceeded, either for extent or manufacture, in the North of Ireland.

A GOOD ASSORTMENT OF

READY-MADE WORK

ALWAYS ON HANDS,

WITH

A VARIETY OF OVERSHOES.

THE PROFESSIONAL
LIFE ASSURANCE COMPANY,

ADMITTING, ON EQUAL TERMS,

Persons of every class and degree to all its advantages.

OFFICES, 76, CHEAPSIDE, LONDON.

By the Deed of Settlement the Directors have power to appropriate one-tenth of the entire profits of the Company—

1st. *For the relief of aged and distressed parties assured for life, who have paid five years' premiums, their widows and orphans;*

2nd. *For the relief of aged and distressed original proprietors, assured or not, their widows and orphans, together with five per cent. per annum on the capital originally invested by them;*

THEREBY SECURING ADVANTAGES

TO THE LIVING

NOT TO BE FOUND IN ANY OTHER EXISTING COMPANY.

INCORPORATED.—CAPITAL, £250,000.

CHAIRMAN, - - - Major HENRY STONES.
DEPUTY-CHAIRMAN, - JAMES A. DURHAM, Esq.
With upwards of 1,400 Shareholders.

ALL POLICIES INDISPUTABLE, AND NO CHARGE FOR STAMPS.

Medical Men, in all cases, remunerated for their Reports.

ANNUAL PREMIUM FOR INSURING £100, VIZ.:

Age.	For One Year.	For Seven Years.	Whole Term of Life.
	£ s. d.	£ s. d.	£ s. d.
20	0 17 3	0 18 7	1 10 9
30	1 0 7	1 1 5	1 19 6
40	1 4 6	1 6 2	2 13 6
50	1 15 2	2 1 0	3 18 6

INCREASING RATES OF PREMIUM.

Age.	Annual Premium for £100 during the		
	1st Seven Years.	2nd Seven Years.	Remainder of Life.
	£ s. d.	£ s. d.	£ s. d.
20	1 1 6	1 12 3	2 3 0
30	1 7 2	2 0 0	2 14 4
40	1 17 6	2 16 3	3 15 0
50	2 17 6	4 6 3	5 15 0

Prospectuses, with fullest information, may be had at the Offices of the Company, or their Agents.

ED. BAYLIS, Resident Manager and Actuary, 76, Cheapside, London.

T. B. JOHNSON, Solicitor, 27, Arthur Street,

AGENT FOR BELFAST.

Dr. COLLINS, Queen Street, Belfast, Medical Referee.

IMPERIAL FIRE
INSURANCE COMPANY,
1, OLD BROAD STREET,
And No. 10, PALL MALL, LONDON.

INSTITUTED 1803.

For Insuring Houses and other Buildings; Goods, Wares, Merchandise, Manufacturing and Farming Stock; Ships in Port, Harbour, or Dock, and the Cargoes of such Ships; also, Ships Building and Repairing, Barges, and Vessels on navigable Rivers and Canals, and the Goods on board such Vessels throughout Great Britain and Ireland, from Loss or Damage by Fire.

Capital, One Million Six Hundred Thousand Pounds.

The Rates of Annual Premiums on the three ordinary Classes of Insurance:—

> Common..............................1s. 6d. per Cent.
> Hazardous...........................2s. 6d.   do.
> Doubly Hazardous................4s. 6d.   do.

(Except in special cases).

The Rates for all Insurances, not coming under the above heads, are fixed by special agreement.

FARMING STOCK Insured at *Four Shillings* per Cent. without the average clause, which is so often found objectionable to the Assured, and *free of Government Duty.*

AGENTS FOR BELFAST:
JOHN PIM, 20, Waring Street;
THOMAS G. FOLINGSBY, 15, Albert Square.

☞ **JOHN PIM is also Agent to the Imperal Life Insurance Company of London.**

ALLIANCE BRITISH AND FOREIGN LIFE AND FIRE ASSURANCE COMPANY.

BARTHOLOMEW LANE, LONDON.

ESTABLISHED BY ACT OF PARLIAMENT.

Capital Five Millions Sterling. Established March, 1824.

BOARD OF DIRECTION.

Presidents.
SAMUEL GURNEY, Esq.
SIR MOSES MONTEFIORE, Bart.,

Directors.

George H. Barnett, Esq.	Samuel Gurney, jun., Esq.
Sir E. N. Buxton, Bart., M.P.	John Irving, Esq.
Sir R. Campbell, Bart.	Louis Lucas, Esq.
Sir George Carrol.	Thomas Masterman, Esq.
The Right Hon. G. R. Dawson.	Baron L. de Rothschild, M.P.
James Fletcher, Esq.	Sir A. N. de Rothschild, Bart.
Charles Gibbs, Esq.	Oswald Smith, Esq.
William Gladstone, Esq.	Melvil Wilson, Esq.

Auditors.
JAMES COOK, Esq. | ANDREW JOHNSTON, Esq.
JOSEPH MAYER MONTEFIORE, Esq.

Bankers.
MESSRS. BARNET, HOARES, & CO.

Secretary.
ANDREW HAMILTON, Esq.

Actuary.
FRANCIS AUGUSTUS ENGELBACH, Esq.

Physicians.
OHN R. HUME, M.D., Curzon Street.

Solicitor.
JOHN M. PEARCE, Esq.

Surveyor.
THOMAS ALLASON, Esq.

**ROBERT TROTTER, Provincial Bank,
GUSTAVUS HEYN, No. 1, Henry Street.**
AGENTS FOR BELFAST.

LEE AND SON,
JEWELLERS TO THE QUEEN,
Watchmakers, Silversmiths, and Opticians,
57, HIGH STREET, BELFAST.

JOHN M'AFEE,
18, CORN MARKET, BELFAST.

GENTLEMEN'S, LADIES', AND CHILDREN'S

BOOT & SHOE MANUFACTURER.

A GREAT VARIETY OF READY-MADE WORK OF FIRST QUALITY ALWAYS ON HANDS.

THOMAS M'CRACKEN & CO.,
ENGRAVERS, LITHOGRAPHERS,
AND
LINEN ORNAMENT MANUFACTURERS,
5, & 7, CROWN ENTRY,
HIGH STREET, BELFAST.

T. M'C. & CO., IN RETURNING THANKS FOR PAST favours, begs to inform the Linen Merchants of the North of Ireland that they have made every preparation for conducting their branch of Linen Ornament Manufacturing in a more extensive scale, and trust, from their style and newness of Design, combined with cheapness and punctuality, to be able to compete with any other House in the Trade.

☞ *Engraving and Lithography, in all its Branches, executed with Neatness and Despatch.*

FAMILY LINEN,

DAMASK,

AND

FRENCH CAMBRIC

WAREHOUSE,

16, ARTHUR STREET, BELFAST.

JOHN NOCHER

BEGS MOST RESPECTFULLY TO RETURN HIS GRATEFUL thanks to the Nobility, Gentry, and Public generally, for the very liberal share of patronage which has hitherto been bestowed upon his Establishment, and he trusts, by renewed exertions on his part, to merit a continuance of their past favours.

It has been, and will be, his constant endeavour to supply his Customers

WITH

LINEN GOODS,

OF

SUPERIOR MANUFACTURE AND BLEACH,

(THE LATTER SO ESSENTIAL IN LINENS),

ALL OF WHICH

HE WILL SELL AT A LOW FIGURE

FOR PROMPT PAYMENTS.

NORTHERN
CLOTHING EMPORIUM,

CORNER OF

VICTORIA STREET AND HIGH STREET,

BELFAST.

TAILOR,

DRAPER, AND OUTFITTER.

AGENT FOR THE

CELEBRATED

PATENT "GOLD LEAF HAT,"

Warranted impervious to Wet and Grease.

N.B.—A LARGE STOCK OF

READY-MADE CLOTHING

ALWAYS ON HANDS,

WELL AND FASHIONABLY MADE.

TO LARGE EMPLOYERS,

MILL OWNERS, CONTRACTORS, &c., &c.

Insurance against Accident, of all Kinds, wherever happening (including Railway Accidents).

THE

ACCIDENTAL DEATH INSURANCE COMPANY

GRANTS POLICIES, AT VERY MODERATE PREMIUMS, TO Masters, insuring not only all in their employment when the Insurance is effected, but likewise those who may enter their work at any subsequent period, with perfect liberty to change their work-people as often as they may think proper.

EXAMPLE OF RATES.

1. For an Insurance of £100 against Accident or Violence, wherever it may happen (terminating fatally), 2s. 6d. per annum, and upwards, according to the nature of the risk.
2. For an Insurance of £100, as above, accompanied with compensation of £50, in case of the loss of an Arm, a Leg, or an Eye, 6s. per annum, and upwards.
3. For an Insurance of £100, as above, accompanied with compensation of £1 per week, in case of a non-fatal accident, and a sum for Medical Expenses, 12s. per annum, and upwards.
4. For an Insurance of £1,000 against Death by Railway Accident only, accompanied with compensation in case of injury, Annual Premium, 10s.

Premium for the whole of Life, £5 5s.

Prospectuses, together with further information, may be had at the Offices of the Company, or from any of the Company's Agents.

Head Office—7, Bank Buildings, Lothbury, London.

DIRECTORS.

Kenyon S. Parker, Esq., Q.C., Lincoln's Inn, *Chairman.*
Geo. I. Raymond Barker, Esq., Daglingworth, near Cirencester.
The Lord Thomas P. Clinton, Carlton Villas, Edgeware Road.
Geo. Hibbert Deffell, Esq., 7, King's Bench Walk, Temple.
Richard Fawkes, Esq., Laurel Lodge, Barnet.
Thomas Knox Holmes, Esq., Fludyer Street, Westminster.
Hon. Richard E. Howard, Temple.
John Phillipps Judd, Esq., 6, Mark Lane.
Capt. Lowther, M.P., 1st Life Guards.
Henry Blair Mayne, Esq., 3, Chester Street, Grosvenor Place.
Savile C. H. Ogle, Esq., M.P., Kirkley Hall, Newcastle-on-Tyne.
Charles Snell Paris, Esq., Salvador House, Bishopsgate Street.

WILLIAM YOUNG, Secretary.

Office for Belfast, WAREHOUSE LANE, WARING STREET.

RICHARD CREETH & Co., Agents.

Belfast, 12th Mo. 1st, 1851.

ions.

ORIGINAL FLANNEL WAREHOUSE.

GEORGE W. KYLE,
HOSIER, GLOVER, & OUTFITTER,

COMMERCIAL BUILDINGS,

No. 21, Bridge Street, Belfast.

READY-MADE SHIRTS, CHEMISES, NIGHT-GOWNS, &c., &c.,

CARPET BAGS, UMBRELLAS, BRACES, &c.,

Gentlemen's India and British Silk Handkerchiefs, Stocks, Satin Scarfs;

LADIES' AND GENTLEMEN'S UNDER-CLOTHING,

OF EVERY DESCRIPTION.

7-8 and 4-4 *Handspun Real Welsh and English FLANNELS, from 5-8 to 12¼ wide.*

DEALER IN WORSTEDS, YARNS, &c.

Established for the Sale of First-Class Goods.

Shirts made to order on the shortest notice.
Dress Shirts (Linen Collars, Bands, &c.), 3s., 3s. 6d., 4s., 4s. 6d., 5s., very best made 6s. 6d. each.
Shirt Collars (Linen), 4s., 5s., 6s. 6d., best 9s. per doz.

A CARD.

G. W. KYLE having commenced business in the Premises formerly occupied by me, I wish to intimate that he will be regularly supplied with an extensive Assortment of Handspun real Welsh and Lancashire Flannels and Swanskins, similar make and quality to those I was in the habit of keeping. From his intimate knowledge of all the varied departments of the business, and his long experience in some of the first Houses in the kingdom, I can confidently present him to my customers as worthy of a trial.

THOMAS CHERMSIDE.

Belfast, March 8, 1847.

G. W. KYLE,

In returning his most grateful thanks to his friends and the public for the kind and unprecedented encouragement which has been afforded him since his commencement, begs to assure them, that his constant aim shall be to merit a continuance of that support so liberally bestowed on his predecessor.

HOSIERY MADE TO ORDER AT THIS ESTABLISHMENT,
To any size, shape, or quality, in one, two, or three ply, at times prices.

Weekly arrivals from WELSH, MARGETSON, & Co., London, in Silk and Satin Scarfs, Neck and Pocket Kerchiefs, &c., &c.

Scotch Plaids, Railway Wrappers, Cordings, Waterproof Goods.

ADVERTISEMENTS.

WHOLESALE AND RETAIL
BOOT AND SHOE DEPOT.

THE WELLINGTON HOUSE,
VICTORIA STREET,
(BETWEEN HIGH STREET AND ANN STREET),
BELFAST.

B. PRATT & CO.,
Military, Naval, Commercial, and Family Boot and Shoe Manufacturers,

HAVE CONSTANTLY ON HAND, AND MAKE TO ORDER, every description of Ladies', Gentlemen's, and Children's BOOTS and SHOES, for Dress, Walking, Riding, Shooting, Fishing, &c., &c.

N.B. *Appointed Agents for the Sale of the most superior Shoe Blackings and Patent Varnish.*

REPAIRS PROMPTLY ATTENDED TO AND NEATLY EXECUTED.
THE MOST MODERATE CHARGES.

OLD ESTABLISHED
BRASS FOUNDRY,
7 & 9, VICTORIA STREET.

BERNARD M'CANN
STILL CONTINUES TO CARRY ON THE BUSINESS OF

BELL AND BRASS FOUNDER.
Gas-Fitting and Silver Plating, in all its Departments.

B. M'C. HAS ALWAYS ON HAND

A LARGE SUPPLY OF GASALIERS,
Of the Newest and most Improved Designs.

WITH A LARGE STOCK OF

BRASS, COPPER, COMPOSITION, AND MALLEABLE IRON TUBING, KNEES, AND TEES,

Which will be disposed of on the most reasonable terms.

NEW BASKET, TOY, AND LADIES' AND CHILDREN'S
BOOT AND SHOE WAREHOUSE,
No. 8, BRIDGE STREET.

ALEXANDER WILSON

RETURNS HIS SINCERE THANKS TO THE PUBLIC FOR their favour since he commenced business in the above line, and begs to inform them that he will still continue to keep on hands a large and well selected stock of Goods, which, for quality, style, and price, cannot be equalled in Belfast.

THE FOLLOWING IS A BRIEF CATALOGUE OF HIS STOCK:

BASKETS.
Fancy Baskets, all kinds.
Market ditt .
Hand ditt .
Clothes ditto.

SUNDRIES.
Straw Bags.
Wax Cloth.
Leather Reticules.
Writing Desks.
Dressing Cases.
Carpet Bags.
Work Boxes.
Accordeons.
Milliners' Blocks.
Children's Carriages and Cradles.
China Ornaments and Delph Toys.
Dissected Maps.
Puzzles.
Playing Cards of all kinds.
Coral Rattles.
Gold and other Rings.
Brooches of various descriptions.
Silver and other Thimbles.
Needles.
Tea and Table Spoons.
German Silver and Britannia Metal.
Fine Horn Spoons.
Children's Whistle ditto.
Penknives.
Scissors.
Snuff Boxes.

Tobacco Boxes.
Cigar Cases.
Le. Grass Games.
Battle Dores and Shuttle Cocks.
Cricket Bats and Balls.
Bows and Arrows.
Chess Men.
Dominoes and other games.
Clothes Pins.
Butter Cutters.
Butter Rollers.
Butter Prints.
Butter Scopes.
Bone Knives and Forks.
Ditto Egg Spoons.
Salt   ditto.
Mustard ditto.
Bone Apple Scopes.
Babies' Puff Boxes.
A large assortment of Dublin Boots and Shoes for Ladies.
Ladies' Strong Welt Boots and Shoes.
Slight ditto.
Boys' and Girls' Strong and Slight ditto.
Babies' Slight ditto.
Carpet Shoes for Ladies and Children.
All sorts of Gentlemen's Carpet & Leather Morning Slippers.
Girth Web and Leather Slippers, for servants.

Combs, Brushes, & Perfumery.
Hair Brushes.
Tooth ditto.
Nail ditto.
Shaving ditto.
Babies' ditto.
Whisker ditto.
Clothes ditto.
French and German Shell Side Combs.
Tortoise Shell ditto.
Back   ditto.
Neck and Band ditto.
Dressing   ditto.
Pocket   ditto.
Fine Tooth   ditto.
Comb Cleaners.
Honey Soap.
Windsor do. (White and Brown).
Transparent Shaving Soap.
Shaving Cream.
Shaving Glasses.
Shaving Boxes.
Rose Oil.
Marrow Oil.
Honey Cream.
Cold Cream.
Tooth Powder.
Scents of all kinds.
Scent Bottles.
Eau de Cologne.
Ladies' Companions and Pin Cushions.

Also, a very large assortment of Toys, too numerous to mention.

A. W. trusts, from strict attention to orders, together with punctuality and moderate charges, to ensure a continuance of that support he has received since his commencement in business.

ALL KINDS OF BASKET WORK MADE TO ORDER.

☞ *Observe*, 8, *BRIDGE STREET* (*next door to the News-Letter Office*).

SHIRTS! SHIRTS! SHIRTS!

SHIRT-MAKING, AS A BRANCH OF BUSINESS, MAY NOW be considered as having arrived at perfection. It is generally allowed that a good fitting shirt is one of the greatest ornaments of dress. To secure such should, therefore, be a great desideratum with every gentleman. It has long been a matter of regret that shirts could not be procured having that beauty of fit so much to be desired.

GEORGE W. KYLE,

Would beg respectfully to call attention to the fact, that all shirts sold at his establishment are made under his own superintendence by first-class workers, and as he purchases the material from manufacturers of the first standing, he thus secures the following

ADVANTAGES, VIZ.:

Of getting them made upon the most economic principle, combined with elegance and neatness, and with what is as desirable, good work.

G. W. K. can, with the greatest confidence, recommend his present styles' as being made with all the latest improvements, including those so much admired at the Great Exposition of the Industry of all Nations.

N.B.—Gentlemen in the country by sending the exact width of neck and wrist, and breadth across shoulders and chest, may have shirts made to order on the shortest notice, of any quality, and a perfect fit guaranteed.

The following is a statement of prices, 3s., 3s. 6d., 4s., 4s. 6d., 5s., 5s. 6d., and 6s.; the very best made, 6s. 6d.

21, BRIDGE STREET, BELFAST.

GENUINE BALBRIGGAN HOSIERY.

BY ROYAL  AUTHORITY.

HENRY APPLEYARD,

Manufacturing Hosier to Her Majesty, H.R.H. Prince Albert, the Duchess of Kent, His Excellency the Lord Lieutenant, the Countess of Clarendon, the Irish Court, and Court of St. James.

H. A. begs respectfully to intimate to the Nobility, Clergy, and Gentry of the North of Ireland that he has appointed GEO. W. KYLE, 21, Bridge Street, Belfast, Sole Agent for his celebrated make of Hosiery, and requests that all orders be sent, in future, to his establishment, where they will meet with special and prompt attention.

N.B.—The initials of any name will be woven into the Stockings, free of charge. A single Stocking enclosed, or length of foot and top will be quite sufficient for G. W. K. to send a satisfactory fit.

Balbriggan, Dec. 1, 1851.

GEORGE W. KYLE,
21, BRIDGE STREET, BELFAST,

Respectfully intimates that the following celebrated maker's Gloves are always to be had at his establishment:—

Dent and Co's. Super Dundee Kid Gloves—linen sewn.
John Rough's   do.   do.   do.
Thomas Burke's Limerick Gloves—one pair in each Walnut Shell.
Thomas Burke's celebrated Cork sewn Gloves.
Sole Agent for D'Borrelli's Real Paris Kid Gloves.
"   Alexandre's   do.
"   Vavasseur's   do.
"   Caldesaign's   do.
"   Jouvin's   do.
"   Corvoissieurs   do.

JOHN M'DOWELL,

WHOLESALE GROCER,

VICTORIA STREET, BELFAST,

OPPOSITE THE NEW NORTHERN BANK.

WILLIAM DALE,

BROKER,

AND

AUCTIONEER,

COMMERCIAL

AND

FURNITURE SALE ROOMS,

No. 4, DONEGALL STREET,

BELFAST.

London Union Assurance Society.

INSTITUTED IN THE REIGN OF QUEEN ANNE, A.D., 1714.

And empowered by Act of Parliament to grant Annuities and make

INSURANCES FOR LIVES AGAINST FIRE.

WILLIAM SIMMS,

AGENT FOR THE SOCIETY, FOR THE TOWN and Neighbourhood of BELFAST, continues to receive orders, in any of these Departments, at his Office in the Linen Hall.

MEDICAL EXAMINER—WILLIAM BURDEN, ESQ., M.D.

BELFAST, DECEMBER 1, 1851.

ATLAS ASSURANCE COMPANY OF LONDON.

Instituted 1808, and empowered by Act of Parliament of 54th George 3rd. Capital £1,200,000.

Life Department.

PERSONS ASSURED FOR THE WHOLE TERM OF LIFE, for £100 and upwards, will have an addition made to their Policies every Seventh year, or an equivalent reduction will be made in the future payments of premium, at the option of the Assured.

The next valuation will be made at Christmas, 1852, and Policies effected before that date will participate in proportion to the time they may have been in force. Policies may also be effected for the whole term of life by a limited number of yearly payments.

Fire Department.

Assurances are now effected by this Company, except in special cases, at the following rates, viz.:—for risks of the First Class, 1s. 6d. per cent.; Second Class, 2s. 6d. per cent.; and for the Third Class, 4s. 6d. per cent. On all policies for £300 and upwards, continuing in force for five years, the Assured will be entitled to participate in the Surplus Premiums to be ascertained at that period. In addition to the benefit of the returns, this Company offers to Assurers the advantage of an allowance for the loss of rent of Buildings rendered untenantable by fire. Farming Stock can now be assured at this Office, at 3s. per cent., and exempt from duty.

HENRY DESBOROUGH, Secretary, Cheapside, London.

C. B. GRIMSHAW & SON, Agents for Belfast and its Neighbourhood.
30, ROSEMARY STREET, BELFAST.

THE STANDARD
LIFE ASSURANCE COMPANY.

(CONSTITUTED BY ACT OF PARLIAMENT.

HEAD OFFICE:—3, George's Street, Edinburgh.

WILLIAM THOMAS THOMSON, GENERAL MANAGER.

THIS COMPANY WAS ESTABLISHED IN 1825, AND THE success which has attended its business places it among the first Institutions in the Kingdom for the assurance of Lives.

Last year, it transacted the largest business in Scotland. The distinctive feature in this company is, the mode pursued in the DIVISION OF PROFITS among the assured, the Bonus additions, to Policies of long standing, having been in some instances of such large amount that *the Policies have not only been relieved of all future payments, but have received, and will continue to receive, large Additions to the sums assured.* The Rates, which are moderate, (either with or without Profits), are made payable Annually, Half-yearly, or Quarterly, and can be readily obtained, along with every other information, by application to any of the Agents.

☞ ANNUITIES and ENDOWMENTS also granted.

Dublin Office—66, UPPER SACKVILLE STREET.

SAMUEL SKYLIE, Resident Secretary.

BELFAST BRANCH.

LOCAL BOARD OF MANAGEMENT.

SAMUEL G. FENTON, Esq., J.P., (Mayor of Belfast), *Chairman.*

James Macnamara, Esq., J.P.,	The Rev. H. Cooke, D.D., LL.D.
William M'Caw, Esq.,	William Dunville, Esq.,

William Hamilton, Esq.

Medical Adviser:—ROBERT STEPHENSON, Esq., M.D.

AGENT:

JOHN TAYLOR, General Manager of the Ulster Bank.
OFFICE:—16, DONEGALL PLACE.

THE MONARCH FIRE AND LIFE ASSURANCE COMPANY.

Established in 1850, and empowered by Special Acts of Parliament.

Subscribed Capital, £300,000,

In addition to the individual responsibility of a highly numerous and Respectable Proprietary.

HEAD OFFICE, ADELAIDE PLACE, LONDON BRIDGE, LONDON.
BRANCH OFFICE, 29, DONEGALL STREET, BELFAST.

Directors.
CHAIRMAN—The Right Honourable the Lord Mayor.
DEPUTY-CHAIRMAN—John K. Hooper, Esq., Alderman.

John Addis, Esq.	J. G. Hammack, Esq.
C. S. Butler, Esq.	William Knott, Esq.
J. Dudin Brown, Esq.	John Laurie, Esq.
G. Harris Child, Esq.	Robert Main, Esq.
William Game, Esq.	Francis Witham, Esq.

ACTUARY—J. F. Clement, Esq. MANAGER—George H. Jay, Esq.
MEDICAL ADVISER FOR BELFAST—Dr. MOFFAT.

The success which has attended this Institution, arising from its extended connexions, and the safe and liberal principles on which it is founded, has fully equalled, if not surpassed, that of any similar Establishment

FIRE DEPARTMENT.

Property of every description is Insured at rates and conditions as advantageous as those of any Office, and all claims for loss are promptly and liberally settled. *Insurance for Seven Years charged only for Six. Transfer is made without expense to the assured.*

LIFE DEPARTMENT.

In this department the premiums have been calculated on the lowest scale consistent with the fair interests of the Company. *No charge made for entry money* beyond the cost of the stamp. Assurers have the option of sharing in the profits; and one-half of the premium may remain unpaid for the first five years, at interest, at five per cent. per annum. The profits are divided every five years, to parties assured for the whole term of life. The last declaration of profits averaged *twenty-eight per cent.* on the premiums paid. Cash advances will, at all times, be made on policies, proportioned to their acquired value.

ANNUITIES AND ENDOWMENTS GRANTED.

Specimen of Annual Premiums to insure £100 at death.

AGE.	WITHOUT PROFITS.	AGE.	WITH PROFITS.
20	£1 13 0	20	£1 18 10
25	1 15 8	25	2 1 6
30	1 19 8	30	2 5 8
35	2 6 6	35	2 12 6
40	2 14 3	40	3 1 3

Prospectuses and every other information may be obtained, on application at the Office of the Agents,

J. & J. BEATH, 29, Donegall Street, Belfast.

THE OLD ESTABLISHED
ACCOUNT BOOK MANUFACTORY,
STATIONERY,
BOOKBINDING AND PRINTING
ESTABLISHMENT,
6, CORN-MARKET, BELFAST,
MARCUS WARD AND CO.,
PROPRIETORS.

STATIONERY.

THIS DEPARTMENT WILL, AS USUAL, BE FOUND REPLETE in every article connected with the trade, suitable for the *Merchant, Banker, or Solicitor*, the *Professional Gentleman*, or the *Lady's Writing Desk.* Note Paper or Envelopes embossed to order with any Initials, Coat of Arms, Crest, or wording, in a most superior manner, and at a very trifling cost. They have always on hand a large Stock of Papers of every description, Account Books, Patent Copying Presses, &c.

ARTISTS' MATERIALS.

Being *Sole Agents in the North of Ireland* for *Messrs. Winson & Newton, Artists' Colourmen to the Queen and Prince Albert,* they are supplied with every *novelty* in this line as it appears in London, while the *character* of the house is a sufficient guarantee for the *very superior quality* of their Goods. *Oil and Water Colours, Colour Boxes, Easels, Palettes, Brushes, &c., &c.*

ACCOUNT BOOKS

Of every description made to order on the shortest notice, of *any size, style* of *binding*, or *pattern* of *ruling*, with or without printed headings, and, if required, paged consecutively by patent machinery.

BOOKBINDING.

From their large premises, extensive machinery, varied assortment of tools, and experienced workmen, they have unusual facilities for efficiently executing every description of binding, to any pattern, in style NOT *inferior* to *any* house in London, or elsewhere. If required, the binding of libraries undertaken by contract.

LITHOGRAPHY

Of every description executed in the *first style of the art, none but experienced workmen* being employed.

Gold, Silver, Chalk, Line, Tinted and Colour Printing. Exact fac-similes of ancient or modern MSS., Music, Prints, Show Cards, Goods Tickets, Invoice Headings. Note and Letter Tops, Banker's Cheques, Receipts, Bills, Price Lists, Circulars, Cards, &c., &c.

Letterpress and Copperplate Printing of every description executed in any Style.

M. W. & Co. beg to return their sincere thanks to their numerous friends and customers, for the patronage which they have so liberally bestowed, and trust by *unremitting attention, punctuality,* and *strictly moderate charges,* still to merit a continuance of their favours.

C

North of England Insurance Company

Incorporated.—Established 1844.
CAPITAL, £500,000.
CHIEF OFFICE, OLD HAYMARKET, SHEFFIELD.

Trustees.

THE RIGHT HON. EARL FITZWILLIAM,
THE RIGHT HON. LORD WHARNCLIFFE,
THE RIGHT HON. LORD MILTON,
SIR H. G. WARD, KNIGHT,
JOHN PARKER, ESQ. M.P.
CORDEN THOMSON, ESQ. M.D.
JOHN CARR, ESQ. MAYOR OF SHEFFIELD.

Directors.

W. J. BAGSHAWE, ESQ. of the Oaks, Derbyshire, *Chairman.*
JOHN CARR ESQ. *Deputy Chairman.*

JOSEPH WARD, ESQ.
CHARLES SHELDON, ESQ.
GEORGE WILTON CHAMBERS, ESQ.
THOMAS WHEATLEY ESQ.
JOHN BROWN, ESQ.
LIEUT. JOHN ROBERTS, R.N.
HENRY WILKINSON, ESQ.
GEORGE WALL ESQ.
JOHN HALL, ESQ.
EDWARD VICKERS ESQ.

Manager & Actuary, GEORGE STEWART, ESQ.

Agent for Belfast: Mr JOSEPH FAREN,

at Messrs Richardson, Brothers & Co., Corporation St.

FIRE DEPARTMENT.

Insurances are granted against Loss by Fire at the following moderate Rates of Premium:—

Common Risks .... 1s 6d per Cent.
Hazardous Risks .... 2s 6d per Cent.
Doubly Hazardous Risks .... 4s 6d per Cent.

The Directors are at all times desirous to give effect to a prompt and liberal adjustment of Claims.

LIFE DEPARTMENT.

Policies may either be placed on the system of Mutual Assurance, with Right of Participating in the Profits, or be effected at a Reduced Rate of Premium, without such Right of Participation.

Annual Investigations & Divisions of Profits.—In order to obtain a Proper Average, the first Investigation has been delayed to 1852.

All Policies on the Mutual System are entitled to share to the extent of Eighty per cent in the Profits arising from Assurances of this class.

Claims are Paid Three Months after Proof of Death, and when the amount insured does not exceed £300, one-fourth part is payable on production of the evidence and the balance at the end of one month.

Prospectuses & further information may be had by applying to the Agent

Joseph Faren,
Corporation Street, Belfast

M'KENZIE, BROTHERS,

BEG LEAVE TO RETURN THEIR SINCERE THANKS TO their numerous Customers and the Public for the large amount of business with which they have been favoured during the last Eleven Years; and also beg to inform them that they have Opened a Warehouse in

REGENT BUILDINGS,

(Within two doors of the new Corn Exchange) for the Sale of every description of Goods in the

BRASS-FOUNDING & GAS-FITTING
DEPARTMENTS.

A LARGE SUPPLY ALWAYS ON HANDS, INCLUDING

Gasaliers, Pendants, Brackets; Brass, Copper, Iron, and Composition Tubing, &c., &c.,

AND TO BE HAD ON THE MOST REASONABLTE TERMS.

They would respectfully invite the attention of PLUMBERS to their Assortment of

WATER-CLOSETS, PUMPS, VALVES, &c.;

SHIP BUILDERS, to their

Bells, Rudder-Bands, Spikes, Nails & Cabin-Mountings;

MILL-OWNERS, to their

BRASS CASTINGS; STEAM, WATER, & GAS-FITTINGS;

SPIRIT MERCHANTS, to their

COCKS OF ALL SIZES, SODA WATER MACHINES, &c.

OLD BRASS AND COPPER TAKEN IN EXCHANGE FOR WORK.

M'KENZIE, BROTHERS, still continue to furnish

PATENT AXLES FOR COACH BUILDERS,

OF SUPERIOR MAKE, AND HAVE ALWAYS A NUMBER IN STOCK.

OLD AXLES REPAIRED.

Brass Foundry and Patent Axle Manufactory, 23, May Street; WAREHOUSE, REGENT BUILDINGS.

STEWART R. M'CLEAVE,

STONE SEAL ENGRAVER,

AND

STEEL DIE CUTTER,

18, CORN MARKET, BELFAST.

THOMAS & JOHN M'QUISTON,

House, Sign, and Ornamental

PAINTERS,

14, ARTHUR STREET,
BELFAST.

STARCH.

GREAT EXHIBITION.

Pro Bono Publico.

EDWARD TUCKER,

BELFAST,

CONTINUES TO MANUFACTURE AND SUPPLY TO

BLEACHERS AND DEALERS

THE DESCRIPTION OF

STARCH,

For which he has been awarded a MEDAL, and "Honourable Mention," by the Jury appointed by her Majesty's Commissioners, in

CLASS 3, No. 122.

ESTABLISHED 1818.

S. FARRELL & Co.,
SEEDSMEN, NURSERYMEN, AND FLORISTS,

BEG TO STATE, THAT THE GREATEST CARE AND ATTENTION is paid to every department of their Business; and they consider that no House in the Trade can excel theirs for superiority of Stock. or moderation in price.

They embrace this opportunity of tendering their best thanks to their kind friends who have so long patronised them, and to whom they are indebted for their present standing; and assure them, that it will be their high ambition to retain the position they now hold in the SEED and NURSERY Trade.

They have much pleasure in stating, that, notwithstanding the general depression (particularly in the Nursery line), their Trade is steadily increasing in this department, as well as in every other branch of their profession.

2, High Street, Belfast, and Nurseries, Ballycloughan, Co. Down.

☞ *The County Down Railway has a Station at the Nurseries.*

WHOLESALE WINE AND SPIRIT MERCHANT.

HUGH CELSTON,

IN returning thanks to his friends and customers, who have honoured him with their patronage since his commencing business, would beg to inform them that he has

REMOVED FROM NORTH STREET,

TO THOSE COMMODIOUS PREMISES,

No. 7, UPPER CHURCH LANE,

WHERE HE WILL CONTINUE TO CARRY ON THE

WHOLESALE
WINE AND SPIRIT BUSINESS,

IN ALL ITS BRANCHES.

JOHN REYNOLDS'
TOY AND FANCY GOODS WAREHOUSE,
NO. 45, DONEGALL STREET, BELFAST,

CONTAINS A SPLENDID SELECTION OF

TOYS OF EVERY DESCRIPTION,
WRITING-DESKS, WORK-BOXES,
DRESSING-CASES,
BROOCHES, BRACELETS,
JEWELLERY IN ENDLESS VARIETY,
ACCORDIONS, FLUTES, AND VIOLINS,

CUTLERY

And all kinds of London, Birmingham, and Sheffield Goods.

TORTOISE SHELL & OTHER COMBS,
BRUSHES AND PERFUMERY,

FRENCH AND BERLIN BASKETS, &c.,

Those wishing to save money will do well to make a trial of the above Goods, as the Subscriber feels confident, from his long experience in the Trade, of *being able to Sell* at prices *which, for cheapness,* HAVE BEEN UNPRECEDENTED IN BELFAST.

JOHN REYNOLDS.

SCHOOL AND COLLEGE BOOKS,
Paper and General Stationery,

Will be Sold equally Cheap.

ADVERTISEMENTS.

JAMES H. SMYTH & CO.,
Glass, Paint, Oil, and Colour Merchants,
7, NORTH STREET,

(WITHIN A FEW DOORS OF THE BELFAST BANK,)

BELFAST.

Sole Agents for PARSONS & Co.'s. Celebrated Matches.

STATIONERY.

HILL SMYTH,
WHOLESALE AND RETAIL

STATIONER, BOOKBINDER

AND

Lithographic, Letterpress and Copperplate
PRINTER,
AND

ARTISTS' COLOURMAN,
No. 1, DONEGALL STREET, BELFAST.

HAS ALWAYS ON HANDS A LARGE AND WELL-ASSORTED STOCK OF THE FOLLOWING GOODS AT REMARKABLY LOW PRICES:

LETTER AND NOTE PAPER;
ENVELOPES TO SUIT.

SCHOOL PAPERS.

Ledgers, Day-Books, Journals, and Cash Books,
STRONGLY AND WELL BOUND,
IN ALL THE DIFFERENT AND MOST APPROVED RULING.

STEEL PENS, INK,
SEALING WAX, COLOURED AND RED.
Every description of Artists' Materials.

ELECTRICAL AND OPTICAL WAREHOUSE,

168

NORTH STREET, BELFAST.

GALVANIC BATTERIES, OF EVERY DESCRIPTION,
MADE TO ORDER.

ELECTRO-MAGNETIC MACHINES FOR ADMINISTERING MEDICAL GALVANISM.

COPPER WIRE COVERED OF ANY THICKNESS.

New or Old Articles Electro Plated or Gilded.

SPECTACLES, OF EVERY DESCRIPTION.

Air Pumps, Magic Lanterns, Telescopes, Microscopes, and Mathematical Instruments, cleaned and repaired.

J. A. CUMINE, Manufacturer.

J. B. YOUNG,

GLASGOW HOUSE,  **14, NORTH STREET,**

UMBRELLA AND PARASOL
MANUFACTORY,
AND

GUTTA PERCHA, PORTMANTEAU, AND TRUNK DEPOT.

UMBRELLAS AND PARASOLS COVERED AND REPAIRED.

Gutta Percha Soles put on, warranted to adhere.

INDIA RUBBER SLIPPERS REPAIRED AND SOLED WITH GUTTA PERCHA.

Terms, Cash—No Second Price. "*Honesty is the best Policy.*"

☞ **Please observe, 'Glasgow House,' 14, North Street,**
(Nearly opposite the Belfast Bank).

BRITANNIA
LIFE ASSURANCE COMPANY,
No. 1, PRINCES STREET, BANK, LONDON.
ESTABLISHED AUGUST 1, 1837.

Empowered by Special Act of Parliament, 4 Vict. Cap. ix.

DIRECTORS.

Colonel Robert Alexander, Blackheath Park, *Chairman*.
William Bardgett, Esq., Fenchurch Street.
George Bevington, Esq., Neckinger Mills, Bermondsey.
Fortescue P. Cockerell, Esq., Shadwell, and Twickenham.
George Cohen, Esq., Shacklewell.
Millis Coventry, Esq., White Hart Court, Lombard Street.
John Drewett, Esq., 50, Cornhill.
Thomas Samuel Girdler, Esq., Tokenhouse Yard.
Henry Lewis Smale, Esq., Doctors' Commons.
Erasmus Robert Foster, Esq., *Resident Director*.

THIS INSTITUTION IS EMPOWERED BY A *SPECIAL ACT of Parliament*, and is so constituted as to afford the benefits of Life Assurance in their fullest extent to Policy-holders, and to present greater facilities and accommodation than are usually offered by any other Companies.

Among others, the following important advantages may be enumerated:—

Increasing Rates of Premium, on a new and remarkable plan, for securing Loans or Debts—*a less immediate payment being required on a Policy for the whole Term of Life than in any other Office.*

CREDIT TABLE.—By this Table, the Premiums may remain unpaid for seven years, upon satisfactory security being given for the liquidation of the same at the expiration of that period.

MUTUAL ASSURANCE BRANCH.

The decided and powerful support which has been continually afforded to this Institution by the public has induced the Directors still further to extend the benefits hitherto offered to policy holders, by the establishment of a *Mutual Assurance Branch* on a plan peculiarly advantageous to the Assured.

The Division of the Profits *Annually* among the policy holders, and the application of such Profits in *Reduction of the future Premiums* having been ascertained, by experience, not only to be a more *equitable*, but, at the same time a *safer* mode of distribution than any other, this Method of appropriating the Profits of the Mutual Branch will invariably be adopted.

E. R. FOSTER, Resident Director.
ANDREW FRANCIS, Secretary.

Detailed prospectuses, and every requisite information as to the mode of affecting Assurances, may be obtained on application to

EDWARD & GEORGE PIM,
29, HIGH STREET, AGENTS FOR BELFAST; OR

GEORGE C. PIM & CO.,
DONEGALL QUAY.

BANBRIDGE SEED HOUSE.

Agent for the China Tea Company,

F. O'FLAHERTY

IS REGULARLY SUPPLIED FROM THE ENGLISH and Foreign Markets with

GARDEN, FLOWER, AND FARM

SEEDS,

In every Variety suitable to their Seasons;

And has always on hand a Stock of Teas, Coffees, Sugars, Spices; Wax, Sperm, and Dublin Mould Candles; Oils, Colours, Alabaster, Roman Cement, Stationery, Dartford Gunpowder, Patent Shot, &c., &c.

And for Messrs. Du Barry & Co.'s Revalenta.

CHANTER & CO.'S

Patent Metallic Composition, for preventing the rapid destruction of Metal or Copper, by sea friction, on Ships' bottoms, and on single-bottomed Ships.

THIS FLUID HAS PROVED MOST EFFECTUAL IN PREVENTING worms and other animalculæ from adhering to or destroying the wood, by which, in either case, an immense saving is secured to the Ship-owner. Numerous testimonials and certificates, from those who have used it, may be seen by application the Patentees, Lime House, London; or to their Agents, THOMAS G. FOLINGSBY & Co., Belfast, who are always supplied with the Composition.

They have also on hand a good supply of that invaluable substitute for Copper and Yellow Metal, PATENT GALVANIZED IRON, for Sheathing Ships' Bottoms, for which it has been found a valuable substitute, of much greater strength, and costing about one-third of the price of Copper. For Roofing, Pumps, Fences, and all other purposes to which Iron is applicable, the Patent Galvanized Iron is also very valuable for its property of resisting Rust.

The New Houses of Parliament and other Public Buildings are Roofed with this Metal, and several of the Railway Termini.

AGENTS FOR BELFAST AND THE NORTH OF IRELAND,

THOMAS G. FOLINGSBY, & CO.,
COMMISSION MERCHANTS, SHIP AND INSURANCE AGENTS,
15, ALBERT SQUARE, BELFAST.

GEORGE MACOUN,
23 & 25, CASTLE PLACE, BELFAST,

IMPORTER OF

Furs,	Feathers.	Corsets,
Bonnets,	Blonds,	Armlets,
Millinery,	Velvets,	Silk Neck Hfs.
Ribbons,	Silks,	Cambric Hfs.
Flowers,	Crapes,	

COMMUNICATION WITH ENGLAND,
VIA HOLYHEAD.

THREE TIMES EACH WAY ON WEEK DAYS,
TWICE ON SUNDAYS.

THE SEA PASSAGE IS FROM 4 TO 4½ HOURS; AND owing to the great acceleration of the Trains in connexion with the Holyhead Route, the whole journey from Dublin to Liverpool is made in 9½ hours; to Manchester 10½ hours; to Birmingham 11¼ hours; and to London in 13½ hours. Passengers by the Half-past Seven .P.M. boat from Kingstown now reach Liverpool at 6 the following morning; Manchester at 6-15; Birmingham at 7-45; Huddersfield at 8; Leeds and Sheffield at 9; and London at 11.

The following Fares include the whole charge of conveyance to or from Belfast to the places named. Children under 12 years of age pay half-fares only. The time allowed for the Single Journey Tickets is the day of issue and the two following days. The journey may be broken at Dublin, Holyhead, Bangor, or Chester.

The Return Tickets to or from London are available for Fourteen days after date of issue; those to the other stations, for Seven Days. The holder may break the journey at the same places as the holder of a Single Journey Ticket.

A Second Class Passenger can travel in the Saloon and After-Deck of the Steam-Boats by paying 3s. extra.

To or from	Single Fare.		Return Ticket.	
BELFAST	1st Class.	2nd Class.	1st Class.	2nd Class.
and	s. d.	s. d.	s. d.	s. d.
London	70 0	50 0	105 0	75 0
Birmingham ...	52 0	40 0	78 0	60 0
Manchester	37 0	28 0	56 0	42 0
Chester	32 0	23 0	48 0	35 0
Liverpool	32 0	23 0	48 0	35 0

DUBLIN OFFICE, 52, WESTLAND ROW,

Where every information, personally, or by letter, will be afforded.

See also, *Bradshaw's Guide*, page 122; *Walsh's Guide*, page 20; and *Fisher's Guide*.

NOTICE.

HAVING DETERMINED TO CLEAR OUT THE STOCK OF BERLIN WOOLS and PATTERNS, I intend, early in the Spring, purchasing a Stock of RIBBONS, LACES, FLOWERS, SEWED MUSLINS, &c., in their stead; with which I will be regularly supplied, along with my present Stock of

HOSIERY, GLOVES, SMALLWARES,

Corset, Ladies' & Children's Boots & Shoes,

HANDKERCHIEFS, BRACES, TIES,
UMBRELLAS, &c., &c.

CHARLES MORGAN,

26, CASTLE PLACE, BELFAST.

WHOLESALE AND RETAIL SHIRT WAREHOUSE.

HENRY ROBINSON,

CHEMIST AND DRUGGIST,

114, HIGH STREET,

(OPPOSITE VICTORIA STREET), BELFAST.

ALL DRUGS AND CHEMICALS SUPPLIED AT THIS Establishment are of the most

PURE AND GENUINE

DESCRIPTION,

And all Orders Executed under the strict Superintendence of the Proprietor.

SEA AND FAMILY

MEDICINE CHESTS

CAREFULLY FITTED UP.

JOHN G. M'GEE & CO.,
MERCHANT CLOTHIERS;

Embroidered Vest Manufacturers;

ROBE AND GOWN MAKERS,

For the Pulpit, the Bar, or the College,

TAILORS, BY APPOINTMENT, TO THE QUEEN, H.R.H. PRINCE ALBERT, THE LORD LIEUTENANT OF IRELAND.

GENERAL OUTFITTERS

TO ALL PARTS OF THE GLOBE.

PANTECHNETHECA,

46 & 48, HIGH STREET, BELFAST.

BOOKS OF PRICES, containing directions for Measures, also patterns of New Materials, forwarded GRATIS on application.

DONEGALL PLACE AND DONEGALL STREET
BAKERIES.

BERNARD HUGHES

BEGS TO RETURN HIS SINCERE THANKS TO HIS FRIENDS and the PUBLIC in general for the extraordinary support he has received since he commenced business; *and although he is only eleven years in the trade, he is enabled to bake between 500 and 600 Bags of Flour per week constantly,* and sell it all for Cash; even sometimes his customers are not fully supplied.

The Weight and Price of his Bread for the last sixteen months has been as follows:

    Best Superfine Loaf 9 lbs., ...   for 1s.
    Household   Do. 8 lbs., ...   for 9d.

SMALL BREAD AT PROPORTIONATE PRICES.

A PROMISE MADE TO THE PUBLIC, AND FULFILLED,

That the inhabitants of Belfast and Vicinity, from their kind and unceasing support, would have Bread manufactured, pure and unadulterated, as cheap, or cheaper, than any part of the United Kingdom, or even of the world. This has been tested by eleven years' experience; and it has been a great source of pleasure to the Proprietor to find, from the French, English, and American papers, that his exertions have been successful.

BREAD HAS BEEN SOLD 2d. TO 4d. PER SHILLING CHEAPER IN BELFAST THAN IN AMERICA, FRANCE, ENGLAND, SCOTLAND, OR IN MANY PARTS OF IRELAND.

From the immense support he has received, he is now enabled to import FLOURS of a quality superior to that heretofore used by Bakers, viz.:—

Extra Superfine Bordeaux FLOUR, per Edward and Henry.

Extra   do.   Nantz   do.,   per Marie Rosalie, &c.

Extra   do.   Parisian   do.,   per Tintern and Annie.

Extra Dantzic do., manufactured by Pim & Co., Dublin, per Ruby and Enterprise.

Also, John Alexander & Co.'s Silk-dressed FLOUR, made from three of the best-selected Wheats known, viz.:—Fren American, and Dantzic.

The Bread manufactured in these Establishments is made from the above-named Flours, on the most improved principles.

Ladies and Gentlemen desirous of seeing Bread manufactured, free from adulteration, may visit the Bake-houses at any time they may find it convenient. The Proprietor or Foreman will feel great pleasure in showing them the various processes.

These Bakeries have connected with them Storage for upwards of 12,000 Bags or Sacks of Flour, and have 14 Ovens constantly at work, which produced, on the two days preceding Christmas, the immense quantity of 126 Batches, and 60 Ovens-full of Small Bread, consuming 710 cwt. of Flour, and amounting to £482 6s. 9d. Sterling. In addition, there were sold 260 Bags of Flour, Oatmeal, &c. The number of persons employed in connexion with the manufacture and sale of same was 107.

On hands, the following descriptions of OATMEAL:—

CARLOW OATMEAL, COARSE AND FINE,

Manufactured by JOHN ALEXANDER & Co., Carlow;

PATENT OATMEAL, COARSE AND FINE,

Manufactured by WM. LANGTRY & Co., Portadown.

Also, a few Tons of PATENT EXHIBITION OATMÉAL, by M'CANN & Co., of Drogheda, of which the Subscriber earnestly recommends a trial to Families desirous of using a very superior Oatmeal

BERNARD HUGHES.

Belfast, 9th January, 1852.

N.B.—B. HUGHES also continues the Commission Departments in the Grain Trade, for which he has taken a stand in the NEW CORN EXCHANGE, where either he or his representative will be in constant attendance.

TO MERCHANTS, MILLERS, AND OTHERS,

Who may favour him with their orders, he begs to state that he advances three-fourths in Cash on the Goods received, and holds a discretionary power to sell, advising them a post previous.

In consequence of the great advance in the price of Flour, and Coarse Flours being now dearer in proportion than fine, the Subscriber considers it more advantageous to the Public to use finer descriptions of Flours, and change the weight and price as follows, viz.:

Best Superfine Loaf 8lbs.,	...	...	for 1s.
Household Do. 4 lbs.,	...	...	for 5d.

THE

QUEEN'S

TEA, COFFEE,

FOREIGN FRUIT,

AND

ITALIAN WAREHOUSE,

CORNER OF

YORK STREET, AND DONEGALL STREET,

JOHN M'KENNA,

PROPRIETOR.

WHOLESALE AND RETAIL

WINE AND SPIRIT MERCHANT.

WHOLESALE AGENT, FOR THE NORTH OF IRELAND, FOR

Brocksopp, Son's and Co.'s Celebrated Teas and Coffees.

EDWARD & GEORGE PIM,
WINE MERCHANTS,
29, HIGH STREET,
BELFAST,

BEG TO CALL THE ATTENTION OF THEIR FRIENDS and CUSTOMERS, to the following List of Superior WINES, imported from the First Houses in Oporto, Cadiz, &c., &c.:—

PRICES OF WINE IN BOTTLE.

Per Doz.

Port, rare and curious, very old and particular,	38s. 40s.
Do., very superior, old, and particular, rich Burgundy flavour,	35s. 36s.
Do., superior old,	33s.
Do., good rich full bodied,	30s.
Do., good rich ditto,	28s.
Sherry, Golden, extra fine, and very old,	40s.
Do., Golden and Pale, very old and superior,	35s. 36s.
Do., do., do., fine old,	30s. 33s.
Do., do., good old,	26s. 28s.
Madeira,	48s. 50s.
Calcavellos, rich and sweet,	30s.
Lisbon, old and dry,	26s.
Marsala, finest imported,	23s. 24s.
Teneriffe, London particular,	28s.
Bucellas,	30s.
Cape Madeira (Collison's Best),	18s.
Ginger Wine,	14s. 16s.

Two Shillings per dozen allowed on all Ports fresh bottled.
All Bottles and Hampers charged for until returned.

French and Rhenish Wines, Cogniac, Burgundy, &c.

(BOTTLES INCLUDED MARKED *)

Per Doz.

Moët's Celebrated Champaigne, in dozen cases,	70s.
Claret, Chateau Margaux, first quality,	74s.
Ditto, Lafitte, very choice,	72s.
Ditto, Leoville, an excellent Wine,	48s.
Do. do., a superior Summer Wine,	42s.
Sparkling Hock,	60s.
Red Burgundy,	84s. 90s.
Red Hermitage,	44s.
Vin de Grave, superior,	54s.
Sauterne, ditto,	54s.
*Moselle, good light,	36s.
*Hockheim, Vintage, 1794,	90s.
*Rudesheim, do., 1811,	62s. 70s.
Rich sparkling Moselle,	60s.
St. Julian Claret,	32s.
Do. do., in pints,	17s.
*2nd Quality Champaigne, recommended,	50s.

Per Gal.

Finest Old Cogniac Brandy,	26s. 28s.
Do. do. do., in doz. cases, containing two gallons,	56s.
Finest Holland Geneva,	24s.
Do. Jamaica Rum,	10s. 11s.

PRIME
OLD CORK, DUNDALK, AND ISLAY MALT
WHISKEY.

J. ARNOLD,

Woollendraper, Clothier, and Hatter,

HEIMATEMPORION,

45, HIGH STREET,

RESPECTFULLY INTIMATES THAT HIS ESTABLISHMENT is always supplied with an Extensive and Fashionable Stock of

WOOLLENDRAPERY,

TO WHICH ALMOST DAILY ADDITIONS ARE MADE.

The Ready-Made Department

EMBRACES EVERY STYLE OF GARMENT,

FASHIONABLY AND SUBSTANTIALLY

GOT UP, WHILST QUALITY AND PRICE ARE SO ARRANGED AS TO SUIT THE TASTES AND WISHES OF ALL CLASSES.

The Proprietor has engaged a FOREMAN from one of the leading West End LONDON-HOUSES, to superintend

The Bespoke Department,

Whereby he is enabled to execute every order entrusted to his care in that superior manner for which those Houses are so justly celebrated, while he REDUCES THE PRICES TO THE LOWEST REMUNERATIVE PROFIT.

HATS.

A general assortment of FRENCH SATIN VELVET HATS, from the first makers, always on hand, THE BEST SATIN HAT BEING ONLY FIFTEEN SHILLINGS IN PRICE.

☞ *Umbrellas, Gloves, Neck Ties, &c.*

BRITISH ASSURANCE COMPANY,

2, KING STREET, CHEAPSIDE, LONDON.

The Capital of the Company actually subscribed for, and paid upon, exceeds £300,000.

DIRECTORS.

Chairman—SYDNEY SMIRKE, Esq., A.R.A.
Deputy Chairmen { ANTHONY SALVIN, Esq., F.S.A.
GEORGE SMITH, Esq., F.S.A.
Physician—Sir JAMES EYRE, MD.   Bankers—The Union Bank of London.
Solicitor—WM. S. VARDY, Esq.   Manager and Actuary—JOHN REDDISH, Esq.

FIRE DEPARTMENT.

RATES, WITH CERTAIN EXCEPTIONS.

Class 1.—Not Hazardous, ...1s. 6d. per cent. per an
Class 2.—Hazardous, ...2s. 6d.   „   „
Class 3.—Doubly Hazardous, ...4s. 6d.   „   „

Special Risks at moderate rates, according to circumstances.

Seven Years' Assurances charged the Premium and Duty for Six Years only.

Short Period Assurances on the usual terms, the Duty being taken for the exact number of Months.

Losses by Fire, occasioned by Lightning, will be paid, and all claims will be settled with as little delay as possible.

REMOVAL AT FIRES.—A reasonable allowance will be made for the Removal of Goods, in case of Fire.

RENT.—Assurances will be granted against the Loss which would be occasioned by Buildings being rendered untenantable by Fire.

LIFE DEPARTMENT.

DIVISION OF PROFITS.—At the end of every five years, four-fifths will be paid to the holders of Policies of two or more years' duration, or will be applied to increase the sums assured, or to decrease the annual premiums.

CREDIT.—Half the annual premiums of Assurances, "WITH PROFITS," may be left unpaid for seven years, or one-third for the whole of life.

Assignments will be registered and acknowledged.

IMPAIRED HEALTH.—Assurances will be granted on terms proportioned to the supposed extra risk.

PURCHASE OF POLICIES.—Policies for the whole term of life, which have been in force two or more years, and on which no premiums are in arrear, will be purchased on equitable terms.

Full particulars may be had at the Chief Office, King Street, Cheapside, London, where attendance is given from Ten to Four o'clock daily, or from any of the Agents.

AGENT FOR BELFAST,

MR. HUGH REA,

Messrs. Sinclair & Boyd's, 45, Donegall Quay.

Medical Referee,....................................R. F. DILL, Esq., M.D.

TAILORING ESTABLISHMENT,

No. 3, ORR'S ENTRY,

(OFF HIGH STREET.)

P. KERNS

BEGS LEAVE TO REQUEST THAT HIS NUMEROUS AND respectable customers will accept his best thanks for the liberal encouragement he has received from them, particularly since his removal to the above Premises; and now wishes to inform them that he has made every arrangement for the execution of Orders in the shortest possible time; and he trusts, from strict attention to business, to be always found deserving of a continuance of their kind support.

January, 1852.

Engraving, Lithographic, Copperplate,

AND

GENERAL PRINTING ESTABLISHMENT,

25, CASTLE STREET, BELFAST.

J. & T. SMYTH

EXECUTE EVERY DESCRIPTION OF ENGRAVING AND PRINTING in the best style, and on the most Moderate Terms.

Business Cards, Invoices, Forms of Bills, Show Cards, Circulars, Maps, Plans, Ornaments and Tickets for Linen, &c.

Envelopes and Note Paper Embossed with Arms, Crests, Initials, &c., in a superior style.

Seals, of all kinds, for Linen, Dies, Woodcuts, Office Seals; Door and Window Plates, in Brass and Zinc.

Marriage and Visiting Cards Engraved and furnished in the best London style.

Specimens sent to the Country on Application.

THE OLD ESTABLISHED
BOOT AND SHOE WAREHOUSE,
2, ANN STREET, BELFAST.

GEORGE M'AFEE, PROPRIETOR,

BEGS MOST RESPECTFULLY TO RETURN HIS GRATEFUL thanks to his Customers and the Public, for the liberal encouragement he has received during the last Thirteen Years; and to assure them that he is determined to pursue the same course he has hitherto adopted, of supplying the Best Articles at the Lowest Remunerating Prices, and of giving to those who may favour him with their Orders all the advantages arising from the reductions in the price of Leather.

G. M'A. begs further to state, that his Stock at present is Large, and comprises what is Fashionable and Substantial in Ladies', Gentlemen's, and Children's BOOTS and SHOES; and, also, that no exertion shall be wanting on his part to have all orders with which he may be favoured executed with punctuality, and in the very best manner, and hopes, by strict attention to Business, to merit a continuance of Public patronage.

TO BUILDERS, &c.

ALEXANDER M'DONALD,
NEWTOWNARDS,

BEGS TO INFORM BUILDERS, &c., IN BELFAST AND NEIGHBOURHOOD, that he is enabled to supply them with

GOOD RUBBLE STONE,
FOR BUILDING;
TOGETHER WITH EVERY OTHER DESCRIPTION OF

SCRABO STONE.

He Supplies them, delivered by Rail, at the BALLYMACARRETT STATION, and, when required, Carts them from thence,

AT THE LOWEST POSSIBLE RATE OF CHARGES.
ORDERS SENT TO HIS YARDS,

POLICE SQUARE, OR YORK STREET, BELFAST,
SHALL BE ATTENDED TO MOST CAREFULLY.

Any kind of STONE WORK attended to, at the Shortest Notice, and executed with the utmost despatch.

GREAT EXHIBITION
OF 1851.

"11, Warwick Lane, Newgate Street, London, 10th Mo., 3, 1851.

"T. C. S. CORRY, of Victoria Street, Belfast, has purchased the large SODA WATER MACHINE, made expressly by us for the Great Exhibition, and which is more complete and highly finished than any Soda Water Machine previously made. It is engraved in the *Illustrated Catalogue* Class 6. (Signed)

"J. TAYLOR & SON."

CORRY'S ÆRATED WATERS

Are prepared in Silver Cylinders from the purest ingredients, by Patent Machinery, manufactured expressly for the Great Exhibition of All Nations; it being the earnest desire of the Proprietor, by every practical means, to retain and extend that character which has gained for his beverages such decided preference. He is, therefore, now prepared to supply an article, which, for purity, strength, and delicacy of flavour, cannot be surpassed by any Manufacturer in the Universe; his

Ærated Lemonade

Possesses in a high degree the agreeable cooling properties of the fresh Lemon, and is recommended as a refreshing draught in febrile affections; whilst, as a winter beverage, his

Ginger Ale

Is agreeably stimulating, invigorating, and stomachic. He also begs to direct attention to a new preparation which he has recently introduced, viz. :—

Fruit Nectar.

This exquisite compound combines the delicious flavour of the Pine Apple with the rich delicacy of the ripe Citron, forming a most agreeable and exhilarating beverage. His

Soda Water

Is prepared with great care from PURE CRYSTALIZED CARBONATE OF SODA; in addition to which he now supplies, principally for family use, a

Double Soda Water,

Containing a larger proportion of the Carbonate, delicately flavoured with Lemon, which renders it much more agreeable to the taste, and in no way detracts from its antacid and stomachic qualities; he also prepares for medicinal use, an

Aperient Solution of Magnesia,

a most valuable and efficacious compound.

The Trade supplied on liberal terms, and Price Lists forwarded free to any part of the kingdom. Country orders, accompanied by a remittance, punctually attended to.

Prepared at CORRY's *Steam Ærated Water-Works, and*
Sold Wholesale and Retail, at Victoria Street Medical Hall, Belfast'

VICTORIA STREET MEDICAL HALL,
BELFAST.
SURGEON CORRY,

PROPRIETOR.

Established in 1849, for the Sale of Pure Drugs, Chemicals, Perfumery, Mineral Waters, &c., &c.

AGENT FOR

BUTTON'S PURE CHEMICALS, AND CHEMICAL APPARATUS; Ede's Laboratories and Preparations; Wood's Philosophical Apparatus; Rowland's, Patey's, Ede's, Beetham's, Rimmel's, Hendrie's, Grossmith's, Jackson's, and Stedman's Perfumery; Bertram's, Cleaver's, and Kendall's Toilet Soaps, and all Patent Medicines of repute.

JOSEPH WAUGH,
WHOLESALE GROCER,
VICTORIA BUILDINGS, VICTORIA STREET,
BELFAST.

CHARLES HOWDEN,
SEEDSMAN, NURSERYMAN, AND FLORIST,

No. 53, HIGH STREET, BELFAST.

NURSERIES, MALONE.

OYSTERS.

JAMES BRADLEY,
LEGG'S LANE,

INFORMS HIS FRIENDS AND THE PUBLIC, THAT HIS arrangements are made so as to ensure a Fresh Supply Twice a week during the Season, of the real Greencastle and Redcastle Oysters. Always on hand, Carrickfergus and Bangor Oysters. No Whitehaven Oysters Received.

TO FAMILIES FURNISHING.

JAMES GIRDWOOD

BEGS TO ANNOUNCE HIS RETURN FROM PARIS, LONDON, and the different manufacturing districts of England, where he has made LARGE ADDITIONS to his STOCK, in all the departments, and wich he is determined to Sell at the LOWEST POSSIBLE PRICE, for CASH The Stock consists of—

EAST INDIA CARPETS,

From the famous Manufactory at Mauslipatam, varying in sizes from 10 feet by 7, to 27 feet by 17 feet.

These Carpets are well adapted for either Dining-Rooms or Drawing-Rooms; Fine and Rich in texture; subdued in colours; and patterns similar to real Persian Carpets.

REAL TURKEY CARPETS.

Sizes from 10 feet by 12 feet, to 28 feet by 20 feet.

AXMINSTER CARPETS, made to order, any size without Seam.

Velvet, Tapestry, Saxony, Brussels, Kidderminster, Versailles, Dutch, and Scotch CARPETINGS.

French Tapestry; Taboret; Tournai Cloth; Silk, Worsted, and Washing Damasks; Moreens; Tammies; Brocatelles; Pictorial Satin Chair and Ottoman Covers.

A SPLENDID ASSORTMENT OF

RICH FIGURED LACE,

EMBROIDERED SWISS NET & MUSLIN CURTAINS

OF THE NEWEST PATTERNS OF THE SEASON.

Magnificent VELVET, FRENCH SILK, London Printed, Embroidered and Brocaded Bordered

TABLE COVERS.

London and French Chintzes and Furniture Covers, in all the Exhibition Patterns.

Well-seasoned Hall Oil-Cloths, from one-half yard to eight yards wide.

India, Cocoa, Fibre, Manilla, and Rush-Matting, all widths.

LONDON AND PARIS ROOM-PAPERS

suitable for Dining-Rooms, Drawing-Rooms, Halls, Libraries, Bed-Rooms, &c.; in Flocks, Gold Panels, Satins, and Plain Papers.

Hearth-Rugs, Door-Screens, Bell-Pulls, Door and Carriage Mats, Toilet Covers, Dimity.

Marseilles Quilts and Counterpanes, Bath Blankets, &c.

44, HIGH STREET, BELFAST.

ADVERTISEMENTS. 49

CHARLES & WILLIAM FINLAY,
WHOLESALE TEA MERCHANTS,
5, WARING-STREET,
BELFAST.

THE
PATRIOTIC ASSURANCE COMPANY
OF IRELAND,
(ESTABLISHED UNDER ACT OF PARLIAMENT.)
CAPITAL—ONE AND A-HALF MILLION, STERLING.

FOR ALL DESCRIPTIONS OF

LIFE AND FIRE INSURANCE,
AND FOR
PURCHASING AND GRANTING ANNUITIES,
HEAD OFFICE, 9, COLLEGE GREEN, DUBLIN.

Treasurers:
John Barton, Thomas Kirwan, Solomon Watson.

Directors:

John Barton,	Wm. M. Geoghegan,	Val. O'B. O'Connor,
Joshua M. Chayter,	Edward A. Gibbon,	Richard O'Gorman,
Joseph Cowper,	Charles Halliday,	William Harvey Pim,
Jeremiah Dunne,	James Haughton,	James Power,
Isaac English,	Thomas Kirwan,	Joseph Watkins,
John Ennis,	George M'Bride,	Joshua Watson,
Alexander Ferrier,	James Murphy,	Solomon Watson.

Auditors—John Allingham, Samuel Newsom, Joseph Webb.
Solicitor—Richard Cathcart. *Secretary*—James J. Fisher.

The Directors feel bound to express their thanks to the Irish Public, and to their Fellow-Citizens in particular, for the confidence and preference which they have evinced toward this Establishment, and which the Directors trust will be continued, and they assure the Public that their patronage and support shall be met by a sincere desire to render every facility and despatch in the transaction of business, and promptitude and liberality in the adjustment of claims.

IN THE FIRE DEPARTMENT, commonly hazardous risks are only 1s. 6d. per cent., and all others proportionately moderate. THE LIFE DEPARTMENT, presents every possible advantage to the assured.

Prospectuses, containing Tables of the Company's Rates, can be had on application at the office, No. 9, College Green, Dublin, where every information will be supplied, or at

ROBERT ATKINSON'S Office,
No. 10, Hill-Street, Belfast.

JOHN LAMB, Agent.

E

NORTHERN
BOOT AND SHOE HOUSE,
JAMES COEY,
12, DONEGALL PLACE,

BELFAST.

MacADAM AND CO.'S
IMPROVED
FLAX SCUTCHING MACHINERY.

ALL THE MOST IMPROVED KINDS OF

BREAKING, SCUTCHING,

AND FINISHING MACHINERY.

For Preparing the *Flax Fibre* from the straw, after the Hot or Cold Water Steeping, supplied by the Makers,

MacADAM, BROTHERS, AND CO., ENGINEERS,

SOHO FOUNDRY,

BELFAST.

P.S.—Competent Workmen provided, if required, to accompany the Machinery to any part of the country, and act as scutchers; also, Foremen scutchers to take charge of Mills, and instruct others.

I OFFER TO THE TRADE

THE

LARGEST AND BEST ASSORTED
STOCK IN ULSTER,

CONSISTING OF

Drugs, Chemicals, Patent Medicines, Perfumery, Spices, Pickles, Sauces, Foreign Fruits, Confectionery,

SUGARS, TEAS, COFFEES, COCOAS,

DRYSALTERIES, DYESTUFFS, PAINTS,

OILS, COLOURS, VARNISHES, BRUSHES,

&c., &c., &c.; ALSO,

Slater's Celebrated Carlisle Biscuits.	Paterson's Patent Fire Lighters.
Carr's Celebrated Carlisle Biscuits.	Superior Table Salt in Delph Pots.
The Celebrated Glenfield Patent Starch.	Bell's New Patent Congreves.
	Bell's New Gas Matches.
Hale's Composite Candles.	Bell's Patent Wax Vestas.
Field's Night Lights.	Martindale's Liquid and Paste Blacking.
Smith's Essence of Coffee.	
Mackay's Essence of Coffee.	Martindale's Congreves.
Allan's Waterproof Harness Liquid.	Cooney's Paste Blacking.
Cox's Patent Gelatine.	Day and Martin's Liquid and Paste Blacking.
Nelson's Patent Gelatine.	
Maccaroni and Vermicelli.	Warren's Liquid and Paste Blacking.
Arrow Root, Tapioca and Semolina.	Lapping Papers.
Candied Citron, Lemon, and Orange Peel.	Black and Red Lead Pencils.
	Round and Square Slate Pencils.
Singleton's Package Coffees.	Sealing Wax and Wafers.
Greenwood's Package Coffees.	Stone and Common Marbles.
Sinclair's Package Coffees.	Emery, Corn and Flour.
Robinson's Package Coffees.	Emery and Glass Cloth.
Green's Celebrated Washing Powder.	Emery and Glass Paper.
Down's Farmer's Friend.	Tin Foil and Foil Paper.
Arnold's Superior Inks.	Machinery Grease.
Maleham's Furniture Lustre.	Charcoal, Lump and Powder.

WILLIAM DOBBIN,
WHOLESALE DRUGGIST,

AND

GENERAL MERCHANT,

18 AND 20, AND 45 AND 47,

NORTH STREET, BELFAST.

NATHANIEL FERGUSON'S

Woollendrapery and Hat Warehouse,

38, HIGH STREET, BELFAST.

BLANKETS, CORDUROYS, MOLESKINS, LAMB'S WOOL VESTS and DRAWERS, VESTINGS, UMBRELLAS, GLOVES, SILK and NECK POCKET HANDKERCHIEFS, STOCKS, BRACES, GLOVES, TIES, &c., &c.

NORTHERN
COACH FACTORY.

MILLER & SONS,
COACH-BUILDERS,
GLOUCESTER STREET, BELFAST,

TAKE THIS OPPORTUNITY OF RETURNING THANKS to the Nobility and Gentry of Ulster for the very decided and encouraging support they have received from them. They also assure their patrons and the public in general that they will persevere in the course they have adopted, of having

Painting, Trimming, and Repairing,

OF ALL DESCRIPTIONS,

Entrusted to them, promptly executed, in a style equal to any work done in Belfast, by respectable Workmen, at Prices that will be found

AS MODERATE AS ANY IN THE TRADE.

N.B.—Old Work taken in Exchange, or Sold on Commission.

VICTORIA STREET PRINTING HOUSE.

NEW PRINTING OFFICE,

BOOKSELLING AND STATIONERY
ESTABLISHMENT,
Victoria Street, Corner of Waring Street,
BELFAST.

JAMES REED

RESPECTFULLY SOLICITS THE ATTENTION OF THE Clergy, Gentry, Merchants, &c., of Belfast and surrounding districts to his New and Extensive PRINTING OFFICE, BOOKSELLING, and FANCY STATIONERY Establishment.

His Printing Materials embrace the newest designs of Type for Bookwork and every description of Plain and Ornamental Printing, and his attention to business, anxiety to give satisfaction, combined with moderate charges, will, he hopes, secure for him a share of public patronage.

☞ Always on hand a large Stock of B O O K S and General STATIONERY, which he offers at very low prices.

⁎ LITHOGRAPHIC PRINTING, BOOKBINDING, &c., executed with neatness, accuracy, and despatch.

Victoria Street, January, 1852.

MITRE
GENERAL LIFE ASSURANCE ASSOCIATION,
Offices—23, PALL MALL, LONDON.

TABLES BASED ON THE EXPERIENCE OF 62,000 ASSURERS. Half Credit allowed for Seven Years.

NON-PARTICIPATION PREMIUM FOR ASSURING £1,000.

AGE.	£	s.	d.
Twenty, … … … … …	15	15	10
Thirty, … … … … …	20	7	6
Forty, … … … … …	27	16	8

Thus, the sum usually charged at the age of Twenty to Assure £1,000, in such Offices as adopt exclusively the principle of granting Bonuses at stated intervals, will assure nearly £1,400 in the MITRE. Here is an immediate Bonus which it generally requires twenty years to attain in other cases.

W. BRIDGES, Actuary and Secretary.

AGENT FOR BELFAST,

JOHN F. TEELING, Solicitor, Castle Lane.

THE IMPERIAL HOTEL,

FOR THE ACCOMMODATION OF COMMERCIAL GENTLEMEN AND PRIVATE FAMILIES,

DONEGALL PLACE, BELFAST,

Continues to be conducted in the same style and manner which gained for it, from its commencement, the distinction of being the FIRST HOTEL IN THE NORTH OF IRELAND.

THE DRAWING & SITTING ROOMS

Are Superbly Furnished, having a *Piano-Forte in each.*

THE COFFEE ROOM,

For the reception of Private and Professional Gentlemen, is Tastefully and Fashionably Fitted-up.

THE COMMERCIAL ROOM

Is confessedly the BEST IN IRELAND, being not only completed with every comfort and convenience for Commercial Gentlemen, but is the only one in Belfast *kept exclusively for their use;* and

THE BED ROOMS

Are Furnished in the Newest Style of Fashion, combining Comfort with Elegance.

THERE ARE ALSO COMMODIOUS

SHOW-ROOMS,

Set apart for the use of Commercial Gentlemen.

☞ Notwithstanding the admitted superiority of the "IMPERIAL," and the many advantages it thus possesess,

THE CHARGES ARE STRICTLY MODERATE.

Hot, Cold, and Shower Baths;

Livery Stables, Post Horses, Chaises, Cars, Gigs, &c.

Gentlemen, whose time may be limited, will find Despatch and Economy at the

IMPERIAL CAFE AND RESTAURANT,

Attached to the Hotel (Entrance by Castle Lane only), where BREAKFASTS, LUNCHEONS, DELICIOUS SOUPS, DINNERS, COFFEE, &c., &c., may be had at all hours of the day, and at a minute's notice.

N.B.—This Hotel has Omnibuses in attendance, at all times, to convey Travellers and their Luggage to and from the Railways and Packets.

GEORGE C. HYNDMAN,

AUCTIONEER & VALUATOR;

AGENT FOR THE

MANCHESTER FIRE AND PELICAN LIFE

ASSURANCE COMPANIES,

OFFERS FOR SALE, AT HIS

AUCTION AND COMMISSION MART,

No. 7, CASTLE-PLACE, BELFAST,

AN EXTENSIVE

STOCK OF FURNITURE,

COMPRISING PEDESTAL SIDEBOARDS; PILLAR DINING and Breakfast Tables; Rosewood and Mahagony Loo, Sofa, and Card Tables; Rosewood and Mahogany Cabinets; Devonports; solid Rosewood Drawing-Room Chairs; Mahogany Dining-Room and Drawing-Room Chairs; Sofas; Couches; Easy Chairs; Beadsteads, in great variety; Feather Beds and Hair Mattresses; *New Beds of prime seasoned Feathers; Hair and Flock Mattresses made to order;* Mahogany Drawers; handsome large Winged Wardrobes; Mahogany and Painted Wardrobes; Dressing Tables; Basin Stands; Cane-seated and other Bed-Room Chairs; Cheval and Dressing Glasses; Work and Ornamental Tables; Writing Desks; Work Boxes; Dressing-Cases; Bagatelle and Backgammon Tables; large Folding Screens; with numerous other articles.

A COMPLETE ASSORTMENT OF

HARDWARE AND IRONMONGERY,

Including Steel, Bronzed, and Brass Fenders; Fire-Irons; Hat and Umbrella Stands; Table, Hall, and Staircase Lamps; Chandeliers; best Sheffield Plated Ware and Cutlery; British Plate; Britannia Metal Goods; Tea Urns; Japanned Trays; Tin Ware; Patent Metal Boilers; Fish Kettles; Oval and Round Pots; Saucepans; Kettles, &c., &c.

LIKEWISE,

Patent and Common Mangles; Wrought-Iron Fire-Proof Safes; London Floor-Cloth, and Painted Table Baize; India Rush and Hemp Matting; Hemp and Fancy Foot Mats; Brushes and Whisks; Baize for Carpet Covers; Hearth Rugs; Leather Portmanteaus; Carpet Bags; real Barbadoes Filtering Stones; Perforated Zinc Meat Safes, &c., &c.

A VARIETY OF PIANO-FORTES ALWAYS ON SALE.

Sales attended in the Country. Valuations made for Probate and Legacy Duties.

BILLSLAND,
GLASS & CHINA WAREHOUSE,
4, DONEGALL PLACE,
BELFAST.

HENRY LOUGHRAN,
GROCER,
TEA, WINE, AND SPIRIT MERCHANT,
41, YORK STREET,
BELFAST.

ULSTER COACH FACTORY.

EVERY DESCRIPTION OF CARRIAGE

BUILT TO ORDER, ON MODERATE TERMS.

Always on hands,

NEW CLARENCES, LANDAUS, PHÆTONS,

CARRIAGE & OUTSIDE CARS, GIGS, &c., &c:

OLD VEHICLES TAKEN IN EXCHANGE, OR SOLD ON COMMISSION,

ULSTER COACH FACTORY.

MONTGOMERY STREET,

BELFAST.

JOHN KENNEDY,
PROPRIETOR.

WILLIAM LOW'S
MARBLE AND STONEYARD,
11, MONTGOMERY STREET.
CEMENT AND ALABASTER STORES,
24, CHICHESTER STREET,
BELFAST.

JOHN NEILL,
(LATE OF PURDEY'S, LONDON).
GUN AND PISTOL MAKER,
78, HIGH STREET, BELFAST.

FISHING TACKLE WAREHOUSE.
GUNPOWDER AND PATENT SHOT.

Guns Restocked to any Pattern, in the best London style.
Agent for the Sale of JOHNSTON'S CELEBRATED FIRE-WORKS.
N.B.—Birds, &c., preserved.

BELFAST UNDERTAKING,
POSTING ESTABLISHMENT, AND LIVERY STABLES,
6, MONTGOMERY STREET,
At the corner of May Street and Montgomery Street.

HUGH MORRISON,

BEGS TO RETURN HIS SINCERE THANKS TO THE Nobility, Gentry, the inhabitants of Belfast, and the North of Ireland generally, for the very liberal patronage with which he has been favoured for so many years past, and having greatly extended his Premises and considerably increased his Stock of Machines, viz., Hearses, Open and Close Carriages, Covered, Sociable, and Outside Cars, &c., &c., all of the very best and newest description, he trusts by strict attention, and reasonable charges, to merit their future support.

N.B.—Coffins of all descriptions on hands, or made to order, mounted and finished in the best style. A large assortment of Shoulder-Scarfs, Hat-Bands, Gloves, &c., always ready for use.

☞ In connexion with the above is a large room called the Wellington Hall, 57 feet by 32 wide, with Retiring Room, &c., suitable for Public Meetings, Concerts, &c., to be let on reasonable terms.

… ADVERTISEMENTS.

WILLIAM HOWARD,
WIRE WORKER.

Manufacturer of Flour Machines, Brushes,

WIRE WEB, SCREENS, CORN SEPARATORS, &c.

15, CHURCH LANE, BELFAST.

MR. H., IN RETURNING THANKS TO HIS NUMEROUS customers, begs to say that he never was in a better position to give satisfaction, and is determined that every exertion shall be used on his part to continue that confidence with which he has been hitherto favoured. In addition to the above branches he has invented a Machine for punching Tin Plates for Oatmeal Sifters, which turns out work not to be equalled in the three kingdoms.

RIDDLES AND SEIVES, OF EVERY SIZE AND FINENESS.

MEARNS & CO.,
WHOLESALE
ROOM-PAPER MANUFACTURERS,
LOW LODGE, OLD PARK.

IMPORTERS OF

ENGLISH AND FOREIGN PAPER HANGINGS;

A CHOICE AND SUPERIOR STOCK OF

HOME-MANUFACTURED PAPERS;

LAMINATED LEAD AND FELT FOR DAMP WALLS;

HALL OIL CLOTHS; OIL BAIZE,

For Table Covers, in Imitation of Woods and Marbles;

DOOR MATS, &c., &c.

SHOW ROOMS, 22, DONEGALL STREET, BELFAST.

ADVERTISEMENTS.

A LARGE AND ELEGANT ASSORTMENT OF

Papier Mache Tables,

DEVOTIONAL CHAIRS,

WORK BOXES, DESKS, &C.,

AT

MACARTNEY'S,

JEWELLER, WATCHMAKER, & OPTICIAN,

No. 6, DONEGALL PLACE,

BELFAST.

REPAIRING IN ALL THE DEPARTMENTS.

JOHN LOW,

TIMBER MERCHANT,

PROPRIETOR OF THE PATENT STEAM SAW MILLS,
PLANING MACHINE AND BOBBIN MANUFACTORY,

PRINCE'S DOCK, BELFAST,

HAS ON HAND PREPARED FLOORING (SEASONED), and CUT DEALS, in Stock, fit for Cloth Boxes, or other purposes where dry wood is wanted.

All Sorts of Sawing and Planing done in the Neatest Style.

Orders for Flax and Cotton Rove and Spinning Bobbins, with Skewers, Thread, and Machine Spools, promptly attended to.

BONDED AND COMMISSION

STORES,

10, HILL STREET, BELFAST.

I BEG RESPECTFULLY TO INFORM YOU, THAT, IN addition to my Agency Business for the undernoted respectable Houses, whom I continue to represent in Belfast, and North of Ireland generally, I have made arrangements with Messrs. BASS & CO., Burton-on-Trent, for the Sale of their celebrated PALE INDIA ALE, with which I will be constantly supplied—in Hogsheads, Barrels, and Kilderkins—and can deliver the same from stock here, or direct from the Brewery, as desired, on same terms to the Trade as all other goods I sell on commission—viz., *at the Makers' Prices*, cost of transit only added. Bottlers and the Trade will find it their interest to order through me, as I neither break bulk nor otherwise interfere with their business—and sell every article genuine. I take charge of all empty Packages, thereby saving much trouble and risk. Your orders will oblige, and shall have my very best attention.

ROBERT ATKINSON,

AGENT AND BROKER.

A. Guinness, Son, and Co.,	Dublin,	XXX, XX, and X Porter
Archibald Campbell and Co.,	Edinburgh,	Mild and Pale Ales, &c.
Clyde Bottle Work Co.,	Glasgow,	Wine and other Bottles.
Hyde Park Pottery,	Do.,	Stoneware Spirit Jars, &c.
James Moore, Esq.,	Coleraine Distillery,	Pure Malt Whiskey.
J. & A. Gairdner,	Jura Distillery,	Do. Do. Do.
Greenock Distillery Co.,	Greenock,	Do. Do. Do.
Hoyle, Martin, & Co.,	Do.	Sugar Refiners.
A. & T. Anderson,	Do.	Do. Do.
Muller & Reese,	Amsterdam,	Do. Do.
De Beer & Co.,	Rotterdam,	Shippers of General Dutch Produce.
Denis, Henry, Mounie & Co.,	Cogniac,	Brandies.
Sir Robert Burnett & Co.,	London,	Pale and Brown Vinegars.

☞ Brokerage Business attended to promptly as heretofore.

ADVERTISEMENTS. 61

SHAKSPEARE HOTEL,

AND LONDON CHOP HOUSE,

21, CASTLE LANE, BELFAST,

EDWARD GREY,

PROPRIETOR.

This long-established Hotel will be found replete with every convenience and accommodation that can be found. It is situated in the centre of the town, and near all the Banks and Public Offices.

THE COFFEE ROOM

in connexion with this Establishment is fitted up in the best manner, and will be found to be a most convenient and economical place of resort for parties from the country, during their stay in town.

BREAKFASTS, DINNERS, SUPPERS, SOUPS,

TEA, COFFEE, STEAKS, &c,

AT A MOMENT'S NOTICE.

CHARGES MODERATE.

WELL AIRED BEDS.

THE CONCERT HALL.

The Proprietor respectfully begs leave to call the attention of Gentlemen and the Public to his CONCERT ROOM, which is open FREE to all respectable parties every evening. The Concert consists of Comic and Sentimental Songs, Glees, &c., by the most talented Artistes.

Wines of the most celebrated vintage and character; splendid Malt Beverages on Draught or in Bottle. Spirits matured by age and of the finest description, at the most moderate scale of charges, it being the ambition of the Proprietor to meet the times, and to secure a large return of patronage to this old-established and celebrated Hotel.

The Exhibition Sutherland Music Chair.

Back of Chair.

Winchester Circular Footstool.

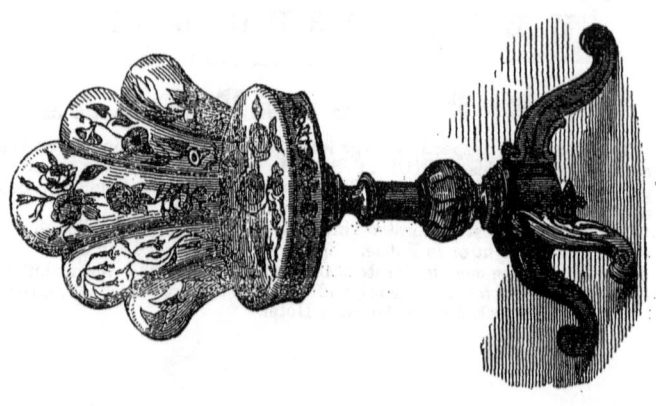

Front of Chair.

ADVERTISEMENTS.

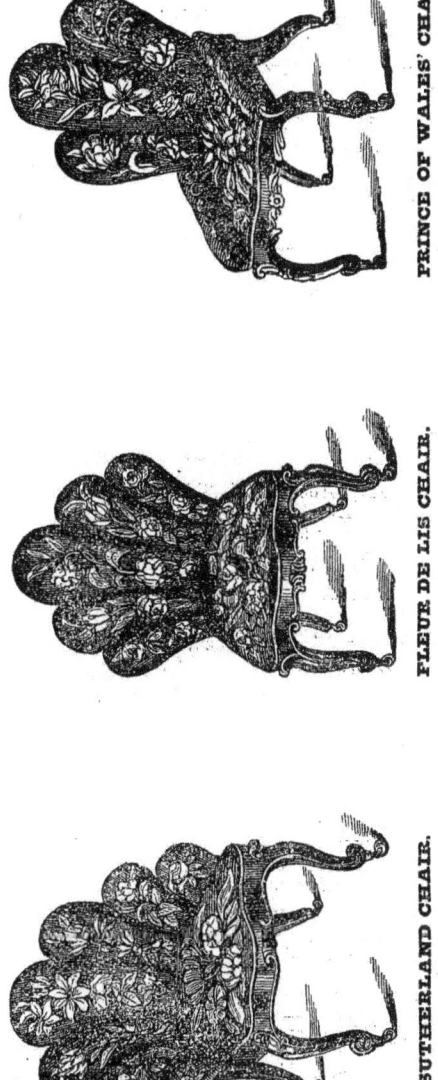

SUTHERLAND CHAIR.   FLEUR DE LIS CHAIR.   PRINCE OF WALES' CHAIR.

THE LADIES'
TRIMMING, BERLIN WOOL, FANCY, AND HABERDASHERY
WAREHOUSE,
H. RIDDEL,
5, CASTLE BUILDINGS, CORNER OF DONEGALL PLACE.

STEAM COMMUNICATION.

First Class Iron Steam-Ships are appointed to Sail from DONEGALL QUAY, BELFAST,

To Fleetwood, London, Plymouth, Glasgow, Ardrossan, Whitehaven, Liverpool, Londonderry, and Stranraer; also, between Glasgow and New York,

AS UNDERMENTIONED:

FLEETWOOD,
The Royal Mail Steam-ships, "PRINCE OF WALES" and "ROYAL CONSORT," every MONDAY, WEDNESDAY, THURSDAY, and FRIDAY, from each Port.

LONDON AND PLYMOUTH.
The new Screw Steam-ships, "OSCAR" and "ERIN'S QUEEN," every FRIDAY, from BELFAST, and THURSDAY, from London. These vessels call at PLYMOUTH, on their passage from BELFAST to LONDON.

GLASGOW *via* ARDROSSAN.
The favourite Steam-ship, "FIRE-FLY," from BELFAST, every TUESDAY and THURSDAY, at NINE o'clock Evening, and SATURDAY, at ONE o'clock, p.m. From ARDROSSAN, every MONDAY, WEDNESDAY, and FRIDAY, at TEN o'clock evening. Passengers leave GLASGOW, by EXPRESS TRAIN, at HALF-PAST EIGHT o'clock, p.m.

WHITEHAVEN AND LIVERPOOL.
The Splendid Steam-ships "WHITEHAVEN" and "QUEEN," from BELFAST for WHITEHAVEN, every FRIDAY, and from WHITEHAVEN for BELFAST, every WEDNESDAY. These vessels carry Goods between LIVERPOOL and BELFAST, and *vice versa*, at very reasonable rates; Loading in LIVERPOOL on TUESDAYS, and in BELFAST on FRIDAYS.

STRANRAER.
The Superior Steam-ship "ALBION," from BELFAST every SATURDAY, and from STRANRAER every FRIDAY.

LONDONDERRY.
The Powerful First-Class Steam-ship, "FENELLA," from BELFAST every WEDNESDAY, from DERRY, every MONDAY.

GLASGOW AND NEW YORK.
The Magnificent Steam-ships, "GLASGOW," and "NEW YORK" are intended to Sail regularly ONCE-A-MONTH from each Port.

For full particulars, see Monthly Bills, or apply to

ROBERT HENDERSON,
Steam Packet, Forwarding, and General Commission Agent.

Offices and Stores, 23 & 25, DONEGALL QUAY, BELFAST.

FORTNIGHTLY STEAM COMMUNICATION FROM LIVERPOOL
TO
NEW YORK, BALTIMORE, PITTSBURGH
CINCINNATI, CHARLESTON,
HAVANNA, &c.
BY WAY OF PHILADELPHIA.

The Steam Ships comprising this Line are the

CITY OF MANCHESTER,	2,125 Tons	Capt. Robt Leitch.
CITY OF PITTSBURGH,	2,200 Tons	Capt. W. C. Stolesbury.
CITY OF GLASGOW,	1,610 Tons	Capt. Wm Wylie.
CITY OF PHILADELPHIA,	2,222 Tons	Capt. _____

Sailing from Liverpool each alternate Wednesday.
" Philadelphia " Thursday.

RATES OF PASSAGE.

FROM LIVERPOOL, First Cabin, 22 Guineas. Second Cabin, 13 Guineas.
FROM PHILADELPHIA, First Cabin, 100 Dollars. Second Cabin, 60 Dollars.
Including all Provisions & Stewards' Fee.

Passengers can procure First Class Railway Tickets, by Mail Trains as under, from Philadelphia.—

			£	s	d
TO NEW YORK & BALTIMORE	3 Dollars,	or	0	12	6
TO PITTSBURGH, OHIO,	11 "	"	2	5	10
TO CINCINNATI, OHIO *(and by River Boat)*	16 "	"	3	6	8
TO CHARLESTON, S.C. *(and by Steam Boat)*	20 "	"	4	3	4
TO HAVANNA *(by Steam, via Charleston,)*	60 "	"	12	10	0

An experienced Surgeon is attached to each Ship.

Freight on Fine Goods 60/ per ton; and Coarse Goods, Hardware &c. will be taken, subject to agreement, payable here, or in Philadelphia, at 4 dols. 80 cents per pound sterling.

Goods sent to the Agents at Liverpool, or Philadelphia, will be forwarded with economy and despatch.

Apply, in Philadelphia and New York, to Thomas Richardson, in Liverpool, to Richardson, Brothers & Co., in Glasgow, to Patrick Henderson & Co., and to

Richardson, Brothers & Co.,
Corporation Street, Belfast.

North of England Insurance Company.

Incorporated.— Established 1844.
CAPITAL, £500,000.
CHIEF OFFICE, OLD HAYMARKET, SHEFFIELD.

Trustees.

THE RIGHT HON. EARL FITZWILLIAM,	SIR H. G. WARD, KNIGHT,
THE RIGHT HON. LORD WHARNCLIFFE,	JOHN PARKER, ESQ. M.P.
THE RIGHT HON. LORD MILTON,	CORDEN THOMSON, ESQ. M.D.

JOHN CARR, ESQ. MAYOR OF SHEFFIELD.

Directors.

W. J. BAGSHAWE, ESQ. of the Oaks, Derbyshire, *Chairman.*
JOHN CARR ESQ. *Deputy Chairman.*

JOSEPH WARD, ESQ.	LIEUT. JOHN ROBERTS, R.N.
CHARLES SHELDON, ESQ.	HENRY WILKINSON, ESQ.
GEORGE WILTON CHAMBERS, ESQ.	GEORGE WALL ESQ.
THOMAS WHEATLEY ESQ.	JOHN HALL, ESQ.
JOHN BROWN, ESQ.	EDWARD VICKERS ESQ.

Manager & Actuary, GEORGE STEWART, ESQ.

Agent for Belfast, Mr. JOSEPH FAREN,
at Messrs. Richardson, Brothers & Co's Corporation St.

FIRE DEPARTMENT.

Insurances are granted against Loss by Fire at the following moderate Rates of Premium.

Common Risks	1s 6d per Cent.
Hazardous Risks	2s 6d per Cent.
Doubly Hazardous Risks	4s 6d per Cent.

The Directors are at all times desirous to give effect to a prompt and liberal adjustment of Claims.

LIFE DEPARTMENT.

Policies may either be placed on the system of Mutual Assurance, with Right of Participating in the Profits, or be effected at a Reduced Rate of Premium, without such Right of Participation.

Annual Investigations & Divisions of Profits.—In order to obtain a Proper Average, the first Investigation has been delayed to 1852.

All Policies on the Mutual System are entitled to share to the extent of Eighty per cent in the Profits, arising from Assurances of this class.

Claims are Paid Three Months after Proof of Death, and when the amount insured does not exceed £300, one fourth part is payable on production of the evidence and the balance at the end of one month.

Prospectuses & further information may be had by applying to the Agent,

Joseph Faren,
Corporation Street, Belfast

GEORGE ADDEY,
47, GRAFTON STREET, DUBLIN,

BEGS LEAVE TO INFORM HIS CUSTOMERS AND THE Public, that he has made such arrangements for this Season as will enable him to supply the newest patterns of UNDERCLOTHING of every description, in great variety, at very moderate prices.

LADIES' INSIDE VESTS AND DRAWERS.—G. A. is desirous that Ladies should inspect his Stock before making their purchases.

THE MILLINERY DEPARTMENT

Is at all times supplied with the newest and most recherche styles of the season from 1s. 10d. to 7s. 6d.

THE UNDERCLOTHING DEPARTMENT

Is supplied with the newest and most useful Patterns in
CHEMISES, DRAWERS, NIGHT DRESSES, DRESSING GOWNS, CORDED, MOHAIR, MOREEN, AND FLANNEL PETTICOATS, &c.. &o.
BABY LINEN, OF EVERY DESCRIPTION.

THE STAY DEPARTMENT.

PRICES—French Cotille, 5s. 6d. to 8s. 6d.; Nursing Stays, 7s. 6d.; French Wove Stays, 11s. The Cotille Stays, at 5s. 6d., are excellent value, and have given much satisfaction.

THE SHIRT DEPARTMENT.

G. A. has confidence in asserting that the above Department will bear comparison with any similar one in Europe. As G. A. pays strict personal attention to it, and purchases his shirtings from the most eminent manufacturers, for cash, and has secured the services of a shirt cutter who is second to none, Gentlemen may depend upon securing a perfect fit.

Prices of Shirts, 3s. 6d.—4s.—5s. and 6s.; Veined Dress and Fancy Shirts, from 6s.; Irish Linen Shirts, 5s. to 10s. 6d.; Night Shirts, 2s. 2d. to 3s. 6d.; do. for Boys, from 1s. 4d.; Boys' Day Shirts, from 2s. to 3s. 6d.

If the following plan of Self-Measurement be strictly adhered to, it will insure a perfect fit:—Round the Neck at A.; round the Wrist at C.; round the Chest under the Arms; length of Shoulder, A. to B.; length of Arm B. to C.; entire length, A. to D.

Neck-Cloths, Stocks, and Ties, in the most improved variety

Vests and Drawers; Mufflers, Hosiery, and Gloves.—N.B. None but the best quality of Gloves kept.

As GEORGE ADDEY gives strict personal attention to every branch of his business, thereby preventing much extra expense —purchases his goods in the best markets, and transacts his business for cash only, he is in a position to secure to his customers the best possible value.

Gentlemen and ladies requiring marriage or foreign outfits will effect a considerable saving of time, trouble, and expense, by purchasing from G. Addy's ready-made stock, which is always supplied with the newest and most useful patterns, in sound materials and superior work.

GEORGE ADDEY'S
General Outfitting Establishment,
47, GRAFTON STREET, DUBLIN.

BOOKS
PUBLISHED BY SAMUEL B. OLDHAM,
8, SUFFOLK STREET, DUBLIN,
AND SOLD BY ALL BOOKSELLERS.

QUAKERISM; or, THE STORY OF MY LIFE. By Mrs. J. R. GREER. Second Edition, with Appendix, Notes, &c. Small 8vo, Cloth, Lettered, Price Five Shillings.

THE VOICE OF THE NEW YEAR. By SIDNEY O. MOORE. Second Edition, with Frontispiece and Vignette Title; 18mo, Cloth, Lettered, Price 1s. 6d.—[The profits to be applied to the support of Destitute Orphans in the West of Ireland.]

THE IRISH PEARL; a Tale of the time of Queen Anne. With Frontispiece and Vignette Title. Royal 16mo, Cloth, Lettered, Price 2s.—[The profits to be applied towards supplying home occupation for the female peasantry, in a comparatively unfriended district in the South of Ireland.]

THE RECTORY OF GLENMURRAGH; a Tale. Small 8vo, Cloth, Lettered, with Illustrations, Price 2s. 6d.

OLD JAMES, THE IRISH PEDLAR; a Tale of 1848. By M. B. TUCKEY, Author of "The Great Exemplar." Square 16mo, with Illustrations, Cloth, Lettered, 1s.

THE ARTIFICIAL PREPARATION OF TURF, Independent of season or weather, and with economy of labour and time. By ROBERT MALLET, C.E., M.R.I.A. 8vo, with Plates, Cloth, 2s. 6d.

THE ORIGIN AND RECLAMATION OF PEAT BOG, with observations on the construction of Roads, Railways, and Canals in Bogs. By B. MULLINS, C.E., and M. B. MULLINS, C.E. 8vo, with Plates, Cloth, 3s. 6d.

THE PRESERVATION OF THE COW AND SHEEP, Being the experience and practice of several generations in the causes, symptoms, and cures of all diseases incident to these Animals. By DANIEL MAHER. Foolscap 8vo, Price 1s. 6d.

ROMANISM QUESTIONED. The Leading Errors of the Church of Rome questioned and refuted out of the Douay Version of the Scriptures. Price One Halfpenny, or Four Shillings per hundred.

THE PROTESTANT CATECHISM. The Leading Errors of the Church of Rome exposed and refuted in a Catechetical Form. Price One Halfpenny, or Four Shillings per hundred

EXTRACTS FROM DENS' THEOLOGY; With Remarks to show the Unscriptural Nature and Destructive Tendency of the Doctrines of the Church of Rome. Third Thousand, Price Sixpence.

THE IRISH SUNDAY SCHOOL MAGAZINE, For 1850 and 1851. Cloth, lettered, 2s. 6d. The Magazine is published on the 1st of each Month. Annual Subscription, Two Shillings; when sent by Post, Three Shillings.

W. H. SMITH AND SON'S
EXPRESS NEWSPAPER OFFICE,
1, EDEN-QUAY, SACKVILLE-STREET, DUBLIN,
(JOHNSTON'S)
ESTABLISHED, MAY 1819.

Patronised by His Excellency the Lord Lieutenant; the Irish Government; H. R. H. the Duke of Cambridge; Right Honourable the Lieutenant-General Commanding the Forces; the Adjutant-General, &c., &c.; the Right Honourable and Honourable the Judges; the Bars; the Kildare and Sackville-street, United Service, University, Leinster, and Stephen's Green Clubs; Friendly Brothers; the Chamber of Commerce; Dublin Library; Nobility and Gentry, &c.; as,also by all the principal News and Commercial Bodies throughout Ireland.

The Late and Express Editions of the London Newspapers always sent to Subscribers.

PRICE CURRENTS, TRADE LISTS, BILLS OF ENTRY, PACKET LISTS, SUPPLIED.

Subscriptions received for Foreign Newspapers, and all the Irish and English Newspapers sent to any part of the world.

THE DUBLIN NEWSPAPERS
SUPPLIED IN TOWN AND COUNTRY
UPON THE RESPECTIVE TERMS OF EACH PAPER.

LONDON AND DUBLIN NEWSPAPERS EXCHANGED AT PLEASURE, OR THE ADDRESS ALTERED AT ANY TIME DURING SUBSCRIPTION, WITHOUT EXPENSE.

All Books, Periodicals, &c., supplied to order.

W. H. SMITH and SON have made arrangements with the Railway Companies in Ireland for forwarding Newspapers by Trains leaving Dublin previous to the Mail.

W. H. SMITH and SON, London, Dublin, General, and Foreign Newspaper and Advertising Agents, 1, Eden-quay, Sackville-street, Dublin, 136, Strand, London, beg to assure their Patrons that not only the facilities for

EXPRESSING NEWS,

which they placed at Mr. JOHNSTON's command for Twenty Years, and which earned for this Establishment the highly reputation it has so long enjoyed, shall be continued, but all the resources which Enterprise and Capital, together with the great additional advantages they possess from their connection with the London and North-Western and Chester and Holyhead Railway Companies, and sole Agents for Ireland for the Electric Telegraph, shall be brought into active operation for their benefit.

HODGES' BELL FOUNDRY,

UPWARDS OF HALF A CENTURY ESTABLISHED.

CHURCH, TURRET, HOUSE, AND FARM BELLS,

CAST TO ANY SIZE, OF SUPERIOR QUALITY AND TONE.

JURY 22.—GREAT EXHIBITION.

PRIZE MEDAL.

London, 16th October, 1851.

MY DEAR SIR,—I am happy to tell you that your Bells have got the Medal for Merit.

In haste, yours truly,

JOHN LENTAIGNE.

To Thomas Hodges, Esq., Bell Founder,
Abbey Street, Dublin.

TO PERSONS VISITING DUBLIN.

PHŒNIX HOTEL, TAVERN & COFFEE HOUSE,

17 D'OLIER STREET & 2 HAWKINS STREET,

DUBLIN

The above Hotel is within two minutes' walk of the Kingstown and Drogheda Railway, and combines every accommodation and comfort with moderate charges. It is in the most central situation in Dublin for gentlemen who may have occasion to transact business in any of the public Offices, Banks, or of a mercantile nature.

Dinner, Soup, and Fruit, 1s. per head,

FROM FIVE TO SEVEN O'CLOCK EACH DAY.

FINE ART ESTABLISHMENT,
REMOVED TO DONEGALL PLACE.

JAMES MAGILL,
PRINTSELLER & STATIONER,
ARTISTS' COLOURMAN,

AND

PICTURE FRAME MAKER,
7, CASTLE BUILDINGS,
DONEGALL PLACE, BELFAST.

BIBLES AND PRAYER BOOKS,
CHURCH SERVICES,
MONTHLY VOLUMES,
DAVIDSON'S CHEAP MUSIC,
DE LA RUE'S BEST PLAYING CARDS,
LETTER AND NOTE PAPERS,
VISITING AND WEDDING CARDS,
ENVELOPES, &c., &c.

ELEGANT TOILET REQUISITES,

UNDER THE ESPECIAL PATRONAGE OF

HER MAJESTY
H. R. H. Prince Albert,
The Court and Royal Family
of Great Britain.

THE QUEEN,
the
Several Sovereigns and Courts
of Europe.

AND UNIVERSALLY PREFERRED AND ESTEEMED.

ROWLANDS' MACASSAR OIL.

The unprecedented success of this discovery, in restoring, improving, and beautifying the Human Hair, is too well known and appreciated to need comment. Price 3s 6d—7s—Family Bottles (equal to 4 Small), 10s 6d, and Double that size, 21s per Bottle.

ROWLANDS' KALYDOR.

An Oriental Botanical Preparation, of unfailing efficacy in thoroughly purifying the SKIN *from all* PIMPLES, SPOTS, BLOTCHES, REDNESS, FRECKLES, TAN, and DISCOLORATIONS; in producing *a healthy freshness and transparency* of COMPLEXION; and a softness and delicacy of the HANDS and ARMS. During the heat and dust of summer, or frost and bleak winds of winter; and in cases of sunburn, stings of Insects, chilblains, chapped skin, or incidental inflammation, its virtues have long and extensively been acknowledged. Price 4s 6d and 8s 6d per Bottle.

ROWLANDS' ODONTO, or PEARL DENTIFRICE.

A WHITE POWDER, compounded of the choicest and most recherché ingredients of the Oriental Herbal, of inestimable value in *preserving* and *beautifying* the TEETH, *strengthening* the GUMS, and in giving sweetness and perfume to the breath. Price 2s 9d per Box.

ROWLANDS' AQUA D'ORO.

This is the most fragrant and refreshing Perfume ever yielded by the " Souls of Flowers." It retains its fresh and delightful odorousness for days. It is invigorating, gently stimulating, yet sedative; and is an unrivalled quintessential spirituous product. For fainting fits, fatigues of dancing, oppression from overcrowded rooms, or intense summer heat, its uses cannot be over-estimated. Price 3s 6d per Bottle.

ROWLANDS' EUPLYSIA.

A Preparation from the choicest ORIENTAL HERBS, of peculiarly mild and detersive properties. It pleasingly and effectually cleanses the Hair and Skin of the Head from Scurf and every species of Impurity. It is particularly recommended to be used after bathing, as it will prevent the probability of catching cold in the head, and will render the hair dry in a few minutes. Price 2s 6d per Bottle.

IMPORTANT INFORMATION.

UNPRINCIPLED SHOPKEEPERS, for the sake of gaining a trifle more profit, vend the most SPURIOUS COMPOUNDS, under the same names; it is therefore highly necessary to see that the word "ROWLANDS" is on the Wrapper or Label of each Article.

SOLD BY THE PROPRIETORS,

A. Rowland and Sons, 20, Hatton Garden, London,

AND BY CHEMISTS AND PERFUMERS.

IMPORTANT NOTICE TO THE

INHABITANTS OF BELFAST AND ITS VICINITY.

EIGHT MONTHS SINCE WE OPENED AN ESTABLISHMENT in Belfast, entitled the ORIGINAL CHINESE TEA COMPANY, on principles which have been so long *tried, and so justly appreciated in Scotland*, that we did not doubt they would be similarly *received by a discerning public* in Belfast. Nor have we been deceived. The success which has attended our endeavours has exceeded our most sanguine expectations; we, therefore, deemed it necessary to make an addition to our Premises, to enable us more fully to meet the wants of a daily-increasing business. Our object, however, is not only to afford greater accommodation *to our customers*, but also with a view to *the further extension of our Trade*.

The experience we have had as *buyers* enables us to purchase, on the most advantageous terms, from the London and Liverpool Markets; and from the late favourable state of the *Tea Trade*, we have selected some of the Finest descriptions, which we shall offer at unusually *Low Prices*, viz.:—

Finest Lapsang Souchong, 4s. 2d. per lb., or 1s. 0½d. the qr. (*Usually sold at 4s. 8d. per lb.*) The

Best Black Tea imported from China. (*Pay no higher price, as it is unnecessary.*)

QUALITY IS THE TRUE TEST OF CHEAPNESS.—COMPARE AND JUDGE FOR YOURSELVES.

The Finest Souchong Congou, 3s. 10d. per lb., or 11½d. the qr. (*A famous Family Tea, of the true old-fashioned kind, very strong, with fine Pekoe flavour.*)

For the accommodation of Families, we supply Catty Packages, in Lead, containing 4lbs. 2oz., of the finest kind, for 16s. 8d.; also, **Finest Pekoe Souchong Congou**, much recommended, for 15s. 4d. Order, by Post, accompanied with a remittance, or reference in town, will have our best attention, and be forwarded without delay.

Strong and fine-flavoured Congou (*strongly recommended*), 3s. 6d. per lb.
Strong Breakfast Congou, ... 3s. 4d. per lb.
Good Sound Congou, ... 3s. 3d. per lb.

COFFEE.

Finest Imported (*very choice*), ... 1s. 6d. per lb.
Fine Jamaica, ... 1s. 4d. per lb.
Fine Costa Rica ... ... 1s. 0d. per lb.
Fine Ceylon ... ... 10d. per lb.

TO COUNTRY SHOPKEEPERS.

We offer great advantages in TEAS, COFFEES, SUGARS, and FRUITS, as one trial will prove. Our terms are *Cash*, as small profits will not admit of credit being given.

CAUTION.—We hereby give PUBLIC NOTICE, that we have NO connexion with, or interest in, any other House in Belfast.

P.S.—To prevent disappointment to our Customers, we beg to inform them, that we keep no article in Stock which is at all detrimental or injurious to the fine flavour of our Teas—such as Soap, Candles, Cheese, &c.; but to those of our country friends requiring same, we shall be happy to supply them from other establishments, at cost price.

ARMSTRONG AND COMPANY,

5, Donegall Place Buildings, corner of Castle Street, Belfast.

www.ingramcontent.com/pod-product-compliance
Lightning Source LLC
Chambersburg PA
CBHW071307150426
43191CB00007B/538